A Social Studies Learning System

CHOOSE how you want to teach

- All print
- All digital
- Your own custom print and digital mix

MEETS YOU ANYWHERE —
TAKES YOU EVERYWHERE

ORGANIZE with everything in one place

- Upload personal resources
- Search Resource Library
- Create class rosters
- File and Save

McGraw-Hill
netw⦿rks™

MEETS YOU ANYWHERE —
TAKES YOU EVERYWHERE

CUSTOMIZE everything for your students – easy, quick, and efficient

- Personalize lessons
- Create tests
- Modify assignments

DIFFERENTIATE instruction to meet the needs of all your students

- Assign different reading levels
- Access full audio
- Use PDFs or modify worksheets
- Print or assign online

start **network**ing

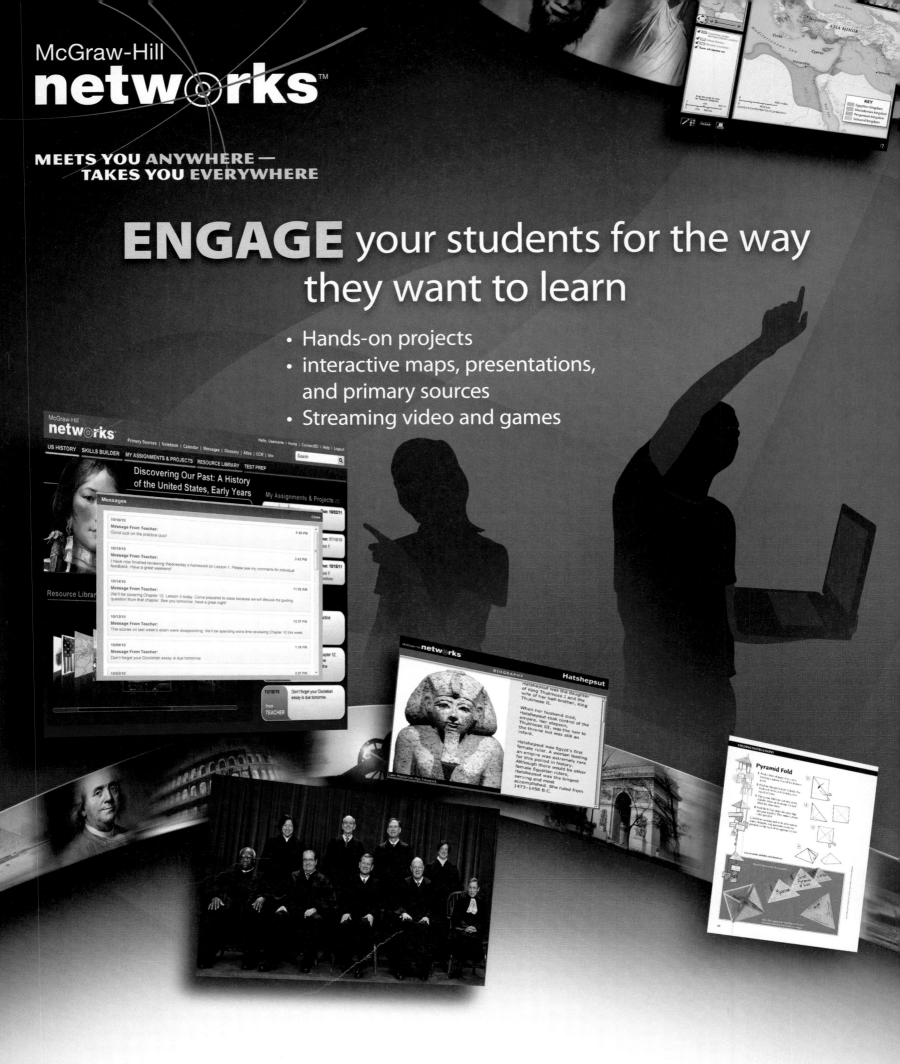

ENGAGE your students for the way they want to learn

- Hands-on projects
- interactive maps, presentations, and primary sources
- Streaming video and games

COMMUNICATE with your students

- Assign homework and tests
- Send messages
- Track and print student results

start **netw⊕rk**ing

McGraw-Hill
networks™

MEETS YOU ANYWHERE — TAKES YOU EVERYWHERE

CONNECT with colleagues, students, experts, and content

1. Log on to the Internet and go to ***connected.mcgraw-hill.com***.
2. Enter User Name and Password.
3. Click on your **Networks** book.
4. Select your chapter and lesson.

start networking

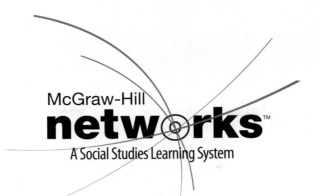

McGraw-Hill

netw✪rks™

A Social Studies Learning System

Teacher Edition

DISCOVERING
OUR PAST

A HISTORY
of the **UNITED**
STATES

Early Years

Joyce Appleby, Ph.D.

Alan Brinkley, Ph.D.

Albert S. Broussard, Ph.D.

James M. McPherson, Ph.D.

Donald A. Ritchie, Ph.D.

Mc Graw Hill Education

Bothell, WA • Chicago, IL • Columbus, OH • New York, NY

connected.mcgraw-hill.com

Send all inquiries to:
McGraw-Hill Education
8787 Orion Place
Columbus, OH 43240

Teacher Edition:
ISBN: 978-0-07-659727-7
MHID: 0-07-659727-X

Student Edition:
ISBN: 978-0-07-659726-0
MHID: 0-07-659726-1

Printed in the United States of America.

5 6 7 8 9 DOW 16 15

Joyce Appleby, Ph.D., is Professor Emerita of History at UCLA. She is the author of several books, including her most recent, *The Relentless Revolution: A History of Capitalism.* She served as president of the Organization of American Historians and the American Historical Association, and she chaired the Council of the Institute of Early American History and Culture at Williamsburg. Appleby has been elected to the American Philosophical Society and the American Academy of Arts and Sciences, and she is a Corresponding Fellow of the British Academy.

Alan Brinkley, Ph.D., is Allan Nevins Professor of American History at Columbia University. His published works include *Voices of Protest: Huey Long, Father Coughlin, and the Great Depression,* which won the 1983 National Book Award. Other titles include *The End of Reform: New Deal Liberalism in Recession and War* and *Liberalism and Its Discontents.* He received the Levenson Memorial Teaching Prize at Harvard University.

Albert S. Broussard, Ph.D., is Professor of History at Texas A&M University, where he was selected as the Distinguished Faculty Lecturer for 1999–2000. He also served as the Langston Hughes Professor of American Studies at the University of Kansas in 2005. Before joining the Texas A&M faculty, Broussard was Assistant Professor of History and Director of the African American Studies Program at Southern Methodist University. Among the books he has published are *Black San Francisco: The Struggle for Racial Equality in the West, 1900–1954* and *African American Odyssey: The Stewarts, 1853–1963.* Broussard has also served as president of the Oral History Association.

James M. McPherson, Ph.D., is George Henry Davis Professor Emeritus of American History at Princeton University. He is the author of 11 books about the Civil War era, including *Tried by War: Abraham Lincoln as Commander in Chief,* for which he won a second Lincoln Prize in 2009. McPherson is a member of many professional historical associations, including the Civil War Preservation Trust.

Donald A. Ritchie, Ph.D., is Historian of the United States Senate. Ritchie received his doctorate in American history from the University of Maryland after service in the U.S. Marine Corps. He has taught American history at various levels, from high school to university. He edits the Historical Series of the Senate Foreign Relations Committee and is the author of several books, including *Press Gallery: Congress and the Washington Correspondents,* which received the Organization of American Historians' Richard W. Leopold Prize. Ritchie has served as president of the Oral History Association and as a council member of the American Historical Association.

Contributing Authors

Jay McTighe has published articles in a number of leading educational journals and has coauthored 10 books, including the best-selling *Understanding by Design* series with Grant Wiggins. McTighe also has an extensive background in professional development and is a featured speaker at national, state, and district conferences and workshops. He received his undergraduate degree from The College of William and Mary, earned a Masters degree from the University of Maryland, and completed post-graduate studies at the Johns Hopkins University.

Dinah Zike, M.Ed., is an award-winning author, educator, and inventor recognized for designing three-dimensional, hands-on manipulatives and graphic organizers known as Foldables®. Foldables are used nationally and internationally by teachers, parents, and other professionals in the education field. Zike has developed more than 150 supplemental educational books and materials. Her two latest books, *Notebook Foldables®* and *Foldables®, Notebook Foldables®, & VKV®s for Spelling and Vocabulary 4th–12th* were each awarded *Learning Magazine's* Teachers' Choice Award for 2011. In 2004, Zike was honored with the CESI Science Advocacy Award. She received her M.Ed. from Texas A&M, College Station, Texas.

Doug Fisher, Ph.D., and Nancy Frey, Ph.D., are professors in the School of Teacher Education at San Diego State University. Fisher's focus is on literacy and language, with an emphasis on students who are English Learners. Frey's focus is on literacy and learning, with a concentration in how students acquire content knowledge. Both teach elementary and secondary teacher preparation courses, in addition to their work with graduate and doctoral programs. Their shared interests include supporting students with diverse learning needs, instructional design, and curriculum development. They are coauthors of numerous articles and books, including *Better Learning Through Structured Teaching, Checking for Understanding, Background Knowledge,* and *Improving Adolescent Literacy.* They are coeditors (with Diane Lapp) of the NCTE journal *Voices from the Middle.*

CONSULTANTS AND REVIEWERS

ACADEMIC CONSULTANTS

David Berger, Ph.D.
Ruth and I. Lewis Gordon
  Professor of Jewish History
Dean, Bernard Revel Graduate
  School
Yeshiva University
New York, New York

Stephen Cunha, Ph.D.
Professor of Geography
Humboldt State University

Tom Daccord
Educational Technology Specialist
Co-Director, EdTechTeacher
Boston, Massachusetts

Sylvia Kniest
Social Studies Teacher
Tucson Unified School District
Tucson, Arizona

Bernard Reich, Ph.D.
Professor of Political Science and
  International Affairs
George Washington University
Washington, D.C.

Justin Reich
Educational Technology Specialist
Co-Director, EdTechTeacher
Boston, Massachusetts

TEACHER REVIEWERS

Laura Abundes
Jefferson Middle School
Waukegan, Illinois

Debbie Clay
Brink Junior High
Moore, Oklahoma

Wendy Blanton
Berkeley Middle School
St. Louis, Missouri

Michael Frint
Fort Riley Middle School
Fort Riley, Kansas

Brian M. Gibson
Highland East Junior High School
Moore, Oklahoma

Carol V. Gimondo
Jefferson Middle School
Waukegan, Illinois

Mark Hamann
Perrysburg Junior High School
Perrysburg, Ohio

Norman Jackson
Frontier Middle School
O'Fallon, Missouri

Connie K. Simmonds
Ferguson Middle School
Ferguson, Missouri

Mary Beth Whaley
Highland West Junior High School
Moore, Oklahoma

CONTENTS

Buyenlarge/Archive Photos/Getty Images

CHAPTER 1

The Art Archive / General Archive of the Indies Seville / Gianni Dagli Orti

CHAPTER 2

CCSS

This icon indicates where reading skills and writing skills from the *Common Core State Standards for English Language Arts & Literacy in History/Social Studies, Science, and Technical Subjects* are practiced and reinforced.

CONTENTS

CONTENTS

The Granger Collection, NYC

CHAPTER 9

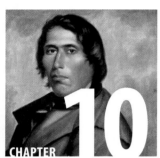

The Granger Collection, NYC

CHAPTER 10

Bettmann/CORBIS

CHAPTER 11

Superstock/Getty Images

CHAPTER **12**

The Granger Collection, NYC

CHAPTER **13**

The Granger Collection, NYC

CHAPTER **14**

CONTENTS

Bettmann/CORBIS

CHAPTER **18**

FEATURES

Thinking Like a HISTORIAN

Connections to TODAY

THEN AND NOW

ECONOMICS SKILLS

MAPS, CHARTS, AND GRAPHS

CHARTS AND GRAPHS

Videos

Interactive Graphs and Charts

Slide Shows

⌄ Interactive Graphic Organizers

⌄ Maps

All maps that appear in your printed textbook are also available in an interactive format in your Online Student Edition.

Presentation Resources

INTERACTIVE WHITEBOARD ACTIVITIES

Chapter 2 Spanish Conquistadores

Chapter 3 New England Colonies
Middle Colonies

Chapter 5 Taxation without Representation

Chapter 7 Contributors to the Constitutional Convention

Chapter 9 The First Party System

Chapter 10 The War of 1812
Dates in History

Chapter 11 The Textile Industry

Chapter 14 Morse Code
Life on a Plantation

Chapter 15 The Life of Frederick Douglass

Chapter 16 Time Line of Events Toward Civil War

LECTURE SLIDES

Chapter 1 Land Bridge Appears
Mayan Civilization
Aztec Civilization
Mound Builders
Eastern Peoples

Chapter 2 The Renaissance
Age of Exploration
The Empires of West Africa
Early Portuguese Explorers
Mexico and Peru
Class Systems in Spain's Empire
Northwest Passage

Chapter 3 Jamestown's Success
New Colonies
The Middle Colonies
The Southern Colonies

Chapter 4 Economies of the Colonies
Mercantilism
The Great Awakening
George Washington

Chapter 5 British Tax Laws
Coercive Acts
Patrick Henry
Second Continental Congress

Chapter 6 Revolutionary War Fighting Forces
Colonial Figures
Revolutionary Battles
Steps to Surrender

Chapter 7 Articles of Confederation
Becoming a New State
Abolishing Slavery
Finding Compromise
Framing the Constitution
Checks and Balances

Chapter 8 Federal System of Powers
Constitutional Rights

Chapter 9 Bank of the United States
George Washington and Foreign Affairs
Political Parties

Chapter 10 Thomas Jefferson
Supreme Court Decisions
The Louisiana Purchase
Lewis and Clark
Tecumseh
The War of 1812

Chapter 11 Technological Advances
Corporation
Steam Power
National Banking System
A New Relationship with the "Old World"
Seminoles

Chapter 12 Andrew Jackson and Changes to Politics
Five Civilized Tribes
Andrew Jackson Economics

Chapter 13 The Cayuse
The Santa Fe Trail
Joseph Smith
Brigham Young

Chapter 14 Agricultural Innovations
Travel Innovations
Working Conditions
Port Cities: Trade
The Cotton Gin
Southern Cities

Chapter 15 Six Major Transcendentalists
Prominent Abolitionists
Women's Education

Chapter 16 The Compromise of 1850
The Kansas-Nebraska Act
Bleeding Kansas
Political Parties in 1856
Lincoln-Douglas Debates
Dred Scott v. *Sandford*
The Election of 1860

Chapter 17 Strengths and Weaknesses of the North and South
Strategies of Winning the War
Who went to war?
Biography of Ulysses S. Grant
Biography of Robert E. Lee
War Democrats and Peace Democrats
Union Generals
Commanders of Civil War
Biography of William Tecumseh Sherman
Outcome of Civil War

Chapter 18 Freedmen's Bureau
Black Codes
The Reconstruction Acts
Carpetbaggers and Scalawags
The New South's Rural Economy
Voting Restrictions for African Americans

networks TEACHER ONLINE RESOURCES

∨ Presentation Resources (continued)

GAMES

Chapter 1 North American Peoples
Chapter 2 Competing for Colonies
Chapter 3 The Middle Colonies
The Southern Colonies
Chapter 4 Early Colonial Government
Culture and Society

Chapter 5 A Call to Arms
Chapter 7 Ratifying the Constitution
A New Plan of Government
Chapter 9 The First President
Early Challenges
Chapter 10 A Time of Conflict
Chapter 17 The War's Final Stages

∨ Worksheets

These printable worksheets are available for every lesson or chapter and can be edited on eAssessment.

- **What Do You Know?**
- **Guided Reading Activity**
- **Vocabulary Builder**
- **Chapter Summaries**
- **Spanish Chapter Summaries**

These printable worksheets are for point-of-use instruction and can be edited on eAssessment.

Chapter 1 Geography and History Activity | Understanding Location: Machu Picchu
21st Century Skills Activity | Communication: Write a Blog Entry

Chapter 2 Geography and History Activity | Cultural Diffusion: Kingdom and Empires in Africa
Geography and History Activity | Understanding Place: Vinland
Geography and History Activity | Understanding Place: Europeans in the Americas
Primary Source Activity | The Conquest of Mexico

Chapter 3 Geography and History Activity | Understanding Place: Jamestown
Geography and History Activity | Dutch Names in New York
Economics of History Activity | Forced Labor and Carolina Rice Plantations

Chapter 4 Economics of History Activity | The Triangular Trade and Mercantilism
Primary Source Activity | The Magna Carta
Geography and History Activity | Understanding Movement: Westward Movement and the Proclamation of 1763

Chapter 5 21st Century Skills Activity | Critical Thinking and Problem Solving: Drawing Conclusions
Primary Source Activity | Boston Massacre Trial
Geography and History Activity | Understanding Movement: "The British Are Coming!"

Chapter 6 Geography and History Activity | Understanding Location: Albany and the Hudson River
Economics of History Activity | The United States and Public Debt
Primary Source Activity | Cornwallis and Greene

Chapter 7 Geography and History Activity | Settlement of Northwest Territory
Primary Source Activity | Shays's Rebellion

Chapter 8 21st Century Skills Activity | Information Literacy: Recognizing Historical Perspectives

Chapter 9 21st Century Skills Activity | Information Literacy: Recognizing Historical Perspectives
Economics of History Activity | The National Debt
Geography and History Activity | Understanding Location: Treaties and Forts of the Northwest Territory

Chapter 10 21st Century Skills Activity | Learning and Innovation: Identify Problems and Solutions
Geography and History Activity | Understanding Human-Environment Interaction: Flora and Fauna of the Louisiana Territory
Primary Source Activity: The Question of War with England

Chapter 11 Geography and History Activity | Understanding Human-Environment Interaction: Industrial Growth
Primary Source Activity | Why We Need a Protective Tariff

Chapter 12 Primary Source Activity | Nullification
Geography and History Activity | Movement: Native American Removal
21st Century Skills | Communication: Writing in Expository Style

Chapter 13 Primary Source Activity | Life on the Trail
Economics of History Activity | Boomtown Economics

Chapter 14 Geography and History Activity | A Landscape for Industry
Primary Source Activity: A Life in Slavery

Chapter 15 Geography and History Activity | Understanding Regions: Religion and Reform
21st Century Skills Activity | Critical Thinking and Problem Solving: Drawing Inferences and Conclusions
Primary Source Activity | Rules for Husbands and Wives

Chapter 16 Geography and History Activity | Understanding Regions: Expansion of Slavery
Primary Source Activity | Speaking on Slavery
21st Century Skills Activity | Critical Thinking and Problem Solving: Distinguish Fact from Opinion

Chapter 17 21st Century Skills Activity | Communication: Write a Letter
Primary Source Activity | Lincoln's Gettysburg Address
Primary Source Activity | Lincoln's Inaugural Addresses

Chapter 18 Primary Source Activity | "Cause of Attack: None Whatever"
21st Century Skills Activity | Analyze Primary Sources: Photographs
Geography and History Activity | Understanding Movement: The Exodusters

Hands-On Chapter Projects and Technology Extensions

Planning the Chapter

Understanding By Design®

All Networks programs have been created using the approach developed by Jay McTighe, coauthor of *Understanding By Design®*.

- The main goal is to focus on the desired results before planning each chapter's instruction.
- The Chapter Planner lists the Enduring Understandings and the Essential Questions that students will learn and use as they study the chapters.
- Identifying the Predictable Misunderstandings will help you anticipate misconceptions students might have as they read the chapters.
- Every chapter provides assessment options to help you measure student understanding.

Standards

Each Chapter Planner identifies the National Council for the Social Studies standards that are covered in the chapter.

CHAPTER 7
A More Perfect Union Planner

UNDERSTANDING BY DESIGN®

Enduring Understanding
- *People, places, and ideas change over time.*

Essential Questions
- *Why do people form governments?*
- *How do new ideas change the way people live?*
- *How do governments change?*

Predictable Misunderstandings
Students may think:
- *The U.S. Constitution was the first document outlining the nation's government.*
- *There was general agreement about the language of the U.S. Constitution.*
- *That there was unanimous popular support for the U.S. Constitution.*

Assessment Evidence
Performance Tasks:
- *Hands-On Chapter Project*
Other Evidence:
- *Interactive Graphic Organizers*
- *What Do You Know? activity*
- *Primary Source Activity*
- *Geography and History Activity*
- *What Do You Think? questions*
- *Written paragraphs*
- *Creating a Constitution Simulation*
- *Online Self-Check Quizzes*
- *Lesson Reviews*
- *Chapter Activities and Assessment*

NCSS Standards covered in "A More Perfect Union"

Learners will understand:

2 TIME, CONTINUITY, AND CHANGE
8. The history of democratic ideals and principles, and how they are represented in documents, artifacts, and symbols
9. The influences of social, geographic, economic, and cultural factors on the history of local areas, states, nations, and the world

3 PEOPLE, PLACES, AND ENVIRONMENTS
5. The concept of regions identifies links between people in different locations according to specific criteria (e.g., physical, economic, social, cultural, or religious)
6. Patterns of demographic and political change, and cultural diffusion in the past and present (e.g., changing national boundaries, migration, and settlement, and the diffusion of and changes in customs and ideas)

6 POWER, AUTHORITY, AND GOVERNANCE
1. Rights are guaranteed in the U.S. Constitution, the supreme law of the land;
2. Fundamental ideas that are the foundation of American constitutional democracy (including those of the U.S. Constitution, popular sovereignty, the rule of law, separation of powers, checks and balances, minority rights, the separation of church and state, and Federalism);
3. Fundamental values of constitutional democracy (e.g., the common good, liberty, justice, equality, and individual dignity)

10 CIVIC IDEALS AND PRACTICES
5. Key documents and excerpts from key sources that define and support democratic ideals and practices (e.g., the U.S. Declaration of Independence, the U.S. Constitution, the Gettysburg Address, the Letter from Birmingham Jail; and international documents such as the Declaration of the Rights of Man and the Universal Declaration of the Rights of Children)
6. The origins and function of major institutions and practices developed to support democratic ideals and practices
7. Key past and present issues involving democratic ideals and practices, as well as the perspectives of various stakeholders in proposing possible solutions to these issues

SUGGESTED PACING GUIDE

Introducing the Chapter	½ Day	Feature: What Do You Think?	½ Day
Lesson 1	1 Day	Lesson 3	1 Day
Lesson 2	1 Day	Chapter Activities and Assessment	½ Day

TOTAL TIME   4 ½ Days

Key for Using the Teacher Edition

SKILL-BASED ACTIVITIES

Types of skill activities found in the Teacher Edition.

V Visual Skills require students to analyze maps, graphs, charts, and photos.
R Reading Skills help students practice reading skills and master vocabulary.
W Writing Skills provide writing opportunities to help students comprehend the text.
C Critical Thinking Skills help students apply and extend what they have learned.
T Technology Skills require students to use digital tools effectively.

Letters are followed by a number when there is more than one of the same type of skill on the page.

DIFFERENTIATED INSTRUCTION

All activities are written for the on-level student unless otherwise marked with the leveled labels below.
BL Beyond Level
AL Approaching Level
ELL English Language Learners
All students benefit from activities that utilize different learning styles. Many activities are marked as below when a particular learning style is highlighted.
Intrapersonal   Naturalist
Logical/Mathematical   Kinesthetic
Visual/Spatial   Auditory/Musical
Verbal/Linguistic   Interpersonal

Chapter 7 Planner   173A

Pacing Guide

Time management suggestions for teaching the chapter are provided.

Skills-Based Activities

Each lesson includes a variety of print-based and digital activities designed to teach a range of skills, including:

C Critical Thinking Skills
V Visual Skills
R Reading Skills
T Technology Skills
W Writing Skills

Differentiated Instruction

Activities are designed to meet the needs of:

BL Beyond Level
AL Approaching Level
ELL English Language Learners

In addition, activities are designed to address a range of *learning styles*.

Don't forget! You can customize all your Lesson Plans online.

Planning the Chapter (continued)

Planners
The Chapter Opener and Lesson Planners provide a snapshot of the resources available to enhance and extend learning. The activities are organized by skill type, level, and learning style.

Student Objectives
Using *Understanding By Design®* as the framework, the planners outline the content and skills that students will be expected to know.

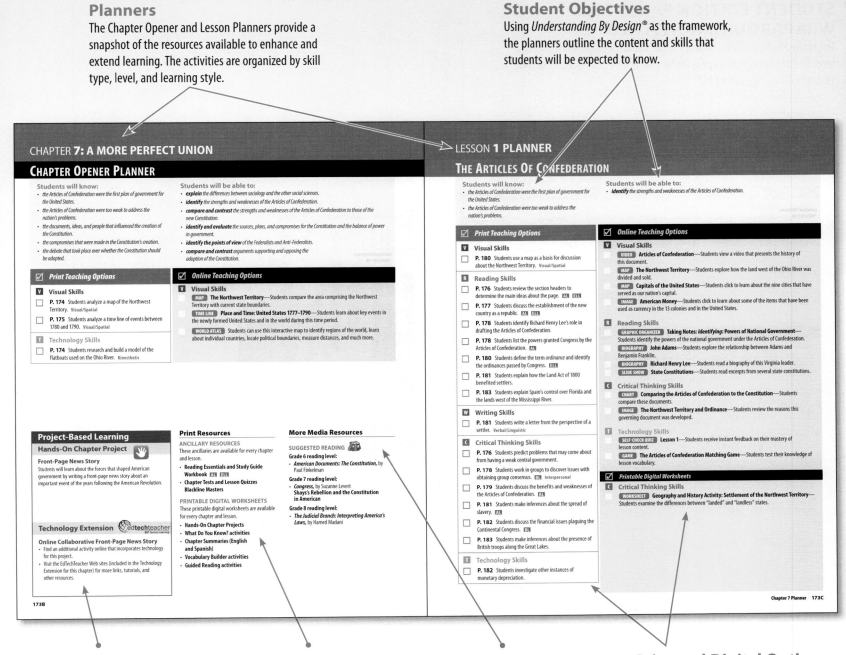

CHAPTER 7: A MORE PERFECT UNION

CHAPTER OPENER PLANNER

LESSON 1 PLANNER

THE ARTICLES OF CONFEDERATION

Project-Based Learning
Cumulative projects bring the subject to life for the student and help you assess your students' level of understanding. The program includes Hands-On Projects as well as Digital Hands-On Projects.

Print Resources
Every chapter includes printable worksheets, including tests, quizzes, and materials to build vocabulary and improve reading comprehension.

Make It Relevant
Enrich and extend the content with videos and books.

Print and Digital Options
Each planner has two columns listing print-based activities and online digital assets.

Digital assets include:
- interactive maps
- photos
- animations
- slide shows
- whiteboard activities
- lesson videos
- worksheets

Using the Wraparound Resources and Activities

STUDENT EDITION PAGES AND WRAPAROUND ACTIVITIES

The entire Student Edition appears in the Teacher Edition. Activities and recommended resources appear in the side and bottom margins of the Teacher Edition, at point of use.

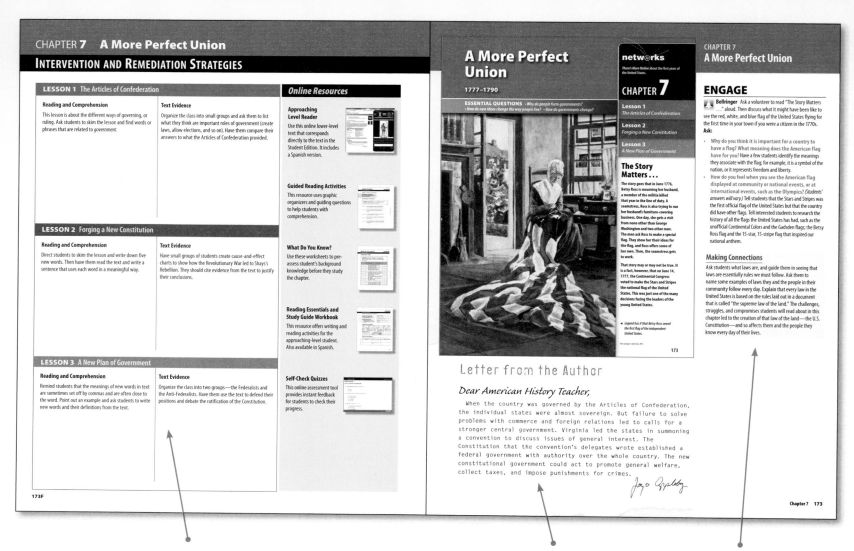

Intervention and Remediation
Each Chapter Planner concludes with intervention and remediation strategies for every lesson, as well as Online Resources that can be used to help students understand the content.

Author Letter
Each chapter begins with the author's perspective about key concepts found in the chapter.

Introduce the Chapter
Each chapter begins with activities to engage students' interest in the chapter's content.

Don't forget! You can customize all your Lesson Plans online.

Using the Wraparound Resources and Activities (continued)

Step Into The Place/Step Into The Time

These two pages of the Chapter Opener are designed to help students locate the region in the world that they will learn about, along with important historical events that took place in that region.

The Teacher Edition contains activities and discussion questions for these features.

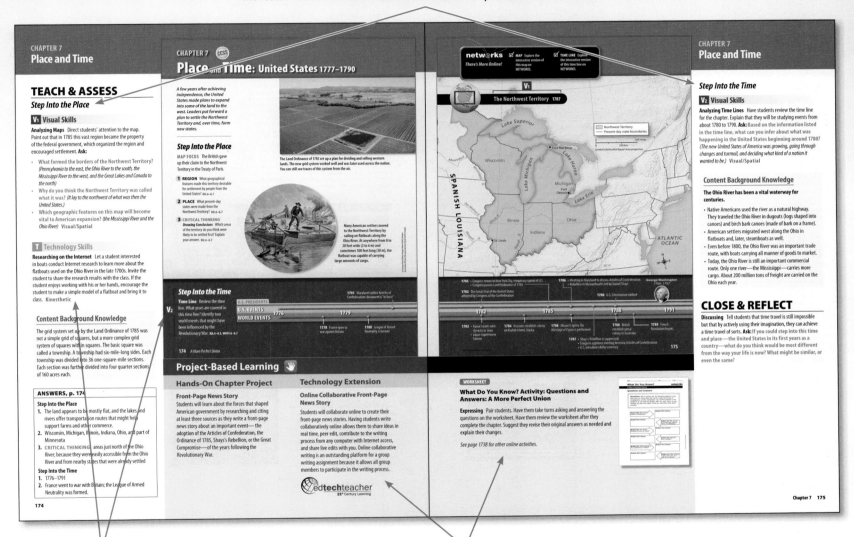

Print-Based Activities

Activities in the margins correspond to the text in the Student Edition. These activities are coded to indicate their level and the learning style they support.

Online Digital Activities

Online digital activities for the lesson appear at the bottom of each page. The gray icon indicates the type of activity available in the online Teacher Center. Activities include interactive whiteboard activities, animations, videos, interactive maps, images, and worksheets. Activities can be projected or used on your classroom whiteboard. Worksheets can be edited and printed, or assigned online, depending on student access to technology.

Using the Wraparound Resources and Activities (continued)

ENGAGE

Every lesson begins with an Engage activity designed to motivate students and focus their attention on the lesson topic.

Guiding Questions

Guiding Questions in the Student Edition point out key knowledge that students need to acquire to be able to answer the chapter's Essential Questions.

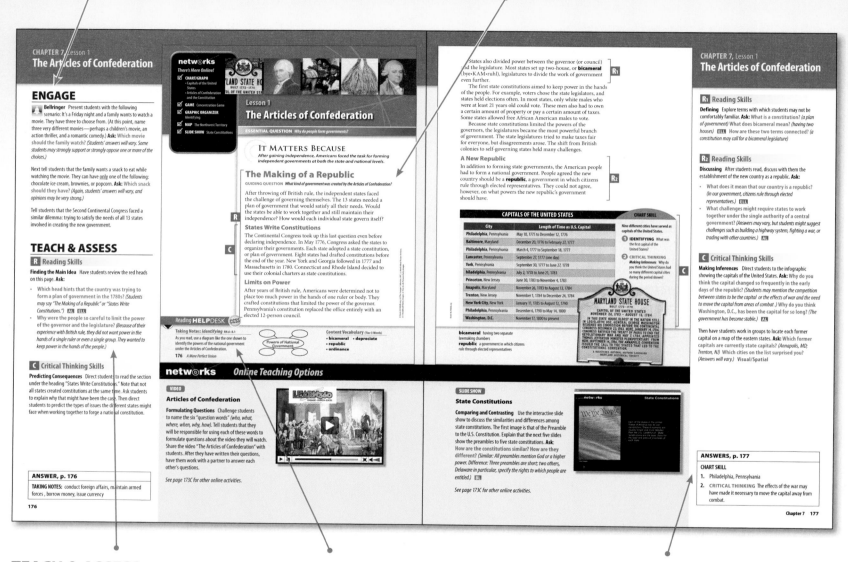

TEACH & ASSESS

Teach & Assess is the core of the lesson. It contains activities, lecture notes, background information, and discussion questions to teach the lesson.

Reading Help Desk

- Content Vocabulary
- Academic Vocabulary
- Note-Taking Activity and Graphic Organizer

Answers

Answers to questions and activities in the Student Edition appear in the bottom corner of the Teacher Edition pages.

networks

Don't forget! You can customize all your Lesson Plans online.

Using the Wraparound Resources and Activities (continued)

Brackets

Brackets on the Student Edition page correspond to teaching strategies and activities in the Teacher Edition. As you teach the lesson, the brackets show you where to use these activities and strategies.

Progress Check

A progress check appears at the end of each topic in the Student Edition to help gauge student reading comprehension.

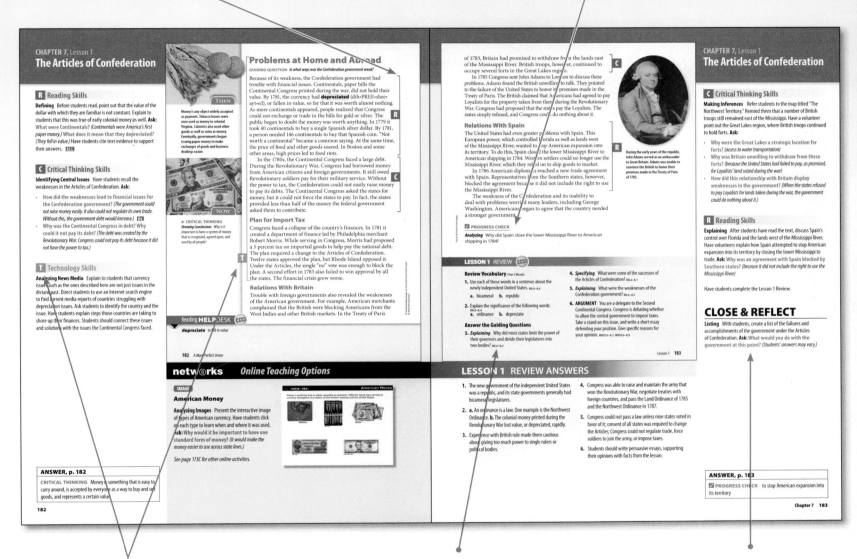

Letters

The letters on the reduced Student Edition page identify the type of activity. See the key on the first planning page of each chapter to learn about the different types of activities.

Common Core State Standards

Questions and activities throughout the Student Edition are correlated to the Reading Standards for Literacy in History/Social Studies 6–8 (RH.6–8) and the Writing Standards for Literacy in History/Social Studies 6–8 (WH.6–8).

CLOSE & REFLECT

Each lesson ends with activities designed to help students link the content to the lesson's Guiding Questions and the chapter's Essential Questions.

Special Features

America's Literature

This program includes *America's Literature* features which represent a wide range of time periods. Each *America's Literature* feature analyzes an excerpt from a famous piece of American fiction and describes its historical lessons.

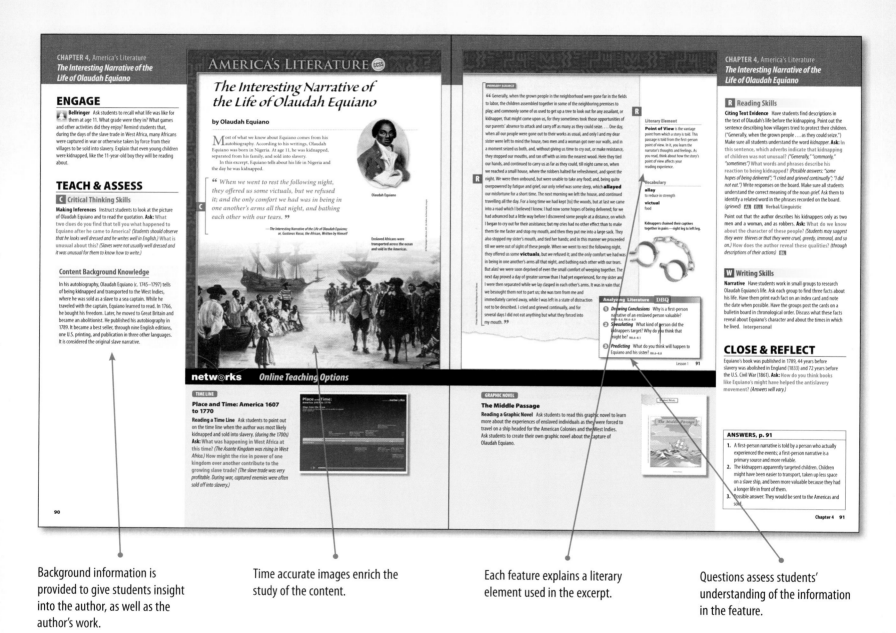

Background information is provided to give students insight into the author, as well as the author's work.

Time accurate images enrich the study of the content.

Each feature explains a literary element used in the excerpt.

Questions assess students' understanding of the information in the feature.

Special Features (continued)

What Do You Think?

This program includes a number of *What Do You Think?* features. Students are asked to analyze different points of view on current world issues and events.

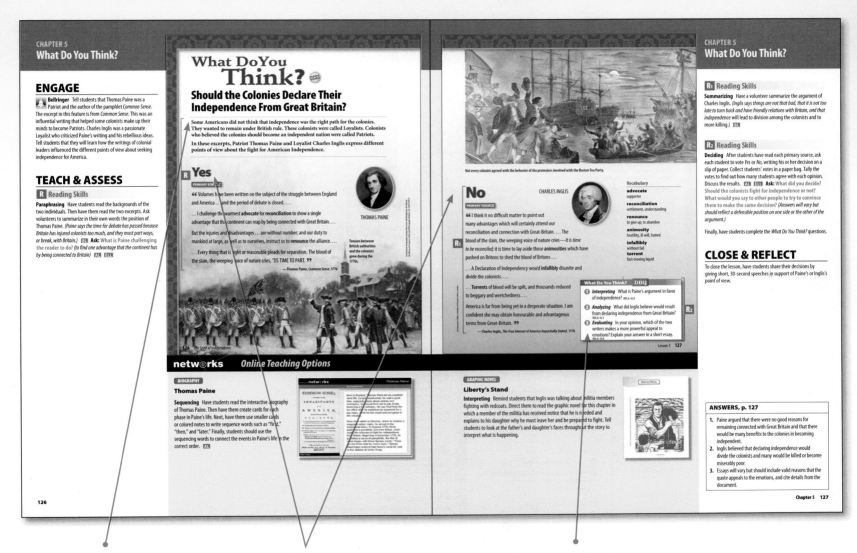

Background information is provided to help students understand why there are opposing viewpoints about the issue or event.

Two primary sources are presented that answer the *What Do You Think?* question.

Questions assess students' understanding of both points of view and ask students to make comparisons between the arguments.

HOW TO USE THE TEACHER EDITION

Activities and Assessment

Chapter Activities

Each chapter ends with the following:

- Exploring the Essential Question Writing Activity
- 21st Century Skills Activity
- Thinking Like a Historian Activity
- Visual Literacy Activity

Chapter Assessment

Each chapter ends with the following:

- Review the Guiding Questions Standardized Test Practice
- Analyzing Documents Questions and Writing Activities

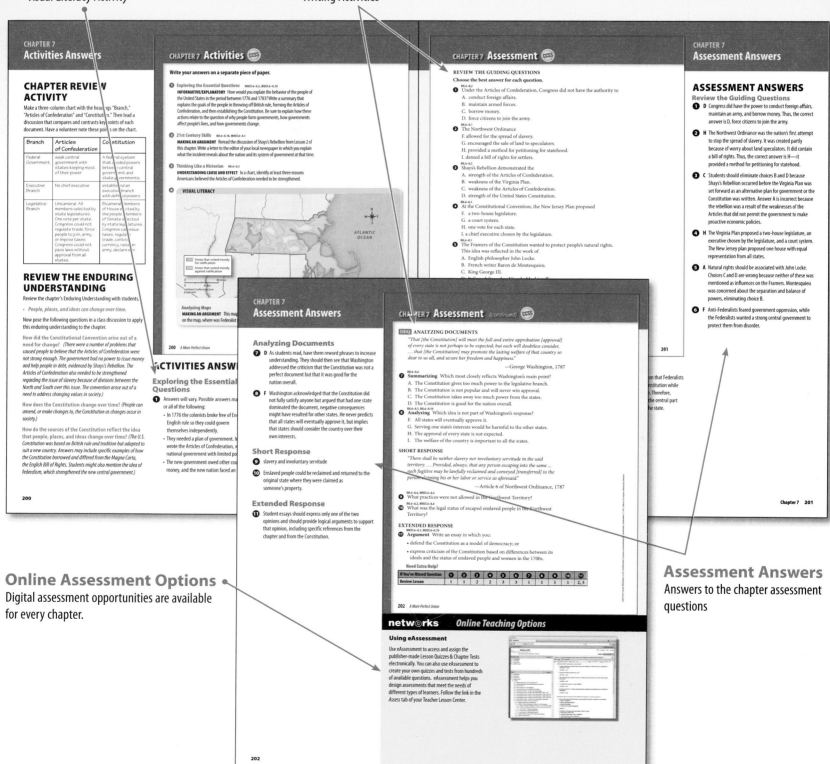

Online Assessment Options

Digital assessment opportunities are available for every chapter.

Assessment Answers

Answers to the chapter assessment questions

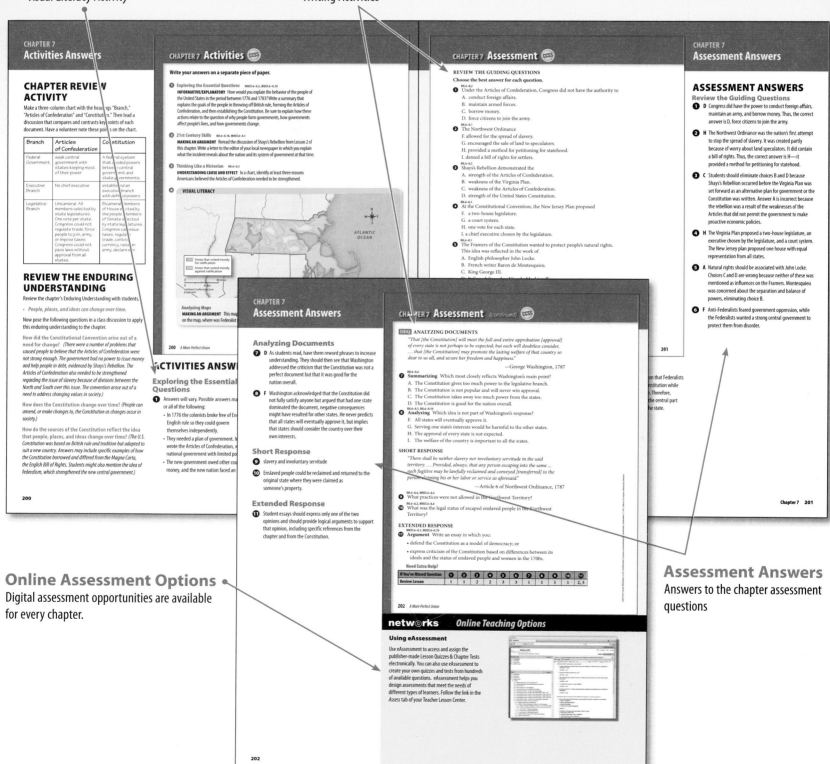

Correlation of *Discovering Our Past: A History of the United States, Early Years* to the Revised NCSS Thematic Strands

The revised standards continue to be focused on ten themes, like the original standards. They represent a way of categorizing knowledge about the human experience, and they constitute the organizing strands that should thread through a social studies program.

Theme and Learning Expectation	Student Edition Chapter/Lesson
1. CULTURE	
1. "Culture" refers to the socially transmitted behaviors, beliefs, values, traditions, institutions, and ways of living together for a group of people	**Ch 1** L2–3; **Ch 4** L3; **Ch 12** L2
2. Concepts such as beliefs, values, institutions, cohesion, diversity, accommodation, adaptation, assimilation, and dissonance	**Ch 2** L3; **Ch 12** L2; **Ch 14** L2, L4
3. How culture influences the ways in which human groups solve the problems of daily living	**Ch 1** L2–L3; **Ch 3** L1; **Ch 4** L3; **Ch 14** L4
4. That the beliefs, values, and behaviors of a culture form an integrated system that helps shape the activities and ways of life that define a culture	**Ch 1** L2–L3; **Ch 3** L2–L3; **Ch 4** L3; **Ch 14** L4
5. How individuals learn the elements of their culture through interactions with others, and how individuals learn of other cultures through communication and study	**Ch 3** L1; **Ch 4** L3; **Ch 10** L2
6. That culture may change in response to changing needs, concerns, social, political, and geographic conditions	**Ch 2** L3; **Ch 11** L2; **Ch 12** L2
7. How people from different cultures develop different values and ways of interpreting experience	**Ch 1** L3; **Ch 2** L3; **Ch 10** L2
8. That language, behaviors, and beliefs of different cultures can both contribute to and pose barriers to cross-cultural understanding	**Ch 2** L3; **Ch 10** L2
2. TIME, CONTINUITY, AND CHANGE	
1. The study of the past provides representation of the history of communities, nations, and the world	**Ch 4** L3; **Ch 5** L2; **Ch 10** L2; **Ch 17** L5
2. Concepts such as: chronology, causality, change, conflict, complexity, multiple perspectives, primary and secondary sources, and cause and effect	**Ch 4** L3; **Ch 5** L4; **Ch 6** L1–L4; **Ch 17** L5
3. That learning about the past requires the interpretation of sources, and that using varied sources provides the potential for a more balanced interpretive record of the past	**Ch 5** L3 WDYT; **Ch 7** L2 WDYT; **Ch 13** L2 WDYT; **Ch 16** L3 WDYT
4. That historical interpretations of the same event may differ on the basis of such factors as conflicting evidence from varied sources, national or cultural perspectives, and the point of view of the researcher	**Ch 5** L3 WDYT; **Ch 13** L2 WDYT; **Ch 16** L3 WDYT
5. Key historical periods and patterns of change within and across cultures (e.g., the rise and fall of ancient civilizations, the development of technology, the rise of modern nation-states, and the establishment and breakdown of colonial systems)	**Ch 2** L1; **Ch 6** L1–L4; **Ch 17** L5
6. The origins and influences of social, cultural, political, and economic systems	**Ch 2** L3; **Ch 9** L1; **Ch 10** L1
7. The contributions of key persons, groups, and events from the past and their influence on the present	**Ch 5** L1, L3–L4; **Ch 6** L1–L4; **Ch 10** L1; **Ch 15** L1–L3; **Ch 16** L2–L3; **Ch 17** L2–L4
8. The history of democratic ideals and principles, and how they are represented in documents, artifacts and symbols	**Ch 5** L4; **Ch 7** L2–L3; **Ch 8** L1; **Ch 9** L1
9. The influences of social, geographic, economic, and cultural factors on the history of local areas, states, nations, and the world	**Ch 2** L1, L4; **Ch 7** L1; **Ch 10** L2; **Ch 14** L2, L4; **Ch 16** L3

Theme and Learning Expectation	Student Edition Chapter/Lesson
3. PEOPLE, PLACES, AND ENVIRONMENTS	
1. The theme of people, places, and environments involves the study of the relationships between human populations in different locations and geographic phenomena such as climate, vegetation, and natural resources	**Ch 1** L1; **Ch 2** L1–L2; **Ch 3** L1; **Ch 11** L2; **Ch 13** L1–L2, L4
2. Concepts such as: location, region, place, migration, as well as human and physical systems	**Ch 3** L1; **Ch 13** L1–L2, L4
3. Past and present changes in physical systems, such as seasons, climate, and weather, and the water cycle, in both national and global contexts	**Ch 1** L1; **Ch 3** L1–L2, L4
4. The roles of different kinds of population centers in a region or nation	**Ch 13** L1–L2, L4; **Ch 14** L2, L4; **Ch 18** L3
5. The concept of regions identifies links between people in different locations according to specific criteria (e.g., physical, economic, social, cultural, or religious)	**Ch 4** L1; **Ch 7** L1; **Ch 13** L1–L2, L4; **Ch 18** L3
6. Patterns of demographic and political change, and cultural diffusion in the past and present (e.g., changing national boundaries, migration, and settlement, and the diffusion of and changes in customs and ideas)	**Ch 2** L1–L4; **Ch 3** L2; **Ch 7** L1; **Ch 11** L2; **Ch 12** L1–L2; **Ch 13** L1–L2, L4
7. Human modifications of the environment	**Ch 11** L2; **Ch 13** L1–L2, L4
8. Factors that contribute to cooperation and conflict among peoples of the nation and world, including language, religion, and political beliefs	**Ch 2** L1, L4; **Ch 3** L2; **Ch 4** L1; **Ch 6** L1, L4; **Ch 8** L1–L2; **Ch 12** L2; **Ch 13** L3; **Ch 17** L1
9. The use of a variety of maps, globes, graphic representations, and geospatial technologies to help investigate the relationships among people, places, and environments	**Ch 1** L1–L3 ; **Ch 2** L1; **Ch 10** L2; **Ch 13** L1–L3; **Ch 17** L1
4. INDIVIDUAL DEVELOPMENT AND IDENTITY	
1. The study of individual development and identity helps us know that individuals change physically, cognitively, and emotionally over time	**Ch 2** L3–L4; **Ch 4** L1; **Ch 15** L2
2. Concepts such as: development, change, personality, learning, individual, family, groups, motivation, and perception	**Ch 1** L2–L3; **Ch 4** L3; **Ch 5** L2; **Ch 11** L2
3. How factors such as physical endowment, interests, capabilities, learning, motivation, personality, perception, and beliefs influence individual development and identity	**Ch 2** L3–L4; **Ch 5** L3; **Ch 6** L2
4. How personal, social, cultural, and environmental factors contribute to the development and the growth of personal identity	**Ch 2** L3; **Ch 11** L2; **Ch 14** L4
5. That individuals' choices influence identity and development	**Ch 2** L2–L3; **Ch 3** L1
6. That perceptions are interpretations of information about individuals and events, and can be influenced by bias and stereotypes	**Ch 9** L3; **Ch 12** L1
5. INDIVIDUALS, GROUPS, AND INSTITUTIONS	
1. This theme helps us know how individuals are members of groups and institutions, and influence and shape those groups and institutions	**Ch 4** L3–L4; **Ch 5** L4; **Ch 6** L4; **Ch 17** L1
2. Concepts such as: mores, norms, status, role, socialization, ethnocentrism, cultural diffusion, competition, cooperation, conflict, race, ethnicity, and gender	**Ch 1** L3; **Ch 2** L4; **Ch 4** L4; **Ch 16** L1
3. Institutions are created to respond to changing individual and group needs	**Ch 7** L1–L3; **Ch 9** L1–L3; **Ch 17** L3
4. That ways in which young people are socialized include similarities as well as differences across cultures	**Ch 4** L3; **Ch 11** L1; **Ch 15** L1
5. That groups and institutions change over time	**Ch 1** L2–L3; **Ch 2** L3; **Ch 4** L1–L3; **Ch 7** L1–L3
6. That cultural diffusion occurs when groups migrate	**Ch 2** L1, L3; **Ch 4** L3–L4

Theme and Learning Expectation	Student Edition Chapter/Lesson
7. That institutions may promote or undermine social conformity	**Ch 4** L3; **Ch 7** L1; **Ch 8** L1–L2; **Ch 16** L1; **Ch 17** L1
8. That when two or more groups with differing norms and beliefs interact, accommodation or conflict may result	**Ch 2** L1, L3; **Ch 9** L3; **Ch 10** L3–L4; **Ch 12** L2; **Ch 16** L1
9. That groups and institutions influence culture in a variety of ways	**Ch 4** L3; **Ch 7** L1; **Ch 8** L1–L2; **Ch 11** L3
6. POWER, AUTHORITY, AND GOVERNANCE	
1. Rights are guaranteed in the U.S. Constitution, the supreme law of the land	**Ch 7** L1–L3; **Ch 8** L1–L2; **Ch 18** L2
2. Fundamental ideas that are the foundation of American constitutional democracy (including those of the U.S. Constitution, popular sovereignty, the rule of law, separation of powers, checks and balances, minority rights, the separation of church and state, and Federalism)	**Ch 7** L1–L3; **Ch 8** L1, L2; **Ch 9** L1; **Ch 18** L2
3. Fundamental values of constitutional democracy (e.g., the common good, liberty, justice, equality, and individual dignity)	**Ch 7** L1–L3; **Ch 8** L1–L2; **Ch 18** L2
4. The ideologies and structures of political systems that differ from those of the United States	**Ch 8** L1–L2; **Ch 10** L3–L4; **Ch 18** L1, L3–L4
5. The ways in which governments meet the needs and wants of citizens, manage conflict, and establish order and society	**Ch 9** L1–L2; **Ch 12** L2; **Ch 16** L2; **Ch 18** L1–L3
7. PRODUCTION, DISTRIBUTION, AND CONSUMPTION	
1. Individuals, government, and society experience scarcity because human wants and needs exceed what can be produced from available resources	**Ch 2** L1, L3; **Ch 11** L1; **Ch 17** L3
2. How choices involve trading off the expected value of one opportunity gained against the expected value of the best alternative	**Ch 10** L1, L4
3. The economic choices that people make have both present and future consequences	**Ch 3** L4; **Ch 4** L1; **Ch 12** L1–L2; **Ch 14** L1, L3; **Ch 18** L4
4. Economic incentives affect people's behavior and may be regulated by rules or laws	**Ch 10** L3; **Ch 11** L3; **Ch 14** L1, L3; **Ch 18** L4
5. That banks and other financial institutions channel funds from savers to borrowers and investors	**Ch 11** L3; **Ch 12** L3
6. The economic gains that result from specialization and exchange as well as the trade-offs	**Ch 11** L1; **Ch 14** L1
7. How markets bring buyers and sellers together to exchange goods and services	**Ch 3** L4; **Ch 4** L1; **Ch 11** L1
8. How goods and services are allocated in a market economy through the influence of prices on decisions about production and consumption	**Ch 9** L1; **Ch 10** L3; **Ch 11** L1
9. How the overall levels of income, employment, and prices are determined by the interaction of households, firms, and the government	**Ch 9** L1; **Ch 10** L3
8. SCIENCE, TECHNOLOGY, AND SOCIETY	
1. Science is a result of empirical study of the natural world, and technology is the application of knowledge to accomplish tasks	**Ch 2** L1–L2; **Ch 11** L1; **Ch 14** L1
2. Society often turns to science and technology to solve problems	**Ch 4** L1; **Ch 11** L2
3. Our lives today are media and technology dependent	**Ch 11** L1–L2
4. Science and technology have had both positive and negative impacts upon individuals, societies, and the environment in the past and present	**Ch 11** L1–L2; **Ch 14** L1, L3
5. Science and technology have changed peoples' perceptions of the social and natural world, as well as their relationship to the land, economy and trade, their concept of security, and their major daily activities	**Ch 2** L1; **Ch 11** L1–L2; **Ch 14** L1, L3

Theme and Learning Expectation	Student Edition Chapter/Lesson
6. Values, beliefs, and attitudes that have been influenced by new scientific and technological knowledge (e.g., invention of the printing press, conceptions of the universe, applications of atomic energy, and genetic discoveries);	**Ch 2** L1; **Ch 11** L1
7. How media are created and received depends upon cultural contexts	**Ch 4** L3; **Ch 15** L1
8. Science and technology sometimes create ethical issues that test our standards and values	**Ch 14** L1, L3
9. The need for laws and policies to govern scientific and technological applications	**Ch 11** L1; **Ch 14** L1
10. That there are gaps in access to science and technology around the world	**Ch 2** L2; **Ch 14** L1, L4
9. GLOBAL CONNECTIONS	
1. Global connections have existed in the past and increased rapidly in current times	**Ch 2** L1–L2; **Ch 4** L1
2. Global factors such as cultural, economic, and political connections are changing the places in which people live (e.g., through trade, migration, increased travel, and communication)	**Ch 2** L4; **Ch 13** L1–L4
3. Spatial relationships that relate to ongoing global issues (e.g., pollution, poverty, disease, and conflict) affect the health and well-being of Earth and its inhabitants	**Ch 2** L3–L4; **Ch 4** L3
4. Global problems and possibilities are not generally caused or developed by any one nation	**Ch 2** L1–L4
5. Global connections may make cultures more alike or increase their sense of distinctiveness	**Ch 2** L1–L4; **Ch 4** L1
6. Universal human rights cut across cultures but are not necessarily understood in the same way in all cultures	**Ch 2** L3; **Ch 15** L2
10. CIVIC IDEALS AND PRACTICES	
1. The theme of civic ideals and practices helps us to learn about and know how to work for the betterment of society	**Ch 8** L1–L2; **Ch 15** L1–L3; **Ch 18** L1–L2
2. Concepts and ideals such as: individual dignity, liberty, justice, equality, individual rights, responsibility, majority and minority rights, and civil dissent	**Ch 8** L1–L2; **Ch 15** L1–L2; **Ch 18** L1–L2
3. Key practices involving the rights and responsibilities of citizenship and the exercise of citizenship (e.g., respecting the rule of law and due process, voting, serving on a jury, researching issues, making informed judgments, expressing views on issues, and collaborating with others to take civic action)	**Ch 8** L1–L2; **Ch 15** L3; **Ch 18** L1–L2
4. The common good, and the rule of law	**Ch 8** L1–L2; **Ch 10** L1
5. Key documents and excerpts from key sources that define and support democratic ideals and practices (e.g., the U.S. Declaration of Independence, the U.S. Constitution, the Gettysburg Address, the Letter from Birmingham Jail; and international documents such as the Declaration of the Rights of Man, and the Universal Declaration of the Rights of Children)	**Ch 5** L4; **Ch 7** L2–L3; **Ch 8** L1–L2; **Ch 15** L3
6. The origins and function of major institutions and practices developed to support democratic ideals and practices	**Ch 7** L2–L3; **Ch 8** L1–L2; **Ch 9** L1; **Ch 12** L3
7. Key past and present issues involving democratic ideals and practices, as well as the perspectives of various stakeholders in proposing possible solutions to these issues	**Ch 7** L2–L3; **Ch 16** L2
8. The importance of becoming informed in order to make positive civic contributions	**Ch 5** L3 WDYT; **Ch 7** L2 WDYT; **Ch 8** L2; **Ch 13** L2 WDYT; **Ch 16** L3 WDYT

Common Core State Standards for English Language Arts and Literacy in History/Social Studies, Science, and Technical Subjects

The following pages contain correlation charts to the Common Core State Standards. The first chart contains the College and Career Readiness (CCR) Anchor Standards for Reading. The chart that follows the CCR Anchor Standards for Reading chart identifies specifically what students should understand and be able to do by the end of grades 6–8. The CCR and grade-specific standards are necessary complements—the former providing broad standards, the latter providing additional specificity—that together define the skills and understandings that all students must demonstrate.

College and Career Readiness Anchor Standards for Reading

Key Ideas and Details

1. Read closely to determine what the text says explicitly and to make logical inferences from it; cite specific textual evidence when writing or speaking to support conclusions drawn from the text.

Student Edition:
Step into the Place: Critical Thinking: 322
Reading Help Desk: Taking Notes: 28, 34, 42, 49, 60, 64, 69, 112, 116, 144, 152, 164, 176, 194, 206, 268, 272, 278, 285, 296, 336, 360, 365, 404, 408, 428, 465, 474, 504; Reading Strategy: 269, 462
Progress Check: 11, 17, 21, 30, 33, 45, 66, 68, 70, 72, 104, 155, 157, 169, 179, 211, 214, 248, 255, 261, 271, 277, 282, 286, 329, 361, 381, 386, 393, 397, 406, 409, 435, 438, 442, 443, 461, 475, 484, 496, 497, 500
Critical Thinking: 9, 10, 21, 35, 37, 44, 53, 72, 85, 105, 122, 159, 167, 168, 190, 254, 270, 275, 279, 288, 289, 306, 327, 328, 367, 380, 395, 396, 413, 436, 438, 463, 500, 502
Thinking Like a Historian: 145, 165, 280
America's Literature: Analyzing: 473; Recalling: 421; Speculating: 91
What Do You Think? feature: Analyzing: 127
Lesson Review: Analyzing: 53, 77, 95, 119, 329, 335, 352, 407, 419, 432, 443, 464, 503; Describing: 7, 13, 21, 41, 63, 72, 125; Discussing: 271; Evaluating: 329; Explaining: 21, 41, 48, 100, 133, 151, 183, 357, 419, 438; Identifying: 105, 157, 163, 199, 301, 364, 381, 390; Listing: 33, 169, 315, 369, 386, 432; Making Inferences: 438; Recalling: 261; Specifying: 183, 191, 199, 352, 364, 438, 443; Summarizing: 471
Chapter Activities & Assessment: Thinking Like a Historian: 106, 216, 446; Review the Guiding Questions: 23, 55, 79, 107, 135, 171, 201, 217, 263, 291, 319, 343, 371, 399, 423, 447, 489, 515; DBQ: 24, 202; Short Response: 344, 424

Teacher Edition:
ENGAGE: 1, 25, 42, 57, 141, 203, 243, 265, 272, 293, 358, 401, 449, 458, 481, 491, 498
TEACH & ASSESS: R7, C7, R$_1$8, R$_2$8, R$_1$9, C$_1$10, R11, R$_1$12, C12, R$_2$12, R13, C$_1$15, R16, O18, R$_2$19, C19, C20, O20, R21, C30, O30, V34, R35, O35, V36, R$_1$37, C39, V40, C$_1$40, C$_2$40, C41, R42, O44, R45, V46, C48, C50, R51, R53, R60, C61, O62, C64, R64, O65, O66, R69, R71, R72, O75, C76, R77, C77, R2 84, R85, C86, C$_2$89, R91, R93, R95, C96, C97, R$_1$102, C104, R111, R112, C$_2$113, C116, R120, R121, R$_2$122, R$_1$124, O124, R$_2$127, R129, C$_1$131, C$_2$131, O131, O132, R133, O143, C144, R145, C146, C147, R$_2$149, C151, C152, O154, C$_1$156, R158, R161, C$_1$162, C$_2$163, C166, C167, R168, C176, C177, R$_2$178, O178, C179, C181, R181, C183, C188, O188, O192, C197, R$_2$197, O197, R207, O207, C$_1$209, O209, C211, R$_2$211, R$_3$213, V214, R215, C215, C245, C246, O247, C249, C250, R253, C$_2$254, C257, O257, C258, C$_2$259, R259, C$_1$260, R260, O260, O268, R269, W269, R$_1$270, C$_1$271, C$_2$271, R272, C$_2$275, O278, C279, R$_2$281, O281, W284, R$_1$287, R$_2$287, C$_1$288, C$_2$288, O295, R296, C297, C301, C304, C$_1$307, C$_2$307, C309, R310, R311, O312, C313, R313, C$_1$316, C$_2$316, C$_1$317, V324, O327, C$_1$328, R329, MC329, R331, C332, R333, O333, C$_1$334, R$_1$335, R338, R339, R340, C349, C$_2$350, R353, R$_1$354, R$_2$354, R355, O355, R357, R$_1$360, R$_2$360, R364, R$_2$365, C$_1$366, R367, C$_1$367, R$_1$368, C$_1$369, R377, R$_1$378, C380, R$_1$381, R382, C382, C383, O383, C384, R386, R$_2$387, C387, O388, O389, R390, R391, C$_1$392, R393, O394, C395, O395, R$_2$397, O403, C404, R$_1$405, V410, C410, C416, O416, C418, R418, C$_1$421, C426, R$_2$428, O430, C432, R434, C435, C436, C438, C442, R$_1$443, C443, C451, C453, O453, C454, R456, C460, R460, R464, R465, R466, R467, C$_1$468, C$_2$468, R471, C472, C$_2$473, R$_2$475, O475, R477, C477, R482, O482, C483, C484, R$_2$485, C486, C493, R494, C495, R496, C496, R497, R$_1$499, C499, R$_2$499, O500, R501, R502, C503, C504, R504, R$_1$506, R$_2$506, R507, R$_2$508, C510, R510, R$_2$512
CLOSE & REFLECT: 63, 68, 89, 119, 127, 133, 157, 163, 169, 175, 183, 191, 199, 215, 245, 251, 255, 261, 267, 277, 284, 289, 307, 315, 329, 341, 352, 357, 359, 364, 438, 443, 464, 471, 493, 507, 513
CHAPTER ASSESSMENT: CRA 54, REU 216, CRA 262, CRA 318, CRA 342, CRA 370, CRA 398, CRA 422, CRA 514
INTERVENTION AND REMEDIATION STRATEGIES: 1F, 25G, 57G, 81G, 109G, 141G, 173F, 203E, 243F, 265G, 293F, 321F, 345G, 373G, 401F, 425F, 449H, 491G

Codes used for the Teacher Edition pages are the initial caps of the activities.

College and Career Readiness Anchor Standards for Reading

2. Determine central ideas or themes of a text and analyze their development; summarize the key supporting details and ideas.

Student Edition:

Reading Help Desk: Taking Notes: 4, 8, 14, 84, 101, 120, 128, 246, 330, 382, 391, 415, 433, 494, 508; Reading Strategy: 18, 104, 312, 340, 410, 456, 466
Progress Check: 6, 7, 13, 37, 41, 48, 53, 61, 77, 87, 89, 95, 98, 105, 114, 117, 119, 121, 123, 125, 133, 147, 150, 159, 181, 189, 191, 199, 254, 284, 306, 307, 315, 333, 338, 341, 350, 352, 357, 364, 369, 384, 396, 419, 455, 463, 466, 467, 469, 480, 503, 507, 511
Critical Thinking: 52, 186, 249, 356, 418
Economics Skill: Describing: 349
America's Literature: Explaining: 317, 473; Expressing: 317
What Do You Think? feature: Making Inferences: 445
Lesson Review: Analyzing: 364; Comparing: 471; Describing: 115, 163, 191, 215, 255, 307, 315, 335, 341, 432, 503, 507; Discussing: 386, 397, 414; Drawing Conclusions: 443; Evaluating: 457, 464, 471, 480, 487; Explaining: 7, 21, 33, 53, 63, 68, 77, 95, 105, 115, 119, 125, 157, 183, 199, 211, 215, 255, 271, 277, 284, 289, 301, 315, 329, 335, 352, 364, 369, 381, 386, 390, 397, 407, 432, 443, 464, 471, 480, 487, 497, 507, 513; Identifying: 33, 115, 438; Identifying the Main Ideas: 89; Making Connections: 357; Making Generalizations: 48; Making Inferences: 315, 480; Recalling: 251; Specifying: 357; Speculating: 497; Summarizing: 48, 72, 100,105, 133, 151, 163, 251, 255, 277, 284, 289, 307, 381, 513
Chapter Activities & Assessment: 21st Century Skills: 318; Thinking Like a Historian: 170, 422; Review the Guiding Questions: 23, 55, 79, 107, 135, 171, 201, 217, 263, 291, 319, 343, 371, 399, 423, 447, 489, 515; DBQ: 24, 172, 218, 264, 292, 320, 372, 400, 424, 490, 516; Short Response: 24, 80, 108, 172, 202, 218, 372, 448, 490, 516

Teacher Edition:

ENGAGE: 109, 365, 425, 474, 508
TEACH & ASSESS: $R_2$4, R5, C6, C9, $C_2$10, O10, R14, C16, $R_1$19, R28, $R_1$30, R31, O31, C35, O37, R38, V45, O45, R49, $R_1$66, R70, O70, O74, R76, $R_1$84, $R_1$86, O86, R89, O91, R97, $R_2$98, R103, R114, R116, O121, R123, R125, R130, R146, $R_1$149, $R_2$155, $C_2$156, O156, O160, $R_1$164, $R_2$167, O167, O175, R176, $R_2$177, R179, O180, C182, R185, $R_2$188, R189, O190, $R_1$192, $R_1$195, C196, C198, $C_2$209, R212, C212, $R_1$213, O213, O214, R248, R250, R251, R252, R258, O259, O273, R280, R282, $R_1$283, R285, O297, O297, R304, O306, R309, R311, R312, C312, C325, $R_1$327, $R_2$327, $C_3$328, O328, $R_3$335, $R_2$348, R349, O349, R351, $R_2$352, C354, R359, R361, O363, O366, O368, $R_2$383, $R_1$384, O384, $R_1$387, R394, R396, O396, $R_1$397, R404, R405, C407, R409, R411, O411, R412, R413, O417, $C_2$419, R421, $C_2$421, O421, $R_2$429, $R_1$435, O436, R437, $R_2$443, R444, $C_2$444, O444, O445, $R_2$452, R453, O455, R457, O459, O461, C465, R468, $C_2$469, R479, C479, O486, O496, R500, O501, O502, R503, C506, R511, O511, $R_1$512, C512
CLOSE & REFLECT: 7, 53, 77, 105, 151, 271, 397, 407, 419, 480, 497
CHAPTER ASSESSMENT: REU 22, REU 54, REU 78, CRA 106, REU 134, REU 170, CRA 200, REU 200, CRA 216, REU 262, REU 290, REU 318, REU 342, REU 370, REU 398, REU 422, REU 446, CRA 488, REU 488, REU 514
INTERVENTION AND REMEDIATION STRATEGIES: 1F, 25G, 57G, 81G, 109G, 203E, 243F, 265G, 293F, 321F, 345G, 373G, 401F, 425F, 449H, 491G
PROJECT-BASED LEARNING: HOCP 142

3. Analyze how and why individuals, events, or ideas develop and interact over the course of a text.

Student Edition:

Progress Check: 31, 43, 51, 63, 75, 94, 100, 103, 151, 163, 166, 183, 186, 197, 251, 270, 273, 298, 299, 301, 312, 326, 328, 335, 362, 367, 380, 388, 390, 407, 431, 434, 464, 487
Critical Thinking: 70, 118, 146, 154, 182, 198, 215, 309, 412, 440
Infographic: Identifying: 210; Critical Thinking: 31, 210
Lesson Review: Contrasting: 271; Discussing: 211; Summarizing: 215

Teacher Edition:

ENGAGE: 345
TEACH & ASSESS: R5, R7, C7, C8, $R_2$9, C12, C17, C28, R29, $R_1$30, $R_2$30, C32, O32, C34, $R_2$37, O38, C42, C43, C44, O46, R47, O47, R49, C52, O52, C60, R62, R64, $R_2$66, $C_1$68, $C_2$68, R70, C70, R73, O76, $C_1$85, $R_1$86, R87, O87, $C_1$89, R93, O94, C95, R99, C99, R101, C102, $R_2$102, O102, C104, R105, C105, R113, $C_1$115, $C_2$115, $C_1$117, R117, O117, R118, O118, C119, R120, C121, C122, O122, $R_2$124, R128, C130, R130, R132, C145, O145, O147, R148, O149, R150, O150, R151, R153, $R_1$155, O155, C155, $R_1$157, C158, R161, O162, C164, $R_2$165, O165, R166, $R_1$167, $R_1$178, O182, C183, R183, R184, R186, O186, $R_1$188, C190, C191, $C_1$192, R194, C194, C195, O195, C199, R207, C208, O208, R210, O210, $R_1$211, $R_1$247, $R_2$247, O248, $R_2$249, O249, C252, $C_1$254, $R_1$256, $C_1$259, $C_2$260, C261, $R_2$270, C270, $C_1$271, R273, $C_1$274, $C_2$275, O275, O276, R277, O279, O280, $R_1$281, C282, $R_2$283, R284, R286, C286, O286, R288, $C_2$288, O288, R289, C298, $C_1$299, R301, R302, R304, R305, O305, R308, O309, C310, R315, $C_2$326, C333, R336, C337, R337, O337, C338, O338, $C_1$340, $C_2$340, O340, $R_1$341, $R_2$341, $C_1$350, R350, O350, $R_1$352, C353, $R_2$354, R357, R362, C362, R363, R364, $R_1$365, $C_2$366, $C_2$367, R368, $R_2$368, $C_2$369, R377, $R_2$378, O378, C379, $R_1$381, C381, $R_2$384, C388, $C_1$389, O389, C390, $C_2$393, R395, C397, $R_1$406, $R_2$406, O406, C406, C409, O413, C414, R415, O418, $C_1$419, $R_1$429, O431, R432, R433, C434, $R_2$435, O435, O437, $R_1$440, $R_2$440, C458, R458, C463, O466, R474, $R_1$475, C481, R483, R484, C485, R487, C498, C502, $R_1$508, C511
CLOSE & REFLECT: 91, 100, 301
CHAPTER ASSESSMENT: REU 106, REU 290
INTERVENTION AND REMEDIATION STRATEGIES: 265G

Codes used for the Teacher Edition pages are the initial caps of the activities.

College and Career Readiness Anchor Standards for Reading

Craft and Structure

4. Interpret words and phrases as they are used in a text, including determining technical, connotative, and figurative meanings, and analyze how specific word choices shape meaning or tone.

Student Edition:
Reading Help Desk: Taking Notes: 92; Build Vocabulary: 86, 442; Word Origins: 36
Progress Check: 131, 160, 196, 209, 215, 412, 417, 506, 513
Critical Thinking: 475
Connections to Today: 48
Lesson Review: Review Vocabulary: 7, 13, 21, 33, 41, 48, 53, 63, 68, 72, 77, 89, 95, 100, 105, 115, 119, 125, 133, 151, 157, 163, 169, 183, 191, 199, 211, 215, 251, 255, 261, 271, 277, 284, 289, 301, 307, 315, 329, 335, 341, 352, 357, 364, 369, 381, 386, 390, 397, 407, 414, 419, 432, 438, 443, 457, 464, 471, 480, 487, 497, 503, 507, 513; Defining: 352
Chapter Activities & Assessment: Review the Guiding Questions: 55, 79, 135, 217, 291, 319, 399, 423, 515; DBQ: 24

Teacher Edition:
ENGAGE: 243, 278
TEACH & ASSESS: $R_1$4, W6, $R_1$30, R2 30, R33, R47, R49, R53, R64, R69, O74, R2 84, R92, R94, $C_2$100, $R_1$122, C129, C145, R156, R159, C159, R160, R162, $R_1$177, O179, R180, R182, R184, R185, R187, R191, $R_2$192, $R_2$195, $R_1$197, O198, R206, $R_2$211, $R_2$213, T215, C246, $R_1$249, R250, O250, W255, $R_2$256, O260, C270, R278, O278, $R_1$281, O282, R298, R300, $R_1$317, $C_2$326, R338, V338, C349, $R_1$352, C352, $R_2$352, R358, W359, $R_2$365, R376, $R_1$383, C383, $C_2$392, R396, C397, $R_2$405, R408, R412, $R_1$428, R436, C438, R439, O440, C454, R457, R458, R459, V459, O460, O461, $C_2$469, R469, $R_1$470, R471, $R_1$475, R480, R481, C482, $R_1$485, C498, W500, C507, R510, O512, $R_1$513, $R_2$513
CLOSE & REFLECT: 438
INTERVENTION AND REMEDIATION STRATEGIES: 25G, 57G, 109G, 141G, 173F, 243F, 265G, 293F, 321F, 373G, 401F, 425F, 449H, 491G

5. Analyze the structure of texts, including how specific sentences, paragraphs, and larger portions of the text (e.g., a section, chapter, scene, or stanza) relate to each other and the whole.

Student Edition:
Step into the Place: Critical Thinking: 294
Step into the Time: 2, 26, 58, 82, 110, 142, 174, 204, 244, 266, 294, 322, 346, 374, 402, 426, 450, 492
Reading Help Desk: Taking Notes: 73, 96, 158, 184, 252, 256, 302, 308, 324, 348, 353, 376, 387, 439, 452, 458, 481, 498; Reading Strategy: 66, 118, 166, 248
Progress Check: 115, 258, 289, 354, 432, 457, 471, 477
Critical Thinking: 156
Economics Skill: Critical Thinking: 349
Thinking Like a Historian: 153, 352
Lesson Review: Comparing: 68, 390; Comparing and Contrasting: 89, 407, 457; Contrasting: 13, 53, 151, 191, 261, 284, 457; Describing: 513; Determining Cause and Effect: 289, 301; Identifying Cause and Effect: 277, 341, 487; Making Connections: 369; Sequencing: 13, 119, 169
Chapter Activities & Assessment: 21st Century Skills: 262, 370, 514; Thinking Like a Historian: 54, 78, 200, 290, 318, 370, 398, 422, 514; DBQ: 424

Teacher Edition:
TEACH & ASSESS: C11, $C_2$15, C37, O43, C71, $C_2$85, $C_1$113, C114, C125, O126, R152, O177, C189, C281, $C_2$299, C303, $C_2$317, O332, C360, C376, C391, R392, $C_1$393, C408, C441, C470, C471, O485, C505
CLOSE & REFLECT: 13, 414
INTERVENTION AND REMEDIATION STRATEGIES: 173F, 293F, 425F

6. Assess how point of view or purpose shapes the content and style of a text.

Student Edition:
Reading Help Desk: Reading Strategy: 258
Progress Check: 414
Critical Thinking: 157, 214, 311, 362, 418, 482
Thinking Like a Historian: 43, 50, 497
America's Literature: Analyzing: 317, 421; Drawing Conclusions: 91; Interpreting: 473; Making Inferences: 421
What Do You Think? feature: Analyzing: 359; Identifying: 193, 445; Interpreting: 127; Making Inferences: 193; Summarizing: 359
Lesson Review: Argument: 390; Comparing and Contrasting: 414; Identifying Points of View: 414; Interpreting: 125, 133
Chapter Activities & Assessment: 21st Century Skills: 134; DBQ: 24, 172, 202, 218, 264, 292, 320, 344, 372, 400, 424, 490, 516; Short Response: 24, 56, 80, 108, 136, 172, 202, 218, 292, 320, 344, 372, 400, 424, 448, 490, 516; Extended Response: 372

Teacher Edition:
TEACH & ASSESS: W43, W75, R126, $R_1$127, O130, C133, R144, C157, O185, C193, C257, $C_2$274, $C_1$275, C276, C279, $C_1$283, $C_2$283, C287, O310, $R_2$317, $C_2$330, $C_2$334, O334, C352, W358, R359, O359, C417, $C_1$421, $C_2$421, C430, R445, T454, C455, C462, C476, R476, O476
CLOSE & REFLECT: 390, 487
INTERVENTION AND REMEDIATION STRATEGIES: 401F

Codes used for the Teacher Edition pages are the initial caps of the activities.

College and Career Readiness Anchor Standards for Reading

Integration of Knowledge and Ideas

7. Integrate and evaluate content presented in diverse formats and media, including visually and quantitatively, as well as in words.

Student Edition:

Step into the Place: Human-Environment Interaction: 58, 322, 492; Location: 110, 142, 204, 244, 266, 294, 374, 402, 426, 450; Movement: 26, 266, 322; Place: 2, 58, 82, 142, 174, 204, 294, 346, 450, 492; Region: 2, 82, 110, 174, 322, 346, 374, 426; Critical Thinking: 2, 26, 58, 82, 110, 142, 174, 204, 244, 266, 346, 374, 402, 426, 450, 492

Step into the Time: 2, 26, 58, 82, 110, 142, 174, 204, 244, 266, 294, 322, 346, 374, 402, 426, 450, 492

Reading Help Desk: Taking Notes: 4, 8, 14, 28, 34, 42, 49, 60, 64, 69, 73, 84, 92, 96, 101, 112, 158; Reading in the Content Area: 392

Critical Thinking: 61, 148, 163, 199, 255, 332, 337, 350, 405, 411, 430, 435, 437, 442, 457, 460, 470, 477, 479, 495, 496, 505

Chart Skill: Comparing: 189, 260; Describing: 456; Identifying: 121, 177, 196; Summarizing: 179, 260; Critical Thinking: 121, 177, 179, 189, 196, 260, 456

Diagram Skill: Describing: 65; Identifying: 209, 298; Critical Thinking: 38, 65, 209, 298

Economics Skill: Analyzing Visuals: 281; Calculating: 114, 510; Comparing: 250; Contrasting: 389; Identifying: 88; Critical Thinking: 88, 114, 250, 281, 389, 510

Geography Connection: Human-Environment Interaction: 305; Location: 12, 29, 32, 47, 76, 104, 147, 161, 166, 356, 363, 429, 441, 478, 483; Movement: 5, 36, 40, 45, 67, 123, 129, 276, 287, 303, 361; Place: 11, 71, 180, 253, 313, 351, 431, 461, 462, 501; Region: 15, 113, 312, 379, 388, 409; Critical Thinking: 5, 11, 12, 15, 29, 32, 36, 40, 45, 47, 67, 71, 76, 104, 113, 123, 129, 147, 161, 166, 180, 253, 276, 287, 303, 305, 312, 313, 351, 356, 361, 363, 379, 388, 409, 429, 431, 441, 461, 462, 478, 483, 501

Graph Skill: Calculating: 187, 333, 385, 386, 486; Identifying: 74, 392; Summarizing: 454; Critical Thinking: 74, 187, 333, 385, 386, 392, 454, 486

Infographic: Calculating: 87, 325, 326, 453; Describing: 299; Drawing Conclusions: 31; Identifying: 269, 339, 416, 434, 509; Critical Thinking: 87, 269, 299, 325, 326, 339, 416, 434, 453, 509

Thinking Like a Historian: 103, 257, 297

Chapter Activities & Assessment: Thinking Like a Historian: 54, 78, 106, 170; Visual Literacy: 22, 54, 78, 106, 134, 170, 200, 216, 262, 290, 318, 342, 370, 398, 422, 446, 488, 514; DBQ: 56, 80, 108, 136, 448; Short Response: 264

Teacher Edition:

ENGAGE: 1, 81, 144, 158, 293, 302, 321, 348, 391

TEACH & ASSESS: V$_1$2, V$_3$3, O3, O4, V5, O5, V6, O6, O8, O9, V11, O11, O12, O14, V15, O15, V16, O16, O17, O19, V$_1$26, V$_2$27, O27, O28, V29, V32, O34, O36, V39, O39, O40, O42, V47, O49, O50, V51, O51, O52, T52, V$_1$58, V$_2$59, O59, O60, O61, V63, O64, V65, V67, O69, V71, O71, O73, O74, V76, V82, V83, O83, O84, O85, V87, V88, O88, C90, O90, O92, O96, O97, O98, O99, O101, V103, O103, O104, O104, V110, R110, V111, O111, O112, O113, V114, O114, O116, V118, O120, V121, V123, O123, O127, O128, O129, V142, C143, O144, O146, V147, O148, O149, O152, C154, O158, O159, V160, V161, O161, V163, O164, O166, O168, O174, V175, O176, C177, O180, O182, C183, O184, V186, O187, O187, O189, O193, O194, V196, O196, V204, C205, O205, O206, V208, V209, O212, V244, O245, O246, O250, O252, O253, O254, O256, V257, O258, V266, O267, O267, O268, V269, O269, O270, O272, V273, O274, V276, O278, V279, O283, O285, O287, V294, O295, O296, O297, O298, V299, O299, V300, O300, O302, O303, O304, V306, W306, O308, V311, O311, O313, V314, O314, V315, O316, V322, O323, O323, O324, V325, O325, C$_1$326, O326, V327, V331, O331, W332, O336, V338, O339, V346, C347, V347, O347, R$_1$348, O348, V351, O351, O353, O354, R356, V356, O356, O358, O360, V361, O361, O362, V363, O365, O366, O367, V368, O374, R375, O375, O376, O377, V379, O379, O380, O382, V384, O385, O385, V386, O387, V388, O389, O391, V392, O392, O393, V402, O403, O404, V406, O408, O409, O410, W411, V412, O412, O415, V420, V426, C426, V427, C427, O428, O429, V431, C431, O433, V434, O434, V437, V439, O440, V441, O441, V442, V445, V450, C450, V451, O451, R$_1$452, O452, O454, V455, O456, O458, V459, O460, V461, O462, O463, O465, V466, V467, O468, C$_1$469, O469, O470, V471, V472, O473, O474, O476, O477, V478, O478, O481, V483, O483, V486, O492, O493, O494, O495, O498, O499, V501, O504, O505, O506, O508, V509, O509, V510, O510

CLOSE & REFLECT: 3, 21, 27, 48, 59, 111, 205

INTERVENTION AND REMEDIATION STRATEGIES: 57G, 243F, 345G, 449H

8. Delineate and evaluate the argument and specific claims in a text, including the validity of the reasoning as well as the relevance and sufficiency of the evidence.

Student Edition:

America's Literature: Predicting: 91

What Do You Think? feature: Contrasting: 193, 359; Evaluating: 127, 445

Chapter Activities & Assessment: Exploring the Essential Questions: 262; 21st Century Skills: 134; Short Response: 400

Teacher Edition:

TEACH & ASSESS: C$_2$117, R268, C$_1$330, O359, C$_1$444, O472, T509

9. Analyze how two or more texts address similar themes or topics in order to build knowledge or to compare the approaches the author's take.

Student Edition:

Critical Thinking: 39

America's Literature: Drawing Conclusions: 91

Lesson Review: Informative/Explanatory: 329, 507

Chapter Activities & Assessment: Short Response: 292, 320; Extended Response: 344

Teacher Edition:

TEACH & ASSESS: T88, R126, C153, O185, O193, C359, O467, C$_1$473

Codes used for the Teacher Edition pages are the initial caps of the activities.

College and Career Readiness Anchor Standards for Reading

Range of Reading and Level of Text Complexity	
10. Read and comprehend complex literary and informational texts independently and proficiently.	**Student Edition:** *Step into the Place:* Critical Thinking: 2, 26, 58, 82, 110 *America's Literature:* Expressing: 317; Recalling: 421 *What Do You Think?* feature: Contrasting: 193, 359 *Chapter Activities & Assessment:* 21st Century Skills: 200; DBQ: 202, 218, 264, 292, 320, 344, 372, 400, 424 **Teacher Edition:** **TEACH & ASSESS:** 037, 043, 044, 046, 047, W66, 070, 075, 0118, 0130, 0150, 0153, 0177, 0186, 0252, 0334, 0349, 0363, 0366, 0384, 0396, 0405, T414, 0417, 0421, 0431, 0437, 0459, 0475, 0479, 0482, 0484, 0511, W513 **CLOSE & REFLECT:** 473 **PROJECT-BASED LEARNING:** HOCP 402

Codes used for the Teacher Edition pages are the initial caps of the activities.

Common Core State Standards for English Language Arts and Literacy in History/Social Studies, Science, and Technical Subjects

Reading Standards for Literacy in History/Social Studies 6-8	
Key Ideas and Details	**Student Edition**
RH.6-8.1 Cite specific textual evidence to support analysis of primary and secondary sources.	Step Into the Place: *Critical Thinking:* 322 *Reading Help Desk:* Taking Notes: 28, 34, 42, 49, 60, 64, 69, 112, 116, 144, 152, 164, 176, 194, 206, 268, 272, 278, 285, 296, 336, 360, 365, 404, 408, 428, 465, 474, 504 *America's Literature:* Analyzing: 473; Recalling: 421; Speculating: 91 *What Do You Think?* feature: Analyzing: 127 *Lesson Review:* Analyzing: 53, 77, 95, 119, 329, 335, 352, 407, 419, 432, 443, 464, 503; Describing: 7, 13, 21, 41, 63, 72, 125; Discussing: 271; Evaluating: 329; Explaining: 21, 41, 48, 100, 133, 151, 183, 357, 419, 438; Identifying: 105, 157, 163, 199, 301, 364, 381, 390; Listing: 33, 169, 315, 369, 386, 432; Making Inferences: 438; Recalling: 261; Specifying: 183, 191, 199, 352, 364, 438, 443; Summarizing: 471 *Chapter Activities & Assessment:* Thinking Like a Historian: 106, 216, 446; Review the Guiding Questions: 23, 55, 79, 107, 135, 171, 201, 217, 263, 291, 319, 343, 371, 399, 423, 447, 489, 515; DBQ: 24, 202; Short Response: 344, 424
RH.6-8.2 Determine the central ideas or information of a primary or secondary source; provide an accurate summary of the source distinct from prior knowledge or opinions.	*Reading Help Desk:* Taking Notes: 4, 8, 14, 84, 101, 120, 128, 246, 330, 382, 391, 415, 433, 494, 508 *America's Literature:* Explaining: 317, 473; Expressing: 317 What Do You Think? feature: Making Inferences: 445 *Lesson Review:* Analyzing: 364; Comparing: 471; Describing: 115, 163, 191, 215, 255, 307, 315, 335, 341, 432, 503, 507; Discussing: 386, 397, 414; Drawing Conclusions: 443; Evaluating: 457, 464, 471, 480, 487; Explaining: 7, 21, 33, 53, 63, 68, 77, 95, 105, 115, 119, 125, 157, 183, 199, 211, 215, 255, 271, 277, 284, 289, 301, 315, 329, 335, 352, 364, 369, 381, 386, 390, 397, 407, 432, 443, 464, 471, 480, 487, 497, 507, 513; Identifying: 33, 115, 438; Identifying the Main Ideas: 89; Making Connections: 357; Making Generalizations: 48; Making Inferences: 315, 480; Recalling: 251; Specifying: 357; Speculating: 497; Summarizing: 48, 72, 100,105, 133, 151, 163, 251, 255, 277, 284, 289, 307, 381, 513 *Chapter Activities & Assessment:* 21st Century Skills: 318; Thinking Like a Historian: 170, 422; Review the Guiding Questions: 23, 55, 79, 107, 135, 171, 201, 217, 263, 291, 319, 343, 371, 399, 423, 447, 489, 515; DBQ: 24, 172, 218, 264, 292, 320, 372, 400, 424, 490, 516; Short Response: 24, 80, 108, 172, 202, 218, 372, 448, 490, 516
RH.6-8.3 Identify key steps in a text's description of a process related to history/social studies (e.g., how a bill becomes law, how interest rates are raised or lowered).	*Lesson Review:* Contrasting: 271; Discussing: 211; Summarizing: 215
Craft and Structure	
RH.6-8.4 Determine the meaning of words and phrases as they are used in a text, including vocabulary specific to domains related to history/social studies.	*Reading Help Desk:* Taking Notes: 92 *Lesson Review:* Review Vocabulary: 7, 13, 21, 33, 41, 48, 53, 63, 68, 72, 77, 89, 95, 100, 105, 115, 119, 125, 133, 151, 157, 163, 169, 183, 191, 199, 211, 215, 251, 255, 261, 271, 277, 284, 289, 301, 307, 315, 329, 335, 341, 352, 357, 364, 369, 381, 386, 390, 397, 407, 414, 419, 432, 438, 443, 457, 464, 471, 480, 487, 497, 503, 507, 513; Defining: 352 *Chapter Activities & Assessment:* Review the Guiding Questions: 55, 79, 135, 217, 291, 319, 399, 423, 515; DBQ: 24
RH.6-8.5 Describe how a text presents information (e.g., sequentially, comparatively, causally).	*Step Into the Place:* Critical Thinking: 294 *Step Into the Time:* 2, 26, 58, 82, 110, 142, 174, 204, 244, 266, 294, 322, 346, 374, 402, 426, 450, 492 *Reading Help Desk:* Taking Notes: 73, 96, 158, 184, 252, 256, 302, 308, 324, 348, 353, 376, 387, 439, 452, 458, 481, 498 *Lesson Review:* Comparing: 68, 390; Comparing and Contrasting: 89, 407, 457; Contrasting: 13, 53, 151, 191, 261, 284, 457; Describing: 513; Determining Cause and Effect: 289, 301; Identifying Cause and Effect: 277, 341, 487; Making Connections: 369; Sequencing: 13, 119, 169 *Chapter Activities & Assessment:* 21st Century Skills: 262, 370, 514; Thinking Like a Historian: 54, 78, 200, 290, 318, 370, 398, 422, 514; DBQ: 424
RH.6-8.6 Identify aspects of a text that reveal an author's point of view or purpose (e.g., loaded language, inclusion or avoidance of particular facts).	*America's Literature:* Analyzing: 317, 421; Drawing Conclusions: 91; Interpreting: 473; Making Inferences: 421 *What Do You Think?* feature: Analyzing: 359; Identifying: 193, 445; Interpreting: 127; Making Inferences: 193; Summarizing: 359 *Lesson Review:* Argument: 390; Comparing and Contrasting: 414; Identifying Points of View: 414; Interpreting: 125, 133 *Chapter Activities & Assessment:* 21st Century Skills: 134; DBQ: 24, 172, 202, 218, 264, 292, 320, 344, 372, 400, 424, 490, 516; Short Response: 24, 56, 80, 108, 136, 172, 202, 218, 292, 320, 344, 372, 400, 424, 448, 490, 516; Extended Response: 372
Integration of Knowledge and Ideas	
RH.6-8.7 Integrate visual information (e.g., in charts, graphs, photographs, videos, or maps) with other information in print and digital texts.	*Step Into the Place:* Human-Environment Interaction: 58, 322, 492; Location: 110, 142, 204, 244, 266, 294, 374, 402, 426, 450; Movement: 26, 266, 322; Place: 2, 58, 82, 142, 174, 204, 294, 346, 450, 492; Region: 2, 82, 110, 174, 322, 346, 374, 426; Critical Thinking: 2, 26, 58, 82, 110, 142, 174, 204, 244, 266, 346, 374, 402, 426, 450, 492 *Step Into the Time:* 2, 26, 58, 82, 110, 142, 174, 204, 244, 266, 294, 322, 346, 374, 402, 426, 450, 492 *Reading Help Desk:* Taking Notes: 4, 8, 14, 28, 34, 42, 49, 60, 64, 69, 73, 84, 92, 96, 101, 112, 158 *Chapter Activities & Assessment:* Thinking Like a Historian: 54, 78, 106, 170; Visual Literacy: 22, 54, 78, 106, 134, 170, 200, 216, 262, 290, 318, 342, 370, 398, 422, 446, 488, 514; DBQ: 56, 80, 108, 136, 448; Short Response: 264

Reading Standards for Literacy in History/Social Studies 6-8

RH.6-8.8 Distinguish among fact, opinion, and reasoned judgment in a text.	*America's Literature:* Predicting: 91 *What Do You Think?* feature: Contrasting: 193, 359; Evaluating: 127, 445 *Chapter Activities & Assessment:* Exploring the Essential Questions: 262; 21st Century Skills: 134; Short Response: 400
RH.6-8.9 Analyze the relationship between a primary and secondary source on the same topic.	*America's Literature:* Drawing Conclusions: 91 *Lesson Review:* Informative/Explanatory: 329, 507 *Chapter Activities & Assessment:* Short Response: 292, 320; Extended Response: 344
Range of Reading and Level of Text Complexity	
RH.6-8.10 By the end of grade 8, read and comprehend history/social studies texts in the grades 6–8 text complexity band independently and proficiently.	*Step Into the Place:* Critical Thinking: 2, 26, 58, 82,110 *America's Literature:* Expressing: 317; Recalling: 421 *What Do You Think?* feature: Contrasting: 193, 359 *Chapter Activities & Assessment:* 21st Century Skills: 200; DBQ: 202, 218, 264, 292, 320, 344, 372, 400, 424

Common Core State Standards for English Language Arts and Literacy in History/Social Studies, Science, and Technical Subjects

The following pages contain correlation charts to the Common Core State Standards. The first chart contains the College and Career Readiness (CCR) Anchor Standards for Writing. The chart that follows the CCR Anchor Standards for Writing chart identifies specifically what students should understand and be able to do by the end of grades 6–8. The CCR and grade-specific standards are necessary complements—the former providing broad standards, the latter providing additional specificity—that together define the skills and understandings that all students must demonstrate.

College and Career Readiness Anchor Standards for Writing	
Text Types and Purposes	
1. Write arguments to support claims in an analysis of substantive topics or texts using valid reasoning and relevant and sufficient evidence.	**Student Edition:** *Lesson Review:* Argument: 33, 77, 95, 133, 151, 157, 163, 183, 199, 211, 251, 261, 284, 289, 315, 341, 352, 357, 381, 390, 419, 432, 438, 457, 464, 471, 503; Informative/Explanatory: 13, 48, 329, 369, 507; Narrative: 21, 53, 115, 119, 215, 277, 335, 386, 397, 414 *Chapter Activities & Assessment:* Exploring the Essential Questions: 262, 290, 422, 446, 514; 21st Century Skills: 200, 422, 488, 514; Thinking Like a Historian: 22, 262, 488; Short Response: 56, 80, 136, 218, 344; Extended Response: 24, 136, 172, 202, 218, 264, 344, 372, 400, 448, 490, 516 **Teacher Edition:** TEACH & ASSESS: O34, W41, W43, W63, W74, W94, W119, W125, C128, W151, W198, W204, W209, W255, W284, W301, W303, W328, W351, W358, W362, W390, W430, W462, W464, W482 CLOSE & REFLECT: 33, 95, 445 INTERVENTION AND REMEDIATION STRATEGIES: 57G, 81G, 109G, 425F, 491G PROJECT-BASED LEARNING: HOCP 58, HOCP 346, HOCP 426
2. Write informative/explanatory texts to examine and convey complex ideas and information clearly and accurately through the effective selection, organization, and analysis of content.	**Student Edition:** *Reading Help Desk:* Taking Notes: 212 *Lesson Review:* Argument: 407; Informative/Explanatory: 7, 41, 68, 105, 191, 271, 307, 443, 497, 513; Interpreting: 133; Narrative: 72, 89, 100, 125, 169, 255, 301, 480, 487 *Chapter Activities & Assessment:* Exploring the Essential Questions: 22, 54, 78, 106, 134, 170, 200, 216, 318, 370, 398, 488; 21st Century Skills: 216, 318, 398; Short Response: 108, 218; Extended Response: 56, 80, 108, 292, 320, 424 **Teacher Edition:** TEACH & ASSESS: W17, W20, O40, W50, W51, O59, W66, W72, W112, W124, T131, W161, W168, W190, W206, O212, W214, W246, W254, W257, W274, W306, W308, W314, W315, O317, W332, W338, W359, W366, W380, W385, W396, W405, W417, W437, W439, W466, W477, W497, W500, W505 CLOSE & REFLECT: 7, 41, 72 CHAPTER ASSESSMENT: CRA 78 INTERVENTION AND REMEDIATION STRATEGIES: 81G, 203E, 321F, 345G, 401F
3. Write narratives to develop real or imagined experiences or events using effective technique, well-chosen details and well-structured event sequences.	**Student Edition:** *Lesson Review:* Argument: 438, 457; Informative/Explanatory: 443; Narrative: 21, 53, 72, 89, 100, 115, 119, 125, 169, 255, 277, 301, 335, 386, 397, 414, 480, 487 *Chapter Activities & Assessment:* Extended Response: 56, 136, 172, 264, 448 **Teacher Edition:** ENGAGE: 60, 203, 265 TEACH & ASSESS: W6, W10, W31, T 67, W75, W115, W125, W154, W162, W181, W269, V279, W280, C₁283, W289, W294, W296, C₂316, O353, W356, W411, W457, W461, W473, W513 CLOSE & REFLECT: 323, 421 INTERVENTION AND REMEDIATION STRATEGIES: 1F, 57G, 141G, 243F, 265G, 345G, 373G, 401F PROJECT-BASED LEARNING: HOCP 26, HOCP 82

Codes used for the Teacher Edition pages are the initial caps of the activities.

College and Career Readiness Anchor Standards for Writing

Production and Distribution of Writing

4. Produce clear and coherent writing in which the development, organization, and style are appropriate to task, purpose, and audience.

Student Edition:
Lesson Review: Review Vocabulary: 13, 48, 68, 95, 115, 125, 211, 215, 261, 301, 369, 397, 432; Argument: 163, 251, 289; Informative/Explanatory: 41, 513; Narrative: 487
Chapter Activities & Assessment: 21st Century Skills: 78; Visual Literacy: 514; Short Response: 24, 80, 108, 172, 202, 264, 292, 320, 344, 372, 400, 424, 448, 490, 516; Extended Response: 218

Teacher Edition:
ENGAGE: 373
TEACH & ASSESS: W31, W41, O86, O91, R95, R121, O176, C178, W274, W296, W303, W308, W338, W405, W445, V472
CLOSE & REFLECT: 72, 193, 323, 407, 414
INTERVENTION AND REMEDIATION STRATEGIES: 57G, 109G, 401F, 449H
PROJECT-BASED LEARNING: TE 426

5. Develop and strengthen writing as needed by planning, revising, editing, rewriting, or trying a new approach.

Student Edition:
Chapter Activities & Assessment: 21st Century Skills: 22, 78, 290, 446

Teacher Edition:
TEACH & ASSESS: W50, W162, W257, W314, W380, W457, W462
CLOSE & REFLECT: 83
INTERVENTION AND REMEDIATION STRATEGIES: 203E
PROJECT-BASED LEARNING: HOCP 2, TE 174, HOCP 266, HOCP 374

6. Use technology, including the Internet, to produce and publish writing and to interact and collaborate with others.

Student Edition:
Chapter Activities & Assessment: Exploring the Essential Questions: 342; 21st Century Skills: 22, 106, 170; Thinking Like a Historian: 342

Teacher Edition:
TEACH & ASSESS: W20, T36, T44, W50, O205, T211, T215, T248, R268, T272, T363, T383, T413, T414, T418, T436, T463, T467
INTERVENTION AND REMEDIATION STRATEGIES: 57G, 109G
PROJECT-BASED LEARNING: TE 2, TE 26, TE 58, TE 82, TE 110, TE 142, TE 174, TE 204, TE 244, TE 266, TE 294, HOCP 322, TE 322, TE 346, TE 374, TE 402, TE 426, TE 450, TE 492

Research to Build and Present Knowledge

7. Conduct short as well as more sustained research projects based on focused questions, demonstrating understanding of the subject under investigation.

Student Edition:
Chapter Activities & Assessment: 21st Century Skills: 54,106, 342; Thinking Like a Historian: 134

Teacher Edition:
ENGAGE: 64, 285, 293, 373, 491
TEACH & ASSESS: O3, T14, T17, T18, O29, V40, T44, O51, T52, W91, C118, T174, T211, T245, V266, C268, T272, T295, T298, T305, T314, T323, T328, O347, O354, T363, O375, T383, C_1389, C394, O405, V412, V416, T417, V420, O420, T436, T467, MC494, T500, R_2513
CLOSE & REFLECT: 133, 271, 335, 381, 386, 457
INTERVENTION AND REMEDIATION STRATEGIES: 25G, 57G, 81G, 265G, 373G, 491G
PROJECT-BASED LEARNING: TE 2, TE 26, HOCP 110, HOCP 204, HOCP 244, HOCP 450

8. Gather relevant information from multiple print and digital sources, assess the credibility and accuracy of each source, and integrate the information while avoiding plagiarism.

Student Edition:
Thinking Like a Historian: 248
Chapter Activities & Assessment: Exploring the Essential Questions: 342; 21st Century Skills: 54, 170, 342, 398, 446; Thinking Like a Historian: 342

Teacher Edition:
ENGAGE: 358
TEACH & ASSESS: W20, T36, W50, T67, W72, O83, T88, T99, T131, T169, O181, T182, T185, W214, T280, W417, T454, T463, W466, T509
INTERVENTION AND REMEDIATION STRATEGIES: 81G, 373G
PROJECT-BASED LEARNING: HOCP 2, HOCP 58, HOCP 174, HOCP 266, HOCP 294, HOCP 322, HOCP 346, TE 346, HOCP 374, HOCP 426

Codes used for the Teacher Edition pages are the initial caps of the activities.

College and Career Readiness Anchor Standards for Writing

9. Draw evidence from literary or informational texts to support analysis, reflection, and research.	**Student Edition:** *Lesson Review:* Argument: 33, 63, 133, 151, 183, 199, 341, 357, 381, 407, 419, 464; Informative/Explanatory: 7, 13, 68, 105, 191, 271, 307, 364, 369, 443, 497; Narrative: 72, 100, 119 *Chapter Activities & Assessment:* Exploring the Essential Questions: 22, 54, 78, 106, 134, 170, 216, 370, 398, 446, 488; 21st Century Skills: 216, 290, 422; Thinking Like a Historian: 22, 488; Short Response: 24, 56, 136, 172; Extended Response: 24, 108, 320, 400, 516 **Teacher Edition:** TEACH & ASSESS: W10, W74, W91, W154, 0193, W198, C258, W280, W328, W362, W497 CLOSE & REFLECT: 95 INTERVENTION AND REMEDIATION STRATEGIES: 265G, 293F, 345G, 425F, 449H PROJECT-BASED LEARNING: HOCP 26, HOCP 110, HOCP 374, HOCP 402, HOCP 492
Range of Writing	
10. Write routinely over extended time frames (time for research, reflection, and revision) and shorter time frames (a single sitting or a day or two) for a range of tasks, purposes, and audiences.	**Student Edition:** *Lesson Review:* Argument: 63, 77, 95, 157, 211, 261, 284, 315, 352, 432, 438, 457, 471, 503; Informative/Explanatory: 48, 364; Narrative: 21, 53, 89, 115, 125, 169, 215, 255, 277, 301, 335, 386, 397, 414, 480 *Chapter Activities & Assessment:* Exploring the Essential Questions: 200, 290, 318, 422, 514; 21st Century Skills: 488; Thinking Like a Historian: 134, 262; Extended Response: 56, 80, 136, 172, 202, 264, 292, 424, 448, 490 **Teacher Edition:** ENGAGE: 203, 265 TEACH & ASSESS: W6, W43, W51, W63, W66, W75, W112, W115, W119, W125, W168, W181, W190, W206, W209, W212, W269, W289, W294, C$_2$316, 0317, W351, W356, W366, W396, W411, W430, W437, W461, W473, W477, W505 CLOSE & REFLECT: 143, 421 INTERVENTION AND REMEDIATION STRATEGIES: 243F, 265G, 401F PROJECT-BASED LEARNING: HOCP 142, HOCP 174

Codes used for the Teacher Edition pages are the initial caps of the activities.

Common Core State Standards for English Language Arts and Literacy in History/Social Studies, Science, and Technical Subjects

Writing Standards for Literacy in History/Social Studies, Science, and Technical Subjects 6–8

Text Types and Purposes	Student Edition
WHST.6-8.1 Write arguments focused on *discipline-specific content*.	*Lesson Review:* Argument: 33, 77, 95, 133, 151, 157, 163, 183, 199, 211, 251, 261, 284, 289, 315, 341, 352, 357, 381, 390, 419, 432, 438, 457, 464, 471, 503; Informative/Explanatory: 13, 48, 329, 369, 507; Narrative: 21, 53, 115, 119, 215, 277, 335, 386, 397, 414 *Chapter Activities & Assessment:* Exploring the Essential Questions: 262, 290, 422, 446, 514; 21st Century Skills: 200, 422, 488, 514; Thinking Like a Historian: 22, 262, 488; Short Response: 56, 80, 136, 218, 344; Extended Response: 24, 136, 172, 202, 218, 264, 344, 372, 400, 448, 490, 516
WHST.6-8.2 Write informative/explanatory texts, including the narration of historical events, scientific procedures/experiments, or technical processes.	*Reading Help Desk:* Taking Notes: 212 *Lesson Review:* Argument: 407; Informative/Explanatory: 7, 41, 68, 105, 191, 271, 307, 443, 497, 513; Interpreting: 133; Narrative: 72, 89, 100, 125, 169, 255, 301, 480, 487 *Chapter Activities & Assessment:* Exploring the Essential Questions: 22, 54, 78, 106, 134, 170, 200, 216, 318, 370, 398, 488; 21st Century Skills: 216, 318, 398; Short Response: 108, 218; Extended Response: 56, 80, 108, 292, 320, 424
WHST.6-8.3 (See note; not applicable as a separate requirement)	**Note:** Students' narrative skills continue to grow in these grades. The Standards require that students be able to incorporate narrative elements effectively into arguments and informative/explanatory texts. In history/social studies, students must be able to incorporate narrative accounts into their analyses of individuals or events of historical import. In science and technical subjects, students must be able to write precise enough descriptions of the step-by-step procedures they use in their investigations or technical work that others can replicate them and (possibly) reach the same results.
Production and Distribution of Writing	
WHST.6-8.4 Produce clear and coherent writing in which the development, organization, and style are appropriate to task, purpose, and audience.	*Lesson Review:* Review Vocabulary: 13, 48, 68, 95, 115, 125, 211, 215, 261, 301, 369, 397, 432; Argument: 163, 251, 289; Informative/Explanatory: 41, 513; Narrative: 487 *Chapter Activities & Assessment:* 21st Century Skills: 78; Visual Literacy: 514; Short Response: 24, 80, 108, 172, 202, 264, 292, 320, 344, 372, 400, 424, 448, 490, 516; Extended Response: 218
WHST.6-8.5 With some guidance and support from peers and adults, develop and strengthen writing as needed by planning, revising, editing, rewriting, or trying a new approach, focusing on how well purpose and audience have been addressed.	*Chapter Activities & Assessment:* 21st Century Skills: 22, 78, 290, 446
WHST.6-8.6 Use technology, including the Internet, to produce and publish writing and present the relationships between information and ideas clearly and efficiently.	*Chapter Activities & Assessment:* Exploring the Essential Questions: 342; 21st Century Skills: 22, 106, 170; Thinking Like a Historian: 342
Research to Build and Present Knowledge	
WHST.6-8.7 Conduct short research projects to answer a question (including a self-generated question), drawing on several sources and generating additional related, focused questions that allow for multiple avenues of exploration.	*Chapter Activities & Assessment:* 21st Century Skills: 54, 106, 342; Thinking Like a Historian: 134
WHST.6-8.8 Gather relevant information from multiple print and digital sources, using search terms effectively; assess the credibility and accuracy of each source; and quote or paraphrase the data and conclusions of others while avoiding plagiarism and following a standard format for citation.	*Chapter Activities & Assessment:* Exploring the Essential Questions: 342; 21st Century Skills: 54, 170, 342, 398, 446; Thinking Like a Historian: 342
WHST.6-8.9 Draw evidence from informational texts to support analysis reflection, and research.	*Lesson Review:* Argument: 33, 63, 133, 151, 183, 199, 341, 357, 381, 407, 419, 464; Informative/Explanatory: 7, 13, 68, 105, 191, 271, 307, 364, 369, 443, 497; Narrative: 72, 100, 119 *Chapter Activities & Assessment:* Exploring the Essential Questions: 22, 54, 78, 106, 134, 170, 216, 370, 398, 446, 488; 21st Century Skills: 216, 290, 422; Thinking Like a Historian: 22, 488; Short Response: 24, 56, 136, 172; Extended Response: 24, 108, 320, 400, 516
Range of Writing	
WHST.6-8.10 Write routinely over extended time frames (time for reflection and revision) and shorter time frames (a single sitting or a day or two) for a range of discipline-specific tasks, purposes, and audiences.	*Lesson Review:* Argument: 63, 77, 95, 157, 211, 261, 284, 315, 352, 432, 438, 457, 471, 503; Informative/Explanatory: 48, 364; Narrative: 21, 53, 89, 115, 125, 169, 215, 255, 277, 301, 335, 386, 397, 414, 480 *Chapter Activities & Assessment:* Exploring the Essential Questions: 200, 290, 318, 422, 514; 21st Century Skills: 488; Thinking Like a Historian: 134, 262; Extended Response: 56, 80, 136, 172, 202, 264, 292, 424, 448, 490

UNDERSTANDING BY DESIGN®

by Jay McTighe

Understanding by Design® (UbD™) offers a planning framework to guide curriculum, assessment, and instruction. Its two key ideas are contained in the title: 1) focus on teaching and assessing for understanding and transfer, and 2) design curriculum "backward" from those ends.

UbD is based on seven key tenets:

1. UbD is a way of thinking purposefully about curricular planning, not a rigid program or prescriptive recipe.

2. A primary goal of UbD is developing and deepening student understanding: the ability to make meaning of learning via "big ideas" and transfer learning.

3. Understanding is revealed when students autonomously make sense of and transfer their learning through authentic performance. Six facets of understanding—the capacity to explain, interpret, apply, shift perspective, empathize, and self assess—serve as indicators of understanding.

4. Effective curriculum is planned "backward" from long-term desired results though a three-stage design process (Desired Results, Evidence, Learning Plan). This process helps to avoid the twin problems of "textbook coverage" and "activity-oriented" teaching in which no clear priorities and purposes are apparent.

5. Teachers are coaches of understanding, not mere purveyors of content or activity. They focus on ensuring learning, not just teaching (and assuming that what was taught was learned); they always aim and check for successful meaning making and transfer by the learner.

6. Regular reviews of units and curriculum against design standards enhance curricular quality and effectiveness.

7. UbD reflects a continuous improvement approach to achievement. The results of our designs —student performance—inform needed adjustments in curriculum as well as instruction.

Three Stages of Backward Design

In UbD, we propose a 3-stage "backward design" process for curriculum planning. The concept of planning "backward" from desired results is not new. In 1949 Ralph Tyler described this approach as an effective process for focusing instruction. More recently, Stephen Covey, in the best selling book, *Seven Habits of Highly Effective People*, reports that effective people in various fields are goal-oriented and plan with the end in mind. Although not a new idea, we have found that the deliberate use of backward design for planning curriculum units and courses results in more clearly defined goals, more appropriate assessments, more tightly aligned lessons, and more purposeful teaching.

Backward planning asks educators to consider the following three stages:

Stage 1 – Identify Desired Results

What should students know, understand, and be able to do? What content is worthy of understanding? What "enduring" understandings are desired? What essential questions will be explored?

In the first stage of backward design we consider our goals, examine established Content Standards (national, state, province, district), and review curriculum expectations. Since there is typically more "content" than can reasonably be addressed within the available time, teachers must make choices. This first stage in the design process calls for setting priorities.

More specifically, Stage 1 of UbD asks teachers to identify the "big ideas" that we want students to come to understand, and then to identify or craft companion essential questions. Big ideas reflect transferable concepts, principles and processes that are key to understanding the topic or subject. Essential questions present open-ended, thought-provoking inquiries that are explored over time.

More specific knowledge and skill objectives, linked to the targeted Content Standards and Understandings, are also identified in Stage 1. An important point in UbD is to recognize that factual knowledge and skills are not taught for their own sake, but as a means to larger ends. Ultimately, teaching should equip learners to be able to use or transfer their learning; i.e., meaningful performance with content. This is the "end" we always want to keep in mind.

Stage 2 – Determine Acceptable Evidence

How will we know if students have achieved the desired results? What will we accept as evidence of student understanding and proficiency? How will we evaluate student performance?

Backward design encourages teachers and curriculum planners to first "think like an assessor" before designing specific units and lessons. The assessment evidence we need reflects the desired results identified in Stage 1. Thus, we consider in advance the assessment evidence needed to document and validate that the targeted learning has been achieved. Doing so invariably sharpens and focuses teaching.

In Stage 2, we distinguish between two broad types of assessment—Performance Tasks and Other Evidence. The performance tasks ask students to apply their learning to a new and authentic situation as means of assessing their understanding. In UbD, we have identified six facets of understanding for assessment purposes[1]. When someone truly understands, they:

- Can **explain** concepts, principles and processes; i.e., put them in their own words, teach them to others, justify their answers, show their reasoning.

- Can **interpret**; i.e., make sense of data, text, and experience through images, analogies, stories, and models.

- Can apply; i.e., effectively use and adapt what they know in new and complex contexts.

- Demonstrate **perspective**; i.e., can see the big picture and recognize different points of view.

- Display **empathy**; i.e., perceive sensitively and "walk in someone else's shoes."

- Have **self-knowledge**; i.e., show metacognition, use productive habits of mind, and reflect on the meaning of their learning and experience.

These six facets do not present a theory of how people come to understand something. Instead, the facets are intended to serve as indicators of how understanding is revealed, and thus provide guidance as to the kinds of assessments we need to determine the extent of student understanding. Here are two notes regarding assessing understanding through the facets:

1) All six facets of understanding need not be used all of the time in assessment. In social studies, Empathy and Perspective may be added when appropriate.

2) Performance Tasks based on one or more facets are not intended for use in daily lessons. Rather, these tasks should be seen as culminating performances for a unit of study.

In addition to Performance Tasks, Stage 2 includes Other Evidence, such as traditional quizzes, tests, observations, and work samples to round out the assessment picture to

Examples of Essential Questions in Social Studies	
Understandings or Big Ideas	**Essential Questions**
History involves interpretation, and different people may interpret the same events differently.	*Whose "story" is this? How do we know what <u>really</u> happened in the past?*
The geography, climate, and natural resources of a region influence the culture, economy, and lifestyle of its inhabitants.	*How does <u>where</u> we live influence <u>how</u> we live?*
History often repeats itself. Recognizing the patterns of the past can help us better understand the present and prepare for the future.	*Why study the past? What does the past have to do with today?*
Governments can change based on the changing needs of their people, the society, and the world.	*What makes an effective government? Why do/should governments change?*

[1] Wiggins, G. and McTighe, J. (1998, 2005). *Understanding by Design.* Alexandria, VA: The Association for Supervision and Curriculum Development.

UNDERSTANDING BY DESIGN®
(continued)

determine what students know and can do. A key idea in backward design has to do with alignment. In other words, are we assessing everything that we are trying to achieve (in Stage 1) or only those things that are easiest to test and grade? Is anything important slipping through the cracks because it is not being assessed? Checking the alignment between Stages 1 and 2 helps ensure that *all* important goals are appropriately assessed.

Stage 3 – Plan Learning Experiences and Instruction

How will we support learners in coming to an understanding of important ideas and processes? How will we prepare them to autonomously transfer their learning? What enabling knowledge and skills will students need in order to perform effectively and achieve desired results? What activities, sequence, and resources are best suited to accomplish our goals?

In Stage 3 of backward design,

teachers now plan the most appropriate learning activities to help students acquire important knowledge and skills, come to understand important ideas and processes, and transfer their learning in meaningful ways. When developing a plan for learning, we propose that teachers consider a set of instructional principles, embedded in the acronym W.H.E.R.E.T.O. These design elements provide the armature or blueprint for instructional planning in Stage 3 in support of our goals of understanding and transfer.

Each of the W.H.E.R.E.T.O. elements is presented in the form of questions to consider.

W = *How will I help learners know – What they will be learning? Why this is worth learning? What evidence will show their learning? How their performance will be evaluated?*

Learners of all ages are more likely to put forth effort and meet with success when they understand the learning goals and see them as meaningful and personally relevant. The "W" in W.H.E.R.E.T.O. reminds teachers to clearly communicate the goals and help students see their relevance. In addition, learners need to know the concomitant performance expectations and assessments through which they will demonstrate their learning so that they have clear learning targets and the basis for monitoring their progress toward them.

H = *How will I hook and engage the learners?*

There is wisdom in the old adage: "Before you try to teach them, you've got to get their attention." The best teachers have always recognized the value of "hooking" learners through introductory activities that "itch" the mind and engage the heart in the learning process, and we encourage teachers to deliberately plan ways of hooking their learners to the topics they teach. Examples of effective hooks include provocative essential questions, counter-intuitive phenomena, controversial issues, authentic problems and challenges, emotional encounters, and humor. One must be mindful, of course, of not just coming up with interesting introductory activities that have no carry-over value. The intent is to match the hook with the content and

the experiences of the learners—by design—as a means of drawing them into a productive learning experience.

E = *How will I equip students to master identified standards and succeed with the transfer performances? What learning experiences will help develop and deepen understanding of important ideas?*

Understanding cannot be simply transferred like a load of freight from one mind to another. Coming to understand requires active intellectual engagement on the part of the learner. Therefore, instead of merely covering the content, effective educators "uncover" the most enduring ideas and processes in ways that engage students in constructing meaning for themselves. To this end, teachers select an appropriate balance of constructivist learning experiences, structured activities, and direct instruction for helping students acquire the desired knowledge, skill, and understanding. While there is certainly a place for direct instruction and modeling, teaching for understanding asks teachers to engage learners in making meaning through active inquiry.

R = *How will I encourage the learners to rethink previous learning? How will I encourage on-going revision and refinement?*

Few learners develop a complete understanding of abstract ideas on the first encounter. Indeed, the phrase "coming to understand" is suggestive of a process. Over time, learners develop and deepen their understanding by thinking and re-thinking, by examining ideas from a different point of view, from examining underlying assumptions, by receiving feedback and revising. Just as the quality of

writing benefits from the iterative process of drafting and revising, so to do understandings become more mature. The "R" in W.H.E.R.E.T.O. encourages teachers to explicitly include such opportunities.

E = *How will I promote students' self-evaluation and reflection?*

Capable and independent learners are distinguished by their capacity to set goals, self-assess their progress, and adjust as needed. Yet, one of the most frequently overlooked aspects of the instructional process involves helping students to develop the meta-cognitive skills of self-evaluation, self-regulation, and reflection. The second "E" of WHERETO reminds teachers to build in time and expectations for students to regularly self-assess, reflect on the meaning of their learning, and set goals for future performance.

T = *How will I tailor the learning experiences to the nature of the learners I serve? How might I differentiate instruction to respond to the varied needs of students?*

"One size fits all teaching" is rarely optimal. Learners differ significantly in terms of their prior knowledge and skill levels, their interests, talents, and preferred ways of learning. Accordingly, the most effective teachers get to know their students and tailor their teaching and learning experiences to connect to them. A variety of strategies may be employed to differentiate *content* (e.g., how subject matter is presented), *process* (e.g., how students work), and *product* (e.g., how learners demonstrate their learning). The logic of backward design offers a cautionary note here: the Content Standards and Understandings should *not* be differentiated (except for students with Individualized Education Plans

—I.E.P.s). In other words, differentiate means keeping the end in mind for all.

O = *How will I organize the learning experiences for maximum engagement and effectiveness? What sequence will be optimal given the understanding and transfer goals?*

When the primary educational goals involve helping students acquire basic knowledge and skills, teachers may be comfortable "covering" the content by telling and modeling.

However, when we include understanding and transfer as desired results, educators are encouraged to give careful attention to how the content is organized and sequenced. Just as effective story tellers and filmmakers often don't begin in the "beginning," teachers can consider alternatives to sequential content coverage. For example, methods such as the Case Method, Problem or Project-Based Learning, and Socratic Seminars immerse students in challenging situations, even before they may have acquired all of the "basics." They actively engage students in trying to make meaning and apply their learning in demanding circumstances without single "correct" answers.

Conclusion

Many teachers who are introduced to the backward design process have observed that while the process makes sense in theory, it often feels awkward in use. This is to be expected since the principles and practices of UbD often challenge conventional planning and teaching habits. However, with some practice, educators find that backward design becomes not only more comfortable, but a way of thinking. The resources found in this program support teaching and assessing for understanding and transfer.

professional development

WHY TEACH WITH TECHNOLOGY?

by Tom Daccord and Justin Reich, EdTechTeacher

✓ **Technology is transforming the practice of historians and should transform history classrooms as well.** While printed documents, books, maps, and artwork constitute the bulk of the historical record before 1900, the history of the last century is also captured in sound and video recording and in Web sites and other Internet resources. Today's students need to learn how to analyze and build arguments using these multimedia records as well as traditional primary sources.

✓ **So many of the sources that helped historians and history teachers fall in love with the discipline are now available online.** In recent decades, universities, libraries, archives, and other institutions have scanned and uploaded many vast treasure troves of historical sources. The Internet-connected classroom increasingly has access to the world's historical record, giving students a chance to develop critical thinking skills as well as learning historical narratives.

✓ **Whoever is doing most of the talking or most of the typing is doing most of the learning, and the more people listening the better.** Technology allows us to transfer the responsibility for learning from teachers to students, and to put students in the driver's seat of their own learning. Students who are actively engaged in creating and presenting their understandings of history are learning more than students passively listening. Technology also allows students to publish their work to broader audiences of peers, parents, and even the entire Internet-connected world. Students find the opportunities challenging, exciting, and engaging.

✓ **The more ways students have to engage with content, the more likely they are to remember and understand that content.** The Internet can provide students and teachers with access to text documents, images, sounds and songs, video, simulations, and games. The more different ways students engage with historical content, the more likely they are to make meaning of that material.

✓ **Students live in a technology-rich world, and classrooms should prepare students for that world.** When students spend most of their waking hours connected to a worldwide, online network of people, resources, and opportunities, they experience dissonance and disappointment in entering a "powered-down" school. Many students will leave school to go on to workplaces completely transformed by technology, and teachers have a responsibility to prepare students for these environments.

---

edtechteacher
21st Century Learning

Technology Extension
- Find an additional activity online that incorporates technology for this project.
- Visit the EdTechTeacher Web sites (included in the Technology Extension for this chapter) for more links, tutorials, and other resources.

Teaching With Technology

In addition to the many other online resources embedded in this program, EdTechTeacher Technology Extensions are provided for every Hands-On Chapter Project. These detailed instructions and inspiration help history teachers creatively and effectively integrate technology in their classrooms. Each Technology Extension describes a technology project, explains the rationale for the suggested technology, and provides guidelines for classroom teachers to help conduct and facilitate the activity. Each Technology Extension also provides links to pages on Teaching History with Technology (www.thwt.org) with up-to-date tutorials, guides, links to examples, and exemplary projects.

Integrating Technology Effectively

Ben Shneiderman, in his book *Leonardo's Laptop,* lays out a four-part framework for teaching with technology: Collect-Relate-Create-Donate. This framework is a helpful blueprint for designing projects and learning experiences with technology.

Collect Students should begin a project by collecting the resources necessary to produce a meaningful presentation of their understanding. In some cases, students might collect these resources through textbook reading and teacher lecture, but students should also collect resources from online collections, school library Web sites, and online searches.

Relate Technology greatly facilitates the process of students working together socially. The ability to collaborate is essential to the workplace and civic sphere of the future. In creating technology projects, students should have the chance to work together, or at least comment on each other's work, using blogs, wikis, podcasts, and other collaborative publishing tools.

Create Using multimedia publishing tools, students should have the opportunity to design presentations and performances of their historical understanding. They should make historical arguments in linear text, as well as through images, audio and video recordings, and multimedia presentations.

Donate Finally, students should create work not just for their teachers, but for broader audiences. Students who have a chance to share their work with their peers, their families, their community, and the Internet-connected world find that opportunity rewarding. Today's students experience very few barriers to expression in their networked lives, and they crave these opportunities in schools.

Learn More about Teaching History with Technology

EdTechTeacher has several Web sites designed to help social studies and history teachers learn more about teaching with technology. The Best of History Web Sites (www.besthistorysites.net) is the Internet's authoritative directory of history-related resources, Web sites, games, simulations, lesson plans, and activities. Teaching History with Technology (www.thwt.org) has a series of white papers, tutorials, and guides for enriching history teaching strategies (lecturing, discussion, presentations, assessments, and so forth) with educational technology. EdTechTeacher (www.edtechteacher.org) has additional teaching resources and information about learning opportunities such as free webinars and other professional development workshops.

Tom Daccord and Justin Reich are co-Directors of EdTechTeacher. Together they authored Best Ideas for Teaching With Technology: A Practical Guide for Teachers by Teachers.

Guidelines for Successful Technology Projects

1) **Plan for problems.** Things can go wrong when working with technology, and learning how to deal with these challenges is essential for students, and for their teachers. As you start using technology in the classroom, try to have an extra teacher, aide, student-teacher, or IT staff member in the room with you to help troubleshoot problems. When things do go wrong, stay calm, and ask your students to help you resolve challenges and make the most of class time. Always have a back up, "pencil and paper" activity prepared in case there are problems with computers or networks. Over time, teachers who practice teaching with technology experience fewer and fewer of these problems, but they can be very challenging the first time you experience them!

2) **Practice from multiple perspectives.** Whenever you develop a technology project, try to do everything that students will do from a student's perspective. If you create a blog or wiki with a teacher account, create a student account to test the technology.

3) **Adapt to your local technology resources, but don't let those resources keep you from using technology.** Some schools have excellent and ample technology resources—labs and laptop carts—that make completing technology projects straightforward. Other schools have fewer resources, but virtually every student can get access to a networked computer in school, at the library or at home, especially if you give them a few nights to do so. Many technology activities are described as if you could complete them in a few class periods, but if resources are limited, you might consider spreading the activity out over a few days or weeks to give students the chance to get online.

4) **Plan with a partner.** Going it alone can be scary. If possible, have another teacher in your department or on your team, design and pilot technology projects with you to help solve the challenges that crop up whenever trying out new pedagogies.

5) **It's harder, then it gets easier.** Learning new teaching strategies is always hard. With technology, however, once you get past the initial learning curve there are all sorts of ways technology can make teaching more efficient and simultaneously make learning more meaningful for students.

BACKGROUND KNOWLEDGE:
THE KEY TO UNDERSTANDING
by Douglas Fisher, Ph.D., and Nancy Frey, Ph.D.

Mention background knowledge and most middle school educators will tell you that it is an essential component of history and social studies learning. They will discuss the importance of activating it in their students and building it when there are gaps. Yet most will also confess to being unsure of how to accomplish this in a systematic way beyond asking some questions about prior experiences. As for the gaps, how can anyone find the time to build it when there is so much new information to be covered?

The answer is to integrate background knowledge activation, building, and assessment into the heart of the lesson, not just as bookends to new learning. The reasons for this are pretty striking. Background knowledge directly influences a learner's ability to understand new information and act upon it (RAND Reading Study Group, 2002). In addition, background knowledge is demonstrated through the use of academic vocabulary and academic language, an important measure of content learning (Cromley & Azevedo, 2007). Finally, students with strong background knowledge about a topic process text better, especially in their ability to monitor and correct comprehension difficulties (Cakir, 2008).

Cultivating Background Knowledge

The key to understanding new information is to link it to what is already known. A feature of initial learning is that we aren't very good at doing so. Our efforts to focus on what is unfa-miliar temporarily blind us to what we already know. It is helpful to have well-placed reminders about what is already known, because it assists us in marshalling the familiar in order to understand the new.

When we ask questions of students about prior experiences, or invite them to engage in a quickwrite about a previously taught topic, we are activating their background knowledge. More importantly, we are providing the signposts they need to direct them to the most salient information they will need to learn the new material. For example, a study of ancient Rome doesn't merely begin with the legendary founding of a great city by two boys raised by wolves. It also requires knowledge of the influence of ancient Greek civilization on Rome's governance, military, art, and culture. It is easy, however, for students to temporarily forget everything they have learned about Greece in their effort to assimilate new information. Well-placed questions, writing opportunities, and graphic organizers can remind them of what they have previously learned.

Another means for cultivating background knowledge is to assess what students know (or think they know) about a topic. This shouldn't be a quiz of isolated facts, but instead should focus on the anticipated misconceptions that a learner is likely to hold about a new topic. For instance, it is easy for students to confuse what they have learned about Greek mythology when learning about Roman gods and goddesses. Those terms (gods and goddesses) alone suggest that for Romans this was at the heart of their religious beliefs. But Roman mythology differs from Greek mythology. For Greeks, mythology formed the heart of religion. For Romans, the gods and goddesses made for good stories, but weren't necessarily worshiped. Posing questions that are designed to surface misconceptions such as this help to rectify incorrect perceptions before they are ingrained.

Assessing Background Knowledge

Despite the efforts of caring educators, families, and communities, students come to us with gaps in their background knowledge. This can be due to a variety of causes, including frequent moves, second language acquisition, lack of experience with a topic, or difficulty with the content itself. Students at the middle school level face the additional well-documented challenges of transitioning from elementary school, where one teacher made connections for them to background knowledge, to a middle school schedule with many teachers and content areas. These changes require them to make more of their own connections across subjects.

In addition, a middle school schedule leaves us with less time across the day to get to know our students and the background knowledge they possess. It is useful to have formative assessment embedded into lessons in order to gauge where gaps might exist.

Activities that draw on core background knowledge necessary for deep understanding of new information provide these opportunities. Lessons that invite students to construct graphic organizers using both new knowledge and background knowledge give us such a window. A well-placed question invites students to consider what they already know.

If and when students have difficulty with activities like this, the teacher can pause to supply missing background knowledge. This may be done through direct explanation, by drawing their attention to features in the text, and even to returning to a previous chapter to revisit information. These need not be seen as delays, but rather as time well spent to solidify foundational knowledge.

Building Background Knowledge

Effective middle school educators take a proactive stance to building background knowledge by creating opportunities to do so. They conduct read alouds and shared readings of text and provide visual information to build students' mental image banks. Texts and images related to necessary background knowledge are especially useful in history and social studies, where students are required to understand and use primary source documents. A challenge is that many of these are hard for students to make sense of on their own, as they often use archaic language and represent ideas that are not con-

PHOTO: SW Productions/Getty Images

temporary to adolescent lives. Texts and images carefully selected with middle school students in mind can build their background knowledge of the people and times being studied, and help them more fully appreciate the influences one culture has upon another. For example, illustrations of Greek and Roman architecture invite comparison. Maps of the ancient world highlight why empires fought over land.

Student background knowledge is also built through deeper understanding of the academic vocabulary and language that lies at the heart of history and social studies. By using

a think aloud technique, teachers build their students' background knowledge about the derivation of the term, as well as the way they approach an unfamiliar word. This ensures that students will recall the term more precisely while also equipping them with a problem-solving strategy to apply to other new words.

Conclusion

McGraw-Hill **netw⦿rks** learning system offers middle school educators the tools needed to activate, assess, and build student background knowledge by infusing approaches like this into the lesson design. The habit of mind of drawing on what one already knows and seeking information to fill in knowledge gaps begins with educators like you who show students how this is done.

Douglas Fisher, Ph.D., and Nancy Frey, Ph.D., are professors in the School of Teacher Education at San Diego State University.

Cakir, O. (2008). The effect of textual differences on children's processing strategies. *Reading Improvement, 45*(2), 69-83.

Cromley, J. G., & Azevedo, R. (2007). Testing and refining the direct and inferential mediation model of reading comprehension. *Journal of Educational Psychology, 99*(2), 311-325.

RAND *Reading Study Group. (2002). Reading for understanding: Toward an R&D program in reading comprehension.* Office of Educational Research and Improvement. Santa Monica, CA: RAND.

USING FOLDABLES® IN THE CLASSROOM
by Rhonda Meyer Vivian, Ph.D., and Nancy F. Wisker, M.A.

Graphic Organizers

Current research shows that graphic organizers are powerful teaching and learning tools. Most of us are familiar with common graphic organizers such as diagrams, maps, outlines, and charts, all of which are two-dimensional. Foldables® are three-dimensional, interactive graphic organizers that were created more than 30 years ago by educator Dinah Zike.

Graphic organizers are visual representations combining line, shape, space, and symbols to convey facts and concepts or to organize information. Graphic organizers, when designed and used appropriately:

- Speed up communication
- Help organize information
- Are easy-to-understand
- Show complex relationships
- Clarify concepts with few words
- Convey ideas and understanding
- Assess comprehension

Graphic organizers help students organize information in a visual manner. This is a profound concept, especially as the number of non-native English-speaking students increases. A student is able to use graphic organizers to clarify concepts or to convey ideas and understandings with fewer words.

Graphic organizers also make complex relationships or concepts easier to understand, particularly for visual learners. Foldables take that process to the next level, most notably, for tactile/kinesthetic learners.

When to Use Graphic Organizers

Graphic organizers may be used at any point during instruction, but just as with any other instructional strategy, they are most successful when they are built into the instructional plan, rather than presented as an "extra" activity.

Graphic organizers may work better than outline notes in helping students discover or understand relationships between concepts. Foldables help teach students how to take notes by visually and kinesthetically chunking information into sections.

Foldables may be used as an alternative form of assessment in the classroom. Because the Foldable has readily identifiable sections, a teacher can quickly see gaps in student knowledge.

Reading, Writing, and Social Studies

Graphic organizers have been shown to be highly effective in literacy development. In numerous studies, graphic organizers help improve the development of literacy skills—including oral, written, and comprehension.

Graphic organizers have been found to help students organize information from expository social studies texts and comprehend content area reading. They also help students develop critical thinking skills and help transfer these skills to new situations and content areas.

Students With Special Needs

Graphic organizers may help English language learners improve higher-order thinking skills.

Because of their visual organization, graphic organizers seem to be quite beneficial for use with learning disabled students. They appear to help students understand content area material, to organize information, and to retain and recall content.

Conclusions

Graphic organizers may lead to improved student performance, whether measured by classroom-based observation, textbook assessments, or standardized assessments, when compared with more traditional forms of instruction.

When students construct their own graphic organizers, as they do with Foldables, they are active participants in their learning.

Our goal as educators is to help students glean important information and understand key concepts and to be able to relate these concepts or apply them to real-world situations. Graphic organizers help support and develop students' note-taking skills, summarizing skills, reading comprehension, and vocabulary development, which leads to better understanding and application of social studies content.

Dinah Zike is an award-winning author, educator, educational consultant, and inventor, known internationally for graphic organizers known as Foldables®. Based outside of San Antonio, Texas, Zike is a frequent keynote speaker and conducts seminars for over 50,000 teachers and parents annually.

Rhonda Myer Vivian, Ph.D., is CEO of Dinah-Might Adventures, LP, and Nancy F. Whisker, M.A., is Director of Math and Science for Dinah-Might Adventures, L.P.

FOLDABLES®

Notebook Foldables®

Using Foldables® in the *Reading Essentials and Study Guide* will help your students develop note-taking and critical thinking skills while directly interacting with the text.

Templates allow students to make their own Notebook Foldables®.

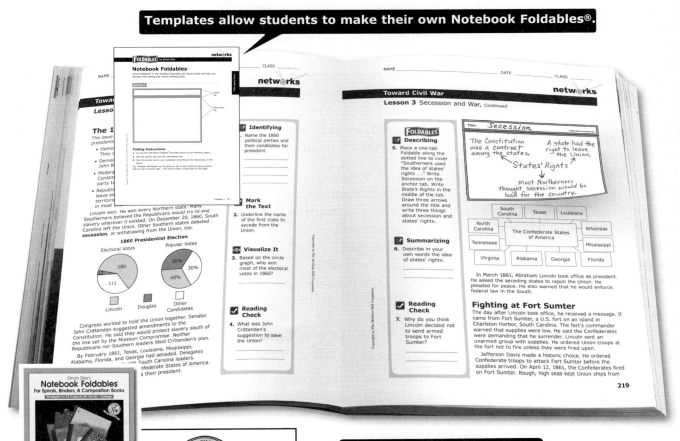

The *Reading Essentials and Study Guide* extends learning with Dinah Zike's award winning Notebook Foldables®. Notebook Foldables are specially designed to fit in workbooks and composition books. In partnership with Dinah, McGraw-Hill has developed the *Reading Essentials and Study Guide* with Notebook Foldables® to engage students more fully in social studies content.

It is easy to make Notebook Foldables®

1. **FOLD** an anchor tab and the desired number of information tabs.

2. **GLUE** the anchor tab.

3. **CUT** information tabs.

Students will master social studies concepts, ideas, and facts as they complete the side margin activities in this workbook, along with the many Notebook Foldables activities placed within the pages.

COLLEGE AND CAREER READINESS

Why Is College & Career Readiness Crucial?

- Only 70% of American students receive a high school diploma.
- Of that 70% of high school graduates, 53% of those who make it to college require remedial help.
- Over 90% of new jobs that will be available to students in the 21st century will require some postsecondary education.
- Most employers today cannot compete successfully without a workforce that has solid academic skills.
- The average difference in salary between someone with a high school degree and someone with postsecondary credentials can be $1 million over their lifetimes.

What Is College & Career Readiness?

Students are college and career ready when they have the level of preparation needed to academically, socially, and cognitively complete a postsecondary course of study without remediation. Students are prepared when they can enter the workforce at a level at which they are in line for promotion and career enhancement.

The ultimate goal of the college & career readiness initiative is to maintain America's competitive edge in the global economy of today. The workforce of the 21st century is an increasingly global, knowledge-based economy that demands the ability to:

- Think critically
- Solve problems
- Create and innovate
- Communicate
- Collaborate
- Learn new skills
- Use ICT (information and communications technology)

Explain College & Career Readiness to Students

One of the first steps you should take is to provide students with a framework that will help them see the relevancy of what they do in school. The three principal elements of College & Career Readiness (CCR) are:

- an understanding of core academic skills and the ability to apply them in educational and employment settings
- familiarity with skills valued by a broad range of employers such as communication, critical thinking, and responsibility
- mastery of the technologies and skill sets associated with a career pathway

Once students have been exposed to these elements, it is critical for them to see how they relate to their own plans for continuing education and career choice. Mention that CCR is more than just a personal issue, and it affects the country and our quality of life.

Most students—as well as many adults—consider work to be an obligation that they must perform in order to have money. Earning a salary is, of course, a central benefit of working, but so is the sense of satisfaction that comes from doing a job well. Moreover, every job contributes to the quality of life in our communities and our nation. Being prepared to pursue an education or get a job after high school is the hallmark of a good citizen.

Recognize That All Careers Are Important

Without question, the greatest challenge faced by educators, parents, and the public is recognizing that all jobs are important. When you discuss careers, be generous with your reflections and encourage your students to do the same. Be sure to mention the enormous variety of opportunities

available to them in diverse fields. The more that students can recognize the rich possibilities of whatever career they pursue, the more likely they will be to enjoy success and personal satisfaction.

Students typically have a relatively narrow perspective on the careers and jobs available to them. As part of the discussion of careers, broaden this perspective by reviewing some opportunities that your students might not be aware of. An interesting place to start is in the high profile industries of sports and entertainment.

Many students dream of being celebrities and have no idea about how unlikely this is. What they don't realize is that for every professional athlete, singer, or movie star, there are a hundred or more fascinating careers including sports trainers, writers, administrative assistants, drivers, and a seemingly endless list of other jobs. Not surprisingly, students usually respond positively when they learn that just in case they are not the next superstar in sports or entertainment, there are other opportunities that will allow them to achieve their dream in a slightly different way.

Students can explore careers in many ways; one way is by reviewing the 16 career clusters. Career clusters are groups of similar occupations and industries. They were developed by the U.S. Department of Education as a way to organize career planning. Students can visit the Career Center at http://ccr.mcgraw-hill.com/ to begin their explorations.

Make It Clear That There Are Various Paths To Success

A surprisingly small percentage of adults reach their careers through a direct and well-planned strategy. Familiarizing students with the vari-

ous paths to success provides them with a realistic view of what life is like after high school and college. It may also give them an anchor in their own lives in the future when they find that they are wandering, which most of them will inevitably do.

Divergence from a direct path to a career is almost inevitable, and in many cases, is a desirable and enriching experience. Helping students to recognize this will make their future challenges seem less intimidating.

Have students investigate and discuss the career paths of people they know personally and by reputation, including celebrities. This discussion will promote engagement while show-

ing the twists and turns that usually lead to success. Be sure to include some common but less-known paths, like the college benefits associated with military service or the arrangements nurses might make with a hospital to exchange tuition payments for a commitment of several years.

Make College & Career Readiness a regular part of interactive classroom discussions.

Unlike many other school subjects, a critical aspect of College & Career Readiness is its focus is on the future of each student, not the content of a course. Perhaps the best way to have students recognize this is to be sure that the time you spend discussing students' future pathways is truly interactive, with at least as much commentary from students as there is from you or other adult participants.

Because students are more willing to participate in discussions that have personal meaning to them, consider using these questions as starting points. These are "self-mentoring" questions that will help students clarify their thinking.

- What is something you really want to do in the next 10 years?
- How do you plan to get there?
- What is your back-up plan?
- What is something that you have done that made you proud?
- In which postsecondary courses do you think you would do best? Why do you think this?
- Imagine that you are going into the military. This choice involves activities that are hard physically and mentally. How would you handle these challenges?
- When you can't make up your mind about something important, what do you do?

Have students explore college & career readiness on their own at http://ccr.mcgraw-hill.com/ .

MEETING THE DIVERSE NEEDS OF OUR STUDENTS

by Douglas Fisher, Ph.D.

Today's classroom contains students from a variety of backgrounds with a variety of learning styles, strengths, and challenges. As teachers we are facing the challenge of helping students reach their educational potential. With careful planning, you can address the needs of all students in the social studies classroom. The basis for this planning is universal access. When classrooms are planned with universal access in mind, fewer students require specific accommodations.

What Is a Universal Access Design for Learning?

Universal design was first conceived in architectural studies when business people, engineers, and architects began making considerations for physical access to buildings. The idea was to plan the environment in advance to ensure that everyone had access.

As a result, the environment would not have to be changed later for people with physical disabilities, people pushing strollers, workers who had injuries, or others for whom the environment would be difficult to negotiate. The Center for Universal Design at <u>www.design.ncsu.edu/cud</u> defines Universal Design as:

The design of products and environments to be usable by all people, to the greatest extent possible, without the need for adaptation or specialized design.

Universal Design and Access in Education

Researchers, teachers, and parents in education have expanded the development of built-in adaptations and inclusive accommodations from architectural space to the educational experience, especially in the area of curriculum.

In 1998, the National Center to Improve the Tools of Educators (NCITE), with the partnership of the Center for Applied Special Technology (CAST), proposed an expanded definition of universal design focused on education:

In terms of learning, universal design means the design of instructional materials and activities that allows the learning goals to be achievable by individuals with wide differences in their abilities to see, hear, speak, move, read, write, understand English, attend, organize, engage, and remember.

How Does Universal Design Work in Education?

Universal design and access, as they apply to education and schooling, suggest the following:

✓ **Inclusive Classroom Participation**
Curriculum should be designed with all students and their needs in mind. The McGraw-Hill social studies print and online texts and materials were designed with a wide range of students in mind. For example, understanding that English learners and students who struggle with reading would be using this text, vocabulary is specifically taught and reinforced. Similarly, the teacher-support materials provide multiple instructional points to be used depending on the needs of the students in the class. Further, the text is written such that essential questions and guiding questions are identified for all learners.

✓ **Maximum Text Readability**
In universally designed classrooms that provide access for all students, texts use direct language, clear noun-verb agreements, and clear construct-based wording. In addition to these factors, the McGraw-Hill social studies texts use embedded

definitions for difficult terms, provide for specific instruction in reading skills, use a number of visual representations, and include note-taking guides.

✓ **Adaptable and Accommodating**
The content in this textbook can be easily translated, read aloud, or otherwise changed to meet the needs of students in the classroom. The lesson and end-of-chapter activities and assessments provide students with multiple ways of demonstrating their content knowledge while also ensuring that they have practice with thinking in terms of multiple-choice questions. Critical thinking and analysis skills are also practiced.

How Is Differentiated Instruction the Key to Universal Access?

To differentiate instruction, teachers must acknowledge student differences in background knowledge and current reading, writing, and English language skills. They must also consider student learning styles and preferences, interests, and needs, and react accordingly. There are a number of general guidelines for differentiating instruction in the classroom to reach all students, including:

✓ **Link Assessment With Instruction**
Assessments should occur before, during, and after instruction to ensure that the curriculum is aligned with what students do and do not know. Using assessments in this way allows you to plan instruction for whole groups, small groups, and individual students. Backward plan-

ning, where you establish the assessment before you begin instruction, is also important.

✓ **Clarify Key Concepts and Generalizations**
Students need to know what is essential and how this information can be used in their future learning. In addition, students need to develop a sense of the big ideas—ideas that transcend time and place.

✓ **Emphasize Critical and Creative Thinking**
The content, process, and products used or assigned in the classroom should require that students think about what they are learning. While some students may require support, additional motivation, varied tasks, materials, or equipment, the overall focus on critical and creative thinking allows for all students to participate in the lesson.

✓ **Include Teacher- and Student-Selected Tasks**
A differentiated classroom includes both teacher- and student-selected activities and tasks. At some points in the lesson or day, the teacher must provide instruction and assign learning activities. In other parts of the lesson, students should be provided choices in how they engage with the content. This balance increases motivation, engagement, and learning.

How Do I Support Individual Students?

The vast majority of students will thrive in a classroom based on universal access and differentiated instruction. However, wise teachers recognize that no single option will work for all students and that there may be students who require unique systems of support to be successful.

Classroom Activity

Display a map of imperialism in Africa around 1914. Discuss with students the map's general information and have them list each country under the European power that controlled it.

To differentiate this activity:

- Have students imagine they are living in the early 1900s. Have them write a letter to a British newspaper about colonial rule in Africa.
- Have students record the number of African countries under European rule. Have them take the data and create a bar graph that shows which European powers were the most active colonizers at the time.
- Have students compose a song or poem about European rule in Africa, from an African's point of view.
- Have students choose a country of modern Africa to research. Have them write a three-page paper discussing how that country was affected by colonialism and how it has changed since the days of European rule.

MEETING THE DIVERSE NEEDS OF OUR STUDENTS
(continued)

Tips For Instruction

The following tips for instruction can support your efforts to help all students reach their maximum potential.

✓ Survey students to discover their individual differences. Use interest inventories of their unique talents so you can encourage contributions in the classroom.

✓ Be a model for respecting others. Adolescents crave social acceptance. The student with learning differences is especially sensitive to correction and criticism, particularly when it comes from a teacher. Your behavior will set the tone for how students treat one another.

✓ Expand opportunities for success. Provide a variety of instructional activities that reinforce skills and concepts.

✓ Establish measurable objectives and decide how you can best help students who meet them.

✓ Celebrate successes and make note of and praise "work in progress."

✓ Keep it simple. Point out problem areas if doing so can help

a student effect change. Avoid overwhelming students with too many goals at one time.

✓ Assign cooperative group projects that challenge all students to contribute to solving a problem or creating a product.

How Do I Reach Students With Learning Disabilities?

✓ Provide support and structure. Clearly specify rules, assignments, and responsibilities.

✓ Practice skills frequently. Use games and drills to help maintain student interest.

✓ Incorporate many modalities into the learning process. Provide opportunities to say, hear, write, read, and act out important concepts and information.

✓ Link new skills and concepts to those already mastered.

✓ If possible, allow students to record answers on audio.

✓ Allow extra time to complete assessments and assignments.

✓ Let students demonstrate proficiency with alternative presentations, including oral reports, role plays, art projects, and musical presentations.

✓ Provide outlines, notes, or recordings of lecture material.

✓ Pair students with peer helpers, and provide class time for pair interaction.

How Do I Reach Students With Behavioral Challenges?

✓ Provide a structured environment with clear-cut schedules,

rules, seat assignments, and safety procedures.

✓ Reinforce appropriate behavior and model it for students.

✓ Cue distracted students back to the task through verbal signals and teacher proximity.

✓ Set goals that can be achieved in the short term. Work for long-term improvement in the big areas.

How Do I Reach Students With Physical Challenges?

✓ Openly discuss with the student any uncertainties you have about when to offer aid.

✓ Ask parents or therapists and students what special devices or procedures are needed and whether any special safety precautions need to be taken.

✓ Welcome students with physical challenges into all activities, including field trips, special events, and projects.

✓ Provide information to assist class members and adults in their understanding of support needed.

How Do I Reach Students with Visual Impairments?

✓ Facilitate independence. Modify assignments as needed.

✓ Teach classmates how and when to serve as visual guides.

✓ Limit unnecessary noise in the classroom if it distracts the student with visual impairments.

✓ Provide tactile models whenever possible.

✓ Foster a spirit of inclusion. Describe people and events as they occur in the classroom. Remind classmates that the student with visual impairments cannot interpret gestures and other forms of nonverbal communication.

✓ Provide recorded lectures and reading assignments for use outside the classroom.

✓ Team the student with a sighted peer for written work.

How Do I Reach Students With Hearing Impairments?

✓ Seat students where they can see your lip movements easily and where they can avoid any visual distractions.

✓ Avoid standing with your back to the window or light source.

✓ Use an overhead projector so you can maintain eye contact while writing information for students.

✓ Seat students where they can see speakers.

✓ Write all assignments on the board, or hand out written instructions.

✓ If the student has a manual interpreter, allow both student and interpreter to select the most favorable seating arrangements.

✓ Teach students to look directly at each other when they speak.

How Do I Reach English Learners?

✓ Remember, students' ability to speak English does not reflect their academic abilities.

✓ Try to incorporate the students' cultural experience into your instruction. The help of a bilingual aide may be effective.

✓ Avoid any references in your instruction that could be construed as cultural stereotypes.

✓ Preteach important vocabulary and concepts.

✓ Encourage students to preview text before they begin reading, noting headings.

✓ Remind students not to ignore graphic organizers, photographs, and maps since there is much information in these visuals.

✓ Use memorabilia and photographs whenever possible to build background knowledge and understanding. An example of this would be coins in a foreign currency or a raw cotton ball to reinforce its importance in history.

How Do I Reach Gifted Students?

✓ Make arrangements for students to take selected subjects early and to work on independent projects.

✓ Ask "what if" questions to develop high-level thinking skills. Establish an environment safe for risk taking in your classroom.

✓ Emphasize concepts, theories, ideas, relationships, and generalizations about the content.

✓ Promote interest in the past by inviting students to make connections to the present.

✓ Let students express themselves in alternate ways such as creative writing, acting, debates, simulations, drawing, or music.

✓ Provide students with a catalog of helpful resources, listing such things as agencies that provide free and inexpensive materials, appropriate community services and programs, and community experts who might be called upon to speak to your students.

✓ Assign extension projects that allow students to solve real-life problems related to their communities.

Classroom Activity

Students respond eagerly to a subject when they can relate it to their own experiences. With the growing number of students who come from other world regions, explaining geography through a global theme (such as volcanoes) can give them a worldwide as well as a regional perspective. To develop this awareness, display a large world map. Have students use the library or the Internet to research the latitude and longitude of 15 major volcanoes around the world. Ask them to mark these locations on the map and answer the following questions:

• What patterns do you see in volcanic activity?

• What causes volcanic activity?

• Where in the world are volcanoes most active?

As a follow-up, suggest students go to http://volcano.und.nodak.edu/vwdocs/kids/legends.html to find legends about the origins of some of the world's volcanoes. Encourage students to share what they find with the class.

development

ACADEMIC VOCABULARY
How Can I Help My Students Learn Academic Vocabulary?

What Is Academic English?

Academic English is the language used in academics, business, and courts of law. It is the type of English used in textbooks, and contains linguistic features associated with academic disciplines like social studies. Proficiency in reading and using academic English is especially related to long-term success in all parts of life.

By reinforcing academic English, teachers can help learners to access authentic, academic texts—not simplified texts that dummy down the content. In this way, they can provide information that will help build their students' background knowledge rapidly.

What Is Academic Vocabulary?

Academic vocabulary is based on academic English. By the time children have completed elementary school, they must have acquired the knowledge needed to understand academic vocabulary. How many words should they acquire to be able to access their texts? A basic 2,000-word vocabulary of high-frequency words makes up 87% of the vocabulary of academic texts. Eight hundred other academic words comprise an additional 8% of the words. Three percent of the remaining words are technical words. The remaining 2% are low-frequency words. There may be as many as 123,000 low-frequency words in academic texts.

Why Should Students Learn Academic Vocabulary?

English learners who have a basic 2,000-word vocabulary are ready to acquire most general words found in their texts.

Knowledge of academic words and general words can significantly boost a student's comprehension level of academic texts. Students who learn and practice these words before they graduate from high school are more likely to master

academic material with increased confidence and speed. They waste less time and effort in guessing words or consulting dictionaries than those who only know the basic 2,000 words that characterize general conversation.

How Do I Include Academic Vocabulary and Academic English in My Teaching?

Teachers can provide students with academic vocabulary and help students understand the academic English of their text.

To develop academic English, learners must have already acquired basic proficiency in everyday English.

Academic English should be taught within contexts that make sense. In terms of instruction, teaching academic English includes providing students with access to core curriculum—in this case social studies.

Academic English arises in part from social practices in which academic English is used. The acquisition of academic vocabulary and grammar is necessary to advance the development of academic English.

Tips for Teaching Academic Vocabulary

✓ **Expose Students to Academic Vocabulary** You do not need to call attention to words students are learning because they will acquire them subconsciously.

✓ **Do Not Correct Students' Mistakes When Using the Vocabulary Words** All vocabulary understanding and spelling errors will disappear once the student reads more.

✓ **Help Students Decode the Words Themselves** Once they learn the alphabet, they should be able to decode words. Decoding each word they don't recognize will help them more than trying to focus on sentence structure. Once they can recognize the words, they can read "authentic" texts.

✓ **Do Not Ignore the English Learner in This Process** They can learn academic vocabulary before they are completely fluent in oral English.

✓ **Helping Students Build Academic Vocabulary Leads to Broader Learning** Students who have mastered the basic academic vocabulary are ready to acquire words from the rest of the groups. To help determine which words are in the 2,000-word basic group, refer to *West's General Service List of English Words,* 1953. The list is designed to serve as a guide for teachers and as a checklist and goal list for students.

Guidelines for Teaching Academic Vocabulary

1. Direct and planned instruction
2. Models—that have increasingly difficult language
3. Attention to form—pointing out linguistic features of words

Classroom Activity

Writing About Modern America

Give students a brief writing assignment. Ask them to write a short essay about one of the topics listed below in the left column. Have students use as many of the academic vocabulary words in the right column as they can in their essay. When completed, ask student volunteers to share their writing. Note which academic vocabulary words they use.

Topic	Academic Vocabulary
The challenges of reducing poverty in America	sufficient minimum medical income
Recent technological advances	innovate technology media potential data transmit

REFERENCE ATLAS

ATLAS KEY

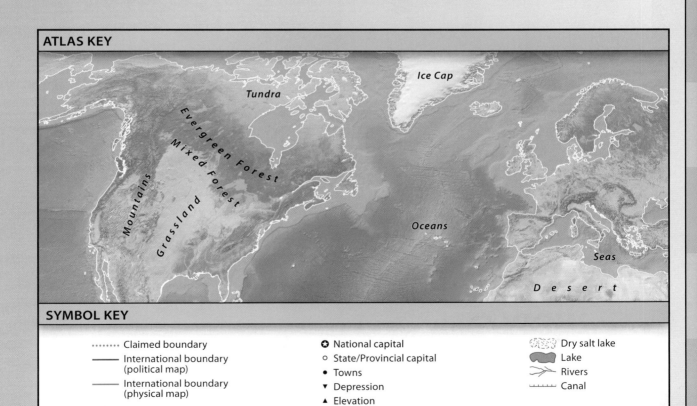

SYMBOL KEY

.... Claimed boundary	✪ National capital	Dry salt lake
—— International boundary (political map)	○ State/Provincial capital	Lake
—— International boundary (physical map)	● Towns	Rivers
	▼ Depression	Canal
	▲ Elevation	

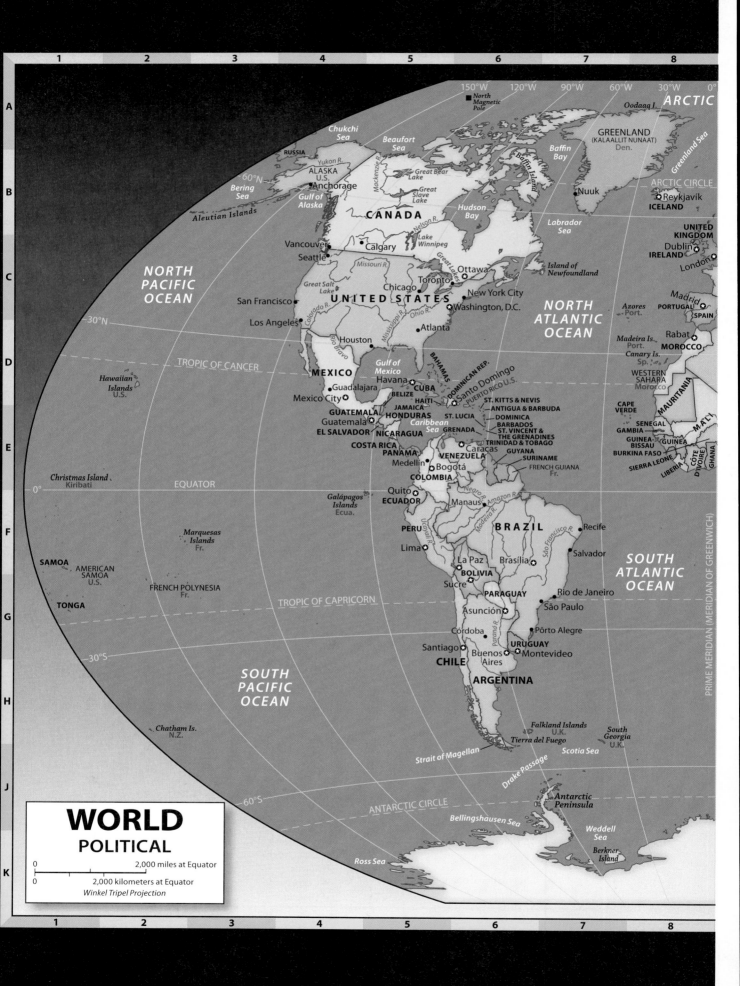

WORLD
POLITICAL

0   2,000 miles at Equator

0   2,000 kilometers at Equator

Winkel Tripel Projection

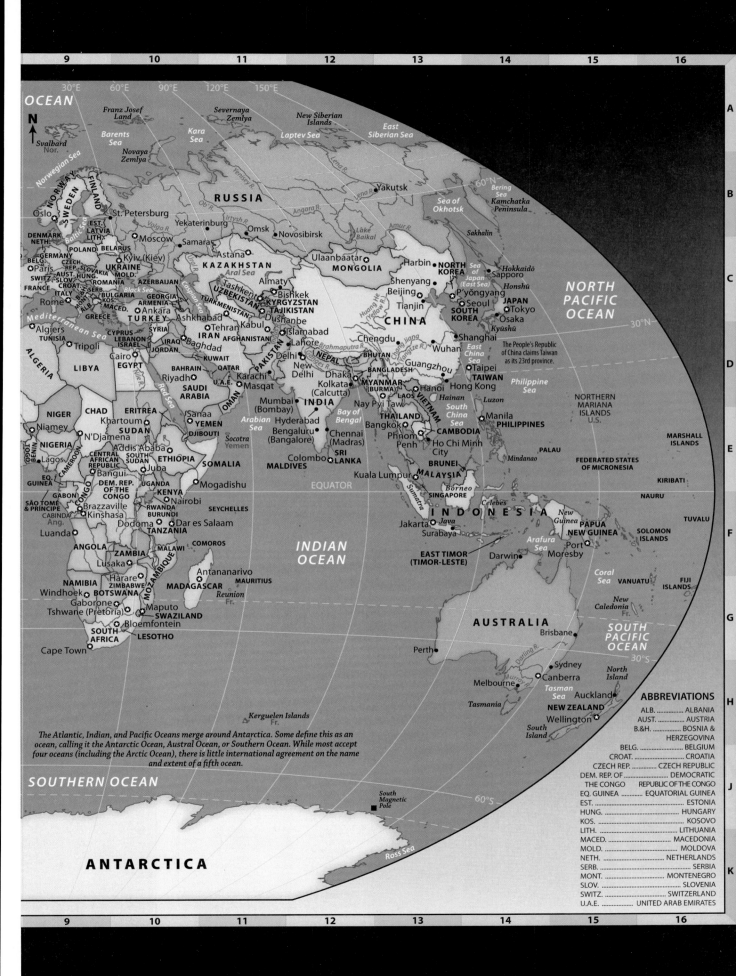

N

OCEAN

30°E   60°E   90°E   120°E   150°E

Svalbard
Nor.

Franz Josef
Land

Severnaya
Zemlya

New Siberian
Islands

East
Siberian Sea

Barents
Sea

Kara
Sea

Laptev Sea

Novaya
Zemlya

NORWEGIAN Sea

NORWAY   SWEDEN   FINLAND

Oslo   St. Petersburg

RUSSIA

Yakutsk

Bering
Sea

Kamchatka
Peninsula

60°N

DENMARK
NETH.
BELG.
GERMANY
Paris
SWITZ.   SLOV.
FRANCE
ITALY
Rome

EST.
LATVIA
LITH.
POLAND   BELARUS
CZECH
REP.   SLOVAKIA
AUST.   HUNG.
ROMANIA
SERB.   BULGARIA
MONT.   MACED.
ALB.
GREECE

Yekaterinburg
Moscow   Samara
Volga R.
UKRAINE
Kyiv (Kiev)
MOLD.
Black Sea
GEORGIA
AZERBAIJAN
ARMENIA

Omsk   Novosibirsk

Ob R.
Irtysh R.

Astana

KAZAKHSTAN
Aral Sea

Yenisey R.

Ulaanbaatar

MONGOLIA

Lake
Baikal

Angara R.

Amur R.

Sakhalin

Sea of
Okhotsk

Harbin

NORTH
KOREA

Shenyang
Beijing
Tianjin

Hokkaidō   Sapporo

Sea
of
Japan
(East Sea)

Honshū

JAPAN

Osaka
Tokyo

NORTH
PACIFIC
OCEAN

30°N

Mediterranean Sea

TUNISIA
Algiers
Tripoli

CYPRUS
LEBANON
ISRAEL
JORDAN
Cairo

TURKEY
Ankara
SYRIA
IRAQ
Baghdad

Almaty
UZBEKISTAN
Tashkent
TURKMENISTAN
Ashkhabad
IRAN
Tehran

Bishkek
KYRGYZSTAN
TAJIKISTAN
Dushanbe

Kabul
AFGHANISTAN

Islamabad
Lahore

Huang He
(Yellow R.)

Chong Jiang
Yangtze R.

CHINA

Chengdu

Wuhan

P'yŏngyang
SOUTH
KOREA   Seoul

Kyūshū

Shanghai

East
China
Sea

The People's Republic
of China claims Taiwan
as its 23rd province.

ALGERIA

LIBYA

EGYPT

SAUDI
ARABIA

KUWAIT
BAHRAIN
QATAR
U.A.E.

Riyadh

Masqat

Karachi
PAKISTAN
New
Delhi
Delhi

NEPAL
BHUTAN

Brahmaputra R.

Dhaka
BANGLADESH

Guangzhou

Hong Kong

Taipei

TAIWAN

Philippine
Sea

NORTHERN
MARIANA
ISLANDS
U.S.

NIGER   CHAD

Khartoum
SUDAN

ERITREA
Sanaa
YEMEN
DJIBOUTI

Red Sea

OMAN

Arabian
Sea

Socotra
Yemen

Mumbai
(Bombay)
INDIA
Hyderabad
Bengaluru
(Bangalore)
Chennai
(Madras)

Kolkata
(Calcutta)

MYANMAR
(BURMA)

Nay Pyi Taw

Hanoi
VIETNAM

LAOS

THAILAND
Bangkok

Hainan

South
China
Sea

Luzon

Manila

PHILIPPINES

MARSHALL
ISLANDS

NIGERIA
Niamey
N'Djamena
Lagos
CENTRAL
AFRICAN
REPUBLIC
Bangui

Addis Ababa
ETHIOPIA
SOUTH
SUDAN
Juba

SOMALIA

Colombo
SRI
LANKA
MALDIVES

Phnom
Penh
CAMBODIA
Ho Chi Minh
City
BRUNEI
MALAYSIA

PALAU

FEDERATED STATES
OF MICRONESIA

KIRIBATI

EQ.
GUINEA
GABON
SÃO TOMÉ
& PRÍNCIPE
CABINDA
Ang.
Luanda

CONGO
Brazzaville
Kinshasa

DEM. REP.
OF THE
CONGO
UGANDA
RWANDA
BURUNDI
Dodoma

KENYA
Nairobi

Mogadishu

SEYCHELLES

EQUATOR

Kuala Lumpur
SINGAPORE

Sumatra

Borneo

Celebes

INDONESIA

New
Guinea

PAPUA
NEW GUINEA

NAURU

TUVALU

SOLOMON
ISLANDS

ANGOLA

NAMIBIA
Windhoek
Gaborone
Tshwane (Pretoria)

ZAMBIA
Lusaka
Harare
ZIMBABWE
BOTSWANA

MALAWI

MOZAMBIQUE

TANZANIA
Dar es Salaam

COMOROS

Antananarivo
MADAGASCAR

MAURITIUS

Reunion
Fr.

INDIAN
OCEAN

Jakarta
Java
Surabaya

EAST TIMOR
(TIMOR-LESTE)

Arafura
Sea
Darwin

Mindanao

Port
Moresby

Coral
Sea

VANUATU

New
Caledonia
Fr.

FIJI
ISLANDS

SOUTH
AFRICA
Cape Town

Maputo
SWAZILAND
Bloemfontein
LESOTHO

AUSTRALIA

Brisbane

SOUTH
PACIFIC
OCEAN

30°S

Perth

Darling R.

Sydney
Canberra
Melbourne
Murray R.

Tasman
Sea

North
Island

Kerguelen Islands
Fr.

The Atlantic, Indian, and Pacific Oceans merge around Antarctica. Some define this as an
ocean, calling it the Antarctic Ocean, Austral Ocean, or Southern Ocean. While most accept
four oceans (including the Arctic Ocean), there is little international agreement on the name
and extent of a fifth ocean.

Tasmania

NEW ZEALAND
Wellington

South
Island

Auckland

SOUTHERN OCEAN

South
Magnetic
Pole

60°S

ANTARCTICA

Ross Sea

ABBREVIATIONS

ALB.	ALBANIA
AUST.	AUSTRIA
B.&H.	BOSNIA & HERZEGOVINA
BELG.	BELGIUM
CROAT.	CROATIA
CZECH REP.	CZECH REPUBLIC
DEM. REP. OF THE CONGO	DEMOCRATIC REPUBLIC OF THE CONGO
EQ. GUINEA	EQUATORIAL GUINEA
EST.	ESTONIA
HUNG.	HUNGARY
KOS.	KOSOVO
LITH.	LITHUANIA
MACED.	MACEDONIA
MOLD.	MOLDOVA
NETH.	NETHERLANDS
SERB.	SERBIA
MONT.	MONTENEGRO
SLOV.	SLOVENIA
SWITZ.	SWITZERLAND
U.A.E.	UNITED ARAB EMIRATES

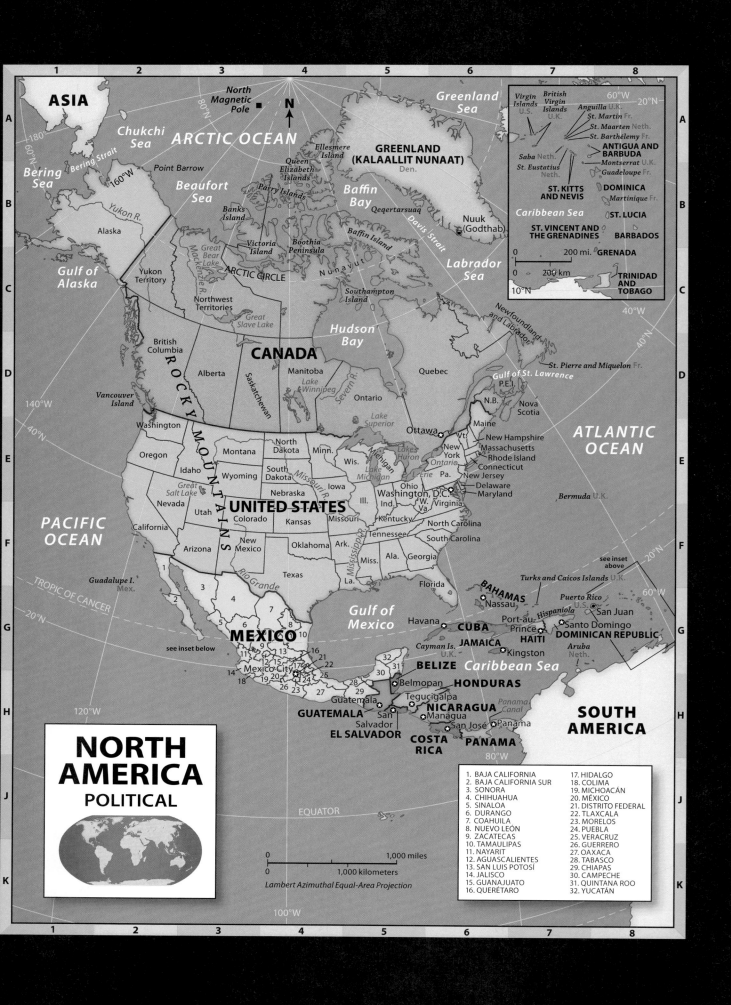

NORTH AMERICA
POLITICAL

ASIA

Chukchi
Sea

ARCTIC OCEAN

North
Magnetic
Pole

N

Greenland
Sea

Bering
Sea

Bering Strait

Point Barrow

Beaufort
Sea

Ellesmere
Island

Queen
Elizabeth
Islands

Baffin
Bay

Qeqertarsuaq

**GREENLAND
(KALAALLIT NUNAAT)**
Den.

Yukon R.

Alaska

Banks
Island

Parry Islands

Gulf of
Alaska

Yukon
Territory

Great Bear
Lake

Victoria
Island

Boothia
Peninsula

Baffin Island

Davis Strait

Nuuk
(Godthab)

ARCTIC CIRCLE

Nunavut

Labrador
Sea

Southampton
Island

British
Columbia

Northwest
Territories

Great
Slave Lake

Hudson
Bay

Newfoundland
and Labrador

CANADA

Alberta

Saskatchewan

Manitoba

Lake
Winnipeg

Quebec

Ontario

Severn R.

St. Pierre and Miquelon Fr.

Gulf of St. Lawrence

Vancouver
Island

Washington

Lake
Superior

Ottawa

P.E.I.

N.B.

Nova
Scotia

**ATLANTIC
OCEAN**

Oregon

Idaho

Montana

North
Dakota

Minn.

Wis.

Lake
Michigan

Lake
Huron

Michigan

Ontario

Lake
Erie

New
York

Vt.

Maine

New Hampshire

Massachusetts

Rhode Island

Connecticut

New Jersey

Pa.

Delaware

Maryland

Wyoming

South
Dakota

Iowa

Missouri R.

Ind.

Ohio

W.
Va.

Washington, D.C.

Virginia

Bermuda U.K.

**PACIFIC
OCEAN**

Nevada

Utah

Great
Salt Lake

Colorado

Nebraska

Kansas

Ill.

Missouri

Kentucky

California

UNITED STATES

North Carolina

Arizona

New
Mexico

Oklahoma

Ark.

Tennessee

South Carolina

TROPIC OF CANCER

Guadalupe I.
Mex.

Rio Grande

Texas

Miss.

Ala.

Georgia

La.

Mississippi

Florida

BAHAMAS

Turks and Caicos Islands U.K.

see inset
above

Puerto Rico
U.S.

Nassau

Gulf of
Mexico

Havana

CUBA

MEXICO

see inset below

Port-au-
Prince

Hispaniola

San Juan

Santo Domingo

DOMINICAN REPUBLIC

Cayman Is.
U.K.

JAMAICA

HAITI

Aruba
Neth.

Kingston

BELIZE

Caribbean Sea

Belmopan

HONDURAS

Tegucigalpa

Panama
Canal

**SOUTH
AMERICA**

GUATEMALA

Guatemala

San
Salvador

NICARAGUA

Managua

San José

Panama

EL SALVADOR

**COSTA
RICA**

PANAMA

EQUATOR

Inset (Caribbean)

Virgin
Islands
U.S.

British
Virgin
Islands
U.K.

60°W

Anguilla U.K.

20°N

St. Martin Fr.

St. Maarten Neth.

St. Barthélemy Fr.

Saba Neth.

St. Eustatius
Neth.

**ANTIGUA AND
BARBUDA**

Montserrat U.K.

Guadeloupe Fr.

Caribbean Sea

**ST. KITTS
AND NEVIS**

DOMINICA

Martinique Fr.

ST. LUCIA

**ST. VINCENT AND
THE GRENADINES**

BARBADOS

10°N

0   200 mi.   **GRENADA**

0   200 km

**TRINIDAD
AND
TOBAGO**

Mexico States Key

1. BAJA CALIFORNIA
2. BAJA CALIFORNIA SUR
3. SONORA
4. CHIHUAHUA
5. SINALOA
6. DURANGO
7. COAHUILA
8. NUEVO LEÓN
9. ZACATECAS
10. TAMAULIPAS
11. NAYARIT
12. AGUASCALIENTES
13. SAN LUIS POTOSÍ
14. JALISCO
15. GUANAJUATO
16. QUERÉTARO
17. HIDALGO
18. COLIMA
19. MICHOACÁN
20. MÉXICO
21. DISTRITO FEDERAL
22. TLAXCALA
23. MORELOS
24. PUEBLA
25. VERACRUZ
26. GUERRERO
27. OAXACA
28. TABASCO
29. CHIAPAS
30. CAMPECHE
31. QUINTANA ROO
32. YUCATÁN

0   1,000 miles
0   1,000 kilometers

Lambert Azimuthal Equal-Area Projection

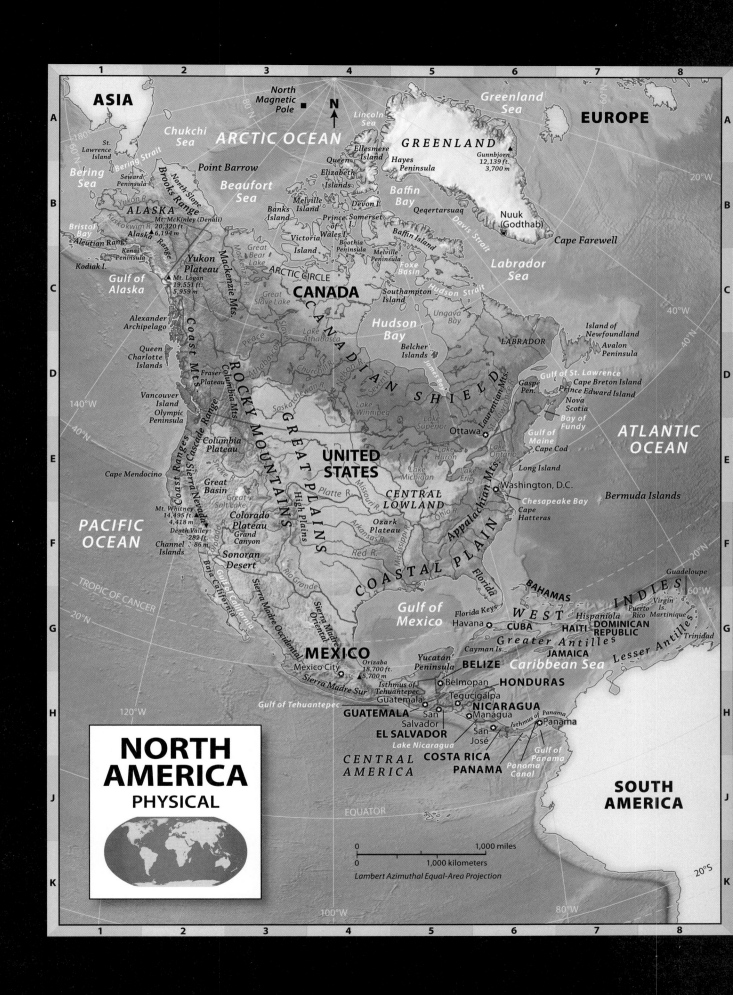

NORTH AMERICA
PHYSICAL

ASIA

EUROPE

ARCTIC OCEAN

Chukchi Sea

Bering Sea

Bering Strait

St. Lawrence Island

Point Barrow

North Slope

Beaufort Sea

Brooks Range

ALASKA

Mt. McKinley (Denali) 20,320 ft. 6,194 m

Seward Peninsula

Yukon R.

Kuskokwim R.

Bristol Bay

Aleutian Range

Kenai Peninsula

Kodiak I.

Gulf of Alaska

Alexander Archipelago

Queen Charlotte Islands

Vancouver Island

Olympic Peninsula

Cape Mendocino

Alaska Range

Mt. Logan 19,551 ft. 5,959 m

Yukon Plateau

Mackenzie Mts.

Great Bear Lake

Mackenzie R.

ARCTIC CIRCLE

CANADA

Great Slave Lake

North Magnetic Pole

N

Lincoln Sea

Greenland Sea

Ellesmere Island

GREENLAND

Gunnbjorn 12,139 ft. 3,700 m

Hayes Peninsula

Queen Elizabeth Islands

Melville Island

Devon I.

Baffin Bay

Banks Island

Prince of Wales I.

Somerset I.

Qeqertarsuaq

Davis Strait

Nuuk (Godthab)

Cape Farewell

Victoria Island

Boothia Peninsula

Melville Peninsula

Foxe Basin

Baffin Island

Labrador Sea

Hudson Strait

Southampton Island

Ungava Bay

Island of Newfoundland

Avalon Peninsula

LABRADOR

Hudson Bay

Belcher Islands

James Bay

C A N A D I A N   S H I E L D

Peace R.

Slave R.

Lake Athabasca

Athabasca R.

Churchill R.

Nelson R.

Saskatchewan R.

Severn R.

Lake Winnipeg

Lake Superior

Lake Huron

Lake Michigan

Lake Erie

Lake Ontario

Ottawa

St. Lawrence R.

Laurentian Mts.

Gulf of St. Lawrence

Gaspé Pen.

Cape Breton Island

Prince Edward Island

Nova Scotia

Bay of Fundy

Gulf of Maine

Cape Cod

Long Island

ATLANTIC OCEAN

R O C K Y   M O U N T A I N S

Fraser Plateau

Columbia Mts.

Columbia Plateau

Coast Mts.

Coast Ranges

Cascade Range

Sierra Nevada

Great Basin

Great Salt Lake

Snake R.

G R E A T   P L A I N S

High Plains

Platte R.

Missouri R.

UNITED STATES

CENTRAL LOWLAND

Washington, D.C.

Appalachian Mts.

Chesapeake Bay

Cape Hatteras

Bermuda Islands

PACIFIC OCEAN

Mt. Whitney 14,495 ft. 4,418 m

Colorado Plateau

Grand Canyon

Death Valley 282 ft. –86 m

Channel Islands

Sonoran Desert

Baja California

Rio Grande

Ozark Plateau

Arkansas R.

Red R.

Mississippi R.

Ohio R.

C O A S T A L   P L A I N

Florida

TROPIC OF CANCER

Gulf of California

Sierra Madre Occidental

Sierra Madre Oriental

MEXICO

Mexico City

Orizaba 18,700 ft. 5,700 m

Sierra Madre Sur

Isthmus of Tehuantepec

Gulf of Tehuantepec

Gulf of Mexico

Havana

Florida Keys

Yucatán Peninsula

BELIZE

Belmopan

Guatemala

GUATEMALA

San Salvador

EL SALVADOR

Tegucigalpa

HONDURAS

San José

Managua

NICARAGUA

Lake Nicaragua

COSTA RICA

PANAMA

Panama Canal

Isthmus of Panama

Panama

Gulf of Panama

CENTRAL AMERICA

BAHAMAS

W E S T   I N D I E S

Hispaniola

Puerto Rico

Virgin Is.

Guadeloupe

Martinique

CUBA

HAITI

DOMINICAN REPUBLIC

JAMAICA

Cayman Is.

Greater Antilles

Caribbean Sea

Lesser Antilles

Trinidad

SOUTH AMERICA

EQUATOR

0 — 1,000 miles
0 — 1,000 kilometers

Lambert Azimuthal Equal-Area Projection

180° 60° N 140° W 40° N 120° W 20° N 100° W 80° W 20° S 60° W 20° N 40° W 40° N 20° W 60° N

1 2 3 4 5 6 7 8

A B C D E F G H J K

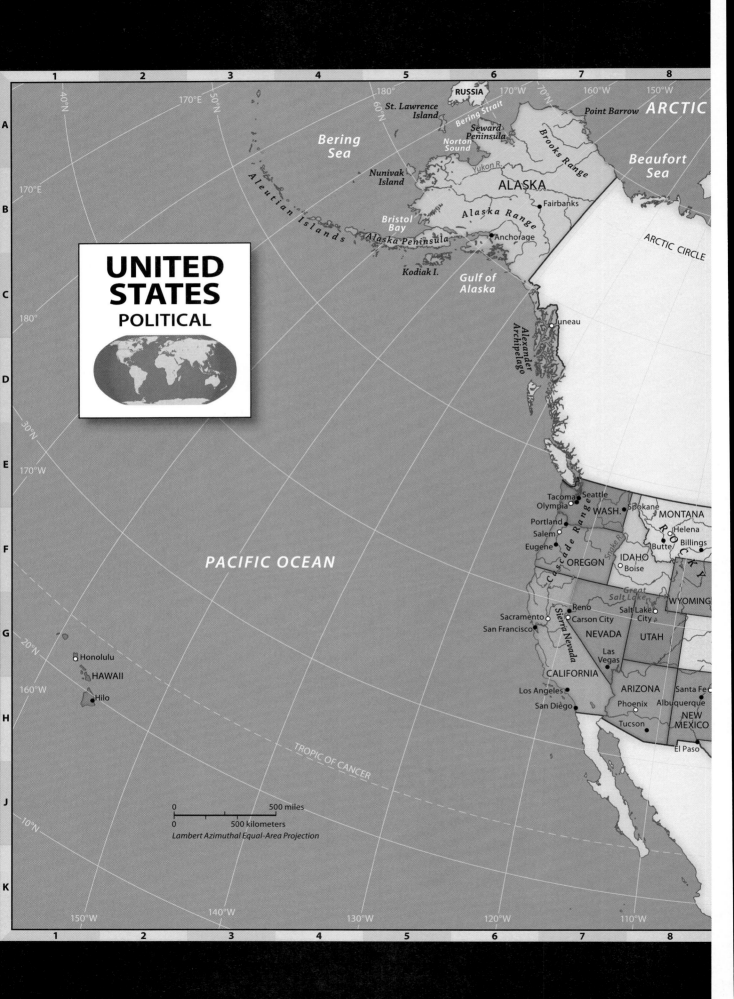

UNITED STATES
STATES
POLITICAL

RUSSIA

ARCTIC

Point Barrow

Beaufort Sea

St. Lawrence Island

Bering Strait

Seward Peninsula

Bering Sea

Norton Sound

Brooks Range

ARCTIC CIRCLE

Yukon R.

ALASKA

Nunivak Island

Fairbanks

Alaska Range

Bristol Bay

Anchorage

Aleutian Islands

Alaska Peninsula

Kodiak I.

Gulf of Alaska

Juneau

Alexander Archipelago

PACIFIC OCEAN

Tacoma   Seattle
Olympia
Portland   Spokane   MONTANA
Salem   WASH.   Helena
Eugene   Billings
         Cascade Range   Butte
         OREGON   IDAHO
                   Boise
                   Snake R.

Great Salt Lake   WYOMING

Reno   Salt Lake City
Sacramento   Carson City
San Francisco   Sierra Nevada   NEVADA   UTAH

Las Vegas
CALIFORNIA
                   ARIZONA   Santa Fe
Los Angeles
         San Diego   Phoenix   Albuquerque
                                  NEW MEXICO
                   Tucson
                              El Paso

TROPIC OF CANCER

Honolulu

HAWAII

Hilo

0   500 miles
0   500 kilometers
Lambert Azimuthal Equal-Area Projection

40°N
50°N
60°N
70°N
170°E
180°
170°W
160°W
150°W
170°E
180°
170°W
160°W
30°N
20°N
10°N
150°W
140°W
130°W
120°W
110°W

1   2   3   4   5   6   7   8
A
B
C
D
E
F
G
H
J
K

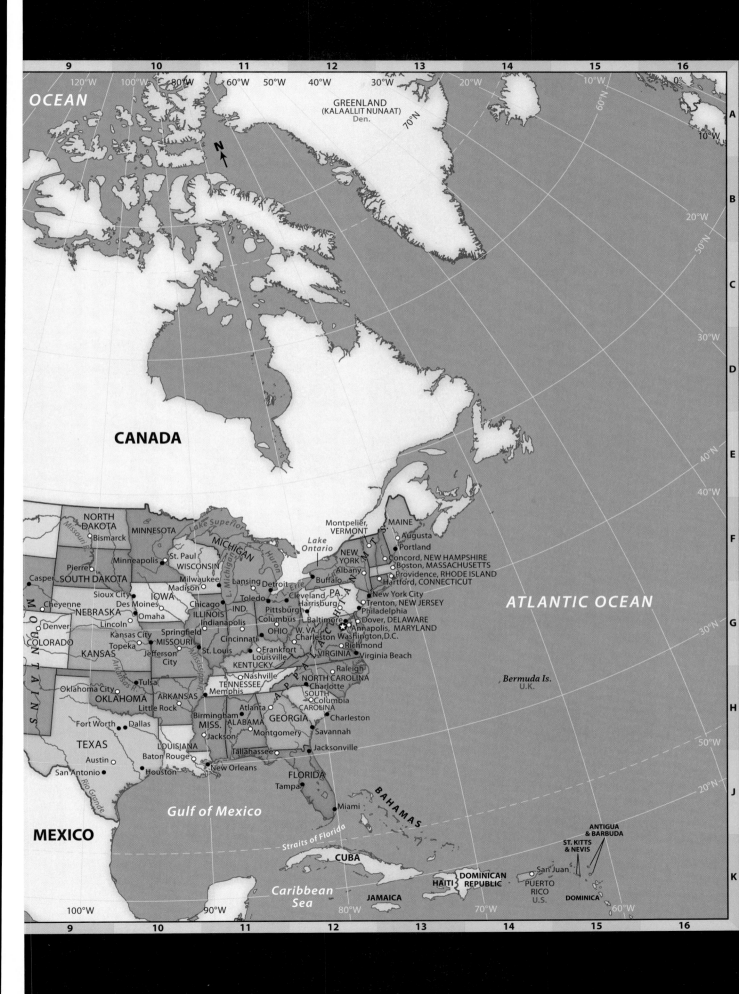

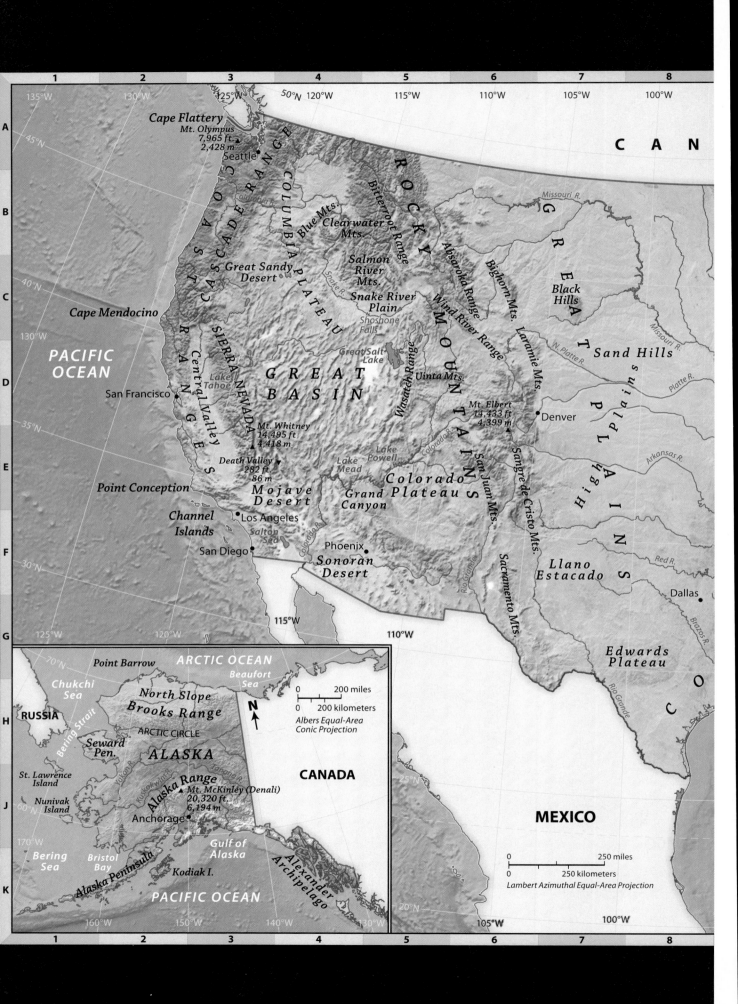

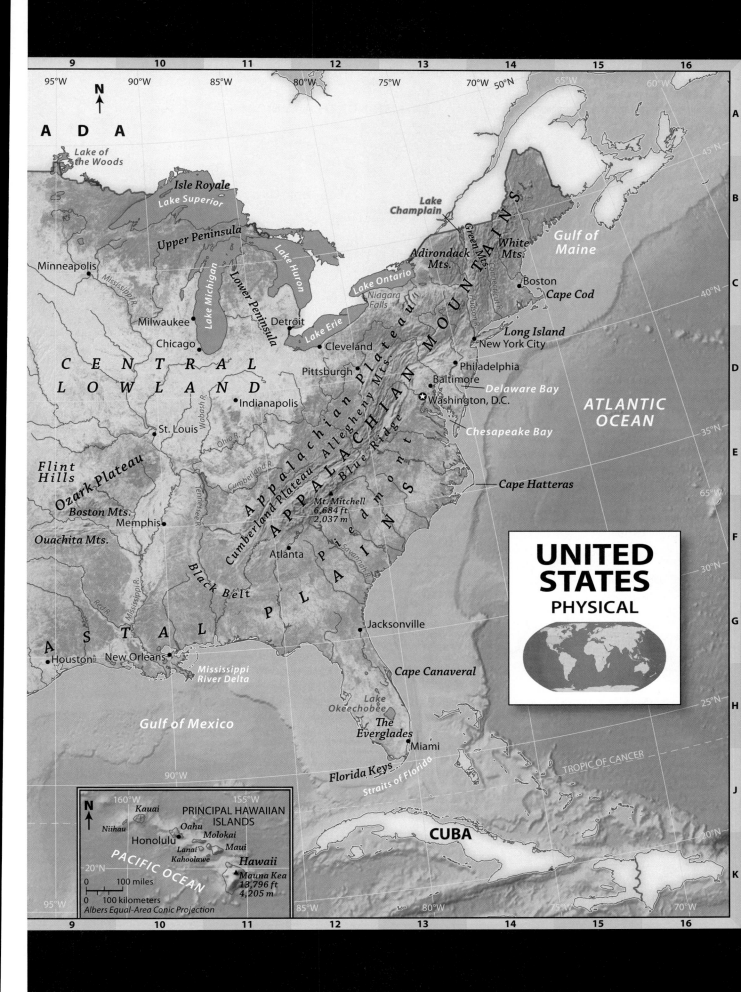

UNITED STATES PHYSICAL

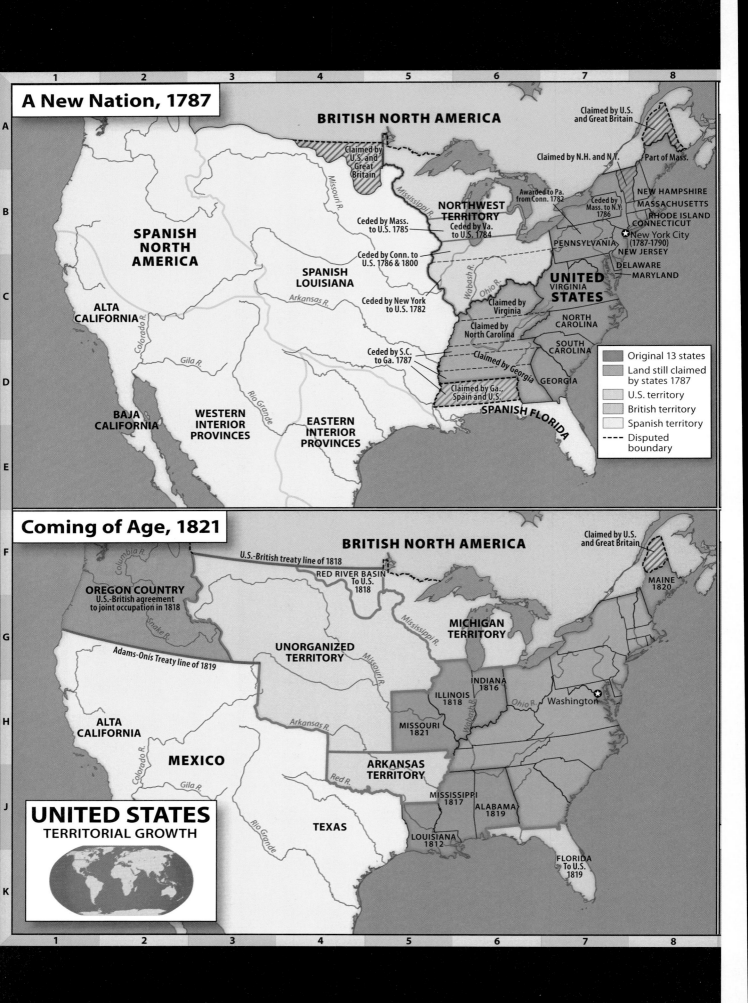

A New Nation, 1787

BRITISH NORTH AMERICA

Claimed by U.S. and Great Britain

Claimed by U.S. and Great Britain

Claimed by N.H. and N.Y.

Part of Mass.

Missouri R.

Mississippi R.

NORTHWEST TERRITORY

Awarded to Pa. from Conn. 1782

Ceded by Mass. to N.Y. 1786

NEW HAMPSHIRE

MASSACHUSETTS

RHODE ISLAND

CONNECTICUT

New York City (1787–1790)

NEW JERSEY

DELAWARE

MARYLAND

SPANISH NORTH AMERICA

Ceded by Mass. to U.S. 1785

Ceded by Va. to U.S. 1784

PENNSYLVANIA

UNITED STATES

Ceded by Conn. to U.S. 1786 & 1800

Wabash R.

Ohio R.

VIRGINIA

SPANISH LOUISIANA

Arkansas R.

Ceded by New York to U.S. 1782

Claimed by Virginia

NORTH CAROLINA

ALTA CALIFORNIA

Colorado R.

Claimed by North Carolina

SOUTH CAROLINA

Gila R.

Rio Grande

Ceded by S.C. to Ga. 1787

Claimed by Georgia

GEORGIA

BAJA CALIFORNIA

WESTERN INTERIOR PROVINCES

EASTERN INTERIOR PROVINCES

Claimed by Ga., Spain and U.S.

SPANISH FLORIDA

Original 13 states

Land still claimed by states 1787

U.S. territory

British territory

Spanish territory

Disputed boundary

Coming of Age, 1821

BRITISH NORTH AMERICA

Claimed by U.S. and Great Britain

Columbia R.

U.S.-British treaty line of 1818

RED RIVER BASIN To U.S. 1818

MAINE 1820

OREGON COUNTRY U.S.-British agreement to joint occupation in 1818

Snake R.

Mississippi R.

MICHIGAN TERRITORY

Adams-Onís Treaty line of 1819

UNORGANIZED TERRITORY

Missouri R.

ALTA CALIFORNIA

Arkansas R.

ILLINOIS 1818

INDIANA 1816

Wabash R.

Ohio R.

Washington

MEXICO

Colorado R.

Gila R.

MISSOURI 1821

ARKANSAS TERRITORY

Red R.

MISSISSIPPI 1817

ALABAMA 1819

Rio Grande

TEXAS

LOUISIANA 1812

FLORIDA To U.S. 1819

UNITED STATES
TERRITORIAL GROWTH

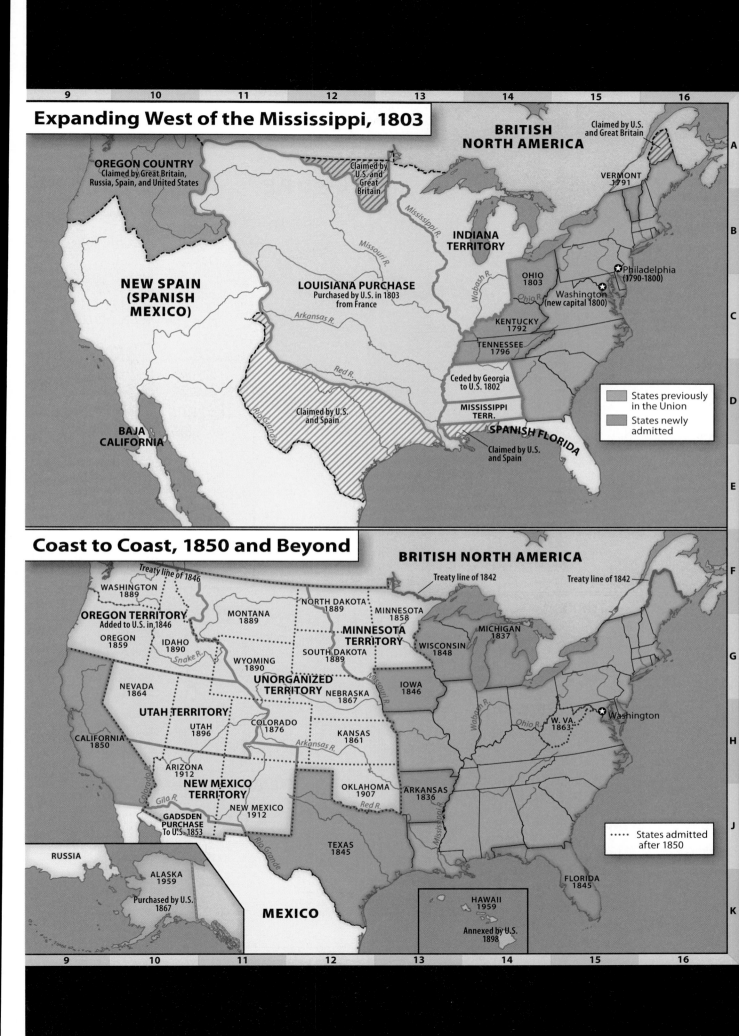

Expanding West of the Mississippi, 1803

BRITISH NORTH AMERICA

Claimed by U.S. and Great Britain

OREGON COUNTRY
Claimed by Great Britain, Russia, Spain, and United States

Claimed by U.S. and Great Britain

VERMONT 1791

Mississippi R.

Missouri R.

INDIANA TERRITORY

Wabash R.

OHIO 1803

Ohio R.

Philadelphia (1790-1800)

Washington (new capital 1800)

NEW SPAIN (SPANISH MEXICO)

LOUISIANA PURCHASE
Purchased by U.S. in 1803 from France

Arkansas R.

KENTUCKY 1792

TENNESSEE 1796

Red R.

Ceded by Georgia to U.S. 1802

Claimed by U.S. and Spain

Rio Grande

BAJA CALIFORNIA

MISSISSIPPI TERR.

SPANISH FLORIDA

Claimed by U.S. and Spain

☐ States previously in the Union
☐ States newly admitted

Coast to Coast, 1850 and Beyond

BRITISH NORTH AMERICA

Treaty line of 1846

Treaty line of 1842

Treaty line of 1842

WASHINGTON 1889

OREGON TERRITORY
Added to U.S. in 1846

OREGON 1859

IDAHO 1890

Snake R.

MONTANA 1889

NORTH DAKOTA 1889

MINNESOTA 1858

MINNESOTA TERRITORY

MICHIGAN 1837

WISCONSIN 1848

WYOMING 1890

SOUTH DAKOTA 1889

Missouri R.

NEVADA 1864

UTAH TERRITORY

UTAH 1896

UNORGANIZED TERRITORY

NEBRASKA 1867

IOWA 1846

Wabash R.

Ohio R.

W. VA. 1863

Washington

CALIFORNIA 1850

COLORADO 1876

KANSAS 1861

Arkansas R.

ARIZONA 1912

NEW MEXICO TERRITORY

Gila R.

Colorado R.

NEW MEXICO 1912

OKLAHOMA 1907

ARKANSAS 1836

Red R.

GADSDEN PURCHASE
To U.S. 1853

Rio Grande

TEXAS 1845

Mississippi R.

RUSSIA

ALASKA 1959

Purchased by U.S. 1867

MEXICO

FLORIDA 1845

HAWAII 1959

Annexed by U.S. 1898

····· States admitted after 1850

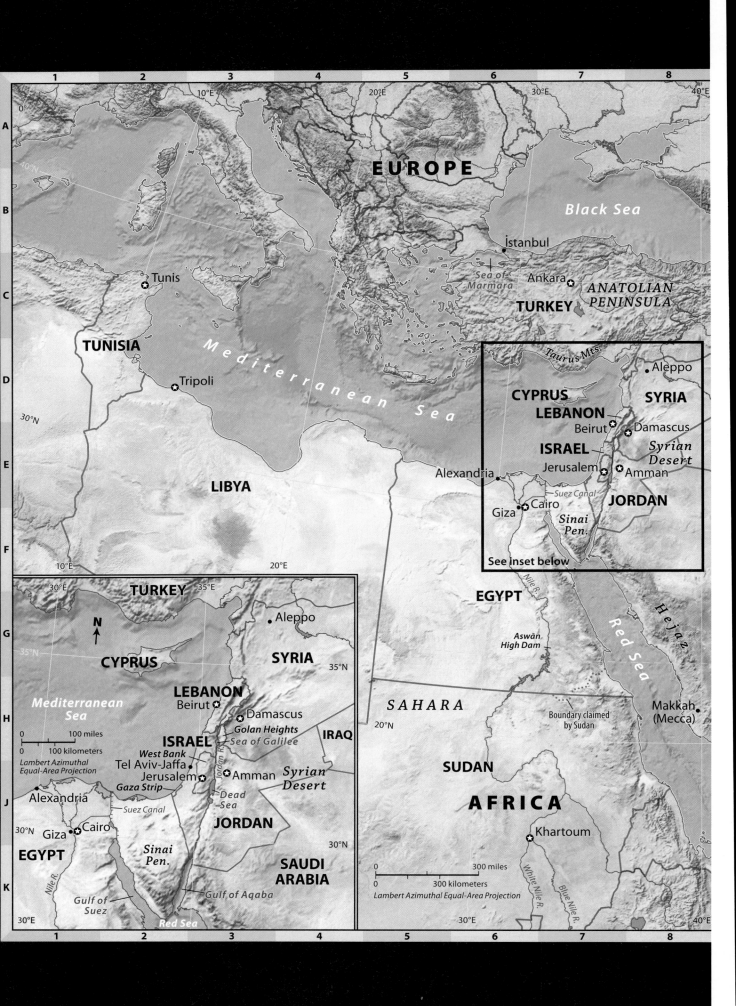

EUROPE

Black Sea

İstanbul

Sea of Marmara

Ankara

TURKEY

ANATOLIAN PENINSULA

Tunis

TUNISIA

M e d i t e r r a n e a n   S e a

Tripoli

LIBYA

30°N

10°E

20°E

Alexandria

Taurus Mts.

Aleppo

CYPRUS

LEBANON

SYRIA

Beirut

Damascus

ISRAEL

Jerusalem

Amman

Syrian Desert

Suez Canal

JORDAN

Giza

Cairo

Sinai Pen.

See inset below

EGYPT

Nile R.

Aswān High Dam

S A H A R A

20°N

Boundary claimed by Sudan

Red Sea

Hejaz

Makkah (Mecca)

SUDAN

AFRICA

Khartoum

White Nile R.

Blue Nile R.

0   300 miles

0   300 kilometers

Lambert Azimuthal Equal-Area Projection

30°E

40°E

Inset map:

30°E

35°E

TURKEY

N

35°N

CYPRUS

SYRIA

Aleppo

35°N

Mediterranean Sea

LEBANON

Beirut

Damascus

Golan Heights

Sea of Galilee

IRAQ

0   100 miles

0   100 kilometers

Lambert Azimuthal Equal-Area Projection

ISRAEL

West Bank

Tel Aviv-Jaffa

Jerusalem

Gaza Strip

Amman

Jordan R.

Syrian Desert

Alexandria

Dead Sea

Suez Canal

JORDAN

30°N

30°N

Giza

Cairo

EGYPT

Sinai Pen.

SAUDI ARABIA

Nile R.

Gulf of Suez

Gulf of Aqaba

Red Sea

30°E

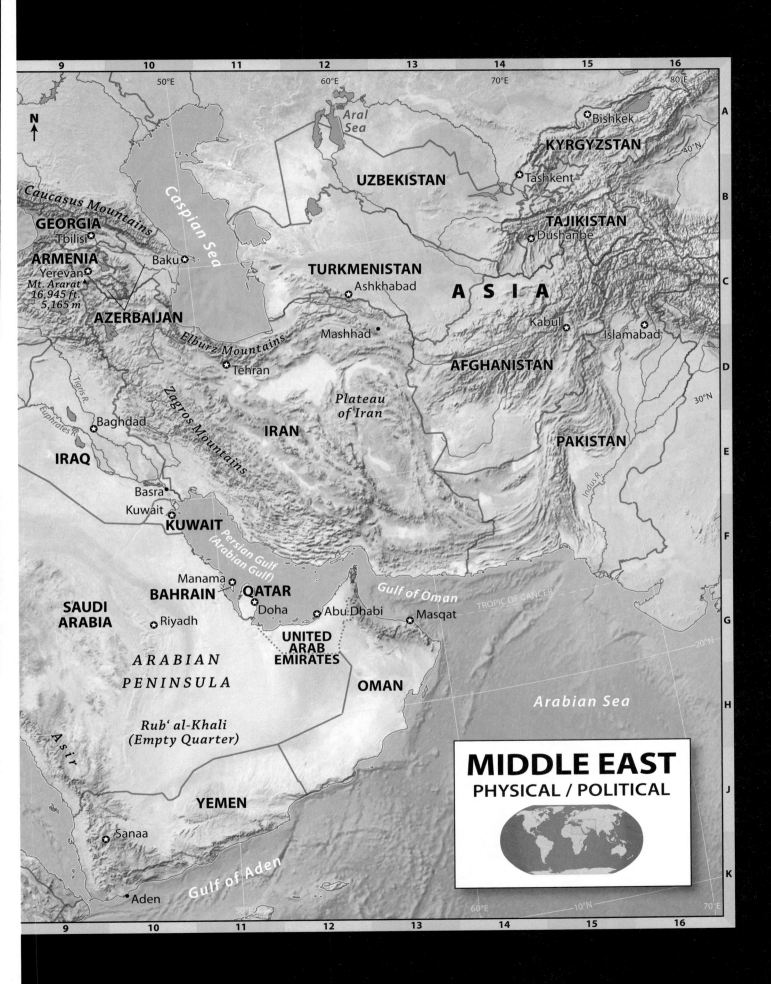

N

9 10 11 12 13 14 15 16

50°E   60°E   70°E   80°E

Aral Sea

• Bishkek   A

KYRGYZSTAN

UZBEKISTAN   40°N   B

✪ Tashkent

Caucasus Mountains

GEORGIA   **TAJIKISTAN**

Tbilisi ✪   ✪ Dushanbe   C

ARMENIA   Baku ✪

Yerevan ✪   **TURKMENISTAN**

Mt. Ararat▲   **A S I A**

16,945 ft.   ✪ Ashkhabad

5,165 m   • Mashhad   Kabul ✪   • Islamabad

AZERBAIJAN   **AFGHANISTAN**   D

Elburz Mountains

✪ Tehran   30°N

Plateau of Iran

Zagros Mountains

Baghdad ✪   **IRAN**   **PAKISTAN**   E

IRAQ

Basra •

Kuwait •   *Indus R.*

KUWAIT ✪

Persian Gulf (Arabian Gulf)   F

Manama ✪   *Gulf of Oman*

BAHRAIN   **QATAR**   TROPIC OF CANCER

Doha •   ✪ Abu Dhabi   • Masqat

SAUDI   G

ARABIA   ✪ Riyadh   **UNITED ARAB EMIRATES**   20°N

A R A B I A N   **OMAN**

P E N I N S U L A

Arabian Sea   H

Rub' al-Khali (Empty Quarter)

A s i r   J

YEMEN   **MIDDLE EAST**

PHYSICAL / POLITICAL

Sanaa ✪

Gulf of Aden   K

• Aden

50°E   60°E   10°N   70°E

9 10 11 12 13 14 15 16

Thinking Like a HIST♦RIAN

WHAT DOES A HISTORIAN DO?

A historian is a person who studies and writes about the people and events of the past. Historians find out how people lived, what happened to them, and what happened around them. They look for the causes of events and the effects of those events.

We study history so we can understand what happened in the past. Understanding what happened to others can help us make sense of current events—things taking place today. It can also help us predict what might happen in the future so we can make better decisions about today and tomorrow.

Have you ever wondered if you could be a historian? To answer that question, you will need to find out how historians conduct research and write about history. Historians use a number of tools to research, or collect information about, their subjects. They also use special tools to organize information. You will learn about these tools in the next few pages and throughout this textbook.

(l) Ira Block/National Geographic/Getty Images, (c) Atlantide Phototravel/Corbis, (r) Dewitt Jones/Corbis

By studying sites where people lived and examining the objects they made and used, we can learn about the lives of people who lived in the past.

MEASURING TIME

One challenge when studying history is knowing when events took place. Which event happened first? How far apart in time did events take place? We use different tools to measure time.

Calendars A calendar is a system for breaking time into units and keeping track of those units. With a calendar, you can measure how much time has passed between events. You can describe that time, for example, in months and years.

The dates in this book are based on the Western calendar. In the Western calendar, a year is 365 days. The calendar begins at the birth of Jesus. The years before this date are known as B.C., or "before Christ." Years after are called A.D., or *anno domini*, which is Latin for "in the year of the Lord." Some people also use C.E., or "common era," and B.C.E., or "before common era."

To date events that took place before B.C., historians count backward from A.D. 1. There is no year 0. The year before A.D. 1 is 1 B.C. The year before that is 2 B.C. To date events after "A.D.," historians count forward. The year after A.D. 1 is A.D. 2.

Throughout history, different cultures have developed different calendars.

Reading a Time Line Historians are interested in chronology, or the order in which events happen. An easy way to keep track of chronology is to use or make a time line. A *time line* is a diagram showing the order of events within a period of time.

Along a time line, each section represents a period of time. A time line also has labels for events. The labels appear near the date on the time line when the event took place.

U.S. AND WORLD HISTORY 1855–1870

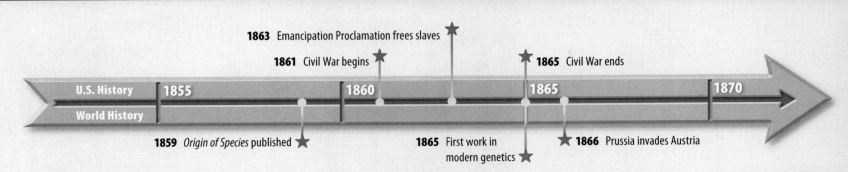

1863 Emancipation Proclamation frees slaves

1861 Civil War begins

1865 Civil War ends

U.S. History   1855   1860   1865   1870

World History

1859 *Origin of Species* published

1865 First work in modern genetics

1866 Prussia invades Austria

ANALYZING SOURCES

Suppose a teacher has asked you to write a paper about the space program. Where would you get the information you need to begin writing? You would look for two types of information—primary and secondary sources.

Primary sources are descriptions or pictures of an event by someone who actually saw or lived through that event. In other words, if you see a rocket launch in person and then write about it, you are creating a primary source. Written impressions of any others who watched at the same time are primary sources, too. Diaries, journals, photographs, and eyewitness reports are examples of primary sources.

Secondary sources usually come from people who were not present at an event. A book about the history of the space program is a secondary source. The author of the book collected information from many sources. He or she then combined this information into something new. Textbooks, biographies, and histories are secondary sources.

Note that a secondary source may use primary sources. In this textbook, you will see and read excerpts from many primary sources. The book itself, however, is a secondary source.

To analyze primary sources, try to answer the five "W" questions:

1. **Who** created the primary source?
2. **Why** was the source created— what was its purpose and its intended audience?
3. **What** is the source about?
4. **Where** was the source created?
5. **When** was the source created?

Answering these questions can help you find the historical significance of a primary source. Ask yourself these questions as you look at the following primary sources.

CLASSIFYING PRIMARY SOURCES

- **Printed publications** include newspapers, magazines, and books. Web sites and e-mails are also printed publications that appear in electronic format.
- **Songs and poems** are often good sources of information because they describe events and reactions to them.
- **Visual materials** include original paintings, drawings, photographs, films, and maps. Political cartoons and other types of cartoons are also visual primary sources.
- **Oral histories** are interviews that are recorded to collect people's memories and observations about their lives and experiences.
- **Personal records** include diaries, journals, and letters.
- **Artifacts** are tools or ornaments that were used by people in the past.

Personal Records and Artifacts

The Native Americans of the Plains used the skins of the animals they hunted to make a number of everyday items. This Sioux deerskin bag (above) is decorated with beads. The mortar, a vessel used for grinding, and the serpent figure (right) are other artifacts left behind by ancient cultures.

The letters from Abraham Lincoln (above right) and Dr. Martin Luther King, Jr., are personal records. The photographs are also examples of primary sources.

Letters and Visual Materials

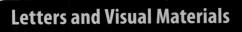

66 We have waited for more than 340 years for our constitutional and God-given rights. . . . [W]e still creep at horse and buggy pace toward gaining a cup of coffee at a lunch counter. Perhaps it is easy for those who have never felt the stinging darts of segregation to say, 'Wait.' . . . Let us all hope that the dark clouds of racial prejudice will soon pass away. 99

—Dr. Martin Luther King, Jr., "Letter from Birmingham Jail," April 1963

As Dr. Martin Luther King, Jr., sat in an Alabama cell, he wrote his famous "Letter from Birmingham Jail."

During the Great Depression of the 1930s, people struggled to survive. This photo shows one example of people affected by tough economic times.

CHARTS, DIAGRAMS, AND GRAPHS

Charts, diagrams, and graphs are ways of displaying types of information such as percentages, numbers, and amounts. They help organize this information and make it easier to read.

Charts Charts present facts and numbers in an organized way. One type of chart is a table. A table arranges data, especially numbers, in rows and columns for easy reference. People also use charts to summarize ideas or main points of broader topics. This allows you to review material and compare main ideas easily.

Chart Skill

Rank	Civil War	World War II 1942	Vietnam War 1965	Iraq War 2007
Private	*$13	$50	$85	$1,203–1,543
Corporal	$14	$66	$210	$1,700
Sergeant	$17	$78	$261	$1,854–2,339
Sergeant Major	$21	$138	$486	$4,110

*Until 1864, African Americans in the Civil War were paid $7 per month.

Source: Bureau of Economic Analysis; *Princeton Review*; www.militaryfactory.com

This chart shows information about monthly army salaries.

▶ **CRITICAL THINKING**

Comparing What two types of comparisons are possible using this chart? **by rank and conflict**

Diagram Skill

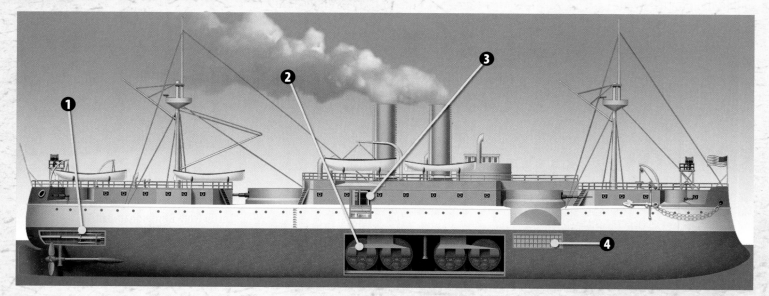

❶ **Torpedo tubes** are devices to launch torpedoes.

❷ **Steam boilers** power the engines.

❸ **Munitions** are stored in the magazine.

❹ **Cowls** provide fresh air below deck.

A diagram is a drawing or an outline that is used to show how things work or to show how parts relate to each other. This diagram shows an old U.S. warship, the USS *Maine* (1895).

▶ **CRITICAL THINKING**

Analyzing Why is a diagram a better choice for displaying this information than a chart? **shows parts of ship and relationships**

Diagrams Diagrams are drawings that show steps in a process, point out the parts of an object, or explain how something works. Diagrams are sometimes called "infographics."

Graphs Graphs present numbers visually. This makes the numbers easier to understand. The types of graphs you will find in this textbook are described and displayed below:
- Circle graphs show how the whole of something is divided.
- Bar graphs use bars to compare numbers visually. They compare different items or groups. Bar graphs can also compare items at different points in time.
- Line graphs can be used to show how something changes over time. Rather than showing data for only specific points in time, line graphs show a continuous line of data.

Graph Skill

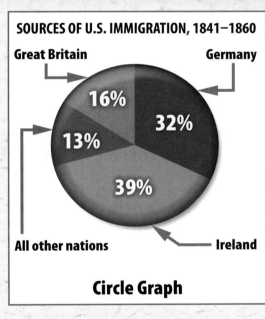

SOURCES OF U.S. IMMIGRATION, 1841–1860

Great Britain — 16%
Germany — 32%
13%
39%
All other nations
Ireland

Circle Graph

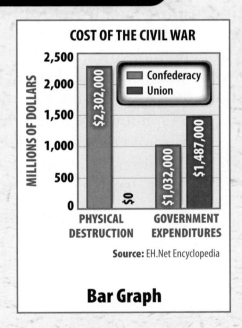

COST OF THE CIVIL WAR

MILLIONS OF DOLLARS

- Confederacy
- Union

PHYSICAL DESTRUCTION: $2,302,000 / $0
GOVERNMENT EXPENDITURES: $1,032,000 / $1,487,000

Source: EH.Net Encyclopedia

Bar Graph

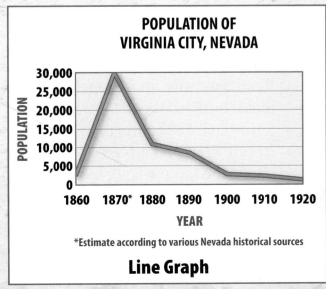

POPULATION OF VIRGINIA CITY, NEVADA

POPULATION

1860 1870* 1880 1890 1900 1910 1920
YEAR

*Estimate according to various Nevada historical sources

Line Graph

CRITICAL THINKING SKILLS

Studying history is about more than reading sources and viewing pictures or graphs. Historians use many thinking skills.

Understanding Cause and Effect A *cause* is an action or a situation that produces an event. What happens as a result of a cause is an *effect*. Understanding cause and effect means thinking about *why* an event occurred. It helps you see how one thing can lead to another. Such an understanding can help you plan to encourage or prevent the same event in the future.

Predicting Consequences Predicting future events is difficult. Sometimes, though, you can use knowledge of how certain causes led to certain effects in the past to make a prediction. For example, if you know that conflicts over borders have often led to war, you might be able to predict the outcome of a current border dispute.

Distinguishing Fact from Opinion To determine the validity of sources and find answers in a text, you need to distinguish facts from opinions. You can check facts using reliable sources to determine whether or not they are accurate. They answer specific questions such as: What happened? Who did it?

Opinions are based on values and beliefs. They are not true, and they are not false. Opinions often begin with phrases such as *I believe . . .*, or they contain words such as *should, ought, best, worst,* or *greatest*.

Drawing Inferences and Conclusions
When you make an *inference*, you "read between the lines" to figure out something that is not stated directly. A *conclusion* is an understanding based on details or facts you read or hear.

Follow these steps to draw inferences and conclusions from a piece of writing:

- Read carefully for key facts and ideas, and list them.
- Summarize the information.
- Recall what you already know about the topic.
- Use your knowledge and insight to develop some inferences and conclusions about the passage.

In 1983, 20 years after Dr. Martin Luther King, Jr.'s March on Washington, a huge crowd gathered once again in the nation's capital. Comparing photographs of the two events can help you see how they were similar and how they were different.

MAKING COMPARISONS

When making comparisons, you examine two or more things. Among the things to compare are documents, events, and images. Compare these two photographs.

▶ **CRITICAL THINKING**
Comparing and Contrasting What similarities do you see? How are the images different? **Students should provide valid comparisons.**

Making Comparisons To make a comparison, look for similarities among ideas or objects. You can also examine contrasts—qualities that make each of the ideas or objects unique. Making comparisons can help you choose among several possible alternatives.

To make comparisons and contrasts, examine the texts, images, or other items and follow these steps:

- Select the items to compare.
- Determine what you are comparing. For example, you might compare a topic or a point of view. Look for similarities within these categories.
- Look for differences that set the items apart from each other.

Thinking Like a HISTORIAN

Review Vocabulary

1. Use the terms *calendar* and *chronology* in a sentence that explains their role in the study of history. **Students will write sentences with correct explanations.**

Answer the Guiding Questions

2. ***Describing*** Describe the role and purpose of the historian. **Answers include: study, write history; help decision-making**

3. ***Explaining*** Why is it important to understand the order in which events occurred? **to understand relationships between events**

4. ***Defining*** Give three examples of primary sources. **letters, diaries, photographs, journals**

5. ***Describing*** What is the purpose of graphs, charts, and diagrams? **analyze and interpret information visually**

6. **PERSONAL WRITING** Write a short essay in which you express why you think it is important to read about, study, and understand the past. **Essays should provide examples and valid reasoning.**

WHAT IS GEOGRAPHY?

Geography is the study of Earth and its people. A geographer tries to understand a place—not just where it is, but what it is like, what takes place there, and how the people there live.

To help them build this understanding, geographers organize their study into themes, or subjects. For example, geographers often speak of the five themes of geography: location, place, regions, movement, and human-environment interaction.

- **Location** describes where something is. Geographers describe location in two ways. Absolute location is the exact position on Earth where a geographic feature, such as a city or mountain, is found. Relative location describes where a geographic feature is located in relation to another feature.
- **Place** explores the physical and human features that make a city, state, or country unique. The Grand Canyon and the Hoover Dam are examples of features that make Arizona a special place.
- **Regions** are areas that share common features. A region may be land, water, or a specific area in a city or state. For instance, New England is a region in the northeastern United States. The West Coast is a region bordering the Pacific Ocean and includes the states of California, Oregon, and Washington.

The technology used for navigation has changed a lot over the centuries. The compass and astrolabe (below right) have given way to the global positioning system (GPS), below.

George Rose/Getty Images Entertainment/Getty Images

Geography explores different places and the people who live in those places.

- **Movement** explains how and why people, things, and ideas move. For instance, a group of people might move for various reasons. Ideas spread from one place to another. Both types of movement lead to change.
- **Human-environment interaction** explores the relationship between people and their environments. For example, early Native Americans in the southwestern United States used materials from plants, animals, and the land to build their homes and to clothe and feed themselves.

MAPS AND GLOBES

The tools of the geographer include maps and globes. These help us learn more about Earth. Globes and maps serve different purposes, and each has its advantages and disadvantages.

Studying geography helps us understand Earth—its people, its natural features, and the ways they interact with each other.

A globe is a round model of Earth. It shows the Earth's shape, its lands, and its bodies of water. The shapes, sizes, and locations of the lands and seas are accurate.

A map is a flat drawing of all or part of Earth's surface. Cartographers, or mapmakers, use complex mathematics to transfer shapes from the round globe to a flat map. Still, all maps distort the shapes of the places they show. Maps can show small areas such as a college campus. They can show the streets in a city, whole continents, or the entire world. Some show places as they exist now. Historical maps show the features of a place at some time in the past.

Understanding Parts of a Map Maps can contain a large amount of information in a small space. In order to understand this information, however, you need to know how to read a map. To read a map, you need to understand the different parts, what they represent, and how they work together. The map on the next page shows some of the most basic map parts.

CHART SKILL

Maps and globes do similar things, but each has advantages and disadvantages.

1. **IDENTIFYING** Do maps or globes give a more accurate representation of the shape, size, and location of places on Earth? **a globe**

2. **CRITICAL THINKING**
   Explaining Why are maps able to show information in greater detail than globes in many cases?
   Maps can represent places at a wide variety of scales.

MAPS AND GLOBES

	Advantages	Disadvantages
Globes	• Represent true land shapes, distances, and directions	• Cannot show detailed information • Difficult to carry or transport
Maps	• Show small areas in great detail • Display different types of information, such as population densities or natural resources • Easy to transport	• Distort, or change, the accuracy of shapes and distances

NASA/Corbis

Physical and Political Maps Maps are useful tools. You can use them to show information and make connections between different facts, such as how the location of towns and cities relates to the location of waterways.

Geographers use many different kinds of maps. Maps that show a wide range of information about an area are known as general purpose maps. Two of the most common general purpose maps are physical maps and political maps.

Physical maps show landforms and water features. Landforms

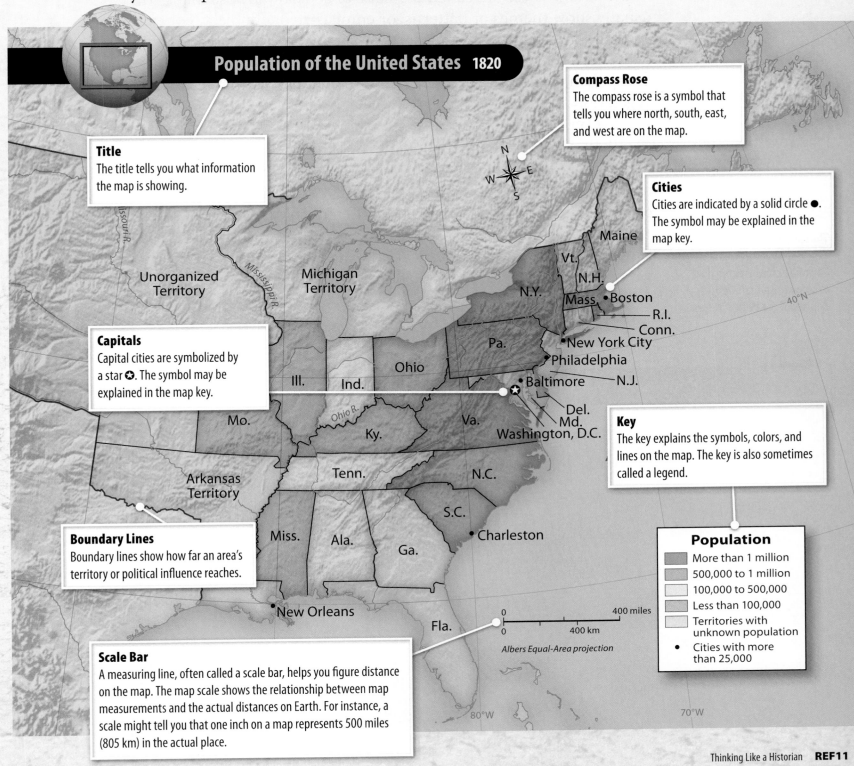

Population of the United States 1820

Title
The title tells you what information the map is showing.

Compass Rose
The compass rose is a symbol that tells you where north, south, east, and west are on the map.

Cities
Cities are indicated by a solid circle ●. The symbol may be explained in the map key.

Capitals
Capital cities are symbolized by a star ✪. The symbol may be explained in the map key.

Key
The key explains the symbols, colors, and lines on the map. The key is also sometimes called a legend.

Boundary Lines
Boundary lines show how far an area's territory or political influence reaches.

Scale Bar
A measuring line, often called a scale bar, helps you figure distance on the map. The map scale shows the relationship between map measurements and the actual distances on Earth. For instance, a scale might tell you that one inch on a map represents 500 miles (805 km) in the actual place.

Unorganized Territory

Michigan Territory

Maine

Vt.

N.H.

N.Y.

Mass. •Boston

R.I.

Conn.

Pa.

•New York City

•Philadelphia

N.J.

Ohio

Ill. Ind.

Mo.

Ohio R.

Ky.

Va.

Del.

Md.

Washington, D.C.

•Baltimore

Arkansas Territory

Tenn.

N.C.

S.C.

Miss. Ala.

Ga.

• Charleston

•New Orleans

Fla.

Mississippi R.

Missouri R.

0   400 miles

0   400 km

Albers Equal-Area projection

Population

More than 1 million

500,000 to 1 million

100,000 to 500,000

Less than 100,000

Territories with unknown population

• Cities with more than 25,000

80°W   70°W

40°N

are natural features on Earth such as deserts, mountains, plains, and plateaus. Physical maps may also show relief, or ups and downs of the Earth's surface, and elevation, the height of an area above sea level.

Political maps show the names and political boundary lines, or borders, of a place. Political maps may also show human-made features, such as cities or transportation routes.

Special Purpose Maps Some maps present specific kinds of information. These are called thematic or special purpose maps. They usually show themes or patterns, or emphasize one subject. For example, special purpose maps may present information on climate or natural resources. They may display where different Native American languages are spoken, what industries are found in an area, or what kind of vegetation grows there.

One type of special purpose map shows population density. A population density map is shown below. Population density refers to how thickly a place is settled—how many people live in each square mile. Cities have a high population density. Rural areas have a low population density. These maps use different colors or dots to show this.

Special purpose maps may also display events that occurred over time. Maps that display historical information, such as voting rights for women (shown top right), are called historical maps. In this textbook, you will study many historical maps.

The special purpose map explores a specific theme. The one below uses red dots to show the population density of the United States.

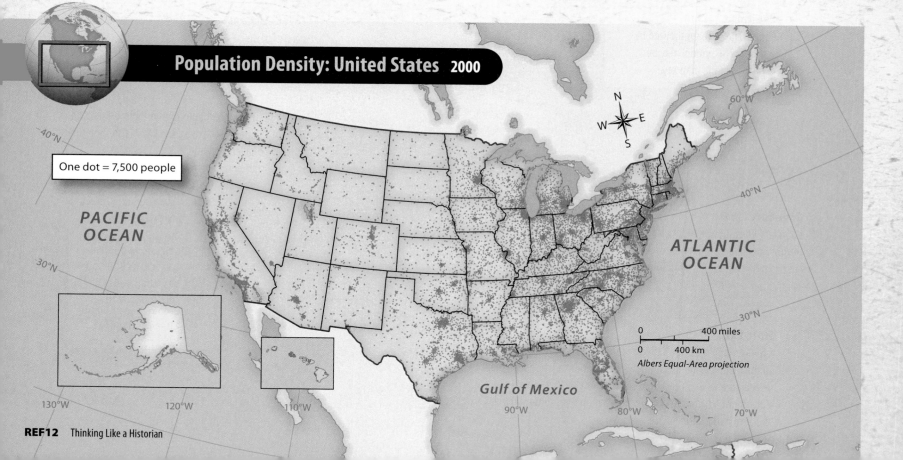

Population Density: United States 2000

One dot = 7,500 people

PACIFIC OCEAN

ATLANTIC OCEAN

Gulf of Mexico

0   400 miles
0   400 km
Albers Equal-Area projection

40°N
30°N
130°W
120°W
110°W
90°W
80°W
70°W
60°W

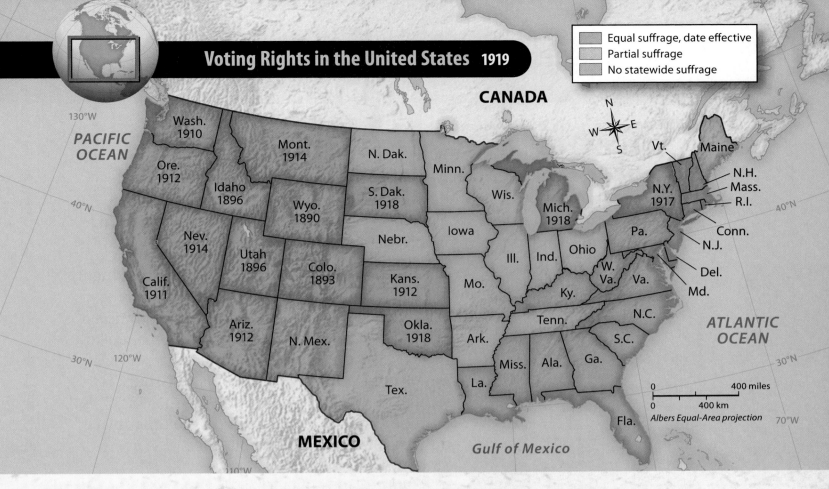

Voting Rights in the United States 1919

Legend:
- Equal suffrage, date effective
- Partial suffrage
- No statewide suffrage

CANADA

PACIFIC OCEAN

130°W
40°N
30°N
120°W
110°W

Wash. 1910
Ore. 1912
Idaho 1896
Mont. 1914
N. Dak.
Minn.
Wis.
Mich. 1918
Vt.
Maine
N.H.
Mass.
R.I.
N.Y. 1917
Conn.
N.J.
Del.
Md.
Nev. 1914
Utah 1896
Wyo. 1890
S. Dak. 1918
Iowa
Ill.
Ind.
Ohio
Pa.
W. Va.
Va.
Calif. 1911
Colo. 1893
Nebr.
Kans. 1912
Mo.
Ky.
N.C.
Ariz. 1912
N. Mex.
Okla. 1918
Ark.
Tenn.
S.C.
ATLANTIC OCEAN
Tex.
Miss.
Ala.
Ga.
La.
Fla.

MEXICO
Gulf of Mexico

40°N
30°N
70°W

0 400 miles
0 400 km
Albers Equal-Area projection

The historical map above gives data about a time in the past and is a type of special purpose map. This map also includes political information about state borders in 1919.

A physical map (below) calls out landforms and water features.

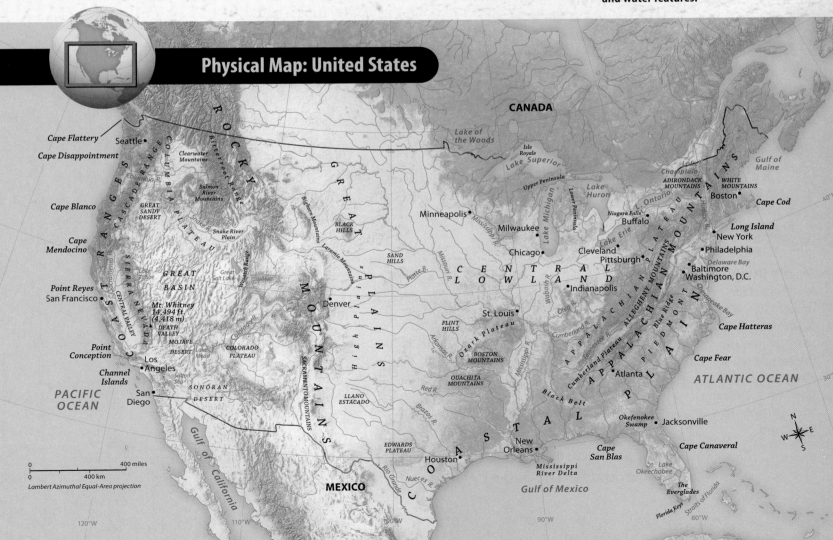

Physical Map: United States

CANADA

Cape Flattery
Seattle
Cape Disappointment
Cape Blanco
Cape Mendocino
Point Reyes
San Francisco
Point Conception
Channel Islands
San Diego
Los Angeles

PACIFIC OCEAN

ROCKY
Clearwater Mountains
Bitterroot Range
Columbia R.
Columbia Plateau
Great Sandy Desert
Salmon River Mountains
Snake River Plain
Snake R.
Bighorn Mountains
Black Hills
Laramie Mountains
Sand Hills
Great Basin
Great Salt Lake
Wasatch Range
Lake Tahoe
Mt. Whitney 14,494 ft. (4,418 m)
Death Valley
Mojave Desert
Lake Mead
Colorado Plateau
Sierra Nevada
Central Valley
Sacramento R.
Salton Sea
Sonoran Desert
Sacramento Mountains
Edwards Plateau
Llano Estacado
Rio Grande
Nueces R.
Houston

Lake of the Woods
Isle Royale
Lake Superior
Upper Peninsula
Lake Michigan
Lower Peninsula
Lake Huron
Minneapolis
Mississippi R.
Milwaukee
Chicago
Missouri R.
Platte R.
High Plains
Great Plains
Mountains
Wabash R.
Ohio R.
St. Louis
Flint Hills
Boston Mountains
Ouachita Mountains
Red R.
Central Lowland
Ozark Plateau
Arkansas R.
Mississippi R.
Black Belt
New Orleans
Cape San Blas
Mississippi River Delta
Gulf of Mexico

Lake Champlain
Adirondack Mountains
White Mountains
Boston
Cape Cod
Lake Ontario
Niagara Falls
Buffalo
Lake Erie
Cleveland
Pittsburgh
Appalachian Plateau
Allegheny Mountains
Appalachian Mountains
Piedmont
Long Island
New York
Philadelphia
Delaware Bay
Baltimore
Washington, D.C.
Hudson R.
Chesapeake Bay
Cape Hatteras
Cumberland Plateau
Cumberland R.
Tennessee R.
Blue Ridge
Atlanta
Coastal Plain
Cape Fear
ATLANTIC OCEAN
Okefenokee Swamp
Jacksonville
Cape Canaveral
Lake Okeechobee
The Everglades
Florida Keys
Straits of Florida

Gulf of Maine

Indianapolis

PACIFIC OCEAN

0 400 miles
0 400 km
Lambert Azimuthal Equal-Area projection

MEXICO

120°W
110°W
100°W
90°W
80°W
40°N
30°N

THE ELEMENTS OF GEOGRAPHY

You have read about the five themes of geography. Geographers have also broken down the study of their subject into six essential elements. Thinking about these six elements is another good way to organize your study and understanding of geography.

Several U.S. cities, such as New York and San Francisco (above), have "Chinatowns"—districts heavily influenced by Chinese culture and immigrants. Canadian cities such as Vancouver and Toronto also have Chinatowns.

The World in Spatial Terms When studying a place, geographers are interested in where it is located. Every place has an absolute location and a relative location. *Absolute location* refers to the exact spot of a place on the Earth's surface. For example, the city of St. Louis, Missouri, is located at a specific spot on the Earth—38°37′ N latitude and 90°13′ W longitude. No other place on Earth has the same absolute location as St. Louis.

Relative location tells where a place is compared with one or more other places. St. Louis is located in the Midwest of the United States, in eastern Missouri, about 295 miles (475 km) southwest of Chicago, Illinois.

Knowing a place's relative location may help a historian understand how it was settled and how its culture developed. For example, Miami, Florida, is the closest large U.S. city to Cuba. This fact helps explain why Miami is home to such a large population of Cuban Americans.

Places and Regions *Place* describes all the characteristics that give an area its own special quality. These can be physical features such as mountains, waterways, climate, and plant or animal life. Places can also be described by human features. These include language, religion, and architecture. If you were trying to tell someone about the town where you live, you would be describing place.

Each place is unique. Still, many places share features in common with others. A *region* is a group of places that share common features.

Physical features, such as a type of landform or plant life, can define regions. Human features, such as religion, language, or industry, also shape regions. For example, the South during the early 1800s was a largely agricultural region. The economy was based on trading agricultural products. The widespread use of slavery also defined the region.

Mitchell Funk/Photographer's Choice/Getty Images

Physical Systems Have you ever wondered where mountains come from or how the oceans formed? What are the factors that cause storms? Earth is subject to powerful forces. These physical systems have shaped the planet.

Physical systems include the complex forces that create weather— wind, rain, snow, and storms. Physical systems make the surface of Earth move and change shape. These forces build mountain ranges, cause earthquakes, and form volcanoes.

Physical systems affect where and how humans live. For example, people will not live on the slopes of an active volcano that could erupt at any time. Almost every place that people choose to live suffers some sort of negative impact from storms, earthquakes, fires, or other physical systems.

Ecosystems are a type of physical system. An ecosystem is a community of living beings and the surroundings in which they live. A lake is an example of an ecosystem. The ecosystem includes the plants, animals, water, and everything that lives beneath the water. Other major ecosystems in the United States include forests, wetlands, grasslands, and deserts.

In an ecosystem, all the creatures and features are connected. A change to one part affects other parts.

Human Systems Geographers are also interested in human systems. A human system includes all the things humans create as they build their lives together on Earth. It includes all the people and their settlements, as well as the cultures they form. It also includes the way different groups of people interact with each other, how they work to get along, and how they settle conflicts when they occur.

Human systems are always changing. Movements of people, ideas, and goods shape the world. At all times of day, people are flying across oceans and continents, delivering goods to distant cities. They are piloting boats filled with goods across the ocean or learning about other cultures through textbooks and the Internet. People move to new places and start new lives. As a result, cultures spread into new areas.

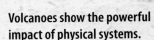

Volcanoes show the powerful impact of physical systems.

Cities like New York City are one form of human system that affects the world. The city has grown significantly over its long history.

Environment and Society As people, we shape the world in which we live. In turn, the world shapes us. People settle in certain places and change their environment to suit them. For example, people create cities with buildings, streets, and homes. People tunnel through mountains to create roads, and they use nonrenewable resources such as coal to make electricity. People also adapt to the world around them. For example, people drive less when gas prices rise. They use renewable energy sources to heat homes during cold weather.

The relationship between people and their surroundings is an important one. Landforms, waterways, climate, and natural resources have helped and hindered human activities.

People respond to their surroundings in different ways. Sometimes they adjust to them. At other times, people change their environment to meet their needs, such as by planting trees to absorb highway noise.

Human beings have a significant impact on the ecosystem they live in. For instance, your school is a building that took a great amount of time and energy to build. The ground had to be leveled. Workers built walls with wood and concrete. Roads were laid to allow people to come and go from the school. These actions affected the environment, destroying plants and forcing animals to find new places to live.

In April 2010, an explosion on an oil-drilling platform in the Gulf of Mexico killed 11 workers. The blast also triggered the worst oil spill—and the worst human-made environmental disaster—in the nation's history. The spill fouled shorelines from Louisiana to the Florida Panhandle.

Even before the spill, pollution, overexploitation, natural disasters, and environmental changes had taxed the Gulf's ecosystems. These factors impacted the region's environment, marine life, and wildlife, as well as the health and well-being of residents. The disaster added to these effects and threatened the people who relied on the Gulf for their livelihood. Jobs and industry in fishing, agriculture, oil, and trade are at risk. Restoration efforts continue, but long-term effects are still unknown.

The Uses of Geography The story of the United States begins with geography—the study of Earth and all of its variety. Geographic factors—including landforms, waterways, and natural resources—have shaped the history of the nation. Wherever people have lived, their lives have been shaped by the geography around them.

Studying geography introduces you to all the elements of geography—people, places, and environments—and how geographers look at our world. The study of geography allows us to make sense out of varied physical environments, diverse cultural systems, why people live where they do, and how they earn a living.

Knowledge of geography helps people understand the relationships among people, places, and the environment. Just as Native Americans and European explorers used knowledge of geography to live in and explore our land, your ability to understand geography and the tools and technology available for its study will equip you for life in our modern world.

An important part of studying geography is learning about the new technologies available for mapping and understanding where and how we live. These technologies have advanced greatly in recent years. You only need to watch automobile television ads to see how Global Positioning Systems (GPSs) and Geographic Information Systems (GISs) have made their way into our everyday lives. These tools give geographers and students new ways of expanding their knowledge.

Thinking Like a HISTORIAN

Review Vocabulary

1. Use the following terms in a sentence that explains the relationship between the terms.

a. globe **b.** map
Students will write sentences with correct explanations.

2. Use the following terms in a sentence that explains the relationship among the terms.

a. landforms **b.** relief **c.** elevation
Students will write sentences with correct explanations.

Answer the Guiding Questions

3. *Identifying* What are the five themes of geography? Why are they important? Students should identify the five themes; understand relationship between people, places, and environment.

4. *Listing* What are the different disadvantages of globes and maps? Answers should provide valid explanations.

5. *Applying* What is the absolute location of your community? What is the relative location? Answers will vary.

6. *Assessing* How do physical systems affect humans? influence where people choose to settle

7. *Speculating* What are two examples of ways that people shape the world they live in? Why do you think people do this? Example: People create reservoirs to control the environment.

8. *Explaining* Why is it important to protect our ecosystems? to protect the health and well-being of people and animal life

9. EXPOSITORY WRITING What is the definition of a place? Give two examples of places you are familiar with. Answers should show valid reasoning and provide examples.

SCAVENGER HUNT

NETWORKS contains a wealth of information. The trick is to know where to look to access all the information in the book. If you complete this scavenger hunt exercise with your teachers or parents, you will see how the textbook is organized and how to get the most out of your reading and studying time. Let's get started!

1 **How many chapters are in this book?**
18

2 **Where in the front of the book can you find a physical map of the United States?** Reference Atlas

3 **What time period does Chapter 3 cover?** Colonial America, 1587–1770

4 **What is the 21st Century Skills Activity for Chapter 5?**
Recognizing Bias. Students look at a poster and create an alternative version that describes the Boston Massacre from the British point of view. Students also write a brief explanation of how the posters differ from each other.

5 **Where can you find the** *Thinking Like a Historian* **activity in each chapter?**
On the Chapter Activities page at the end of each chapter

6 **What is the title of Chapter 9?** The Federalist Era

7 **What Essential Questions will you answer in Chapter 11?**
How does geography influence the way people live? Why does conflict develop?

8 **What are the Academic Vocabulary words in Lesson 3, Chapter 12?**
institution and symbol

9 **Where in the back of the book can you find the meaning of vocabulary words such as** *mercenary***?**
Glossary

10 **Where in the back of the book can you find page numbers for information about Frederick Douglass?**
Index

(t) DEA/A. DAGLI ORTI/Getty Images, (c) Squared Studios/Getty Images, (b) Comstock/PunchStock

CHAPTER **1**
The First Americans Planner

UNDERSTANDING BY DESIGN®

Enduring Understanding

- *Cultures are held together by shared beliefs and common practices and values.*

Essential Questions

- *What are characteristics that make up a culture?*
- *How do civilizations rise and fall?*
- *What makes a culture unique?*

Predictable Misunderstandings

Students may think:

- *The peoples who migrated to North America all arrived at the same time.*
- *The peoples who migrated to North America all came in the same manner, such as across Beringia or by boat along the coast.*
- *There were no great civilizations, with large cities and road systems, among the early cultural groups in the Americas.*
- *There were no great civilizations in North America, in the future United States, before the arrival of European colonists.*

Assessment Evidence

Performance Tasks:

- *Hands-On Chapter Project*

Other Evidence:

- *Interactive Graphic Organizers*
- *Geography and History Activity*
- *21st Century Skills Activity*
- *Written paragraphs*
- *Online Self-Check Quizzes*
- *Lesson Reviews*
- *Chapter Activities and Assessment*

NCSS Standards covered in "The First Americans"

Learners will understand:

1 CULTURE

1. "Culture" refers to the socially transmitted behaviors, beliefs, values, traditions, institutions, and ways of living together for a group of people

3. How culture influences the ways in which human groups solve the problems of daily living

4. That the beliefs, values, and behaviors of a culture form an integrated system that helps shape the activities and ways of life that define a culture

3 PEOPLE, PLACES, AND ENVIRONMENTS

1. The theme of people, places, and environments involves the study of the relationships between human populations in different locations and geographic phenomena such as climate, vegetation, and natural resources

3. Past and present changes in physical systems, such as seasons, climate, and weather, and the water cycle, in both national and global contexts

9. The use of a variety of maps, globes, graphic representations, and geospatial technologies to help investigate the relationships among people, places, and environments

SUGGESTED PACING GUIDE

Introducing the Chapter. . . . . 1 day	Lesson 3 . . . . .2 days
Lesson 1 . . . . 1 day	Chapter Wrap-Up and Assessment. . . . . . 1 day
Lesson 2 . . . . .2 days	

TOTAL TIME 7 Days

Key for Using the Teacher Edition

SKILL-BASED ACTIVITIES

Types of skill activities found in the Teacher Edition.

V Visual Skills require students to analyze maps, graphs, charts, and photos.

R Reading Skills help students practice reading skills and master vocabulary.

W Writing Skills provide writing opportunities to help students comprehend the text.

C Critical Thinking Skills help students apply and extend what they have learned.

T Technology Skills require students to use digital tools effectively.

Letters are followed by a number when there is more than one of the same type of skill on the page.

DIFFERENTIATED INSTRUCTION

All activities are written for the on-level student unless otherwise marked with the leveled labels below.

BL Beyond Level
AL Approaching Level
ELL English Language Learners

All students benefit from activities that utilize different learning styles. Many activities are marked as below when a particular learning style is highlighted.

Intrapersonal	Naturalist
Logical/Mathematical	Kinesthetic
Visual/Spatial	Auditory/Musical
Verbal/Linguistic	Interpersonal

CHAPTER OPENER PLANNER

Students will know:

- *how the first people arrived in North America.*
- *how agriculture allowed the development of unique cultures.*
- *the peoples of the Americas who predated the arrival of the Europeans.*
- *why the Inca were considered to be a developed and well-organized civilization.*
- *the characteristics of various civilizations of early North America.*
- *the special ways early Native Americans adapted to their environments.*

Students will be able to:

- ***identify and evaluate*** *ways in which the first people may have arrived to the Americas.*
- ***explain*** *how agriculture influenced the development of culture.*
- ***Identify*** *some of the people who lived in the Americas before European exploration.*
- ***identify and analyze*** *the characteristics that made the Inca a well-organized civilization.*
- ***describe*** *civilizations of early North America.*
- ***analyze and explain*** *how early Native Americans adapted to their environments.*

UNDERSTANDING
BY DESIGN®

☑ *Print Teaching Options*

V Visual Skills

☐ **P. 2** Students review parts of a map, identify locations, and estimate the size of cultural regions using the scale.
Visual/Spatial Logical/Mathmatical

☐ **P. 3** Students identify events in different parts of the world on two separate time lines spanning the same time period. **BL**

☑ *Online Teaching Options*

V Visual Skills

☐ **MAP** **Native American Cultures c. 1492**—Students use the interactive map to locate the areas populated by various Native American groups around 1492.

☐ **TIME LINE** **Place and Time: The Americas c. 1492**—Students learn about key historical events in the Americas up to 1492.

☐ **WORLD ATLAS** Students can use this interactive map to identify regions of the world, learn about individual countries, locate political boundaries, measure distances, and much more.

☑ *Printable Digital Worksheets*

R Reading Skills

☐ **GRAPHIC NOVEL** *Tenochtitlán*—Describes the legend of the eagle with a snake in its beak, which appears on the Mexican flag.

Project-Based Learning

Hands-On Chapter Project

The First Americans
Students will work in groups to develop a presentation about the La Brea Tar Pits, Beringia/the Bering Strait, Tenochtitlán/Lake Texcoco, Cuzco, Machu Picchu, the Cahokia Mounds, the Great Serpent Mound, Pueblo Bonito, or Mesa Verde.

Technology Extension

Multimedia Presentations
- Find an additional activity online that incorporates technology for this project.
- Visit the EdTechTeacher Web sites (included in the Technology Extension for this chapter) for more links, tutorials, and other resources.

Print Resources

ANCILLARY RESOURCES
These ancillaries are available for every chapter and lesson.

- **Reading Essentials and Study Guide Workbook** **AL** **ELL**
- **Chapter Tests and Lesson Quizzes Blackline Masters**

PRINTABLE DIGITAL WORKSHEETS
These printable digital worksheets are available for every chapter and lesson.

- **Hands-On Chapter Projects**
- **What Do You Know? activities**
- **Chapter Summaries (English and Spanish)**
- **Vocabulary Builder activities**
- **Guided Reading activities**

More Media Resources

SUGGESTED READING

Grade 6 reading level:
- *Ikwa of the Mound-Builder Indians,* by Margaret Zehmer

Grade 7 reading level:
- *Mammoth Bones and Broken Stones: The Mystery of North America's First People,* by David L. Harrison

Grade 8 reading level:
- *Heart of a Jaguar,* by Marc Talbert

MIGRATION TO THE AMERICAS

Students will know:
- *how the first people arrived in North America.*
- *how agriculture allowed the development of unique cultures.*

Students will be able to:
- **_identify and evaluate_** *ways in which the first people may have arrived to the Americas.*
- **_explain_** *how agriculture influenced the development of culture.*

UNDERSTANDING
BY DESIGN®

☑ *Print Teaching Options*

V Visual Skills

☐ **P. 5** Students examine different migration routes and draw conclusions about theories of migration. **BL**
Visual/Spatial

☐ **P. 6** Students analyze an image in order to understand the hunting techniques of the first Americans. **AL**
Visual/Spatial

R Reading Skills

☐ **P. 4** Students explain how scientists have studied ancient American peoples. **AL** **ELL**

☐ **P. 4** Students explain the theory about how the first humans came to the Americas.

☐ **P. 5** Students discuss the land bridge and its contribution to one theory of migration. **BL**

☐ **P. 7** Students discuss the effects of changing from a nomadic to a farming lifestyle. **AL**

W Writing Skills

☐ **P. 6** Students write a narrative about one group of early Americans and their possible reasons for migrating.
AL **ELL** Verbal/Linguistic

C Critical Thinking Skills

☐ **P. 6** Students discuss the effects of climate change that occurred around 15,000 years ago.

☐ **P. 7** Students draw conclusions about the effect climate change had on migration.

☑ *Online Teaching Options*

V Visual Skills

☐ **VIDEO** **Before Columbus**—Students view a video that describes life in what is now Colorado before Columbus.

☐ **MAP** **Routes to the Americas**—Students visualize possible migration routes to the Americas during the last ice age.

☐ **IMAGE** **The Woolly Mammoth**—Students learn about the woolly mammoth and its interactions with early peoples in North America.

R Reading Skills

☐ **GRAPHIC ORGANIZER** **Taking Notes:** *Identifying:* **Reasons Early People Migrated**—Students complete the lesson graphic organizer in which they identify reasons early people migrated.

C Critical Thinking Skills

☐ **WHITEBOARD ACTIVITY** **Early American Tools**—Students match pictures of tools with their names and functions.

T Technology Skills

☐ **SELF-CHECK QUIZ** **Lesson 1**—Students receive instant feedback of their mastery of lesson content.

CITIES AND EMPIRES

Students will know:
- the peoples of the Americas who predated the arrival of the Europeans.
- why the Inca were considered to be a developed and well-organized civilization.
- the characteristics of various civilizations of early North America.

Students will be able to:
- **identify** some of the people who lived in the Americas before European exploration.
- **identify and analyze** the characteristics that made the Inca a well-organized civilization.
- **describe** civilizations of early North America.

UNDERSTANDING
BY DESIGN®

☑ *Print Teaching Options*

V Visual Skills

☐ **P. 11** Students analyze how a road network may have helped shape the Maya civilization. **BL** Visual/Spatial

R Reading Skills

☐ **P. 8** Students identify four advanced civilizations established in the early Americas. **AL** **ELL**

☐ **P. 8** Students describe the history and achievements of the Olmec people.

☐ **P. 9** Students describe Maya trade activities. **AL**

☐ **P. 9** Students explain the decline of Maya civilization.

☐ **P. 11** Students identify important cities of the Inca empire. **AL**

☐ **P. 12** Students discuss the role of war and conquest in the Inca state. **AL**

☐ **P. 12** Students describe different aspects of Incan culture. **AL** **ELL**

☐ **P. 13** Students cite text evidence to describe communication throughout the Inca empire. **AL**

W Writing Skills

☐ **P. 10** Students write personal accounts as if they are early explorers arriving in Tenochtitlán for the first time.
Verbal/Linguistic

C Critical Thinking Skills

☐ **P. 8** Students speculate as to why the Olmec civilization declined and collapsed. **BL**

☐ **P. 9** Students determine how knowledge of astronomy and mathematics contributed to Maya advancements. **BL**

☐ **P. 10** Students discuss religion in Aztec culture. **AL** **ELL**

☐ **P. 10** Students analyze descriptions of the Aztec empire as written by Hernán Cortés and Bernal Díaz del Castillo.

☐ **P. 11** Students create time lines showing the dates of existence for the civilizations they've learned about so far.
Logical/Mathematical

☐ **P. 12** Students infer why neighboring states so easily surrendered to Inca rule. **BL**

☑ *Online Teaching Options*

V Visual Skills

☐ **VIDEO** **Aztec, Maya, and Inca Civilizations**—Students view a video that describes these three great empires of South America and Mexico that were eventually overtaken by Spanish conquistadores.

☐ **IMAGE** **The Maya**—Students learn about Maya religion.

☐ **IMAGE** **The Aztec Calendar**—Students learn about the workings of the Aztec calendar.

☐ **BIOGRAPHY** **Malinche**—Students explore the relationship between the Aztec and the Spanish through this biography.

☐ **IMAGE** **Quipus**—Students explore the use of this tool for record keeping.

R Reading Skills

☐ **GRAPHIC ORGANIZER** **Taking Notes: *Listing:* Accomplishments**—Students list accomplishments of the Olmec, Maya, Aztec, and Inca civilizations.

C Critical Thinking Skills

☐ **MAP** **Civilizations of Mexico and Central America**—Students visualize the areas where the Olmec, Maya, and Aztec people lived.

☐ **MAP** **The Inca Empire, 1532**—Students locate the four provinces that made up the Inca Empire.

T Technology Skills

☐ **SELF-CHECK QUIZ** **Lesson 2**—Students receive instant feedback of their mastery of lesson content.

☑ *Printable Digital Worksheets*

W Writing Skills

☐ **WORKSHEET** **Geography and History Activity: Understanding Location: Machu Picchu**—Students read about this Inca city and answer questions.

NORTH AMERICAN PEOPLES

Students will know:
- the peoples of the Americas who predated the arrival of the Europeans.
- the special ways early Native Americans adapted to their environments.

Students will be able to:
- **Identify** some of the people who lived in the Americas before European exploration.
- **analyze and explain** how early Native Americans adapted to their environments.

UNDERSTANDING BY DESIGN®

☑ Print Teaching Options

V **Visual Skills**

☐ **P. 15** Students locate different mound-building cultures on a map. **Visual/Spatial**

☐ **P. 16** Students analyze an image of a pueblo. **AL** **ELL** **Visual/Spatial**

R **Reading Skills**

☐ **P. 14** Students identify Mound Builder cultures and list different purposes for mounds. **AL**

☐ **P. 16** Students discuss the history and location of the Ancient Puebloan people.

☐ **P. 19** Students describe the Southwestern people who were descendants of the Ancient Puebloans. **AL**

☐ **P. 19** Students examine the importance of buffalo to the Plains peoples.

☐ **P. 21** Students explain why farming was so important to the Southeastern peoples. **AL** **ELL**

W **Writing Skills**

☐ **P. 17** Students describe different regions in the United States today. **AL** **ELL** **Verbal/Linguistic**

☐ **P. 20** Students write about the Great Peace alliance. **AL**

C **Critical Thinking Skills**

☐ **P. 15** Students discuss similarities between the Cahokia site and the great cultures of Mexico. **BL**

☐ **P. 16** Students analyze the environment in which the Hohokam people lived.

☐ **P. 17** Students speculate about the Inuit's ability to survive in frigid temperatures. **BL**

☐ **P. 19** Students compare the Cherokee and Iroquois with our culture today. **AL** **ELL** **Interpersonal**

☐ **P. 20** Students compare the Grand Council of the Iroquois with modern methods of democracy. **BL**

T **Technology Skills**

☐ **P. 14** Students compare earthworks created by the Mound Builders with Maya and Aztec pyramids.

☐ **P. 17** Students research a map and locate the Inuit region. **AL** **ELL** **Visual/Spatial**

☐ **P. 18** Students locate groups who lived on the western coast of North America. **Visual/Spatial**

☑ Online Teaching Options

V **Visual Skills**

☐ **VIDEO** **The Great Plains Native Americans**—Students view a video that provides some insight into the Great Plains Native Americans of North America.

☐ **IMAGE** **Taos Pueblo**—Students learn about the architecture and uses of pueblos built by the Ancient Puebloans.

☐ **IMAGE** **Mesa Verde**—Students learn about cliff dwellings built by Northern Puebloans.

☐ **IMAGE** **Igloos**—Students explore these structures that the Inuits built to live in.

☐ **IMAGE** **Longhouses**—Students explore the construction of these structures.

☐ **IMAGE** **Dekanawidah**—Students learn about the man said to be founder of the Iroquois League.

R **Reading Skills**

☐ **GRAPHIC ORGANIZER** **Taking Notes:** *Describing:* **Native American Cultures**—Students complete the lesson graphic organizer in which they describe characteristics of several early North American cultures.

☐ **IMAGE** **Pueblo Pottery**—Students explore the development of this art form and its uses.

☐ **IMAGE** **Totem Poles**—Students explore the significance of these poles, which were carved by members of some Northwest Native American tribes.

C **Critical Thinking Skills**

☐ **MAP** **Significant Adena, Hopewell, and Mississippian Sites**—Students visualize the areas where the Adena, Hopewell, and Mississippian cultures built mounds.

T **Technology Skills**

☐ **SELF-CHECK QUIZ** **Lesson 3**—Students receive instant feedback of their mastery of lesson content.

☐ **GAME** **Crossword Puzzle: North American Peoples**—Students complete a puzzle to reinforce their knowledge of vocabulary definitions.

☑ Printable Digital Worksheets

W **Writing Skills**

☐ **WORKSHEET** **21st Century Skills Activity: Communication: Write a Blog Entry**—Students learn how to structure the content of a blog entry as they blog about a day in the life of a young Inuit.

INTERVENTION AND REMEDIATION STRATEGIES

LESSON 1 Migration to the Americas

Reading and Comprehension

To ensure student understanding regarding the arrival of the first Americans, ask students to summarize the prevailing theories about how the continent was populated. Ask students to explain not only how the migration happened, but also why historians believe it took place.

Text Evidence

Organize students into groups, and ask each group to conduct research to determine what the settlements of the first Americans may have looked like. Each group should create a diagram that depicts how the settlement may have been laid out. Students should check their understanding against the descriptions in this text.

LESSON 2 Cities and Empires

Reading and Comprehension

Students should work in pairs to outline the accomplishments of each of the major civilizations discussed in this lesson. Each pair should explain to the class which civilization they think created the most substantial accomplishments.

Text Evidence

Ask students to create a narrative depicting life in the Incan civilization. Remind students to use details from the lesson to create the narrative. Students can take turns reading their narratives aloud.

LESSON 3 North American Peoples

Reading and Comprehension

Organize the class into small groups. Ask each group to list each of the peoples discussed in this lesson. Ask students to categorize each group of peoples according to the region of the continent they occupied. For each region, ask students to identify one notable fact.

Text Evidence

Ask students to select a group mentioned in this lesson and to describe how that group adapted to its environment. Students should cite evidence from the text in their description. Then, ask students to note ways the group might have adapted had their environment undergone drastic changes.

Online Resources

Approaching Level Reader

Use this online lower-level text that corresponds directly to the text in the Student Edition. It includes a Spanish version.

Guided Reading Activities

This resource uses graphic organizers and guiding questions to help students with comprehension.

What Do You Know?

Use these worksheets to pre-assess student's background knowledge before they study the chapter.

Reading Essentials and Study Guide Workbook

This resource offers writing and reading activities for the approaching-level student. Also available in Spanish.

Self-Check Quizzes

This online assessment tool provides instant feedback for students to check their progress.

The First Americans

Prehistory to 1492

ESSENTIAL QUESTIONS · *What are characteristics that make up a culture?* · *How do civilizations rise and fall?* · *What makes a culture unique?*

◄ *This Acoma woman lived in what is today western New Mexico.*

Buyenlarge/Archive Photos/Getty Images

netw☉rks

There's More Online about the people of the Americas in the time before Europeans arrived.

CHAPTER 1

The Story Matters . . .

The year is 1905, but this woman and the rest of her Acoma community are living much as their people did in 1305. The Acoma's culture is shaped by the environment that surrounds them. Their mesa-top village provides natural protection from ancient enemies they have outlasted. In the fields below, they grow crops using methods that have sustained their people in this dry land for hundreds of years. Their artwork—in particular their finely crafted pottery—shows the influences of the shapes and colors of the American Southwest that is their home.

The Acoma are just one example of the hundreds of Native American cultures that developed in the time before Europeans arrived. Their story is part of the rich history of the Americas.

1

ENGAGE

🔔 **Bellringer** Have students study the 1905 photograph of the Acoma woman. Then have a volunteer read "The Story Matters . . ." aloud.

Ask: What does the photograph depict? *(a Native American Acoma woman in 1905)* From what you heard in the story, do you think the woman would have been dressed much differently in 1305, more than 700 years ago? Why or why not? *(Answers may vary. Some students may say there would be little difference, based on the language in the first sentence of the story, while others may say she would be dressed a little differently based on the language near the end of the story stating that the people reflect their surroundings. Maybe the Acoma's surroundings had changed a little during the centuries.)*

Ask: Based on what you know, do you think this woman is dressed in her everyday clothes or in her more formal or special clothes? *(Answers may vary but should reflect an analysis of the woman's garb as shown in the photograph.)*

Invite students to browse the chapter, noting headings, photos and captions, and other text features. **Ask:** What do you think you will learn about in this chapter? *(Answers will vary but should reflect the information available to students in the headings, photos and captions, and other text features.)*

Ask: What do you already know about the people who lived in the Americas before the arrival of Christopher Columbus? *(Answers may vary.)*

Making Connections

Read the following information to students:

Hundreds of different cultural groups lived in the Americas at the time of Christopher Columbus's arrival. These peoples migrated primarily from Asia. Today, America's population looks drastically different but still represents a diverse mix of cultures, values, and languages. People have migrated from all over the world to live in America. The diversity in our schools, communities, and nation continues to evolve.

Letter from the Author

Dear American History Teacher,

Today we can travel conveniently between continents and purchase goods made the world over. What may seem obvious today was once new as isolated civilizations of the Americas encountered each other. Exploration by the first Americans led to trade and enlightenment, but also to exploitation and enslavement. Chapter 1 points out the diversity of the peoples of the early Americas. Historians and archaeologists study the remains of these societies—art and artifacts—to better understand what they thought and how they lived.

Donald A. Ritchie

TEACH & ASSESS

Step Into the Place

V1 Visual Skills

Analyzing Maps Review with students the parts of the map, such as the title, compass rose, scale, and legend. **Ask:**

- What information does the legend on this map give? *(regions where Native American groups lived)*
- Which cultural group resided in the northernmost region identified on the map? *(Inuit)*

Then, have volunteers match each color used in the key with its location on the map and explain what it stands for. Ask students to locate specific Native American groups in different regions.

Have student pairs use the map scale to calculate the approximate sizes of the following cultural regions in square miles:

- Great Basin *(about 300,00 square miles)*
- Great Plains *(about 720,000 square miles)*
- Southeast *(about 120,000 square miles)*

(Answers may vary but should demonstrate accurate estimates.)

Ask volunteers to explain how they determined the size of each cultural region. **Visual/Spatial Logical/Mathematical**

Content Background Knowledge

- A land bridge called Beringia once connected northeastern Asia to what is now Alaska.
- The Ancient Puebloan people of the Great Basin region built cliff dwellings in what is now southwestern Colorado.
- Fossils dating back to the last Ice Age were found near the La Brea Tar Pits in what is now Los Angeles, California.

ANSWERS, p. 2

Step Into the Place

1. There are 10 different culture areas shown on the map.
2. the portion of what is now Canada south of the Arctic culture area
3. **CRITICAL THINKING** Answers may vary but might include that differences in climate; landforms, soil, or vegetation; and types of wildlife may have defined different culture regions.

Step Into the Time

Humans arrived in the Americas considerably before the last Ice Age ended. It was at least 16,800 years between the likely arrival of human beings in North America and the emergence of the Olmec civilization.

By the late 1400s, Native American groups had spread out across most of North America. Groups adapted to the different climates and conditions to form unique cultures.

Step Into the Place

MAP FOCUS Each Native American group had its own features, yet groups within certain areas often shared similar characteristics.

1 REGION How many different culture groups are shown on the map? RH.6–8.7

2 PLACE According to this map, which part of North America was not populated by Native Americans? RH.6–8.7

3 CRITICAL THINKING
Speculating What geographic factors do you think might have defined the different culture areas shown on this map? RH.6–8.7, RH.6–8.10

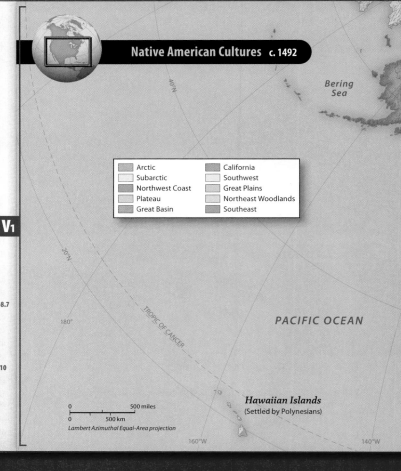

Native American Cultures c. 1492

Bering Sea

Arctic	California
Subarctic	Southwest
Northwest Coast	Great Plains
Plateau	Northeast Woodlands
Great Basin	Southeast

PACIFIC OCEAN

0   500 miles
0   500 km
Lambert Azimuthal Equal-Area projection

Hawaiian Islands
(Settled by Polynesians)

Step Into the Time

TIME LINE Look at the time line. Had human beings reached North America before the end of the last Ice Age? How long after the likely date of human arrival in the Americas did the Olmec civilization emerge? RH.6–8.5, RH.6–8.7

c. 18,000 B.C. Humans have likely reached the Americas

c. 1200 B.C. Olmec civilization develops in Mexico

AMERICAS
WORLD
PREHISTORY

c. 8,000 B.C. Ice Age ends

c. 600s B.C. Construction of Great Wall of China begins

2 *The First Americans*

Project-Based Learning ✋

Hands-On Chapter Project

The First Americans

Students will work in groups to develop a presentation about the La Brea Tar Pits, Beringia/the Bering Strait, Tenochtitlán/Lake Texcoco, Cuzco, Machu Picchu, the Cahokia Mounds, the Great Serpent Mound, Pueblo Bonito, or Mesa Verde. Students will read about the topic in their textbook and then conduct personal research, citing at least three sources and gathering facts and images. Then they will meet in teams to organize research, decide what to include, and create their presentations. Teams deliver their presentations to the class, explaining the significance of their sites.

Technology Extension

Multimedia Presentations

Students will create multimedia presentations about the La Brea Tar Pits, Beringia/the Bering Strait, Tenochtitlán/Lake Texcoco, Cuzco, Machu Picchu, the Cahokia Mounds, the Great Serpent Mound, Pueblo Bonito, or Mesa Verde. Students should research a topic and create slide shows that include images, text, videos, drawings, music, and narration. Presentations can be shared via email, a blog, a Web site, or through media-sharing sites, and students should collect audience feedback.

edtechteacher
21st Century Learning

networks
There's More Online!

☑ **MAP** Explore the interactive version of this map on NETWORKS.

☑ **TIME LINE** Explore the interactive version of this time line on NETWORKS.

Map labels

ARCTIC OCEAN

Baffin Bay

INUIT

INUIT

Labrador Sea

Hudson Bay

TLINGIT

HAIDA

ATLANTIC OCEAN

CHINOOK

YAKIMA

NEZ PERCE

BLACKFOOT

OJIBWA

SHOSHONE

CHEYENNE

DAKOTA

OMAHA

PAWNEE

HURON

IROQUOIS

SAUK

FOX

MIAMI

SHAWNEE

WAMPANOAG

PEQUOT

NARRAGANSETT

IROQUOIS LEAGUE:
CAYUGA
MOHAWK
ONEIDA
ONONDAGA
SENECA

POWHATAN

POMO

ANASAZI

UTE

NAVAJO

KIOWA

ACOMA

APACHE

ZUÑI

COMANCHE

APACHE

OSAGE

CHEROKEE

CHICKASAW

CHOCTAW

CREEK

Gulf of Mexico

TROPIC OF CANCER

ROCKY MTNS.

SIERRA NEVADA

APPALACHIAN MTNS.

Great Lakes

Time line

c. A.D. 1300s Hohokam civilization begins to decline

c. A.D. 1438 Inca Empire begins to expand

c. A.D. 700 Maya Empire reaches its peak

c. A.D. 1200s Drought strikes Ancient Puebloan (Anasazi) communities

A.D. 1492 Christopher Columbus arrives in West Indies

300   600   900   1200   1500

A.D. 313 Roman Empire accepts Christianity

c. A.D. 622 Spread of Islam begins

c. A.D. 1000 Norse voyagers reach Newfoundland

c. A.D. 1400s Astrolabe sailing navigation tool is in wide use

3

Step Into the Time

V₂ Visual Skills

Analyzing Time Lines Have students read through both tiers of events on the time line—those dealing with the Americas and those dealing with the rest of the world. Remind students that a time line is read from left to right. Point out that the time line deals with events that occurred before 1492.

As a class, discuss the time line's major points of interest. **Ask: How did the astrolabe sailing navigation tool affect the people living in the Americas?** *(Answers may include that it gave Europeans a means to travel over the Atlantic Ocean, changing forever the lives of the Native American peoples in the Americas.)* **How might the drought around A.D. 1200 have affected the Ancient Puebloan (Anasazi) communities?** *(It left them with no water for farming, so crops failed.)* **Which cultural group was expanding around the time Christopher Columbus arrived in the West Indies?** *(the Incas)*

Then, have students use an atlas to identify the West Indies and Newfoundland on the map of the Americas. **BL**

Content Background Knowledge

- The Inca civilization of western South America was the largest of all early American civilizations.
- The largest and most advanced civilizations of the early Americas developed in what is now Mexico, Central America, and South America.

CLOSE & REFLECT

Formulating Questions Have each student write a question based on the map, time line, or class discussion about the Americas c. 1492. Collect the questions and answer them as a class. Tell students they will be learning more about the Americas as they study this chapter.

---

networks *Online Teaching Options*

TIME LINE

Place and Time: The Americas c. 1492

Reading a Time Line Display the time line on the white board. Have student volunteers read each event as it is revealed, and discuss it as a class. Ask students to choose one event and research it using the Internet. Then, have students create a more detailed time line that includes events that occurred around the same time as the event that they chose.

See page 1B for other online activities.

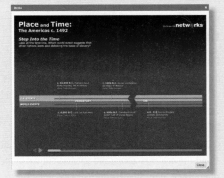

ENGAGE

🔔 **Bellringer** Bring a basin, a metal spoon, and several sponges to class. Place the spoon in the basin and add enough water to cover the spoon completely. Explain that the water in the basin represents the ocean before the most recent Ice Age. Then, put sponges into the basin to soak up enough water to expose the spoon. Explain that when temperatures dropped, a lot of Earth's water froze into glaciers, which caused ocean water levels to drop. The sponges represent glaciers. **Ask:**

- **What do you see now?** *(The spoon is no longer submerged.)*
- **Why is the spoon no longer submerged?** *(The sponges soaked up enough water to lower the water level in the basin.)* **AL** **ELL**
- **How does this resemble what happened during the Ice Age?** *(The spoon represents land that was exposed during the Ice Age because of changes in the climate.)*

TEACH & ASSESS

R1 Reading Skills

Determining Word Meaning Before students read the text, remind them that people lived in the Americas long before European explorers arrived. After they have read, ask students to explain how scientists have studied ancient American peoples. **Ask: What is** *archaeology?* *(the study of ancient peoples)* **What are** *artifacts?* *(items early peoples left behind, such as tools, weapons, and artwork)* **AL** **ELL**

R2 Reading Skills

Explaining After students have read the text, ask them to explain the widely held theory about how the first humans may have come to the Americas about 20,000 years ago. **Ask: What have scientists learned from artifacts of early North American peoples?** *(that the first humans may have come to the Americas across a land bridge connecting Asia to North America)*

ANSWER, p. 4

TAKING NOTES: Some were nomadic hunters. People would move to areas to obtain food through gathering. People were looking for a better climate.

---

networks
There's More Online!

☑ **GRAPHIC ORGANIZER** Reasons Early Peoples Migrated

☑ **MAP** Routes to the Americas

☑ **VIDEO**

NORTH AMERICA

Lesson 1
Migration to the Americas

ESSENTIAL QUESTION *What are characteristics that make up a culture?*

IT MATTERS BECAUSE
Human history in the Americas began thousands of years ago.

The Migration Begins
GUIDING QUESTION *Who were the first Americans and how did they live?*

The written history of the Americas is several hundred years old, yet human beings have been living on these continents for thousands of years. Where did these people come from? How and when did they get here? How did the different corners of North and South America get settled?

Today, scientists are still seeking answers to these questions. Experts in **archaeology** (AHR·kee·ah·luh·jee), the study of ancient peoples, continue to piece together evidence that tells the story of the first Americans.

Archaeologists have learned a lot about the past from **artifacts** (AHR·tih·fakts)—the tools, weapons, and other objects that early people left behind. Based on this and other types of evidence, archaeologists have offered some possible answers to questions about the first Americans. A widely held theory of recent times is that the first humans might have come to the Americas perhaps 20,000 or more years ago. This theory maintains that early people traveled along a strip of land that once linked Asia and the Americas.

A Land Bridge Revealed
Throughout Earth's history, the climate has changed. Several periods of extreme cold have occurred. The most recent of these ice ages began 100,000 years ago and ended about 12,000 years

(c)Gianni Dagli Orti/CORBIS, (r)Kenneth Garrett

Reading HELPDESK (CCSS)

Taking Notes: *Identifying*
As you read, use a chart like this one to record reasons early peoples migrated from place to place. RH.6–8.2, RH.6–8.7

Reasons Early Peoples Migrated
1.
2.

Content Vocabulary (Tier 3 Words)
- **archaeology**
- **artifact**
- **strait**
- **migration**
- **nomad**
- **maize**
- **carbon dating**
- **culture**

4 *The First Americans*

---

networks *Online Teaching Options*

VIDEO

Before Columbus

Drawing Conclusions Play the video about early American life before Columbus. Explain that in this video a tribal administrator and an archeologist help viewers appreciate the complexity and beauty of the Ancient Puebloan culture as it is preserved by contemporary descendants. Have students take notes about the artifacts, tools, and shelters shown in the video. Then, have small groups discuss what these items can teach us about how early Americans lived long ago.

See page 1C for other online activities.

Mesa Verde National Park
Cortez, CO

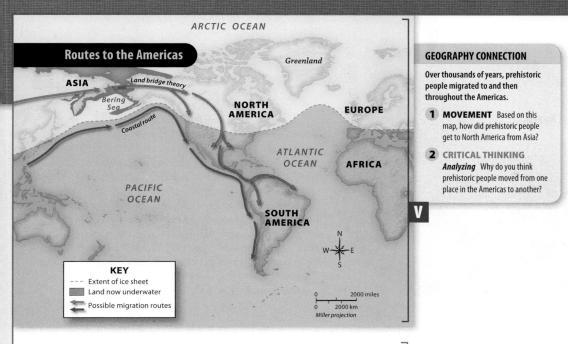

Routes to the Americas

ARCTIC OCEAN

ASIA

Land bridge theory

Bering Sea

Coastal route

Greenland

NORTH AMERICA

EUROPE

ATLANTIC OCEAN

AFRICA

PACIFIC OCEAN

SOUTH AMERICA

KEY
- - - Extent of ice sheet
▨ Land now underwater
⇦ Possible migration routes

0   2000 miles
0   2000 km
Miller projection

GEOGRAPHY CONNECTION

Over thousands of years, prehistoric people migrated to and then throughout the Americas.

1 **MOVEMENT** Based on this map, how did prehistoric people get to North America from Asia?

2 **CRITICAL THINKING**
Analyzing Why do you think prehistoric people moved from one place in the Americas to another?

ago. During these years, a large share of Earth's water formed huge sheets of ice, or glaciers. The glaciers held so much water that ocean levels were lower. The lower sea level exposed a strip of land—a "land bridge"—connecting northeastern Asia to what is now Alaska. Scientists today call this land bridge Beringia. It now lies beneath the Bering Strait, a body of water named for explorer Vitus Bering. A **strait** is a narrow body of water that connects two larger ones.

Many scientists believe early people traveled from Asia to North America across the land bridge. Yet not all scientists agree on how or when this might have happened. For example, some think people might have come to the Americas by boat. This might have allowed humans to spread faster throughout the Americas. As archaeologists discover new artifacts and evidence, new theories emerge to challenge old ones.

Searching for Hunting Grounds

It is clear, of course, that humans arrived in the Americas. Over centuries, they traveled throughout both continents. In time, settlements stretched as far east as the Atlantic Ocean and as far south as the tip of South America.

archaeology the study of the material remains of ancient peoples

artifact a tool, weapon, or other object left behind by early peoples

strait a narrow passage of water between two larger bodies of water

MAP

Routes to the Americas

Analyzing Maps Have students click to reveal the routes prehistoric people took as they migrated to and then throughout the Americas. Then, have students click to reveal the extent of glaciers that covered the Earth during the last Ice Age and the strip of land that is now under water. Have students label the land bridge and use the scale to measure its approximate length.

See page 1C for other online activities.

V Visual Skills

Analyzing Maps Have students study the map "Routes to the Americas." Ask a volunteer to explain what the map shows. After students study the map, ask students the following questions:

- **How many possible migration routes does the map show?** *(two)*

- **What is the difference between the migration routes shown?** *(One route is by land and supports the land bridge theory. The other route is a coastal route, supporting the theory that some people came to the Americas by boat.)*

- **Which migration theory better supports the idea that humans spread very quickly across the Americas?** *(coastal route theory)* **BL** **Visual/Spatial**

R Reading Skills

Explaining After reading, ask student to explain how the last Ice Age exposed the land bridge. **Ask: How did cold temperatures result in the land bridge appearing?** *(The climate caused a large portion of Earth's water to freeze into glaciers, which lowered the sea level. This in turn exposed land that was previously under water.)* Then, discuss with students how the exposure of the land bridge might encourage migration from Asia to the Americas. **Ask: Why are there different theories about how people came to the Americas?** *(Archaeologists discover new artifacts and evidence, which changes how they think about the migration.)* **BL**

Content Background Knowledge

Beringia This land bridge played an important role in the spread of human, plant, and animal life between the continents of Asia and North America. Animal species, including woolly mammoths, mastodons, bears, moose, and fox traversed the land bridge between continents. It is believed that the people who first came to North America followed the movements of these mammals in pursuit of food, resulting in the first population of the northernmost regions of North America. Today, some remaining land is still visible from the central part of Beringia, including the Diomede Islands, the Pribilof Islands of St. Paul and St. George, St. Lawrence Island, and King Island.

ANSWERS, p. 5

GEOGRAPHY CONNECTION

1 by a coastal route or land bridge

2 **CRITICAL THINKING** Answers may include that prehistoric peoples were nomadic and would have moved either to find places where it was more hospitable to live or where food—animals or plants—was more plentiful.

Migration to the Americas

W Writing Skills

Narrative As a class, discuss the definition of the word *migration (a movement of people from one area to another)*. Explain that scientists think migration to the Americas happened over many centuries. **AL** **ELL** As students read, have them record notes about reasons early peoples migrated from place to place. Then, ask students to write a short narrative that imagines the story of one group of early Americans and their reasons for migration. **Verbal/Linguistic**

V Visual Skills

Analyzing Images Use the image of the mammoth to discuss the hunting techniques of the first Americans. Explain that North America was home to large mammals that served as food. **Ask: What were some of these large mammals?** *(mammoths, mastodons, bison)* **Ask: To what modern animal is the mammoth related?** *(elephant)* **AL** **Visual/Spatial**

C Critical Thinking Skills

Analyzing Open a discussion by asking students to consider how they and the plants and animals in their environments are affected when the temperature becomes either dramatically hot or dramatically cold. After students have read the text, ask students to connect what they have read to the opening discussion. **Ask: What happened when the Earth began to warm around 15,000 years ago?** *(Over thousands of years, glaciers began to melt, oceans rose, and the Beringia land strip was covered once again.)*

Then, discuss with students how and why, over those same thousands of years, many of the large mammals disappeared. *(Students may suggest it was climate change, overhunting, disease, some unknown cause, or a combination of these that killed off the animals.)* Students should support their answers with evidence from the text.

A single mammoth, which averaged 12 feet (3.7 m) tall, could provide tons of meat, enough to feed a group of people for months.

What is the reason for this **migration** (my·GRAY·shuhn), or movement of people from one area to another? Why did these early Americans travel such distances? The answer may lie in the search for food. Early peoples were **nomads** (NOH·madz), people who moved from place to place in search of hunting grounds. Although they also ate wild grains and fruits, they depended on hunting for much of their food.

The first Americans did, indeed, find huge mammals to hunt. These included giant, shaggy beasts that resembled modern elephants: mastodons and mammoths. Early Americans were skilled at hunting these and other animals. They stalked herds of bison, mastodons, or mammoths, charging at the animals with spears.

Earth Warms

About 15,000 years ago, the Ice Age began to end. Temperatures started to rise, and the glaciers began to melt. Ocean levels rose, and Beringia disappeared beneath the waves, cutting off the land route between Asia and the Americas.

Around the same time, the large mammals on which humans depended for food began to disappear. This might have been the result of overhunting or changes in the climate. The decline in game populations meant that early Americans had to find other **sources** of food.

✓ **PROGRESS CHECK**

Explaining How did the Ice Age expose a land bridge between Asia and the Americas?

Settlement

GUIDING QUESTION *How did agriculture change the way of life for early Americans?*

The constant search for food meant trying new methods. Early Americans caught fish and hunted smaller animals, while also gathering berries and grains. Farming was another new option that began to emerge. Its development would change the nomadic way of life of many groups.

Reading **HELP**DESK **CCSS**

migration the movement of people into a new area
nomad person who moves from place to place

maize a variety of corn
carbon dating a scientific method of determining the age of an artifact
culture a people's shared values, beliefs, traditions, and behaviors

Academic Vocabulary (Tier 2 Words)
source a supply
estimate a rough calculation of a number

6 The First Americans

netw⚙rks *Online Teaching Options*

WHITEBOARD ACTIVITY

Early American Tools

Analyzing Use the interactive whiteboard activity to match pictures of early artifacts with descriptions of their function. **Ask: What were many of the tools used for?** *(Many were used for food or shelter purposes.)* **AL** **ELL** How can carbon dating help us understand cultures from the past? *(It can help date certain artifacts so we know when people were using them.)* **BL**

Explain that analysis of these artifacts shows that agriculture changed people's lives.

See page 1C for other online activities.

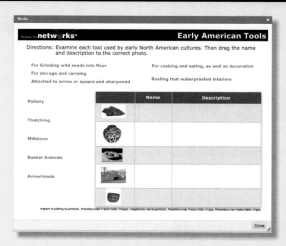

Learning to Farm

Around 10,000 years ago, people in the area now known as Mexico learned to plant an early form of **maize** (MAYZ), which is a type of corn. These early farmers also planted pumpkins, beans, and squash. The crops provided a steady, reliable source of food. The farming people no longer had to move from place to place to find things to eat. Farming also allowed the people to spend time on activities other than finding food. This resulted in an improvement in the lives of early Americans.

Establishing Unique Cultures

Although some early Americans remained nomadic hunters, many others began to settle down. They built permanent shelters from clay, stone, or wood. They also made pottery and cloth.

Scientists have a method of determining how old an artifact is. Using a process called **carbon dating,** scientists can measure the amount of radioactive carbon in an artifact. They can use this measurement to come up with an **estimate** of the artifact's age. Carbon dating has helped scientists to date some settled North American villages to about 5,000 years ago.

Through the study and dating of artifacts from these villages, scientists know that agriculture changed the lives of early Americans. Common customs and beliefs also grew over time. Eventually, the groups of people living in the Americas developed their own **cultures** (KUHL•churz), or shared traditions and behaviors.

PROGRESS CHECK

Identifying What were some changes that affected the nomadic way of life?

Thinking Like a HISTORIAN

Drawing Inferences

R Studying artifacts such as this antler or bone tool helps scientists learn about early cultures. Items like this give important clues about the way ancient people lived. For example, scientists may be able to use this tool to infer how early people worked, what foods they ate, and what other tools they may have used. To learn more about Drawing Inferences, review *Thinking Like a Historian*.

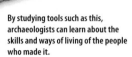

By studying tools such as this, archaeologists can learn about the skills and ways of living of the people who made it.

R Reading Skills

Explaining After reading, ask students to explain the change in food sources and why people began farming. **Ask: What are some foods they planted?** *(maize, pumpkins, beans, and squash)* **AL Ask: How did farming change the nomadic way of life?** *(People did not have to wander to find food, which gave them time to spend on other activities.)* Ask students to explain how changing from a nomadic to a farming lifestyle might change a culture and lead to the formation of civilizations.

C Critical Thinking Skills

Drawing Conclusions The nomadic way of life would have been affected significantly by factors that limited peoples' ability to get to and from familiar places. **Ask: How did the change in climate, which led to the loss of the land bridge, affect those people who had migrated to the Americas?** *(Answers may vary, but should adress the possibility that such a change might have encouraged groups of people to settle into one place, forming their own traditions and shaping their culture apart from their pre-migration influences.)*

Have students complete the Lesson 1 Review.

CLOSE & REFLECT

Summarizing To close the lesson, have students write short essays summarizing how people adapted to changes in their environment as the climate slowly warmed. Ask students to think about how these changes may have led to the diversity of the Americas. Have students reflect on how they themselves have adapted to new situations and circumstance as a result of their changing lives. **BL**

LESSON 1 REVIEW (CCSS)

Review Vocabulary (Tier 3 Words)

1. Examine the three terms below. Then write a sentence explaining what the terms have in common. RH.6–8.4

   a. archaeology
   b. artifact
   c. carbon dating

2. Use the following terms in a sentence about the ancient history of the Americas. RH.6–8.4

   a. nomad   b. migration

Answer the Guiding Questions

3. *Explaining* Why might people have migrated from Asia to the Americas? RH.6–8.2

4. *Explaining* What factors likely led some early Americans to change from hunting to farming? RH.6–8.2

5. *Describing* How does carbon dating help scientists learn about early cultures? RH.6–8.1

6. **INFORMATIVE/EXPLANATORY** Write a short essay describing how farming changed the lives of early people. Include examples of the types of food they grew. WHST.6–8.2, WHST.6–8.9

Lesson 1   **7**

LESSON 1 REVIEW ANSWERS

1. Possible answer: Archaeology is the study of ancient peoples and the artifacts that reveal how these people lived; carbon dating is used to determine the ages.

2. Possible answer: Scientists believe that early nomads followed a migration route from Asia.

3. The people were nomadic hunters who traveled from place to place following, or in search of, game for food.

4. Large mammals, a source of their food, began to disappear. Taking up farming allowed early Americans to create a stable source of food.

5. Carbon dating is a method for estimating the age of artifacts. Linking carbon-dated items to a group of people in certain places and conditions helps scientists determine more about their culture, or the ways they lived.

6. Essays will vary but should reflect understanding that agriculture provided a stable source of food that allowed people to settle down. People in parts of what is now Mexico learned to farm maize, beans, squash, and pumpkins.

ANSWER, p. 7

PROGRESS CHECK Answers may include the warming Earth, the unavailability of large game, and the adaptation to farming.

Kenneth Garrett

ENGAGE

🔔 **Bellringer** Recall with students that groups do not change in a single step—going from nomadic hunters to building large, self-sustaining cities filled with thousands of people. Discuss that this kind of cultural change takes time. **Ask: What do you think are some steps along the path from being nomadic hunters to being city dwellers?** *(Answers may vary.)* `AL` `ELL`

TEACH & ASSESS

R1 Reading Skills

Identifying After students have read the text, discuss with them that several centuries before Europeans arrived, there were highly developed societies living in the Americas. **Ask: What are the names of four of the largest and most advanced of these civilizations?** *(Olmec, Maya, Aztec, Inca)* Be sure that students understand the definition of *civilization*. *(a highly developed society)* `AL` `ELL`

R2 Reading Skills

Describing Ask students to describe the history and achievements of the Olmec people. Prompt students to use evidence from the text to support thier answers. **Ask: Where did the Olmecs live?** *(along the Gulf Coast of what is now Mexico)* **When did they flourish?** *(1200 B.C. to 800 B.C.)* **Ask: What were some of the accomplishments of the Olmec?** *(building stone houses and drainage systems, farming enough to feed thousands, building large stone monuments)*

C Critical Thinking Skills

Speculating Explain to students that the Olmec civilization declined and collapsed for unknown reasons. **Ask: What are some reasons the Olmec society may have collapsed?** *(Answers will vary.)* `BL`

ANSWER, p. 8

TAKING NOTES: Olmec: 1200 B.C.–300 B.C., Along the Gulf Coast of what is now Mexico, farmed and built stone houses and drainage systems; **Maya:** A.D. 250–900; Mexico, Guatemala, Honduras, and Belize; planted maize, beans, squash, and other vegetables; **Aztec:** A.D. 1300–1500; Central Mexico (Lake Texcoco); capital city was Tenochtitlán; military empire with religious focus; **Inca:** capital city Cuzco founded around A.D. 1200, located in Peru, with an empire that stretched from Colombia to northern Argentina and Chile; farmed on terraces in the Andes; military empire with religious focus

---

networks
There's More Online!
☑ **BIOGRAPHY** Malinche
☑ **GRAPHIC ORGANIZER** Early Civilizations of the Americas
☑ **MAP**
• Civilizations of Mexico and Central America
• The Inca Empire
☑ **VIDEO**

Lesson 2
Cities and Empires

ESSENTIAL QUESTION *How do civilizations rise and fall?*

IT MATTERS BECAUSE
Early Americans developed rich cultures and complex civilizations in several locations.

Great Civilizations of Mexico, Central America, and South America

GUIDING QUESTION *What civilizations in Mexico, Central America, and South America predated the arrival of Europeans?*

Centuries before the Europeans arrived, great **civilizations** (sih·vuh·luh·ZAY·shuhnz), or highly developed societies, thrived in Mexico, Central America, and South America. The largest and most advanced of these were the Olmec, Maya, Aztec, and Inca.

Each of these civilizations controlled areas covering hundreds of square miles. They included millions of people and lasted for several centuries. The accomplishments of the Olmec, Maya, Aztec, and Inca rivaled any of the great civilizations in other parts of the world. Their people built grand cities in dense forests and on high mountains. They created spectacular works of art and developed advanced tools. They also came up with **complex** methods for tracking time, counting, and writing.

The Olmec

Along the Gulf Coast of what is now Mexico, a people called the Olmec (OHL·mehk) once flourished. Between 1200 B.C. and 800 B.C., the Olmec built stone houses, monuments, and drainage systems. Their farmers grew food for thousands of people. For

(i) Gianni Dagli Orti/CORBIS, (c) Getty Images, (c) North Wind Picture Archives, (c) The British Museum/Heritage-Images/The Image Works, (d) Manuel Cohen/Getty Images News/Getty Images (r) Science & Society Picture Library/SSPL/Getty Images

---

Reading HELPDESK `CCSS`

Taking Notes: *Listing* RH.6–8.2, RH.6–8.7
As you read, use a chart like this to make note of the features of each of the following civilizations. Include when and where they existed, what they accomplished, and other features of their societies.

OLMEC	MAYA	AZTEC	INCA

Content Vocabulary (Tier 3 Words)
• civilization
• theocracy
• hieroglyphic
• terrace

8 *The First Americans*

---

networks *Online Teaching Options*

VIDEO

Aztec, Maya, and Inca Civilizations

Previewing Show the video about the Aztec, Maya, and Inca civilizations. Encourage students to take notes about the video that they can compare with the content they will be learning in the lesson. Tell them that in this lesson they will learn about important cities and empires that developed in the Americas.

See page 1D for other online activities.

reasons that are not fully understood, the Olmec civilization declined. By about 300 B.C., it had collapsed. Yet the Olmec had a strong influence on the cultures that followed.

The Maya

The Maya (MY•uh) civilization followed the Olmec and reached its peak between A.D. 250 and A.D. 900. Maya farmers planted maize, beans, squash, and other vegetables. These crops helped feed a large population, which may have peaked at 2 million people. These people lived in one of the many large cities the Maya built in the steamy rain forests of present-day Mexico, Guatemala, Honduras, and Belize.

Maya civilization was a **theocracy** (thee•AH•kruh•see), a society ruled by religious leaders. Powerful Maya priests believed the gods were visible in the stars, sun, and moon. Their understanding of astronomy and their advanced mathematics helped them predict eclipses and develop a 365-day calendar. The Maya also developed a system of writing that used **hieroglyphics** (HY•ruh•glih•fihks), symbols or pictures that represent things, ideas, and sounds.

Maya Transport and Trade

The Maya were active traders. Farmers brought maize and vegetables to city markets. They exchanged their goods for items such as cotton cloth, pottery, deer meat, and salt.

Without wheeled vehicles or horses, the Maya carried goods on their backs. Traders traveled on a network of roads that were carved out of the jungle. They also used canoes to ship goods, such as jade statues, turquoise jewelry, and cacao beans used for making chocolate, up and down Mexico's east coast.

Maya Civilization Declines

In time the Maya civilization declined. By about 1200, its once-great cities were nearly deserted. The reason is a mystery. One theory holds that the soil became exhausted and unable to produce enough food for large populations.

Though their civilization declined, the Mayan people did not disappear entirely. Descendants of this great civilization still live in parts of Mexico and Central America today.

This Aztec calendar played an important role in religious as well as daily life. The Maya also had complex calendars.

C

Each Maya city had at least one stone pyramid, some of which reached about 200 feet (61 m)—the height of a 20-story building. The temples on top of the pyramids were religious and governmental centers.

▶ **CRITICAL THINKING**
Drawing Conclusions What can you conclude about Mayan society based on their ability to build such large structures?

R1

R2

civilization highly developed society
theocracy a society that is ruled by religious leaders
hieroglyphic a form of writing that uses symbols or pictures to represent things, ideas, and sounds

Academic Vocabulary (Tier 2 Words)
complex highly detailed

Lesson 2   **9**

(t) Gianni Dagli Orti/CORBIS, (b) Manuel Cohen/Getty Images News/Getty Images

---

C Critical Thinking Skills

Determining Central Ideas Discuss that the Maya were an advanced civilization that created a writing system called hieroglyphics and that they also had an understanding of astronomy and mathematics. **Ask: How did their understanding of astronomy and advanced mathematics lead to some of the Maya's advancements?** *(This helped them predict eclipses and develop a 365-day calendar.)* BL Then, discuss where the Maya were located and when their civilization existed. Discuss with students the different crops the Maya farmed. As students read, have them add more notes to their graphic organizers, noting the features of the Olmec, Maya, Aztec, and Inca civilizations.

R1 Reading Skills

Describing Direct students to read the section titled "Maya Transport and Trade." Then, discuss with students Mayan trade activities, including transportation of their goods. Ask students to explain what farmers brought to market and what they traded for. Have students explain the extent of the Maya's trading network. Have volunteers describe the ways that the Maya would transport their goods. **Ask: What were some items that the Maya would trade?** *(Answers may include maize, vegetables, cotton cloth, pottery, deer meat, salt, jade statues, turquoise jewelry, and cacao beans.)* Students should cite evidence from the text to support their answers. AL

R2 Reading Skills

Explaining After students have read the text, ask them to explain the decline of the Mayan civilization. Be sure to discuss theories about why the civilization declined. **Ask: What became of the Maya?** *(Though the civilization declined, descendants of the Maya still live in parts of Mexico and Central America today.)*

The Maya

Analyzing Visuals Use the interactive image of the Maya to explain that every Mayan city would have had similar tall stone pyramids. Discuss the significance of the temples on top of the pyramids. Then, explain that Mayan society was a theocracy, or a society ruled by religious leaders. AL ELL Ask students to describe the importance of the role of priests in Mayan life. *(Priests were powerful leaders who performed rituals and ceremonies. They had knowledge of astronomy and mathematics.)* AL

See page 1D for other online activities.

Media
McGraw-Hill **netw⊛rks**   The Maya
Manuel Cohen/Getty Images News/Getty Images
More Information
Close

ANSWER, p. 9

CRITICAL THINKING Answers may include that they had developed sophisticated mathematical techniques, engineering skills, construction organization, and labor supply and management. They would also have to have had plenty of food, clothing, and shelter for the workers.

C1 Critical Thinking Skills

Making Connections Discuss with students that the Aztec were a military empire that conquered others and enslaved their enemies. Explain that like Maya culture, the Aztec culture also revolved around religion. **AL** **ELL** **Ask: Why did the Aztec engage in human sacrifice?** (*They believed that it was necessary to please the gods in order to secure an abundant harvest.*)

C2 Critical Thinking Skills

Analyzing Primary Sources Explain to students that the Aztec Empire was still prospering when the Europeans arrived in 1492. Discuss with students that Spanish explorers were very impressed with the beauty and workmanship of the Aztec cities. Have a volunteer read the primary sources from Hernán Cortés and Bernal Díaz del Castillo aloud. Have the class discuss the two descriptions of this empire.

W Writing Skills

Narrative Have students imagine that they are early explorers arriving in the ancient city of Tenochtitlán for the first time. Then, have them write short personal accounts of their experience in a style similar to the primary source accounts of Hernán Cortés in *Five Letters*. Students should include a description of Tenochtitlán, as well as a description of the Aztec people and their culture. Have students include reactions to their experience visiting this great, foreign city for the very first time. Encourage students to conduct some brief research about the capital city of Tenochtitlán in order to add strong detail and description to their stories. **Verbal/Linguistic**

BIOGRAPHY

Malinche (c. 1501–1550)

Much of what we know about individual Native Americans comes from Europeans. Malinche is one example. In 1519 she was enslaved and living under harsh Aztec rule. When the Spanish arrived in 1519, she gave them information about Aztec culture. She also learned Spanish quickly and served as a translator for the Spanish, who called her Doña Marina. Malinche helped build ties between the Spanish and the many unhappy Aztec subjects in the region.

▶ **CRITICAL THINKING**
Making Inferences Why might Malinche have been willing to help the Spanish?

C1

W **C2**

Reading HELPDESK (CCSS)

Academic vocabulary (Tier 2 Words)
link to connect

The Aztec Empire

In 1325, centuries after the fall of the Maya, a group of hunters called the Aztec (AZ•tehk) were wandering through central Mexico. They were searching for a permanent home for their people. One day, they came upon an island in Lake Texcoco (tehs•KOH•koh). There they saw what they thought was a sign from their god: an eagle with a snake in its beak sitting on a cactus. According to Aztec legend, this sign indicated that the island was to be their home. It was on this site that the Aztec would build their capital city, Tenochtitlán (tay•NAWCH•teet•LAHN). Today it is the site of Mexico City.

At its height, Tenochtitlán was the largest city in the Americas—and one of the largest in the world. The city was a center of trade, attracting thousands of merchants to its outdoor marketplaces.

Tenochtitlán's construction was a marvel of building skill, knowledge, and human labor. Workers toiled day and night under the direction of priests and nobles. They dug soil from the bottom of the lake to make causeways, or bridges of earth. These causeways **linked** the island and the shore. Elsewhere, they used earth to fill in parts of the lake, creating fields for growing crops.

Aztec Culture

The Aztec created a military empire. In the 1400s, the Aztec army conquered many neighboring communities. Conquered people had to pay tribute in food and other goods. Some were also forced to work as slaves in Aztec cities and villages.

Like Mayan culture, Aztec culture revolved around its religious beliefs. The Aztec believed they must perform human sacrifices to please the gods and ensure abundant harvests. They sacrificed prisoners of war by the thousands for this purpose.

A Great City Remembered

The Aztec Empire was still going strong when Europeans arrived in the Americas in 1492. The first Europeans to see Tenochtitlán were awed by its splendor. In 1519 Hernán Cortés led 550 Spanish soldiers into the Aztec capital. Cortés wrote:

PRIMARY SOURCE

❝ There are forty towers at the least, all of stout construction and very lofty.... The workmanship both in wood and stone could not be bettered anywhere. ❞

—from *Five Letters*

Northwind Picture Archives

---

netw⊚rks *Online Teaching Options*

BIOGRAPHY

Malinche

Summarizing Have student groups use the interactive image of Malinche to discuss the relationship between the Aztec and the Spanish. Have students describe Malinche. (*a woman held as a slave by a native group under Aztec rule*) Then have them tell why she was important to the Spanish explorers. (*She provided key information about Aztec culture and served as translator for the Spanish and the Aztecs.*)

See page 1D for other online activities.

ANSWER, p. 10

CRITICAL THINKING Answers may include that she did not like the Aztec.

Civilizations of Mexico and Central America

MEXICO

Gulf of Mexico

Chichén
Itzá

*Lake
Texcoco* Tenochtitlán

YUCATÁN
PENINSULA

Palenque

Tikal

PACIFIC OCEAN

	Olmec, c. 900 B.C.
	Maya, c. A.D. 750
	Aztec, c. A.D. 1500

0   250 miles
0   250 km
Lambert Azimuthal Equal-Area projection

GEOGRAPHY CONNECTION

The civilizations that developed in modern-day Mexico and Central America rivaled those that grew in other parts of the world.

1 PLACE Which of the empires shown covered the largest area?

2 CRITICAL THINKING
Drawing Conclusions
Given what you have read about the Aztec, what do you think is the explanation for the small areas within the Aztec Empire that were not under Aztec control?

Bernal Díaz del Castillo, one of the soldiers, marveled at the "great towers and cues [temples] and buildings rising from the water." Some of the Spanish soldiers thought Tenochtitlán was more magnificent than Rome and the other great European capitals of the time.

✓ **PROGRESS CHECK**

Identifying What was the capital city of the Aztec Empire, and where was it located?

The Great Inca Civilization

GUIDING QUESTION *Why were the Inca considered a highly developed culture?*

In the western highlands of South America, the largest of all early American civilizations grew—the Inca. The Inca people founded their capital city of Cuzco (KOOS•koh) around 1200.

In 1438 the emperor Pachacuti (PAH•chah•KOO•tee) came to the throne. He and his son, Topa Inca, expanded the empire by conquering others with their powerful army. At its peak, the Inca Empire stretched for more than 3,000 miles (4,828 km), from present-day Colombia to northern Argentina and Chile.

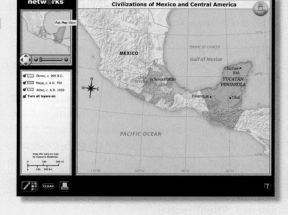

This double-headed serpent is an Aztec wood carving covered in turquoise tiles. It may have been worn as a chest decoration during important occasions.

The British Museum/Heritage-Images/The Image Works

Lesson 2   **11**

Integrating Visual Information Remind students that the Maya created vast networks of roads within their empire. Ask students to study the portion of the map that shows the Maya Empire. Have students explain how a road network may have contributed to the size and shape of this civilization. **BL** Visual/Spatial

C Critical Thinking Skills

Sequencing Have students create time lines showing the dates of existence for the civilizations of Mexico, Central America, and South America that they have learned about so far. *(Time lines should include the following dates and civilizations: 1200 B.C.–300 B.C.—Olmec; A.D. 250–900—Maya; A.D 1325–approximately 1521—Aztec) You may wish to tell students that the Aztec Empire ended when the Spanish captured Tenochtitlán.* **Logical/Mathematical**

R Reading Skills

Identifying Before students read the text, explain that they will be learning about another great civilization: the Inca. Ask students to read the text in order to identify key people and places related to the Inca empire. **Ask:**

- **What was the capital city of the Inca Empire?** *(Cuzco)*
- **When was this city founded?** *(around 1200)*
- **Which emperor expanded the empire by conquering others?** *(Pachacuti)*
- **At its peak, how far did the empire stretch?** *(more than 3,000 miles, from present-day Colombia to northern Argentina and Chile)* **AL**

MAP

Civilizations of Mexico and Central America

Analyzing Maps Use the interactive map of the civilizations to discuss the location of these three civilizations. **Ask: What can you tell about the three civilizations discussed?** *(They were relatively close to one another.)* **AL** Focus on the location of Aztec civilization. Discuss Tenochtitlán, including its size, location, and role as a trade center. **BL Ask: Why is Tenochtitlán's construction impressive?** *(In the middle of a lake, its building required extensive work and innovation.)*

See page 1D for other online activities.

ANSWERS, p. 11

GEOGRAPHY CONNECTION

1 The Maya Empire covered the largest area.

2 CRITICAL THINKING Answers may include that these areas might have been uninhabited or that they were communities that had been conquered by the Aztecs but were allowed to remain free as long as they paid tribute to the Aztecs.

✓ **PROGRESS CHECK** The city was Tenochtitlán, which was located on an island in Lake Texcoco, in central Mexico.

R1 Reading Skills

Explaining Have students read the first paragraph of the text titled "Fearsome Warriors." Then ask students to explain what part war and conquest played in Inca civilization. Discuss the different weapons used by the Inca. **Ask: Who was eligible for the Inca draft?** *(all men between the ages of 25 and 50)*
AL

C Critical Thinking Skills

Making Inferences Ask students to consider what it would be like for a culture to be taken over by a conquering civilization and how that would likely be a difficult event to accept. **Ask: Why do you think some neighboring groups accepted Inca rule without a fight?** *(Answers may vary but should reflect an understanding that the Inca were an intimidating fighting force that others did not want to engage in battle.)* **BL**
Ask: What incentive was there for areas near the Inca state to accept Inca rule? *(The Inca allowed those areas that accepted Inca rule without resistance to participate in governing the Inca Empire.)* **What was in store for areas that resisted or rebelled?** *(harsh treatment by Incas)*

R2 Reading Skills

Describing Direct students to read the section titled "Inca Culture." Have volunteers describe the different aspects of Inca culture and life. Students should mention that the Inca viewed their emperor as a descendant of the sun god. Students should also note the different aspects of Inca art and religion.

Then ask students to describe how the Inca were able to farm in their mountainous region. **Ask: How did the Inca farm in the Andes Mountains?** *(They cut broad platforms called terraces into the mountain slopes to create farmland.)* **What types of crops did the Inca farm?** *(maize, squash, tomatoes, peanuts, chili peppers, cotton, and potatoes)* **AL** **ELL**

GEOGRAPHY CONNECTION

The Inca Empire was divided into four provinces along the western coast of South America. Modern-day countries are bordered and labeled in black.

1 LOCATION In which modern-day countries did the Inca Empire have territory?

2 CRITICAL THINKING *Analyzing* How do you think the Andes Mountains shaped and affected the Inca Empire?

The Inca Empire 1532

Fearsome Warriors

R1 The Inca state was built around war. All men between 25 and 50 years old could be drafted to serve in the army for up to five years. Their weapons included clubs, spears, and spiked copper balls on ropes. Using slings, Inca soldiers could throw stones 30 yards (27 m).

C Rather than fight this fearsome force, many neighboring areas accepted Inca rule. The Inca allowed those who cooperated to take part in the empire's government. Those who resisted or rebelled faced harsh treatment.

Inca Culture

R2 The Inca people believed their emperor was a descendant of the sun god. The Inca made magnificent gold jewelry and temple ornaments as gifts to the sun god. Inca workers also built great cities devoted to religious ceremonies, including Machu Picchu (MAH·choo PEE·choo), a site hidden high in the Andes Mountains.

Reading **HELP**DESK **CCSS**

terrace a broad platform of flat land cut into a slope

12 *The First Americans*

---

netw⊛rks *Online Teaching Options*

MAP

The Inca Empire, 1532

Locating Have students explore the interactive map of the Inca Empire. Explain that the Inca lived in the western highlands of present-day Peru and that the empire covered areas from what is now Colombia to Argentina and Chile. Discuss the four different provinces of the Inca Empire. **Ask: How did the size of the Inca Empire compare to the size of the other three major early American civilizations?** *(It was the largest of the four civilizations.)* **AL ELL How large was the Inca Empire at its peak?** *(It stretched more than 3,000 miles [4,828 km] from north to south along the western coast of what is now South America.)* **Visual/Spatial**

See page 1D for other online activities.

ANSWERS, p. 12

GEOGRAPHY CONNECTION

1 Colombia, Ecuador, Peru, Bolivia, Chile, and Argentina

2 CRITICAL THINKING Answers may include that mountains may have provided protection from other people and made it difficult for the empire to expand farther east.

Supporting the large Inca population required a lot of food. In order to farm their mountainous lands, the Inca cut **terraces,** or broad platforms, into steep slopes. Stone walls on the terraces held the soil and plants in place. Inca farmers grew maize, squash, tomatoes, peanuts, chili peppers, cotton, and potatoes.

Managing and ruling over such a large territory was a great challenge. The Inca built at least 10,000 miles (16,093 km) of stone-paved roads to link distant parts of their empire. The roads crisscrossed mountains, deserts, and dense forests. To cross deep canyons or river valleys, the Inca built rope bridges. Runners carried messages to and from the emperor and linked outposts of the empire to Cuzco. The Inca language, Quechua (KEH•chuh•wuh), became the official language for the entire empire. The Inca had no written language, but they did develop a system of recordkeeping using string called quipus (KEE•poos). By knotting different colors of string in special patterns, quipus helped the Inca record and keep track of information about resources, such as grain supplies.

Like the Aztec, the Inca were thriving in the early 1500s. They, too, would soon come face to face with Spanish soldiers and experience a dramatic change in fortunes.

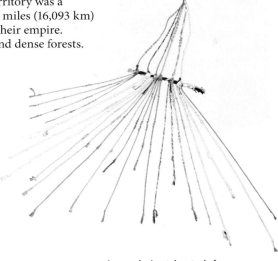

Incas used quipus to keep track of resources, such as food supplies. Different colors and lengths of string and different types of knots made up the system for recording important information.

✔ **PROGRESS CHECK**

Explaining How did the Inca Empire grow so large?

LESSON 2 REVIEW (CCSS)

Review Vocabulary (Tier 3 Words)

1. Use the following terms in a paragraph about the Maya. RH.6–8.4, WHST.6–8.4

   a. civilization
   b. theocracy
   c. hieroglyphic

Answer the Guiding Questions

2. ***Sequencing*** In what chronological order did the great civilizations of Mexico, Central America, and South America appear? RH.6–8.5

3. ***Describing*** What key features did the great civilizations of Mexico, Central America, and South America have in common? RH.6–8.1

4. ***Contrasting*** In what ways were the great civilizations of Mexico, Central America, and South America different? RH.6–8.5

5. **INFORMATIVE/EXPLANATORY** Consider each of the four civilizations detailed in the lesson. Write a short essay discussing what life might have been like in one of these societies. Use facts from the chapter to add details to your writing. WHST.6–8.1, WHST.6–8.9

Lesson 2 **13**

LESSON 2 REVIEW ANSWERS

1. The Maya were one of the great civilizations that emerged in Central and South America. The Maya empire was a theocracy, and among its great achievements was a system of writing that used hieroglyphics.

2. Olmec, Maya, Aztec, Inca

3. The Olmec, Maya, Aztec, and Inca civilizations all covered a wide area and had large populations. They produced great works of art, built spectacular structures, and demonstrated advanced knowledge in many areas.

4. They were all located in different areas. They did not share the same religion. They did not all have writing or systems for keeping records.

5. Essays will vary, but students should draw on information they learned in this lesson.

R Reading Skills

Citing Text Evidence Have students refer to the paragraph. **Ask:** How did the Inca keep their large empire connected? *(They built thousands of miles of roads, as well as rope bridges throughout the empire. Runners carried messages over these roadways.)* **AL**

Discuss with students some of the Inca communication methods, including the development of their own language. **Ask:** What was the official language of the Inca Empire? *(Quechua)* What is one notable feature of Quechua? *(It was a spoken language only—the Inca had no written language.)*

Have students complete the Lesson 2 Review.

CLOSE & REFLECT

Comparing and Contrasting Summarize the reasons that these four cultures were considered advanced: population size, length of time the civilizations lasted, architecture, art, and technological advances. **AL** **ELL** **Ask:** What were some accomplishments of these societies? *(Answers will vary but may include building large structures in challenging geographical areas; devising complex ways of tracking time, counting, and writing; and crafting beautiful works of art.)*

To close the lesson, have students think about the early civilizations in the Americas and how they were similar and how they were different. Make a compare-and-contrast chart on the board and have students give similarities and differences.

ANSWER, p. 13

✔ **PROGRESS CHECK** The Inca civilization was built around war; the Inca had a strong army that conquered other people and expanded the lands and people under their control.

ENGAGE

🔔 **Bellringer** Tell the class that great early American cultures were not limited to Central and South America. North America had its own distinct cultures that developed in the centuries leading up to the arrival of the Europeans. Explain that many artifacts of these peoples can be found in museums. Many dwellings and structures that students will learn about remain standing today and are protected sites at national parks such as Mesa Verde National Park and Chaco Culture National Historical Park. Explain that in this lesson, students will learn why early groups in different areas of North America developed unique cultures.

TEACH & ASSESS

R Reading Skills

Explaining Explain that the Mound Builders were not a single group, but many groups. Explain that the mounds were built in different forms and had different purposes. **Ask: What were two purposes for mounds?** *(burial chambers and as bases for temples)* **What are the three different Mound Builder cultures?** *(the Adena, Hopewell, and Mississippian)* **AL** Direct students to take notes on the key features of these three cultures as they read the lesson.

T Technology Skills

Researching on the Internet Direct students to search the Internet for photographs of the earthworks created by the Mound Builders. Then, have students research images of the pyramids of the Maya and the Aztec. Ask students to describe how the structures are similar and how they are different.

ANSWER, p. 14

TAKING NOTES: Adena: hunters and gatherers, lived in Ohio River valley from 800 B.C. to A.D. 100, built mounds; **Hopewell:** farmers and traders, 200 B.C. to A.D. 500, built mounds; **Mississippians:** present-day Illinois, A.D. 900, farmers and builders; **Hohokam:** A.D. 200 to 1400, present-day Arizona, farmers, dug channels for water; **Ancient Puebloans:** Four Corners, A.D. 1 to 1300, built pueblos and cliff dwellings, farmers

---

networks
There's More Online!

☑ **BIOGRAPHY**
Dekanawidah

☑ **GRAPHIC ORGANIZER**
Describing Ancient Native Americans

☑ **GAME**

☑ **MAP** Significant Adena, Hopewell, and Mississippian Sites

☑ **VIDEO**

Lesson 3
North American Peoples

ESSENTIAL QUESTION *What makes a culture unique?*

IT MATTERS BECAUSE
Early Native American groups of North America adapted to their environments.

Early North American Cultures

GUIDING QUESTION *What did the Adena, Hopewell, Mississippian, Hohokam, and Ancient Puebloan cultures have in common?*

As in Mexico, Central America, and South America, advanced cultures developed in parts of North America that are now the United States long before Europeans arrived in the 1500s. Among these cultures were the Adena, Hopewell, and Mississippians in the central and eastern regions of the present-day United States. The Hohokam and the Ancient Puebloans emerged in the southwestern region.

The Adena, Hopewell, and Mississippian Cultures

In central and eastern North America, prehistoric Native Americans built thousands of earthen mounds, or earthworks. The earthworks were not created by a single group but by many different peoples. Scientists have sometimes referred to these different peoples together as the Mound Builders.

The ancient earthworks take many different forms. One famous example is in the shape of a serpent. Some resemble the pyramids of the Maya and the Aztec. Some contained burial chambers, and others were topped with temples. This seems to indicate that cultures of Mexico and Central America, such as the Maya and Aztec, may have influenced some of these cultures.

(l) Doug Pensinger/Getty Images Sport/Getty Images, (c) SSPL/Getty Images, (c) Chris Cheadle/All Canada Photos/Corbis, (cr) Peabody Essex Museum, Salem, MA/Bridgeman Art Library, (r) Stock Montage/Alamy Images

---

Reading HELPDESK **CCSS**

Taking Notes: *Describing*
As you read, use a chart like this one to make notes about each of the ancient cultures given. RH.6–8.2, RH.6–8.7

Adena, Hopewell, and Mississippians	Hohokam	Ancient Puebloans

Content Vocabulary (Tier 3 Words)
• **irrigate**
• **federation**
• **clan**

14 *The First Americans*

---

networks   *Online Teaching Options*

VIDEO

The Great Plains Native Americans

Discussing Play the video about the Great Plains Native Americans. Explain how the video provides insight into the Crow, Sioux, Cheyenne, Comanche, and Blackfoot tribes. The video also looks at how these peoples hunted buffalo for their meat and hides. After students have watched the video, **ask: How did tepees suit the Native Americans' nomadic lifestyle?** *(The tepees were easy to carry and could be built and broken down quickly.)* **How did the Native Americans use the buffalo to meet their basic needs?** *(They ate the buffalo and used all parts of it to make clothes, weapons, tools, and shelters.)* Then, have partners identify the Great Plains on a map of North America.

See page 1E for other online activities.

Archaeologists have classified these earthwork-building cultures into three groups: the Adena, Hopewell, and Mississippian cultures. Modern-day scientists named the groups. No one knows what these early peoples called themselves.

The Adena were hunters and gatherers who lived in the Ohio River valley from about 800 B.C. to A.D. 100. The Hopewell people came later, between 200 B.C. and A.D. 500. The Hopewell were farmers and traders who built huge burial earthworks in the shapes of birds, bears, and snakes. Within these earthworks, archaeologists have discovered freshwater pearls, shells, cloth, and copper. These finds indicate that the Hopewell trade networks extended for hundreds of miles.

Cahokia

Sometime after A.D. 900, a people now called the Mississippians built the largest known earthworks complex in present-day Illinois. Later named Cahokia (kuh•HOH•kee•uh), the complex might have had 20,000 or more residents. Surrounded by farms and settlements, Cahokia became the center of Mississippian culture.

Cahokia appears to have resembled the ancient cities of Mexico. A great pyramid-shaped earthwork dominated Cahokia. Known as Monks Mound, it rose nearly 100 feet (30 m).

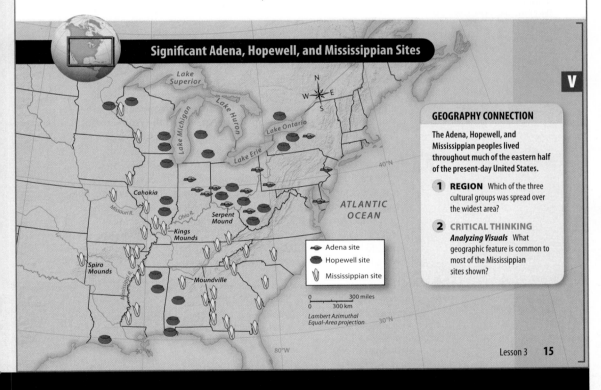

Significant Adena, Hopewell, and Mississippian Sites

GEOGRAPHY CONNECTION

The Adena, Hopewell, and Mississippian peoples lived throughout much of the eastern half of the present-day United States.

1 **REGION** Which of the three cultural groups was spread over the widest area?

2 **CRITICAL THINKING** *Analyzing Visuals* What geographic feature is common to most of the Mississippian sites shown?

Legend:
- Adena site
- Hopewell site
- Mississippian site

0   300 miles
0   300 km
Lambert Azimuthal
Equal-Area projection

Lesson 3   15

G1 Critical Thinking Skills

Drawing Conclusions Discuss with students that there are no written records from any of the Mound Builder cultures and that very few oral traditions have been passed on. **Ask: How do we know that at least one group, the Hopewell people, had extensive trade networks with distant cultures?** *(There is archaeological evidence in the Hopewell mounds that gives us that information.)* **Why do items found inside Hopewell burial mounds indicate widespread trade?** *(Some items, such as freshwater pearls and shells, were not native to the region and had to have come from a location hundreds of miles away.)*

G2 Critical Thinking Skills

Comparing Discuss with students the Mississippian site of Cahokia. Point out important features, such as the population and Monks Mound. Note that Cahokia was reminiscent of great cities in Mexico. **Ask: What clues suggest similarities between the Cahokia site and the great cultures of Mexico?** *(the similarities in design of the pyramid-shaped temples, as well as a possible reference to Mexico in the legends of the native peoples of that region)* **BL** Then, ask students to name the great cultures of Mexico that may have influenced the cultures in the central and eastern parts of the United States. *(Maya and Aztec)*

V Visual Skills

Analyze Maps Review with students the important parts of the map such as the title, legend, and scale. Have students identify each symbol used in the legend and its significance in early North American cultures *(maize or corn—food and farming, clay pottery—artwork and tools, arrowheads—tools for hunting)* **Ask:**

- **What is the northernmost earthwork listed on the map** *(Cahokia)*
- **Which mound-building culture settled around the Great Lakes?** *(Hopewell)*

Ask: Why are the map symbols important? *(to help the reader distinguish the different earthwork sites and give some additional information about early North American cultures)* **Visual/Spatial**

Significant Adena, Hopewell, and Mississippian Sites

Reading a Map Launch the interactive map about the Adena, Hopewell, and Mississippian sites from the textbook to discuss these three important early North American cultures. **Ask: According to the map, where are these three groups located?** *(They are located as far north as Michigan and Canada, and as far south as Florida. They also go as far west as the Mississippi River and as far east as North Carolina.)*

See page 1E for other online activities.

ANSWERS, p. 15

GEOGRAPHY CONNECTION

1 The Hopewell were the most widely distributed.

2 **CRITICAL THINKING** The Mississippian sites are found mostly along major rivers.

C Critical Thinking Skills

Analyzing Discuss with students the history of the Hohokam people, and remind students that the Hohokam lived in a much different environment from that of the Mound Builder groups. Explain that the Hohokam lived in present-day Arizona, in a hot, dry desert region with few sources of water. **Ask: How did the Hohokam adapt to their desert location?** *(by digging hundreds of miles of irrigation channels to water their crops)*

R Reading Skills

Identifying Direct students to read the text titled "The Ancient Puebloans." Then, ask students to discuss the history and location of the Ancient Puebloan people. **Ask: Where did the Ancient Puebloans live?** *(at the Four Corners — the intersection of present-day Utah, Colorado, Arizona, and New Mexico)* Then, discuss with students the ancient settlement of Pueblo Bonito. Have a volunteer describe the Pueblo Bonito based on the information from the textbook. **Ask: Why is Pueblo Bonito believed to be important to the Ancient Puebloans?** *(Archaeologists suggest that it may have been a key center for trade or religion.)*

V Visual Skills

Direct students to the image of the pueblo at the bottom of the page. Explain to students that this image represents the type of structure Ancient Puebloans created. Note with students that each of the cultures discussed so far—the Mound Builders, the Hohokam, and the Ancient Puebloans—created distinct structures that were well suited to their specific environments. Make three categories on the board and label them with each of these cultures. Then, ask students to describe the structures of each group and how they related to the environment in which each group lived. *(Answers will vary.)* **AL** **ELL**
Visual/Spatial

Ancient cliff dwellings are preserved at Mesa Verde National Park in Colorado. The largest cliff dwelling is Cliff Palace, which could shelter up to 250 people.

A temple crowned the summit of Monks Mound. A legend of the Natchez people, descendants of the Mississippians, hints of a direct link to Mexico:

PRIMARY SOURCE

66 Before we came into this land, we lived yonder, under the sun. [the speaker pointed toward Mexico] . . . Our entire nation extended along the great water [the Gulf of Mexico] where this great river (the River St. Louis) loses itself. 99

—Natchez legend

The Hohokam

From about A.D. 200 to A.D. 1400, the Hohokam (hoh•hoh•KAHM) culture flourished in the dry, hot desert of present-day Arizona. As with the Adena, Hopewell, and Mississippian cultures, the name *Hohokam* was given to this culture in modern times.

As desert dwellers, the Hohokam were experts at maximizing their few sources of water. They **irrigated** (IHR•uh•gayt•uhd), or brought water to, their corn, cotton, and other crops by digging hundreds of miles of **channels.** The Hohokam also produced pottery, carved stone, and etched shells with acid. The shells serve as evidence of trade with coastal peoples.

The Ancient Puebloans

The Four Corners is the place where the modern-day states of Utah, Colorado, Arizona, and New Mexico meet. It was in this region that the Ancient Puebloans (PWEH•bloh•uhnz) lived at about the same time as the Hohokam—from about A.D. 1 to A.D. 1300. In the past, these people were called the Anasazi, but descendants of the Ancient Puebloans dislike that name.

The Ancient Puebloans built great stone dwellings that Spanish explorers later called **pueblos** (PWEH•blohs), or villages. Visitors to New Mexico today can still see one of the most spectacular of these ancient settlements, Pueblo Bonito. The huge **structure** was at least four stories high and had hundreds of rooms. Around Pueblo Bonito, archaeologists have found traces of a complex network of roads. These roads linked the pueblo with other villages. They suggest that Pueblo Bonito may have been a center for trade or religion.

(t) Doug Pensinger/Getty Images Sport/Getty Images, (b) Tom Bean/CORBIS

Reading **HELP**DESK **CCSS**

irrigate to supply water to crops by artificial means

Academic Vocabulary (Tier 2)
channel a long, narrow gutter or groove through which water can flow
structure a building

Visual Vocabulary
pueblo a communal Native American structure with a flat roof; a type of Native American village

16 *The First Americans*

---

netw⊙rks *Online Teaching Options*

IMAGE

Taos Pueblo and Mesa Verde

Images Explain that the Ancient Puebloans made two significant types of structures that still exist today: pueblos and cliff dwellings. **AL** **ELL** Describe the structures that Spanish explorers called *pueblos*. Use the interactive image of Taos Pueblo to discuss these structures with many stories and numerous rooms. **Ask: Why were floors set back from the one below?** *(so that the roof could also function as a terrace)* Then, use the interactive image of the cliff dwellings of Mesa Verde to discuss this type of dwelling. **Ask: What were some advantages to building shelters in cliff walls?** *(They were easy to defend and offered protection from the winter weather.)* **Why were the Ancient Puebloans forced to abandon their pueblos and cliff dwellings?** *(The Great Drought of 1276–1299 drove most inhabitants away.)*

See page 1E for other online activities.

The Ancient Puebloans also built dwellings in the walls of steep cliffs. Cliff dwellings were easy to defend and offered protection from winter weather. One of the largest cliff dwellings is Mesa Verde (MAY•suh VUHR•dee) in Colorado. This ancient, complex structure was home to several thousand people.

The Ancient Puebloans began leaving their pueblos and cliff dwellings for smaller communities in about 1300. They might have abandoned their large villages when drought, a long period of little rainfall, destroyed their crops.

☑ **PROGRESS CHECK**

Describing Name two types of dwellings for which the Ancient Puebloans are known.

The Native Americans Circa 1492

GUIDING QUESTION *How did early Native Americans adapt to their environment?*

While the Hohokam, Ancient Puebolan, and the Adena, Hopewell, and Mississippian civilizations eventually faded away, other Native American cultures arose to take their place. In the time before European arrival in the late 1400s, many unique societies flourished throughout North America. Within different regions, different groups shared common features. These features reflected the conditions within each region.

 W

Northern Peoples

A people called the Inuit (IH•noo•wuht) settled the frigid lands at the northernmost part of North America, near the Arctic Ocean. Some scientists believe the Inuit were the last migrants to come from Asia to North America.

 T

The Inuit people of the far North developed tools and techniques for living in a frozen and watery land.

The Inuit may have originally come from the Asian region of Siberia, bringing with them the skills needed to survive the cold climate. In the winter, the Inuit built igloos, low-lying structures of snow blocks, which protected them from severe weather.

The Inuit were skilled hunters and fishers. In the coastal waters, they hunted whales, seals, and walruses in small, skin-covered boats called kayaks. On land they hunted caribou, large deerlike animals that lived in the far North. The Inuit made warm, waterproof clothing from caribou skins and seal skins. They burned seal oil in lamps.

C

SSPL via Getty Images

Build Vocabulary: *Word Origins*

The words *igloo* and *kayak* are two examples of the many English-language words that come from Native American languages. Other examples include the words *tomahawk, moose,* and *moccasin.*

W **Writing Skills**

Informative/Explanatory In a think-pair-share activity, have students create a list of some of the different regions in the United States today. List their responses on the board and discuss. *(Answers might include the South, the East Coast, the Midwest, the Southwest, or the West Coast.)* Then, have students write several sentences describing some of the geographic differences between each region. *(Answers will vary, but students may describe differences in climate, food, and natural resources.)* **AL** **ELL** Have volunteers share their responses with the rest of the class. **Verbal/Linguistic**

T **Technology Skills**

Researching on the Internet Explain that numerous cultures were flourishing in North America around 1492. Northern peoples, such as the Inuit, were located at the very northern part of the continent. Ask students to use the Internet to locate a map of North America. Have students print out the map and identify the location of the Inuit peoples. Students should highlight the northernmost regions of present-day Alaska and Canada. **AL** **ELL** **Ask: Which ocean did the Inuit live near?** *(the Arctic Ocean)* **Visual/Spatial**

C **Critical Thinking Skills**

Speculating Remind students that scientists and students alike can make speculations and draw probable conclusions based on evidence. **Ask: Where do scientists think the Inuit came from?** *(They think that the Inuit arrived from Siberia.)* **How do you think this affected the Inuit's ability to survive in the frigid temperatures?** *(It probably helped because they brought cold-weather survival skills with them from Siberia, which has a very cold climate.)* **BL**

IMAGE

Igloos

Analyzing Images Show the interactive image of the igloo to discuss the structure that the Inuit used to live in. **Ask: What were these structures made of?** *(snow blocks)* **AL** **ELL** **Why do you think the Inuit built houses of snow?** *(The material was readily available.)* **How are the tepee and igloo structurally similar?** *(Both structures are circular in shape and have a small hole at the top to let air in and out).* **AL**

See page 1E for other online activities.

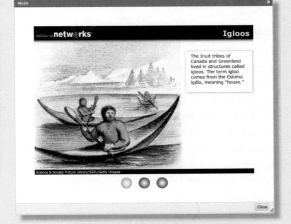

ANSWER, p. 17

☑ **PROGRESS CHECK** The Ancient Puebloans built pueblos and cliff dwellings.

T **Technology Skills**

Researching on the Internet Ask students to use the Internet to locate a map of the western coast of North America. Begin a discussion with students about the groups who lived there. Explain that this area encompassed many different cultural groups. **Ask:** Who were some of the western peoples in the Pacific Northwest? *(the Tlingit, the Haida, and the Chinook)* Who were some of the western peoples from the plateau region? *(the Nez Perce and Yakima)* Who were some of the western peoples from the Great Basin region? *(the Ute and the Shoshone)* Ask students to locate on the map the approximate areas in which these peoples would have lived. **Visual/Spatial**

Content Background Knowledge

Totem Poles Totem poles have been built throughout the Pacific Northwest since ancient times. These symbolic pillars serve many purposes. Some poles show the ancestry of a particular family or the history of a clan. Some totem poles are built to commemorate a person. A totem pole might also illustrate folklore, legends, or the historical experiences and incidents of a certain cultural group. The elaborate pillars often contain images of native animals, such as bears, ravens, and eagles, as well as human figures.

Totem poles are carved wooden pillars made by Native American groups of the Pacific Northwest. Totem poles typically include symbols that represent the history and experience of a family or clan.

Western Peoples

The western coast of North America has a mostly mild climate and dependable food sources. Such favorable conditions helped many native groups in this region thrive.

The Tlingit (TLIHNG•kuht), Haida (HY•duh), and Chinook (shuh•NUK) lived on the northwestern coast of North America in what are now Canada, southern Alaska, Washington, and Oregon. The cultures of this region depended on the forest and the sea for food and materials needed for living. Forests provided wood for houses and canoes as well as tree bark for making baskets and clothing. The rivers and coastal waters were filled with salmon, a main food source. Native Americans preserved salmon by smoking it over fires.

The area between the Cascade Mountains and the Rocky Mountains is known as the plateau region. There, the Nez Perce (NEHZ PUHRS) and Yakima (YAH•keh•muh) peoples also depended on the land, fishing the rivers, hunting deer in forests, and gathering roots and berries. The Native Americans of the plateau region lived in earthen houses.

Present-day California was home to a great variety of cultures. Along the northern coast, Native Americans fished for their food. In the central valley of California, the Pomo (poh•moh) gathered acorns and pounded them into flour. In the more barren southern deserts, nomadic groups collected roots and seeds.

Between the Sierra Nevada and the Rocky Mountains lies the Great Basin region. There, the soil was too hard and rocky for farming. This meant that peoples such as the Ute (YOOT) and Shoshone (shuh•SHOHN) had to travel in search of food. They hunted and gathered small game, pine nuts, juniper berries, roots, and some insects. They crafted temporary shelters from branches and reeds.

Southwestern Peoples

In the Southwest region, descendants of the Ancient Puebloans formed the Hopi (HOH•pee), the Acoma (uh•KOH•muh), the Zuni (ZOO•nee), and other peoples. Farming was central to their cultures, with maize serving as their basic food source.

Chris Cheadle/All Canada Photos/Corbis

Reading **HELP**DESK **CCSS**

Reading Strategy: *Categorizing*
When you categorize information, you organize it into clearly identified categories. As you read the section on Native American Groups Circa 1492, identify the categories of groups presented, such as Northern, Western, or Southwestern peoples. Use these headings to organize notes you take as you read the material.

18 *The First Americans*

---

netw✺rks *Online Teaching Options*

IMAGE

Totem Poles

Interpreting Display the interactive image of the totem pole. Have students describe its characteristics, including its design, size, and color, as well as other images of totem poles they may have seen before. **Ask:** What do the images on some totem poles you have seen symbolize? *(Answers will vary.)* Explain that the word totem means an emblem of a family or clan, or a revered symbol. Then, have students suggest some personal totems that they would choose to represent themselves, their family, or their ancestry. Discuss students' ideas as a class.

See page 1E for other online activities.

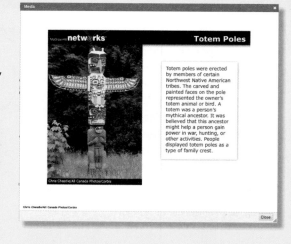

Media

netw✺rks **Totem Poles**

Totem poles were erected by members of certain Northwest Native American tribes. The carved and painted faces on the pole represented the owner's totem animal or bird. A totem was a person's mythical ancestor. It was believed that this ancestor might help a person gain power in war, hunting, or other activities. People displayed totem poles as a type of family crest.

Chris Cheadle/All Canada Photos/Corbis

Chris Cheadle/All Canada Photos/Corbis

Close

They built their homes from dried mud bricks called adobe (uh‧DOH‧bee). They also used irrigation to grow beans, squash, melons, pumpkins, and fruit. Their trade network spread throughout the Southwest and into Mexico.

The Apache (uh‧PAH‧chee) and the Navajo (NAH‧vuh‧hoh) settled in the Southwest region about 1,000 years ago. These new groups were primarily hunters and gatherers. In time, the Navajo settled in villages and built square houses called hogans. They also began to grow maize and beans, and they raised sheep as well.

Plains Peoples

The peoples of the Great Plains were nomadic. Their villages were temporary, lasting only for a growing season or two. The women planted maize, squash, and beans. The men hunted antelope, deer, and buffalo. When the people moved from place to place, they dragged their homes—cone-shaped skin tents called tepees—behind them.

Buffalo were central to the lives of the people of the Plains. Native Americans used buffalo to supply many basic needs. Buffalo meat was a good source of food, and people used the bones to make tools and weapons. Buffalo skins provided shelter and clothing.

Today many people associate Native Americans of the Plains with the use of horses. These animals would transform Plains life—but not until the 1600s, after their arrival from Europe.

Eastern Peoples

Complex societies existed in the woodlands of eastern North America. A similar language connected the many Algonquian (al‧GAHN‧kwee‧uhn) groups. The Cherokee (CHEHR‧uh‧kee) and Iroquois (IHR‧uh‧kwoy) had formal law codes, and formed **federations** (feh‧duh‧RAY‧shuhnz), agreements among different groups to join together.

federation a government that links and unites different groups

For centuries, Native American groups of the Great Plains hunted buffalo. Native Americans often painted buffalo skins and made them into robes.

Peabody Essex Museum, Salem, MA/Bridgeman Art Library

Lesson 3 **19**

R1 Reading Skills

Describing As students read the section titled "Southwestern Peoples," ask them to take notes on the various groups. Then ask students to describe the history of the Southwestern peoples. Explain that the Hopi, Acoma, and Zuni were descendants of the Ancient Puebloans, whom students learned about earlier in the lesson. **Ask: What material did Southwestern peoples use to build their homes?** *(adobe, which was dried mud bricks)* AL

R2 Reading Skills

Discussing Have a student volunteer read the section titled "Plains Peoples." Discuss with students the history of the Plains peoples. **Ask: Why did the Plains peoples use tepees as shelter?** *(Their design made them portable, ideal for nomadic cultures.)* Then, review with students the importance of buffalo to Plains cultures. **Ask: What were the three uses the Plains people had for buffalo?** *(food, use of skins for clothing and shelter, use of bones for weapons)* Remind students to cite evidence from the text to support their answers.

C Critical Thinking Skills

Comparing Explain to students that a similar language connected the different Algonquian groups. Explain that there were agreements among different groups called federations in place among the Eastern peoples, specifically the Cherokee and the Iroquois. **Ask: What aspects of early Cherokee and Iroquois culture are similar to our culture today?** *(These groups had common languages, formal law codes, and agreements just as we do in modern American culture.)* **Interpersonal**

Explain that some Native American languages are still spoken today by small numbers of people. Discuss that as Europeans arrived in the Americas, Native Americans would find their lives changed forever. **Ask: What are some ways to preserve Native American languages when fewer people are speaking them?** *(Answers will vary, but suggestions could include recording them or teaching them in schools.)* AL ELL

Connections to
TODAY

Native American Languages

Many Native American groups still speak their native languages today, though the number of native-language speakers is small. It is estimated that approximately 150,000 people still speak Navajo (nah vuh HO), while only about 2,000 still speak Cherokee.

IMAGE

Longhouses

Analyzing Images Show students the interactive image of the traditional Native American longhouse. Explain that these homes, made from young saplings and covered with tree bark, were common in many Iroquoian villages. Have students work in small groups to fill out a three-column chart listing Native American cultural groups, the type of shelter each built, and the resources used. *(Eastern: longhouses—wood, bark; Plains: tepees—wood, buffalo hides; Southwestern: pueblos—clay or adobe; Northern: igloos—snow blocks; Western: earthen houses—wood, earthen resources)*

See page 1E for other online activities.

McGraw Hill **networks**   Longhouses

Longhouses were the traditional dwellings of Northeast Native Americans. Saplings were used to build a rectangular frame.

Stock Montage/Alamy Images

C Critical Thinking Skills

Comparing Discuss with students the creation of the Grand Council, which was established by the Iroquois constitution. **Ask:** Even though women were not permitted on the council, how did this method of selecting council members give women a strong voice in Iroquois government? *(Women were solely responsible for selecting the male members for the council, so they could choose men who would serve their interests.)* How is this system similar to our modern method of democracy? *(Voters choose representatives who create laws on our behalf. This is similar to clan women selecting clan mothers who, in turn, chose council members.)* **BL**

W Writing Skills

Informative/Explanatory Have students write short informational texts telling about the Great Peace alliance and the Iroquois League. Students should include information about women's roles within the Grand Council; the league's founders, Hiawatha and Dekanawidah; and the similarities, if any, between the Great Peace alliance and other modern constitutions. Students should conduct their research by gathering information from multiple print and digital sources, making sure to assess the credibility of each source. Encourage students to publish their writing using a word-processing program. **AL**

The Iroquois lived in bark-covered longhouses. Each building could shelter several families.

The Iroquois lived near Canada in what is now northern New York State. The original five Iroquois groups, or nations, were the Onondaga (ah•nuhn•DAW•guh), the Seneca (SEH•nih•kuh), the Mohawk (MOH•hawk), the Oneida (oh•NY•duh), and the Cayuga (kay•YOO•guh).

These groups often warred with each other. Then, in the 1500s, they established the Great Peace, an alliance called the Iroquois League. According to Iroquoian tradition, Dekanawidah (deh•kah•nuh•WEE•duh), a tribal elder, and a chief of the Mohawk named Hiawatha (hi•uh•WAH•thuh) founded the league. Worried that war was tearing the nations apart, they urged the people to unite in the spirit of friendship and peace.

The five nations agreed to the Great Binding Law, an oral constitution that defined how the league worked and established the Grand Council. This group of leaders met regularly to settle disputes among the various peoples.

Although Grand Council members were men, women played an important part in choosing delegates to the council.

C

W

Reading **HELP**DESK **CCSS**

clan a group of people who have a common ancestor

Stock Montage/Alamy Images

20 *The First Americans*

netw⊙rks *Online Teaching Options*

IMAGE

Dekanawidah

Explaining Show students the interactive image of Dekanawidah, the Huron leader who is said to have founded the Iroquois League. Discuss with students the formation of the Iroquois League. **Ask:** What were the six Iroquois nations? *(the Mohawk, Oneida, Onondaga, Cayuga, Seneca, and Tuscarora)* **AL** Discuss the discord among these groups. **Ask:** How was the fighting among the Eastern peoples resolved? *(Five Iroquois nations established the Great Peace.)*

See page 1E for other online activities.

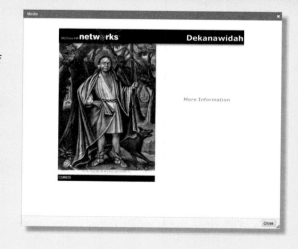

The different members of the Iroquois League were organized according to **clans,** or groups of related families. The women in each clan chose a clan mother. These clan mothers then chose the male members of the Grand Council.

The Tuscarora (tus•kuh•ROR•uh) people joined the league in 1715. With their addition, the five nations became six.

Southeastern Peoples

The Southeast was also a woodlands area, but with a warmer climate than the Eastern Woodlands. Among the Native American groups of the Southeast were the Creek, Cherokee, and Chickasaw (CHIH•kuh•saw). Farming was essential for each of these groups. The Creek lived in loosely knit farming communities in what is now Georgia and Alabama. There they grew corn, squash, tobacco, and other crops. The Cherokee farmed in the mountains of what is now Georgia, Tennessee, and the Carolinas. The Chickasaw spread out across the Southeast, but most of their largest settlements were in present-day Mississippi. There they farmed the fertile river bottomlands.

A Changing World

In whichever part of North America they lived, Native Americans developed rich and varied cultures, and ways of living that were suited to their environments. In the 1500s, however, a new people with vastly different cultures and ways of life would arrive in the Americas: the Europeans. Their arrival would change the Native Americans' world forever.

☑ **PROGRESS CHECK**

Describing How did location affect the culture of different native peoples? Give examples from the text to support your answer.

BIOGRAPHY

Dekanawidah (1500s)

Legend has it that a leader named Dekanawidah founded the Iroquois League. A Huron by birth, Dekanawidah sought an end to the terrible fighting among Native Americans in the Northeast. He drew up the "Great Law," which created a system for making decisions and settling disputes in an orderly manner. The agreement helped the Iroquois become one of the most powerful Native American groups in North America.

▶ **CRITICAL THINKING**
Drawing Conclusions Why do you think Iroquois groups were willing to join together in a federation?

R **Reading Skills**

Identifying Have students read the paragraph. Ask students to note where the various Southeastern peoples lived: the Creek, the Chickasaw, and the Cherokee. Ask students to explain why farming was important to these groups. **Ask: What were some important crops to Southeastern peoples?** *(corn, squash, tobacco)* **AL** **ELL**

Have students complete the Lesson 3 Review.

CLOSE & REFLECT

Locating To close the lesson, use the chapter opener map to summarize the locations of the Native American cultures of the United States. Explain that many names of places in the United States are related to native cultures. The names of states such as Minnesota, North and South Dakota, Oklahoma, Wyoming, Utah, and Missouri all derive from Native American words. **AL** **ELL**

Ask students to think about how Native American groups might have evolved if Europeans had not arrived in the Americas. **BL**

LESSON 3 REVIEW (CCSS)

Review Vocabulary (Tier 3 Words)

1. Examine the two terms below. Then write a sentence explaining how the words are related. RH.6–8.4
   a. federation   b. clan

Answer the Guiding Questions

2. **Describing** Describe the cliff dwellings of the Ancient Puebloans, and explain the advantages those dwellings may have offered. RH.6–8.1

3. **Explaining** How did the Inuit adapt to the cold Arctic climate? RH.6–8.2

4. **Explaining** What was the significance of the Iroquois League? RH.6–8.1

5. **NARRATIVE** Consider the different groups discussed in the lesson. Write a paragraph that describes what life might have been like for a young member of one of these groups. Use details from the lesson to illustrate how your chosen group adapted to the environment where they lived. WHST.6–8.1, WHST.6–8.10

Lesson 3   **21**

LESSON 3 REVIEW ANSWERS

1. A clan was a group of related families. Federations were formal agreements between different groups that linked them together. Five Iroquois groups formed a federation based on clans.

2. The Ancient Puebloans built dwellings in the walls of steep cliffs. The dwellings offered protection from weather and enemies.

3. Inuits adapted to a low-vegetation environment by becoming skilled hunters. They also used snow to build shelters called igloos.

4. The Iroquois League was a federation of Iroquois nations that agreed to exist peacefully. The League created an Iroquois constitution, which established the Grand Council.

5. Paragraphs will vary but students should support their points with details from the lesson.

ANSWERS, p. 21

CRITICAL THINKING Answers may include that they realized fighting was bad for them and that working together to solve problems was in their best interest.

☑ **PROGRESS CHECK** Location affected the types of food that were available, as well as what weather conditions the peoples' structures had to be able to endure. For example, Inuit people lived in a cold environment that could not be farmed. They built igloos to protect themselves from the cold and learned to be skilled hunters on both water and land.

CHAPTER REVIEW ACTIVITY

Lead a discussion on aspects of modern American culture. Have students create a chart with one column titled "Shared Beliefs" and the other titled "Common Practices and Values." Ask students to describe in their own words what might fall into these categories, and record their responses in the chart. Ask how American culture is unique among those around the world. Then ask, based on what they learned from the chapter, why our culture is different from others.

Shared Beliefs	Common Practices and Values

REVIEW THE ENDURING UNDERSTANDING

Review the chapter's Enduring Understanding with students:

- *Cultures are held together by shared beliefs and common practices and values.*

Now pose the following questions in a class discussion to apply it to the chapter.

How did the last Ice Age affect the populating of North America? *(Answers may include how it exposed the Beringia land bridge and allowed nomadic peoples from Asia to traverse the continents in their search for food. When the Ice Age ended, the Beringia land bridge was submerged, cutting off the migration route between Asia and North America.)*

How did the practice of agriculture lead to the establishment of advanced cultures and civilizations? *(Answers may include how nomadic peoples began to settle down and build permanent shelters. Eventually, villages and great civilizations began to form. Crops fed large populations and highly developed, more complex civilizations flourished.)*

How did North America's distinct environments shape early American cultures? *(Answers may include how each culture adapted to their environment by using the different resources their environments provided. Early peoples hunted or grew different types of food, built a variety of unique shelters, and gained varied skills as a result of North America's distinct landscapes.)*

Write your answers on a separate piece of paper.

1 Exploring the Essential Questions WHST.6–8.2, WHST.6–8.9
INFORMATIVE/EXPLANATORY Geography played an important part in the development of North America's Native American cultures. Write an essay in which you explain how factors of geography helped shape cultures. Use specific examples from the chapter in making your argument.

2 21st Century Skills WHST.6–8.5, WHST.6–8.6
CRITICAL THINKING AND PROBLEM SOLVING Use the Internet to research the Iroquois constitution. Read parts 1 and 2 only. Then rewrite these parts of the constitution in your own words, using modern English. Share and compare your rewrites with those of other members of the class. How are they similar? How do they differ?

3 Thinking Like a Historian WHST.6–8.1, WHST.6–8.9
DRAWING INFERENCES AND CONCLUSIONS Consider what you have read about the great Native American civilizations that existed in the Americas prior to the arrival of Europeans. What became of those civilizations? What conclusions can you draw about the nature of civilizations and cultures based on the history of the Native American civilizations?

4 Visual Literacy RH.6–8.7
ANALYZING IMAGES Petroglyphs are paintings or carvings on rock. What can you determine about the cultures that created these petroglyphs in southern Utah?

© Frank Lukasseck/CORBIS

22 *The First Americans*

ACTIVITIES ANSWERS

Exploring the Essential Questions

1 Answers will vary but should include how geography influenced the development of different Native American cultures. References to climate, food sources, and types of dwellings should be reflected in students' responses, along with specific facts from the chapter supporting these points.

21st Century Skills

2 Rewrites will vary, but should reflect an understanding of the first two sections of the Iroquois constitution. Compare students' research to their rewrite for accuracy.

Thinking Like a Historian

3 Answers will vary, but should draw inferences based on facts from the chapter. Responses may note that civilizations rise and fall, making way for other dominant groups, or may argue that civilizations evolve and change, serving as the basis for future civilizations. Students should use specific facts from the chapter to support their inferences.

Visual Literacy

4 Pictures of the deer and the people hunting indicate that people hunted for food. The man hunting appears to be on a horse. Many footprints might indicate travel. Accept other reasonable answers.

REVIEWING THE GUIDING QUESTIONS

Choose the best answer for each question.

RH.6–8.1
1 Which of the following has been a leading theory about how human beings first came to the Americas?

A. They crossed a land bridge from Asia to North America.

B. They swam across the Pacific Ocean from small islands.

C. They sailed from Europe to explore new lands.

D. They crossed glaciers that once linked Antarctica to South America.

RH.6–8.2
2 Why do scientists think people first migrated to the Americas?

F. to escape from harsh rule in their homeland

G. to seek out other ancient peoples for wisdom

H. to search for hunting grounds for food

I. to map the land for future generations

RH.6–8.1
3 Which city was the center of the Aztec Empire?

A. Montezuma

B. Machu Picchu

C. Cuzco

D. Tenochtitlán

RH.6–8.1
4 Which of the following is an example of a key feature of the Inca civilization?

F. farming their land by cutting terraces into the mountainsides

G. building their capital city in the middle of Lake Texcoco

H. creating enormous stone monuments that were up to nine feet tall

I. predicting eclipses and creating a 365-day calendar

RH.6–8.2
5 Which of the following correctly describes the Adena, Hopewell, and Mississippian cultures, and the Hohokam and Ancient Puebloans?

A. These were the dominant cultures of North America in 1492.

B. These cultures thrived and then faded before the arrival of Europeans.

C. These cultures influenced the development of the great empires of Mexico, Central America, and South America.

D. These cultures were competitors that eventually destroyed one another.

RH.6–8.2
6 The Native American groups living in North America around 1492

F. varied according to the environments in which they lived.

G. were remarkably similar.

H. had developed advanced farming techniques.

I. were dependent on hunting and gathering for all their food.

23

ASSESSMENT ANSWERS
Review the Guiding Questions

1 **A** A land bridge was uncovered during the most recent Ice Age, and ancient peoples from Asia crossed over it into the Americas. There is no evidence that ancient peoples swam to the Americas, so B is incorrect. When Europeans arrived in the Americas in the 1500s, people already inhabited the land, ruling out choice C. Ancient peoples did not live in Antarctica, so D is also incorrect.

2 **H** There is no indication that ancient people sought to escape harsh rule or seek out others for wisdom, making both F and G incorrect. There is no evidence that the nomads were interested in mapping the land. The most likely explanation is that people were searching for food, making H the correct answer.

3 **D** Montezuma was not a city, so A is incorrect. Both Machu Picchu and Cuzco were located in the Inca Empire, so they are incorrect. Tenochtitlán was the center of the Aztec Empire.

4 **F** Choice G was an accomplishment of the Aztec people. The Olmec were responsible for building huge stone monuments, making H incorrect. Choice I reflects an accomplishment of the Maya people.

5 **B** These cultures had faded by 1492, so A is incorrect. It is likely that any influence came from the empires of Mexico, Central America, and South America, not the other way around, so C is incorrect. These cultures were separated by time and geography, so D is not correct.

6 **F** The Native American groups in North America around 1492 were distinct, and varied according to their environments, so G is wrong. While some had advanced farming techniques, not all groups did, so H is incorrect. Likewise, while some depended on hunting and gathering, others farmed, so I is incorrect.

Analyzing Documents

7 A The roots are from the Tree of Great Peace and spread in all directions. The confederate lords are planting the symbolic tree, not being represented by it, making B incorrect. The excerpt references peace, not war, spreading out in all directions, so there is no desire to keep the Five Nations apart. This rules out choices C and D.

8 H The purpose of the Iroquois constitution is to establish peace among the Five Nations. There is no reference to appointing a leader of the confederate lords, ruling out choice F. Choice G is wrong because it refers to actual trees. Choice I is wrong because the desire is to secure peace.

Short Response

9 so his feet would never touch the ground

10 Answers will vary, but should include details that show an understanding of the level of respect and reverence Montezuma was given.

Extended Response

11 Answers will vary but essays should discuss how various groups secured food. Discussions should note how the environment influenced available food sources, specifically the roles of both climate and geography. Essays should also note the role that farming played in the transition many Native American groups had from nomadic to settled lifestyles. Students should use specific facts from the chapter to support their discussions.

CHAPTER 1 Assessment (continued)

DBQ ANALYZING DOCUMENTS

This excerpt is from the Iroquois constitution.

> "I am Dekanawidah and with the Five Nations' Confederate Lords I plant the Tree of Great Peace. ... Roots have spread out from the Tree of the Great Peace, one to the north, one to the east, one to the south, and one to the west."
>
> —From the Iroquois constitution

RH.6–8.1, RH.6–8.4

7 Analyzing What do you think the roots mentioned in the excerpt represent?

A. a peace that grows and spreads out in all directions

B. each of the Five Nations' confederate lords

C. the desire to start wars with other peoples in different areas

D. the separation that keeps the Five Nations apart

RH.6–8.2, RH.6–8.6

8 Drawing Conclusions The main purpose of the Iroquois constitution as explained in the excerpt is to

F. appoint the leader of the confederate lords.

G. plant trees that will create a forest.

H. establish peace among the Five Nations.

I. begin a war with other cultures.

SHORT RESPONSE

Spaniard Bernal Díaz del Castillo was among the first Europeans to meet Montezuma, the ruler of the Aztec Empire. This excerpt describes how Montezuma was treated by his subjects.

> "[T]here were ... Lords who walked before the Great Montezuma, sweeping the ground where he would tread and spreading cloths on it, so that he should not tread on the earth. Not one of these chieftains dared even to think of looking him in the face, but kept their eyes lowered with great reverence."
>
> —From The True History of the Conquest of New Spain

RH.6–8.2, WHST.6–8.4

9 Why did the lords spread cloths on the ground where Montezuma was to walk?

RH.6–8.6, WHST.6–8.9

10 How did the Aztec people apparently feel about Montezuma? Give specific details to support your response.

EXTENDED RESPONSE

WHST.6–8.1, WHST.6–8.9

11 Informative/Explanatory Write an essay exploring how the quest for food and the way it was obtained helped shape and define various Native American civilizations. Use examples from the chapter to make your argument.

Need Extra Help?

If You've Missed Question	1	2	3	4	5	6	7	8	9	10	11
Review Lesson	1	1	2	2	3	3	3	3	2	2	1–3

---

networks   *Online Teaching Options*

Using eAssessment

Use eAssessment to access and assign the publisher-made Lesson Quizzes & Chapter Tests electronically. You can also use eAssessment to create your own quizzes and tests from hundreds of available questions. eAssessment helps you design assessments that meet the needs of different types of learners. Follow the link in the *Assess* tab of your Teacher Lesson Center.

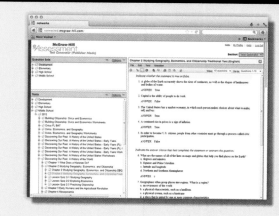

Exploring the Americas Planner

UNDERSTANDING BY DESIGN®

Enduring Understanding

- *The movement of people, goods, and ideas causes societies to change over time.*

Essential Questions

- *How do new ideas change the way people live?*
- *Why do people trade?*
- *What are the consequences when cultures interact?*

Predictable Misunderstandings

Students may think:

- *Every country had the same basic reasons for exploring and colonizing new lands.*
- *Travel was very different during the Age of Exploration, but students may not realize how slow it was.*
- *The Americas have always had large areas of developed land.*

Assessment Evidence

Performance Tasks:

- *Hands-On Chapter Project*

Other Evidence:

- *Interactive Graphic Organizers*
- *What Do You Know? activity*
- *Geography and History Activities*
- *Primary Source Activity*
- *Class discussion responses about European exploration of the Americas*
- *Written paragraphs*
- *Online Self-Check Quizzes*
- *Lesson Reviews*
- *Chapter Activities and Assessment*

SUGGESTED PACING GUIDE

Introducing the Chapter	1 day	Lesson 3	2 days
Lesson 1	2 days	Lesson 4	2 days
Lesson 2	2 days	Chapter Wrap-Up and Assessment	1 day

TOTAL TIME   10 Days

Key for Using the Teacher Edition

SKILL-BASED ACTIVITIES

Types of skill activities found in the Teacher Edition.

V **Visual Skills** require students to analyze maps, graphs, charts, and photos.

R **Reading Skills** help students practice reading skills and master vocabulary.

W **Writing Skills** provide writing opportunities to help students comprehend the text.

C **Critical Thinking Skills** help students apply and extend what they have learned.

T **Technology Skills** require students to use digital tools effectively.

*Letters are followed by a number when there is more than one of the same type of skill on the page.

DIFFERENTIATED INSTRUCTION

All activities are written for the on-level student unless otherwise marked with the leveled labels below.

BL Beyond Level
AL Approaching Level
ELL English Language Learners

All students benefit from activities that utilize different learning styles. Many activities are marked as below when a particular learning style is highlighted.

Intrapersonal	Naturalist
Logical/Mathematical	Kinesthetic
Visual/Spatial	Auditory/Musical
Verbal/Linguistic	Interpersonal

Learners will understand:

2   Time, Continuity, and Change

5. Key historical periods and patterns of change within and across cultures (e.g., the rise and fall of ancient civilizations, the development of technology, the rise of modern nation-states, and the establishment and breakdown of colonial systems)

6. The origins and influences of social, cultural, political, and economic systems

9. The influences of social, geographic, economic, and cultural factors on the history of local areas, states, nations, and the world.

3   PEOPLE, PLACES, AND ENVIRONMENTS

1. The theme of people, places, and environments involves the study of the relationships between human populations in different locations and geographic phenomena such as climate, vegetation, and natural resources

6. Patterns of demographic and political change, and cultural diffusion in the past and present (e.g., changing national boundaries, migration, and settlement, and the diffusion of and changes in customs and ideas)

8. Factors that contribute to cooperation and conflict among peoples of the nation and world, including language, religion, and political beliefs

9. The use of a variety of maps, globes, graphic representations, and geospatial technologies to help investigate the relationships among people, places, and environments

5   INDIVIDUALS, GROUPS, AND INSTITUTIONS

6. That cultural diffusion occurs when groups migrate

8. That when two or more groups with differing norms and beliefs interact, accommodation or conflict may result

7   PRODUCTION, DISTRIBUTION, AND CONSUMPTION

1. Individuals, government, and society experience scarcity because human wants and needs exceed what can be produced from available resources

8   SCIENCE, TECHNOLOGY, AND SOCIETY

5. Science and technology have changed peoples' perceptions of the social and natural world, as well as their relationship to the land, economy and trade, their concept of security, and their major daily activities

9   GLOBAL CONNECTIONS

1. Global connections have existed in the past and increased rapidly in current times

2. Global factors such as cultural, economic, and political connections are changing the places in which people live (e.g., through trade, migration, increased travel, and communication)

CHAPTER OPENER PLANNER

Students will know:

- *that advances in technology paved the way for European exploration.*
- *why Europeans explored and colonized the Americas.*
- *the positive and negative contributions of the Europeans in the Americas.*
- *how the reforms of Martin Luther brought about religious change.*

Students will be able to:

- **compare and contrast** *information about European explorers and explorations.*
- **analyze** *relationships between European explorers and Native Americans.*
- **understand** *the impact and importance of events, such as the defeat of the Aztec Empire or the establishment of Spanish missions.*
- **identify and describe** *geographical places and regions such as north and central Africa or southwestern North America.*
- **explain** *events of the Age of Exploration both graphically and orally.*

UNDERSTANDING
BY DESIGN®

☑ *Print Teaching Options*

V **Visual Skills**

☐ **P. 26** Students trace the routes of several famous explorers. **AL** **Visual/Spatial Logical/Mathematical**

☐ **P. 27** Students examine historical events that occurred in the Americas and the rest of the world during this period.

☑ *Online Teaching Options*

V **Visual Skills**

☐ **MAP** **European Exploration 1487–1611**—Students use the interactive map to investigate the routes Europeans took during their explorations.

☐ **TIME LINE** **Place and Time: The Americas 1400 to 1625**—Students learn about key events related to European exploration of the Americas between 1400 and 1625.

☐ **WORLD ATLAS** Students can use this interactive map to identify regions of the world, learn about individual countries, locate political boundaries, measure distances, and much more.

☑ *Printable Digital Worksheets*

R **Reading Skills**

☐ **GRAPHIC NOVEL** *The Sea of Possibilities*—Two sailors readying the *Santa Maria* discuss the upcoming voyage.

Project-Based Learning

Hands-On Chapter Project

Exploring the Americas
To better understand early exploration of the Americas, students will create an illustrated piece of historical fiction for children about an important person or event from this era.

Technology Extension

VoiceThread Picture Books
- Find an additional activity online that incorporates technology for this project.
- Visit the EdTechTeacher Web sites (included in the Technology Extension for this chapter) for more links, tutorials, and other resources.

Print Resources

ANCILLARY RESOURCES
These ancillaries are available for every chapter and lesson.

- **Reading Essentials and Study Guide Workbook** **AL** **ELL**
- **Chapter Tests and Lesson Quizzes Blackline Masters**

PRINTABLE DIGITAL WORKSHEETS
These printable digital worksheets are available for every chapter and lesson.

- **Hands-On Chapter Projects**
- **What Do You Know? activities**
- **Chapter Summaries (English and Spanish)**
- **Vocabulary Builder activities**
- **Guided Reading activities**

More Media Resources

SUGGESTED READING

Grade 6 reading level:
- *Voices from Colonial America: Florida, 1513–1821,* by Matthew C. Cannavale
- *Voices from Colonial America: New York, 1609–1776,* by Michael Burgan
- *Peter Stuyvesant: New Amsterdam and the Origins of New York,* by L.J. Krizner, Lisa Sita

Grade 7 reading level:
- *Who Was First? Discovering America,* by Russell Freedman

Grade 8 reading level:
- *1491,* by Charles Mann
- *The World Made New: Why the Age of Exploration Happened and How It Changed the World,* by Marc Aronson, John W. Glenn

LESSON 1 PLANNER

A CHANGING WORLD

Students will know:
- *that advances in technology paved the way for European exploration.*

Students will be able to:
- *identify and describe geographical places and regions such as north and central Africa or southwestern North America.*
- *explain events of the Age of Exploration both graphically and orally.*

UNDERSTANDING BY DESIGN®

☑ Print Teaching Options

V Visual Skills

☐ **P. 29** Students trace the overland routes that were used to carry goods between Asia and Europe.

☐ **P. 32** Students explore the locations of three West African Trading Kingdoms and compare and contrast overland and sea trade routes. **Visual/Spatial**

R Reading Skills

☐ **P. 28** Students discuss the initial purpose of the Crusades. **AL**

☐ **P. 29** Students explain how trade led to the exchange of ideas as well as goods. **BL**

☐ **P. 30** Students summarize the accomplishments that come with the development of powerful nations. **BL**

☐ **P. 30** Students discuss the meaning of *technology.* **AL** **ELL**

☐ **P. 31** Student pairs analyze a passage from the text.

☐ **P. 33** Students explore the meaning of the word *pilgrimage.* **BL** **Verbal/Linguistic**

W Writing Skills

☐ **P. 31** Students listen to passages from Marco Polo's *Travels* and write descriptive passages about his adventures in Asia. **AL** **Verbal/Linguistic**

C Critical Thinking Skills

☐ **P. 28** Students identify unplanned effects of trade.

☐ **P. 30** Students consider whether worldwide trade today has the same effect as trade during the 1500s.

☐ **P. 31** Students construct a compass and draw conclusions as to how this tool aids in navigation. **Kinesthetic**

☐ **P. 32** Students sequence events in three West African kingdoms. **BL** **Logical/Mathematical**

☑ Online Teaching Options

V Visual Skills

☐ **VIDEO** **Leonardo da Vinci**—Students view a video that explains how Leonardo da Vinci defined the Renaissance.

☐ **MAP** **Trade Routes to Asia, 300 B.C. to A.D. 1500**—Students trace the land and sea routes used by Europeans to access goods in Asia.

☐ **IMAGE** **Caravels**—Students explore advancements in ship design.

☐ **MAP** **West African Trading Kingdoms, A.D. 400–1600**—Students visualize the kingdoms of Ghana, Mali, and Songhai and trace the trade routes from these empires to the Mediterranean Sea.

R Reading Skills

☐ **GRAPHIC ORGANIZER** **Taking Notes: *Identifying:* Technological Advances**—Students identify the advances in technology that paved the way for European voyages of exploration.

C Critical Thinking Skills

☐ **SLIDE SHOW** **The Compass**—Students explore the workings of a compass.

☐ **SLIDE SHOW** **Mansa Musa**—Students explore the kingdom of Mali and its great king.

T Technology Skills

☐ **SELF-CHECK QUIZ** **Lesson 1**—Students receive instant feedback of their mastery of lesson content.

☑ Printable Digital Worksheets

W Writing Skills

☐ **WORKSHEET** **Geography and History Activity: Exploring the Americas, A Changing World**—Students read about the Berber traders and write about how they affected the trading centers in West Africa.

EARLY EXPLORATION

Students will know:
- why Europeans explored and colonized the Americas.

Students will be able to:
- **compare and contrast** information about European explorers and explorations.
- **identify and describe** geographical places and regions such as north and central Africa or southwestern North America.
- **explain** events of the Age of Exploration both graphically and orally.

UNDERSTANDING
BY DESIGN®

☑ *Print Teaching Options*

V Visual Skills

☐ **P. 34** Students map known landmasses and oceans at the time of Columbus's voyage. **BL** Visual/Spatial

☐ **P. 36** Students speculate and role-play the difficulties encountered by sailors onboard ships. **ELL**

☐ **P. 38** Students imagine sailing on the ships of European explorers. **ELL** Visual/Spatial

☐ **P. 39** Students explore the location of San Salvador. Visual/Spatial

☐ **P. 40** Students create a time line of Columbus's voyages. **AL** Logical/Mathematical

R Reading Skills

☐ **P. 37** Students identify and rank the importance of major achievements of Portuguese explorers. **AL**

☐ **P. 37** Students assess Ptolemy's effect on Columbus and other explorers.

☐ **P. 38** Students analyze a passage about the Vikings in North America.

W Writing Skills

☐ **P. 41** Students outline arguments as to whether they think Columbus "discovered" America.

C Critical Thinking Skills

☐ **P. 34** Students speculate about what Columbus expected to find across the Atlantic Ocean.

☐ **P. 35** Students analyze Portugal's motives for wanting to find a new route to Asia. **AL** **BL**

☐ **P. 37** Students identify how the route taken by Cabral differed from those of Dias and da Gama.

☐ **P. 39** Students connect Columbus's first voyage to life in the United States today.

☐ **P. 40** Students identify people who were significantly affected by the connection of New and Old Worlds. **BL**

☐ **P. 41** Students consider whether Columbus's journeys were successful. **BL**

T Technology Skills

☐ **P. 36** Students research the Cape of Good Hope as it is today. **AL** Visual/Spatial

☑ *Online Teaching Options*

V Visual Skills

☐ **VIDEO** **Journey to the New World: Christopher Columbus**—Students view a video that describes how Christopher Columbus's voyage to the New World opened a new era of exploration.

☐ **MAP** **Early Portuguese Exploration**—Students trace the sea routes of Dias and da Gama.

☐ **MAP** **European Exploration 1487–1611**—Students reexamine the sea routes followed by Dutch, English, French, Portuguese, and Spanish explorers.

☐ **BIOGRAPHY** **Queen Isabella**—Students view an image of Queen Isabella and learn about her background.

☐ **IMAGE** **The Santa Maria**—Students learn about the three ships used in Columbus's first voyage to the Americas.

☐ **IMAGE** **Vasco Núñez de Balboa**—Students learn about Balboa's sighting of the Pacific Ocean.

R Reading Skills

☐ **GRAPHIC ORGANIZER** **Taking Notes:** *Identifying:* **Explorers**—Students complete the lesson graphic organizer in which they identify the explorers who were sponsored by Spain and Portugal.

☐ **PRIMARY SOURCE** **Vasco da Gama**—Students analyze an excerpt from Vasco da Gama's description of the trials of sailing around the Cape of Good Hope.

C Critical Thinking Skills

☐ **CHART** **Isabella of Spain**—Students learn about Isabella's views on exploration, religion, human rights, education, and the arts.

☐ **WHITEBOARD ACTIVITY** **Spanish Conquistadors**—Students match the names of explorers with their accomplishments.

T Technology Skills

☐ **SELF-CHECK QUIZ** **Lesson 2**—Students receive instant feedback of their mastery of lesson content.

SPAIN IN AMERICA

Students will know:
- *why Europeans explored and colonized the Americas.*
- *the positive and negative contributions of the Europeans in the Americas.*

Students will be able to:
- **compare and contrast** *information about European explorers and explorations.*
- **analyze** *relationships between European explorers and Native Americans.*
- **understand** *the impact and importance of events, such as the defeat of the Aztec Empire or the establishment of Spanish missions.*
- **identify and describe** *geographical places and regions such as north and central Africa or southwestern North America.*

UNDERSTANDING BY DESIGN®

☑ *Print Teaching Options*

V Visual Skills

☐ **P. 45** Students use a map to reinforce lesson concepts. **Visual/Spatial**

☐ **P. 46** Students examine the social classes in Spanish colonial society. **AL BL**

☐ **P. 47** Students locate Spanish missions on a map of California. **Visual/Spatial**

R Reading Skills

☐ **P. 42** Students discuss the pressures of being a conquistador.

☐ **P. 45** Student discuss the travels of Juan de Oñate. **ELL Logical/Mathematical**

☐ **P. 47** Students determine the meaning of words as they are used in the text. **AL ELL**

W Writing Skills

☐ **P. 43** Students write a paragraph to justify or reject Cortés's mission. **BL Verbal/Linguistic**

C Critical Thinking Skills

☐ **P. 42** Students connect how the discovery of wealth led civilizations to more exploration of the Americas. **BL**

☐ **P. 43** Students connect the death of many Native Americans to their lack of immunity against European diseases.

☐ **P. 44** Students consider how the rumors of the Seven Cities of Gold affected exploration of the New World. **AL**

☐ **P. 48** Students evaluate the treatment of Native Americans by the Spanish.

T Technology Skills

☐ **P. 44** Students research the fabled fountain of youth. **BL Interpersonal**

☑ *Online Teaching Options*

V Visual Skills

☐ **VIDEO** **Hernando de Soto**—Students join de Soto in his search for cities of gold in the New World.

☐ **MAP** **Spanish Explorers 1513–1542**—Students trace land and sea routes of several Spanish explorers of North America.

☐ **IMAGE** **Spanish Missions in the Americas**—Students learn about the building and uses of missions built by the ancient Puebloans.

☐ **BIOGRAPHY** **Bartolomé de Las Casas**—Students reflect on the treatment of Native Americans under Spanish rule.

☐ **BIOGRAPHY** **Father Junípero Serra**—Students explore the background and motives of one of the builders of several California missions.

☐ **MAP** **Spanish Missions in California**—Students explore the location of missions in relation to modern cities.

R Reading Skills

☐ **GRAPHIC ORGANIZER** **Taking Notes:** *Describing:* **Spanish Conquistadors**—Students complete the lesson graphic organizer in which they identify three Spanish conquistadors and the regions they explored.

☐ **PRIMARY SOURCE** **Cortés and the Aztecs**—Students analyze an excerpt from *The Broken Spears.*

☐ **PRIMARY SOURCE** **Cabeza de Vaca**—Students analyze an excerpt from an account of de Vaca's years in the Americas that describes a storm that struck Trinidad.

☐ **PRIMARY SOURCE** **Juana Inés de la Cruz**—Students analyze an excerpt from the poem "Phyllis."

T Technology Skills

☐ **SELF-CHECK QUIZ** **Lesson 3**—Students receive instant feedback of their mastery of lesson content.

☑ *Printable Digital Worksheets*

W Writing Skills

☐ **WORKSHEET** **Primary Source Activity: Exploring the Americas, Spain in America**—Students respond to an eyewitness account of Aztec objects of worship.

COMPETING FOR COLONIES

Students will know:
- why Europeans explored and colonized the Americas.
- the positive and negative contributions of the Europeans in the Americas.
- how the reforms of Martin Luther brought about religious change.

Students will be able to:
- **identify and describe** geographical places and regions such as north and central Africa or southwestern North America.
- **explain** events of the Age of Exploration both graphically and orally.

UNDERSTANDING
BY DESIGN®

☑ *Print Teaching Options*

V Visual Skills

☐ **P. 51** Students analyze a painting of Hudson meeting the Native Americans. **Visual/Spatial**

☐ **P. 52** Students examine the image of Marquette and Joliet.

R Reading Skills

☐ **P. 49** Students identify important points and vocabulary in the text. **AL** **ELL** **Verbal/Linguistic**

☐ **P. 51** Students discuss the motivations of Cartier.

☐ **P. 53** Students discuss the colony of New France. **AL** **ELL**

W Writing Skills

☐ **P. 50** Students research and write about the battle that defeated the Spanish Armada. **Auditory/Musical** **Verbal/Linguistic**

☐ **P. 51** Students write raps or songs as ways to remember lesson content. **ELL** **Auditory/Musical**

C Critical Thinking Skills

☐ **P. 50** Students discuss the motivations of Marie Guyard. **AL**

☐ **P. 52** Students consider how French goals in North America paved the way for French settlements. **AL** **ELL**

☐ **P. 53** Students contrast New Amsterdam and today's Manhattan Island.

T Technology Skills

☐ **P. 52** Students use maps to trace the direction of U.S. rivers. **BL** **Visual/Spatial**

☑ *Online Teaching Options*

V Visual Skills

☐ **VIDEO** **Henry Hudson and the New World**—Students view a video that recounts Henry Hudson's exploration of the northern coast of the New World.

☐ **IMAGE** **The Northwest Passage**—Students learn about the bodies of water explorers hoped would provide a Northwest Passage.

☐ **IMAGE** **Jacques Marquette and Louis Joliet**—Students explore the backgrounds of these explorers who were the first to chart the course of the Mississippi River.

☐ **BIOGRAPHY** **Sieur de La Salle**—Students learn about the background of this Mississippi River explorer.

☐ **IMAGE** **New Amsterdam**—Students learn about the Dutch settlement that eventually became New York City.

R Reading Skills

☐ **GRAPHIC ORGANIZER** **Taking Notes: *Listing:* Search for the Northwest Passage**—Students complete the lesson graphic organizer in which they list explorers who tried to find the Northwest Passage.

C Critical Thinking Skills

☐ **MAP** **European Exploration 1487–1611**—Students trace the routes of explorers during this time period.

☐ **GAME** **Competing for Colonies Column Game**—Students complete a sorting game to reinforce their knowledge of Catholicism and Protestantism.

T Technology Skills

☐ **SELF-CHECK QUIZ** **Lesson 4**—Students receive instant feedback of their mastery of lesson content.

☑ *Printable Digital Worksheets*

W Writing Skills

☐ **WORKSHEET** **Geography and History Activity: Exploring the Americas, Competing for Colonies**—Students examine different points of view related to exploration and colonization.

LESSON 1 A Changing World

Reading and Comprehension

Have students skim the lesson looking for the terms in bold and those both bold and highlighted. Have them write down those terms that are unfamiliar and then use dictionaries to define the terms. Pair students. Have one student read a definition and the other identify the term and use the term in a sentence.

Text Evidence

To help students understand the importance of the Renaissance, organize the class into three groups—art, architecture, and science. Have groups do research to determine how these aspects of society changed as Europeans rediscovered classical Greek and Roman ideas. Students should address these questions in their analyses: What important changes occurred in (art/architecture/science) during this period? Who were the important historical figures driving these changes? How did other parts of society react to the changes?

LESSON 2 Early Exploration

Reading and Comprehension

Write the term *circumnavigate* on the board. Have students identify the prefix *(circum-)* and base *(navigate)*. Point out that *circum-* means "round about" or "around. *Navigate* means to move over or through, in this case, through water. Have students identify other words with the prefix *circum-* and compile a list of their meanings. Examples might include circumference *(distance around a circle)*, circumscribe *(to draw a line around or encircle)*, and circumpolar *(surrounding or located near either of Earth's poles)*.

Text Evidence

Organize students into small groups. Have each group take a position and create a list of reasons why Columbus should (or should not) be considered the greatest explorer in history. Have each group present their lists and defend their arguments.

LESSON 3 Spain in America

Reading and Comprehension

Have students work in pairs to outline the early history of Spain in America. Students should include explorers, the dates of their explorations, their accomplishments, and any other important facts that students wish to include. Have students use their outlines to write a sentence or two that summarizes each section of the lesson.

Text Evidence

Students may confuse the different classes in Spanish colonial society. Assign groups of students to read their text and other sources to find information on the way of life of the peninsulares (Spanish-born people, landowners, heads of the church and government), Creoles (people born of Spanish parents), mestizos (people of Spanish and Native American ancestry, the Native Americans, and enslaved Africans. Have groups role-play a scene where several of these different classes of people interact.

LESSON 4 Competing for Colonies

Reading and Comprehension

After students read the lesson, have them work with a small group to look back through the text. Have students take turns sharing important facts about each section of the lesson. If students cannot remember what parts of the lesson were about, have the group reread sections looking for the main ideas. Have students restate these main ideas in their own words.

Text Evidence

Have students use the information in the text to make a map of North America showing where the different religious groups concentrated as they settled. Have them use a different color or symbol to represent the dominant religion in each area. Discuss why people coming to the New World often settled in areas where others that held their beliefs were already living.

Online Resources

Approaching Level Reader

Use this online lower-level text that corresponds directly to the text in the Student Edition. It includes a Spanish version.

Guided Reading Activities

This resource uses graphic organizers and guiding questions to help students with comprehension.

What Do You Know?

Use these worksheets to pre-assess student's background knowledge before they study the chapter.

Reading Essentials and Study Guide Workbook

This resource offers writing and reading activities for the approaching-level student. Also available in Spanish.

Self-Check Quizzes

This online assessment tool provides instant feedback for students to check their progress.

How Do I Apply
Understanding By Design®?

All materials developed for this program incorporate Understanding By Design® (UBD™) as a planning framework to guide content development, assessment, and instruction. Often referred to as "backward design," the goal of Understanding By Design is to plan with the end in mind. This ensures more clearly defined goals, more appropriate assessments, more tightly aligned lessons, and more purposeful teaching. Consider these three stages as you integrate UBD into your planning.

Stage 1 Identify Desired Results

- What should students know, understand, and be able to do?

- Identify the "big ideas" that you want students to understand and then craft companion "essential questions." Big ideas are transferable concepts, principles, and processes that are key to understanding the topic or subject. Essential questions present open-ended, thought-provoking inquiries that are explored over time.

- Consider the appropriate teaching goals, examine relevant content standards, and make choices on what content to emphasize during teaching.

Stage 2 Determine Acceptable Evidence

- How will you know if students have achieved the desired results? What will you accept as evidence of student understanding and proficiency? How will you evaluate student performance?

- Identify in advance the evidence that will verify that expected levels of learning and content mastery have been achieved.

- There are two types of UBD assessment: Performance Tasks and Other Evidence. "Performance Tasks" require students to apply their learning to an authentic situation to assess their understanding. "Other Evidence" includes traditional assessment materials, such as quizzes, tests, observations, and daily work. Examples of "Assessment Evidence" can be found in the Chapter Planners of your print and online Teacher Editions.

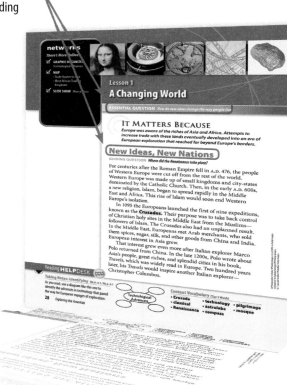

Stage 3 Plan Learning Experiences and Instruction

- What knowledge and skills will students need to perform effectively and achieve desired results? What activities, sequence, and resources are best suited to accomplish these goals?

- The McGraw-Hill Networks Learning System offers a variety of print and digital teaching materials to help your students acquire important knowledge and skills, understand important ideas and processes, and transfer their learning in meaningful ways. Choose from any of these teaching resources with the confidence that you will create a learning plan that meets your students' needs and matches your teaching goals.

Exploring the Americas

1400–1625

ESSENTIAL QUESTIONS • *How do new ideas change the way people live?*
• *Why do people trade?* • *What are the consequences when cultures interact?*

◄ *Queen Isabella of Spain supported early explorations of the Americas.*

The Art Archive / General Archive of the Indies Seville / Gianni Dagli Orti

networks

There's More Online about how the Europeans explored and colonized the Americas.

CHAPTER 2

Lesson 1
A Changing World

Lesson 2
Early Exploration

Lesson 3
Spain in America

Lesson 4
Competing for Colonies

The Story Matters . . .

The year is 1492—a good year for Queen Isabella. After centuries of struggle, Catholic forces have driven the Muslim invaders from Spain. She is grateful to God—and determined to use her power for God's glory.

Full of these thoughts, Isabella recalls a visit she received the year before. A sailor named Christopher Columbus said he knew of a new route to faraway Asia. She ignored him then. Now she is ready to listen. She knows if Columbus succeeds, it will bring glory to God—and untold wealth to Spain.

Queen Isabella agrees to give Columbus the ships and sailors he needs. Before long, he is ready to set sail. The European exploration of the Americas is about to begin.

25

ENGAGE

Bellringer Have students read "The Story Matters . . ." to themselves. Explain that it is written almost in the style of a biography. Help students identify the qualities of royalty during a time of absolute monarchy. **Ask:**

- When was Queen Isabella first approached by Christopher Columbus for money? *(in 1491)*
- Why did Queen Isabella ignore Columbus at that time? *(She wanted to use her power for God's glory since the Catholic forces were finally able to drive the Muslim invaders out of Spain.)*
- What is one reason Isabella sent Columbus to the New World? *(gold)* How does Isabella's purpose relate to Columbus's request for funds for his exploration? *(They are both in search of something great. Columbus wants to find a new route to Asia and Queen Isabella wants riches and glory to Spain.)* Have students role-play a conversation between Isabella and Columbus, based on the information gathered from the questions.

Making Connections

Read the following information to students:

Christopher Columbus sought funding for his voyage across the Atlantic Ocean as early as 1484. He failed twice in his requests for support from King Ferdinand and Queen Isabella. In the summer of 1491, he befriended the Spanish treasurer and a Franciscan friar who had contact with Queen Isabella. Many historians believe that this connection also contributed to the 1492 decision to support Columbus's expedition.

Letter from the Author

Dear American History Teacher,

Powerful motives drove the explorers of the Americas. European explorers claimed vast new territories despite ancient civilizations already occupying those lands. Missionaries brought religion; adventurers sought riches in metals and land. The powerful motives of the explorers clashed with native cultures. Exploration turned to conquest and idealism to exploitation. The conquest of the Americas also pitted the exploring nations against each other. Exploration both succeeded and failed in unexpected ways, and often produced unintended consequences.

Donald A. Ritchie

TEACH & ASSESS

Step Into the Place

V1 Visual Skills

Analyzing Maps Review with students the parts of the map, such as the title, compass rose, scale, and legend. **Ask:**

- **What information does the legend on this map give?** *(different routes that explorers took on their voyages)*
- **In which direction do most of the explorers travel?** *(west)*

Have students study the map and explain the main areas that each nation explored. *(Answers will vary but should demonstrate accurate use of the map and map legend.)* **AL** Then have volunteers match each explorer's route with its locations on the map. Ask students to point out which routes were similar among nations and explorers. **Visual/Spatial**

Have pairs use the map scale to estimate or compare the distances explorers traveled. **Logical/Mathematical**

- **How far did Cortés sail during his voyage in 1519?** *(about 2,000 miles)*
- **Which of Hudson's voyages was longer, the one in 1609 or the one in 1610–1611?** *(1609)*
- **Whose route around the globe appears longer, that of Drake or Magellan and Elcano?** *(Drake)*

Ask volunteers to explain how they determined which routes were longer. Have students use a globe to trace the route of one of the explorers, using their text as a guide. Then have students answer the Map Focus questions.

Content Background Knowledge

- Portugal was the only country that sent explorers southward along the African coast.
- It was common for explorers to sail for more than one country and sometimes they sailed for a country different from their own.
- Explorers did not always live long enough to enjoy their accomplishments. Magellan, for example, died before he circumnavigated the globe, but Elcano finished the voyage for him.

ANSWERS, p. 26

Step Into the Place
1. Four: England, France, the Netherlands, and Spain all sent explorers.
2. **CRITICAL THINKING** Possible answer: They were competing against one another to seize territory, secure resources, and make money for their countries. They also had new technology to help them sail long distances.

Step Into the Time
Ponce de Leon arrived in Florida 21 years after Columbus had landed in America.

Place and Time: The Americas 1400 to 1625

Starting in the late 1400s, Europeans explored the oceans, hoping to find a direct sea route to the East Indies. Instead, they found what to them was a "New World." Over the next few centuries, they explored and settled the Americas.

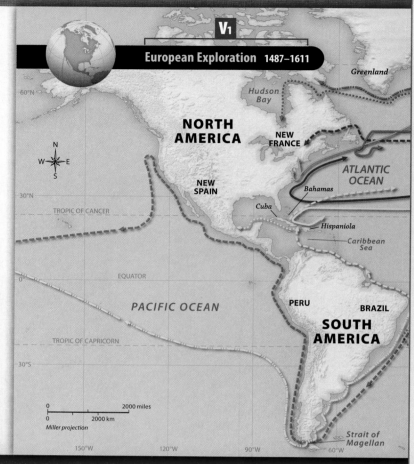

Step Into the Place

MAP FOCUS This map shows the different routes taken by different explorers.

1. **MOVEMENT** How many European nations made explorations of North and South America? RH.6–8.7

2. **CRITICAL THINKING** *Drawing Conclusions* Why do you think so many nations sent out voyages of exploration at this time? RH.6–8.7, RH.6—8.10

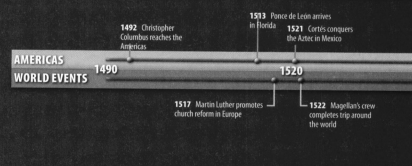

Step Into the Time

TIME LINE Study the time line. How much time passed after Europeans first arrived in the Americas before they explored Florida? RH.6–8.5, RH.6–8.7

V2

AMERICAS

WORLD EVENTS 1490 — 1520

1492 Christopher Columbus reaches the Americas

1513 Ponce de León arrives in Florida

1521 Cortés conquers the Aztec in Mexico

1517 Martin Luther promotes church reform in Europe

1522 Magellan's crew completes trip around the world

26 *Exploring the Americas*

Project-Based Learning

Hands-On Chapter Project

Exploring the Americas

Student groups will create an illustrated piece of historical fiction for children about an important person or event from this era. They will discuss the characteristics of an effective historical children's story and how it should be structured, research their topic to ensure historical accuracy, write and illustrate their stories, and share their children's stories with the class.

Technology Extension

VoiceThread Picture Books

Students will create a VoiceThread picture book of an explorer's story. Students will select key events from the explorer's story and collect images that go with the story either by searching online or drawing them. Pictures that are drawn can be scanned and uploaded. Students will then record a narrative over those images. Students will then share their VoiceThreads with younger students and record their questions and comments.

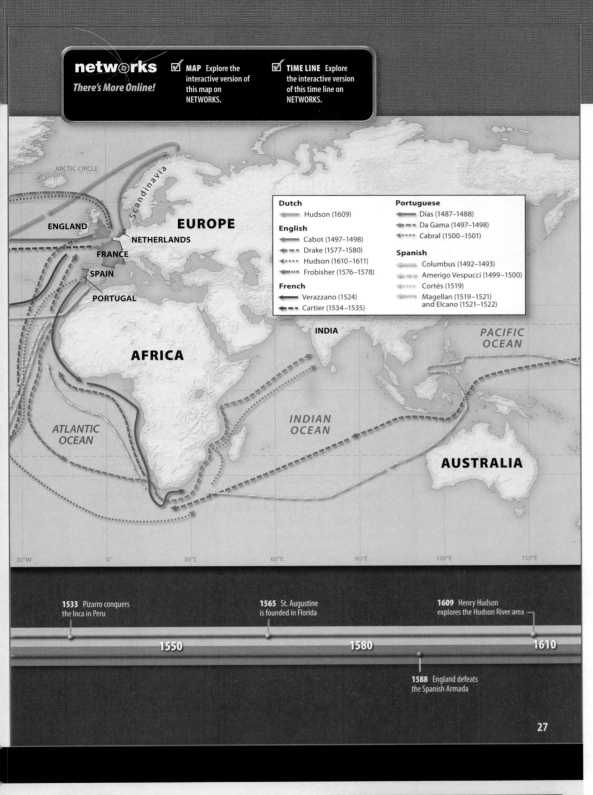

networks MAP Explore the interactive version of this map on NETWORKS.

There's More Online! TIME LINE Explore the interactive version of this time line on NETWORKS.

Map Legend

Dutch
- Hudson (1609)

English
- Cabot (1497–1498)
- Drake (1577–1580)
- Hudson (1610–1611)
- Frobisher (1576–1578)

French
- Verazzano (1524)
- Cartier (1534–1535)

Portuguese
- Dias (1487–1488)
- Da Gama (1497–1498)
- Cabral (1500–1501)

Spanish
- Columbus (1492–1493)
- Amerigo Vespucci (1499–1500)
- Cortés (1519)
- Magellan (1519–1521) and Elcano (1521–1522)

1533 Pizarro conquers the Inca in Peru

1565 St. Augustine is founded in Florida

1609 Henry Hudson explores the Hudson River area

1550   1580   1610

1588 England defeats the Spanish Armada

27

Step Into the Time

V2 Visual Skills

Analyzing Time Lines Have students read through both tiers of events on the time line—those dealing with the Americas and those dealing with the rest of the world. Remind students that the time line is read from left to right. **Ask:** What general statement can you make about European contact with the Americas? *(Possible answer: European contact with the Americas covered two continents—a huge area of land.)*

Have students review the time line and then discuss its major points of interest as a class.

Ask: What was unique about Portugal's explorations? What can you conclude about Portugal from its explorations? *(Portugal was the only country that sent explorers southward along the African coast. Possible Conclusions: Portugal had a different reason for sending out explorers than Spain, England, and France.)*. **Ask:**

- How did Columbus's voyages affect other explorers? *(They were encouraged to explore after Columbus's success. They followed shortly thereafter.)*
- How do you think the defeat of the Spanish Armada affected Spanish exploration? *(Possible answer: It probably hurt Spain's ability to send explorers on expeditions.)*

Have students answer the time line questions and share their answers with the class.

Content Background Knowledge

- Some explorers were driven to find riches such as gold and silver; others were seeking shorter routes to Asia.
- The prices for goods such as silk, spices, coffee, and tea were high and often required a "middle man." Europeans hoped that finding a shorter route to Asia would make the goods less expensive to buy.
- Spices were important to Europeans because few spices grew in Europe. Bland food could be spiced and perfume scented with spices from Asia.

TIME LINE

Place and Time: The Americas 1400 to 1625

Determining Cause and Effect Display the time line on the white board. Have student volunteers read each event as it is revealed, and discuss it as a class. Ask students to compare and contrast the types of events in the Americas versus in the world. Have them choose one world event and write a sentence to explain how it affected European exploration.

See page 25B for other online activities.

CLOSE & REFLECT

Formulating Questions Have each student write a question based on the map, time line, or class discussion about European Exploration, 1487–1611. Collect the questions and answer them as a class. Tell students they will be learning more about European exploration of the Americas as they study this chapter.

ENGAGE

 Bellringer Tell students that in Europe, centuries ago, explorers sailed to find a sea route to Asia.

Ask: What kinds of dangers do you think they faced? *(Possible answers: storms, hunger, despair, sickness)*

Discuss with students that Europeans wanted to reach Asia by sea because it was so hard to reach by land, but many died in the process. **Ask: Why do you think they went so far to get something they thought was valuable?** *(Possible answer: because they wanted to improve their lives or become rich)*

TEACH & ASSESS

R Reading Skills

Discussing Have students skim the paragraph. Discuss the growing European interest in Asia. **Ask: What was the initial purpose of the Crusades?** *(to take back control of Christian holy sites in the Middle East from Muslims)* **AL**

C Critical Thinking Skills

Determining Cause and Effect Point out that all of the effects of the Crusades were not directly associated with religious objectives. **Ask: How did the Crusades influence trade?** *(While in the Middle East, Europeans met Arab merchants who sold them spices, sugar, silk, and other goods from China and India.)* Explain to students that this interest grew even stronger after Marco Polo returned from China. **Ask: How would Marco Polo's return spark interest in goods from China?** *(Possible answer: Marco Polo's book probably included a lot of detail about the amazing goods he saw in China. His descriptions of the riches were enticing.)*

---

netw**rks**
There's More Online!

☑ **GRAPHIC ORGANIZER**
Technological Advances

☑ **MAP**
• Trade Routes to Asia
• West African Trading Kingdoms

☑ **SLIDE SHOW** Mansa Musa

Lesson 1
A Changing World

ESSENTIAL QUESTION *How do new ideas change the way people live?*

IT MATTERS BECAUSE
Europe was aware of the riches of Asia and Africa. Attempts to increase trade with these lands eventually developed into an era of European exploration that reached far beyond Europe's borders.

New Ideas, New Nations

GUIDING QUESTION *Where did the Renaissance take place?*

For centuries after the Roman Empire fell in A.D. 476, the people of Western Europe were cut off from the rest of the world. Western Europe was made up of small kingdoms and city-states dominated by the Catholic Church. Then, in the early A.D. 600s, a new religion, Islam, began to spread rapidly in the Middle East and Africa. This rise of Islam would soon end Western Europe's isolation.

R In 1095 the Europeans launched the first of nine expeditions, known as the **Crusades.** Their purpose was to take back control of Christian holy sites in the Middle East from the Muslims— followers of Islam. The Crusades also had an unplanned result. In the Middle East, Europeans met Arab merchants, who sold them spices, sugar, silk, and other goods from China and India. European interest in Asia grew.

C That interest grew even more after Italian explorer Marco Polo returned from China. In the late 1200s, Polo wrote about Asia's people, great riches, and splendid cities in his book, *Travels*, which was widely read in Europe. Two hundred years later, his *Travels* would inspire another Italian explorer— Christopher Columbus.

(l) Photographer's Choice RF/Getty Images, (cl, cr) SSPL via Getty Images, (c) Stephane De Sakutin/Stringer/AFP/Getty Images, (r) C squared Studios/ Photodisc/ Getty Images

Reading HELPDESK **CCSS**

Taking Notes: *Identifying* RH.6–8.1, RH.6–8.7
As you read, use a diagram like this one to identify the advances in technology that paved the way for European voyages of exploration.

Technological Advances

Content Vocabulary (Tier 3 Words)
• Crusade   • technology   • pilgrimage
• classical   • astrolabe   • mosque
• Renaissance • compass

28 *Exploring the Americas*

---

netw**rks** *Online Teaching Options*

VIDEO

Leonardo da Vinci

Expressing Ask students if they have ever heard the term "Renaissance man." Invite them to speculate on what qualities such a person would have. Then play the video about Leonardo da Vinci. Afterwards, explain to students that a "Renaissance man" is a person, like da Vinci, who had many different interests. Organize students into small groups, and direct each group to write a paragraph, prepare a brief speech, or otherwise express how the spirit of the Renaissance helped set the stage for an age of exploration.

See page 25C for other online activities.

ANSWER, p. 28

TAKING NOTES: printing press (provided more people with access to information), more accurate maps, better navigational tools (astrolabe, magnetic compass), improved ship design

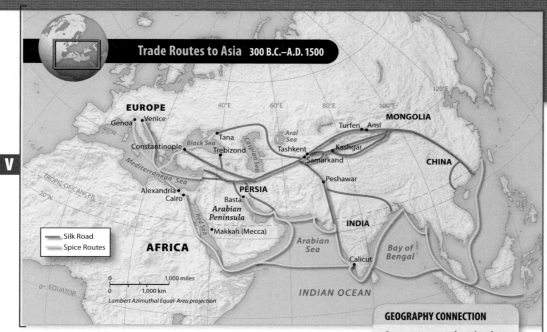

Trade Routes to Asia 300 B.C.–A.D. 1500

EUROPE
Genoa • Venice
Constantinople • Tana
Trebizond
Black Sea
Tashkent
Samarkand
Aral Sea
Kashgar
Turfen Ansi
MONGOLIA
CHINA
Peshawar
Alexandria •
Cairo
Basta
Arabian Peninsula
• Makkah (Mecca)
PERSIA
INDIA
Red Sea
Calicut
Arabian Sea
Bay of Bengal
AFRICA
INDIAN OCEAN
TROPIC OF CANCER
Mediterranean Sea
Caspian Sea
EQUATOR

— Silk Road
— Spice Routes

0   1,000 miles
0   1,000 km
Lambert Azimuthal Equal-Area projection

The Growth of Trade

Merchants in Europe knew they could make a lot of money selling goods from Asia. Wealthy Europeans were eager to buy Asian spices, perfumes, silks, and precious stones.

Merchants first bought these goods from Arab traders in the Middle East. The merchants then sent the goods overland by caravan to the Mediterranean Sea. From there, the goods traveled by ship to Italian ports in Venice, Genoa, and Pisa. These cities prospered as centers of the growing trade. However, Arab traders charged high prices. This led Europeans to look for a route to the East that would not require them to buy from Arab merchants.

The Growth of Ideas

By the 1300s, several Italian city-states had become strong economic and cultural centers. Their influence spread across Europe. Newly powerful bankers and merchants in Pisa, Venice, and Genoa studied **classical** works—those of ancient Greece and Rome.

Science was another area in which change occurred. Many scholars tested new and old theories of science. They performed experiments and evaluated the results.

GEOGRAPHY CONNECTION

Caravans, or groups of travelers, from Asia carried silks and spices overland to markets in the West. At the shores of the Mediterranean and Black Seas, the goods were loaded onto ships and transported to Europe.

1 LOCATION How would you describe the location of Genoa and Venice?

2 CRITICAL THINKING
Making Connections Based on the information on this map, why do you think European traders charged high prices for silks and spices?

Crusade one of a series of expeditions Europeans made to regain control of Christian holy sites in the Middle East from the A.D. 1000s to the 1200s
classical related to the culture of ancient Greece and Rome

Reading in the Content Area: *Understanding Visuals*

When a map shows a historical event or era, you will not always find present-day boundaries. Sometimes you can identify where things are taking place today by using natural features, such as bodies of water. Historical maps provide a sense of time and help us to understand which cities and countries existed hundreds of years ago and which still exist today.

Lesson 1   **29**

V Visual Skills

Analyzing Maps Point to the map of trade routes to Asia. Have students trace the overland routes that were used to carry Asian goods to Europe. Discuss the growth of trade between Europe and Asia. **Ask:**

• **About how far is the east coast of China from Genoa and Venice?** *(roughly 4,000 miles)*

• **What do you think the long, difficult journey meant for the price and availability of Asian goods in Europe?** *(They were expensive and rare.)*

• **Why did Europeans want to find a sea route?** *(It would take less time to get the items from Asia.)*

R Reading Skills

Explaining After students have read the sections on the growth of trade and ideas, discuss with them how trade involved not only the exchange of goods, but also led to the sharing of ideas. **Ask: How did trade foster new ideas among different peoples and groups?** *(Possible answer: It led to cultural interaction, not just economic. Trade brought people from different parts of the world to the same ports or trade centers where they could share new ideas and inventions, as well as exchange trade goods.)* **BL**

Content Background Knowledge

• The Silk Road was so called because of the large amounts of silk produced in China that traders carried along the route. Most traders traveled in camel caravans.

• The Silk Road was about 4,000 miles long—close to one-fifth the distance around the Earth at the equator. However, it was not one continuous route. It was a series of routes that were collectively called the "Silk Road."

• Trade along the Silk Road thrived from about A.D. 100 to A.D. 1500.

MAP

Trade Routes to Asia, 300 B.C. to A.D. 1500

Researching Ask students to identify the trade routes on the map and describe their paths on land and water. Point out that the spice routes were largely sea routes, but to connect Europe and Asia a land route was necessary in northeastern Africa along the Red Sea. Ask students to work with a partner and research what modern technology was used to connect the Red Sea and the Mediterranean. Ask them to locate the answer to this research question on the map and then to explain what route it shortened. *(Students should point to the Suez Canal and explain that it vastly shortened the sea route around Africa that the European explorers pioneered.)*

See page 25C for other online activities.

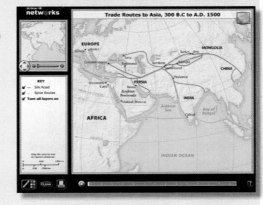

ANSWERS, p. 29

GEOGRAPHY CONNECTION

1 They are located on the coast, on either side of the Italian peninsula.

2 CRITICAL THINKING Possible answer: They had to bring these goods from very far away; they had to carry the goods over land and then transfer them onto ships.

A Changing World

R1 Reading Skills

Summarizing After students have read the text, point out that in the 1400s and 1500s, Europe was going through a period known as the *Renaissance*. Write *rebirth* on the board. Have students write a sentence to explain its meaning. **Ask: What does rebirth have to do with the Renaissance?** *(There was a rebirth of interest in classical learning and in discovering new things.)*

Point out that at this time, too, powerful nations emerged in Europe. Have students name some of these nations. Explore students' knowledge of the politics and cultures of these powerful nations. **Ask: What resulted from the development of powerful nations?** *(Answers may include the establishment of armies, national laws, courts, taxes, and the expansion of trade.)* **BL**

C Critical Thinking Skills

Making Connections Point out to students that trade with Asian and Middle Eastern peoples also allowed for the exchange of cultural ideas. Explain that it also influenced science and art. **Ask: Do you think trade has the same impact today? Explain.** *(Possible answer: No, I think that trade does not have the same influence today because we live in a hi-tech world in which we often learn about new things and ideas on the Internet or through social media. Also, because of economic agreements, trade is limited among some countries but encouraged among others.)*

R2 Reading Skills

Defining Have a volunteer read the text. Then review the meaning of *technology*. **ELL** Discuss the introduction of the printing press as an important piece of technology. **Ask: Why was the printing press important to the Age of Exploration?** *(The printing press made it easier to print books and more people had access to information. People read Polo's book and it encouraged them to travel.)* **AL**

The Mona Lisa, painted by Leonardo da Vinci, is a masterpiece of the Renaissance. From what we know, the portrait features a woman from Florence who was 24 years old when da Vinci began the painting.

The arts were also influenced by classical forms and new ideas. Authors wrote about the individual's place in the universe. Artists studied classical sculpture and architecture. They admired the harmony and balance in Greek art. **C**

The Renaissance

This period of intellectual and artistic creativity is known as the **Renaissance** (reh•nuh•SAHNTS). The word *renaissance* means "rebirth" in French. It refers to the rebirth of interest in classical Greek and Roman ideas. As the Renaissance spread across Europe over the next two centuries, it changed the way Europeans thought about themselves and the world. It also set the stage for an age of exploration and discovery.

The Rise of Powerful Nations

For centuries, Europe had been a patchwork of small states. By the 1400s, however, a new, larger type of state had developed in Western Europe. Strong monarchs rose to power in Spain, Portugal, England, and France. They began to establish national laws, courts, taxes, and armies to replace those of the local rulers. These ambitious monarchs sought ways to increase trade and make their countries even stronger and wealthier. **R1**

As early as the mid-1400s, powerful countries such as Portugal and Spain began to search for sea routes to Asia. They, too, wanted to engage in foreign trade. This placed them in direct competition with the Italian port cities that had become so powerful a century earlier. As a result, a new era of exploration began.

☑ **PROGRESS CHECK**

Drawing Conclusions In what way did trade help to bring about the Renaissance?

The Effects of New Technology

GUIDING QUESTION *What technological advancements paved the way for European voyages of exploration?*

Advances in **technology**—the use of scientific knowledge for practical purposes—helped to make European voyages of exploration possible. In the 1450s, the introduction of the printing press made it much easier to print books. More people had access to books and to new information. Many Europeans read Marco **R2**

Reading HELPDESK CCSS

Renaissance a reawakening of culture and intellectual curiosity in Europe from the 1300s to the 1600s
technology the use of scientific knowledge for practical purposes

astrolabe an instrument used to plan a course, using the stars
compass an instrument that shows the direction of magnetic north

netw⊚rks · *Online Teaching Options*

GRAPHIC ORGANIZER

Taking Notes: *Identifying:* Technological Advances

Identifying Have students work in pairs to complete the interactive graphic organizer and identify the advances in technology that paved the way for European voyages of exploration. Ask students to share their graphic organizers with another pair of students to compare their answers.

See page 25C for other online activities.

ANSWER, p. 30

☑ **PROGRESS CHECK** The merchants in Pisa, Venice, and Genoa became wealthy, and the city-states became wealthy, too. With their riches came influence, so when they decided to improve their knowledge of the ancient world, those ideas spread.

AIDS TO NAVIGATION

Compass

Astrolabe

Quadrant

With the compass, sailors could tell which direction they were sailing. The astrolabe and quadrant (QWAH • druhnt) allowed sailors to measure the angle of a star to the horizon, which helped them find their location on the sea.

INFOGRAPHIC

1 DRAWING CONCLUSIONS Explain how the compass, astrolabe, and quadrant could make a long ocean voyage possible.

W

2 CRITICAL THINKING *Making Connections* What tools might sailors use to find their position at sea today?

Polo's *Travels* when it appeared in printed form in 1477. This book gave people descriptions of faraway places, such as modern-day areas of Iraq, Siberia, Japan, India, Ethiopia, and Madagascar. Whether the descriptions were entirely accurate is open to debate. However, Polo's *Travels* led European readers to realize that there were many spectacular sights beyond their immediate world.

Better Maps and Instruments

Most early maps were not accurate. This was because they were drawn based on the points of view of traders and travelers. Little by little, cartographers, or mapmakers, improved their accuracy. Using reports of explorers and information from Arab and Chinese scholars and astronomers, mapmakers made more accurate land and sea maps. These maps showed the directions of ocean currents. They also showed lines of latitude, which measured the distance north and south of the Equator.

People also improved instruments for navigating the seas. Sailors could find their latitude with an **astrolabe** (AS•truh•layb), which measured the positions of stars. In the 1200s, Europeans **acquired** the magnetic **compass** from China. The compass allowed sailors to accurately determine their direction.

C

Better Ship Design

Advances in ship design allowed sailors to make long ocean voyages. The stern rudder and triangular sail enabled ships to sail into the wind. The Portuguese three-masted caravel (KER• uh•vehl) became the most famous ship of the European age of exploration. Caravels could sail faster and carry more cargo and supplies than earlier ships. These advances and competition for foreign trade led countries such as Portugal and Spain to search for sea routes to Asia. Portugal began its explorations along the west coast of Africa, an area Europeans had never visited before.

R

☑ PROGRESS CHECK

Determining Cause and Effect How did the caravel affect exploration in a positive way?

Lesson 1 **31**

W Writing Skills

Narrative Review with students how the reports of travelers such as Marco Polo made Europeans aware of the riches in Asia. Research and read excerpts of Polo's book, *Travels*, to students to discuss how these reports could be influential. **Ask:** What did Europeans do with this knowledge? *(They searched for ways to obtain these riches.)*

Have students write a story from the perspective of Marco Polo on his travels to Asia based on his book, *Travels*. Remind them to use vivid verbs and dialogue to make their narratives interesting. Point out that using good transitions will help their narratives flow from one event to the next. Invite students to share their narratives with the class. **AL** Verbal/Linguistic

C Critical Thinking Skills

Drawing Conclusions Have students work in small groups to make their own compasses. Provide each group with a straightened paper clip, the bottom of a foam cup, a bar magnet, and a shallow pan filled with water. Demonstrate how to magnetize the paper clip by stroking it in the same direction 25 times. Have students place the paper clip flat across the floating foam cup. The clip will rotate until it points north. Suggest that students slowly rotate the pan and observe what happens. **Ask:** How would such a device aid in navigation? *(If you know which direction is north, you can determine all the other directions.)* Kinesthetic

R Reading Skills

Summarizing Point out to students the heading "Better Ship Design," and ask them to read the section aloud to a partner. Have the partner who is listening take notes. **Ask:** What new kind of ship was developed at this time? *(the caravel)* What was better about the caravel? *(Caravels could sail faster and carry more cargo and supplies than earlier ships. They could float in shallow water, so sailors could explore inlets and sail their ships up to the beach for repairs.)*

The Compass

Comparing Use the interactive slide show to help students understand what a compass is and how it works. **AL** **ELL** **Ask:** How does a compass help sailors at sea? *(A compass points out magnetic north, which allows sailors to determine their direction at sea.)* Pause at slide 2 and discuss the Earth's magnetic field and how it interacts with the compass. **BL** Review slides 1, 3, and 5 about the different types of compasses. **Ask:** How is the compass in slide 1 similar to the one in slide 5? How is it different? *(Students' responses should be based on the images.)* **AL** **ELL**

See page 25C for other online activities.

McGraw-Hill netw❂rks™   The Compass

Navigators discovered something unusual in the 1100s. They found that when a small magnetic needle was suspended freely, it would always point north. They used this knowledge to create the first compasses.

SSPL via Getty Images

ANSWERS, p. 31

INFOGRAPHIC
1. The compass allowed sailors to know what direction they were sailing even when they were out of sight of land; the astrolabe and quadrant made it possible for sailors to know their location while out of sight of land.
2. **CRITICAL THINKING** Answers might include radar, radio, satellite communications, computers, GPS navigation systems, and cell phones, as well as compasses and modern quadrants.

☑ **PROGRESS CHECK** The caravel made ship travel much easier: It could sail faster and hold more cargo and supplies. Because it could float in shallow water, sailors (and explorers) could get very close to land without having to leave the ship.

V Visual Skills

Analyzing Maps Focus students' attention on the map of West African Trading Kingdoms. Have students identify the absolute and relative locations of the three kingdoms on the map. **Ask:**

- **What geographic feature lay between these empires and their North African trading partners?** *(the Sahara)*
- **What does the map show you about Timbuktu?** *(It is a place where many trade routes cross.)*
- **How did this affect the culture of Timbuktu?** *(Possible answers: It was a center of learning; trade with North Africa led people there to adopt Islamic ideas and customs.)*

After students have studied the map on this page, have them turn back a few pages and review the map of the trade routes of Asia. **Ask: How are the trade routes in Asia and Africa similar and different?** *(Possible answer: The trade routes in Asia are more spread out and cover longer distances, from east to west. The trade routes in Africa are concentrated in the north and west, and are closer together.)* **Visual/Spatial**

C Critical Thinking Skills

Sequencing Have students work in small groups to create sequencing charts that trace the rise and fall of the kingdoms of Ghana, Mali, and the Songhai Empire. Students should include how long each kingdom or empire existed, what it traded, and what happened to it. **BL Logical/Mathematical**

GEOGRAPHY CONNECTION

Trade routes across Earth's largest desert, the Sahara, provided West African kingdoms with access to the Mediterranean coast.

1 LOCATION What West African kingdom extended the farthest west?

2 CRITICAL THINKING
Draw Conclusions Other than the information on trade routes, what key historic information does the map show?

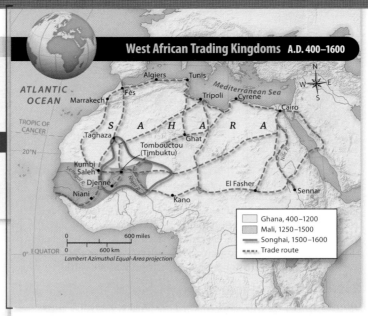

West African Trading Kingdoms A.D. 400–1600

Ghana, 400–1200
Mali, 1250–1500
Songhai, 1500–1600
Trade route

Kingdoms and Empires in Africa

GUIDING QUESTION *What were the most powerful empires in Africa?*

Between A.D. 400 and 1600, powerful kingdoms and city-states flourished in Africa south of the Sahara. Much of their power and wealth came from mining and trade.

Arab traders traveled Africa's east coast exchanging cotton, silk, and porcelain for African ivory and metals. West Africans mined and traded gold, copper, and iron ore. Trade with North Africa's Islamic societies brought wealth and Islamic customs to the West African kingdoms. The kingdoms also traded directly with Europe. The Portuguese set up trading posts along Africa's western coast in the mid-1400s.

Ghana—A Trading Empire

Between A.D. 400 and 1100, a vast trading empire known as Ghana emerged in West Africa. Ghana grew wealthy from the taxes it placed on trade. Caravans carrying gold, ivory, and enslaved people crossed the desert to North Africa and returned with salt, cloth, and brass. Such trading contacts led many West Africans to become Muslim.

Reading **HELP**DESK CCSS

pilgrimage a journey to a holy place
mosque a Muslim house of worship

Academic Vocabulary (Tier 2 Words)

acquire to get possession or control of

---

netw⊙rks *Online Teaching Options*

WORKSHEET

Geography and History Activity: Exploring the Americas, A Changing World

Analyzing Have student pairs take turns reading paragraphs from "Cultural Diffusion: Kingdoms and Empires in Africa." If students need help interpreting the map, direct them to the color version shown in their textbooks. Before pairs work together to complete the questions, ask: **With whom did these kingdoms conduct most of their trade?** *(cities in North Africa)* **What occurred as a result of this trading relationship?** *(Answers will vary but students should recognize that ideas were also exchanged, such as the principles of Islam.)* **BL**

See page 25C for other online activities.

ANSWERS, p. 32

GEOGRAPHY CONNECTION

1 Mali

2 CRITICAL THINKING It shows the location and size of three significant African trading kingdoms, as well as the location of their North African trading partners.

In 1076 North African people called Almoravids (al•muh•RAH•vihdz) attacked Ghana, disrupting the trade routes in the region. Soon new trade routes bypassed Ghana altogether. The drop in trade led to Ghana's decline, and new kingdoms emerged in the region.

Mali—Wealth and Power

Mali, one of the new kingdoms, grew very powerful. Mali developed trade routes across the desert to North Africa. By the late 1200s, Mali's territory was huge. One traveler reported that it took four months to cross it from north to south.

In 1324 Mali's great king, Mansa Musa, a Muslim, traveled to the Muslim holy city of Makkah (Mecca) in what is now Saudi Arabia. He returned from this religious journey, or **pilgrimage** (PIHL•gruh•mihj), with an Arab architect. The architect built great **mosques** (MAHSKS), Muslim houses of worship, in Timbuktu, Mali's capital. Timbuktu became a center of Islamic art and learning.

The Songhai Empire

In time, the Songhai (sawng•GEYE) people, who lived along the Niger River, overthrew Mali rule. They captured Timbuktu in 1468. Askiya Muhammad, leader of the Songhai Empire, divided Songhai into provinces, each with its own officials. Everyone in the empire followed a legal system based on the teachings of Islam. In the late 1500s, North Africa's kingdom of Morocco defeated—and ended—the Songhai Empire.

☑ **PROGRESS CHECK**

Drawing Conclusions What did the Middle East and Africa have that Europeans wanted?

R

Gold was one of the valuable trade items that helped enrich the great trading empires of West Africa.

R Reading Skills

Using Context Clues As students read the paragraph, point out the word *pilgrimage*. Ask them what root word they recognize in this term. *(pilgrim)* Explain that a pilgrim is a person who goes on a journey, often one of a religious nature. **Ask: Why would the journey that Mansa Musa undertook to Makkah be considered a pilgrimage?** *(It was a journey to a sacred place.)* **Why might the word pilgrim be used to describe the settlers that came to the Massachusetts Colony in 1620?** *(They were travelers who were on a type of religious journey to escape religious persecution in Europe.)* **BL** Verbal/Linguistic

Have students complete the Lesson 1 Review.

CLOSE & REFLECT

To close the lesson, ask students to think about the changes that resulted from trade in Europe, Asia, and Africa. Have them write one or two sentences to explain what they think was the most important change. Invite volunteers to share and defend their answers. Verbal/Linguistic

---

LESSON 1 REVIEW (CCSS)

Review Vocabulary (Tier 3 Words)

1. Examine the two terms that follow. Then write a sentence based on what you have read that explains the connection between the terms. RH.6–8.4

   a. astrolabe   b. technology

2. Write a sentence about the classical ideas that were rediscovered during the Renaissance. RH.6–8.4

Answer the Guiding Questions

3. ***Explaining*** How did the rise of Italian city-states help lead to the Renaissance? RH.6–8.2

4. ***Identifying*** How did new technology pave the way for European voyages of exploration? RH.6–8.2

5. ***Listing*** What were the three most powerful empires in West Africa between the 400s and 1500s? RH.6–8.1

6. **ARGUMENT** Which of the following do you think was the most important innovation, and why?
   • the compass
   • improved maps
   • the printing press
   WHST.6–8.1, WHST.6–8.9

Lesson 1   **33**

LESSON 1 REVIEW ANSWERS

1. Possible answer: The astrolabe was an example of new technology that allowed better navigation on the oceans.

2. Possible answer: During the Renaissance, Europeans rediscovered the classical teachings of ancient Greece and Rome, which influenced art, science, literature, and thought.

3. The Renaissance began in the Italian city-states of Venice, Genoa, and Pisa, and spread throughout Europe.

4. Better maps; navigation aids such as the astrolabe, quadrant, and compass; and improved ship design, especially the caravel, enabled ships to sail longer distances and to navigate effectively even when out of sight of land.

5. Ghana, Mali, Songhai

6. Students' essays should argue that one innovation was most important and use details and facts from the lesson to support that choice.

ANSWER, p. 33

☑ **PROGRESS CHECK** Possible answer: The African kingdoms had salt, gold, and other metals to trade. Both Africa and the Middle East had easier access to Asian goods, such as silk and spices.

C squared Studios/ Photodisc/ Getty Images

ENGAGE

🔔 **Bellringer** To help students understand how intrepid and motivated the explorers and their crews were, draw a parallel between the voyages of early explorers and possible future planetary exploration. **Ask: What kinds of equipment would you need?** *(Answers may vary but should suggest equipment that they could use to determine speed, distance, and time.)* **What are the risks of such a voyage?** *(no easy landmarks, no way to survive outside a space capsule, no way to travel to safety if something goes wrong)* Remind students that at the time of the first European ocean explorations, there were no ways to track ships or communicate with sailors. Discuss with students what it must have been like to travel into a situation that was truly unknown. **Ask: What would make people want to make such a voyage anyway?** *(Exploration of oceans was for curiosity, finding resources and wealth, and claiming land for the explorer's country or supporters, possibly for colonization. Exploration of planets would be for exactly the same reasons.)*

TEACH & ASSESS

C Critical Thinking Skills

Speculating Point out to students that explorers had different reasons for exploring and had only limited knowledge of the world. Mapmaking and knowledge of the geography around the globe was also limited. **Ask: What did Columbus expect to find on the other side of the Atlantic Ocean?** *(Answers may include Asia, India, the Indies, riches, and spices.)*

V Visual Skills

Creating Maps Remind students that early European explorers did not know about the Americas at the time Columbus sailed west. Have them draw a map of the oceans and Europe, Asia, and Africa known at that time. *(The map may show one huge landmass—Europe, Asia, and Africa—bordered by the Western and Eastern Oceans.)* **BL** Visual/Spatial

---

ANSWER, p. 34

TAKING NOTES: Portugal: Bartolomeu Dias, Vasco da Gama, Pedro Álvares Cabral, Amerigo Vespucci; **Spain:** Columbus, Vasco Núñez de Balboa, Ferdinand Magellan, Amerigo Vespucci

---

netw🌐rks
There's More Online!

☑ **BIOGRAPHY**
• Vasco da Gama
• Queen Isabella
• Christopher Columbus

☑ **GRAPHIC ORGANIZER**
Explorers and Their Sponsors

☑ **MAP** Early Portuguese Exploration

☑ **PRIMARY SOURCE**
Vasco da Gama

☑ **VIDEO**

Lesson 2
Early Exploration

ESSENTIAL QUESTION *Why do people trade?*

IT MATTERS BECAUSE
The arrival of the Europeans in the Americas in the fifteenth century changed the lives of people in both the Americas and Europe forever.

The Search for New Trade Routes

GUIDING QUESTION *Which country took the lead in finding a trade route to India?*

C

In 1492 Christopher Columbus led 90 sailors in three ships on a voyage into the unknown. As the voyage dragged on, the sailors grew angry. Columbus wrote: "I am told ... that if I persist in going onward, the best course of action will be to throw me into the sea some night." Before that could happen, a lookout from the ship *Pinta* made the signal that he had spotted land. On October 12, 1492, Columbus left his ship, the *Santa María*, and went ashore.

V

Columbus believed he had arrived in the Indies—islands located southeast of China. Actually, he had reached North America. How did Columbus get it so wrong? The maps that he and other European explorers used at the time did not include the Americas because no one in Europe knew they existed. All maps showed three continents—Europe, Asia, and Africa—merged into a huge landmass and bordered by oceans. Some explorers thought that the Western (Atlantic) and Eastern (Pacific) Oceans ran together to form what they called the "Ocean Sea." No one realized the true size of the oceans or the existence of other continents.

(l) Keystone/Stringer/Hulton Archive/Getty Images; (c) Gianni Dagli/The Art Archive at Art Resource, NY; (cr) Bridgeman-Giraudon/Art Resource, NY; (r) North Wind Picture Archive /North Wind Picture Archives

Reading **HELP**DESK (CCSS)

Taking Notes: *Identifying* RH.6–8.1, RH.6–8.7

As you study the lesson, use a diagram such as this one to identify the explorers who were sponsored by Portugal and those who were sponsored by Spain.

```
            Explorers
           /         \
  Sponsored by    Sponsored by
   Portugal          Spain
```

Content Vocabulary (Tier 3 Words)
• cape
• circumnavigate

34 *Exploring the Americas*

---

netw🌐rks *Online Teaching Options*

VIDEO

Journey to the New World: Christopher Columbus

Finding the Main Idea Play the video "Journey to the New World: Christopher Columbus" for students. Tell students that historians sometimes organize history into "pre-contact" era (before the Old World— Europe—came into ongoing contact with the New World—the Americas) and a "post-contact" era (after ongoing contact was established). Challenge students to write a sentence that succinctly states why Columbus's voyages were such a pivotal point in human history.

See page 25D for other online activities.

Columbus was sailing on behalf of Spain, but Portugal was the first European power to explore the boundaries of the known world by sea. Unlike Spain, Portugal did not have a port on the Mediterranean Sea. This meant the Portuguese could not use the existing trade routes between Asia and Europe. Portugal's rulers wanted to find a new route to China and India.

The Portuguese also knew about the great riches in the West African kingdoms. These riches were carried by caravan across the desert to North Africa and then by ship across the Mediterranean. Portuguese traders needed a better route so that they, too, could get West African gold and other riches.

C

The Beginning of Portuguese Exploration

Portugal's Prince Henry laid the groundwork for the era of exploration. In about 1420, he set up a center for exploration at Sagres (SAW•grish), on the southwestern tip of Portugal, "where endeth land and where beginneth sea."

Known as Henry the Navigator, the prince never intended to become an explorer himself. Instead, he planned the voyages and then analyzed the reports that his crews brought home. At Sagres, Prince Henry set up a school of navigation. There, astronomers, geographers, and mathematicians came to share their knowledge with Portuguese sailors, shipbuilders, and mapmakers. As each successful voyage brought back new information, Henry's expert mapmakers updated the charts.

R

Portuguese ships sailed south along the coast of West Africa. As they went south, they traded for gold and ivory and set up trading posts in the region. Because of its abundance of gold, Africa's west coast came to be known as the "Gold Coast." In the mid-1400s, Portuguese traders began to buy enslaved Africans there as well.

King John II of Portugal launched new efforts to create a Portuguese trading empire in Asia. All the Portuguese had to do was find a sea route around Africa. If they succeeded, they would be able to trade directly with India and China. They could bypass the North African and Asian caravans and Mediterranean merchants. With that goal in mind, in the 1480s King John urged Portuguese sea captains to explore farther south along the African coast.

The *Santa María* was a sturdy vessel built to survive a long ocean voyage.

▶ **CRITICAL THINKING**
Making Inferences What traits would make a person a good crew member on the *Santa María*?

Reading Strategy: *Reading in the Content Area*

Answers to the questions "What happened?" and "Why did it happen?" fill the pages of history books. Look for the answers to these questions as you read. It can help your understanding of history to think of the situations you encounter as a series of cause-and-effect relationships.

See page 25D for other online activities.

C **Critical Thinking Skills**

Identifying Central Issues Discuss with students that even though Columbus was sailing on behalf of Spain, Portugal was the first European power to explore the boundaries of the world by sea. **Ask: Why did Portugal want to find a new route to China and India?** *(They did not have access to a port on the Mediterranean Sea and could not use existing trade routes.)* **AL** **Why did the Portuguese not want to travel overland to Asia?** *(They wanted to bypass Arab merchants because they charged high prices. They also knew it took too long.)* **BL**

R **Reading Skills**

Identifying After students have read about Portuguese exploration, **ask: Who was Henry the Navigator?** *(a Portuguese prince who promoted exploration by setting up a school of navigation)* **What did sailors learn at Henry the Navigator's school?** *(information about astronomy, geography, mathematics, cartography, and navigation)* **How did the Portuguese decide to try to reach Asia?** *(by sailing around Africa)*

Content Background Knowledge

Henry the Navigator's expeditions were not very successful as a whole. Even his hopes to spread Christianity among the people he encountered in West Africa did not pan out. What he is most remembered for, however, is lighting a spark that contributed to the birth of the era of European exploration. The era of European exploration produced a wealth of discovery and global interaction that changed the world.

GRAPHIC ORGANIZER

Taking Notes: *Identifying:* Explorers

Identifying As students read about each Portuguese and Spanish explorer in their textbook, encourage them to use the interactive graphic organizer to record the explorers sponsored by each country. Challenge students to come up with mnemonic devices to help them associate each explorer with the country who sponsored him. **Auditory/Musical**

McGraw-Hill **networks**

Name: _____ Date: _____

TAKING NOTES: *Identifying*
ACTIVITY As you read, use the diagram to identify the explorers who were sponsored by Portugal and Spain.

Explorers

Sponsored by Portugal   Sponsored by Spain

ANSWER, p. 35

CRITICAL THINKING Possible answers: courage, physical strength, stamina, desire for adventure, curiosity

Early Exploration

V Visual Skills

Visualizing Invite a volunteer to read aloud the second paragraph on this page ("They sailed for days. . . .") Point out that this brief paragraph is just a tiny summation of what was truly a harrowing story. The men in the ships, far from home, sailing along an exotic coast and then facing monstrous winds and waves, surely feared for their lives. Lead a class discussion in which you invite students to speculate what it was truly like for the sailors and what emotions they must have felt. Provide an opportunity for students to role-play what it was like for the sailors on the ship. **ELL**

T Technology Skills

Researching on the Internet Direct two or three students to conduct online research about the Cape of Good Hope today. What is there? What does it look like? How's the weather? Students should organize written information, maps, photographs, and other media onto a poster or Web page entitled "The Cape of Good Hope Today." **AL** Visual/Spatial

---

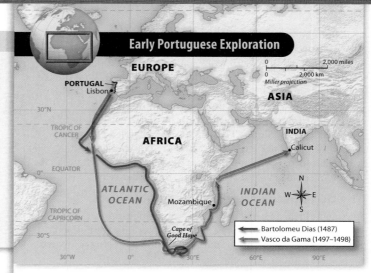

GEOGRAPHY CONNECTION

In order to reach Asia, ships from Europe had to sail south, all the way around Africa, and then north again to Asia.

1 **MOVEMENT** Study the map. Trace da Gama's route with your finger. Then describe where it began, the oceans through which it passed, and where it ended.

2 **CRITICAL THINKING** *Speculating* What can you conclude from the fact that Bartolomeu Dias's route hugged the coast of Africa and Vasco da Gama's route did not?

Early Portuguese Exploration

→ Bartolomeu Dias (1487)
→ Vasco da Gama (1497–1498)

Bartolomeu Dias

In 1487 Bartolomeu Dias set out from Lisbon with two small caravels and a supply ship. King John had sent Dias to explore the southernmost part of Africa. From there, Dias was to sail northeast into the Indian Ocean. This expedition included some of Portugal's best pilots.

They sailed for days, staying close to the coast of Africa. After passing the mouth of the Orange River in South Africa, the expedition met with a fierce storm that carried it southward, off course, and out of sight of land. When the winds finally died down, Dias steered east and then north until he found land again. Excitedly, Dias realized that he had already sailed past the southernmost part of Africa. On the way, he had passed a landform called a **cape,** a piece of land that juts into the water.

Dias set a course back to Portugal. On the return journey, after passing that piece of land again, he wrote that he had been around the "Cape of Storms." King John renamed it the "Cape of Good Hope." The king hoped that the passage around Africa might provide a new route to India.

Vasco da Gama

Portugal's voyages to India began years later. In July 1497, after much preparation, Vasco da Gama set sail from Portugal with four ships, headed for Africa. Da Gama's ships did not hug the

Reading HELPDESK (CCSS)

cape a point of land that sticks out into water, much like a peninsula

Word Origins: *Changing Meanings*
The word *pilot* used to mean *navigator.* What does it mean today?

---

networks   *Online Teaching Options*

MAP

Early Portuguese Exploration

Analyzing Maps Display the interactive map about early Portuguese exploration. Have students identify the Cape of Good Hope. **Ask:** **What dangers did Dias encounter there?** *(fierce storm, wind)* Use the map to display and discuss the routes of Bartolomeu Dias and Vasco da Gama. Point out the different routes the explorers followed in the southeast Atlantic Ocean. **How did they differ?** *(Dias's route followed the coast of Africa; da Gama's traveled the open ocean.)* **What accounts for these differences?** *(Da Gama was seeking ocean currents he hoped would help him round the Cape of Good Hope.)*

See page 25D for other online activities.

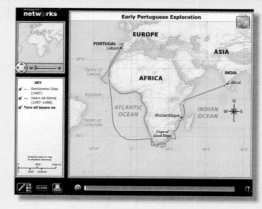

ANSWERS, p. 36

GEOGRAPHY CONNECTION

1 The route begins in Portugal and tracks southward through the Atlantic Ocean until about 30 degrees south of the Equator. Then it rounds the Cape of Good Hope in Africa, continues north until the Equator, and then heads sharply northeast until it reaches India.

2 **CRITICAL THINKING** Possible answer: Vasco da Gama's route suggests that he had navigation equipment that did not require him to stay within sight of land at all times.

Word Origins Possible answer: a person who flies a plane

African coast, as Dias's ships had. Instead, they sailed in a wide arc south and west of Africa. They were out of sight of land for more than three months. The purpose of this detour was to reach ocean currents that would help the sailors travel safely around the Cape of Good Hope.

After rounding the cape on November 22, da Gama was on Africa's eastern coast. He made many stops, including one at Mombasa (mahm•BAH•suh), part of present-day Kenya. There, he met a pilot from India who guided him the rest of the way. Da Gama reached the port of Calicut, in India, in May 1498. Portugal's long-held dream of a sea route to Asia was now reality.

Portugal's Trading Empire

Events moved quickly. Within six months of da Gama's return to Portugal, 13 ships set sail out of Lisbon and headed for India. The ships were commanded by a nobleman, Pedro Álvares Cabral (PEH•droo AWL•vuh ruhsh kuh•BRAWL).

Cabral planned to follow da Gama's westward-then-southward course. Instead, he went so far west that he reached Brazil. Cabral claimed Brazil for his king and sent one of the ships back to Portugal with the good news that Portugal now had a foothold in the Americas.

Cabral then continued to India and returned with spices, porcelain, and other valuable cargo. Other Portuguese fleets soon made the journey to India, where Portugal set up permanent forts. Portuguese fleets began to make yearly voyages to India. Their cargoes made the Portuguese capital of Lisbon the marketplace of Europe.

☑ **PROGRESS CHECK**

Analyzing What was the importance of the voyages of Dias and da Gama?

Columbus Crosses the Atlantic

GUIDING QUESTION *How did Spain and Portugal protect their claims in the Americas?*

Born in Genoa, Italy, in 1451, Christopher Columbus became a sailor for Portugal. He traveled as far north as the Arctic Circle and as far south as Africa's Gold Coast. To reach Asia, Christopher Columbus had a different route in mind than the one used by his Portuguese comrades. He planned to sail west.

In the 1400s, most educated people believed the world was round. People were less certain about the Earth's size. Columbus was among those who based their estimates on the works of Ptolemy (TAHL•uh•mee), an ancient Greek astronomer. Columbus believed Asia was about 2,760 miles (4,441 km) from Portugal—a voyage of about two months by ship. However, Ptolemy had underestimated Earth's size and, by using Ptolemy's estimate, Columbus did, too.

Keystone/Stringer/Hulton Archive/Getty Images

BIOGRAPHY

Vasco da Gama (c. 1460–1524)

Vasco da Gama, who was the son of a Portuguese noble, led two voyages of exploration for Portugal. During the second, he landed at Goa, which later became Portugal's base of power in India. In 1524 the king of Portugal made da Gama Portugal's viceroy, or governor, in India, and he returned to Goa.

C

▶ **CRITICAL THINKING**
Making Inferences Why do you think the king appointed Vasco da Gama his viceroy in India?

R1

R2

C Critical Thinking Skills

Contrasting Discuss with students how the routes followed by Pedro Alvares Cabral differed from those of Dias and da Gama. **Ask:**

- **Which direction did he travel in?** *(west)* **How far west did he go?** *(He went far enough to discover Brazil.)*
- **Where did he go after that?** *(He went on to India.)*
- **How did this impact Portugal?** *(The cargo from the trips to India made Lisbon, Portugal's capital, a marketplace of Europe.)*

R1 Reading Skills

Theorizing After students have read the text, have them identify each of the major Portuguese explorers (Dias, da Gama, Cabral) and identify their signature achievements (rounding the Cape of Good Hope, reaching India, claiming Brazil, respectively). **Ask: Which achievement do you think is the most important? Why?** *(Answers may vary but should be supported by facts from the lesson.)* **AL**

R2 Reading Skills

Assessing Refer students to the paragraph that begins "In the 1400s..." Underscore the importance of Ptolemy, an ancient Greek astronomer, to exploration in the 1400s. **Ask: How did Ptolemy affect Columbus's travels?** *(Columbus used Ptolemy's measurements, which were underestimated. This meant that Columbus's measurements were inaccurate.)*

Vasco da Gama

Paraphrasing Display the Vasco da Gama primary source excerpt. Have a volunteer read the journal entry from his voyage. Have students paraphrase the entry describing da Gama's journey around the Cape of Good Hope. **AL ELL**

See page 25D for other online activities.

networks — Vasco de Gama
ANALYZING PRIMARY SOURCES

Vasco da Gama rounded the Cape of Good Hope in November 1497. His journal of the event reveals that it was not an easy task.

❝ At daybreak of Thursday the 16th of November . . . we set sail. At that time we did not know how far we might be abaft [from] the Cape of Good Hope. . . . We therefore stood out towards S.S.W., and late on Saturday (November 18) we beheld the Cape. On that same day we again stood out to sea, returning to the land in ❞

—from *Round Africa to India*, in *The Library of Original Sources, Vol. V* by Vasco de Gama

Source: http://www.fordham.edu/halsall/mod/1497dagama.html

ANSWERS, p. 37

CRITICAL THINKING Possible answer: Vasco da Gama had experience with the place and people when he was there before.

☑ **PROGRESS CHECK** **Dias:** The king of Portugal sent him to sail around Africa to the Indian Ocean, and he became the first person to sail around the southern tip of Africa, the Cape of Good Hope, before returning to Europe.
Da Gama: In rounding the cape, he became the first European to sail out of sight of land for such a long time; he was the first European to sail up the east coast of Africa and the first Portuguese pilot to reach India by sea.

V Visual Skills

Simulating Discuss with students the technology of the caravel as depicted in the diagram. Point out that, although it was a remarkable piece of technology that changed history, students today would find such a ship remarkably small, especially for an ocean voyage. Explain that Christopher Columbus's flagship, the *Santa Maria*, was not a caravel. It was actually larger than the other two ships (both caravels) that accompanied it. Yet the *Santa Maria* was only about 117 feet long and 25 feet wide at its greatest width. If possible, use sidewalk chalk to draw a rough outline of the deck of the *Santa Maria* on an appropriate outdoor surface. Have students walk around the "deck" and discuss what the voyage must have been like on such a small ship in a vast, unknown ocean. **ELL** Visual/Spatial

R Reading Skills

Finding the Main Idea From the text, discuss with students the exploration of the Vikings, or Norsemen. Explain that after settling in Greenland for a brief time, they went on to explore lands west of Greenland and referred to this land as "Vinland." **Ask:**

- Where was Vinland located? *(northeastern Canada)*
- Why weren't the Vikings given credit for discovering America? *(They weren't well-known to other Europeans.)*

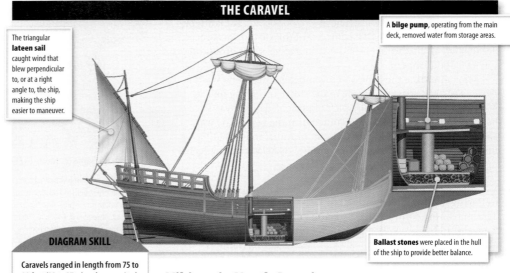

THE CARAVEL

The triangular **lateen sail** caught wind that blew perpendicular to, or at a right angle to, the ship, making the ship easier to maneuver.

A **bilge pump**, operating from the main deck, removed water from storage areas.

Ballast stones were placed in the hull of the ship to provide better balance.

DIAGRAM SKILL

Caravels ranged in length from 75 to 90 feet (23 to 27 m) and were suited for sailing along shallow coastlines.

▶ **CRITICAL THINKING**
Explaining How did the caravel's lateen sail help sailors?

Vikings in North America

Several centuries before the voyages of da Gama, Cabral, and Columbus, northern Europeans had sailed to North America. Known as Vikings, or Norsemen, their ships sailed from present-day Scandinavia to Iceland and Greenland in the 800s and 900s, and established settlements there for a brief period of time. According to Norse sagas, or traditional stories, a Viking sailor named Leif Eriksson explored lands west of Greenland in about the year 1000. The sagas refer to this land as "Vinland." Ruins from around that period exist in northeastern Canada, which could support the sagas. The Vikings' voyages were not well-known throughout Europe, however. Other Europeans did not "discover" the Americas until Columbus made his historic voyage.

Columbus and Queen Isabella

Columbus had a plan for reaching Asia, but he still needed money to finance his expedition. He visited European monarchs, looking for support. Finally, he found a sponsor in Spain.

For most of the 1400s, Spanish monarchs **devoted,** or committed, their energy to driving the Muslims out of Spain. Muslims had invaded Spain in the 700s, but their power had been declining for centuries. The last Muslim kingdom in Spain

Reading **HELP**DESK **CCSS**

Academic Vocabulary (Tier 2 Words)
devote to commit oneself or one's resources to something
alter to change

Reading Strategy: *Reading a Diagram*
Diagrams may include a cutaway view. This provides a view of the outside and part of the inside of an object at the same time.

38   *Exploring the Americas*

netw⊙rks   *Online Teaching Options*

CHART

Isabella of Spain

Identifying Use the chart about Queen Isabella of Spain to introduce her to students and to help them understand why she might have wanted to fund Columbus's voyages. **AL** Ask:

- What were two reasons Isabella wanted Columbus to sail across the ocean? *(If Spain found a sea route to Asia, Spain would become very wealthy. Columbus promised to bring Christianity to any lands he found.)*

See page 25D for other online activities.

netw⊙rks*   Isabella of Spain

Directions: Isabella of Spain was a remarkable woman who greatly influenced the course of history. Click each question mark below to learn more about her life.

Area of Influence	Event
Exploration	?
Human Rights	?
Religion	?
Education	?
The Arts	?

ANSWER, p. 38

DIAGRAM SKILL

CRITICAL THINKING With it, the ship was able to take advantage of wind even when it was blowing perpendicular to the direction the crew wanted to go.

fell in 1492. This freed Spain's monarchs to focus on other goals. The Spanish observed the seafaring and trading successes of neighboring Portugal with envy. They, too, wanted the riches of Asian trade.

King Ferdinand and Queen Isabella of Spain agreed to support Columbus's expedition for two reasons. One reason was that Columbus promised to bring Christianity to any lands he found. As a devout Catholic, this was important to Isabella. Another reason was that if he succeeded in finding a route to Asia, Spain would become wealthy from trade with that region. Queen Isabella promised Columbus a share of any riches gained from lands he discovered on his way to Asia.

Columbus's First Voyage

On August 3, 1492, Columbus set sail from Palos, Spain. He had two small ships, the *Niña* and the *Pinta*, and a larger one, the *Santa María*. Columbus was captain of the *Santa María*, his lead ship, or flagship. The three ships carried about 90 sailors and a six-month supply of food and water.

The small fleet stopped at the Canary Islands off the coast of West Africa for repairs and supplies. Columbus then began the difficult voyage westward across unknown and mysterious stretches of the Atlantic Ocean.

After a few weeks at sea, the sailors grew nervous about the distance they had traveled. Columbus refused to **alter** his course. Instead, he encouraged the crew by describing the riches he believed they would find. He urged them on, saying that, "with the help of our Lord" they would arrive in the Indies.

On October 12, 1492, at two o'clock in the morning, a lookout shouted, *"Tierra! Tierra!"* "Land! Land!" He had spotted a small island in the chain now called the Bahamas. Columbus went ashore, claimed the island for Spain, and named it "San Salvador." Although he did not know it, Columbus had reached the Americas.

Columbus believed he had arrived in the East Indies, the islands off the coast of Asia. This is why today we call the Caribbean Islands "the West Indies." It also explains why Columbus called the local people "Indians." He noted that the natives regarded the Europeans with wonder and often touched the crew members to find out "if they were flesh and bones like themselves."

When Columbus returned to Spain, Queen Isabella and the Spanish king, Ferdinand, received him with great honor. They made him Admiral of the Ocean Sea, and agreed to provide funds for his future voyages.

Lesson 2 **39**

Queen Isabella (1451–1504)

Queen Isabella was a Catholic of strong faith. She insisted Columbus treat Native Americans fairly and ordered him to release several enslaved Native Americans he brought to Spain. Isabella hoped to convert the Native Americans to Christianity. She also wanted their labor. She ordered that the Native Americans be forced "to work on . . . buildings, to mine and collect gold . . . and to work on . . . farms and crop fields."

C

Christopher Columbus (1451–1506)

Columbus proved himself to be a great navigator and sailor. He believed he would discover great riches and new lands. He also knew he could win rich rewards for himself. Columbus wrote in 1492: "Your Highnesses commanded me . . . [to] go to . . . India, and for this accorded me great rewards and ennobled me [raised me to the rank of nobility]."

V

▶ CRITICAL THINKING
Comparing and Contrasting How were the goals of Queen Isabella and Columbus similar and different?

C Critical Thinking Skills

Making Connections Challenge students to find information on this page about Columbus's first voyage that has a direct connection to life in the United States today. Guide them in identifying:

• the use of the term "Indians" for Native Americans and the use of the geographical term "the West Indies"
• the celebration of Columbus Day
• tens of millions of people of European descent living in the United States today

V Visual Skills

Reading a Map Invite a volunteer to find the absolute location of San Salvador, where Columbus landed on his first voyage, on a world map or a map of the Western Hemisphere, and indicate the location to the rest of the class. Have students describe the island's relative location. Point out that Columbus returned to Europe without realizing he was relatively close to the two giant continents of North and South America. **Visual/Spatial**

The Santa Maria

Analyzing Images Have students view the interactive image of the *Santa Maria* and the other two ships of Columbus's first voyage, the *Niña* and the *Pinta*. Point out that the ship in the photograph is a recreation of the *Santa Maria*. **Ask: What adjectives would you use to describe these famous vessels?** *(small, frail, cramped, and so on.)* **Are you surprised that not all three returned to Spain?** *(probably not, because the ships were frail and the voyage long and hazardous)* **Verbal/Linguistic**

See page 25D for other online activities.

McGraw-Hill **netw⊙rks** The Santa Maria

CORBIS

○ ○ ○ ○

ANSWER, p. 39

CRITICAL THINKING Both Isabella and Columbus were eager to discover new lands and acquire wealth. Queen Isabella hoped to convert the native people to Catholicism and to take advantage of their labor to achieve wealth for Spain. Columbus sought wealth and personal glory.

Early Exploration

V Visual Skills

Creating Time Lines Direct students to create a time line of Columbus's voyages. Have them use colored markers or clip art to illustrate it, using the general themes of old ships, navigational instruments, and the Spanish flag. **Ask: How many voyages did Columbus make?** *(four)* Check students' time lines for correct chronological order, scale, and appropriateness of illustrations. Columbus made four voyages for Spain: 1492, 1493, 1498, 1502. **AL Logical/ Mathematical**

G Critical Thinking Skills

Speculating Point out to students that Columbus had "found a part of the world unknown to Europeans." **Ask: How significant do you think Columbus's voyages to America were in the course of world history? Why?** *(Answers may vary but should acknowledge the historic importance of the meeting of the Old and New Worlds.)* Tell students that many historians consider Columbus's voyages, which led to further exploration and European colonization of much of the world, among the most important events in all of human history.

C₂ Critical Thinking Skills

Making Connections Challenge students to name the many groups of people to be significantly affected by the connecting of the Old and New Worlds. *(Answers will vary but should at least include Native Americans, affected by European encroachment; Africans, brought to the New World as slaves by Europeans; and Europeans, enriched by growing overseas empires.)* **BL**

European Voyages of Exploration 1492–1609

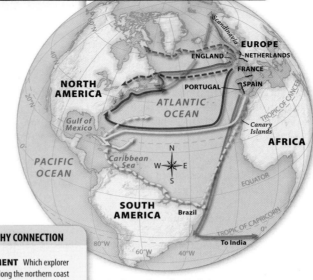

GEOGRAPHY CONNECTION

1 **MOVEMENT** Which explorer traveled along the northern coast of South America? For which country did he sail?

2 **CRITICAL THINKING**
Analyzing Visuals Study Cabral's route. Based on what you know about Portugal and the information in the map key, explain why his route is labeled, "To India."

Columbus's Achievements

V Columbus made three more voyages for Spain, in 1493, 1498, and 1502. He explored the Caribbean islands of Hispaniola (present-day Haiti and the Dominican Republic), Cuba, and Jamaica. He also sailed along the coasts of Central America and northern South America. He claimed these lands for Spain and started settlements. He also mapped the coastline of Central America.

C₁ Columbus had not reached Asia, but instead had found a part of the world that was unknown to Europeans, Asians, and Africans. In the years that followed, the Spanish went on **C₂** to explore most of the Caribbean, and to establish the Spanish Empire in the Americas.

Dividing the Americas

Both Spain and Portugal wanted to protect their claims in the Americas. They turned to Pope Alexander VI for help. In 1493 he ordered a line of demarcation, an imaginary line that reached from the North Pole to the South Pole, and cut through the middle of the Atlantic Ocean. Spain was to control all lands west of the line, and Portugal would control all lands east of the line.

Reading HELPDESK CCSS

circumnavigate to travel completely around something, usually by water

---

networks   *Online Teaching Options*

MAP

European Exploration 1487–1611

Analyzing Maps Have students view the map of European Exploration at least three times. Challenge them to write a sentence that best summarizes the meaning and message of the map. *(Example: "Just before, during, and after the 16th century, Europeans sent explorers to many parts of the world.")* **ELL**

See page 25D for other online activities.

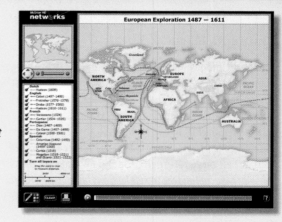

European Exploration 1487 — 1611

ANSWERS, p. 40

GEOGRAPHY CONNECTION

1 Amerigo Vespucci, who made two voyages, one for Spain and a later one for Portugal

2 **CRITICAL THINKING** A few years earlier, Portuguese explorer Vasco da Gama had successfully sailed around the southern tip of Africa to reach India. Cabral's goal was to reach India. He followed da Gama's route, but swung farther west—all the way to Brazil—before turning toward India.

Portugal objected, saying that the division gave more land to Spain. In 1494 the two countries signed an agreement called the Treaty of Tordesillas (tohr•day•SEE•yuhs), which moved the line farther west. The two countries had divided the entire unexplored world between themselves.

Further Explorations

After Columbus, other voyagers explored the Americas. In 1499 Italian Amerigo Vespucci (veh•SPOO•chee) led a voyage funded by Spain. On this and a later journey for Portugal, he explored the coast of South America. Vespucci realized South America was a separate continent, and not part of Asia. European geographers began to call the continent "America" in his honor.

A Spaniard, Vasco Núñez de Balboa (bal•BOH•uh), heard stories of the "great waters" beyond the mountains of Panama, in Central America. He hiked through steamy rain forests to find them. At the coast in 1513, Balboa saw a vast body of water, which he claimed for Spain, along with the adjoining lands. Balboa was the first European to see the Pacific Ocean from the Americas.

Sailing Around the World

In 1520 Ferdinand Magellan, a Portuguese explorer who was sailing for Spain, reached the southernmost tip of South America. He sailed through the stormy waters of a narrow sea passage, or strait. The strait led him into a calm ocean—the same one Balboa had seen. The waters were so peaceful—*pacifico* in Spanish—that Magellan named the ocean the Pacific Ocean. Magellan died in the Philippine Islands, but his crew continued to sail westward, arriving back in Spain in 1522. Magellan's crew were the first people known to **circumnavigate,** or sail around, the world.

The strait that led Magellan (above) from the Atlantic to the Pacific Ocean is now called the Strait of Magellan.

✅ **PROGRESS CHECK**

Evaluating What did Spain have to gain by supporting Columbus and his voyage?

LESSON 2 REVIEW CCSS

Review Vocabulary (Tier 3 Words)

1. Use the term *cape* in a sentence about the explorations of Portugal in the late 1800s. RH.6–8.4

2. Write a sentence about why it was such an achievement for someone to circumnavigate the globe. RH.6–8.4

Answer the Guiding Questions

3. *Describing* Describe the geographic factors that led Portugal to begin its ocean explorations. RH.6–8.1

4. *Explaining* What was the purpose of the Treaty of Tordesillas? RH.6–8.1

5. **INFORMATIVE/EXPLANATORY** Write a paragraph explaining why Americans might celebrate Eriksson Day rather than Columbus Day. WHST.6–8.2, WHST.6–8.4

LESSON 2 REVIEW ANSWERS

1. Possible answer: To reach India, Portuguese ships sailed down the west coast of Africa, around the cape, and then up Africa's east coast.

2. Possible answer: Magellan's crew, which circumnavigated the globe, showed that they had great skill at sailing and also proved that the Earth was a sphere.

3. Portugal did not have a Mediterranean port, so it needed to find a different sea route to Asia.

4. To protect their claims, Spain and Portugal asked Pope Alexander VI for help. He first drew a line of demarcation, which divided all lands between Spain and Portugal. However, Portugal protested that the line did not divide the lands evenly. In 1494, the two countries signed the Treaty of Tordesillas to move the line farther west. All unexplored lands were divided between Spain and Portugal.

5. Students' paragraphs should include the fact that evidence proves the existence of a Viking settlement in North America around the year 1000, when the Viking sailor Leif Eriksson was exploring lands west of Greenland.

C Critical Thinking Skills

Theorizing Remind students that the first explorers to reach the Americas were not sure what they had discovered. Have students work in pairs for a few minutes to evaluate the outcomes of the explorer's journeys, even though many of them did not end up at the destinations that they had planned. Consider using the Chapter Opener map to retrace the outcomes of the explorers discussed so far. **Ask: Do you think these voyages were successful despite their outcomes? Explain.** *(Answers may vary but should reflect the fact that these voyages, although they did not result in new routes to Asia, provided countries with extensive land and other riches.)* **BL**

W Writing Skills

Argument Ask: Why do we often think of Columbus as the one who "discovered" America? *(Students should realize that his visit began European settlement of the Americas, while Viking settlements in North America did not last.)* Then ask students whether they think that Columbus earned the title of the one who "discovered" America or not. Remind students that native peoples had already been living in the Americas for centuries. Have students write an outline for an argument in which they develop a thesis, provide supporting points, address the counterargument, and restate their argument in the conclusion. If possible, hold a debate on the issue, with students using their outlines as prompts.

Have students complete the Lesson 2 Review.

CLOSE & REFLECT

To close the lesson, have students write a short essay or annotate a blackline master of a world map to explain and illustrate the extent of European exploration during this time and how it affected the Americas. Have students reflect on the effects of these changes over the next century.

ANSWER, p. 41

✅ **PROGRESS CHECK** Whatever he found would belong to Spain, and they hoped he would find great riches. Also, he could convert the native people he met to Christianity.

ENGAGE

Bellringer Review with students the reasons for European exploration. **Ask:** **What were the three main reasons explorers made ocean voyages in the late 1400s and early 1500s?** *(to trade, to gain riches for their countries, to spread Christianity)* **What new technology made exploration possible?** *(faster, stronger ships such as the caravel; new instruments: compass, astrolabe, quadrant; better maps)* Point out to students that Spanish exploration was fueled by similar reasons and Spanish explorers used similar navigation technology.

TEACH & ASSESS

R Reading Skills

Discussing Ask students what pressures they face at school or even among friends. Explain that conquistadors had pressures, too. Have students read the paragraph. Then, **ask:** **What happened when a conquistador failed?** *(He lost his own fortune.)* Discuss with students what kind of pressure conquistadors must have faced knowing the consequences of failure.

C Critical Thinking Skills

Determining Cause and Effect Discuss with students the goals of early Spanish explorers. **Ask:** **How did the discovery of gold treasures among the Aztec and Inca lead to more exploration in the Americas?** *(After Cortés and Pizarro shipped back large amounts of Aztec and Inca gold, Europeans decided to explore southeastern and southwestern parts of North America.)* **BL**

ANSWER, p. 42

TAKING NOTES: Answers may include Cortés, Mexico; Pizarro, Peru; Ponce de León, Florida; and de Soto, Southeastern United States (Florida), Oklahoma.

---

networks
There's More Online!

☑ **BIOGRAPHY**
Sor Juana Inés de la Cruz

☑ **MAP**
• Spanish Explorers
• California's Missions

☑ **PRIMARY SOURCE**
• Cortés and the Aztecs
• Sor Juana Inés de la Cruz
• Cabeza de Vaca

☑ **VIDEO**

Lesson 3
Spain in America

ESSENTIAL QUESTION *What are the consequences when cultures interact?*

IT MATTERS BECAUSE
Spanish explorers in the Americas conquered people and searched for gold. Spain became richer, while many Native Americans suffered from harsh treatment at the hands of the Spaniards.

European Explorers and Conquerors

GUIDING QUESTION *What were the goals of early Spanish explorers?*

When Spanish explorers reached the Americas, natives told tales of gold, silver, and kingdoms wealthy beyond belief. The Spanish listened eagerly, and they traveled far and wide in search of these riches.

These explorers, known as **conquistadors** (kahn•KEES•tah•dohrz), got encouragement from Spanish rulers. The rulers gave conquistadors the right to explore and create settlements in the Americas. In return, the conquistadors agreed to give Spain one-fifth of any treasure they found. This deal allowed Spanish rulers to explore the Americas with little risk. If a conquistador failed, he lost his own fortune. If he succeeded, both he and Spain gained wealth and glory.

The Conquest of Mexico and Peru

Although many of the tales of gold and riches proved to be false, some were true. Two wealthy empires—the Aztec in what is now Mexico and Central America and the Inca in South America—were among the richest prizes the conquistadors claimed.

Reading **HELP**DESK **CCSS**

Taking Notes: *Describing* RH.6–8.1, RH.6–8.7
As you study the lesson, use a graphic organizer like this one to identify three Spanish conquistadors and describe the regions they explored.

Explorer	Region Explored

Content Vocabulary (Tier 3 Words)
• conquistador • mission
• immunity • presidio
• pueblo • plantation

42 *Exploring the Americas*

---

networks   *Online Teaching Options*

VIDEO

Hernando de Soto

Discussing Play the video about Hernando de Soto for students. Afterwards, discuss with them what type of man de Soto was. **Ask:** **What qualities did de Soto possess?** *(Possible answer: He was strong, intelligent, and well organized but also ruthless and cruel.)* Tell students that many historians view de Soto as the epitome, or perfect example, of a conquistador, and that many of the qualities students saw in de Soto were shared by other conquistadors.

See page 25E for other online activities.

In 1519 Hernán Cortés landed on the east coast of present-day Mexico. Within two years, Cortés conquered the Aztec Empire that had ruled the region. Huge amounts of Aztec gold made Cortés and Spain wealthy.

Cortés's success encouraged other conquistadors. Twelve years after the Aztec conquest, Francisco Pizarro led an army into the Inca capital in Cuzco, Peru. The Spanish arrested and later executed the Inca ruler. Without their leader, the Inca were not able to fight effectively. Pizarro soon controlled most of the vast and wealthy Inca Empire.

Why Spain Won

The conquistadors' victories over the Aztec and Inca were quick and lasting. How did Cortés and Pizarro conquer such mighty empires with their small forces?

First, the Spanish had weapons and animals the Aztec and Inca had never seen. The Spanish had guns and cannons. They rode horses and had huge, ferocious dogs. To the Native Americans, the Spanish seemed almost like gods. One Aztec recalled the fear that spread at the soldiers' approach: "[T]heir weapons clashed and rattled. ... [T]hey terrified everyone who saw them." Cortés received help from some native people who disliked their harsh rulers and were happy to help overthrow them. Finally, disease played a large role. For many native groups, **contact** with the Europeans was deadly. With no **immunity,** or resistance, to European diseases, the Aztec and the Inca suffered terrible epidemics. Illnesses weakened them in their struggle against the Spanish.

☑ **PROGRESS CHECK**

Analyzing How were the Spanish able to defeat Native American empires?

Spain in North America

GUIDING QUESTION *What did Spain hope to find in the Americas?*

Mexico and Peru were lands rich in silver and gold. Hoping to find similar wealth to the north, conquistadors explored the southeastern and southwestern parts of what is today the United States.

conquistador Spanish explorer
immunity resistance, such as to disease

The Granger Collection, NYC

Thinking Like a
HISTORIAN
Analyzing Primary Sources

In 1519 Hernán Cortés prepared to leave Cuba for Mexico with 11 ships carrying about 550 Spanish soldiers and 16 horses. Before setting off, Cortés said to his men:

"I know in my heart that we shall take vast and wealthy lands, people such as have never before been seen. ... If you do not abandon me, as I shall not abandon you, I shall make you in a very short time the richest of all men who have crossed the seas."

—from *The Life of the Conqueror by His Secretary,* trans. Lesley Byrd Simpson

Based on this quote, what inspired the conquistadors?

For more about analyzing primary sources, review *Thinking Like a Historian.*

Cortés accepts the surrender of the Aztec ruler.

W Writing Skills

Argument Invite a volunteer to read the "Thinking Like a Historian" primary source quote aloud to the class. **Ask: Does Cortés clearly state his intention? If so, what is it?** *(Yes; to take wealth and land)* Ask students why they think he believed it was acceptable to be a conqueror. Direct students to write a paragraph, arguing either from the perspective of Cortés or the Aztec, justifying or rejecting the conquistador's mission. Remind them to state their argument clearly, use strong supporting points, address the counterargument, and restate their argument in the conclusion. **BL** **Verbal/Linguistic**

C Critical Thinking Skills

Determining Cause and Effect Explain to students that the effects of disease on the Aztec (and on other Native American groups) were horrific. Some historians think that diseases unknowingly brought by Europeans killed the vast majority of some Native American groups. **Ask: Why did so many Native Americans fall ill when the Spanish arrived?** *(They had no immunity to European diseases.)* **What do people now do that helps them resist many diseases?** *(They are immunized.)*

Content Background Knowledge

The Inca civilization thrived in present-day Peru before Spanish conquistador Francisco Pizarro conquered the area. By the 1530s, the empire was large, stretching the full span of the Andes Mountains, about 2,500 miles. To get messages from one part of the empire to the other, the Inca used special runners. They built a complex series of roads throughout the empire on which the messengers ran.

PRIMARY SOURCE

Cortés and the Aztecs

Sequencing Discuss the quotation from *The Broken Spears.* Invite students to tell the events of the surrender in sequence. Remind them to use sequence clue words, such as *first, next,* and *last.* **ELL** As students describe the events, make notes in a time line on the board. **AL** **Visual/Spatial**

See page 25E for other online activities.

networks   **Cortés and the Aztecs**
ANALYZING PRIMARY SOURCES

Although Aztec ruler Montezuma II welcomed Cortés as a fellow leader, Cortés took him captive and seized control of the Aztec's capital city, Tenochtitlán. Cortés and his men, with the help of other Native American groups, seized the Aztecs' wealth on behalf of Spain.

The Granger Collection, NYC

"They came in battle array, as conquerors. ... Their spears glinted in the sun, and their pennons (banners) fluttered like bats. They made a loud clamor as they marched, for their coats of mail (armor) and their weapons clashed and rattled. ... [T]hey terrified everyone who saw them."

—from *The Broken Spears*

Source: Broken Spears New York Edited by Miguel León-Portilla, Beacon Press, 1962

ANSWERS, p. 43

Thinking Like a Historian Conquest and treasure (riches) inspired the conquistadors.

☑ **PROGRESS CHECK** The Spanish had many weapons; many Native Americans helped the Spanish fight their Aztec rulers; Native Americans were weakened by European diseases.

T Technology Skills

Researching on the Internet Students may not be aware that the search for the fountain of youth was not limited to Ponce de León. Rumors of such a water source have been recorded in writings by Herodotus, Alexander the Great, and others. Have students work in small groups to conduct Internet research to discover these stories. Suggest they compile their research into a presentation—a speech, a short skit with acts for the different searchers, or poster session—that they can share with the class. **BL** Interpersonal

C Critical Thinking Skills

Interpreting Point out that rumors had a significant influence on early exploration. **Ask: How did Cabeza de Vaca learn about the Seven Cities of Gold?** *(He was part of a Spanish expedition that became stranded on an island near Texas. While traveling across the Southwest toward Mexico, which was Spanish territory, he heard about the Seven Cities of Gold from Native Americans.)* **How did stories of riches and wealth affect the exploration of North America?** *(Rumors of these cities resulted in conquistadors exploring large portions of the Americas.)* **AL**

BIOGRAPHY

Sor Juana Inés de la Cruz (1651?–1695)

Juana Inés de la Cruz was born in New Spain, the daughter of a Spanish father and a Creole mother. She became a famous writer in a culture where most women were not taught to read. Her intelligence and thirst for learning led her to seek religious training, which allowed her time to study and write. Her private library was one of the largest in the Americas. In addition to books, she also collected musical and scientific instruments. Recognized as a great writer in her own lifetime, her poems, plays, and stories were published in the Americas and in Spain. Today, de la Cruz is seen as one of the greatest Mexican colonial writers.

▶ **CRITICAL THINKING**
Speculating Why do you think it might have been difficult for de la Cruz to become a successful writer?

C

Juan Ponce de León (pahn·suh day lee·OHN) made the first Spanish landing on the east coast of present-day Florida in 1513. According to legend, Ponce de León was not looking only for gold. He also hoped to find the legendary fountain of youth. This had been described by a historian of that time as, "a spring of running water of such marvelous virtue" that drinking it "makes old men young again." Ponce de León's exploration led to the first Spanish settlement in what is now the United States—a fort the Spanish built at St. Augustine, Florida, in 1565.

T

The Seven Cities of Gold

Still other conquistadors searched for quick riches, and several lost their lives in the process. Álvar Núñez Cabeza de Vaca (cuh·BAY·suh duh VAH·cuh) was part of a Spanish expedition to Florida in 1528. After coming into conflict with Native Americans in Florida, the expedition sailed south toward Mexico in November, led by Pánfilo de Narváez (nahr·VAH·ays). Three of its five boats were lost in a storm.

The two boats that made it through the storm became stuck on a beach on an island near present-day Texas. Within a few months, only a handful of the Spanish explorers were still alive. To survive among the Native Americans, de Vaca and an enslaved African named Estevanico (es·TAY·vahn·EE·koh) persuaded the Native Americans that they had healing powers. Cabeza de Vaca later wrote that their method of healing was "to bless the sick, breathing upon them," and to recite Latin prayers.

In 1533 the Spaniards set off on a long trek across the Southwest. While traveling, they often heard stories about seven rich cities in the region. When Cabeza de Vaca finally arrived in Mexico in 1536, he told eager listeners about the "Seven Cities of Cíbola"—seven cities of gold.

De Soto Searches for Gold

Excited by these stories, Hernando de Soto led an expedition to explore Florida and what is today the southeastern United States. For three years they traveled, following stories of gold. Their encounters with the native people often turned violent.

De Soto crossed the Mississippi River in 1541, describing it as "swift, and very deep." After traveling as far west as present-day Oklahoma, de Soto died of fever. His men buried him in the waters of the Mississippi.

© Alfredo Dagli Orti/The Art Archive/Corbis

▼ Reading **HELP**DESK **CCSS**

Academic Vocabulary (Tier 2 Words)

contact when two or more groups or objects come together

Reading in the Content Area: *Map Keys*

A map key shows what symbols and colors on the map mean. In the map on the next page, the key explains the colors of the lines on the map. For example, the yellow line represents Ponce de León's route in 1513.

netw⊙rks *Online Teaching Options*

PRIMARY SOURCE

Cabeza de Vaca

Making Inferences Project the interactive primary source excerpt from Cabeza de Vaca. After reading the text, have a volunteer locate the island of Trinidad on a map or globe. Discuss what type of storm these sailors might have experienced, using evidence from the source as well as their own prior knowledge of weather events to support their conclusion. *(Students should infer that the storm the men experienced was a hurricane.)*

See page 25E for other online activities.

netw⊙rks **Cabeza de Vaca**
ANALYZING PRIMARY SOURCES

This excerpt from Cabeza de Vaca's account of his years in the Americas, *La Relación*, describes a great storm that struck the island of Trinidad.

The Granger Collection, NYC

" An hour after I departed [the ship] the sea began to be very stormy. . . . At that time the rain and the storm began to increase so much that it was just as strong in the town as on the sea, for all the houses and churches were blown down, and it became necessary for us to go about in groups of seven or eight men locking our arms together so that we could keep the wind from blowing us away. . . . In this storm and danger we went about all night without finding a place nor a spot where we "

—from *La Relación*, by Álvar Núñez Cabeza de Vaca

ANSWER, p. 44

CRITICAL THINKING Possible answer: She was a woman and a Creole in a culture where the most important people were Spanish-born men.

Spanish Explorers 1513–1542

Ponce de León 1513
Cabeza de Vaca 1528–1536
De Soto 1539–1542
Coronado 1540–1542
Present-day boundaries

NORTH AMERICA

Santa Fe
El Paso
Mexico City

Gulf of Mexico

St. Augustine

ATLANTIC OCEAN

From Spain

Havana
Cuba

PACIFIC OCEAN

TROPIC OF CANCER

0   800 miles
0   800 km
Lambert Azimuthal Equal-Area projection

GEOGRAPHY CONNECTION

In 1513 Juan Ponce de León made the first Spanish landing on the North American mainland.

1 MOVEMENT Which conquistador explored areas along the southern half of the Mississippi River?

2 CRITICAL THINKING
Drawing Conclusions Why do you think the Spanish made their first landing on the North American mainland in Florida?

V

Coronado Takes Up the Search

Another conquistador who searched for the Seven Cities of Cíbola was Francisco Vásquez de Coronado (kawr•oh•NAH•doh). His travels took him through northern Mexico and present-day Arizona and New Mexico, until his expedition reached a Zuni (ZOO•nee) settlement in 1540. Finally convinced that there was no gold, members of the expedition traveled west to the Colorado River and east into what is now Kansas. They found no gold—only "windswept plains" and strange "shaggy cows" (buffalo).

C

☑ PROGRESS CHECK

Speculating Why do you think that the encounters between de Soto's party and Native Americans were sometimes violent?

Life Under Spanish Rule

GUIDING QUESTION *What effect did Spanish rule have on society?*

Spanish law set up three kinds of settlements in the Americas—pueblos, missions, and presidios. **Pueblos,** or towns, were centers of trade. **Missions** were religious communities. They included a church, a small town, and fields for crops. A **presidio** was a type of fort, and was usually built near a mission.

Juan de Oñate (day ohn•YAH•tay) traveled up from Mexico to establish a Spanish presence in the lands to the north. He was also assigned to convert the native people to Christianity.

R

The Granger Collection, NYC

CHAPTER 2, Lesson 3
Spain in America

V Visual Skills

Synthesizing Focus students' attention on the map of Spanish explorers. Be sure to highlight with students the explorers de Vaca, de Soto, and de Coronado. Create a list with students of the Spanish explorers discussed in this lesson. List where they explored and what happened to them. **Ask: What did they look for?** *(All looked for gold. Ponce de León also looked for the fountain of youth.)* **Why did they expect to find gold?** *(Possible answers: They had found it in Central and South America; they had heard tales of cities of gold from Cabeza de Vaca.)* **Visual/Spatial**

R Reading Skills

Identifying Have a volunteer read the text. Then, **ask:** **Who was Juan de Oñate?** *(He was the man who founded the province of New Mexico.)* Discuss with students why de Oñate traveled from Mexico to establish a Spanish presence in the lands to the north. Invite one volunteer to locate on a map where de Oñate traveled and another volunteer to explain why he probably chose that area. **ELL** **Logical/Mathematical**

Content Background Knowledge

The exact route that Coronado followed through the Southwest has been debated by historians and archaeologists for decades. One of his campsites in Texas was confirmed by the finding of crossbow bolt points, horseshoe nails, and the remains of a chain-mail glove, which was worn by many conquistadors to protect their hands in battle.

IMAGE

Spanish Missions in the Americas

Explaining Show the interactive image of a Spanish mission. Discuss with students how pueblos, presidios, and missions were set up throughout the area, including the American Southwest, that was colonized by Spain. Have volunteers define each item of Spanish settlement. **AL** **ELL** **Ask: Why did the Spanish set up missions?** *(They set up missions to spread the Spanish way of life and the Catholic religion among Native Americans.)* **What would you find at a Spanish mission?** *(a small town, some farmland, and a church)* **AL**

See page 25E for other online activities.

netw@rks   **Spanish Missions in the Americas**

Mission Loreto, founded in Baja California in 1697, is the first of the California missions.

PoodlesRock/CORBIS

○ ○ ○ ○

ANSWERS, p. 45

GEOGRAPHY CONNECTION

1 De Soto

2 CRITICAL THINKING Possible answer: This land was close to the islands in the Caribbean where the Spanish were already established.

☑ PROGRESS CHECK Possible answer: The Spaniards were searching for riches that did not exist. On top of that, a language barrier existed between the Spaniards and native peoples. Neither group had a way to communicate the important things they needed to say.

V Visual Skills

Visualizing As students discuss the social classes in Spanish colonial society, draw a triangle on the board. Review with students the different levels of Spanish colonial society. Help them visualize the structure and organization of this society. **Ask:**

- Where on the triangle would each group be? *(At the top would be peninsulares, then the creoles, the mestizos, and, at the bottom, the Native Americans and the enslaved Africans.)* **AL**

- What was the distinction between a Creole and a mestizo? *(Creoles were people born in the Americas to Spanish parents. Mestizos were the people who had Spanish and Native American parents.)*

- Why do you think mestizos ranked higher than Native Americans in Spanish colonial society? *(Mestizos had one Native American parent and one Spanish parent, and since Spain was in charge, they were ranked higher than if they were Native American with no Spanish parent.)* **BL**

Content Background Knowledge

In 1598 the Spanish and Mexicans came to present-day New Mexico on a road called the *El Camino Real de Tierra Adentro* ("Royal Road of the Interior"). Settlers made the six-month journey from Mexico City to Santa Fe until about 1885. Extending some 1,500 miles, the road brought caravans of people, goods, and ideas to New Spain. It served as a confluence of cultures—Mexican, Native American, European, and American. A monument and heritage center, which opened in 2005, features artifacts from the period.

Mission Santa Clara de Asís was California's eighth mission. All missions had the same basic plan and were located near wood, water, and land for farming and grazing. There was a church, housing for the priests and Native American converts, grain fields with irrigation ditches, and corrals for cattle, sheep, and goats.

In 1598 Oñate **founded,** or established, the province of New Mexico. He introduced cattle and horses to the Pueblo people. The first Spanish city in the southwest, Santa Fe, was established in 1607. Santa Fe became the capital of the province in 1610.

Spanish Colonial Society

There was a very clear class system in Spanish colonial society. The highest level of society was made up of the *peninsulares*, people who were born in Spain. They were the landowners, leaders of government, and heads of the Catholic Church. Next in rank were the Creoles, people born in the Americas whose parents were Spanish. The next level below were the mestizos (meh·STEE·zohs), people with one Spanish and one Native American parent. Still lower were the Native Americans, most of whom lived in great poverty, and enslaved Africans.

The Spanish government granted conquistadors who settled in the Americas the right to demand either taxes or labor from Native Americans living on the land. This system forced the Native Americans into a form of slavery.

For example, in the 1540s, when the Spanish discovered silver ore in northern Mexico, they set up mining camps. They then forced Native Americans to dig for silver. The damp mineshafts were a grueling environment in which to work. Many Native Americans died there from malnutrition and disease.

Reading **HELP**DESK (CCSS)

pueblo a town in the Spanish-ruled lands
mission a religious community where farming was carried out and Native Americans were converted to Christianity

presidio a fort
plantation a large farm

Academic Vocabulary (Tier 2 Words)

found to start, to establish

netw⊙rks *Online Teaching Options*

BIOGRAPHY

Bartolomé de Las Casas

Analyzing Display the biography of Bartolomé de Las Casas, and discuss with students the treatment of Native Americans under Spanish rule. Discuss the passage of the New Laws in 1542. **Ask:** What do you think made Bartolomé de Las Casas speak out about how the Native Americans were treated by the Spanish? *(Possible answer: Treatment of the Native Americans was so cruel that he could not keep silent.)* **AL**

See page 25E for other online activities.

A Spanish priest, Bartolomé de Las Casas, spoke out against such cruel treatment of Native Americans and pleaded for laws to protect them. He claimed that millions had died because the Spanish "made gold their ultimate aim, seeking to load themselves with riches in the shortest possible time."

Las Casas's reports convinced Spanish leaders to pass the New Laws in 1542. These laws forbade enslaving Native Americans. Unfortunately, the laws were not always enforced.

The Plantation System

Not all Spaniards sought gold. Some found wealth shipping crops to Spain. In the West Indies, key exports were tobacco and sugarcane. The Spanish developed the **plantation** system to raise these crops. A plantation is a large farm.

The Spanish first used Native American labor to work their plantations. Las Casas suggested that they be replaced by enslaved Africans—a suggestion he bitterly regretted later. As a result, thousands of enslaved Africans were brought from West Africa to the Americas. Those who survived the brutal voyage were sold to plantation owners. By the late 1500s, slave labor was an essential part of the economy of the colonies.

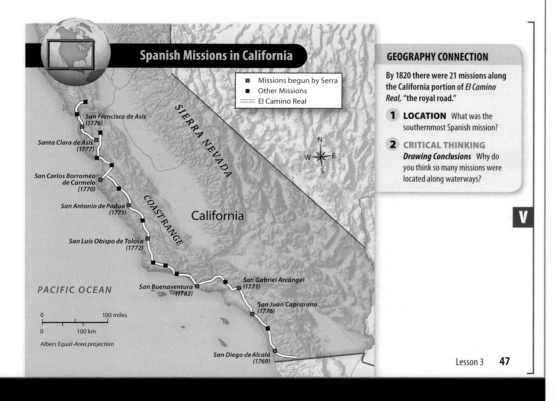

Spanish Missions in California

- Missions begun by Serra
- Other Missions
- El Camino Real

San Francisco de Asís (1776)
Santa Clara de Asís (1777)
San Carlos Borroméo de Carmelo (1770)
San Antonio de Padua (1771)
San Luis Obispo de Tolosa (1772)
San Buenaventura (1782)
San Gabriel Arcángel (1771)
San Juan Capistrano (1776)
San Diego de Alcalá (1769)

SIERRA NEVADA
COAST RANGE
California
PACIFIC OCEAN

0   100 miles
0   100 km
Albers Equal-Area projection

GEOGRAPHY CONNECTION

By 1820 there were 21 missions along the California portion of *El Camino Real,* "the royal road."

1 LOCATION What was the southernmost Spanish mission?

2 CRITICAL THINKING
Drawing Conclusions Why do you think so many missions were located along waterways?

R Reading Skills

Defining After students have read about the plantation system, ask a student volunteer to define the term *plantation.* **AL** **ELL** **Ask: Why did Spanish colonists set up plantations?** *(They set up plantations to raise sugar cane and tobacco.)*

Explain to students that the Spanish began to settle in the Southwest in the 1600s and 1700s. Discuss that Juan Cabrillo sighted what is now California, but for 200 years, the Spanish left it alone. **Ask: Why did that policy change?** *(The Spanish needed a larger number of colonists to hold on to their territory, and they wanted to convert more Native Americans to Christianity.)* Discuss how the missions in California became economically profitable.

V Visual Skills

Reading a Map Direct students attention to the map of Spanish missions in California. **Ask: Where are most of these missions located?** *(on the coast of California)* **Which names are still in use today?** *(San Diego, San Luis Rey, San Juan Capistrano, Los Angeles, Santa Barbara, San Luis Obispo, Santa Cruz, Santa Clara, San Francisco)* **Visual/Spatial**

Father Junípero Serra

Identifying Display the biography of Father Junípero Serra, and discuss his background and accomplishments. **Ask:**

- **What were Serra's goals for his work with Native Americans?** *(to convert them to Christianity and make them a part of Spanish culture)*
- **How many Spanish missions in California did he found?** *(nine)*

See page 25E for other online activities.

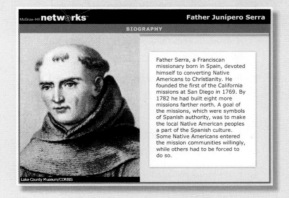

McGraw-Hill **networks** — Father Junípero Serra

BIOGRAPHY

Father Serra, a Franciscan missionary born in Spain, devoted himself to converting Native Americans to Christianity. He founded the first of the California missions at San Diego in 1769. By 1782 he had built eight more missions farther north. A goal of the missions, which were symbols of Spanish authority, was to make the local Native American peoples a part of the Spanish culture. Some Native Americans entered the mission communities willingly, while others had to be forced to do so.

Lake County Museum/CORBIS

ANSWERS, p. 47

GEOGRAPHY CONNECTION

1 San Diego de Alcalá

2 CRITICAL THINKING Possible answer: Mission life involved farming, where crops are grown and animals are pastured. The housing was permanent and had a European look. Each mission had a church.

Spain in America

C Critical Thinking Skills

Evaluating Discuss with students the use of Native Americans by the Spanish as laborers on the plantations. Also discuss the impact of the Spanish on Native American life. **Ask:** Overall, do you think that Spanish missions were good or bad for Native Americans? Explain your answer. *(Answers will vary but should demonstrate student understanding of the challenges that Native Americans faced at the missions.)*

Have students complete the Lesson 3 Review.

CLOSE & REFLECT

To close the lesson, display a map of the United States. Call on volunteers to locate the Southwest and New England regions. **Ask:** What do you see in the place names in these regions? *(the languages of other countries)* Guide students to conclude that European nations explored and settled in North America and that we can tell some of the history of these explorations and settlements by looking at modern place names.

Finally, call attention to such locations as Tallahassee and Mississippi. Tell students that these are Native American names. If time permits, allow students to identify names of places from other languages. **Ask:** What can you conclude by looking at the place names in our country? *(The history of the United States is the history of Native Americans and of European settlers such as those from Spain, England, and France.)* **BL** Visual/Spatial

---

The Spanish influence in the United States is strong. Many Spanish words have been incorporated into the language, such as fiesta and canyon. The Spanish, who were expert ranchers, introduced animals such as horses, sheep, pigs, and beef cattle into the American Southwest. Many place names in the United States today are Spanish in origin. Some examples in the text are Santa Fe and San Diego. Can you think of any others?

Spanish Settlement in the Southwest

In the 1600s and 1700s, the Spanish, with much help from Native Americans, settled the Southwest, including present-day New Mexico, Texas, and California.

The Spanish explorer Juan Cabrillo (kuh•BREE•yoh) first sighted what is now California in 1542. However, for 200 years the Spanish had left the area alone. Around 1769, that policy changed. California was the northern frontier of the Spanish Empire in North America, and Spain needed a large number of colonists to solidify its hold on the region. Spain also wanted to convert more Native Americans to Christianity.

Spanish settlement in California consisted mostly of mission building. The Spaniards trained Native Americans who lived on the mission as farmers. They learned how to grow crops, irrigate farmland, and perform other tasks usually carried out on a ranch. Eventually, the missions became economically profitable enough to sell some of their goods, such as wine, olive oil, and leather.

Effect on Native American Life

C California's many Native American groups had well-ordered societies before the Spanish arrived. They hunted, fished, and gathered plants for food. The arrival of the Spanish disrupted this way of life. The Spanish forced native peoples to convert to Christianity and to live and work at the missions.

✓ **PROGRESS CHECK**

Summarizing What kinds of settlements did the Spanish build in the Americas?

LESSON 3 REVIEW

Review Vocabulary (Tier 3 Words)

1. Use the following content vocabulary terms to write a short paragraph about Spanish settlement in the Americas. RH.6–8.4, WHST.6–8.4

   a. pueblo   b. mission
   c. presidio   d. plantation

Answer the Guiding Questions

2. ***Summarizing*** What did most conquistadors hope to accomplish in the Americas? RH.6–8.2

3. ***Explaining*** Why was 1513 a significant year in the history of the United States? RH.6–8.1

4. ***Making Generalizations*** What effect do you think Spanish settlement had on Native Americans? RH.6–8.2

5. **INFORMATIVE/EXPLANATORY** The conquistadors are often described as possessing both good and bad qualities. Write a paragraph in which you express what you think were the qualities, both good and bad, of the Spanish conquistadors. WHST.6–8.1, WHST.6–8.10

LESSON 3 REVIEW ANSWERS

1. Possible answer: Spanish settlements included towns, called *pueblos*; forts, called *presidios*; and religious centers, called *missions*. The Spanish also set up a plantation system.

2. to acquire riches for themselves and for Spain; to claim lands for Spain; to convert Native Americans to Christianity

3. Juan Ponce de León first set foot on the Florida coast and claimed the territory for the Spanish crown.

4. Possible answer: Spanish settlement resulted in much suffering and hardship; it turned many Native Americans into slaves and killed millions of them through battle, mistreatment, and disease.

5. Possible answer: The good qualities of the conquistadors were that they were courageous and took tremendous risks in their exploration—both in their personal safety and in their personal wealth. If their expeditions failed, they would lose everything. On the other hand, they thought little of killing or enslaving the Native Americans.

ANSWERS, p. 48

Connections to Today Possible answers: Boca Raton, Florida, Los Angeles, Las Vegas. Accept all correct answers.

✓ **PROGRESS CHECK** plantations, pueblos, missions, presidios

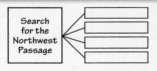

networks
There's More Online!
☑ **GRAPHIC ORGANIZER**
The Northwest Passage

Lesson 4
Competing for Colonies

ESSENTIAL QUESTION *What are the consequences when cultures interact?*

IT MATTERS BECAUSE
The European competition for colonies in the Americas led to settlement and exploration in many parts of North America.

Religious Rivalries

GUIDING QUESTION *What were the religious motives behind the Age of Exploration?*

The Europeans who explored and settled in North America in the 1500s sought wealth. They also wanted to spread their Christian faith. The first to arrive were Roman Catholics—the only Christian church in the western part of Europe at that time. Not long after Columbus made his first voyage across the Atlantic, however, religious conflict shook Europe. New rivalries based on religious beliefs emerged.

Luther and the Reformation
In 1517 a German priest named Martin Luther nailed a list of complaints on the door of a local Catholic church, questioning the power and authority of Catholic leaders—including the pope, the head of the Catholic Church. Luther hoped to spark reform within the Church, but Pope Leo X rejected his ideas. Others agreed with Luther. His ideas helped launch a movement called the **Reformation** (reh•fuhr•MAY•shuhn). The movement led to a new form of Christianity called **Protestantism** (PRAH•tuhs•tuhn•tih•zuhm). Among the differences between Protestants and Catholics was that Protestants did not accept the leadership of the pope. The Reformation led to **widespread** conflict within and between the nations of Europe.

R

(l) Bettmann/CORBIS, (c) PoodlesRock/Corbis, (r) The Granger Collection, NYC

Reading **HELP**DESK **CCSS**

Taking Notes: *Listing* RH.6–8.1, RH.6–8.7
As you study the lesson, use a diagram like this to list the explorers who tried to find a Northwest Passage.

> Search for the Northwest Passage → [ ] [ ] [ ] [ ]

Content Vocabulary (Tier 3 Words)
- **Reformation**
- **Protestantism**
- **armada**
- **Northwest Passage**
- **tenant farmer**

Lesson 4 **49**

CHAPTER 2, Lesson 4
Competing for Colonies

ENGAGE

Bellringer To help students get a feeling for Luther's rebellion against the Catholic Church, have them imagine that they live in a small town, where everyone knows everyone else and holds the same beliefs and attitudes. One angry member of the town has decided to air the community's more serious problems by posting a list of them in a public place. **Ask:**

- What would happen in the town? *(Answers may vary, but students might suggest that some people would be upset with the person; some might support him or her.)*
- Should the community change how it operates, or should those who are dissatisfied leave? *(Students should explain their answers.)*

TEACH & ASSESS

R Reading Skills

Finding the Main Idea After students have read the text, **ask: Who was Martin Luther?** *(a German priest who was dissatisfied with the teachings and leadership of the Catholic Church)* **What did he do?** *(He nailed a list of his complaints to a church door.)* Point out to students that many people, even entire nations, left the Catholic Church in the wake of Luther's actions.

Discuss with students how England broke with the Roman Catholic Church and became a Protestant nation. **Ask: What conflict did this cause with Spain?** *(Spain was a Catholic country and decided to invade Protestant England. They sent an armada and were defeated.)* If needed, clarify the meaning of the term *armada*, and then check student understanding by asking them to orally provide the definition or write it on a piece of paper. **AL ELL Verbal/Linguistic**

VIDEO

Henry Hudson and the New World

Analyzing Use the video to introduce students to the search for the Northwest Passage. Remind students that, although virtually all of Earth is mapped today, most of it was completely unknown to Europeans in the 1500s and 1600s. **Ask: What mistakes did Hudson make in his search for the Northwest Passage?** *(He thought the Hudson River might be the Northwest Passage.)* **AL How could explorers continue to make this kind of mistake in different parts of North America?** *(There was no way to see the whole continent.)* **BL**

See page 25F for other online activities.

ANSWER, p. 49

TAKING NOTES: John Cabot, Giovanni de Verrazano, Jacques Cartier, Henry Hudson

Competing for Colonies

C Critical Thinking Skills

Analyzing Primary Sources Review with students the life of Marie Guyard, the French nun who brought her faith to the settlement of Quebec. Then have a volunteer read aloud the excerpt from *Word from New France* in Thinking Like a Historian. **Ask:**

- **Why do you think Marie Guyard went to Quebec?** *(Possible answer: to convert Native Americans to Catholicism)*
- **Why do you think someone might question her decision to learn a new language at age 50?** *(Possible answers: She was grown up, out of school, and had a life as a nun. Traveling to the Americas and learning a strange language—especially one so different from her own language—might have been considered unusual; it would have been a big undertaking.)*

Discuss with students the desire by France to introduce Catholicism to the Native Americans. **Ask: What other country wanted to spread the Catholic religion to Native Americans?** *(Spain)* **AL**

W Writing Skills

Informative/Explanatory Direct students to research the battle that defeated the Spanish Armada. What types of ships were involved? What tactics were used? Did weather play a role? Students should write a multi-paragraph essay to inform the reader of the essential aspects of the battle. Remind them to plan out their writing before they begin and to take notes and cite their sources accurately as they research. Discuss with students what constitutes a good, reliable source.

After students have completed their essays, you may choose for them to use computer presentation software to present them to the class. Allow five minutes for each student to present his or her essay. Have students in the audience evaluate the presentations. Then ask students to make revisions to their essays based on the evaluations from their peers. **Auditory/ Musical Verbal/Linguistic**

ANSWER, p. 50

Thinking Like a Historian Possible answers: She was 50 years old and had led a life as a nun, not as an explorer. She was probably adventurous, religious, and unconventional. She accepted the challenge of learning Native American languages to help convert Native Americans to Catholicism.

Thinking Like a HISTORIAN

Analyzing Primary Sources

In 1639 a French woman named Marie Guyard, or Marie of the Incarnation, arrived in Quebec, New France's first colony. Later, she wrote religious books in the languages of the native peoples she met there. In a letter, Guyard wrote:

"You will perhaps laugh that at the age of fifty years I am beginning to study a new tongue [language], but one must undertake all things for the service of God and the salvation of one's neighbour."

—from *Word From New France*, by Marie Guyard

From her letter, what do you know about the person and character of Marie Guyard?

For more about analyzing primary sources, review *Thinking Like a Historian.*

Religious Rivalry in Europe

In 1533 the English king, Henry VIII, left the Catholic Church. Later, during the rule of his daughter Elizabeth I, further reforms established England as a Protestant nation. At that time, it was common for kings and queens to insist that their subjects follow their religion. Subjects who did not could lose their lands and fortunes. In England, many people were unhappy about leaving the Catholic Church, but they had little power to resist.

England's Protestantism caused conflict with Spain. Beginning in 1585, King Philip of Spain made plans to invade England. A successful invasion could mean the overthrow of Protestantism. In May 1588, Philip sent an **armada** (ahr·MAH· duh), or war fleet, of 132 ships to England. With 30,000 troops and more than 2,000 guns, the Spanish Armada was the mightiest naval force in the world. Yet the smaller, faster English ships quickly gained the upper hand.

The defeat of Spain's armada marked the end of Spanish control of the seas. Now the way was clear for the English to start colonies in North America.

Religious Rivalries in the Americas

Catholics from Spain and France worked to spread their faith among the Native Americans. The Spanish settled in the southwestern and southeastern regions of North America, and the French settled in the northeast. Dutch and English Protestants set up colonies along the Atlantic coast between the French and the Spanish settlements. Religious differences contributed to the rivalries between these settlements.

Search for a Northwest Passage

In the 1500s and early 1600s, England, France, and the Netherlands sent explorers to map the coast of North America and, later, establish trade and colonies. Explorers also hoped to discover a **Northwest Passage** to Asia, a direct water route through the Americas.

England sent John Cabot, an Italian, to look for a northern sea route to Asia in 1497. Cabot probably landed on the coast of present-day Newfoundland. In 1524 France hired another Italian, Giovanni de Verrazano, to look for a northern route. Verrazano explored the coast of North America from present-day Nova Scotia down to the Carolinas.

Reading HELPDESK (CCSS)

Reformation a sixteenth-century religious movement rejecting or changing some Roman Catholic teachings and practices and establishing the Protestant churches

Protestantism a form of Christianity that was in opposition to the Catholic Church
armada a fleet of warships

Academic Vocabulary (Tier 2 Words)
widespread over a wide area

50 *Exploring the Americas*

---

netw⊙rks *Online Teaching Options*

GAME

Competing for Colonies Column Game

Classifying Review with students how to play the interactive game. Organize the class into two teams. Have students play the game by sorting terms related to the Protestants and Catholics. To add a challenge, use the timing option for teams to see which team is able to select all of the correct answers in the shortest amount of time. **AL ELL**

See page 25F for other online activities.

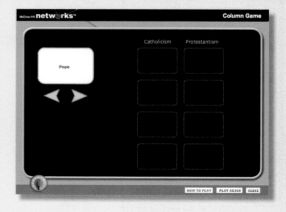

In 1535 French explorer Jacques Cartier (kahr•tee•AY) sailed up the St. Lawrence River, hoping it would lead to the Pacific. Cartier did not make it to the Pacific, but he discovered a mountain peak that he named Mont-Royal, which means "royal mountain." This is the site of the present-day city of Montreal.

The Netherlands also wanted to find a passage through the Americas. The Dutch hired English sea explorer and navigator Henry Hudson to look for it. In 1609 he discovered the river that now bears his name. In his ship, the *Half Moon*, Hudson sailed north on the Hudson River as far as the site of present-day Albany, New York. Deciding that he had not found a passage to India, he turned back.

The following year England sent Hudson to try again. On this trip, Hudson discovered a huge bay—now called Hudson Bay. Thinking he had reached the Pacific, Hudson spent months looking for an outlet. His crew became impatient and rebelled. They set Hudson, his son, and a few sailors adrift in a small boat, never to be seen again.

In 1609 Henry Hudson and his crew landed on the shores of Delaware Bay. The native people offered goods for trade.

☑ **PROGRESS CHECK**

Analyzing Why did nations want to find a Northwest Passage?

Northwest Passage a sea passage between the Atlantic and the Pacific along the north coast of North America

Bettmann/CORBIS

Lesson 4 **51**

V Visual Skills

Analyzing Images Direct students' attention to the painting of Henry Hudson and the native people. **Ask: What do you think the native people thought of Henry Hudson and his crew?** *(Answers will vary, but students may say the painting shows the native people reacted favorably.)* **Visual/Spatial**

R Reading Skills

Identifying After students have read the text, discuss the background of Jacques Cartier with them. Have them identify Montreal on the Chapter Opener map. **Ask:**

- **Why do you think Cartier decided he might have found the Northwest Passage?** *(He was sailing on the St. Lawrence River, which is quite long.)*
- **What is the name of this lesson?** *(Competing for Colonies)*
- **Name the countries that were competing to find a Northwest Passage.** *(England, France, and the Netherlands)*

W Writing Skills

Informative/Explanatory Have students work in small groups to write a short rap or song to help them remember which countries were competing for the Northwest Passage and which explorers came to the area. Invite students to share their songs or raps with the class. **ELL** **Auditory/Musical**

Content Background Knowledge

It was not uncommon for explorers to return home after a voyage of exploration with riches and gifts from interactions with native peoples of the area. Some even returned with Native Americans themselves. Jacques Cartier, for example, brought back two Native Americans to France after exploring the St. Lawrence River.

IMAGE

The Northwest Passage

Discussing Display and review the interactive image about explorers searching for the Northwest Passage. Have students locate the area of this passage on a map or globe. Discuss the barriers to travel through this passage. As an extension, you may wish to have students research the melting of ice mentioned in the passage and what this may mean for navigation and trade.

See page 25F for other online activities.

McGraw-Hill **networks** The Northwest Passage

The Northwest Passage is an east-to-west sea passage across North America. The passage connects the Atlantic Ocean to the Pacific Ocean via a route through Canada's Arctic islands.

Stocktrek Images

ANSWER, p. 51

☑ **PROGRESS CHECK** They wanted to find a shorter, less difficult route to Asia so trade and commerce would be more profitable.

Analyzing Use the image of Jacques Marquette and Louis Joliet to launch a discussion with students about the men's exploration of the Mississippi River. **Ask: What did they hope to find?** *(precious metals and the Northwest Passage)* **What made them turn around?** *(They realized that the Mississippi River flowed south rather than west.)*

C **Critical Thinking Skills**

Determining Cause and Effect Point out that French goals in North America were different from Spanish goals. **Ask: How did fishing and trapping pave the way for French settlements?** *(French trappers and missionaries went far into the interior of North America to trade with the Native Americans, and they built forts and trading posts to protect their trade.)* Have students define the word *trapping*. **AL** **ELL**

T **Technology Skills**

Using Visual Aids Have students trace the flow of the Mississippi River on a map. As a challenge, ask students to research, using the Internet or other digital media, another river in North America that generally flows southwest. *(Possible answer: Colorado River)* **BL** **Visual/Spatial**

ANSWER, p. 52

CRITICAL THINKING Students should point out that Marquette and Joliet were unsuccessful in that they did not find precious metals or a Northwest Passage. However, they did locate a river that flowed the entire way to the Gulf of Mexico, which would be extremely important for trade for centuries to come.

In 1673 Father Jacques Marquette and Louis Joliet located the great Mississippi River. They hoped to find that the river led to the Pacific Ocean.

▶ **CRITICAL THINKING**
Explaining In what way was Marquette and Joliet's expedition successful? Unsuccessful?

French and Dutch Settlements

GUIDING QUESTION *How did French and Dutch settlements compare to the Spanish colonies?*

French explorers and settlers trailed the Spanish by many years, but the French did establish settlements in North America. At first, the French were most interested in natural resources, including fish and furs. French trappers went far into the interior of North America and traded with Native Americans. France built forts to protect their trade. French missionaries followed the traders.

In 1663 New France became a royal colony. The new royal governor supported expanded exploration.

Exploring the Mississippi River

In the 1670s, two French explorers—a fur trader, Louis Joliet, and a priest, Jacques Marquette—traveled the Mississippi River by canoe. Joliet and Marquette hoped to find precious metals. They were also looking for a Northwest Passage. When they realized that the Mississippi flowed south into the Gulf of Mexico rather than west into the Pacific, they headed back upriver.

In 1682 Robert Cavelier de La Salle followed the Mississippi all the way to the Gulf of Mexico. He claimed the region for France, calling it Louisiana in honor of Louis XIV. In 1718 the French founded New Orleans. French explorers and missionaries traveled west to the Rocky Mountains and the Rio Grande.

Reading **HELP**DESK **CCSS**

tenant farmer settler who pays rent or provides work to a landowner in exchange for the right to use the landowner's land

Academic Vocabulary (Tier 2 Words)
pose to present; to offer

52 *Exploring the Americas*

---

netw✺rks *Online Teaching Options*

Sieur de La Salle

Identifying Display the biography of Sieur de La Salle and discuss his accomplishment of navigating the Mississippi River. **Ask:**

- **Who was Robert Cavelier, Sieur de La Salle?** *(a French explorer)*
- **What role did he play in French settlement of America?** *(He followed the Mississippi River all the way to the Gulf of Mexico, discovering new territory along the way.)*

See page 25F for other online activities.

McGraw-Hill **netw✺rks** **Sieur de La Salle**

BIOGRAPHY

Sieur de La Salle

René-Robert Cavelier, Sieur de La Salle was the first person to travel the Mississippi River to the Gulf of Mexico. This famous expedition resulted in his claiming the entire Mississippi Valley for France. La Salle named the territory Louisiana after King Louis XIV of France.

New France and New Netherland

French settlement in North America advanced slowly. New France was made up of estates along the St. Lawrence River. Estate holders brought in settlers in exchange for land. These **tenant** (TEH·nuhnt) **farmers** paid rent and worked for their lord for a set period each year.

The French got along well with the Native Americans. French trappers and missionaries lived among them, learned their languages, and respected their ways. The missionaries had come to convert Native Americans to Catholicism, but they did not try to change their customs. Because the French colony grew slowly, it did not seem to **pose** a threat to the Native Americans and their lands.

The Netherlands was a small country with few natural resources and limited farmland. This is why the Dutch were anxious to set up a North American colony. After Hudson's voyage in 1609, the Dutch began to explore North America.

The Netherlands also had a large fleet of trading ships that sailed all over the world. In 1621 the Netherlands created the Dutch West India Company to run its trade between the Americas and Africa. In 1623 the company took over control of the Dutch colony in North America, called "New Netherland."

The heart of the colony was New Amsterdam. The town was built on the tip of Manhattan Island. In 1626 governor Peter Minuit bought the island from the Manhattoes people for 60 Dutch guilders (about $24) worth of trade goods.

☑ **PROGRESS CHECK**

Explaining What were France's goals in North America?

The Dutch hoped New Amsterdam, located where the Hudson River enters what is now New York Harbor, would become an important center for their trade.

▶ CRITICAL THINKING
Analyzing Which characteristics of the region of New Amsterdam might encourage trade for the Dutch settlers?

The Granger Collection, NYC

LESSON 4 REVIEW (CCSS)

Review Vocabulary (Tier 3 Words)

1. Explain the meaning of the terms *armada* and *Protestantism* by using both in a sentence. RH.6–8.4

2. Explain the significance of the term *tenant farmer*. RH.6–8.4

Answer the Guiding Questions

3. *Explaining* What were the key religious differences between the European nations that explored the Americas? RH.6–8.2

4. *Analyzing* What was the effect on England of the defeat of the Spanish Armada? RH.6–8.1

5. *Contrasting* How did the French attitude toward Native Americans differ from that found in the Spanish colonies? RH.6–8.5

6. **NARRATIVE** Write a letter to a relative in Europe from the point of view of an early French or Dutch settler in North America. Describe what life is like and what your goals are in North America. WHST.6–8.1, WHST.6–8.10

Lesson 4   **53**

R Reading Skills

Discussing Have a volunteer read the text aloud. Then, discuss with students that the colony of New France developed in what is now Canada. **Ask: What type of settlement did the French establish along the St. Lawrence River?** *(New France was made up of estates along the St. Lawrence River.)* **How did estate holders receive their land?** *(They received land in North America by bringing settlers.)*

Point out that some farmers did not own their land. **Ask: What is the meaning of the word tenant?** *(someone who rents property from a landlord)* **AL ELL How did tenant farmers pay rent?** *(Part of the year they worked for their lord, and they paid their lord an annual rent. But the rest of the year they worked for themselves.)*

C Critical Thinking Skills

Contrasting Help student contrast New Amsterdam and today's Manhattan. Draw a T-chart on the board. Invite students who have visited Manhattan to share their experiences. Show students a modern-day picture of Manhattan Island to help them see the differences between past and present. If possible, show them an image that reflects Dutch influence, either in architecture or in a place name or sign.

Have students complete the Lesson 4 Review.

CLOSE & REFLECT

To close this lesson, have students think about early settlements mentioned in this chapter, such as St. Augustine and New Amsterdam. **Ask: Why were the first settlements on waterways?** *(They needed access to the ocean for trading goods.)* **What might happen when they started moving away from the coast?** *(They would have to find or create ways to get access to the oceans.)*

LESSON 4 REVIEW ANSWERS

1. The Spanish sent an *armada*, a fleet of ships, to fight England and perhaps strike a blow at the spread of Protestantism.

2. A *tenant farmer* is a person who farms land that belongs to someone else, to whom the tenant farmer gives money or labor, just as the tenant of an apartment pays rent to the landlord.

3. France and Spain were Catholic, and England and the Netherlands were Protestant.

4. The defeat of Spain's armada marked the end of Spanish control of the seas. The victory cleared the way for England to start colonies in North America.

5. The French treated the Native Americans with respect, learned their languages, and lived among them. The Spanish often enslaved or killed the Native Americans and took their wealth.

6. Students' letters should make use of information in the lesson to discuss daily life, as well as the settlers' and French/Dutch goals in North America.

ANSWERS, p. 53

CRITICAL THINKING Answers will vary but may include characteristics such as that Manhattan Island was on a river and had a good harbor, the fort could defend the trading business of the Dutch up the Hudson River and the interests of the Dutch East India Company, and that the island had good soil and would support a settlement.

☑ **PROGRESS CHECK** France had little interest in establishing settlements and was in North America mainly for fishing and fur trading; the French wanted to develop trade and commerce, including trade and commerce with Native Americans.

CHAPTER REVIEW ACTIVITY

Have students create a two-column chart like the one below and write "European Country" above the left column and "Area Explored" above the right column. Have students identify at least one area explored per country. A volunteer should note student responses in the chart. *(Possible answers have been provided in the table below.)*

European Country	Area Explored
(Portugal)	(Africa, South America)
(Spain)	(Central and South America; southern regions of North America)
(France)	(St. Lawrence River, Mississippi River)
(Great Britain)	(Eastern regions of North America)
(The Netherlands)	(Manhattan Island; Hudson River)

REVIEW THE ENDURING UNDERSTANDING

Review this chapter's Enduring Understanding with students:

- *The movement of people, goods, and ideas causes societies to change over time.*

Now pose the following questions in a class discussion to apply these to the chapter.

Why did Europeans want to explore west to Asia? *(They were looking for a shorter route to Asia and for riches such as gold and silver.)*

How did exploring the Americas and the quest for resources affect interaction among different peoples and countries? *(Possible answer: It led to many countries and groups in Europe, Asia, and Africa interacting through trade, which led to the exchange of goods and new ideas.)*

Write your answers on a separate piece of paper.

❶ **Exploring the Essential Question**   WHST.6–8.2, WHST.6–8.9

INFORMATIVE/EXPLANATORY Choose one of the main topics discussed in this chapter: the Renaissance, the trading empires of Africa, the Age of Exploration, Spain in the Americas, the Protestant Reformation, or the colonization of the Americas by France or the Netherlands. For the topic you chose, identify one new idea and one way in which it caused a change for people living at that time. Explain whether it was a positive or a negative change, and why. Use examples from the text to support your opinion.

❷ **21st Century Skills**   WHST.6–8.7, WHST.6–8.8

INFORMATION LITERACY Working in small groups, research the factors and events that contributed to the decline in the population of Native Americans. Then, research the factors and events that contributed to the increase in the population of Africans in the Americas. Create a time line or other kind of diagram that charts the development of these two historical trends. Present your findings to the class.

❸ **Thinking Like a Historian**   RH.6–8.5, RH.6–8.7

UNDERSTANDING CAUSE AND EFFECT Create a diagram like the one to the right to examine how the exploration and conquest of the Americas may have affected Europe.

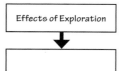

Effects of Exploration

❹ **Visual Literacy**   RH.6–8.7

ANALYZING PAINTINGS In the painting below, Coronado heads an expedition into New Mexico. What does this image suggest about the way the Spanish conquistadors viewed their role in the lands they explored? Explain your answer.

MPI/Stringer/Getty Images

ACTIVITIES ANSWERS

Exploring the Essential Question

❶ For the topic chosen, students' essays should identify one new idea and one way in which that idea changed the lives of people in that period. Essays should include information from the text to support students' opinions as to whether they think this change was good or not.

21st Century Skills

❷ Projects should be done in small groups; tasks within the project can be individual or group tasks. Discuss your expectations when assigning the project. Students' diagrams should clearly show the factors and events they have identified in their research.

Thinking Like a Historian

❸ Possible answers: **Effects of Exploration** → gains in European nations' wealth → gains in resources and influence → the effect of increased or decreased power within Europe and in the Americas

Visual Literacy

❹ Possible answers: The image suggests that the Spanish conquistadors thought of themselves as conquerors and as rulers of the lands they explored. They rode horses, they carried rifles, and they appeared to be in charge.

REVIEW THE GUIDING QUESTIONS

Choose the best answer for each question.

RH.6–8.4
1 The tool of navigation that showed the direction of magnetic north was the

  A. caravel.

  B. compass.

  C. carrack.

  D. quadrant.

RH.6–8.1
2 Between A.D. 400 and 1100, many West Africans decided to become Muslim through trading contact with

  F. Asia.

  G. Europe.

  H. North Africa.

  I. North America.

RH.6–8.1
3 Vasco da Gama fulfilled Portugal's goal of a sea route to Asia when he reached

  A. the coast of Brazil.

  B. the Cape of Good Hope.

  C. Calicut in India.

  D. Mombasa in eastern Africa.

RH.6–8.4
4 Spanish settlements that served as centers for teaching Native Americans the Spanish religion and ways of living were called

  F. pueblos.

  G. missions.

  H. presidios.

  I. plantations.

RH.6–8.2
5 What was one result from the defeat of the armada sent by Spain?

  A. The Reformation began.

  B. Spain controlled the world's sea trade.

  C. France became the world's largest empire.

  D. The way was clear for England to start colonies in North America.

RH.6–8.1
6 Joliet and Marquette

  F. condemned the treatment of Native Americans.

  G. founded the settlement of New Amsterdam.

  H. explored the Mississippi River for France.

  I. led the battle against the Spanish Armada.

55

ASSESSMENT ANSWERS
Review the Guiding Questions

1 **B** Point out to students that the caravel and carrack are ships. The quadrant is a device sailors used to calculate their location on the sea. Ask students if they have ever used a compass to find their way. Explain that sailors use the compass to navigate because it indicates magnetic north and allows them to determine what direction they are sailing.

2 **H** If students are having difficulty finding the correct answer, have them review lesson 1. North Africa was Islamic, and West Africans became familiar with Islam through their trade with that region. Some Asians also adopted Islam after establishing trade with North Africa. Europeans were Christian. There was no trade between North Africa and North America at that time.

3 **C** Students should recognize that, while da Gama sailed past the Cape of Good Hope and stopped in Mombasa, these places are not in Asia. Have students check this on a map or globe. Da Gama did not reach Asia until he reached Calicut. It was Cabral who reached Brazil before continuing to India.

4 **G** Refer students to lesson 2 to review the section on da Gama. Students should understand that pueblos are towns, presidios are forts, and plantations are large farms. Only missions, which were run by priests, combined churches, living accommodations, and small farms, and were established to teach Native Americans Christianity and European ways of life.

5 **D** Point out the word *defeat* to students in the question. Understanding of this word can rule out answer choice B. Explain that the Reformation occurred much later, ruling out answer choice A. Explain that Spain had lost its domination of the seas after the defeat of the armada. This cleared the way for England to become the great sea power. Being able to travel unchallenged on the seas was an important prerequisite to sending settlers and carrying on trade between North America and Great Britain.

6 **H** If students cannot remember what role Joliet and Marquette played during this time period, point them to page 52. Joliet, a priest, and Marquette, a trader, traveled the Mississippi by canoe. They explored for France.

Analyzing Documents

7 **A** St. Augustine is in North America and was therefore in New Spain, which was the only viceroyalty that included settlements in North America.

8 **I** The first three choices are in South America: Lima, Peru; La Paz, Bolivia; and Santiago, Chile.

Short Response

9 The Spanish did not regard the Native Americans to be persons worthy of respect, good treatment, or even life itself.

10 The Spanish regarded the Native Americans as a source of labor and as uncivilized people from whom land, wealth, and labor could be taken.

Extended Response

11 Letters should include examples of contact with the French and may include trading, contact with missionaries, and so forth. From the Native American person's perspective, the purpose of the French settlers might appear to be to propagate their faith, to establish mutually beneficial trade with Native Americans, and to live peacefully wherever they share lands. Students should mention that the French learned Native Americans' languages and respected their way of life.

DBQ **ANALYZING DOCUMENTS**
RH.6–8.7

7 **Locating** According to the map, St. Augustine is located in
A. New Spain.
B. New Granada.
C. Peru.
D. the Rio de la Plata.

RH.6–8.7

8 **Analyzing Visuals** Spanish settlements in North America include
F. Lima.
G. La Paz.
H. Santiago.
I. Santa Fe.

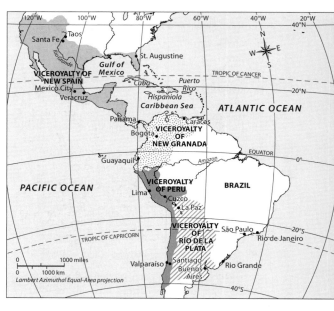

SHORT RESPONSE

In 1541, the Spanish priest Bartolomé de Las Casas wrote:

"The pattern established at the outset has remained unchanged to this day, and the Spaniards still do nothing save tear the natives to shreds, murder them and inflict upon them untold misery, suffering and distress, tormenting ... and persecuting them mercilessly."

—from *A Short Account of the Destruction of the Indies* by Bartolomé de Las Casas

RH.6–8.6, WHST.6–8.9

9 What does this passage suggest about Spanish attitudes toward the Native Americans they encountered?

RH.6–8.6, WHST.6–8.1

10 Why did the Spanish treat the Native Americans as described here?

EXTENDED RESPONSE
RH.6–8.2, WHST.6–8.10

11 **Narrative** Write a letter to a friend from the perspective of a Native American living in lands that the French have recently settled. How has life changed for you and your people since the French arrived? What are they doing to your people? What appears to be their purpose?

Need Extra Help?

If You've Missed Question	**1**	**2**	**3**	**4**	**5**	**6**	**7**	**8**	**9**	**10**	**11**
Review Lesson	1	1	2	3	4	4	3	3	3	3	4

---

netw⊙rks   *Online Teaching Options*

More Assessment Resources

The *Assess* tab in the online Teacher Lesson Center includes resources to help students improve their test-taking skills. It also contains many project-based rubrics to help you assess students' work.

CHAPTER 3
Colonial America Planner

NCSS Standards covered in "Colonial America"

Learners will understand:

1 CULTURE

4. That the beliefs, values, and behaviors of a culture form an integrated system that helps shape the activities and ways of life that define a culture

3 PEOPLE, PLACES, AND ENVIRONMENTS

1. The theme of people, places, and environments involves the study of the relationships between human populations in different locations and geographic phenomena such as climate, vegetation, and natural resources

2. Concepts such as: location, region, place, migration, as well as human and physical systems

6. Patterns of demographic and political change, and cultural diffusion in the past and present (e.g., changing national boundaries, migration, and settlement, and the diffusion of and changes in customs and ideas)

8. Factors that contribute to cooperation and conflict among peoples of the nation and world, including language, religion, and political beliefs

7 PRODUCTION, DISTRIBUTION, AND CONSUMPTION

3. The economic choices that people make have both present and future consequences

7. How markets bring buyers and sellers together to exchange goods and services

UNDERSTANDING BY DESIGN®

Enduring Understanding
- *People, places, and ideas change over time.*

Essential Questions
- *How does geography influence the way people live?*
- *How do new ideas change the way people live?*

Predictable Misunderstandings

Students may think:
- *All settlers and colonists were Pilgrims.*
- *Pilgrims and Puritans were just different names for the same group.*
- *Founding the colonies and helping them grow was easily accomplished.*

Assessment Evidence

Performance Tasks:
- *Hands-On Chapter Projects*

Other Evidence:
- *Interactive Graphic Organizers*
- *What Do You Know? activity*
- *Geography and History Activities*
- *Primary Source Activity*
- *Economics of History Activity*
- *Written Paragraphs*
- *Lesson Reviews*
- *Online Self-Check Quizzes*
- *Chapter Activities and Assessment*

SUGGESTED PACING GUIDE

Introducing the Chapter.............. 1 day	Lesson 3 .... 1 day
Lesson 1 .... 1 day	Lesson 4 ....2 days
Lesson 2 ....2 days	Chapter Wrap-Up and Assessment...... 1 day

TOTAL TIME   8 Days

Key for Using the Teacher Edition

SKILL-BASED ACTIVITIES

Types of skill activities found in the Teacher Edition.

V Visual Skills require students to analyze maps, graphs, charts, and photos.

R Reading Skills help students practice reading skills and master vocabulary.

W Writing Skills provide writing opportunities to help students comprehend the text.

C Critical Thinking Skills help students apply and extend what they have learned.

T Technology Skills require students to use digital tools effectively.

*Letters are followed by a number when there is more than one of the same type of skill on the page.

DIFFERENTIATED INSTRUCTION

All activities are written for the on-level student unless otherwise marked with the leveled labels below.

BL Beyond Level
AL Approaching Level
ELL English Language Learners

All students benefit from activities that utilize different learning styles. Many activities are marked as below when a particular learning style is highlighted.

Intrapersonal	Naturalist
Logical/Mathematical	Kinesthetic
Visual/Spatial	Auditory/Musical
Verbal/Linguistic	Interpersonal

CHAPTER OPENER PLANNER

Students will know:
- the reasons colonists migrated to the Americas.
- the complex relationship between colonists and Native Americans.
- the challenges that the colonists at Jamestown and Plymouth faced.
- the society, culture, and economy of the New England, Middle, and Southern colonies.

Students will be able to:
- **analyze** historical and political maps.
- **analyze and sequence** information about early Colonial America.
- **demonstrate** connections between events.
- **analyze and evaluate** primary source readings.
- **evaluate and use** appropriate resources to obtain factual information.
- **identify and locate** on a map the original thirteen English colonies.
- **compare and contrast** the New England, Middle, and Southern colonies.
- **identify points of view** of the leaders of the colonies and explain their impact on the colony.
- **analyze** the contributions of key groups to colonial society.

UNDERSTANDING
BY DESIGN®

☑ *Print Teaching Options*

V Visual Skills

☐ **P. 58** Students describe the British Colonies while looking at a map of Colonial America. **AL** **ELL**
Visual/Spatial

☐ **P. 59** Students examine historical events during the colonial America period.

☑ *Online Teaching Options*

V Visual Skills

☐ **MAP** **Land Claims, 1750**—Students use the interactive map to investigate the extent of British, French, and Spanish land claims in 1750.

☐ **TIME LINE** **Place and Time: Colonial America 1587–1770**—Students learn about key historical events related to Colonial America and the world between 1587 and 1770.

☐ **WORLD ATLAS** Students can use this interactive map to identify regions of the world, learn about individual countries, locate political boundaries, measure distances, and much more.

☑ *Printable Digital Worksheets*

R Reading Skills

☐ **GRAPHIC NOVEL** *The Gentlemen of Jamestown*—The men of Jamestown recount some of their adventures.

Project-Based Learning

Hands-On Chapter Project

Create Presentations
To understand how geography influenced the development of the American colonies, students will create an illustrated presentation about one of six possible locations for the Jamestown settlement.

Technology Extension

Mapping Possible Jamestown Locations with Google™ Maps
- Find an additional activity online that incorporates technology for this project.
- Visit the EdTechTeacher Web sites (included in the Technology Extension for this chapter) for more links, tutorials, and other resources.

Print Resources

ANCILLARY RESOURCES
These ancillaries are available for every chapter and lesson.
- **Reading Essentials and Study Guide Workbook** **AL** **ELL**
- **Chapter Tests and Lesson Quizzes Blackline Masters**

PRINTABLE DIGITAL WORKSHEETS
These printable digital worksheets are available for every chapter and lesson.
- **Hands-On Chapter Projects**
- **What Do You Know? activities**
- **Chapter Summaries (English and Spanish)**
- **Vocabulary Builder activities**
- **Guided Reading activities**

More Media Resources

SUGGESTED VIDEOS
Watch clips of popular culture films about early America, such as *Pocahontas, The New World,* or *Squanto: A Warrior's Tale.* (NOTE: Preview any clips for age-appropriateness.)

SUGGESTED READING
Grade 6 reading level:
- *The Adventurous Life of Myles Standish and the Amazing-But-True Survival Story of Plymouth Colony,* by Cheryl Harness

Grade 7 reading level:
- *Where the Great Hawk Flies,* by Liza Ketchum

Grade 8 reading level:
- *Voices from Colonial America,* by the National Geographic Society

LESSON 1 PLANNER

ROANOKE AND JAMESTOWN

Students will know:
- the reasons colonists migrated to the Americas.
- the complex relationship between colonists and Native Americans.
- the challenges that the colonists at Jamestown and Plymouth faced.

Students will be able to:
- *analyze and evaluate* primary source readings.
- *demonstrate* connections between events.
- *identify points of view* of the leaders of the colonies and explain their impact on the colony.
- *analyze* the contributions of key groups to colonial society.

UNDERSTANDING
BY DESIGN®

☑ *Print Teaching Options*

V Visual Skills

☐ **P. 63** Students discuss how Pocahontas's life changed when she married Rolfe. **BL** Visual/Spatial

R Reading Skills

☐ **P. 60** Students identify the role of Walter Raleigh.

☐ **P. 62** Students identify Captain John Smith's role in Jamestown. **BL**

W Writing Skills

☐ **P. 63** Students write a position paragraph about the portrayal of Pocahontas.

C Critical Thinking Skills

☐ **P. 60** Students sequence events in the history of the Roanoke Colony. **AL**

☐ **P. 61** Students consider the mystery of Roanoke Island.

☑ *Online Teaching Options*

V Visual Skills

☐ **VIDEO** **Life in Jamestown**—Students view a video that explains what life was like for the early Jamestown settlers.

☐ **BIOGRAPHY** **John White**—Students learn the background of John White, an artist and early English colonist.

☐ **BIOGRAPHY** **Pocahontas**—Students learn the contributions of Pocahontas to the English colonists at Jamestown.

R Reading Skills

☐ **GRAPHIC ORGANIZER** **Taking Notes:** *Listing:* **Hardships for Jamestown Settlers**—Students complete the lesson graphic organizer in which they list the hardships faced by the Jamestown settlers.

C Critical Thinking Skills

☐ **CHART** **The Mystery of the Lost Colony**—Students analyze clues and identify likely theories for why colonists disappeared from Roanoke.

☐ **GRAPH** **The Golden Crop**—Students compare the value of tobacco in the 1600s and the 2000s.

T Technology Skills

☐ **SELF-CHECK QUIZ** **Lesson 1**—Students receive instant feedback of their mastery of lesson content.

☑ *Printable Digital Worksheets*

W Writing Skills

☐ **WORKSHEET** **Geography and History Activity: Colonial America, Roanoke and Jamestown**—Students read about the physical characteristics of the areas around Jamestown, analyze maps of the area, and write about how physical geography affected the success of the settlement.

THE NEW ENGLAND COLONIES

Students will know:
- the reasons colonists migrated to the Americas.
- the complex relationship between colonists and Native Americans.
- the society, culture, and economy of the New England, Middle, and Southern colonies.

Students will be able to:
- *analyze and sequence* information about early Colonial America.
- *identify points of view* of the leaders of the colonies and explain their impact on the colony.
- *analyze* the contributions of key groups to colonial society.

UNDERSTANDING
BY DESIGN®

☑ *Print Teaching Options*

V Visual Skills

☐ **P. 65** Students examine a cut-away diagram of the *Mayflower.*

☐ **P. 67** Students compare a map of the New England colonies with a map of modern New England.
Visual/Spatial

R Reading Skills

☐ **P. 64** Students identify groups of people who resisted becoming Anglicans. **AL**

☐ **P. 66** Students discuss the development of the Mayflower Compact. **AL** **ELL**

☐ **P. 66** Students discuss the role of Squanto and Samoset. **BL**

W Writing Skills

☐ **P. 66** Students research and write paragraphs about important documents similar to the Mayflower Compact. **BL** **Verbal/Linguistic**

C Critical Thinking Skills

☐ **P. 64** Students imagine the effect of being told they must change how they worship.

☐ **P. 68** Students discuss the Puritans' intolerance of religious dissent.

☐ **P. 68** Students describe the war waged by Metacomet.

T Technology Skills

☐ **P. 67** Students research reasons why Hooker and his followers left Boston. **BL** **Verbal/Linguistic**

☑ *Online Teaching Options*

V Visual Skills

☐ **IMAGE** The *Mayflower*—Students view an image of the *Mayflower* and learn about its voyage.

☐ **MAP** The New England Colonies—Students use a map to analyze the products produced by the three New England colonies.

☐ **VIDEO** **Bitter Conflict Grows Between New England Colonists and Native Americans**—Students view a video that describes how the Puritans' expansion into land used by Native American tribes led to conflict.

R Reading Skills

☐ **GRAPHIC ORGANIZER** **Taking Notes: *Describing:* Cooperation and Conflict**—Students complete the lesson graphic organizer in which they describe examples of cooperation and conflict between Native Americans and English colonists.

☐ **PRIMARY SOURCE** **Anne Hutchinson**—Students analyze a description of Anne Hutchinson written by John Winthrop in the mid-1600s.

C Critical Thinking Skill

☐ **SLIDE SHOW** **Plymouth Colony**—Students explore the voyage of the *Mayflower* and the colonists' first year.

☐ **WHITEBOARD ACTIVITY** **New England Colonies**—Students drag and drop terms onto the colonies to which they apply.

T Technology Skills

☐ **SELF-CHECK QUIZ** **Lesson 2**—Students receive instant feedback of their mastery of lesson content.

☑ *Printable Digital Worksheets*

W Writing Skills

☐ **WORKSHEET** **Primary Source Activity: Colonial America, The New England Colonies**—Students analyze various points of view about land and land use in the colonies.

THE MIDDLE COLONIES

Students will know:
- *the reasons colonists migrated to the Americas.*
- *the society, culture, and economy of the New England, Middle, and Southern colonies.*

Students will be able to:
- ***analyze and sequence*** *information about early Colonial America.*
- ***compare and contrast*** *the New England, Middle, and Southern colonies.*
- ***identify points of view*** *of the leaders of the colonies and explain their impact on the colony.*
- ***analyze*** *the contributions of key groups to colonial society.*

UNDERSTANDING BY DESIGN®

☑ *Print Teaching Options*

V Visual Skills

☐ **P. 71** Students analyze a map of the Middle Colonies. **AL** **ELL** Visual/Spatial

R Reading Skills

☐ **P. 69** Students explore why the Dutch West India Company controlled New Netherland. **ELL** Kinesthetic

☐ **P. 70** Students find the main idea of a selection from the text. **AL** **BL**

☐ **P. 71** Students discuss the role of William Penn. **AL**

☐ **P. 72** Students discuss the founding of Delaware.

W Writing Skills

☐ **P. 72** Students write essays reflecting what they have learned about New York's ethnic heritage. **BL** Interpersonal

C Critical Thinking Skills

☐ **P. 70** Students evaluate the advantages of the New Jersey colony.

☐ **P. 71** Students contrast Pennsylvania with the other colonies. **BL**

☑ *Online Teaching Options*

V Visual Skills

☐ **VIDEO** **New Jersey**—Students view a video depicting the ethnic and religious diversity of Middle Colony immigrants.

☐ **IMAGE** **The Middle Colonies**—Students read an overview of the makeup of the Middle Colonies.

☐ **BIOGRAPHY** **Peter Stuyvesant**—Students learn of Stuyvesant's background and his role in New Netherland becoming New York.

☐ **MAP** **The Middle Colonies**—Students locate the Middle Colonies with respect to the other colonies and identify the products produced in each colony.

R Reading Skills

☐ **GRAPHIC ORGANIZER** **Taking Notes:** *Identifying:* **The New York and Pennsylvania Colonies**—Students complete the lesson graphic organizer in which they illustrate how the New York and Pennsylvania colonies split to form the four middle colonies under British rule.

☐ **PRIMARY SOURCE** **Excerpt from New Amsterdam's Citizens to Peter Stuyvesant**—Students analyze an excerpt from a letter from the inhabitants of New Amsterdam to Peter Stuyvesant regarding the English attack on the town.

C Critical Thinking Skills

☐ **WHITEBOARD ACTIVITY** **Middle Colonies**—Students sort terms in order to describe New York, New Jersey, and Pennsylvania.

T Technology Skills

☐ **GAME** **The Middle Colonies Vocabulary Game**—Students review lesson vocabulary using online flash cards.

☐ **SELF-CHECK QUIZ** **Lesson 3**—Students receive instant feedback of their mastery of lesson content.

☑ *Printable Digital Worksheets*

W Writing Skills

☐ **WORKSHEET** **Geography and History Activity: Colonial America, The Middle Colonies**—Students analyze a chart containing Dutch-origin place names and answer questions about the places and names.

THE SOUTHERN COLONIES

Students will know:
- the reasons colonists migrated to the Americas.
- the complex relationship between colonists and Native Americans.
- the society, culture, and economy of the New England, Middle, and Southern colonies.

Students will be able to:
- *analyze and sequence* information about early Colonial America.
- *compare and contrast* the New England, Middle, and Southern colonies.
- *identify points of view* of the leaders of the colonies and explain their impact on the colony.
- *analyze* the contributions of key groups to colonial society.

UNDERSTANDING
BY DESIGN®

☑ *Print Teaching Options*

V Visual Skills

☐ **P. 76** Students examine a map of the Southern Colonies. **BL**

R Reading Skills

☐ **P. 73** Students review what they have already learned about Jamestown. **AL**

☐ **P. 74** Students discuss the establishment of the colony of Maryland. **AL** **BL**

☐ **P. 76** Students summarize a quote by John Locke.

☐ **P. 77** Students identify people of the Southern Colonies. **AL**

W Writing Skills

☐ **P. 74** Students write a short essay that defends the Calvert brothers or William Penn. **AL** **Verbal/Linguistic**

☐ **P. 75** Students write short narratives from the perspective of each group who played a role in Bacon's Rebellion. **Verbal/Linguistic**

C Critical Thinking Skills

☐ **P. 76** Students consider the role of agriculture in the Southern Colonies. **AL**

☐ **P. 77** Students discuss the establishment of Georgia.

☑ *Online Teaching Options*

V Visual Skills

☐ **VIDEO** **The Caribbean Connection**—Students view a video that explains the link between South Carolina and Barbados.

☐ **MAP** **The Southern Colonies**—Students locate the Southern Colonies with respect to the other colonies and identify the products produced in each colony.

☐ **IMAGE** **Indigo**—Students discover the important crops grown in the Southern Colonies.

☐ **IMAGE** **Plantations**—Students examine how the growth of plantations contributed to the rise of slavery.

R Reading Skills

☐ **GRAPHIC ORGANIZER** **Taking Notes:** *Determining Cause and Effect:* **Causes and Effects of Bacon's Rebellion**—Students complete the lesson graphic organizer in which they list the causes and effects of Bacon's Rebellion.

☐ **PRIMARY SOURCE** **Nathaniel Bacon**—Students discuss Bacon's Rebellion.

C Critical Thinking Skills

☐ **CHART** **Enslaved People in the Colonies 1650–1710**—Students compare and contrast characteristics of enslaved Africans and indentured servants.

T Technology Skills

☐ **SELF-CHECK QUIZ** **Lesson 4**—Students receive instant feedback of their mastery of lesson content.

☐ **GAME** **The Southern Colonies Identification Game**—Students complete a matching game to reinforce their understandings of the New England, Middle, and Southern colonies.

☑ *Printable Digital Worksheets*

W Writing Skills

☐ **WORKSHEET** **Economics of History Activity: Colonial America, The Southern Colonies**—Students respond to a selection that describes labor in South Carolina.

INTERVENTION AND REMEDIATION STRATEGIES

LESSON 1 Roanoke and Jamestown

Reading and Comprehension

To ensure comprehension of the concepts in the lesson, have students write sentences using the new lesson vocabulary. Sentences should show an understanding of the meaning of each word and how it applies to the lesson content.

Text Evidence

Ask students to analyze the settlements at Roanoke and Jamestown. Students should list similarities and differences they identify in the text, and supplement their findings with independent research. Students should address these questions in their analyses: Why did the earliest settlers come to Virginia? What did they find waiting for them? What makes a colony successful?

LESSON 2 The New England Colonies

Reading and Comprehension

Understanding diagrams is essential when reading informational text. Direct students to the cut-away diagram of the *Mayflower*. Have students working in groups of five take turns reading one of the extended captions and pointing out salient details of that portion of the ship. Have students look up unknown words such as *forecastle* and *whipstaff* and share the definitions with others in the group.

Text Evidence

Organize the students into an even number of small groups. Have each group discuss this statement: Religious persecution was the most important reason driving people to move to America in the 1600s. Assign half the groups to argue *for* this statement, and half to argue *against*. After allowing time for discussion, have groups with the same position meet to pool their arguments and craft a position statement. Have groups present their statement and their reasons to the class.

LESSON 3 The Middle Colonies

Reading and Comprehension

Using visuals as clues to meanings can aid in comprehension. Pair students, and have them skim the lesson, stopping to look at each visual. Suggest they read the heads on the page on which the visual appears and its caption. Then have students write sentences predicting what the lesson will be about, using the information they have discovered.

Text Evidence

The similarities and differences among the middle colonies can be confusing for students. Organize the class into four groups, and assign each group a colony. Have each group use evidence from the text as well as additional research they undertake to prepare a description of their colony that they can share with the class. Allow students to use varied formats for their presentations, such as slide shows, posters, skits, or poems/songs.

LESSON 4 The Southern Colonies

Reading and Comprehension

Provide a structure for note taking. Suggest that students turn each red title into a question. After they read a section, have them write the answer to the question they wrote. Have pairs of students share their questions and answers on the same sections.

Text Evidence

Students may not realize the important role indentured servants played in the development of the early colonies. After researching the role of these early colonists, have students write and perform a three-act skit detailing the life of an indentured servant. Act 1 should be the servant's arrival in America and introduction to his or her master; Act 2 should be a scene from daily life; and Act 3 should be the servant's emancipation.

Online Resources

Approaching Level Reader

Use this online lower-level text that corresponds directly to the text in the Student Edition. It includes a Spanish version.

Guided Reading Activities

This resource uses graphic organizers and guiding questions to help students with comprehension.

What Do You Know?

Use these worksheets to pre-assess student's background knowledge before they study the chapter.

Reading Essentials and Study Guide Workbook

This resource offers writing and reading activities for the approaching-level student. Also available in Spanish.

Self-Check Quizzes

This online assessment tool provides instant feedback for students to check their progress.

How Do I Use the
btw: Stuff You Should Know
Current Events Web Site?

Using social media in the classroom sounds like a great idea. But where do you start?

The articles on McGraw-Hill's btw Web site offer engaging, student-centric coverage of current events. These articles can be used in your classroom in a number of ways.

Option **1** ## Use as a Bellringer Activity

- Start your class by having students read an article on *btw*. Then, launch a discussion by having students respond to the questions that accompany that article.

- Or, post the article on your classroom blog or discussion board and have the students respond to the questions as homework before you teach the content.

Option **2** ## Activate Critical Thinking

- Assign an article and the accompanying questions to encourage analysis of a specific topic.

- Use accompanying activities for group work during class time.

Option **3** ## Engage Students in High-Interest Projects

- Ask students to analyze different points of view and take a stand on current domestic and world issues in the "You Decide" feature.

- In the "Be an Active Citizen!" section, encourage students to link to the iCivics Web site inspired by Justice Sandra Day O'Connor.

- Tap into the btw "Teacher Page" to find tools to help you create more digitally-driven projects.

Visit <u>http://blog.glencoe.com</u> to keep up to date with the btw Current Events Web site.

Colonial America

1587–1770

networks

There's More Online about the people and events of early colonial America.

CHAPTER 3

ESSENTIAL QUESTIONS • *How does geography influence the way people live?* • *How do new ideas change the way people live?*

The Story Matters . . .

She has three names, and she lives in two worlds. She is born Matoak, daughter of the chief of the Powhatan people. Yet she is such a fun-loving child that she is called "Pocahontas," or "playful one."

In 1607, bold Pocahontas—not yet a teenager—befriends the English colonists who settle nearby. She convinces her father to aid the colonists. In time she receives the English name Rebecca and marries a Briton. Their son is Thomas. The family travels to England, where Rebecca is presented to King James as a princess. Sadly, before her return to America, she falls ill. "Tis enough that [our] child liveth," she tells her husband before she dies.

◄ *Pocahontas played a key role in the early history of colonial Virginia.*

W. Langdon Kihn/National Geographic Society/Corbis

57

Letter from the Author

Dear American History Teacher,

The thirteen colonies established between 1607 and 1733 formed three regions. Virginia, Britain's first colony in the New World, experienced great wealth from growing tobacco. This commercial agriculture used enslaved laborers and differentiated the Southern colonies from other colonies. The Massachusetts Bay Colony was founded by Puritans seeking a place to establish churches. With tight-knit communities, disciplined workers, and strong leaders, the Puritan colonies flourished. Pennsylvania acquired a mixed European population, making the Middle Colonies the most diverse.

Joyce Appleby

ENGAGE

Bellringer Draw a T-chart on the board, with column heads *Legend* and *Fact*. Ask students what they have heard about Pocahontas, and where they heard that information. As students respond, explain that many legends have grown up about this woman who lived four centuries ago, but that her real life was even more interesting than the fictitious accounts.

Ask a volunteer to read "The Story Matters . . ." aloud. Have students raise their hands every time a fact about Pocahontas is revealed. Record these facts in the chart. Then explain that Pocahontas was almost 12 years old when she first befriended the English colonists. William Strachey, Jamestown's official historian, wrote that Pocahontas used to turn cartwheels through the middle of her village. But despite her youth, she quickly became a diplomat, acting as an ambassador between her father and the Jamestown settlers. She acted as a peacemaker and even negotiated with the settlers to arrange the release of Powhatan captives. Then she, herself, was kidnapped and married to an Englishman, ushering in the "peace of Pocahontas," which was to last for her lifetime.

Ask: In what three worlds did Pocahontas live? (*her own Powhatan culture, that of the Jamestown settlers, and then England itself*) Tell students that London was a city of a quarter million people when Pocahontas visited. She had likely never been to a place with more than a few hundred people before.

Ask: What emotions might she have felt? (*excitement, nervousness*)

Making Connections

Explain that vaccination campaigns are the result of medical advances in the twentieth century. For most of history, the only way to be "immunized" against a disease was to be exposed to it directly by spending time with someone who was ill or who was acting as a carrier for a virus or bacteria, or by handling objects that had been contaminated with a disease. Tell students that Pocahontas, who lived only to about the age of 21, is believed to have died of a disease that she did not have natural immunity to because she had not grown up in England. It was no coincidence that at home many other Powhatan were dying of similar diseases.

Ask: Why has it become unusual for people in our society to die of diseases such as smallpox? (*Possible answers: vaccination campaigns, better public hygiene, safe drinking water*)

TEACH & ASSESS

Step Into the Place

V1 Visual Skills

Analyzing Maps Review the map with students, pointing out the early British colonial cities. Remind students that the British colonies were in areas inhabited by Native Americans, and that the colonists were surrounded by Native Americans. **Ask: What information is missing from this map?** *(the areas in which Native American nations lived)* **How would you describe the British colonies in relation to North America?** *(The early colonies were limited to an area along the Atlantic coast. They constituted a small region compared to British and French landholdings at this particular time.)*

Remind students that European explorers did not know the full extent of the territories they were exploring. **Ask: Why do you think France extended so far inland, rather than claiming as much land along the coast as Great Britain did?** *(French explorers took a more northern route and used the Great Lakes as a transportation network.)* **AL** **What physical features do you see that might have aided French explorers to travel long distances?** *(In addition to the Great Lakes, there were rivers that could be traveled for long distances.)*

Have students work in pairs to compare the map shown here with a current map of the United States. Have students make a list of states that fall within each territorial area. Remind students that some states have boundaries that fall within more than one of the areas shown here. *(Answers will vary but should demonstrate accurate use of the map.)* **ELL** Ask volunteers to discuss each land claim area, describing which states fall within that area today. Then have students answer the Map Focus questions. **Visual/Spatial**

Making Connections

Explain that although European powers claimed the areas of land shown here, they did not control these areas or govern them in their entirety. The land claims reflected a European vision of the future, not the present.

ANSWERS, p. 58

Step Into the Place
1. France
2. Britain's land appears to be the most settled/populated.
3. **CRITICAL THINKING** Answers will vary, but students might suggest that conflicts over land claims would probably have lead to conflict between the nations.

Step Into the Time
Less than 20 years after the defeat of the Spanish Armada, England began establishing colonies in North America. Students might infer that the defeat of the Spanish Armada freed England to focus on colonization.

Place and Time: Colonial America 1587 to 1770

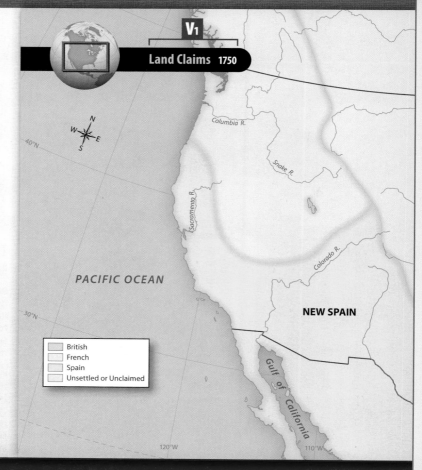

Although several European nations had claims in North America, it was the British who eventually dominated the continent. England's early attempts at colonizing ended in failure, but by 1750, British colonies stretched for hundreds of miles along the Atlantic Coast.

V1 Land Claims 1750

Step Into the Place

MAP FOCUS Several European powers claimed parts of North America in the mid-1700s.

1. **PLACE** Which European power claimed the largest territory in North America? RH.6–8.7

2. **HUMAN-ENVIRONMENT INTERACTION** Which nation's land claims seem to be the most settled and populated? RH.6–8.7

3. **CRITICAL THINKING**
   Predicting What effect do you think these nations' land claims in North America might have on relations between them?
   RH.6–8.7, RH.6–8.10

Legend:
- British
- French
- Spain
- Unsettled or Unclaimed

PACIFIC OCEAN

NEW SPAIN

Columbia R.
Snake R.
Sacramento R.
Colorado R.
Gulf of California

40°N
30°N
120°W
110°W

Step Into the Time

TIME LINE Look at the time line. The Spanish Armada was a fleet of warships Spain sent to attack England. How might this event be related to what happened in North America at about that time? RH.6–8.5, RH.6–8.7

V2

AMERICAS
WORLD EVENTS 1550

1600

1607 English establish first permanent settlement at Jamestown

1612 Tobacco planted in Virginia

1620 Pilgrims land at Plymouth Rock

1588 England defeats Spanish Armada

c. 1605 Shakespeare writes *King Lear*

58 *Colonial America*

Project-Based Learning 🖐

Hands-On Chapter Project

Create Presentations

Students work in groups to create illustrated presentations about one of six possible locations for the Jamestown settlement. Students will review the information about colonial America in their textbook and then conduct personal research, citing at least three sources. They will choose the site they think is best, create a presentation supporting their position, and deliver their presentation to the class.

Technology Extension

Mapping Possible Jamestown Locations with Google™ Maps

Students will create an interactive online map of options for locating Jamestown. Students may use an online mapping platform, such as Google Maps™. Students work in small groups to research locations and to provide three reasons and a conclusion as to why the location they choose is best. They can annotate the online map with this information. As groups present their maps to the class, ask students to compare and contrast the locations selected.

edtechteacher
21st Century Learning

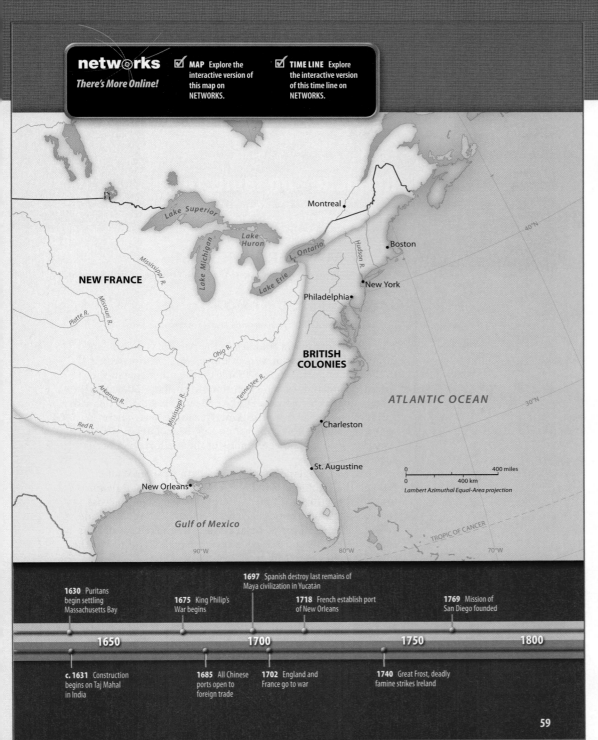

NEW FRANCE

BRITISH COLONIES

Montreal

Boston

New York

Philadelphia

Charleston

St. Augustine

New Orleans

Gulf of Mexico

ATLANTIC OCEAN

Lake Superior
Lake Huron
Lake Michigan
Lake Erie
L. Ontario
Hudson R.
Mississippi R.
Missouri R.
Platte R.
Arkansas R.
Red R.
Ohio R.
Tennessee R.

40°N
30°N
90°W
80°W
70°W
TROPIC OF CANCER

0   400 miles
0   400 km
Lambert Azimuthal Equal-Area projection

1630 Puritans begin settling Massachusetts Bay

1675 King Philip's War begins

1697 Spanish destroy last remains of Maya civilization in Yucatán

1718 French establish port of New Orleans

1769 Mission of San Diego founded

c. 1631 Construction begins on Taj Mahal in India

1685 All Chinese ports open to foreign trade

1702 England and France go to war

1740 Great Frost, deadly famine strikes Ireland

1650   1700   1750   1800

59

Step Into the Time

V₂ Visual Skills

Analyzing Time Lines Have students examine the time line for the chapter. Point out that this chapter deals with events from the late 1500s to the late 1700s. **Ask:**

- Where would Pocahontas's lifetime fall on this time line? How can you tell? *(by the 1607 marker; because she interacted with the Jamestown settlers)* **Visual/Spatial**
- Which events on the time line might affect life in the English colonies during that period? *(all events on the U.S. time line; on the world time line: England defeats Spanish Armada; England and France go to war)*

Content Background Knowledge

- Millions of Native Americans, including hundreds of Native American nations, lived in North America at the time of European contact. One reason that European settlers described North America as sparsely populated was that traders and explorers had brought diseases that killed, according to most estimates, about 95 percent of the local native people. The Native American population decline began about 1500 and continued until about 1900.
- Though Pocahontas died in England, it was for many of the same reasons that Native Americans were dying in epidemic numbers at home.
- In areas that had been decimated by disease, it was hard for Native Americans to muster strong resistance to European conquest.

CLOSE & REFLECT

Formulating Questions On separate pieces of paper, have each student write a question about an event on the time line and on the back write the name of the event. Use students' questions as an opportunity for them to work individually, in small groups, or as a class to review the key events they will be reading about in the chapter.

TIME LINE

Place and Time: Colonial America 1587–1770

Comparing and Contrasting Display the time line on the white board. Have volunteers compare and contrast the events of the 1600s to those of the 1700s. Ask students to choose one event from each time frame. Then have them write a paragraph to compare and contrast the events.

See page 57B for other online activities.

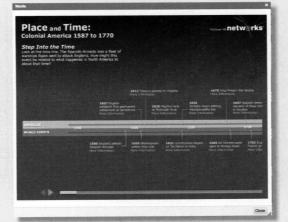

ENGAGE

🔔 **Bellringer** If possible, take students outside. Have them brainstorm how they would survive in their own outdoor environment, without the infrastructure of grocery stores and public transportation. Have students write a narrative paragraph reflecting on what strategies they might use to survive in such a situation. Encourage students to draw illustrations to support their strategies. **ELL** **Ask:**

- What challenges would you face if you had to support yourself by living off the land at this time of the year? *(Students should mention survival-related challenges, such as finding food and water, and making shelter.)*
- What resources do you see around you that you could use as tools to help you survive? *(Students might mention making tools or weapons from branches or rocks, or gathering seeds from edible plants.)*
- What if you not only had to support yourself, but also care for children? What additional challenges might you face? *(Students might mention such challenges as foraging for food or hunting while keeping a baby safe, or losing members of one's family to disease or starvation.)*

TEACH & ASSESS

R Reading Skills

Identifying After students have read the text, explain that colonists did not organize their own trips to the Americas. The founding of each colony had to be organized and financed by someone with government connections. In Great Britain, this meant someone with connections in Queen Elizabeth's court. **Ask: Who was Sir Walter Raleigh?** *(He was an explorer who sent settlers to Roanoke Island.)* **How was Raleigh significant to American history?** *(He helped establish one of the first colonies in America.)*

C Critical Thinking Skills

Sequencing Ask students to name and locate the first English colony in North America. On the board, list events in the history of the Roanoke Colony. **Ask: In what order did the main events in the colony's history occur?** **AL** *(1584—Raleigh's scouts recommend location; 1585—first settlers start settlement on Roanoke but return to England; 1587—second group of settlers establish settlement on Roanoke, leader John White returns to England; 1590—White returns from England, colony is gone and settlers have disappeared)*

ANSWER, p. 60

TAKING NOTES: disease, hunger, hostile Native Americans

netw⊙rks
There's More Online!

☑ **CHART/GRAPH**
- The Golden Crop
- The Mystery of the Lost Colony

☑ **GRAPHIC ORGANIZER**
Listing

☑ **VIDEO**

Lesson 1
Roanoke and Jamestown

ESSENTIAL QUESTION *How does geography influence the way people live?*

IT MATTERS BECAUSE
Jamestown was the first successful English colony in North America.

The Mystery of Roanoke

GUIDING QUESTION *What problems did the Roanoke settlers encounter?*

The success of Spain's colonies in the Americas did not go unnoticed. The great powers of Europe were all interested in the rich opportunities available on the other side of the Atlantic. England was no exception. In the late 1500s, English pirates such as Sir Francis Drake had success stealing Spanish treasure on its way from the Americas to Europe. There were even some efforts to start an English colony in North America. By 1584, however, none of these efforts had been successful.

R That year, England's Queen Elizabeth gave Sir Walter Raleigh the right to claim land in North America. Raleigh took up this effort with great energy. He sent scouts across the ocean to find a good place for a colony. The scouts made an enthusiastic report of a place called Roanoke Island. This island lies off the coast of what is now North Carolina. At the time, Raleigh called this area Virginia.

C Raleigh sent settlers to Roanoke Island twice. The first group arrived in 1585. While they were there, artist John White explored the area and drew pictures of what he saw. In a book illustrated by White, another colonist described the Native American towns:

(l) The Granger Collection, NYC, (c) National Park Service, (r) Library of Congress Prints & Photographs Division, [LC-DIG-det-4a26409]

Reading **HELP**DESK **CCSS**

Taking Notes: *Listing* RH.6–8.1, RH.6–8.7
As you read, use a diagram like this one to list hardships the people of Jamestown faced.

Hardships for Jamestown Settlers

Content Vocabulary (Tier 3 Words)
- charter
- joint-stock company
- headright
- burgess

60 *Colonial America*

---

netw⊙rks   *Online Teaching Options*

VIDEO

Life in Jamestown

Identifying Evidence Show the video to students, and then discuss how the colony on Roanoke is often called the "Lost Colony." Explain that the fate of the colonists is one of history's mysteries. Use the interactive chart entitled "The Mystery of the Lost Colony" to discuss each of the clues on the chart and how those clues might provide evidence to support the various theories of what happened to the colony. **BL**

See page 57C for other online activities.

PRIMARY SOURCE

" Their townes are but small, & neere the sea coast but few, some containing but 10 or 12 houses: some 20, the greatest that we [have] seene [have] bene but of 30 houses: if they be walled it is only done with barks of trees made fast to stakes. "

—from *A Briefe and True Report of the New Found Land of Virginia*, 1588

The 1585 expedition produced some valuable information about the people and places of Virginia. Their colony, however, did not survive. After suffering through a difficult winter, the colonists gave up and returned to England.

Then, in 1587 Raleigh sent 91 men, 17 women, and 9 children to Roanoke. John White led this group. Shortly after arriving on the island, White's daughter, who was part of the expedition, gave birth. Virginia Dare was the first English child born in North America.

Nine days after his granddaughter's birth, White returned to England for supplies. Although he had hoped to be back within a few months, White was delayed. His country was at war with Spain. This war featured England's great naval battle with the Spanish Armada. The fighting between England and Spain made it impossible for White to sail back to Roanoke for nearly three years.

When he returned to Roanoke, White found his colony deserted. The only clue he found was a tree with the word *Croatoan* carved on it. White thought perhaps the colonists had gone to Croatoan Island, about 50 miles (80 km) to the south. Bad weather kept White from **investigating**. The Roanoke colonists were never seen again.

C

☑ PROGRESS CHECK

Explaining Why did the English decide to settle in Roanoke?

Success at Jamestown

GUIDING QUESTION *Why did the Jamestown settlement succeed?*

For a time, the failure at Roanoke discouraged the English from settling in North America. The idea emerged again in 1606. By then, England had a new king, James I. He wanted to renew England's quest for a colony in North America. Several merchants pressed him for a **charter**—a document that granted the right to form a colony.

charter a document granting the recipient the right to settle a colony

Academic Vocabulary (Tier 2 Words)

investigate to try to discover facts and other information about something

Thinking Like a HISTORIAN

Analyzing Primary Sources

John White drew pictures of the plants, animals, and people of the region in order to help educate Europeans about North America. For more information about analyzing primary sources, read *Thinking Like a Historian*.

▶ CRITICAL THINKING

Analyzing Visuals Do you think John White's sketches are a primary source? Why or why not?

The Granger Collection, NYC

C Critical Thinking Skills

Speculating Explain that historians have never stopped trying to solve the puzzle of Roanoke Island. In 2012 scientists working at the British Museum used infrared light, x-ray spectroscopy, and other modern imaging techniques to examine a map drawn by John White. They discovered two small patches—one of which covered a marking that is now thought to have represented another fort. **Ask:**

- Why do you think scientists were so excited to discover another settlement location? *(because the settlers may have moved there temporarily after leaving Roanoke)*
- Why do you think the patch might have been placed over the location of the fort on White's map? *(Students' answers may vary, but some scholars think that the fort's location on the map was hidden deliberately.)*

Content Background Knowledge

- When the Virginia Company chose the site for the Jamestown colony, they took into consideration possible attacks by the Powhatan, and possible attacks by the Spanish. Jamestown was far enough inland to be difficult for the Spanish to attack. It was protected by a strong fort with several pieces of artillery.
- The water in the harbor at Jamestown was deep enough for a ship to moor there, which was important for possible trade with Great Britain and the rest of Europe and important in case the colony needed to be evacuated.
- During the early years at Jamestown, the settlers could not have survived without food from the Powhatan.

BIOGRAPHY

John White

Analyzing Visuals Use the interactive image of John White's art to discuss White, his role in the Roanoke colony, and his sketches of the region. **Ask: Who was John White?** *(He was the man who led the group that Raleigh sent to Roanoke.)* **Why did he leave Roanoke?** *(He returned to England for supplies.)* **What did he discover when he returned?** *(He found the colony deserted, and his only clue as to what happened was the word* CROATOAN *carved into a tree.)* **Would the illustration in the slide be considered a primary or a secondary source?** *(a primary source)* BL

See page 57C for other online activities.

ANSWERS, p. 61

CRITICAL THINKING yes, because White was drawing things that he actually saw

☑ PROGRESS CHECK Sir Walter Raleigh's scouts said it was a good place for a colony.

R Reading Skills

Identifying Have a volunteer read the text. Then, discuss Captain John Smith's role in Jamestown. **Ask:**

- **How did Smith's leadership help the colony survive?** *(Smith knew that without hard work the colony would not last. He forced the settlers to work.)* **BL**
- **What were the first two years like for the Jamestown colonists?** *(They faced hardships and hunger.)*
- **How did the colony's relations with Native Americans affect its success?** *(At first Native Americans helped the colonists and provided food, but later they stopped doing this.)*

Making Connections

Explain that the Virginia Company was a joint-stock company, similar to companies today that are traded on the stock market. Stocks are shares in a company. The company's owners, or shareholders, provide money to get the company started or keep it operating, and they receive profits if the company succeeds in making money. However, in the 1600s, shares in companies were not traded on a stock market. In addition, companies in the 1600s could not form freely. They had to receive a charter from the legislature, which would be granted only if the company was going to do something regarded as a public work, or a work that was for the good of the country.

The Virginia Company

The Virginia Company was a **joint-stock company**, in which investors bought shares, or part ownership. Investors bought shares hoping the company would make money and that they would share in the profits. The plan was for the company's settlers to find gold and establish trade in fish and furs.

James I granted a charter to the Virginia Company of London. In December 1606, the company sent 144 settlers in three ships to build a new colony in North America. In April 1607, the ships entered Chesapeake Bay. They sailed up a river flowing into the bay. The colonists named the river the James and their new settlement Jamestown to honor their king.

Jamestown Survives

R The colonists did not find gold or riches in Virginia. Instead they faced severe hardships, including disease and hunger. The colony survived its first two years in part because of 27-year-old Captain John Smith. Smith forced the settlers to work. He also built ties with—and got food from—the local Powhatan people and their chief, who was also named Powhatan.

In late 1609, Smith was injured and had to return to England. The colony struggled. The Powhatan stopped providing food. The winter of 1609–1610 was called "the starving time."

Soon after landing, the Jamestown colonists began building a fort for protection. The surrounding forest provided the materials they needed for this project.

joint-stock company a company in which investors buy stock in return for a share of its future profits

headright a 50-acre grant of land given to colonial settlers who paid their own way
burgess elected representative to an assembly

Academic Vocabulary (Tier 2 Words)
expand to increase in size or number

netw⊚rks *Online Teaching Options*

GRAPHIC ORGANIZER

Taking Notes: *Listing:* **Hardships for Jamestown Settlers**

Listing Use the interactive graphic organizer to list hardships that the people of Jamestown faced. Students may write words or draw sketches with labels in each circle of the graphic organizer. **Ask: Would you want to have been one of those colonists? Why or why not?** *(Possible answer: No, I think it would have been too challenging.)* **AL ELL Interpersonal**

See page 57C for other online activities.

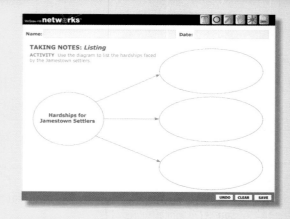

Somehow Jamestown survived this terrible time. More colonists arrived to replace those who had died. The colonists also found a way to make money for the investors. They began growing a type of tobacco using seeds from the West Indies. Soon planters all along the James River were raising this valuable crop.

More Settlers Come to Virginia

The colony of Virginia began to **expand**. Relations with the Powhatan improved after a colonist, John Rolfe, married the chief's daughter, Pocahontas. The Virginia Company sent women to Jamestown. As a result, marriage and children became a part of life in the colony. The Virginia Company also began giving a **headright** (HEHD·RYT), or land grant, of 50 acres to settlers who paid their own way to the colony. The headright system helped the colony succeed. The chance to own land lured many settlers to Virginia and gave them a reason to work hard.

The Virginia Company also gave the colonists the right to take part in their own government. In 1619 land-owning male colonists cast ballots for **burgesses** (BUHR·juhs·uhz), or representatives. The burgesses helped make laws for the colony. The House of Burgesses was the first legislature in North America elected by the people.

The Virginia Colony was growing in size, but it was not making any money for the shareholders of the Virginia Company. In fact, the company faced financial troubles. In 1624 King James took away the company's charter. Virginia became a royal colony, meaning it was directly under the control of the government in England.

☑ **PROGRESS CHECK**

Analyzing Why was the House of Burgesses important?

Pocahontas, shown here in English-style clothes for a visit to England, served as a link between the colonists and the Native Americans of Virginia.

Library of Congress Prints & Photographs Division, [LC-DIG-det-4a26409]

LESSON 1 REVIEW (CCSS)

Review Vocabulary (Tier 3 Words)

1. Examine the meaning of *charter* and *joint-stock company* by using each term in a sentence. RH.6–8.4

2. Write a sentence about the early years of the Virginia colony that use the following terms. RH.6–8.4
   a. headright   **b.** burgess

Answer the Guiding Questions

3. *Describing* What did John White find when he returned to Roanoke after several years in England? RH.6–8.1

4. *Explaining* Why was the Jamestown colony able to prosper in spite of many hardships? RH.6–8.2

5. **ARGUMENT** Using primary and secondary source images and descriptions in this lesson, write an advertisement for a newspaper in England that encourages people to come to America in the 1600s. WHST.6–8.9, WHST.6–8.10

Lesson 1   **63**

LESSON 1 REVIEW ANSWERS

1. Possible answers: A charter was a document from the king that gave a group the right to organize a settlement. A joint-stock company was a company in which people bought shares of ownership.

2. Possible answer: Colonists could own land through the headright system, and male property owners began electing burgesses to represent them in a new colonial legislature.

3. The colony was deserted and the word *Croatoan* was carved on a tree trunk.

4. John Smith's leadership, growing tobacco, Rolfe's marriage to Pocahontas, the headright system, the House of Burgesses

5. Advertisements will vary but should demonstrate an understanding of the colonists' motivations.

W Writing Skills

Argument In movies, Pocahontas appears as a romantic image, and she is often portrayed as being in love with John Smith. On the other hand, history portrays Pocahontas as a diplomat who entered into a marriage with a different Englishman, John Rolfe, in order to start an alliance between Jamestown and the Powhatan.

Have students write a paragraph arguing for the portrayal of Pocahontas as a young girl who fell in love with John Smith or for the portrayal of a diplomat who was instrumental in forming and strengthening relations between the English and the Powhatan. Encourage students to state their arguments clearly, using strong, supporting points. *(Students' paragraphs will vary but should clearly state their arguments and supporting points. They should use a logical sequence and restate the argument in the concluding sentence.)*

V Visual Skills

Analyzing Images Use the image of Pocahontas to stimulate a discussion of the ways in which Pocahontas's life changed when she married John Rolfe and joined the Jamestown settlement. **Ask: How did Pocahontas affect the success of the Jamestown settlement?** *(When Pocahontas married settler John Rolfe, relations with Native Americans improved.)* **How did this help the colony of Virginia to expand?** *(The improvement of the relationship between the Native Americans and the colonists allowed the colony to expand, because it was a time of peace and people felt safe. Women were sent to the colony. People began to get married and have children.)* **BL** Visual/Spatial

Have students complete the Lesson 1 Review.

CLOSE & REFLECT

To close the lesson, remind students that Jamestown was primarily a business venture. Have students characterize whether the settlement would have been regarded as a success or a failure according to modern business guidelines. *(Possible response: No, the settlement was initially established to make money for shareholders of The Virginia Company. The settlement failed to do that and was eventually taken over by the English government.)*

ANSWER, p. 63

☑ **PROGRESS CHECK** It was the first legislature in North America elected by the people.

ENGAGE

Bellringer Invite volunteers to share current events about religious refugees around the world. Allow time for students to work together in small groups to research an event that was shared or a different event that deals with modern-day religious refugees. Ask them to summarize the event, including its causes and its effects on people's freedom to practice their religion. Ask a spokesperson from each group to present their summary orally to the class. As part of the presentation, have each student locate the news event on a map. After students have completed their presentations, discuss religious persecution. **Ask: What religions or religious groups are in conflict in the world today?** *(Answers will vary.)* **How do persecuted religious groups react to oppression in their home countries?** *(Answers will vary.)*

TEACH & ASSESS

C Critical Thinking Skills

Determining Cause and Effect Discuss with students that in 1534, King Henry VIII of England not only broke away from the Roman Catholic Church, he also formed the Anglican Church. **Ask: If you and your family had been Roman Catholics for several generations, what reaction would you have had when you were told you had to become an Anglican?** *(Student responses may vary but should include understandable reactions that were caused by forcing a state religion on people.)*

R Reading Skills

Identifying As students read the text, discuss with them the two groups of people who did not like being forced to be a part of King Henry's new church. **Ask:**

- **What two groups of people opposed King Henry's church?** *(Separatists and Puritans)* **To which group did the Pilgrims belong?** *(the Separatists)*
- **Why were these people called Separatists?** *(because they wanted to set up their own churches separate from the Anglican church)*
- **What is the basic reason the Separatists known as Pilgrims went to America?** *(They wanted religious freedom.)* **AL**

ANSWER, p. 64

TAKING NOTES: Possible answers: Plymouth colonists learned how to grow corn, beans, and pumpkins; colonists learned where to hunt and fish; treaty with Wampanoag allowed settlers and Native Americans to live in harmony; colonists' settlement on Native American land led to a conflict known as King Philip's War.

---

netw⊙rks
There's More Online!

☑ **CHART/GRAPH**
King Philip's War

☑ **GRAPHIC ORGANIZER**
Cooperation and Conflict between Colonists and Native Americans

☑ **MAP** The New England Colonies

☑ **SLIDE SHOW** The Pilgrims

Lesson 2
The New England Colonies

ESSENTIAL QUESTION *How do new ideas change the way people live?*

IT MATTERS BECAUSE

Seeking freedom to pursue their own religion, English settlers started colonies in New England. Many people still come to the Americas in search of religious freedom.

Seeking Religious Freedom

GUIDING QUESTION *Why did the Puritans settle in North America?*

The Jamestown settlers had come to America in search of wealth. The next wave of English colonists arrived in search of religious freedom.

England had been a Protestant country since 1534, when the king, Henry VIII, broke away from the Roman Catholic Church and formed the Anglican Church. Not everyone in England was happy with the new church. Many people **dissented** (dih·SEHNT·uhd), disagreeing with Anglican beliefs or practices. Some English people remained Catholic. Others were Protestants who wanted to reform the Anglican Church. Still others wanted to break away from it altogether. The Protestants who wished to reform the Anglican Church were called Puritans. Those who sought to set up their own churches were known as Separatists.

The Separatists were **persecuted** (PUHR·sih·kyoot·uhd)—mistreated because of their beliefs—in England. Some fled to the Netherlands. There they found freedom to practice their religion, but they had difficulty finding work. They also worried that their children were losing their religious values and their English way of life.

(c) Swerer/Alamy Images, (r) Bettmann/CORBIS.

Reading HELPDESK **CCSS**

Taking Notes: *Describing* RH.6–8.1, RH.6–8.7
Use a diagram like this one to describe examples of cooperation and conflict between Native Americans and English colonists.

Cooperation and Conflict

Content Vocabulary (Tier 3 Words)
- dissent
- persecute
- tolerance

64 *Colonial America*

---

netw⊙rks *Online Teaching Options*

VIDEO

Bitter Conflict Grows Between New England Colonists and Native Americans

Giving Examples After showing the video on conflict between New England colonists and Native Americans, ask students to describe examples of cooperation and conflict between Native Americans and English colonists. **Ask: Do you think the Plymouth colonists would have survived if they had not found peace with the Wampanoag?** *(Possible answer: Perhaps not. Working and learning how to live together in peace may have led to their survival.)* **AL**

See page 57D for other online activities.

LEARN360
ENGAGE · ENRICH · EXCEL

The Pilgrims Settle Plymouth

In 1620 a group of Separatists decided to move to America. They became known as the Pilgrims. A pilgrim is someone who undertakes a religious journey. The Pilgrims were able to get grants of land from the Virginia Company. They got permission to settle in Virginia and to practice their religion freely. They boarded a ship called the *Mayflower* and left to begin new lives.

The *Mayflower* drifted off course on its journey across the Atlantic. The first land the Pilgrims sighted was Cape Cod, well north of their target. It was November, and winter was fast approaching. The colonists decided to drop anchor in Cape Cod Bay. They went ashore on a cold, bleak day in December at a place they called Plymouth.

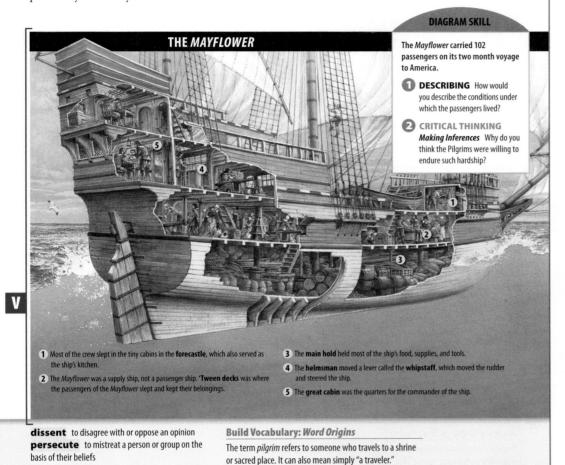

THE *MAYFLOWER*

DIAGRAM SKILL

The *Mayflower* carried 102 passengers on its two month voyage to America.

1 DESCRIBING How would you describe the conditions under which the passengers lived?

2 CRITICAL THINKING *Making Inferences* Why do you think the Pilgrims were willing to endure such hardship?

1 Most of the crew slept in the tiny cabins in the **forecastle**, which also served as the ship's kitchen.

2 The *Mayflower* was a supply ship, not a passenger ship. **'Tween decks** was where the passengers of the *Mayflower* slept and kept their belongings.

3 The **main hold** held most of the ship's food, supplies, and tools.

4 The **helmsman** moved a lever called the **whipstaff**, which moved the rudder and steered the ship.

5 The **great cabin** was the quarters for the commander of the ship.

dissent to disagree with or oppose an opinion
persecute to mistreat a person or group on the basis of their beliefs

Build Vocabulary: *Word Origins*

The term *pilgrim* refers to someone who travels to a shrine or sacred place. It can also mean simply "a traveler."

Lesson 2 **65**

V Visual Skills

Analyzing Images Use the cut-away diagram in the textbook to further discuss the voyage of the *Mayflower*. Have volunteers point out and describe different sections of the ship. Draw a T-chart on the board and discuss with students the reasons and ways that people come to the United States today, and analyze the hardships that individuals endure for freedom.

Content Background Knowledge

- It took the *Mayflower* about two months to cross the Atlantic. It was supposed to be joined by the *Speedwell*, in which some of the Pilgrims had traveled to England from the Netherlands. The *Speedwell* turned out not to be seaworthy and had to turn back, so the *Mayflower* took some of its passengers and supplies.

- Shortly after the Pilgrims anchored at Plymouth, Wampanoag leader Massasoit stopped by to visit. Over the next couple of months, he was able to gain the trust of the Pilgrims.

- The first "Thanksgiving" was a feast that lasted for days and included about 50 Pilgrims and about 100 Wampanoag. Historians are not sure whether turkey was served, but primary documents from the time state that the men "went fowling."

IMAGE

The *Mayflower*

Analyzing Use the interactive image of the *Mayflower* to discuss its voyage with students. **Ask:** What words would you use to describe the Pilgrims' voyage? *(long, crowded, difficult, dangerous)* Continue eliciting opinions on what it must have been like to make this arduous voyage. **AL ELL**

See page 57D for other online activities.

The Mayflower was originally a wine ship before it was used by the Pilgrims. The ship had three masts, weighed 180 tons, and was 90-feet long and 26-feet wide. It originally departed from England with another ship, the Speedwell, but ended up sailing to North America alone on September 16, 1620, because the Speedwell was not seaworthy and had to return to port.

ANSWERS, p. 65

DIAGRAM SKILL

1. The conditions were crowded and noisy; there was little room for privacy.

2. **CRITICAL THINKING** The Pilgrims were committed to gaining their freedom.

R1 Reading Skills

Discussing Have a volunteer read the text. Then, discuss with students the creation of the Mayflower Compact. **Ask: What did the Mayflower Compact establish?** *(It established a government for the new colonists who lived outside the Virginia Company.)* AL ELL

R2 Reading Skills

Explaining After students have read the text, discuss with them how the Pilgrims suffered hunger and illness until two Native Americans, Squanto and Samoset, befriended the colonists. Squanto had previously been kidnapped and taken to England, where he learned to speak English. Samoset had learned English from English explorers in Maine. Discuss the impact of these two Native Americans on the Pilgrims. **Ask:**

- **How did Squanto and Samoset help the Pilgrims?** *(They helped the Pilgrims survive by teaching them how to grow corn, beans, and pumpkins, and where to hunt and fish.)*

- **Why do you think the Pilgrims would need help from Squanto and Samoset to keep peace with the Wampanoag people?** *(The Pilgrims needed someone to interpret for them. In addition, the Wampanoag people were probably upset with the Pilgrims for settling on their land and hunting and fishing in the same places. The Wampanoag probably distrusted the Pilgrims but would be more likely to trust Squanto and Samoset.)* BL

W Writing Skills

Informative/Explanatory To extend the lesson, have students research and find a copy of the Mayflower Compact. Then have them use the Resource Library to find primary sources that are similar in structure and purpose to the Mayflower Compact. Suggest to students that they could use primary source documents such as the Magna Carta, the English Bill of Rights, and the U.S. Constitution. Have students compare and contrast the two documents in a two-paragraph essay. BL **Verbal/Linguistic**

ANSWERS, p. 66

☑ **PROGRESS CHECK** It was a step in the development of representative government in America.

Reading Strategy Possible entries on time line: **1621:** Pilgrims feast with Wampanoag people; **1629:** Puritans form Massachusetts Bay Company; **1630s:** Great Migration; **1630:** Boston founded; **1636:** Hartford founded; **1638:** Exeter founded; **1639:** Fundamental Orders of Connecticut adopted; **1675:** King Philip's War begins; **1679:** New Hampshire becomes independent colony

---

R1
W

The Mayflower Compact

Plymouth was outside the territory of the Virginia Company and its laws. While they were still onboard ship, the Pilgrims signed a document they called the Mayflower Compact. This document set up an organized, orderly government. Each signer promised to obey the laws passed "for the general good of the colony." The Mayflower Compact was a key step in the development of representative, democratic government in America.

Native American Help

R2

During their first winter in America, almost half the Pilgrims died. Illness, hunger, and cold took a terrible toll. In the spring, however, two Native Americans, Squanto and Samoset, befriended the colonists. They taught the Pilgrims to grow corn, beans, and pumpkins and showed the colonists where to hunt and fish. Without their help, the Pilgrims might not have survived.

Squanto and Samoset also helped the Pilgrims make peace with the Wampanoag people who lived in the area. For a time, the two groups lived together in harmony. In the fall of 1621, the Pilgrims included their new Wampanoag friends in a feast of thanksgiving.

☑ **PROGRESS CHECK**

Analyzing What was the significance of the Mayflower Compact?

New Colonies

GUIDING QUESTION *What role did religion play in founding the various colonies?*

In 1629 a group of Puritans formed the Massachusetts Bay Company. They received a royal charter to establish a colony north of Plymouth. The company chose John Winthrop to be the colony's governor. In 1630 Winthrop led about 900 men, women, and children to Massachusetts Bay. Most of them settled in a place they called Boston.

More settlers followed. During the 1630s, more than 15,000 Puritans journeyed to Massachusetts to escape religious persecution and economic hard times in England. This movement of people became known as the Great Migration.

At first Winthrop and his assistants made the colony's laws. In 1634 settlers demanded a larger role in the government. Adult male church members were allowed to vote for the governor and for representatives to the government. Later, property ownership became a requirement for voting.

Connections to
TODAY

Plimoth Plantation

Plimoth Plantation, shown here, is an outdoor museum and a popular tourist site. Located in present-day Plymouth, Massachusetts, it uses actors to portray life as it was in 1627.

Reading **HELPDESK** CCSS

Reading Strategy: Sequencing

Sequencing means arranging events in the order in which they occur. Create a time line for the years 1620 to 1700, then place the events discussed in this lesson in their proper place along this line.

66 *Colonial America*

---

netw⊙rks *Online Teaching Options*

Plymouth Colony

Describing Use the interactive slide show about the Plymouth colony to show students the voyage of the *Mayflower* and what the Pilgrims did when they arrived in Plymouth. **Ask: Do you think you would have gone with the Pilgrims on their voyage? Why or why not?** *(Answers will vary but should be explained.)*

See page 57D for other online activities.

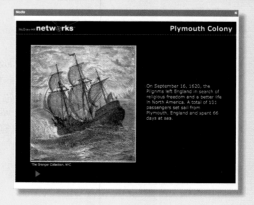

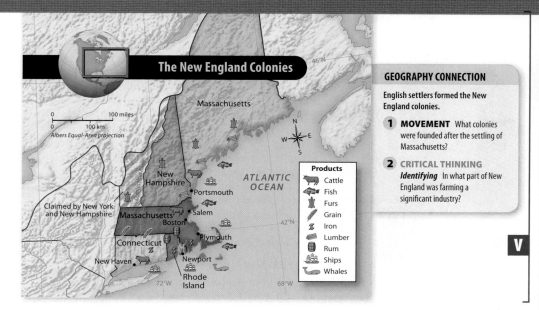

The New England Colonies

GEOGRAPHY CONNECTION

English settlers formed the New England colonies.

1 **MOVEMENT** What colonies were founded after the settling of Massachusetts?

2 **CRITICAL THINKING** *Identifying* In what part of New England was farming a significant industry?

Products

- Cattle
- Fish
- Furs
- Grain
- Iron
- Lumber
- Rum
- Ships
- Whales

The Puritans came to America to put their religious beliefs into practice. At the same time, they themselves had little **tolerance** (TAH·luh·ruhnts) for different beliefs. They criticized or persecuted people who did not agree with their views. They strictly **enforced** their own religious rules. This lack of tolerance led people to form new colonies.

Connecticut and Rhode Island

To the west of Boston is land we now call the Connecticut River Valley. This rich land is better for farming than the stony soil around Boston. In the 1630s colonists began to settle this area.

A leader of this movement was Massachusetts minister Thomas Hooker. He did not like how Winthrop and other Puritan leaders ran the colony. In 1636 Hooker led his congregation to the Connecticut River Valley. There he founded the town of Hartford. Other nearby towns were soon established. Three years later these towns formed a colony called Connecticut. In 1639 they adopted a plan of government called the Fundamental Orders of Connecticut. This was the first written constitution in America. The document described the organization of representative government in detail. Like the Mayflower Compact, it reflected a belief in democratic principles.

tolerance the ability to accept or put up with different views or behaviors

Academic Vocabulary (Tier 2 Words)

enforce to apply a rule or law
policy a statement of ideals or plan of action

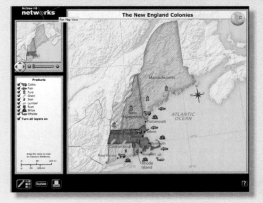

C1 Critical Thinking Skills

Analyzing Lead the class in a discussion about the Puritans' intolerance of religious dissent, considering their own role as dissenters and their quest for religious freedom. **Ask: Why was Hutchinson banned from the Massachusetts Bay Colony?** *(She held meetings in her home to discuss and give her views on religion. Winthrop disliked this and helped to have her banned.)*

C2 Critical Thinking Skills

Describing Discuss the war waged in 1675 by Metacomet, who was known to settlers as King Philip. Discuss with students the impact of King Philip's War on the Wampanoag population. **Ask:**

- **How long did King Philip's War last?** *(14 months)*
- **What was the outcome of this conflict?** *(The colonists defeated the Wampanoag.)*
- **What was the larger result of King Philip's War?** *(The war destroyed the power of the Native Americans of New England.)*

Have students complete the Lesson 2 Review.

CLOSE & REFLECT

To close the lesson, have students identify and discuss the two steps toward democratic government addressed in this lesson. *(Mayflower Compact: agreement to form government; Fundamental Orders of Connecticut: America's first written constitution)*

Then ask students to create a list that names each new colony, the leader of that colony, their occupations, and their reasons for creating new colonies. **Ask: Who were the leaders of these three groups of dissenters, and what did these leaders all have in common?** *(Connecticut: Thomas Hooker; Rhode Island: Roger Williams; New Hampshire: John Wheelwright; they were all ministers.)* Ask volunteers to name some other ways the new colonies were similar.

A minister named Roger Williams founded the colony of Rhode Island. Williams felt that government should not force people to worship in a certain way. He also believed it was wrong for settlers to take land away from the Native Americans. Forced by Massachusetts leaders to leave the colony, Williams found refuge with the Narragansett, a Native American people. They later sold him land, where Williams founded the town of Providence. With its **policy** of religious toleration, Rhode Island became a safe place for dissenters. It was the first place in America where people of all faiths could worship freely.

Others followed Williams's example. In 1638 John Wheelwright led a group of dissidents from Massachusetts to found the town of Exeter in New Hampshire. New Hampshire became an independent colony in 1679.

Conflict With Native Americans

As settlers spread across New England, they met the Native Americans who lived there—Wampanoags, Narragansett, and other groups. Native Americans traded furs for settlers' goods, but conflicts arose. Usually settlers moved onto Native American lands without permission or payment. Throughout the colonial period, settlers and Native Americans competed fiercely for land.

In 1675 Wampanoag leader Metacomet waged war against the New England colonies. Known to settlers as King Philip, Metacomet enlisted the help of other Native American groups. King Philip's War raged for 14 months. In the end, the colonists defeated Metacomet. The war destroyed the power of the Native Americans in New England. Colonial settlement expanded.

C1 Anne Hutchinson held meetings in her home to discuss and give her views on religious teachings. Puritan leaders charged her with "dishonoring" the Massachusetts Bay Colony. They banished Hutchinson in 1637.

☑ **PROGRESS CHECK**

Identifying Which colony was first to let people of all faiths worship freely?

LESSON 2 REVIEW (CCSS)

Review Vocabulary (Tier 3 Words)

1. Examine the words below. Then write a paragraph explaining what the words have in common.
RH.6–8.4, WHST.6–8.4
a. dissent **b.** persecute **c.** tolerance

Answer the Guiding Questions

2. *Explaining* Why did the Separatists and Puritans leave England and settle in North America?
RH.6–8.2

3. *Comparing* What did the colonies of Connecticut, Rhode Island, and New Hampshire have in common? RH.6–8.5

4. **INFORMATIVE/EXPLANATORY** Write a paragraph describing the importance of the search for religious freedom in the settling of America. Describe the founding of at least two colonies. WHST.6–8.2, WHST.6–8.9

68 *Colonial America*

LESSON 2 REVIEW ANSWERS

1. Possible answer: In England, Puritans were persecuted because they dissented, and disagreed with the beliefs of the Anglican Church. In New England, however, they themselves did not show tolerance for other faiths.

2. to escape religious persecution and maintain their religious values and way of life

3. They were all settled by groups escaping religious persecution in Massachusetts.

4. Paragraphs will vary, but should accurately describe the role of religious freedom in the founding of at least two of the following: Massachusetts, Rhode Island, Connecticut, or New Hampshire.

ANSWER, p. 68

☑ **PROGRESS CHECK** Rhode Island

networks

There's More Online!

☑ **CHART/GRAPH** The Middle Colonies

☑ **GRAPHIC ORGANIZER** Dividing Colonies

☑ **MAP** The Middle Colonies

☑ **PRIMARY SOURCE** Attack on New Amsterdam

Lesson 3
The Middle Colonies

ESSENTIAL QUESTION *How does geography influence the way people live?*

IT MATTERS BECAUSE
The Middle Colonies drew a diverse population to North America.

New York and New Jersey

GUIDING QUESTION *Why did the Middle Colonies grow?*

By 1660, England had two groups of colonies in North America. In the north were the New England colonies. In the south was Virginia, and also the colony of Maryland, which was settled in 1634. Between these two groups of colonies were lands under Dutch control. This area was called New Netherland.

The main settlement of New Netherland was New Amsterdam, on Manhattan Island. This location combined a good seaport with access to the Hudson River. The river served as a major transportation link to a rich land of farms, forests, and furs. As a result, New Amsterdam became a center of shipping to and from the Americas.

The Dutch West India Company controlled New Netherland. It wanted to increase the colony's population. To do this, the company offered large grants of land to anyone who could bring at least 50 settlers to work the land. The landowners who received these grants were called **patroons** (puh·TROONS). The patroons ruled like kings. They had their own courts and laws. Settlers owed the patroons labor and a share of their crops.

R

(t) Bloomberg/Getty Images, (c) Allan Baxter/The Image Bank/Getty Images, (r) Art Resource, NY.

Reading **HELP**DESK **CCSS**

Taking Notes: *Identifying* RH.6–8.1, RH.6–8.7

As you read, use a diagram like this one to illustrate how the New York and Pennsylvania colonies split to form the four middle colonies under British rule.

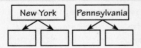

New York → ☐ ☐
Pennsylvania → ☐ ☐

Content Vocabulary (Tier 3 Words)
• **patroon**
• **pacifist**

Lesson 3 **69**

See page 57E for other online activities.

VIDEO

New Jersey

Comparing and Contrasting Play the video of New Jersey for students. Have each student work with a partner to complete a Venn diagram that compares and contrasts the New Jersey colony with the New England Colonies. Have pairs share their diagrams in small groups and then use them in a class discussion. **AL** **ELL**

ENGAGE

🔔 **Bellringer** Ask students what they know about New York City. If anyone in the class has visited New York City, have him or her describe what the city was like. Provide images or video of the city in case no one has been there. **Ask: Why do you think this large city has always attracted people?** *(Answers may vary but should demonstrate understanding that a large city would have many opportunities for people.)* Tell students that in this lesson they will learn about the development of the Middle Colonies, where New York City (then New Amsterdam) was one of the most important early settlements.

TEACH & ASSESS

R **Reading Skills**

Discussing Ask students to scan the text. Discuss the goals the Dutch West India Company had for New Netherland. Be sure students understand that this company wanted to increase the population of the colony. **Ask:**

- **What incentive did the Dutch West India Company offer to people who brought settlers?** *(They offered large grants of land to people who could bring at least 50 settlers to work the land.)*

- **What were the landowners called?** *(patroons)* Discuss the rule of the patroons over the colony, including that they established their own courts and that the settlers owed the patroons labor and a share of the crops. Have students take turns role-playing what patroons did and might say to settlers. **ELL** Kinesthetic

R Reading Skills

Finding the Main Idea Explain to students that to find the main idea in reading text, you look for a central, or key, idea that is supported by details. Point out that sometimes a section of text will have more than one main idea. Have students read the section "New Netherland Becomes New York." **Ask:**

- **Who started the colony that became New York?** *(the Dutch)* **What did the Dutch call the colony?** *(New Netherland)* **Why?** *(The Netherlands was the name of the country in Europe that the Dutch came from.)* **BL**
- **Why would the English have wanted New Netherland?** *(The colony was successful, and it separated New England from England's colonies to the south.)*
- **How did New Netherland become an English colony?** *(The English captured New Amsterdam.)* **AL**

C Critical Thinking Skills

Evaluating Discuss the founding of New Jersey and what the colony offered as compared to others. **Ask:**

- **How did Berkeley and Carteret attract settlers?** *(They offered large tracts of land and provided freedom of religion, trial by jury, and a representative assembly.)*
- **Was their offer effective? Explain your answer.** *(Yes, it was effective because it attracted a lot of different kinds of people who sought a variety of opportunities in North America.)*

THEN

New Amsterdam, which later became New York City, was a prosperous and diverse city. Its population was around 8 thousand in 1664. Today, the city is home to 8 million people. The population is still diverse. Some 3 million New York City residents were born in another country.

R

NOW

▶ CRITICAL THINKING
Speculating Why do you think New York City draws such a diverse population?

C

New Netherland Becomes New York

New Netherland's success did not go unnoticed. The English wanted to gain control of the valuable Dutch colony. England insisted it had a right to the land based on John Cabot's explorations in the late 1400s. In 1664 the English sent a fleet to attack New Amsterdam. Peter Stuyvesant, governor of the colony, surrendered it to the English forces without a fight.

England's King Charles gave the colony to his brother, the Duke of York, who renamed it New York. New York was a proprietary colony. This was a colony in which an owner, or proprietor, owned all the land and controlled the government. Not until 1691 did the English government allow citizens of New York to elect their legislature.

New York continued to prosper under English control. It had a diverse population made up of Dutch, German, Swedish, and Native American people. Also among the population were people of the Jewish religion. They were the first Jews to settle in North America.

In 1664 New York had about 8,000 residents, including at least 300 enslaved Africans. By 1683 the population had swelled to about 12,000 people. New Amsterdam, which had been renamed New York City, was one of the fastest-growing places in the colonies.

Founding New Jersey

The Duke of York decided to divide his colony. He gave the land between the Hudson and Delaware Rivers to Lord John Berkeley and Sir George Carteret. The two proprietors named their colony New Jersey, after the English Channel island of Jersey, where Carteret was born. To attract settlers, the proprietors offered large tracts of land and also promised freedom of religion, trial by jury, and a representative assembly.

Like New York, New Jersey had a diverse population. There were people of many different racial, religious, and national backgrounds—that is, many different **ethnic** groups. New Jersey had no natural harbors, so it did not develop a major port or city like New York. New Jersey's proprietors made few profits. Both eventually sold their shares in the colony. By 1702, New Jersey had become a royal colony. However, the colonists continued to make local laws.

☑ **PROGRESS CHECK**

Explaining Why did no major city develop in New Jersey?

Reading **HELP**DESK **CCSS**

patroon landowner in the Dutch colonies who ruled over large areas of land

Academic Vocabulary (Tier 2 Words)

ethnic of or relating to national, tribal, racial, religious, language, or cultural background

networks   *Online Teaching Options*

PRIMARY SOURCE

Excerpt from New Amsterdam's Citizens to Peter Stuyvesant

Analyzing Primary Sources Display the interactive primary source excerpt of the letter from New Amsterdam's citizens to Peter Stuyvesant. Have a student read the excerpt aloud, and discuss how this letter explains the reasons behind Stuyvesant surrendering New Amsterdam to the English without firing a shot. **BL**

See page 57E for other online activities.

ANSWERS, p. 70

CRITICAL THINKING Possible answer: It has a history and tradition of being diverse, it has always been a busy seaport, and it offers many opportunities for newcomers to make their way in a new land.

☑ **PROGRESS CHECK** New Jersey had no natural harbors.

Pennsylvania and Delaware

GUIDING QUESTION *How did Pennsylvania differ from the other English colonies?*

The Quakers, a Protestant group that had been persecuted in England, founded the colony of Pennsylvania. In 1680 William Penn, a wealthy English Quaker, received the land in payment for a debt King Charles owed Penn's father. Pennsylvania, or "Penn's Woods," stretched inland from the Delaware River. The new colony was nearly as large as England.

William Penn saw Pennsylvania as a "holy experiment," a chance to put his Quaker ideals into practice. The Quakers, or Society of Friends, believed that everyone was equal. People could follow their own "inner light" rather than the teachings of a religious leader. Quakers were also **pacifists** (PA·suh·fihsts), or people who refuse to use force or fight in wars.

Penn was an active proprietor. In 1682 he sailed to America to supervise the building of Philadelphia, a name that means "city of brotherly love." Penn designed the city himself. He also wrote Pennsylvania's first constitution. Penn believed that the land belonged to the Native Americans and that settlers should pay for it. He negotiated several treaties with local Native Americans.

R **C**

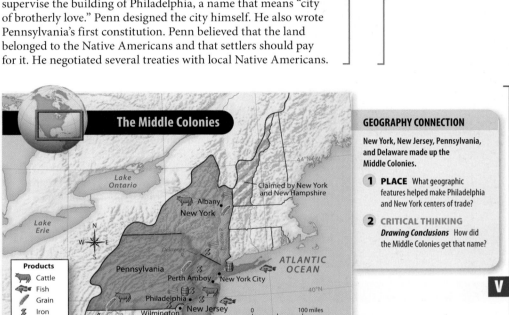

The Middle Colonies

Products
- Cattle
- Fish
- Grain
- Iron
- Lumber
- Rum

GEOGRAPHY CONNECTION

New York, New Jersey, Pennsylvania, and Delaware made up the Middle Colonies.

1 **PLACE** What geographic features helped make Philadelphia and New York centers of trade?

2 **CRITICAL THINKING**
Drawing Conclusions How did the Middle Colonies get that name?

V

pacifists people opposed to the use of war or violence to settle disputes

Academic Vocabulary (Tier 2 Words)
function to be in action; to operate

IMAGE

The Middle Colonies

Analyzing Visuals Use the interactive image of the Middle Colonies to discuss the location of New York, New Jersey, Pennsylvania, and Delaware with students. **Ask: Where are Pennsylvania and Delaware located in relation to New York and New Jersey?** (*Pennsylvania is more inland and is west of New Jersey and south of New York. Delaware is south of New Jersey.*) **Why are these four colonies called the Middle Colonies?** (*They were located in the "middle" of the strip of colonies that lined the Atlantic Coast—between New England and the Southern Colonies.*) **Where was the main settlement of New Netherland located?** (*on Manhattan Island*)

See page 57E for other online activities.

C Critical Thinking Skills

Contrasting Invite students to differentiate Pennsylvania from the other middle colonies. **Ask: What are some differences between the development of Pennsylvania and the other colonies?** (*Student responses may vary but could include that Pennsylvania was developed with Quaker ideals in mind. Because of this, the relationship with Native Americans was one of peace, respect, and the feeling that the land belonged to them.*) **BL**

R Reading Skills

Identifying After students have read the text, discuss with them the idea that William Penn was a figure of significance in the Middle Colonies. **Ask: Who was William Penn?** (*the founder of Pennsylvania*) **AL** **What other roles did he play in this colony?** (*He helped to build Philadelphia, he wrote the colony's constitution, and he negotiated the treaty with local Native Americans.*) Discuss how Penn attracted a wide variety of people to his colony. Discuss with students that Penn advertised his new colony to increase diversity. **Ask: What did Penn promise to new colonists in the Charter of Privileges?** (*He granted colonists the right to elect representatives.*)

V Visual Skills

Analyzing Maps Have students analyze the map of the Middle Colonies. Have a volunteer discuss the location of the Middle Colonies in relation to the New England Colonies, using direction words (*north, south, above, below,* and so forth). **AL** **ELL** Use the map to discuss the goods that the Middle Colonies produced. Then create a list that compares and contrasts the goods of both areas. **Ask: Why do you think the Middle Colonies did not produce as many goods that relied on using the ocean?** (*Answers may vary but should suggest that the Middle Colonies had a wider variety of economic opportunities than New England did and because Philadelphia was a commercial port, not a fishing port. Also, Delaware had limited access to the ocean and did not develop a fishing industry.*) **Visual/Spatial**

ANSWERS, p. 71

GEOGRAPHY CONNECTION

1 located on water with good harbors, located between northern and southern colonies

2 **CRITICAL THINKING** They were in the middle of the strip of English colonies along the coast.

The Middle Colonies

R Reading Skills

Describing As students read this paragraph, discuss with them how the colony of Delaware was created. **Ask: What groups of people helped to found Delaware?** *(the Swedish, the Dutch, and the English)* Be sure to explain to students that before the Dutch and the English settled in the area south of Pennsylvania, there were people from Sweden already living there. Discuss with students that Delaware remained under the control of Pennsylvania's governor even though it functioned as a separate colony.

W Writing Skills

Informative/Expository Point out that there are many reminders of New York's Dutch heritage still today. Ask students to work in pairs to research examples of other heritages in New York, such as Chinatown and Little Italy. Instruct students to use the Internet to gather information and print out pictures that illustrate the group's heritage for a digital presentation. After pairs have presented, have each student in the pair write an expository essay explaining what he or she learned about the group's heritage and how it is reflected in New York today. Remind students to make their essays engaging and to use vivid verbs, strong transition words, and clear and concise sentences in their essays. **BL** Interpersonal

Have students complete the Lesson 3 Review.

CLOSE & REFLECT

To close the lesson, have students write a paragraph that compares and contrasts the Middle Colonies and the New England Colonies. Ask volunteers to share their paragraphs with the class.

Rich farmland lured immigrants from throughout Europe to the Middle Colonies. These colonists produced important agricultural exports.

▶ **CRITICAL THINKING**
Identifying What farm products were important in Pennsylvania?

W Penn advertised his colony throughout Europe. By 1683, more than 3,000 English, Welsh, Irish, Dutch, and German settlers had arrived. In 1701, in the Charter of Privileges, Penn granted colonists the right to elect representatives to the legislature. Philadelphia quickly became America's most prosperous city and its most popular port.

R People from Sweden had settled land in southern Pennsylvania before the Dutch and then the English took over the area. Penn allowed these southern counties to form their own legislature. The counties then **functioned**, or worked, as a separate colony known as Delaware. However, Delaware remained under the authority of Pennsylvania's governor.

☑ **PROGRESS CHECK**

Inferring What was William Penn's main purpose for founding the colony of Pennsylvania?

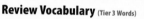

LESSON 3 REVIEW

Review Vocabulary (Tier 3 Words)
1. Explain the significance of the words. RH.6–8.4
   a. patroon   b. pacifist

Answer the Guiding Questions
2. *Describing* How was the colony of New York governed? RH.6–8.1

3. *Summarizing* What policies of Pennsylvania reflected Quaker beliefs? RH.6–8.2

4. **NARRATIVE** Think about what you read about New Amsterdam: It was a bustling seaport with many different types of people. Write a paragraph that describes what it might have been like to walk down one of its busy streets. What might you have seen? Heard? Felt? WHST.6–8.2, WHST.6–8.9

LESSON 3 REVIEW ANSWERS

1. A patroon was a landowner in the Dutch colonies. Patroons were important in the settlement of New Netherland. A pacifist is someone, such as the Quakers, who refuses to fight in wars or use force to settle disputes.

2. New York was first controlled by a proprietor; later it had an elected legislature.

3. Answers will vary, but may include that everyone was considered equal; the colony allowed citizens to elect representatives, treated Native Americans fairly, and welcomed diversity.

4. Descriptions will vary, but should appeal to the senses and demonstrate an appreciation of New Amsterdam as a busy and diverse seaport in which many different types of people were present and welcome.

ANSWERS, p. 72

CRITICAL THINKING grain, cattle
☑ PROGRESS CHECK to put his Quaker ideals into practice

netw rks
There's More Online!

☑ **CHARTS/GRAPHS**
Indentured Servants and
Enslaved Africans

☑ **GAME** Founding of the
Colonies

☑ **GRAPHIC ORGANIZER**
Cause and Effect of Bacon's
Rebellion

☑ **MAP** The Economy of the
Southern Colonies

☑ **PRIMARY SOURCE**
Bacon's Rebellion

Lesson 4
The Southern Colonies

ESSENTIAL QUESTION *How does geography influence the way people live?*

IT MATTERS BECAUSE
A warm climate, long growing season, and rich soil spurred the growth of large-scale agriculture in the Southern Colonies.

Virginia and Maryland

GUIDING QUESTION *What problems faced Maryland and Virginia?*

The settlement of Jamestown marked the beginning of English colonization in North America—and of the Virginia Colony. After its difficult beginnings, Virginia began to grow. The demand for workers was high. It took a great deal of labor to plant, tend, and harvest the tobacco crop on which the colony depended.

White landowners helped meet this need through the use of enslaved Africans. The first group of 20 Africans arrived in 1619 aboard a Dutch trading vessel. In the years to follow, many more shiploads of this human cargo would arrive in North America. You will learn more about this terrible trade in enslaved Africans in other chapters.

The story of Virginia's first Africans shows that not all people came to work in the colonies of their own free will. England also shipped criminals and prisoners of war to the colonies. They could earn their release by working for a period of time—usually seven years.

Many people also came to the colonies as **indentured servants** (ihn·DEHN·shuhrd SIR·vuhnts). To pay for their passage to America, they agreed to work without pay for a certain length of time.

R

Reading **HELP**DESK **CCSS**

Taking Notes: *Determining Cause and Effect*
Use a diagram like this one to list the causes and effects of Bacon's Rebellion. RH.6–8.5, RH.6–8.7

Causes → Bacon's Rebellion → Effects

Content Vocabulary (Tier 3)
• **indentured servant**
• **constitution**
• **debtor**

Lesson 4   **73**

VIDEO

The Caribbean Connection

Identifying Central Issues Show the video to students, and then discuss the unusual set of circumstances that led to the development of the African and Caribbean slave trade. Tell students that initially, settlers in North America made attempts to enslave Native Americans. However, epidemics of diseases brought from Europe killed more than 90 percent of them in the Caribbean and elsewhere—and those Native Americans who did not die of disease knew their own environment well enough to escape.

See page 57F for other online activities.

ENGAGE

🔔 **Bellringer** Begin the lesson by asking students about the economic activities in their community. Have students make a list of ways in which people in their community earn a living. Then, next to each job on the list, have students write about the working conditions associated with each job.
Ask:

• **What economic activities are there in this area?** *(Student responses will vary but might include activities such as farming, tourism, or manufacturing.)*

• **What are working conditions like in each line of work?** *(Student responses will vary but should include factors such as working environment, the type of work, and hours.)*

• **Why do people work?** *(Because working provides money to pay for basic survival needs such as food and shelter, and because money can be used to improve the quality of life in many ways.)*

• **How does the market for products affect the availability of jobs in an area?** *(The more of a product that there is a demand for in the market, the more jobs are available.)*

TEACH & ASSESS

R **Reading Skills**

Identifying After students have read the text, review information about Jamestown that was discussed in Lesson 1.
Ask: On what crop did the settlers of Jamestown, and then all of Virginia, come to rely? *(tobacco)* Why did growing tobacco lead to the start of the slave trade? *(Tobacco took a lot of labor to plant, grow, and harvest. Farmers believed that it was more cost-effective to rely on enslaved labor to grow and harvest the crop, because, rather than paying wages, they paid for food and shelter, at a very minimal level, for enslaved workers.)* **AL**

ANSWER, p. 73

TAKING NOTES: Causes: Westerners resented domination of Virginia's government by Easterners and the governor's pledge forbade settlement of Native American lands. **Effects:** More western land was opened to settlement, supported by militia force.

The Southern Colonies

R Reading Skills

Summarizing Have students read the text. Then, discuss with them the establishment of the colony of Maryland. **Ask:**

- **Who was Sir George Calvert?** *(An English lord who was given a proprietary colony north of Virginia; he died, and his son inherited the colony and named it Maryland.)* **AL**
- **Why did Calvert believe that Catholics needed a religious haven?** *(They were persecuted in England.)*

Explain to students that Maryland was established as that safe haven.

- **How was the land in Maryland distributed?** *(Large estates were given to English aristocrats, smaller pieces to other settlers.)*
- **How did this increase the need for indentured servants and enslaved Africans?** *(Many workers were needed to work the large plantations.)*

Discuss that eventually Maryland became home to both Protestants and Catholics. Discuss the creation of the Acts of Toleration to protect the Catholic settlers. **Ask:**

- **Do you think that Maryland served the purpose for which it was founded?** *(Answers may vary.)* **BL**
- **What were the Acts of Toleration?** *(Maryland laws ensuring Protestants and Catholics the right to worship freely)*
- **How successful was Maryland as a safe haven?** *(Catholics faced the same restrictions on worship after Maryland became a royal colony in 1692 and established an official Protestant church.)*

W Writing Skills

Argument Discuss the argument between the Calvert brothers and William Penn over the border between Maryland and Pennsylvania. **Ask: How did they resolve this dispute?** *(They hired Charles Mason and Jeremiah Dixon to map the boundary, which became known as the Mason-Dixon Line.)* Have students write a short essay that defends the Calvert brothers or William Penn over the border issue. Remind students to cite evidence from the text or from additional research they conduct, support their arguments with clear points, address the counterargument, and conclude their essays by restating their opening statements. **AL** **Verbal/Linguistic**

ANSWERS, p. 74

GRAPH SKILL

1. In about 1670, the gap between slavery in the North and South began to widen significantly.

2. **CRITICAL THINKING** Slavery was practiced at a similar level from about 1650 to 1670, but then the number of enslaved people in the South shot up.

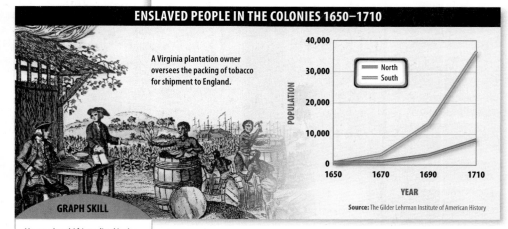

ENSLAVED PEOPLE IN THE COLONIES 1650–1710

A Virginia plantation owner oversees the packing of tobacco for shipment to England.

POPULATION / YEAR

Source: The Gilder Lehrman Institute of American History

GRAPH SKILL

Most enslaved Africans lived in the Southern Colonies, where they were forced to work on plantations. Northern Colonies had fewer enslaved people but also profited from the international slave trade.

1 **IDENTIFYING** In about what year did the South begin relying on slavery in a much larger way than the North?

2 **CRITICAL THINKING** *Comparing and Contrasting* Describe how the number of enslaved people in the South compared to those in the North during the time period shown in this graph.

Founding Maryland

Maryland arose from the dream of Sir George Calvert, Lord Baltimore. Calvert wanted a safe place for his fellow Catholics who faced persecution in England. England's king, Charles I, gave Calvert a proprietary colony north of Virginia. Soon after receiving this grant, Calvert died. His son, Cecilius, inherited the colony and named it Maryland. Cecilius sent two of his brothers to start the colony. They reached America in 1634.

Cecilius gave large **estates** to English aristocrats. He also granted smaller pieces of land to other settlers. As the number of plantations grew, so did the need for workers. The colony imported indentured servants and enslaved Africans.

For years the Calvert and Penn families argued over the boundary between Maryland and Pennsylvania. In the 1760s, they hired two men named Charles Mason and Jeremiah Dixon to map the boundary between the colonies. This boundary line became known as the Mason-Dixon Line.

Religion was another source of conflict. The Calverts welcomed Protestants as well as Catholics. Protestant settlers outnumbered Catholics. To protect Catholics, the colony established the Act of Toleration in 1649. The act ensured Protestants and Catholics the right to worship freely.

Tensions, however, continued. In 1692 Maryland—now a royal colony—established an official Protestant church. As a result, Catholics faced the same restrictions they had in England.

Reading HELPDESK CCSS

indentured servant laborer who agrees to work without pay for a certain period of time in exchange for passage to America

Academic Vocabulary (Tier 2 Words)

estate large area of land that has one owner
dominate to control

74 *Colonial America*

---

networks   *Online Teaching Options*

CHART

Enslaved People in the Colonies 1650–1710

Comparing and Contrasting Use the interactive chart to discuss the difference between indentured servants and enslaved Africans. Ask students to explain how the two groups were similar and how they differed. **Ask:**

- **Who were indentured servants?** *(laborers who worked for a specified time in exchange for passage to America)* **AL** **ELL**
- **What other individuals did England ship to the colonies to work for the colonists?** *(criminals and prisoners of war)* **How could they earn their freedom?** *(by working for a certain period of time, usually seven years)*

See page 57F for other online activities.

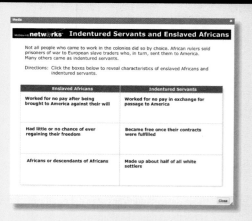

networks **Indentured Servants and Enslaved Africans**

Not all people who came to work in the colonies did so by choice. African rulers sold prisoners of war to European slave traders who, in turn, sent them to America. Many others came as indentured servants.

Directions: Click the boxes below to reveal characteristics of enslaved Africans and indentured servants.

Enslaved Africans	Indentured Servants
Worked for no pay after being brought to America against their will	Worked for no pay in exchange for passage to America
Had little or no chance of ever regaining their freedom	Became free once their contracts were fulfilled
Africans or descendants of Africans	Made up about half of all white settlers

Rebellion in Virginia

Virginia also experienced conflict. As the colony grew, settlers moved west—and onto Native American lands. In the 1640s, Virginia governor William Berkeley made a pledge to Native Americans. In exchange for a large piece of land, he agreed to keep settlers from pushing farther into their territory. Berkeley's goal was to prevent the outbreak of a war with the Native Americans.

Nathaniel Bacon was a young planter in western Virginia. He opposed the colonial government because it was **dominated** by easterners. Many westerners also resented Berkeley's pledge to stay out of Native American territory. Some settled in the forbidden areas. They then blamed the government for not clearing the colony of Native Americans.

In 1676 Bacon led attacks on Native American villages. His army also marched to Jamestown to drive out Berkeley, and they burned the town to the ground. Bacon seemed on the verge of taking over the colony when he suddenly became ill and died. With his death, the rebellion faded. England recalled Berkeley and sent troops to restore order. Bacon's Rebellion showed that government could not ignore the demands of its people.

☑ **PROGRESS CHECK**

Analyzing Why did Nathaniel Bacon oppose the colonial government?

Bettmann/CORBIS

Lesson 4 **75**

W Writing Skills

Identifying Points of View Discuss Bacon's Rebellion with students. **Ask: Who were the people and groups who played a role in the development of Bacon's Rebellion?** *(Bacon himself and the settlers who sided with him, Governor William Berkeley, and the Native Americans whose land the settlers coveted)*

Have students write a short narrative from the perspective of each group or person who played a role in the unfolding events: Governor William Berkeley, Nathaniel Bacon, and the Native Americans whose villages Bacon attacked. Have students write their narratives in first person, explaining the point of view as if they were the person speaking. **Verbal/Linguistic**

Content Background Knowledge

Nathaniel Bacon was a strong supporter of territorial expansion, which led him to mount an attack against Native Americans in 1676. What led him to migrate to North America was two-fold. First, he tried to take financial advantage of a neighbor while still living in England. His father-in-law did not care for him and paid for his voyage across the ocean. In fact, his father-in-law also provided him with two estates of prime real estate near the James River.

PRIMARY SOURCE

Nathaniel Bacon

Analyzing Primary Sources Point out to students that this excerpt about Bacon's Rebellion is all one sentence. Encourage students to break the sentence down into parts to find its meaning. **Ask:**

- **To whom does the word** *heathen* **refer?** *(Native Americans)* **What other words in this declaration contain clues that Bacon was upset about not being able to expand the settlement into Native American lands?** *("by a loss of a greate part of this His Colony")*
- **How did Bacon justify his rebellion to himself and others? Use evidence to support your answer.** *(Bacon accused Virginia's governor of being a traitor because of the treaty he made with Native Americans to respect their land boundaries.)* **BL**

See page 57F for other online activities.

ANSWER, p. 75

☑ **PROGRESS CHECK** Bacon lived in western Virginia and wanted settlers to be able to expand west onto Native American land. He believed the colonial government was dominated by people who lived in eastern Virginia, who were not responding to the demands of the western settlers.

Chapter 3 75

V Visual Skills

Analyzing Maps Refer students to the map of the Southern Colonies on this page. Use the map to discuss with students the location of these new colonies and the features of the region. **Ask:**

- **What colonies are included in the Southern Colonies?** *(Georgia, North Carolina, South Carolina, Virginia, and Maryland)*
- **How was the economy of the Southern Colonies different from that of the New England and Middle Colonies?** *(Students should note that the Southern Colonies relied more on agriculture than the other colonies.)*

Then have students compare and contrast the economy of Virginia with the economies of North and South Carolina. **Ask:**

- **Why were ocean ports important in the development of the Carolinas?** *(Farmers needed to ship their crops.)*
- **Which crops greatly increased the demand for slave labor?** *(tobacco and rice)* **BL**
- **How did the geography of the Carolinas affect agricultural development?** *(Rice grew well in the wet coastal area.)*

R Reading Skills

Summarizing Have students read the quotation from the Carolina constitution written by John Locke. Ask volunteers to summarize it in their own words. **Ask: How do you think this idea differed from the social divisions in England at the time?** *(It emphasized that every man might have property and own the products of his labor.)* **Ask: How did Locke's statement differ from common practices in Carolina at the time?** *(The values expressed in the statement are the opposite of the rationale for slavery.)*

C Critical Thinking Skills

Evaluating Focus students' attention on the vital role of agriculture in the English colonies. **Ask: On a scale of one to ten, how important was agriculture to the Southern Colonies?** *(ten)* **Why?** *(It was the major economic activity.)* **AL**

ANSWERS, p. 76

GEOGRAPHY CONNECTION

1 Georgia

2 **CRITICAL THINKING** The map shows tobacco as a major product of three colonies—Maryland, Virginia, and North Carolina.

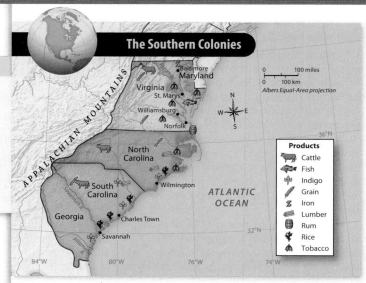

The Southern Colonies

GEOGRAPHY CONNECTION

The Southern Colonies were Maryland, Virginia, North and South Carolina, and Georgia.

1 **LOCATION** Which was the southernmost colony?

2 **CRITICAL THINKING** *Analyzing Visuals* How does the map show the importance of tobacco in the Southern Colonies?

Products
- Cattle
- Fish
- Indigo
- Grain
- Iron
- Lumber
- Rum
- Rice
- Tobacco

The Carolinas and Georgia

GUIDING QUESTION *What factors contributed to the growth of the Carolinas?*

In 1663 King Charles II created a proprietary colony south of Virginia called Carolina—Latin for "Charles's land." The king gave the colony to eight nobles. The proprietors set up estates and sold or rented land to settlers brought from England.

John Locke, an English philosopher, wrote a **constitution** (kahn•stuh•TOO•shuhn), a plan that outlined the jobs and powers of the colony's government. The constitution covered topics such as land divisions and social rank. Locke stated, "Every man has a property in his own person. … The labour of his body, and the work of his hands … are properly his."

Two Carolinas

Carolina did not develop as planned. It split into northern and southern Carolina.

Farmers from inland Virginia settled northern Carolina. They grew tobacco and sold timber and tar. Northern Carolina lacked a good harbor, so farmers used Virginia's ports.

Settlers in southern Carolina took advantage of fertile land and the harbor at Charles Town (later Charleston). Settlements there spread, and trade in deerskin, lumber, and beef thrived.

---

constitution a list of fundamental laws to support a government
debtor person or country that owes money

Visual Vocabulary
indigo The *indigofera* plant, often called just indigo, was used to make indigo dye.

76 *Colonial America*

---

net**works** *Online Teaching Options*

IMAGE

Plantations

Analyzing Visuals Use the interactive images of plantations to discuss with students their role in the economy of the Southern Colonies. **Ask: How did the growth of plantations contribute to the rise of slavery?** *(As agriculture increased, farms became larger plantations. Plantation owners wanted to increase their profits by using workers they would not have to pay. This led to an increasing dependency on the labor of enslaved people.)* **BL**

See page 57F for other online activities.

Plantations

Crops grown on plantations included cotton, coffee, tobacco, rice, indigo, and sugar cane, among others.

Two crops came to dominate Carolina agriculture. In the 1680s planters discovered that rice grew well in the wet coastal lowlands. Growing rice required much labor, and the demand for slave labor rose. Another important crop was **indigo**. A young English woman named Eliza Lucas developed this crop in the 1740s. Indigo, a blue flowering plant, was used to dye cloth.

By the early 1700s, Carolina's settlers were growing tired of proprietor rule. In 1719 settlers in southern Carolina took control from the proprietors. In 1729 Carolina became two royal colonies—North Carolina and South Carolina.

Georgia

Georgia, founded in 1733, was the last British colony set up in America. James Oglethorpe received a charter from George II for a colony where debtors and poor people could make a fresh start. In Britain, **debtors** (DEH·tuhrs)—those who had debts—could be imprisoned if they were unable to pay what they owed.

The British also hoped Georgia would block any Spanish attack on the colonies from Florida. Oglethorpe and his settlers built the forts and town of Savannah to discourage such attacks.

Georgia did not develop as Oglethorpe planned. Hundreds of poor people came from Britain, but few debtors settled there. Religious refugees from Central Europe and a small group of Jews also arrived. Many settlers complained about Oglethorpe's rules, especially the limits on landholding and the bans on slave labor and rum. A frustrated Oglethorpe finally agreed to their demands. Disappointed with the colony's slow growth, he gave up and turned Georgia over to the king in 1751.

By that time, the British had been in eastern North America for almost 150 years. They had lined the Atlantic coast with colonies.

☑ **PROGRESS CHECK**

Explaining Why was Georgia founded?

LESSON 4 REVIEW (CCSS)

Review Vocabulary (Tier 3 Words)

1. Examine the terms below. Write a sentence explaining what the terms have in common. RH.6–8.4
   a. indentured servant   **b.** debtor

2. Use the word *constitution* in a sentence. RH.6–8.4

Answer the Guiding Questions

3. *Explaining* Why did George Calvert establish the colony of Maryland? RH.6–8.2

4. *Analyzing* Why did demand for enslaved workers increase in the Carolinas? RH.6–8.1

5. **ARGUMENT** Take the role of James Oglethorpe. Write a letter to the king asking for a charter for a colony. Explain why you are founding Georgia and how it might benefit England. WHST.6–8.1, WHST.6–8.10

Lesson 4   **77**

R Reading Skills

Identifying After students have read the text, lead a discussion about significant figures in the establishment of the colony of Georgia. **Ask: Who was Eliza Lucas?** *(She was a young English woman who developed the indigo crop.)* **Ask: Who was James Oglethorpe?** *(He received the charter that established the colony of Georgia.)* **AL**

C Critical Thinking Skills

Evaluating Discuss the establishment of Georgia, the last British colony in America. Remind students that Georgia was a debtors' colony. **Ask:**

- **How were the laws concerning debts different from modern laws?** *(Modern laws do not imprison people for debts but allow them to work to pay off the debt.)* Note that the British also hoped the colony of Georgia would block Spain from moving north from Florida. Discuss James Oglethorpe's plans for Georgia.

- **Was Oglethorpe's plan for a colony successful?** *(Some students may say that Oglethorpe failed because not many debtors came to his colony and he eventually gave up. Other students may say that Oglethorpe was successful because he started a new colony, even though it did not work out as he had planned.)*

Have students complete the Lesson 4 Review.

CLOSE & REFLECT

To close this lesson, hold a discussion of the importance of African Americans to the economy of the Southern Colonies. Discuss with students the different ways in which each colonial area developed. **Ask: How does the establishment and growth of the different colonies reflect the growth of America and the reasons people come here?** *(Answers may vary but should suggest that each colony developed for a unique purpose. The desire for religious freedom, better government, land, and self rule inspired their establishment and growth, and inspired people to come to America.)*

LESSON 4 REVIEW ANSWERS

1. Sentences will vary but should indicate that both terms refer to people who owe something to another. An indentured servant owes labor, and a debtor owes money.

2. Possible answer: John Locke wrote a constitution for Carolina that set up a plan of government, including topics such as land division.

3. Calvert wanted to establish a safe haven for persecuted Catholics.

4. Rice became an important crop, and it required a great deal of labor to grow. Enslaved workers could provide the necessary labor.

5. Letters will vary but should reflect an understanding of Georgia as a place where debtors and poor people could get a new start, as well as how the colony could serve as a buffer against the Spanish. On the one hand, the colony would take people who might be a burden to England (debtors and poor people) away from English society. On the other hand, these same people would serve as a useful shield against any Spanish expansion toward the English colonies.

ANSWER, p. 77

☑ **PROGRESS CHECK** Georgia was founded as a place to give debtors and poor people a fresh start and to act as a barrier against any Spanish attacks from Florida.

CHAPTER REVIEW ACTIVITY

Ask students to sketch a rough outline of the contiguous United States on a sheet of paper. Have them mark an *X* where Roanoke and Jamestown were. Then have them draw rough outlines of the English colonies on the map.

Have students analyze the maps they have drawn by writing a paragraph to explain how the English influence grew from small settlements to a string of colonies along the eastern coast of the North America. *(Students' maps should show the correct locations of both Roanoke, in present-day northeastern North Carolina, and Jamestown, in present-day southeastern Virginia. Paragraphs will vary but should demonstrate understanding that successful settlements and available resources enabled England to expand its colonial possessions in this region of North America.)*

REVIEW THE ENDURING UNDERSTANDING

Review this chapter's Enduring Understanding with students:

- *People, places, and ideas change over time.*

To apply this to the chapter, pose the following questions in a class discussion:

Why did different groups from England want to start new settlements in North America? *(Many came to escape religious persecution. They wanted to practice their religion freely. Others sought economic opportunities and land.)*

How were the English colonies similar and different? *(Sample answer: Colonies were set up differently, but some were established for similar reasons. For example, there were royal, charter, and proprietary colonies, as well as joint-stock colonies. The type of colony determined who had control of the colony and its government, such as an individual, a group, or the king. Many of the colonies were set up for economic gain and potential, but some were started so that groups could practice their religion without persecution. The Pennsylvania colony, for example, was religiously diverse, but other colonies, such as Massachusetts, were stricter and religious freedom was not granted to other groups.)*

CHAPTER 3 Activities CCSS

Write your answers on a separate piece of paper.

❶ **Exploring the Essential Questions**   WHST.6–8.2, WHST.6–8.9
   INFORMATIVE/EXPLANATORY   Write an essay in which you answer this question: How did geography, religion, and government affect how people in the English colonies lived? Use examples from the chapter to help you organize your essay.

❷ **21st Century Skills**   WHST.6–8.4, WHST.6–8.5
   ORGANIZING IDEAS   Working with a small group, read the Mayflower Compact. Rewrite the Compact in your own words. Then compare the rewritings done by various groups of your classmates. How do they differ from the original document?

❸ **Thinking Like a Historian**   WHST.6–8.5, WHST.6–8.7
   UNDERSTANDING CAUSE AND EFFECT   In about 150 years, the population of the English colonies in America increased from about 100 to about 1,000,000. What is one reason the population may have increased? What are two effects this increase may have had?

Causes	→	Population Increase	→	Effects

❹ **Visual Literacy**   RH.6–8.7
   ANALYZING PAINTINGS   This painting shows William Penn meeting with Native Americans in the colony of Pennsylvania. What details in the painting give you clues about the Native Americans' relationship with William Penn?

William Penn's Treaty with the Indians by Edward Hicks, 1830–1840

The Granger Collection, NYC.

78   *Colonial America*

ACTIVITIES ANSWERS

Exploring the Essential Questions

❶ Essays will vary but should identify separate geographic, religious, and governmental factors that affected life in the English colonies. For example, students might mention the religious influences of the Puritans, Pilgrims, Quakers, and Roman Catholics, or the different types—royal, charter, proprietary, or joint-stock —of colony formation and organization.

21st Century Skills

❷ Rewritings will vary but should accurately convey the meaning of the Mayflower Compact. Ensure students understand that the word *meet* as used in the Compact ("as shall be thought most meet and convenient for the General good of the Colony") means "fit" or "suitable." Focus student attention on the phrase "the general Good of the Colony" and remind them of its echo, "the general welfare," in the Preamble to the U.S. Constitution.

REVIEW THE GUIDING QUESTIONS

Choose the best answer for each question.

RH.6–8.4
1 A document that grants the right to organize a settlement in an area is called a

A. charter.

B. compact.

C. headright.

D. policy.

RH.6–8.1
2 What crop was important in making Jamestown and early Virginia an economic success?

F. indigo

G. tobacco

H. potatoes

I. rice

RH.6–8.2
3 Roger Williams clashed with Massachusetts Puritans because

A. he converted to Roman Catholicism.

B. he did not think government should require certain religious beliefs.

C. he wanted Native American land.

D. his views were considered too intolerant.

RH.6–8.1
4 In which type of colony does a person or persons own all the land and control the colony's government?

F. a royal colony

G. a charter colony

H. a proprietary colony

I. a joint-stock colony

RH.6–8.4
5 Men and women who signed contracts to pay for their passage to the Americas were called

A. Separatists.

B. burgesses.

C. indentured servants.

D. tenant farmers.

RH.6–8.1
6 What role did Eliza Lucas play in the Southern Colonies?

F. She wrote a constitution.

G. She divided the Carolinas into two colonies.

H. She developed indigo as an important crop.

I. She founded Charles Town (later Charleston).

79

ASSESSMENT ANSWERS
Review the Guiding Questions

1 **A** Point out to students that a compact is an agreement, a headright is a land grant, and a policy is a course of action. A chart, which is the correct answer choice, was a document that granted the right to organize a settlement.

2 **G** Explain to students that indigo and rice were important colonial crops, but at a later time and in the Carolinas. Potatoes were not an important cash crop at Jamestown. Tobacco was the key in making Jamestown and Virginia's early economy successful.

3 **B** Remind students that the religious intolerance of the Massachusetts Puritans led some of its colonists, including Williams, to move elsewhere.

4 **H** Review with students that a charter is a document granting the recipient the right to settle a colony. A royal colony is directly under the control of the government in England. A joint-stock colony is owned as a business by two or more shareholders. Have students look back at Lesson 2 for further clarification.

5 **C** Review the meaning of *indentured* with students. Point out that Separatists were people who wanted to separate from the Anglican Church. Burgesses were elected representatives in Virginia. Tenant farmers pay a landowner an amount in exchange for the right to farm a piece of land.

6 **H** Explain to students that they can go back to the text to find the answer or eliminate answer choices to find the correct answer. For example, no colonial women were allowed to write a constitution or make political decisions, such as dividing or founding a colony on their own. The only correct answer choice possible is H. Eliza Lucas, a young English woman, developed indigo as a crop in the 1740s.

Thinking Like a Historian

3 Answers may vary. Causes of growth include the birth of children to the early immigrants and continued immigration to the colonies for a variety of reasons, such as to escape persecution, find religious freedom, or make a profit. Effects might include the growth of cities, westward expansion, and conflict with Native Americans.

Causes → **Population Increase** → **Effects**

Visual Literacy

4 Answers will vary. The relationship is friendly, fair, and probably trustworthy. Clues include people facing each other, pleasant facial expressions, eye contact, Penn's outstretched arms, respectful body language, and the presentation of gifts.

Analyzing Documents

7 **C** The map shows that the periods of rapid growth in Virginia, North Carolina, and New Hampshire came later.

8 **I** There were already colonies to the north and south, and the Atlantic Ocean was to the east. The natural direction of growth was to the "unpopulated" west.

Short Response

9 Answers will vary, but students might suggest that Bradford wanted to document the early hardships and to commend those who helped Plymouth to survive.

10 Answers will vary but should be explained. Those who say it is typical might point out that the lack of "houses and other comforts" was the lot of many early colonists. Those who say it is not typical might point out the large numbers of sick and dead colonists.

Extended Response

11 Students' papers will vary, but they should note that the quest for the freedom to practice one's religion led to the founding of some of the colonies and that those religious colonies did not always tolerate religious diversity.

CHAPTER 3 **Assessment** (continued)

DBQ ANALYZING DOCUMENTS

RH.6–8.7

7 **Analyzing Visuals** The map at the right shows the settlement of the British Colonies. Which colony was the most heavily settled before 1660?

A. Virginia

B. North Carolina

C. Massachusetts

D. New Hampshire

RH.6–8.7

8 **Analyzing Visuals** Which of the following best describes what happened to English settlement over time?

F. It spread to the north.

G. It spread to the south.

H. It spread to the east.

I. It spread to the west.

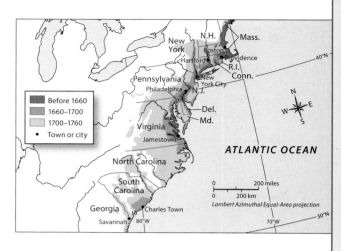

SHORT RESPONSE

William Bradford was governor of the Plymouth Colony in 1621.

"[I]n two or three months' time half of their company died, especially in ... the depth of winter, and wanting houses and other comforts; being infected with the scurvy and other diseases. ... there died sometimes two or three of a day ... of 100 and odd persons, scarce 50 remained. And of these ... there was but six or seven sound persons who to their great commendation [took care of the sick people] ... and ... willingly and cheerfully ... showing herein their true love unto their friends.

—from *Of Plymouth Plantation*, by William Bradford, c. 1650

RH.6–8.6, WHST.6–8.4

9 Why do you think Bradford recorded this information about the Pilgrims?

RH.6–8.2, WHST.6–8.1

10 Do you think this scene is typical of the hardships early colonists faced? Why or why not?

EXTENDED RESPONSE

WHST.6–8.2, WHST.6–8.10

11 **Informative/Explanatory** What role did religion play in the establishment and life of the English colonies? Write your answer in a one-page paper.

Need Extra Help?

If You've Missed Question	1	2	3	4	5	6	7	8	9	10	11
Review Lesson	1	1	2	3	4	4	1–4	1–4	2	2	2

---

networks *Online Teaching Options*

Help students use the Skills Builder resources

Your students can practice important 21st Century skills such as geography, reading, writing, and critical thinking by using resources found in the Skills Builder tab of the online Student Learning Center. Resources include templates, handbooks, and slide shows. These same resources are also available in the Resource Library of the Teacher Lesson Center.

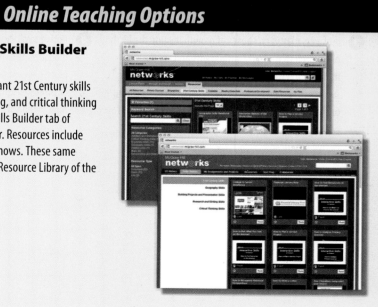

Life in the American Colonies
Planner

UNDERSTANDING BY DESIGN®

Enduring Understanding

- *People, places, and ideas change over time.*

Essential Questions

- *How does geography influence the way people live?*
- *How do new ideas change the way people live?*
- *Why does conflict develop?*

Predictable Misunderstandings

Students may think:

- *The same crops were grown throughout the colonies.*
- *The same industries existed throughout the colonies.*
- *There were no European models for colonial government.*
- *The French and Indian War occurred between Native American tribes and the French.*

Assessment Evidence

Performance Tasks:

- *Hands-On Chapter Project*

Other Evidence:

- *Interactive Graphic Organizers*
- *What Do You Know? activity*
- *Economics of History Activity*
- *Primary Source Activity*
- *Geography and History Activity*
- *America's Literature questions*
- *Written Paragraphs*
- *Analyzing Images*
- *Lesson Reviews*
- *Online Self-Check Quizzes*
- *Chapter Activities and Assessment*

SUGGESTED PACING GUIDE

Introducing the Chapter.............. 1 day	Lesson 3 ....2 days
Lesson 1 ....2 days	Lesson 4 ....2 days
America's Literature .... 1 day	Chapter Wrap-Up and Assessment...... 1 day
Lesson 2 .... 1 day	

TOTAL TIME   10 Days

NCSS Standards covered in "Life in the American Colonies"

Learners will understand:

1   CULTURE

5. How individuals learn the elements of their culture through interactions with others, and how individuals learn of other cultures through communication and study

2   TIME, CONTINUITY, AND CHANGE

1. The study of the past provides representation of the history of communities, nations, and the world

2. Concepts such as: chronology, causality, change, conflict, complexity, multiple perspectives, primary and secondary sources, and cause and effect

3   PEOPLE, PLACES, AND ENVIRONMENTS

4. The concept of regions identifies links between people in different locations according to specific criteria (e.g., physical, economic, social, cultural, or religious)

8. Factors that contribute to cooperation and conflict among peoples of the nation and world, including language, religion, and political beliefs

5   INDIVIDUALS, GROUPS, AND INSTITUTIONS

1. This theme helps us know how individuals are members of groups and institutions, and influence and shape those groups and institutions

7   PRODUCTION, DISTRIBUTION, AND CONSUMPTION

3. The economic choices that people make have both present and future consequences

Key for Using the Teacher Edition

SKILL-BASED ACTIVITIES

Types of skill activities found in the Teacher Edition.

V **Visual Skills** require students to analyze maps, graphs, charts, and photos.

R **Reading Skills** help students practice reading skills and master vocabulary.

W **Writing Skills** provide writing opportunities to help students comprehend the text.

C **Critical Thinking Skills** help students apply and extend what they have learned.

T **Technology Skills** require students to use digital tools effectively.

*Letters are followed by a number when there is more than one of the same type of skill on the page.

DIFFERENTIATED INSTRUCTION

All activities are written for the on-level student unless otherwise marked with the leveled labels below.

BL Beyond Level
AL Approaching Level
ELL English Language Learners

All students benefit from activities that utilize different learning styles. Many activities are marked as below when a particular learning style is highlighted.

Intrapersonal	Naturalist
Logical/Mathematical	Kinesthetic
Visual/Spatial	Auditory/Musical
Verbal/Linguistic	Interpersonal

CHAPTER OPENER PLANNER

Students will know:

- how geography played a role in the development of the economies of the colonies.
- the values and beliefs that the colonists developed about government.
- the traditional beliefs and values associated with American culture.
- the causes and consequences of the French and Indian War.

Students will be able to:

- **compare** the economic diversity of the three regions of the thirteen colonies.
- **draw conclusions** about the role geography played in the colonies' economic development.
- **identify and analyze** the triangular trade route that includes the Middle Passage and the trade of enslaved Africans.
- **describe** life for a plantation owner, his family, and enslaved Africans in the Southern Colonies.
- **identify** the values and beliefs that the colonists had about government.
- **explain** the principles of limited government and representative government.
- **identify** the traditional beliefs and values associated with life in the colonies.
- **analyze** Britain's economic policies and the reactions of the colonists.
- **identify** the causes and significant events of the French and Indian War.

UNDERSTANDING
BY DESIGN®

☑ *Print Teaching Options*

V **Visual Skills**

☐ **P. 82** Students identify distinct regions within the thirteen colonies. Visual/Spatial

☐ **P. 83** Students evaluate the effect of world events on life in the colonies.

☑ *Online Teaching Options*

V **Visual Skills**

☐ **MAP** **The Colonial Economy c. 1750**—Students explore the regions of the thirteen colonies and their major industries.

☐ **TIME LINE** **Place and Time: America 1607 to 1770**—Students learn about key historical events related to pre-revolution America.

☐ **WORLD ATLAS** Students can use this interactive map to identify regions of the world, learn about individual countries, locate political boundaries, measure distances, and much more.

☑ *Printable Digital Worksheets*

R **Reading Skills**

☐ **GRAPHIC NOVEL** *The Middle Passage*—The experiences of two enslaved African sisters are recounted as they endure the journey to America.

Project-Based Learning

Hands-On Chapter Project

Colonial Journal

To understand forces that shaped life in colonial America, student groups will create a journal written from the perspective of one of the figures in this chapter.

Technology Extension edtechteacher
21st Century Learning

Create a Google™ Apps Journal

- Find an additional activity online that incorporates technology for this project.
- Visit the EdTechTeacher Web sites (included in the Technology Extension for this chapter) for more links, tutorials, and other resources.

Print Resources

ANCILLARY RESOURCES

These ancillaries are available for every chapter and lesson.

- **Reading Essentials and Study Guide Workbook** AL ELL
- **Chapter Tests and Lesson Quizzes Blackline Masters**

PRINTABLE DIGITAL WORKSHEETS

These printable digital worksheets are available for every chapter and lesson.

- **Hands-On Chapter Projects**
- **What Do You Know? activities**
- **Chapter Summaries (English and Spanish)**
- **Vocabulary Builder activities**
- **Guided Reading activities**

More Media Resources

SUGGESTED READING

Grade 6 reading level:

- *The Adventurous Life of Myles Standish and the Amazing-But-True Survival Story of Plymouth Colony,* by Cheryl Harness

Grade 7 reading level:

- *The Amazing Mr. Franklin: Or the Boy Who Read Everything,* by Ruth Ashby

Grade 8 reading level:

- *Worlds Apart,* by Kathleen Karr

Students will know:
- how geography played a role in the development of the economies of the colonies.

Students will be able to:
- **compare** the economic diversity of the three regions of the thirteen colonies.
- **draw conclusions** about the role geography played in the colonies' economic development.
- **identify and analyze** the triangular trade route that includes the Middle Passage and the trade of enslaved Africans.
- **describe** life for a plantation owner, his family, and enslaved Africans in the Southern Colonies.

UNDERSTANDING BY DESIGN®

☑ *Print Teaching Options*

V Visual Skills

☐ **P. 87** Students extract data about slavery from a chart and diagram. **Visual/Spatial**

☐ **P. 88** Students explore Triangular Trade routes. **Visual/Spatial**

R Reading Skills

☐ **P. 84** Students explain how geographical features of a region affect agriculture.

☐ **P. 84** Students identify types of work and businesses in Colonial New England and evaluate their economic effects. **AL** **ELL**

☐ **P. 85** Students discuss conditions and crops in the Middle Colonies. **AL**

☐ **P. 86** Students associate agriculture in the Southern Colonies with slavery. **ELL**

☐ **P. 87** Students consider factors that contributed to the growth of slavery. **AL**

☐ **P. 89** Students describe the work of enslaved peoples. **AL**

C Critical Thinking Skills

☐ **P. 85** Students determine how farming conditions led to new industries.

☐ **P. 85** Students differentiate agriculture in different regions.

☐ **P. 86** Students infer reasons and factors in the development of Southern Colony plantations.

☐ **P. 89** Students consider the origins of slave codes. **BL**

☐ **P. 89** Students propose reasons for colonial opposition to slavery. **BL**

T Technology Skills

☐ **P. 88** Students research primary source accounts of the slave trade. **BL**

☑ *Online Teaching Options*

V Visual Skills

☐ **MAP** **The Colonial Economy, c. 1750**—Students identify the three regions of colonial America and the goods produced in each region.

☐ **VIDEO** **New York's Early History**—Students view a video that explains how the colony flourished under Dutch rule and examines events that led to the colony's takeover by the British.

☐ **IMAGE** **Colonial Philadelphia**—Students examine the importance of this city as a business and shipping center.

☐ **MAP** **Triangular Trade**—Students explore the "legs" of the triangular trade routes.

R Reading Skills

☐ **GRAPHIC ORGANIZER** **Taking Notes: *Describing:* The Triangle Trade Route**—Students use a three-part diagram to describe the triangular trade route.

☐ **PRIMARY SOURCE** **Life on a Colonial Plantation**—Students read about a slave's life on a plantation.

C Critical Thinking Skills

☐ **WHITEBOARD ACTIVITY** **The African Slave Trade**—Students match terms and definitions.

☐ **CHART** **The African Slave Trade**—Students examine statistics related to the African Slave Trade.

T Technology Skills

☐ **SELF-CHECK QUIZ** **Lesson 1**—Students receive instant feedback of their mastery of lesson content.

☑ *Printable Digital Worksheets*

W Writing Skills

☐ **WORKSHEET** **Economics of History Activity: The Triangular Trade and Mercantilism**—Students respond to a passage that describes how the triangular trade supported mercantilism.

COLONIAL GOVERNMENT

Students will know:
- the values and beliefs that the colonists developed about government.

Students will be able to:
- **identify** the values and beliefs that the colonists had about government.
- **explain** the principles of limited government and representative government.
- **analyze** Britain's economic policies and the reactions of the colonists.

UNDERSTANDING
BY DESIGN®

☑ *Print Teaching Options*

R Reading Skills

☐ **P. 92** Students define protected rights and representative government.

☐ **P. 93** Students discuss the Glorious Revolution and the English Bill of Rights.

☐ **P. 94** Students define mercantilism. **AL** **ELL**

☐ **P. 95** Students list effects of the Navigation Acts. **AL** **BL**

W Writing Skills

☐ **P. 94** Students argue the advantages and disadvantages of limited voting rights in colonial government. **AL** **BL**

C Critical Thinking Skills

☐ **P. 93** Students examine the Bill of Rights. **BL**

☐ **P. 95** Students analyze the colonists' changing relationship with the British government. **BL**

☑ *Online Teaching Options*

V Visual Skills

VIDEO **Society, Community, and Justice in the Northern Colonies**—Students view a video that describes the social order of the New England colonies.

MAP **Mercantilism**—Students use a map to discuss the European economic policy of mercantilism.

IMAGE **The House of Burgesses**—Students learn how members were elected to the Virginia House of Burgesses and contrast New England's style of government with Virginia's.

R Reading Skills

GRAPHIC ORGANIZER **Taking Notes: *Explaining*: Protected Rights and Representative Government**—Students use a diagram to explain protected rights and representative government.

T Technology Skills

SELF-CHECK QUIZ **Lesson 2**—Students receive instant feedback of their mastery of lesson content.

GAME **Early Colonial Government Crossword Puzzle**—Students solve clues to review the lesson's concepts and content vocabulary.

☑ *Printable Digital Worksheets*

W Writing Skills

WORKSHEET **Primary Source Activity: The Magna Carta**—Students respond after reading excerpts from the Magna Carta.

Students will know:
- the traditional beliefs and values associated with American culture.

Students will be able to:
- **identify** the traditional beliefs and values associated with life in the colonies.

UNDERSTANDING
BY DESIGN®

☑ *Print Teaching Options*

R Reading Skills

☐ **P. 97** Students determine roles of colonial family members.

☐ **P. 98** Students compare current American beliefs and values to those of the colonists.

☐ **P. 98** Students paraphrase colonial sentiments about education and make comparisons with the present. **Verbal/Linguistic**

☐ **P. 99** Students cite evidence showing how the Great Awakening affected the colonies.

C Critical Thinking Skills

☐ **P. 96** Students evaluate factors affecting colonial population. **ELL Logical/Mathematical**

☐ **P. 97** Students infer causes that brought about a change in American spirit. **BL**

☐ **P. 99** Students discuss main ideas about the Enlightenment Movement. **BL**

☐ **P. 100** Students debate pros and cons of a free press. **BL Verbal/Linguistic**

☐ **P. 100** Students examine behaviors that constitute civic virtue. **AL ELL Intrapersonal**

T Technology Skills

☐ **P. 99** Students take notes on Internet research about important figures in the Great Awakening.

☑ *Online Teaching Options*

V Visual Skills

☐ **IMAGE Smallpox**—Students learn the history of smallpox and discuss how disease can affect populations.

☐ **VIDEO The Great Awakening**—Students hear excerpts from emotional sermons given by two influential orators during the Great Awakening.

R Reading Skills

☐ **GRAPHIC ORGANIZER Taking Notes: *Determining Cause and Effect:* The Great Awakening and the Enlightenment**—Students explain how the Great Awakening and the Enlightenment affected the colonists.

☐ **PRIMARY SOURCE The New-York Weekly Journal**—Students analyze the order for the burning of Zenger's journals and discuss his role in establishing freedom of the press.

C Critical Thinking Skills

☐ **SLIDE SHOW Colonial Children**—Students examine scenes from colonial family life and compare them with their own experiences.

☐ **SLIDE SHOW The Inventions of Benjamin Franklin**—Students examine some of the inventions of Benjamin Franklin and connect them to the ideas of the enlightenment.

T Technology Skills

☐ **SELF-CHECK QUIZ Lesson 3**—Students receive instant feedback of their mastery of lesson content.

☐ **GAME Culture and Society–Periods of Change Sorting Game**—Students sort terms into categories to reinforce their understanding of the Enlightenment and the Great Awakening.

RIVALRY IN NORTH AMERICA

Students will know:
- the causes and consequences of the French and Indian War.

Students will be able to:
- **analyze** Britain's economic policies and the reactions of the colonists.
- **identify** the causes and significant events of the French and Indian War.

UNDERSTANDING
BY DESIGN®

☑ *Print Teaching Options*

V Visual Skills

☐ **P. 103** Students interpret the meaning of a political cartoon. **Visual/Spatial**

☐ **P. 104** Students use a map to understand locations and disputed territories associated with the French and Indian War. **BL** **Visual/Spatial**

R Reading Skills

☐ **P. 101** Students identify issues that sparked British and French rivalries. **AL** **BL**

☐ **P. 102** Students identify roles of Native Americans in the French and Indian War.

☐ **P. 102** Students explain the Albany Plan. **AL**

☐ **P. 103** Students make inferences about the potential outcome of the French and Indian War. **BL**

☐ **P. 105** Students explain the effects of colonists' movement west of the Appalachian Mountains. **AL**

☐ **P. 105** Students restate key ideas about Pontiac and Pontiac's War. **AL**

C Critical Thinking Skills

☐ **P. 102** Students evaluate significant events in the French and Indian War. **AL** **BL**

☐ **P. 104** Students examine the attack and capture of Quebec.

☐ **P. 105** Students assess the Proclamation of 1763.

☑ *Online Teaching Options*

V Visual Skills

☐ **MAP** **The French and Indian War, 1754–1763**—Students use the map to identify regions under French, British, and Native American control and the movement of troops during the war.

☐ **IMAGE** **George Washington and the French and Indian War**—Students learn of Washington's contributions during the French and Indian War.

☐ **IMAGE** **The Battle of Quebec**—Students learn of the British capture of this city and its strategic location.

☐ **VIDEO** **The Proclamation of 1763**—Students view a video that describes how British policies after the French and Indian War caused conflicts with both Native Americans and the colonists.

R Reading Skills

☐ **GRAPHIC ORGANIZER** **Taking Notes:** *Summarizing:* **Native American Relations**—Students summarize why Native Americans had better relations with the French than with the British.

C Critical Thinking Skills

☐ **IMAGE** **Political Cartoon: Unite or Die**—Students analyze a cartoon originally drawn and published by Benjamin Franklin.

T Technology Skills

☐ **SELF-CHECK QUIZ** **Lesson 4**—Students receive instant feedback of their mastery of lesson content.

☑ *Printable Digital Worksheets*

W Writing Skills

☐ **WORKSHEET** **Geography and History Activity: Understanding Movement: Westward Movement and the Proclamation of 1763**—Students analyze a reading selection and maps and then apply this knowledge to writing about the role of mercantilism in the colonies.

INTERVENTION AND REMEDIATION STRATEGIES

LESSON 1 Colonial Economy

Reading and Comprehension

Ask students to create a three-column chart, labeling the columns *New England Colonies, Middle Colonies,* and *Southern Colonies.* Have students write important details describing each of these regions of colonial America.

Text Evidence

Ask students to choose one aspect of slavery and do Internet research to learn more about it. Examples might be the middle passage, slave ships, and life on a plantation. Have them do the research, take notes, and give a two- or three-minute presentation.

LESSON 2 Colonial Government

Reading and Comprehension

Ask students to write two or three paragraphs summarizing the section, "English Principles of Government."

Text Evidence

Tell students that the Magna Carta is considered one of the most important documents in the history of democracy. Have students research the document and write a paragraph giving reasons to support this claim.

LESSON 3 Culture and Society

Reading and Comprehension

Ask students to create an outline of Lesson 3. Have them use the major heads to organize their outlines and include all main ideas for each topic.

Text Evidence

The text describes Benjamin Franklin as "a shining example of civic virtue." Have students write a paragraph explaining why he was such an example. They can do research as necessary.

LESSON 4 Rivalry in North America

Reading and Comprehension

Have students write and deliver a short speech they might give to fourth grade students explaining the rivalry between Great Britain and France.

Text Evidence

Ask students to research the Iroquois Confederacy and to write an essay answering these questions:

- What was the Iroquois Confederacy?
- Why was it important?

Online Resources

Approaching Level Reader

Use this online lower-level text that corresponds directly to the text in the Student Edition. It includes a Spanish version.

Guided Reading Activities

This resource uses graphic organizers and guiding questions to help students with comprehension.

What Do You Know?

Use these worksheets to pre-assess student's background knowledge before they study the chapter.

Reading Essentials and Study Guide Workbook

This resource offers writing and reading activities for the approaching-level student. Also available in Spanish.

Self-Check Quizzes

This online assessment tool provides instant feedback for students to check their progress.

How Do I Incorporate the
Common Core State Standards
in My Lessons?

The Common Core State Standards (CCSS), are national standards focused on ensuring that students master language arts skills by the time they complete high school. In grades 6 through 12, the standards require that some of this skill development and skill practice be part of other subjects, such as social studies.

Step 1 Familiarize Yourself with the Standards.

- The Common Core Solutions Web site, **http://www.commoncoresolutions.com**, has several free training modules on the CCSS.

- The Common Core State Standards Toolbox Web site, **http://www.mhecommoncoretoolbox.com**, has articles and tips from other teachers and professionals that you can refer to throughout the year.

Step 2 Incorporate the Standards into Your Lessons.

- Common core activities are clearly marked in the McGraw-Hill print teacher and student editions and online teacher lesson plans to help you incorporate the standards into your lessons.

- Activities are correlated to the Common Core State Standards.

Step 3 Use Resources in the Online Resource Library to Promote Student Skill Mastery.

Slide Shows that help students learn how to:
- Identify main ideas
- Understand cause and effect
- Compare and contrast
- Draw conclusions
- Analyze visuals, documents, videos

Writing and Analyzing Templates to help students:
- Write drafts
- Evaluate writing samples
- Write persuasive text
- Create expository text
- Compose narrative

Life in the American Colonies

1607–1770

ESSENTIAL QUESTIONS • *How does geography influence the way people live?* • *How do new ideas change the way people live?* • *Why does conflict develop?*

© Burstein Collection/CORBIS

81

networks

There's More Online about life in the American colonies.

CHAPTER 4

Lesson 1
Colonial Economy

Lesson 2
Colonial Government

Lesson 3
Culture and Society

Lesson 4
Rivalry in North America

The Story Matters . . .

At first glance, the painting is simple—just a woman and her small baby. Look deeper, however, and you can see more.

The portrait dates from the 1670s, just 50 years after the Pilgrims first arrived in New England. It shows Elizabeth Freake, wife of a Boston merchant and lawyer John Freake, with baby Mary. Notice the fine fabrics mother and child are wearing.

For many colonial Americans such as the Freakes, life is no longer a struggle for survival. In fact, it is increasingly prosperous and comfortable.

ENGAGE

Bellringer Ask a student volunteer to read "The Story Matters . . ." aloud. Then ask these questions:

- **How are Pilgrims often depicted?** *(The stereotype is someone dressed in severe or austere grays, blacks, or browns, without lace, jewelry, or fine fabrics.)*
- **How does this portrait differ from the usual picture of Pilgrims?** *(Elizabeth Freake is dressed in a green dress made of some fine material. She is wearing strands of pearls around her neck and a bracelet on her wrist. Baby Mary is similarly dressed in fine fabrics and lace.)*
- **Based on this portrait and passage, what did Elizabeth Freake value in her life?** *(Answers will vary but may include husband, family, her role as a mother, piety or religion, fine clothing and possessions, financial security or success, respect within the community, and so on.)* Record responses on the board.
- **Which of these values would you say are commonly held by people in the United States today?** *(Students should explain the reasons for their answers.)*

Remind students that part of who we are as a nation today was built upon the lives and values of the colonists who first settled here. What the colonists thought, how they lived, and their customs and traditions are woven into the fabric of the nation. As students read the chapter, remind them to look for threads that can be traced from the colonial past to our present day.

Making Connections

Read the following information to students:

The unknown artist who painted this portrait probably did so around 1670. About nine other paintings depicting people who lived in Boston during the early 1670s have been attributed to this artist, who is commonly referred to as the "Freake Painter."

Letter from the Author

Dear American History Teacher,

The American colonies were controlled by England, the economic leader of the world. The Southern colonies were economically the most important. Their commercial agriculture tied the colonies closer to slavery. Being on the North American continent also made the colonies Britain's line of defense against the French empire in Canada. When France and England went to war in 1756, the colonies were drawn together by fighting the French and Indian War.

Joyce Appleby

TEACH & ASSESS

Step Into the Place

V1 Visual Skills

Analyzing Maps Review the map with students, explaining that it shows the different regions of the thirteen colonies, along with their major industries. Briefly discuss the map icons and what they represent. Ask students to recall and point out where the earliest English settlers arrived in North America and to explain what happened to those colonists. **Visual/Spatial**

Explain to students that in this chapter they will read about the development of the colonial economy, government, and society, and learn how tensions among groups of people in North America (English colonists, French colonists, and Native Americans) led to conflict. Have students study the key to the map. Then, as a class, discuss the Map Focus questions.

Content Background Knowledge

Early in life, Benjamin Franklin became a printer. He was so successful that he was able to retire in 1748 at the age of 42 and then devote his life to being a "gentleman." This enabled him to participate in the activities for which he is best known, including politics and science. His study of electricity led to his book *Experiments and Observations on Electricity*, which was published in four languages and included many important breakthroughs in the science. He became famous at a time when people in many parts of the world looked down on the American colonies as a primitive backwater.

ANSWERS, p. 82

Step Into the Place
1. in the New England Colonies
2. wheat and corn
3. **CRITICAL THINKING** Possible answer: The land was hard to farm. Other resources were more readily available.

Step Into the Time
Bacon's Rebellion and the French and Indian War show there was conflict in colonial North America.

CHAPTER 4 (CCSS)

Place and Time: America 1607 to 1770

Colonial America was rich in natural resources, such as lumber, fish, and furs. In many of the colonies, the land was well-suited to agriculture, producing crops like wheat, corn, tobacco, rice, and indigo. In some colonies, industries developed to process and transport the wealth of the new land.

The kitchen was the heart of the American home in colonial times. Maintaining the fire was an important task. The fire was used to cook the food, provide warmth, and boil the water for washing the clothes.

Step Into the Place

MAP FOCUS The Colonial Economy map shows the different regions of the thirteen colonies along with their major industries.

1 PLACE Where was shipbuilding a major industry? RH.6–8.7

2 REGION What crops were common to both the Middle Colonies and the Southern Colonies? RH.6–8.7

3 CRITICAL THINKING
Drawing Conclusions Why do you think the New England Colonies developed industries that were not based in agriculture? RH.6–8.7, RH.6–8.10

Perhaps no other person represented the rise of the American colonies better than Benjamin Franklin. A successful businessperson, a scientific genius, and a skilled political leader—Franklin showed many of the best traits of the growing colonial society.

Step Into the Time

V2 **TIME LINE** Which events on the time line hint at conflict in colonial North America? RH.6–8.5, RH.6–8.7

| AMERICAS | | c. 1570 Iroquois Confederacy forms | 1619 The first Africans arrive in Virginia |
| WORLD EVENTS | 1550 | 1600 | |

Project-Based Learning

Hands-On Chapter Project

Colonial Journal
To understand forces that shaped colonial life, student teams will write a journal from the perspective of one of the figures in this chapter. Students will read about life in colonial America in their textbooks, discuss aspects of colonial life to write about, research their historical figures, meet with their team to organize research, produce the journals, and share the journals with the class.

Technology Extension

Create a Google™ Apps Journal
Students will work in groups to create a Google Apps multimedia slide show presentation that may include text, images, videos, drawings, and tables. They will combine their presentations into a whole-class product, which they will then share with an audience via email, blog, Web site, or wiki, or through slide-sharing sites.

edtechteacher
21st Century Learning

networks
There's More Online!

☑ **MAP** Explore the interactive version of this map on NETWORKS.

☑ **TIME LINE** Explore the interactive version of this time line on NETWORKS.

V1

The Colonial Economy c. 1750

Lake Huron
Lake Michigan
L. Ontario
Lake Erie
Wabash R.
Ohio R.
Mississippi R.
Tennessee R.
APPALACHIAN MOUNTAINS

Mass.
N.H.
Falmouth
Portsmouth
Albany
N.Y.
Mass.
Boston
Conn.
Newport
R.I.
NEW ENGLAND COLONIES
Delaware
New York
Pa.
New Castle
Baltimore
N.J.
Md.
Del.
MIDDLE COLONIES
Susquehanna R.
Virginia
Chesapeake Bay
York R.
Williamsburg
James R.
Norfolk
North Carolina
New Bern
South Carolina
Wilmington
SOUTHERN COLONIES
Georgia
Charleston
Ocmulgee R.
Savannah

ATLANTIC OCEAN

Gulf of Mexico

45°N
40°N
65°W
35°N
75°W
70°W
30°N
85°W
80°W

Legend:
- Wheat and corn
- Tobacco
- Rice and indigo
- Fishing and whaling
- Cattle
- Fur trapping
- Ironworks
- Lumber
- Rum distillery
- Shipbuilding

0   200 miles
0   200 km
Lambert Azimuthal Equal-Area projection

Time line:

1651 First Navigation Act regulates colonial trade

1676 Bacon's Rebellion takes place in Virginia

c. 1740 Great Awakening peaks

1754 French and Indian War begins

1763 King George issues Proclamation of 1763

1650   1700   1750   1800

1644 Qing Dynasty established in China

1689 English Bill of Rights signed

c. 1700 Asante Kingdom rises in West Africa

1748 Montesquieu publishes *The Spirit of Laws*

1756 Seven Years' War begins

1762 Catherine the Great begins rule in Russia

83

Step Into the Time

V2 Visual Skills

Analyzing Time Lines Have students examine the time line for the chapter. Point out that this chapter deals with events from the early 1600s to the mid-1700s. **Ask: Which events on the time line might affect life in the English colonies during that period?** *(all events on the U.S. time line; on the world time line: English Bill of Rights is signed, Seven Years' War begins)* Make sure students realize that world events such as the signing of the English Bill of Rights and the Seven Years' War had an effect on England's colonies in North America.

Content Background Knowledge

Bacon's Rebellion was orchestrated by Nathaniel Bacon, who organized an army to attack the Indians in order to open the frontier. The Virginia governor feared the consequences of an all-out war with the Indians and opposed Bacon's plan. Bacon then directed his army against the governor. For a short time, he controlled most of Virginia. Bacon died in the midst of the rebellion, however, and the movement disintegrated.

CLOSE & REFLECT

Formulating Questions Assign students to work in pairs and write two or three questions about the map and the time line. Have them briefly discuss possible answers to their questions. Then call on volunteers to read the questions. Discuss the proposed answers as a class. **Interpersonal**

TIME LINE

Place and Time: America 1607 to 1770

Reading a Time Line Have students explore the interactive time line by clicking on "More Information" to learn more about each event. Then have each student choose one event to investigate online. Ask students to write a paragraph describing the social, political, or economic consequences of the event.

See page 81B for other online activities.

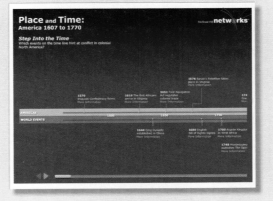

ENGAGE

 Bellringer Ask students to describe the economy of their region.

Ask: Is it based on agriculture, manufacturing, service, tourism, or something else? *(Answers will vary based on local conditions.)* Invite students to discuss why their region relies on certain industries rather than on others.

Tell students that they will be reading about the economies of the three main regions of colonial America and why each region developed the industries it did.

TEACH & ASSESS

R1 Reading Skills

Explaining Have students read the text to explain what life was like for the colonists. **Ask: What was the basis of colonial life?** *(agriculture)* **Ask: What are some general geographical features that influence the type of agriculture practiced in a region?** *(Possible answers: type of soil, rainfall and other water sources, type of terrain, and climate and weather.)* Students should support their answers with evidence from the text.

R2 Reading Skills

Identifying Have students read the text to identify the role farming played in New England's economy. **Ask: What is subsistence farming?** *(farming that produces only enough to meet the needs of the family, leaving little to sell or trade)* Discuss subsistence farming and why New England colonists practiced it. **Ask: How much did this type of farming contribute to the prosperity of a region?** *(none because the food raised was for the farmer and his family)* **AL** **ELL**

Have students use the text to determine the kinds of work that people did in New England. **Ask: What work was typically done by the families of New England farmers?** *(spinning yarn, and making cloth, garments, candles, and soaps)* **What were some of the small businesses of New England?** *(mills for grinding grain and sawing lumber, blacksmithing, shoemaking, furniture making, gunsmithing)* Point out that both on the farms and in the towns, efforts applied to producing basic goods. People tried to make all that was needed in order to live. Ask students to find evidence in the text that supports this assertion.

ANSWER, p. 84

TAKING NOTES: Possible answers: **West Indies to American Colonies:** sugar and molasses; **American Colonies to West Africa:** rum, iron, and tools; **Africa to the West Indies:** enslaved persons, gold, and pepper

---

---

networks
There's More Online!

- ☑ **BIOGRAPHY**
  Olaudah Equiano
- ☑ **CHART/GRAPH**
  The African Slave Trade
- ☑ **GRAPHIC ORGANIZER**
  The Triangular Trade
- ☑ **MAP** The Triangular Trade
- ☑ **PRIMARY SOURCE**
  · Life on a Plantation
  · Conditions on a Slave Ship

Lesson 1
Colonial Economy

ESSENTIAL QUESTION *How does geography influence the way people live?*

IT MATTERS BECAUSE
The unique resources and conditions that existed in each colony helped shape colonial economies and ways of living.

Making a Living in the Colonies

GUIDING QUESTION *How did the economic activity of the three regions reflect their geography?*

R1 Life in colonial America was based largely on agriculture. Most colonists farmed or made their livings from businesses related to farming, such as milling flour. Geography played an important role in the colonies' economic development. Colonists learned to adapt to the climate and terrain of the region where they lived.

Commercial New England

R2 In New England, long winters and thin, rocky soil made large-scale farming difficult. Most farmers here practiced **subsistence farming** (suhb·SIS·tuhns)—producing enough to meet the needs of their families, with little left over to sell or trade. New England farmers often depended on their children for labor. Everyone in the family worked—spinning yarn, milking cows, fencing fields, and sowing and harvesting crops. Women made cloth, garments, candles, and soaps for their families.

    Throughout New England were many small businesses. Nearly every town had a mill for grinding grain or sawing lumber. People used waterpower from streams to run the mills. Large towns attracted skilled craftspeople. Among them were blacksmiths, shoemakers, furniture makers, and gunsmiths.

Reading HELPDESK **CCSS**

Taking Notes: *Describing* RH.6–8.2, RH.6–8.7
As you read, use a diagram like this one to describe the triangular trade routes.

Content Vocabulary (Tier 3 Words)
- subsistence farming
- triangular trade
- cash crop
- slave code
- diversity

84 *Life in the American Colonies*

---

networks *Online Teaching Options*

VIDEO

New York's Early History

Evaluating Show the Learn360 video about the early history of New York. Discuss with students New York's importance as a port city. Have students explain how the significance of the port changed as trade with England and other countries grew.

See page 81C for other online activities.

Shipbuilding was an important New England industry. The lumber for building ships came from the region's forests. Workers floated the lumber down rivers to shipyards in coastal towns. The Northern coastal cities served as centers of the colonial shipping trade, linking the Northern Colonies with the Southern Colonies—and America with other parts of the world.

Fishing was also important. Some New Englanders ventured far out to sea to hunt whales for oil and whalebone.

The Middle Colonies

Most people in the Middle Colonies were farmers. This region enjoyed more fertile soil and a slightly milder climate than New England. Farmers here plowed and planted larger areas of land and produced bigger harvests than did New Englanders. In New York and Pennsylvania, farmers grew large quantities of wheat and other **cash crops**—crops that could be sold easily in markets in the colonies and overseas.

Farmers sent wheat and livestock for shipment to New York City and Philadelphia, which became busy ports. By 1760, New York, with 14,000 people, and Philadelphia, with 19,000 people, were two of the largest cities in the American colonies.

Like the New England Colonies, the Middle Colonies also had industries. Some were home-based crafts, such as carpentry and flour making. Others were larger businesses—lumber mills, mines, ironworks, small-scale manufacturing, and so on.

The Middle Colonies attracted many Scotch-Irish, German, Dutch, and Swedish settlers. Using agricultural methods developed in Europe, these immigrants became successful farmers. They gave the Middle Colonies a cultural **diversity** (duh·VUHR·suh·tee), or variety, not found in New England.

Life in the Southern Colonies

The Southern Colonies had rich soil and a warm climate well suited to certain kinds of farming. Southern farmers could plant large areas and produce harvests of cash crops, such as tobacco or rice. Most settlers in the Southern Colonies made their living from farming.

New York City, shown here in the late 1750s, was a bustling center of trade and population in the American colonies.

▶ CRITICAL THINKING
Analyzing What geographic features helped New York thrive as a seaport?

Collection of the New-York Historical Society/Bridgeman Art Library

subsistence farming producing just enough to meet immediate needs
cash crop a crop that can be sold easily in markets

diversity variety, such as of ethnic or national groups

<image-block> C1

R

C2 </image-block>

C1 Critical Thinking Skills

Determining Cause and Effect Discuss the development of the shipping and fishing industries in the New England Colonies. **Ask: How did poor farming conditions lead to the development of other industries in New England?** *(Colonists were forced to search for other economic opportunities in order to survive and prosper.)*

R Reading Skills

Discussing After students have read the text, discuss conditions in the Middle Colonies. **Ask: How did the soil quality and climate in the Middle Colonies affect the development of farming there?** *(The soil was more fertile, and the climate was milder than in New England, which made it easier to grow crops. Large areas were planted, and these produced big harvests. Farmers grew cash crops and sold their produce.)* **AL**

Discuss the cash crops grown in the Middle Colonies. **Ask: What was the main cash crop of the Middle Colonies?** *(wheat)* **What were two large markets for the farmers' cash crops?** *(Philadelphia and New York)* Direct students to cite evidence from the text to support their answers.

C2 Critical Thinking Skills

Comparing and Contrasting Remind students that agriculture was the basis of the economies of the colonies but that differences in climate and soil affected the kinds of farming practiced. **Ask: What cash crops were grown in both the Middle Colonies and the South?** *(wheat and tobacco)* **What additional cash crop was produced in the South?** *(rice)*

Content Background Knowledge

In 1760, the largest cities in the colonies, and their populations, were:

1. Philadelphia, 19,000
2. Boston, 16,000
3. New York, 14,000
4. Charleston, South Carolina, 8,000
5. New Port, Rhode Island, 7,000

IMAGE

Colonial Philadelphia

Recognizing Relationships Use the interactive image of colonial Philadelphia to discuss the importance of this city as a business and shipping center. Tell students to click on each bullet to read information about Philadelphia. **Ask: What was the result of Philadelphia being a successful seaport?** *(Philadelphia became one of the two largest cities in the American colonies.)*

See page 81C for other online activities.

networks   Colonial Philadelphia

Bettmann/CORBIS
○ ○ ○

ANSWER, p. 85

CRITICAL THINKING New York's location on a river near the Atlantic Ocean made it a seaport. It was also surrounded by fertile farmland, so farmers could easily bring goods to the city for shipment.

Colonial Economy

C Critical Thinking Skills

Making Inferences Discuss the plantations of the Southern Colonies. **Ask:** Why do you think the plantations came to resemble small villages? *(The plantations were very large with many people living on them who needed the services of a small town. It was probably practical to provide them on the plantation.)* **Ask:** Why do you think the large plantations developed mainly in the Tidewater rather than in the backcountry? *(The land was richer and flatter, making it easier to plant and harvest large fields.)*

R Reading Skills

Explaining Have students read the section titled "Tobacco and Rice," then discuss the effects of tobacco and rice on the Southern Colonies. Ask these questions:

- How did rice farmers change the geography of the land to accommodate their farming needs? *(They built dams to create fields, called paddies, that could be flooded or drained as necessary.)*
- Why is cultivation of rice such difficult work? *(Workers must stand in knee-deep mud with no protection from the hot sun or insects.)*
- How did the popularity of rice and tobacco lead to the growth of slavery in the Southern Colonies? *(Demand for these products increased. More workers were needed for planting and harvesting. Enslaved people filled this need.)*

Ensure that all students understand the concept of slavery. **Ask: What is slavery?** *(a condition in which one person has absolute authority over another, controlling the person's life and liberty)* Students should cite evidence from the text to support their answers. **ELL**

Little commerce or industry developed there. For the most part, London merchants rather than local merchants from the colonies managed Southern trade.

C   Most large plantations were located in the Tidewater, a region of flat, low-lying plains along the seacoast. Planters built their plantations on rivers so they could ship their crops to market by boat. A plantation was like a small village. It had fields stretching out around a cluster of buildings, including cabins, barns, and stables, as well as carpenter and blacksmith shops, storerooms, and kitchens. A large plantation might have its own chapel and school. Small plantations often had fewer than 50 enslaved workers. Large ones typically had 200 or more.

Between the Tidewater and the Appalachian Mountains lay a region of hills and forests known as the backcountry. Its settlers included hardy newcomers to the colonies. They grew corn and tobacco on small family farms. Some had one or two enslaved Africans to help with the work. Backcountry farmers greatly outnumbered large plantation owners. Still, the plantation owners were wealthier and more powerful. They controlled the economic and political life of the region.

Tobacco and Rice

Tobacco was the **principal** cash crop in Maryland and Virginia. Growing tobacco and preparing it for sale required a lot of labor. At first, planters used indentured servants to work in the fields. These servants worked for a time and then went free. When indentured servants became scarce and expensive, Southern planters began using enslaved Africans instead.

R   Slaveholders with large farms grew wealthy by growing tobacco. They sold most of it in Europe. Sometimes, though, there was too much tobacco on the market—more than buyers wanted. To sell the extra tobacco, planters had to lower their prices. As a result, their profits fell. Some planters switched to other crops, such as corn and wheat.

The geography of South Carolina and Georgia helped make rice the main cash crop there. In low-lying areas along the coast, planters built dams to create rice fields, called paddies. Planters flooded the fields when the rice was young and drained them when the rice was ready to harvest.

Work in the rice paddies was very hard. It involved standing knee-deep in the mud with no protection from the blazing sun or biting insects. To do this hard work, rice growers **relied** on slave labor.

Reading HELPDESK (CCSS)

Academic Vocabulary (Tier 2)
principal most important
rely to depend upon

Build Vocabulary: *Related Words*
If the word *principal* means "most important," what can you say about the principal of your school?

---

net**w**rks   *Online Teaching Options*

LECTURE SLIDE

The Economies of the Early Colonies

Summarizing Have students write one sentence about each of the three regions in colonial America. In each sentence, they should describe how geography played a role in the economy of that region. Then show the lecture slide about the economies of the early colonies and summarize the economy of each region. **Ask:** Why was geography so important to the economic development of a region? *(Colonial society was based on agriculture. Geography—soil, water sources, and terrain—determined the size of farms and the type of farming that could be done. It determined the kind of crops that could be planted and the size of the harvest.)*

See page 81C for other online activities.

---

networks   **Economies of Colonies**

The Economies of the Early Colonies

- New England Colonies: The economy of the New England Colonies relied on commercial industries, such as textile production and shipbuilding.

- Middle Colonies: The economy of the Middle Colonies relied on agriculture. The fertile soil and mild temperatures made the conditions ideal for farming.

- Southern Colonies: The economy of the Southern Colonies relied on the harvest of cash crops. Cash crops such as tobacco, cotton, and rice could be sold easily in markets. The rich soil and warm climate made the land suitable for certain types of farming.

ANSWER, p. 86

Build Vocabulary Possible answer: The principal is the most important person in the school.

Colonial Economy

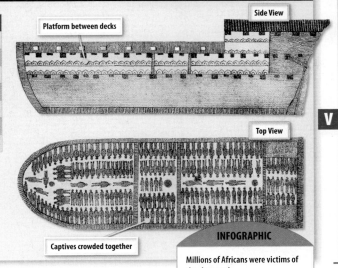

AFRICAN SLAVE TRADE 1450–1870

Destination	Total
British America/United States	427,000
Mexico and Central America	224,000
West Indies	4,040,000
Spanish South America	522,000
Guianas	531,000
Brazil	3,647,000
Europe	175,000

Side View

Platform between decks

Top View

Captives crowded together

Captains of slave ships added platforms between decks to fit more captives onto their ships. In the filthy, crowded slave compartments, disease—and rebellion—spread rapidly. On some ships, as many as half of the Africans died.

V

INFOGRAPHIC

Millions of Africans were victims of the slave trade.

1 CALCULATING
What was the total number of Africans shipped from Africa to the countries and regions shown?

2 CRITICAL THINKING
Drawing Conclusions What do you think was the impact of the slave trade on African cultures?

Rice proved to be an even more profitable crop than tobacco. Prices rose steadily as rice became popular in Europe. By the 1750s, South Carolina and Georgia had the fastest-growing economies in the colonies.

☑ **PROGRESS CHECK**

Summarizing Why was agriculture so important to the economy of the Southern Colonies?

The Growth of Slavery

GUIDING QUESTION *Why were enslaved Africans brought to the colonies?*

By the time Europeans were sailing to the Americas, slavery was widely practiced in West Africa. Many West African kingdoms enslaved those they defeated in war. Slave traders from Arab lands bought some of these enslaved people. Others were forced to work in gold mines or farm fields.

The arrival of Europeans in the Americas created a huge new demand for enslaved workers. Colonists needed a large labor force to work on their plantations. West African slave traders met this need. They sold captives they gained through wars and raids. Slavery and the slave trade became major parts of the colonial economy.

For enslaved Africans, the voyage to America usually began with a march to a European fort on the West African coast. There, they were sold to Europeans, who loaded them on ships.

R

Lesson 1   **87**

V Visual Skills

Analyzing Images Direct students' attention to the chart. Ask the following questions:

- **During what period of time was the slave trade carried out?** *(1450–1870)*
- **How many slaves were sent to British America and the United States?** *(427,000 slaves)*
- **Where were most slaves sent?** *(West Indies)*

Now ask students to examine the diagram of the slave ship. Point out the very tight crowding in the ship, explaining that the slaves could hardly stand up straight. **Ask: How many full levels were filled with slaves?** *(2 full levels)* **Visual/Spatial**

R Reading Skills

Discussing After students read the text, discuss the development of slavery in Africa and Arab lands. **Ask: Where did the West African kingdoms get many of these first slaves?** *(They were enemies captured in war and in raids.)* **Why did the American colonies become a large new market for slaves?** *(They needed a large workforce for the plantations.)* Students should support their responses with evidence from the text. **AL**

WHITEBOARD ACTIVITY

The African Slave Trade

Explaining Use the interactive whiteboard activity to discuss with students the different aspects of the African slave trade. **Ask: How did slavery become a part of this economic system?** *(Farmers and plantation owners needed a large and inexpensive labor force to work in the fields.)* **How were enslaved Africans supplied to the colonies?** *(Slave traders brought people kidnapped from West Africa to the colonies by ship.)*

See page 81C for other online activities.

networks   The African Slave Trade

Directions: Drag and drop each definition to the correct row of the table.

Term	Definition
West Africa	
Cheap Labor	
The Middle Passage	
Plantations	
Slave Codes	

- The slave-trading route from Africa to the Americas
- Where many enslaved people worked as laborers
- The origin of many slave-trading operations
- The rules governing the behavior of enslaved people
- The main purpose of slavery

ANSWERS, p. 87

☑ **PROGRESS CHECK** Agriculture provided crops they could sell to make a profit.

INFOGRAPHIC

1. more than 9.5 million people

2. **CRITICAL THINKING** Possible answer: The capture and sale of millions of people must have done terrible damage to societies throughout Africa.

V Visual Skills

Analyzing Maps Discuss the Triangular Trade map. Point out that there were several triangular routes. Have students trace the red, blue, and green routes to find the triangles. Explain that each route carried different goods, many of them to different destinations. Ask the following questions:

- What goods were sent from the British Colonies to Great Britain? *(rice, tobacco, indigo, and furs)*
- What were rice, tobacco, indigo, and fur traded for? *(cloth and other manufactured goods)*
- What was shipped from Great Britain to be exchanged for slaves? *(cloth, manufactured goods)*
- Have students locate the Middle Passage. Ask: How long was the passage? *(about 9,200 miles)*
Visual/Spatial

T Technology Skills

Researching on the Internet Discuss the conditions the slaves endured during their passage from Africa to the Americas. Then challenge students to research primary source accounts of the slave trade. Have students share what they learn in class discussion. **BL**

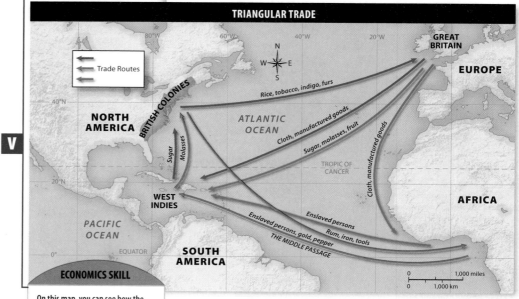

TRIANGULAR TRADE

ECONOMICS SKILL

On this map, you can see how the trade routes between the colonies, Great Britain, and Africa formed triangles. The triangular trade supported the economies of all three regions—though at a terrible human cost. The map shows which goods and products came from which locations.

1 IDENTIFYING From where did the American colonies receive molasses?

2 CRITICAL THINKING
Analyzing What was the main role of Great Britain in the triangular trade?

The Middle Passage

The trip across the ocean was called the "Middle Passage." This name came from the fact that it was often the second, or middle, leg of the three-part route known as the **triangular trade** (try·ANG·gyuh·luhr). People called this route "triangular" because, as the ships traveled between their destinations, their paths formed the three sides of a triangle.

The Middle Passage was a terrible ordeal. Chained together for more than a month, prisoners could hardly sit or stand. They received little food or water. Africans who died or became sick were thrown overboard. Those who refused to eat were whipped.

Those who survived the Middle Passage faced another terror when they reached American ports—the slave market. There they were put up for sale as laborers to plantation owners.

The Life of the Slave

Some enslaved Africans on plantations did housework, but most worked in the fields. Many enslaved workers suffered great cruelty. Owners of large plantations hired overseers, or bosses, to keep the enslaved Africans working hard.

Reading **HELP**DESK **CCSS**

triangular trade trade route between three destinations, such as Britain, West Africa, and the West Indies

slave code rules focusing on the behavior and punishment of enslaved people

netw⊙rks *Online Teaching Options*

MAP

Triangular Trade

Analyzing Maps Display the interactive map titled *Triangular Trade*. Have students click on titles on the map to initiate audio clips. **Ask:** Why was the route followed by these slave ships called the triangular trade? *(It was a three-legged route with three destinations that formed a triangle.)* What was the Middle Passage? *(the trade route from West Africa to the colonies that brought the slaves to America)*

See page 81C for other online activities.

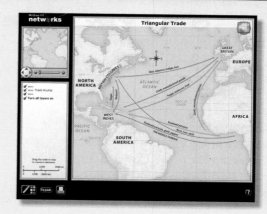

ANSWERS, p. 88

ECONOMICS SKILL

1. from the West Indies
2. **CRITICAL THINKING** Great Britain received raw materials and used them to make manufactured goods for trade.

Many colonies had **slave codes**, rules governing the behavior and punishment of enslaved people. Some did not allow enslaved workers to leave the plantation without the slaveholder's written permission. Some made it illegal to teach enslaved people to read or write. Enslaved people were seldom allowed to move about freely or gather in large groups. Punishments ranged from whipping for even minor misdeeds to hanging or burning to death for more serious crimes. Enslaved workers who ran away were punished severely when caught.

Although enslaved Africans had strong family ties, their families were often torn apart when a slaveholder sold a spouse, parent, or child. Many of the enslaved found strength in their African roots. They developed a culture that drew on the languages, customs, and religions of their African homelands.

Some enslaved Africans learned trades, such as carpentry, blacksmithing, or weaving. Skilled workers could sometimes set up shops, sharing their profits with the slaveholders. Those lucky enough to be able to buy their freedom joined the small population of free African Americans.

On large plantations, the owner or a hired overseer looked on while enslaved workers worked in the fields from sunrise to sunset.

Critics of Slavery

Not all colonists believed in slavery. Many Puritans, for example, refused to hold enslaved people. In Pennsylvania, Quakers and Mennonites condemned slavery. Eventually, the debate over slavery would spark a bloody war between North and South.

✔ **PROGRESS CHECK**

Describing What role did Africans play in the economy of the Southern Colonies?

The Granger Collection, NYC

LESSON 1 REVIEW (CCSS)

Review Vocabulary (Tier 3 Words)

1. Define the following terms by using them in a sentence about colonial farming. RH.6–8.4
   a. subsistence farming   b. cash crop

2. Explain the significance of the following terms by using each in a sentence. RH.6–8.4
   a. triangular trade   b. diversity
   c. slave code

Answer the Guiding Questions

3. *Comparing and Contrasting* How did agriculture differ in the three colonial regions? RH.6–8.5

4. *Identifying Main Ideas* What was the Middle Passage, and what made it so horrible? RH.6–8.2

5. **NARRATIVE** As a New England farmer, write a letter to relatives in Europe describing your family's daily life as subsistence farmers. WHST.6–8.2, WHST.6–8.10

Lesson 1 **89**

LESSON 1 REVIEW ANSWERS

1. Possible answer: Farmers in New England practiced subsistence farming, while farmers in other parts of the colonies were able to raise valuable cash crops such as rice and tobacco.

2. **a.** The three-part pattern of trade among the Americas, Great Britain, and Africa is an example of triangular trade. **b.** There was great diversity of population in the Middle Colonies. **c.** Slave codes placed harsh limits on the lives of enslaved Africans.

3. In New England, the land and climate supported mainly subsistence farming. In the Middle Colonies and the Southern Colonies, farmers grew cash crops because the land and climate could support them.

4. The Middle Passage was the second leg of the triangular trade, the ocean journey of enslaved Africans from Africa to the Americas. It involved terrible physical and emotional hardships for enslaved Africans.

5. Students' letters should use descriptive language and include details about the many chores involved with meeting all the needs of a family.

G1 Critical Thinking Skills

Speculating Ask a volunteer to define the term *slave code*. **Ask: Why would slaveholders have devised and used such codes?** *(Answers may vary. Students may suggest that slaveholders wished to keep the slaves under tight control to limit their ability to escape or rebel.)* **BL**

R Reading Skills

Describing After students have read the text, ask students to describe the work enslaved people performed. **AL** **Ask: What kinds of work did enslaved people do?** *(Most of them worked in the fields. Some worked in the house or learned a trade, like carpentry or blacksmithing.)*

G2 Critical Thinking Skills

Hypothesizing Discuss with students those groups who opposed slavery. **Ask: Why would Quakers object to slavery?** *(Their religious beliefs condemn the practice.)* **BL**

Have students complete the Lesson 1 Review.

CLOSE & REFLECT

Ask how many students are familiar with the hymn "Amazing Grace." On the board, write the first verse of the hymn (or make copies to distribute). Explain that the hymn was written by John Newton (1725–1807). Newton was a former slave trader until a near-death experience caused him to question his actions. He later fought for the end of slavery and wrote the hymn "Amazing Grace." Encourage students to offer interpretations of the lyrics.

ANSWER, p. 89

✔ **PROGRESS CHECK** Enslaved Africans provided almost all of the hard labor on the farms and plantations of the Southern Colonies.

ENGAGE

Bellringer Ask students to recall what life was like for them at age 11. What grade were they in? What games and other activities did they enjoy? Remind students that, during the days of the slave trade in West Africa, many Africans were captured in war or otherwise taken by force from their villages to be sold into slavery. Explain that even young children were kidnapped, like the 11-year-old boy they will be reading about.

TEACH & ASSESS

C Critical Thinking Skills

Making Inferences Instruct students to look at the picture of Olaudah Equiano and to read the quotation. **Ask: What two clues do you find that tell you what happened to Equiano after he came to America?** *(Students should observe that he looks well dressed and he writes well in English.)* **What is unusual about this?** *(Slaves were not usually well dressed and it was unusual for them to know how to write.)*

Content Background Knowledge

In his autobiography, Olaudah Equiano (c. 1745–1797) tells of being kidnapped and transported to the West Indies, where he was sold as a slave to a sea captain. While he traveled with the captain, Equiano learned to read. In 1766, he bought his freedom. Later, he moved to Great Britain and became an abolitionist. He published his autobiography in 1789. It became a best seller, through nine English editions, one U.S. printing, and publication in three other languages. It is considered the original slave narrative.

AMERICA'S LITERATURE

The Interesting Narrative of the Life of Olaudah Equiano

by Olaudah Equiano

Most of what we know about Equiano comes from his autobiography. According to his writings, Olaudah Equiano was born in Nigeria. At age 11, he was kidnapped, separated from his family, and sold into slavery.

In this excerpt, Equiano tells about his life in Nigeria and the day he was kidnapped.

C

> ❝ *When we went to rest the following night, they offered us some victuals, but we refused it; and the only comfort we had was in being in one another's arms all that night, and bathing each other with our tears.* ❞

Olaudah Equiano

—*The Interesting Narrative of the Life of Olaudah Equiano; or, Gustavus Vassa, the African, Written by Himself*

Enslaved Africans were transported across the ocean and sold in the Americas.

networks *Online Teaching Options*

(t) The Granger Collection, NYC. (b) Hulton Archives/Getty Images

---

TIME LINE

Place and Time: America 1607 to 1770

Reading a Time Line Ask students to point out on the time line when the author was most likely kidnapped and sold into slavery. *(during the 1700s)* **Ask: What was happening in West Africa at this time?** *(The Asante Kingdom was rising in West Africa.)* **How might the rise in power of one kingdom over another contribute to the growing slave trade?** *(The slave trade was very profitable. During war, captured enemies were often sold off into slavery.)*

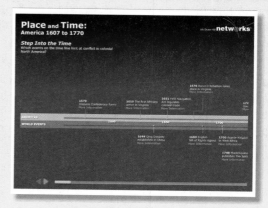

R

" Generally, when the grown people in the neighborhood were gone far in the fields to labor, the children assembled together in some of the neighboring premises to play; and commonly some of us used to get up a tree to look out for any assailant, or kidnapper, that might come upon us, for they sometimes took those opportunities of our parents' absence to attack and carry off as many as they could seize. . . . One day, when all our people were gone out to their works as usual, and only I and my dear sister were left to mind the house, two men and a woman got over our walls, and in a moment seized us both, and, without giving us time to cry out, or make resistance, they stopped our mouths, and ran off with us into the nearest wood. Here they tied our hands, and continued to carry us as far as they could, till night came on, when we reached a small house, where the robbers halted for refreshment, and spent the night. We were then unbound, but were unable to take any food; and, being quite overpowered by fatigue and grief, our only relief was some sleep, which **allayed** our misfortune for a short time. The next morning we left the house, and continued travelling all the day. For a long time we had kept [to] the woods, but at last we came into a road which I believed I knew. I had now some hopes of being delivered; for we had advanced but a little way before I discovered some people at a distance, on which I began to cry out for their assistance; but my cries had no other effect than to make them tie me faster and stop my mouth, and then they put me into a large sack. They also stopped my sister's mouth, and tied her hands; and in this manner we proceeded till we were out of sight of these people. When we went to rest the following night, they offered us some **victuals**, but we refused it; and the only comfort we had was in being in one another's arms all that night, and bathing each other with our tears. But alas! we were soon deprived of even the small comfort of weeping together. The next day proved a day of greater sorrow than I had yet experienced, for my sister and I were then separated while we lay clasped in each other's arms. It was in vain that we besought them not to part us; she was torn from me and immediately carried away, while I was left in a state of distraction not to be described. I cried and grieved continually, and for several days I did not eat anything but what they forced into my mouth. "

Chicago History Museum/The Bridgeman Art Library

R

Literary Element

Point of View is the vantage point from which a story is told. This passage is told from the first-person point of view. In it, you learn the narrator's thoughts and feelings. As you read, think about how the story's point of view affects your reading experience.

Vocabulary

allay
to reduce in strength

victual
food

Kidnappers chained their captives together in pairs—right leg to left leg.

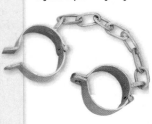

Analyzing Literature · DBQ

❶ **Drawing Conclusions** Why is a first-person narrative of an enslaved person valuable? RH.6–8.6, RH.6–8.9

❷ **Speculating** What kind of person did the kidnappers target? Why do you think that might be? RH.6–8.1

❸ **Predicting** What do you think will happen to Equiano and his sister? RH.6–8.8

Lesson 1 **91**

The Middle Passage

Reading a Graphic Novel Ask students to read this graphic novel to learn more about the experiences of enslaved individuals as they were forced to travel on a ship headed for the American Colonies and the West Indies. Ask students to create their own graphic novel about the capture of Olaudah Equiano.

GRAPHIC NOVEL

The Middle Passage

R Reading Skills

Citing Text Evidence Have students find descriptions in the text of Olaudah's life before the kidnapping. Point out the sentence describing how villagers tried to protect their children. ("Generally, when the grown people . . . as they could seize.") Make sure all students understand the word *kidnapper*. **Ask: In this sentence, which adverbs indicate that kidnapping of children was not unusual?** *("Generally," "commonly," "sometimes")* **What words and phrases describe his reaction to being kidnapped?** *(Possible answers: "some hopes of being delivered"; "I cried and grieved continually"; "I did not eat.")* Write responses on the board. Make sure all students understand the correct meaning of the noun *grief*. Ask them to identify a related word in the phrases recorded on the board. *(grieved)* **AL ELL** Verbal/Linguistic

Point out that the author describes his kidnappers only as two men and a woman, and as robbers. **Ask: What do we know about the character of these people?** *(Students may suggest they were thieves or that they were cruel, greedy, immoral, and so on.)* **How does the author reveal these qualities?** *(through descriptions of their actions)* **BL**

W Writing Skills

Narrative Have students work in small groups to research Olaudah Equiano's life. Ask each group to find three facts about his life. Have them print each fact on an index card and note the date when possible. Have the groups post the cards on a bulletin board in chronological order. Discuss what these facts reveal about Equiano's character and about the times in which he lived. **Interpersonal**

CLOSE & REFLECT

Equiano's book was published in 1789, 44 years before slavery was abolished in England (1833) and 72 years before the U.S. Civil War (1861). **Ask: How do you think books like Equiano's might have helped the antislavery movement?** *(Answers will vary.)*

ANSWERS, p. 91

1. A first-person narrative is told by a person who actually experienced the events; a first-person narrative is a primary source and more reliable.
2. The kidnappers apparently targeted children. Children might have been easier to transport, taken up less space on a slave ship, and been more valuable because they had a longer life in front of them.
3. Possible answer: They would be sent to the Americas and sold.

ENGAGE

Bellringer Read the first sentence of the U.S. Constitution, and ask if students recognize it:

"We the People of the United States, in Order to form a more perfect Union, establish Justice, insure domestic Tranquility, provide for the common defence, promote the general Welfare, and secure the Blessings of Liberty to ourselves and our Posterity, do ordain and establish this Constitution for the United States of America."

If students do not recognize the sentence, explain that it is the first sentence of the Constitution, which established the United States government.

Explain that ideas like these developed over time. Tell students they will be learning about ideas that formed the basis of government in Great Britain and the colonies. Some of these ideas go back many hundreds of years and now shape our current government and serve as our guiding principles.

TEACH & ASSESS

R **Reading Skills**

Defining As they read, have students describe the terms "protected rights" and "representative government." **Ask: In what document and what year did these ideas first appear?** *(the Magna Carta, in 1215)* **What did the Magna Carta do to the power of the government?** *(It limited the power of the king.)* Discuss the principle of representative government, the power wielded by the English Parliament, and how both houses, Commons and Lords, are representative houses.

ANSWER, p. 92

TAKING NOTES: Protected Rights: The people have certain rights that government must respect.
Representative Government: a government in which people elect delegates to make laws and govern

---

networks
There's More Online!

☑ **CHART/GRAPH**
Literacy Rates

☑ **GRAPHIC ORGANIZER**
• Principles of Government
• Colonial Government

☑ **TIME LINE** Principles of British Government

☑ **VIDEO**

Lesson 2
Colonial Government

ESSENTIAL QUESTION *How do new ideas change the way people live?*

IT MATTERS BECAUSE
Using ideas from England and their own experiences, American colonists began developing their beliefs about the proper form and role of government.

English Principles of Government

GUIDING QUESTION *Why are protected rights and representative government important principles?*

When English colonists came to North America, they brought with them English ideas about government. These ideas had been developing in England over hundreds of years. By the 1600s, the English people had won political liberties, such as trial by jury, that were largely unknown elsewhere.

At the heart of the English system were two principles of government—protected rights and representative legislatures. These two principles greatly influenced the development of the United States and are important parts of the U.S. Constitution.

Protected Rights

R

The colonists believed that government must respect civil liberties, or rights. In fact, the protection of people's rights was a central idea in the English system of government. It first appeared in the Magna Carta, or Great Charter, which King John signed on June 15, 1215. This document gave English people protection against unjust treatment or punishment. For the English, even kings and queens were bound by the law.

© and ©The Granger Collection, NYC; (c) Erin Paul Donovan / Alamy

---

Reading HELPDESK **CCSS**

Taking Notes: *Explaining*
As you read, use a diagram like this one to explain protected rights and representative government. RH.6–8.4, RH.6–8.7

| Protected Rights | → | |
| Representative Government | → | |

Content Vocabulary (Tier 3 Words)
• **representative government**   • **import**
• **mercantilism**
• **export**

92 *Life in the American Colonies*

---

networks *Online Teaching Options*

VIDEO

Society, Community, and Justice in the Northern Colonies

Recognizing Relationships Explain to students that a distinctly American society emerged in the New England colonies. Ask them to watch the video and learn how the tightly knit communities bound by town covenants developed a fairly egalitarian social order. After they view the video, guide a discussion of what can be learned about New England values from court records.

See page 81D for other online activities.

Representative Government

The English had a tradition of **representative government**, in which people elect delegates to make laws and conduct government. The English Parliament was a representative assembly. It had the power to legislate, or make laws.

Parliament had two chambers, or houses: the House of Lords and the House of Commons. Only the eldest sons of England's aristocracy—the upper, ruling class—could sit in the House of Lords. The House of Commons included commoners—mostly merchants or property owners elected by other property owners. American legislatures grew in part from this English model.

R In the mid-1600s, Parliament and King James II began a struggle for power. In 1688, Parliament removed King James II from power and crowned William and Mary to rule. William and Mary promised to govern England according to the "statutes [laws] in Parliament agreed upon, and the laws and customs of the same." The English called this peaceful transfer of power the Glorious Revolution. It brought a major change in the idea of government in England. From that time forward, no ruler would have more power than the legislature.

The English Bill of Rights

C To set clear limits on a ruler's powers, Parliament drew up the English Bill of Rights in 1689. The Bill of Rights stated that the ruler could not **suspend** Parliament's laws, **impose** taxes, or raise an army without Parliament's consent. Members of Parliament had to be freely elected. Citizens of England had the right to a fair trial by jury in court cases. The Bill of Rights also banned cruel and unusual punishments.

Government in America

The thirteen colonies began as either charter or proprietary colonies. Charter colonies were based on a charter, a grant of rights by the English monarch to a company. Massachusetts was a charter colony.

Established in 1619, the Virginia House of Burgesses was the first legislature in the English Colonies. It became a foundation for the principle of self-government in colonial America and, later, the United States.

The Granger Collection, NYC

representative government
a system by which people elect delegates to make laws and conduct government

Academic Vocabulary (Tier 2 Words)

suspend to set aside or temporarily stop operation of something
impose to force on others

Lesson 2 **93**

R Reading Skills

Citing Text Evidence After students have read the text, discuss the Glorious Revolution and the English Bill of Rights. **Ask:**

- **What was the Glorious Revolution and how did it begin?** *(It was the peaceful transfer of power from King James II to William and Mary in 1688. It began when Parliament removed King James II and crowned William and Mary, who promised to rule according to Parliament's laws.)*
- **How did it change the idea of government?** *(From that time forward, no ruler would have more power than the legislature.)*
- **Why was the English Bill of Rights written?** *(After the Glorious Revolution, Parliament drew up the Bill of Rights to state the rights gained during the revolution.)*
- **How did the English Bill of Rights help English subjects?** *(It guaranteed that members of Parliament would be freely elected, that citizens would get a fair trial by jury, and that there would be no cruel or unusual punishments.)* Students should support their answers with evidence from the text.

C Critical Thinking Skills

Making Connections Point out that almost exactly one hundred years after the English Bill of Rights was instituted, the United States added its own Bill of Rights to the U.S. Constitution. Explain that our Bill of Rights is the first ten amendments. The U.S. Bill of Rights goes further in protecting rights, but there are clear similarities, including guarantees of freedom of speech, the right to bear arms, protections against quartering soldiers in citizens' homes, the right to a trial by jury, and protections against cruel and unusual punishment. **BL**

IMAGE

The House of Burgesses

Comparing Have students view the image and scroll down to read more about the House of Burgesses. Guide a discussion comparing the House of Burgesses to present-day legislative bodies in local, state, and national government.

See page 81D for other online activities.

McGraw-Hill **networks** The House of Burgesses

The Granger Collection, NYC

The first legislature to be established in the American colonies was in Virginia. Called the House of Burgesses, it held its first meeting on July 30, 1619. The main order of business was to set a minimum price for selling tobacco. In time, the House of Burgesses became a symbol of representative government in America. It could make

W Writing Skills

Argument Review with students how colonial governments were established in the English colonies. Discuss how ideas based on English government helped to form the government of America. Discuss colonists' participation in government. **Ask: Among the colonists, who was allowed to vote?** *(white men who owned property)* **Which groups could not vote in the colonies?** *(women, indentured servants, landless poor, and African Americans)* **AL How might some of these groups still have participated in local government?** *(Possible responses include attending town meetings, becoming informed about issues, sharing opinions and suggestions, and so on.)* **BL**

Instruct students to prepare pro/con lists of the advantages and the disadvantages of the colonists permitting only white male landowners to vote. Discuss the lists as a class.

R Reading Skills

Defining Write the term *mercantilism* on the board, and ask students to define it. **AL** **ELL** After students have read the text, discuss the role that imports and exports play in mercantilism.

Making Connections

Town meetings were widely used in colonial times, especially in New England. They have survived in New England and continue to function as the primary form of government for many local communities.

- Town meetings represent a working example of a pure, or direct, democracy. In a town meeting, all eligible voters in a community vote directly on laws for the community. Most other democratic governments are representative, or indirect, democracies: voters vote for representatives who pass laws and govern.

In New England, town meetings were held in meeting houses like this one in Pelham, Massachusetts. Built in 1743, Pelham's Old Meeting House is the oldest town hall in continuous use in the nation.

Proprietary colonies were the property of an owner or group of owners. These proprietors ruled more or less as they wished. For example, they named their own governors and many other colonial officials. Pennsylvania was a proprietary colony.

Some colonies later became royal colonies, under direct English control. Virginia became the first royal colony in 1624. In a royal colony, Parliament appointed a governor and council, known as the upper house. The colonists selected an assembly, or lower house. The governor and council usually did as the English king and Parliament told them. This often led to conflicts with the assembly. For example, colonists got angry when officials enforced tax or trade laws.

W

Not all colonists had a voice in government. In general, only white men who owned property could vote. Most women, indentured servants, landless poor, and African Americans could not vote. Still, compared to Europe, the share of the colonial population taking part in government was large. This training proved valuable when the colonies became independent.

Local Government in the Colonies

Over time, townspeople began discussing local issues at town meetings. These developed into local governments, with landowners holding the right to vote and pass laws. Because colonists in many areas took part in local government, they developed a strong belief in their right to govern themselves. Town meetings helped set the stage for the American Revolution.

✓ PROGRESS CHECK

Making Connections How did the Magna Carta influence government in the colonies?

English Economic Policies

GUIDING QUESTION *How did the colonists react to England's economic policies?*

R

Beginning in the 1600s, many European nations followed a theory known as **mercantilism** (MUHR•kuhn•tuh•lih•zuhm). Mercantilism holds that a country builds wealth and power by building its supplies of gold and silver. To achieve this goal, a country must **export**, or sell to other countries, more than it

Erin Paul Donovan / Alamy

Reading **HELP**DESK **CCSS**

mercantilism an economic theory whose goal is building a state's wealth and power by increasing exports and accumulating precious metals in return

export to sell abroad
import to bring in from foreign markets

94 *Life in the American Colonies*

netw⭕rks *Online Teaching Options*

MAP

Mercantilism

Explaining Have students view the map. Use it to discuss the European economic policy of mercantilism. **Ask: Why were the colonies important to the success of mercantilism?** *(They provided raw materials to England and were a market for its manufactured goods.)* **Were the colonies the only market for England's manufactured goods? Why or why not?** *(No. England exported its goods to foreign markets as well. In the colonies, England traded manufactured goods for more raw materials. In order to make a profit and build wealth, England also would have had to sell goods to other markets.)*

See page 81D for other online activities.

ANSWER, p. 94

✓ **PROGRESS CHECK** It introduced the idea that the rights of citizens should be protected.

imports, or buys from other countries. A country must also seek colonies, which could supply raw materials and serve as a market for exports.

The English followed a mercantilist policy. They looked to the American colonies for raw materials, such as tobacco, rice, indigo, wheat, lumber, fur, leather, fish, and whale products. They also wanted the colonists to buy English manufactured goods, such as tools, clothing, and furniture.

To control this trade, England began passing a series of laws called Navigation Acts in the 1650s. The laws forced colonists to sell their raw materials to England even if they could get a better price elsewhere. Goods bought by the colonies from other countries in Europe had to go to England first and be taxed. All trade goods had to be carried on ships built in England or the colonies. The crews on the ships had to be English as well.

Many items in a colonial kitchen were tinware imported from England. Because of its silvery color, tinware was often called "poor man's silver." Although it was thought to be inferior to china or silver, tinware goods were less breakable than china and easier to clean than silverware.

Colonial Resistance

The colonists at first accepted the Navigation Acts because the laws guaranteed them a place to sell their raw materials. Later, the colonists came to resent English restrictions. With their population growing, colonists wanted to manufacture their own goods rather than import them from England. They also wanted to sell their products to buyers other than England. Colonial merchants began smuggling, or shipping goods without government permission or payment of taxes. Controls on trade would later cause conflict between the American colonies and England.

The Granger Collection, NYC

☑ **PROGRESS CHECK**

Making Generalizations What was the purpose of the Navigation Acts?

LESSON 2 REVIEW (CCSS)

Review Vocabulary (Tier 3 Words)

1. Use the words *import, export,* and *mercantilism* in a paragraph about the colonies. RH.6–8.4, WHST.6–8.4

2. Write a sentence about the political ideas of the English colonists using the term *representative government*. RH.6–8.4

Answer the Guiding Questions

3. ***Analyzing*** Where did the colonists get their ideas and attitudes about government? RH.6–8.1

4. ***Explaining*** How did the colonists react to Britain's economic policies? RH.6–8.2

5. **ARGUMENT** Write a speech from the perspective of a merchant, urging colonists to support your idea of free trade with countries other than Britain. WHST.6–8.1, WHST.6–8.10

Lesson 2   **95**

R Reading Skills

Listing After students read the text, discuss the Navigation Acts, including what they were and why they were passed. Remind students that the Navigation Acts required any goods bought by the colonies from other countries to go to England first. **Ask:** Why was this part of the acts? (so the goods could be taxed before being sent to the colonies) Why do you think the government of England insisted on this? (It wanted the tax money to pay its debts.) **AL**

Have students list ways in which the Navigation Acts restricted the trade of goods by the colonists and ways in which both the colonies and Britain profited from them. **BL**

C Critical Thinking Skills

Analyzing Discuss the colonists' changing attitudes toward British rule. **Ask:** Why did the colonists begin to resist the trade laws? (Colonists wanted to make their own manufactured goods instead of importing everything from England. They also wanted to be able to sell their products to foreign markets.) How was the colonists' relationship with their government in Britain changing? (There was growing resentment among the colonists over the way in which they were being governed.) **BL**

Have students complete the Lesson 2 Review.

CLOSE & REFLECT

Review the emerging colonial system of government and mercantilism, and their effects on the colonies. Ask students to consider these developments and to write a paragraph predicting what may happen next. Instruct them to use details from the lesson to support their predictions.

LESSON 2 REVIEW ANSWERS

1. Sample answer: British mercantilism greatly affected the colonial economy. British laws forced colonists to send all of their export goods to Britain. The colonists also had to buy all of their imports from or through Britain.

2. Sample answer: The English colonists arrived in America with a belief in the value of a representative government such as Parliament.

3. The colonists got their ideas from the Magna Carta, the English Parliament, the English Bill of Rights, and their history of representative government.

4. At first, they liked the guarantee of their goods being bought, but later they wanted to sell to other markets and get higher prices.

5. Speeches should explain why free trade could lead to more money for colonists.

ANSWER, p. 95

☑ **PROGRESS CHECK** The acts sought to impose limits on colonial trade to fit with Britain's mercantilist system and its goals.

ENGAGE

Bellringer Ask students how they think a change in the population might affect the community in which they live. **Ask: If the population in the neighborhoods around the school grew dramatically, what changes might take place in your neighborhood and classrooms?** *(Possible answers: more students per class; the need for more places to live, more food, more jobs, and so on)* Tell students that they will be reading about the reasons for population growth in the regions of colonial America and the effect it had on life in the colonies.

TEACH & ASSESS

C Critical Thinking Skills

Reasoning Discuss the growth in population in the thirteen colonies between 1700 (approx. 250,000) and the mid-1770s (approx. 2.5 million). Point out that much of this growth occurred because of immigration. **Ask: What are some reasons that people would immigrate to the colonies in such large numbers?** *(Answers may include for economic opportunity; for more freedom, including freedom of religion; for the chance for a better life; and to escape oppression.)* **ELL** Logical/Mathematical

Discuss with students how other factors, such as disease, affect population change. **Ask: How could an outbreak of smallpox affect the population?** *(It could kill a large segment of a city's population.)*

ANSWER, p. 96

TAKING NOTES: Great Awakening: led to formation of many new churches; religion contributed to a new American culture, the colonies united; **Enlightenment:** increased interest in science and observation of nature; increased belief in popular government and freedom of expression

---

networks
There's More Online!

☑ **CHART/GRAPH** Great Awakening and the Enlightenment

☑ **GRAPHIC ORGANIZER** Great Awakening and the Enlightenment

☑ **PRIMARY SOURCE** Freedom of the Press

☑ **SLIDE SHOW** A Child's Life in the Colonies

Lesson 3
Culture and Society

ESSENTIAL QUESTION *How do new ideas change the way people live?*

IT MATTERS BECAUSE
An American culture, influenced by religion and education, began to develop in the colonies.

Life in the Colonies

GUIDING QUESTION *What was life like for people living in the thirteen colonies?*

The number of people living in the thirteen colonies rose from about 250,000 in 1700 to approximately 2.5 million by the mid-1770s. The population of African Americans increased at an even faster rate—from about 28,000 to more than 500,000.

Immigration (im·ih·GRAY·shuhn)—the permanent moving of people into one country from other countries—was important to this growth. Between 1607 and 1775, an estimated 690,000 Europeans came to the colonies. Also during this time, traders brought in 278,000 enslaved Africans to the colonies.

There was another reason for the growing population. Colonial women tended to marry early and have large families. In addition, the colonies—especially New England—turned out to be a very healthy place to live compared to other parts of the world.

Still, compared to today, life was fragile. For example, women often died in childbirth. Outbreaks of serious diseases such as smallpox were common. Many people died in **epidemics** (eh·puh·DEH·mihks), outbreaks that affect large numbers of people. In 1721, for example, a smallpox epidemic in the city of Boston killed about 850 people, or 15 percent of the city's population.

Reading **HELP**DESK (CCSS)

Taking Notes: *Determining Cause and Effect*
As you read, use a diagram like this one to explain how the Great Awakening and the Enlightenment affected the colonists. RH.6–8.5, RH.6–8.7

Great Awakening →

The Enlightenment →

Content Vocabulary (Tier 3 Words)
• **immigration** • **civic virtue**
• **epidemic**
• **apprentice**

96 *Life in the American Colonies*

---

networks *Online Teaching Options*

VIDEO

The Great Awakening

Analyzing Have students view the video and learn about two of the great evangelists of the eighteenth century, Jonathan Edwards and George Whitefield. Edwards, known for his fire and brimstone sermons, and Whitefield, known for his ability to move people to tears, aimed to bring people back to their faith. Guide a discussion of how their efforts in the Great Awakening would, in the years ahead, influence the new nation's emphasis on the separation of church and state.

See page 81E for other online activities.

A New American Spirit

Many Americans were born in other countries. They brought with them different languages and ways of thinking. Yet in the colonies, immigrants became something new and different—they became Americans. In 1782 French writer J. Hector St. John De Crèvecoeur (krev•KUHR) described this new type of person:

PRIMARY SOURCE

❝ He is an American, who, leaving behind him all his ancient prejudices and manners, receives new ones from the new mode of life he has embraced, the new government he obeys, and the new rank he holds. . . . Here individuals of all races are melted into a new race of man, whose labors and posterity will one day cause great changes in the world. ❞

—from *Letters from an American Farmer*

C

A spirit of independence developed early in the history of the American people. Far from the rules and limits of their home countries, settlers began to develop their own ways of doing things. Throughout the colonies, people **adapted** their traditions to the new conditions of life.

Religion, education, and the arts contributed to a new American culture. The family, however, formed the basic foundation of colonial society—for those who were not enslaved, at least.

Family Roles

Men were the formal heads of the households. They managed the farm or business and represented the family in the community. On the farm, men worked in the fields and built barns, houses, and fences. Sons might work as indentured servants for local farmers or become apprentices. An **apprentice** (uh•PREHN•tuhs) agrees to work with a skilled craftsperson as a way of learning a trade.

R

Women ran their households and cared for children. Many worked in the fields with their husbands. Married women had few rights. Unmarried women might work as maids or cooks.

Bettmann/Corbis

In 1721, Boston clergyman Cotton Mather suggested a daring answer to smallpox—inoculation, or injecting smallpox virus into healthy people. Often, inoculation causes only mild disease and leaves the body protected from illness in the future. In 1796, Edward Jenner, shown inoculating a child, developed a safer smallpox vaccine.

---

immigration the permanent movement of people into one country from other nations
epidemic an illness that affects large numbers of people

apprentice a young person who learns a trade from a skilled craftsperson

Academic Vocabulary (Tier 2 Words)

adapt to change in response to a new set of conditions

C Critical Thinking Skills

Making Inferences Discuss the new American spirit that arose as people from other countries settled in America. **Ask:** *What influences brought about this new spirit? (Answers will vary, but students should note the effect of living on a frontier in an egalitarian society.)* Guide a discussion of why these factors brought about changes and created the new American spirit. **BL**

R Reading Skills

Depicting After students have read the text, work with them to generate a class list of the parental roles in the colonial family. **Ask:** *What roles did the father and mother play in the colonial family? (The father was the formal head of the household, managed the farm or business, and represented the family in the community. The mother ran the household, cared for the children, often worked in the fields with her husband, and was under his authority.)*

Content Background Knowledge

Smallpox was a dreadful killer in the eighteenth century. It was sometimes combated by infecting healthy persons with matter from a lesion on the skin of someone who had a milder case of smallpox. A healthy person would usually get somewhat sick but then develop immunity to severe cases. This treatment was not reliable though; sometimes the inoculation provoked a severe and deadly case of smallpox. Plus, the inoculated person could infect those around him or her.

Edward Jenner recognized that people who got cowpox—a similar disease that had only a small effect on humans—did not get smallpox. Jenner inoculated a healthy eight-year-old boy with cowpox. A couple of months later, he inoculated the boy with smallpox. When the boy didn't develop smallpox, Jenner knew he had found a new and safer means of combating this disease.

IMAGE

Smallpox

Analyzing Visuals Emphasize to students that throughout much of history, smallpox was one of the most devastating of all diseases. Have students view the interactive image on smallpox, clicking on "more information" to reveal further details. **Ask:** *Why do you think smallpox remained a dangerous disease even after Jenner's discovery of a vaccine? (Students may suggest that not enough people received the vaccine.)*

See page 81E for other online activities.

McGraw-Hill **networks** — Smallpox

Smallpox is one of the world's most dangerous diseases. It is spread through saliva or mucus from an infected person. Symptoms of the disease include fever, aches, and fatigue. A rash of puss-filled blisters breaks out on the skin. Up to 30 percent of people infected with smallpox died from the disease. In 1796, Edward Jenner discovered a vaccine for the disease. Although it was effective, millions of cases of smallpox were still occurring. In 1967, the World Health Organization began a global vaccination campaign to eliminate smallpox. In 1980, the organization declared the disease extinct.

Bettmann/CORBIS

R1 Reading Skills

Listing Before students read the text, ask them to provide examples of current American beliefs and values. *(a commitment to education, strong religious beliefs, openness to new ideas; responses may also include freedom, rights of the individual, free speech, family, community, and so on.)* Record responses on the board. Explain that these values developed over time and began when the American colonies were young. As students read the text, ask them to compare today's beliefs and values with those of the colonists.

R2 Reading Skills

Paraphrasing After students have read the text, have them paraphase what they have read about education in the colonies. **Ask:**

- **How did children learn to read and write?** *(Parents taught them at home.)*
- **What special purpose did schools in Pennsylvania and New England have?** *(to teach people to read so they could study the Bible)*
- **What was the result of this focus on education?** *(high literacy rates, especially in New England)*
- **How did the first colleges differ from colleges today?** *(They focused on training ministers, while colleges today educate people in a wide variety of fields.)* **Verbal/Linguistic**

Connections to
TODAY

Colleges and Universities

Several colleges and universities founded in colonial times are still educating students today. For example, Harvard University in Massachusetts got its start in 1636 as a school for training ministers. Next came Virginia's College of William and Mary, founded in 1693. Yale University in Connecticut started as a school in 1701. The University of Pennsylvania in Philadelphia began as a charity school in 1740.

A hornbook, made of a wooden paddle with lessons tacked onto it, helped young students learn to read.

The Granger Collection, NYC

Widows and older women who never married might work as teachers, nurses, or seamstresses. They could run businesses and own property, but they could not vote.

Even children as young as four or five often had jobs. When they played, they enjoyed simple games, such as hopscotch or leap frog. Their toys were usually made from common objects.

✔ PROGRESS CHECK

Finding the Main Idea What was the role of the family in colonial life?

American Beliefs

GUIDING QUESTION *What values and beliefs were important to the American colonists?*

The American spirit and the family served as a foundation for life in the colonies. In addition, Americans shared a commitment to education, strong religious beliefs, and openness to new ideas.

Colonial Education

Most colonists valued education. Parents often taught their children to read and write at home. In New England and Pennsylvania, in particular, people set up schools to make sure everyone could read and study the Bible. In 1647 the Massachusetts Puritans passed a public education law requiring communities with 50 or more homes to have a public school.

The result was a high level of literacy in New England. By 1750, about 85 percent of the men and about half of the women were able to read. Many learned from *The New England Primer*.

Most schools in the Middle Colonies were private. Widows or unmarried women ran many of those schools. Quakers and other religious groups ran others. In towns and cities, craftspeople often set up night schools for their apprentices. The earliest colleges in the colonies were founded to train ministers.

The Great Awakening

Religion had a strong influence in colonial life. In the 1730s and 1740s, a religious revival called the Great Awakening swept through the colonies. In New England and the Middle Colonies, ministers called for "a new birth," a return to the

---

Reading HELPDESK CCSS

Reading in the Content Area: *Percentages*

Many social studies texts give information in percentages. A percentage gives information as a fraction—how many out of 100. For instance, 12 percent, which may also be written 12%, means 12 out of every 100. Twelve percent of 200 would be 24, and twelve percent of 1,000 would be 120. Percentages allow for easy comparison of different numbers.

---

netw⊙rks   *Online Teaching Options*

SLIDE SHOW

Colonial Children

Analyzing Visuals Have students view the interactive slide show about colonial children. Ask volunteers to read the texts aloud. After students view the slides, discuss the different activities. **Ask: Which aspects of colonial life do you think you might like? Which ones do you think you would dislike? Why?** *(Answers will vary.)*

See page 81E for other online activities.

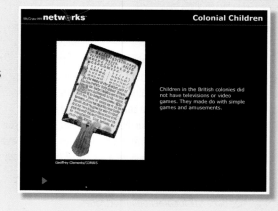

McGraw-Hill netw⊙rks   **Colonial Children**

Children in the British colonies did not have televisions or video games. They made do with simple games and amusements.

Geoffrey Clements/CORBIS

ANSWER, p. 98

✔ PROGRESS CHECK It was the foundation of the society.

strong faith of earlier days. One of these was Jonathan Edwards of Massachusetts, who gave powerful and convincing sermons. George Whitefield, an English preacher who arrived in the colonies in 1739, inspired worshipers in churches and open fields from New England to Georgia.

T

The Great Awakening inspired greater religious freedom. It led to the formation of many new types of churches. The new churches placed an **emphasis** on having personal faith rather than on church rituals. More colonists began choosing their own faiths, and the strength of established official churches declined. As a Baptist preacher noted soon after the Great Awakening, "The common people now claim as good a right to judge and act in matters of religion as civil rulers or the learned clergy."

R

The Great Awakening also united colonists from north to south in a common experience. The colonists overcame regional barriers, and this helped pave the way for the rapid spread of revolutionary ideas and excitement during the struggle for independence.

The Enlightenment

By the middle of the 1700s, many educated colonists were also influenced by the Enlightenment. This movement, which began in Europe, spread the idea that knowledge, reason, and science could improve society. In the colonies, the Enlightenment increased interest in science. People observed nature, staged experiments, and published their findings, much as Benjamin Franklin did. The Enlightenment also promoted freedom of thought and expression, a belief in equality, and the idea of popular government.

C

Ideas of Freedom

Freedom of the press became an important issue in colonial America. Newspapers in colonial cities, such as Boston and Philadelphia, carried political news and often faced government censorship. Censorship is the banning of printed materials because they contain unpopular or offensive ideas.

Ministers such as George Whitefield (shown below) and Jonathan Edwards swayed crowds with their vivid, emotional style of preaching.

Francis G. Mayer/CORBIS

Academic Vocabulary (Tier 2 Words)

emphasis a special stress or indication of importance

R Reading Skills

Identifying As students read the text, ask them to find evidence that the Great Awakening helped feelings of unity to develop among the colonies. **Ask:** How did the Great Awakening affect the role of churches in the colonies? *(It emphasized personal faith rather than church rituals; people chose their own faiths and the role of the church was reduced.)* **Ask:** Who were two of the preachers who were influential in this movement? *(Jonathan Edwards, George Whitefield)*

T Technology Skills

Research on the Internet Assign students to do research on the Internet to learn about Jonathan Edwards, George Whitefield, and other important figures of the Great Awakening. You may wish to assign this as homework, having students take notes and report back to the class the next day.

C Critical Thinking Skills

Making Connections Discuss the main ideas that formed the basis of the Enlightenment Movement, including:

- emphasis on knowledge, reason, and science
- promotion of freedom of thought and expression
- equality
- a government supported by the common people

Guide students to further understand that these views lay at the foundation of the American Revolution and the U.S. Constitution, and they continue to influence our society today. **BL**

GAME

Culture and Society—Periods of Change Sorting Game

Making Comparisons Have students play the game, individually or with partners, to compare key terms and important people related to the Enlightenment and the Great Awakening. Afterwards, discuss as a class the terms and people introduced in the game.

See page 81E for other online activities.

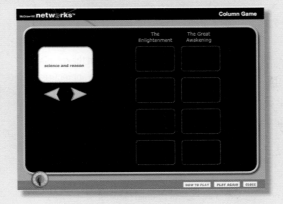

C1 Critical Thinking Skills

Defending Talk about Zenger's role in establishing freedom of the press and a ban on censorship. Then guide a discussion of freedom of the press today. Explain the differences among strict reporting of the news, editorials, and opinion pieces. Invite students to suggest the pros and cons of having a free press and the dangers of irresponsible or deceptive reporting. **BL** **Verbal/Linguistic**

C2 Critical Thinking Skills

Making Decisions Define *civic virtue* and provide examples to students. Discuss why civic virtue is important in a free society. Present students with the list of behaviors such as voting, having respect for others, helping a neighbor, tossing trash on the street, being part of the neighborhood watch, using offensive language in public, tolerance, and public rudeness. **Ask: How do such behaviors help or hurt the community in which students live?** *(Answers will vary but should reflect some civic and moral awareness.)* **AL** **ELL** **Which behaviors represent the idea of civic virtue?** *(those that benefit the community, like voting, volunteering, donating, and so forth)* Discuss the individual's responsibility for practicing and upholding civic virtue. **Intrapersonal**

Have students complete the Lesson 3 Review.

CLOSE & REFLECT

Review the ideas central to the Enlightenment— that knowledge, reason, and science can improve society. Discuss the influence these ideas may have had on emerging ideas of civic virtue. Discuss the connection between a person's role and responsibilities in society and his or her virtues and character. **Ask: Do you think a person can be of good character and not contribute much to society? Do you think a person can have bad character and still make some contribution to society?** *(Students' answers will vary, but they should be supported by good reasons and defensible examples.)*

ANSWER, p. 100

☑ **PROGRESS CHECK** The Great Awakening was a religious revival that led to the formation of many new churches. It also led to an increase in religious freedom and a growing unity among the colonies.

John Peter Zenger's newspaper, the *New-York Weekly Journal,* was the battleground in an early case about freedom of the press.

civic virtue the democratic ideas, practices, and values that are at the heart of citizenship in a free society

In 1733 publisher John Peter Zenger, in his newspaper the *New-York Weekly Journal,* accused New York's governor of corruption. For criticizing the governor, officials charged Zenger with a crime and threw him in jail. Zenger argued that the statements written about the governor were true. Therefore, he claimed, he had the right to publish them. Zenger's lawyer, Andrew Hamilton, made a stirring defense:

PRIMARY SOURCE   **C1**

❝ The loss of liberty in general would soon follow the suppression of the liberty of the press; for it is an essential branch of liberty, so perhaps it is the best preservative of the whole. ❞

—from *The Trial of John Peter Zenger and the Birth of Freedom of the Press,* by Doug Linder

The jury found Zenger not guilty. The case is seen as a key step in the development of a free press in this country.

Civic Virtue

Colonists were beginning to form new ideas of freedom. They began thinking in terms of **civic virtue** (SI•vihk VUHR•choo)—democratic ideas, practices, and values that form a truly free society. De Crèvecoeur was writing about these ideals when he described the spirit of the new American. Benjamin Franklin was a shining example of civic virtue at its best. Colonists would soon put their belief in civic virtue into action. These ideas and actions would become the building blocks of a new nation.

☑ **PROGRESS CHECK**

Analyzing In what ways did the Great Awakening influence culture in the colonies?

LESSON 3 REVIEW

Review Vocabulary (Tier 3 Words)

1. Describe how each of the following terms relates to culture and society in the thirteen colonies. RH.6–8.4

   a. immigration   **b.** epidemic
   c. apprentice   **d.** civic virtue

Answer the Guiding Questions

2. *Summarizing* How did the size of the colonial population change in the 1700s, and what contributed to this development? RH.6–8.2

3. *Explaining* Describe some of the central values and beliefs that helped shape the emerging culture of the American colonies. RH.6–8.1

4. **NARRATIVE** Imagine you are a student in a colonial town. Write three journal entries that describe a typical day in school. WHST.6–8.2, WHST.6–8.9

100   *Life in the American Colonies*

LESSON 3 REVIEW ANSWERS

1. **a.** *Immigration* is the moving of people from one country into another, and it was a major cause of the growth of the colonial population. **b.** Epidemics such as smallpox took many lives in the colonial era. **c.** Many young boys became apprentices, which was a system for training them in a trade. **d.** The American colonists developed ideas of civic virtue—the basic ideas of how citizens should act in society.

2. The colonial population increased greatly, mostly as the result of immigration, the growth of slavery, and the large size of colonial families.

3. Colonists believed in education, the free press, religious freedom, certain Enlightenment ideas, and an emerging notion of civic virtue.

4. Essays should reflect the information provided in the chapter, such as the likelihood that the teacher was a widowed or unmarried woman, an emphasis on religious teaching, and the use of the *New England Primer.*

networks
There's More Online!

☑ **BIOGRAPHY**
George Washington

☑ **GRAPHIC ORGANIZER**
Native American Relations
With the Europeans

☑ **MAP** The French and Indian War

☑ **PRIMARY SOURCE**
Political Cartoons

☑ **VIDEO**

Lesson 4
Rivalry in North America

ESSENTIAL QUESTION *Why does conflict develop?*

IT MATTERS BECAUSE
Rivalry between Great Britain and France led to a war for control of North America and set the stage for a dispute between the colonists and Great Britain.

Rivalry Between the French and the British

GUIDING QUESTION *How did competition for land in North America lead to the French and Indian War?*

In the 1700s, Britain and France were leading European powers. They competed for wealth and empire in different parts of the world. In North America, their rivalry was very strong.

This rivalry turned especially bitter in the mid-1700s. The British began to show interest in the Ohio River valley. This vast land beyond the Appalachian Mountains was rich in resources. The British believed they had a right to this land. The French also viewed the valley as theirs. The French enjoyed a thriving fur trade with the Native Americans of the region. They did not want to share this business with British settlers.

To protect their claims in the valley, the French built a chain of forts from Lake Ontario south to the Ohio River. The British responded by starting to build a fort in what is now western Pennsylvania. Before they could finish, the French seized the site. On it, they built their own fort, calling it Fort Duquesne (doo•KAYN).

R

Reading **HELP**DESK **CCSS**

Taking Notes: *Summarizing* RH.6–8.2, RH.6–8.7

As you read, use a diagram like this one to summarize why Native Americans had better relations with the French than with the British.

Native Americans	
Relations With the British	Relations With the French

Content Vocabulary (Tier 3 Words)
- **militia**
- **Iroquois Confederacy**
- **alliance**

Lesson 4 **101**

© Artist Robert Griffing/ Paramount Press Inc., (c) Art Archive/ General Wolfe Museum, Quebec House/ Eileen Tweedy, (r) The Granger Collection, NYC

Video block

VIDEO

The Proclamation of 1763

Assessing Following the French and Indian War, the British had a great deal more land in the New World, and they set out to gain stronger control over their holdings. Have students view the video to discover how British mistakes created conflicts with both Native Americans and the colonials. Conduct a follow-up discussion. **Ask: What could the British have done differently to maintain better relations with the Native Americans? With the colonials?** *(Answers will vary, and might include observations about greater compromise or diplomacy.)*

See page 81F for other online activities.

ENGAGE

🔔 **Bellringer** Discuss the French and British influence in America. Ask students to consider current place names in the United States that reflect French and British influence *(St. Louis, New Orleans, New England, Carolina, and so forth).*

TEACH & ASSESS

R Reading Skills

Identifying Before students read the text, remind them that France and Great Britain had long been rivals in Europe and in their competition for colonizing other parts of the world. As students read, ask them to note how that rivalry came to a head in North America in the mid-1700s. **Ask: What issue sparked the conflict between the British and French in North America?** *(They both claimed rights to the Ohio River Valley.)* **AL What did the British and the French do to protect their claims?** *(The French built forts from Lake Ontario south to the Ohio River. The British began to build a fort in western Pennsylvania.)*

Remind students that this land was already occupied by Native Americans. **Ask: What view might the Native Americans have taken toward this land in the Ohio River Valley that was being disputed by the French and British?** *(They considered the land their own and did not want to lose it to either the French or the British.)* **BL**

ANSWER, p. 101

TAKING NOTES: Relations with the British: The British wanted to seize Native American land; **Relations with the French:** The French established a fur trade; married Native Americans and adopted their customs; shared Christianity

---

C Critical Thinking Skills

Determining Cause and Effect Explain that the conflict over Fort Duquesne was the opening conflict in what would be called the French and Indian War. **Ask: Why was the loss of Fort Duquesne significant for the British?** *(The French seized the site and built the fort, adding it to the numerous forts the French had already built.)* **What role did George Washington play in the French and Indian War?** *(He led the Virginia militia in a failed attempt to drive the French out of Fort Duquesne.)* **AL** **Why do you think colonists considered Washington a hero even though he lost the attack at Fort Necessity?** *(It was the first blow struck against the French, despite the loss.)* **BL**

R1 Reading Skills

Citing Text Evidence After students read the text, discuss the role Native Americans would play in this war. **Ask: Why did the Native Americans regard the British as a bigger threat than the French?** *(The British wanted to allow settlers to build farms and villages, which meant the Native Americans would lose their land. The French didn't come to stay; they only wanted to trade with the Native Americans.)* Students should support their responses with evidence from the text.

R2 Reading Skills

Explaining After students read the text, ask them to explain the Albany Plan. **Ask: When and where was the Albany Plan proposed?** *(It was proposed as war with the French became a certainty. Delegates from the colonies met in Albany, New York, to discuss a treaty with the Iroquois. The Albany Plan arose as part of the discussion.)* **Who proposed it?** *(Benjamin Franklin)* **AL** **What was its purpose?** *(to unite the colonies in the fight against the French)* **Why did the plan fail?** *(It required colonies to give up power to a central government, and none of them wanted to do that.)*

Although Washington suffered defeat at Fort Necessity, the colonists viewed him as the hero who had struck the first blow against the French.

In spring 1754, the governor of Virginia sent a **militia** (muh•LIH•shuh)—a military force made up of ordinary citizens—to drive out the French. Leading this force was a young Virginian. His name was George Washington.

After marching to Fort Duquesne, Washington set up a small fort of his own nearby. He called it Fort Necessity. **C**

Washington's outpost soon came under attack by the French and their Native American allies. This combined army won the battle and forced Washington's soldiers to surrender. The French later released the soldiers, who returned to Virginia.

Native American Alliances

R1 As the conflict got underway, the French and the British both sought Native American help. The French had a big advantage. They already had many Native American allies. Native Americans generally distrusted the British and their hunger for land. In contrast, the French were more interested in fur trading than in land. French trappers and fur traders often married Native American women. French missionaries **converted** many Native Americans to Catholicism. For these reasons, Native Americans helped the French and raided British settlements.

To counter the threat of the French and their Native American friends, the British colonists tried to make a treaty with the Iroquois. The **Iroquois Confederacy** (EER•uh•kwoy kuhn•FEH•duh•ruh•see) was the most powerful group of Native Americans in eastern North America. At that time, the confederacy included six nations—the Mohawk, Seneca, Cayuga, Onondaga, Oneida, and Tuscarora. Delegates—representatives—from seven colonies met with Iroquois leaders at Albany, New York, in June 1754. The Iroquois refused an **alliance** (uh•LY•uhns), or partnership, with the British. They did, however, **R2** promise to remain **neutral**—that is, to take no side.

The Albany delegates also talked about how the colonies might work together more closely against the French. They decided to adopt Benjamin Franklin's Albany Plan of Union for a united colonial government. To form a colonial government, each colony would have to give up some of its powers. Not one

Artist Robert Griffing/ Paramount Press Inc.

Reading **HELP**DESK **CCSS**

militia a military force made up of ordinary citizens
Iroquois Confederacy a group of Native American nations in eastern North America joined together under one general government

alliance partnership

Academic Vocabulary (Tier 2 Words)
convert to change the religious beliefs of someone
neutral taking no side

102 *Life in the American Colonies*

---

net**w**rks   *Online Teaching Options*

IMAGE

George Washington and the French and Indian War

Analyzing Visuals Have students explore the interactive image and read more about George Washington's role in the French and Indian War by scrolling down the text. **Ask: What led to George Washington's promotion to colonel and title as commander-in-chief of the Virginia militia?** *(He proved his leadership during an assignment to warn the French commander at Fort Le Boeuf against further advances into British territory.)*

See page 81F for other online activities.

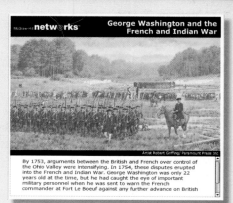

George Washington and the French and Indian War

By 1753, arguments between the British and French over control of the Ohio Valley were intensifying. In 1754, these disputes erupted into the French and Indian War. George Washington was only 22 years old at the time, but he had caught the eye of important military personnel when he was sent to warn the French commander at Fort Le Boeuf against any further advance on British

colonial assembly was willing to do so. Disappointed, Franklin wrote, "Everybody cries, a Union is absolutely necessary; but when they come to the manner and form of the union, [they] are perfectly distracted."

The Albany meeting failed to unify the colonists. Meanwhile, the conflict between the British and the French expanded into full-scale war—the French and Indian War.

☑ **PROGRESS CHECK**

Determining Cause and Effect Why did hostilities between the French and British increase during the mid-1700s?

The French and Indian War

GUIDING QUESTION *What was the turning point in the French and Indian War?*

The French enjoyed early success in the war. They captured several British forts. Meanwhile, their Native American allies carried out raids on the frontier, or edges, of the colonies. They killed colonists, burned farmhouses and crops, and drove many families back toward the coast.

The turning point came in 1757, when William Pitt became prime minister, the head of the British government. Pitt was a great military planner. He sent more trained British troops to fight in North America. To stop colonial complaints about the cost of the war, Pitt decided that Britain would pay for it. He knew that, after the war, the British would raise colonists' taxes to help pay the large bill. Pitt had only delayed the time when the colonists would have to pay their share of the military costs.

Pitt's goal was not just to open the Ohio River valley. He also wanted to conquer French Canada. In 1758 British forces won a key victory at Fort Louisbourg, in present-day Nova Scotia.

After a month-long siege, Major General James Wolfe ordered British forces to cross the St. Lawrence River and climb the cliffs near the city of Quebec. In less than an hour, French troops fled, and the city fell.

Thinking Like a ― HISTORIAN

Analyzing Primary Sources

America's first political cartoon, drawn by Benjamin Franklin in 1754, promoted his Albany Plan of Union. Each section represents a colony. The New England Colonies are combined as one section. What warning does the cartoon convey about the approaching war with France? For more information about analyzing primary sources, read *Thinking Like a Historian.*

V Visual Skills

Interpreting Call students' attention to Benjamin Franklin's "Unite or Die" political cartoon. Discuss the cartoon in the context of the looming war with the French and Franklin's Albany Plan.

Ask: **How does the phrase "Unite or Die" relate to the segmented snake?** *(Cut apart, the snake would die. If the pieces were to unite, the snake could survive.)* **What do the letters represent?** *(They are the initials of different colonies.)* **Visual/Spatial**

R Reading Skills

Making Inferences Direct students to read the section titled "The French and Indian War." Have students recall which nations were involved in the French and Indian War. *(France and Great Britain)* **Ask: With which nation were most of the Native Americans allied?** *(Most Native Americans were allied with France.)*

After they have read the section, divide the class into small groups. Direct each group to discuss the potential for defeat of the colonial troops by the French. Groups should also discuss factors that favored a French victory, such as their alliances with Native Americans and the fortifications they had built. Remind students to cite text evidence to support their assertions. **BL**

Content Background Knowledge

The French and Indian War was one part of a worldwide war between France and Great Britain that ultimately involved all of the great powers of Europe. Known as the Seven Years' War, the war began when Prussia attacked Saxony, setting off a domino effect as different powers were drawn into the war as a result of political alliances. For long-time rivals France and Britain, the war spilled over to their colonies and ended with the Treaty of Paris, which granted Britain undisputed possession of North America and India.

IMAGE

Unite or Die

Analyzing Images Have students view the interactive image showing Benjamin Franklin's political cartoon advocating a union of the colonies. Have students click on the arrow to reveal a text giving more specific information about the context of the cartoon. Ask students to summarize their interpretation of the cartoon during a follow-up discussion.

See page 81F for other online activities.

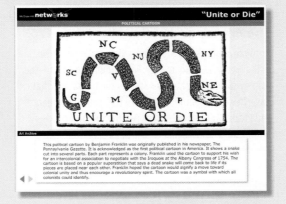

ANSWERS, p. 103

Thinking Like a Historian The colonies must unite or they will not succeed.

☑ **PROGRESS CHECK** The British tried to control the Ohio River Valley, which the French regarded as theirs.

V Visual Skills

Analyzing Maps Have students examine the map of the French and Indian War. Ask students to study the map key and find the locations of the disputed territories, the forts, the British and French victories, and the troop movements. Explain that the names accompanying the troop movement arrows are those of the commanders of those forces. **Ask: What can you tell from the map about how the British attacked Montreal?** (They attacked from three directions at once with troops coming from Fort Oswego, Quebec, and the forts at Crown Point, Ticonderoga, and William Henry.) **BL What route did General Wolfe follow on his approach to Quebec?** (He followed the St. Lawrence River) **Visual/Spatial**

C Critical Thinking Skills

Drawing Conclusions Explain that Quebec was the capital of New France, France's largest and most important province in Canada. As a result, it was an important target for the British. Ask students to describe the attack on Quebec by the British troops. **Ask: Why were the attack and capture of Quebec a surprise to the French?** (Due to its location, Quebec was thought to be impossible to capture.) **What happened as a result of the fall of Quebec and Montreal?** (The French were defeated in North America.)

Remind students that the French and Indian War was just one part of the greater war between France and Britain, most of which took place in Europe. Explain that the Treaty of Paris of 1763 formally ended that war. **Ask: How did the signing of the Treaty of Paris affect North America?** (It ended the French and Indian War and ceded French territory to Britain and Spain.)

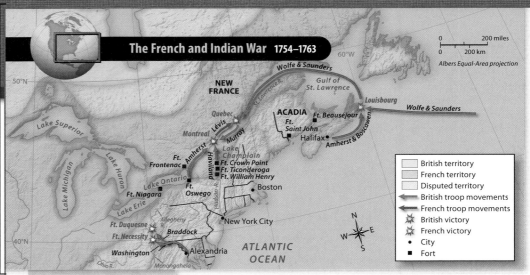

The French and Indian War 1754–1763

GEOGRAPHY CONNECTION

During the French and Indian War, the British and the French fought for control of the lands between their North American territories.

1 **LOCATION** Where are the cities of Quebec and Montreal located?

2 **CRITICAL THINKING**
Analyzing Why do you think Quebec and Montreal were related to French dominance in the Ohio River valley?

The same year a British force, made up mostly of New York and New England militia, captured Fort Frontenac at Lake Ontario. Another British force finally took Fort Duquesne. The British renamed it Fort Pitt.

Quebec, the capital of New France, sat on a cliff above the St. Lawrence River. Because of its position, Quebec was thought to be impossible to attack. In September 1759, British scouts spotted a poorly guarded path along the back of the cliff. At night, Wolfe's soldiers overwhelmed the French guards and scrambled up the path. The British troops then surprised and defeated the French army on a field called the Plains of Abraham. The fall of Quebec and of Montreal the next year marked the defeat of France in North America.

The war in Europe finally ended with the Treaty of Paris of 1763. This treaty forced France to give Canada and most of its lands east of the Mississippi River to Great Britain. Great Britain also received Florida from France's ally, Spain. Spain acquired French lands west of the Mississippi River—called Louisiana—as well as the port of New Orleans.

The Treaty of Paris marked the end of France as a power in North America. In its aftermath, North America was in the hands of two European powers—Great Britain and Spain.

☑ **PROGRESS CHECK**

Explaining Why was William Pitt successful at managing the war for Britain?

Reading **HELP**DESK **CCSS**

Reading Strategy: *Identifying the Main Idea*

In most paragraphs, the main idea appears near the beginning. The rest of the paragraph often gives examples or details to help you understand the main idea. Read the first paragraph under the Guiding Question on the next page. Identify the main idea of the paragraph and three supporting details.

104 *Life in the American Colonies*

net**w**◉rks   *Online Teaching Options*

MAP

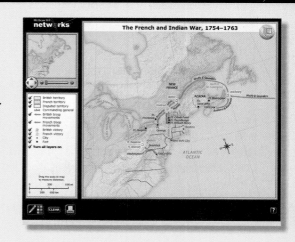

The French and Indian War 1754–1763

Analyzing Maps Have students view the interactive map of the French and Indian War. Ask students to explore the map by clicking on the key to reveal the map's information. Have students identify forts, trace the troop movements, and locate the sites of battles. Ask them to notice where Britain and France held territory before the war. **Ask: Where was most of the disputed land?** (west of the colonies, northeast of the colonies near New France, and northwest of New France.)

See page 81F for other online activities.

New British Policies

GUIDING QUESTION *How did the American colonists react to new British policies?*

The French defeat was a blow to Native Americans in the Ohio River Valley. They had lost their French allies and trading partners and now had to deal with the British. The British raised the prices of their goods. Unlike the French, the British refused to pay Native Americans to use their land. Worst of all, more colonists began settling in Native American lands.

Many Native Americans saw the settlers as a threat to their way of life. One of these was Pontiac, the chief of an Ottawa village near Detroit. In 1763, Pontiac and his forces captured the British fort at Detroit and other British outposts. During Pontiac's War, Native Americans killed settlers along the Pennsylvania and Virginia frontiers.

The same year as Pontiac's War began, Britain's King George declared that colonists were not to settle west of the Appalachian Mountains. To enforce the new rule, the British planned to keep 10,000 troops in America. The Proclamation of 1763 helped removed a source of conflict with Native Americans. It also kept colonists on the coast—where the British could control them.

Colonists believed the proclamation limited their freedom of movement. They feared that the large number of British troops might interfere with their liberties. As a result, distrust began to grow between Britain and its American colonies.

Britain's financial problems also led to trouble. Deeply in debt as a result of the war with France, the British government made plans to tax the colonies and tighten trade rules. These efforts would lead to conflict—and eventually revolution.

✓ **PROGRESS CHECK**

Examining Why did the Proclamation of 1763 anger colonists?

BIOGRAPHY

Pontiac, c. 1720–1769

Pontiac became an Ottawa chief while still a young man. A born leader, he brought together three tribes—the Ottawa, the Potawatomi, and the Ojibwa—in an alliance. As more British settlers moved into their lands, he convinced more tribes to join. Based on Pontiac's plans, these tribes attacked British forts and settlements. Pontiac himself led the successful attack on the fort at Detroit. Pontiac agreed to peace with the British in July 1766. Afterward, his allies turned against him.

▶ **CRITICAL THINKING**
Drawing Conclusions Why do you think Pontiac's former allies turned against him?

LESSON 4 REVIEW (CCSS)

Review Vocabulary (Tier 3 Words)

1. Write a sentence using the terms *alliance* and *Iroquois Confederacy*. RH.6–8.4

2. Write a sentence about the colonies using the word *militia*. RH.6–8.4

Answer the Guiding Questions

3. *Explaining* What was the role of the Ohio River valley in the growing conflict between the French, Native Americans, and British in the mid-1700s? RH.6–8.2

4. *Identifying* What was the role of William Pitt in the French and Indian War? RH.6–8.1

5. *Summarizing* Why were the American colonists dissatisfied with the outcome of the war? RH.6–8.2

6. **INFORMATIVE/EXPLANATORY** Write a paragraph that summarizes the Albany Plan of Union, including the problems it was meant to address and the response it received among the colonies. WHST.6–8.2, WHST.6–8.9

Lesson 4 **105**

LESSON 4 REVIEW ANSWERS

1. Sample answer: The Iroquois Confederacy did not make an alliance with either the French or the British at the start of the French and Indian War.

2. Sample answer: George Washington led a Virginia militia to fight the French.

3. Both the French and the British claimed the valley. The Native Americans lived on this land, and many of them favored the French.

4. Pitt became prime minister of Great Britain during the war, and he helped turn the tide of the conflict by sending many more British soldiers to fight in North America.

5. They were denied the opportunity to move onto the lands west of the Appalachians, and then they were subjected to new taxes.

6. Paragraphs should describe that the Albany Plan of Union was an effort to unite the colonies and make them into a more effective force against the French and their Native American allies. It was rejected by the colonies because it required individual colonies to give up authority.

R1 Reading Skills

Explaining Have students read the text to discuss the westward movement into Native American lands following the Treaty of Paris. **Ask: When colonists moved west of the Appalachian Mountains, where did they settle?** *(in Native American territory)* **How did Native Americans view the new settlers?** *(They saw the settlers as a threat to their way of life.)* AL

R2 Reading Skills

Restating Have students read the biography of Pontiac and then restate the important details. **Ask: Who was Pontiac?** *(an Ottawa chief who brought several Native American tribes into an alliance against the British)* **What happened during Pontiac's War?** *(He captured British outposts, such as their fort at Detroit; Native Americans attacked and killed settlers along the Pennsylvania and Virginia frontiers.)* **How did the war end?** *(Pontiac made peace with the British in July 1766.)* AL

C Critical Thinking Skills

Determining Cause and Effect Describe the increasing friction between the British government and the colonies. **Ask: How did the Proclamation of 1763 help the economy of Great Britain?** *(It kept colonists from moving from colonies along the coast, protecting British markets and investments. It averted another costly war, this one with the Native Americans.)* Discuss how the Proclamation of 1763 added to the growing dissension. **Ask: How was the attitude of colonists toward British rule changing?** *(Distrust began to grow between Britain and its American colonies.)* **What other actions did the British take that angered colonists?** *(They brought more troops to the colonies to enforce the proclamation; they created new taxes.)*

Have students complete the Lesson 4 review.

CLOSE & REFLECT

Summarizing Have students summarize the French and British rivalry in North America and how it eventually led to rising tensions between colonists and England. **Ask: What do you think will happen next?** *(Answers may vary.)*

ANSWERS, p. 105

CRITICAL THINKING Possible answer: Pontiac's allies were angry because settlers were still taking their lands.

✓ **PROGRESS CHECK** The Proclamation of 1763 prevented further westward expansion, which many colonists believed was their right.

CHAPTER REVIEW ACTIVITY

Instruct students to create a chart with two columns and five rows, and to label the rows as shown below. Then guide a class discussion reviewing the main points of the chapter. Have students list the main ideas and important details in their charts. **Ask: What did each of these groups want or need during the colonial period in America?** *(Possible answers have been provided in the sample table.)*

English Government	• *raw materials*
	• *market for manufactured goods*
	• *tax revenues*
Colonists	• *access to non-English markets*
	• *cheap labor*
	• *free press*
French Settlers	• *trade with Native Americans*
	• *land claims in the Ohio River Valley*
Native Americans	• *settlers staying off their land*
	• *trade for goods*
African Americans	• *freedom*
	• *opportunity for land and jobs*

REVIEW THE ENDURING UNDERSTANDING

Review this chapter's Enduring Understanding with students:

• *People, places, and ideas change over time.*

Now pose the following questions in a class discussion to apply these to the chapter.

How did the lives of the colonists change as events of the seventeenth and eighteenth centuries unfolded? *(At first, the colonists were content to settle the land along the coast and earn a living by farming and building small businesses. Plantation owners in the Southern Colonies needed more labor and imported slaves to work their lands. Many colonists in the North opposed slavery. The colonists had a clear sense of their rights to self-government, so when Britain imposed the Navigation Acts, many colonists resented the restrictions. Meanwhile, immigration continued and the population of the colonies grew quickly. New immigrants brought new values and languages, but they melded into Americans, creating a new American spirit. Religious leaders initiated the Great Awakening, which emphasized personal faith and united colonists in a common experience. The Enlightenment spread the idea that knowledge, reason, and science could improve society. In the mid-1700s, Britain won a war with France and took over all of France's lands in North America. Britain then imposed new policies to control the colonies and to raise revenues to pay the war debt. The colonists began to resent the British government more and more.)*

Write your answers on a separate piece of paper.

1 **Exploring the Essential Questions**   WHST.6–8.2, WHST.6–8.9
INFORMATIVE/EXPLANATORY How did geography shape the lives of the American colonists? Write a summary essay in which you consider how geographic factors shaped the development of life in the colonies, but also how it led to conflict, including conflicts with Great Britain.

2 **21st Century Skills**   WHST.6–8.6, WHST.6–8.7
CREATE AND GIVE A PRESENTATION Use presentation software or a poster to create a presentation that illustrates how life in colonial America was influenced and shaped by geography. Use illustrations of life in the different colonies and colonial regions, and include explanations of how the illustrations show geographic differences and factors.

3 **Thinking Like a Historian**   WHST.6–8.1, WHST.6–8.7
DRAWING INFERENCES AND CONCLUSIONS Create a diagram such as the one here to identify the factors in colonial America that caused conflict with Great Britain.

4 **Visual Literacy**   RH.6–8.7
ANALYZING IMAGES This painting shows methods used in whaling in colonial times. Explain how this picture demonstrates the effects of geography on the economy of the colonies.

Growing Conflict with Great Britain

Collection of the New-York Historical Society/Bridgeman Art Library

ACTIVITIES ANSWERS

Exploring the Essential Questions

1 Essays should include details about how geography influenced the development of agriculture and other industries in the colonies, and also how conflict—between settlers and Native Americans, between different nations, and between colonists and their home countries—emerged over control of land and where colonists could live.

21st Century Skills

2 Students' presentations will vary but should reflect an understanding of how geography, such as soil, climate, and rivers, shaped life in colonial America.

Thinking Like a Historian

3 Students might identify factors such as "growing sense of independence," "Proclamation of 1763," "trade policies," and "taxes." Allow other ideas, depending on students' ability to defend them.

Visual Literacy

4 The colonists used the resources available to them to build their economies. Colonists who lived near the ocean used its resources, including whales, to build their economies.

REVIEW THE GUIDING QUESTIONS

Choose the best answer for each question.

RH.6–8.2
❶ The Middle Colonies were known for

A. poor farmland.   C. plantations.

B. a diverse population.   D. their whaling industry.

RH.6–8.2
❷ The success of the large plantations of the Southern Colonies depended upon

F. the region's many large ports.   H. slavery.

G. large families.   I. rocky soil.

RH.6–8.1
❸ The concept of protected rights began with the

A. Magna Carta.   C. English Bill of Rights.

B. Enlightenment.   D. Great Awakening.

RH.6–8.2
❹ Merchants in the American colonies began smuggling goods because

F. the Navigation Act allowed merchants to choose the buyer.

G. Britain always offered the colonists the best price.

H. they had more goods than Britain could buy.

I. they could sometimes get better prices from customers in other countries.

RH.6–8.1
❺ The Great Awakening resulted in a renewed interest in

A. science.   C. mercantilism.

B. religion.   D. conflict.

RH.6–8.2
❻ Benjamin Franklin is an example of an American colonist strongly influenced by

F. traditional medicine.   H. the unfairness of censorship.

G. the Great Awakening.   I. the Enlightenment.

RH.6–8.1
❼ The Albany Plan of Union was not approved by the colonies because

A. it called for the colonies to declare their independence from Britain.

B. most colonists did not consider the western lands valuable.

C. it diminished the strength of the united colonial government.

D. colonies were not willing to give up any of their power.

RH.6–8.2
❽ How did the British victory over the French affect the Native Americans of the Ohio River valley?

F. It helped them because the British, unlike the French, paid Native Americans for the use of their land.

G. It hurt them because so many French refugees fled to their lands.

H. It hurt them because they lost their French allies and trading partners.

I. It helped them because the British lowered the prices of their goods.

107

ASSESSMENT ANSWERS
Review the Guiding Questions

❶ **B** Farmland was fertile in the Middle Colonies. The Southern Colonies were known for plantations. New England was known for whaling.

❷ **H** Ports would not help to produce goods, only to transport them. Plantations required far more labor than even a large family could provide. Rocky soil would not permit much more than small-scale, subsistence farming.

❸ **A** King John signed the Magna Carta in 1215; Parliament drew up the English Bill of Rights, which provided further details about protected rights, in 1689. The Great Awakening was a religious movement, and the Enlightenment was a philosophical movement.

❹ **I** Colonists could sometimes get better prices from customers in other countries. The Navigation Acts did not allow merchants to choose their own buyers. The colonists had no choice but to sell to Britain regardless of the price paid or the level of demand.

❺ **B** The Great Awakening was a religious movement emphasizing personal faith. The Enlightenment was a movement that focused on rational thought. Mercantilism was an economic policy.

❻ **I** Benjamin Franklin was a scientist and inventor. The Enlightenment was a movement that focused on science to improve society. The work of Franklin demonstrated goals of the Enlightenment.

❼ **D** Colonies were not willing to give up any of their power. The purpose of the Albany Plan was to unite the colonies in a common effort against the French. However, the plan would have required each colony to give up some of its power for the common cause.

❽ **H** It hurt the Native Americans because they lost their French allies and trading partners. Unlike the French, the British did not pay the tribes for use of their land, and they increased the price of goods sold to the tribes. There was no flood of French refugees into tribal lands. When the French lost all claims to land in North America, including land inhabited by native tribes, they withdrew.

Analyzing Documents

9 **C** rice and indigo

10 **F** Philadelphia

Short Response

11 the formation of a single government made up of the different American colonies

12 It would have included the colonies within the authority of a single government but would have left each of them with their existing constitutions.

Extended Response

13 Students' papers should explore the role Franklin demonstrated as a successful, hardworking business owner, an Enlightenment-inspired thinker, and an advocate of colonial unity.

CHAPTER 4 **Assessment** *(continued)*

DBQ ANALYZING DOCUMENTS

RH.6–8.7
9 **Identifying** This map illustrates trade and industry in the American colonies around 1750. Based on the map, what trade and industry was found only in the Southern Colonies?

A. lumber

B. fur and skins

C. rice and indigo

D. fishing

Cattle and grain
Tobacco
Rice and indigo
Fur and skins
Fishing
Lumber
Shipbuilding
Ironworks

ATLANTIC OCEAN

Boston
Newport
New-York City
Philadelphia
Baltimore
Richmond
Williamsburg
New Bern
Charleston
Savannah

APPALACHIAN MTS.

0   500 miles
0   500 km
Lambert Azimuthal Equal-Area projection

Source: Historical Atlas of the United States

RH.6–8.7
10 **Locating** Near which major city were ironworks found?

F. Philadelphia

G. Richmond

H. Williamsburg

I. Savannah

SHORT RESPONSE

"It is proposed that humble application be made for an act of Parliament of Great Britain, by virtue of which one general government may be formed in America, including all the said colonies, within and under which government each colony may retain its present constitution."

—from *Albany Plan of Union*

RH.6–8.6, WHST.6–8.4
11 What is being proposed here?

RH.6–8.2, WHST.6–8.2
12 How would the resulting government have affected the individual colonies?

EXTENDED RESPONSE

WHST.6–8.2, WHST.6–8.9
13 **Informative/Explanatory** Benjamin Franklin served a number of roles in the American colonies in the 1700s. Write an essay about the way he represented key qualities of the colonies.

Need Extra Help?

If You've Missed Question	**1**	**2**	**3**	**4**	**5**	**6**	**7**	**8**	**9**	**10**	**11**	**12**	**13**
Review Lesson	1	1	2	2	3	3	4	4	1	1	4	4	2,3,4

---

netw⊙rks   *Online Teaching Options*

Using eAssessment

Use eAssessment to access and assign the publisher-made Lesson Quizzes & Chapter Tests electronically. You can also use eAssessment to create your own quizzes and tests from hundreds of available questions. eAssessment helps you design assessments that meet the needs of different types of learners. Follow the link in the *Assess* tab of your Teacher Lesson Center.

CHAPTER 5
The Spirit of Independence Planner

UNDERSTANDING BY DESIGN®

Enduring Understanding
- *Conflict can lead to change.*

Essential Questions
- *Why does conflict develop?*
- *What motivates people to act?*

Predictable Misunderstandings
Students may think:
- *All colonists wanted independence.*
- *Only a few colonists remained loyal to Britain.*
- *Only Thomas Jefferson was responsible for the Declaration of Independence.*
- *The colonists' desire for independence appeared suddenly.*

Assessment Evidence
Performance Tasks:
- *Hands-On Chapter Project*

Other Evidence:
- *Interactive Graphic Organizers*
- *What Do You Know? activity*
- *21st Century Skills Activity*
- *Primary Source Activity*
- *Geography and History Activity*
- *What Do You Think? questions*
- *Written Paragraphs*
- *Lesson Reviews*
- *Online Self-Check Quizzes*
- *Chapter Activities and Assessment*

SUGGESTED PACING GUIDE

Introducing the Chapter	1 day	*What Do You Think?*	1 day
Lesson 1	1 day	Lesson 4	2 days
Lesson 2	1 day	Declaration of Independence	1 day
Lesson 3	2 days	Chapter Wrap-Up and Assessment	1 day

TOTAL TIME   10 Days

Key for Using the Teacher Edition

SKILL-BASED ACTIVITIES

Types of skill activities found in the Teacher Edition.

V **Visual Skills** require students to analyze maps, graphs, charts, and photos.

R **Reading Skills** help students practice reading skills and master vocabulary.

W **Writing Skills** provide writing opportunities to help students comprehend the text.

C **Critical Thinking Skills** help students apply and extend what they have learned.

T **Technology Skills** require students to use digital tools effectively.

*Letters are followed by a number when there is more than one of the same type of skill on the page.

DIFFERENTIATED INSTRUCTION

All activities are written for the on-level student unless otherwise marked with the leveled labels below.

BL **Beyond Level**
AL **Approaching Level**
ELL **English Language Learners**

All students benefit from activities that utilize different learning styles. Many activities are marked as below when a particular learning style is highlighted.

Intrapersonal	Naturalist
Logical/Mathematical	Kinesthetic
Visual/Spatial	Auditory/Musical
Verbal/Linguistic	Interpersonal

Learners will understand:

2   TIME, CONTINUITY, AND CHANGE

1. The study of the past provides representation of the history of communities, nations, and the world

2. Concepts such as: chronology, causality, change, conflict, complexity, multiple perspectives, primary and secondary sources, and cause and effect

3. That learning about the past requires the interpretation of sources, and that using varied sources provides the potential for a more balanced interpretive record of the past

4. That historical interpretations of the same event may differ on the basis of such factors as conflicting evidence from varied sources, national or cultural perspectives, and the point of view of the researcher

7. The contributions of key persons, groups, and events from the past and their influence on the present

8. The history of democratic ideals and principles, and how they are represented in documents, artifacts, and symbols

5   INDIVIDUALS, GROUPS, AND INSTITUTIONS

1. This theme helps us know how individuals are members of groups and institutions, and influence and shape those groups and institutions

10   CIVIC IDEALS AND PRACTICES

5. Key documents and excerpts from key sources that define and support democratic ideals and practices (e.g., the U.S. Declaration of Independence, the U.S. Constitution, the Gettysburg Address, the Letter from a Birmingham Jail; and international documents such as the Declaration of the Rights of Man, and the Universal Declaration of the Rights of Children)

CHAPTER OPENER PLANNER

Students will know:

- the causes for the development of conflict between Britain and the colonies.
- the consequences of that conflict and how it motivated colonial leaders and others to act.

Students will be able to:

- **explain** the Proclamation of 1763.
- **analyze** why Britain began to enact harsher trade laws and taxes.
- **understand cause and effect relationships** as they relate to the reaction of the colonists.
- **identify** those individuals and groups that began to rebel against British policy.
- **draw conclusions** about tensions between the colonists and the British that led up to the Boston Massacre.
- **analyze** the role of propaganda in the colonies.
- **identify** the Founders and recognize their contributions.
- **evaluate** the battles of Lexington and Concord.
- **compare points of view** held by Patriots and Loyalists.
- **evaluate** the reaction of the colonies to the rejection of the Olive Branch Petition.
- **summarize** the steps taken that led to the writing of the Declaration of Independence.
- **understand** the four parts of the Declaration of Independence.

UNDERSTANDING BY DESIGN®

☑ *Print Teaching Options*

V Visual Skills

☐ **P. 110** Students interpret a map showing Loyalist and Patriot presence. **BL** Visual/Spatial

☐ **P. 111** Students deduce the reasons for protests in port cities. **BL** Visual/Spatial

R Reading Skills

☐ **P. 110** Students read a time line. **AL** Visual/Spatial

☐ **P. 111** Students interpret a listing on a time line. **BL**

☑ *Online Teaching Options*

V Visual Skills

☐ **MAP** **North America 1775**—Students review the three geographic regions of the colonies and identify locations of major battles.

☐ **TIME LINE** **Place and Time: Revolutionary America 1775 to 1783**—Students learn about key historical events related to the time period that encompasses the Revolutionary War.

☐ **WORLD ATLAS** Students can use this interactive map to identify regions of the world, learn about individual countries, locate political boundaries, measure distances, and much more.

☑ *Printable Digital Worksheets*

R Reading Skills

☐ **GRAPHIC NOVEL** **Liberty's Stand**—A member of the colonial militia explains to his daughter why he must leave her and be prepared to fight.

Project-Based Learning

Hands-On Chapter Project

The American Revolution

To understand how the American Revolution began, student groups will memorize, summarize, and recite one or more stanzas from Henry Wadsworth Longfellow's poem "Paul Revere's Ride."

Technology Extension *edtechteacher*
21ˢᵗ Century Learning

Online Interactive Multimedia Posters

- Find an additional activity online that incorporates technology for this project.
- Visit the EdTechTeacher Web sites (included in the Technology Extension for this chapter) for more links, tutorials, and other resources.

Print Resources

ANCILLARY RESOURCES

These ancillaries are available for every chapter and lesson.

- **Reading Essentials and Study Guide Workbook** **AL** **ELL**
- **Chapter Tests and Lesson Quizzes Blackline Masters**

PRINTABLE DIGITAL WORKSHEETS

These printable digital worksheets are available for every chapter and lesson.

- **Hands-On Chapter Projects**
- **What Do You Know? activities**
- **Chapter Summaries (English and Spanish)**
- **Vocabulary Builder activities**
- **Guided Reading activities**

More Media Resources

SUGGESTED VIDEOS

Watch clips of popular films about the coming of the American Revolution, such as **Johnny Tremain** and **1776**.

- **Discuss:** What do these films tell us about the American spirit of independence?
- **Discuss:** Can fictional movies capture historical events accurately?

(Note: Preview clips for age-appropriateness.)

SUGGESTED READING

Grade 6 reading level:

- **The Second Continental Congress (We the People),** by Jessica S. Gunderson

Grade 7 reading level:

- **Give Me Liberty: The Story of the Declaration of Independence,** by Russell Freedman

Grade 8 reading level:

- **Declaration: The Nine Tumultuous Weeks When America Became Independent, May 1–July 4, 1776,** by William Hogeland

NO TAXATION WITHOUT REPRESENTATION

Students will know:
- the causes for the development of conflict between Britain and the colonies.
- the consequences of that conflict and how it motivated colonial leaders and others to act.

Students will be able to:
- **explain** the Proclamation of 1763.
- **analyze** why Britain began to enact harsher trade laws and taxes.
- **understand cause and effect relationships** as they relate to the reaction of the colonists.
- **identify** those individuals and groups that began to rebel against British policy.

UNDERSTANDING
BY DESIGN®

☑ *Print Teaching Options*

V **Visual Skills**

☐ **P. 114** Students analyze a chart showing the growth of debt after the French/Indian War. **BL** Visual/Spatial

R **Reading Skills**

☐ **P. 112** Students list three benefits the British expected to gain from the Proclamation of 1763. **AL**

☐ **P. 113** Students identify why Grenville wanted to end smuggling. **AL**

☐ **P. 114** Students write a famous quote in their own words. **AL** **ELL**

W **Writing Skills**

☐ **P. 112** Students write a short paragraph that explains why the British enacted the Proclamation of 1763. **AL** **ELL**

☐ **P. 115** Students write a letter from the point of view of a Boston colonist. **BL** Verbal/Linguistic

C **Critical Thinking Skills**

☐ **P. 113** Students order events surrounding the enforcement of trade laws. **BL** Visual/Spatial

☐ **P. 113** Students predict how colonists may have reacted to soldiers invading their homes. **AL**

☐ **P. 114** Students compare and contrast the Sugar Act and Stamp Act. **BL**

☐ **P. 115** Students analyze the formation of the Sons of Liberty. **BL**

☐ **P. 115** Students discuss the passage of the Townshend Act. **AL**

☑ *Online Teaching Options*

V **Visual Skills**

☐ **MAP** **The Proclamation of 1763**—Students analyze the effect of the proclamation on westward expansion.

☐ **VIDEO** **British Tyranny in Boston**—Students view a video that explains the Stamp Act and why colonists were opposed to it.

R **Reading Skills**

☐ **GRAPHIC ORGANIZER** **Taking Notes:** *Identifying:* **British Policies**—Students identify British policies that affected the colonists and the colonists' view of those policies.

C **Critical Thinking Skills**

☐ **GRAPH** **A Growing Debt**—Students analyze how British debt after the French and Indian War led to England imposing taxes on the colonies.

☐ **WHITEBOARD ACTIVITY** **Taxation Without Representation**—Students complete an activity to compare the different taxation acts passed by the British.

T **Technology Skills**

☐ **SELF-CHECK QUIZ** **Lesson 1**—Students receive instant feedback on their mastery of lesson content.

☑ *Printable Digital Worksheets*

C **Critical Thinking Skills**

☐ **WORKSHEET** **21st Century Skills Activity: Critical Thinking and Problem Solving**—Students draw conclusions using information from a chart.

UNITING THE COLONISTS

Students will know:
- the causes for the development of conflict between Britain and the colonies.
- the consequences of that conflict and how it motivated colonial leaders and others to act.

Students will be able to:
- **draw conclusions** about tensions between the colonists and the British that led up to the Boston Massacre.
- **analyze** the role of propaganda in the colonies.

UNDERSTANDING
BY DESIGN®

☑ *Print Teaching Options*

V Visual Skills

☐ **P. 118** Students analyze a painting depicting the Boston Tea Party. **BL** Visual/Spatial

R Reading Skills

☐ **P. 116** Students explain tension between the colonists and British soldiers. **AL**

☐ **P. 118** Students explain the importance of the Tea Act. **AL**

W Writing Skills

☐ **P. 119** Students write a persuasive speech. **BL** Auditory/Musical

C Critical Thinking Skills

☐ **P. 116** Students infer reasons for the colonists' anger and British occupation in Boston. **BL**

☐ **P. 117** Students connect the use of propaganda to influence public opinion among the colonists. **AL**

☐ **P. 117** Students investigate how propaganda uses inflammatory language to sway opinion. **BL** Verbal/Linguistic

☐ **P. 118** Small groups of students reenact the Boston Tea Party. **BL** Kinesthetic

☐ **P. 119** Students fill in a graphic organizer about the Coercive Acts and then discuss them as a group. **AL** **BL** **ELL** Interpersonal

☑ *Online Teaching Options*

V Visual Skills

☐ **VIDEO** **The Boston Massacre and Escalating Anger in the Colonies**—Students view a video about the Boston Massacre and compare attitudes of different colonists toward the British.

R Reading Skills

☐ **GRAPHIC ORGANIZER** **Taking Notes: *Describing:* Intolerable Acts**—Students describe how the Intolerable Acts changed life for the colonists.

☐ **BIOGRAPHY** **Crispus Attucks**—Students learn about the first colonist killed by the British in the Boston Massacre.

C Critical Thinking Skills

☐ **PRIMARY SOURCE** **The Boston Tea Party**—Students read an excerpt from George Hewes's account of the event and discuss the causes of the Boston Tea Party.

T Technology Skills

☐ **SELF-CHECK QUIZ** **Lesson 2**—Students receive instant feedback on their mastery of lesson content.

☑ *Printable Digital Worksheets*

W Writing Skills

☐ **WORKSHEET** **Primary Source Activity: Uniting the Colonies**—Boston Massacre Trial—Students respond to an excerpt from John Adams's closing statements to the jury at the trial of British troops arrested after the Boston Massacre.

A CALL TO ARMS

Students will know:
- *the causes for the development of conflict between Britain and the colonies.*
- *the consequences of that conflict and how it motivated colonial leaders and others to act.*

Students will be able to:
- ***identify*** *the Founders and recognize their contributions.*
- ***evaluate*** *the battles of Lexington and Concord.*
- ***compare points of view*** *held by Patriots and Loyalists.*

UNDERSTANDING
BY DESIGN®

☑ *Print Teaching Options*

V Visual Skills

☐ **P. 121** Students analyze a chart showing purchases for a Massachusetts militia. **BL** **Visual/Spatial**

☐ **P. 122** Students locate key places on a map. **AL** **Visual/Spatial**

☐ **P. 123** Students review map keys and labels on a map showing locations of armed conflict during the American Revolution. **AL** **Visual/Spatial**

R Reading Skills

☐ **P. 120** Students identify the organization of the Continental Congress. **AL**

☐ **P. 121** Students write a list of actions taken by the Continental Congress. **BL** **Intrapersonal**

☐ **P. 122** Students investigate the term "minutemen." **AL** **ELL**

☐ **P. 124** Students speculate on what may have happened if Fort Ticonderoga had not been taken by the Allen's and Arnold's forces and then share their scenarios with the class. **BL** **Auditory/Musical**

☐ **P. 124** Students explain the role of Benedict Arnold. **AL**

☐ **P. 125** Students summarize the events at Bunker Hill. **AL** **ELL**

W Writing Skills

☐ **P. 124** Students write about why more volunteers joined the militias after Lexington and Concord. **BL** **Intrapersonal**

☐ **P. 125** Students write a journal entry from the point of view of a Loyalist or Patriot. **BL**

C Critical Thinking Skills

☐ **P. 120** Students recognize important individuals and their contributions to working toward independence for the colonists. **AL**

☐ **P. 121** Students recognize why delegates sought to repeal certain laws. **AL** **BL**

☐ **P. 122** Students interpret a quote by Patrick Henry. **AL** **BL** **ELL**

☐ **P. 125** Students compare and contrast the beliefs of the Loyalists and Patriots. **AL**

☑ *Online Teaching Options*

V Visual Skills

☐ **VIDEO** **Boston Tea Party and the Intolerable Acts**—Students view a video that explains how the Boston Tea Party led to the Intolerable Acts and prompted the formation of the First Continental Congress.

☐ **IMAGE** **Militia, Minutemen, and the Continental Army**—Students learn the differences among these three groups.

☐ **MAP** **Battles of Lexington and Concord, April 1775**— Students use the map to trace the movements of troops and messengers in these battles.

☐ **IMAGE** **The North Bridge**—Students learn the history of the North Bridge, where Patriots first came face-to- face with British troops.

☐ **IMAGE** **The Battle of Bunker Hill**—Students analyze a painting of this famous battle.

R Reading Skills

☐ **GRAPHIC ORGANIZER** **Taking Notes:** *Summarizing:* **Continental Congress**—Students summarize three key actions of the Continental Congress.

☐ **BIOGRAPHY** **Patrick Henry**—Students learn about Henry's background and beliefs, and how he inspired other colonists to fight for freedom.

C Critical Thinking Skills

☐ **CHART** **Choosing Sides**—Students contrast the beliefs of Loyalists and Patriots.

T Technology Skills

☐ **SELF-CHECK QUIZ** **Lesson 3**—Students receive instant feedback on their mastery of lesson content.

☐ **GAME** **A Call to Arms Concentration Game**—Students match cards to review key lesson concepts.

☑ *Printable Digital Worksheets*

W Writing Skills

☐ **WORKSHEET** **Geography and History Activity: Understanding Movement: "The British Are Coming!"**—Students answer questions after analyzing a map showing the routes of colonial messengers.

DECLARING INDEPENDENCE

Students will know:
- the causes for the development of conflict between Britain and the colonies.
- the consequences of that conflict and how it motivated colonial leaders and others to act.

Students will be able to:
- **evaluate** the reaction of the colonies to the rejection of the Olive Branch Petition.
- **summarize** the steps taken that led to the writing of the Declaration of Independence.
- **understand** the four parts of the Declaration of Independence.

UNDERSTANDING
BY DESIGN®

☑ *Print Teaching Options*

R Reading Skills

☐ **P. 128** Students identify individuals who were part of the Second Continental Congress. AL

☐ **P. 129** Students evaluate the steps the Continental Congress took toward independence. BL

☐ **P. 130** Students discuss the Continental Army's movements in Montreal, Quebec, and Boston. AL

☐ **P. 130** Students paraphrase parts of *Common Sense.* AL ELL

☐ **P. 132** Students discuss how John Locke inspired Thomas Jefferson's ideas. BL

☐ **P. 132** Students make connections between the wording in the Declaration and the events that had transpired leading up to it. BL

C Critical Thinking Skills

☐ **P. 128** Students argue why having colonial government experience made men more or less qualified to serve on the Second Continental Congress. BL

☐ **P. 129** Students evaluate the expression "extending the olive branch." BL Verbal/Linguistic

☐ **P. 130** Students discuss Thomas Paine's work *Common Sense.* AL BL

☐ **P. 131** Students predict what the Americans will do after their success during the American Revolution. BL

☐ **P. 131** Students discuss Lee's proposal to the Second Continental Congress. AL

☐ **P. 132** Students analyze documents that inspired Jefferson while he was writing the Declaration. AL

☐ **P. 133** Students interpret a quote made by Thomas Jefferson in reference to the Declaration. BL

T Technology Skills

☐ **P. 131** Students research why Adams considered himself too unpopular to write the Declaration of Independence. BL

☑ *Online Teaching Options*

V Visual Skills

☐ **MAP** **The Siege of Boston, 1775–1776**—Students use the map to trace troop placement, battles, and the retreat of the British.

☐ **IMAGE** **The Lee Resolution**—Students learn how Lee's resolution led to the writing of the Declaration of Independence.

☐ **SLIDE SHOW** **The Committee of Five**—Students view photos of the men tasked with writing the Declaration of Independence.

☐ **VIDEO** **Declaration of Independence**—Students view a video that describes this important American document.

R Reading Skills

☐ **GRAPHIC ORGANIZER** **Taking Notes:** *Organizing:* **Declaration of Independence**—Students detail the four parts of the Declaration of Independence.

☐ **BIOGRAPHY** **Thomas Paine**—Students learn about this writer in a short biography.

☐ **PRIMARY SOURCE** **Reaction to the Declaration**—Students read how the Patriot troops reacted to the reading of the Declaration.

☐ **IMAGE** **The Declaration of Independence**—This image provides an annotated version of the Declaration to aid student comprehension.

C Critical Thinking Skills

☐ **PRIMARY SOURCE** **George Washington on Lexington and Concord**—Students analyze an excerpt from a letter Washington wrote to George Fairfax about fighting in Massachusetts in April of 1775.

T Technology Skills

☐ **SELF-CHECK QUIZ** **Lesson 4**—Students receive instant feedback on their mastery of lesson content.

LESSON 1 No Taxation Without Representation

Reading and Comprehension

Students should work in pairs or small groups to outline the colonists' complaints against the British. Students should write a few sentences explaining why the colonists were angry.

Text Evidence

Ask students to analyze the relationship between taxes and smuggling. Students should select various aspects covered in the text to explain the cyclical nature of the relationship.

LESSON 2 Uniting the Colonists

Reading and Comprehension

Tell students to look up the meanings of *coercive* and *intolerable*. Have them make lists of synonyms for each of those words.

Text Evidence

Students should research Samuel Adams and his propaganda posters. Have students prepare a short digital presentation featuring images of the posters and explaining their arguments.

LESSON 3 A Call to Arms

Reading and Comprehension

Students can make a two-column chart to take notes as they read the section "Choosing Sides." This will help them compare and contrast Patriots and Loyalists.

Text Evidence

Have students form two debate teams to argue whether Benedict Arnold should ultimately be remembered as a patriot or a traitor. Each team should research and organize the facts that support its arguments. Then hold a formal debate in class.

LESSON 4 Declaring Independence

Reading and Comprehension

Explain to students that lesson titles and subtitles can help them preview what they are about to read. Have students copy the title and subtitles from this lesson and write one sentence, predicting what they think each one will be about. After students have finished the lesson, refer them back to their predictions, to see how accurate they were.

Text Evidence

Remind students that a preamble is an introduction. The preamble to the Declaration of Independence explains the reasons the colonists wanted to form a new country. Ask students to think of something they want to do very strongly. Then have them write a "preamble" that introduces the idea and lays out their reasons.

Online Resources

Approaching Level Reader

Use this online lower-level text that corresponds directly to the text in the Student Edition. It includes a Spanish version.

Guided Reading Activities

This resource uses graphic organizers and guiding questions to help students with comprehension.

What Do You Know?

Use these worksheets to pre-assess student's background knowledge before they study the chapter.

Reading Essentials and Study Guide Workbook

This resource offers writing and reading activities for the approaching-level student. Also available in Spanish.

Self-Check Quizzes

This online assessment tool provides instant feedback for students to check their progress.

How Do I Teach with
Hands-On Chapter Projects?

Would you like your students to explore a more complicated bit of chapter content that could take more than a class period? Do you want to teach group work rather than assign individual homework? The Hands-On Chapter Project option can help you meet such teaching goals. Each chapter features a cumulative project that brings the content to life for students in different ways. Here are some steps for running project-based teaching more effectively.

Step **1** Gather the right resources

- Projects require student research outside of the student textbook. Familiarize them with the proper tools and research techniques.

- Sources could include online collections, reference materials in your school library, or additional Web sites.

Step **2** Collaboration Skills

- Students need to be aware that group projects require interaction with classmates and review of each other's work.

- Build in time and methods for group members to review the assigned product throughout the project. This may be done in class, digitally outside of school, or in another agreed-upon method.

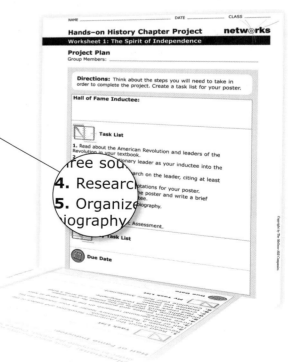

Step **3** Producing the Final Project

- Students may choose to utilize technology for the final project. Today's students are skilled creators. Provide them with the tools and the opportunity to be as creative in class as they can.

The Spirit of Independence

1763–1776

ESSENTIAL QUESTIONS · *Why does conflict develop?*
· *What motivates people to act?*

The Story Matters . . .

He stands proud and tall, this minuteman, part of a colonial militia. Citizen soldiers like him were the first responders of their time. A call to arms could come day or night. The minutemen were out the door on a minute's notice, ready to protect their communities.

Few would doubt the minutemen's bravery. But if the growing tension between the colonies and Great Britain led to war, how would these farmers, clerks, and shopkeepers stand up to a force of skilled British soldiers? This was one of many troubling questions that the colonies faced as they moved closer to declaring their independence.

◄ *This portrait of a minuteman was created in 1876 to celebrate 100 years of American independence.*

Bettmann/CORBIS

109

ENGAGE

🔔 **Bellringer** Call on a student to read "The Story Matters . . ." aloud. Remind students that the minutemen were a citizen militia, not a regular military force. No colony needed an army, and no colony could have afforded one. The militias were sufficient to meet the needs of the colonists and their communities. **Then ask:** Why did the colonies need militias? *(so the colonists could protect themselves)* Why were some militia called minutemen? *(They could be ready to fight in a very short time, with little notice.)* Invite students to browse the chapter, noting headings, photos and captions, and other text features. **Ask:** What do you think you will learn about in this chapter? *(Answers may vary.)* **Ask:** What do you already know about the American colonists' fight for independence? *(Answers may vary.)*

Making Connections

Read the following information to students:

Independence is about having rights and responsibilities. When young people reach certain ages, they are granted increasing independence.

- The age at which young people can start working outside their homes for pay is 14, but the hours that teenagers can work are restricted to allow time for schoolwork and other activities.
- Between the ages of 15 and 16, young people have the right to obtain a driver's license. However, this comes with other responsibilities, such as buying auto insurance and maintaining good driving habits.
- By age 18, teenagers are legally adults. They can vote, sign legal documents, and enlist in the armed forces. But many young people will not be financially independent — that is, fully responsible for their own well-being — for several years after that.

Explain to students that minutemen were often 25 years of age or younger. Ask students to draw parallels between the responsibilities of a teenager or young adult during the Revolutionary Way and today's young people. **BL**

Letter from the Author

Dear American History Teacher,

Through a decade of angry exchanges, it became obvious that the colonies and Britain had different ideas and goals. When the sides could not find a compromise, colonial representatives met in Philadelphia to boldly declare independence. During the next six years, mighty Great Britain sent armies of mercenaries while the colonies scrounged to keep an army in the field. George Washington kept his army intact until an opportunity arose to capture the British Army at Yorktown. The British government had to give in when its people lost heart in this long battle.

Joyce Appleby

TEACH & ASSESS

Step Into the Place

V1 Visual Skills

Reading a Map Tell students to look at the map. **Ask: Where was the strongest Loyalist presence?** (North Carolina) **How do you know?** (It is the largest of the dark-pink shaded areas.) **BL** Visual/Spatial

R1 Reading Skills

Expressing Have students take turns reading aloud the dates and information on the time line. Remind students that the time line is read from left to right. **Ask: What is the difference between the red and blue lines on the time line?** (The blue line is a time line of events in the Americas, and the red line shows events happening in other parts of the world at the same time.) **AL** Visual/Spatial

Content Background Knowledge

The British Army in the eighteenth century was one of the strongest in the world. Known as "redcoats" for their distinctive uniforms, these soldiers had already driven European rivals France and Spain out of some colonial territory in the Americas and the Caribbean.

The British colonies extended along the coast of the Atlantic Ocean. In the middle of this strip was Philadelphia. This city would become a gathering place for colonial leaders as they discussed the growing conflict with Great Britain.

Step Into the Place

MAP FOCUS By 1775, British policies had caused unrest in the colonies and a growing movement toward independence.

V2

1 REGION Which colonial region appears to have the largest area of Loyalist support? RH.6–8.7

2 LOCATION What lay beyond the borders of British territory in North America? RH.6–8.7

3 CRITICAL THINKING
Making Connections In which colonies do you think the movement for independence might have been the strongest? What makes you think so? RH.6–8.7, RH.6–8.10

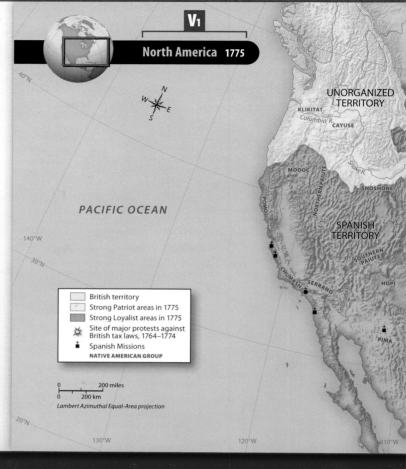

North America 1775

PACIFIC OCEAN

UNORGANIZED TERRITORY

KLIKITAT
Columbia R.
CAYUSE

MODOC
Snake R.

SHOSHONE

SPANISH TERRITORY

POMO
NORTHERN PAIUTE

CHUMASH
SERRANO
SOUTHERN PAIUTE

HOPI

PIMA

- British territory
- Strong Patriot areas in 1775
- Strong Loyalist areas in 1775
- ☀ Site of major protests against British tax laws, 1764–1774
- ⚑ Spanish Missions
- NATIVE AMERICAN GROUP

0   200 miles
0   200 km
Lambert Azimuthal Equal-Area projection

Step Into the Time

R1

TIME LINE Review the time line. What was taking place in Europe at about the same time the First Continental Congress met in America? RH.6–8.5, RH.6–8.7

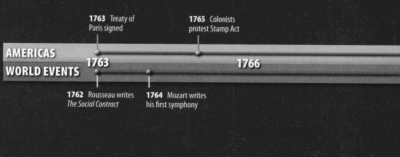

1763 Treaty of Paris signed

1765 Colonists protest Stamp Act

AMERICAS
WORLD EVENTS 1763   1766

1762 Rousseau writes *The Social Contract*

1764 Mozart writes his first symphony

110 *The Spirit of Independence*

Project-Based Learning ✋

Hands-On Chapter Project

The American Revolution
To learn about the lives of people who led American colonists on the road to revolution, students will create a Spirit of Independence Hall of Fame. They will read about the American Revolution and leaders of the Revolution in their textbook, choose a Revolutionary leader as their inductee into the Hall of Fame, and then create and display their posters.

Technology Extension

Online Interactive Multimedia Posters
Posters allow students to present information in a visual medium by incorporating text, images, and color. By creating online posters, students can add multimedia (audio and video) and incorporate hyperlinks to additional Web sites that relate to their presentation topic. Interactivity makes the poster much more dynamic than a traditional two-dimensional presentation.

edtechteacher
21st Century Learning

ANSWERS, p. 110

Step Into the Place
1. the southern colonies
2. Spanish Louisiana
3. **CRITICAL THINKING** The movement was most likely strongest in New England, especially Massachusetts and Connecticut, because the map shows that the greatest concentration of protests occurred in those colonies.

Step Into the Time
Louis XVI became king of France.

networks
There's More Online!
☑ **MAP** Explore the interactive version of this map on NETWORKS.
☑ **TIME LINE** Explore the interactive version of this time line on NETWORKS.

HUDSON'S BAY COMPANY

BLACKFOOT

CROW

DAKOTA SIOUX

YANKTONAI

SANTEE

CHEYENNE

Lake Superior

OJIBWA

WINNEBAGO

Lake Michigan

POTAWATOMI

Lake Huron

Province of Québec

Lake Ontario

Lake Erie

ERIE

• Québec

• Montréal

Nova Scotia • Halifax

N.H.

New York Mass. • Boston

R.I.

Conn.

• New York

N.J.

• Philadelphia

Md. Del.

Pa.

IROQUOIS

ARAPAHO

IOWA

Missouri R.

ILLINOIS BRITISH TERRITORY

Ohio R.

UTE

NAVAJO

SPANISH LOUISIANA

• St. Louis

SHAWNEE

Virginia • Williamsburg

North Carolina

KIOWA

OSAGE

Arkansas R.

CHICKASAW

Indian Reserve

CHEROKEE

CATAWBA

South Carolina

• Wilmington

ATLANTIC OCEAN

Red R.

WICHITA

CADDO

COMANCHE

Bravos R.

Rio Grande

MESCALERO

NATCHEZ

CHOCTAW

• Natchez

West Florida

• Pensacola

MUSKOGEE

Georgia

YAMASEE

• Charleston

• Savannah

• New Orleans

TIMUCUA

• St. Augustine

Florida

CALUSA

Gulf of Mexico

90°W   80°W   70°W

60°N

50°N

40°N

30°N

50°W

1770 Boston Massacre occurs

1773 Boston Tea Party takes place

1774 First Continental Congress meets

1775 Battles of Lexington and Concord occur

1776 Colonies issue the Declaration of Independence

1769 **R2** 1772 1775 1778

1769 James Watt introduces his steam engine

1770 James Cook explores coast of Australia

1772 Poland divided among Russia, Prussia, and Austria

1774 Louis XVI becomes king of France

111

Step Into the Time

R2 Reading Skills

Explaining Ask students to note the listing on the time line for 1772 about the division of Poland. **Ask: What might American colonists have thought about the division of Poland?** (Possible answer: They might have identified with the Polish people being ruled by another country instead of being independent.) **BL**

V2 Visual Skills

Analyzing Maps Direct students to the tax protests shown on this map. **Ask: What do all these protests have in common? Use the map to help you answer the question.** (They all took place along the coast.) **Why do you think that might be?** (Answers will vary but should include the idea that taxes on imports and exports would be important in port cities.) **BL** Visual/Spatial

CLOSE & REFLECT

To close the lesson, ask students to study the map and share what it indicates about where they live — whether it was British or Spanish territory, or near the site of an early colonial protest.

MAP

North America 1775

Location Project the Chapter Opener map of North America on the whiteboard. Point out the map key and review its use. Have students read and identify what each symbol stands for. Discuss that the map shows the regions of colonial protest. Have volunteers match each key symbol with its location on the map and explain what each symbol stands for. **Ask: What does the map tell you about the spirit of independence in the colonies by 1775?** (There was strong Patriot support in every colony and protests over British taxes in most of them.) As a class, discuss the Map Focus questions. **AL** Visual/Spatial

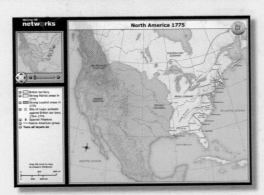

See page 109B for other online activities.

ENGAGE

🔔 **Bellringer** To help students understand why the American colonists began to resent the British and their tax policies, ask students how some people today react to taxes. **Ask:** How are people's reactions to taxes today similar to what colonists felt? *(Many people dislike paying taxes, whether those taxes are justified or not.)* Tell students that the colonists in America believed they should have a say in the taxes they had to pay.

TEACH & ASSESS

W Writing Skills

Informative/Explanatory Have students review the Guiding Question. Organize them into small groups, and have them read the first section of the chapter aloud, with each student reading one sentence. Then direct students to write a short paragraph that explains why the British government issued the Proclamation of 1763. `AL` `ELL`

R Reading Skills

Listing Have students review the text to list the three benefits the British expected to gain from the Proclamation of 1763. **Ask:** What do these three benefits have in common? *(They made it easier for the British government to control what happened in the colonies.)* Why might the colonists be angry about this? *(The Proclamation benefited only the British government, while the colonists were restricted.)* `AL`

ANSWER, p. 112

TAKING NOTES: Policy: Sugar Act; **View:** Writs of assistance violated colonists' security in their homes, and new trial procedures violated their right to be considered "innocent until proven guilty." **Policy:** Stamp Act; **View:** Parliament had no right to tax colonists directly or without their consent. **Policy:** Townshend Acts; **View:** Only colonial representatives had the right to tax the colonists.

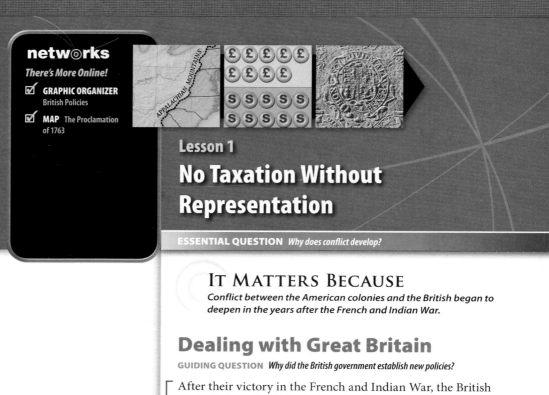

net⊚rks
There's More Online!

☑ **GRAPHIC ORGANIZER**
British Policies

☑ **MAP** The Proclamation of 1763

Lesson 1
No Taxation Without Representation

ESSENTIAL QUESTION *Why does conflict develop?*

IT MATTERS BECAUSE
Conflict between the American colonies and the British began to deepen in the years after the French and Indian War.

Dealing with Great Britain

GUIDING QUESTION *Why did the British government establish new policies?*

After their victory in the French and Indian War, the British controlled much of North America. Now they had to protect all this territory. To meet this challenge, King George III issued the Proclamation of 1763. This order **prohibited**, or barred, colonists from living west of the Appalachian Mountains, on Native American land. For the British, the proclamation offered several advantages. It helped keep peace between Native Americans and settlers. It also kept colonists near the Atlantic Coast, where British authority was stronger. Finally, it allowed Britain to control westward expansion and the fur trade in the region. The king sent 10,000 troops to the colonies to enforce the Proclamation of 1763 and keep the peace with Native Americans.

Enforcing Trade Laws

Great Britain needed new **revenue**, or income, to pay for the troops. The British also had large debts from the French and Indian War. The king and Parliament felt the colonists should pay part of these

(t) The Granger Collection, NYC

Reading HELPDESK (CCSS)

Taking Notes: *Identifying* RH.6–8.1, RH.6–8.7
As you read, identify British policies that affected the colonists. Record each policy in a chart like this one. Then record the colonists' views of each policy.

British Policy		Colonists' View
	→	
	→	
	→	

Content Vocabulary (Tier 3 Words)
- revenue
- writ of assistance
- resolution
- effigy
- boycott
- repeal

112 *The Spirit of Independence*

---

net⊚rks *Online Teaching Options*

VIDEO

British Tyranny in Boston

Explaining Show the Learn360 video about the Stamp Act. Discuss with students the passage of the Stamp Act and why it was opposed. **Ask:** What did the Stamp Act tax? *(all printed materials, including newspapers, wills, and playing cards)* How did the colonists react to the Stamp Act? *(They opposed it.)* `AL`

Discuss the resolution that the House of Burgesses passed. Call on volunteers to explain how this resolution was related to the idea of "No Taxation Without Representation." `BL`

See page 109C for other online activities.

costs, so the British government issued new taxes on the colonies. It also enforced old taxes more strictly. To avoid taxes, some colonists resorted to smuggling. This caused British revenues to fall.

In 1763 Britain's prime minister, George Grenville, set out to stop the smuggling. Parliament passed a law to have accused smugglers tried by royally appointed judges rather than local juries. Grenville knew that American juries often found smugglers innocent. Parliament also empowered customs officers to obtain **writs of assistance**. These documents allowed the officers to search almost anywhere—shops, warehouses, and even private homes—for smuggled goods.

The Sugar Act

In 1764 Parliament passed the Sugar Act, which lowered the tax on the molasses the colonists imported. Grenville hoped this change would convince the colonists to pay the tax instead of smuggling. The act also allowed officers to seize goods from accused smugglers without going to court.

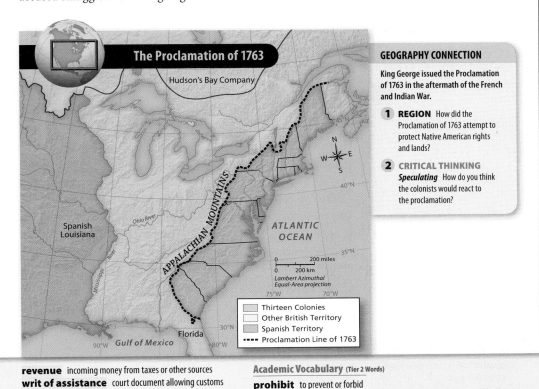

The Proclamation of 1763

GEOGRAPHY CONNECTION

King George issued the Proclamation of 1763 in the aftermath of the French and Indian War.

1. **REGION** How did the Proclamation of 1763 attempt to protect Native American rights and lands?

2. **CRITICAL THINKING** *Speculating* How do you think the colonists would react to the proclamation?

Thirteen Colonies
Other British Territory
Spanish Territory
---- Proclamation Line of 1763

revenue incoming money from taxes or other sources
writ of assistance court document allowing customs officers to enter any location to search for smuggled goods

Academic Vocabulary (Tier 2 Words)

prohibit to prevent or forbid

Lesson 1 **113**

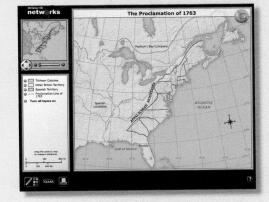

V Visual Skills

Analyzing Charts Use the chart about the growing debt to discuss the financial consequences of the French and Indian War. **Ask:** Why did Britain need to raise money? *(to pay for troops and to repay a big debt from the war)* How did Britain plan to raise the revenue it needed? *(by taxing the colonists)* Why did British leaders believe that this policy was "fair"? *(because the colonists' share of the debt was much smaller than the British people's share, while the war had been fought in the colonies and for the colonists)* **BL** Visual/Spatial

R Reading Skills

Paraphrasing Have students read the quote from *The Rights of the British Colonies* and then rewrite it in their own words. **AL** **ELL**

C Critical Thinking Skills

Comparing and Contrasting Remind students that the Stamp Act came after the Sugar Act. **Ask:** How are the Stamp Act and the Sugar Act similar? *(Answers may vary. Sample answers: They are both taxes, they were both used to raise money for the British, they both made the colonists angry.)* Then ask: How are they different? *(Answers may vary. Sample answers: One is a tax on goods, the other is a tax on documents; one was aimed at smugglers, the other was aimed at anybody who needed paper or official documents.)* **BL**

Content Background Knowledge

The Sugar Act did more than just tax sugar and molasses. It also restricted the trade of specific goods, such as lumber. Before the law, the colonists could trade those goods with any country. After the law was enacted, they could sell those goods *only* to Britain. This limited the colonists' market and gave Britain more control over the cost of goods from the Americas.

ANSWERS, p. 114

ECONOMICS SKILL

1. The average citizen in Britain paid 17 pounds (or 340 shillings); colonists paid an average of 18 shillings (less than 1 pound).
2. **CRITICAL THINKING** They paid taxes to the British government.

☑ **PROGRESS CHECK** to convince the colonists to pay the lower tax on imported molasses rather than smuggle it and to allow officials to seize goods from smugglers without a trial

---

V

ECONOMICS SKILL

1 **CALCULATING** Did British or colonial subjects pay more toward the debt? What was the difference in pounds and shillings?

2 **CRITICAL THINKING**
Identifying Central Issues
How did residents of Britain and the American colonists pay their shares of the debt?

A GROWING DEBT

Share of the debt per person:

Britain: £ £ £ £ £ £ £ £ £ £ £ £ £ £ £ £ £

Colonies: S S S S S S S S S S S S S S S S

£ = 1 British pound   S = 1 British shilling
1 Pound (£) = 20 Shillings

Great Britain's national debt soared as a result of the French and Indian War. Subjects living in Great Britain paid more on this debt per person than people living in the colonies. British efforts to get colonists to pay a bigger share of war-related debt led to sharp conflict.

Source: Don Cook. *The Long Fuse: How England Lost the American Colonies, 1760–1785*

The Sugar Act angered many colonists. They believed this and other new laws **violated** their rights. As British citizens, colonists argued, they had a right to a trial by jury and to be viewed as innocent until proved guilty, as stated in British law. Colonists also believed they had the right to be secure in their homes—without the threat of officers barging in to search for smuggled goods.

British taxes also alarmed the colonists. James Otis, a lawyer in Boston, argued:

PRIMARY SOURCE

❝ No parts of [England's colonies] can be taxed without their consent ... every part has a right to be represented. ❞

—from *The Rights of the British Colonies*, 1763

☑ **PROGRESS CHECK**

Explaining Why did Parliament pass the Sugar Act?

New Taxes on the Colonies

GUIDING QUESTION *How did the American colonists react to British policies?*

In 1765 Parliament passed the Stamp Act. This law taxed almost all printed materials. Newspapers, wills, and even playing cards needed a stamp to show that the tax had been paid.

Opposition to the Stamp Act

The Stamp Act outraged the colonists. They argued that only their own assemblies could tax them. Patrick Henry, a member of the Virginia House of Burgesses, got the burgesses to take

Reading HELPDESK (CCSS)

resolution an official expression of opinion by a group
effigy a mocking figure representing an unpopular individual

boycott to refuse to buy items in order to show disapproval or force acceptance of one's terms
repeal to cancel an act or law

Academic Vocabulary (Tier 2 Words)
violate to disregard or go against

114 *The Spirit of Independence*

---

netw⊙rks   *Online Teaching Options*

WHITEBOARD ACTIVITY

Taxation Without Representation

Comparing and Contrasting Use the interactive whiteboard activity about taxation without representation to compare and contrast the different acts passed by the British. **Ask:** What do all the acts have in common? *(They all have to do with taxes.)* How was the Stamp Act different from the Sugar Act and Townshend Acts? *(The Sugar Act and Townshend Acts were taxes on imports.)* **AL** **ELL** Why might the British have believed the colonists would accept the Townshend Acts? *(Students should realize that unlike the Stamp Act, which was an internal tax, the Townshend Acts were taxes on trade.)* **BL**

See page 109C for other online activities.

Directions: Read each statement. Then drag and drop the statement to the correct column in the table.

	The Stamp Act	The Sugar Act	The Townshend Acts
Taxed glass, tea, and paper			
An internal tax within the colonies that raised money for Britain			
Tax applied only to imported goods			
Lowered tax on imported molasses			
Taxed most printed materials			
Allowed officers to seize goods from accused smugglers without going to court			
Tax paid at port of entry			
Stamp was applied when tax was paid			
Attempted to reduce smuggling of molasses from non-British colonies			

action. The assembly passed a **resolution**—a formal expression of opinion—declaring that it had "the only and sole exclusive right and power to lay taxes" on its citizens.

In Boston, Samuel Adams helped start the Sons of Liberty. Its members took to the streets to protest the Stamp Act. Protesters burned **effigies** (EH·fuh·jeez)—stuffed figures—made to look like unpopular tax collectors.

Colonial leaders decided to work together. In October, delegates from nine colonies met in New York at the Stamp Act Congress. They sent a statement to the king and Parliament declaring that only colonial assemblies could tax the colonists.

People in colonial cities urged merchants to **boycott**—refuse to buy—British goods in protest. As the boycott spread, businesses in Britain lost so much money that they demanded Parliament **repeal**, or cancel, the Stamp Act. In March 1766, Parliament repealed the law. However, it also passed the Declaratory Act, stating that it had the right to tax and make decisions for the British colonies "in all cases."

The Townshend Acts

The Stamp Act taught the British that the colonists would resist internal taxes—those paid inside the colonies. As a result, in 1767 Parliament passed the Townshend Acts to tax imported goods, such as glass, tea, and paper. The tax was paid when the goods arrived—before they were brought inside the colonies.

By then, *any* British taxes angered the colonists. Protests of the Townshend Acts began immediately. In towns throughout the colonies, women protested by supporting another boycott of British goods. They also urged colonists to wear homemade fabrics rather than buying fabric made in Britain. Some women's groups called themselves the Daughters of Liberty.

☑ **PROGRESS CHECK**

Contrasting How did the Townshend Acts differ from the Stamp Act?

A British government official placed this seal, or stamp, on certain paper items in the colonies to show that the tax on them had been paid.

The Granger Collection, NYC

LESSON 1 REVIEW (CCSS)

Review Vocabulary (Tier 3 Words)

1. Write a paragraph about the 1760s in the American colonies in which you use these vocabulary words: RH.6–8.4, WHST.6–8.4

   a. revenue   b. resolution   c. effigy
   d. boycott   e. repeal

Answer the Guiding Questions

2. ***Describing*** What advantages did the British hope to gain by limiting westward settlement in 1763? RH.6–8.2

3. ***Explaining*** Why did some colonists smuggle goods in the 1760s? RH.6–8.2

4. ***Identifying*** Why did colonists oppose the Stamp Act? RH.6–8.2

5. **NARRATIVE** Write a conversation between two colonists who disagree over Britain taxing the colonies to help pay off its debts from the French and Indian War. WHST.6–8.1, WHST.6–8.10

Lesson 1   **115**

LESSON 1 REVIEW ANSWERS

1. Possible answer: In an effort to raise revenue, Britain began to impose new taxes on the colonies. This caused widespread protest. Colonial legislatures passed resolutions against the taxes. Colonists burned effigies of tax collectors and organized boycotts of British goods. Parliament repealed some of the taxes.

2. to avoid conflict with Native Americans, keep colonists where British authority was stronger, and control the fur trade

3. Colonists smuggled imported goods to avoid paying taxes on them.

4. They argued that they could be directly taxed only by their own assemblies.

5. Answers will vary; students should express both sides of the argument in their dialogues.

C1 Critical Thinking Skills

Analyzing Discuss the formation of groups to protest British policies. **Ask: Why do you think Samuel Adams and others formed the Sons of Liberty instead of just acting alone to express anger at the British policies?** (*Possible answers: They could build a stronger resistance because there is strength in numbers. A group has a louder, more forceful voice than one person.*) **BL**

C2 Critical Thinking Skills

Discussing Discuss with students the passage of the Townshend Acts. **Ask: What did the Townshend Acts do?** (*They taxed imported goods such as glass, tea, and paper. The tax was paid before the goods entered the colonies.*) **How did the colonists protest these acts?** (*They boycotted British goods and wore homemade fabrics. Women formed a group called the Daughters of Liberty to protest.*) **AL**

W Writing Skills

Narrative Ask students to write a letter to a relative from the point of view of an American merchant, soldier, or farmer living in colonial times. In their letters, have students describe the Stamp Act or the Townshend Acts and reflect on how these acts specifically affected them in their particular occupation. **BL** **Verbal/Linguistic**

Have students complete the Lesson 1 Review.

CLOSE & REFLECT

To close the lesson, ask students to think about which changes in British policy would have angered them the most if they had lived in the colonies at that time. They should discuss their answers and their reasons.

ANSWER, p. 115

☑ **PROGRESS CHECK** The Stamp Act tax was paid inside the colonies; the Townshend Acts applied taxes only to imported goods, to be paid at the port of entry.

ENGAGE

🔔 **Bellringer** Discuss with students the economic challenges that the colonists were facing and how they would feel toward the British if they were colonists. Tell students that they will learn in this lesson how tensions with Britain united the colonists.

TEACH & ASSESS

R Reading Skills

Citing Text Evidence Have students cite text evidence that demonstrates that tensions continued to grow between the British and the colonists. **Ask: Why did Boston colonists think the British soldiers had gone too far?** *(The soldiers set up camp in occupied colonial cities, stole goods, fought with locals, and competed for colonial jobs.)* **AL**

C Critical Thinking Skills

Making Inferences Remind students that the colonists were still British citizens. **Ask: Why do you think the colonists were angry about the encampment in the center of Boston?** *(because their own government was sending the army against them)* **Why do you think the British army set up camp where it did?** *(Answers may vary. Sample answers: to show that they controlled the city; to be able to reach any trouble spots quickly)* **BL**

Content Background Knowledge

Colonial Boston was one of the oldest and most important cities in the American colonies. A center of learning, shipping, and trade, control of Boston had great symbolic value for both the British and the colonists.

ANSWER, p. 116

TAKING NOTES: Any three of the following are acceptable: closed Boston Harbor; other colonies unified to support Boston; town meetings were banned; Bostonians were forced to shelter British soldiers.

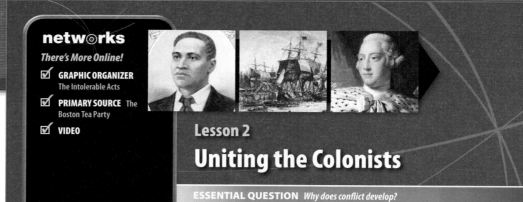

netw⊙rks
There's More Online!

☑ **GRAPHIC ORGANIZER** The Intolerable Acts

☑ **PRIMARY SOURCE** The Boston Tea Party

☑ **VIDEO**

Lesson 2
Uniting the Colonists

ESSENTIAL QUESTION *Why does conflict develop?*

IT MATTERS BECAUSE

Harsh British actions aimed at controlling the colonies united them instead.

Trouble in Massachusetts

GUIDING QUESTION *How did the American colonists react to the Boston Massacre?*

Protests continued to flare in the colonies, making British officials nervous. In 1768 they sent word to Britain that the colonies were on the brink of **rebellion**—a rejection of British authority. Parliament sent troops to Boston. As angry colonists jeered, the "redcoats" set up camp in the center of the city.

For many colonists, this British act went too far. First the colonists were convinced that the British had passed laws that violated colonial rights. Now Britain had sent an army to **occupy,** or take control of, colonial cities.

To make matters worse, the soldiers in Boston acted rudely. The redcoats, who were mostly poor men, earned little pay. Some stole from local shops and got into fights with colonists. Also, in their off-hours, the soldiers competed for jobs that Bostonians wanted.

Tension in the Streets

On March 5, 1770, violence erupted. A fight broke out between some Bostonians and soldiers. As British officers tried to calm the crowd, a man shouted, "We did not send for you. We will not have you here. We'll get rid of you, we'll drive you away!"

(l) Library of Congress [LC-DIG-ppmsca-15704], (c) Time & Life Pictures/Getty Images (r) Apic/Hulton Archive/Getty Images

---

Reading HELPDESK **CCSS**

Taking Notes: *Describing* RH.6–8.1
As you read, use a diagram like this one to record how the Intolerable Acts changed life for the colonists.

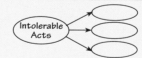

Intolerable Acts

Content Vocabulary (Tier 3 Words)
• **rebellion**
• **propaganda**
• **committee of correspondence**

116 *The Spirit of Independence*

---

netw⊙rks *Online Teaching Options*

VIDEO

The Boston Massacre and Escalating Anger in the Colonies

Connecting Show the Learn360 video about the Boston Massacre and colonists' anger. Discuss the video and how the event might have affected the colonists' attitudes toward British authority. Clarify any unfamiliar terms or concepts. **AL** **ELL**

See page 109D for other online activities.

The angry townspeople surged forward. They began throwing sticks and stones at the soldiers. "Come on, you rascals, you bloody backs, you lobster scoundrels, fire, if you dare," someone in the crowd shouted.

After one soldier was knocked down, the nervous redcoats did fire. They killed five colonists. Among the dead was Crispus Attucks, a dockworker who was part African, part Native American. One Bostonian cried: "Are the inhabitants to be knocked down in the streets? Are they to be murdered ... ?" The colonists called the tragic **encounter** "the Boston Massacre."

Spreading the News

Colonial leaders used the killings as **propaganda**—information designed to influence opinion. Samuel Adams put up posters that described the Boston Massacre as a slaughter of innocent Americans by bloodthirsty redcoats. Paul Revere made an engraving that showed a British officer giving the order to open fire on an orderly crowd.

The Boston Massacre led colonists to call for stronger boycotts of British goods. Troubled by the growing opposition in the colonies, Parliament repealed all the Townshend Acts taxes on British imported goods, except the one on tea. In response, the colonists ended their boycotts, except on tea. Trade with Britain resumed.

Still, some colonists continued to call for resistance to British rule. In 1772 Samuel Adams revived the Boston **committee of correspondence**, a group used in earlier protests. The group circulated calls for action against Britain. Soon committees of correspondence sprang up throughout the colonies, bringing together protesters opposed to British measures.

☑ **PROGRESS CHECK**

Explaining How did the Boston Massacre affect the relations between the colonists and Britain?

Crisis in Boston

GUIDING QUESTION *How did the British government react to the actions of the colonists?*

The British East India Company was vital to the British economy. Colonial refusal to import British East India tea had nearly driven the company out of business. To help save the company and protect the British economy, Parliament passed the Tea Act.

Crispus Attucks was the first colonist killed by the British in the Boston Massacre.

C2

C1

Library of Congress [LC-DIG-ppmsca-15704]

C1 Critical Thinking Skills

Making Connections Discuss the growing tensions between Britain and the colonists that resulted from the Boston Massacre. Discuss how the colonists used propaganda to influence opinion about the Boston Massacre. **Ask:** How did the Boston Massacre affect British policies and relations between the two sides? *(Fearing more trouble, Parliament repealed the Townshend Acts taxes, except on tea, and the colonists ended their boycotts, except of tea.)* **AL**

C2 Critical Thinking Skills

Recognizing Bias Review the meaning of the word propaganda with students. Explain that when colonists called the deaths a "massacre," rather than a more neutral word, they were seeking to sway opinion. As a class, ask students to suggest more neutral ways to describe the event. Then ask them for ways to describe it that would indicate bias for the British. **BL** **Verbal/Linguistic**

Then discuss Samuel Adams's reaction. **Ask:** What was Samuel Adams's reaction to the Boston Massacre? *(He revived the Boston committee of correspondence.)* How did this help to spread propaganda against Great Britain? *(Committees shared writings about concerns, and many colonists read and were influenced by the anti-British opinions.)* **BL**

rebellion open defiance of authority	**Academic Vocabulary** (Tier 2)	**Build Vocabulary:** *Multiple Meaning Words*
propaganda ideas or information intentionally spread to harm or help a cause	**occupy** to move into and take control of a place, especially by force	As a verb, the word *encounter* means "to come across or meet." As a noun, *encounter* can mean "a chance meeting" or "a sudden, often violent, meeting between hostile people."
committee of correspondence an organization that spread political ideas and information through the colonies	**encounter** a sudden, often violent clash	Lesson 2 **117**

BIOGRAPHY

Crispus Attucks

Discussing Use the interactive image of Crispus Attucks, a victim in the Boston Massacre, to discuss with students how the massacre began and the end results. **Ask:** How did the Boston Massacre begin? *(as a fight between Bostonians and British soldiers)* Who was Crispus Attucks? *(He was one of the five victims; a dockworker who was part African, part Native American.)* Tell students that John Adams, a lawyer and future Founder, defended the British soldiers in their trial. **Ask:** Why do you think Adams defended them? *(because even though he might not have agreed with their actions, he believed they deserved a fair trial)* **BL**

See page 109D for other online activities.

McGraw-Hill **netw⊙rks**   Crispus Attucks
BIOGRAPHY

Crispus Attucks
Little is known about Crispus Attucks, but it is thought that he probably spent much of his life aboard whaling ships. During the Boston Massacre on March 5, 1770, Attucks was among the first to fall. He therefore became one of the first men to die for the cause of American independence. On March 8, Attucks and the others killed with him were buried in a common grave.

Library of Congress/ LC-DIG-ppmsca-15704

ANSWER, p. 117

☑ **PROGRESS CHECK** Anger over the Boston Massacre prompted colonists to boycott British goods, which led Britain to repeal all but one of the Townshend Acts' taxes and drove more colonists to call for resistance to British rule.

V

V Visual Skills

Analyzing images Direct students to the painting of the Boston Tea Party. **Ask: What is being shown in this painting?** (angry colonists cheering the Sons of Liberty throwing tea into Boston Harbor) **How can you tell the ships are British?** (The flags are British.) Tell students that artists often place the focus of a painting in the front, or foreground. **Ask: What is in the foreground of this painting?** (cheering colonists) **What does that tell you about the artist's possible point of view?** (The point of view is sympathetic toward the colonists.) **BL** Visual/Spatial

R Reading Skills

Explaining Have students use evidence from the text to explain the importance of the Tea Act. **Ask: Why was the Tea Act passed?** (to try to force colonists to buy British East India Company tea to keep the company from failing) **What did the act do?** (It gave the company almost total control of the tea market in the colonies. It lowered the tax on tea so colonists would buy it.) **How did the Daughters of Liberty react?** (They stopped drinking tea.) **AL**

C Critical Thinking Skills

Collaborating Organize the class into small groups. Assign each group to role-play one of the major players in the Boston Tea Party: the East India Company, the British government, the angry colonists, and the Sons of Liberty. Instruct each group to work together to determine how they will dramatize their part of the story. Then have the students act out the Boston Tea Party. **BL** Kinesthetic

Colonists angry at the restrictions of the Tea Act staged a dramatic protest. They threw three shiploads of British tea into Boston Harbor.

▶ **CRITICAL THINKING**
Analyzing Why were American colonists especially angry with the Tea Act?

R

It gave the company nearly total control of the market for tea in the colonies. The Tea Act also removed some—but not all—of the taxes on tea, making it less expensive for colonists. Yet the colonists remained angry. They did not want to pay any tax, and they did not want to be told what tea they could buy.

Colonial merchants called for a new boycott. Colonists vowed to stop East India Company ships from unloading. The Daughters of Liberty issued a pamphlet declaring that rather than part with freedom, "We'll part with our tea."

A Tea Party

C

Despite warnings of trouble, the East India Company continued shipping tea to the colonies. Colonists in New York and Philadelphia forced the tea ships to turn back. In 1773, three ships loaded with tea arrived in Boston Harbor. The royal governor ordered that they be unloaded. The Boston Sons of Liberty acted swiftly. At midnight on December 16, colonists dressed as Native Americans boarded the ships and threw 342 chests of tea overboard. As word of the "Boston Tea Party"

Time & Life Pictures/Getty Images

Reading HELPDESK (CCSS)

Reading Strategy: *Determining Cause and Effect*

A cause is an event or action that makes something else happen. That something else that happens is an effect. Determining causes and effects can help you see relationships between events and find patterns in history. As you read, identify one cause and one effect of the Boston Tea Party.

118 *The Spirit of Independence*

networks *Online Teaching Options*

The Boston Tea Party

Analyzing Primary Sources Use the primary source excerpt from George Hewes to discuss the Boston Tea Party. **What was the Boston Tea Party?** (Colonists opposed to the Tea Act destroyed three shiploads of tea by throwing the tea into Boston Harbor.) **Who owned the tea that was destroyed?** (the British East India Company) **Who threw it overboard?** (members of the Boston Sons of Liberty disguised as Native Americans) **AL**

Why did they do this? (They resented the advantage the British gave this company over colonial tea sellers.) **BL**

See page 109D for other online activities.

McGraw-Hill **networks** The Boston Tea Party
ANALYZING PRIMARY SOURCES

During what became known as the Boston Tea Party, American patriots boarded ships and threw 342 chests of tea belonging to the British East India Company into Boston Harbor. The Americans were protesting taxation without representation and a monopoly by the East India Company.

Time & Life Pictures/Getty Images

❝ It was now evening, and I immediately dressed myself in the costume of [a Native American], equipped with a small hatchet . . . [A]fter having painted my face and hands with coal dust in the shop of a blacksmith, I repaired to Griffin's wharf, where the ships lay that contained the tea. . . . I fell in with many who were dressed, equipped and painted as I was. . . . ❞

—from *George Hewes account of the Boston Tea Party,* by George Hewes

ANSWERS, p. 118

CRITICAL THINKING The colonists were angry about the Tea Act because they did not want to pay any tax or be told what they could buy.

Reading Strategy Possible answer: **Cause** – Britain gave nearly total control of the market for tea to the British East India Company; **Effect** – Parliament passed the Coercive Acts.

spread, colonists gathered to celebrate the bold act. Yet no one spoke out against British rule itself. Most colonists still saw themselves as loyal British citizens.

The Intolerable Acts

W

When news of the Boston Tea Party reached London, King George III realized that Britain was losing control of the colonies. He declared, "We must either master them or totally leave them to themselves."

In 1774 Parliament responded by passing a series of laws called the Coercive Acts. *Coercive* (co•UHR•sihv) means to force someone to do something. These laws were meant to punish the colonists for resisting British authority. One Coercive Act applied to all the colonies. It forced the colonies to let British soldiers live among the colonists. Massachusetts, though, received the harshest treatment.

One of the Coercive Acts banned town meetings in Massachusetts. Another closed Boston Harbor until the colonists paid for the ruined tea. This stopped most shipments of food and other supplies to the colony. Parliament was trying to cut Massachusetts off from the other colonies. Instead, the Coercive Acts drew the colonies together. Other colonies sent food and clothing to support Boston.

C

Following the Coercive Acts, Parliament also passed the Quebec Act. This law created a government for Canada and extended its territory south all the way to the Ohio River. This action ignored the colonies' claims to that region.

The colonists believed all of these new laws violated their rights as English citizens. They expressed their feelings about the laws by calling them the Intolerable Acts. *Intolerable* means painful and unbearable.

Apic/Hulton Archive/Getty Images

☑ **PROGRESS CHECK**

Summarizing List the effects of the Coercive Acts on the citizens of Boston.

King George's determination to take a firm stand against the colonies after the Boston Tea Party failed to resolve the growing crisis. In fact, colonial anger grew.

Evaluating Explore a series of probing questions with students. **Ask: Why did Britain pass these laws?** *(to punish the colonies for resisting British authority)* **Why was Massachusetts singled out for especially harsh treatment?** *(It was a center of resistance to British rule and because of the Boston Tea Party.)* **BL** **Why did the British close Boston Harbor?** *(to keep ships from bringing in goods until the destroyed tea was paid for)* **What democratic right did the Coercive Acts take away from Massachusetts colonists?** *(the colonists' right to hold town meetings)* **Ask: What was the name by which colonists called the Coercive Acts?** *(the Intolerable Acts)* **Why? AL ELL Interpersonal**

W Writing Skills

Argument Have students write a short speech designed to persuade people to resist the Intolerable Acts. Instruct them to use both persuasive language and facts to back up their arguments. Invite volunteers to deliver their speeches to the class. **BL Auditory/Musical**

Have students complete the Lesson 2 Review.

CLOSE & REFLECT

To close the lesson, have students recall what they learned about Crispus Attucks. Then ask students to reflect on why he is still remembered today and his importance as an early American.

ANSWER, p. 119

☑ **PROGRESS CHECK** As a result of the Coercive Acts, the citizens of Boston had limited access to food and supplies that arrived by ship, town meetings were banned, and they had to provide shelter for British soldiers.

Review Vocabulary (Tier 3 Words)

1. Explain the significance of the following terms:
   RH.6–8.4
   a. rebellion **b.** propaganda
   c. committee of correspondence

Answer the Guiding Questions

2. *Sequencing* List the events leading up to and following the Boston Massacre in the order that they occurred.
   RH.6–8.5

3. *Analyzing* How did Samuel Adams and Paul Revere use propaganda to rally colonists after the Boston Massacre? RH.6–8.1

4. *Explaining* How did the British punish the colonists for the Boston Tea Party? RH.6–8.2

5. **NARRATIVE** Write an account of the Boston Massacre from the point of view of a British soldier involved in the event. WHST.6–8.1, WHST.6–8.9

LESSON 2 REVIEW ANSWERS

1. Possible answer: **a.** *Rebellion* means the rejection or the fight against authority, and it describes what the British feared the colonists were preparing for. **b.** *Propaganda* is information designed to encourage a particular view; an example is the handling of reports about the Boston Massacre. **c.** *Committees of correspondence* were groups of colonists in different colonies who called for action against the British and shared political ideas with each other.

2. Wording will vary but events in order are: 1. British troops were stationed in Boston. 2. Some soldiers were rude or fought with residents. 3. On March 5, 1770, a fight broke out between the soldiers and residents of Boston. 4. Nervous soldiers fired on the crowd. 5. Five colonists were killed. 6. Colonial leaders used the event to influence public opinion and unify colonists.

3. They portrayed the Boston Massacre as a deliberate British slaughter of innocent colonists. This heightened colonial resistance to British laws that colonists considered unjust.

4. It gave the British East India Company nearly total control of the tea market in the colonies, limiting citizens' choices. It also removed some taxes on tea, but the colonists did not want to pay any tax on tea.

5. Students' narratives should include information about the angry crowd, the soldiers' attempts to calm the crowd, and the soldiers' fear and nervousness.

ENGAGE

Bellringer Ask students to think of some causes or issues they are passionate about. Have them share their thoughts and tell what actions they have taken to bring about change in these areas. Tell students that in this lesson they will learn what some passionate colonists did to bring about change in the relationship between the colonies and Great Britain.

TEACH & ASSESS

R Reading Skills

Identifying Ask students to read the section titled "A Meeting in Philadelphia." Then ask students to identify the organization of the First Continental Congress and the delegates who were asked to join. **Ask: Which colony was not represented?** *(Georgia)* **Who were some of the important delegates?** *(Students' answers may include John Adams, Samuel Adams, John Jay, George Washington, Richard Henry Lee, and Patrick Henry.)* **AL**

C Critical Thinking Skills

Recognizing Relationships Have students recall what they have learned about how some of these individuals were involved in the earlier troubles between the colonies and Britain. *(Samuel Adams with the Sons of Liberty, Patrick Henry in the Virginia House of Burgesses, John Adams in the trial of the Boston Massacre)* **AL**

ANSWER, p. 120

TAKING NOTES: drafted a statement of grievances calling for a repeal of 13 laws; voted to boycott trade with Britain; endorsed resolutions calling for people to arm themselves against the British

---

networks

There's More Online!

☑ **BIOGRAPHY**
Patrick Henry

☑ **GRAPHIC ORGANIZER**
Key Actions of the Continental Congress

☑ **MAP** Battles of Lexington and Concord

Lesson 3

A Call to Arms

ESSENTIAL QUESTION *What motivates people to act?*

IT MATTERS BECAUSE

As anger toward the British grew, Americans began to consider the possibility of independence.

A Meeting in Philadelphia

GUIDING QUESTION *What role did key individuals play in the movement toward independence?*

In September 1774, fifty-five delegates gathered in Philadelphia. They had come to set up a political body that would represent Americans and challenge British control. The delegates called this body the Continental Congress.

Leaders from twelve of the thirteen colonies attended the meeting. Only Georgia did not send a representative. Massachusetts sent fiery Samuel Adams and his lawyer cousin, John Adams. New York sent John Jay, another lawyer. Virginia sent George Washington as well as Richard Henry Lee and Patrick Henry, two outspoken defenders of colonial rights. Patrick Henry wanted the colonies to unite in firm resistance to Britain. He summed up the meaning of the meeting when he addressed the delegates on its second day:

PRIMARY SOURCE

❝ The distinctions between Virginians, Pennsylvanians, New Yorkers, and New Englanders are no more. I am not a Virginian, but an American. ❞

—Patrick Henry, at the Continental Congress, 1774

Reading **HELP**DESK **CCSS**

Taking Notes: *Summarizing* RH.6–8.2
As you read, use a diagram like this one to list three key actions of the Continental Congress.

Continental Congress

Content Vocabulary (Tier 3 Words)
• **minuteman**
• **Loyalist**
• **Patriot**

120   *The Spirit of Independence*

---

networks *Online Teaching Options*

VIDEO

Boston Tea Party and the Intolerable Acts

Determining Cause and Effect Show the Learn360 video about the Boston Tea Party and the Intolerable Acts. Afterward, have students draw diagrams that show the chain of cause and effect between the tea tax, the Boston Tea Party, and the new, harsher treatment from the British. **AL** **ELL**

See page 109E for other online activities.

The Delegates Vote

The delegates discussed complaints against the British. Then they voted. In a statement of grievances, the delegates called for the repeal of 13 acts of Parliament. They believed these laws violated the "laws of nature, the principles of the English constitution, and the several charters" of the colonies. The delegates also voted to boycott British trade. The colonies would not import or use any British goods, nor would they sell their goods in Great Britain.

Continental Congress delegates also decided to endorse the Suffolk Resolves, prepared by the people of Boston and other Suffolk County towns in Massachusetts. These resolutions declared the Coercive Acts to be illegal. They called on the county's residents to arm themselves against the British. After delegates endorsed the resolves, other colonies also organized militias—groups of citizen soldiers.

The Colonial Militias

American colonists had a long tradition of serving and protecting their communities in militias. Members of a militia were an important part of each town's defense. Militia members trained and had drills with the other citizen soldiers. They practiced using muskets and cannons. Each member was required to provide his own weapon—usually a musket—and ammunition. Later, as tension between Britain and the colonies grew, towns began to gather and store military supplies.

☑ **PROGRESS CHECK**

Explaining What was the purpose of the Continental Congress?

© Kevin Fleming/CORBIS

A MASSACHUSETTS COMMUNITY PREPARES

Purchases authorized by Salem Provincial Congress, October 1774	
20 tons grape- and round shot, from 3 to 24 lb. @ £15	£300
10 tons bomb shells @ £20	£200
5 tons lead balls @ £33	£165
1,000 barrels of powder @ £8	£8,000
5,000 arms and bayonets @ £2	£10,000
75,000 flints	£100

CHART SKILL

This chart shows military supplies that the town of Salem, Massachusetts, purchased for its militia in 1774.

1 **IDENTIFYING** About how many soldiers does Salem appear prepared to equip?

2 **CRITICAL THINKING** *Making Inferences* What does this list suggest about this community's expectations about relations with the British?

Build Vocabulary: *Multiple Meaning Words*

The word *resolves*, as used on this page, means "something that is decided." As a noun, the word *resolve* can also mean "firmness of purpose," as in "The Patriots showed resolve against the British." As a verb, *resolve* can mean "to decide something" or "to solve a problem."

Lesson 3 **121**

C Critical Thinking Skills

Making Connections Remind students that laws are not permanent. They do change as legislators respond to the concerns of the electorate. **Ask:** Why did the delegates call for the repeal of certain laws? *(The laws violated their natural and constitutional rights as British citizens, as well as colonial charters.)* **BL** What other actions did the delegates take? *(They voted to boycott British goods coming into the colonies and colonial goods going to Britain, and they endorsed the right of citizens to form militias. They also endorsed the Suffolk Resolves.)* **AL**

R Reading Skills

Citing Text Evidence Have students read the section titled "The Delegates Vote." Then have them write out a list of actions taken by the Second Continental Congress in response to the Intolerable Acts. Remind students that if they quote directly from the book, they must use quotation marks. **BL** Intrapersonal

V Visual Skills

Analyzing Charts Refer students to the chart in their textbooks containing information about purchases for a Massachusetts militia. Ask students what a colonist who saw this list might think. **BL** Visual/Spatial

---

IMAGE

Militia, Minutemen, and the Continental Army

Describing Show students the interactive image Militia, Minutemen, and the Continental Army. Make sure everyone understands these terms. **AL** **ELL**

Ask: How did the New England colonists prepare to fight? *(Militias drilled, made bullets, and stockpiled weapons.)* What did the British do to prepare? *(They sent more troops to New England, with orders to seize the militias' weapons.)* **AL**

See page 109E for other online activities.

McGraw-Hill **networks** Militia, Minutemen, and the Continental Army

Minutemen were members of the militia that trained more than the regular militia. These men were trained so they could be ready for military duty immediately.

Kevin Fleming/CORBIS

ANSWER, p. 121

CHART SKILL

1. Salem is purchasing 5,000 weapons, suggesting it plans to arm at least that many soldiers.

2. **CRITICAL THINKING** Possible answer: It appears Salem is convinced there will be conflict because it is taking the step to ensure its citizens are armed.

☑ **PROGRESS CHECK** to represent Americans and challenge British control

Chapter 5 **121**

R Reading Skills

Determining Word Meanings Remind students that some militias were known as "minutemen." Have students break the word apart to better understand its meaning. **Ask: Why would the colonists have wanted to use words like this to describe their forces?** *(Answers may vary. Sample answer: to show the British that they were prepared to fight)* **AL ELL**

C Critical Thinking Skills

Interpreting Call students' attention to the words of Patrick Henry. Make sure everyone understands his famous quote. **AL ELL**

Discuss how his words echoed the feelings of some of the men in the Continental Congress. **Ask: What effect do you think these words might have had on other colonists?** *(Many were probably inspired by Henry's call for unity, but others might have been disturbed by his identification of the colonists as "Americans" rather than Englishmen.)* **BL**

V Visual Skills

Visualizing As students read this paragraph, have them note each of the specific places mentioned. **Ask: Where did Dr. Joseph Warren see British troops on the march?** *(Boston)* **Where were the colonial weapons stored?** *(Concord)* **Where did Paul Revere and William Dawes ride to in order to warn the colonists?** *(Lexington)* Direct students to locate each place on the map on the next page. **AL** **Visual/Spatial**

BIOGRAPHY

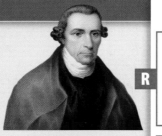

Patrick Henry (1736–1799)

Henry was one of the first members of the Virginia House of Burgesses to argue for independence from Britain. His speaking ability inspired many colonists. In a debate over whether the Virginia Colony should form a militia, he said, "Give me liberty or give me death!" His stirring cry gave voice to the independence movement.

▶ **CRITICAL THINKING**
Analyzing Is good speaking ability an important quality of a leader? Explain.

Reading **HELP**DESK **CCSS**

minuteman during Revolutionary era, civilian sworn to be ready to fight with only one minute's notice

122 *The Spirit of Independence*

Fighting Begins

GUIDING QUESTION *Why were the battles at Lexington and Concord important?*

Many colonists believed that if fighting with the British were to break out, it would happen in New England. Militias in Massachusetts held drills, made bullets, and stockpiled weapons. Some militias were known as **minutemen** because they boasted they would be ready to fight at a minute's notice. In the winter of 1774–1775, a British officer stationed in Boston noted in his diary:

PRIMARY SOURCE

❝ The people are evidently making every preparation for resistance. They are taking every means to provide themselves with Arms. **❞**

—from *Diary of Frederick Mackenzie*, 1775

Great Britain Sends Troops

The British also got ready for a fight. King George told Parliament that the New England Colonies were "in a state of rebellion" and that "blows must decide" who would control America. By April 1775, several thousand British troops were in and around Boston, with more on the way. British general Thomas Gage had orders to seize the weapons from the Massachusetts militia and arrest the leaders.

Gage learned that the militia stored arms and ammunition at Concord, a town about 20 miles (32 km) northwest of Boston. He ordered 700 troops under Lieutenant Colonel Francis Smith "to Concord, where you will seize and destroy all the artillery and ammunition you can find."

The British on the Move

On the night of April 18, 1775, colonial protest leader Dr. Joseph Warren walked through Boston. Watching for any unusual activity by the British, he saw troops marching out of the city.

Warren alerted Paul Revere and William Dawes, members of the Sons of Liberty. Revere and Dawes rode to Lexington, a town east of Concord, to spread the word that the British were coming. Revere galloped across the countryside, shouting his warning of the approaching troops. Hearing the news, Samuel Adams said, "What a glorious morning this is!" He was ready to fight. A British patrol later captured Dawes and Revere. Another rider named Samuel Prescott carried the warning to Concord.

National Portrait Gallery, Smithsonian Institution/Art Resource, NY

---

networks   *Online Teaching Options*

BIOGRAPHY

Patrick Henry

Discussing Use the interactive image of Patrick Henry to discuss his background and beliefs, and how he might have inspired other colonists to join the fight for freedom. Have students list the important roles that Patrick Henry played in the colonies. **AL**

See page 109E for other online activities.

McGraw-Hill **networks** — **Patrick Henry**
BIOGRAPHY

Patrick Henry was Virginia's first governor. Before the age of 10, he received some education in a local school and was later tutored by his father. He owned two stores that failed, and he was also unsuccessful as a farmer. After marrying Sarah Shelton, Henry needed to find a way to support his growing family. He decided to study law. He used his wit, speaking skills, and wisdom about people to succeed.

In the years leading up to the American Revolution, Patrick Henry became an influential leader who opposed British rule. He was convinced that war with Britain was inevitable. Henry will always be remembered for his famous words, "I know not what

National Portrait Gallery, Smithsonian Institution/Art Resource, NY

ANSWER, p. 122

CRITICAL THINKING Possible answer: Yes. Inspiring and encouraging the public would be important in a long, difficult struggle against a powerful adversary.

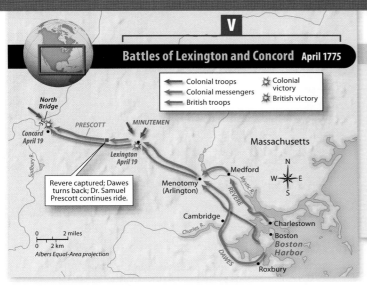

Battles of Lexington and Concord April 1775

- ← Colonial troops
- ← Colonial messengers
- ← British troops
- ✦ Colonial victory
- ✦ British victory

North Bridge
PRESCOTT
MINUTEMEN
Concord April 19
Lexington April 19
Revere captured; Dawes turns back; Dr. Samuel Prescott continues ride.
Menotomy (Arlington)
Medford
Massachusetts
Cambridge
Charlestown
Boston
Boston Harbor
Roxbury

0 2 miles
0 2 km
Albers Equal-Area projection

GEOGRAPHY CONNECTION

The first fighting between British troops and the colonial militia took place at Lexington and Concord, Massachusetts.

1 MOVEMENT Which towns did Paul Revere warn on his ride to Lexington?

2 CRITICAL THINKING
Analyzing How might the starting point of the British forces in Boston have affected the outcome of these battles?

Lexington and Concord

Meanwhile, the British continued their march. At dawn, the redcoats **approached** Lexington. There they ran into about 70 waiting minutemen. Led by Captain John Parker, the minutemen stood on the town common with muskets in hand. Badly outnumbered, the minutemen were about to give way to the redcoats. Just then, a shot was fired—from where is still not clear. Both sides let loose an exchange of bullets. When the shooting ended, eight minutemen lay dead.

The British continued on to Concord. While some troops burned the few weapons they found, the others met a group of minutemen waiting at the North Bridge. In a short battle, the British took heavy losses. They began to make their way back to Boston.

All along the road, colonists hid behind trees and fired on the soldiers. By the time the redcoats reached Boston, at least 174 were wounded and 73 were dead.

About 60 years later, poet Ralph Waldo Emerson wrote in "The Concord Hymn" that the Americans at Lexington and Concord had fired the "shot heard 'round the world." The battle for independence had begun.

☑ PROGRESS CHECK

Explaining Why did British troops march to Concord?

Academic Vocabulary (Tier 2 Words)

approach to draw near to something

V Visual Skills

Reading a Map Students should review map labels for information. **Ask:** What state is being shown on the map? *(Massachusetts)* How do you know that? *(The name is in larger, bolder type.)* How many rivers are labeled on the map? *(three)* What other body of water is shown? *(Boston Harbor)*

Tell students that this map shows the first armed conflicts of the American Revolution. **Ask:** How do you know which symbol on the map indicates a battle? *(by reading the map key)* Why do you think the mapmaker chose that symbol? *(Answers will vary but may include the fact that it denotes an impact or something being hit, such as in a conflict.)* **AL** Visual/Spatial

Content Background Knowledge

- The idea of the American Revolution as the "shot heard 'round the world" is a reference to the way it inspired other democratic revolutions.
- In 1789, the people of France revolted against their king under the slogan "Liberty, Equality, and Brotherhood." Today, this is the national motto of France.
- In 1791, slaves in the French colony of Haiti revolted. These men and women won an end to slavery, the withdrawal of French rule, and the establishment of the Republic of Haiti.

MAP

Battles of Lexington and Concord, April 1775

Analyzing Visuals Have students trace the movements on the interactive map. Then ask them to describe in their own words the rides of Paul Revere, William Dawes, and Dr. Samuel Prescott. **ELL** **Ask:** How were the results of the battle at Lexington different from the results at Concord? *(At Lexington, some militia died in a brief skirmish and the British moved on; at Concord, the British took heavy losses in a pitched battle and on their march back to Boston.)*

See page 109E for other online activities.

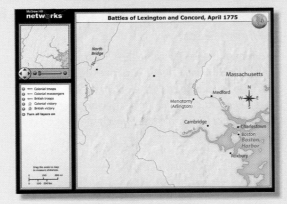

ANSWERS, p. 123

GEOGRAPHY CONNECTION

1 Charlestown, Medford, and Menotomy (Arlington)

2 CRITICAL THINKING The British had to march out a long way through enemy territory to reach Lexington and then Concord.

☑ PROGRESS CHECK to destroy militia arms and ammunition stored there

R1 Reading Skills

Speculating In small groups, have students read the section "More Military Action" aloud. Then have them speculate on what might have happened if Allen and Arnold's forces had not succeeded in taking Fort Ticonderoga. Ask volunteers to share their group's scenario with the class. **BL** Auditory/Musical

R2 Reading Skills

Explaining Have students read the section titled "More Military Action." **Ask:** What role did Benedict Arnold play in both helping and hurting the American cause? *(He joined Ethan Allen and his men to take Fort Ticonderoga from the British. Later he sold military information to the British and led raids against the Americans in Virginia and Connecticut.)* Have students cite evidence from the text to support their answers. **AL**

W Writing Skills

Informative/Explanatory Remind students that more volunteers joined the colonial militias after the battles at Lexington and Concord. Ask students to write a few sentences in which they infer why this occurred. **BL** Intrapersonal

This painting shows the British charge at what historians call the Battle of Bunker Hill—which actually took place on Breed's Hill.

More Military Action

GUIDING QUESTION *What were the beliefs of the Loyalists and Patriots?*

After the battles at Lexington and Concord, armed conflict with British forces quickly spread. Benedict Arnold, a captain in the Connecticut militia, raised a force of 400 to seize Fort Ticonderoga near Lake Champlain in New York. Ticonderoga occupied a key location. It was also rich in military supplies. Arnold learned that Ethan Allen of nearby Vermont also planned to attack the fort. So Arnold joined forces with Allen's men—the **so-called** Green Mountain Boys. Together, they took the British by surprise. Fort Ticonderoga surrendered on May 10, 1775.

Later, Arnold became a traitor to the Patriot cause. He sold military information to the British. When his crime was discovered in September 1780, he fled to British-controlled New York City. There he commanded British troops and led raids against the Americans in Virginia and Connecticut.

The Battle of Bunker Hill

Following Lexington and Concord, more volunteers joined the colonial militias. Soon militia around Boston numbered about 20,000 strong.

The British remained in control of the city, with the militia camped nearby. On June 16, 1775, militia commanded by Colonel William Prescott set up posts on Bunker Hill and Breed's Hill, across the harbor from Boston.

North Wind Picture Archives

Reading **HELP**DESK (CCSS)

Loyalist American colonist who remained loyal to Britain and opposed the war for independence
Patriot American colonist who favored American independence

Academic Vocabulary (Tier 2 Words)
so-called known as

netw⊙rks   *Online Teaching Options*

CHART

Choosing Sides

Speculating Use the interactive chart to discuss the beliefs of Loyalists and Patriots. **Ask:** Why might it have been hard for people to decide which side to support? *(influence from other family members, fear of losing position or job, fear of losing friends, fear of retaliation if the other side won)* **BL**

See page 109E for other online activities.

netw⊙rks™   Choosing Sides

The Battle of Bunker Hill was the first major battle of the American Revolution. It was fought in Charlestown, Massachusetts, on June 17, 1775. Even though the British won the battle, it ignited the revolutionary cause. Click the chart to learn more about the loyalists and the patriots.

Loyalists	Patriots

The next day, the redcoats assembled at Breed's Hill. Bayonets drawn, they charged. Low on ammunition, Prescott reportedly ordered, "Don't fire until you see the whites of their eyes." The Americans opened fire, forcing the British to retreat. Twice more the redcoats charged, receiving furious fire from above. Finally, the Americans ran out of gunpowder and had to withdraw.

The battle on Breed's Hill—which became known as the Battle of Bunker Hill—was a British victory. Yet the British suffered heavy losses of more than 1,000 dead and wounded. They were learning that defeating the Americans on the battlefield would be neither quick nor easy.

Choosing Sides

As news spread about these battles, the colonists each faced a major decision—to join the rebels or remain loyal to Great Britain.

Those who sided with Britain, the **Loyalists**, did not think unfair taxes and laws justified a rebellion. Some were officeholders who felt a responsibility to uphold British rule. Others had not suffered from British policies and saw no reason to break with Britain. Still others believed Britain would win the war and did not want to be on the losing side.

The **Patriots**, on the other hand, supported the war. They believed that the colonists should have the right to govern themselves. The Patriots were determined to fight the British until American independence was won.

The American Revolution was not just a war between America and Britain. It was also a civil war—Patriots against Loyalists.

☑ **PROGRESS CHECK**

Describing What did the British learn from the Battle of Bunker Hill?

Thinking Like a
HISTORIAN

Making Predictions

Loyalists came from all parts of American society. Political differences divided communities and even split families. Benjamin Franklin's son, William, served as Royal Governor of New Jersey. When the Revolution began, William remained loyal to Britain and quarreled with his father. Do you think Benjamin Franklin and William Franklin resolved their differences? For more about making predictions, review *Thinking Like a Historian*.

R **Reading Skills**

Summarizing After students have read the text, have them summarize what happened at Bunker Hill, including the outcome and what the British learned about the Americans. **Ask:** Why did the British want Bunker Hill and Breed's Hill? *(They were strategic locations overlooking the city.)* **AL** **ELL**

C **Critical Thinking Skills**

Comparing and Contrasting Have students make a T-chart to compare and contrast the beliefs of Loyalists and Patriots. Lead the class in a discussion about the similarities and differences. **AL**

W **Writing Skills**

Argument Direct students to write a journal entry from the point of view of either a Loyalist or a Patriot. Have them focus on describing why they chose to join that particular side. Invite volunteers to share their journal entries with the class. **BL**

Have students complete the Lesson 3 Review.

CLOSE & REFLECT

To close the lesson, stress that the American Revolution was not only a war of Americans against the British, but it was also a civil war of Americans—between Patriots and Loyalists. Discuss how this would have affected families and friendships.

LESSON 3 REVIEW

Review Vocabulary (Tier 3 Words)

1. Write a paragraph explaining what the words below have in common. RH.6–8.4, WHST.6–8.4

    a. minuteman **b.** Loyalist **c.** Patriot

Answer the Guiding Questions

2. *Explaining* How did support for the Suffolk Resolves by the Continental Congress push the colonies closer to war? RH.6–8.2

3. *Describing* What fighting methods did the colonists use against the British troops marching back to Boston from Concord? RH.6–8.1

4. *Interpreting* Reread Patrick Henry's quote about the Continental Congress. What change was taking place in how the colonists saw themselves? RH.6–8.6

5. **NARRATIVE** Write a scene from a play in which colonists in a small town react to the news of the Battle of Lexington. Remember, not all colonists wanted independence from Britain. WHST.6–8.2, WHST.6–8.10

LESSON 3 REVIEW ANSWERS

1. Possible answer: The Patriots wanted independence from Britain. Many of them served as minutemen, colonial militia who were ready to fight on short notice. But not all colonists joined the cause. The Loyalists supported Britain.

2. By endorsing the Suffolk Resolves, the Continental Congress was supporting the call to arms against the British and the forming of militias.

3. The colonists hid behind fences and trees, and fired on the British without being seen.

4. They were beginning to see themselves as citizens of one country instead of individual colonies and as entitled to freedom from British rule, something they were willing to die to achieve.

5. Dialogue in students' scenes should include reaction to the news from both Loyalist and Patriot points of view.

ANSWERS, p. 125

Thinking Like a Historian Answers will vary. Some students may say that father and son reconciled because they were family, while others will say it is unlikely they were able to reconcile because of their strong beliefs.

☑ **PROGRESS CHECK** that defeating the Americans would not be quick or easy

ENGAGE

Bellringer Tell students that Thomas Paine was a Patriot and the author of the pamphlet *Common Sense*. The excerpt in this feature is from *Common Sense*. This was an influential writing that helped some colonists make up their minds to become Patriots. Charles Inglis was a passionate Loyalist who criticized Paine's writing and his rebellious ideas. Tell students that they will learn how the writings of colonial leaders influenced the different points of view about seeking independence for America.

TEACH & ASSESS

R Reading Skills

Paraphrasing Have students read the backgrounds of the two individuals. Then have them read the two excerpts. Ask volunteers to summarize in their own words the position of Thomas Paine. *(Paine says the time for debate has passed because Britain has injured colonists too much, and they must part ways, or break, with Britain.)* **BL Ask: What is Paine challenging the reader to do?** *(to find one advantage that the continent has by being connected to Britain)* **AL ELL**

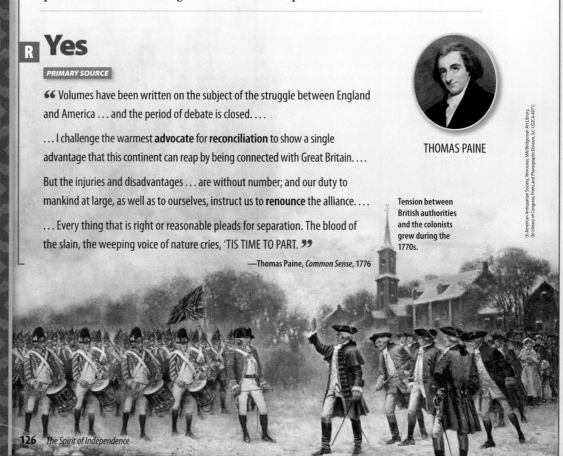

What Do You Think? CCSS

Should the Colonies Declare Their Independence From Great Britain?

Some Americans did not think that independence was the right path for the colonies. They wanted to remain under British rule. These colonists were called Loyalists. Colonists who believed the colonies should become an independent nation were called Patriots.

In these excerpts, Patriot Thomas Paine and Loyalist Charles Inglis express different points of view about the fight for American Independence.

R Yes

PRIMARY SOURCE

❝ Volumes have been written on the subject of the struggle between England and America . . . and the period of debate is closed. . . .

. . . I challenge the warmest **advocate** for **reconciliation** to show a single advantage that this continent can reap by being connected with Great Britain. . . .

But the injuries and disadvantages . . . are without number; and our duty to mankind at large, as well as to ourselves, instruct us to **renounce** the alliance. . . .

. . . Every thing that is right or reasonable pleads for separation. The blood of the slain, the weeping voice of nature cries, 'TIS TIME TO PART. ❞

—Thomas Paine, *Common Sense*, 1776

THOMAS PAINE

Tension between British authorities and the colonists grew during the 1770s.

126 *The Spirit of Independence*

(t) American Antiquarian Society, Worcester, MA/Bridgeman Art Library, (b) Library of Congress, Prints and Photographs Division, [LC-USZC4-4971]

netw⊕rks *Online Teaching Options*

BIOGRAPHY

Thomas Paine

Sequencing Have students read the interactive biography of Thomas Paine. Then have them create cards for each phase in Paine's life. Next, have them use smaller cards or colored notes to write sequence words such as "first," "then," and "later." Finally, students should use the sequencing words to connect the events in Paine's life in the correct order. **AL**

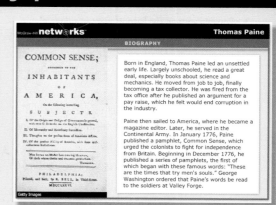

McGraw-Hill **netw⊕rks** Thomas Paine

BIOGRAPHY

Born in England, Thomas Paine led an unsettled early life. Largely unschooled, he read a great deal, especially books about science and mechanics. He moved from job to job, finally becoming a tax collector. He was fired from the tax office after he published an argument for a pay raise, which he felt would end corruption in the industry.

Paine then sailed to America, where he became a magazine editor. Later, he served in the Continental Army. In January 1776, Paine published a pamphlet, Common Sense, which urged the colonists to fight for independence from Britain. Beginning in December 1776, he published a series of pamphlets, the first of which began with these famous words: "These are the times that try men's souls." George Washington ordered that Paine's words be read to the soldiers at Valley Forge.

Getty Images

Not every colonist agreed with the behavior of the protesters involved with the Boston Tea Party.

No

CHARLES INGLIS

PRIMARY SOURCE

❝ I think it no difficult matter to point out many advantages which will certainly attend our reconciliation and connection with Great-Britain. . . . The blood of the slain, the weeping voice of nature cries—*It is time to be reconciled;* it is time to lay aside those **animosities** which have pushed on Britons to shed the blood of Britons . . .

. . . A Declaration of Independency would **infallibly** disunite and divide the colonists. . . .

. . . **Torrents** of blood will be spilt, and thousands reduced to beggary and wretchedness. . . .

America is far from being yet in a desperate situation. I am confident she may obtain honourable and advantageous terms from Great-Britain. ❞

—Charles Inglis, *The True Interest of America Impartially Stated,* 1776

(l) Bettmann/CORBIS, (b) National Portrait Gallery, London

Vocabulary

advocate
supporter

reconciliation
settlement, understanding

renounce
to give up, to abandon

animosity
hostility, ill will, hatred

infallibly
without fail

torrent
fast-moving liquid

What Do You Think?   DBQ

1 ***Interpreting*** What is Paine's argument in favor of independence? RH.6–8.6

2 ***Analyzing*** What did Inglis believe would result from declaring independence from Great Britain? RH.6–8.1

3 ***Evaluating*** In your opinion, which of the two writers makes a more powerful appeal to emotions? Explain your answer in a short essay. RH.6–8.8

Lesson 3   **127**

R1 Reading Skills

Summarizing Have a volunteer summarize the argument of Charles Inglis. *(Inglis says things are not that bad, that it is not too late to turn back and have friendly relations with Britain, and that independence will lead to division among the colonists and to more killing.)* **BL**

R2 Reading Skills

Deciding After students have read each primary source, ask each student to vote *Yes* or *No,* writing his or her decision on a slip of paper. Collect students' votes in a paper bag. Tally the votes to find out how many students agree with each opinion. Discuss the results. **AL ELL Ask: What did you decide? Should the colonists fight for independence or not? What would you say to other people to try to convince them to make the same decision?** *(Answers will vary but should reflect a defensible position on one side or the other of the argument.)*

Finally, have students complete the *What Do You Think?* questions.

CLOSE & REFLECT

To close the lesson, have students share their decisions by giving short, 30-second speeches in support of Paine's or Inglis's point of view.

GRAPHIC NOVEL

Liberty's Stand

Interpreting Remind students that Inglis was talking about militia members fighting with redcoats. Direct them to read the graphic novel for this chapter in which a member of the militia has received notice that he is needed and explains to his daughter why he must leave her and be prepared to fight. Tell students to look at the father's and daughter's faces throughout the story to interpret what is happening.

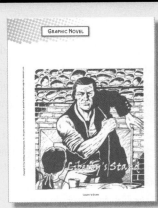

GRAPHIC NOVEL

ANSWERS, p. 127

1. Paine argued that there were no good reasons for remaining connected with Great Britain and that there would be many benefits to the colonies in becoming independent.
2. Inglis believed that declaring independence would divide the colonists and many would be killed or become miserably poor.
3. Essays will vary but should include valid reasons that the quote appeals to the emotions, and cite details from the document.

ENGAGE

Bellringer List on the board some of the most important figures in the American Revolution, such as George Washington, Thomas Jefferson, and Benjamin Franklin. Ask students to share what they learned about these people in earlier grades. **Ask: How do Americans view these people today?** *(Students are likely to suggest that they have , especially Washington, become "legends".)* **Who are some legends like these in our times?** *(Students may mention important political leaders, sports figures, or other celebrities.)* Tell students that in this lesson they will learn about the important figures who played a part in declaring our independence.

TEACH & ASSESS

R Reading Skills

Identifying Using evidence from the text, ask students to identify men who were part of the Second Continental Congress. *(Students' answers should include John Adams, Samuel Adams, Patrick Henry, Richard Henry Lee, Benjamin Franklin, and George Washington.)* **Ask: Why do you think the delegates chose John Hancock to be president of the Second Continental Congress?** *(Possible answer: He was a wealthy merchant who helped to fund many Patriot groups, including the Sons of Liberty.)* **AL**

C Critical Thinking Skills

Defending Remind students that many of the delegates to the Second Continental Congress had colonial government experience. Ask students to write two or three sentences explaining why this might make them more or less qualified to serve. **BL**

ANSWER, p. 128

TAKING NOTES: Part 1: an introduction, or preamble, explains why the people wanted to form a new country; **Part 2:** a list of the rights colonists believed they should have; **Part 3:** a list of grievances against the British king and Parliament; **Part 4:** an announcement of independence

---

networks
There's More Online!

☑ **BIOGRAPHY**
Thomas Paine

☑ **GRAPHIC ORGANIZER**
Declaration of
Independence

☑ **MAP** The Siege of Boston

☑ **PRIMARY SOURCE**
• Battles of Lexington and Concord
• Reaction to Declaration of
Independence

Lesson 4
Declaring Independence

ESSENTIAL QUESTION *What motivates people to act?*

IT MATTERS BECAUSE
The decision to declare independence came only after all other options had been exhausted.

The Second Continental Congress

GUIDING QUESTION *How did individuals and events impact efforts for independence?*

In 1774 the Continental Congress agreed to meet again if the British did not address their complaints. In fact, as the battles at Lexington and Concord in 1775 showed, the dispute between the British and the colonies had worsened.

Distinguished Leaders

The Second Continental Congress met on May 10, 1775. The delegates included some of the greatest leaders in the colonies. Among them were John and Samuel Adams, Patrick Henry, Richard Henry Lee, and George Washington—all delegates to the First Continental Congress. Several new delegates came as well.

Benjamin Franklin, one of the most respected men in the colonies, had been a leader in the Pennsylvania legislature. In 1765 he represented the colonies in London and helped win repeal of the Stamp Act. John Hancock of Massachusetts was a wealthy merchant. He funded many Patriot groups, including the Sons of Liberty. The delegates chose Hancock to be president of the Second Continental Congress. Thomas Jefferson, only 32, was also a delegate. He served in the Virginia legislature. Jefferson was already known as a brilliant thinker and writer.

(c) North Wind Picture Archives, (c) MPI/Archive Photos/Getty Images, (cr) SuperStock (r) © Bettmann/CORBIS

Reading HELPDESK CCSS

Taking Notes: *Organizing* RH.6–8.2
As you read, use a diagram like this one to describe the parts of the Declaration of Independence.

128 *The Spirit of Independence*

Declaration of Independence
Part 1:
↓
Part 2:
↓
Part 3:
↓
Part 4:

Content Vocabulary (Tier 3 Words)
• **petition**
• **preamble**

---

networks *Online Teaching Options*

VIDEO

Declaration of Independence

Determining Central Ideas Students should watch the lesson video about the Declaration of Independence. Then divide the class into small groups, and have each group discuss what they think is the central idea of the Declaration, based on what they just watched. Have a representative from each group share their answers, and write them on the interactive whiteboard. Then discuss the differences and similarities as a class. **BL Interpersonal**

See page 109F for other online activities.

The delegates at the Second Continental Congress had much to discuss. Though American and British blood had been spilled, they were not ready to vote for a break from Britain. It would be another year before Jefferson would write the Declaration of Independence.

Key Actions

The Continental Congress did take steps to begin governing the colonies. It authorized the printing of money and set up a post office, with Franklin in charge. The Congress also formed committees to handle relations with Native Americans and foreign countries. Most important, it created the Continental Army. Unlike local militias, such a force could form and carry out an overall strategy for fighting the British. The Congress unanimously chose George Washington to command this army. Washington was an experienced soldier and a respected Southern planter. He left Philadelphia at once to take charge of the forces in Boston.

R

The delegates then offered Britain a last chance to avoid war. They sent a **petition**, or formal request, to George III. Called the Olive Branch Petition, it assured the king that the colonists wanted peace. It asked him to protect the colonists' rights. The king rejected the petition. Instead, he prepared for war. He hired more than 30,000 German troops, called Hessians (HEH•shuhnz), to fight alongside British troops.

C

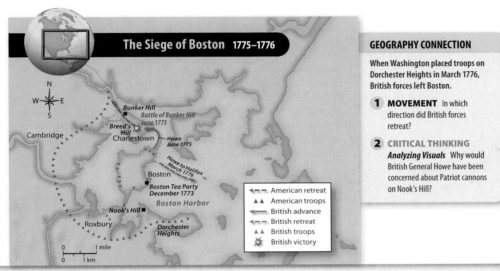

The Siege of Boston   1775–1776

American retreat
American troops
British advance
British retreat
British troops
British victory

GEOGRAPHY CONNECTION

When Washington placed troops on Dorchester Heights in March 1776, British forces left Boston.

1 MOVEMENT In which direction did British forces retreat?

2 CRITICAL THINKING
Analyzing Visuals Why would British General Howe have been concerned about Patriot cannons on Nook's Hill?

petition a formal request

R Reading Skills

Identifying Ask a student volunteer to review the steps the Second Continental Congress took to govern the colonies. Then have students identify which of these actions were steps toward independence and why. **Ask: Which step do you think was most important?** *(Students should be able to defend their answers. Most will likely say setting up an army with Washington to lead it.)* **Which step did the delegates eventually take that is not shown on this list?** *(They accepted declaring independence or writing the Declaration of Independence.)* **BL**

C Critical Thinking Skills

Determining Word Meanings Explain to students that the expression "extending the olive branch" means an offer of peace from one person or group to another. **Ask: Why did the delegates name their document the Olive Branch petition?** *(because it was an offer from the delegates to the British to keep peace instead of going to war)* Have students think of another expression that they hear frequently and share its meaning with the class. **BL** **Verbal/Linguistic**

MAP

The Seige of Boston, 1775–1776

Analyzing Visuals Have students locate Nook's Hill on the map and explain why it was a critical position for the Continental Army. *(It gave Washington's artillery the ability to bombard the British troops in Boston.)* **Ask: Why do you think the British boarded their ships and sailed away?** *(Students should note that Washington's command of the heights around Boston was a threat to the British and that the only escape route available to them was by sea, as the Patriots were surrounding the rest of the city.)* **BL**

See page 109F for other online activities.

ANSWERS, p. 129

GEOGRAPHY CONNECTION

1 to the southeast, by ship

2 **CRITICAL THINKING** Washington could bombard the city and British forces from this position.

Declaring Independence

R1 Reading Skills

Explaining After students have read the text, discuss the mounting offensive by the Continental Army, including the capture of Montreal, the attack on Quebec, and the siege in Boston. **Ask: Why did the Americans attack Montreal?** *(They heard that British troops in that area planned to attack New York.)* **Why was Fort Ticonderoga significant to the battle in Boston?** *(The fort had weapons that were needed by Washington's army.)* **How did George Washington use his newly trained troops?** *(to drive the British out of Boston)* **AL**

C Critical Thinking Skills

Making Connections Ask students to consider the kinds of people who tend to have influence on public opinion. Then, **ask: Who was Thomas Paine?** *(He was the author of the pamphlet* Common Sense.*)* **AL**

Remind students that not all colonists were in favor of independence. **Ask: How do you think Thomas Paine's Common Sense influenced people? Why was it such an important writing?** *(Possible answer: He gave powerful, persuasive reasons that the colonies should separate from Britain. More people were inspired to join the cause for independence.)* **BL**

R2 Reading Skills

Paraphrasing Provide a copy of *Common Sense* to students. Ask volunteers to read selections from the document. To make sure students understand Paine's arguments, work with them to paraphrase each passage. Have students speculate how Paine's message affected public opinion and strengthened support for independence. **AL** **ELL**

General George Washington commanded the Continental Army in their battles with the British. **R1**

Thomas Paine's *Common Sense* had a great influence on public opinion in the colonies.

R2

The War Heats Up

Congress learned that British troops in Canada were planning to invade New York. The Americans decided to strike first. A unit of Patriots marched north from Fort Ticonderoga and captured Montreal. However, an American attack on Quebec, led by Benedict Arnold, failed.

Washington reached the Boston area in July 1775, a few weeks after the Battle of Bunker Hill. The British held Boston, but Patriot militia ringed the city. Although the size of the colonial force grew every day, Washington realized that the men were disorganized and lacked **discipline**—the ability to follow strict rules and procedures. Washington began the task of turning armed civilians into soldiers.

Washington also needed weapons. He arranged to have dozens of cannons hauled 300 miles (483 km) from Fort Ticonderoga. Moving the heavy guns was a huge effort.

In March 1776, Washington believed his army was ready to fight. Under the cover of darkness, he moved soldiers and cannons into position overlooking Boston, while the redcoats slept.

The move surprised the British, who realized they were now within easy reach of Washington's big guns. British General William Howe commanded his soldiers to board ships and withdraw from Boston. On March 17, Washington led his jubilant troops into the city. They watched as the British troops sailed away to Halifax, Nova Scotia, a part of Canada.

Moving Toward Independence

Many colonists held on to hope that the colonies could remain part of Great Britain. Still, support for independence was growing. It was inspired in no small part by writer Thomas Paine. Paine arrived in the colonies from England in 1774. He soon caught the revolutionary spirit. In January 1776, he published a pamphlet called *Common Sense*. In bold language, Paine called for a complete break with British rule. **C**

PRIMARY SOURCE

❝ Every thing that is right or reasonable pleads for separation. The blood of the slain, the weeping voice of nature cries, 'TIS TIME TO PART. ❞

—from *Common Sense*, 1776

Reading **HELP**DESK **CCSS**

Academic Vocabulary (Tier 2 Words)

discipline the ability to follow strict rules and procedures
debate a discussion of opposing points of view

130 *The Spirit of Independence*

net**w**orks *Online Teaching Options*

PRIMARY SOURCE

George Washington on Lexington and Concord

Analyzing Primary Sources Use the interactive primary source excerpt of George Washington's letter to George William Fairfax to discuss how Washington may have felt about the events that had taken place in Massachusetts. Have volunteers point out words or phrases that might tell a reader how Washington felt about the events. **AL** **ELL**

See page 109F for other online activities.

net**w**orks George Washington on Lexington and Concord

ANALYZING PRIMARY SOURCES

George Fairfax was one of George Washington's closest friends. In this letter to Fairfax, Washington describes the fighting that took place in Massachusetts in April, 1775.

North Wind Picture Archives

❝ Before this Letter can reach you, you must, undoubtedly, have received an Account of the engagement in the Massachusetts Bay between the Ministerial Troops (for we do not, nor cannot yet prevail upon ourselves to call them the king's Troops) and the Provincials. . . . ❞

—from *George Washington to George William Fairfax*, by George Washington, May 31, 1775

Common Sense listed powerful reasons why Americans would be better off free from Great Britain. The pamphlet greatly influenced opinions throughout the colonies.

✅ **PROGRESS CHECK**

Explaining What was the significance of the Olive Branch Petition?

Declaring Independence

GUIDING QUESTION *Why did the American colonies declare independence?*

The Second Continental Congress was filled with spirited **debate**: Should the colonies declare themselves an independent nation or stay under British rule? In June 1776, Virginia's Richard Henry Lee offered a bold resolution:

PRIMARY SOURCE

❝ That these United Colonies are, and of right ought to be, free and independent States … and that all political connection between them and the State of Great Britain is, and ought to be, totally dissolved. ❞

—Richard Henry Lee, resolution for independence, 1776

The Congress debated Lee's resolution. Some delegates still thought the colonies should not form a separate nation. Others argued that war had already begun and they should be free from Great Britain. Still others feared Britain's power to crush the rebellion.

Writing the Declaration

While delegates debated, Congress chose a committee to write a declaration of independence. John Adams, Benjamin Franklin, Thomas Jefferson, Robert Livingston, and Roger Sherman formed the committee. Adams asked Jefferson to write the first draft. Jefferson hesitated, but Adams persuaded him, saying:

PRIMARY SOURCE

❝ Reason first—You are a Virginian, and a Virginian ought to appear at the head of this business. Reason second—I am obnoxious, suspected, and unpopular. You are very much otherwise. Reason third—you can write ten times better than I can. ❞

—from *The Writings of Thomas Jefferson*, 1822

Jefferson agreed that he would do the writing for the great project. He drew on ideas from English philosopher John Locke to explain why the 13 colonies were proclaiming their freedom. In the

Committee members Benjamin Franklin, Thomas Jefferson, and John Adams examine Jefferson's changes to his draft of the Declaration.

Lesson 4 131

C1 Critical Thinking Skills

Hypothesizing Review with students what they have learned so far about the Second Continental Congress. **Ask: What do you predict the Americans will do next?** After students share their predictions, explain that they will discover why and how the Declaration of Independence was written. **BL**

C2 Critical Thinking Skills

Analyzing Primary Sources Discuss with the class the decision of the Second Continental Congress to seek independence. **Ask: What did Richard Henry Lee propose at the Second Continental Congress?** *(that the colonies be independent states free from Great Britain)* **AL**

T Technology

Researching on the Internet Read to students the quote from John Adams to Thomas Jefferson about his insistence that Jefferson write the Declaration. Have students use the Internet to research the reasons Adams may have considered himself "obnoxious, suspected, and unpopular." Have students write a paragraph based on their research that explains Adams's reasons. **BL**

SLIDE SHOW

The Committee of Five

Identifying Note that the Second Continental Congress created a committee to write a declaration of independence. Use the interactive image of the Committee of Five to discuss these five men and their contributions to the Declaration of Independence. **Ask: Who was on the committee chosen to write the Declaration of Independence?** *(John Adams, Benjamin Franklin, Thomas Jefferson, Robert Livingston, and Roger Sherman)* **Who was asked to write the first draft?** *(Jefferson)* **AL** **ELL**

See page 109F for other online activities.

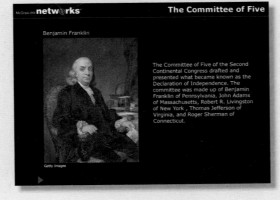

McGraw-Hill **netw⊚rks**   The Committee of Five

Benjamin Franklin

The Committee of Five of the Second Continental Congress drafted and presented what became known as the Declaration of Independence. The committee was made up of Benjamin Franklin of Pennsylvania, John Adams of Massachusetts, Robert R. Livingston of New York , Thomas Jefferson of Virginia, and Roger Sherman of Connecticut.

Getty Images

ANSWER, p. 131

✅ **PROGRESS CHECK** Congress wanted to give the king a way to avoid war, but he responded with a buildup of troops.

Declaring Independence

Jefferson and the rest of the committee present the completed Declaration of Independence to the Second Continental Congress.

R1 Reading Skills

Discussing After students have read the text, discuss the ideas and writers that inspired Thomas Jefferson. **Ask: Whose ideas inspired Jefferson?** *(English philosopher John Locke)* **What were Locke's ideas?** *(that people are born with certain natural rights to life, liberty, and property)* Review with students some of Locke's ideas that are mentioned in the textbook. Challenge students to point out elements that are contained in the Declaration of Independence. **BL**

C Critical Thinking Skills

Analyzing Discuss the work by Jefferson to draft the Declaration of Independence. Help students connect other documents that inspired Jefferson while drafting this document. Jefferson used documents, such as the Virginia Declaration of Rights and his own draft of the Virginia state constitution, to craft a statement about the rights of the colonists in the Declaration. **AL**

R2 Reading Skills

Discussing Direct students to read the section titled "The Declaration of Independence." Then discuss with students how the Declaration provides context for the colonists' experiences. **Ask: Does the document describe what was going on in the colonies at that time?** *(Yes, it tells how the colonists believed they had been wronged by Britain. It explains the rights that the colonists should have. Then it states that the colonies are a new nation.)* **BL**

R1 1690s Locke expressed the idea that people are born with certain natural rights to life, liberty, and property. Locke wrote that people form governments to protect those rights, and that a government interfering with those rights could rightfully be overthrown. Jefferson and other Patriots agreed with Locke.

On July 2, 1776, the Second Continental Congress voted on Lee's resolution for independence. Twelve colonies voted for independence. New York did not vote but later announced its support.

C Next, the delegates discussed Jefferson's draft of the Declaration of Independence. After making some changes, delegates approved the document on July 4, 1776. John Hancock signed the Declaration first. He remarked that he wrote his name large enough for King George to read without his glasses. Eventually 56 delegates signed the document announcing the birth of the United States.

Copies of the Declaration of Independence were printed and sent out to people in the newly declared states. George Washington had the Declaration read to his troops in New York City on July 9. In Worcester, Massachusetts, a public reading of the Declaration of Independence led to "repeated [cheers], firing of musketry and cannon, bonfires, and other demonstrations of joy."

The Declaration of Independence

R2 The Declaration has four major sections. The **preamble**, or introduction, states that people who wish to form a new country should explain their reasons for doing so. The next two sections of the Declaration list the rights that the colonists believed they should have and their complaints against Great Britain. The final section proclaims the existence of the new nation.

John Adams expected the day Congress voted on Lee's resolution for independence to be celebrated as a national holiday. He wrote, "The Second Day of July 1776 ... ought to be

© Bettmann/CORBIS

Reading **HELP**DESK **CCSS**

preamble the introduction to a formal document that often tells why the document was written

Academic Vocabulary (Tier 2 Words)
status rank or place as compared to others

netw◉rks   *Online Teaching Options*

PRIMARY SOURCE

The Declaration of Independence

Hypothesizing Use the interactive primary source excerpt to discuss the reading of the Declaration to citizens and soldiers, and their reactions to the Declaration. **Ask: What kind of reaction did the Declaration receive when it was read in public?** *(People cheered and fired muskets.)* **How do you think you would have reacted to the reading of the Declaration if you were a citizen or a soldier during this historical event?** *(Answers may vary.)* **AL**

See page 109F for other online activities.

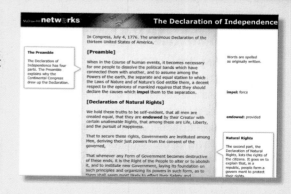

solemnized with Pomp and Parade … and Illuminations from one End of this Continent to the other." Instead, July 4, the date the delegates actually adopted the Declaration of Independence, is celebrated as Independence Day.

The Declaration of Independence states what Jefferson and many Americans thought were universal principles—that is, principles that apply to all people in all situations. It begins by describing what had long been viewed as basic English rights:

PRIMARY SOURCE

 We hold these truths to be self-evident, that all men are created equal, that they are endowed by their Creator with certain unalienable [not to be denied] Rights, that among these are Life, Liberty, and the pursuit of Happiness. 99

—*Declaration of Independence*, 1776

The Declaration states that government exists to protect these rights. If government fails, "it is the Right of the People to alter or to abolish it and to institute new Government." The document goes on to list grievances against the king and Parliament. These include "cutting off our trade with all parts of the world" and "imposing taxes on us without our consent." Americans had "Petitioned for Redress" of these grievances. The British had ignored or rejected these petitions.

Finally, the Declaration announces America's new **status** (STAY·tuhs). Pledging "to each other our Lives, our Fortunes, and our sacred Honor," the Americans declared themselves a new nation. The struggle for independence—the American Revolution—had begun.

☑ PROGRESS CHECK

Summarizing According to John Locke, what is the purpose of government?

 LESSON 4 REVIEW

Review Vocabulary (Tier 3 Words)

1. Use the term *petition* in a sentence about the colonists' struggles with Britain. RH.6–8.4

2. Use *preamble* in a sentence that helps explain its meaning. RH.6–8.4

Answer the Guiding Questions

3. *Explaining* What actions did the Second Continental Congress take to begin governing the colonies? RH.6–8.1

4. *Summarizing* What grievances against King George III were included in the Declaration of Independence? RH.6–8.2

5. *Interpreting* Reread the Primary Source quote from the Declaration of Independence above. Rewrite this quote in your own words and explain its significance. RH.6–8.6, WHST.6–8.2

6. ARGUMENT Who did the most to promote the cause of independence: George Washington, Thomas Jefferson, or Thomas Paine? Give reasons for your choice. WHST.6–8.1, WHST.6–8.9

Lesson 4 **133**

C **Critical Thinking Skills**

Explaining Explain to students that Jefferson believed that the Declaration simply stated universal principles that were not upheld for Americans. Have a volunteer interpret Jefferson's call on Americans to pledge "to each other our Lives, our Fortunes, and our sacred Honor." **BL**

Have students complete the Lesson 4 Review.

CLOSE & REFLECT

To close the lesson, ask students which phrases in the Declaration of Independence they think are most important. To extend the lesson, have students research what sections were taken out of the Declaration, the reasons they were removed, and the impact those passages could have had on the development of the United States.

LESSON 4 REVIEW ANSWERS

1. Possible answer: In a final effort to avoid war, the colonists sent a petition to the king in hopes of settling their differences.

2. Possible answer: The preamble of the Declaration of Independence introduces the reason that the document was written.

3. authorized the printing of money, established a post office, set up committees to work with Native Americans and foreign countries, and created the Continental Army with George Washington as commander

4. Grievances included cutting off the colonies' trade with other countries, taxing colonists without their consent, and ignoring their petitions.

5. Possible answer: All human beings are equal and they have certain rights that cannot be taken away, including the rights to live, be free, and to pursue happiness.

6. Possible answers: Washington, because he fought the battles; Jefferson, because he helped write the Declaration of Independence; Thomas Paine, because he rallied people to the cause

---

ANSWER, p. 133

☑ **PROGRESS CHECK** to protect people's natural rights to life, liberty, and property

CHAPTER REVIEW ACTIVITY

Have students create a two-column chart like the one below and write "Before the Declaration" in one column header and "After the Declaration" in the other. Then lead a discussion that allows students to recall how conflict led to the Declaration and changed colonists' lives. Allow student volunteers to write the changes on the chart.

Before the Declaration	After the Declaration

REVIEW THE ENDURING UNDERSTANDING

Review this chapter's Enduring Understanding with students.

- *Conflict can lead to change.*

Now pose the following questions in a class discussion to apply these to the chapter.

How did the geographic distance between Britain and the colonies lead to conflict? *(Answers may include that the British government didn't understand the situation or problems in the American colonies; the American colonists felt less connected to the British, which made them more independent; the time it took for communication made it easy to misunderstand one another.)*

What were the issues that led to conflict between Britain and the American colonies? *(Answers may include taxation without representation, the cost of defending the colonies, the right to self government, trade restrictions, and occupying soldiers in colonial towns and cities.)*

CHAPTER 5 Activities

Write your answers on a separate piece of paper.

❶ Exploring the Essential Questions   WHST.6–8.2, WHST.6–8.9

INFORMATIVE/EXPLANATORY The conflict that led to the Declaration of Independence took many years to develop. Write a brief summary of the events leading up to the Declaration that explains the basic views of the British and of the colonists. Use examples from the chapter to support your answer.

❷ 21st Century Skills   RH.6–8.6, RH.6–8.8

RECOGNIZING BIAS Look at this poster, which was created after the Boston Massacre. Create an alternative version that describes the event from the British point of view. Write a brief explanation of how your poster differs from the one shown here.

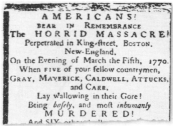

❸ Thinking Like a Historian   WHST.6–8.7, WHST.6–8.10

DRAWING INFERENCES AND CONCLUSIONS The Declaration of Independence guarantees "unalienable rights" to life, liberty, and "the pursuit of happiness." What exactly does "pursuit of happiness" mean? Does it mean that you can do anything you want to as long as it makes you happy? Take a survey of friends and neighbors. Ask them what it means to them. Prepare a short report on your findings for the class.

❹ Visual Literacy   RH.6–8.7

ANALYZING POLITICAL CARTOONS This 1774 cartoon shows some Patriots pouring tea down the throat of John Malcolm, a British tax collector. What message is the artist trying to send? How do the Patriots seem to feel toward the tax collector?

134   *The Spirit of Independence*

ACTIVITIES ANSWERS

Exploring the Essential Questions

❶ Students' summaries should include views from both the British and the colonists about events that led to the colonists' decision to separate from England and issue their Declaration of Independence.

21st Century Skills

❷ Posters and explanations should include information to convey the British belief that the colonists provoked the situation and caused the Boston Massacre.

Thinking Like a Historian

❸ Students' reports will vary but should reflect their survey results. Reports may contain quotations from some of those surveyed.

Visual Literacy

❹ The depiction of these colonists' harsh treatment of Malcolm suggests that the artist is pro-British and does not condone their actions. It is clear that the colonists do not like the tax collector or the tax. Accept any answer a student can justify.

REVIEW THE GUIDING QUESTIONS

Choose the best answer for each question.

RH.6–8.1
1. What British regulation prohibited colonists from moving west of the Appalachian Mountains?
   A. Townshend Acts
   B. Coercive Acts
   C. Proclamation of 1763
   D. Stamp Act

RH.6–8.1
2. Why did colonists object to the Sugar Act?
   F. It prevented colonists from trading with other nations.
   G. It violated colonists' right to be secure in their homes.
   H. It taxed colonists with their consent.
   I. It made sugar much more expensive.

RH.6–8.4
3. What was the purpose of the committees of correspondence?
   A. to write protests to the king
   B. to oversee trials in British courts
   C. to handle problems with Native Americans
   D. to share information among the colonies

RH.6–8.1
4. What resulted from the Coercive Acts?
   F. Boston Harbor was closed until the colonists paid for tea dumped at the Boston Tea Party.
   G. The area west of the Appalachians and north of the Ohio River became part of Quebec.
   H. The tax on molasses imported into the colonies was raised.
   I. A tax was collected on almost all printed material sold in the colonies.

RH.6–8.4
5. What name was given to American colonists who sided with Great Britain during the American Revolution?
   A. Sons of Liberty   C. Loyalists
   B. minutemen   D. Patriots

RH.6–8.2
6. What did the preamble to the Declaration of Independence say?
   F. It spelled out the colonists' complaints against Britain.
   G. It listed the rights the colonists believed they should have.
   H. It proclaimed the existence of the new nation.
   I. It stated that people who wish to form a new country should explain their reasons for doing so.

135

ASSESSMENT ANSWERS
Review the Guiding Questions

1. **C** Choices A, B, and D are all British laws passed after the Proclamation.

2. **G** The writs of assistance authorized by the Sugar Act allowed citizens' homes to be searched for smuggled goods. Choice F was imposed by the Tea and Townshend Acts. Choice H is incorrect because the colonists did not consent to the tax. Choice I is incorrect because the Sugar Act made sugar less expensive.

3. **D** The committees circulated colonists' ideas to rally other colonists to work for independence. Choices A and B involve protests and courts. Choice C is wrong because colonists did not correspond with Native Americans through committees.

4. **F** Britain closed Boston Harbor to punish the colonists for the Boston Tea Party. The law that established choice G was not part of the Coercive Acts. Choice H never took place, and choice I was the goal of the Stamp Act.

5. **C** These were American colonists who remained loyal to the king. Choices A, B, and D are all colonists who supported freedom from Britain.

6. **I** The preamble is the introduction, stating that people who plan a new country should explain why. Choices F and G are the second and third parts of the Declaration. Choice H is the last part, which proclaims a new nation.

Analyzing Documents

7 **C** The dates on the map show that the battles took place on the same day.

8 **I** The colonial troops traveled in a southeasterly direction to reach Concord. The British troops traveled northwest to reach Concord. The minutemen traveled to Lexington, not to Concord. Of the colonial messengers, only Dr. Prescott traveled to Concord; he traveled in a northwesterly direction to get there.

Short Response

9 He addresses the colonists' complaint that they were being denied their right as British citizens to elect the leaders who tax them.

10 They might say that a citizen's rights do not change just because of where he or she lives, so British citizens cannot be denied their privileges because they moved to America.

Extended Response

11 Letters should identify ways in which both sides were being stubborn.

DBQ ANALYZING DOCUMENTS
RH.6–8.7

7 **Drawing Conclusions**
According to the map, the battles of Lexington and Concord were fought

A. three days apart.

B. at the same location.

C. on the same day.

D. in New York.

RH.6–8.7

8 **Identifying** Based on the map, who traveled in a southeasterly direction to the battle at Concord?

F. the Loyalists

G. the British troops

H. the colonial messengers

I. the colonial troops

SHORT RESPONSE

British writer Samuel Johnson said in his 1775 pamphlet, *Taxation No Tyranny:*

"He who goes voluntarily to America, cannot complain of losing what he leaves in Europe. … By his own choice he has left a country where he had a vote and little property, for another where he has great property, but no vote."

—*The Works of Samuel Johnson*

RH.6–8.6, WHST.6–8.9

9 What complaint does Johnson's statement appear to address?

RH.6–8.6, WHST.6–8.1

10 How might colonists respond to Johnson's statement?

EXTENDED RESPONSE
WHST.6–8.1, WHST.6–8.10

11 **Narrative** It is the 1770s and you are visiting the colonies from a country other than Great Britain. How would you describe the conflict between the colonists and the British? Write a letter to a friend back in your country giving your impressions of the disagreement.

Need Extra Help?

If You've Missed Question	**1**	**2**	**3**	**4**	**5**	**6**	**7**	**8**	**9**	**10**	**11**
Review Lesson	1	1	2	2	3	4	3	3	1,2,3	1,2,3	2,3,4

---

networks *Online Teaching Options*

More Assessment Resources

The *Assess* tab in the online Teacher Lesson Center includes resources to help students improve their test-taking skills. It also contains many project-based rubrics to help you assess students' work.

THE DECLARATION of INDEPENDENCE

In Congress, July 4, 1776. The unanimous Declaration of the thirteen United States of America,

[Preamble]

When in the Course of human events, it becomes necessary for one people to dissolve the political bands which have connected them with another, and to assume among the Powers of the earth, the separate and equal station to which the Laws of Nature and of Nature's God entitle them, a decent respect to the opinions of mankind requires that they should declare the causes which **impel** them to the separation.

[Declaration of Natural Rights]

We hold these truths to be self-evident, that all men are created equal, that they are **endowed** by their Creator with certain unalienable Rights, that among these are Life, Liberty, and the pursuit of Happiness.

That to secure these rights, Governments are instituted among Men, deriving their just powers from the consent of the governed,

That whenever any Form of Government becomes destructive of these ends, it is the Right of the People to alter or to abolish it, and to institute new Government, laying its foundation on such principles and organizing its powers in such form, as to them shall seem most likely to effect their Safety and Happiness. Prudence, indeed, will dictate that Governments long established should not be changed for light and transient causes; and accordingly all experience hath shown, that mankind are more disposed to suffer, while evils are sufferable, than to right themselves by abolishing the forms to which they are accustomed. But when a long train of abuses and **usurpations**, pursuing invariably the same Object evinces a design to reduce them under absolute **Despotism**, it is their right, it is their duty, to throw off such Government, and to provide new Guards for their future security.

[List of Grievances]

Such has been the patient sufferance of these Colonies; and such is now the necessity which constrains them to alter their former Systems of Government. The history of the present King of Great Britain is a history of repeated injuries and usurpations, all having in direct object the establishment of an absolute Tyranny over these States. To prove this, let Facts be submitted to a candid world.

Words are spelled as originally written.

The Preamble The Declaration of Independence has four parts. The Preamble explains why the Continental Congress drew up the Declaration.

impel: force

Natural Rights The second part, the Declaration of Natural Rights, lists the rights of the citizens. It goes on to explain that, in a republic, people form a government to protect their rights.

endowed: provided

usurpations: unjust uses of power

despotism: unlimited power

List of Grievances The third part of the Declaration lists the colonists' complaints against the British government. Notice that King George III is singled out for blame.

R

C

Getty Images

The Declaration of Independence **137**

ENGAGE

Bellringer Inform students that at the signing of the Declaration of Independence, Benjamin Franklin remarked to John Hancock, "We must indeed all hang together, or most assuredly, we shall all hang separately." Have students suggest what Franklin meant by the comment. *(If the colonists did not work together for independence and succeed, they would all be hanged for treason.)*

TEACH & ASSESS

R Reading Skills

Paraphrasing Ask students to read the Preamble and rewrite it in their own words. English language learners may struggle with the wording used in the Declaration of Independence, so pair English learners with more proficient students who can guide them through the language of the Preamble.
ELL Verbal/Linguistic

Ask: What is the main point of the Preamble? *(It states the reasons for the colonists' severing their ties with Great Britain.)*

C Critical Thinking Skills

Analyzing Primary Sources Tell students that statements in the Declaration of Independence proclaim some of the most important ideas on which democratic government is based.
Ask: What statements in the Declaration of Independence are important values in a democracy? *(all people are created equal; all people possess certain basic rights; the purpose of government is to secure or protect people's rights; the power and authority of governments come from the people)*

PRIMARY SOURCE

The Declaration of Independence

A copy of the Declaration of Independence can be found online in **networks** in the Chapter 5: Chapter Resources at a Glance: Lesson 4 Resources and in the Resource Library under "Primary Sources."

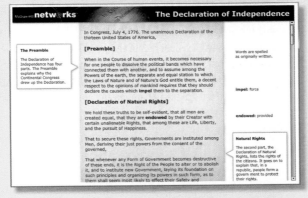

The Declaration of Independence

138

T Technology Skills

Using Visual Aids Organize students into small groups, and assign each group several of the grievances listed in the Declaration. Have the groups conduct research on the Internet to find specific events, acts, or statements made by the king or Parliament that relate to at least one of their grievances. Have students put their findings into a graphic organizer, such as a cause-and-effect diagram. Then have students create a slide show using multimedia presentation software to share their graphic organizer with the class. **BL** **Visual/Spatial**

C Critical Thinking Skills

Making Inferences Remind students that at the time, transportation was limited and slow, and people either depended on horses or traveled on foot. **Ask:** Why might holding government meetings in unusual and inconvenient places have offended the colonists? *(Students should note that the king was trying to make it so difficult for legislators to meet that they would simply give up. The colonists would feel that their views were not valued.)*

relinquish: give up
inestimable: priceless

annihilation: destruction

convulsions: violent disturbances

Laws for Naturalization of Foreigners: process by which foreign-born persons become citizens

tenure: term

quartering: lodging

T

He has refused his Assent to Laws, the most wholesome and necessary for the public good.

He has forbidden his Governors to pass Laws of immediate and pressing importance, unless suspended in their operation till his Assent should be obtained; and when so suspended, he has utterly neglected to attend to them.

He has refused to pass other Laws for the accommodation of large districts of people, unless those people would **relinquish** the right of Representation in the Legislature, a right **inestimable** to them and formidable to tyrants only.

C

He has called together legislative bodies at places unusual, uncomfortable, and distant from the depository of their Public Records, for the sole purpose of fatiguing them into compliance with his measures.

He has dissolved Representative Houses repeatedly, for opposing with manly firmness his invasions on the rights of the people.

He has refused for a long time, after such dissolutions, to cause others to be elected; whereby the Legislative Powers, incapable of **Annihilation**, have returned to the People at large for their exercise; the State remaining in the mean time exposed to all the dangers of invasion from without, and **convulsions** within.

He has endeavoured to prevent the population of these States; for that purpose obstructing the **Laws for Naturalization of Foreigners;** refusing to pass others to encourage their migrations hither, and raising the conditions of new Appropriations of Lands.

He has obstructed the Administration of Justice, by refusing his Assent to Laws for establishing Judiciary Powers.

He has made Judges dependent on his Will alone, for the **tenure** of their offices, and the amount and payment of their salaries.

He has erected a multitude of New Offices, and sent hither swarms of Officers to harass our people, and eat out their substance.

He has kept among us, in times of peace, Standing Armies without the Consent of our legislature.

He has affected to render the Military independent of and superior to the Civil Power.

He has combined with others to subject us to a jurisdiction foreign to our constitution, and unacknowledged by our laws; giving his Assent to their acts of pretended legislation: For **quartering** large bodies of troops among us:

© Bettmann/CORBIS

---

networks *Online Teaching Options*

The Declaration of Independence in the News

Researching on the Internet Tell students that although the Declaration of Independence was written hundreds of years ago, it is still relevant in today's society. Have pairs of students search an Internet news database and enter the search term "Declaration of Independence." Tell students to pick three news stories that reference the Declaration and note the context in which the document is mentioned. Have the pairs share their findings during a class discussion.

For protecting them, by a mock Trial, from Punishment for any Murders which they should commit on the Inhabitants of these States:

For cutting off our Trade with all parts of the world:

For imposing taxes on us without our Consent:

For depriving us in many cases, of the benefits of Trial by Jury:

For transporting us beyond Seas to be tried for pretended offences:

For abolishing the free System of English Laws in a neighbouring Province, establishing therein an Arbitrary government, and enlarging its Boundaries so as to **render** it at once an example and fit instrument for introducing the same absolute rule into these Colonies:

render: make

For taking away our Charters, abolishing our most valuable Laws, and altering fundamentally the Forms of our Governments:

For suspending our own Legislature, and declaring themselves invested with Power to legislate for us in all cases whatsoever.

He has **abdicated** Government here, by declaring us out of his Protection and waging War against us.

abdicated: given up

He has plundered our seas, ravaged our Coasts, burnt our towns, and destroyed the lives of our people.

He is at this time transporting large armies of foreign mercenaries to compleat the works of death, desolation and tyranny, already begun with circumstances of Cruelty & **perfidy** scarcely parrelleled in the most barbarous ages, and totally unworthy the Head of a civilized nation.

R **perfidy:** violation of trust

He has constrained our fellow Citizens taken Captive on the high Seas to bear Arms against their Country, to become the executioners of their friends and Brethren, or to fall themselves by their Hands.

He has excited domestic **insurrections** amongst us, and has endeavoured to bring on the inhabitants of our frontiers, the merciless Indian Savages, whose known rule of warfare, is an undistinguished destruction of all ages, sexes and conditions.

insurrections: rebellions

In every stage of these Oppressions We have **Petitioned for Redress** in the most humble terms: Our repeated Petitions have been answered only by repeated injury. A Prince, whose character is thus marked by every act which may define a Tyrant, is unfit to be the ruler of a free People.

petitioned for redress: asked formally for a correction of wrongs

C

Nor have We been wanting in attention to our British brethren. We have warned them from time to time of attempts by their legislature to extend an **unwarrantable jurisdiction** over us. We have reminded them of the circumstances of our emigration and settlement here. We have appealed to their native justice and magnanimity, and we have conjured them by the ties of our common kindred to disavow these usurpations, which, would inevitably interrupt our connections and correspondence. They too have been deaf to the voice of justice and of **consanguinity**.

unwarrantable jurisdiction: unjustified authority

W

consanguinity: originating from the same ancestor

The Declaration of Independence **139**

R Reading Skills

Defining Remind students that in the 1700s, many words we use today were spelled differently. Point out the word *compleat* in the paragraph. Have students identify the modern spelling of the word *(complete)* and give its definition as both an adjective and as a verb. *(whole, to bring to an end)*
ELL Verbal/Linguistic

C Critical Thinking Skills

Making Inferences Have students read the paragraph. **Ask:** What does the paragraph mean? *(The colonists have tried to ask for relief from these problems, but their efforts were ignored; the king is not fit to rule.)* **Ask:** What is the purpose of making this statement? *(to show that the colonists did not simply jump into the rebellion, but had no choice)*

W Writing Skills

Argument Tell students to take the role of a Patriot or a Loyalist newspaper editor in 1776, and write an editorial reacting to the Declaration of Independence. You might wish to have volunteers share their editorials with the class or in small groups and use the writings as a basis for class discussion about the role of the Patriots and Loyalists in establishing the Constitution and fighting the Revolutionary War.

Declaration of the Rights of Man and Citizen

Comparing and Contrasting Tell students that France's Declaration of the Rights of Man and Citizen was as important to the French Revolution as the Declaration of Independence was to the American Revolution. The French document was written by the Marquis de Lafayette and was partly inspired by the American Declaration. In fact, Thomas Jefferson was the U.S. minister to France at the time the document was drafted. Lafayette and Jefferson were friends and often discussed Lafayette's work.

Have students read the translation of France's Declaration online. As they read, students should note the differences and similarities between the ideas in the two documents. Have students share their findings with the class. As a class, make a Venn diagram that shows how the two documents are the same and different.

The Declaration of Independence

R1 Reading Skills

Listing Have students list the powers the new and free independent states planned to claim. *(to levy war, to conclude peace, to make alliances, to establish commerce, and all other things that governments do)* **AL**

R2 Reading Skills

Explaining Have a volunteer read aloud the last paragraph with some dramatic intonation. **Ask: What does the closing of the document mean, in which the signers "mutually pledge to each other our Lives, our Fortunes and our sacred Honor"?** *(The delegates promise their lives, their wealth, and their reputations to one another in a vow to carry out the work of independence.)* **Ask: Why do you think the word "mutually" was inserted into this last sentence of the Declaration of Independence?** *(Possible answer: The delegates understood the importance of the act they were undertaking, and that they would have to agree and stand together to face Great Britain.)*

Content Background Knowledge

Signers of the Declaration included brothers Richard Henry Lee and Francis Lightfoot Lee, from Virginia, and cousins John and Samuel Adams, from Massachusetts. At age 26, Edward Rutledge, from South Carolina, was the youngest signer of the Declaration of Independence. Despite his age, Rutledge was an influential member of the Congress. However, he was initially opposed to independence for the colonies. He even worked to delay the vote for declaring independence. When a vote finally took place, the South Carolina and New Hampshire delegations voted no. After Rutledge realized he was in the minority, he encouraged the South Carolina legislators to reconsider their vote to support independence.

CLOSE & REFLECT

Assessing Have students explain the purposes of the Declaration of Independence. *(It justified the revolution and put forth the principles on which the new nation was founded.)*

Resolution of Independence The final section declares that the colonies are "Free and Independent States" with the full power to make war, to form alliances, and to trade with other countries.

rectitude: rightness

Signers of the Declaration The signers, as representatives of the American people, declared the colonies independent from Great Britain. Most members signed the document on August 2, 1776.

We must, therefore, acquiesce in the necessity, which denounces our Separation, and hold them, as we hold the rest of mankind, Enemies in War, in Peace Friends.

[Resolution of Independence by the United States]

We, therefore, the Representatives of the united States of America, in General Congress, Assembled, appealing to the Supreme Judge of the world for the **rectitude** of our intentions, do, in the Name, and by Authority of the good People of these Colonies, solemnly publish and declare, That these United Colonies are, and of Right ought to be Free and Independent States; that they are Absolved from all Allegiance to the British Crown, and that all political connection between them and the State of Great Britain, is and ought to be totally dissolved; and that as Free and Independent States, they have full Power to levy War, conclude Peace, contract Alliances, establish Commerce, and to do all other Acts and Things which Independent States may of right do.

And for the support of this Declaration, with a firm reliance on the Protection of Divine Providence, we mutually pledge to each other our Lives, our Fortunes and our sacred Honor.

John Hancock
President from Massachusetts

Georgia
Button Gwinnett
Lyman Hall
George Walton

North Carolina
William Hooper
Joseph Hewes
John Penn

South Carolina
Edward Rutledge
Thomas Heyward, Jr.
Thomas Lynch, Jr.
Arthur Middleton

Maryland
Samuel Chase
William Paca
Thomas Stone
Charles Carroll
*   of Carrollton*

Virginia
George Wythe
Richard Henry Lee
Thomas Jefferson
Benjamin Harrison
Thomas Nelson, Jr.
Francis Lightfoot Lee
Carter Braxton

Pennsylvania
Robert Morris
Benjamin Rush
Benjamin Franklin
John Morton
George Clymer
James Smith
George Taylor
James Wilson
George Ross

Delaware
Caesar Rodney
George Read
Thomas McKean

New York
William Floyd
Philip Livingston
Francis Lewis
Lewis Morris

New Jersey
Richard Stockton
John Witherspoon
Francis Hopkinson
John Hart
Abraham Clark

New Hampshire
Josiah Bartlett
William Whipple
Matthew Thornton

Massachusetts
Samuel Adams
John Adams
Robert Treat Paine
Elbridge Gerry

Rhode Island
Stephen Hopkins
William Ellery

Connecticut
Samuel Huntington
William Williams
Oliver Wolcott
Roger Sherman

Bettmann/CORBIS

---

networks   *Online Teaching Options*

The Declaration as a Force of Change

Making Presentations Inform students that the Declaration of Independence has been a force for change in the United States and also influenced independence movements in other countries. Americans used the Declaration's ideas to promote measures such as the abolition of slavery and equal rights for women. International leaders such as Ho Chi Minh in Vietnam and Jawaharlal Nehru in India also cited the Declaration as an inspiration for the independence movements in their own countries.

Organize students into small groups. Have students conduct research online to find three examples of individuals or groups, in the United States or elsewhere, who used the Declaration to promote reform or independence. Have groups create a slide show presentation with their findings.

CHAPTER 6
The American Revolution Planner

UNDERSTANDING BY DESIGN®

Enduring Understanding
- Conflict can lead to change.

Essential Questions
- Why does conflict develop?

Predictable Misunderstandings
Students may think:
- All colonists were Patriots.
- The War for Independence was an easy victory for the Patriots.
- The Patriots defeated the British without the help of foreign allies.
- African Americans did not fight in the Revolutionary War.
- Women did not contribute to the American war effort.

Assessment Evidence
Performance Tasks:
- Hands-On Chapter Project

Other Evidence:
- Interactive Graphic Organizers
- What Do You Know? activity
- Economics of History Activity
- Geography and History Activity
- Primary Source Activity
- Written Paragraphs
- Lesson Reviews
- Online Self-Check Quizzes
- Chapter Activities and Assessment

Learners will understand:
2 TIME, CONTINUITY, AND CHANGE
   2. Concepts such as: chronology, causality, change, conflict, complexity, multiple perspectives, primary and secondary sources, and cause and effect
   7. The contributions of key persons, groups, and events from the past, and their influence on the present
3 PEOPLE, PLACES, AND ENVIRONMENTS
   8. Factors that contribute to cooperation and conflict among peoples of the nation and world, including language, religion, and political beliefs
5 INDIVIDUALS, GROUPS, AND INSTITUTIONS
   1. This theme helps us know how individuals are members of groups and institutions, and influence and shape those groups and institutions.

SUGGESTED PACING GUIDE

Introducing the Chapter	1 day	
Lesson 1	2 days	
Lesson 2	2 days	
Lesson 3	2 days	
Lesson 4	2 days	
Chapter Wrap-Up and Assessment	1 day	

TOTAL TIME   10 Days

Key for Using the Teacher Edition

SKILL-BASED ACTIVITIES

Types of skill activities found in the Teacher Edition.

V **Visual Skills** require students to analyze maps, graphs, charts, and photos.

R **Reading Skills** help students practice reading skills and master vocabulary.

W **Writing Skills** provide writing opportunities to help students comprehend the text.

C **Critical Thinking Skills** help students apply and extend what they have learned.

T **Technology Skills** require students to use digital tools effectively.

*Letters are followed by a number when there is more than one of the same type of skill on the page.

DIFFERENTIATED INSTRUCTION

All activities are written for the on-level student unless otherwise marked with the leveled labels below.
BL Beyond Level
AL Approaching Level
ELL English Language Learners
All students benefit from activities that utilize different learning styles. Many activities are marked as below when a particular learning style is highlighted.
Intrapersonal   Naturalist
Logical/Mathematical   Kinesthetic
Visual/Spatial   Auditory/Musical
Verbal/Linguistic   Interpersonal

CHAPTER OPENER PLANNER

Students will know:
- the causes of the American Revolution.
- the opposing sides in the American Revolution.
- the significant battles of the Revolutionary War and the strategies of both sides.
- how the Americans gained allies in the war.
- what helped the Patriots win independence.

Students will be able to:
- **identify** the opposing sides in the American Revolution.
- **compare and contrast** the advantages of the British and the Patriots.
- **identify and evaluate** the Patriot defeats and victories.
- **analyze and evaluate** the British plan for victory.
- **analyze** how the Americans gained allies.
- **describe** life on the home front during the Revolutionary War.
- **identify and evaluate** events and elements of the war.
- **analyze** the victory at Yorktown.
- **identify and analyze** what helped the Patriots win independence.

UNDERSTANDING
BY DESIGN®

☑ *Print Teaching Options*

V **Visual Skills**

☐ **P. 142** Students focus on the major battles of the American Revolutionary War. **Visual/Spatial**

C **Critical Thinking Skills**

☐ **P. 143** Students analyze events in U.S. and world history between 1776 and 1783.

☑ *Online Teaching Options*

V **Visual Skills**

☐ **MAP** **Place and Time: Revolutionary America 1775–1783**—Students analyze a map that shows the original 13 colonies and major battles of the Revolutionary War.

☐ **TIME LINE** **Place and Time: Revolutionary America 1775–1783**—Students learn about key American and world events during this time period.

☐ **WORLD ATLAS** Students can use this interactive map to identify regions of the world, learn about individual countries, locate political boundaries, measure distances, and much more.

☑ *Printable Digital Worksheets*

R **Reading Skills**

☐ **GRAPHIC NOVEL** **America's Citizen Soldiers**—Students learn more about the American Revolution and the summer of 1776.

Project-Based Learning

Hands-On Chapter Project

Performances on the American Revolution
Students will work in groups to present "Paul Revere's Ride" by Henry Wadsworth Longfellow to the class.

Technology Extension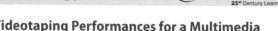

Videotaping Performances for a Multimedia Presentation
- Find an additional activity online that incorporates technology for this project.
- Visit the EdTechTeacher Web sites (included in the Technology Extension for this chapter) for more links, tutorials, and other resources.

Print Resources

ANCILLARY RESOURCES
These ancillaries are available for every chapter and lesson.

- **Reading Essentials and Study Guide Workbook** **AL** **ELL**
- **Chapter Tests and Lesson Quizzes Blackline Masters**

PRINTABLE DIGITAL WORKSHEETS
These printable digital worksheets are available for every chapter and lesson.

- **Hands-On Chapter Projects**
- **What Do You Know? activities**
- **Chapter Summaries (English and Spanish)**
- **Vocabulary Builder activities**
- **Guided Reading activities**

More Media Resources

SUGGESTED VIDEOS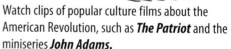
Watch clips of popular culture films about the American Revolution, such as *The Patriot* and the miniseries *John Adams.*
- **Ask:** Can fictional movies capture historically accurate events?

(NOTE: Preview clips to ensure age-appropriateness.)

SUGGESTED READING
Grade 6 reading level:
- *Five Smooth Stones: Hope's Revolutionary War Diary,* by Kristiana Gregory

Grade 7 reading level:
- *Letters for Freedom: The American Revolution,* by Douglas M. Rife and Gina Capaldi

Grade 8 reading level:
- *John Paul Jones: The Pirate Patriot,* by Armstrong Sperry

LESSON 1 PLANNER

THE WAR FOR INDEPENDENCE

Students will know:
- the causes of the American Revolution.
- the opposing sides in the American Revolution.
- the significant battles of the American Revolution and the strategies of both sides.

Students will be able to:
- **identify** the opposing sides in the American Revolution.
- **compare and contrast** the advantages of the British and the Patriots.
- **identify and evaluate** the Patriot defeats and victories.
- **analyze and evaluate** the British plan for victory.

UNDERSTANDING
BY DESIGN®

☑ Print Teaching Options

V Visual Skills

☐ **P. 147** Students compare and contrast numbers and locations of British and American victories. **Visual/Spatial**

☐ **P. 148** Students analyze a graph showing numbers of British and American troops. **Logical/Mathematical**

☐ **P. 149** Pairs analyze an image of the Battle of Bunker Hill. **Visual/Spatial**

R Reading Skills

☐ **P. 144** Students summarize the views of people before the war. **AL** **ELL**

☐ **P. 145** Students use a web to organize reasons why some colonists were Loyalists. **AL** **BL** **ELL** **Visual/Spatial**

☐ **P. 146** Students discuss why it was difficult for the colonies to raise an army.

☐ **P. 148** Students discuss early battle strategies. **AL**

☐ **P. 149** Students identify reasons for the Continental Army's near collapse. **AL** **ELL**

☐ **P. 149** Students discuss the role of African Americans in the American Army.

☐ **P. 150** Students explain the British plan to take Albany. **AL** **ELL**

☐ **P. 151** Students discuss the capture of Philadelphia and the results of the plan to capture Albany. **BL**

W Writing Skills

☐ **P. 151** Pairs work together to decide which battle they think was most important, and then individually write paragraphs explaining their reasoning. **Interpersonal**

C Critical Thinking Skills

☐ **P. 144** Students discuss differing points of view about the war.

☐ **P. 145** Students compare the position of the Patriots to a home-court advantage in sports. **BL**

☐ **P. 146** Students consider the role of the Hessians.

☐ **P. 147** Students speculate as to how the age of officers affects an army.

☐ **P. 151** Students analyze how the defeat of the British at Saratoga aided the American cause. **BL**

☑ Online Teaching Options

V Visual Skills

☐ **VIDEO** **Women of the Revolution**—Students watch a video that shows the life of Mary Hays, as she recounts to a reporter her journey from soldier's wife to folk hero Molly Pitcher during the Revolutionary War.

☐ **MAP** **The Revolutionary War, 1776–1777**—Students view a map that shows the major battles of the Revolutionary War.

☐ **IMAGE** **The Liberty Bell**—Students explore the history of the Liberty Bell.

☐ **IMAGE** **The Continental Army**—Students explore the history of the Continental Army.

☐ **IMAGE** **Hessian Soldiers**—Students explore the background of these British mercenaries.

R Reading Skills

☐ **GRAPHIC ORGANIZER** **Taking Notes:** *Categorizing:* **Early Battles**—Students list the Patriot defeats and victories during the early years of the revolution.

☐ **PRIMARY SOURCE** **The Battle of Trenton**—Students analyze an excerpt from *The Battle of Trenton* by Henry K. How.

☐ **BIOGRAPHY** **Peter Salem**—Students click to learn about this African American soldier.

C Critical Thinking Skills

☐ **GRAPH** **The Fighting Forces, 1777**—Students click to reveal data about the fighting forces of the British Regular Army and the Continental Army.

☐ **SLIDE SHOW** **Women of the Revolution**—Students view a slide show of the role of women during the Revolutionary War.

T Technology Skills

☐ **SELF-CHECK QUIZ** **Lesson 1**—Students receive instant feedback on their mastery of lesson content.

☑ Printable Digital Worksheets

C Critical Thinking Skills

☐ **WORKSHEET** **Geography and History Activity: Understanding Location: The War for Independence**—Students answer questions based on a reading passage and a map.

THE WAR CONTINUES

Students will know:
- how the Americans gained allies in the war.

Students will be able to:
- **analyze** how the Americans gained allies.
- **describe** life on the home front during the Revolutionary War.
- **identify and evaluate** events and elements of the war.

UNDERSTANDING
BY DESIGN®

☑ *Print Teaching Options*

R Reading Skills

☐ **P. 152** Students contrast the different approaches of France and Spain. **AL** **ELL**

☐ **P. 153** Students identify the hardships faced at Valley Forge.

☐ **P. 155** Students discuss the contributions of two Polish men.

☐ **P. 155** Students identify the role of foreign individuals in the war effort. **AL** **ELL**

☐ **P. 156** Students compare the inflation of a balloon to inflation in the economy. **BL** Visual/Spatial

☐ **P. 157** Students discuss how the Revolutionary War affected attitudes toward slavery.

W Writing Skills

☐ **P. 154** Students write a journal entry from the perspective of a soldier at Valley Forge. Intrapersonal

C Critical Thinking Skills

☐ **P. 152** Students infer why the French kept their involvement in the war secret. **BL**

☐ **P. 153** Students consider the faithfulness of the soldiers at Valley Forge. **BL**

☐ **P. 154** Students compare a description of conditions with a painting of solders at Valley Forge. Visual/Spatial

☐ **P. 155** Students reflect on how Baron von Steuben affected the troops.

☐ **P. 156** Students imagine how war affected the people left at home. **BL** **ELL**

☐ **P. 156** Students discuss women's roles in society during the war. **AL**

☐ **P. 157** Students discuss points of view of Loyalists and Patriots.

☑ *Online Teaching Options*

V Visual Skills

☐ **VIDEO** **Turning Point of the Revolutionary War**—Students view a video that explains how the battles at Trenton and Princeton restored the morale of the American people.

☐ **BIOGRAPHY** **Baron von Steuben**—Students learn about this Prussian who helped train Patriot soldiers.

☐ **BIOGRAPHY** **Juan de Miralles**—Students click to learn about the first Spanish diplomatic representative to the United States

☐ **PRIMARY SOURCE** **Early U.S. Currency**—Students view an image of early paper currency.

R Reading Skills

☐ **GRAPHIC ORGANIZER** **Taking Notes:** *Identifying:* **Sources of Aid to the Patriots**—Students use a diagram to record sources of aid to the Patriots during the Revolutionary War.

☐ **BIOGRAPHY** **Abigail Adams**—Students learn about her role in supporting the revolutionary cause and women's rights.

☐ **BIOGRAPHY** **Benjamin Franklin**—Students learn of Franklin's life and accomplishments.

☐ **BIOGRAPHY** **Martha Washington**—Students learn about America's first First Lady.

C Critical Thinking Skills

☐ **TIME LINE** **Thaddeus Kościuszko**—Students read about the events of his life.

☐ **PRIMARY SOURCE** **The Winter at Valley Forge**—Students analyze an excerpt from Washington's letter to Governor George Clinton.

☐ **PRIMARY SOURCE** **The Letters of Abigail Adams**—Students analyze an excerpt from Abigail Adams's letters to her husband, John Adams.

T Technology Skills

☐ **SELF-CHECK QUIZ** **Lesson 2**—Students receive instant feedback on their mastery of lesson content.

☑ *Printable Digital Worksheets*

C Critical Thinking Skills

☐ **WORKSHEET** **Economics of History Activity: The United States and Public Debt**—Students analyze the growth of public debt over time.

BATTLEGROUNDS SHIFT

Students will know:
- *the significant battles of the American Revolution.*

Students will be able to:
- ***identify** and **evaluate** events and elements of the war.*

☑ *Print Teaching Options*

V Visual Skills

☐ **P. 160** Students use visuals as a prompt to discuss John Paul Jones. **Visual/Spatial**

☐ **P. 161** Students infer why Savannah was an important city. **Visual/Spatial**

☐ **P. 163** Students analyze a political cartoon. **BL**

R Reading Skills

☐ **P. 158** Students identify details from the text. **AL**

☐ **P. 159** Students discuss the meaning of the word "blockade."

☐ **P. 160** Students use context to identify meaning of figurative words. **BL** **ELL**

☐ **P. 161** Students find text evidence to support several statements. **AL** **ELL**

☐ **P. 162** Students discuss the meaning of "hit-and-run."

W Writing Skills

☐ **P. 161** Students write about the move of the battlefields to the south. **Verbal/Linguistic**

☐ **P. 162** Students write letters from the point of view of mountain people told to join the British. **Interpersonal**

C Critical Thinking Skills

☐ **P. 158** Students identify the effect of colonists wanting more land.

☐ **P. 159** Students speculate why fishermen were eager to become privateers. **BL**

☐ **P. 162** Students consider the advantage of hit-and-run attacks. **BL**

☐ **P. 163** Students discuss Green's army.

☑ *Online Teaching Options*

V Visual Skills

☐ **VIDEO** **Victory at Yorktown**—Students view a video that describes this shared triumph of the French and American armies.

☐ **TIME LINE** **Bernardo de Gálvez, 1746–1786**—Students explore the events of his life.

☐ **MAP** **The Revolutionary War in the West and South, 1778–1781**—Students trace the movement of troops between 1778 and 1781.

R Reading Skills

☐ **GRAPHIC ORGANIZER** **Taking Notes:** *Determining Cause and Effect:* **British Defeats in the South**—Students use a diagram to show why the British lost control in the South.

☐ **BIOGRAPHY** **John Paul Jones**—Students read a biography of this naval hero.

C Critical Thinking Skills

☐ **CHART** **Native American Alliances in the Revolutionary War**—Students identify the tribes that sided with the British and the Patriots.

☐ **POLITICAL CARTOON** **The Horse, America, Throwing His Master**—Students analyze a political cartoon.

T Technology Skills

☐ **SELF-CHECK QUIZ** **Lesson 3**—Students receive instant feedback on their mastery of lesson content.

☑ *Printable Digital Worksheets*

C Critical Thinking Skills

☐ **WORKSHEET** **Primary Source Activity: Cornwallis and Greene**—Students compare points of view of these two generals.

THE FINAL YEARS

Students will know:
- *what helped the Patriots win independence.*

Students will be able to:
- **analyze** *the victory at Yorktown.*
- **identify and analyze** *what helped the Patriots win independence.*

UNDERSTANDING
BY DESIGN®

☑ *Print Teaching Options*

R Reading Skills

☐ **P. 164** Students use text headings to provide clues to what they will learn.

☐ **P. 165** Students discuss Washington's strategy at Yorktown. **AL BL ELL**

☐ **P. 166** Students describe details of the surrender at Yorktown. **BL** Musical/Auditory

☐ **P. 167** Students analyze how the battle at Yorktown affected the outcome of the war. **BL**

☐ **P. 167** Students explain how the war ended and describe the beginning of the peace process.

☐ **P. 168** Students consider George Washington's departure from the army. **AL**

W Writing Skills

☐ **P. 168** Students list reasons the Americans won the war. Verbal/Linguistic

C Critical Thinking Skills

☐ **P. 164** Students consider why the initial plan for an attack on New York City was revised. **AL BL ELL**

☐ **P. 166** Students consider how the British must have felt after their defeat at Yorktown.

☐ **P. 167** Students consider the time between the defeat of the British at Yorktown and the end of the war. **BL** Interpersonal

T Technology Skills

☐ **P. 169** Students conduct Internet research on the French Revolution.

☑ *Online Teaching Options*

V Visual Skills

☐ **VIDEO** **Colonial Leader and General**—Students explore Washington's leadership roles.

☐ **MAP** **Siege at Yorktown 1781**—Students visualize the staging of troops and ships at this decisive battle.

☐ **IMAGE** **Yankee Doodle**—Students examine a painting showing patriots in the Revolutionary War.

R Reading Skills

☐ **GRAPHIC ORGANIZER** **Taking Notes:** *Describing:* **Treaty of Paris**—Students list details of the Treaty of Paris.

☐ **BIOGRAPHY** **Comte de Rochambeau**—Students read of this general's life and accomplishments.

C Critical Thinking Skills

☐ **IMAGE** **Revolution in Haiti**—Students learn about Toussaint Louverture, who spearheaded the revolution that resulted in independence in 1804.

☐ **AUDIO** **Yankee Doodle**—Students listen to children singing this period song.

T Technology Skills

☐ **SELF-CHECK QUIZ** **Lesson 4**—Students receive instant feedback on their mastery of lesson content.

LESSON 1 The War for Independence

Reading and Comprehension

This section is about *independence*. Ask students to skim the chapter and find words or phrases that are related to the word *independence*.

Text Evidence

Ask students to create a T-chart with *British* and *Patriots* as the column heads. Under each head, have them list possible resources and attributes that each group had (clothing, discipline, money, shoes, an important cause, leadership, etc.). They should support their answers by using the text.

LESSON 2 The War Continues

Reading and Comprehension

Ask students to skim the lesson and write the names of three people they know nothing about. Then have them read the text and write a short description of each person.

Text Evidence

Divide the class into groups and ask them to talk about the nationalities of people who helped the colonists. Each group should mark the locations of these allies' countries on a map in the classroom. Have students return to the lesson to check their answers.

LESSON 3 Battlegrounds Shift

Reading and Comprehension

Ask students to skim the chapter and find three words that are new to them. They should use a dictionary to find the meaning and then use the word in a sentence.

Text Evidence

Divide the class into groups and tell them to list some of the major battles mentioned in this lesson. Ask them to create a map and mark the locations of as many of the battles as they can. Have them refer to the text and the map to check answers.

LESSON 4 The Final Years

Reading and Comprehension

Ask students to skim the chapter and find three words that are new to them. They should use a dictionary to find the meaning and then use the word in a sentence.

Text Evidence

Ask students to write a letter from the perspective of a British soldier who is corresponding with his family in England. They should explain in the letter why the British lost the war. Ask students to use evidence in the text to help them craft their letters.

Online Resources

Approaching Level Reader

Use this online lower-level text that corresponds directly to the text in the Student Edition. It includes a Spanish version.

Guided Reading Activities

This resource uses graphic organizers and guiding questions to help students with comprehension.

What Do You Know?

Use these worksheets to pre-assess student's background knowledge before they study the chapter.

Reading Essentials and Study Guide Workbook

This resource offers writing and reading activities for the approaching-level student. Also available in Spanish.

Self-Check Quizzes

This online assessment tool provides instant feedback for students to check their progress.

How Do I Teach with
Graphic Novels?

Graphic novels cannot replace reading for content, but they can be used effectively to build a student's background knowledge, to motivate students, to provide a different access route to the content, and to allow students to check and review their work. A variety of graphic novels can be found in the online Teacher and Student Resource Libraries of each McGraw-Hill program.

Teaching Strategy **1** Previewing Content

- Before reading textbook narrative, assign appropriate graphic novels to activate background knowledge.

- Project the digital graphic novel on the classroom whiteboard and discuss it with the class.

Teaching Strategy **2** Narrative and Summary Writing

- Ask students to read one of the graphic novels, paying attention to details and imagery presented in the story.

- Then ask students to write their own summary of the story being told in the graphic novel. This strategy can be especially useful in the graphic novels that are very illustrative and don't use much character dialogue.

Teaching Strategy **3** Improving Content Analysis Skills

- Graphic novels often have a thematic strand that illustrates a specific point about the content being studied. This may take the form of irony, humor, or a more direct and formal approach to an event.

- Have students read a graphic novel with the intention of trying to understand the main point the author is trying to convey. This approach is particularly useful after students have covered the content in the main textbook. Pose these questions to help students uncover the main points:

  a) Why did the author choose this topic?

  b) What does the graphic novel tell me about the people or events we have studied?

  c) Does the author portray the characters in a positive or a negative way?

  d) Is the tone of the story humorous or serious?

  e) What conclusions can I draw about the author's intentions in creating this graphic novel?

The American Revolution

1776–1783

ESSENTIAL QUESTION · *Why does conflict develop?*

◄ *General George Washington led the Continental Army in the War for Independence.*

Samuel King/The Bridgeman Art Library/Getty Images

The Story Matters ...

It is December 25, 1776. General George Washington is preparing to lead 2,400 troops across the Delaware River to launch a surprise attack on the British troops stationed in Trenton. The river is filled with huge chunks of ice. The weather is terrible, and hurricane-force winds pound at Washington's troops. After crossing the Delaware River, General Washington and his troops will have to march 9 miles (14 km) to meet their enemy. General Washington is well aware how important a victory in Trenton could be. The young United States is in desperate need of some battlefield success in its war against the British.

141

ENGAGE

🔔 **Bellringer** Ask students to name wars or conflicts they have heard of. *(Arab Spring, Gulf Wars, World War I & II, the Civil War)* List their responses on the board. **Ask: Where were these wars fought? What were some of the conditions that soldiers had to endure?** *(Answers will vary.)* Tell students they are going to look at the causes, conditions, and locations of early battles in the Revolutionary War.

Making Connections

Have students read "The Story Matters . . . " to themselves. Discuss the weather conditions (the cold and the high winds), the icy water, and the huge chunks of ice that confronted Washington as he tried to move 2,400 troops across the river and prepare for battle. Remind students that once the army crossed the river they still had to march 9 miles (14.5 km) before they could engage the British. **Ask:**

- Why did General Washington choose to cross the Delaware River under such harsh conditions? *(General Washington braved the harsh weather and difficult circumstances to launch a surprise attack. He knew the importance of winning the battle at Trenton.)*
- Are there things that you would brave similar conditions to protect? *(Some students might say that there are things worth fighting and facing danger for, such as family and freedom.)*

Letter from the Author

Dear American History Teacher,

The American Revolution should fascinate students when they realize the dim prospects for success the Americans had in 1776. All the advantages of soldiers, wealth, and weaponry lay with the British, but the Americans were driven by their cause, and they knew the terrain on which the battles would take place. Washington turned out to be a very wise military tactician, and he kept his army in the field against great odds.

Joyce Appleby

TEACH & ASSESS

Step Into the Place

V Visual Skills

Analyzing Maps Direct students to the map that shows the major battles in the War for Independence. Have students recall that the thirteen colonies are often organized into three geographic regions: New England, Middle, and Southern Colonies and the geographic and economic differences among the geographic regions. Explain to students that the American Revolution was fought on many fronts. Focus on the regions of some of the most important battles, especially the battles that involved harbors and sea ports. As a class, discuss the Map Focus questions. **Visual/Spatial**

Content Background Knowledge

The theories in Adam Smith's influential book of 1776, *The Wealth of Nations,* are still used today. His ideas of limited government intervention in the economy are part of the underlying platform of the modern Republican Party. His arguments against restrictions on international trade have been used in debates on the North American Free Trade Agreement (NAFTA) and importing of Japanese automobiles.

CHAPTER 6 CCSS

Place and Time: Revolutionary America 1775 to 1783

After a period of growing tension, the American colonies rebelled against the British. Soon, Patriot soldiers were fighting against British redcoats up and down the East Coast as well as in the West. The map on the next page shows many of the major battles of the Revolutionary War.

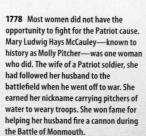

1776 Nathan Hale (standing, left) was an officer of the Continental Army, but his greatest contribution was as a spy—and as a symbol of the Patriot spirit of freedom. Captured by the British during a mission and sentenced to die, Hale is said to have declared, "I only regret that I have but one life to lose for my country."

Step Into the Place

MAP FOCUS This map shows some of the major battles fought during the American Revolution.

1 **PLACE** Which two battles were fought in New Jersey? RH.6–8.7

2 **LOCATION** Which was the southernmost battle? RH.6–8.7

3 **CRITICAL THINKING** *Identifying* Where did most of the battles in the Revolutionary War take place? RH.6–8.7

1778 Most women did not have the opportunity to fight for the Patriot cause. Mary Ludwig Hays McCauley—known to history as Molly Pitcher—was one woman who did. The wife of a Patriot soldier, she had followed her husband to the battlefield when he went off to war. She earned her nickname carrying pitchers of water to weary troops. She won fame for helping her husband fire a cannon during the Battle of Monmouth.

Step Into the Time

C **TIME LINE** This era is dominated by war between Britain and its American colonies. Why do you think Great Britain hired German mercenaries in 1775? RH.6–8.5, RH.6–8.7

| U.S. EVENTS | | | |
| WORLD EVENTS | 1774 | | 1776 |

1774 Joseph Priestley discovers oxygen

1775 The British hire German soldiers to fight for them in North America

1776 Adam Smith publishes *Wealth of Nations*

1776 Thomas Jefferson writes the Declaration of Independence

1777 Americans and British fight Battle of Saratoga

The Granger Collection, NY; The Bettmann/CORBIS

Project-Based Learning

Hands-On Chapter Project

Performances on the American Revolution

Student groups will memorize a stanza (or two or three) of "Paul Revere's Ride" by Henry Wadsworth Longfellow. Students will utilize Tips for Reading Poetry to help understand the poem and will discuss its meaning as a group. Using their discussion points, each group will write a summary of its stanza(s) to present to the class along with their memorized stanzas.

Technology Extension

Videotaping Performances for a Multimedia Presentation

Turn your students' recitations of Henry Wadsworth Longfellow's "Paul Revere's Ride," into a multimedia presentation. As each group recites their stanzas, video record their performance. Have each group design slides for their stanza(s) that include the written stanza(s), their summary, and definitions to aid the viewer in better understanding the poem. Finally, students will add their public performances to complete the multimedia presentation slides.

edtechteacher
21st Century Learning

ANSWERS, p. 142

Step Into the Place
1. Trenton and Princeton
2. Savannah
3. **CRITICAL THINKING** Most battles took place in the Middle or Southern Colonies.

Step Into the Time
The British were facing the war in the colonies, and perhaps they also anticipated the coming wars with Spain and Holland, so they needed additional troops.

The War for Independence 1775–1781

Lake Superior

Lake Michigan

Lake Huron

L. Ontario

Lake Erie

St. Lawrence R.

Lake Champlain
Ft. Ticonderoga

Lake George

N.H.
Bennington

Saratoga

New York

Bunker Hill
Mass.
Boston
Conn.
Lexington & Concord
R.I.

Delaware

Susquehanna R.

New York City
Pa.
Trenton
Long Island
Princeton
N.J.
Philadelphia
Hudson R.

Md.
Del.

Wabash River

Cahokia   Vincennes

Kaskaskia

Ohio River

APPALACHIAN MOUNTAINS

Virginia
York R.
James R.
Yorktown
Chesapeake Bay

ATLANTIC OCEAN

Guilford Courthouse

NorthCarolina
Kings Mtn.

Cowpens
Camden
South
Carolina

Georgia
Charles Town

Savannah

Tennessee River

Mississippi River

Gulf of Mexico

0   200 miles

0   200 km

Lambert Azimuthal Equal-Area projection

60°W

45°N

40°N

35°N

30°N

95°W   90°W   85°W   80°W   75°W   70°W   65°W

N W E S

Original 13 Colonies
Major battle

1778 Act of Congress prohibits import of enslaved people into U.S.

1780 British forces capture Charles Town, South Carolina

1781 British surrender at Yorktown

1782 Spain completes conquest of Florida

1783 Treaty of Paris is signed

1778   **1780**   **1782**   **1784**

1779 Spain declares war on Great Britain

1780 Great Britain declares war on Holland

1783 Japan suffers famine

143

Step Into the Time

C Critical Thinking Skills

Making Inferences Have students review the time line for the chapter. Explain that they will be studying events from around 1776 to 1783. **Ask: According to the time line, how many wars was Great Britain fighting during the American Revolution?** *(The time line notes indicate wars with the United States, Spain, and Holland.)* **How might this have affected Great Britain's war effort in the colonies?** *(This could have overstretched the British fighting forces and made it harder to focus their efforts on winning the American Revolution.)*

Content Background Knowledge

In 1782, Spain won Florida from the British. This territory was important because of its trees. Francis Philip Fatio was Swiss and had lived in Italy, France, and Britain. He started three plantations in Florida to produce turpentine, indigo, oranges, and sheep. He realized the value of the forests on the East Coast, and lumber, timber, staves, and shingles made of pine and cedar were some of the area's first exports.

CLOSE & REFLECT

Ask students to write down one thing they knew about this time period before today's lesson, one thing they learned during the lesson, and something they'd like to learn in the chapter.

WORKSHEET

What Do You Know? Activity: The Spirit of Independence

Reasoning Have students complete the Opinionnaire® activity before they study the chapter. Direct students to read the statements carefully before deciding whether they strongly agree, agree, disagree, or strongly disagree with each statement. Next take a class poll so that you can tailor your lessons to focus on students' ideas and feelings.

After students complete the chapter, have them take the survey again to see if any of their ideas have changed. Invite students who have changed their responses to explain why they did so. *(Students should cite facts from the chapter.)*

See page 141B for other online activities.

ENGAGE

Bellringer Use the Chapter Opener map depicting the battles of the Revolutionary War to discuss the location of the war in America. Tell students that in this lesson they will learn about the early years of the war for independence. **Ask: On which continent did the war take place?** (*North America*) **On which coast?** (*the East Coast*) **In which colonies?** (*Many colonies saw battles, as shown on the map.*)

How can the location of a war and its many battles affect the outcome? (*It can help the people whose land or country is being attacked because they are more familiar with the terrain and are fighting to protect their homes. On the other hand, it is their land and homes that will be destroyed.*)

TEACH & ASSESS

R Reading Skills

Summarizing Discuss with students what they think people thought about the prospect of war. Then direct them to read the first paragraph of the lesson. **Ask: What was John Adams's opinion on the human cost of the war?** (*Adams thought it would be a long war with many deaths.*) **Did people agree or disagree with him?** (*Few people agreed because each side thought they would win quickly.*) **AL** **ELL**

C Critical Thinking Skills

Drawing Conclusions Use the description of the fighting forces of the British and the Patriots to discuss the advantages of each side and opinions of the British and the Patriots about the war. **Ask: Which side seems to have the greater chance of winning a war? Why?** (*The British have a far superior fighting force, larger population, organized fighting forces, and greater wealth, which should indicate a greater likelihood of success in a war.*)

ANSWER, p. 144

TAKING NOTES: Defeats: Battle of Long Island, Battle of Brandywine, Battle of Paoli, capture of Philadelphia, Battle of Germantown, Battle of Fort Ticonderoga; **Victories:** Battle of Trenton, Battle of Princeton, Battle of Fort Stanwix, Battle of Saratoga

---

networks
There's More Online!
- ☑ **GRAPHIC ORGANIZER** Early Battles
- ☑ **SLIDE SHOW** Famous Women of the Revolutionary War

Lesson 1
The War for Independence

ESSENTIAL QUESTION *Why does conflict develop?*

IT MATTERS BECAUSE
The Patriots used skill, cunning, and determination to survive early defeats and win a key victory at Saratoga.

The Two Armies Face Off

GUIDING QUESTION *Who were the opposing sides in the American Revolution?*

R In April 1776, colonial leader John Adams predicted "We shall have a long … and bloody war to go through." Few people agreed with him. Each side thought they would win the war quickly. The British planned to crush the colonists by force. Most Patriots—Americans who supported independence—believed the British would give up after losing one or two major battles.

British Advantages

As the war began, the British seemed to have a big advantage. They had the strongest navy in the world. The British also had a well-trained army. They were supported by the wealth of their empire. Great Britain also had more people. More than 8 million people lived in Britain. There were only 2.5 million Americans.

C The Patriots did not seem to be a match for the British. They had no regular army and a weak navy. American soldiers also lacked experience and weapons for fighting. Much of the Patriot military force was in the form of militia groups. These volunteer soldiers fought only for short periods of time and then returned home.

(l) Painting by Don Troiani, courtesy of Historical Art Prints, Ltd. (cl) Bob Krist/CORBIS, (c) Blend Images / SuperStock, (cr) The Granger Collection, NYC, (r) SuperStock

Reading HELPDESK CCSS

Taking Notes: *Categorizing* RH.6–8.1
Use a diagram like this one to list the Patriot defeats and victories during the early years of the American Revolution.

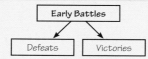
Early Battles → Defeats / Victories

Content Vocabulary (Tier 3 Words)
- **mercenary**
- **recruit**

144 *The American Revolution*

---

networks *Online Teaching Options*

VIDEO

Women of the Revolution

Speculating Ask students what historical figures they associate with the Revolutionary War. Point out how many—or how few—of them are women. Ask students why they think this is so. Before students watch "Women of the Revolution," challenge them to predict the types of women's roles the film will depict. After sharing the video, guide students in comparing what they predicted they would see with what they saw.

See page 141C for other online activities.

In addition, not all Americans supported the struggle for independence. Some Americans remained loyal to Britain. Others, such as the Quakers, were neutral. They would not take part in the war because they opposed all armed conflict.

Loyalists in the Colonies

At least one in five Americans was thought to be a "Loyalist" or "Tory." The number may have been as high as one in three. These Americans remained loyal to Britain and opposed independence. Some Americans changed sides during the war. Loyalist support also varied from region to region. In general, support for Britain was strongest in the Carolinas and Georgia and weakest in New England.

Loyalists had reasons to support Britain. Some depended on the British for their jobs. Some feared the Revolution would throw America into chaos. Others simply could not understand why the colonies wanted independence. For them, Patriot complaints seemed minor and not worth fighting over.

The British actively sought the support of African Americans. Virginia's royal governor, Lord Dunmore, promised freedom to those African Americans who joined the British cause. Many men answered his call. Eventually some of them ended up free in Canada. Others settled in the British colony of Sierra Leone in Africa.

Loyalty to Britain divided friends and family. For example, William Franklin, son of Patriot Benjamin Franklin, was a Loyalist who had served as a royal governor of New Jersey. This disagreement caused lasting damage to their relationship. As one Connecticut man observed: "Neighbor [was] ... against neighbor, father against son and son against father, and he that would not thrust his own blade through his brother's heart was called an infamous villain."

Advantages of the Patriots

The Patriots did hold some advantages. They were fighting on their own ground. The British, on the other hand, had to fight from thousands of miles across the Atlantic Ocean. It took time and money to ship soldiers and supplies.

R

C

The Continental Army was made up mostly of inexperienced soldiers.

Thinking Like a HISTORIAN

Drawing Inferences and Conclusions

Made in the 1750s, the Liberty Bell hung in the Pennsylvania State House (now Independence Hall). Legend has it that on July 8, 1776, the bell's ringing announced the first public reading of the Declaration of Independence. The Liberty Bell also rang every Fourth of July and for many public events until a crack appeared in about 1846. Today, the Liberty Bell stands as a symbol of freedom. Why do you think such symbols are important to the people of a country? For more about drawing inferences and conclusions, review *Thinking Like a Historian.*

(t) Bob Kreist/CORBIS
(b) Painting by Don Troiani, courtesy of Historical Art Prints, Ltd.

Build Vocabulary: *Word Parts*

The suffix *-ist* means "one who is." Adding this suffix to an adjective creates a noun. Adding *-ist* to the word *loyal* makes the word *loyalist*—one who is loyal. During the Revolution, Loyalists were Americans who were loyal to Great Britain.

Lesson 1 **145**

CHAPTER 6, Lesson 1

The War for Independence

R Reading Skills

Identifying Draw a concept web on the board, and write "Reasons for Remaining Loyal to England" in the center. As students read the section titled "Loyalists in the Colonies," have a volunteer record information from the text in the web. *(Students should record that some people depended on the British for jobs; some feared the chaos war would bring; some did not think the problems of the colonies were worth fighting over.)*

Ask: Why do you think that many African Americans gave their loyalties to the British? *(Most African Americans were enslaved. They probably hoped that the British would give them their freedom.)* **AL** **BL** **ELL** Visual/Spatial

C Critical Thinking Skills

Evaluating Ask students to raise their hands if they play sports. **Ask:**

- **What does the term "home-court advantage" mean?** *(The correct answer should reflect that there is a level of comfort and familiarity associated with playing on your home court.)* **BL**
- **Did home-court advantage play a role in the American Revolution?** *(The Patriots did have the advantage of fighting on their own land, making them more familiar with the terrain. The British forces also had to ship troops and supplies across the Atlantic Ocean to fight the war.)*

Content Background Knowledge

The Quakers Quakers is the popular name for a group called the Religious Society of Friends. This group broke away from the Church of England in the 17th century to establish a simpler, more spiritual style of worship. They are known for pacifism and humanitarian activities. A Quaker, William Penn, founded the colony of Pennsylvania in 1682. Quakers governed Pennsylvania until 1756.

IMAGE

The Liberty Bell

Using Visual Aids Use the interactive image of the liberty bell to discuss the history of the bell and its role as a symbol of freedom. Ask students to name other American symbols. *(Students might mention bald eagles, the statue of liberty, and the American Flag, among others.)* **AL** **ELL**

See page 141C for other online activities.

McGraw-Hill **networks** The Liberty Bell

The Liberty Bell was ordered from a company in London in 1751. The bell first cracked from the stroke of the clapper when it was being tested. John Pass and John Stow melted down the bell and cast a new bell in 1753. It rang to announce the first public reading of the Declaration of Independence on July 8, 1776.

Bob Krist/CORBIS

ANSWER, p. 145

Thinking Like a Historian Students might mention the role of symbols in representing and reinforcing shared values or ideals.

Chapter 6 **145**

The War for Independence

Drawing Conclusions Encourage students to consider how differences in motivation could affect the outcome of a conflict. **Ask: Who were the Hessians, and what role did they play during the war?** *(Hessians were mercenaries, or hired soldiers. Great Britain hired them to fight against the Americans.)* **Why did the Hessians have less motivation than the Patriots?** *(The Patriots were fighting for their own rights and freedoms; the Hessians were paid to fight.)*

R Reading Skills

Explaining Direct students to read the section titled "The Continental Army." Discuss with students why it was difficult to raise an army. Remind students that Congress had limited power and could not raise money through taxation. **Ask: Did the colonies have an army established before the start of the war?** *(Though individual colonies had militias, there had never been a unified army before.)* Ask students to discuss why the colonists were not able to unite the Continental Army with the local militia forces. Remind students to support their responses with evidence from the text.

THEN

During the Revolutionary War, women could not officially join the army. A few managed to fight in disguise. Many more served as cooks, nurses, or even spies.

NOW

Today, about 400,000 women serve in the American armed forces, reserves, and National Guard.

▶ **CRITICAL THINKING**
Comparing and Contrasting How have attitudes about women in the military changed since the 1770s?

R

The Patriot soldier also had greater motivation, or sense of purpose. The British relied on **mercenaries** (MUHR·suh·nehr·eez) to fight for them. The Americans called these mercenaries "Hessians" (HEH·shuhnz) after the region in Germany from which most of them came. The Patriots fought for the freedom of their own land. This gave them a greater stake in the war's outcome than soldiers who fought for money. The Americans also lured the Hessians away with promises of land.

C

The Patriots' greatest advantage was probably their leader, George Washington. Few could match him for courage and determination. The war might have taken a different turn without Washington.

The Continental Army

After the Declaration of Independence, the Continental Congress served as the national government. However, the Congress lacked the power to raise money through taxes. Delegates led by James Madison of Virginia called for a stronger national government to bind the colonies together. They believed that winning independence was possible only under a strong national government.

Not every American agreed. They placed great value on liberty and personal freedom. After rejecting the rule of the British Parliament, they were unwilling to **transfer** power to their own Continental Congress. As a result, the American Revolution was in some ways 13 separate wars, with each state fighting for its own interests. This made it hard for the Congress to get soldiers and raise money.

Local militia made up a key part of the Patriot forces. These troops were limited. Many were farmers who needed to provide for their families and did not want to leave their fields unattended. The Patriots also needed well-trained soldiers who could fight the British throughout the colonies. To meet this need, the Congress established the Continental Army, which depended on the states to **recruit** (ree·KROOT) soldiers.

At first, soldiers signed up for just one year, but General Washington asked for longer terms. "If we ever hope for success," he said, "we must have men enlisted for the whole term of the war." Eventually the Continental Congress invited soldiers to sign up for three years or until the war ended. Most soldiers, however, still signed up for only one year.

Reading **HELP**DESK **CCSS**

mercenary hired soldier
recruit to enlist in the military

Academic Vocabulary (Tier 2 Words)
transfer to move
previous earlier

(l) The Granger Collection, New York, (c) Blend Images / SuperStock

---

netw⊙rks *Online Teaching Options*

IMAGE

The Continental Army

Contrasting Use the interactive image to help students identify the difference between colonial militias and the permanent army. **Ask: How were the militia forces different from Continental Army soldiers?** *(Militia forces were local individuals who would come to fight when called upon. They were often farmers who did not want to leave their farms for long periods of time. Continental Army forces were professional soldiers who were being paid to fight wherever they were ordered to.)* **Why were militias important to the revolution?** *(The Continental Army was not able to get as many regular soldiers as Washington would have liked. Local militias knew the land and were motivated to protect their homes and families.)* **BL**

See page 141C for other online activities.

McGraw-Hill **netw⊙rks** · The Continental Army

The Second Continental Congress established the Continental Army, America's first regular army, in 1775.

Led by General George Washington, this army was made up of two groups: a "standing" permanent army and supplemental soldiers from each state, known as militias.

The state militias were temporary and only fought for a specific amount of time. Following the Treaty of Paris (1783) at the end of the war, the Continental Army was officially disbanded.

Historical Art Prints, Ltd.

ANSWER, p. 146

CRITICAL THINKING Today women are allowed to serve openly in the military, even in combat positions, while in the 1770s they had to serve secretly or in support roles in the military.

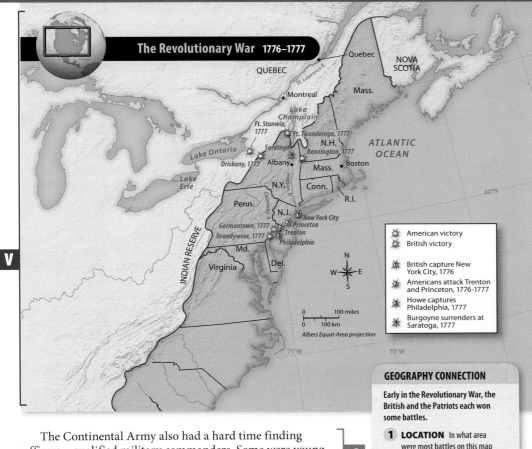

The Revolutionary War 1776–1777

QUEBEC
Quebec
NOVA SCOTIA
Montreal
Mass.
Lake Champlain
Ft. Stanwix, 1777
Ft. Ticonderoga, 1777
Lake Ontario
Saratoga
N.H.
Bennington, 1777
ATLANTIC OCEAN
Oriskany, 1777
Albany
Mass.
Boston
Lake Erie
N.Y.
Conn.
R.I.
40°N
Penn.
N.J.
New York City
Germantown, 1777
Princeton
Brandywine, 1777
Trenton
Philadelphia
Md.
Del.
INDIAN RESERVE
Virginia
75°W
70°W

American victory
British victory
British capture New York City, 1776
Americans attack Trenton and Princeton, 1776-1777
Howe captures Philadelphia, 1777
Burgoyne surrenders at Saratoga, 1777

0   100 miles
0   100 km
Albers Equal-Area projection

The Continental Army also had a hard time finding officers—qualified military commanders. Some were young men who were recruited from the ranks. The best officers had experience from **previous**, or earlier, wars.

Men did all the fighting—with a few exceptions. For example, Margaret Corbin of Pennsylvania went with her husband when he joined the Continental Army. After he died in battle, she took his place. Mary Ludwig Hays McCauley joined her husband in battle as well. The soldiers called her "Moll of the Pitcher," or "Molly Pitcher," because she carried water pitchers to the soldiers. Legend has it she also took part in combat. On February 21, 1822, Pennsylvania recognized Molly Pitcher's service by granting her an annual payment of $40. Deborah Sampson of Massachusetts took a different route to the battlefield. She joined up as a soldier by disguising herself as a man.

✓ PROGRESS CHECK

Summarizing What disadvantages did the Patriots face in fighting the British?

GEOGRAPHY CONNECTION

Early in the Revolutionary War, the British and the Patriots each won some battles.

1 **LOCATION** In what area were most battles on this map fought?

2 **CRITICAL THINKING** *Sequencing* According to this map, which British victory occurred just before the Battle of Saratoga?

V Visual Skills

Analyzing Maps Ask students to examine the map and compare and contrast the numbers and locations of the American and British victories. *(Students may mention that there were more British victories near the coast than inland and that the Americans won equal numbers of battles near the coast and inland. Overall, the British had more victories than the Americans.)* **Visual/Spatial**

C Critical Thinking Skills

Predicting Consequences Point out to students that many of the officers in the Continental Army were young. **Ask: How might the age of the officers affect the army?** *(The officers were expected to be experienced leaders. It is unlikely that young soldiers had enough time in battle to be good commanders.)*

SLIDE SHOW

Women of the Revolution

Discussing Discuss the active roles some women played in combat in the American Revolution. Introduce Margaret Corbin, Mary Ludwig Hays McCauley, Molly Pitcher, and Deborah Sampson. **Ask:**

- What actions did these women take to help in the war? *(They fought in battle and helped the soldiers on the battlefield.)*
- Why might these women have wanted to participate in dangerous battle zones? *(Answers will vary but may include that they wanted to be near their loved ones or to fight for independence.)*

See page 141C for other online activities.

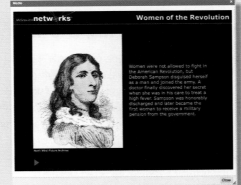

McGraw-Hill networks™   Women of the Revolution

Women were not allowed to fight in the American Revolution, but Deborah Sampson disguised herself as a man and joined the army. A doctor finally discovered her secret when she was in his care to treat a high fever. Sampson was honorably discharged and later became the first woman to receive a military pension from the government.

North Wind Picture Archives

ANSWERS, p. 147

GEOGRAPHY CONNECTION

1 **LOCATION** in Pennsylvania, New Jersey, and New York

2 **CRITICAL THINKING** New York

✓ PROGRESS CHECK The Patriots did not have a strong navy or a regular army with experience, were short on weapons and ammunition, and did not have support from all Americans.

R Reading Skills

Identifying Direct students to read the section titled "Early Campaigns." Discuss with students the ways in which battle differed as the war advanced. **Ask: What strategy did the British use after the Battle of Bunker Hill?** *(The British sent 32,000 troops to America in the hopes that the large number of men would intimidate the Patriots.)* **AL**

V Visual Skills

Analyzing Graphs Direct students to the circle graph that compares Great Britain's fighting forces with those of the Americans. **Ask: According to the chart, how did the number of troops on each side compare?** *(The British had about twice as many troops as the Americans,)* **Given these statistics, did Great Britain have good reason to be confident about winning?** *(Yes, the British forces outnumbered the Patriots two to one.)* **Given this data, why did the Patriots think the war would be over quickly?** *(They thought the British would give up easily after losing a few battles.)* **Logical/Mathematical**

Making Connections

Explain that early battles of the American Revolution made the British realize that controlling the colonies would not be as easy as they had thought. **Ask: Have you ever been doing something and then realized that it was going to be harder than you thought it would be?** *(Answers will vary.)* Then ask students what they might have done differently if they had prepared properly.

Early Campaigns

GUIDING QUESTION *What were significant battles in the early years of the American Revolution?*

R Relatively few soldiers fought in the war's early battles. At Bunker Hill, for example, about 2,200 British soldiers fought 1,200 Americans. The British had not yet won a clear victory. They realized they were going to need more troops.

During the summer of 1776, Britain sent 32,000 troops across the Atlantic to New York. The British commander, General William Howe, hoped the sheer size of his army would convince the Patriots to give up. He was soon disappointed.

Patriot Defeat on Long Island

Only 20,000 soldiers made up the Patriot force under George Washington. Yet the Americans were determined to fight. The two sides clashed in the Battle of Long Island in late August 1776. The British badly defeated the outnumbered Continental Army.

One Patriot, Nathan Hale, showed his bravery at Long Island. Hale disguised himself as a Dutch schoolteacher and went to spy on British troops. The British caught Hale and hanged him as punishment. According to legend, Hale went to his death saying, "I only regret that I have but one life to lose for my country."

The Patriots fought hard on Long Island but could not overcome the larger and better-equipped British army. A British officer wrote that many Patriot soldiers killed on Long Island had not been wearing shoes, socks, or jackets. "They are also in great want of blankets," he said, predicting that the rebels would suffer during the winter.

After the defeat, Washington retreated from New York, which became a Loyalist stronghold. The British chased the Continental Army across New Jersey into Pennsylvania. Satisfied that Washington was beaten, the British let him go.

A Low Point for the Patriots

Washington and his forces had managed to escape the British. As winter approached, however, the Patriots' cause was near collapse. The Continental Army had fewer than 5,000 soldiers. Many had completed their terms. Others had run away.

V

▶ **CRITICAL THINKING**
Analyzing What is the approximate ratio of British army forces to the Continental Army and colonial militias?

THE FIGHTING FORCES 1777

20,000

42,000

British regular army

Continental Army and colonial militias

Reading **HELP**DESK **CCSS**

Reading in the Content Area: *Circle Graphs*

Circle, or pie, graphs show how a whole is divided into parts. In the case of the graph above, the "whole" is fighting forces in the Revolutionary War. Often, circle graphs visually show how the whole is divided. They often have numbers and labels, as well.

148 *The American Revolution*

---

netw⊙rks *Online Teaching Options*

MAP

The Revolutionary War, 1776–1777

Explaining Discuss the events of the Battle of Long Island. Have students review the interactive map for the location and surroundings of this battle. **Ask: Who won the Battle of Long Island and why?** *(The British won. They outnumbered the Patriots. The British were also better equipped. Some of the Patriots even lacked shoes, socks, and jackets.)* **AL** **Why did the British let General Washington escape after the Battle of Long Island?** *(After chasing him across New Jersey into Pennsylvania, they thought he was beaten).*

See page 141C for other online activities.

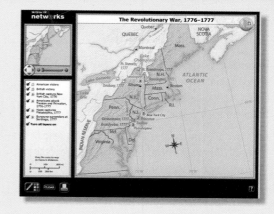

ANSWER, p. 148

CRITICAL THINKING 2:1

Enslaved African American Peter Salem appears in the far right of this painting of the Battle of Bunker Hill.

Washington wrote his brother that if new soldiers were not found soon, "I think the game is pretty near up." Yet he remained hopeful that the fight for freedom would succeed.

Washington begged the Continental Congress for more troops. He suggested allowing free African Americans to enlist, but many Americans opposed this idea. Early in the war, the Southern Colonies had persuaded the Congress not to take this step. Many white people in the South worried about giving guns and training to African Americans. They feared the possibility of revolt among the enslaved population.

African Americans in Battle

The growing need for soldiers led some states to ignore the ban on African Americans. Rhode Island raised an all-African American regiment in 1778. By the war's end, every state except South Carolina enlisted African Americans to fight.

Historians believe that as many as 5,000 African Americans joined the Patriots. One example was Peter Salem, an enslaved African American from Massachusetts. Salem fought at Concord and at the Battle of Bunker Hill, and he served the Patriot cause throughout the war. In return for his service, Salem won his freedom.

African Americans had many reasons to fight. Some fought because they believed in the Patriot cause. Others may have joined up for the chance to earn money. Some were enslaved Africans who had run away or who, like Salem, were allowed by their owners to enlist.

Lesson 1 **149**

R1 Reading Skills

Identifying After students have read the section titled "A Low Point for the Patriots," discuss with students the low point for Washington's army during the winter after the battle of Long Island. Have volunteers identify the reasons the Continental Army was near collapse. Remind them to use words like *because* and *since* in their answers. **AL ELL**

V Visual Skills

Analyzing Images Direct pairs of students to examine the painting of the Battle of Bunker Hill, and discuss what they see. **Ask:** Do you think this painting is a realistic portrayal of the Battle of Bunker Hill? Explain, using evidence from the painting. *(Possible answer: No; the highly stylized painting was created for dramatic effect.)* Point out the illustration of Peter Salem in the bottom right corner of the painting. Have pairs talk about that image and what the painter may have been trying to portray. **Visual/Spatial**

R2 Reading Skills

Specifying After students read the text, ask them to identify the role of African Americans in the Patriot's cause. Remind students that the British had offered African Americans freedom if they would remain loyal. **Ask:** About how many African Americans joined the Patriots? *(5,000)* Elicit reasons from students why African Americans might have chosen one side rather than the other. Remind students to cite text evidence to support their answers.

BIOGRAPHY

Peter Salem

Describing Use the interactive image of Peter Salem to reinforce why General Washington asked Congress to allow free African Americans to enlist in the Continental Army. **Ask:** What were some of the reasons that African Americans fought in the American Revolution? *(Possible answers: They believed in the Patriot cause; they wanted a chance to earn money; some may have been enslaved people who had run away; others may have been allowed to enlist.)* **AL**

See page 141C for other online activities.

Peter Salem was an African American soldier in the Revolutionary War.

The War for Independence

Reading Skills

Explaining After students read the text, discuss with them the British plan to take Albany, New York. **Ask: Why was Albany so important to the British?** *(If the British could control Albany, then they could control the Hudson River.)* **Which three British leaders were essential to the plan to take Albany?** *(General Howe, Lieutenant Colonel St. Leger, and General Burgoyne)* Have students explain each part of the three-pronged approach the British planned to take. **AL** **ELL**

Content Background Knowledge

Washington Crossing the Delaware This famous painting was created by Emanuel Leutze, a German American painter, in 1851. The painting does a magnificent job of capturing the idea of heroic men fighting nature and superior forces to advance a noble cause. Yet, interestingly, nearly every other aspect of the painting is historically inaccurate. The crossing was made at night and during a storm. It is doubtful that a flag would have been raised, and, even if it were, the flag used at the time was almost certainly not the one pictured. The ice was in sheets upon the water, the boats used were not like the one in the picture (the actual boats had much higher sides and no seats), and George Washington did not yet have gray hair.

Washington's forces made a daring crossing of the icy Delaware River, surprising the enemy at Trenton and delivering a key Patriot victory.

The Battles of Trenton and Princeton

While the Patriots were struggling through the winter, the main British force was settled in New York. The British also left some troops in Princeton and Trenton, New Jersey. Washington saw a chance to catch the British by surprise.

Washington was camped in Pennsylvania, across the Delaware River from the British camp in New Jersey. On Christmas night 1776, Washington led 2,400 troops across the icy river to surprise the enemy at Trenton the next day. Washington then escaped and marched to Princeton; his army scattered the British force there.

☑ **PROGRESS CHECK**

Explaining Why was the winter of 1776–1777 significant?

British Strategy

GUIDING QUESTION *Was the British plan for victory successful?*

In early 1777, the British began a three-pronged battle plan. Their goal was to seize Albany, New York, and gain control of the Hudson River. If they controlled the Hudson, they would cut off New England from the Middle Colonies.

Reading **HELP**DESK **CCSS**

Build Vocabulary: *Multiple Meaning Words*
Some words have more than one meaning. *Late* most commonly means "not on time." It can also mean "recent."

---

net**w**⊙rks   *Online Teaching Options*

The Battle of Trenton

Analyzing Use the primary source excerpt to review the poem about the Battle of Trenton and to discuss the events leading up to the Battles of Trenton and Princeton. **Ask: Why was Washington's attack on Trenton a surprise?** *(It was Christmas night. The British did not expect an attack.)* **Why were the Battles of Trenton and Princeton so important to the American Revolution?** *(The surprise battles were a great strategic success for George Washington, and they also raised the hope and morale of the Continental Army.)*

See page 141C for other online activities.

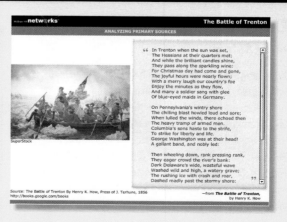

ANSWER, p. 150

☑ **PROGRESS CHECK** The Patriot's cause was near collapse, but Washington's successful attacks around Christmas of 1776 rekindled his army's fighting spirit.

First, General John Burgoyne would lead troops south from Canada. At the same time, Lieutenant Colonel Barry St. Leger would move east from Lake Ontario. A third group, under General Howe, would move north up the Hudson. The three British forces would then attack Patriot troops at Albany.

The British Capture Philadelphia

Before the attack on Albany, Howe sought to capture Philadelphia—the home of the Continental Congress. Howe won battles in September 1777 at Brandywine and Paoli, near Philadelphia. Then Howe's troops captured Philadelphia, forcing the Continental Congress to flee. By now, winter was coming. Howe decided to stay in Philadelphia instead of going to Albany.

R

The Battle of Saratoga

Meanwhile, the British plan for taking Albany was in trouble. In August, American soldiers led by Benedict Arnold stopped St. Leger at Fort Stanwix, New York.

General Burgoyne's army hadn't reached Albany either. In July he captured Fort Ticonderoga, but he needed supplies. He sent a force to the American supply base at Bennington, Vermont. A local militia group, the Green Mountain Boys, defeated them. Burgoyne retreated to Saratoga, New York.

Here Burgoyne found himself in serious trouble—and alone. Patriots had stopped St. Leger at Fort Stanwix. Howe was still in Philadelphia. Now American troops under General Horatio Gates blocked and surrounded Burgoyne's army. Burgoyne made a desperate attack on October 7. The Patriots held firm.

C

On October 17, 1777, General Burgoyne surrendered. The British plan had failed. The Continental Army had won an enormous victory that changed the course of the war.

W

✔ PROGRESS CHECK

Analyzing Why did Howe's Philadelphia victory lead to defeat at Saratoga?

LESSON 1 REVIEW (CCSS)

Review Vocabulary (Tier 3 Words)

1. Use each of the following words in a sentence that demonstrates its meaning. RH.6–8.4

    a. mercenary   **b.** recruit

Answer the Guiding Questions

2. *Contrasting* How did the two sides in the American Revolution differ? RH.6–8.5

3. *Summarizing* How did the Continental Army fare in the early battles of the war? RH.6–8.2

4. *Explaining* What key factors led to the American victory at Saratoga? RH.6–8.1

5. **ARGUMENT** As a Patriot, write a letter to the editor of your local newspaper. Point out the Patriot strengths and why you think the Patriots will win the war for independence. WHST.6–8.1, WHST.6–8.9

Lesson 1　**151**

LESSON 1 REVIEW ANSWERS

1. a. The British paid mercenaries to do some of their fighting. **b.** The Continental Army struggled to recruit soldiers,.

2. The British had a larger population, a far better trained army, and great wealth, but they were fighting far from their country, often using hired soldiers. The American force was smaller, ill equipped, and fairly untrained, but they were fighting for their own freedom in their own land.

3. The Continental Army suffered some bad defeats, such as at Long Island, but managed to win some victories, such as at Trenton and Princeton.

4. The British plan to bring three armies together did not work because one of the armies was beaten and the other was delayed. Burgoyne's army was left alone and vulnerable.

5. Students' letters should use the colonies' strengths described in the lesson to argue persuasively that the Patriots will win the war.

R Reading Skills

Discussing After students read the text, discuss with them the British plan to capture Philadelphia and the results of the plan to capture Albany. **Ask: How did Howe's victory in Philadelphia change his strategy?** *(He decided to camp in comfort in Philadelphia instead of going to Albany as planned.)* **BL** **Why did the British plan fail?** *(None of the three commanders was able to proceed as planned. Howe stayed in Philadelphia, St. Leger was stopped at Fort Stanwix, and Burgoyne was left alone with low supplies.)*

C Critical Thinking Skills

Predicting Consequences Remind students that the Patriots had been pretty much alone in their fight for independence. **Ask: What was the outcome of the Battle of Saratoga?** *(The British, under General Burgoyne, suffered a serious defeat. This marked a turning point in the war.)* **How do you think the Continental Army's victory at Saratoga might change the course of the war?** *(Possible answers: The victory might shake British confidence and inspire more American support for the war, and it might persuade other countries, such as France, to support the American cause.)* **BL**

W Writing Skills

Argument Remind students that they have read about several different battles of the Revolutionary War. Some were British victories; others were Patriot victories. Some were larger; some were smaller. Have partners work together to answer this question: **Does any battle strike you as being the most important, or among the most important, of the war? Explain.** After partners come to a decision, direct them to each write a paragraph identifying the battle and explaining their reasoning. **Interpersonal**

Have students complete the Lesson 1 Review.

CLOSE & REFLECT

Summarizing Have students summarize the battles thus far in the war. Have them compare this to their experiences in sports or other competitions. Ask them if they ever had a small lead that made them believe they could win in the end.

ANSWER, p. 151

✔ **PROGRESS CHECK** Howe's victory delayed his progress north, which left Burgoyne vulnerable.

ENGAGE

🔔 **Bellringer** Ask students to work in small groups to list their favorite celebrities. Suggest they organize them into sports figures, entertainers, musicians, and any other categories they feel are relevant. Bring the class back together, and make a master list of people whom students have listed. **Ask: How do celebrities influence culture?** *(Answers will vary. Students may mention hair and clothing styles, and mannerisms, among other things.)* Explain that the Patriots also had celebrities who influenced popular culture. In this lesson, they will learn about perhaps the most important Patriot celebrity, Benjamin Franklin.

TEACH & ASSESS

C Critical Thinking Skills

Making Inferences Point out to students that the French secretly supported the American Patriots. **Ask: Why might the French have kept secret the monetary support of the American revolutionaries?** *(Possible answer: The French did not want to get formally involved in the war. They supported the American cause but did not want to anger the British, who were a powerful force in Europe.)* **BL**

R Reading Skills

Contrasting As they read the text, have students contrast the different approaches France and Spain took to supporting the American revolutionaries. **Ask: How did Spain and France take different approaches to aiding the Patriots?** *(France supported the Patriots secretly at first and then declared war on Britain. Spain did not directly aid the Patriots but declared war on Britain, fighting British troops in other parts of North America.)* **AL** **ELL**

ANSWERS, p. 152

TAKING NOTES: Possible answers: **Allies:** France, Spain, other European nations, Mexico, Cuba; **Individuals:** Lafayette, Kościuszko, Pulaski, von Steuben, de Miralles; **Volunteers:** Martha Washington and others who made clothes or cared for the sick

---

netw⊕rks
There's More Online!

☑ **BIOGRAPHY**
 • Franklin and the Revolution
 • Martha Washington

☑ **GRAPHIC ORGANIZER**
 Sources of Aid to Patriots

☑ **PRIMARY SOURCE**
 • Abigail Adams
 • Winter at Valley Forge

☑ **TIME LINE**
 Thaddeus Kościuszko

Lesson 2
The War Continues

ESSENTIAL QUESTION *Why does conflict develop?*

IT MATTERS BECAUSE
The ideals of liberty and freedom helped attract key support and helped the colonists overcome difficult challenges.

Gaining Allies

GUIDING QUESTION *How did America gain allies?*

By late 1777, Benjamin Franklin had been in France for a year. He was trying to get the French to support the Americans' fight for independence. With his skill and charm, Franklin gained many friends for the United States. The French had secretly given the Americans money, but they had not entered the war.

The Continental Congress sent Jonathan Austin of Boston to France to deliver the news of the American victory at Saratoga. As soon as Austin arrived, Franklin asked if the British had taken Philadelphia. Austin answered, "Yes sir. ... But sir, I have greater news than that. General Burgoyne and his whole army are prisoners of war!"

Franklin surely understood the importance of this news. The victory at Saratoga was a turning point in the American Revolution. France and other nations now realized that the Americans might actually win their war against Great Britain. France decided to help the Americans. In February 1778, France declared war on Britain and sent money, equipment, and troops to **aid** the American Patriots.

Like France, Spain also decided to help the Americans. Spain did not form an alliance with the United States, but it did declare war on Great Britain in 1779. Spanish forces fought the British

Reading **HELP**DESK **CCSS**

Taking Notes: *Identifying* RH.6–8.1
Use a diagram like the one here to determine what aid the Patriots received during the American Revolution.

Sources of Aid to the Patriots

Content Vocabulary
• **inflation** (Tier 3)

Academic Vocabulary (Tier 2)
aid to help
desert to leave without permission

152 *The American Revolution*

---

netw⊕rks *Online Teaching Options*

VIDEO

The Turning Point of the Revolutionary War

Integrating Visual Information Write the word *morale* on the board, and invite students to define it. *(the confidence and enthusiasm of a group)* Tell students to keep the definition in mind as they view *The Turning Point of the Revolutionary War.* Then have students explain the relationship between the idea of morale and the video they watched. *(Americans had lost enthusiasm for the war by the winter of 1776, so George Washington used the battles at Trenton and Princeton to restore morale.)*

See page 141D for other online activities.

in present-day Louisiana, Mississippi, Alabama, and Florida. This fighting kept many British troops out of action against the Americans.

Winter at Valley Forge

In 1778 news traveled slowly across the Atlantic. People in the United States did not learn of the French-American alliance until the spring. Meanwhile, British general Howe and his forces spent the winter in comfort in Philadelphia. Washington set up camp at Valley Forge, about 20 miles (32 km) to the west. There, Washington and his troops suffered through a terrible winter. They lacked decent food, clothing, shelter, and medicine. Washington's greatest challenge at Valley Forge was keeping the Continental Army together.

Snowstorms and damaged roads slowed delivery of supplies. The Continental Army built huts and gathered supplies from the countryside. Several volunteers—including Washington's wife, Martha—made clothes for the troops and cared for the sick. Washington declared that no army had ever put up with "such uncommon hardships" with such spirit. "Naked and starving as they are," he wrote, "we cannot enough admire the incomparable patience and fidelity [faithfulness] of the soldiery."

North Wind Picture Archives

Thinking Like a HISTORIAN

Understanding Cause and Effect

R

Benjamin Franklin served as America's first ambassador to France. French nobles and thinkers greatly admired the American. Much like a singer or actor today, Franklin became a star in America and Europe. Fashionable women even wore a hairstyle meant to look like a fur cap Franklin wore. How might Franklin's popularity have helped the Patriot cause? For more about understanding cause and effect, review *Thinking Like a Historian*.

C

Martha Washington, shown here on the arm of George Washington, helped lift the spirits of the army during the bitter winter at Valley Forge.

Lesson 2 **153**

R Reading Skills

Stating Direct students to read the section titled "Winter at Valley Forge." Have students explain the hardships that Washington's troops faced. **Ask: How did Martha Washington and other volunteers help at Valley Forge?** *(They made clothes for the soldiers and tended to the sick.)*

C Critical Thinking Skills

Analyzing Primary Sources Have a volunteer read Washington's quote. Have students identify another sentence in the previous paragraph that also addresses the problem of faithfulness. *("Washington's greatest challenge at Valley Forge was keeping the Colonial Army together.)* **Ask: How might Washington be surprised that his troops were faithful?** *(The troops were suffering under terrible weather conditions and lack of food, clothing, and medicine.)* **BL**

Content Background Knowledge

Ask students if they know some of Ben Franklin's achievements. They may mention flying a kite in a storm to prove that lightning was electricity. Although Franklin never actually performed that feat, he was a very accomplished person. Among other things, he

- was a printer and publisher.
- founded newspapers.
- worked as an editor and reporter.
- founded "Poor Richard's Almanac."
- worked with insurance companies.
- improved communication and transportation in Philadelphia.
- invented the Franklin stove.
- founded the University of Pennsylvania.

PRIMARY SOURCE

The Winter at Valley Forge

Analyzing Primary Sources Use the interactive primary source excerpt from General Washington's letter to discuss the winter at Valley Forge. **Ask: How were the conditions encountered by Washington's army different from those experienced by Howe's army in Philadelphia?** *(Washington's army lacked decent food, clothing, shelter, and medicine. Howe's army enjoyed all the comforts of being in a large city.)*

See page 141D for other online activities.

networks   The Winter at Valley Forge
ANALYZING PRIMARY SOURCES

SuperStock

" Head Quarters, Valley Forge, February 16, 1778

Dear Sir,—

It is with great reluctance I trouble you on a subject, which does not properly fall within your province; but it is a subject that occasions me more distress, than I have felt since the commencement of the war; and which loudly demands the most zealous exertions of every person of weight and authority, who is interested in the success of our affairs; I mean the present dreadful situation of the army, for want of "

—from *George Washington's letter to Governor George Clinton* (February 16, 1778), by George Washington

Source: The Life of General Washington: First President of the United States, Volume 1 By Charles Wentworth Upham, Office of the National Illustrated Library, 1851

ANSWER, p. 153

Thinking Like a Historian Students might suggest that Franklin could use his charm and popularity to gain allies and aid from other nations. A celebrity is a famous person, so Franklin could be considered a celebrity. Students might name musicians who give concerts to benefit a charity or sports stars who use their fame in advertisements to persuade people to buy products.

W Writing Skills

Narrative Refer to the description of the conditions at Valley Forge. Ask students to write a journal entry from the perspective of a soldier there. They should include descriptions of and feelings about the weather, the supplies, and the interactions with George and Martha Washington. **Intrapersonal**

C Critical Thinking Skills

Analyzing Primary Sources Have students read the excerpt from *A Narrative of a Revolutionary Soldier* by Joseph Martin. Have students compare the excerpt to the image of the soldiers at Valley Forge at the top of the page. **Ask: How are Martin's words visually expressed in the painting? Visual/ Spatial**

Making Connections

Discuss how the troops must have received the news of the promise of France's help. **Ask: Have you ever been in a situation in which things looked hopeless, and then help came from an unexpected source?** Allow volunteers to share their experiences.

Washington and the Continental Army lived through a terrible winter at Valley Forge.

▶ CRITICAL THINKING
Determining Cause and Effect How did the difficult winter at Valley Forge affect the Continental Army?

W

Joseph Martin, a young soldier from Connecticut, spent the winter at Valley Forge. "We had hard duty to perform," he wrote years later, "and little or no strength to perform it with." Most of the men lacked blankets, shoes, and shirts. Martin made a pair of rough shoes for himself out of a scrap of cowhide, which hurt his feet.

C

PRIMARY SOURCE

❝ [T]he only alternative I had, was to endure this inconvenience or to go barefoot, as hundreds of my companions had to, till they might be tracked by their blood upon the rough frozen ground. ❞

—Joseph Martin, in *A Narrative of a Revolutionary Soldier*

Many soldiers became sick and died. Other men **deserted** (duh•ZERT•ed), or left without permission. Some officers quit. The Continental Army seemed to be falling apart.

Yet the Continental Army did survive the winter. Spring came, and conditions gradually improved. New soldiers joined the ranks. "The army grows stronger every day," one officer wrote. "There is a spirit of discipline among the troops that is better than numbers."

Then, in April 1778, Washington told his troops of France's help. Everyone's spirits rose at the thought. The Continental Army celebrated with a religious service and a parade.

Reading **HELP**DESK (CCSS)

Academic Vocabulary (Tier 2 Words)

desert to leave without permission or intent to come back

Build Vocabulary: *Related Words*

Some words sound the same despite different spellings and meanings. Still, *aid* and *aide* have related meanings. The word *aide* is a noun meaning "helper." The Academic Vocabulary *aid* is a verb meaning "to help."

154 *The American Revolution*

---

netw⊙rks *Online Teaching Options*

GRAPHIC ORGANIZER

Taking Notes: *Identifying:* **Sources of Aid to the Patriots**

Identifying Point out that George Washington told his troops of France's help in April of 1778, at the end of the terrible winter at Valley Forge. Use the interactive graphic organizer to identify the sources of the aid the Patriots received during the Revolutionary War.

See page 141D for other online activities.

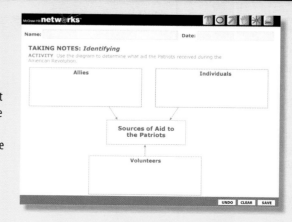

ANSWER, p. 154

CRITICAL THINKING The number of soldiers decreased as some deserted and some became sick and died. The army suffered with cold and lack of supplies.

Foreigners Help on the Battlefield

The Patriot cause had supporters around the world. A number of individuals from other nations gave their talents to the cause.

One leader at Valley Forge was Marquis de Lafayette (lah•fee•EHT) of France. He had come to the United States as a 19-year-old volunteer in June 1777. Lafayette was excited about the ideas expressed in the Declaration of Independence, and he wanted to join the battle for freedom. He believed that the American cause represented the future of humankind.

When he reached the United States, Lafayette offered his services to General Washington. He agreed to serve without pay and became a trusted aide to Washington.

Other Europeans volunteered to work for the Patriot cause. Two Polish men—Thaddeus Kościuszko (THAD•ee•uhs kawsh•CHUSH•KOH) and Casimir Pulaski (KAH•sih•meer poo•LAHS•kee)—supported American efforts. Kościuszko helped build important defenses for the Americans. Pulaski won promotion to the rank of general. He died in 1779, fighting for the Continental Army.

Friedrich von Steuben (FREE•drihk vahn STOO•buhn) also came to help Washington. Von Steuben had been an officer in the Prussian army. He helped to train the Patriot troops at Valley Forge and shape the ragged Continental Army into a more effective fighting force.

In 1778 Spaniard Juan de Miralles (mee•RAH•yays) arrived in Philadelphia. He had persuaded Spain, Cuba, and Mexico to send money to the United States. Miralles became friends with many Patriot leaders and loaned money to the cause.

Europeans who had recently moved to the United States also joined the Patriot cause. For example, almost two-thirds of the Pennsylvania regiments were foreign-born.

Even with the help of foreign nations and individuals, the Patriots faced a huge challenge. The Continental Army still needed large amounts of money to fight the war and defeat the British.

C

R1

R2

Thaddeus Kościuszko of Poland was a big contributor to the Patriot cause.

Baron von Steuben trained American recruits at Valley Forge, 1778.

✓ PROGRESS CHECK

Describing How did Lafayette help the Patriot cause?

(t) Bettmann/CORBIS, (b) SuperStock

Lesson 2   **155**

BIOGRAPHY

Juan de Miralles

Identifying Discuss Juan de Miralles and his contributions to the Patriot cause. **Ask: Which nations did Juan de Miralles persuade to help the United States?** *(Miralles persuaded Spain, Cuba, and Mexico to send money to the colonies.)*

See page 141D for other online activities.

MyGraw-Hill **netw⊕rks**   Juan de Miralles

BIOGRAPHY

Juan de Miralles was the first Spanish diplomatic representative to the United States of America. Miralles and George Washington also became personal friends and professional correspondents. This is a photo of his home.

Historical Marker Database

Close

CHAPTER 6, Lesson 2
The War Continues

R1 Reading Skills

Discussing After students examine the image of Thaddeus Kościuszko of Poland and read the text, discuss Kościuszko's contributions to the Patriot's cause. **Ask: What other Polish man played a vital role in helping the Patriots?** *(Casimir Pulaski)* **How did Kościuszko and Pulaski contribute to the Continental Army?** *(They fought for the army and helped build defenses.)*

C Critical Thinking Skills

Speculating Direct students' attention to the image of Baron von Steuben training troops. Discuss his role and the role of Marquis de Lafayette at Valley Forge. **Ask: How do you think Baron von Steuben's presence at Valley Forge affected the morale of the Continental Army?** *(Von Steuben had been a professional soldier in the Prussian army. By training the Patriot troops, he probably improved their morale.)* **Who was Marquis de Lafayette, and what role did he play in the American Revolution?** *(Lafayette was a young French volunteer who believed in Patriot ideals and became a trusted aide to General Washington.)*

R2 Reading Skills

Identifying After students read the text, point out that not every foreign individual who helped the Continental Army was a famous person. **Ask: How did "regular" individuals contribute to the Patriot cause?** *(They joined the army and helped fight against the British.)* **AL** **ELL**

ANSWER, p. 155

✓ **PROGRESS CHECK** He was excited about the cause and became a trusted aide to General Washington.

Chapter 6   155

C₁ Critical Thinking Skills

Speculating Ask students to think about the lives of those who were not actively fighting the war. **Ask: How do you think the war affected the families that stayed home when soldiers went to war?** *(Student responses will vary but should indicate that the war caused problems raising families and running the family farm or business.)* Have a volunteer describe the hardships for soldiers and how the lives of Americans changed during the war. **BL** **ELL**

R Reading Skills

Defining Before students read the text, help them define the concept of inflation. Bring in a balloon, and blow it up in front of the class. Explain that you have *inflated* the balloon. Ask students to describe what happens as the balloon is inflated. *(It gets larger.)* Make the tie between the balloon getting larger as it inflates, and the larger amount of money needed to purchase goods when inflation occurs in the economy. **Ask: Why did the value of the paper money fall?** *(There was more paper money printed than there was gold or sliver to back its worth)* You may want to share with students that our money is no longer directly tied to the amount of gold or silver owned by the government. **BL** **Visual/Spatial**

C₂ Critical Thinking Skills

Evaluating Discuss why some women began to question their role in American society. **Ask: What was expected of women on the home front? How was this different from usual?** *(Women had to care for their families by themselves. They also ran businesses or farms , jobs that men usually did, if their husbands or others were away.)* **AL**

Life on the Home Front

GUIDING QUESTION *What was life like on the home front during the American Revolution?*

The hardships of the soldiers involved in fighting the war were considerable. However, the war changed the lives of all Americans, even those who stayed at home. For example, wives of soldiers had to take care of families by themselves. They had to run a farm or a business without a husband's help. Children had to make do without a father present.

Problems in the Economy

For the young United States, getting the money to pay for the war was a great challenge. The Continental Congress had no power to raise money through taxes. The Congress did get some money from the states and from foreign countries. Yet this amount fell far short of the need.

To meet this need, the Congress and the states simply printed hundreds of millions of dollars' worth of paper money. The paper money quickly lost its value. The amount of bills was greater than the supply of gold and silver backing them. This led to **inflation** (in•FLAY•shun), which means that it took more and more money to buy the same amount of goods. People began to have doubts about how much their paper bills were worth. Congress stopped printing paper money because no one would use it. This left the Americans with no way to finance their fight for independence.

During the war, Congress and the states printed paper money. Over time, people came to question the value of this paper money, and the amounts required to make purchases rose.

▶ CRITICAL THINKING
Determining Cause and Effect What happened when people began to question the value of the paper money?

New Ways of Thinking

The ideals of liberty and freedom inspired the American Revolution. These same ideals also caused some women to question their role in American society.

Abigail Adams was one example. She wrote to her husband, John Adams, a member of Congress:

PRIMARY SOURCE

❝ I can not say that I think you [are] very generous to the Ladies, for whilst you are proclaiming peace and good will to Men, Emancipating all Nations, you insist upon retaining an absolute power over Wives. ❞

—from *Adams Family Papers*

North Wind Picture Archives

Reading **HELP**DESK **CCSS**

inflation when it takes more and more money to buy the same amount of goods

Academic Vocabulary (Tier 2 Words)

issue subject that people have different views about

---

net**w**orks — *Online Teaching Options*

WORKSHEET

Economics of History Activity: The United States and Public Debt

Analyzing Pair students, and have them complete the Economics of History activity. Suggest that students sketch a rough time line of the events described as they read. **Ask: How did the amount of U.S. debt change over time?** *(It increased.)*

See page 141D for other online activities.

Economics of History Activity net**w**orks
The American Revolution

Lesson 2 *The War Continues*

The United States and Public Debt

Debt means something that is owed. During times of war, governments have a greater need to purchase goods than during peacetime. During the American Revolution, the brand new national government relied on loans and credit to secure the necessary goods and services needed to win the war. The debts of the nation came to over $77 million by 1782.

Alexander Hamilton was appointed the nation's very first secretary of the treasury. In 1790, he wrote to Congress the "First Report on Public Credit." In it he said, "The United States debt, foreign and domestic, was the price of liberty."

During the nation's early years, the debt of the United States was reduced. An expansion of the United States (the Louisiana Purchase) and another war (the War of 1812) added to the debt once again. At the beginning of 1812, the debt totaled over $45 million. Just three years later, in 1815, the debt had skyrocketed to $119 million.

President Andrew Jackson, who was elected in 1828, was determined to erase the national debt. Through his efforts, for the first and only time in history, the United States government had no interest-bearing debt at the beginning of 1835.

By 1899, the dawning of the new century, the debt was at $1.9 billion. Currently, the public debt is nearing $14 trillion.

Directions: Answer the following questions on a separate piece of paper.

1. **Defining** Define the word debt.

2. **Explaining** Name two different reasons that the public debt has increased over the years.

3. **Explaining** What did Alexander Hamilton mean when he said the public debt "was the price of liberty"?

ANSWER, p. 156

CRITICAL THINKING The value of money decreased, and prices, or the amounts required to make purchases, increased.

Questioning Slavery

The revolutionary quest for freedom and liberty led some white Americans to question slavery. In 1778 Governor William Livingston of New Jersey asked his government to free all enslaved people. He said slavery was "utterly inconsistent with the principles of Christianity and humanity."

African Americans made similar arguments. In New Hampshire enslaved people asked the government for their freedom so "that the name of slave may not be heard in a land gloriously contending for the sweets of freedom."

As you have read, African Americans fought for the American cause and hoped the Revolution would help end slavery. The Pennsylvania legislature in 1780 adopted a plan to gradually free enslaved people—the first legislature in the world to take such action against slavery. Other northern states soon took similar measures. Still, the **issue** of slavery would remain unsettled for many years.

Treatment of Loyalists

Not all Americans supported the Patriot cause. During the war, thousands of Loyalists fought on the side of the British. Some Loyalists spied on the Patriots. Many Loyalists fled, packing their belongings and selling whatever they could. Some left hurriedly for England. Others took off for Spanish-owned Florida.

Known Loyalists who remained in the United States faced difficult times. Their neighbors often shunned them. Some became victims of violence. Loyalists who actively helped the British faced arrest. In a few rare cases, Patriots executed Loyalists.

R

C

☑ PROGRESS CHECK

Describing How were Loyalists treated by the Patriots during the war?

Bettmann/CORBIS

BIOGRAPHY

Abigail Adams (1744–1818)

Abigail Adams was the wife of John Adams, delegate to the Continental Congress. She had a close relationship with her husband, and the two wrote often about the political issues of the day. Abigail Adams famously argued for women's rights in a letter to her husband, telling him, "If [particular] care and attention is not paid to the Ladies we are determined to [start] a [rebellion], and will not hold ourselves bound by any Laws in which we have no voice, or Representation."

▶ CRITICAL THINKING
Analyzing Primary Sources On what basis did Abigail Adams suggest women might not hold themselves bound by laws?

LESSON 2 REVIEW (CCSS)

Review Vocabulary (Tier 3 Words)

1. Explain the significance of the following terms from this lesson. RH.6–8.4

   a. desert   b. inflation

Answer the Guiding Questions

2. *Identifying* Who were the key European allies of the Patriots? RH.6–8.1

3. *Explaining* Explain some of the ways that the war affected women. RH.6–8.2

4. **ARGUMENT** Take the perspective of a foreign soldier volunteering to serve in the United States in the fight against the British. Write a letter to family back home explaining why you have decided to risk your life in this cause. WHST.6–8.1, WHST.6–8.10

Lesson 2   **157**

R Reading Skills

Explaining Have students read the text before discussing how the ideals of liberty and freedom began to affect African-Americans and how some people began to question the practice of slavery. **Ask: How did ideas about slavery begin to change around this time?** *(People began to question if it was right to seek their own freedom while keeping some people enslaved.) Students should support their responses using evidence from the text.*

C Critical Thinking Skills

Identifying Points of View Have a volunteer explain what positions a Loyalist might have taken during the Revolution. **Ask: What were some consequences of being a Loyalist during the American Revolution?** *(They faced difficult times, including being shunned, becoming victims of violence, having their property taken away, and facing arrest and possibly even execution for spying.)* **Why were Patriots so hard on Loyalists?** *(They viewed them as traitors.)*

Have students complete the Lesson 2 Review.

CLOSE & REFLECT

Making Connections Organize the class into small groups. Have half of the groups consider reasons why the roles of women began to change as a result of the war. Have the other groups consider changing attitudes towards African Americans and slavery. Have groups share their ideas with the class.

LESSON 2 REVIEW ANSWERS

1. **a.** To *desert* means to leave without permission. Desertion was a problem that occurred within the Continental Army at times. **b.** *Inflation* is the rising of prices or the dropping of the value of money. It was a problem that occurred during the war as a result of the money-printing practices of the Continental Congress and the colonies.

2. The French were an official ally, who offered financial and military support. The Spanish more quietly supported the Patriot cause. In addition, a number of individuals from different countries supported the Patriot cause.

3. In a few cases, the war directly affected women—those who fought or were involved directly with helping soldiers. Many other women had to adjust to more work without the men in their lives. The war also affected some women's attitudes about their own freedom and liberty.

4. Letters might discuss the importance of freedom and liberty, and why these are worth fighting and perhaps even dying for.

ANSWERS, p. 157

CRITICAL THINKING Women had no representation in making laws. Adams's suggestion echoes the Declaration of Independence, which argues that men are not bound by laws if they have no representation making those laws.

☑ PROGRESS CHECK Neighbors frequently shunned them. Some Loyalists suffered violence or were arrested.

ENGAGE

🔔 **Bellringer** Use the map, "Revolutionary War in the West and the South" shown in this lesson to discuss the shift in battlegrounds. Ask students to speculate why the battlegrounds may have shifted from the Northeast. Tell students that in this lesson they will learn more about the changing battlegrounds in the Revolutionary War.

TEACH & ASSESS

C Critical Thinking Skills

Determining Cause and Effect Remind students that actions have both intended and unintended consequences. **Ask:** **What was the result of the colonists' desire to take land from the Native Americans?** *(The Native Americans mostly sided with the British because the colonists had taken their lands and they wanted them to leave.)*

R Reading Skills

Identifying As students read, remind them that the British made allies of the Native Americans. **Ask: Who was Chief Joseph Brant?** *(Brant was a Mohawk war chief who led brutal attacks against the Americans in New York and Pennsylvania.)* Have a volunteer explain the role Brant played in the war in the West. **Ask: What was Henry Hamilton's nickname and how did he get it?** *(Hamilton was known as the "hair buyer" because he paid Native Americans for the scalps of settlers.)* **AL**

ANSWERS, p. 158

TAKING NOTES: Possible answers: The British received less help from the Loyalists than expected; hit-and-run attacks by Patriots; help for Patriots from Spain and Gálvez

---

networks
There's More Online!

☑ **BIOGRAPHY**
John Paul Jones

☑ **CHART/GRAPH**
Native American Alliances

☑ **GRAPHIC ORGANIZER**
British Defeats in the South

☑ **PRIMARY SOURCE**
Political Cartoons

☑ **TIME LINE**
Bernardo de Gálvez

Lesson 3
Battlegrounds Shift

ESSENTIAL QUESTION *Why does conflict develop?*

IT MATTERS BECAUSE
Important battles of the War for Independence took place along the western frontier, at sea, and in the South.

Fighting in the West

GUIDING QUESTION *How did the war in the West develop?*

The Revolutionary War was of great interest to many Native American groups living in and around the 13 states. Some Native Americans helped the Patriots. More sided with the British. For them, the British seemed less of a threat than the Americans, who lived in their midst and took their land.

West of the Appalachian Mountains, the British and their Native American allies raided American settlements. Mohawk war chief Joseph Brant led a number of brutal attacks in southwestern New York and northern Pennsylvania. Farther west, Henry Hamilton, British commander at Detroit, paid Native Americans for settlers' scalps. This practice earned him the nickname, the "hair buyer."

Virginia militia leader George Rogers Clark set out to end attacks in the West. In July 1778, Clark led a force of 175 westward down the Ohio River and over land. The Patriots captured a British post at Kaskaskia (ka•SKAS•kee•uh) in present-day Illinois. They then took the British town of Vincennes (vin•SEHNZ) in present-day Indiana. British troops under Hamilton recaptured Vincennes that December. Clark vowed to get it back. In February 1779, Clark and his troops

Reading **HELP**DESK **CCSS**

Taking Notes: *Determining Cause and Effect*
Use a diagram like the one here to show why the British lost control in the South. RH.6–8.5, RH.6–8.7

British Defeats in the South

Content Vocabulary (Tier 3 Words)
• blockade
• privateer

158 *The American Revolution*

---

networks *Online Teaching Options*

Victory at Yorktown

Discussing Discuss with students the retreat of Cornwallis to Virginia, the raids for supplies carried out by his troops in the region and his eventual arrival at Yorktown. Then play the video, which provides an introduction to Cornwallis.

See page 141E for other online activities.

braved harsh winter conditions to surprise the British and force their surrender. Clark's victory strengthened the American position in the West.

☑ **PROGRESS CHECK**

Summarizing What victories did the American forces win in the West?

The War at Sea

GUIDING QUESTION *What was the result of the war at sea?*

The Revolutionary War also took place at sea. Here Great Britain's powerful navy enjoyed a major advantage. British vessels formed an effective **blockade** (blo•KAYD), keeping ships from entering or leaving American harbors. The blockade limited delivery of supplies and troops to Patriot forces.

R

Privateers

To break the blockade, Congress ordered 13 warships, but only two of the ships made it to sea. Several were quickly captured by the British. The American navy was too weak to operate well.

Congress also authorized some 2,000 ships to sail as privateers. A **privateer** (pry•vuh•TEER) is a privately owned merchant ship outfitted with weapons. The goal of the privateer is to capture enemy merchant ships and cargo.

Finding crews for these ships was not difficult. Sailors from the whaling and fishing ports of New England signed on eagerly for the profitable privateering trade. During the war, privateers captured more British ships than the American navy did.

C

At the time of the Revolution, about 200,000 Native Americans lived along the western frontier. Here they attack an American settlement in Pennsylvania's Wyoming Valley in 1778.

▶ **CRITICAL THINKING**
Speculating Why do you think many Native Americans supported the British rather than the Americans?

---

blockade measure that keeps a country from communicating and trading with other nations
privateer privately owned ship outfitted with weapons

Lesson 3 **159**

Painting by Don Troiani, Military & Historical Image Bank

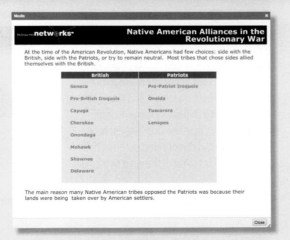

V Visual Skills

Integrating Visual Information Use the images of John Paul Jones and the battle between the *Bonhomme Richard* and the Serapis to discuss with students the encounter. **Ask: Who was the captain of the Bonhomme Richard?** *(John Paul Jones)* **What did Jones mean when he said, "I have not yet begun to fight"?** *(Even though there had been a long battle, he was nowhere near giving in.)* **Visual/Spatial**

R Reading Skills

Using Context Clues Have a volunteer read aloud the paragraph that begins with "In the early years…" **Ask: What do the words *crushed* and *key* mean in this paragraph?** Explain that these words are not literal; they are figurative, meaning they may not necessarily mean what they seem to mean. Ask students to use context clues to determine synonyms for these words. *(crushed: defeated, conquered; key: important).* **BL** **ELL**

The warships *Bonhomme Richard* and *Serapis* meet in one of the most famous naval battles of the war. American naval officer, John Paul Jones, led the crew of the *Bonhomme Richard* in the conflict.

V

An American Naval Hero

The war at sea produced one of the war's great heroes. A daring American naval officer, John Paul Jones, won his first successes raiding British ports. Near the coast of Great Britain in September 1779, Jones's ship, *Bonhomme Richard*, met the British warship *Serapis*. The *Bonhomme Richard* and the *Serapis* fought for hours. The British captain asked whether Jones wished to surrender. Jones is said to have answered, "I have not yet begun to fight."

In the end, it was the *Serapis* that surrendered. The naval victory made John Paul Jones a hero to the Patriots.

✓ **PROGRESS CHECK**

Describing How did privateers contribute to the American war effort?

Fighting in the South

GUIDING QUESTION *What was the result of the war in the South?*

In the early years of the war, the Americans had won several battles in the South. In 1776 Patriot forces crushed Loyalists at the Battle of Moore's Creek, near Wilmington, North Carolina. They also saved the key port of Charles Town, South Carolina, from the British. Although this was a small battle, its **impact** on the rest of the war was great.

R

Reading **HELP**DESK **CCSS**

Academic Vocabulary (Tier 2 Words)
impact an effect

160 *The American Revolution*

networks *Online Teaching Options*

BIOGRAPHY

John Paul Jones

Discussing Have volunteers take turns reading the paragraphs describing the life of John Paul Jones. Discuss how amazing it was that a 12-year-old could bring a ship safely home. Remind students that at this time ships did not have engines. They had complicated sails that had to be carefully set to catch the wind or the boat would tip.

See page 141E for other online activities.

ANSWER, p. 160

✓ **PROGRESS CHECK** Privateers captured more British ships at sea than the American navy.

By 1778, these results, along with Patriot victories such as Saratoga, had convinced the British that bringing their old colonies back into the empire would not be easy. As a result, the British came up with a new plan to finish the war.

The new British plan focused on the South, where there were many Loyalists. The British hoped to use sea power and the support of the Loyalists to win important victories in the Southern states. At first, the strategy worked.

W

Early British Success

In late 1778, British general Henry Clinton sent 3,500 troops from New York to take Savannah, Georgia. The British occupied the coastal city and controlled most of the state.

Clinton himself led a force into the South in early 1780. In May, he led a second British attack on Charles Town. This time the South Carolina city surrendered, and the British took thousands of prisoners. It marked the worst American defeat of the war.

After Clinton's victory, he returned to New York. He left General Charles Cornwallis in command of British forces in the South. The Continental Congress sent forces under General Horatio Gates to face Cornwallis. The two armies met at Camden, South Carolina, in August 1780. The British won this first encounter. Yet Cornwallis soon found that he could not control the area he had conquered. He and his troops faced a new kind of warfare.

R

GEOGRAPHY CONNECTION

Starting in 1778, many Revolutionary War battles took place in the West and the South.

1 **LOCATION** Based on this map, what was the southernmost battle between the Patriots and the British?

2 **CRITICAL THINKING** *Analyzing Visuals* Why do you think the British wanted to capture ports at Savannah and Charles Town?

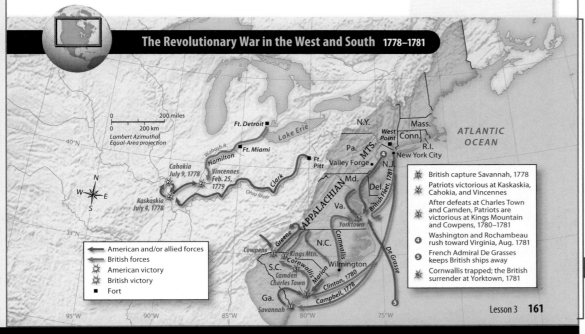

The Revolutionary War in the West and South 1778–1781

- ← American and/or allied forces
- ← British forces
- ✸ American victory
- ✸ British victory
- ■ Fort

British capture Savannah, 1778

Patriots victorious at Kaskaskia, Cahokia, and Vincennes

After defeats at Charles Town and Camden, Patriots are victorious at Kings Mountain and Cowpens, 1780–1781

4 Washington and Rochambeau rush toward Virginia, Aug. 1781

5 French Admiral De Grasses keeps British ships away

Cornwallis trapped; the British surrender at Yorktown, 1781

Lesson 3 **161**

W Writing Skills

Informative/Explanatory Point out to students that the British decided to move the fighting to the southern part of the colonies. Ask them to write a few sentences detailing why this was a good strategy. *(The victories in the North had left the British thinking they might not win. So they decided to focus on the Southern Colonies, where there were many Loyalists. If they could win the favor of these Loyalists, then perhaps their forces would be strengthened and they could win the war.)* **Verbal/Linguistic**

R Reading Skills

Citing Text Evidence Explain that Savannah was an important city in Georgia. **Ask:** **What information can you find in the text to defend this statement?** *("In late 1778, British general Henry Clinton sent 3,500 troops from New York to take Savannah, Georgia. The British occupied the coastal city and controlled most of the state.")* **AL** **ELL**

Ask: **Who was General Cornwallis, and what was his role in the war?** *(General Cornwallis was a British commander who was the leader of British forces in the South.)*

V Visual Skills

Interpreting Direct students to locate Savannah on the map on this page. **Ask:** **What natural feature made Savannah an important city in Georgia?** *(Possible answers: Students may say that Savannah's location on the ocean meant that it would have received and shipped a lot of goods, so it was important for trade. It was also located on a river and so would have controlled trade in the state.)* **Visual/Spatial**

V

MAP

The Revolutionary War in the West and South, 1778–1781

Explaining Use the interactive map to discuss early British successes in the South at the Battles of Savannah and Charles Town. **Ask:** **Why was the surrender of Charles Town considered the worst American defeat of the war?** *(Charles Town was a key city, and the British took thousands of prisoners upon its surrender.)*

See page 141E for other online activities.

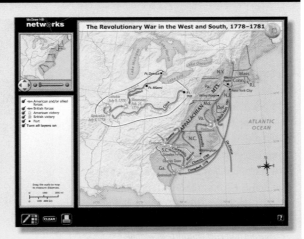

ANSWERS, p. 161

GEOGRAPHY CONNECTION

1 The southernmost battle was the Battle of Savannah.

2 **CRITICAL THINKING** Blocking ports would keep the Patriots from getting supplies. The Patriots would not be able to move large numbers of troops easily.

R Reading Skills

Using Context Clues Direct students to read the section titled "Hit-and-Run Tactics." Ask students to explain why Cornwallis had won at Camden, South Carolina but could not control the area. **Ask:**

- **What was the new kind of warfare he faced in the South?** *(the hit-and-run tactics of the Patriots)*
- **Explain the meaning of "hit-and-run" in this context.** *(Bands of Patriots appeared suddenly, attacked, and then disappeared.)*
- **What South Carolina Patriot leader used this technique to harass the British?** *(Francis Marion)*
- **In what other context have you heard the phrase "hit-and-run" used?** *(Students will likely mention auto accidents where a pedestrian or another car is hit and the person at fault drives away without stopping.)*

C Critical Thinking Skills

Reasoning Why are hit-and-run attacks a good strategy when you are outnumbered? *(If outnumbered, using surprise hit-and-run style attacks can help preserve your own force while doing maximum damage to the opposing side.)* **BL**

W Writing Skills

Narrative Have partners brainstorm ideas about what the mountain people who were threatened and told to join the British must have felt, based on how they reacted. Have pairs work together to write a letter from one of these mountain people to an imaginary relative in Savannah, Georgia. Encourage them to use expressive language as they convey their feelings. **Interpersonal**

Hit-and-Run Tactics

R The British had counted on strong Loyalist support in the South. They received less help than expected. Instead, as British forces moved through the countryside, small forces of Patriots attacked them. These bands of soldiers appeared suddenly, fired their weapons, and then disappeared. This hit-and-run technique caught the British off guard.

C Francis Marion was one successful Patriot leader. Marion, who was known as the "Swamp Fox," operated out of the swamps of eastern South Carolina. He was quick and smart. One British colonel grumbled that "the devil himself" could not catch Marion.

Spain's Help

Great Britain also found itself with another new enemy. Spain declared war on Britain in 1779. The Spanish governor of Louisiana, Bernardo de Gálvez (GAHL•ves), had tons of supplies and ammunition shipped up the Mississippi River to American troops in the Northwest Territory. It was with this help that George Rogers Clark captured the key posts of Kaskaskia and Vincennes. Gálvez also raised an army to fight the British. Gálvez's forces drove the British out of the Gulf of Mexico region.

American Successes

After their victory at Camden, South Carolina, the British moved northward through the Carolinas in September 1780. Along the way, the British warned the local people to give up the fight for independence and join the British. If they refused, the British threatened to "hang their leaders, and lay their country waste …"

W The Americans who received this warning were mountain people. Fiercely independent, they had been neither Patriots nor Loyalists until the British warning angered them. They formed a militia army and set out to force the British from their land. At Kings Mountain, the American militia force killed or captured a British-led Loyalist force of about 1,000. The Patriot victory brought new support for independence from Southerners.

In October 1780, Nathanael Greene replaced Gates as commander of the Continental forces in the South. Rather than lead one attack on Cornwallis's forces, Greene split his army in two. In January 1781, one section defeated the British at Cowpens, South Carolina. Another section joined Francis Marion's raids. Greene combined his forces in March. Then, he

Spaniard Bernardo de Gálvez fought against the British during the American Revolution.

Richard Cummins / SuperStock

Reading HELPDESK (CCSS)

Academic Vocabulary (Tier 2 Words)

sustain to suffer or experience

Build Vocabulary: *Word Origins of Sayings*

Today, people refer to the hit-and-run tactics used by some patriot forces as guerrilla warfare.

162 *The American Revolution*

---

networks   *Online Teaching Options*

TIME LINE

Bernardo de Gálvez, 1746–1786

Identifying Project the interactive time line showing the life of Bernardo de Gálvez to discuss the help that the Patriots received from Spain and its impact on the war in the South. **Ask:**

How did Gálvez help the United States? *(He sent supplies and ammunition to Americans up the Mississippi River and raised an army to fight the British. He drove the British out of the Gulf of Mexico. He defeated the British on Manchac, Baton Rouge, and Natchez, and captured Fort Georgia at Pensacola and Fort Charlotte at Mobile.)*

See page 141E for other online activities.

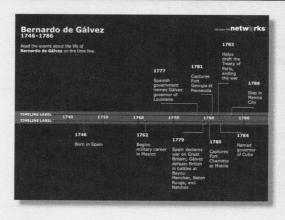

This British cartoon dates from 1779, before the American Revolution ended. It shows a rider being thrown off a horse. The horse represents the former colonies. The rider represents Great Britain, and the man on the ground represents a Revolutionary War soldier.

▶ CRITICAL THINKING
Analyzing Political Cartoons
What outcome of the war does the cartoonist predict?

met Cornwallis's army at Guilford Courthouse, in present-day Greensboro, North Carolina. Greene's army was forced to retreat, but the British **sustained** great losses in the process. General Cornwallis gave up the campaign to conquer the Carolinas.

Cornwallis Retreats

Cornwallis realized the British had to act quickly to win the war. More French troops were coming to North America, and the Patriots held Virginia. Troops and supplies were moving south.

In April 1781, Cornwallis marched north to Virginia. His troops carried out raids throughout the region. General Washington sent Lafayette and General Anthony Wayne south to push Cornwallis back. Meanwhile, Cornwallis took shelter at Yorktown, on the Virginia coast. The battle for the South was entering its final phase.

✅ PROGRESS CHECK

Evaluating What effect did the Patriot victory at Kings Mountain produce?

LESSON 3 REVIEW (CCSS)

Review Vocabulary (Tier 3 Words)

1. Use each of the following words in a sentence about the Revolutionary War. RH.6–8.4
   a. blockade   b. privateer

Answer the Guiding Questions

2. *Describing* What role did many Native Americans take during the war in the West? RH.6–8.2

3. *Identifying* Who was John Paul Jones, and what was his significance in the war? RH.6–8.1

4. *Summarizing* What happened during the British campaign in the South? RH.6–8.2

5. **ARGUMENT** You read about several military leaders in this lesson. Which leader do you think most helped the Patriot cause? Write a short essay to explain your answer. WHST.6–8.1, WHST.6–8.4

Lesson 3 **163**

C Critical Thinking Skills

Evaluating Discuss with students the new leader of the Continental Army in the south, Nathanael Greene. **Ask: Was Greene a successful commander in the Carolinas? Why or why not?** (*Greene did not successfully rout Cornwallis at Guilford Courthouse, but his army caused a large number of British losses. He also defeated the British at Cowpens.*)

V Visual Skills

Analyzing Images Ask students to read the political cartoon's caption. **Ask: How did people in 1779 know that the rider in the cartoon was British?** (*The color of his coat; the British wore red coats.*) Explain that the cartoon was published two years before the war ended and four years before the Treaty of Paris was signed. **Ask: If the cartoon was published in London before the war ended, what might have been its purpose?** (*Possible answers: to explain to people how many Americans felt about British rule, to alert people that Americans were serious about ending British domination of the colonies*) BL

Have students complete the Lesson 3 Review.

CLOSE & REFLECT

Evaluating Review with students the impact of the victories in the West, South, and on the sea. Have volunteers recall the advantages and disadvantages for both sides and discuss whether they have made a difference. **Ask: Why do you think the Patriots are proving victorious despite their disadvantages?** (*Answers may vary, but students could suggest that their passion and inspiration for the cause could be encouraging them.*)

LESSON 3 REVIEW ANSWERS

1. To fight the British blockade, the Continental Congress authorized the use of privateers.

2. Many Native Americans took on the role of ally to the British forces, although some Native American groups took the side of the Americans.

3. John Paul Jones was an American naval hero who successfully raided British ports and took part in a famous sea duel.

4. The British won some early victories, but the Patriots eventually managed to frustrate the campaign and force the British to give up their plans to conquer the Carolinas.

5. The account should explain the role of the leader, his accomplishments, and the results of battles.

ANSWERS, p. 163

CRITICAL THINKING The horse is in the process of throwing the rider, suggesting that the colonists will succeed in throwing off British rule.

✅ PROGRESS CHECK It brought new support to the Patriot cause from Southerners.

ENGAGE

🔔 **Bellringer** Discuss how succeeding at any serious goal takes many steps and actions. Explain that athletes incorporate many different actions into their training in order to succeed at an event in the future. Each of these actions contributes to the outcome. Explain that at the end of the Revolutionary War, many successful actions added up to a final victory. Tell students that they will learn about people and actions that played a part in defeating General Cornwallis at Yorktown in the final years of the war.

TEACH & ASSESS

R1 Reading Skills

Using Context Clues Point out to students the headings on these two pages. Ask students to think about how they can use the headings to frame their reading. The name of the lesson, "The Final Years," tells students that they will be reading about the end of the Revolutionary War. The heading "Victory at Yorktown" communicates what the end result of the war will be. The two subheadings, "Washington Leaves for Virginia" and "A Trap at Yorktown," imply that Yorktown is in Virginia and states that Washington engineers a trap for the British there. **Ask: What meaning can you construct from the headings alone?** *(The end of the Revolutionary War is brought about by General Washington achieving victory, using a trap at Yorktown in Virginia.)* Encourage students to actively use the headings in their textbooks to preview, understand, and review what they read.

C Critical Thinking Skills

Making Connections Discuss with students the meeting between Rochambeau and Washington in New York City. Have a volunteer describe the plan of attack on New York City and how and why that plan was eventually shifted to Yorktown. **Ask:**

- **Who did Comte de Rochambeau meet with in New York?** *(Rochambeau met General George Washington in New York. Washington was the commander of the Continental Army.)* `AL` `ELL`
- **What did Washington plan to do once the second French fleet arrived?** *(He planned to attack a British army base in New York under the command of General Clinton.)*
- **How did the strategy change once they realized that the second French fleet was not going to arrive in New York?** *(The focus shifted to the British in Yorktown.)* `BL`

ANSWER, p. 164

TAKING NOTES: United States: granted British merchants the right to collect debts owed to them by Americans, would advise states to return Loyalist property; **Great Britain:** recognized the United States as an independent nation, promised to withdraw all troops from American territory, granted Americans the right to fish in Canadian coastal waters.

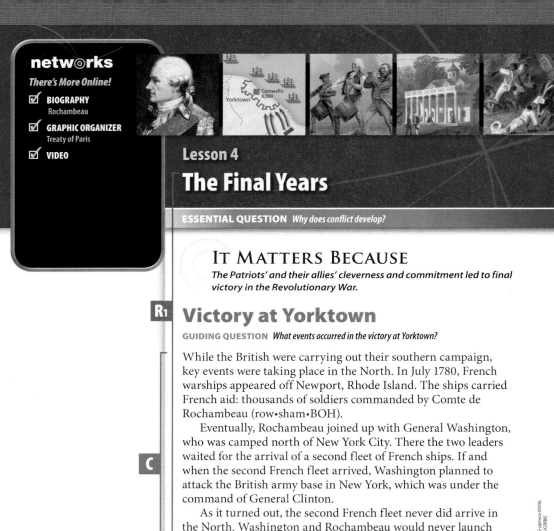

networks
There's More Online!
☑ **BIOGRAPHY**
Rochambeau
☑ **GRAPHIC ORGANIZER**
Treaty of Paris
☑ **VIDEO**

Lesson 4
The Final Years

ESSENTIAL QUESTION *Why does conflict develop?*

IT MATTERS BECAUSE
The Patriots' and their allies' cleverness and commitment led to final victory in the Revolutionary War.

R1
Victory at Yorktown

GUIDING QUESTION *What events occurred in the victory at Yorktown?*

While the British were carrying out their southern campaign, key events were taking place in the North. In July 1780, French warships appeared off Newport, Rhode Island. The ships carried French aid: thousands of soldiers commanded by Comte de Rochambeau (row•sham•BOH).

Eventually, Rochambeau joined up with General Washington, who was camped north of New York City. There the two leaders waited for the arrival of a second fleet of French ships. If and when the second French fleet arrived, Washington planned to attack the British army base in New York, which was under the command of General Clinton.

As it turned out, the second French fleet never did arrive in the North. Washington and Rochambeau would never launch the attack on Clinton. Instead, both the ships and the troops would find a better opportunity to strike at the British. That opportunity would come farther south—at Yorktown, Virginia.

Washington Leaves for Virginia

As he waited outside New York, Washington had followed reports of fighting in the South. In 1781 he sent Lafayette and Anthony Wayne to Virginia to stop Cornwallis. The results were

Reading HELPDESK (CCSS)

Taking Notes: *Describing* RH.6–8.1
Use a diagram like this one to show what the United States and Great Britain agreed to in the Treaty of Paris.

| United States | → | |
| Great Britain | → | |

164 *The American Revolution*

Content Vocabulary (Tier 3 Words)
- **siege**
- **ratify**
- **ambush**

---

networks **Online Teaching Options**

VIDEO

Colonial Leader and General

Interpreting Share with students the video about George Washington. **Ask: What experiences helped George Washington be an effective military leader?** *(He was a surveyor who knew the land, an officer who studied military science, a military leader who knew how to lead troops, and a landowner and businessman who knew how to manage a large organization.)* **Interpersonal**

See page 141F for other online activities.

positive. Lafayette had Cornwallis pinned down on a peninsula, a piece of land surrounded by water on three sides. The place was called Yorktown.

Washington also got important news about the French fleet he was waiting for: The ships were heading toward Chesapeake Bay instead of New York. They were going to join in the fight to defeat Cornwallis. With this news, Washington quickly changed his plans. He and Rochambeau would advance on the British at Yorktown rather than at New York.

Washington kept his new **strategy**, or plan of action, secret. He wanted Clinton to think the Patriots still planned to attack at New York. This, he hoped, would keep Clinton from sending aid to Cornwallis.

Washington and Rochambeau then rushed south with their armies. Secrecy was strict. Most soldiers did not know where they were going. Wrote one, "We do not know the object of our march, and are in perfect ignorance whether we are going against New York, or … Virginia."

The French and American troops marched 200 miles (322 km) in 15 days. General Clinton did not learn they were gone until it was too late. There was nothing he could do to stop the three forces—Lafayette's troops, Washington's and Rochambeau's army, and the French fleet—from meeting at Yorktown.

A Trap at Yorktown

Washington's plan worked perfectly. By the end of September, 14,000 American and French troops stood against Cornwallis's 8,000 British and Hessian troops at Yorktown. Meanwhile, the French fleet kept guard at Chesapeake Bay. British ships could not get in to help Cornwallis escape by sea. General Clinton and the rest of the British army sat helplessly in New York. They were unable to help Cornwallis. The British were trapped. American and French forces began a **siege** (SEEJ)—they blocked off the British supply and escape routes. In this way, they hoped to force the British to surrender.

In August 1781, Comte de Rochambeau joined Washington's Continental Army in its march to Yorktown.

Archivo Iconografico, SA/CORBIS

siege an attempt to force surrender by blocking the movement of people or goods into or out of a place

Academic Vocabulary (Tier 2 Words)
strategy a plan of action

Lesson 4 **165**

Thinking Like a HISTORIAN

Predicting Consequences

Throughout the Revolutionary War, Washington succeeded in holding his army together, despite many difficulties. One of these difficulties was political meddling. The Continental Congress often interfered with his military operations. During the gloomy winter at Valley Forge, some members of Congress and army officers plotted to replace Washington as commander in chief. How might Washington's removal or resignation have affected the war? For more about predicting consequences, review *Thinking Like a Historian*.

R2 Reading Skills

Discussing After students read the text, discuss with them Washington's secret march to Virginia and the eventual arrival of the French fleet. Remind students to support their responses with evidence from the text. **Ask:**

- Why did Washington keep his plan to march to Virginia a secret? *(It prevented General Clinton from sending help to General Cornwallis.)*
- How far and long did the French and the Patriots march? *(200 miles in 15 days)*
- How did this secrecy turn out to be successful? *(General Clinton did not learn about where the French and the Patriots had gone until it was too late. By then there was nothing they could do.)*

Next, discuss Washington's strategy at Yorktown. **Ask:** What is a siege? *(A siege is an attempt to force surrender by blocking the movement of people or goods into or out of a place.)* AL ELL

Discuss with students the trap at Yorktown, the fact that the British were outnumbered, and the Patriots' siege against the British. **Ask:**

- How did the Americans employ a siege against Cornwallis? *(The Americans had Cornwallis blocked and stopped supplies, troops, and aid from coming in or going out.)*
- How might the siege affect the British forces at this time? *(Answers will vary, but students might suggest that the siege left the British low on supplies, weak, and vulnerable to the attack.)* BL

Comte de Rochambeau

Identifying Use the biography of Comte de Rochambeau to discuss his role in preparing for the Battle of Yorktown. **Ask:** What advantage did Rochambeau bring to the Americans and the Continental Army? *(Rochambeau was an experienced military leader with thousands of troops at his command.)*

See page 141F for other online activities.

netw rks
BIOGRAPHY
Comte de Rochambeau

The Comte de Rochambeau was born in France in 1725. As an adult, he was active in the French military for many years. In 1780, he commanded thousands of French troops sailing to America to join the Continental Army. When Rochambeau and his troops reached Rhode Island in July, their journey was delayed for almost a year.

In June 1781, Rochambeau's forces finally headed south and met General George Washington's army in New York. The combined group marched to Virginia and put Yorktown under siege. On October 19, 1781, the British army surrendered.

Rochambeau returned to Europe in 1783 and was appointed commander of Calais by King Louis XVI for his service during the Revolutionary War.

Archivo Iconografico, SA/CORBIS

ANSWER, p. 165

Thinking Like a Historian Answers will vary. Students may argue that Washington was replaceable, but others may suggest that he was key to the success of the Patriot cause.

Chapter 6 **165**

166   *The American Revolution*

R Reading Skills

Explaining Have students read the text, and then discuss the surrender ceremony at Yorktown and the songs "Yankee Doodle" and "The World Turned Upside Down." **Ask:**

- Why did Cornwallis choose to surrender at Yorktown? *(He could see that his situation was hopeless.)* **BL**
- Why did the French band play "Yankee Doodle" at the surrender ceremony? *(Playing this was ironic because it was a song the British had used to tease the Americans.)* **Musical/Auditory**

C Critical Thinking Skills

Making Inferences Prompt students to consider the significance of the title "The World Has Turned Upside Down." **Ask:** Why do you think the British may have felt that "the world was upside down"? *(Students may indicate that the strong British army would find it strange to be trapped by the Americans, whom the British expected to beat easily. The British at Yorktown may have also finally understood that defeat at Yorktown would have very serious ramifications for the war.)*

Siege at Yorktown 1781

- ■ British troops
- ⌐⌐⌐ British defensive lines
- ← American and French attacks October 6–15
- ■ American troops
- ■ French troops
- ⚓ French fleet
- ⚔ French and American artillery

0 — 1 mile
0 — 1 km
Polyconic projection

York River
Gloucester
Swamp
Yorktown
Cornwallis 8,000
Rochambeau 9,000
French lines
American lines
Mill Pond
Field of British Surrender
General Lincoln
Lafayette's Headquarters
General von Steuben
General Lafayette 8,000
Washington's Headquarters

GEOGRAPHY CONNECTION

General Cornwallis and his army left the Carolinas for Virginia in 1781. He wound up at Yorktown, on the shores of the Chesapeake Bay.

1 LOCATION How would you describe the type of land on which Cornwallis and his forces camped at Yorktown?

2 CRITICAL THINKING
Analyzing Does this location seem like it would be easy or difficult to defend? Explain.

Victory Over Cornwallis

R The siege began to take effect. The British ran low of supplies and many soldiers were wounded or sick. On October 14, Washington's aide, Alexander Hamilton, led an attack that captured key British defenses. Cornwallis could see that the situation was hopeless. On October 19, he surrendered his troops. The Patriots had won the Battle of Yorktown. They took nearly 8,000 British prisoners and captured more than 200 guns.

C At the surrender ceremony, the British marched between rows of French and American troops. A French band played "Yankee Doodle." This was a song the British had used to taunt the Americans. A British band responded with a children's tune, "The World Turned Upside Down." With the mighty British surrendering to the upstart Americans, it seemed a fitting song for the situation.

☑ **PROGRESS CHECK**

Explaining Why did Washington advance on Yorktown?

Reading **HELP**DESK **CCSS**

Reading Strategy: *Sequence of Events*
Describe the sequence of events from October 9 to October 19 that led to the victory over Cornwallis.

netw⊙rks   *Online Teaching Options*

MAP

Seige at Yorktown 1781

Analyzing Maps Use the interactive map of the siege at Yorktown to discuss how the siege began to work in the Patriots' favor, blocking supplies from the British. Have students describe the features of the map, and discuss how the map displays the effectiveness of the attack. **Ask:** Who led an attack to capture key British defenses? *(Alexander Hamilton)* Why did Cornwallis finally surrender? *(He saw that the situation was hopeless.)* How many prisoners did the Patriots capture? *(8,000)*

See page 141F for other online activities.

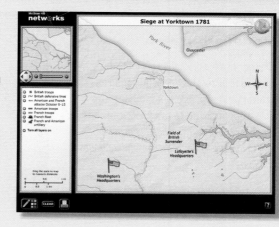

ANSWERS, p. 166

GEOGRAPHY CONNECTION

1 along the shore or next to water

2 CRITICAL THINKING Possible answer: It may be difficult for the enemy to attack from water, but it is possible to become completely surrounded.

☑ PROGRESS CHECK Washington advanced because Lafayette was keeping Cornwallis bottled up at Yorktown, and the French fleet was heading there instead of to New York.

166

Independence Achieved

GUIDING QUESTION *What helped the Patriots win independence?*

The Patriot victory at Yorktown was a terrible blow to the British and their war effort. Still, the fighting went on after Cornwallis surrendered. The British still held Savannah, Charles Town, and New York. There would be a few more clashes on land and sea. However, the defeat at Yorktown convinced the British that the war was too costly to **pursue**, or proceed with.

The Americans and British sent delegates to Paris to work out a treaty. Benjamin Franklin, John Adams, and John Jay represented the United States. The American Congress **ratified** (RAT•ih•fyed), or approved, the first draft of the treaty in April 1783. The final Treaty of Paris was signed on September 3, 1783. By that time Britain had also made peace with France and Spain.

Under the Treaty of Paris, Great Britain recognized the United States as an independent nation. The British also promised to withdraw all their troops from American territory. They gave Americans fishing rights to the waters off the coast of nearby Canada.

In turn, the United States promised that Americans would pay to British merchants what they owed. The treaty also stated that the Congress would advise the new states to return property taken from Loyalists.

A Conspiracy Against Congress

Many months passed between the end of fighting in the Revolutionary War and the signing of the peace treaty. During that time, Washington was unwilling to dissolve the army. Instead, he camped his idle troops in Newburgh, New York.

Many of these soldiers believed they were owed pay from the Congress. When this pay did not come, the soldiers grew angry. Some officers sent a letter around in March 1783. If their demands were not met, the letter said, the army should use force against the Congress.

Washington realized that this threat of revolt was dangerous. The new nation could be destroyed. In a dramatic speech, he asked the angry soldiers to be patient. Then Washington urged the Congress to meet their just demands.

Library of Congress, Prints & Photographs Division, LC Dig-ppmsca-05936

ratify to approve officially

Academic Vocabulary (Tier 2 Words)

pursue to proceed with

British forces first sang "Yankee Doodle" to poke fun at what they considered the awkward ways of the Americans. The Americans, however, quickly made "Yankee Doodle" their own. They created new verses that made fun of the British and praised George Washington.

▶ CRITICAL THINKING
Explaining Why might songs and other forms of music be important in fighting a war? Explain.

Lesson 4 **167**

R1 Reading Skills

Analyzing As students read the text, remind them that Yorktown was not the final battle of the war. Discuss that the British still held Savannah, Charles Town, and New York. **Ask:** How did Yorktown affect the outcome of the war? *(The loss made the British realize that continuing the war would be too costly.)* **BL**

R2 Reading Skills

Explaining Have a volunteer read the text aloud. Ask another volunteer to explain how the war ended and what the beginning of the peace process was like. **Ask:**

- **What was the Treaty of Paris?** *(It was an agreement between the United States and Great Britain to end the Revolutionary War.)*
- **Who were the delegates sent by America to negotiate the treaty?** *(Benjamin Franklin, John Adams, and John Jay)*
- **When was the Treaty of Paris signed?** *(September 3, 1783)* Explain that the end of a war can be a complicated matter. In the case of the Revolutionary War, a particular battle (Yorktown) led to the end of the conflict in 1781. However, the formal treaty between the United States and Great Britain was not signed for almost another two years
- **Why do you think it took so long to finalize the treaty that ended the war?** *(Answers may vary but can include the slower means of communication in the 1780s and the need to negotiate terms favorable to both parties.)*

C Critical Thinking Skills

Making Inferences Remind students that nearly two years passed between Yorktown and the official end of the war. **Ask:** Why might Washington have insisted that the army not be disbanded during this time? *(Students might note concern over a resurgence of British attacks).* How do you think it might have felt to be one of Washington's soldiers during this time? *(Answers will vary.)* **BL** Interpersonal

GRAPHIC ORGANIZER

Taking Notes: *Describing:* The Treaty of Paris

Categorizing Use the interactive graphic organizer to describe the agreements of the United States and Great Britain in the Treaty of Paris. Discuss the terms of the treaty. Have students sort the provisions into columns or into a graphic organizer. **Ask:** What benefits did each side receive under the Treaty of Paris? *(America received recognition as an independent nation, withdrawal of all British troops, fishing rights to the waters off the coast of Canada. Americans would pay their debts to British merchants, and states would return property taken from Loyalists.)*

See page 141F for other online activities.

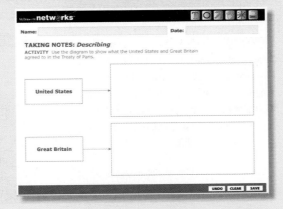

McGraw-Hill **netw rks**

Name: _____ Date: _____

TAKING NOTES: Describing
ACTIVITY Use the diagram to show what the United States and Great Britain agreed to in the Treaty of Paris.

| United States | → | |
| Great Britain | → | |

UNDO CLEAR SAVE

ANSWER, p. 167

CRITICAL THINKING Students might state that songs and music help unite people and build spirit and enthusiasm.

Chapter 6 **167**

R Reading Skills

Discussing Discuss with students Washington's departure from the army. Consider finding a copy of his farewell address and reading it to the students. **Ask:** What were Washington's plans after the war? *(to settle in Mount Vernon)* Why do you think he wanted to retire from public life? *(Answers may vary but should suggest that his involvement in establishing America went all the way back to the French and Indian War, and he may have wanted time to live a private life.)* **AL**

W Writing Skills

Informative/Explanatory Create a list with students that addresses how the Americans managed to win the Revolutionary War. Have students list advantages the Americans had and advantages the British had. Discuss other reasons that the Patriots may have been victorious. Be sure to include elements like home-field advantage, fighting tactics, help from allies, and the determination and spirit of the American people. Direct students to use their lists and notes as prewriting exercises for informative papers that explain why the Americans won the Revolutionary War. **Verbal/Linguistic**

After the war, Washington looked forward to a return to his home, Mount Vernon, in Virginia. He planned to take no role in the new government.

▶ **CRITICAL THINKING**
Speculating Why do you think Washington hoped to get away from public life?

The Congress agreed. Washington's leadership ended the threat to the new nation.

Washington Returns Home

In late November 1783, the war truly ended. The last British troops left New York City. Washington could at last give up his command. The soldiers could return to their homes and their lives.

On December 4, Washington said farewell to his troops. Three weeks later he formally resigned, or gave up his position, at a meeting of the Congress. Washington said, "Having now finished the work assigned me, I retire … and take my leave of all the employments of public life."

Washington returned home to Mount Vernon, Virginia. There he planned to remain and live quietly with his family.

Why the Americans Won

How did the Americans defeat powerful Great Britain? Remember, the Americans had several advantages in the war. First, they fought on their own land. The British had to move troops and supplies across an ocean. It was harder for them to get reinforcement, as the siege of Yorktown showed. When their ships were blocked, the British troops had no support.

Also, the Americans knew the land. They knew where to lay an **ambush** (AM·bush), or surprise attack. They were expert at wilderness fighting. The British, in contrast, had much difficulty controlling the American countryside once they occupied the cities. The Battle of Kings Mountain, which you read about in Lesson 3, illustrates this point. The rural people did not like being told what to do. They also had wilderness fighting skills that could defeat their new enemies.

Help from other countries contributed to the American victory. The success at Yorktown would not have been possible without French soldiers and ships. Spain gave aid when they

Reading **HELP**DESK **CCSS**

ambush an attack in which the attacker hides and surprises the enemy

netw⊙rks *Online Teaching Options*

IMAGE

Revolution in Haiti

Analyzing Images Use the interactive image of the revolution in Haiti to discuss how the American Revolution inspired other countries. Discuss with students the French Revolution and the revolution in Saint Domingue, which is present-day Haiti. **BL**

See page 141F for other online activities.

Toussaint Louverture was born into slavery but became a great military leader. He led the fight for the independence of Haiti, which was granted in 1804.

ANSWER, p. 168

CRITICAL THINKING Washington may have believed he had done more than his share to help the new nation and that he had earned the right to the quiet enjoyment of his family and home.

attacked the British. Individuals, such as Lafayette and von Steuben, came to America to provide vital services to the Patriot cause.

Perhaps most important, the American Revolution was a people's movement. Its outcome depended not on any one battle or event but on the determination and spirit of all Patriots. As Washington remarked about the patriotic crowds, "Here is an army they [the British] will never conquer."

In 1776 the American colonists began a revolution. In the Declaration of Independence they outlined the principles of freedom and the rights they felt all peoples and nations should have. These ideas inspired people in other parts of the world. For example, French rebels in 1789 fought a revolution in defense of "Liberty, Equality, and Fraternity." The French upheld these principles: "Men are born and remain free and equal in rights."

In 1791 there was revolution in the French colony of Saint Domingue. Inspired by the ideals of the American and French revolutions, enslaved Africans took up arms. They were led by a man named Toussaint L'Ouverture (too•SAN loo•vuhr•TOOR) and soon shook off French rule. In 1804 Saint Domingue—present-day Haiti—became the second nation in the Americas to achieve independence from colonial rule. "We have asserted our rights," declared the revolutionaries. "We swear never to yield them to any power on earth."

T

The ideals of the American Revolution helped inspire the enslaved people of Haiti, who fought for the independence of their French colony.

Bettmann/CORBIS

☑ **PROGRESS CHECK**

Explaining Why did Washington take action to end the Newburgh Conspiracy?

LESSON 4 REVIEW (CCSS)

Review Vocabulary (Tier 3 Words)

1. Define each of the following terms and use it in a sentence. RH.6–8.4

   a. siege   **b.** ratify   **c.** ambush

Answer the Guiding Questions

2. *Sequencing* Describe Washington's actions leading up to and during the Patriot victory at Yorktown. RH.6–8.5

3. *Listing* What elements were key to the Patriots' victory in the war? RH.6–8.1

4. **NARRATIVE** Take the perspective of Deborah Sampson, who joined the Patriots in the conflict by disguising herself as a man. Write a short autobiography describing what you went through to become a soldier and why taking part in the war was important to you. WHST.6–8.2, WHST.6–8.10

Lesson 4 **169**

T **Technology Skills**

Researching on the Internet   Instruct students to conduct independent research on the French Revolution mentioned on this page. Ask students to use their findings to create a Venn diagram comparing the French Revolution and the American Revolutionary War. Ask students to focus on how these movements were both similar and different.

Have students complete the Lesson 4 Review.

CLOSE & REFLECT

Discussing   Prompt students to consider the American Revolution from the perspective of the newly liberated colonists. **Ask:** What steps do you think the colonists needed to take to protect their newly acquired independence? *(Answers may vary.)* Discuss with students that the colonists needed to establish a new government and that the next chapters will discuss the creation of our federal government.

LESSON 4 REVIEW ANSWERS

1. a. A *siege* is a military attempt to force surrender by blocking people and goods from going into or out of a city or fort. **b.** To *ratify* something, such as a treaty, is to formally approve of it. **c.** An *ambush* is a surprise attack.

2. Washington waited for word of the arrival of a French fleet. When Washington learned that the fleet was headed to the Chesapeake Bay to fight against Cornwallis, he joined with Rochambeau on a surprise march to Virginia.

3. First, the Patriots fought on their own land. Second, help from other nations supported the Patriots' cause. Third, the Revolutionary War was a people's movement that depended on the Patriots' determination and spirit, not on any particular battle or event.

4. Answers will vary. Students may mention the desire to be a part of, and contribute to, an effort even when one is not expected to, or is discouraged from doing so. They may also relate the physical difficulties Sampson would have gone through to disguise herself and maintain a false identity.

ANSWER, p. 169

☑ **PROGRESS CHECK**   He realized that an angry army could lead to a revolt, which could destroy the new nation.

CHAPTER REVIEW ACTIVITY

Organize the class into two groups. Tell them that each group is fighting over the same area of land. Group one relies on the land for hunting and food, while group two considers the land a holy area. Have each group brainstorm different ways that they can resolve the dispute. *(Answers may include dividing the land, going to war over the land, trying to solve the problem peacefully, and calling a truce.)* Have students from each group use the following graphic organizer to present each possible solution. As each possibility is raised, have the class make inferences about how that solution would affect each side. *(Example: If the two groups went to war, possible effects include people dying and the land being ruined.)*

Explain that these effects would be caused by the conflict between the parties.

REVIEW THE ENDURING UNDERSTANDING

Review the chapter's Enduring Understanding with students.

- *Conflict can lead to change.*

Now pose the following questions in a class discussion to apply this enduring understanding to the chapter.

How did warfare lead to change for African Americans in the colonies? *(The need for soldiers in the Revolutionary War led some states to ignore the ban on African Americans, who joined the ranks of the militias. In the case of Pennsylvania, this led to the adoption of a plan to free slaves.)*

How was the difficult winter at Valley Forge important to the revolutionary cause? *(It made the soldiers firmer in their resolve. Positive interactions with George and Martha Washington during this winter led them to trust their leaders more.)*

How were the military tactics of the British troops different from those of the Patriot militias? How did this affect the way the British conducted battle? *(The British tended to fight in an orderly, disciplined fashion, whereas the Patriots used surprise and disorganized hit-and-run tactics. The British needed to change the way they fought in order to repel a militia attack.)*

Write your answers on a separate piece of paper.

1 **Exploring the Essential Question**   WHST.6–8.2, WHST.6–8.9

INFORMATIVE/EXPLANATORY How did the experiences of the Patriots and the experiences of the British differ in the war? How did these differences contribute to the outcome? Use examples from the chapter to help you organize your essay.

2 **21st Century Skills**   WHST.6–8.6, WHST.6–8.8

COMPARING AND CONTRASTING Working in small groups, use the Internet or other sources to research the French Revolution, which began not long after the American Revolution and which involved the key Patriot ally, France. Together, create a poster that compares and contrasts the features of these two revolutions. Present the poster to the class.

3 **Thinking Like a Historian**   RH.6–8.2, RH.6–8.7

DRAWING INFERENCES AND CONCLUSIONS Use a diagram like the one at the right to explain why Loyalists supported Britain rather than the Patriot cause.

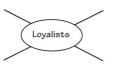

4 **Visual Literacy**   RH.6–8.7

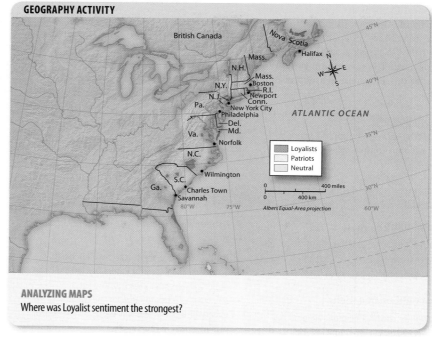

GEOGRAPHY ACTIVITY

ANALYZING MAPS
Where was Loyalist sentiment the strongest?

ACTIVITIES ANSWERS

Exploring the Essential Question

1 Answers should explore the different experiences and motivations of the two sides in the war. The British were fighting to control colonies that they viewed as economic assets. The Patriots were fighting for their own freedom and rights. The British were traveling a long distance to assert control. The Patriots were defending their own land. These differences gave the colonists the few advantages they enjoyed in the conflict.

21st Century Skills

2 Possible focus: Both revolutions were about personal freedom, citizens having a voice, and proper representation within each government. Each revolution was influenced by Enlightenment ideas and involved armed conflict. The American Revolution occurred in the thirteen colonies, while the French Revolution occurred within France. American colonists rejected the authority of King George and the Parliament of Great Britain, while French citizens rejected absolute monarchy under Louis XVI. The French Revolution was also triggered by a financial crisis that was caused by French participation in the American Revolution.

REVIEW THE GUIDING QUESTIONS

Choose the best answer for each question.

RH.6–8.1
1 Washington's surprise attack across the Delaware River on Christmas night

   A. was the last battle of the Revolutionary War.

   B. boosted the morale of the Patriots.

   C. was followed by calls for his resignation.

   D. was successful but caused a great number of American casualties.

RH.6–8.2
2 Americans had problems getting enough money to finance the war because

   F. Congress did not have the power to raise money through taxes.

   G. the states were against the war.

   H. no foreign countries would help the Patriots pay for the war.

   I. the British closed all colonial banks at the start of the war.

RH.6–8.2
3 Why were African Americans at first banned from serving in the army?

   A. General Washington had forbidden African Americans from serving.

   B. All African Americans were loyal to the British.

   C. African Americans were needed to serve the war effort in factories.

   D. Some Southern colonies feared arming African Americans.

RH.6–8.2
4 How did the war affect attitudes toward slavery in the United States?

   F. African Americans were seen as too valuable as soldiers to be enslaved people.

   G. Loyalists had to free enslaved people as punishment for supporting the British.

   H. Slavery was outlawed in the United States immediately following the war.

   I. The ideals of freedom and liberty led some white Americans to question slavery.

RH.6–8.2
5 During the war, Native Americans generally supported the

   A British because the British promised to free enslaved African Americans.

   B British because the British seemed less of a threat to their way of life.

   C Patriots because the Patriots seemed less of a threat to their way of life.

   D Patriots because the Patriots promised to return Native American lands.

RH.6–8.1
6 What role did the French play in the Patriot victory at Yorktown?

   F. They prevented the British navy from leaving New York.

   G. They tricked the British into fighting them before arriving at Yorktown.

   H. They provided troops and ships to help contain the British at Yorktown.

   I. They sank British ships in Newport Harbor.

171

Thinking Like a Historian

3 Loyalists were often members of the Anglican Church, depended on Britain for work, feared disorder, and thought the causes for the rebellion were trivial.

Visual Literacy

4 While Loyalist support was present in multiple states, students should recognize that the Carolinas and New York had larger regions of Loyalist support than other states.

ASSESSMENT ANSWERS
Review the Guiding Questions

1 **B** The surprise attack on Trenton took place early in the war, so A is incorrect. Since it was a surprise, the Patriots were able to take the British forces quickly and with relatively few casualties, so D is incorrect. Given the success of the mission, there were no calls for General Washington to resign, and Patriot morale was boosted. Thus, B is the correct answer.

2 **F** Though the Continental Congress was acting as a national government, colonists had been reluctant to transfer authority to it. This meant that the Congress did not have the power to tax the colonists to raise money for the war. The states were not at war, and other nations (such as France and Spain) did contribute to the American efforts, so G and H are incorrect. F is therefore the correct answer.

3 **D** General Washington did not forbid African Americans from fighting, so A is incorrect. While some African Americans sided with the Loyalists, not all of them did, which makes B incorrect. Southern states were wary of arming enslaved African Americans. This makes D the correct answer.

4 **I** The Revolutionary War was based on freedom and equality. This made some people question slavery. However, slavery did continue after the war. Therefore, answers F and H are incorrect. Loyalists were not forced to free their enslaved people, so G is also incorrect. I is the correct answer.

5 **B** More Native Americans supported the British. This was because they viewed the Patriots as those who had taken their land and represented a threat to their way of life. This makes B the best answer choice.

6 **H** The first French fleet that arrived to assist the Patriots marched on Yorktown with General Washington. The second French fleet blocked a British escape through Chesapeake Bay. Therefore, H is the correct answer.

Analyzing Documents

7 **C** They looked upon the miserable condition of their children with horror, knowing that they were being raised and trained to live a life as enslaved people as well. Therefore, C is the correct answer.

8 **H** The passage does not mention the fighting aspects of the war, nor does it indicate a time when enslaved people should be freed. Therefore, neither F nor G is the correct answer. There is also no indication that enslaved people were needed to win the war, making I incorrect. H, however, asks whether the fight for American independence and equality should apply to enslaved African Americans as well. This makes H the correct answer.

Short Response

9 He was 13. Between battles, his job was to serve the officers. During a battle, he was expected to carry ammunition to a particular gun.

10 In addition to the ordinary dangers of being at sea and fulfilling his job serving the officers of the ship, he faced battle dangers of getting wounded or killed.

Extended Response

11 Students' answers will vary based on the famous Patriot they select. Students' questions should relate to the experience of the specific individual selected. Students may suggest that the United States has made more progress toward equality since slavery has been abolished and voting rights have expanded. Other students may acknowledge the improvements made in society but may suggest that the United States is still making additional efforts toward equality.

DBQ ANALYZING DOCUMENTS

"And we not only groan under our own Burden, but with Concern, & Horror, look forward, & Contemplate, the miserable Condition of our Children, who are training up, and kept in Preparation, for a like State of Bondage, and Servitude. [We ask] your Honours serious Consideration, whether it is consistent with the present Claims, of the united States to hold so many Thousands … in perpetual Slavery."

—from *Connecticut Slaves Petition for Freedom, 1779*

RH.6–8.6
7 **Analyzing** According to the writer, what did enslaved Africans look upon with "horror"?

A. their own burdens   C. the condition of their children

B. perpetual slavery   D. the consideration of his audience

RH.6–8.2
8 **Summarizing** Which of the following best summarizes this excerpt?

F. Enslaved Africans have been fighting alongside the Patriots during the war.

G. Enslaved Africans should be freed after the war is over.

H. Slavery is not in agreement with the ideals of freedom on which the United States is based.

I. The Patriots need enslaved Africans in order to win the war.

SHORT REPONSE

"I was not yet fourteen years of age. … The boys were employed in waiting on the officers, but in time of action a boy was quartered [assigned] to each gun to carry cartridges."

—from Andrew Sherburne's *Experiences on a Privateer During the Revolutionary War*

RH.6–8.2, WHST.6–8.9
9 How old was Sherburne, and what were his duties aboard the ship?

RH.6–8.6, WHST.6–8.4
10 What dangers do you think Andrew Sherburne faced while on a privateer?

EXTENDED RESPONSE

WHST.6–8.1, WHST.6–8.10
11 **Narrative** Write a letter to a famous Patriot of your choice who helped the United States win the Revolution. Thank the Patriot for his or her service, and ask questions about the war effort. Finally, tell him or her about America in the modern era. State your view about whether the United States has lived up to the ideals upon which it was founded.

Need Extra Help?

If You've Missed Question	1	2	3	4	5	6	7	8	9	10	11
Review Lesson	1	2	1	2	3	4	1	1	3	3	1–4

---

netw⊙rks   *Online Teaching Options*

Help students use the Skills Builder resources

Your students can practice important 21st Century skills such as geography, reading, writing, and critical thinking by using resources found in the Skills Builder tab of the online Student Learning Center. Resources include templates, handbooks, and slide shows. These same resources are also available in the Resource Library of the Teacher Lesson Center.

UNDERSTANDING BY DESIGN®

Enduring Understanding

- *People, places, and ideas change over time.*

Essential Questions

- *Why do people form governments?*
- *How do new ideas change the way people live?*
- *How do governments change?*

Predictable Misunderstandings

Students may think:

- *The U.S. Constitution was the first document outlining the nation's government.*
- *There was general agreement about the language of the U.S. Constitution.*
- *That there was unanimous popular support for the U.S. Constitution.*

Assessment Evidence

Performance Tasks:

- *Hands-On Chapter Project*

Other Evidence:

- *Interactive Graphic Organizers*
- *What Do You Know? activity*
- *Primary Source Activity*
- *Geography and History Activity*
- *What Do You Think? questions*
- *Written paragraphs*
- *Creating a Constitution Simulation*
- *Online Self-Check Quizzes*
- *Lesson Reviews*
- *Chapter Activities and Assessment*

SUGGESTED PACING GUIDE

Introducing the Chapter	1 day	What Do You Think?	1 day
Lesson 1	2 days	Lesson 3	2 days
Lesson 2	2 days	Chapter Wrap-Up and Assessment	1 day

TOTAL TIME   9 Days

Key for Using the Teacher Edition

SKILL-BASED ACTIVITIES

Types of skill activities found in the Teacher Edition.

V **Visual Skills** require students to analyze maps, graphs, charts, and photos.

R **Reading Skills** help students practice reading skills and master vocabulary.

W **Writing Skills** provide writing opportunities to help students comprehend the text.

C **Critical Thinking Skills** help students apply and extend what they have learned.

T **Technology Skills** require students to use digital tools effectively.

*Letters are followed by a number when there is more than one of the same type of skill on the page.

DIFFERENTIATED INSTRUCTION

All activities are written for the on-level student unless otherwise marked with the leveled labels below.

BL Beyond Level
AL Approaching Level
ELL English Language Learners

All students benefit from activities that utilize different learning styles. Many activities are marked as below when a particular learning style is highlighted.

Intrapersonal	Naturalist
Logical/Mathematical	Kinesthetic
Visual/Spatial	Auditory/Musical
Verbal/Linguistic	Interpersonal

NCSS Standards covered in "A More Perfect Union"

Learners will understand:

2   TIME, CONTINUITY, AND CHANGE

  8. The history of democratic ideals and principles, and how they are represented in documents, artifacts, and symbols

  9. The influences of social, geographic, economic, and cultural factors on the history of local areas, states, nations, and the world

3   PEOPLE, PLACES, AND ENVIRONMENTS

  5. The concept of regions identifies links between people in different locations according to specific criteria (e.g., physical, economic, social, cultural, or religious)

  6. Patterns of demographic and political change, and cultural diffusion in the past and present (e.g., changing national boundaries, migration, and settlement, and the diffusion of and changes in customs and ideas)

6   POWER, AUTHORITY, AND GOVERNANCE

  1. Rights are guaranteed in the U.S. Constitution, the supreme law of the land;

  2. Fundamental ideas that are the foundation of American constitutional democracy (including those of the U.S. Constitution, popular sovereignty, the rule of law, separation of powers, checks and balances, minority rights, the separation of church and state, and Federalism);

  3. Fundamental values of constitutional democracy (e.g., the common good, liberty, justice, equality, and individual dignity)

10 CIVIC IDEALS AND PRACTICES

  5. Key documents and excerpts from key sources that define and support democratic ideals and practices (e.g., the U.S. Declaration of Independence, the U.S. Constitution, the Gettysburg Address, the Letter from Birmingham Jail; and international documents such as the Declaration of the Rights of Man and the Universal Declaration of the Rights of Children)

  6. The origins and function of major institutions and practices developed to support democratic ideals and practices

  7. Key past and present issues involving democratic ideals and practices, as well as the perspectives of various stakeholders in proposing possible solutions to these issues

CHAPTER OPENER PLANNER

Students will know:

- the Articles of Confederation were the first plan of government for the United States.
- the Articles of Confederation were too weak to address the nation's problems.
- the documents, ideas, and people that influenced the creation of the Constitution.
- the compromises that were made in the Constitution's creation.
- the debate that took place over whether the Constitution should be adopted.

Students will be able to:

- **explain** the differences between sociology and the other social sciences.
- **identify** the strengths and weaknesses of the Articles of Confederation.
- **compare and contrast** the strengths and weaknesses of the Articles of Confederation to those of the new Constitution.
- **identify and evaluate** the sources, plans, and compromises for the Constitution and the balance of power in government.
- **identify the points of view** of the Federalists and Anti-Federalists.
- **compare and contrast** arguments supporting and opposing the adoption of the Constitution.

UNDERSTANDING BY DESIGN®

☑ *Print Teaching Options*

Ⅴ Visual Skills

☐ **P. 174** Students analyze a map of the Northwest Territory. **Visual/Spatial**

☐ **P. 175** Students analyze a time line of events between 1780 and 1790. **Visual/Spatial**

Ⅰ Technology Skills

☐ **P. 174** Students research and build a model of the flatboats used on the Ohio River. **Kinesthetic**

☑ *Online Teaching Options*

Ⅴ Visual Skills

☐ **MAP** The Northwest Territory—Students compare the area comprising the Northwest Territory with current state boundaries.

☐ **TIME LINE** Place and Time: United States 1777–1790—Students learn about key events in the newly formed United States and in the world during this time period.

☐ **WORLD ATLAS** Students can use this interactive map to identify regions of the world, learn about individual countries, locate political boundaries, measure distances, and much more.

Project-Based Learning

Hands-On Chapter Project

Front-Page News Story

Students will learn about the forces that shaped American government by writing a front-page news story about an important event of the years following the American Revolution.

Technology Extension  edtechteacher
21st Century Learning

Online Collaborative Front-Page News Story

- Find an additional activity online that incorporates technology for this project.
- Visit the EdTechTeacher Web sites (included in the Technology Extension for this chapter) for more links, tutorials, and other resources.

Print Resources

ANCILLARY RESOURCES

These ancillaries are available for every chapter and lesson.

- **Reading Essentials and Study Guide Workbook** **AL** **ELL**
- **Chapter Tests and Lesson Quizzes Blackline Masters**

PRINTABLE DIGITAL WORKSHEETS

These printable digital worksheets are available for every chapter and lesson.

- **Hands-On Chapter Projects**
- **What Do You Know? activities**
- **Chapter Summaries (English and Spanish)**
- **Vocabulary Builder activities**
- **Guided Reading activities**

More Media Resources

SUGGESTED READING

Grade 6 reading level:

- *American Documents: The Constitution,* by Paul Finkelman

Grade 7 reading level:

- *Congress,* by Suzanne Levert
- *Shays' Rebellion and the Constitution in American,* by Mary E. Hull

Grade 8 reading level:

- *The Judicial Branch: Interpreting America's Laws,* by Hamed Madani

Students will know:
- the Articles of Confederation were the first plan of government for the United States.
- the Articles of Confederation were too weak to address the nation's problems.

Students will be able to:
- *identify* the strengths and weaknesses of the Articles of Confederation.

UNDERSTANDING
BY DESIGN®

☑ Print Teaching Options

V Visual Skills

☐ **P. 180** Students use a map as a basis for discussion about the Northwest Territory. **Visual/Spatial**

R Reading Skills

☐ **P. 176** Students review the section headers to determine the main ideas about the page. **AL ELL**

☐ **P. 177** Students discuss the establishment of the new country as a republic. **AL ELL**

☐ **P. 178** Students identify Richard Henry Lee's role in drafting the Articles of Confederation.

☐ **P. 178** Students list the powers granted Congress by the Articles of Confederation. **AL**

☐ **P. 180** Students define the term *ordinance* and identify the ordinances passed by Congress. **ELL**

☐ **P. 181** Students explain how the Land Act of 1800 benefited settlers.

☐ **P. 183** Students explain Spain's control over Florida and the lands west of the Mississippi River.

W Writing Skills

☐ **P. 181** Students write a letter from the perspective of a settler. **Verbal/Linguistic**

C Critical Thinking Skills

☐ **P. 176** Students predict problems that may come about from having a weak central government.

☐ **P. 178** Students work in groups to discover issues with obtaining group consensus. **BL Interpersonal**

☐ **P. 179** Students discuss the benefits and weaknesses of the Articles of Confederation. **BL**

☐ **P. 181** Students make inferences about the spread of slavery. **AL**

☐ **P. 182** Students discuss the financial issues plaguing the Continental Congress. **BL**

☐ **P. 183** Students make inferences about the presence of British troops along the Great Lakes.

T Technology Skills

☐ **P. 182** Students investigate other instances of monetary depreciation.

☑ Online Teaching Options

V Visual Skills

☐ **VIDEO** **Articles of Confederation**—Students view a video that presents the history of this document.

☐ **MAP** **The Northwest Territory**—Students explore how the land west of the Ohio River was divided and sold.

☐ **MAP** **Capitals of the United States**—Students click to learn about the nine cities that have served as our nation's capital.

☐ **IMAGE** **American Money**—Students click to learn about some of the items that have been used as currency in the 13 colonies and in the United States.

R Reading Skills

☐ **GRAPHIC ORGANIZER** **Taking Notes:** *Identifying:* **Powers of National Government**—Students identify the powers of the national government under the Articles of Confederation.

☐ **BIOGRAPHY** **John Adams**—Students explore the relationship between Adams and Benjamin Franklin.

☐ **BIOGRAPHY** **Richard Henry Lee**—Students read a biography of this Virginia leader.

☐ **SLIDE SHOW** **State Constitutions**—Students read excerpts from several state constitutions.

C Critical Thinking Skills

☐ **CHART** **Comparing the Articles of Confederation to the Constitution**—Students compare these documents.

☐ **IMAGE** **The Northwest Territory and Ordinance**—Students review the reasons this governing document was developed.

T Technology Skills

☐ **SELF-CHECK QUIZ** **Lesson 1**—Students receive instant feedback on their mastery of lesson content.

☐ **GAME** **The Articles of Confederation Matching Game**—Students test their knowledge of lesson vocabulary.

☑ Printable Digital Worksheets

C Critical Thinking Skills

☐ **WORKSHEET** **Geography and History Activity: Settlement of the Northwest Territory**—Students examine the differences between "landed" and "landless" states.

FORGING A NEW CONSTITUTION

Students will know:
- the documents, ideas, and people that influenced the creation of the Constitution.
- the compromises that were made in the Constitution's creation.

Students will be able to:
- **explain** the differences between sociology and the other social sciences.
- **compare and contrast** the strengths and weaknesses of the Articles of Confederation to those of the new Constitution.

UNDERSTANDING
BY DESIGN®

☑ *Print Teaching Options*

V Visual Skills

☐ **P. 186** Students analyze a painting of Southern life. **Visual/Spatial**

☐ **P. 187** Students analyze a circle graph of the professions of the 55 Framers. **BL** **Logical/Mathematical**

R Reading Skills

☐ **P. 184** Students list reasons why there was a depression following the Revolutionary War. **AL** **BL** **ELL**

☐ **P. 185** Students restate a primary source quote in their own words. **ELL**

☐ **P. 187** Students discuss the meaning of *convention*. **ELL**

☐ **P. 188** Students identify James Madison as the "Father of the Constitution." **AL**

☐ **P. 188** Students discuss *proportional representation*.

☐ **P. 189** Students identify the motivation behind the New Jersey plan.

☐ **P. 191** Students define bill of rights. **AL** **ELL**

W Writing Skills

☐ **P. 190** Students write a one-page paper about the role of compromise at the Constitutional Convention. **Verbal/Linguistic**

C Critical Thinking Skills

☐ **P. 186** Students analyze how attitudes toward slavery were changing. **AL** **ELL**

☐ **P. 188** Students infer the importance of public trust in the Convention.

☐ **P. 189** Students compare and contrast the Virginia and New Jersey plans. **AL** **ELL** **Visual/Spatial**

☐ **P. 190** Students list the compromises made that allowed the writing of the Constitution to proceed. **AL** **BL** **ELL** **Intrapersonal**

☐ **P. 191** Students identify why a proposal for a bill of rights was voted down.

T Technology Skills

☐ **P. 185** Students research the Springfield Armory National Historic Site.

☑ *Online Teaching Options*

V Visual Skills

☐ **VIDEO** **Shays's Rebellion**—Students view a video that describes the struggle to preserve and fund a strong central government.

☐ **CHART** **The 55 Framers**—The occupations of the Framers of the Constitution are presented in a circle graph.

R Reading Skills

☐ **GRAPHIC ORGANIZER** **Taking Notes:** *Comparing and Contrasting:* **Leaders and Their Roles**—Students note details about different leaders' plans for creating a new government.

☐ **BIOGRAPHY** **George Washington**—Students learn about Washington's role at the Constitutional Convention.

☐ **BIOGRAPHY** **James Madison**—Students learn more about Madison's role at the Constitutional Convention.

☐ **PRIMARY SOURCE** **Plantation Life**—Students read an excerpt from *Adventures and Escape of Moses Roper.*

☐ **IMAGE** **The Great Compromise: Virginia and New Jersey Plans**—Students examine the debate that lead to the establishment of a bicameral legislature.

C Critical Thinking Skills

☐ **CHART** **Framers of the Constitution**—Students click to learn the occupations and states of origin of the 55 Framers of the Constitution.

☐ **WHITEBOARD ACTIVITY** **Contributors to the Constitutional Convention**—Students match Framers with their contributions.

T Technology Skills

☐ **SELF-CHECK QUIZ** **Lesson 1**—Students receive instant feedback on their mastery of lesson content.

☐ **GAME** **Ratifying the Constitution Identification Game**—Students match ideas related to ratifying the Constitution.

☑ *Printable Digital Worksheets*

C Critical Thinking Skills

☐ **WORKSHEET** **Primary Source Activity: Shays's Rebellion**—Students contrast points of view presented in several primary sources.

A NEW PLAN OF GOVERNMENT

Students will know:
- the documents, ideas, and people that influenced the creation of the Constitution.
- the debate that took place over whether the Constitution should be adopted.

Students will be able to:
- **identify and evaluate** the sources, plans, and compromises for the Constitution and the balance of power in government.
- **identify the points of view** of the Federalists and Anti-Federalists.
- **compare and contrast** arguments supporting and opposing the adoption of the Constitution.

UNDERSTANDING
BY DESIGN®

☑ *Print Teaching Options*

V Visual Skills

☐ **P. 196** Students use a chart to identify powers given to the federal and state governments. **Visual/Spatial**

R Reading Skills

☐ **P. 194** Students discuss background information that the Framers drew upon while writing the Constitution.

☐ **P. 195** Students summarize the key influencers of the framers' political thinking. **BL ELL**

☐ **P. 195** Students define federalism and give examples of federalism from current events. **BL ELL**

☐ **P. 197** Students explain the three branches of government and how electors in the Electoral College are chosen. **BL ELL**

☐ **P. 197** Students discuss whether or not government leaders should be limited in what they can or cannot do.

W Writing Skills

☐ **P. 198** Students argue for the Bills of Rights from a modern perspective. **Verbal/Linguistic**

C Critical Thinking Skills

☐ **P. 194** Students discuss how European tradition influenced the framing of the Constitution.

☐ **P. 195** Students reflect on how Montesquieu's ideas about separation of powers affected the Framers of the Constitution. **BL**

☐ **P. 196** Students identify "the supreme law of the land" and explain why the Constitution is referred to in this way.

☐ **P. 197** Students analyze the role of the Supreme Court within the judicial branch.

☐ **P. 198** Students differentiate between the Federalists and the Anti-Federalists.

☐ **P. 199** Students discuss the debates over the ratification of the Constitution and Virginia's objection. **BL Interpersonal**

☑ *Online Teaching Options*

V Visual Skills

☐ **VIDEO Who Were the Framers of the Constitution?**—Students view a video that recounts the events leading up to the Constitutional Convention and describes several of its Framers.

☐ **IMAGE State of the Union Address Milestones**—Students click to learn how the presentation of the address has changed over time.

R Reading Skills

☐ **GRAPHIC ORGANIZER Taking Notes: *Categorizing:* Three Branches of Government**—Students use the chart to identify ways that each branch of the federal government can limit the power of the other branches.

C Critical Thinking Skills

☐ **WHITEBOARD ACTIVITY A Bicameral Legislature**—Students match descriptors to the chamber of Congress to which it applies.

☐ **POLITICAL CARTOON The Ninth Pillar Erected**—Students examine a political cartoon showing the struggle for ratification of the Constitution.

☐ **BIOGRAPHY Locke & Montesquieu**—Students read biographies of these philosophers.

T Technology Skills

☐ **SELF-CHECK QUIZ Lesson 3**—Students receive instant feedback on their mastery of lesson content.

☐ **GAME A New Plan of Government Column Game**—Students sort powers of government by Federal, State, and Both.

☐ **GAME A New Plan of Government Matching Game**—Students match terms and definitions to review lesson vocabulary.

LESSON 1   The Articles of Confederation

Reading and Comprehension

This lesson is about the different ways of governing, or ruling. Ask students to skim the lesson and find words or phrases that are related to *government*.

Text Evidence

Organize the class into small groups and ask them to list what they think are important roles of government (create laws, allow elections, and so on). Have them compare their answers to what the Articles of Confederation provided.

LESSON 2   Forging a New Constitution

Reading and Comprehension

Direct students to skim the lesson and write down five new words. Then have them read the text and write a sentence that uses each word in a meaningful way.

Text Evidence

Have small groups of students create cause-and-effect charts to show how the Revolutionary War led to Shays's Rebellion. They should cite evidence from the text to justify their conclusions.

LESSON 3   A New Plan of Government

Reading and Comprehension

Remind students that the meanings of new words in text are sometimes set off by commas and are often close to the word. Point out an example and ask students to write new words and their definitions from the text.

Text Evidence

Organize the class into two groups—the Federalists and the Anti-Federalists. Have them use the text to defend their positions and debate the ratification of the Constitution.

Online Resources

Approaching Level Reader

Use this online lower-level text that corresponds directly to the text in the Student Edition. It includes a Spanish version.

Guided Reading Activities

This resource uses graphic organizers and guiding questions to help students with comprehension.

What Do You Know?

Use these worksheets to pre-assess student's background knowledge before they study the chapter.

Reading Essentials and Study Guide Workbook

This resource offers writing and reading activities for the approaching-level student. Also available in Spanish.

Self-Check Quizzes

This online assessment tool provides instant feedback for students to check their progress.

A More Perfect Union

1777–1790

ESSENTIAL QUESTIONS • Why do people form governments?
• How do new ideas change the way people live? • How do governments change?

◀ Legend has it that Betsy Ross sewed the first flag of the independent United States.

The Granger Collection, NYC.

networks

There's More Online about the first years of the United States.

CHAPTER 7

Lesson 1
The Articles of Confederation

Lesson 2
Forging a New Constitution

Lesson 3
A New Plan of Government

The Story Matters ...

The story goes that in June 1776, Betsy Ross is mourning her husband, a member of the militia killed that year in the line of duty. A seamstress, Ross is also trying to run her husband's furniture-covering business. One day, she gets a visit from none other than George Washington and two other men. The men ask Ross to make a special flag. They show her their ideas for the flag, and Ross offers some of her own. Then, the seamstress gets to work.

That story may or may not be true. It is a fact, however, that on June 14, 1777, the Continental Congress voted to make the Stars and Stripes the national flag of the United States. This was just one of the many decisions facing the leaders of the young United States.

173

CHAPTER 7
A More Perfect Union

ENGAGE

🔔 **Bellringer** Ask a volunteer to read "The Story Matters ..." aloud. Then discuss what it might have been like to see the red, white, and blue flag of the United States flying for the first time in your town if you were a citizen in the 1770s.
Ask:

- Why do you think it is important for a country to have a flag? What meaning does the American flag have for you? Have a few students identify the meanings they associate with the flag; for example, it is a symbol of the nation, or it represents freedom and liberty.
- How do you feel when you see the American flag displayed at community or national events, or at international events, such as the Olympics? *(Students' answers will vary.)* Tell students that the Stars and Stripes was the first official flag of the United States but that the country did have other flags. Tell interested students to research the history of all the flags the United States has had, such as the unofficial Continental Colors and the Gadsden flags; the Betsy Ross flag and the 15-star, 15-stripe flag that inspired our national anthem.

Making Connections

Ask students what laws are, and guide them in seeing that laws are essentially rules we must follow. Ask them to name some examples of laws they and the people in their community follow every day. Explain that every law in the United States is based on the rules laid out in a document that is called "the supreme law of the land." The challenges, struggles, and compromises students will read about in this chapter led to the creation of that law of the land—the U.S. Constitution—and so affects them and the people they know every day of their lives.

Letter from the Author

Dear American History Teacher,

When the country was governed by the Articles of Confederation, the individual states were almost sovereign. But failure to solve problems with commerce and foreign relations led to calls for a stronger central government. Virginia led the states in summoning a convention to discuss issues of general interest. The Constitution that the convention's delegates wrote established a federal government with authority over the whole country. The new constitutional government could act to promote general welfare, collect taxes, and impose punishments for crimes.

Joyce Appleby

Chapter 7 173

TEACH & ASSESS

Step Into the Place

V1 Visual Skills

Analyzing Maps Direct students' attention to the map. Point out that in 1785 this vast region became the property of the federal government, which organized the region and encouraged settlement. **Ask:**

- **What formed the borders of the Northwest Territory?** *(Pennsylvania to the east, the Ohio River to the south, the Mississippi River to the west, and the Great Lakes and Canada to the north)*
- **Why do you think the Northwest Territory was called what it was?** *(It lay to the northwest of what was then the United States.)*
- **Which geographic features on this map will become vital to American expansion?** *(the Mississippi River and the Ohio River)* **Visual/Spatial**

T Technology Skills

Researching on the Internet Let a student interested in boats conduct Internet research to learn more about the flatboats used on the Ohio River in the late 1700s. Invite the student to share the research results with the class. If the student enjoys working with his or her hands, encourage the student to make a simple model of a flatboat and bring it to class. **Kinesthetic**

Content Background Knowledge

The grid system set up by the Land Ordinance of 1785 was not a simple grid of squares, but a more complex grid system of squares within squares. The basic square was called a township. A township had six-mile-long sides. Each township was divided into 36 one-square-mile sections. Each section was further divided into four quarter sections of 160 acres each.

ANSWERS, p. 174

Step Into the Place
1. The land appears to be mostly flat, and the lakes and rivers offer transportation routes that might help support farms and other commerce.
2. Wisconsin, Michigan, Illinois, Indiana, Ohio, and part of Minnesota
3. **CRITICAL THINKING** areas just north of the Ohio River; because they were easily accessible from the Ohio River and from nearby states that were already settled

Step Into the Time
1. 1776–1791
2. France went to war with Britain; the League of Armed Neutrality was formed.

Place and Time: United States 1777–1790

A few years after achieving independence, the United States made plans to expand into some of the land to the west. Leaders put forward a plan to settle the Northwest Territory and, over time, form new states.

Step Into the Place

MAP FOCUS The British gave up their claim to the Northwest Territory in the Treaty of Paris.

1. **REGION** What geographical features made this territory desirable for settlement by people from the United States? RH.6–8.7

2. **PLACE** What present-day states were made from the Northwest Territory? RH.6–8.7

3. **CRITICAL THINKING** *Drawing Conclusions* Which areas of the territory do you think were likely to be settled first? Explain your answer. RH.6–8.7

The Land Ordinance of 1785 set up a plan for dividing and selling western lands. The new grid system worked well and was later used across the nation. You can still see traces of this system from the air.

Many American settlers moved to the Northwest Territory by sailing on flatboats along the Ohio River. At anywhere from 8 to 20 feet wide (2 to 6 m) and sometimes 100 feet long (30 m), the flatboat was capable of carrying large amounts of cargo.

(t) George Rose/Getty Images News/Getty Images
(b) Archive Photos/George Eastman House/Getty Images

Step Into the Time

V2 **Time Line** Review the time line. What years are covered in this time line? Identify two world events that might have been influenced by the Revolutionary War. RH.6–8.5, WHST.6–8.7

U.S. PRESIDENTS		
U.S. EVENTS		
WORLD EVENTS	1776	1779

1781 Maryland ratifies Articles of Confederation; document is "in force"

1778 France goes to war against Britain

1780 League of Armed Neutrality is formed

Project-Based Learning

Hands-On Chapter Project

Front-Page News Story

Students will learn about the forces that shaped American government by researching and citing at least three sources as they write a front-page news story about an important event— the adoption of the Articles of Confederation, the Ordinance of 1785, Shays's Rebellion, or the Great Compromise—of the years following the Revolutionary War.

Technology Extension

Online Collaborative Front-Page News Story

Students will collaborate online to create their front-page news stories. Having students write collaboratively online allows them to share ideas in real time, peer edit, contribute to the writing process from any computer with Internet access, and share live edits with you. Online collaborative writing is an outstanding platform for a group writing assignment because it allows all group members to participate in the writing process.

edtech**teacher**
21st Century Learning

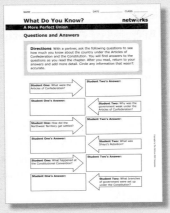

networks
There's More Online!

☑ **MAP** Explore the interactive version of this map on NETWORKS.

☑ **TIME LINE** Explore the interactive version of this time line on NETWORKS.

V1

The Northwest Territory 1787

Lake Superior

Northwest Territory
Present-day state boundaries

St. Lawrence R.

Fort Mackinac

Minnesota R.

Wisconsin

Lake Michigan

Lake Huron

Michigan

Fort Detroit

Lake Erie

0   200 miles
0   200 km
Lambert Azimuthal Equal-Area projection

S P A N I S H   L O U I S I A N A

Mississippi R.

Des Moines R.

Illinois R.

Illinois

Indiana

Missouri R.

St. Louis

Wabash R.

Ohio

Ohio R.

ATLANTIC OCEAN

N
W   E
S

90°W   80°W

1785 • Congress moves to New York City, temporary capital of U.S.
• Congress passes Land Ordinance of 1785

1786 • Meeting in Maryland to discuss Articles of Confederation
• Rebellion in Massachusetts led by Daniel Shays

George Washington 1789–1797

1782 The Great Seal of the United States adopted by Congress of the Confederation

1788 U.S. Constitution ratified

1782   **1785**   **1788**   **1791**

1782 • Rama I starts new dynasty in Siam
• Japan experiences famine

1784 Russians establish colony on Kodiak Island, Alaska

1786 Mozart's opera *The Marriage of Figaro* is performed

1788 British establish penal colony in Australia

1789 French Revolution begins

1787 • Shays's Rebellion is suppressed
• Congress approves meeting to revise Articles of Confederation
• U.S. introduces dollar currency

White House Historical Association

175

Step Into the Time

V2 Visual Skills

Analyzing Time Lines Have students review the time line for the chapter. Explain that they will be studying events from about 1780 to 1790. **Ask: Based on the information listed in the time line, what can you infer about what was happening in the United States beginning around 1780?** *(The new United States of America was growing, going through changes and turmoil, and deciding what kind of a nation it wanted to be.)* **Visual/Spatial**

Content Background Knowledge

The Ohio River has been a vital waterway for centuries.

• Native Americans used the river as a natural highway. They traveled the Ohio River in dugouts (logs shaped into canoes) and birch bark canoes (made of bark on a frame).

• American settlers migrated west along the Ohio in flatboats and, later, steamboats as well.

• Even before 1800, the Ohio River was an important trade route, with boats carrying all manner of goods to market.

• Today, the Ohio River is still an important commercial route. Only one river—the Mississippi—carries more cargo. About 200 million tons of freight are carried on the Ohio each year.

CLOSE & REFLECT

Discussing Tell students that time travel is still impossible but that by actively using their imagination, they can achieve a time travel of sorts. **Ask: If you could step into this time and place—the United States in its first years as a country—what do you think would be most different from the way your life is now? What might be similar, or even the same?**

WORKSHEET

What Do You Know? Activity: Questions and Answers: A More Perfect Union

Expressing Pair students. Have them take turns asking and answering the questions on the worksheet. Have them review the worksheet after they complete the chapter. Suggest they revise their original answers as needed and explain their changes.

See page 173B for other online activities.

What Do You Know?
A More Perfect Union
networks

Questions and Answers

Directions With a partner, ask the following questions to see how much you know about the country under the Articles of Confederation and the Constitution. You will find answers to the questions as you read the chapter. After you read, return to your answers and add more detail. Circle any information that wasn't accurate.

ENGAGE

Bellringer Present students with the following scenario: It's a Friday night and a family wants to watch a movie. They have three to choose from. (At this point, name three very different movies—perhaps a children's movie, an action thriller, and a romantic comedy.) **Ask: Which movie should the family watch?** *(Students' answers will vary. Some students may strongly support or strongly oppose one or more of the choices.)*

Next tell students that the family wants a snack to eat while watching the movie. They can have <u>only</u> one of the following: chocolate ice cream, brownies, or popcorn. **Ask: Which snack should they have?** *(Again, students' answers will vary, and opinions may be very strong.)*

Tell students that the Second Continental Congress faced a similar dilemma: trying to satisfy the needs of all 13 states involved in creating the new government.

TEACH & ASSESS

R Reading Skills

Finding the Main Idea Have students review the red titles on this page. **Ask:**

- **Which head hints that the country was trying to form a plan of government in the 1780s?** *(Students may say "The Making of a Republic" or "States Write Constitutions.")* **AL** **ELL**

- **Why were the people so careful to limit the power of the governor and the legislature?** *(Because of their experience with British rule, they did not want power in the hands of a single ruler or even a single group. They wanted to keep power in the hands of the people.)*

C Critical Thinking Skills

Predicting Consequences Direct students to read the section under the heading "States Write Constitutions." Note that not all states created constitutions at the same time. Ask students to explain why that might have been the case. Then direct students to predict the types of issues the different states might face when working together to forge a national constitution.

ANSWER, p. 176

TAKING NOTES: conduct foreign affairs, maintain armed forces , borrow money, issue currency

---

networks
There's More Online!
- ☑ **CHART/GRAPH**
  - Capitals of the United States
  - Articles of Confederation and the Constitution
- ☑ **GAME** Concentration Game
- ☑ **GRAPHIC ORGANIZER** Identifying
- ☑ **MAP** The Northwest Territory
- ☑ **SLIDE SHOW** State Constitutions

Lesson 1
The Articles of Confederation

ESSENTIAL QUESTION *Why do people form governments?*

IT MATTERS BECAUSE

After gaining independence, Americans faced the task for forming independent governments at both the state and national levels.

The Making of a Republic

GUIDING QUESTION *What kind of government was created by the Articles of Confederation?*

After throwing off British rule, the independent states faced the challenge of governing themselves. The 13 states needed a plan of government that would satisfy all their needs. Would the states be able to work together and still maintain their independence? How would each individual state govern itself?

States Write Constitutions

The Continental Congress took up this last question even before declaring independence. In May 1776, Congress asked the states to organize their governments. Each state adopted a state constitution, or plan of government. Eight states had drafted constitutions before the end of the year. New York and Georgia followed in 1777 and Massachusetts in 1780. Connecticut and Rhode Island decided to use their colonial charters as state constitutions.

Limits on Power

After years of British rule, Americans were determined not to place too much power in the hands of one ruler or body. They crafted constitutions that limited the power of the governor. Pennsylvania's constitution replaced the office entirely with an elected 12-person council.

Reading HELPDESK (ccss)

Taking Notes: *Identifying* RH.6–8.1
As you read, use a diagram like the one shown to identify the powers of the national government under the Articles of Confederation.

Powers of National Government

Content Vocabulary (Tier 3 Words)
- **bicameral** • **depreciate**
- **republic**
- **ordinance**

176 *A More Perfect Union*

---

networks ***Online Teaching Options***

VIDEO

Articles of Confederation

Formulating Questions Challenge students to name the six "question words" *(who, what, where, when, why, how)*. Tell students that they will be responsible for using each of these words to formulate questions about the video they will watch. Share the video "The Articles of Confederation" with students. After they have written their questions, have them work with a partner to answer each other's questions.

See page 173C for other online activities.

States also divided power between the governor (or council) and the legislature. Most states set up two-house, or **bicameral** (bye•KAM•ruhl), legislatures to divide the work of government even further.

The first state constitutions aimed to keep power in the hands of the people. For example, voters chose the state legislators, and states held elections often. In most states, only white males who were at least 21 years old could vote. These men also had to own a certain amount of property or pay a certain amount of taxes. Some states allowed free African American males to vote.

Because state constitutions limited the powers of the governors, the legislatures became the most powerful branch of government. The state legislatures tried to make taxes fair for everyone, but disagreements arose. The shift from British colonies to self-governing states held many challenges.

A New Republic

In addition to forming state governments, the American people had to form a national government. People agreed the new country should be a **republic**, a government in which citizens rule through elected representatives. They could not agree, however, on what powers the new republic's government should have.

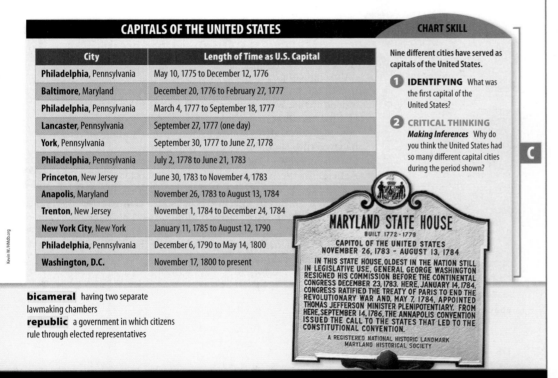

CAPITALS OF THE UNITED STATES

City	Length of Time as U.S. Capital
Philadelphia, Pennsylvania	May 10, 1775 to December 12, 1776
Baltimore, Maryland	December 20, 1776 to February 27, 1777
Philadelphia, Pennsylvania	March 4, 1777 to September 18, 1777
Lancaster, Pennsylvania	September 27, 1777 (one day)
York, Pennsylvania	September 30, 1777 to June 27, 1778
Philadelphia, Pennsylvania	July 2, 1778 to June 21, 1783
Princeton, New Jersey	June 30, 1783 to November 4, 1783
Anapolis, Maryland	November 26, 1783 to August 13, 1784
Trenton, New Jersey	November 1, 1784 to December 24, 1784
New York City, New York	January 11, 1785 to August 12, 1790
Philadelphia, Pennsylvania	December 6, 1790 to May 14, 1800
Washington, D.C.	November 17, 1800 to present

Kevin W./HMdb.org

CHART SKILL

Nine different cities have served as capitals of the United States.

1 **IDENTIFYING** What was the first capital of the United States?

2 **CRITICAL THINKING** *Making Inferences* Why do you think the United States had so many different capital cities during the period shown?

bicameral having two separate lawmaking chambers

republic a government in which citizens rule through elected representatives

MARYLAND STATE HOUSE
BUILT 1772 - 1779
CAPITOL OF THE UNITED STATES
NOVEMBER 26, 1783 - AUGUST 13, 1784
IN THIS STATE HOUSE, OLDEST IN THE NATION STILL IN LEGISLATIVE USE, GENERAL GEORGE WASHINGTON RESIGNED HIS COMMISSION BEFORE THE CONTINENTAL CONGRESS DECEMBER 23, 1783. HERE, JANUARY 14, 1784, CONGRESS RATIFIED THE TREATY OF PARIS TO END THE REVOLUTIONARY WAR AND, MAY 7, 1784, APPOINTED THOMAS JEFFERSON MINISTER PLENIPOTENTIARY. FROM HERE, SEPTEMBER 14, 1786, THE ANNAPOLIS CONVENTION ISSUED THE CALL TO THE STATES THAT LED TO THE CONSTITUTIONAL CONVENTION.

A REGISTERED NATIONAL HISTORIC LANDMARK
MARYLAND HISTORICAL SOCIETY

SLIDE SHOW

State Constitutions

Comparing and Contrasting Use the interactive slide show to discuss the similarities and differences among state constitutions. The first image is that of the Preamble to the U.S. Constitution. Explain that the next five slides show the preambles to five state constitutions. **Ask:** **How are the constitutions similar? How are they different?** *(Similar: All preambles mention God or a higher power. Difference: Three preambles are short; two others, Delaware in particular, specify the rights to which people are entitled.)* **BL**

See page 173C for other online activities.

McGraw-Hill **netw⊕rks**   State Constitutions

We the People

Each of the states in the United States of America has its own constitution. These documents are usually longer and more detailed than the U.S. Constitution. State constitutions are the basic plans for the legal and political processes of each state.

Tetra Images

R1 **Reading Skills**

Defining Explore terms with which students may not be comfortably familiar. **Ask:** **What is a constitution?** *(a plan of government)* **What does bicameral mean?** *(having two houses)* **ELL** **How are these two terms connected?** *(a constitution may call for a bicameral legislature)*

R2 **Reading Skills**

Discussing After students read, discuss with them the establishment of the new country as a republic. **Ask:**

- **What does it mean that our country is a republic?** *(In our government, citizens rule through elected representatives.)* **ELL**

- **What challenges might require states to work together under the single authority of a central government?** *(Answers may vary, but students might suggest challenges such as building a highway system, fighting a war, or trading with other countries.)* **AL**

C **Critical Thinking Skills**

Making Inferences Direct students to the infographic showing the capitals of the United States. **Ask:** **Why do you think the capital changed so frequently in the early days of the republic?** *(Students may mention the competition between states to be the capital or the effects of war and the need to move the capital from areas of combat.)* **Why do you think Washington, D.C., has been the capital for so long?** *(The government has become stable.)* **AL**

Then have students work in groups to locate each former capital on a map of the eastern states. **Ask:** **Which former capitals are currently state capitals?** *(Annapolis, MD; Trenton, NJ)* **Which cities on the list surprised you?** *(Answers will vary.)* **Visual/Spatial**

ANSWERS, p. 177

CHART SKILL

1. Philadelphia, Pennsylvania

2. **CRITICAL THINKING** The effects of the war may have made it necessary to move the capital away from combat.

The Articles of Confederation

Identifying Before students read, remind them that the Constitution was not the first or only important document in the formation of the nation. As students read the next few lessons, ask them to identify the many steps that led to the Constitution's development. **Ask: What did Virginia's Richard Henry Lee do that helped make the Articles of Confederation a reality?** *(He made a motion at the Second Continental Congress to create a plan of confederation to send to the colonies for approval.)*

R2 Reading Skills

Listing After reading, ask students to identify the challenges of the Continental Congress in assigning enough power to the government to make it effective but also of limiting the government's power. **Ask: What powers did the Articles of Confederation give Congress?** *(to conduct foreign affairs, maintain armed forces, borrow money, and issue currency)* **How might these limited powers affect Congress as the nation developed?** *(Answers will vary, but students should note the challenges Congress may face in getting states to pay for troops and getting citizens to join an army.)* **AL**

C Critical Thinking Skills

Problem-Solving Organize the class into groups. Have each group create a list of classroom rules that they would like to see implemented. After each group has finished its list, have members of the group appoint one member to work with representatives of other groups to develop a single list of classroom rules. Explain to students that the challenges they face in coming to consensus on the classroom rules are similar to the challenges faced by the committee that authored the Articles of Confederation. **BL** **Interpersonal**

R1 On June 7, 1776, Virginia's Richard Henry Lee moved that "a plan of confederation be prepared and transmitted to the respective colonies, for their consideration and approbation [approval]."

At first, most Americans wanted a weak central government. They expected each state would remain free to act independently on most issues. The states would rely on a central government only to wage war and handle relations with other countries.

The Articles of Confederation

In 1776 the Second Continental Congress appointed a committee to draw up a plan for a new central government. The result of this committee's work was the Articles of Confederation. After much discussion, Congress adopted the Articles—the nation's first constitution—in November 1777.

The Articles of Confederation established a weak central government. The states kept most of their power. For the states, the Articles of Confederation were "a firm league of friendship" in which each state retained "its sovereignty, freedom and independence."

R2 The Articles of Confederation gave the Congress limited powers. Congress could conduct foreign affairs, maintain armed forces, borrow money, and issue currency. Congress did not have the power to regulate trade, force citizens to join the army, or impose taxes. If Congress needed to raise money or troops, it had to ask the states. States were not required to contribute.

The new central government had no chief executive. This is an official, such as a president or a governor, who carries out the laws and leads the government in its day-to-day operations. Under the Articles of Confederation government carried on its business, such as selling western lands, through congressional committees.

All the states had to approve the Articles and any amendments. Yet not every state supported the Articles of Confederation at first. Under the new plan, each state had one vote regardless of population. States with large populations believed they should have more votes.

Disputes over land also threatened to block approval of the Articles. By the 1780s, seven of the original states lay claim to areas in the West. Maryland refused to approve the Articles until New York, Virginia, and other states **abandoned** their land claims west of the Appalachian Mountains. This done, Maryland joined the other 12 states in approving the Articles. On March 1, 1781, the Confederation formally became the government of the United States of America. **C**

Reading **HELP**DESK **CCSS**

Academic Vocabulary (Tier 2 Words)
abandon to give up

---

netw⊙rks   *Online Teaching Options*

GRAPHIC ORGANIZER

Taking Notes: *Identifying***: Powers of National Government**

Identifying Have student pairs use the interactive graphic organizer to identify the powers of the national government under the Articles of Confederation. **Ask: What powers did Congress have under the Articles of Confederation?** *(conduct foreign affairs, maintain armed forces, borrow money, and issue currency)* **What were weaknesses of the Articles?** *(Congress did not have power to regulate trade, force citizens to join the army, or impose taxes; it could not pass a law unless nine states voted in favor of it; it lacked a chief executive.)* **What might be the result of Congress not having power to tax?** *(The government would be weak because it would not have money.)* **AL**

See page 173C for other online activities.

netw⊙rks

Name: _____   Date: _____

TAKING NOTES: *Identifying*
ACTIVITY At you read, use the diagram to identify the powers of the national government under the Articles of Confederation.

Powers of National Government

UNDO   CLEAR   SAVE

WEAKNESSES OF THE ARTICLES OF CONFEDERATION
Congress had no authority to raise money by collecting taxes.
Congress had no control over foreign trade.
Congress could not force states to carry out its laws.
All 13 states had to agree to any amendments, making it nearly impossible to correct problems.

CHART SKILL

The Articles of Confederation had several key weaknesses.

1 SUMMARIZING
Summarize the basic problem with the Articles of Confederation.

2 CRITICAL THINKING
Speculating Why do you think getting 13 states to agree on decisions and actions was so difficult?

C

The Confederation Government

The next several years were critical ones for the young republic. It soon became clear that the new national government was too weak to handle the problems facing the United States. The weak Congress could not pass a law unless nine states voted in favor of it. Changing the Articles required the approval of all 13 states. This made it hard for Congress to pass laws when there was any disagreement.

R

Even with these challenges, the new government managed some key achievements. Under the Confederation government, Americans negotiated a peace treaty with Britain and expanded the country's foreign trade. The Confederation also helped with settling and governing the country's western lands.

☑ PROGRESS CHECK

Specifying How many votes did each state have in the new Congress?

Policies for Western Lands

GUIDING QUESTION *What process allowed new states to join the union?*

The Articles of Confederation did not propose a way to add new states to the United States. Yet there were settlers living west of the Appalachian Mountains, outside the existing states. These Western settlers wanted to organize their lands as states and join the Union.

Under the terms of the Treaty of Paris, the British gave up control of the land north of the Ohio River and west of the Appalachian Mountains. Many Americans were eager to settle in this region. The new United States government had to establish policies for settlement of these western lands. Another challenge was to come up with an orderly process by which new territories could achieve the status of statehood.

Reading in the Content Area: *Charts*

Charts can take many forms. The simple chart on this page lists a series of statements or facts. It presents a clear, short summary of key information. The title of the chart indicates the common theme that unites the items in the chart.

C Critical Thinking Skills

Evaluating As a class, discuss the strengths and weaknesses of the Articles of Confederation. Have students decide which weaknesses might pose the greatest problems for the country. Then have students put the weaknesses listed on the chart in that order. *(Order will vary.)* **BL**

R Reading Skills

Paraphrasing After researching a copy, have volunteers read some sections of the Articles of Confederation to the class. Ask additional volunteers to paraphrase the section or article that was read aloud. Then have the class discuss those articles. **BL** Ask students to read "The Confederation Government" and to apply their knowledge of the Articles of Confederation in order to explain why the government would have faced the issues outlined in this section of the text.

The Articles of Confederation

Defining Have students play the Articles of Confederation matching game to test their knowledge of key vocabulary words used in this section of the text. Instruct students to find the term and then match the definition to that term. Allow students to play multiple times until they are able to correctly define all key terms. **ELL**

See page 173C for other online activities.

ANSWERS, p. 179

☑ PROGRESS CHECK one vote, regardless of population

CHART SKILL

1. The basic problem with the Articles of Confederation was that the central government had very limited powers and was too weak to solve the problems of the new United States.

2. **CRITICAL THINKING** They all had their own interests and were in some ways in competition with each other.

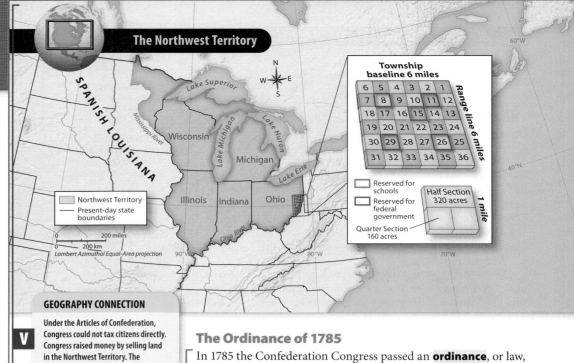

The Northwest Territory

Township baseline 6 miles

6	5	4	3	2	1
7	8	9	10	11	12
18	17	16	15	14	13
19	20	21	22	23	24
30	29	28	27	26	25
31	32	33	34	35	36

Range line 6 miles

Reserved for schools
Reserved for federal government

Half Section 320 acres

Quarter Section 160 acres

1 mile

☐ Northwest Territory
— Present-day state boundaries

0   200 miles
0   200 km
Lambert Azimuthal Equal-Area projection

V Visual Skills

Analyzing Maps Use the map "The Northwest Territory" and the text on this page as a basis for discussion. **Ask:**

- What was the major provision of the Ordinance of 1785? *(It set up a process to survey and sell the western lands north of the Ohio River.)*
- What current states were once part of the Northwest Territory? *(Ohio, Michigan, Indiana, Illinois, Wisconsin, and part of Minnesota)* **Visual/Spatial**

R Reading Skills

Defining Have students read the text on this page. **Ask:** What is an ordinance? *(a law)* **ELL** Tell students that Congress passed two ordinances dealing with western lands. **Ask: Which two ordinances did Congress pass?** *(the Ordinance of 1785; the Northwest Ordinance)* Remind students to support their answers with evidence from the text.

C Critical Thinking Skills

Analyzing Ask students what they think the government should require from a group of people who want the territory they settled to become a state in the Union. Tell students that in this section they will learn what was required.

GEOGRAPHY CONNECTION

Under the Articles of Confederation, Congress could not tax citizens directly. Congress raised money by selling land in the Northwest Territory. The Ordinance divided land into townships, 6 miles (10 km) to a side. This created 36 square miles, or "sections."

1 PLACE Which rivers acted as borders for the Northwest Territory?

2 CRITICAL THINKING
Explaining Why do you think Congress set up such a precise system for measuring out and dividing up the land?

The Ordinance of 1785

In 1785 the Confederation Congress passed an **ordinance**, or law, that set up a process to survey and sell the lands north of the Ohio River. The new law divided this large area into townships 6 miles long (9.7 km) and 6 miles wide (9.7 km). These townships were to be further divided into 36 sections of 640 acres (259 ha). The government would sell each section at public auction, or sale, for at least a dollar an acre. Concerned about lawless people moving into western lands, Richard Henry Lee, the president of the Congress, urged that "the rights of property be clearly defined" by the government. Congress drafted another law to protect the interests of hardworking settlers.

The Northwest Ordinance

The Northwest Ordinance, passed in 1787, created a single Northwest Territory from lands north of the Ohio River and east of the Mississippi River. The lands were to be divided into three to five smaller territories. When a territory had 60,000 residents, the people could seek statehood. Each new state would have the same standing as the original 13 states.

Reading HELPDESK (CCSS)

ordinance law

Academic Vocabulary (Tier 2 Words)
clause a special condition in a formal document

netw⊙rks   *Online Teaching Options*

MAP

The Northwest Territory

Discussing Discuss ways in which the government encouraged settlement of the Northwest Territory. **Ask: Why would the government encourage settlement of these and other western lands?** *(The government may have wanted to prevent other countries from taking the lands away from the United States by making sure the area was settled. The government may also have wanted to develop resources available in the new lands. One way to accomplish its goals was to make land available to settlers.)* **How did the Northwest Territory change between 1800 and 1820?** *(Its population grew very quickly. In just 20 years, the total settler population grew from about 51,000 to almost 793,000.)*

See page 173C for other online activities.

ANSWERS, p. 180

GEOGRAPHY CONNECTION

1 the Mississippi River and the Ohio River

2 CRITICAL THINKING Creating specific plots of land with defined boundaries made it easier for the land to be sold. This land could be sold to fund education.

The Northwest Ordinance had a bill of rights for the settlers in the territory. It guaranteed freedom of religion and trial by jury. It also stated, "There shall be neither slavery nor involuntary servitude in said territory." This **clause**, or condition added to a document, marked the first attempt to stop the spread of slavery in the United States. The Ordinance of 1785 and the Northwest Ordinance attempted to make possible the settlement of the Northwest Territory in a peaceful and orderly way. In general, the laws were successful.

The United States Congress would later take a similar step in the South. In 1798 it created the Mississippi Territory from land west of Georgia. Congress organized the government of the territory in the same basic way as in the Northwest Territory—except that slavery was allowed.

Land Act of 1800

The Ordinance of 1785 and the Northwest Ordinance aimed to encourage settlement in the Northwest Territory. In time it became clear that people needed even more help. In 1800 Congress passed the Land Act. This law made it easier for people to buy land in the territory. For example, the act made it possible for people to pay for land a little at a time. Under the terms of this law, a person was required to buy at least 320 acres of land at a price of $2 per acre. The buyer could pay half of the money at the time of purchase and the rest in four yearly payments.

☑ **PROGRESS CHECK**

Explaining What did the Northwest Ordinance say about slavery?

Much of the land in the West was sold to pay off debts from the Revolutionary War. The sale of these lands also provided opportunity for many settlers, who eagerly moved West.

North Wind Picture Archives

Lesson 1 **181**

See page 173C for other online activities.

C Critical Thinking Skills

Making Inferences Explain to students that the Northwest Ordinance included a clause that marked the first attempt to stop the spread of slavery in the United States. **Ask: What can you infer from this about the history of the United States in the late 1700s and early 1800s?** *(that more attempts will be made to stop the spread of slavery)* **AL**

R Reading Skills

Explaining Have students read the passage and explain how home ownership worked in the early 1800s. **Ask:**

- How did the Land Act of 1800 benefit settlers? *(It made it easier for people to buy land. For example, they could pay for it a little at a time.)*
- How did the payment process work? *(Settlers could buy 320 acres at two dollars an acre, with half the payment up front and the other half paid over four years.)*

W Writing Skills

Narrative Direct students to the image of the settlers on this page. Encourage students to discuss what life might have been like for these settlers moving into new territories. Ask a student volunteer to record the details from the class discussion on the board. Then instruct students to use the details from the class discussion, as well as details from the image on this page, to write a letter from a settler to a relative in one of the thirteen colonies. The letter should explain what life is like in the territories, including any challenges the settlers faced. **Verbal/Linguistic**

IMAGE

The Northwest Territory and Ordinance

Researching on the Internet Display the interactive image of the Northwest Ordinance, and have students read the accompanying text. Direct students to use the Internet to learn more about the lives of settlers in these territories. Have students create a fact sheet listing five things they learned from their research.

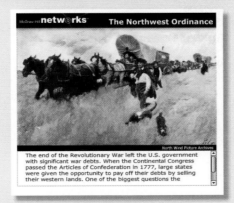

McGraw-Hill **netw⊚rks** The Northwest Ordinance

North Wind Picture Archives

The end of the Revolutionary War left the U.S. government with significant war debts. When the Continental Congress passed the Articles of Confederation in 1777, large states were given the opportunity to pay off their debts by selling their western lands. One of the biggest questions the

---

ANSWER, p. 181

☑ **PROGRESS CHECK** It banned slavery in the Northwest Territory.

The Articles of Confederation

R | Reading Skills

Defining Before students read, point out that the value of the dollar with which they are familiar is not constant. Explain to students that this was true of early colonial money as well. **Ask: What were Continentals?** *(Continentals were America's first paper money.)* **What does it mean that they depreciated?** *(They fell in value.)* Have students cite text evidence to support their answers. **ELL**

C | Critical Thinking Skills

Identifying Central Issues Have students recall the weaknesses in the Articles of Confederation. **Ask:**

- **How did the weaknesses lead to financial issues for the Confederation government?** *(The government could not raise money easily. It also could not regulate its own trade. Without this, the government debt would increase.)* **BL**
- **Why was the Continental Congress in debt? Why could it not pay its debt?** *(The debt was created by the Revolutionary War. Congress could not pay its debt because it did not have the power to tax.)*

T | Technology Skills

Analyzing News Media Explain to students that currency issues such as the ones described here are not just issues in the distant past. Direct students to use an Internet search engine to find current media reports of countries struggling with depreciation issues. Ask students to identify the country and the issue. Have students explain steps those countries are taking to shore up their finances. Students should connect these issues and solutions with the issues the Continental Congress faced.

THEN

Money is any object widely accepted as payment. Tobacco leaves were once used as money in colonial Virginia. Colonists also used other goods as well as coins as money. Eventually, governments began issuing paper money to make exchanges of goods and business dealings easier.

NOW

▶ **CRITICAL THINKING**
Drawing Conclusions Why is it important to have a system of money that is recognized, agreed upon, and used by all people?

Problems at Home and Abroad

GUIDING QUESTION *In what ways was the Confederation government weak?*

Because of its weakness, the Confederation government had trouble with financial issues. Continentals, paper bills the Continental Congress printed during the war, did not hold their value. By 1781, the currency had **depreciated** (dih•PREE•shee•ayt•ed), or fallen in value, so far that it was worth almost nothing. As more continentals appeared, people realized that Congress could not exchange or trade in the bills for gold or silver. The public began to doubt the money was worth anything. In 1779 it took 40 continentals to buy a single Spanish silver dollar. By 1781, a person needed 146 continentals to buy that Spanish coin. "Not worth a continental" became a common saying. At the same time, the price of food and other goods soared. In Boston and some other areas, high prices led to food riots.

In the 1780s, the Continental Congress faced a large debt. During the Revolutionary War, Congress had borrowed money from American citizens and foreign governments. It still owed Revolutionary soldiers pay for their military service. Without the power to tax, the Confederation could not easily raise money to pay its debts. The Continental Congress asked the states for money, but it could not force the states to pay. In fact, the states provided less than half of the money the federal government asked them to contribute.

Plan for Import Tax

Congress faced a collapse of the country's finances. In 1781 it created a department of finance led by Philadelphia merchant Robert Morris. While serving in Congress, Morris had proposed a 5 percent tax on imported goods to help pay the national debt. The plan required a change to the Articles of Confederation. Twelve states approved the plan, but Rhode Island opposed it. Under the Articles, the single "no" vote was enough to block the plan. A second effort in 1783 also failed to win approval by all the states. The financial crisis grew worse.

Relations With Britain

Trouble with foreign governments also revealed the weaknesses of the American government. For example, American merchants complained that the British were blocking Americans from the West Indies and other British markets. In the Treaty of Paris

Reading **HELP**DESK (CCSS)

depreciate to fall in value

---

netw**o**rks *Online Teaching Options*

IMAGE

American Money

Analyzing Images Present the interactive image of types of American currency. Have students click on each type to learn when and where it was used. **Ask: Why would it be important to have one standard form of money?** *(It would make the money easier to use across state lines.)*

See page 173C for other online activities.

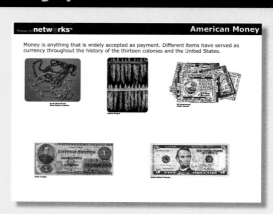

netw**o**rks™   **American Money**

Money is anything that is widely accepted as payment. Different items have served as currency throughout the history of the thirteen colonies and the United States.

ANSWER, p. 182

CRITICAL THINKING Money is something that is easy to carry around, is accepted by everyone as a way to buy and sell goods, and represents a certain value.

of 1783, Britain had promised to withdraw from the lands east of the Mississippi River. British troops, however, continued to occupy several forts in the Great Lakes region.

In 1785 Congress sent John Adams to London to discuss these problems. Adams found the British unwilling to talk. They pointed to the failure of the United States to honor its promises made in the Treaty of Paris. The British claimed that Americans had agreed to pay Loyalists for the property taken from them during the Revolutionary War. Congress had proposed that the states pay the Loyalists. The states simply refused, and Congress could do nothing about it.

Relations With Spain

The United States had even greater problems with Spain. This European power, which controlled Florida as well as lands west of the Mississippi River, wanted to stop American expansion into its territory. To do this, Spain closed the lower Mississippi River to American shipping in 1784. Western settlers could no longer use the Mississippi River, which they relied on to ship goods to market.

In 1786 American diplomats reached a new trade agreement with Spain. Representatives from the Southern states, however, blocked the agreement because it did not include the right to use the Mississippi River.

The weakness of the Confederation and its inability to deal with problems worried many leaders, including George Washington. Americans began to agree that the country needed a stronger government.

☑ **PROGRESS CHECK**

Analyzing Why did Spain close the lower Mississippi River to American shipping in 1784?

C

R

During the early years of the republic, John Adams served as an ambassador to Great Britain. Adams was unable to convince the British to honor their promises made in the Treaty of Paris of 1783.

C Critical Thinking Skills

Making Inferences Refer students to the map titled "The Northwest Territory." Remind them that a number of British troops still remained east of the Mississippi. Have a volunteer point out the Great Lakes region, where British troops continued to hold forts. **Ask:**

- **Why were the Great Lakes a strategic location for forts?** *(access to water transportation)*
- **Why was Britain unwilling to withdraw from these forts?** *(because the United States had failed to pay, as promised, for Loyalists' land seized during the war)*
- **How did this relationship with Britain display weaknesses in the government?** *(When the states refused to pay Loyalists for lands taken during the war, the government could do nothing about it.)*

R Reading Skills

Explaining After students have read the text, discuss Spain's control over Florida and the lands west of the Mississippi River. Have volunteers explain how Spain attempted to stop American expansion into its territory by closing the lower Mississippi to trade. **Ask: Why was an agreement with Spain blocked by Southern states?** *(because it did not include the right to use the Mississippi River)*

Have students complete the Lesson 1 Review.

CLOSE & REFLECT

Listing With students, create a list of the failures and accomplishments of the government under the Articles of Confederation. **Ask: What would you do with the government at this point?** *(Students' answers may vary.)*

LESSON 1 REVIEW (CCSS)

Review Vocabulary (Tier 3 Words)

1. Use each of these words in a sentence about the newly independent United States. RH.6–8.4

    a. bicameral **b.** republic

2. Explain the significance of the following words: RH.6–8.4
    a. ordinance **b.** depreciate

Answer the Guiding Questions

3. *Explaining* Why did most states limit the power of their governors and divide their legislatures into two bodies? RH.6–8.2

4. *Specifying* What were some of the successes of the Articles of Confederation? RH.6–8.1

5. *Explaining* What were the weaknesses of the Confederation government? RH.6–8.1

6. **ARGUMENT** You are a delegate to the Second Continental Congress. Congress is debating whether to allow the central government to impose taxes. Take a stand on this issue, and write a short essay defending your position. Give specific reasons for your opinion. WHST.6–8.1, WHST.6–8.9

Lesson 1 **183**

LESSON 1 REVIEW ANSWERS

1. The new government of the independent United States was a republic, and its state governments generally had bicameral legislatures.

2. **a.** An ordinance is a law. One example is the Northwest Ordinance. **b.** The colonial money printed during the Revolutionary War lost value, or depreciated, rapidly.

3. Experience with British rule made them cautious about giving too much power to single rulers or political bodies.

4. Congress was able to raise and maintain the army that won the Revolutionary War, negotiate treaties with foreign countries, and pass the Land Ordinance of 1785 and the Northwest Ordinance in 1787.

5. Congress could not pass a law unless nine states voted in favor of it; consent of all states was required to change the Articles; Congress could not regulate trade, force soldiers to join the army, or impose taxes.

6. Students should write persuasive essays, supporting their opinions with facts from the lesson.

ANSWER, p. 183

☑ **PROGRESS CHECK** to stop American expansion into its territory

ENGAGE

🔔 **Bellringer** Ask students what they have done on an occasion when plans they had made for a day's activity did not work out. Did they go home disappointed, or did they make a new plan for a different activity? Tell students that the early leaders of our country realized that the plan of government they had made, the Articles of Confederation, was not working. They had to make a new plan of government.

TEACH & ASSESS

R Reading Skills

Explaining Have a volunteer read the section on economic issues. **Ask:** What is an economic depression? *(a period when economic activity is slow and unemployment increases)* **ELL** Have another student volunteer explain the reasons that the nation was facing an economic depression after the Revolutionary War. **Ask:**

- What were two reasons that trade decreased at this time? *(Damaged plantations resulted in a drop in rice exports; the British closed the West Indies market to American trade.)*
- What did the Confederation government need to do with the little money that it had? *(pay debts to foreign countries)* **AL**
- Why was the Confederation government too weak to deal with the country's economic problems? *(Under the Articles of Confederation, the government did not have the power to tax citizens in order to raise money, it could not compel states to pay debts, and it had no control over foreign trade.)* **BL**

ANSWERS, p. 184

TAKING NOTES: Randolph: introduced the Virginia Plan; Madison: author of the Virginia Plan, known as the "Father of the Constitution"; Sherman: proposed Great Compromise, calling for a two-house legislature; Morris: published final draft of the Constitution.

---

networks

There's More Online!

- ☑ **CHART/GRAPH**
  - Leaders and Their Roles
  - Framers of the Constitution
- ☑ **GAME** Crossword Puzzle
- ☑ **GRAPHIC ORGANIZER** Comparing and Contrasting
- ☑ **PRIMARY SOURCE** Plantation Life
- ☑ **VIDEO**

Lesson 2
Forging a New Constitution

ESSENTIAL QUESTION *How do new ideas change the way people live?*

IT MATTERS BECAUSE
Bold action helped the nation overcome the serious shortcomings of the Articles of Confederation.

The Need for Change

GUIDING QUESTION *What problems did the government face under the Articles of Confederation?*

A growing number of Americans became convinced that the government under the Articles of Confederation was too weak to deal with the country's problems. Among these problems were serious economic difficulties.

After the Revolutionary War, the United States went through a **depression**, a period when economic activity slows and unemployment increases. Wartime damage to Southern plantations led to a sharp drop in rice exports. Trade also fell off when the British closed the West Indies market to American merchants. The little money the government did have went to pay debts to foreign countries. This resulted in a serious shortage of money in the United States.

Shays's Rebellion

Economic troubles hit farmers hard. Unable to sell their goods, they could not pay their taxes and debts. This led state officials to seize farmers' lands and throw them in jail. This treatment angered many farmers. Some began to view the new government as just another form of tyranny. They wanted the

(i) Bettmann/CORBIS,(cl and c) The Granger Collection, NYC, (cr) Tom Grill/Corbis, (r) Visions of America/Joe Sohm/ Getty Images.

Reading **HELP**DESK CCSS

Taking Notes: *Comparing and Contrasting*
As you read, use a diagram like the one shown to take notes about each individual's plan for creating a new government. RH.6–8.5

Leader	Role
Edmund Randolph	
James Madison	
Roger Sherman	
Gouverneur Morris	

Content Vocabulary (Tier 3 Words)
- **depression**
- **manumission**
- **proportional**
- **compromise**

184 *A More Perfect Union*

---

networks *Online Teaching Options*

VIDEO

Shays's Rebellion

Determining Cause and Effect Show students the video about Shays's Rebellion. Ask: What was the cause of Shays's Rebellion? (When farmers could not pay their debts, state officials seized farmers' lands and threw many farmers in jail. Farmers' anger over this treatment grew.) What was the effect of the rebellion? (Four farmers were killed; Americans were frightened and more worried than ever that their government was too weak to deal with problems.)

See page 173D for other online activities.

government to issue paper money and make new policies to help those in debt. A group of farmers in Massachusetts made this plea to state officials:

66 Surely your honours are not strangers to the distresses [problems] of the people but ... know that many of our good inhabitants are now confined in [jail] for debt and taxes. 99

—from "Petition from the Town of Greenwich, Massachusetts"

Resentment boiled in Massachusetts. In 1786 angry farmers led by former Continental Army captain Daniel Shays forced courts in the western part of the state to close. The goal was to stop judges from legally taking away farmers' lands.

The farmers' revolt grew. In January 1787, Shays led a force of about 1,200 supporters toward the federal arsenal, or weapons storehouse, in Springfield, Massachusetts. The farmers wanted to seize guns and ammunition. The state militia ordered the advancing farmers to halt and then fired over their heads. The farmers did not stop. The militia fired again, killing four farmers.

Shays and his followers fled, and the uprising was over. Still, Shays's Rebellion frightened Americans. Concern grew that the government could not handle unrest and prevent violence. On hearing of the rebellion, George Washington wondered whether "mankind, when left to themselves, are unfit for their own government."

Shays's Rebellion divided the young country during the difficult 1780s.

Slavery in the New Republic

The Revolutionary War called attention to the clash between the American belief in liberty and the practice of slavery. Between 1776 and 1786, 11 states—all except South Carolina and Georgia—outlawed or taxed the importation of enslaved people.

Slavery existed and was legal in every state. In the North, however, it was not a major source of labor. People in that region began working to end slavery in America. In 1774 Quakers in Pennsylvania founded the first American antislavery society.

Bettmann/CORBIS

depression a period when economic activity slows and unemployment increases

---

R Reading Skills

Paraphrasing Invite a volunteer to read the primary source aloud, omitting the bracketed words. Then guide the class in paraphrasing the statement, using more modern and informal language. ELL

T Technology Skills

Researching on the Internet Invite interested students to conduct Internet research to learn about the Springfield Armory National Historic Site. Students should attempt to answer the following questions:

- **What is it?** *(It is the site of the nation's first armory. It includes the worlds' largest historic U.S. military small arms collections.)*
- **What do visitors see?** *(Visitors can tour the grounds and the historic buildings, as well as view the gun collection housed in the Main Arsenal building.)*
- **How does it commemorate Shays's Rebellion?** *(It protects the site where Daniel Shays and like-minded farmers tried to seize arms stored in the armory.)* Have student share with the class what they learn.

Primary Source Activity: Shays's Rebellion

Identifying Points of View Pair students, and have them take turns reading the primary sources to each other. If students need extra help, point out the reader's dictionary at the bottom of the page. Allow students to work together to answer the questions as they analyze the points of view of the writers.

See page 173D for other online activities.

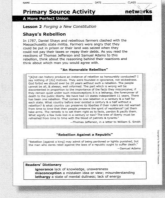

Forging a New Constitution

V Visual Skills

Analyzing Visuals Have small groups of students study the painting of the Southern plantation. As they talk about their reactions, **ask:** **Do you think this painting accurately reflects the treatment of African Americans in the South? Explain.** *(Students will likely point out that this picture shows an idealized view of Southern life. In reality, life was very difficult for enslaved African Americans.)* **Visual/Spatial**

C Critical Thinking Skills

Identifying Problems Discuss the differences between the North and the South in attitudes toward slavery. Ask:

- **What was the purpose of the manumission law in Virginia?** *(The law encouraged slaveholders to free individual enslaved persons.)* **AL ELL**
- **What problems did freed slaves face, even in states such as Pennsylvania and New Jersey?** *(They faced discrimination and were forced to attend separate schools. Many were denied the right to vote.)*
- **How might the question of slavery make strengthening the Articles of Confederation more difficult?** *(Answers will vary. Slavery was important in the South, and some people were working to end slavery. Perhaps the legality of slavery would divide Americans as they worked to strengthen the Articles of Confederation.)*

V

In the South, much of the wealth came from large plantations that used slave labor to grow valuable crops such as tobacco, rice, and later, cotton. The reliance on slavery tended to keep Southern states from investing in other parts of their economy. Southern cities remained smaller than those in the North because there were fewer businesses in the South. The South also did not devote itself to improving its transportation systems or training its people to build new businesses and industries.

▶ **CRITICAL THINKING**
Identifying Central Issues Why do you think the white South was so committed to keeping a slave-based economy?

Six years later Pennsylvania passed a law that provided for the gradual freeing of enslaved people. Between 1783 and 1804, Connecticut, Rhode Island, New York, and New Jersey passed laws that gradually ended slavery there.

Still, free African Americans faced discrimination. They were barred from many public places. Only a few states gave them the right to vote. Most of their children had to attend separate schools from white children. In response, free African Americans set up their own churches, schools, and aid groups.

C

Slavery continued to spread south of Pennsylvania. The plantation system depended on slave labor, and many white Southerners feared their economy could not survive without it.

That fear did not stop a number of slaveholders from freeing enslaved people. The number of free African Americans increased in Virginia after that state passed a law that encouraged **manumission** (man·yuh·MIH·shuhn), the freeing of individual enslaved persons.

Around this time, American leaders were deciding that the Articles of Confederation needed to be strengthened. The question of slavery would make those discussions more difficult.

☑ **PROGRESS CHECK**

Explaining Why did farmers in Massachusetts rebel in 1787?

The Granger Collection, NYC

Reading **HELP**DESK **CCSS**

manumission the freeing of individual enslaved persons

---

networks *Online Teaching Options*

PRIMARY SOURCE

Plantation Life

Analyzing Primary Sources Use the interactive primary source excerpt about plantation life in the South to discuss this topic with students. **Ask:** **Why did the South cling to the practice of slavery?** *(The plantation system relied on slave labor, and Southerners were afraid their economy would collapse without it.)*

See page 173D for other online activities.

networks Plantation Life

ANALYZING PRIMARY SOURCES

Moses Roper wrote one of the first important books about life as an enslaved person in the United States.

❝ Mr. Gooch, the cotton planter, he purchased me at a town called Liberty Hill, about three miles from his home. As soon as he got home, he immediately put me on his cotton plantation to work, and put me under overseers, gave me allowance of meat and bread with the other slaves, which was not half enough for me to live upon, and very laborious work. Here my heart was almost broke with grief at leaving my fellow slaves. Mr. Gooch did not mind my grief, for he flogged me nearly every day, and very severely. Mr. Gooch bought me for his son-in-law, Mr. Hammans, about five miles from his residence. This man had but two slaves besides myself; he treated me very kindly for a week or two, but in summer, when cotton was ready to hoe, he gave me task work connected with this department, which I could not get done, not having worked on cotton farms before. When I failed in my task, he commenced ❞

—from the *Adventures and Escape of Moses Roper* (1838)
by Moses Roper

Source: http://www.spartacus.schoolnet.co.uk/USAScotton.htm

ANSWERS, p. 186

CRITICAL THINKING Slavery was a key part of the Southern agricultural economy, which relied heavily on the use of enslaved persons as a source of labor. The South's reliance on slavery tended to keep the region from investing in other parts of its economy and limited its growth and development.

☑ **PROGRESS CHECK** When farmers couldn't pay taxes or debts, the states were taking their land and throwing them into jail.

The Constitutional Convention

GUIDING QUESTION *How did leaders reshape the government?*

Although the American Revolution led to a union of 13 states, it had not yet created a nation. Some leaders were satisfied with independent state governments that were similar to the old colonial governments. Others wanted a strong national government. They demanded a change in the Articles of Confederation. Among the leading Americans supporting reform were James Madison, a Virginia planter, and Alexander Hamilton, a New York lawyer.

The Convention Begins

In September 1786, Hamilton called for a **convention**, or meeting, in Philadelphia to discuss trade issues. He also suggested that this convention consider what possible changes were needed to make "the Constitution of the Federal Government adequate to the exigencies [needs] of the Union."

George Washington at first was not enthusiastic about the meeting. Then, news of Shays's Rebellion made Washington change his mind. He agreed to attend the Philadelphia convention, and the meeting took on greater importance.

The Convention began in May 1787 and continued through one of the hottest summers on record. The 55 delegates included planters, merchants, lawyers, physicians, generals, governors, and a college president. Three of the delegates were under 30 years of age, and one, Benjamin Franklin, was over 80. Many of the delegates were well educated. At a time when few people went to college, 26 of the delegates had college degrees. Native Americans, African Americans, and women were not represented at the Convention. These groups were not considered part of the political process at that time.

Having Washington and Franklin at the Convention guaranteed public trust.

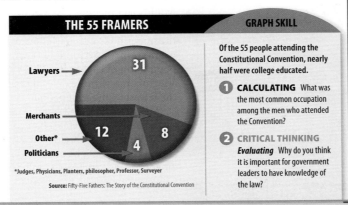

THE 55 FRAMERS

Lawyers → 31
Merchants → 12
Other* → 4
Politicians
8

*Judges, Physicians, Planters, philosopher, Professor, Surveyer

Source: Fifty-Five Fathers: The Story of the Constitutional Convention

GRAPH SKILL

Of the 55 people attending the Constitutional Convention, nearly half were college educated.

1. **CALCULATING** What was the most common occupation among the men who attended the Convention?

2. **CRITICAL THINKING** *Evaluating* Why do you think it is important for government leaders to have knowledge of the law?

Reading in the Content Area: *Circle Graphs*

Circle or pie graphs show how a whole is divided into different parts. To read a circle graph, imagine that the circle is a pie. Compare the different sizes of the different pieces. Use any numbers or labels to help you measure and compare the sizes of each piece.

Academic Vocabulary (Tier 2)

convention meeting

Lesson 2 **187**

R Reading Skills

Defining As students read, ensure that they understand key terminology in the passage. **Ask:** What is a convention? *(a meeting)* **ELL** What other conventions are you aware of? *(Students may mention political conventions and conventions for businesses or entertainment.)*

V Visual Skills

Analyzing Graphs Direct students to the graph and the portion of the text that describes the make-up of the Framers of the Constitution. Have a volunteer describe the people's professions represented in the graph. Explain that at this time, you did not need a college degree to be a lawyer. Instead, the 26 delegates with college degrees were distributed among all the occupations. **Ask:**

- What would a circle graph of the genders of the Framers look like? *(It would be a circle with no divisions, representing all males.)*
- What would a circle graph of the ethnicities of the Framers look like? *(It too would be circle with no divisions, showing that all the Framers were white.)*

Remind students that at this time, Native Americans, most African Americans, and all women were denied the vote and a voice in government. **BL** Logical/Mathematical

CHART

Framers of the Constitution

Identifying Display the interactive chart, and have students take turns clicking on names to reveal their occupation and state from which they hailed. You may wish to turn this into a game by allowing students to guess the state before clicking to reveal a particular Framer's information.

See page 173D for other online activities.

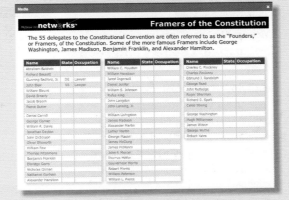

Media

McGraw-Hill **networks** — **Framers of the Constitution**

The 55 delegates to the Constitutional Convention are often referred to as the "Founders," or Framers, of the Constitution. Some of the more famous Framers include George Washington, James Madison, Benjamin Franklin, and Alexander Hamilton.

ANSWERS, p. 187

GRAPH SKILL

1. lawyer

2. **CRITICAL THINKING** Students may suggest that a legal background is vital to shaping the laws and policies for the nation.

188

R1 Reading Skills

Identifying After students read the text, prompt them to consider what types of personality traits and actions would have been prized in such a challenging time as during the framing of the Constitution. **Ask: Who was called the "Father of the Constitution," and what made his contribution valuable?** *(James Madison; he was the author of the basic plan of government that the Convention adopted.)* AL ELL

C Critical Thinking Skills

Making Inferences Ask students to consider modern advertising and what influence it has on them when they see a product or event connected in some way to a popular person or a celebrity whom they admire. **Ask: Why do you think the presence of George Washington would make people trust the Convention's work?** *(He led the battle for independence and was a respected leader.)* **Why was this trust important?** *(The Convention was not just amending the Articles of Confederation, they were writing an entirely new document.)*

R2 Reading Skills

Explaining Ask a volunteer to explain proportional representation as it is described in the text. *(The number of representatives would correspond in size to the population of each state.)* **Ask: Why was the issue of representation so difficult to resolve?** *(States had very different populations and wanted to be fairly represented.)*

Trust was important, because the convention did not just **amend,** or revise, the Articles of Confederation. It produced an entirely new constitution. Some questioned whether the Convention had such authority.

Yet the work went on. Two men from Philadelphia also had key roles. James Wilson did important work on the details of the Constitution, and Gouverneur Morris polished the final draft. James Madison, who was a keen supporter of a strong national government, kept a record of the convention's work. Madison is often called the "Father of the Constitution" because he was the author of the basic plan of government that the Convention adopted.

The Convention Organizes

The delegates chose George Washington to lead the meetings. Delegates also decided that each state would have one vote on all questions. Decisions would be based on a majority vote of the states present. Sessions were not open to the public. In fact, the windows were closed in the sweltering heat to keep anyone from listening in. This made it possible for the delegates to talk freely.

The Virginia Plan

Edmund Randolph of Virginia opened the Convention with a surprise. He proposed the Virginia Plan that called for a strong national government. The plan, which was largely the work of James Madison, created a government with three branches: a two-house legislature, a chief executive chosen by the legislature, and a court system. The legislature would have powers to tax, regulate trade, and veto state laws. Voters would elect members of the lower house of the legislature. The members of the lower house would then choose members of the upper house. In both houses the number of representatives would be **proportional**, or corresponding in size, to the population of each state. This would give a state such as Virginia many more delegates than Delaware, the state with the fewest number of people.

Delegates from the small states objected. They preferred a system in which all states had equal representation. Opponents of the Virginia Plan rallied around William Paterson of New Jersey. On June 15, he presented another plan. This plan amended the Articles of Confederation, which was all the Convention had the power to do.

Reading **HELP**DESK (CCSS)

proportional having the proper size in relation to other objects or items

Academic Vocabulary (Tier 2 Words)

amend to change or revise

---

netw⊙rks *Online Teaching Options*

GRAPHIC ORGANIZER

Taking Notes: *Comparing and Contrasting:* **Leaders and Their Roles**

Identifying Have students use the interactive graphic organizer as a recording tool for identifying the plans key players at the Constitutional Convention had for a new government. You may wish to have students work in pairs or small groups to complete the graphic organizer.

See page 173D for other online activities.

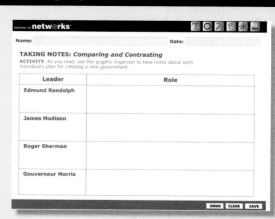

McGraw-Hill netw⊙rks

Name: _____ Date: _____

TAKING NOTES: *Comparing and Contrasting*
ACTIVITY As you read, use the graphic organizer to take notes about each individual's plan for creating a new government.

Leader	Role
Edmund Randolph	
James Madison	
Roger Sherman	
Gouverneur Morris	

UNDO CLEAR SAVE

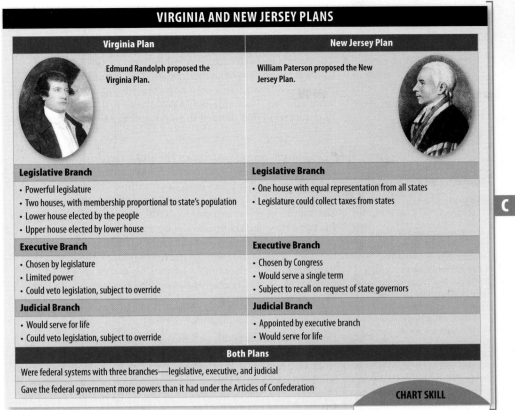

VIRGINIA AND NEW JERSEY PLANS

Virginia Plan	New Jersey Plan
Edmund Randolph proposed the Virginia Plan.	William Paterson proposed the New Jersey Plan.
Legislative Branch	**Legislative Branch**
• Powerful legislature • Two houses, with membership proportional to state's population • Lower house elected by the people • Upper house elected by lower house	• One house with equal representation from all states • Legislature could collect taxes from states
Executive Branch	**Executive Branch**
• Chosen by legislature • Limited power • Could veto legislation, subject to override	• Chosen by Congress • Would serve a single term • Subject to recall on request of state governors
Judicial Branch	**Judicial Branch**
• Would serve for life • Could veto legislation, subject to override	• Appointed by executive branch • Would serve for life
Both Plans	
Were federal systems with three branches—legislative, executive, and judicial	
Gave the federal government more powers than it had under the Articles of Confederation	

CHART SKILL

Delegates at the Constitutional Convention considered different plans.

1 **COMPARING** In what ways were the two plans similar?

2 **CRITICAL THINKING** *Explaining* Explain how proportional representation favored larger states.

The New Jersey Plan

Under this plan, the legislature would have a single house, with each state having one vote. Paterson argued that the Convention should not deprive smaller states of the equality they had under the Articles. The New Jersey plan gave Congress the power to set taxes, regulate trade, and elect an executive branch made up of more than one person. In sum, the New Jersey Plan favored a more powerful government than existed under the Articles—but a less powerful government than the Virginia Plan proposed.

✔ **PROGRESS CHECK**

Explaining Why did New Jersey's delegates object to the Virginia Plan?

(l) The Granger Collection, NYC, (r) The Granger Collection, NYC

C **Critical Thinking Skills**

Comparing and Contrasting Lead a class discussion that compares and contrasts the Virginia and New Jersey plans. Direct students to compare them point by point, identify which plan's position on each point they prefer, and explain why. Encourage students who have differing positions on a point to discuss and debate the matter. Challenge them to develop a compromise. **AL** **ELL** **Visual/Spatial**

R **Reading Skills**

Identifying Central Issues As students read about the New Jersey Plan, ask them to consider the varying sizes of the states today. **Ask:** Why did William Paterson want each state to have a vote in the new government? *(He thought the Convention should not deprive smaller states of the equality they had under the Articles.)*

Contributors to the Constitutional Convention

Identifying Write the names of the Framers on slips of paper, and place them in a hat. Organize the class into two teams. As you draw a name from the hat, have teams take turns determining which characteristic should be matched with that Framer.

See page 173D for other online activities.

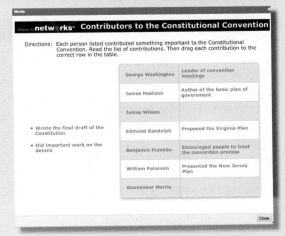

ANSWERS, p. 189

CHART SKILL

1. Both were federal systems with three branches—legislative, executive, and judicial. Both gave the federal government more power than it had before.

2. **CRITICAL THINKING** The larger states would have more votes than the smaller states, which would give the larger states more power to pass the legislation they favored.

✔ **PROGRESS CHECK** Representation was proportional, so a small state like New Jersey would have fewer votes in Congress than a larger state.

C Critical Thinking Skills

Analyzing Have students take turns reading aloud the areas upon which compromise allowed the new Constitution to take shape. **Ask:** What is a compromise? *(an agreement between two or more sides in which each side gives up some of what it wants)* Have volunteers give examples of times they have had to compromise with siblings or friends. **What did each party have to give up to reach an agreement?** **AL** **ELL** Intrapersonal

Then, **ask:**

- **What did the Great Compromise state about the upper house and lower house of the legislature?** *(In the upper house, each state would have two members. In the lower house, the number of seats for each state would vary based on the state's population.)* **AL**
- **In what way was the Great Compromise an agreement in which each side gives up something?** *(The smaller states wanted equal representation, which they would have in the Senate but not in the House of Representatives. The larger states favored proportional representation, which they would have in the House of Representatives but not in the Senate.)* **BL**
- **Why did the Southern states want to count enslaved people as part of their population?** *(This would increase their population count and give them more seats in the House of Representatives.)* **What was the Three-Fifths Compromise?** *(Every five enslaved persons would equal three free persons.)*

W Writing Skills

Informative/Explanatory Direct students to write a one-page paper, "The Role of Compromise at the Constitutional Convention," in which they define *compromise* and describe the Great Compromise and the Three-Fifths Compromise. Guide students in prewriting their papers to focus on logical organization and the order of presentation of their ideas.
Verbal/Linguistic

BIOGRAPHY

George Washington (1732–1799)

George Washington's military service is well known. He also became a key political leader in his later years. Washington did not want to attend the Constitutional Convention, but he did because he worried that the nation would not survive under the weak Articles of Confederation. The delegates unanimously chose him as the presiding officer, or leader, of the Convention. Washington said very little during the debates but later became one of the new Constitution's strongest supporters. He argued that later generations could make any changes necessary. **W**

▶ **CRITICAL THINKING**
Making Inferences What can you infer from the fact that the other delegates chose Washington as the leader of the Convention?

Reading **HELP**DESK **CCSS**

compromise a settlement of a dispute by each party giving up some demands

---

Agreeing to Compromise

GUIDING QUESTION *What compromises were reached in the new Constitution?*

The delegates had to decide whether to revise the Articles of Confederation or write a new constitution. On June 19, the states voted to work toward a new constitution based on the Virginia Plan. They still had to deal with the difficult issue of representation that divided the large and small states.

The Great Compromise

The Convention appointed a committee to settle the disagreement. Roger Sherman of Connecticut suggested what would later be called the Great Compromise. A **compromise** is a settlement of a dispute by each party giving up some demands. Sherman's compromise proposed different representation in the two-house legislature. In the upper house—the Senate—each state would have two members. That is, the states would be equal in representation. In the lower house—the House of Representatives—the number of seats for each state would vary based on the state's population. Larger states would have more representation.

The Three-Fifths Compromise

Delegates from the South and North disagreed on whether—and how—to count each state's enslaved population. Including enslaved people as part of a state's population would increase each Southern state's size. This would give Southern states more seats in Congress. The Southern states liked this, and the Northern states did not. At the same time, larger populations would increase each Southern state's taxes, because states were to be taxed based on their populations. The South was not happy about this.

As a solution to this dispute, delegates agreed to what was called the Three-Fifths Compromise. As part of this compromise, every five enslaved persons would count as three persons in the state's population total. This population total would be the basis for setting taxes and representation in Congress.

The Question of the Slave Trade

The Northern states had already banned the slave trade. They wanted to prohibit it nationwide. Southern states considered slavery central to their economy. Northerners agreed to keep the new Congress from interfering with the slave trade until 1808.

Museum of the City of New York/CORBIS

---

netw⊚rks   *Online Teaching Options*

IMAGE

The Great Compromise

Summarizing Present the interactive image The Great Compromise. Explain that the portrait shows Roger Sherman, who was the author of the compromise. Use the text and image to reiterate that this compromise produced a legislature with two houses: the Senate, in which each state would have equal representation, and the House of Representatives, in which states would have representation based on population.

See page 173D for other online activities.

McGraw-Hill **netw⊚rks**   **The Great Compromise**

One of the major areas of disagreement at the Constitutional Convention was the number of representatives each state would be allowed in Congress. The larger states were in favor of the Virginia Plan, which said that a state's representatives would be determined by the state's population. The smaller states were in favor of the New Jersey Plan, which said that the number of representatives would be the same for each state. Roger Sherman, a delegate from Connecticut, proposed a bicameral legislature, consisting of a Senate and a House of Representatives. The Senate would have the same number of representatives from each state. The House of Representatives would include one representative for every 30,000 people in a state. The delegates to the Convention approved this plan, which became

Réunion des Musées Nationaux/Art Resource, NY

ANSWER, p. 190

CRITICAL THINKING They trusted his judgment and his leadership abilities.

Debating a Bill of Rights

State constitutions such as those of Virginia and Massachusetts had a listing of key rights and freedoms. These are known as a declaration of rights, or a bill of rights. At the Convention, some delegates worried that without a bill of rights, the new national government might abuse its power. George Mason of Virginia proposed a bill of rights to be included in the Constitution. The delegates defeated this idea. Most of the delegates believed that the Constitution carefully defined government powers and provided enough protection of individual rights.

R

Approving the Constitution

C

On September 17, 1787, the delegates assembled to sign the Constitution they had created. Three delegates refused to sign— Elbridge Gerry of Massachusetts, and Edmund Randolph and George Mason of Virginia. Gerry and Mason would not sign because the Constitution did not have a bill of rights. Randolph, who had put forth the Virginia Plan, felt the final document strayed too far from his own beliefs.

The other delegates did sign the document. The approved draft of the Constitution went out to the states for their approval. Under the Articles of Confederation, all 13 states would have had to accept any change. The drafters of the new Constitution decided, however, that the document would go into effect with the approval of just 9 of the 13 states.

☑ **PROGRESS CHECK**

Explaining What compromises were reached concerning enslaved people?

LESSON 2 REVIEW

Review Vocabulary

1. Use each of the two words below in a sentence that shows their meaning in this lesson. RH.6–8.4

   a. depression   **b.** manumission

2. Write a sentence about the Constitutional Convention that uses both of these terms. RH.6–8.4

   a. proportional   **b.** compromise

Answer the Guiding Questions

3. ***Specifying*** What weaknesses in the national government did Shays's Rebellion reveal? RH.6–8.1

4. ***Contrasting*** What was the difference between the Virginia Plan and the New Jersey Plan concerning the legislature? RH.6–8.5

5. ***Describing*** On what key issues did delegates have to compromise in order to create a Constitution that most states would accept? RH.6–8.2

6. **INFORMATIVE/EXPLANATORY** You have been asked to write a short announcement to inform your community about the Great Compromise. Summarize the key points of the agreement. Include any other details you think are important. WHST.6–8.2, WHST.6–8.9

Lesson 2   **191**

LESSON 2 REVIEW ANSWERS

1. Possible answers: Unemployment is high in a time of depression, a period of slow economic activity. Enough people in Virginia believed in manumission to pass a law that could free enslaved persons.

2. Possible answer: At the Constitutional Convention, delegates from both large and small states had to compromise on the question of proportional representation.

3. The national government could not respond to the economic crisis nor to an armed threat to the government.

4. The Virginia Plan called for two houses with proportional representation in the legislature; the New Jersey Plan called for one house in the legislature with equal representation for all states.

5. number of houses in the legislature, states' representation in the legislature, and how enslaved persons would count toward representation

6. Students should identify the key points as the two houses in the legislature and how seats in each house are to be allotted to the states.

R Reading Skills

Defining To help students understand the concepts in the Bill of Rights, have a volunteer read the text, then lead a discussion encouraging students to consider the simple meanings in a concept often taken for granted. **Ask: What is a bill of rights?** *(a listing of people's rights and freedoms)* **AL ELL Why did some delegates believe a bill of rights was necessary?** *(to keep the government from abusing its power)*

C Critical Thinking Skills

Determining Cause and Effect Point out that the rights with which we are familiar in the present day were not established under unanimous agreement. **Ask: Why was the proposal for a bill of rights for the Constitution voted down?** *(Most delegates thought that the Constitution carefully defined government powers and provided enough protection of individual rights.)* **Why did delegates Gerry and Mason oppose the new Constitution and refuse to sign it?** *(because it did not include a bill of rights)*

Have students complete the Lesson 2 Review.

CLOSE & REFLECT

Discussing As a class, discuss the compromises that the nation's leaders reached to resolve issues in order to write a new constitution. **Ask: Why did these leaders push so hard for compromise?** *(Students' answers may vary.)*

ANSWER, p. 191

☑ **PROGRESS CHECK** Under the Three-Fifths Compromise, each enslaved person would count as three-fifths of a free person for determining both taxation and representation. To keep the Southern states in the nation, Northerners agreed that the new Congress would not interfere with the slave trade for 20 years.

ENGAGE

Bellringer Ask students if they listen to the different sides of an argument before they decide what they think or what they will do. Have volunteers give examples from their lives. Have students discuss whether it is important to listen to and consider all sides of a situation or an argument when there is a decision to be made.

TEACH & ASSESS

R1 Reading Skills

Discussing Remind students that in 1787, the country was still finding its way after declaring independence. The federal government was small. The economy was in a depression. Lead a class discussion on why there was still disagreement over whether a new government was needed. Have volunteers read the introductory section about this debate to the class. Be sure to discuss any difficult vocabulary in the activity.

R2 Reading Skills

Identifying Remind students that the word *federal* refers to the central, or federal, government. Federalists were in favor of a strong central government. The prefix anti- means "against." Anti-Federalists, therefore, were against a strong central government. **Ask: Who were the Anti-Federalists?** *(people who opposed the Constitution)* **What did the Anti-Federalists fear?** *(They feared a strong national government that would be able to take away the rights of citizens.)* **AL**

C Critical Thinking Skills

Analyzing Primary Sources Have students read the excerpt from Mercy Otis Warren. **Ask: Why did Mercy Otis Warren oppose the proposed new Constitution?** *(She believed the Constitution was a bad plan and would enslave people to the government by doing away with their rights and freedoms.)*

What Do You Think? CCSS

Should the Constitution Be Ratified?

After the delegates in Philadelphia wrote the U.S. Constitution, it went before the American people for approval. Delegates in each state met at special conventions to decide whether to accept or reject the Constitution. In order for the Constitution to become the new plan for the government of the United States, nine of the 13 states had to ratify, or approve, it.

Those who opposed the Constitution were called Anti-Federalists. They feared a strong national government that would be able to take away the rights of citizens. Federalists supported the Constitution. They believed that the Constitution would give the national government power to manage the problems facing the United States. At the same time, the Federalists argued, the Constitution would protect the right of the individual.

The Constitutional Convention met at Independence Hall.

No
PRIMARY SOURCE

MERCY OTIS WARREN

❝ Our situation is truly delicate & critical. On the one hand we are in need of a strong federal government founded on principles that will support the prosperity & union of the colonies. On the other we have struggled for liberty & made lofty sacrifices at her shrine: and there are still many among us who **revere** her name too much to **relinquish** (beyond a certain medium) the rights of man for the Dignity of Government. ❞

C

192 *A More Perfect Union*

---

networks   *Online Teaching Options*

CHART

Comparing the Articles of Confederation and the Constitution

Identifying Use the interactive chart to help students identify the differences between the two documents. Use these differences to underscore the positions the Federalists and Anti-Federalists held.

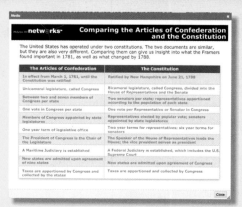

V This is the Assembly Room, where delegates signed the United States Constitution.

V Visual Skills

Analyzing Images Ask students to look at the image of the Assembly Room. **Ask:**

- **How is this room similar to modern meeting rooms?** *(It contains tables, chairs, writing materials, windows, and a place for a speaker in the front.)*
- **How is it different?** *(It has quills, candles, wooden chairs, fireplaces, and a bare floor.)* **Visual/Spatial**

C Critical Thinking Skills

Drawing Conclusions Have students read the excerpt from James Wilson. Address any vocabulary questions students may have. **Ask: Why did Wilson seem satisfied with the Constitution?** *(Wilson believed nothing else could have been better. If the Constitution had problems, it could be amended.)* **BL**

Yes

PRIMARY SOURCE

C

JAMES WILSON

❝ I am satisfied that anything nearer to perfection could not have been accomplished. If there are errors, it should be remembered, that the seeds of **reformation** are sown in the work itself, and the **concurrence** of two-thirds of the Congress may at any time introduce alterations and amendments. ... I am bold to assert, that it is the BEST FORM OF GOVERNMENT WHICH HAS EVER BEEN OFFERED TO THE WORLD. ❞

Vocabulary

revere   deeply love and respect
relinquish   give up
reformation   change
concurrence   agreement

What Do You Think? DBQ

❶ *Making Inferences* What does Warren suggest is more important than the "dignity of government"? RH.6–8.6

❷ *Identifying* According to Wilson, how can the Constitution be changed? RH.6–8.6

❸ *Contrasting* How would you summarize the difference between Warren's and Wilson's views on the risks involved with ratifying the Constitution? RH.6–8.8, RH.6–8.10

Lesson 2   **193**

CLOSE & REFLECT

Identifying Points of View Have each student write a statement about the Constitution from a Federalist or Anti-Federalist perspective. Ask students to exchange slips and then decide if the paper they are holding is a Federalist or Anti-Federalist opinion. Review them as a class.

CHART

Graphic Organizer: Elliptical Chart

Identifying Give each student pair two copies of the graphic organizer. Have them collaborate to complete one organizer for each primary source in the feature.

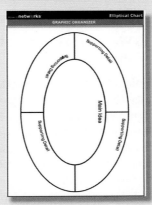

ANSWERS, p. 193

What Do You Think?
1. **Making Inferences**   protecting the rights of man and freedoms that have been so hard-won
2. **Identifying**   It can be amended with the support of two-thirds of Congress.
3. **Contrasting**   Warren suggests that adopting a less-than-perfect document may not be worth sacrificing rights and freedoms, while Wilson thinks that the document is nearly perfect and if it isn't, the method of changing it, to make adjustments in the future, is contained in the document itself.

ENGAGE

🔔 **Bellringer** Ask volunteers to tell the class about people they see as role models in their community. Have them explain why they chose the people they did. Tell students that the Framers of the Constitution needed role models as well. They looked at political writers from other countries to help them find models for ways of thinking about government.

TEACH & ASSESS

R Reading Skills

Discussing After students have read the text, discuss the backgrounds of the Framers. **Ask: What country provided the Framers with most of their background knowledge?** *(Britain)* Have students discuss why Americans may have still respected British traditions, although they were no longer part of England.

C Critical Thinking Skills

Making Connections Remind students that although America was a new country, a lot of ideas about how to govern came from the European tradition. **Ask: How did the English Magna Carta influence colonial rule in America?** *(The Magna Carta placed limits on the power of the king; the lawmaking body took some control over spending. In the same way, colonial assemblies controlled funds so that they had some control over governors.)*

ANSWER, p. 194

TAKING NOTES: Executive: carries out the nation's laws and policies, such as collecting and administering the taxes that are enacted into law by the legislative branch, operating the nation's military, and administering other departments. **Legislative:** makes laws; has power to impose taxes, makes laws related to coining money, and regulates trade. **Judicial:** hears cases involving the Constitution, federal laws, and disputes between states.

netw⊙rks
There's More Online!

☑ **GAME** State or Federal
☑ **GRAPHIC ORGANIZER** Categorizing
☑ **PRIMARY SOURCE** The Ninth Pillar

Lesson 3
A New Plan of Government

ESSENTIAL QUESTION *How do governments change?*

IT MATTERS BECAUSE
The Constitution contains features that came from the best political thinkers and that have helped the nation survive and thrive.

The Constitution's Sources

GUIDING QUESTION *From where did the Framers of the Constitution borrow their ideas about government?*

Although an American document, the Constitution has roots in other civilizations. The delegates who wrote the document studied the history of political thought in an effort to avoid the mistakes of the past. Many ideas found in the Constitution came from European political institutions and writers.

R The Framers who shaped the document were familiar with the parliamentary system of Britain. Many had taken part in their colonial or state assemblies. They valued the individual rights guaranteed by the British judicial system. Although the Americans broke away from British rule, they respected many British **traditions**, or cultural beliefs and practices.

European Influences
The English Magna Carta (1215) placed limits on the power of the monarch. Parliament, England's lawmaking body, became **C** a force that the king or queen had to depend on to pay for wars and the royal government. Like Parliament, colonial assemblies controlled their colonies' funds. The assemblies had some control over colonial governors.

(l) DEA PICTURE LIBRARY/Getty Images, (c) Brooks Kraft/Corbis, (r) The Granger Collection, NYC

Reading HELPDESK (CCSS)

Taking Notes: *Categorizing* RH.6–8.1
As you read, use a chart like this one to identify the powers of each branch of the federal government.

Branch	Example
Executive	
Legislative	
Judicial	

Content Vocabulary (Tier 3 Words)
- **federalism**
- **legislative branch**
- **executive branch**
- **Electoral College**
- **judicial branch**
- **checks and balances**
- **amendment**

194 *A More Perfect Union*

---

netw⊙rks *Online Teaching Options*

VIDEO

Who Were the Framers of the Constitution?

Depicting As students watch the video, have them note the different points of view represented at the convention. **Ask: How were the Framers a diverse group?** *(There were aristocratic planters from the South and pragmatic Puritans from New England. They represented a diverse range of ages and professions.)* **What does it mean that the Framers were regarded in Europe as "provincials"?** *(They were looked upon by Europeans as unsophisticated farmers and merchants who lived far from the city centers of the day.)*

See page 173E for other online activities.

The English Bill of Rights of 1689 was another model for Americans. In fact, many people in the United States felt the Constitution also needed a bill of rights. The Framers believed in the ideas about the nature of people and government put forth by European writers of the Enlightenment. The Enlightenment was a movement of the 1700s that promoted knowledge, reason, and science as a means of improving society. James Madison and other Framers of the Constitution were familiar with the work of John Locke and Baron de Montesquieu (mahn•tuhs•KYOO), two philosophers of the Enlightenment.

The English philosopher Locke wrote that all people have natural rights. He stated that these natural rights include the rights to life, liberty, and property. In his *Two Treatises of Civil Government* (1690), he wrote that government is based on an agreement, or contract, between the people and the ruler. Americans interpreted natural rights to mean the rights of Britons defined in the Magna Carta and the English Bill of Rights. The Framers viewed the Constitution as a contract between the American people and their government. The contract protected people's natural rights by limiting government power.

The French writer Montesquieu declared in *The Spirit of Laws* (1748) that the powers of government should be separated and balanced against each other. This separation would prevent any one person or group from gaining too much power. The Framers of the Constitution carefully spelled out and divided the powers of government.

Federalism

The Constitution created a federal system of government that divided powers between the national, or federal, government and the states. In the Articles of Confederation, the states held most powers. Under the Constitution, the states gave up some powers to the federal government and kept others. **Federalism** (FE•duh•ruh•lih•zuhm), or sharing power between the federal and state governments, is one of the key features of the United States government. Under the Constitution, the federal government gained wide-ranging powers to tax, regulate trade, control the currency, raise an army, and declare war. It could also pass laws that were "necessary and proper" for carrying out its responsibilities. This power would allow Congress to make laws as needed to deal with new situations.

John Locke influenced many of the Framers of the Constitution. His views on natural rights are reflected in the Constitution.

federalism sharing power between the federal and state governments

Academic Vocabulary (Tier 2 Words)
tradition longstanding cultural belief and practice

Reading Skills

Summarizing Ask students to read the section on Locke and Montesquieu. Have students name the key points in John Locke's political thinking. (*All people have natural rights; these natural rights include the rights to life, liberty, and property; government is based on a contract between the people and the ruler.*) **Ask:** What is a contract? (*A contract is a type of legal agreement that creates a relationship between the parties.*) ELL

Then have students name the key points in Montesquieu's political thinking. (*The powers of government should be separated and balanced against each other; this separation would prevent any one person or group from gaining too much power.*) BL

Critical Thinking Skills

Making Connections Remind students that many of the Framers of the Constitution were as influenced by French ideas as English ones. **Ask:** How did Montesquieu's idea about separating the powers of government influence the Framers of the Constitution? (*The Framers adopted Montesquieu's idea of the separation of powers and divided the powers of the American government.*) Have students predict how these concepts were integrated into the United States government. BL

Reading Skills

Defining Help students connect to the text by explaining that the powers of the federal government are still being discussed today. **Ask:** What is federalism? (*sharing of power between the federal and state governments*) ELL

Have students give examples of federalism from current events. (*Examples could include education, environmental protection, and road construction.*) BL

CHAPTER 7, Lesson 3
A New Plan of Government

BIOGRAPHY

Locke & Montesquieu

Comparing Use the image to discuss and compare the philosophies of John Locke and Baron de Montesquieu. **Ask:** How are Locke's ideas about government similar to Montesquieu's ideas? (*Both believed in republican government based on the consent of the governed. They both supported ideas about individual rights and freedoms.*)

See page 173E for other online activities.

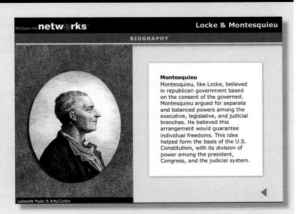

networks   Locke & Montesquieu
BIOGRAPHY

Montesquieu
Montesquieu, like Locke, believed in republican government based on the consent of the governed. Montesquieu argued for separate and balanced powers among the executive, legislative, and judicial branches. He believed this arrangement would guarantee individual freedoms. This idea helped form the basis of the U.S. Constitution, with its division of power among the president, Congress, and the judicial system.

A New Plan of Government

A New Plan of Government

C Critical Thinking Skills

Making Connections Have students read the first three paragraphs on this page. **Ask:**

- **What is the supreme law of the land?** *(the Constitution and the laws that Congress passes)*
- **Why is it called this?** *(A state can make no laws that go against the Constitution.)* Prompt students to cite examples from current events of the federal courts settling disputes between the federal government and the states.

V Visual Skills

Analyzing Charts Have students use the chart in their textbooks to identify powers given to the federal government. *(powers to regulate trade, control the currency, raise an army, declare war, and pass laws)* Have students identify powers given to state governments. *(powers to control trade inside their borders, set up local governments and schools, and set marriage and divorce laws)* Then ask which powers are shared by both. *(power to tax and power to set up court systems)*
Visual/Spatial

The Constitution left some important powers to the states. The states kept the power to control trade inside their borders. They also could set up local governments and schools and establish marriage and divorce laws.

The Constitution also called for the sharing of some powers between the federal and state governments. Both federal and state governments would have the power to tax and to establish criminal justice.

While states had powers and shared others with the federal government, the Constitution and the laws of Congress were to be "the supreme law of the land." No state could make laws or take actions that went against the Constitution. Federal courts would settle disputes between the federal government and the states on the basis of the Constitution.

✓ PROGRESS CHECK

Describing What is the principle of federalism?

Government Structure

GUIDING QUESTION *How does the Constitution limit the power of the government?*

The Framers of the Constitution used Montesquieu's idea of a division of powers. They divide the federal government into three branches—legislative, executive, and judicial. The first three articles, or parts, of the Constitution describe each branch's powers and responsibilities. They detail the methods for electing or selecting key members of each branch.

CHART SKILL

The Constitution gives exclusive powers to the state and federal governments, and it also calls for some powers to be shared.

1 IDENTIFYING What is an example of a power shared by the federal and state governments?

2 CRITICAL THINKING
Explaining Why do you think both the national and state governments have the power to collect taxes?

FEDERAL AND STATE POWERS

National Government	National and State Governments	State Governments
Coin money	Establish courts	Regulate trade within a state
Maintain army and navy	Enforce laws	Protect public welfare and safety
Declare war	Collect taxes	Conduct elections
Regulate trade between states and with foreign nations	Borrow money	Establish local governments
Carry out all expressed powers	Provide for general welfare	

Reading HELPDESK (CCSS)

legislative branch lawmaking branch of government

executive branch branch of government that executes, or carries out, the law; headed by the president

Electoral College special group of electors chosen to vote for president and vice president

---

netw⊙rks *Online Teaching Options*

GAME

A New Plan of Government Column Game

Sorting In this game, students sort powers by whether they are reserved for the state or federal government, or are shared by both. Use the game as a review or as a team experience in which one team calls out the power, and the other must decide where the power resides.

See page 173E for other online activities.

ANSWERS, p. 196

✓ PROGRESS CHECK In federalism, the powers of government are divided and shared between states and the national government.

CHART SKILL

1. Answers may include power to establish courts, collect taxes, or provide for the general welfare.

2. **CRITICAL THINKING** Each level of government needs to raise money through taxes to pay for what it provides to citizens.

Congress, shown here listening to the president deliver the State of the Union speech, consists of both the House of Representatives and the Senate. Congress currently has 100 senators and 435 representatives.

Government Branches

Article I of the Constitution declares Congress to be the **legislative** (LEH·juhs·lay·tiv) **branch**, or lawmaking branch, of the government. Congress is made up of the House of Representatives and the Senate. The powers of Congress include establishing taxes, coining money, and regulating trade.

Article II of the Constitution sets up the **executive branch**, to carry out the nation's laws and policies. At the head of this branch are the president and vice president. A special group called the **Electoral** (ee·lehk·TAWR·uhl) **College** elects the president and vice president. Voters in each state choose the electors who make up the Electoral College.

Article III deals with the **judicial** (joo·DIH·shuhl) **branch**, or court system. The nation's judicial power **resides** in "one supreme Court" and any lower federal courts Congress creates. The Supreme Court and other federal courts hear cases involving the Constitution, federal laws, and disputes between states.

 R1

 C

Checks and Balances

The Constitution contains a system of **checks and balances**. This means each branch of government has ways to check, or limit, the power of the other branches. With this system, no single branch can gain too much power in the government. You will learn more about this system in another chapter.

R2

✓ PROGRESS CHECK

Explaining Why does the Constitution divide power among branches of government?

Brooks Kraft/Corbis

---

judicial branch the branch of government that includes the courts that settle disputes and questions of the law

checks and balances a system by which each branch of government limits power of other branches

Academic Vocabulary (Tier 2 Words)

reside to exist in

R1 Reading Skills

Explaining After students have read the section on government branches, ask them to name and explain the three branches of the federal government. *(The legislative branch is the lawmaking branch; the executive branch is headed by the president and carries out the laws; the judicial branch is the court system, which says what the law is.)* **ELL**

Explain to students the concept and ideas behind the Electoral College. **Ask: How are electors chosen?** *(Voters in each state choose them.)* **Why do you think the Electoral College was created?** *(Answers may vary. Students will probably suggest that the Framers did not trust the general public to directly elect the president.)* **BL**

C Critical Thinking Skills

Analyzing Remind students of the concept of checks and balances as a means to keep power evenly distributed among the three branches of government. **Ask: What is the function of the judicial branch and the Supreme Court?** *(The judicial branch is the nation's court system; to hear cases involving the Constitution, federal laws, and disputes between states.)* Lead a class discussion on current or recent cases tried before the Supreme Court. Ask students what they know of these cases. Next work with students to help them understand how these cases are preserving the balance of power within the government.

R2 Reading Skills

Discussing Before they read, inform students that in this section they will read about checks and balances on power in the federal government. **Ask: Do you think government leaders should be limited in what they can or cannot do?** *(Require students to justify their responses.)*

GRAPHIC ORGANIZER

Taking Notes: *Categorizing:* Three Branches of Government

Categorizing Use the interactive graphic organizer to identify the powers of each branch of government as you move through this part of the lesson. Then present the interactive whiteboard activity to students. Have students sort the information under the appropriate chamber of Congress. Be sure that students explain their choices in their own words.
Ask: Why does the Senate have fewer members than the House of Representatives? *(The Senate has two members from each state, while the House has proportional representation based on the population of each state.)*

See page 173E for other online activities.

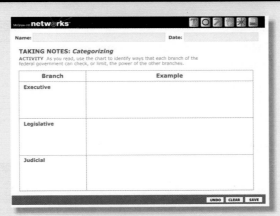

McGraw-Hill **networks**

Name: _____   Date: _____

TAKING NOTES: *Categorizing*
ACTIVITY As you read, use the chart to identify ways that each branch of the federal government can check, or limit, the power of the other branches.

Branch	Example
Executive	
Legislative	
Judicial	

UNDO   CLEAR   SAVE

ANSWER, p. 197

✓ **PROGRESS CHECK** to keep any one branch from gaining too much power

C Critical Thinking Skills

Differentiating Have students identify the Federalists and the Federalist Papers. *(Federalists were supporters of the Constitution. Three of them—Madison, Hamilton, and Jay—wrote a series of essays, called the Federalist Papers, explaining and defending the Constitution.)* **Ask:**

- **Who were the Anti-Federalists?** *(people who opposed the Constitution)*
- **What did the Anti-Federalists fear about the Constitution?** *(Anti-Federalists feared that a strong national government would take away liberties Americans had fought for and that the government would ignore the will of the states and favor the wealthy few over the many common people.)*

W Writing Skills

Argument Direct students to review the section titled "A Bill of Rights." Review with students the major amendments in the Bill of Rights. Then ask students to write a letter to the Framers of the Constitution. In their letters, students should draw from what they know of their rights today to justify why the Bills of Rights is a necessary set of amendments to the Constitution. **Verbal/Linguistic**

Content Background Knowledge

- The biggest controversy of the Constitutional Convention involved the question of how the states were to be represented in the national legislature. One question involved the issue of whether the states ought to be represented equally or in proportion to their population – hence the compromise in which states are represented equally in the Senate and according to their population in the House of Representatives.
- Another question concerned how to count enslaved persons: as persons for the purpose of determining a state's representation in the House of Representatives, or as property for purposes of determining taxation. In 1783 the Founders worked out a compromise in which enslaved persons were counted at the ratio of 3:5.

ANSWER, p. 198

CRITICAL THINKING Lawmakers today refer to the Bill of Rights when they are trying to pass legislation because they know Americans value the rights in the Constitution. If they can make voters believe that their legislation rises to the level of the Bill of Rights, they know they can get voters' support.

Debate and Adoption

GUIDING QUESTION *How was the Constitution ratified?*

Before the Constitution could go into effect, nine states had to ratify, or approve, it. Americans debated the arguments for and against the Constitution in newspapers, at meetings, and in everyday conversations.

Federalists and Anti-Federalists

People who supported the new Constitution were called Federalists. They took this name to stress that the Constitution would create a system of federalism, a government in which power is divided between the national government and the states. Among them were George Washington and Benjamin Franklin. James Madison, Alexander Hamilton, and John Jay wrote a series of essays explaining and defending the Constitution. Called the Federalist Papers, these essays were later published in newspapers and sent to delegates at state conventions. They made a powerful argument in favor of ratification.

Those who opposed the Constitution were called Anti-Federalists. They wrote their own essays, which later came to be known as the Anti-Federalist Papers. Anti-Federalists argued that a strong national government would take away liberties Americans had fought for in the American Revolution. They warned that the government would ignore the will of the states and favor the wealthy few over the common people. Anti-Federalists favored local government that was controlled more closely by the people.

A Bill of Rights

The strongest criticism of the Constitution may have been that it lacked a bill of rights to protect individual freedoms. Several state conventions announced that they would not ratify it unless a bill of rights was included. George Mason expressed the problem:

PRIMARY SOURCE

66 There is not a declaration of rights, and the laws of the general government being paramount to the laws and constitutions of the several States, the declarations of rights in the separate States are no security. 99

—from "Objections to This Constitution of Government," September 1787

Connections to
TODAY

The Bill of Rights

Various groups have drafted their own specialized versions of the Bill of Rights. For instance, in 2010 New Jersey lawmakers drafted an "Anti-Bullying Bill of Rights." This legislation was designed to protect students from bullying and cyberbullying. The bill calls for anti-bullying training for teachers and gives school administrators tools for responding to bullying.

▶ **CRITICAL THINKING**
Drawing Conclusions Why do you think lawmakers today refer to the Bill of Rights when proposing and promoting legislation?

Reading **HELP**DESK **CCSS**

amendment a change, correction, or improvement added to a document

198 *A More Perfect Union*

---

netw⊚rks *Online Teaching Options*

GAME

A New Plan of Government Identification Game

Defining Present the interactive vocabulary game to give students an opportunity to review the vocabulary for this lesson. **ELL**

See page 173E for other online activities.

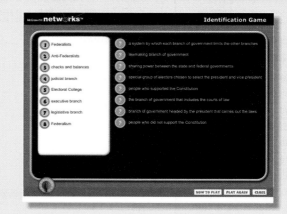

The Ninth PILLAR erected !
" The Ratification of the Conventions of nine States, fhall be fufficient for the eftablifh-
ment of this Conftitution, between the States fo ratifying the fame." *Art.* vii.
INCIPIENT MAGNI PROCEDERE MENSES.

☞If it is not up
it will rife.

The Attraction muft
be irrefiftible

The pillars in this cartoon
represent the ratifying vote
by each state convention.

▶ CRITICAL THINKING
Drawing Conclusions Why
is the ninth pillar significant?

Ratifying the Constitution

On December 7, 1787, Delaware became the first state to approve
the Constitution. By June 21, 1788, the ninth state—New
Hampshire—ratified it. In theory, this made the Constitution
law. However, without the support of the largest states—New
York and Virginia—the new government could not succeed.

In Virginia, Patrick Henry claimed the Constitution did not
place enough limits on government power. Still, Virginia did
ratify the document after promises that there would be a bill of
rights **amendment** (uh•MEHND•muhnt)—something added
to a document. This promise was met in 1791. In July 1788, New
York ratified the Constitution, followed by North Carolina in
November 1789 and Rhode Island in May 1790.

☑ PROGRESS CHECK

Explaining Why was it important that the largest states ratify
the Constitution?

The Granger Collection, NYC

LESSON 3 REVIEW

Review Vocabulary (Tier 3 Words)

1. Explain the relationship between the
   following terms. RH.6–8.4

   a. Electoral College   **b.** executive branch

2. Explain the significance of the following terms.
   RH.6–8.4
   a. federalism
   b. legislative branch
   c. judicial branch
   d. checks and balances
   e. amendment

Answer the Guiding Questions

3. *Identifying* What features of the Constitution
   developed from the ideas of Montesquieu? RH.6–8.1

4. *Explaining* What is the purpose of the first three
   articles of the Constitution? RH.6–8.2

5. *Specifying* Why did Virginia finally ratify
   the Constitution? RH.6–8.1

6. **ARGUMENT** Take the role of James Madison. Write
   an essay for the Federalist Papers, urging states to
   ratify the Constitution. Use details about the
   Constitution to support your argument. WHST.6–8.1, WHST.6–8.9

Lesson 3   **199**

C Critical Thinking Skills

Determining Cause and Effect Discuss with students the
debates over ratification of the Constitution. **Ask:**

• **What was Virginia's objection that prevented the
  Constitution from going into effect?** *(Virginia claimed
  there were not enough limits on federal power. They refused to
  ratify until a bill of rights was promised.)*

• **Why was it important for large states such as
  Virginia and New York to approve the Constitution—
  even though only nine states needed to approve?**
  *(Large states meant large populations of people supporting the
  new government, and the government needed the support to
  succeed.)* **BL** **Interpersonal**

Have students complete the Lesson 3 Review.

CLOSE & REFLECT

Speculating To close the lesson, have students think about
what it would have been like to be a citizen of the United States
at the time of the ratification of the Constitution. **Ask: Do you
think the American people were hopeful about their
government? How do you think the Framers might view
the government today?** *(Students' answers may vary.)*

LESSON 3 REVIEW ANSWERS

1. Possible response: The executive branch of government
   is headed by the president. The Electoral College is a
   group of people who have the responsibility of electing
   the president.

2. **a.** Federalism is the system in which power is shared
   between state and federal governments. **b.** The
   legislative branch of the government makes laws.
   c. The judicial branch includes the courts, and it settles
   questions involving laws. **d.** Checks and balances is
   the system by which each branch checks and thereby
   balances the power of the other branches. **e.** An
   amendment is a change, such as a formal change to
   the Constitution.

3. dividing the powers of government between separate
   branches, each with defined powers; and the system
   of checks and balances that keeps one branch from
   becoming too powerful

4. to describe and establish the powers and
   responsibilities of each branch of the
   federal government

5. Virginia was promised that a bill of rights would be
   added to the Constitution.

6. Essays should include the need for a strong central
   government and safeguards such as checks and
   balances, shared powers, and a bill of rights.

ANSWERS, p. 199

CRITICAL THINKING The ninth pillar is the ninth state to
ratify the Constitution, meaning that America has an
approved government.

☑ **PROGRESS CHECK** Virginia and New York were the
two states with the largest populations.

CHAPTER REVIEW ACTIVITY

Make a three-column chart with the headings "Branch," "Articles of Confederation" and "Constitution." Then lead a discussion that compares and contrasts key points of each document. Have a volunteer note these points on the chart.

Branch	Articles of Confederation	Constitution
Federal Government	weak central government with states keeping most of their power	A federal system that divided powers between central government and state governments.
Executive Branch	No chief executive	established an executive branch with defined powers
Legislative Branch	Unicameral. All members selected by state legislatures. One vote per state. Congress could not regulate trade, force people to join, army, or impose taxes. Congress could not pass laws without approval from all states.	Bicameral Members of House elected by the people. Members of Senate selected by state legislatures. Congress can issue taxes, regulate trade, control currency, raise an army, declare war.

REVIEW THE ENDURING UNDERSTANDING

Review the chapter's Enduring Understanding with students.

• *People, places, and ideas can change over time.*

Now pose the following questions in a class discussion to apply this enduring understanding to the chapter.

How did the Constitutional Convention arise out of a need for change? *(There were a number of problems that caused people to believe that the Articles of Confederation were not strong enough. The government had no power to issue money and help people in debt, evidenced by Shays's Rebellion. The Articles of Confederation also needed to be strengthened regarding the issue of slavery because of divisions between the North and South over this issue. The convention arose out of a need to address changing values in society.)*

How does the Constitution change over time? *(People can amend, or make changes to, the Constitution as changes occur in society.)*

How do the sources of the Constitution reflect the idea that people, places, and ideas change over time? *(The U.S. Constitution was based on British rule and tradition but adapted to suit a new country. Answers may include specific examples of how the Constitution borrowed and differed from the Magna Carta, the English Bill of Rights. Students might also mention the idea of federalism, which strengthened the new central government.)*

Write your answers on a separate piece of paper.

❶ Exploring the Essential Questions WHST.6–8.2, WHST.6–8.10

INFORMATIVE/EXPLANATORY How would you explain the behavior of the people of the United States in the period between 1776 and 1783? Write a summary that explains the goals of the people in throwing off British rule, forming the Articles of Confederation, and then establishing the Constitution. Be sure to explain how these actions relate to the question of why people form governments, how governments affect people's lives, and how governments change.

❷ 21st Century Skills RH.6–8.10, WHST.6–8.1

MAKING AN ARGUMENT Reread the discussion of Shays's Rebellion from Lesson 2 of this chapter. Write a letter to the editor of your local newspaper in which you explain what the incident reveals about the nation and its system of government at that time.

❸ Thinking Like a Historian RH.6–8.5

UNDERSTANDING CAUSE AND EFFECT In a chart, identify at least three reasons Americans believed the Articles of Confederation needed to be strengthened.

❹ VISUAL LITERACY

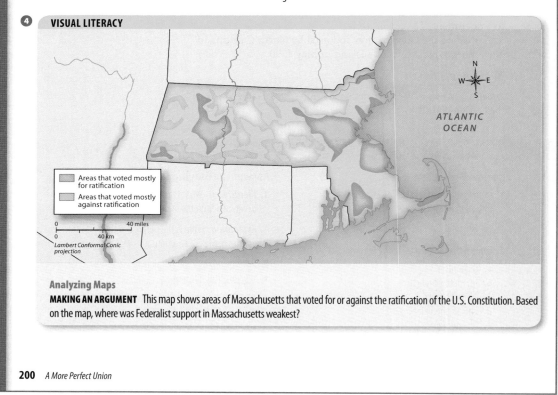

Analyzing Maps

MAKING AN ARGUMENT This map shows areas of Massachusetts that voted for or against the ratification of the U.S. Constitution. Based on the map, where was Federalist support in Massachusetts weakest?

ACTIVITIES ANSWERS

Exploring the Essential Questions

❶ Answers will vary. Possible answers may include some or all of the following:

• In 1776 the colonists broke free of England and English rule so they could govern themselves independently.

• They needed a plan of government. In 1777 they wrote the Articles of Confederation, which included a national government with limited powers.

• The new government owed other countries a lot of money, and the new nation faced an economic crisis.

• Farmers rebelled against the policies of higher taxes and putting people in jail if they could not pay their taxes.

• The Confederation government was too weak to handle internal problems with the economy and external problems with Britain and Spain.

• The Constitutional Convention was called; the delegates decided to replace the Articles of Confederation with a constitution.

• The delegates had to compromise on issues of power distribution, representation, and slavery. The Constitution was finally approved on the promise of the inclusion of a bill of rights, which some states insisted upon before ratifying.

REVIEW THE GUIDING QUESTIONS

Choose the best answer for each question.

RH.6–8.2
1. Under the Articles of Confederation, Congress did not have the authority to
   A. conduct foreign affairs.
   B. maintain armed forces.
   C. borrow money.
   D. force citizens to join the army.

RH.6–8.1
2. The Northwest Ordinance
   F. allowed for the spread of slavery.
   G. encouraged the sale of land to speculators.
   H. provided a method for petitioning for statehood.
   I. denied a bill of rights for settlers.

RH.6–8.2
3. Shays's Rebellion demonstrated the
   A. strength of the Articles of Confederation.
   B. weakness of the Virginia Plan.
   C. weakness of the Articles of Confederation.
   D. strength of the United States Constitution.

RH.6–8.1
4. At the Constitutional Convention, the New Jersey Plan proposed
   F. a two-house legislature.
   G. a court system.
   H. one vote for each state.
   I. a chief executive chosen by the legislature.

RH.6–8.1
5. The Framers of the Constitution wanted to protect people's natural rights. This idea was reflected in the work of
   A. English philosopher John Locke.
   B. French writer Baron de Montesquieu.
   C. King George III.
   D. Italian philosopher Niccolo Machiavelli.

RH.6–8.2
6. In the debate over the ratification of the Constitution, the Anti-Federalists most feared
   F. government oppression.
   G. the establishment of a state religion.
   H. disorder without a strong central government.
   I. a national sales tax.

201

ASSESSMENT ANSWERS
Review the Guiding Questions

1. **D** Congress did have the power to conduct foreign affairs, maintain an army, and borrow money. Thus, the correct answer is D, force citizens to join the army.

2. **H** The Northwest Ordinance was the nation's first attempt to stop the spread of slavery. It was created partly because of worry about land speculators. It did contain a bill of rights. Thus, the correct answer is H—it provided a method for petitioning for statehood.

3. **C** Students should eliminate choices B and D because Shays's Rebellion occurred before the Virginia Plan was set forward as an alternative plan for government or the Constitution was written. Answer A is incorrect because the rebellion was a result of the weaknesses of the Articles that did not permit the government to make proactive economic policies.

4. **H** The Virginia Plan proposed a two-house legislature, an executive chosen by the legislature, and a court system. The New Jersey plan proposed one house with equal representation from all states.

5. **A** Natural rights should be associated with John Locke. Choices C and D are wrong because neither of these was mentioned as influences on the Framers. Montesquieu was concerned about the separation and balance of powers, eliminating choice B.

6. **F** Anti-Federalists feared government oppression, while the Federalists wanted a strong central government to protect them from disorder.

21st Century Skills

2. Students should write letters reflecting that the nation was in the midst of economic turmoil. The federal government was unable to address either the financial crisis that was at the heart of the unrest or the unrest itself.

Thinking Like a Historian

3. Congress could not pass a law unless 9 states voted for it; consent of all 13 states was required to change the Articles; Congress could not regulate trade; Congress could not force people to join the army; Congress could not impose taxes.

Analyzing Maps

4. Students should make the connection that Federalists supported ratification of the U.S. Constitution while Anti-Federalists opposed ratification. Therefore, Federalist support was strongest in the central part and weakest in the eastern part of the state.

Analyzing Documents

7 **D** As students read, have them reword phrases to increase understanding. They should then see that Washington addressed the criticism that the Constitution was not a perfect document but that it was good for the nation overall.

8 **F** Washington acknowledged that the Constitution did not fully satisfy anyone but argued that had one state dominated the document, negative consequences might have resulted for other states. He never predicts that all states will eventually approve it, but implies that states should consider the country over their own interests.

Short Response

9 slavery and involuntary servitude

10 Enslaved people could be reclaimed and returned to the original state where they were claimed as someone's property.

Extended Response

11 Student essays should express only one of the two opinions and should provide logical arguments to support that opinion, including specific references from the chapter and from the Constitution.

DBQ ANALYZING DOCUMENTS

"That [the Constitution] will meet the full and entire approbation [approval] of every state is not perhaps to be expected; but each will doubtless consider, … that [the Constitution] may promote the lasting welfare of that country so dear to us all, and secure her freedom and happiness."

—George Washington, 1787

RH.6–8.6

7 **Summarizing** Which most closely reflects Washington's main point?

A. The Constitution gives too much power to the legislative branch.

B. The Constitution is not popular and will never win approval.

C. The Constitution takes away too much power from the states.

D. The Constitution is good for the nation overall.

RH.6–8.1, RH.6–8.10

8 **Analyzing** Which idea is not part of Washington's response?

F. All states will eventually approve it.

G. Serving one state's interests would be harmful to the other states.

H. The approval of every state is not expected.

I. The welfare of the country is important to all the states.

SHORT RESPONSE

"There shall be neither slavery nor involuntary servitude in the said territory. … Provided, always, that any person escaping into the same … such fugitive may be lawfully reclaimed and conveyed [transferred] to the person claiming his or her labor or service as aforesaid."

—Article 6 of Northwest Ordinance, 1787

RH.6–8.6, WHST.6–8.4

9 What practices were not allowed in the Northwest Territory?

RH.6–8.2, WHST.6–8.4

10 What was the legal status of escaped enslaved people in the Northwest Territory?

EXTENDED RESPONSE

WHST.6–8.1, WHST.6–8.10

11 **Argument** Write an essay in which you:

- defend the Constitution as a model of democracy; or

- express criticism of the Constitution based on differences between its ideals and the status of enslaved people and women in the 1700s.

Need Extra Help?

If You've Missed Question	❶	❷	❸	❹	❺	❻	❼	❽	❾	❿	⓫
Review Lesson	1	1	2	2	3	3	1	1	1	1	2, 3

Letter from George Washington to the Confederation Congress, accompanying the Constitution, September 17, 1877, Library of Congress, Manuscript Division.

---

networks *Online Teaching Options*

Using eAssessment

Use eAssessment to access and assign the publisher-made Lesson Quizzes & Chapter Tests electronically. You can also use eAssessment to create your own quizzes and tests from hundreds of available questions. eAssessment helps you design assessments that meet the needs of different types of learners. Follow the link in the *Assess* tab of your Teacher Lesson Center.

CHAPTER 8

The Constitution Planner

UNDERSTANDING BY DESIGN®

Enduring Understanding

- *Governments are formed to establish and maintain order within a society.*

Essential Questions

- *Why do people form governments?*
- *How do new ideas change the way people live?*

Predictable Misunderstandings

Students may think:

- *The Constitution never changes.*
- *The meaning of the Constitution never changes.*
- *All groups of people were treated equally at the time the Constitution was written.*

Assessment Evidence

Performance Tasks:

- *Hands-On Chapter Project*

Other Evidence:

- *Interactive Graphic Organizers*
- *What Do You Know? activity*
- *21st Century Skills Activity*
- *Written Paragraphs*
- *Class discussion answers about the Constitution and its provisions*
- *Lesson Reviews*
- *Online Self-Check Quizzes*
- *Chapter Activities and Assessment*

SUGGESTED PACING GUIDE

Introducing the Chapter . . . . 1 Day	Lesson 2 . . . . 2 Days
Lesson 1 . . . . 2 Days	Chapter Activities and Assessment . . . . . . 1 Day

TOTAL TIME   6 Days

Key for Using the Teacher Edition

SKILL-BASED ACTIVITIES

Types of skill activities found in the Teacher Edition.

V **Visual Skills** require students to analyze maps, graphs, charts, and photos.

R **Reading Skills** help students practice reading skills and master vocabulary.

W **Writing Skills** provide writing opportunities to help students comprehend the text.

C **Critical Thinking Skills** help students apply and extend what they have learned.

T **Technology Skills** require students to use digital tools effectively.

Letters are followed by a number when there is more than one of the same type of skill on the page.

DIFFERENTIATED INSTRUCTION

All activities are written for the on-level student unless otherwise marked with the leveled labels below.

BL **Beyond Level**
AL **Approaching Level**
ELL **English Language Learners**

All students benefit from activities that utilize different learning styles. Many activities are marked as below when a particular learning style is highlighted.

Intrapersonal	Naturalist
Logical/Mathematical	Kinesthetic
Visual/Spatial	Auditory/Musical
Verbal/Linguistic	Interpersonal

Learners will understand:

2 Time, Continuity, and Change

8. The history of democratic ideals and principles, and how they are represented in documents, artifacts and symbols

6 Power, Authority, and Governance

1. Rights are guaranteed in the U.S. Constitution, the supreme law of the land

2. Fundamental ideas that are the foundation of American constitutional democracy (including those of the U.S. Constitution, popular sovereignty, the rule of law, separation of powers, checks and balances, minority rights, the separation of church and state, and Federalism)

3. Fundamental values of constitutional democracy (e.g., the common good, liberty, justice, equality, and individual dignity)

10 Civic Ideals and Practices

1. The theme of civic ideals and practices helps us to learn about and know how to work for the betterment of society.

2. Concepts and ideals such as: individual dignity, liberty, justice, equality, individual rights, responsibility, majority and minority rights, and civil dissent

3. Key practices involving the rights and responsibilities of citizenship and the exercise of citizenship (e.g., respecting the rule of law and due process, voting, serving on a jury, researching issues, making informed judgments, expressing views on issues, and collaborating with others to take civic action)

4. The common good and the rule of law

5. Key documents and excerpts from key sources that define and support democratic ideals and practices (e.g., the U.S. Declaration of Independence, the U.S. Constitution, the Gettysburg Address, the Letter from Birmingham Jail; and international documents such as the Declaration of the Rights of Man and the Universal Declaration of the Rights of Children)

6. The origins and function of major institutions and practices developed to support democratic ideals and practices

8. The importance of becoming informed in order to make positive civic contributions

CHAPTER OPENER PLANNER

Students will know:
- the structure of the Constitution.
- the principles contained in the Constitution.
- the process of amending the Constitution.
- the importance of Constitutional interpretation.
- the responsibilities of the three branches of the federal government.

Students will be able to:
- **analyze and describe** the structure of the Constitution.
- **identify and evaluate** the principles contained in the Constitution and their importance.
- **analyze and evaluate** the process of amending the Constitution.
- **draw conclusions** about the importance of interpreting the Constitution instead of amending it.
- **analyze and describe** the separation of powers.

UNDERSTANDING
BY DESIGN®

☑ *Print Teaching Options*

V Visual Skills

☐ **P. 204** Students read a map of Washington, D.C.
AL ELL Visual/Spatial

W Writing Skills

☐ **P. 204** Students write a persuasive paragraph giving their own opinions about statehood for the District of Columbia.

C Critical Thinking Skills

☐ **P. 205** Students review the chapter time line and consider how these events are related to changes to the Constitution made over time.

☑ *Online Teaching Options*

V Visual Skills

☐ **MAP** **Washington D.C. Today**—Students examine the extent and location of our nation's capital.

☐ **TIME LINE** **The Constitution**—Students learn about key events in the evolution of the Constitution between 1788 and the present.

☐ **WORLD ATLAS** Students can use this interactive map to identify regions of the world, learn about individual countries, locate political boundaries, measure distances, and much more.

☑ *Printable Digital Worksheets*

R Reading Skills

☐ **GRAPHIC NOVEL** *In the House*—Students get a tour of the White House.

Project-Based Learning

Hands-On Chapter Project

Constitution Flip Chart
Students will learn about key components of the U.S. Constitution and the basic principles reflected in the document by creating and presenting an educational Web page.

Technology Extension

Constitution Web Page
- Find an additional activity online that incorporates technology for this project.
- Visit the EdTechTeacher Web sites (included in the Technology Extension for this chapter) for more links, tutorials, and other resources.

Print Resources

ANCILLARY RESOURCES
These ancillaries are available for every chapter and lesson.
- **Reading Essentials and Study Guide Workbook** **AL ELL**
- **Chapter Tests and Lesson Quizzes Blackline Masters**

PRINTABLE DIGITAL WORKSHEETS
These printable digital worksheets are available for every chapter and lesson.
- **Hands-On Chapter Projects**
- **What Do You Know? activities**
- **Chapter Summaries (English and Spanish)**
- **Vocabulary Builder activities**
- **Guided Reading activities**

More Media Resources

SUGGESTED VIDEOS **MOVIES**
Watch clips of popular culture films about the making of the U.S. Constitution, such as *The American Constitution: The Road from Runnymede* (a documentary film narrated by Christopher Reeve) and *1776*, a movie that gives glimpses of the Founders as they pushed toward independence from Great Britain.

Discuss Compare and contrast documentary films to films made for entertainment. **Ask: What are possible benefits and drawbacks of each type of film?** (NOTE: Preview clips for age-appropriateness.)

SUGGESTED READING
Grade 6 reading level:
- *A More Perfect Union: The Story of Our Constitution,* by Betsy Maestro

Grade 7 reading level:
- *The Founders: The 39 Stories Behind the U.S. Constitution,* by Dennis Brindell Fradin

Grade 8 reading level:
- *Our Constitution,* by Hal Marcowitz

PRINCIPLES OF THE CONSTITUTION

Students will know:
- the structure of the Constitution.
- the principles contained in the Constitution.
- the process of amending the Constitution.
- the importance of Constitutional interpretation.

Students will be able to:
- *analyze and describe* the structure of the Constitution.
- *identify and evaluate* the principles contained in the Constitution and their importance.
- *analyze and evaluate* the process of amending the Constitution.
- *draw conclusions* about the importance of interpreting the Constitution instead of amending it.

UNDERSTANDING
BY DESIGN®

☑ *Print Teaching Options*

V Visual Skills

☐ **P. 208** Students make a chart showing the three branches of government. **Visual/Spatial**

☐ **P. 209** Students analyze how the legislative branch could act as a check on the executive branch. **Visual/Spatial**

R Reading Skills

☐ **P. 206** Students define *popular sovereignty* and *republic.*

☐ **P. 207** Students explain why the Framers wanted to establish a limited government.

☐ **P. 210** Students explain how the Constitution can be regarded as a flexible document.

☐ **P. 211** Students explain the amendment process. **AL**

☐ **P. 211** Students identify the clauses that are the source for the idea of implied power. **BL**

W Writing Skills

☐ **P. 206** Students write a paragraph translating the Preamble to the Constitution into modern language. **AL ELL Verbal/Linguistic**

☐ **P. 209** Students pick one right that is especially meaningful to them and write a paragraph explaining why they feel it is so important. **Verbal/Linguistic**

C Critical Thinking Skills

☐ **P. 207** Students categorize the powers of the states and the federal government.

☐ **P. 208** Students discuss the separation of powers and checks and balances.

☐ **P. 209** Students discuss ways in which they have exercised their rights under the Bill of Rights. **ELL**

☐ **P. 209** Students identify what different amendments to the Constitution have in common.

☐ **P. 211** Students consider how certain Constitutional amendments have changed lives.

T Technology Skills

☐ **P. 211** Students use video cameras and interview an elderly family member about changes to the Constitution. **AL**

☑ *Online Teaching Options*

V Visual Skills

☐ **VIDEO** **Checks, Balances, and the Exercise of Power**—Students view a video that explains how our system of checks and balances works to ensure that power is exercised fairly.

☐ **IMAGE** **The Federal Court System**—Students click to see a visual representation of the levels of the federal courts.

☐ **CHART** **Amending the Constitution**—Students click to reveal facts on the process of amending the Constitution.

R Reading Skills

☐ **GRAPHIC ORGANIZER** **Taking Notes:** *Listing:* **Major Principles of the Constitution**—Students record in a web diagram the seven major principles on which the Constitution is based.

☐ **PRIMARY SOURCE** **The Constitution**—Students can click through the pages to read the preamble, articles, and amendments to the Constitution.

☐ **IMAGE** **The U.S. Department of the Treasury**—Students read about the establishment and roles of the DOT.

C Critical Thinking Skills

☐ **DIAGRAM** **The Amendment Process**—Students identify how amendments are proposed and ratified.

T Technology Skills

☐ **SELF-CHECK QUIZ** **Lesson 1**—Students receive instant feedback on their mastery of lesson content.

☑ *Printable Digital Worksheets*

W Writing Skills

☐ **WORKSHEET** **21st Century Skills Activity: Information Literacy: Recognizing Historical Perspectives**—Students write definitions for each of the principles that the Constitution embodies and then apply those definitions to quotes from the constitutional Framers.

GOVERNMENT AND THE PEOPLE

Students will know:
- the responsibilities of the three branches of the federal government.

Students will be able to:
- *analyze and describe* the separation of powers.

☑ *Print Teaching Options*

R Reading Skills

☐ **P. 212** Students make a list of information about the Senate and the House of Representatives.
AL Visual/Spatial

☐ **P. 213** Students summarize the roles of the vice president and other members of the executive branch.
BL **ELL** Visual/Spatial

☐ **P. 213** Students consider whether the three branches of government are equal.

☐ **P. 214** Students explain what a judicial review is.
AL **ELL**

☐ **P. 215** Students create a list of different ways a person can become a U.S. citizen.

W Writing Skills

☐ **P. 214** Students prepare a class display or website in which they provide a news story, along with an annotation or caption analyzing how the story relates to these constitutional issues. **BL** Visual/Spatial Interpersonal

C Critical Thinking Skills

☐ **P. 212** Students explain why it is important for people to be represented fairly in the legislature. **BL** Interpersonal

☐ **P. 215** Students list patriotic songs and consider why people write them. **AL** **ELL** Auditory/Musical

T Technology Skills

☐ **P. 215** Students use word processing software to make a chart showing the duties and responsibilities of citizenship.

☑ *Online Teaching Options*

V Visual Skills

☐ **VIDEO** **The New Congress Designs a Bill of Rights**—Students examine historical and modern issues surrounding the first ten amendments to the Constitution.

☐ **SLIDE SHOW** **The Oval Office**—Students click to see images of the president's office.

☐ **DIAGRAM** **The Federal Court System**—Students click to see a visual representation of the levels of the federal courts.

R Reading Skills

☐ **GRAPHIC ORGANIZER** **Taking Notes:** *Summarizing:* **The Three Branches of the U.S. Government**—Students summarize the jobs of the three branches of the federal government.

☐ **BIOGRAPHY** **Sandra Day O'Connor**—Students read a biography of the first woman Supreme Court justice.

C Critical Thinking Skills

☐ **CHART** **Naturalization Test**—Students test themselves on sample questions included on the naturalization test administered to those wishing to become U.S. citizens.

☐ **CHART** **Landmark Supreme Court Cases**—Students click to learn details of four cases decided by the Supreme Court between 1803 and 1969.

☐ **IMAGE** **Voting Rights**—Students click to learn about the five Constitutional amendments that expanded and protected voting rights.

T Technology Skills

☐ **SELF-CHECK QUIZ** **Lesson 2**—Students receive instant feedback on their mastery of lesson content.

LESSON 1   Principles of the Constitution

Reading and Comprehension

This section is about the principles on which the Constitution is based. Tell students that the Constitution is, in a sense, the philosophy behind the nation's system of laws. It provides guidance to legislators as they write laws, and it provides guidance to courts when they determine whether a given law can be upheld and enforced or whether it must be struck down. Have students preview the lesson and write down any questions that they have.

Text Evidence

Divide the class into small groups and ask students to list what they believe are important functions of government (e.g., protect the country, provide services to citizens). Then have students look through the lesson or through the Constitution itself, to find the powers of government that relate to each function. Next to each function of government on students' lists, have them write the corresponding power or powers. For example, next to "protect the country," students might write "maintain a standing military."

LESSON 2   Government and the People

Reading and Comprehension

This section explains the three branches of government and the duties and responsibilities of citizenship. Give students a copy of the K-W-L-H chart and have them preview the lesson and complete the two left columns of the chart. After students have finished the lesson, have them complete the two right columns.

Text Evidence

Divide the class into small groups. Assign each group one power of government, such as the power to tax. Then have students write a paragraph explaining what each branch of government has to do with the assigned power. For example, in the case of the power to tax, the legislative branch must pass a law imposing the tax. The executive branch must collect the tax from citizens. The judicial branch must handle any disputes that arise related to the collection of the tax.

Online Resources

Approaching Level Reader

Use this online lower-level text that corresponds directly to the text in the Student Edition. It includes a Spanish version.

Guided Reading Activities

This resource uses graphic organizers and guiding questions to help students with comprehension.

What Do You Know?

Use these worksheets to pre-assess student's background knowledge before they study the chapter.

Reading Essentials and Study Guide Workbook

This resource offers writing and reading activities for the approaching-level student. Also available in Spanish.

Self-Check Quizzes

This online assessment tool provides instant feedback for students to check their progress.

How Do I Use
Primary Sources
in My Classroom?

A primary source is an oral or written account obtained from people who witnessed or experienced an event. Examples of primary sources can include official government documents; speeches, interviews, and oral histories; diaries; autobiographies; advertisements; physical historical objects; and songs or audio recordings.

Using primary sources transforms students into active participants in the examination of a subject. Students can use primary sources to think critically about events, issues, and concepts.

Step 1 How Do I Introduce Students to Primary Sources?

- Alert students to the fact that primary sources contain biases and prejudices and should be examined cautiously. Every primary source reflects the creator's point of view, which is only one interpretation of an event, a document, or an issue.

- Students can use questions such as *Who created the source? What was the purpose for doing so?*

Step 2 Choosing Primary Sources

- Expose students to a variety of primary sources.

- Be aware that many documents include challenging vocabulary, or unfamiliar sentence structure. You may need to explain how to interpret these things before students can really begin to understand the source's content.

Step 3 Using Primary Sources in a Variety of Ways

- Use these types of sources in multiple ways to keep learners engaged.

- As a **prereading activity**, you can provide primary sources to introduce content at the start of the chapter or topic. Have students analyze the source and ask questions about it. Then ask students to make predictions about what they may learn when studying the main content.

- As an **evaluation activity**, ask students to compare what they learn in a primary source against the information provided by the textbook or in digital assets. Is the content the same? Does the primary source have a limited perspective of events that the narrative challenges or supports? Does the primary source increase student understanding on the human impact of the event, document, or issue?

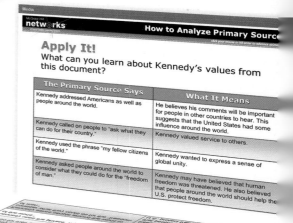

The Constitution

1788–Today

ESSENTIAL QUESTIONS • Why do people form governments?
• How do new ideas change the way people live?

◄ James Madison earned the nickname
"Father of the Constitution."

The Bridgeman Art Library /Getty Images

networks

There's More Online about the United States Constitution.

CHAPTER 8

Lesson 1
Principles of the Constitution

Lesson 2
Government and the People

The Story Matters . . .

The early years of the United States and the Constitution produced many great leaders and heroes. Of that group, none stands taller than James Madison.

It is Madison's Virginia Plan that provides the basic framework and many of the central ideas of the Constitution. It is his detailed notes taken throughout the months of debate that serve as a record of the convention. Then, as the nation debates ratification, Madison's contributions to the *Federalist Papers* help persuade many to accept the new document. Later, he sponsors the Bill of Rights, the first 10 amendments to the Constitution, which help protect the basic liberties Americans enjoy to this day.

203

ENGAGE

🔔 **Bellringer** Ask a volunteer to read "The Story Matters . . ." aloud. Explain that students will learn a great deal about the Bill of Rights in this chapter, including that it recognizes and protects basic rights such as freedom of religion, freedom of speech, freedom of the press, and freedom of association.

Ask: What documents was Madison involved in writing that contained ideas related to the Constitution? *(Students should mention the Virginia Plan, the Federalist Papers, and possibly the Constitution and Bill of Rights themselves.)* **Ask:** Based on Madison's story, what can you infer about the process of developing a Constitution? *(Students should note that the Constitution was developed over a long period of time, that the ideas in the Constitution were drawn from other related documents, and that the Framers engaged in a protracted debate over the issues as part of the process of developing the final document.)*

Making Connections

Have students brainstorm about what Madison's personality must have been like based on what we learn about him here. Have students make a list of adjectives or short phrases that likely applied to Madison. *(organized, careful, attention to detail, educated, scholarly, legible handwriting, etc.)* **Ask:** What if "Father of the Constitution," a nickname often given to Madison, was a job for which Madison were applying? Have students write a creative cover letter for applicant Madison to use in applying for this job, making use of the adjectives and short phrases on their brainstormed lists.

Letter from the Author

Dear American History Teacher,

The United States Constitution is this nation's fundamental law. It is made up of three parts: the Preamble, the articles, and the amendments. The Constitution establishes the basic organization of the nation's government and the powers of its various branches. The Bill of Rights was eventually added to safeguard individual liberties and rights. Additional amendments ended slavery, defined citizenship to include African Americans, guaranteed men their voting rights, provided the right of women to vote, and lowered the voting age.

Joyce Appleby

TEACH & ASSESS

Step Into the Place

V Visual Skills

Reading a Map Direct students' attention to the Chapter Opener map. Ask students to identify what the map shows. Verify that it shows the location of the capital of the United States, Washington, D.C. Remind students that "D.C." stands for "District of Columbia" and that the District of Columbia is not in, or a part of, any state. It is a separate entity. **Ask: Is there any advantage to having a national capital that is not in any state?** *(Possible answer: Yes; no state can control the capital.)* Next, as a class, discuss the Map Focus questions. **AL** **ELL** **Visual/Spatial**

W Writing Skills

Informative/Explanatory Have students write a persuasive paragraph giving their own opinions about statehood for the District of Columbia. **Ask: Why might the Founders have decided to deny the residents of Washington, D.C., voting representatives in the national Congress?** *(Answers will vary, but students might suggest that the Founders did not want the federal government to be subordinate to state laws or to risk the chance of a clash between federal law and state law.)*

Content Background Knowledge

- The name "District of Columbia" is a reference to Christopher Columbus.
- Congress first gathered together in Washington, D.C., on Dec. 1, 1800.
- The residents of Washington, D.C., do not have representatives in the U.S. Senate and have only a nonvoting representative in the House of Representatives.

ANSWERS, p. 204

Step Into the Place
1. Washington, D.C., is located on the Potomac River between Maryland and Virginia.
2. Washington Monument, U.S. Supreme Court building, U.S. Capitol, the White House, and so forth
3. **CRITICAL THINKING** Placing the national capital at the center of the country would make it equally available to all states and would not make one part or region any more important than another for having the capital in it. In addition, giving the capital a central location would make it more accessible to citizens who would need to travel there either to serve in public office or to lobby elected officials.

Step Into the Time
1870: The Fifteenth Amendment protects African American voting rights.
1920: The Nineteenth Amendment establishes women's right to vote.

Place and Time: The Nation's Capital 1788 to Today

The Constitution established a strong central government. The home of that government is the District of Columbia— Washington, D.C.

Step Into the Place

MAP FOCUS Washington, D.C. serves as the capital of the United States and the home to many important buildings and offices.

1 LOCATION Between what two states is the district located? RH.6–8.7

2 PLACE What are some of the buildings or institutions of national importance located in Washington, D.C.? RH.6–8.7

3 CRITICAL THINKING
Drawing Conclusions One of the reasons that the site of Washington, D.C., was chosen as the capital was that it was in the center of the country as it existed in 1790. What are the advantages of such a location? RH.6–8.7

A joint session of Congress—including both the House and the Senate—listens to the president deliver the State of the Union Address.

In the United States, immigrants can become citizens—and accept the rights and responsibilities that go along with it.

Step Into the Time

TIME LINE What two amendments protect the right to vote? When were they ratified? RH.6–8.5, RH.6–8.7

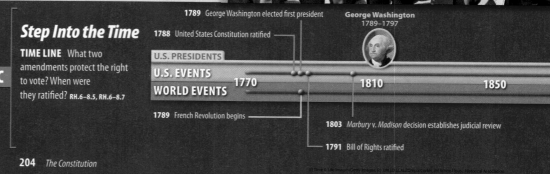

1789 George Washington elected first president

George Washington
1789–1797

1788 United States Constitution ratified

U.S. PRESIDENTS
U.S. EVENTS
WORLD EVENTS   1770   1810   1850

1789 French Revolution begins

1803 *Marbury v. Madison* decision establishes judicial review

1791 Bill of Rights ratified

204 The Constitution

Project-Based Learning

Hands-On Chapter Project

Constitution Flip Chart

Students will learn about key components of the U.S. Constitution and the basic principles reflected in the document by creating an educational flip chart. Students will choose a section of the Constitution to research and will then plan and prepare a flip chart that shows their understanding of the section of the Constitution that they selected. The flip chart should include a variety of elements such as photos, drawings, graphs, and quotes. Once the flip charts are completed, students should present them to the class and evaluate using a class-developed assessment rubric.

Technology Extension

Constitution Web Page

Have students create U.S. Constitution Web pages from their research to be published and shared. Students can take advantage of the growing number of resources available online by linking to research, multimedia, video, and images on the Web. There are a number of free hosting services that allow students and educators to create Web sites by simply dragging and dropping page elements (such as text, images, and multimedia content) into a page template.

edtechteacher
21st Century Learning

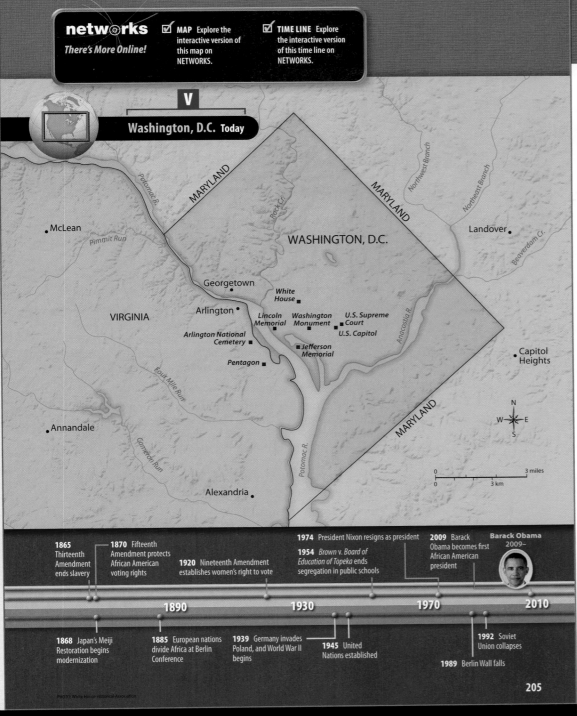

networks
There's More Online!

☑ **MAP** Explore the interactive version of this map on NETWORKS.

☑ **TIME LINE** Explore the interactive version of this time line on NETWORKS.

Washington, D.C. Today

MARYLAND

Northwest Branch

MARYLAND

Northeast Branch

Potomac R.

Rock Cr.

McLean

Pimmit Run

WASHINGTON, D.C.

Landover

Beaverdam Cr.

Georgetown

White House

VIRGINIA

Arlington

Lincoln Memorial

Washington Monument

U.S. Supreme Court

Anacostia R.

Arlington National Cemetery

U.S. Capitol

Jefferson Memorial

Capitol Heights

Pentagon

Four Mile Run

MARYLAND

N W E S

Potomac R.

Cameron Run

0   3 miles
0   3 km

Annandale

Alexandria

Time line:

1865 Thirteenth Amendment ends slavery

1870 Fifteenth Amendment protects African American voting rights

1920 Nineteenth Amendment establishes women's right to vote

1974 President Nixon resigns as president

1954 *Brown v. Board of Education of Topeka* ends segregation in public schools

2009 Barack Obama becomes first African American president

Barack Obama 2009–

1890   1930   1970   2010

1868 Japan's Meiji Restoration begins modernization

1885 European nations divide Africa at Berlin Conference

1939 Germany invades Poland, and World War II begins

1945 United Nations established

1992 Soviet Union collapses

1989 Berlin Wall falls

PHOTO: White House Historical Association

205

What Do You Know? Activity: The Constitution

Using Digital Tools Have students use the interactive time line to find out more about each event. If there is time, have students prepare their own illustrated time lines (either in print or html/Web site form), adding photos and other images from their research. You may wish to have students make a time line that can be added to the class Web site, with each student or pair of students preparing one entry on the time line. **AL** Visual/Spatial

See page 203B for additional online activities.

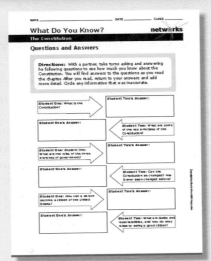

NAME _____ DATE _____ CLASS _____

What Do You Know? networks
The Constitution
Questions and Answers

Directions: With a partner, take turns asking and answering the following questions to see how much you know about the Constitution. You will find answers to the questions as you read the chapter. After you read, return to your answers and add more detail. Circle any information that was inaccurate.

Step Into the Time

Making Inferences Have students review the time line for the chapter. Explain to students that many of the events on the time line are related to how the Constitution has been interpreted and changed over time.

Ask: Which time line events support the view that groups of people achieved greater equality as a result of constitutional changes? *(The Thirteenth Amendment ended slavery and the Nineteenth Amendment gave women the right to vote.)* Point out to students that even after the Constitution has been changed, it sometimes takes society some time to catch up. **Ask:** Find the point on the time line when voting rights were extended to all adult male Americans. *(1870, passage of the Fifteenth Amendment)* How many years after passage of the Fifteenth Amendment did Americans finally elect their first African American president? *(138 years)* How many years after passage of the Fifteenth Amendment did it take before an amendment was passed ensuring women the right to vote? *(fifty years)* Then have students complete the time line question on page 204.

Content Background Knowledge

- The District of Columbia's official seal is related to its geographical location. The seal's background shows the Potomac River separating D.C. from Virginia. The seal also depicts the Capitol itself, to the left of a figure of Justice and a statue of George Washington. To Justice's right are an eagle and some agricultural products. The seal also includes the district's motto, *Justitia omnibus* (Justice for all), and the date 1871.

- The District occupies 69 square miles (179 square kilometers). It is bounded by Maryland on the north, east, and south, and on the west by the Potomac River (beyond which lies Virginia).

- Some parts of Maryland and Virginia are today counted as part of the Washington, D.C., metropolitan area for the purpose of gathering statistics about the city.

CLOSE & REFLECT

Predicting Consequences Ask: What tourist attractions can you see on the map? *(White House, Lincoln Memorial, Washington Monument, Jefferson Memorial, the Supreme Court, and the Capital)* **Ask:** Why do you think it is productive to encourage citizens to visit our nation's capital? *(Seeing government at work can help promote civic education and civic pride.)*

ENGAGE

Bellringer Have students consider the rules that they must follow in all the different contexts of their lives: at home, at school, in extracurricular activities, and in sports. Have students make a list of the different rules that they follow in different settings. Then ask students to try to find the guiding principles behind the rules. For example, the guiding principles behind many sports-related rules are safety and good sportsmanship. The guiding principles behind many of the rules at school are creating a proper learning environment and respecting others. Have students think of others and share them with the class.

Ask: If you were creating a nation, what rules and laws would you establish? Why? *(Answers will vary but might include laws to collect taxes, establish and sustain a military, guarantee and protect personal rights of various kinds, and make certain behaviors or actions crimes.)*

TEACH & ASSESS

W Writing Skills

Narrative Discuss the preamble as the beginning of the Constitution. Ask a volunteer to read the preamble to the class. **Ask:** Which three words do you think are the most important part of the preamble? *(Answers may vary but should suggest that "We the People" are the most important words. This expresses the idea that the government will be based on the free choices of its citizens.)* Have students write a paragraph in which they "translate" the preamble into modern language. **AL** **ELL** Verbal/Linguistic

R Reading Skills

Defining Direct the students to read the subsections titled "Popular Sovereignty" and "The Nation Is a Republic." **Ask:** What is popular sovereignty? *(a form of government in which citizens are in control)* **Ask:** How does the preamble present the argument that the people should be in control of their government? *(The preamble states that the people hold the power and can establish a system of government for their own well-being.)* Discuss *republicanism* with students. **Ask:** What is a *republic*? *(a government in which people rule through chosen or elected representatives)* Why is this important? *(Answers may vary.)* Lead a class discussion in which students debate the merits of popular sovereignty and the republican form of government.

ANSWER, p. 206

TAKING NOTES: (1) popular sovereignty, (2) republican form of government, (3) limited government, (4) federalism, (5) separation of powers, (6) checks and balances, and (7) individual rights

---

---

netw⊕rks
There's More Online!
☑ **CHART/GRAPH**
 • Amending the Constitution
 • The Federal Court System
☑ **GAME**
 "We the People" Concentration
☑ **GRAPHIC ORGANIZER**
 Major Principles of the Constitution
☑ **VIDEO**

Lesson 1
Principles of the Constitution

ESSENTIAL QUESTION *Why do people form governments?*

IT MATTERS BECAUSE
The Constitution is the foundation of our country's government.

Our Constitution

GUIDING QUESTION *What basic principles of government are set forth by the Constitution?*

The United States Constitution presents the American solution to the challenge of government. This solution is based on seven key principles: (1) popular sovereignty, (2) a republican form of government, (3) limited government, (4) federalism, (5) separation of powers, (6) checks and balances, and (7) individual rights.

Popular Sovereignty

W The Constitution begins with an introduction, or preamble. With its first words—"We the People"—the preamble lays the foundation of the American system of government: **popular sovereignty** (PAH•pyuh•luhr SAHV•rihn•tee), or the authority of the people. The preamble makes clear that it is the people of the United States who hold the power and who establish a system of government for their own well-being.

The Nation Is a Republic

How do the people rule in the United States? The Constitution establishes a republican form of government. A republic is a government in which the people rule through elected representatives. Those representatives make laws and conduct government on behalf of the people. In general, the terms *republic* and *representative government* mean the same thing.

(tl) James Leynse/CORBIS (tcl) WireImage/Getty Images

Reading HELPDESK **CCSS**

Taking Notes: *Listing* RH.6–8.1
As you read, use a diagram like the one shown to identify the seven major principles on which the Constitution was based.

[Diagram: Major Principles]

206 The Constitution

Content Vocabulary (Tier 3 Words)
• popular sovereignty • concurrent power
• limited government • separation of
• enumerated power   powers
• reserved power • implied power

---

netw⊕rks *Online Teaching Options*

VIDEO

Checks, Balances, and the Exercise of Power

Making Connections Present the video that discusses the separation of powers and checks and balances. **Ask:** How do the separation of powers and the checks and balances system in the Constitution prevent power from building up in any one branch of government? *(Separating powers gives each branch different duties; checks and balances allow one branch to limit the power of the other two.)* **BL**

See page 203C for other online activities.

Limited Government

The Framers were wary of a government that might take away people's rights or favor certain groups. At the same time, they realized that the nation needed a stronger government than the Articles of Confederation had provided. Their goal was to establish **limited government**, in which the powers of government are strictly defined. A limited government has only those powers that are given to it by the people.

R

Federalism

The original thirteen states had fought hard to win independence from Great Britain. The Articles of Confederation protected that independence, but it failed to create a national government strong enough to deal with many challenges the young nation faced. The United States has a federal government, where the many state governments and the single federal government share power. This system is known as federalism.

The Constitution creates the federal system. It explains how powers are distributed among different levels of government. The Constitution spells out the powers given to Congress and establishes the executive and judicial branches.

The Constitution lists **enumerated** (ee•NOO•muh•ray•tuhd) **powers,** or those powers that are specifically given to Congress. Enumerated powers include the power to coin money, regulate interstate and foreign trade, maintain the armed forces, and create federal courts. The states cannot exercise these powers.

Reserved powers are those powers that belong to the states. The Constitution does not specifically list the reserved powers. The Tenth Amendment declares that all powers not specifically granted to the federal government "are reserved to the States." The reserved powers include the power to establish schools, pass marriage and divorce laws, and regulate trade within a state.

Under the Constitution, the federal government and the state governments share certain powers. These are the **concurrent** (kuhn•KUHR•hnt) **powers.** Examples of concurrent powers are the right to raise taxes, borrow money, provide for public welfare, and carry out criminal justice. Each state and the federal government can exercise these powers at the same time.

The power to coin money is an enumerated power. Congress also has the power to print currency, such as the paper bills shown here.

James Leynse/CORBIS

C

---

popular sovereignty the belief that government is subject to the will of the people
limited government government with limited powers strictly defined by law

enumerated power power specifically given Congress in the Constitution
reserved power power belonging only to the states

concurrent power power shared by the states and federal government

Lesson 1 **207**

GRAPHIC ORGANIZER

Taking Notes: *Listing:* Major Principles of the Constitution

Listing Introduce the Constitution as the document that established our nation's laws and rules. Explain that students will learn about the Constitution. Have students use the interactive graphic organizer to list the seven basic principles upon which the Constitution is based. **AL** **ELL**

See page 203C for other online activities.

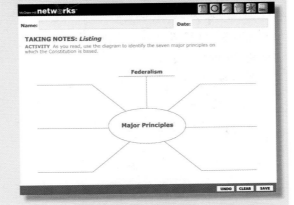

McGraw-Hill **networks**

Name: _____ Date: _____

TAKING NOTES: *Listing*
ACTIVITY As you read, use the diagram to identify the seven major principles on which the Constitution is based.

Federalism

Major Principles

UNDO   CLEAR   SAVE

R Reading Skills

Explaining Direct students to read the paragraph. Then ask a volunteer to explain the worries that the Framers had about government. **Ask:** Why did the Framers want to establish a limited government? *(to prevent the government from gaining too much power, as they thought Britain had)* Then read students the axiom "Power corrupts, and absolute power corrupts absolutely." **Ask:** Do you think this statement is true? Can even a democratic government have too much power? Lead a discussion in which students reflect on this point. Relate students' discussion to the Framers' concerns about limited government.

C Critical Thinking Skills

Categorizing Discuss with students the powers that are granted to the federal government and the powers that belong to the states. **Ask:** What is *federalism*? *(the division of power between a federal government and the state governments)* Make space for two lists on the board. **Ask:** What powers does the federal government have? *(Answers should include the power to coin money, to regulate interstate and foreign trade, to handle foreign policy, to maintain the armed forces, and to create and operate federal courts.)* **Ask:** What powers do the states have? *(Answers should include the power to set up school systems, police, and other emergency powers; the power to handle marriages and divorces, etc. Students may also mention some powers not referred to in the text, such as the power to license drivers.)* **Ask:** What powers are shared concurrently by the federal government and the states? *(Answers should include the power to tax, to borrow money, to operate court systems, to provide for the public welfare, etc.)* Lead a discussion in which students continue to think of other powers of government that they know of, and categorize these powers according to whether the power is a power of the federal government, the state, or is shared concurrently.

Content Background Knowledge

- A federal system is not the same as a confederation. In a confederation, states join together as allies with related interests, but each state is still sovereign unto itself. In a federal system of government, the states' power is subordinate to that of the national government, although the states still retain certain powers of their own.
- A federal system of government has a stronger centralized government than a confederacy does.
- Not only did the young American nation form a confederacy (under the Articles of Confederation), but the states of the South also formed a confederacy when they seceded, bringing about the Civil War.

Wirelmage/Getty Images

C Critical Thinking Skills

Predicting Consequences Discuss the separation of powers and checks and balances with the class. **Ask: Why did the Founders provide for power to be separated among different branches of government?** *(They wanted to make sure that no one branch had too much power.)* **Ask: What is a possible consequence of the separation of powers?** *(In democracies with separation of powers, governmental decisions are often made and executed very slowly.)* Lead a discussion in which the class explores what consequences might result if a particular branch of government had too much unchecked power.

V Visual Skills

Creating Charts Have students make a chart that shows the three branches of government. **Ask: Which branch of government is the least democratic? Explain your answer.** *(The judicial branch; federal judges are appointed, not elected.)* **Why is it important for democracies to have a branch of government that is not democratic?** *(In theory, the judicial branch should protect minorities from oppression by the majorities who have more power in the other branches.)* **Visual/Spatial**

The right to carry out criminal justice is a concurrent power, and the federal government and the states have their own justice systems.

While states have their own laws and powers, the Constitution is "the supreme Law of the Land." If a state law **contradicts** the Constitution or federal law, the Constitution or federal law prevails. This is stated in Article VI, Clause 2, of the Constitution—the "Supremacy Clause."

Separation of Powers

V

To make sure no person or group in government has too much power, the Constitution provides for a **separation of powers**. This means the Constitution separates the legislative, executive, and judicial powers of government. It then places these powers in three different branches of government. Each branch has different—and limited—powers, duties, and responsibilities.

Checks and Balances

The Framers did more than separate the powers of government. They set up a system of checks and balances. Under this system, each branch of government can check, or limit, the power of the other branches. This system helps maintain a balance in the power of the three branches.

Here is an example of how the system of checks and balances works: Congress (legislative branch) has the power to pass a law. If the president (executive branch) disagrees with the law, he or she can reject it through the presidential power of the veto. This veto power checks the power of Congress. At the same time, Congress can override the veto. This checks the power of the executive branch.

C

The United States Supreme Court (judicial branch) also has important checks on the other branches. The Supreme Court has the power to interpret the Constitution and to decide whether or not actions by the legislative and executive branches are allowed.

Congress can check decisions made by the courts by beginning the process of changing the Constitution itself. For example, the Supreme Court ruled in the 1857 *Dred Scott* v. *Sandford* decision that enslaved African Americans were not citizens. In 1866 Congress proposed the Fourteenth Amendment. The amendment was meant to grant full citizenship to formerly enslaved African Americans. When ratified by the states in 1868, the Fourteenth Amendment had the effect of overruling the *Dred Scott* decision.

There are several other ways in which the branches of government check and balance one another. The diagram on the next page shows the system in detail.

Reading **HELP**DESK **CCSS**

separation of powers a principle by which powers are divided among different branches of government to make sure no one branch has too much power

Academic Vocabulary (Tier 2 Words)

contradict to go against or state the opposite

---

network Online Teaching Options

IMAGE

The U.S. Department of the Treasury

Analyzing Images Use the interactive image of the U.S. Department of the Treasury to discuss enumerated powers. **Ask: Why was the power of coining money and regulating trade given to Congress?** *(The Articles of Confederation gave these powers to the states and this proved to be a weakness of that government.)* **Visual/Spatial**

See page 203C for other online activities.

McGraw-Hill **networks** The U.S. Department of the Treasury

The Department of the Treasury (DOT) was established in 1789. It is the division of the federal government that is responsible for fiscal (monetary) policy. Among its many functions, the DOT manufactures U.S. currency and supervises the nation's banks.

James Leynse/CORBIS

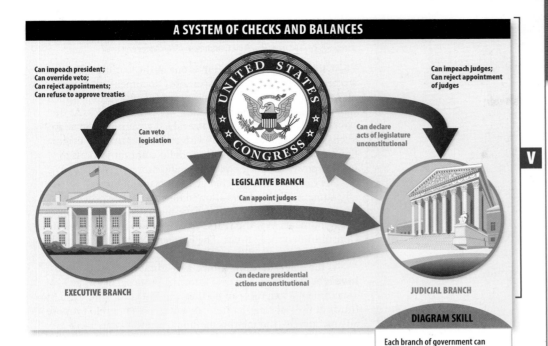

A SYSTEM OF CHECKS AND BALANCES

UNITED STATES
CONGRESS

LEGISLATIVE BRANCH

Can impeach president;
Can override veto;
Can reject appointments;
Can refuse to approve treaties

Can veto
legislation

Can declare
acts of legislature
unconstitutional

Can impeach judges;
Can reject appointment
of judges

Can appoint judges

Can declare presidential
actions unconstitutional

EXECUTIVE BRANCH

JUDICIAL BRANCH

DIAGRAM SKILL

Each branch of government can check and balance the power of the other branches in several ways.

1 IDENTIFYING What is an example of a legislative branch check on the judicial branch?

2 CRITICAL THINKING
Analyzing Do you think the different branches of government are truly balanced? Why or why not?

Individual Rights

The Constitution that the Framers wrote in Philadelphia in 1787 did not have a Bill of Rights. These ten amendments became part of the Constitution in 1791. They guarantee basic freedoms and liberties including:

- Freedom of religion
- Freedom of speech and of the press
- Freedom to assemble in groups and to protest against the government
- The right to bear arms
- The right to a speedy and public trial by jury
- The right to be free from unreasonable searches and seizures by the government
- Freedom from "cruel and unusual" punishments.

Since 1791, other constitutional amendments have expanded on the rights of the American people. For example, amendments have abolished slavery, defined citizenship, guaranteed "equal protection of the law" for all people, and guaranteed the right to vote for people aged 18 and older. Amendments have also authorized the direct, popular election of senators.

☑ **PROGRESS CHECK**

Describing What is the purpose of the system of checks and balances?

Lesson 1   **209**

V Visual Skills

Analyzing Images Discuss the diagram "A System of Checks and Balances." **Ask:** Based on this diagram, how do you think the legislative branch could stop the president (who is part of the executive branch) when legislators disagree with a policy or an action? *(Legislators can veto legislation that the president supports, refuse to approve treaties, refuse to provide a budget for presidentially supported activities, reject the appointment of judges, etc.)* **Visual/Spatial**

C1 Critical Thinking Skills

Making Connections Discuss that these first 10 amendments to the Constitution are called the Bill of Rights. **Ask:** What are ways that you have exercised some of these rights? *(Answers will vary but should give specific examples of how someone might exercise a right.)* Lead the class in a discussion of how the rights of the individual can affect daily life and why these rights are important. **ELL**

W Writing Skills

Argument Remind students that the Bill of Rights guarantees basic freedoms and liberties. **Ask:** What are some of the individual rights protected under the Bill of Rights? *(Answers may include freedom of speech, freedom of religion, the right to bear arms, and the right to a speedy public trial.)* Have students pick one right that is especially meaningful to them and write a paragraph explaining why they believe the right they have chosen is so important. **Verbal/Linguistic**

C2 Critical Thinking Skills

Identifying Central Issues Have students consider the different amendments to the Constitution that have been ratified over the years. **Ask:** What do most of these amendments have in common? *(Most of these amendments made the government more democratic by expanding the number of citizens who had access to basic civil rights such as voting.)*

Standard Venn Diagram: Federal System of Powers

Creating Visuals Give students the Venn diagram graphic organizer. Have them fill out the diagram, labeling one circle "Federal Powers" and the other circle "State Powers." Point out that the overlapping area should include those powers that the state and federal governments share concurrently. Then have students fill in the diagram. **AL** **Visual/Spatial**

See page 203C for other online activities.

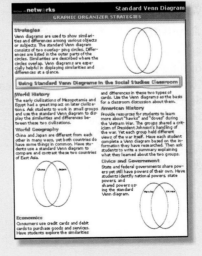

ANSWERS, p. 209

DIAGRAM SKILL

1. Congressional checks on the judicial branch include the power to reject nominees to the federal courts and to impeach and convict judges under certain circumstances.

2. **CRITICAL THINKING** Some students may say the system of checks and balances is truly balanced; others may argue that one branch has a more or less effective check. Students' answers will vary but should include information from the lesson to support whichever position they take.

☑ **PROGRESS CHECK** The system of checks and balances helps make sure that no branch of government acquires too much power over the others.

Principles of the Constitution

C Critical Thinking Skills

Contrasting Have students list ways that society is different from the time when the Constitution was written. **Ask: What are some laws that exist today that did not exist at the time the Constitution was written?** *(Answers may vary.)* Explain to students that it is necessary for the government to develop new laws to address changes in society over time.

R Reading Skills

Explaining After students have read the text, ask them to explain how the Constitution can still be effective almost 225 years after it was first created. **Ask: How is the Constitution a flexible document?** *(Answers should describe how the Constitution can be interpreted and changed.)*

Amending the Constitution

GUIDING QUESTION *How is the Constitution able to change over time?*

The United States Constitution is one of the world's oldest written Constitutions. It is also a short document compared to many other constitutions. Its clear, direct language has helped **C** support stable government for well over two centuries. At the same time, the Constitution has enabled government to adapt to changing times and to deal with challenges that the original Framers never dreamed of—from radio communications to nuclear power to space exploration and more.

The Constitution has changed as a result of formal amendment. The Framers allowed for this process when they wrote the Constitution. People have suggested many hundreds **R** of amendments over the years. Yet the nation has amended its Constitution only 27 times. The Framers deliberately made the amendment process difficult.

As the diagram below shows, amending the Constitution **involves** two steps. The first is formal proposal of an amendment. Congress can do this by two-thirds' vote. Also, two-thirds of the state legislatures can call a convention to propose an amendment, though this method has never been used.

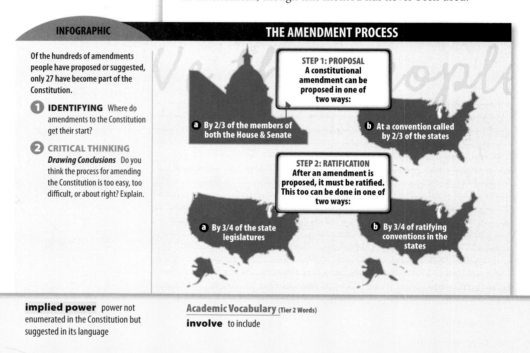

INFOGRAPHIC — **THE AMENDMENT PROCESS**

Of the hundreds of amendments people have proposed or suggested, only 27 have become part of the Constitution.

1 IDENTIFYING Where do amendments to the Constitution get their start?

2 CRITICAL THINKING *Drawing Conclusions* Do you think the process for amending the Constitution is too easy, too difficult, or about right? Explain.

STEP 1: PROPOSAL A constitutional amendment can be proposed in one of two ways:
- **a** By 2/3 of the members of both the House & Senate
- **b** At a convention called by 2/3 of the states

STEP 2: RATIFICATION After an amendment is proposed, it must be ratified. This too can be done in one of two ways:
- **a** By 3/4 of the state legislatures
- **b** By 3/4 of ratifying conventions in the states

implied power power not enumerated in the Constitution but suggested in its language

Academic Vocabulary (Tier 2 Words)
involve to include

networks *Online Teaching Options*

CHART

Amending the Constitution

Analyzing Charts Present the interactive chart that discusses amending the Constitution. **Ask: How can the Constitution deal with modern problems that the Framers could never have imagined?** *(The Framers made it possible to amend the Constitution so it can change as the country changes.)* **BL** Visual/Spatial

See page 203C for other online activities.

McGraw netw@rks™ — Amending the Constitution

Proposal	Ratification
Proposed amendments may be recommended by:	*Proposed amendments are adopted if approved by:*
OR	OR

ANSWERS, p. 210

INFOGRAPHIC

1. Amendments are proposed in Congress or when two-thirds of the state legislatures call for a constitutional convention.

2. CRITICAL THINKING Students' answers will vary but should include information from the lesson to support whichever position they take.

R1 The second step in the amendment process is ratification. Ratification of an amendment requires approval by three-fourths of the states. States can ratify the amendment at either a state convention or through a vote by the state legislature.

Amendments have brought significant changes to the nation. In addition to protecting our rights, amendments have extended the right to vote to a larger share of the population. The Fifteenth Amendment sought to ensure that African American men would have the right to vote. The Nineteenth Amendment extended voting rights to women. The Twenty-Fourth Amendment outlawed poll taxes, giving more people the ability to vote. The Twenty-Sixth Amendment lowered the voting age to 18.

Formal amendment is one way the Constitution has changed. The language of the Constitution has also been subject to different interpretations.

For example, over history, Congress has claimed for itself certain **implied** (ihm•PLYD) **powers**. These are powers that are suggested but not directly stated in the Constitution. The source of the implied powers is Article I, Section 8 of the Constitution. Here is found the "necessary and proper clause," or the "elastic clause." This clause directs Congress to "make all Laws which shall be necessary and proper" for carrying out its duties.

Also in Article I, Section 8, is the "commerce clause." This gives Congress power to "regulate Commerce with foreign Nations, and among the several States." Congress has used this clause to expand its powers into areas, such as the regulation of television, that do appear in the Constitution.

✅ **PROGRESS CHECK**

Calculating How many constitutional amendments have been ratified?

Thinking Like a HISTORIAN

Understanding Cause and Effect

Over the course of American history, some unwritten customs of government have become so strong that they seem to have the effect of law. For example, until the 25th Amendment, which was ratified in 1967, the Constitution did not specify that the vice president would assume the office of president in the event of a president's death. Yet on eight occasions, that is exactly what happened. Each time the custom was applied, it acquired more force. For more information about understanding cause and effect, read *Thinking Like a Historian*.

R1 Reading Skills

Explaining After students have read the section about amending the Constitution, remind them that the Constitution has been amended only 27 times. Ask students to explain the amendment process, either verbally or in a diagram. **Ask: Who can propose an amendment to the Constitution?** *(either Congress or state legislatures)* **AL**

C Critical Thinking Skills

Making Connections Discuss which amendments to the Constitution have significantly changed the nation. Have students preview the Constitution for ideas. **Ask: Which Constitutional amendments significantly changed aspects of life?** *(Answers may vary but might include voting rights, prohibition, free speech, and freeing enslaved people.)*

T Technology Skills

Using Digital Tools Have students use video cameras such as the cameras in cell phones to record an interview with an elderly family member. Encourage students to ask their family members what they remember about the ways in which the Constitution has changed in their lifetimes. Have students share the video interviews with the class and/or post them on the class Web site. **AL**

R2 Reading Skills

Identifying Review with students the meaning of the word *imply*. **Ask: What three clauses are the source for the idea of implied power?** *(the necessary and proper clause, the elastic clause, and the commerce clause)* **What is the effect on the Constitution of these three clauses?** *(The "necessary and proper clause" allows Congress to make laws to carry out its duties. The "elastic clause" and the "commerce clause" have been interpreted to give Congress broad implied powers.)* **BL**

Have students complete the Lesson 1 Review.

LESSON 1 REVIEW (CCSS)

Review Vocabulary (Tier 3 Words)

1. Write a paragraph in which you explain the difference between the following: RH.6–8.4, WHST.6–8.4
   a. enumerated power   b. reserved power
   c. concurrent power   d. implied power

2. Explain the significance of the following terms: RH.6–8.4
   a. popular sovereignty   b. limited government

Answer the Guiding Questions

3. *Explaining* What was the challenge that the Framers faced when setting out to write the Constitution, and how did they meet it? RH.6–8.2

4. *Discussing* Why do you think the Framers made the Constitution difficult to amend? RH.6–8.3

5. **ARGUMENT** Should Congress have the power to interpret the Constitution? Write a paragraph in which you argue for or against the wide application of the implied powers. WHST.6–8.1, WHST.6–8.10

Lesson 1   **211**

CLOSE & REFLECT

Discussing Have students consider the idea of "implied power" in terms of their own lives. **Ask: Which people in your life have power over you?** *(Parents/guardians, teachers, coaches, babysitters, etc.)* **What powers do the authorities in your life have that are explicit (spelled out)? What powers do they have that are implied? What powers do they share concurrently?** *(Students' answers will vary.)* **BL**

LESSON 1 REVIEW ANSWERS

1. Enumerated powers are granted to the federal government in the Constitution. Reserved powers are retained by the states. The federal government and the states share concurrent powers. Finally, some congressional powers are implied but not stated, as under the "necessary and proper clause."

2. **a.** Popular sovereignty means that power to govern belongs to the people and government gets its authority from the people. **b.** A limited government's powers are defined and restricted by law . The U.S. government is limited with checks and balances.

3. The Framers needed to form a government that would meet the needs of the country better than the Articles of Confederation did. They wanted to avoid abuses and threats to freedom that a powerful government might present. The Framers established a democratic republic, allowing citizens to participate in government and elect representatives. It is based on seven basic principles: **(1)** popular sovereignty, **(2)** republicanism, **(3)** limited government, **(4)** federalism, **(5)** separation of powers, **(6)** checks and balances, and **(7)** individual rights.

4. The Framers made the Constitution difficult to amend so that it could not be changed to reflect a whim or a passing fad in public opinion.

5. Students may suggest that Congress should not have power to interpret the Constitution because it would give the legislative branch too much power. Others could suggest that Congress should have the power to interpret the Constitution because it is the lawmaking body of the federal government.

ANSWER, p. 211

✅ **PROGRESS CHECK** Twenty-seven amendments have been ratified.

ENGAGE

Bellringer Have students discuss a sports team with which they are familiar. Have them identify the role each player fills. **Ask: How are the different branches of government like the different positions on a team?** *(Each branch of the United States government has separate duties.)* **Interpersonal**

TEACH & ASSESS

R Reading Skills

Listing After reading, have students create a two-column list, one column entitled "Senate" and the other entitled "House of Representatives." Discuss the legislative branch. Ask students to compile a list of information for both houses. **Ask: How many people are in the House? The Senate? How are those numbers determined? What are other guidelines about the two houses?** *(House of Representatives: 435 members; number from each state determined by population in each state. Senate: 100 members; each state has two senators. House apportions seats every 10 years, and members serve two-year terms. Senators serve six-year terms.)* **AL Visual/Spatial**

C Critical Thinking Skills

Identifying Central Issues Direct students to read the subsection on the nation's legislature. **Ask: Why is it important for people from every part of the United States to be represented fairly in the legislature?** *(Fair representation is the basis for democratic government. If representation were not fair, people from one part of the country might have more political power than people from another part of the country.)* **Ask: Do you think that every part of the United States is represented fairly in Congress? Why or why not?** Encourage the class to explore this issue fully. *(Answers will vary but should be well thought out.)* **BL Interpersonal**

ANSWER, p. 212

TAKING NOTES: Legislative: Makes the laws; Executive: Carries out the laws; Judicial: Interprets the laws; Comparing/contrasting: Each branch has a different role and makes sure the other branches are maintaining the balance of power.

networks *There's More Online!*
- ☑ **BIOGRAPHY** Sandra Day O'Connor
- ☑ **CHART/GRAPH** Landmark Supreme Court Cases
- ☑ **GAME** Crossword Puzzle
- ☑ **GRAPHIC ORGANIZER** Branches of Government
- ☑ **SLIDE SHOW** The Oval Office

Lesson 2
Government and the People

ESSENTIAL QUESTION *How do new ideas change the way people live?*

IT MATTERS BECAUSE
In a nation where the people rule, citizens must understand their government and their rights and responsibilities.

The Federal Government

GUIDING QUESTION *What are the three branches of government?*

To achieve a separation of powers, the Constitution divides the federal government into three branches. They are called the legislative, executive, and judicial branches.

The Nation's Legislature

Congress is the legislative branch of government. It has two houses—the House of Representatives and the Senate. Currently the House has 435 voting members and 6 nonvoting delegates from the District of Columbia, Puerto Rico, Guam, American Samoa, the Virgin Islands, and the Northern Mariana Islands. Representatives, who must be at least 25 years old, serve two-year terms. There is no limit to the number of terms a person can serve.

The number of representatives from each state is based on the state's population. States with more people have more representatives in Congress, though every state has at least one representative. The federal government resets each state's share of the 435 House seats every 10 years. A state's number of representatives may go up or down depending on population changes.

Reading **HELP**DESK (CCSS)

Taking Notes: *Summarizing* WHST.6–8.2
Write a short summary of the job of each branch of government as you read along. Then compare how each branch differs from the other two.

212 *The Constitution*

Content Vocabulary (Tier 3 Words)
- **judicial review** • **naturalization**
- **due process**
- **equal protection**

---

networks   *Online Teaching Options*

VIDEO

The New Congress Designs a Bill of Rights

Informative/Explanatory As students watch the lesson video, have them listen carefully to the discussion of why James Madison was against having a Bill of Rights. Explain that Madison had three reasons for being against the Bill of Rights: (1) he worried that listing these rights implied that the federal government had more power than it ought to have; (2) he worried that words could not protect rights; and (3) he worried that rights not mentioned in the Bill of Rights could later be denied by government. Have students pick one of these reasons and write an essay explaining why it was a legitimate concern. **BL Visual/Spatial**

See page 203D for other online activities.

The Senate has 100 senators, two from each state. Senators must be 30 years old, and they serve six-year terms. Only a third of the seats come up for election every two years. As with House members, there are no term limits for Senators.

Article I of the Constitution describes the role of Congress. Congress makes the nation's laws. These laws are not just rules for behavior. Congress passes laws that impose taxes, authorize the spending of money, and create government programs. Congress also has the job of declaring war.

Both houses of Congress must agree on a bill, or proposed law. Once both houses do this, the bill goes to the president. If the president signs the bill, it becomes law.

The Executive Branch

The executive branch is led by the president and vice president, who each serve four-year terms. It also includes the president's cabinet, or top advisers, and many other offices, departments, and agencies. The executive branch's main job is to **administrate,** or carry out, the laws passed by Congress. The president does, however, propose laws to Congress.

The president has many other powers laid out in Article II of the Constitution. These include directing foreign policy, naming ambassadors, and negotiating treaties with other nations. The president is also the commander-in-chief of the armed forces.

The Judicial Branch

Article III of the Constitution establishes a Supreme Court and allows for Congress to create lower courts. Congress has established district courts, which are the main trial courts for the federal government, and appeals courts, which hear cases on appeal from lower courts. There are several other types of federal courts as well. For example, there are special federal courts for hearing bankruptcy cases. Bankruptcy is a legal process for people or businesses that cannot pay off their debts.

The Supreme Court is at the top of the United States legal system. It rules on only the most difficult legal questions, and its rulings are never appealed.

The Supreme Court also has the power of **judicial review.** This means that the Court can review the actions of the executive and legislative branches to determine whether or not they violate the Constitution.

The Oval Office is the official office of the president of the United States.

AP/Getty Images

judicial review power of the court to judge whether or not actions of other branches are constitutional

Academic Vocabulary (Tier 2 Words)

administrate to carry out

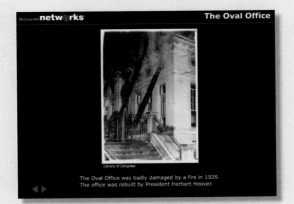

R1 Reading Skills

Summarizing Have students read the section titled "The Executive Branch." **Ask:** What are the roles played by the president and other members of the executive branch? *(The president is the chief executive officer of the country. He or she makes sure that Congress's laws are properly carried out and also makes decisions as Commander in Chief of the nation's military. Other executive officers, such as the cabinet members, assist the president in carrying out laws.)* If time permits, have students make a list of functions of the executive branch and illustrate their lists with photos and examples drawn from newspapers, news magazines, and online news. BL ELL Visual/Spatial

R2 Reading Skills

Expressing After students have read about all three government branches, ask students if they think that the branches of government are equal. **Ask:** If you think the branches are not equal, which branch do you think has more power than the others? What do you think could be done to rebalance the branches? Students should support their answers with details from the text.

Content Background Knowledge

- The president and vice president are elected, but the members of the president's cabinet are appointed by the president.
- The judicial branch is considered the least democratic branch of government because federal judges are appointed by the president, not elected.

SLIDE SHOW

The Oval Office

Discussing Launch the slide show presentation from the interactive images of the Oval Office. Discuss the executive branch. **Ask:** Whose office is this? *(the president's)* What is the role of the executive branch as defined in the Constitution? *(to administer the laws passed by Congress, conduct foreign affairs, negotiate treaties, and act as commander-in-chief of the armed forces)* BL ELL Visual/Spatial

See page 203D for other online activities.

McGraw-Hill **networks** The Oval Office

Library of Congress

The Oval Office was badly damaged by a fire in 1929. The office was rebuilt by President Herbert Hoover.

Government and the People

R **Reading Skills**

Explaining After students have read the text, discuss that there are nine members of the Supreme Court: the chief justice of the United States and eight associate justices. **Ask**: What is judicial review? *(the power of the Court to review actions of the executive and legislative branches to determine if they are constitutional.)* Ask students if they can name any justices.
AL **ELL**

W **Writing Skills**

Informative/Explanatory Discuss with students that due process and equal protection are two of the most important ideas in the Constitution. Discuss the constitutional amendments that provide these rights. **Ask:** How do due process and equal protection help guarantee your constitutional rights? *(Due process prohibits the government from restricting or taking away your rights unless it follows very strict rules. Equal protection means that each person will be treated by the law the same as every other person.)* **Ask:** What are some of the basic freedoms that are guaranteed by the Constitution? *(Answers will vary but may include freedom of speech and the press; the right to bear arms; the right to a speedy, public trial; and freedom from cruel and unusual punishment.)* Then have students work together in pairs or small groups to research stories in the news that relate to due process and/or equal protection. Have students prepare a class display or Web site in which they provide the news story, along with an annotation or a caption analyzing how the story relates to these constitutional issues. **BL** **Visual/Spatial** **Interpersonal**

BIOGRAPHY

**Sandra Day O'Connor
(1930 –)**

In his 1980 election campaign, Ronald Reagan promised to name the first woman justice to the Supreme Court. During his first year in office, a vacancy opened on the Court. Reagan chose Sandra Day O'Connor, an Arizona appeals court judge, to fill the vacancy. O'Connor served as a justice until 2006. In an interview, she discussed the increased opportunities for women she had witnessed: "When I went to law school, about 1 percent of all law students were women. And last year, over 50 percent were."

▶ **CRITICAL THINKING**
Describing What view does Sandra Day O'Connor express about the progress of women's opportunities? Explain.

Members are nominated by the president and approved by Congress. Today the Supreme Court is made up of nine justices—the chief justice and eight associate justices. The Constitution gave Congress the power to set this number. Justices serve no fixed term. Unless removed for bad behavior, they stay on the bench until they retire or die. **R**

The main duties of the justices are to hear and rule on cases they choose from among the thousands that are presented to them each year. They listen to arguments, and then they must present and explain their decision—called the Court's opinion. This opinion is then used by lower courts in making their rulings.

☑ **PROGRESS CHECK**

Identifying What parts of the Constitution discuss the establishment and duties of the three branches of our federal government?

What it Means to be a Citizen

GUIDING QUESTION *What are the rights and elements of participation of American citizens?*

Citizens of the United States enjoy certain rights and liberties. Being a citizen also involves some responsibilities.

Our Rights

Our rights fall into three main categories: The right to be protected from unfair government actions, the right to be treated equally with others, and the right to enjoy basic freedoms.

Our government must treat people fairly and according to clear rules. This is spelled out in the Fifth Amendment, which says no one shall "be deprived of life, liberty, or property, without due process of law." **Due process** means the government must follow established procedures in taking action against a citizen.

The Fourteenth Amendment guarantees all people **equal protection** of the laws. This principle means all people, regardless of race, religion, or political beliefs, must receive the same treatment under the law.

The First Amendment outlines many of our basic freedoms. These include freedom of religion, freedom of speech and of the press, freedom of assembly, and freedom to petition the government. The Framers knew that in a free society in which the people rule, people must be able to share ideas.

 W

Wally McNamee/CORBIS

Reading **HELP**DESK **CCSS**

due process the legal rules and procedures the government must observe before depriving a person of life, liberty, or property
equal protection the equal application of the law regardless of a person's race, religion, political beliefs, or other qualities

naturalization the process of becoming a citizen of another country

Academic Vocabulary (Tier 2 Words)
diminish reduce, make smaller

netw⊙rks *Online Teaching Options*

IMAGE

Voting Rights

Discussing Use the interactive image about voting rights to recall the voting rights that have been established. Explain that voting is a major responsibility. **Ask:** What happens if you neglect your responsibilities? *(If citizens are not actively responsible, the quality of government and society will be diminished.)* Why is voter turnout higher in some years than in other years? *(In some years, the presidential election or a policy issue gets people's attention. In other years, there may be less interest in the election or issues.)* **BL** **Visual/Spatial**

See page 203D for other online activities.

McGraw-Hill **netw⊙rks**
Voting Rights

William Hogarth/Getty Images

ANSWERS, p. 214

CRITICAL THINKING O'Connor said that women's opportunities had increased because from the time she went to law school until the time of the interview, the percentage of women law students grew from about 1 percent to more than 50 percent.

☑ **PROGRESS CHECK** The first three articles create the three branches of the federal government: Article I, the legislative branch; Article II, the executive branch, and Article III, the judicial branch.

Our rights and freedoms have some limits. For example, government can limit our freedom of speech or our right to hold a protest if it threatens public health or safety. Also, one person's exercise of his or her rights cannot take away the rights of other people. Limits on rights and freedoms must be applied equally to all people.

The Duties and Responsibilities of Citizenship

A citizen is a person who owes loyalty to a nation and is entitled to its protection. For the most part, anyone born on U.S. soil is automatically a U.S. citizen. U.S. soil includes American territories and military bases around the world.

Citizenship is also granted to anyone born outside of the United States if one parent is a U.S. citizen. A person who was born in another country can become a citizen through the process called **naturalization** (NA•chuh•ruh•lih•ZAY•shuhn).

With citizenship comes duties and responsibilities. Duties are things we must do, while responsibilities are things we should do. Citizens have a duty to obey the law, to pay taxes, and to sit on a jury if called. Another key duty is defending the country. All males 18 and older must register with the government in case they are needed to serve in the military.

Responsibilities are things a person should do, though they may not be required by law. However, if people do not fulfill their responsibilities as citizens, the quality of our government and communities is **diminished.** Exercising the right to vote is probably the most important responsibility of a citizen. Voting allows you to participate in government and guide its direction.

☑ **PROGRESS CHECK**

Contrasting What is the difference between a duty and a responsibility? Why should citizens fulfill both?

THEN

NOW

Early in United States history, voting was generally limited to white men who owned property. Today, the right to vote is available to most citizens 18 years of age or older.

▶ **CRITICAL THINKING**
Drawing Conclusions Why do you think the people of the United States have steadily expanded the eligibility to vote?

(t) William Hogarth/ Getty Images
(b) Zach Boyden-Holmes/Getty Images

LESSON 2 REVIEW (CCSS)

Review Vocabulary (Tier 3 Words)

1. Write a brief paragraph that includes the following terms: RH.6–8.4, WHST.6–8.4
   a. due process   b. equal protection

2. Explain the significance of these terms: RH.6–8.4
   a. judicial review   b. naturalization

Answer the Guiding Questions

3. ***Summarizing*** How does a person become a citizen of the United States? RH.6–8.3

4. ***Describing*** What are the three branches of government, and what are their roles in the government? RH.6–8.2

5. ***Explaining*** Explain how our freedoms help people become more effective and knowledgeable citizens. RH.6–8.2

6. **NARRATIVE** In the United States, voting is considered a responsibility. Should the United States make voting a duty and require all citizens to vote? Write a short essay that supports your position. WHST.6–8.1, WHST.6–8.10

Lesson 2   **215**

LESSON 2 REVIEW ANSWERS

1. **a.** The Constitution protects many types of individual rights, including due process and equal protection. Due process means that the government has to follow certain rules before it can act against a person. **b.** Equal protection means that everyone must be treated equally under the law, regardless of race, religion, or other factors.

2. **a.** Judicial review is the power of the judicial branch to review the acts of the other branches to make sure they meet constitutional standards. It is one of the checks in our checks and balances system. **b.** Naturalization is a process by which a person who is not an American citizen can become an American citizen.

3. A person can be a citizen by being born on U.S. soil or by having a parent who is a citizen. People who

move to this country can become citizens by a process called naturalization.

4. The three branches of the government are the legislative branch, which makes the laws; the executive branch, which carries out the laws; and the judicial branch, which decides whether actions of the other two branches are constitutional.

5. Answers will vary but may include freedom of speech, freedom of the press, and freedom of assembly, which all support the open exchange of information and opinion, and help citizens to be more knowledgeable and therefore more effective.

6. Answers may vary. Essays should consider the pros and cons of requiring all citizens to vote.

R **Reading Skills**

Listing After students have read the text, ask them to create a list of different ways a person can become a U.S. citizen. **Ask: Are people born on U.S. soil citizens?** *(yes)* **How can a person who is a citizen of another country become a U.S. citizen?** *(If one of that person's parents was a U.S. citizen, the person is also a U.S. citizen; if not, the person can go through the naturalization process.)*

T **Technology Skills**

Using Digital Tools Discuss the duties and responsibilities of American citizens. **Ask: What is the difference between a duty and a responsibility?** *(A duty is mandatory while a responsibility is not.)* **Ask: What are some duties Americans have?** *(Answers will vary but may include obeying laws, paying taxes, possibly defending the nation, and serving on a jury if called.)* Have students use word processing software to make a chart showing the duties and responsibilities of citizenship.

C **Critical Thinking Skills**

Making Connections Have students make a list of patriotic songs that they know. **Ask: What rights and duties of citizens appear in these songs? Why do you think that people write patriotic songs? How do songs help people to be better citizens?** *(Answers will vary, but students should justify their answers.)* **AL** **ELL** Auditory/Musical

Have students complete the Lesson 2 Review.

CLOSE & REFLECT

Speculating Tell students that although voting is a responsibility of citizenship, voting turnout during elections is often low. Many people choose not to vote. **Ask: Why do you think some people choose not to vote?** *(People often say they do not have time, they do not know enough about the candidates or the issues, or they do not like any of the choices.)* **What might happen if citizens do not meet their responsibilities, educate themselves, and vote?** *(Our system depends on citizen participation, and if citizens do not participate, the whole system could be subject to corruption or manipulation.)*

ANSWERS, p. 215

CRITICAL THINKING The United States is a representative democracy. That means citizens choose representatives by voting. The more inclusive the right to vote is, the more representative and better able the government will be to address concerns of all people.

☑ **PROGRESS CHECK** A duty is something a person must do. A responsibility is something a person should do. Citizens should fulfill both their duties and responsibilities as part of being an active citizen, taking part in government and their communities. By taking part, citizens help protect the Constitutional rights guaranteed to them and other citizens.

CHAPTER REVIEW ACTIVITY

Have students create a chart similar to the one below showing the seven main ideas of the United States Constitution. Then have students write a definition/explanation of each idea in their own words. Call on volunteers to provide examples, again using their own words, of how each idea is present in our government system.

Main Ideas of U.S. Constitution	
popular sovereignty	The people of a country control the government and give it the powers to govern.
republicanism	People rule through elected officials. In the U.S., citizens choose their government by voting.
limited government	The powers of government are restricted by and subject to the rule of law. For example, before you can be convicted of certain crimes, the government must give you a trial by jury and must follow procedures that make sure you get a fair trial.
federalism	Power is shared between the federal government and states. For example, the U.S. Congress has the sole power to declare war. States cannot declare war.
separation of powers	Powers of government are divided among the legislative, executive, and judicial branches to prevent any branch from becoming too powerful. The president cannot make laws.
checks and balances	Each branch of government can prevent the others from becoming too powerful. The Supreme Court can strike down laws that it determines are unconstitutional, but Congress can pass a new law.
individual rights	Basic rights and freedoms, such as freedom of speech, are guaranteed in the Constitution. For example, the government cannot generally stop someone from standing on a street corner and making a speech.

REVIEW THE ENDURING UNDERSTANDING

Review the chapter's Enduring Understanding with students.

- *Governments are formed to establish and maintain order within a society.*

Discuss with students that not all forms of disorder are unwelcome in a democratic society. For example, political campaigns and rallies can be very disorderly, as can political protests.

Write your answers on a separate piece of paper.

1 **Exploring the Essential Questions**   WHST.6–8.2, WHST.6–8.9

INFORMATIVE/EXPLANATORY After gaining independence, Americans were concerned about the new government having too much power. Write an essay in which you explain the measures taken by the Framers of the Constitution to prevent the government from becoming too powerful. Consider different features of the Constitution and Bill of Rights.

2 **21st Century Skills**   WHST.6–8.2, WHST.6–8.9

CREATING A PUBLIC SERVICE ANNOUNCEMENT Recall what you have read about the duties and responsibilities of citizenship. Write a public service announcement that stresses the key role citizens play in our society. Address the difference between duties and responsibilities, and explain why both are important. Link the need for all citizens to do their part with the idea that in the United States, the people rule.

3 **Thinking Like a Historian**   RH.6–8.1

ANALYZING AND INTERPRETING INFORMATION Create a graphic organizer such as the one shown that shows the three branches of the federal government. Add details about how one branch acts as a check for the other two.

LEGISLATIVE

EXECUTIVE   JUDICIAL

4 **Visual Literacy**   RH.6–8.7

ANALYZING MAPS The Constitution authorized the federal government to determine the population, or take a census, every 10 years. This map shows the results of the first census in 1790. The count included states and future states. Under the Constitution, what states or future states would have the fewest representatives in Congress based on the 1790 population figures? Explain how you arrived at your answer.

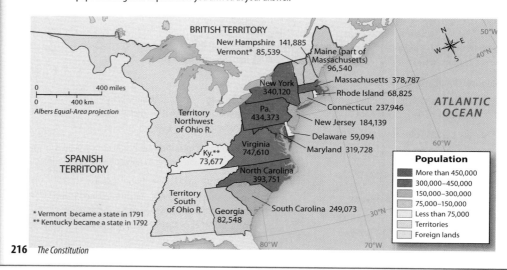

BRITISH TERRITORY
New Hampshire 141,885
Vermont* 85,539
Maine (part of Massachusetts) 96,540
New York 340,120
Massachusetts 378,787
Rhode Island 68,825
Connecticut 237,946
Pa. 434,373
New Jersey 184,139
Delaware 59,094
Territory Northwest of Ohio R.
Virginia 747,610
Maryland 319,728
Ky.** 73,677
SPANISH TERRITORY
North Carolina 393,751
Territory South of Ohio R.
Georgia 82,548
South Carolina 249,073
ATLANTIC OCEAN

0 400 miles
0 400 km
Albers Equal-Area projection

* Vermont became a state in 1791
** Kentucky became a state in 1792

Population
- More than 450,000
- 300,000–450,000
- 150,000–300,000
- 75,000–150,000
- Less than 75,000
- Territories
- Foreign lands

216   *The Constitution*

Now pose the following questions in a class discussion to apply these to the chapter.

What types of disorder are unwelcome in a democratic society? *(Forms of disorder that violate the rights of individuals, such as violent crime, or that form a public safety hazard, such as disorderly traffic, unsanitary sewers, or fires. Another type of disorder can occur if people are uneducated or cannot find the information they need. Still another type of disorder involves public crises such as epidemics and earthquakes.)*

What are some ways that governments promote order? *(Governments promote order by creating departments whose function is to address disorder: fire and police departments, libraries, schools, departments of motor vehicles, departments that provide aid to people in crisis, etc.)*

ACTIVITIES ANSWERS

Exploring the Essential Questions

1 The Framers established a government with sufficient power to meet the needs of the nation. At the same time, they included safeguards against abuse of power, ensuring that no branch of government would get too powerful and guaranteeing key rights and liberties.

21st Century Skills

2 Students should identify duties as required activities and responsibilities as generally optional. Both are necessary to a healthy society. The Framers recognized that a democratic republic requires active, involved, knowledgeable citizens.

REVIEW THE GUIDING QUESTIONS

Choose the best answer for each question.

RH.6–8.2
❶ What is federalism?

  A. a series of articles written in response to the *Federalist Papers*

  B. a major political party in the early years of the United States

  C. a set of powers that belong only to the federal government

  D. a system in which state and national governments share power

RH.6–8.4
❷ What are enumerated powers?

  F. powers belonging only to the states

  G. powers not directly mentioned in the Constitution

  H. powers belonging to Congress listed in the Constitution

  I. powers shared between the states and federal government

RH.6–8.1
❸ What is the name used for the first 10 constitutional amendments?

  A. the Articles of Confederation

  B. the Preamble

  C. the Declaration of Independence

  D. the Bill of Rights

RH.6–8.1
❹ Which are the two houses of Congress?

  F. the House of Commons and the House of Lords

  G. the Senate and the National Assembly

  H. the House of Representatives and the Senate

  I. the Legislative Council and the City Council

RH.6–8.2
❺ The way that two branches keep the third from gaining too much power is known as

  A. federalism.

  B. checks and balances.

  C. due process.

  D. naturalization.

RH.6–8.4
❻ What is due process?

  F. procedures the government must follow when taking any action against a person

  G. requirements a foreign-born person must fulfill to become a citizen of the United States

  H. procedures the federal government must follow when selecting a Supreme Court justice

  I. steps the members of the legislative branch must follow when creating laws

217

ASSESSMENT ANSWERS
Review the Guiding Questions

❶ **D** Federalism refers to the division of power between a strong federal government and the many individual state governments. This makes D the best answer.

❷ **H** Powers expressly given to Congress by the Constitution are enumerated powers. F refers to reserved powers, G to implied powers, and I to concurrent powers.

❸ **D** The first 10 amendments are called the Bill of Rights. The Articles of Confederation and the Declaration of Independence were not amended. The Preamble is the introduction to the Constitution.

❹ **H** The United States has a bicameral legislature with a Senate and a House of Representatives. The other choices are either incorrect or fictitious.

❺ **B** Choices A, C, and D relate to other parts of the Constitution. B, checks and balances, is the correct answer.

❻ **F** Choice G describes the process of naturalization. Choices H and I discuss other procedures. Choice F reflects the correct definition of due process.

Thinking Like a Historian

❸ Legislative: Can check executive veto by 2/3 vote of both houses. Can overrule judicial decision by proposing amendments. Executive: Can use veto power to reject laws. Can nominate members of the Supreme Court. Judicial: Can review acts of both the legislative and executive branches for compliance with the Constitution.

Visual Literacy

❹ Rhode Island, Delaware, and Kentucky had the lowest populations. They would have had the fewest members in the House of Representatives as this number is based on population.

Analyzing Documents

7 **C** The authors state that if people are not able to form a government based on reflection and choice, they will have a government based on accident and force.

8 **F** The authors imply that the people of the colonies are ready to form a government based on reflection and choice, and will set an example for the rest of the world.

Short Response

9 Franklin meant that a democratic republic takes work: the people must take part in and support the government in order for it to be successful.

10 A republic is a government in which the people choose their government officials, so it depends on the actions by and participation of the people to make it work.

Extended Response

11 Answers may vary but should provide well-reasoned arguments as to whether being able to amend a constitution is a positive or a negative feature. Positive arguments may note that the Constitution has been amended 27 times, allowing it to change with the times. A negative argument is that a bad idea could become popular and be added to the Constitution, which might harm freedom.

DBQ ANALYZING DOCUMENTS

"It has been … remarked that it seems to have been reserved to the people of this country … to decide … whether societies of men are really capable or not of establishing good government from reflection and choice, or whether they are forever destined to depend for their political constitutions on accident and force. If there be any truth in the remark, the crisis at which we are arrived may … be regarded as the era in which that decision is to be made; and a wrong election of the part we shall act may … deserve to be considered as the general misfortune of mankind."

Source: *The Federalist,* No. 1

RH.6–8.2

7 **Identifying Central Issues** According to the authors, what is the alternative to support for the Constitution?

A. good government based on reflection and choice

B. a return to the status of a British colony

C. government based on accident and force

D. the rise of an American Empire

RH.6–8.6, RH.6–8.10

8 **Inferring** What can you infer about the beliefs of the authors?

F. They thought the U.S. would be an example for the world.

G. They thought the British Empire was the worst in history.

H. They thought the people were not capable of making rational decisions.

I. They thought all mankind shared the same misfortunes.

SHORT RESPONSE

As Benjamin Franklin was leaving the last session of the Constitutional Congress, a woman asked, "Well, Doctor, what have we got: a republic or a monarchy?" Franklin answered, "A republic, if you can keep it."

RH.6–8.6, WHST.6–8.1

9 What do you think Franklin meant by his remark?

RH.6–8.2, WHST.6–8.2

10 What does he suggest about citizen rights and responsibilities in a republic?

EXTENDED RESPONSE

WHST.6–8.1, WHST.6–8.4

11 **Argument** The Constitution contains features that allow for it to be changed and to be interpreted. Do you consider this to be a strength or a weakness of the Constitution? Write an essay to explain your view.

Need Extra Help?

If You've Missed Question	1	2	3	4	5	6	7	8	9	10	11
Review Lesson	1	1	1	2	2	2	1	1	2	2	1, 2

---

networks *Online Teaching Options*

More Assessment Resources

The *Assess* tab in the online Teacher Lesson Center includes resources to help students improve their test-taking skills. It also contains many project-based rubrics to help you assess students' work.

THE CONSTITUTION of the UNITED STATES

The Constitution of the United States is truly a remarkable document. It was one of the first written constitutions in modern history. The Framers wanted to devise a plan for a strong central government that would unify the country, as well as preserve the ideals of the Declaration of Independence.

The entire text of the Constitution and its amendments follows. For easier study, those passages that have been set aside or changed by the adoption of amendments are printed in blue. Also included are explanatory notes that will help clarify the meaning of each article and section.

219

PRIMARY SOURCE

The Constitution of the United States

A copy of the Constitution can be found online in Networks™ in the Chapter 8: Chapter Resources at a Glance and in the Resource Library under "Primary Sources."

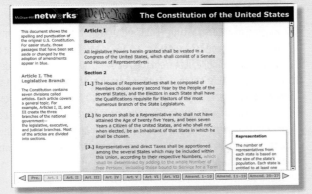

ENGAGE

🔔 **Bellringer** Point out the phrase "We the People" in the image of the Constitution on this opening page. Explain to students that these are the first three words of the Constitution.

Ask: **What is the significance of the phrase "We the People"?** (*Answers may include: These words show that the Constitution belongs to the citizens--the people--of the United States. These words mean that U.S. citizens created the U.S. government. The words demonstrate that the Constitution will cover all citizens, etc.*)

Have students note the size of the words "We the People" compared to the rest of the text in the image.

Ask: **Why might the authors of the Constitution have made these words so much bigger than the rest of the text?** (*Students might say that these are the most important words in the document or that the words are emphasized because they represent one of the ideals of the American democracy and form the basis of the Constitution.*)

TEACH & ASSESS

R Reading Skills

Finding the Main Idea The Constitution is reproduced in its original language, some of which can be difficult for students because of the complex sentence structure and the vocabulary. The explanatory notes should help students grasp the purpose of major sections. Many of the Constitution's difficult words are defined in margin notes on the page where they appear. Suggest that students substitute the definitions for the original words to help them understand the point of the document.

AL ELL Verbal/Linguistic

Content Background Knowledge

The final draft of the Constitution was prepared by a group of five delegates called the Committee of Style. Chaired by William Samuel Johnson of Connecticut, the committee included Alexander Hamilton of New York, Rufus King of Massachusetts, James Madison of Virginia, and Gouverneur Morris of Pennsylvania. The committee worked for five days, completing its task on September 12. Morris did most of the work of styling the document.

The Constitution of the United States

G1 Critical Thinking Skills

Making Connections Ask students to read the Preamble to the Constitution or have a volunteer read it aloud. Review the wording with students to ensure that all students understand the meaning of the Preamble. Have students identify which purpose of the Constitution is personally most important to them and to explain why. **AL** Intrapersonal

G2 Critical Thinking Skills

Making Inferences Point out to students that Article I, Section 1, of the Constitution establishes Congress, which consists of the Senate and the House of Representatives. Section 2 deals with the House of Representatives. **Ask:** What is the significance of discussing the legislative branch first? *(Answers may include the idea that the lawmaking power is the most important or that the lawmaking power logically comes first because Congress must pass laws before the president can execute them or before judges can interpret them.)* **BL**

The Preamble introduces the Constitution and sets forth the general purposes for which the government was established. The Preamble also declares that the power of the government comes from the people.

The printed text of the document shows the spelling and punctuation of the parchment original.

G1

Article I. The Legislative Branch
The Constitution contains seven divisions called articles. Each article covers a general topic. For example, Articles I, II, and III create the three branches of the national government—the legislative, executive, and judicial branches. Most of the articles are divided into sections.

G2

Representation The number of representatives from each state is based on the size of the state's population. Each state is entitled to at least one representative. *What are the qualifications for members of the House of Representatives?*

Vocabulary
preamble: introduction
constitution: principles and laws of a nation
enumeration: census or population count

Preamble

We the People of the United States, in Order to form a more perfect Union, establish Justice, insure domestic Tranquility, provide for the common defence, promote the general Welfare, and secure the Blessings of Liberty to ourselves and our Posterity, do ordain and establish this **Constitution** for the United States of America.

Article I

Section 1

All legislative Powers herein granted shall be vested in a Congress of the United States, which shall consist of a Senate and House of Representatives.

Section 2

[1.] The House of Representatives shall be composed of Members chosen every second Year by the People of the several States, and the Electors in each State shall have the Qualifications requisite for Electors of the most numerous Branch of the State Legislature.

[2.] No person shall be a Representative who shall not have attained the Age of twenty five Years, and been seven Years a Citizen of the United States, and who shall not, when elected, be an Inhabitant of that State in which he shall be chosen.

[3.] Representatives and direct Taxes shall be apportioned among the several States which may be included within this Union, according to their respective Numbers, which shall be determined by adding to the whole Number of free Persons, including those bound to Service for a Term of Years, and excluding Indians not taxed, three fifths of all other Persons. The actual **Enumeration** shall be made within three Years after the first Meeting of the Congress of the United States, and within every subsequent Term of ten Years, in such Manner as they shall by Law direct. The Number of Representatives shall not exceed one for every thirty Thousand, but each State shall have at Least one Representative; and until such enumeration shall be made, the State of New Hampshire shall be entitled to chuse three; Massachusetts eight, Rhode-Island and Providence Plantations one, Connecticut five, New-York six, New Jersey four, Pennsylvania eight, Delaware one, Maryland six, Virginia ten, North Carolina five, South Carolina five, and Georgia three.

---

networks *Online Teaching Options*

The Census

Comparing and Contrasting Point out to students that the Constitution calls for the nation to conduct a census every ten years. Have students use the Internet to research and compile data from the 2000 and 2010 censuses. Students should first create a spreadsheet that identifies the populations of each state and the number of representatives each state had in 2000. Then students should list the population of each state in 2010 and show whether the state lost or gained representation in the House of Representatives. Have students use the census data to create or fill in a map of the United States to illustrate the numbers of seats lost or gained by each state. Have students identify which states lost the most and which states gained the most. Have students speculate as to why those states are losing or gaining population. Finally, ask students to speculate how these changes might affect the balance of power in the House of Representatives.

ANSWER, p. 220

Representation A member of the House must be at least 25 years old, be a United States citizen for at least seven years, and be an inhabitant of the state from which he or she was elected.

[4.] When vacancies happen in the Representation from any State, the Executive Authority thereof shall issue Writs of Election to fill such Vacancies.

[5.] The House of Representatives shall chuse their Speaker and other Officers; and shall have the sole Power of **Impeachment**.

Section 3

[1.] The Senate of the United States shall be composed of two Senators from each State, chosen by the Legislature thereof, for six Years; and each Senator shall have one Vote.

[2.] Immediately after they shall be assembled in Consequence of the first Election, they shall be divided as equally as may be into three Classes. The Seats of the Senators of the first Class shall be vacated at the Expiration of the second Year, of the second Class at the Expiration of the fourth Year, and of the third Class at the Expiration of the sixth Year, so that one third may be chosen every second Year; and if Vacancies happen by Resignation, or otherwise, during the Recess of the Legislature of any State, the Executive thereof may make temporary Appointments until the next Meeting of the Legislature, which shall then fill such Vacancies.

[3.] No Person shall be a Senator who shall not have attained to the Age of thirty Years, and been nine Years a Citizen of the United States, and who shall not, when elected, be an Inhabitant of that State for which he shall be chosen.

[4.] The Vice President of the United States shall be President of the Senate, but shall have no Vote, unless they be equally divided.

[5.] The Senate shall chuse their other Officers, and also a **President pro tempore**, in the Absence of the Vice President, or when he shall exercise the Office of the President of the United States.

[6.] The Senate shall have the sole Power to try all Impeachments. When sitting for that Purpose, they shall be on Oath or Affirmation. When the President of the United States is tried, the Chief Justice shall preside: And no Person shall be convicted without the Concurrence of two thirds of the Members present.

[7.] Judgment in Cases of Impeachment shall not extend further than to removal from Office, and disqualification to hold and enjoy any Office of honor, Trust or Profit under the United States: but the Party convicted shall nevertheless be liable and subject to **Indictment**, Trial, Judgment and Punishment, according to Law.

Electing Senators Originally, senators were chosen by the state legislators of their own states. The Seventeenth Amendment changed this, so that senators are now elected by the people. There are 100 senators, 2 from each state. The vice president serves as president of the Senate.

Impeachment One of Congress's powers is the power to impeach—to accuse government officials of wrongdoing, put them on trial, and if necessary remove them from office. *Which body has the power to decide the official's guilt or innocence?*

Vocabulary

impeachment: bringing charges against an official

president pro tempore: presiding officer of Senate who serves when the vice president is absent

indictment: charging a person with an offense

The Constitution **221**

G1 Critical Thinking Skills

Comparing Tell students that Article 1, Section 3, deals with the Senate. Remind students that the Articles of Confederation created a one-house legislature in which each of the original 13 states had one representative. **Ask: How many votes does each state get in the Senate?** *(two)* **How many votes did each state have under the Articles of Confederation?** *(one)*

G2 Critical Thinking Skills

Comparing and Contrasting Have students read Section 3, Clause 2. **Ask: How much of the Senate is elected every two years?** *(one-third)* **How many seats in the House of Representatives are subject to an election every two years?** *(all)* **Which house might be more responsive to voters' wishes? Why?** *(the House; because members who want to be reelected must face voters more often)*

R Reading Skills

Explaining Remind students that the vice president presides over the Senate. **Ask: What happens if the Senate ties when holding a vote?** *(The vice president has the right to cast the deciding vote.)* **Ask: Why do you think the issue of tie votes is discussed in the Constitution?** *(Because each state has two voting senators, there will always be an equal number of senators; thus, having a process for casting a deciding vote is needed.)* **BL** **Logical/Mathematical**

The Impeachment Clause

Analyzing Draw students' attention to Article 1, Section 3, Clause 6. Read it aloud and begin a discussion of the impeachment clause. Tell students that only two sitting presidents have been impeached: Andrew Johnson and William Clinton. The House started impeachment proceedings on President Richard Nixon, but he resigned before the vote took place.

Have students work in groups to research both presidential impeachments. Although neither President Johnson nor President Clinton was convicted by the Senate, the impeachment is part of their historical records. Have students discuss how this affects each president's place in history.

ANSWER, p. 221

Impeachment the Senate

The Constitution of the United States

R1 Reading Skills

Applying Direct students to the bottom of the page for the definition of quorum. **Ask: How many members of the 100-person Senate are needed for a quorum?** *(51)* **Logical/Mathematical**

C Critical Thinking Skills

Drawing Conclusions Refer to Section 5, Clause 3. **Ask: Why is Congress required to make its proceedings public?** *(to let people know what members said about particular issues)* **Why is Congress allowed to keep some discussions secret?** *(Answers may include the need to maintain security.)*

R2 Reading Skills

Defining Have students read Section 5, Clause 3. **Ask: What is meant by the "Yeas and Nays"?** *(the yes and no votes that members of Congress register on a bill)* Guide students in a discussion of the reasons congressional votes are made public. You might ask interested students to examine the voting record of their own congressional representative and share it with the class. **AL** **ELL**

Section 4

[1.] The Times, Places and Manner of holding Elections for Senators and Representatives, shall be prescribed in each State by the Legislature thereof; but the Congress may at any time by Law make or alter such Regulations, except as to the Places of chusing Senators.

[2.] The Congress shall assemble at least once in every Year, and such Meeting shall be on the first Monday in December, unless they shall by Law appoint a different Day.

Section 5

R1

[1.] Each House shall be the Judge of the Elections, Returns and Qualifications of its own Members, and a Majority of each shall constitute a **Quorum** to do Business; but a smaller Number may **adjourn** from day to day, and may be authorized to compel the Attendance of absent Members, in such Manner, and under such Penalties as each House may provide.

[2.] Each House may determine the Rules of its Proceedings, punish its Members for disorderly Behaviour, and, with the Concurrence of two thirds, expel a Member.

C

[3.] Each House shall keep a Journal of its Proceedings, and from time to time publish the same, excepting such Parts as may in their Judgment require Secrecy; and the Yeas and Nays of the Members of either House on any question shall, at the Desire of one fifth of those Present, be entered on the Journal. **R2**

[4.] Neither House, during the Session of Congress, shall, without the Consent of the other, adjourn for more than three days, nor to any other Place than that in which the two Houses shall be sitting.

Section 6

[1.] The Senators and Representatives shall receive a Compensation for their Services, to be ascertained by Law, and paid out of the Treasury of the United States. They shall in all Cases, except Treason, Felony and Breach of the Peace, be privileged from Arrest during their Attendance at the Session of their respective Houses, and in going to and returning from the same; and for any Speech or Debate in either House, they shall not be questioned in any other Place.

[2.] No Senator or Representative shall, during the Time for which he was elected, be appointed to any civil Office under the Authority of the United States, which shall have been created, or the **Emoluments** whereof shall have been increased during such time; and no Person holding any Office under the United States, shall be a Member of either House during his Continuance in Office.

Congressional Salaries To strengthen the federal government, the Founders set congressional salaries to be paid by the United States Treasury rather than by members' respective states. Originally, members were paid $6 per day. In 2006, all members of Congress received a base salary of $165,200.

Vocabulary

quorum: minimum number of members that must be present to conduct sessions

adjourn: to suspend a session

emoluments: salaries

---

netw✺rks   *Online Teaching Options*

The Daily Life of a Member of Congress

Drawing Conclusions Have students use the Internet and other sources to find out what representatives and senators do on a daily basis. Organize students into small groups and instruct students to being their research with a list of questions, such as: Do new senators and representatives get training? What do they do each day? What kind of work constitutes a typical day? How long does it take to learn all the rules? How often are they involved in actually casting a vote on pending legislation?

Encourage students to e-mail their representatives or senators to get a personal answer to their questions. Have students document the results of their research in a slide show or multimedia presentation.

Section 7

[1.] All **Bills** for raising **Revenue** shall originate in the House of Representatives; but the Senate may propose or concur with Amendments as on other Bills.

[2.] Every Bill which shall have passed the House of Representatives and the Senate, shall, before it become a Law, be presented to the President of the United States; If he approve he shall sign it, but if not he shall return it, with his Objections to that House in which it shall have originated, who shall enter the Objections at large on their Journal, and proceed to reconsider it. If after such Reconsideration two thirds of that House shall agree to pass the Bill, it shall be sent, together with the Objections, to the other House, by which it shall likewise be reconsidered, and if approved by two thirds of that House, it shall become a Law. But in all such Cases the Votes of both Houses shall be determined by yeas and Nays, and the Names of the Persons voting for and against the Bill shall be entered on the Journal of each House respectively. If any Bill shall not be returned by the President within ten Days (Sundays excepted) after it shall have been presented to him, the Same shall be a Law, in like Manner as if he had signed it, unless the Congress by their Adjournment prevent its Return, in which Case it shall not be a Law.

[3.] Every Order, **Resolution**, or Vote to which the Concurrence of the Senate and House of Representatives may be necessary (except on a question of Adjournment) shall be presented to the President of the United States; and before the Same shall take Effect, shall be approved by him, or being disapproved by him, shall be repassed by two thirds of the Senate and House of Representatives, according to the Rules and Limitations prescribed in the Case of a Bill.

Section 8 **V₂**

[1.] The Congress shall have the Power To lay and collect Taxes, Duties, **Imposts** and Excises, to pay the Debts and provide for the common Defence and general Welfare of the United States; but all Duties, Imposts and Excises shall be uniform throughout the United States;

[2.] To borrow Money on the credit of the United States;

[3.] To regulate Commerce with foreign Nations, and among the several States, and with the Indian Tribes;

[4.] To establish an uniform Rule of **Naturalization**, and uniform Laws on the subject of Bankruptcies throughout the United States;

[5.] To coin Money, regulate the Value thereof, and of foreign Coin, and fix the Standard of Weights and Measures;

[6.] To provide for the Punishment of counterfeiting the Securities and current Coin of the United States;

[7.] To establish Post Offices and post Roads;

Where Tax Laws Begin All tax laws must originate in the House of Representatives. This ensures that the branch of Congress that is elected by the people every two years has the major role in determining taxes.

How Bills Become Laws A bill may become a law only by passing both houses of Congress and by being signed by the president. The president can check Congress by rejecting—vetoing—its legislation. *How can Congress override the president's veto?*

V₁

Powers of Congress Expressed powers are those powers directly stated in the Constitution. Most of the expressed powers of Congress are listed in Article I, Section 8. These powers are also called enumerated powers because they are numbered 1–18. *Which clause gives Congress the power to declare war?*

C

Vocabulary

bill: draft of a proposed law
revenue: income raised by government
resolution: legislature's formal expression of opinion
impost: tax
naturalization: procedure by which a citizen of a foreign nation becomes a citizen of the United States.

The Constitution **223**

V₁ Visual Skills

Creating Maps, Graphs, Charts, Time Lines Have students work in pairs to create a flowchart or sequence diagram of how a bill becomes a law. **BL**

V₂ Visual Skills

Creating Maps, Graphs, Charts, Time Lines Have students construct a chart categorizing the legislative powers of Congress, as listed in Section 8. Suggest they list powers under the following categories: *Monetary, Commerce, Regulatory, Judicial, War, Implied.*

C Critical Thinking Skills

Identifying Central Issues Both the first and fourth clauses of Section 8 point out that laws Congress passes on particular subjects should be uniform. **Ask: What problem with the Articles of Confederation were the Framers trying to solve by using the word** *uniform*? *(the difficulties caused by having different laws from state to state)*

Congressional Committees

Researching on the Internet To carry out their many expressed powers, both houses of Congress form committees to oversee all bills in certain areas, such as banking, defense, or agriculture. Those committees are often divided further into subcommittees that focus on specific parts of the broader area. Have students work in pairs to research the representative from their district and the senators from their state to find out what committees and subcommittees they serve on and whether they have leadership roles. Encourage students to e-mail their representative and senators asking for information about the committees on which they serve. Invite volunteers to share the replies they receive. You might invite students to create an online flowchart showing the committees and subcommittees on which their representative and senator serve.

ANSWERS, p. 223

How Bills Become Laws A bill can become a law, despite not being signed by the president, if two-thirds of the House of Representatives and two-thirds of the Senate approve the bill.

Powers of Congress Article 1, Section 8, Clause 11

The Constitution of the United States

C1 Critical Thinking Skills

Defending Discuss with students how on some occasions when the United States has intervened militarily, Congress has not issued a formal declaration of war. These undeclared wars are typically called *conflicts*; for example, the Vietnam Conflict. Other wars—the Korean, Gulf, and Iraq wars—have been fought with the president's authority. Have students discuss their views on these military actions. During the discussion, ask guiding questions to help students elaborate their views and provide supporting details. **Ask: Should the executive branch have the power to use military force without a declaration of war by Congress? If Congress authorizes military appropriations, is that acceptable?**

C2 Critical Thinking Skills

Analyzing Information Ask: Is the term *elastic clause* appropriate for Section 8, Clause 18? Why or why not? *(Students may say that it is appropriate because Congress can "stretch" the clause to cover many actions.)*

C3 Critical Thinking Skills

Making Connections Remind students that creating a Constitution that all the states would accept required compromises. One compromise was with the Southern states, whose economy depended on the labor of enslaved persons. Explain that Section 9, Clause 1, prevented Congress from passing any law banning the importation of Africans as enslaved persons before 1808. This language was a compromise between delegates who wanted to ban the importation of enslaved persons and those who wished to continue the practice. **Ask: Which part of the country was represented by proslavery delegates?** *(the South)*

R Reading Skills

Discussing Section 9, Clause 2, prohibits suspension of the writ of habeas corpus. Discuss with students the protection this clause offers. Ask students if they think this is an outdated principle today or still necessary to the Constitution. *(Most students will see this as a major principle of our legal system.)*

ANSWER, p. 224

Habeas Corpus Congress cannot pass such bills.

224

Elastic Clause The final enumerated power is often called the "elastic clause." This clause gives Congress the right to make all laws "necessary and proper" to carry out the powers expressed in the other clauses of **Article I.** It is called the elastic clause because it lets Congress "stretch" its powers to meet situations the Founders could never have anticipated.

What does the phrase **"necessary and proper"** in the elastic clause mean? Almost from the beginning, this phrase was a subject of dispute. The issue was whether a strict or a broad interpretation of the Constitution should be applied. The dispute was first addressed in 1819, in the case of *McCulloch* v. *Maryland*, when the Supreme Court ruled in favor of a broad interpretation.

Habeas Corpus A writ of habeas corpus issued by a judge requires a law official to bring a prisoner to court and show cause for holding the prisoner. A bill of attainder is a bill that punished a person without a jury trial. An "ex post facto" law is one that makes an act a crime after the act has been committed. *What does the Constitution say about bills of attainder?*

Vocabulary
tribunal: a court
insurrection: rebellion

224 *The Constitution*

[8.] To promote the Progress of Science and useful Arts, by securing for limited Times to Authors and Inventors the exclusive Right to their respective Writings and Discoveries;

[9.] To constitute **Tribunals** inferior to the supreme Court;

[10.] To define and punish Piracies and Felonies committed on the high Seas, and Offences against the Law of Nations;

C1 [11.] To declare War, grant Letters of Marque and Reprisal, and make Rules concerning Captures on Land and Water;

[12.] To raise and support Armies, but no Appropriation of Money to that Use shall be for a longer Term than two Years;

[13.] To provide and maintain a Navy;

[14.] To make Rules for the Government and Regulation of the land and naval Forces;

[15.] To provide for calling forth the Militia to execute the Laws of the Union, suppress **Insurrections** and repel Invasions;

[16.] To provide for organizing, arming, and disciplining, the Militia, and for governing such Part of them as may be employed in the Service of the United States, reserving to the States respectively, the Appointment of the Officers, and the Authority of training the Militia according to the discipline prescribed by Congress;

[17.] To exercise exclusive Legislation in all Cases whatsoever, over such District (not exceeding ten Miles square) as may, by Cession of particular States, and the Acceptance of Congress, become the Seat of Government of the United States, and to exercise like Authority over all Places purchased by the Consent of the Legislature of the State in which the Same shall be, for the Erection of Forts, Magazines, Arsenals, dock-Yards, and other needful Buildings, —And

[18.] To make all Laws which shall be necessary and proper for carrying into Execution the foregoing Powers, and all other Powers vested by this Constitution in the Government of the United States, or in any Department or Officer thereof. **C2**

Section 9

[1.] The Migration or Importation of such Persons as any of the States now existing shall think proper to admit, shall not be prohibited by the Congress prior to the Year one thousand eight hundred and eight, but a Tax or duty may be imposed on such Importation, not exceeding ten dollars for each Person. **C3**

[2.] The Privilege of the Writ of Habeas Corpus shall not be suspended, unless when in Cases of Rebellion or Invasion the public Safety may require it.

[3.] No Bill of Attainder or ex post facto Law shall be passed.

[4.] No Capitation, or other direct, Tax shall be laid, unless in Proportion to the Census or Enumeration herein before directed to be taken.

[5.] No Tax or Duty shall be laid on Articles exported from any State.

---

networks   *Online Teaching Options*

Copyright and Patent Laws

Researching on the Internet Read aloud Section 8, Clause 8. Explain that this clause establishes copyright as well as patents. Illustrate this by showing students the copyright information at the front of their textbook and other books in the classroom. **Ask: What does the phrase "securing for limited Times" mean in Section 8, Clause 8?** *(that copyright does not last forever)* Explain that books and other materials that are no longer protected by copyright are in the public domain.

Have students use the Internet to find out how long copyright protections are currently guaranteed in the United States. Have volunteers share what they find. Organize students into groups and assign each group a list of popular books from a variety of eras. Have students work collaboratively to find out if each book is still copyrighted or if it is in the public domain.

[6.] No Preference shall be given by any Regulation of Commerce or Revenue to the Ports of one State over those of another: nor shall Vessels bound to, or from, one State, be obliged to enter, clear, or pay Duties in another.

[7.] No Money shall be drawn from the Treasury, but in Consequence of **Appropriations** made by Law; and a regular Statement and Account of the Receipts and Expenditures of all public Money shall be published from time to time.

R1

[8.] No Title of Nobility shall be granted by the United States: And no Person holding any Office of Profit or Trust under them, shall, without the Consent of the Congress, accept of any present, Emolument, Office, or Title, of any kind whatever, from any King, Prince, or foreign State.

Section 10

[1.] No State shall enter into any Treaty, Alliance, or Confederation; grant Letters of Marque and Reprisal; coin Money; emit Bills of Credit; make any Thing but gold and silver Coin a Tender in Payment of Debts; pass any Bill of Attainder, ex post facto Law, or Law impairing the Obligation of Contracts, or grant any Title of Nobility.

[2.] No State shall, without the Consent of the Congress, lay any Imposts or Duties on Imports or Exports, except what may be absolutely necessary for executing its inspection Laws: and the net Produce of all Duties and Imposts, laid by any State on Imports and Exports, shall be for the Use of the Treasury of the United States; and all such Laws shall be subject to the Revision and Controul of the Congress.

V1

[3.] No State shall, without the Consent of Congress, lay any Duty of Tonnage, keep Troops, or Ships of War in time of Peace, enter into any Agreement or Compact with another State, or with a foreign Power, or engage in War, unless actually invaded, or in such imminent Danger as will not admit of delay.

Article II **V2**

Section 1

[1.] The executive Power shall be vested in a President of the United States of America. He shall hold his Office during the Term of four Years, and, together with the Vice President, chosen for the same Term, be elected, as follows.

R2

[2.] Each State shall appoint, in such Manner as the Legislature thereof may direct, a Number of Electors, equal to the whole Number of Senators and Representatives to which the State may be entitled in the Congress: but no Senator or Representative, or Person holding an Office of Trust or Profit under the United States, shall be appointed an Elector.

Limitations on the States Section 10 lists limits on the states. These restrictions were designed, in part, to prevent an overlapping in functions and authority with the federal government.

Article II. The Executive Branch Article II creates an executive branch to carry out laws passed by Congress. Article II lists the powers and duties of the presidency, describes qualifications for office and procedures for electing the president, and provides for a vice president.

Vocabulary
appropriations: funds set aside for a specific use

The Constitution **225**

R1 **Reading Skills**

Explaining Have a student read aloud Clause 7. **Ask:** What limits does Section 9, Clause 7, place on the federal government? *(It prevents it from spending any money unless authorized by Congress.)*

V1 **Visual Skills**

Creating Maps, Graphs, Charts, Time Lines Have students create a two-column chart in which they list the powers denied the states in one column and the clause in which that power is granted to the federal government in the other.

V2 **Visual Skills**

Creating Maps, Graphs, Charts, Time Lines As students read Article II, have them create and fill in a chart that categorizes the powers of the president as "Executive," "Legislative," "Diplomatic," "Military," and "Judicial."

R2 **Reading Skills**

Identifying Have students read Article 2, Section 1, Clause 1. **Ask:** Who are the only two members of the executive branch specified in the Constitution? *(the president and the vice president)* **AL**

Content Background Knowledge

The Constitution originally did not limit the number of terms the Chief Executive could serve. George Washington served two terms; no president served more than two until Franklin D. Roosevelt. Many people opposed Roosevelt's four terms in office. The opposition eventually led to ratification of the Twenty-second Amendment in 1951, which limited presidents to two terms.

Gallup Polls

Evaluating One of the most important traditional measures of the president's standing with the public is the Gallup presidential approval survey, or poll. Since 1945 the Gallup Organization has polled members of the public each month— and sometimes more often—about whether they approve or disapprove of the president's handling of the job.

Have students conduct outside research to find the most recent Gallup poll results for the current president. Discuss the poll results with students. **Ask:** Is the number what you expected it to be? Why or why not?

Have students look up Gallup poll results for Congress. Have students compare the two sets of results. **Ask:** What do these results say about the public's opinion of Congress and the president? *(Answers will vary depending on the poll numbers.)*

The Constitution of the United States

C Critical Thinking Skills

Making Inferences Ask: As the Constitution was originally written, how did the Electoral College choose the president and vice president? *(The candidate with the most electoral votes became president; the candidate with the second-highest number of electoral votes became vice president.)* What potential problems might this create? *(Students may point out the perils of having a president and vice president from competing political parties.)*

R Reading Skills

Determining Word Meanings Point out the word *chuse* in the last line of Clause 3. **Ask:** What is the modern spelling of this word? *(choose)* What does it mean? *(to decide among options)* Have students name the corresponding noun. *(choice)*
ELL Verbal/Linguistic

W Writing Skills

Argument Have students write an essay in which they argue whether, in modern times, a person who is 35 years old is adequately prepared for the complex demands of serving as president of the United States. If they believe 35 is not old enough, ask them to specify the minimum age they would set and explain why. You might wish to tell students that the youngest elected president was John F. Kennedy, who was 43; the oldest was Ronald Reagan, who was almost 70.

T Technology Skills

Making Presentations Have students work in small groups to research and create a slide show presentation about the vice presidents who later became president. Have students explain why these people were chosen as vice presidents, how they became presidents, and whether or not they were elected to the presidency.

Previous Elections The Twelfth Amendment, added in 1804, changed the method of electing the president stated in Article II, Section 3. The Twelfth Amendment requires that the electors cast separate ballots for president and vice president.

Qualifications The president must be a citizen of the United States by birth, at least 35 years of age, and a resident of the United States for 14 years.

Vacancies If the president dies, resigns, is removed from office by impeachment, or is unable to carry out the duties of the office, the vice president becomes president. The Twenty-fifth Amendment sets procedures for presidential succession.

Salary Originally, the president's salary was $25,000 per year. The president's current salary is $400,000 plus a $50,000 nontaxable expense account per year. The president also receives living accommodations in two residences—the White House and Camp David.

C **[3.]** The Electors shall meet in their respective States, and vote by Ballot for two Persons, of whom one at least shall not be an Inhabitant of the same State with themselves. And they shall make a List of all the Persons voted for, and of the Number of Votes for each; which List they shall sign and certify, and transmit sealed to the Seat of the Government of the United States, directed to the President of the Senate. The President of the Senate shall, in the Presence of the Senate and House of Representatives, open all the Certificates, and the Votes shall then be counted. The Person having the greatest Number of Votes shall be the President, if such Number be a Majority of the whole Number of Electors appointed; and if there be more than one who have such Majority, and have an equal Number of Votes, then the House of Representatives shall immediately chuse by Ballot one of them for President; and if no person have a Majority, then from the five highest on the List the said House shall in like Manner chuse the President. But in chusing the President, the Votes shall be taken by States, the Representation from each State having one Vote; A quorum for this Purpose shall consist of a Member or Members from two thirds of the States, and a Majority of all the States shall be necessary to a Choice. In every Case, after the Choice of the President, the Person having the greatest Number of Votes of the Electors shall be the Vice President. But if there should remain two or more who have equal Votes, the Senate shall **R** chuse from them by Ballot the Vice President.

[4.] The Congress may determine the Time of chusing the Electors, and the Day on which they shall give their Votes; which Day shall be the same throughout the United States.

[5.] **W** No Person except a natural born Citizen, or a Citizen of the United States, at the time of the Adoption of this Constitution, shall be eligible to the Office of President; neither shall any Person be eligible to that Office who shall not have attained to the Age of thirty five Years, and been fourteen Years a Resident within the United States.

[6.] **T** In Case of the Removal of the President from Office, or of his Death, Resignation, or Inability to discharge the Powers and Duties of the said Office, the Same shall devolve on the Vice President, and the Congress may by Law provide for the Case of Removal, Death, Resignation or Inability, both of the President and Vice President, declaring what Officer shall then act as President, and such Officer shall act accordingly, until the Disability be removed, or a President shall be elected.

[7.] The President shall, at stated Times, receive for his Services, a Compensation, which shall neither be encreased nor diminished during the Period for which he shall have been elected, and he shall not receive within that Period any other Emolument from the United States, or any of them.

---

netw⊙rks   *Online Teaching Options*

The Perfect President

Making Generalizations The Constitution outlines the basic qualifications of the president of the United States and how elections should be run. It does not, however, provide a list of traits the president should have.

Have students write a blog post in which they describe the perfect president. Blog posts should include personality traits, work experience, and principles they think a person should possess to run as president. Ask students if any past or current presidents measure up to the standards they have created. Then have students discuss whether the traits needed to serve effectively as president change according to the times and conditions in the nation.

[8.] Before he enter on the Execution of his Office, he shall take the following Oath or Affirmation:—"I do solemnly swear (or affirm) that I will faithfully execute the Office of President of the United States, and will to the best of my Ability, preserve, protect and defend the Constitution of the United States."

R

Section 2

[1.] The President shall be Commander in Chief of the Army and Navy of the United States, and of the Militia of the several States, when called into the actual Service of the United States; he may require the Opinion, in writing, of the principal Officer in each of the executive Departments, upon any Subject relating to the Duties of their respective Offices, and he shall have Power to grant Reprieves and Pardons for Offences against the United States, except in Cases of Impeachment.

C₁
C₂
C₃

[2.] He shall have Power, by and with the Advice and Consent of the Senate, to make Treaties, provided two thirds of the Senators present concur; and he shall nominate, and by and with the Advice and Consent of the Senate, shall appoint Ambassadors, other public Ministers and Consuls, Judges of the supreme Court, and all other Officers of the United States, whose Appointments are not herein otherwise provided for, and which shall be established by Law: but the Congress may by Law vest the Appointment of such inferior Officers, as they think proper, in the President alone, in the Courts of Law, or in the Heads of Departments.

[3.] The President shall have Power to fill up all Vacancies that may happen during the Recess of the Senate, by granting Commissions which shall expire at the End of their next Session.

Section 3

He shall from time to time give to the Congress Information of the State of the Union, and recommend to their Consideration such Measures as he shall judge necessary and expedient; he may, on extraordinary Occasions, convene both Houses, or either of them, and in Case of Disagreement between them, with Respect to the Time of Adjournment, he may adjourn them to such Time as he shall think proper; he shall receive Ambassadors and other public Ministers; he shall take Care that the Laws be faithfully executed, and shall Commission all the Officers of the United States.

The Cabinet Mention of "the principal officer in each of the executive departments" is the only suggestion of the president's cabinet to be found in the Constitution. The cabinet is an advisory body, and its power depends on the president. Section 2, Clause 1 also makes the president—a civilian—the head of the armed services. This established the principle of civilian control of the military.

Presidential Powers An executive order is a command issued by a president to exercise a power which he or she has been given by the U.S. Constitution or by a federal statute. In times of emergency, presidents sometimes have used the executive order to override the Constitution and Congress. During the Civil War, President Lincoln suspended many fundamental rights, such as closing down newspapers that opposed his policies and imprisoning people who disagreed with him. Lincoln said that these actions were justified to preserve the Union.

The Constitution **227**

R Reading Skills

Explaining Have students read Clause 8. **Ask: What pledge does the president make when taking the oath of office?** *(to preserve, protect, and defend the Constitution)* **What does the pledge mean?** *(Answers may include that the president's actions should uphold the Constitution and not undermine it.)* **AL**

C₁ Critical Thinking Skills

Determining Cause and Effect Point out that one of the difficult questions for the Framers of the Constitution concerned the Chief Executive—exactly how much power should the president have? Have students discuss why the Framers set up an office of president with limited powers. (Discussion should focus on the Framers' fear of a single leader with uncontrolled powers.)

C₂ Critical Thinking Skills

Making Inferences Ask students to discuss why the Framers of the Constitution made the president commander in chief of the armed forces and any state militias called to serve the United States. *(The Framers wanted to ensure civilian control of the military.)*

C₃ Critical Thinking Skills

Evaluating Discuss examples showing the growth in presidential power during the last century. For example, increasing globalization has expanded the president's foreign relations responsibilities, such as negotiating international treaties, military and humanitarian interventions, and waging "undeclared wars" (without the authorization of Congress). Write the following statement on the chalkboard: "The increase in presidential power during the last century has been largely related to crises, whether domestic or foreign." **Ask: Do you think this is the true cause of the increase in presidential power? Why or why not? If not, what do you think caused the increase?**

State of the Union message

Determining Central Ideas It is the president's responsibility to inform Congress of the status of the country as well as to recommend actions that Congress should consider taking in the next year. Article II, Section 3, of the United States Constitution does not specify how often State of the Union messages should be delivered, but George Washington set the precedent by delivering an address every year he was in office.

For homework, have students find and watch an online video of a State of the Union address. State of the Union addresses by the current president are archived on the White House Web site (www.whitehouse.gov) under the Photos & Video tab. State of the Union addresses by previous presidents should be available through an Internet search.

Have students write a summary of the State of the Union address they watched. In their summaries, students should identify major themes and ideas mentioned by the president.

R1 Reading Skills

Explaining Have students read Article III, Section 1. **Ask:** What does the Constitution mean by saying that judges "hold their Offices during good Behaviour"? If students are unable to answer, explain that it means federal judges hold office for life unless they retire, resign, or are impeached and removed from office.

C1 Critical Thinking Skills

Defending Refer to Article III, Section 1. **Ask:** As long as judges are on good behavior they can serve. This is interpreted as serving for life. Do you think Supreme Court justices should have such long terms? How does this affect our laws? (Answers will vary. Because they are appointed for life, justices do not have to run for election, and therefore, can be less political in their approach to problems and cases that come before them. Appointment of Supreme Court justices does not occur frequently. Students may consider this advantageous or detrimental.)

C2 Critical Thinking Skills

Contrasting Have students think about Articles I, II, and III. **Ask:** Which branch of the government is described in more detail in the Constitution, the legislative or the judicial? (legislative) Explain that as a result, Congress had to pass laws, starting with the Judiciary Act of 1789, to set up the federal courts. **AL**

R2 Reading Skills

Describing Have students read Article III, Section 2. **Ask:** What kinds of cases are heard in federal courts? (disputes involving officials of the federal government; cases about ships; cases involving the government; cases that involve two state governments, a citizen of one state and the government of another state, or citizens of different states; cases involving land grants by different states; cases between a citizen or state and a foreign person or government) **AL**

Article III. The Judicial Branch The term judicial refers to courts. The Constitution set up only the Supreme Court, but provided for the establishment of other federal courts. The judiciary of the United States has two different systems of courts. One system consists of the federal courts, whose powers derive from the Constitution and federal laws. The other includes the courts of each of the 50 states, whose powers derive from state constitutions and laws.

Statute Law Federal courts deal mostly with "statute law," or laws passed by Congress, treaties, and cases involving the Constitution itself.

The Supreme Court A Court with "original jurisdiction" has the authority to be the first court to hear a case. The Supreme Court has "appellate jurisdiction" and mostly hears cases appealed from lower courts.

Vocabulary
original jurisdiction: authority to be the first court to hear a case
appellate jurisdiction: authority to hear cases that have been appealed from lower courts

228 *The Constitution*

Section 4

The President, Vice President and all civil Officers of the United States, shall be removed from Office on Impeachment for, and Conviction of, Treason, Bribery, or other high Crimes and Misdemeanors.

Article III
Section 1

The judicial Power of the United States, shall be vested in one supreme Court, and in such inferior Courts as the Congress may from time to time ordain and establish. The Judges, both of the supreme and inferior Courts, shall hold their Offices during good Behaviour, and shall, at stated Times, receive for their Services, a Compensation, which shall not be diminished during their Continuance in Office. **R1**

Section 2

[1.] The judicial Power shall extend to all Cases, in Law and Equity, arising under this Constitution, the Laws of the United States, and Treaties made, or which shall be made, under their Authority;—to all Cases affecting Ambassadors, other public Ministers and Consuls;—to all Cases of admiralty and maritime Jurisdiction;—to Controversies to which the United States shall be a Party;—to Controversies between two or more States;—between a State and Citizens of another State;—between Citizens of different States,—between Citizens of the same State claiming Lands under Grants of different States, and between a State, or the Citizens thereof, and foreign States, Citizens or Subjects. **R2**

[2.] In all Cases affecting Ambassadors, other public Ministers and Consuls, and those in which a State shall be Party, the supreme Court shall have **original Jurisdiction**. In all the other Cases before mentioned, the supreme Court shall have **appellate Jurisdiction**, both as to Law and Fact, with such Exceptions, and under such Regulations as the Congress shall make.

[3.] The Trial of all Crimes, except in Cases of Impeachment, shall be by Jury; and such Trial shall be held in the State where the said Crimes shall have been committed; but when not committed within any State, the Trial shall be at such Place or Places as the Congress may by Law have directed.

---

networks *Online Teaching Options*

The Supreme Court

Identifying Points of View Until the late 1900s, all Supreme Court justices were white males. Lead a discussion on how this may have influenced Supreme Court decisions. Point out that the first African American justice was Thurgood Marshall, the first woman was Sandra Day O'Connor, and the first Hispanic justice was Sonia Sotomayor.

Have students create a slide show or a poster about the justices currently serving on the Supreme Court. Students should note when each justice joined the Court and which president made the appointment. Have them include a thesis or conclusion about the Supreme Court and diversity based on their findings.

Section 3

[1.] **Treason** against the United States, shall consist only in levying War against them, or in adhering to their Enemies, giving them Aid and Comfort. No Person shall be convicted of Treason unless on the Testimony of two Witnesses to the same overt Act, or on Confession in open Court.

[2.] The Congress shall have Power to declare the Punishment of Treason, but no Attainder of Treason shall work Corruption of Blood, or Forfeiture except during the Life of the Person attainted.

Article IV

Section 1

Full Faith and Credit shall be given in each State to the public Acts, Records, and judicial Proceedings of every other State. And the Congress may by general Laws prescribe the Manner in which such Acts, Records and Proceedings shall be proved, and the Effect thereof.

Section 2

[1.] The Citizens of each State shall be entitled to all Privileges and Immunities of Citizens in the several States.

[2.] A Person charged in any State with Treason, Felony, or other Crime, who shall flee from Justice, and be found in another State, shall on Demand of the executive Authority of the State from which he fled, be delivered up, to be removed to the State having Jurisdiction of the Crime.

[3.] No Person held to Service of Labour in one State, under the Laws thereof, escaping into another, shall, in Consequence of any Law or Regulation therein, be discharged from such Service or Labour, but shall be delivered up on Claim of the Party to whom such Service or Labour may be due.

Section 3

[1.] New States may be admitted by the Congress into this Union; but no new State shall be formed or erected within the Jurisdiction of any other State; nor any State be formed by the Junction of two or more States, or Parts of States, without the Consent of the Legislatures of the States concerned as well as of the Congress.

[2.] The Congress shall have Power to dispose of and make all needful Rules and Regulations respecting the Territory or other Property belonging to the United States; and nothing in this Constitution shall be so construed as to Prejudice any Claims of the United States, or of any particular State.

Article IV. Relations Among the States Article IV explains the relationship of the states to one another and to the national government. This article requires each state to give citizens of other states the same rights as its own citizens, addresses admitting new states, and guarantees that the national government will protect the states.

New States Congress has the power to admit new states. It also determines the basic guidelines for applying for statehood. Two states, Maine and West Virginia, were created within the boundaries of another state. In the case of West Virginia, President Lincoln recognized the West Virginia government as the legal government of Virginia during the Civil War. This allowed West Virginia to secede from Virginia without obtaining approval from the Virginia legislature.

Vocabulary

treason: violation of the allegiance owed by a person to his or her own country, for example, by aiding an enemy

The Constitution **229**

R1 Reading Skills

Discussing Have students read the definition of treason. **Ask:** What standard must be met to convict someone of treason? *(the testimony of two eyewitnesses or a confession)* Do you think this standard is fair? Why or why not? Point out that the standard of proof today is higher than that laid out in the Constitution. Congress and the courts expect to see physical evidence, such as electronic records or surveillance photographs, to secure a conviction for treason. **AL**

R2 Reading Skills

Applying Have students read Section 3, Clause 1. **Ask:** If North Dakota and South Dakota wanted to combine to become the single state of Dakota, what would have to happen? *(The North Dakota and South Dakota legislatures would have to approve the merger, and so would Congress.)* How would such a merger change Congress? *(There would be fewer senators, because the Senate is made up of two representatives from each state.)* **BL** Logical/Mathematical

The Route to Statehood

Creating Maps, Graphs, Charts, Time Lines Have students draw a current map of the United States showing all 50 states. They should fill in each state's name and the year in which it became a state. Students should look online for the necessary information. Have students share their drawings and research. Ask students to name the last two states to join the Union *(Hawaii and Alaska, both in 1959)*. Ask students if they think geography played a role in the route to statehood and how being so far away from the mainland United States affected their ability to become states. Then use the maps to discuss Article IV, Section 3, of the Constitution.

The Constitution of the United States

V Visual Skills

Creating Visuals Have students review the definitions of the types of governments listed in the box: autocracy, oligarchy, democracy, republic. Then have students create illustrated flash cards for each type of government. Have students share and explain their drawings. **ELL** Visual/Spatial

C Critical Thinking Skills

Contrasting Remind students that all the states were needed to approve an amendment to the Articles of Confederation. **Ask: How many states are needed to amend the Constitution?** *(two-thirds of the states in Congress or in the state legislatures for proposing amendments; three-fourths for approving one)*

Have students speculate as to why the Framers of the Constitution established the amendment process as they did. *(The Framers wanted to make the Constitution flexible, but not so easy to amend that the document would not be respected.)* Ask students to discuss the following questions: **Should the amendment process be made easier? Why or why not?**

R Reading Skills

Discussing A political scientist once named the supremacy clause "the most important single provision of the Constitution." **Ask: Do you agree or disagree with this statement? Why?** Discuss students' answers as a class.

Republic Government can be classified in many different ways. The ancient Greek philosopher Aristotle classified government based on the question "who governs?" According to Aristotle, all governments belong to one of three major groups: (1) autocracy—rule by one person; (2) oligarchy—rule by a few persons; or (3) democracy—rule by many persons. A republic is a form of democracy in which the people elect representatives to make the laws and conduct government.

Article V. The Amendment Process Article V spells out the ways that the Constitution can be amended, or changed. All of the 27 amendments were proposed by a two-thirds vote of both houses of Congress. Only the Twenty-first Amendment was ratified by constitutional conventions of the states. All other amendments have been ratified by state legislatures. **What is an amendment?**

Article VI. National Supremacy Article VI contains the "supremacy clause." This clause establishes that the Constitution, laws passed by Congress, and treaties of the United States "shall be the supreme Law of the Land." The "supremacy clause" recognized the Constitution and federal laws as supreme when in conflict with those of the states.

Vocabulary
amendment: a change to the Constitution
ratification: process by which an amendment is approved

V

Section 4

The United States shall guarantee to every State in this Union a Republican Form of Government, and shall protect each of them against Invasion; and on Application of the Legislature, or of the Executive (when the Legislature cannot be convened) against domestic Violence.

Article V

C

The Congress, whenever two thirds of both Houses shall deem it necessary, shall propose **Amendments** to this Constitution, or, on the Application of the Legislatures of two thirds of the several States, shall call a Convention for proposing Amendments, which, in either Case, shall be valid to all Intents and Purposes, as Part of this Constitution, when ratified by the Legislatures of three fourths of the several States, or by Conventions in three fourths thereof, as the one or the other Mode of **Ratification** may be proposed by the Congress; Provided that no Amendment which may be made prior to the Year One thousand eight hundred and eight shall in any Manner affect the first and fourth Clauses in the Ninth Section of the first Article; and that no State, without its Consent, shall be deprived of its equal Suffrage in the Senate.

Article VI

[1.] All Debts contracted and Engagements entered into, before the Adoption of this Constitution, shall be as valid against the United States under this Constitution, as under the Confederation.

R

[2.] This Constitution, and the Laws of the United States which shall be made in Pursuance thereof; and all Treaties made, or which shall be made, under the Authority of the United States, shall be the supreme Law of the Land; and the Judges in every State shall be bound thereby, any Thing in the Constitution or Laws of any State to the Contrary notwithstanding.

[3.] The Senators and Representatives before mentioned, and the Members of the several State Legislatures, and all executive and judicial Officers, both of the United States and of the several States, shall be bound by Oath or Affirmation, to support this Constitution; but no religious Test shall ever be required as a Qualification to any Office or public Trust under the United States.

---

networks   *Online Teaching Options*

Constitutional Amendments

Creating Maps, Graphs, Charts, Time Lines Have students conduct outside research to find out when each of the Constitution's 27 amendments were ratified. Then have students work in pairs to create a time line of the amendments. Ask students to create an illustration showing the purpose of each amendment.

ANSWER, p. 230

Article V. The Amendment Process a change to the Constitution

Article VII

The Ratification of the Conventions of nine States, shall be sufficient for the Establishment of this Constitution between the States so ratifying the Same.

Done in Convention by the Unanimous Consent of the States present the Seventeenth Day of September in the Year of our Lord one thousand seven hundred and Eighty seven and of the Independence of the United States of America the Twelfth. In witness whereof We have hereunto subscribed our Names,

> **Article VII. Ratification** Article VII addresses ratification and declares that the Constitution would take effect after it was ratified by nine states.

Signers

George Washington,
President and Deputy from
Virginia

New Hampshire
John Langdon
Nicholas Gilman

Massachusetts
Nathaniel Gorham
Rufus King

Connecticut
William Samuel Johnson
Roger Sherman

New York
Alexander Hamilton

New Jersey
William Livingston
David Brearley
William Paterson
Jonathan Dayton

Pennsylvania
Benjamin Franklin
Thomas Mifflin
Robert Morris
George Clymer
Thomas FitzSimons
Jared Ingersoll
James Wilson
Gouverneur Morris

Delaware
George Read
Gunning Bedford, Jr.
John Dickinson
Richard Bassett
Jacob Broom

Maryland
James McHenry
Daniel of St. Thomas Jenifer
Daniel Carroll

Virginia
John Blair
James Madison, Jr.

North Carolina
William Blount
Richard Dobbs Spaight
Hugh Williamson

South Carolina
John Rutledge
Charles Cotesworth
Pinckney
Charles Pinckney
Pierce Butler

Georgia
William Few
Abraham Baldwin

Attest: William Jackson,
Secretary

The Constitution of the United States

W1 Writing Skills

Argument Explain that three members of the Constitutional Convention did not sign the Constitution because they objected to the lack of a Bill of Rights. Have students write an essay explaining why they, themselves, would or would not have signed the Constitution as written. Remind students to draw attention to specific articles and clauses to support their arguments. **BL**

W2 Writing Skills

Informative/Explanatory Have each student write a brief biography of one of the signers of the Constitution and present their findings orally.

Content Background Knowledge

Of the 55 delegates who attended the Constitutional Convention, only 38 signed the document. A thirty-ninth signature—that of John Dickinson—was written by George Read at Dickinson's request. Elbridge Gerry of Massachusetts and Edmund Randolph and George Mason of Virginia refused to sign, while 14 other delegates left the Convention early.

Main Ideas in the Constitution

Creating Visuals The first seven articles of the Constitution provide our country with a framework for the national government. Have students create a collage that illustrates the main ideas set forth in Articles I–VII of the Constitution. Students can find pictures online or in magazines, or draw their own images. Ask students to present and explain their work to the class.

The Constitution of the United States

Content Background Knowledge

Critics of the Constitution believed it did not go far enough in protecting individual rights and liberties. To answer these objections, supporters of the Constitution promised to introduce a series of amendments listing the rights of individuals. On June 8, 1789, James Madison kept his promise by proposing 12 amendments to the Constitution, 10 of which were adopted and are now known as the Bill of Rights. One amendment not adopted concerned pay raises for members of Congress. It eventually became the Twenty-seventh Amendment to the Constitution.

R Reading Skills

Applying Give students the following situations, and have them identify which part of the First Amendment applies:

- A magazine column criticizes the president. *(freedom of the press)*
- Protesters gather outside city hall. *(right of assembly)*
- People call a radio show to express their thoughts on a public issue. *(freedom of speech)*
- Muslims go to a mosque without being bothered. *(freedom of religion)*
- Citizens ask the government to change a tax law. *(right of petition)*

C Critical Thinking Skills

Identifying Central Issues Explain that the Fourth Amendment is aimed at protecting the rights of a person accused of a crime. **Ask:** What limits does this amendment place on law enforcement officials? *(They cannot search a person or his or her property without having a reason.)*

Bill of Rights The first 10 amendments are known as the Bill of Rights (1791). These amendments limit the powers of government. The First Amendment protects the civil liberties of individuals in the United States. The amendment freedoms are not absolute, however. They are limited by the rights of other individuals. *What freedoms does the First Amendment protect?*

Rights of the Accused This amendment contains important protections for people accused of crimes. One of the protections is that government may not deprive any person of life, liberty, or property without due process of law. This means that the government must follow proper constitutional procedures in trials and in other actions it takes against individuals. *According to Amendment V, what is the function of a grand jury?*

Vocabulary

quarter: to provide living accommodations

warrant: document that gives police particular rights or powers

probable cause: a reasonable basis to believe a person is linked to a crime

common law: law established by previous court decisions

bail: money that an accused person provides to the court as a guarantee that he or she will be present for a trial

Amendment I

R Congress shall make no law respecting an establishment of religion, or prohibiting the free exercise thereof; or abridging the freedom of speech, or of the press; or the right of the people peaceably to assemble, and to petition the Government for a redress of grievances.

Amendment II

A well regulated Militia, being necessary to the security of a free State, the right of the people to keep and bear Arms, shall not be infringed.

Amendment III

No Soldier shall, in time of peace be **quartered** in any house, without the consent of the Owner, nor in time of war, but in a manner to be prescribed by law.

Amendment IV

C The right of the people to be secure in their persons, houses, papers, and effects, against unreasonable searches and seizures, shall not be violated, and no **Warrants** shall issue, but upon **probable cause**, supported by Oath or affirmation, and particularly describing the place, to be searched, and the persons or things to be seized.

Amendment V

No person shall be held to answer for a capital, or otherwise infamous crime, unless on a presentment or indictment of a Grand Jury, except in cases arising in the land or naval forces, or in the Militia, when in actual service in time of War or public danger; nor shall any person be subject for the same offence to be twice put in jeopardy of life or limb; nor shall be compelled in any criminal case to be a witness against himself, nor be deprived of life, liberty, or property, without due process of law; nor shall private property be taken for public use without just compensation.

networks   *Online Teaching Options*

Amendments Reflected in Today's News

Analyzing News Media Organize students into pairs. Assign each pair an amendment from Amendments I, II, IV, and V. Have students use an online news source to find an article (or articles) related to their assigned amendment. Partners should summarize the news article and then write a brief explanation of how their article relates to or reflects their assigned amendment. Have students share their writings with the class. Use the information as a springboard for discussion about the significance of these amendments in the everyday lives of Americans.

Amendment VI

In all criminal prosecutions, the accused shall enjoy the right to a speedy and public trial, by an impartial jury of the State and district wherein the crime shall have been committed, which district shall have been previously ascertained by law, and to be informed of the nature and cause of the accusation; to be confronted with the witnesses against him; to have compulsory process for obtaining Witnesses in his favor, and to have the assistance of counsel for his defence.

R

C

Amendment VII

In Suits at **common law**, where the value in controversy shall exceed twenty dollars, the right of trial by jury shall be preserved, and no fact tried by a jury, shall be otherwise reexamined in any Court of the United States, than according to the rules of common law.

Amendment VIII

Excessive **bail** shall not be required, nor excessive fines imposed, nor cruel and unusual punishments inflicted.

Amendment IX

The enumeration in the Constitution, of certain rights, shall not be construed to deny or disparage others retained by the people.

Amendment X

The powers not delegated to the United States by the Constitution, nor prohibited by it to the States, are reserved to the States respectively, or to the people.

Amendment XI

The Judicial power of the United States shall not be construed to extend to any suit in law or equity, commenced or prosecuted against one of the United States by Citizens of another State, or by Citizens or Subjects of any Foreign State.

Rights to a Speedy, Fair Trial A basic protection is the right to a speedy, public trial. The jury must hear witnesses and evidence on both sides before deciding the guilt or innocence of a person charged with a crime. This amendment also provides that legal counsel must be provided to a defendant. In 1963, the Supreme Court ruled, in *Gideon* v. *Wainwright*, that if a defendant cannot afford a lawyer, the government must provide one to defend him or her. **Why is the right to a "speedy" trial important?**

Powers of the People This amendment prevents government from claiming that the only rights people have are those listed in the Bill of Rights.

Powers of the States The final amendment of the Bill of Rights protects the states and the people from an all-powerful federal government. It establishes that powers not given to the national government—or denied to the states—by the Constitution belong to the states or to the people.

Suits Against States The Eleventh Amendment (1795) limits the jurisdiction of the federal courts. The Supreme Court had ruled that a federal court could try a lawsuit brought by citizens of South Carolina against a citizen of Georgia. This case, *Chisholm* v. *Georgia*, decided in 1793, raised a storm of protest, leading to passage of the Eleventh Amendment.

The Constitution **233**

The Constitution of the United States

R Reading Skills

Paraphrasing On the board, write the four phrases in the Sixth Amendment beginning with "to be informed of the nature and cause of the accusation" to the end of the amendment. Then read each of the following rewordings and ask which phrase it applies to:

- A person accused of a crime has the right to a lawyer. (*to have the assistance of counsel for the defense*)
- A person must be able to hear the words of anyone who testifies against him in court. (*to be confronted with the witnesses against him*)
- A person must be told what crime he or she is accused of. (*to be informed of the nature and cause of the accusation*)
- The court can order people to appear as witnesses for an accused person. (*to have compulsory process for obtaining Witnesses*) **AL**

C Critical Thinking Skills

Defending Some defense lawyers say the large amount of media coverage of some trials threatens the accused person's Sixth Amendment rights. Have students debate the issue. If necessary, students may wish to conduct outside research so they can cite recent cases in their debates, or you may wish to bring in news articles about recent cases that had heavy media coverage.

The Bill of Rights

Using Digital Tools Guide students in a general discussion of the rights granted in the first ten Amendments. Then organize students into small groups. Have each group create a set of four or five scenarios or situations to illustrate the freedoms or rights in the first 10 Amendments. (You may want to assign particular amendments to each group.) Have groups make video recordings of their scenarios and show them to the class. The class will decide to which amendment the situation applies. If students do not agree or reach consensus about which amendment is being demonstrated, have the group that created the scenario defend and explain why they chose that scenario and how it relates to the amendment.

ANSWER, p. 233

Rights to a Speedy, Fair Trial The requirement of a "speedy" trial ensures that an accused person will not be held in jail for a lengthy period as a means of punishing the accused without a trial.

The Constitution of the United States

C Critical Thinking Skills

Defending Review with students the role of the Electoral College, as students may believe that presidents are elected by popular vote. Point out that in recent years and during close elections, the Electoral College has been criticized as being obsolete. Various ideas have been suggested for changing it or abolishing it altogether. **Ask: Should the Electoral College be abolished and the president elected by popular vote?** Have students debate the question. Point out that those in favor must address the concern of states with smaller populations—that they would have no voice, or a smaller voice, in a system that relied solely on popular vote.

Content Background Knowledge

The 1888 presidential election was extremely close. The Democratic candidate, President Grover Cleveland, won the popular election by 95,713 votes, but lost the Electoral College vote by 65 votes. As a result, Benjamin Harrison was elected as the 23rd president of the United States.

Today, a president must have the majority of electoral votes, 270, to be elected. In situations where no candidate has the majority of electoral votes, the House of Representatives selects the president. This has happened only twice. The House voted for Thomas Jefferson in 1801 and John Quincy Adams in 1825.

Election of President and Vice President The Twelfth Amendment (1804) corrects a problem that had arisen in the method of electing the president and vice president. This amendment provides for the Electoral College to use separate ballots in voting for president and vice president. *If no candidate receives a majority of the electoral votes, who elects the president?*

Amendment XII

The electors shall meet in their respective states and vote by ballot for President and Vice-President, one of whom, at least, shall not be an inhabitant of the same state with themselves; they shall name in their ballots the person voted for as President, and in distinct ballots the person voted for as Vice-President, and they shall make distinct lists of all persons voted for as President, and of all persons voted for as Vice-President, and of the number of votes for each, which lists they shall sign and certify, and transmit sealed to the seat of the government of the United States, directed to the President of the Senate;—The President of the Senate shall, in the presence of the Senate and House of Representatives, open all the certificates and the votes shall then be counted;—The person having the greatest number of votes for President, shall be the President, if such number be a majority of the whole number of Electors appointed; and if no person have such majority, then from the persons having the highest numbers not exceeding three on the list of those voted for as President, the House of Representatives shall choose immediately, by ballot, the President. But in choosing the President, the votes shall be taken by states, the representation from each state having one vote; a quorum for this purpose shall consist of a member or members from two-thirds of the states, and a **majority** of all the states shall be necessary to a choice. And if the House of Representatives shall not choose a President whenever the right of choice shall **devolve** upon them, before the fourth day of March next following, then the Vice-President shall act as President, as in the case of the death or other constitutional disability of the President. The person having the greatest number of votes as Vice-President, shall be the Vice-President, if such number be a majority of the whole number of Electors appointed, and if no person have a majority, then from the two highest numbers on the list, the Senate shall choose the Vice-President; a quorum for the purpose shall consist of two-thirds of the whole number of Senators, and a majority of the whole number shall be necessary to a choice. But no person constitutionally ineligible to the office of President shall be eligible to that of Vice-President of the United States.

C

Vocabulary
majority: more than half
devolve: to pass on

---

netwⓞrks *Online Teaching Options*

The Electoral College and the Popular Vote

Researching on the Internet Have students use the Internet to find the results of the most recent presidential election. Students should locate the data for the popular and Electoral College votes. Then have students create graphs with the election data they found. Encourage students to create online, interactive, illustrated maps of the United States showing the results of the popular and Electoral College votes in each state. Allow class time for volunteers to project their maps and share their work with the class.

ANSWER, p. 234

Election of President and Vice President The House of Representatives elects the president; the Senate elects the vice president.

Amendment XIII

Section 1

Neither slavery nor involuntary servitude, except as a punishment for crime whereof the party shall have been duly convicted, shall exist within the United States, or any place subject to their jurisdiction.

Section 2

Congress shall have power to enforce this article by appropriate legislation.

Amendment XIV

Section 1

All persons born or naturalized in the United States, and subject to the jurisdiction thereof, are citizens of the United States and of the State wherein they reside. No State shall make or enforce any law which shall **abridge** the privileges or immunities of citizens of the United States; nor shall any State deprive any person of life, liberty, or property, without due process of law; nor deny to any person within its jurisdiction the equal protection of the laws.

Section 2

Representatives shall be apportioned among the several States according to their respective numbers, counting the whole number of persons in each State, excluding Indians not taxed. But when the right to vote at any election for the choice of electors for President and Vice President of the United States, Representatives in Congress, the Executive and Judicial officers of a State, or the members of the Legislature thereof, is denied to any of the male inhabitants of such State, being twenty-one years of age, and citizens of the United States, or in any way abridged, except for participation in rebellion, or other crime, the basis of representation therein shall be reduced in the proportion which the number of such male citizens shall bear to the whole number of male citizens twenty-one years of age in such State.

Section 3

No person shall be a Senator or Representative in Congress, or elector of President and Vice President, or hold any office, civil or military, under the United States, or under any State, who, having previously taken an oath, as a member of Congress, or as an officer of the United States, or as a member of any State legislature, or as an executive or judicial officer of any State, to support the Constitution

Abolition of Slavery Amendments Thirteen (1865), Fourteen (1868), and Fifteen (1870) often are called the Civil War amendments because they grew out of that great conflict. The Thirteenth Amendment outlaws slavery.

Rights of Citizens The Fourteenth Amendment (1868) originally was intended to protect the legal rights of the freed slaves. Today it protects the rights of citizenship in general by prohibiting a state from depriving any person of life, liberty, or property without "due process of law." In addition, it states that all citizens have the right to equal protection of the law in all states.

Representation in Congress This section reduced the number of members a state had in the House of Representatives if it denied its citizens the right to vote. Later civil rights laws and the Twenty-fourth Amendment guaranteed the vote to African Americans.

Vocabulary
abridge: to reduce

The Constitution of the United States

Content Background Knowledge

The Thirteenth, Fourteenth, and Fifteenth Amendments represent attempts to use the Constitution to end slavery, to extend citizenship to former enslaved persons, and to guarantee African Americans the right to vote. Literacy tests, poll taxes, and grandfather clauses, however, continued to keep large numbers of African Americans from voting in many Southern states even after Reconstruction.

C Critical Thinking Skills

Making Connections Tell students that Section 1 of the Fourteenth Amendment sets out two of the three alternative requirements of American citizenship. **Ask: What are the two requirements for citizenship listed here?** *(birth on American soil and naturalization)* Tell students the third possible requirement is birth to a parent who is an American citizen.

This section also concerns the rights of citizens. **Ask: What two principles of the Constitution regarding the legal rights of citizens are stated in Section 1 of the Fourteenth Amendment?** *(grants to all citizens due process of the law and equal protection of the law)*

Fights for Equality

Identifying Evidence Explain that Amendment XIV, especially Section 1, has been used in the fight for civil rights, woman's suffrage, rights for those with disabilities, and immigrants' rights. Have students choose a group of people and research that group's fight for equality. Then have students write an editorial connecting Amendment XIV to the group's cause. Encourage students to add visuals to their editorials and to include information about the people who led the group's efforts for equal rights.

The Constitution of the United States

R Reading Skills

Identifying Read aloud or have a volunteer read aloud the Sixteenth Amendment. Point out to students that it changed Article I, Section 9, Clause 4 of the Constitution. The amendment was ratified in 1913 and is still the basis for federal income tax laws. **Ask: What new power did the Sixteenth Amendment grant Congress?** *(the right to levy an income tax)* **AL**

C Critical Thinking Skills

Analyzing Primary Sources Have students glance through the Constitution pages. **Ask: How were senators chosen before the Seventeenth Amendment became law?** *(U.S. senators were chosen by the state legislatures)* You may wish to refer students to Article I, Section 3, Clause 2 of the Constitution. **Ask: Did the Seventeenth Amendment make the Senate more or less democratic? Why?** *(more; because all the voters in a state can choose senators, and they are elected by direct vote)*

Public Debt The public debt acquired by the federal government during the Civil War was valid and could not be questioned by the South. However, the debts of the Confederacy were declared to be illegal. *Could former slaveholders collect payment for the loss of their slaves?*

Right to Vote The Fifteenth Amendment (1870) prohibits the government from denying a person's right to vote on the basis of race. Despite the law, many states denied African Americans the right to vote by such means as poll taxes, literacy tests, and white primaries. During the 1950s and 1960s, Congress passed successively stronger laws to end racial discrimination in voting rights.

Election of Senators The Seventeenth Amendment (1913) states that the people, instead of state legislatures, elect United States senators. *How many years are in a Senate term?*

Vocabulary
emancipation: freedom from slavery

of the United States, shall have engaged in insurrection or rebellion against the same, or given aid or comfort to the enemies thereof. But Congress may by a vote of two-thirds of each House, remove such disability.

Section 4
The validity of the public debt of the United States, authorized by law, including debts incurred for payment of pensions and bounties for service in suppressing insurrection or rebellion, shall not be questioned. But neither the United States nor any State shall assume or pay any debt or obligation incurred in aid of insurrection or rebellion against the United States, or any claim for the loss or **emancipation** of any slave; but all such debts, obligations and claims shall be held illegal and void.

Section 5
The Congress shall have power to enforce, by appropriate legislation, the provisions of this article.

Amendment XV
Section 1
The right of citizens of the United States to vote shall not be denied or abridged by the United States or by any State on account of race, color, or previous condition of servitude.

Section 2
The Congress shall have power to enforce this article by appropriate legislation.

Amendment XVI
R The Congress shall have power to lay and collect taxes on incomes, from whatever source derived, without apportionment among the several States and without regard to any census or enumeration.

Amendment XVII
Section 1
C The Senate of the United States shall be composed of two Senators from each State, elected by the people thereof, for six years; and each Senator shall have one vote. The electors in each State shall have the qualifications requisite for electors of the most numerous branch of the State legislatures.

---

netw⊙rks *Online Teaching Options*

Income Tax

Creating Maps, Graphs, Charts, Time Lines Explain to students that as population grows, so do government spending and taxes. Have students create a line graph. One line will show how the average income of Americans has increased since 1915. A second line will indicate tax increases. Students should look online for information to complete their graph. Encourage students to use a spreadsheet program to generate their graph. When students have finished their graphs, ask students to show them to family members or friends and to note personal reactions. Have students share responses with the class. **Ask: Do you agree that income tax is necessary? Should everyone pay the same rate, or should it be a progressive tax (rates rise with income), as it is now?** Engage students in a discussion of the relationship between growing population and increasing government expenditures.

ANSWERS, p. 236

Public Debt No, they could not.

Election of Senators six years

Section 2

When vacancies happen in the representation of any State in the Senate, the executive authority of such State shall issue writs of election to fill such vacancies: *Provided,* That the legislature of any State may empower the executive thereof to make temporary appointments until the people fill the vacancies by election as the legislature may direct.

Section 3

This amendment shall not be so construed as to affect the election or term of any Senator chosen before it becomes valid as part of the Constitution.

R

Amendment XVIII

Section 1

After one year from ratification of this article, the manufacture, sale, or transportation of intoxicating liquors within, the importation thereof into, or the exportation thereof from the United States and all territory subject to the jurisdiction thereof for beverage purposes is hereby prohibited.

C

Section 2

The Congress and the several States shall have concurrent power to enforce this article by appropriate legislation.

Section 3

This article shall be inoperative unless it shall have been ratified as an amendment to the Constitution by the legislatures of the several States, as provided in the Constitution, within seven years from the date of the submission hereof to the States by the Congress.

Amendment XIX

Section 1

The right of citizens of the United States to vote shall not be denied or abridged by the United States or by any State on account of sex.

Section 2

Congress shall have power by appropriate legislation to enforce the provisions of this article.

Prohibition The Eighteenth Amendment (1919) prohibited the production, sale, or transportation of alcoholic beverages in the United States. Prohibition proved to be difficult to enforce. This amendment was later repealed by the Twenty-first Amendment.

Woman Suffrage The Nineteenth Amendment (1920) guaranteed women the right to vote. By then women had already won the right to vote in many state elections, but the amendment put their right to vote in all state and national elections on a constitutional basis.

R **Reading Skills**

Paraphrasing Have students rephrase the Seventeenth Amendment, Section 3, in their own words. *(Senators elected under the old system will continue to serve their terms.)* **BL**

C **Critical Thinking Skills**

Defending The Eighteenth Amendment made the production, sale, or transportation of alcohol illegal. **Ask: What legislative power gave Congress the right to pass this amendment?** *(the power to regulate commerce)*

Organize students into groups to debate the pros and cons of Prohibition. Give groups time to prepare their arguments and encourage each group member to be responsible for a different part of the research. As each group presents its argument, note major points on the board. When groups have completed the debate, lead the class in a discussion by asking: **Is Prohibition an issue that should have been addressed in a Constitutional amendment? Why or why not?**

Woman's Suffrage

Creating Maps, Graphs, Charts, Time Lines Point out that several states and local municipalities gave women the right to vote before the federal government did. Have students conduct research on the Internet and create a map that shows when women gained suffrage in different states. Have students share their work with the class. Then guide students in a discussion of why it might have been easier for women to gain the right to vote locally before they were granted the right to vote through a Constitutional amendment.

The Constitution of the United States

R1 Reading Skills

Defining Students who are learning the English language are probably not familiar with the expression "lame duck." **Ask:** What does "lame duck" mean in terms of elected officials? *(people who have announced they will retire or who have lost their bid for reelection but whose original term of office still has time remaining)* Explain to students that these officials are called "lame ducks" because—like injured ducks that cannot fly—they are not able to do much. **ELL**

R2 Reading Skills

Defining Direct students' attention to the bottom of the page, where *president elect* is defined. **Ask:** What does *vice president elect* mean? *(a vice president who has been elected but has not yet begun serving his or her term)* **ELL**

"Lame-Duck" Amendments The Twentieth Amendment (1933) sets new dates for Congress to begin its term and for the inauguration of the president and vice president. Under the original Constitution, elected officials who retired or who had been defeated remained in office for several months. For the outgoing president, this period ran from November until March. Such outgoing officials had little influence and accomplished little, and they were called lame ducks because they were so inactive. *What date was fixed as Inauguration Day?* **R1**

Succession This section provides that if the president-elect dies before taking office, the vice president-elect becomes president.

Amendment XX

Section 1

The terms of the President and Vice President shall end at noon on the 20th day of January, and the terms of the Senators and Representatives at noon on the 3d day of January, of the years in which such terms would have ended if this article had not been ratified; and the terms of their successors shall then begin.

Section 2

The Congress shall assemble at least once in every year, and such meeting shall begin at noon on the 3d day of January, unless they shall by law appoint a different day.

Section 3

If, at the time fixed for the beginning of the term of the President, the **President elect** shall have died, the Vice President elect shall become President. If a President shall not have been chosen before the time fixed for the beginning of his term, or if the President elect shall have failed to qualify, then the Vice President elect shall act as President until a President shall have qualified; and the Congress may by law provide for the case wherein neither a President elect nor a Vice President elect shall have qualified, declaring who shall then act as President, or the manner in which one who is to act shall be selected, and such person shall act accordingly until a President or Vice President shall have qualified.

Section 4

The Congress may by law provide for the case of the death of any of the persons from whom the House of Representatives may choose a President whenever the right of choice shall have devolved upon them, and for the case of the death of any of the persons from whom the Senate may choose a Vice President whenever the right of choice shall have devolved upon them.

Section 5

Section 1 and 2 shall take effect on the 15th day of October following the ratification of this article.

Vocabulary
president elect: individual who is elected president but has not yet begun serving his or her term **R2**

---

networks   *Online Teaching Options*

Lame-Duck Cartoons

Analyzing Primary Sources Have groups search online for current or historical political cartoons that address lame-duck congressional sessions or presidents. Have each group make a slide show of cartoons and share the final product with the class. Remind students to include citations for the cartoons so the reader will know where and when the cartoon was created, as well as the name of the cartoonist. Students should discuss the meanings of the cartoons. Encourage students to make their own political cartoons to add to their slide show. You might also wish to encourage students to create a series of cartoons, showing both sides of particular issues.

ANSWER, p. 238

"Lame-Duck" Amendments January 20

Section 6

This article shall be inoperative unless it shall have been ratified as an amendment to the Constitution by the legislatures of three-fourths of the several States within seven years from the date of its submission.

C

Amendment XXI

Section 1

The eighteenth article of amendment to the Constitution of the United States is hereby repealed.

Section 2

The transportation or importation into any State, Territory, or possession of the United States for delivery or use therein of intoxicating liquors, in violation of the laws thereof, is hereby prohibited.

Section 3

This article shall be inoperative unless it shall have been ratified as an amendment to the Constitution by conventions in the several States, as provided in the Constitution, within seven years from the date of the submission hereof to the States by the Congress.

R1

> **Repeal of Prohibition** The Twenty-first Amendment (1933) repeals the Eighteenth Amendment. It is the only amendment ever passed to overturn an earlier amendment. It is also the only amendment ratified by special state conventions instead of state legislatures.

Amendment XXII

Section 1

No person shall be elected to the office of the President more than twice, and no person who had held the office of President, or acted as President, for more than two years of a term to which some other person was elected President shall be elected to the office of the President more than once. But this Article shall not apply to any person holding the office of President when this Article was proposed by the Congress, and shall not prevent any person who may be holding the office of President, or acting as President, during the term within which this Article becomes operative from holding the office of President or acting as President during the remainder of such term.

R2

W

> **Term Limit** The Twenty-second Amendment (1951) limits presidents to a maximum of two elected terms. It was passed largely as a reaction to Franklin D. Roosevelt's election to four terms between 1933 and 1945.

Section 2

This article shall be inoperative unless it shall have been ratified as an amendment to the Constitution by the legislatures of three-fourths of the several States within seven years from the date of its submission to the States by the Congress.

The Constitution of the United States

C Critical Thinking Skills

Predicting Consequences This was the first amendment that was ratified that put a time limit on ratification of constitutional amendments. **Ask: Do you expect later amendments to include this language? Why or why not?** *(Students are likely to answer yes because once the idea of time limits was introduced, people would probably want to repeat it.)* Have students read Amendment XXI, Section 3, and Amendment XXII, Section 2, to confirm their predictions.

R1 Reading Skills

Using Context Clues Have students read the note explaining the Twenty-first Amendment. **Ask: What does** *repeal* **mean?** *(to cancel an earlier law)*

R2 Reading Skills

Explaining Make sure that students understand the differences in the term limits. **Ask: How many times can someone be elected as president?** *(two)* **How many times can someone be elected as president if he or she first is a vice president who succeeds to the presidency and serves two or more years?** *(one)* **AL**

W Writing Skills

Argument Have students write a persuasive essay in which they argue that the two-term limit on presidents is a good or bad idea. Remind students to write a coherent statement of their thesis and have a well-supported conclusion. Ask them to cite historical evidence to support their positions.

Presidential Terms

Researching on the Internet The Twenty-second Amendment became law in 1951. Give students a list of presidents, 1951 to the present. Have students work with a partner to identify which of these presidents and vice presidents were subject to the amendment—presidents who served two terms and vice presidents who succeeded to the presidency, served two or more years, and were then elected as president in their own right. Students should use the Internet as their primary research tool. Have students use the data to create an interactive table or chart showing their research results.

The Constitution of the United States

G1 Critical Thinking Skills

Analyzing Point out that although the people of the District of Columbia have presidential electors, they do not have members with full voting rights in the House or Senate. Have students discuss whether this situation is fair for the people of the District. Remind students to provide reasons that support their opinions.

W Writing Skills

Argument Imagine you are a resident of Washington, D.C. You have only recently been allowed to vote in presidential elections (1963). Yet, presently, you do not have representation in Congress. No one represents the District of Columbia in the House or in the Senate. Write a letter to the Supreme Court or to the president, urging them to support you in your fight to win representation in Congress. You might wish to suggest that students consider some of the slogans from the Revolutionary War era: is this taxation without representation?

G2 Critical Thinking Skills

Making Connections In 1966, the Supreme Court ruled that poll taxes violated the Fourteenth Amendment. **Ask: How would requiring someone to pay a poll, or voting, tax violate that person's Fourteenth Amendment rights?** *(Students may say that the Fourteenth Amendment says the states cannot reduce the privileges of U.S. citizens. Voting is one of those privileges, and a poll tax reduces or eliminates the ability of some citizens to exercise that privilege. Students might also cite the amendment's equal protection clause.)*

V Visual Skills

Creating Maps, Graphs, Charts, Time Lines Have students find the order of succession in case of a president's death and create a flowchart illustrating the sequence. **AL**
ELL Visual/Spatial

Content Background Knowledge

The assassination of President John F. Kennedy made apparent the need for a constitutional amendment on presidential disability. Kennedy's successor, Lyndon Johnson, had once suffered a heart attack, and the two men in line of succession after Johnson were both more than 70 years old. Congress quickly passed the Twenty-fifth Amendment, which was submitted to the states in mid-1965 and was ratified early in 1967.

ANSWER, p. 240

The Vice President the president pro tempore of the Senate (the vice president) and the Speaker of the House of Representatives

---

240

Electors for the District of Columbia The Twenty-third Amendment (1961) allows citizens living in Washington, D.C., to vote for president and vice president, a right previously denied residents of the nation's capital. The District of Columbia now has three presidential electors, the number to which it would be entitled if it were a state.

Abolition of Poll Tax The Twenty-fourth Amendment (1964) prohibits poll taxes in federal elections. Prior to the passage of this amendment, some states had used such taxes to keep low-income African Americans from voting. In 1966 the Supreme Court banned poll taxes in state elections as well.

The Vice President The Twenty-fifth Amendment (1967) established a process for the vice president to take over leadership of the nation when a president is disabled. It also set procedures for filling a vacancy in the office of vice president.

This amendment was used in 1973, when Vice President Spiro Agnew resigned from office after being charged with accepting bribes. President Richard Nixon then appointed Gerald R. Ford as vice president in accordance with the provisions of the Twenty-fifth Amendment. A year later, President Nixon resigned during the Watergate scandal and Ford became president. President Ford then had to fill the vice presidency, which he had left vacant upon assuming the presidency. He named Nelson A. Rockefeller as vice president. Thus individuals who had not been elected held both the presidency and the vice presidency. *Whom does the president inform if he or she cannot carry out the duties of the office?*

240 *The Constitution*

Amendment XXIII

Section 1
The District constituting the seat of Government of the United States shall appoint in such manner as the Congress may direct:
A number of electors of President and Vice President equal to the whole number of Senators and Representatives in Congress to which the District would be entitled if it were a State, but in no event more than the least populous State; they shall be in addition to those appointed by the States, but they shall be considered, for the purposes of the election of President and Vice President, to be electors appointed by a State; and they shall meet in the District and perform such duties as provided by the twelfth article of amendment.

Section 2
The Congress shall have power to enforce this article by appropriate legislation.

Amendment XXIV

Section 1
The right of citizens of the United States to vote in any primary or other election for President or Vice President, for electors for President or Vice President, or for Senator or Representative in Congress, shall not be denied or abridged by the United States or any State by reason of failure to pay any poll tax or other tax.

Section 2
The Congress shall have power to enforce this article by appropriate legislation.

Amendment XXV

Section 1
In case of the removal of the President from office or his death or resignation, the Vice President shall become President.

Section 2
Whenever there is a vacancy in the office of the Vice President, the President shall nominate a Vice President who shall take the office upon confirmation by a majority vote of both Houses of Congress.

---

netw☉rks   *Online Teaching Options*

The Death of a President

Analyzing News Media On a few occasions, the president of the United States has died, been assassinated, or become disabled. The most recent case was the assassination of President John F. Kennedy in 1963. Have students find news coverage—print or video—of Kennedy's assassination and funeral. Have students create print or digital collages or posters with their findings to share with the class. **Ask: Based on the news coverage, how did the people of the United States react to Kennedy's death? How did the world react?** Have students analyze the coverage, noting instances of emotion or bias by the reporter.

Section 3

Whenever the President transmits to the President pro tempore of the Senate and the Speaker of the House of Representatives his written declaration that he is unable to discharge the powers and duties of his office, and until he transmits to them a written declaration to the contrary, such powers and duties shall be discharged by the Vice President as Acting President.

Section 4

Whenever the Vice President and a majority of either the principal officers of the executive departments or of such other body as Congress may by law provide, transmit to the President pro tempore of the Senate and the Speaker of the House of Representatives their written declaration that the President is unable to discharge the powers and duties of his office, the Vice President shall immediately assume the power and duties of the office of Acting President.

Thereafter, when the President transmits to the President pro tempore of the Senate and the Speaker of the House of Representatives his written declaration that no inability exists, he shall resume the powers and duties of his office unless the Vice President and a majority of either the principal officers of the executive department or of such other body as Congress may by law provide, transmit within four days to the President pro tempore of the Senate and the Speaker of the House of Representatives their written declaration that the President is unable to discharge the powers and duties of his office. Thereupon Congress shall decide the issue, assembling within forty-eight hours for that purpose if not in session. If the Congress, within twenty-one days after receipt of the latter written declaration, or, if Congress is not in session, within twenty-one days after Congress is required to assemble, determines by two-thirds vote of both Houses that the President is unable to discharge the powers and duties of his office, the Vice President shall continue to discharge the same as Acting President; otherwise, the President shall resume the power and duties of his office.

Amendment XXVI **T**

Section 1

The right of citizens of the United States, who are eighteen years of age or older, to vote shall not be denied or abridged by the United States or by any State on account of age.

> **Voting Age** The Twenty-sixth Amendment (1971) lowered the voting age in both federal and state elections to 18.

The Constitution **241**

The Constitution of the United States

G₁ Critical Thinking Skills

Making Inferences Ask: Why does Section 4 of the Twenty-fifth Amendment provide a way for someone other than the president to declare that the president cannot serve? *(in case the president is too ill to be able to make the declaration)* **BL**

T Technology Skills

Researching on the Internet Have students use the Internet to look up the history of the Twenty-sixth Amendment. Tell them to find out what major issue facing the nation led to its approval. Discuss with students the ramifications and consequences of this amendment. **Ask: When younger people can vote, does it make them feel more tied to the current political situation? Does it encourage them to enter politics? Are younger people more likely to campaign for candidates or to take more interest in local and national policies?**

G₂ Critical Thinking Skills

Defending Point out that the turnout in elections among people ages 18 to 21 tends to be low. **Ask: If so few young people vote in elections, should they lose the right to vote?** Have students debate the issue. If students have researched the number of younger voters in the past presidential election, have them use that data to support their positions in the debate.

Young Voters

Creating Maps, Graphs, Charts, Time Lines Have students use the Internet to find voter turnout data for the last two or three presidential elections, focusing on voters ages 18 to 21. Have students create a graph to illustrate their data and present their graphs to the class. Discuss as a class any trends the graphs suggest.

The Constitution of the United States

Making Connections

Many people used the Vietnam War to justify adoption of the Twenty-sixth Amendment. These people argued that those old enough to fight and die for their country were also old enough to vote.

CLOSE & REFLECT

Categorizing Have students categorize the articles and amendments of the Constitution on a chart with the following headings: *Process of Government, Personal Freedoms, Relations Among States, Citizenship*. Students should keep in mind the substance of each article and amendment and its effect on American life. Remind students that some articles and amendments might fit in more than one category.

Congressional Pay Raises The Twenty-seventh Amendment (1992) makes congressional pay raises effective during the term following their passage. James Madison offered the amendment in 1789, but it was never adopted. In 1982 Gregory Watson, then a student at the University of Texas, discovered the forgotten amendment while doing research for a school paper. Watson made the amendment's passage his crusade.

Section 2

The Congress shall have power to enforce this article by appropriate legislation.

Amendment XXVII

No law, varying the compensation for the services of Senators and Representatives, shall take effect, until an election of representatives shall have intervened.

▼ Joint meeting of Congress

Time & Life Images/Getty Images

netw⊙rks   *Online Teaching Options*

A School Constitution

Synthesizing Have students work in groups to write a constitution for your school. Students should begin the document with a preamble that lists goals for school government. Each group member should write an article describing one branch of the school government. Be certain that groups list the function of each branch. Have students decide if they think some powers should be denied to the school government and list these in another article. Finally, have students decide if a bill of rights is necessary. If so, have students list the rights they think should be added. Have students type their constitutions using a word processing program and give students the option of publishing their constitutions as wikis or blogs.

CHAPTER 9
The Federalist Era Planner

UNDERSTANDING BY DESIGN®

Enduring Understanding
- *People, places, and ideas change over time.*

Essential Questions
- *What are the characteristics of a leader?*
- *Why does conflict develop?*
- *How do governments change?*

Predictable Misunderstandings

Students may think:
- *Political parties always dominated the American political system.*
- *Western expansion of the United States was easy.*
- *George Washington had a trouble-free presidency.*

Assessment Evidence

Performance Tasks:
- *Hands-On Chapter Project*

Other Evidence:
- *Interactive Graphic Organizers*
- *What Do You Know? activity*
- *Geography and History Activity*
- *Economics of History Activity*
- *21st Century Skills Activity*
- *Class discussions about the Federalists and the Jeffersonian Republicans*
- *Written Paragraphs*
- *Lesson Reviews*
- *Online Self-Check Quizzes*
- *Chapter Activities and Assessment*

NCSS Standards covered in "The Federalist Era"

Learners will understand:

2 TIME, CONTINUITY, AND CHANGE
   6. The origins and influences of social, cultural, political, and economic systems

   8. The history of democratic ideals and principles, and how they are represented in documents, artifacts, and symbols

5 INDIVIDUALS, GROUPS, AND INSTITUTIONS
   3. Institutions are created to respond to changing individual and group needs

   8. That when two or more groups with differing norms and beliefs interact, accommodation or conflict may result

6 POWER, AUTHORITY, AND GOVERNANCE
   2. Fundamental ideas that are the foundation of American constitutional democracy (including those of the U.S. Constitution, popular sovereignty, the rule of law, separation of powers, checks and balances, minority rights, the separation of church and state, and Federalism)

   5. The ways in which governments meet the needs and wants of citizens, manage conflict, and establish order and society

10 CIVIC IDEALS AND PRACTICES
   6. The origins and function of major institutions and practices developed to support democratic ideals and practices

SUGGESTED PACING GUIDE

Introducing the Chapter . . . . 1 day	Lesson 3 . . . . .2 days
Lesson 1 . . . . .2 days	Chapter Wrap-Up and Assessment . . . . . . 1 day
Lesson 2 . . . . 1 day	

TOTAL TIME   7 Days

Key for Using the Teacher Edition

SKILL-BASED ACTIVITIES

Types of skill activities found in the Teacher Edition.

V Visual Skills require students to analyze maps, graphs, charts, and photos.

R Reading Skills help students practice reading skills and master vocabulary.

W Writing Skills provide writing opportunities to help students comprehend the text.

C Critical Thinking Skills help students apply and extend what they have learned.

T Technology Skills require students to use digital tools effectively.

Letters are followed by a number when there is more than one of the same type of skill on the page.

DIFFERENTIATED INSTRUCTION

All activities are written for the on-level student unless otherwise marked with the leveled labels below.

BL Beyond Level
AL Approaching Level
ELL English Language Learners

All students benefit from activities that utilize different learning styles. Many activities are marked as below when a particular learning style is highlighted.

Intrapersonal	Naturalist
Logical/Mathematical	Kinesthetic
Visual/Spatial	Auditory/Musical
Verbal/Linguistic	Interpersonal

CHAPTER OPENER PLANNER

Students will know:
- how the federal government developed under George Washington.
- how the new government responded to internal and external threats.
- how the two-party political system developed in America.

Students will be able to:
- **identify and analyze** the development of the American political system during the Federalist Era.
- **evaluate** decisions made by the new government.
- **draw conclusions** about how the economy developed under Hamilton.
- **identify and analyze** the challenges on the frontier that the new government faced.
- **analyze and explain** American relations with European nations under Washington and Adams.
- **contrast** the views of the developing political parties.
- **identify and analyze** issues that developed during the presidency of John Adams.

UNDERSTANDING BY DESIGN®

Print Teaching Options

V **Visual Skills**

☐ **P. 244** Students analyze a map of the United Stated in 1790 and imagine how their lives would be different if they lived in 1790. **Visual/Spatial**

C **Critical Thinking Skills**

☐ **P. 245** Students review a time line and speculate on how a particular event will affect the future of the nation. **BL**

T **Technology Skills**

☐ **P. 245** Students research the impact of the discovery of the Rosetta Stone.

Online Teaching Options

V **Visual Skills**

☐ **MAP** **United States 1789–1800**—Students locate states, territories, and disputed areas.

☐ **TIME LINE** **Place and Time: United States 1789 to 1800**—Students learn about key events in American history between 1789 and 1800.

☐ **WORLD ATLAS** Students can use this interactive map to identify regions of the world, learn about individual countries, locate political boundaries, measure distances, and much more.

Printable Digital Worksheets

R **Reading Skills**

☐ **GRAPHIC NOVEL** *Election Deadlock*—The novel reports events of the election of 1800, when Jefferson and Burr tied for president.

Project-Based Learning

Hands-On Chapter Project

The Federalist Era

Student groups will research significant events of the Federalist Era and create a time line. Students will then coordinate with other groups to combine time line sections into a coherent, complete time line to display in the classroom.

Technology Extension

Interactive Time Line

- Find an additional activity online that incorporates technology for this project.
- Visit the EdTechTeacher Web sites (included in the Technology Extension for this chapter) for more links, tutorials, and other resources.

Print Resources

ANCILLARY RESOURCES
These ancillaries are available for every chapter and lesson.

- **Reading Essentials and Study Guide Workbook** **AL** **ELL**
- **Chapter Tests and Lesson Quizzes Blackline Masters**

PRINTABLE DIGITAL WORKSHEETS
These printable digital worksheets are available for every chapter and lesson.

- **Hands-On Chapter Projects**
- **What Do You Know? activities**
- **Chapter Summaries (English and Spanish)**
- **Vocabulary Builder activities**
- **Guided Reading activities**

More Media Resources

SUGGESTED READING

Grade 6 reading level
- *Who Was George Washington?* by Roberta Edwards

Grade 7 reading level:
- *George Washington's Socks,* by Elvira Woodruff

Grade 8 reading level:
- *John Adams: Young Revolutionary,* by Jan Adkins

THE FIRST PRESIDENT

Students will know:
- how the federal government developed under George Washington.

Students will be able to:
- **identify and analyze** the development of the American political system during the Federalist Era.
- **evaluate decisions** made by the new government.
- **draw conclusions** about how the economy developed under Hamilton.

UNDERSTANDING
BY DESIGN®

☑ *Print Teaching Options*

R Reading Skills

☐ **P. 247** Students make conclusions about the precedent set by the vote on the president's power over the cabinet.

☐ **P. 247** Students recall the system of checks and balances and how that relates to the Judiciary Act of 1789. **AL**

☐ **P. 248** Students discuss the protection the Bill of Rights provides.

☐ **P. 249** Students discuss Hamilton's argument that the national government should pay national debts. **AL**

☐ **P. 250** Students describe what a bond is and Hamilton's plan for paying back old bonds. **AL** **ELL**

☐ **P. 251** Students discuss the national bank and why some leaders opposed it.

W Writing Skills

☐ **P. 246** Students write a narrative about George Washington's presence in everyday life today. **AL**

C Critical Thinking Skills

☐ **P. 246** Students speculate on what George Washington meant when he said that "no slip" of his "will pass unnoticed."

☐ **P. 247** Students discuss how the president's cabinet today compares with George Washington's cabinet.

☐ **P. 249** Students compare the influence of the treasury secretary today with the influence of Alexander Hamilton. **BL**

☐ **P. 249** Students discuss their experiences with borrowing and lending money with friends or relatives. **AL** **ELL**

☐ **P. 250** Students infer why the Southern leaders' support for Hamilton's plan would be beneficial to the South.

T Technology Skills

☐ **P. 248** Pairs of students make a presentation to the class about the Bill of Rights. **AL** Visual/Spatial

---

☑ *Online Teaching Options*

V Visual Skills

☐ **VIDEO** **The First President: Washington's Legacy**—Students view a video that describes the impressive career of the nation's first president.

☐ **SLIDE SHOW** **The U.S. Supreme Court**—Students learn of important milestones in the court's history.

R Reading Skills

☐ **GRAPHIC ORGANIZER** **Taking Notes:** *Describing:* **Important Figures in the Nation's Early Years**—Students list and identify accomplishments of leaders during the nation's early years.

☐ **BIOGRAPHY** **Alexander Hamilton**—Students read a biography of the first Secretary of the Treasury.

C Critical Thinking Skills

☐ **IMAGE** **The First Cabinet**—Students click to reveal biographical data on the men who made up Washington's cabinet.

☐ **CHART** **Protective Tariffs**—Students interpret graphs that explain how tariffs impact the cost of goods.

T Technology Skills

☐ **SELF-CHECK QUIZ** **Lesson 1**—Students receive instant feedback on their mastery of lesson content.

☐ **GAME** **First President Crossword Puzzle**—Students solve clues to review lesson vocabulary and concepts.

☑ *Printable Digital Worksheets*

W Writing Skills

☐ **WORKSHEET** **Economics of History Activity: The National Debt**—Students research the amount of the national debt over time and write about their findings.

C Critical Thinking Skills

☐ **WORKSHEET** **21st Century Skills Activity: Information Literacy: Recognizing Historical Perspectives**—Students explore how the passage of time can affect how people view a historical event, place, or person.

EARLY CHALLENGES

Students will know:
- *how the new government responded to internal and external threats.*

Students will be able to:
- ***identify and analyze*** *the challenges on the frontier that the new government faced.*
- ***analyze and explain*** *American relations with European nations under Washington and Adams.*

UNDERSTANDING
BY DESIGN®

Print Teaching Options

R Reading Skills

☐ **P. 252** Students explain the Whiskey Rebellion and the use of arms by both protestors and the government. **AL**

☐ **P. 253** Students identify important leaders and events that took place in the Northwest Territory. **AL**

W Writing Skills

☐ **P. 254** Students paraphrase the first paragraph of a section of text.

☐ **P. 255** Students read a line from George Washington's address and write paragraphs arguing either for or against neutrality in foreign policy. **AL**

C Critical Thinking Skills

☐ **P. 252** Students determine the cause of the Whiskey Rebellion.

☐ **P. 254** Students analyze the differing opinions of Americans on the French Revolution.

☐ **P. 254** Students create a list to compare Jay's Treaty to Pinckney's Treaty. **AL** **ELL**

Online Teaching Options

V Visual Skills

VIDEO **George Washington**—Students view a video of an actor playing the part of George Washington on the eve of his second inauguration as he expresses concerns about the nation and his role as president.

MAP **Native American Campaigns, 1791–1795**—Students trace major campaigns against Native Americans in what is now Indiana and Ohio.

R Reading Skills

GRAPHIC ORGANIZER **Taking Notes:** *Determining Cause and Effect:* **Treaties and Their Effects**—Students summarize how three treaties affected the United States.

BIOGRAPHY **John Jay**—Students read biographical information about the first chief justice of the United States.

C Critical Thinking Skills

PRIMARY SOURCE **Little Turtle and the Treaty of Greenville**—Students read biographical information about Little Turtle and an excerpt from the treaty he signed.

T Technology Skills

SELF-CHECK QUIZ **Lesson 2**—Students receive instant feedback on their mastery of lesson content.

GAME **Early Challenges Fill-in-the-Blank Game**—Students complete statements to review lesson concepts.

Printable Digital Worksheets

C Critical Thinking Skills

WORKSHEET **Geography and History Activity: Understanding Location: Treaties and Forts of the Northwest Territory**—Students analyze text and a map in order to answer questions about the Northwest Territory.

THE FIRST POLITICAL PARTIES

Students will know:
- *how the two-party political system developed in America.*

Students will be able to:
- *contrast* the views of the developing political parties.
- *identify and analyze* issues that developed during the presidency of John Adams.

UNDERSTANDING
BY DESIGN®

Print Teaching Options

V Visual Skills

☐ **P. 257** Students review a political cartoon and draw conclusions about the differences in opinion in the country implied by the cartoon. **BL** Visual/Spatial

R Reading Skills

☐ **P. 256** Students identify the leaders whose supporters formed the first two political parties. **AL**

☐ **P. 256** Students compare the definition of the word *factions* in the late 1700s with how it is commonly used today. **ELL**

☐ **P. 258** Students summarize the events and results of the election of 1796. **AL**

☐ **P. 259** Students identify the events of the XYZ Affair and explain how this scandal got its name. **AL**

☐ **P. 260** Students explain why the Virginia and Kentucky Resolutions were created in response to the Alien and Sedition Acts. **AL**

W Writing Skills

☐ **P. 257** Students work in teams to write sentences that show the differences in the interpretation of the Constitution between the two parties. **AL** **ELL** Interpersonal

C Critical Thinking Skills

☐ **P. 257** Students analyze what Hamilton meant when he said that people are "turbulent and changing." **BL**

☐ **P. 258** Students create a T-chart that illustrates where Hamilton and Jefferson stood on the important issues of the time. **AL**

☐ **P. 259** Students predict how John Adams would fare as a president based on what they learned about him in previous chapters.

☐ **P. 259** Students make inferences about the actions of the French agents involved in the XYZ Affair.

☐ **P. 260** Students review the chart on the Alien and Sedition Acts. **BL**

☐ **P. 260** Students examine the principle of states' rights. **AL** **ELL**

☐ **P. 261** Students determine the effects of Adams' decision to send a representative to seek peace with France.

Online Teaching Options

V Visual Skills

☐ **VIDEO** **Electing the President: Political Parties**—Students view a video that describes how the development of political parties affected presidential campaigning.

☐ **IMAGE** **The White House**—Students view an image of the East Room of the White House being used to hang laundry while the building was under construction.

R Reading Skills

☐ **GRAPHIC ORGANIZER** **Taking Notes:** *Comparing and Contrasting:* **Role of the Federal Government**—Students compare and contrast the ideals of the first two U.S. political parties.

☐ **POLITICAL CARTOON** **The Providential Detection**—Students consider the role of political cartoons throughout U.S. history.

C Critical Thinking Skills

☐ **WHITEBOARD ACTIVITY** **The First Party System**—Students sort characteristics by which political party they describe.

☐ **CHART** **Jefferson and Hamilton**—Students click to compare and contrast the views of Jefferson and Hamilton on a number of issues.

☐ **CHART** **The Alien and Sedition Acts**—Students click to reveal information on how these four laws affected the ability of immigrants to become U.S. citizens.

T Technology Skills

☐ **SELF-CHECK QUIZ** **Lesson 3**—Students receive instant feedback on their mastery of lesson content.

INTERVENTION AND REMEDIATION STRATEGIES

LESSON 1   The First President

Reading and Comprehension

Pair students. Direct each pair to create one-sentence summaries of the text under each heading in the lesson.

Text Evidence

Tell students to reread the definition of *precedent*. Then have them reread the lesson and list three *precedents* George Washington set as the first president.

LESSON 2   Early Challenges

Reading and Comprehension

After students have read the lesson, have them scan the lesson, reading only the headings. Discuss with them how and why headings in the text can help them anticipate, understand, and recall what they have read.

Text Evidence

Have students write a one-paragraph speech from George Washington's point of view. The title and subject of the speech should be "Challenges I Faced as President."

LESSON 3   The First Political Parties

Reading and Comprehension

Direct students to review the images that accompany the text in Lesson 3. Tell them to write new captions for each image that help summarize the content of the lesson.

Text Evidence

Remind students that words in boldface are important because they are likely to be words that are new to students or are important terms. Have students list the boldface words in Lesson 3 and identify each as a new vocabulary word or a new term important to their understanding of history.

Online Resources

Approaching Level Reader

Use this online lower-level text that corresponds directly to the text in the Student Edition. It includes a Spanish version.

Guided Reading Activities

This resource uses graphic organizers and guiding questions to help students with comprehension.

What Do You Know?

Use these worksheets to pre-assess student's background knowledge before they study the chapter.

Reading Essentials and Study Guide Workbook

This resource offers writing and reading activities for the approaching-level student. Also available in Spanish.

Self-Check Quizzes

This online assessment tool provides instant feedback for students to check their progress.

The Federalist Era

1789–1800

ESSENTIAL QUESTIONS · *What are the characteristics of a leader?*
· *Why does conflict develop?* · *How do governments change?*

◀ *Abigail Adams played a major role in the career of John Adams, one of the leading figures in early American history.*

The Granger Collection, NYC

network

There's More Online about the people and events of the Federalist Era

CHAPTER 9

Lesson 1
The First President

Lesson 2
Early Challenges

Lesson 3
The First Political Parties

The Story Matters . . .

Abigail Adams is thoughtful and smart. Like other women of her day, she does not lead a public life. Yet to her husband—patriot and now President John Adams—she is a trusted adviser.

During her husband's presidency, she watches with a keen eye as the first political parties form. She helps her husband identify his true friends—and his secret enemies.

Her involvement in politics shocks some. For a time, it even costs her a dear friendship with Thomas Jefferson.

The division of the nation into different political parties was a trying time for the United States. It was one of the challenges facing the young nation in the Federalist Era.

243

CHAPTER 9
The Federalist Era

ENGAGE

Bellringer Ask students what federalist means. *(a supporter of federalism, or a federal system of government)* Remind them that the Federalists of the time were supporters of a strong federal government and belief that the Constitution gave the government "implied" powers, unlike the Democratic-Republicans, who supported the power of the states and a strict reading of the Constitution. Emphasize that Americans, far from being politically united in the early years of their country, had significant differences of opinion about their government. **Ask: How might such differing opinions affect how the government functions?** *(Students' responses may vary. They may say that the different views of the Constitution may lead to disagreements over the amount of power that the federal government has versus the states.)*

Making Connections

Have students read "The Story Matters . . . " to themselves. Then discuss the role of women in politics at the time. Generally, women were not directly involved with political factions, debates, or campaigns. Abigail Adams was unusual in that regard because, although she remained largely behind the scenes, her partnership with her husband was not a secret. **Ask: What might it have been like to be a part of early government in the United States?** *(Answers will vary.)* Encourage students to suggest earlier events that may have affected Abigail Adams and others involved in shaping the new government. Tell the class that even though the Constitution had been ratified, there were still many choices that needed to be made to form a new, working government. Ask students to suggest things that might have been left out of the Constitution or things that might have been described only vaguely. **Ask: How much has the situation changed for presidents' wives? What role do they play in running the country today?** *(Answers will vary.)*

Letter from the Author

Dear American History Teacher,

The beginning of government under the new constitution brought together a number of stars of the revolutionary era: Washington, of course, as president, Alexander Hamilton, Thomas Jefferson, and James Madison. Rarely have revolutionary leaders become statesmen of the first rank. Because of his firm guidance, Washington was able to keep the country on a safe course despite the turmoil caused by renewed European hostilities related to the French Revolution. His rectitude stabilized the frail new government.

Joyce Appleby

TEACH & ASSESS

Step Into the Place

V Visual Skills

Analyzing Maps Draw students' attention to the map of the United States in 1790. Ask a volunteer to identify the map's key symbols and explain what they mean. Remind students that the United States was a very different place during this period from what it is today. **Ask: What is the main difference between the United States of 1790 and the nation today?** *(In 1790 the country did not extend beyond the Mississippi River; the population was much smaller; and people were not as mobile as today's population. There were no motor vehicles, railroads, or airplanes.)* Have student volunteers analyze the map. Ask if they can show where major cities of today would be on the 1790 map. Ask students to speculate about how their lives would be different if they lived in 1790. Then, as a class, discuss the Map Focus questions. **Visual/Spatial**

Content Background Knowledge

The United States of 1790 was a very rural nation—95 percent of the people lived in the country. In 1790, the United States:

- had a total population of 3,929,214.
- had 3,727,559 people living in rural areas.
- had only 201,655 people living in towns and cities.

Chapter 9 CCSS

Place and Time: United States 1789 to 1800

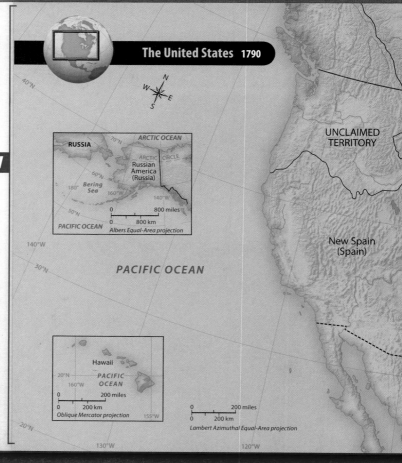

In 1790 the United States occupied the eastern areas of the continent, but people were moving to the West. There were fewer states than today, but some were larger than they are now. Other countries controlled much of the land that now makes up the nation. Some areas were claimed by more than one country. **V**

The United States 1790

UNCLAIMED TERRITORY

RUSSIA
ARCTIC OCEAN
ARCTIC CIRCLE
Russian America (Russia)
Bering Sea
PACIFIC OCEAN
0   800 miles
Albers Equal-Area projection

New Spain (Spain)

PACIFIC OCEAN

Hawaii
PACIFIC OCEAN
0   200 miles
0   200 km
Oblique Mercator projection

0   200 miles
0   200 km
Lambert Azimuthal Equal-Area projection

Step Into the Place

MAP FOCUS The United States in 1790 was concentrated on the East Coast and surrounding areas.

1 **LOCATION** Look at the map. Where is your state located? Did your state exist in 1790? **RH.6–8.7**

2 **LOCATION** What other countries had territory near the new United States? **RH.6–8.7**

3 **CRITICAL THINKING**
Making Inferences What does this map suggest about why settlers in the United States were moving west? **RH.6–8.7**

Step Into the Time

TIME LINE What events on this time line suggest that the United States was early in its history as a nation? **RH.6–8.5, RH.6–8.7**

U.S. PRESIDENTS		
U.S. EVENTS		
WORLD EVENTS		

1789 • Washington becomes first president
• Judiciary Act passes

1791 Bill of Rights added to Constitution

1788   1790   1792

1789 • Lavoisier's table of 33 elements published
• French Revolution begins

1792 France declares war on Austria

244   *The Federalist Era*

Project-Based Learning 🖐

Hands-On Chapter Project

The Federalist Era
Students will identify and learn about key events that happened during the Federalist Era by creating a time line of significant events. Students will read about the topic in their textbook; research their group's section of the time line, citing at least three sources; and find maps, photos, or other visuals to add to the time line. Then students will meet with their group to organize research and decide what information to include in their time line and create their time line. Students should coordinate with other groups to combine time line sections into a coherent, complete time line and display it.

Technology Extension

Interactive Time Line
Turn your students' time line into a Web-based resource. Online time lines allow students to put specific events on a time line and also add images, locations, hyperlinks, and even embedded video. The nature of online time lines allows students to share their work with others.

edtechteacher
21st Century Learning

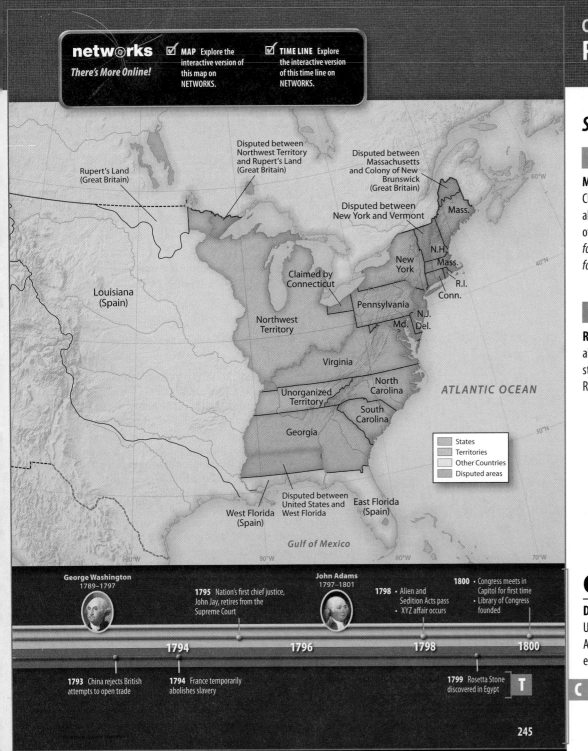

Disputed between Northwest Territory and Rupert's Land (Great Britain)

Rupert's Land (Great Britain)

Disputed between Massachusetts and Colony of New Brunswick (Great Britain)

Disputed between New York and Vermont

Mass.

N.H.

Louisiana (Spain)

Claimed by Connecticut

New York

Mass.

R.I.

Conn.

Pennsylvania

N.J.

Md. Del.

Northwest Territory

Virginia

ATLANTIC OCEAN

North Carolina

Unorganized Territory

South Carolina

Georgia

Legend:
- States
- Territories
- Other Countries
- Disputed areas

West Florida (Spain)

Disputed between United States and West Florida

East Florida (Spain)

Gulf of Mexico

Time line:

George Washington 1789–1797

1795 Nation's first chief justice, John Jay, retires from the Supreme Court

John Adams 1797–1801

1798 • Alien and Sedition Acts pass • XYZ affair occurs

1800 • Congress meets in Capitol for first time • Library of Congress founded

1794   1796   1798   1800

1793 China rejects British attempts to open trade

1794 France temporarily abolishes slavery

1799 Rosetta Stone discovered in Egypt **T**

245

Step Into the Time

C Critical Thinking Skills

Making Inferences Have students review the time line in the Chapter Opener. Ask students to select one event and speculate about what lasting effects that event would have on the future of the nation. *(Possible answers: 1789–Washington was a model for later presidents; 1791–the Bill of Rights continues to be a guide for people and governments.)* **BL**

T Technology Skills

Researching on the Internet Point out the time line entry about the discovery of the Rosetta Stone. Direct a pair of students to conduct a quick Internet search to find out what the Rosetta Stone is and why its discovery was so important.

Content Background Knowledge

In 1790, the total area of the United States was 864,746 square miles. Today, the country covers 3,537,379 square miles—an area about four times the earlier size

CLOSE & REFLECT

Describing Have students take turns stating facts about the United States that describe the country either in 1790 or today. After each statement the rest of the class should say aloud either "1790" or "today." **C**

TIME LINE

Place and Time: United States 1789 to 1800

Making Presentations Organize a small group of students (2 to 4) to create a three-minute presentation of the interactive chapter time line and present it to the class. They should review the time line, familiarize themselves with the events of the Federalist Era (both in the United States and the world), and decide how best to present and highlight selected events of the era to other students. **Interpersonal**

See page 243B for other online activities.

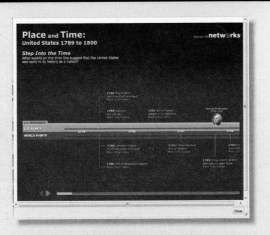

ENGAGE

Bellringer Tell students to think about what steps would be necessary for them to set up a successful club. First, they would have to decide what type of club they wanted; then they would need to think about what type of organization and structure their club would have. Last, but not least, their club would need a leader. **Ask:** What are some different ways you could use to pick a leader? *(Students may say that a group could appoint a leader, one could be elected by the members, or members could flip a coin or pull a leader's name from a hat.)* How would you recommend picking a leader for your club? *(Students might suggest that a leader of the club should be elected.)*

Tell students that the first president of the United States, George Washington, was elected. They will be learning about actions he took when he entered office.

TEACH & ASSESS

W Writing Skills

Narrative Remind students that George Washington is known as "the Father of Our Country." **Ask:** How did he earn this nickname? *(because he led the fight for independence and was the country's first president)* Tell students that George Washington remains a giant of American history and that his influence is still felt today. As homework, have students note the presence of Washington in everyday life (his face on money, towns and schools named for him, and so on). Direct them to write one-page papers that describe George Washington's presence in popular culture and everyday life today. **AL**

C Critical Thinking Skills

Speculating Tell students that, as the first president, George Washington said that "no slip" of his "will pass unnoticed." **Ask:** What is a synonym for the word slip? *(mistake)* Why did Washington say this? *(because he was in a highly visible and powerful position, and knew many people were watching him closely)*

ANSWER, p. 246

TAKING NOTES: George Washington, President; John Adams, Vice President; Thomas Jefferson, head of State Department; Alexander Hamilton, head of Department of Treasury; Henry Knox, Secretary of War; Edmund Randolph, Attorney General; John Jay, Chief Justice of the United States.

---

networks
There's More Online!

☑ **CHARTS/GRAPHS**
The First Cabinet

☑ **GAME**
Leaders Crossword

☑ **GRAPHIC ORGANIZER**
Leaders and Roles

☑ **SLIDE SHOW**
The Supreme Court

Lesson 1
The First President

ESSENTIAL QUESTION *What are the characteristics of a leader?*

IT MATTERS BECAUSE
George Washington and his administration established many customs and processes that are still in place today.

Washington Takes Office

GUIDING QUESTION *What decisions did Washington and the new Congress have to make about the new government?*

Under the Articles of Confederation, the United States had several presidents. Their job was to lead Congress, and they were not strong chief executives. The government under the Articles was weak and ineffective. When delegates met to reform the government, they wrote a new Constitution that included a strong executive branch headed by a single president.

On April 30, 1789, George Washington took the oath of office as the first president of the United States under that new Constitution. John Adams became vice president.

Washington knew that his actions and decisions would set **precedents** (PREH·suh·duhnts), or traditions, that would help shape the nation's future. "No slip will pass unnoticed," he said. Washington worked closely with Congress to create an effective government. In those first years, the president and Congress created departments within the executive branch and set up the court system. Congress added the Bill of Rights to the Constitution. Washington set the standard for how long a president should serve and for how the nation should relate to other nations.

Reading HELPDESK CCSS

Taking Notes: *Describing* RH.6–8.2
As you read, use a table like this one to describe important figures in the nation's early years. Use as many as seven rows.

Name	Role
George Washington	
	Vice President

Content Vocabulary (Tier 3 Words)
• precedent
• cabinet
• bond

246 *The Federalist Era*

---

networks   *Online Teaching Options*

VIDEO

The First President: Washington's Legacy

Identifying Share the video with the class. Recall the point when Richard Brookhiser states, "Everyone needs stories, but with Washington you didn't need to make up many because the actual stories of what he did were very impressive." Have a student name one of the stories or myths (for example, chopping down the cherry tree) and then call on another student to name something Washington actually did (for example, a victory in the Revolutionary War). Repeat for several myths and accomplishments. **Interpersonal**

See page 243C for other online activities.

The Cabinet

The executive branch of government took shape during the summer of 1789. Congress set up three departments and two offices within the executive branch. Washington chose leading political figures to head them. He picked Thomas Jefferson to head the State Department, which handles relations with other nations. He named Alexander Hamilton to manage the nation's money at the Department of the Treasury. Henry Knox was the choice to look after the nation's defense as the secretary of the Department of War. To address the government's legal affairs, Washington chose Edmund Randolph to be attorney general. Congress also created the office of postmaster general.

The three department heads and the attorney general had many important duties. Among them was giving advice to the president. Together, this group of top executive advisers formed what is called a **cabinet**.

Congress was unsure how much power the president ought to have over the cabinet. In a vote on this question, senators were evenly divided. Vice President John Adams broke the tie. He voted to allow the president the power to dismiss cabinet officers without Senate approval. This established presidential power over the whole executive branch.

Establishing the Court System

The first Congress also faced the job of forming the nation's court system. Some favored a **uniform** legal system for the entire nation. Others favored keeping the existing state systems. The two sides reached an agreement in the Judiciary Act of 1789. This act established a federal court system. The states kept their own laws and courts, but the federal courts had the power to reverse state decisions. The act marked a first step in creating a strong and independent national judicial system.

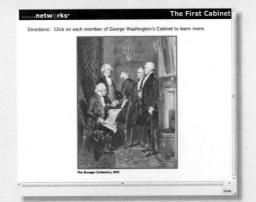

President Washington (far right) relied on the expert advice of this cabinet. Henry Knox is seated at left. Next to him are Thomas Jefferson, Edmund Randolph (back turned), and Alexander Hamilton.

The Granger Collection, NYC

---

precedent something done or said that becomes an example for others to follow
cabinet a group of advisers to a president

Academic Vocabulary (Tier 2 Words)
uniform of the same form with others

C Critical Thinking Skills

Speculating Remind students that the executive branch today is similar to the one that George Washington formed in 1789. **Ask:** How do you think the president's cabinet today compares with George Washington's cabinet? *(Answers will vary. It is much larger because of the growth of the executive branch; today it includes the vice president and the heads of 15 executive departments.)*

R1 Reading Skills

Discussing After students have read the text, discuss the fact that Congress was divided on how much power the president should have over the cabinet. Have a volunteer explain the issue and how the issue was resolved. *(Students may mention that senators were equally divided over whether the president should be able to dismiss cabinet officers without Senate approval. Vice President John Adams broke the tie.)* **Ask:** What precedent did the vote set? *(It allowed the president the authority to dismiss cabinet officers without Senate approval, strengthening the president's position with authority over the executive branch.)* Be sure students understand the meaning of the term *precedent*.

R2 Reading Skills

Recalling Before students read, remind them that in 1789, there were no federal courts. Then ask a volunteer to recall the system of checks and balances discussed in previous chapters. **AL Ask:** How does the Judiciary Act of 1789 fit into the system of checks and balances? *(The Judiciary Act created the Supreme Court, which is the final authority on constitutional issues and rulings from other courts.)*

IMAGE

The First Cabinet

Making Connections Use the interactive image to discuss the first cabinet. Ask volunteers to name these cabinet members and any current cabinet members they know. **Ask:** What qualities would make a good cabinet member? *(Students may say that patience, an ability to listen and compromise, strength, and courage are some of the qualities that cabinet members should have.)* **Visual/Spatial**

See page 243C for other online activities.

netw rks   The First Cabinet
Directions: Click on each member of George Washington's Cabinet to learn more.

The Granger Collection, NYC

Thinking Like a HISTORIAN

Making Comparisons

In 1791 Congress created a federal court system with three levels. Those three levels today include the district courts at the lower level, the appeals courts in the middle, and the Supreme Court at the top. Use the Internet to research this system, and create a chart or diagram that compares the powers of each level. For more information about making comparisons, read *Thinking Like a Historian.*

The Supreme Court Building, built in 1935, is the seat of the Supreme Court of the United States.

The Constitution established the Supreme Court as the final authority on many issues. President Washington chose John Jay to lead the Supreme Court as chief justice. The Senate approved Jay's nomination.

The Bill of Rights

Americans had fought a revolution to gain independence from British control. They did not want to replace one unjust government with another one. As protection from the powers of a strong national government, many Americans wanted the Constitution to include a bill of rights. It would guarantee civil liberties. In fact, some states had agreed to ratify the Constitution only with the promise that a bill of rights be added.

To fulfill this promise, James Madison introduced a set of amendments during the first session of Congress. Congress passed 12 amendments, and the states ratified 10 of them. In December 1791, these 10 amendments, together called the Bill of Rights, became part of the Constitution.

The Bill of Rights limits the power of government. It protects individual liberty, including freedom of speech and the rights of people accused of crimes. The Tenth Amendment says that any power not listed in the Constitution belongs to the states or the people. Madison hoped this amendment would help protect Americans against a national government that was too powerful.

✓ **PROGRESS CHECK**

Listing What were three important actions taken by Washington and the first Congress?

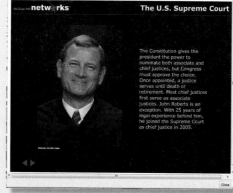

Reading **HELP**DESK **CCSS**

Reading Strategy: *Determining Cause and Effect*

A cause is an event that triggers some event. An effect is the event that occurs as a result of the cause. Read about the Bill of Rights. Identify the cause that triggered the effect—the ratification of the Bill of Rights.

bond certificate that promises to repay borrowed money in the future—plus an additional amount of money, called interest.

net**w**orks *Online Teaching Options*

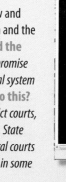

The U.S. Supreme Court

The Constitution gives the president the power to nominate both associate and chief justices, but Congress must approve the choice. Once appointed, a justice serves until death or retirement. Most chief justices first serve as associate justices. John Roberts is an exception. With 25 years of legal experience behind him, he joined the Supreme Court as chief justice in 2005.

The New Economy

GUIDING QUESTION *How did the economy develop under the guidance of Alexander Hamilton?*

As president, Washington focused on foreign affairs and military matters. He rarely suggested new laws and almost always approved the bills that Congress passed. For the government's economic policies, the president depended on Alexander Hamilton, secretary of the treasury. Hamilton was in his early thirties when he took office, but he had bold plans and clear policies in mind.

Hamilton faced a difficult task. The federal and state governments had borrowed money to pay for the American Revolution. They now owed millions of dollars to other countries and to American citizens. As a result, the nation faced serious financial trouble. Hamilton tried to improve the government's finances and strengthen the nation at the same time.

Hamilton's Plan

The House of Representatives asked Hamilton to make a plan for the "adequate support of the public credit." This meant that the United States needed a way to borrow money for its government and economy. To be able to borrow in the future, the government had to prove it could pay back the money it already owed.

Hamilton proposed that the federal government take over and pay off the states' wartime debts. He argued that paying off the debt as a nation would build national credit and make it easier for the nation to borrow money. Hamilton also believed that federal payment of state debts would give the states a strong interest in the success of the national government.

The Plan Faces Opposition

Congress agreed to part of Hamilton's plan—to pay the money owed to other nations. However, Hamilton's plan to pay off the debt owed to American citizens caused protest.

When borrowing money from citizens during the American Revolution, the government issued **bonds**. These are notes that promise repayment of borrowed money in the future.

Alexander Hamilton shaped the new nation's economy.

▶ CRITICAL THINKING

Explaining Why did Hamilton propose that the federal government pay off the states' wartime debts?

Library of Congress [LC-DIG-pga-03160]

Lesson 1 **249**

CHAPTER 9, Lesson 1
The First President

G1 Critical Thinking Skills

Evaluating Tell students that in this section they will learn about America's first secretary of the treasury and the nation's first national bank. **Ask:** Do you think the person holding this office today has more or less influence on the country than Alexander Hamilton did? *(Students may say that the treasury secretary has less influence today because policies have been in effect for a long time. Hamilton was establishing the initial procedures and policies and creating the first national bank.)* **BL**

G2 Critical Thinking Skills

Making Connections Before students read the text, **ask:** Have you ever borrowed money from family or friends, or lent them money? *(Answers may vary.)* Lead a discussion about how and when the money was paid back. Explain that the act of lending and borrowing money creates a debt. A debt is an amount of money that needs to be paid back. **AL ELL** Remind students that the United States ran up a large debt when it was fighting for its independence.

R Reading Skills

Explaining Direct students to read the text. Have them explain Hamilton's plan and his belief that it was important for the federal government—not the states—to pay back the national debts. **Ask:** Why did Hamilton argue that the national government should pay the national wartime debts? *(Hamilton believed that federal payment of national debts would help the country build national credit and give the states a strong interest in the success of the national government.)* Students should cite evidence from the text to support their answers. **AL**

BIOGRAPHY

Alexander Hamilton

Discussing Display the biography of Alexander Hamilton and note that his influence on the early economy was profound. **Ask:** How did Alexander Hamilton become secretary of the treasury? *(George Washington appointed him to the position.)*

See page 243C for other online activities.

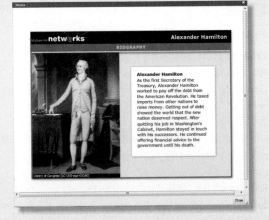

ANSWER, p. 249

CRITICAL THINKING It would build national credit, make it easier to borrow money, and give states an interest in the success of the government.

Chapter 9 **249**

R Reading Skills

Describing Have a student volunteer read the section aloud. Then, ask another volunteer to describe what a bond is and how it works. **AL** **ELL** Then discuss with students the role that bonds played in Hamilton's plan. **Ask:** Why was Hamilton's plan to pay off old bonds controversial? *(Speculators would get rich and the original bond owners would get nothing.)* Why did Southern states oppose Hamilton's plan? *(They had less debt and Hamilton wanted the nation to pay all the debts together.)*

C Critical Thinking Skills

Making Inferences Explain to students that Hamilton had to be creative when coming up with a plan to get Southern leaders on board with his proposal to pay off debts as a nation. **Ask:** What did Alexander Hamilton offer Southern leaders in exchange for supporting his plan? *(to locate the nation's capital in the South)* Why would this be attractive to Southern leaders? *(Hosting the capital would be an honor that would give the South more prestige; there would likely be significant economic development in and around a capital city.)*

PROTECTIVE TARIFFS

In the late 1700s, American industries lacked experience. As a result, it often cost American manufacturers more to make a product than it cost foreign makers. To raise the price of imported products, the U.S. government used tariffs. This helped protect American industries by making foreign-made goods more expensive and, therefore, less attractive to American buyers.

BREAKDOWN OF COST

U.S.: Profit: $1; Cost to produce: $5
Britain: Tariff: $2; Profit: $1; Cost to produce: $4

Hat made in U.S. — $6
Hat made in Britain — $7

ECONOMICS SKILL

Tariffs affected the price consumers paid for goods.

1. **COMPARING** Use the figures above to create a line graph for the cost of producing 100 hats in the United States and 100 hats in Britain. Which is greater?

2. **COMPARING** Now graph the cost of buying 100 American-made and 100 British-made hats with the tariff. Which is greater?

3. **CRITICAL THINKING** *Speculating* How might the issue of U.S.-imposed tariffs impact U.S. relations with Britain?

While waiting for repayment, many bond owners—shopkeepers, farmers, and soldiers—sold their bonds. They accepted less money than the bonds' stated value. Often, the buyers of these bonds were speculators, people who risk money in hopes of making a large profit in the future.

Now, Hamilton was proposing to pay off the old bonds at full value. This would make the speculators rich. The original bondholders would get nothing. Many people were upset by this idea. One newspaper said Hamilton's plan was "established at the expense of national justice, gratitude, and humanity."

Even stronger opposition came from the Southern states. These states had **accumulated**, or built up, much less debt than the Northern states. Several had already repaid their debts. Yet Hamilton wanted the entire nation to pay all the debt together. Southern states complained about having to help pay other states' debts.

Compromise and a Capital

To win support for his plan, Hamilton worked out a **compromise** with Southern leaders. If they voted for his plan to pay off the state debts, he would support locating the nation's capital in the South.

Congress ordered a special district to be laid out between Virginia and Maryland along the banks of the Potomac River. There, George Washington chose the site for the new capital city, later named Washington, D.C., in his honor. While workers prepared the new city, the nation's capital shifted from New York to Philadelphia.

Reading **HELP**DESK **CCSS**

Academic Vocabulary (Tier 2 Words)

accumulate to build up or collect
compromise a settlement of a disagreement reached by each side giving up some of what it wants in order to reach an agreement

---

net**works** *Online Teaching Options*

CHART

Protective Tariffs

Explaining Use the interactive chart to explain to students that a tariff is a kind of tax. **AL** **ELL** Discuss why Hamilton proposed high tariffs. **Ask:** What is a tariff? *(a tax on imports)* **AL** **ELL** Why were Hamilton's tariffs important to the country? *(They made U.S. manufacturers' goods cheaper for Americans to buy, and the money collected on imported goods helped the country pay off its debt from the Revolutionary War.)* Why did the South oppose tariffs? *(The South had little industry.)*

See page 243C for other online activities.

ANSWERS, p. 250

Economics Skill 1. Cost to produce 100 hats: U.S. hats, $500; British hats, $400. **2.** Cost to buy 100 hats: U.S. hats, $600 ($500 cost plus $100 profit); British hats, $700 ($400 cost plus $100 profit plus $200 in tariffs).
3. **CRITICAL THINKING** Tariffs might anger the British because they would increase the price—and decrease the sale—of British manufactured goods for sale in the United States.

The Fight for a National Bank

Hamilton also asked Congress to create a national bank—the Bank of the United States. The proposed bank would hold government funds and make debt payments. It would also issue a single form of money for use throughout the nation. At that time, different states and banks issued their own currencies. Having a national currency would make trade and all other financial actions much easier.

Madison and Jefferson opposed a national bank, believing it would help the wealthy. They argued that the Constitution did not give Congress the power to create a bank. Hamilton believed the Constitution indirectly gave Congress power to create a bank when it gave Congress power to collect taxes and borrow money. Washington agreed, and Congress created the national bank.

Tariffs and Taxes

Hamilton believed that the United States needed more manufacturing. He proposed high tariffs—taxes on imports. The tariffs would raise money for the government and protect American industries from foreign competition. The South had little industry and opposed such tariffs. Congress passed only low tariffs. Hamilton also called for national taxes to help the government pay the national debt. Congress approved several taxes, including a tax on whiskey made in the United States.

Hamilton's ideas created conflict. Jefferson and Madison worried that Hamilton was building a dangerously powerful government run by the wealthy. They began to organize opposition to Hamilton and the policies he favored.

✓ PROGRESS CHECK

Explaining Why did some people oppose Hamilton's plan to pay off government bonds?

LESSON 1 REVIEW CCSS

Review Vocabulary (Tier 3 Words)

1. Use the following two words in a sentence about the first Washington presidency. RH.6–8.4

   a. precedent   **b.** cabinet

2. Explain the significance of the word *bond* to this era of United States history. RH.6–8.4

Answer the Guiding Questions

3. ***Recalling*** What decisions did Washington and the first Congress have to make about the new government? RH.6–8.2

4. ***Summarizing*** How did the economy develop under the guidance of Alexander Hamilton? RH.6–8.2

5. **ARGUMENT** Why do you think George Washington's presidency was so important in the development of the young nation? Write a paragraph to explain. WHST.6–8.1, WHST.6–8.4

Lesson 1   **251**

R Reading Skills

Discussing Have students review the section about national banks. As a class, discuss the purpose of the national bank, who supported it, who opposed it, and why. **Ask:** Who opposed the national bank? Why? *(The bank was opposed by Madison and Jefferson. They believed it would benefit the wealthy and thought it was unconstitutional because the Constitution did not specifically authorize a bank.)*

Have students complete the Lesson 1 Review.

CLOSE & REFLECT

Ask: Why do you think Hamilton's ideas caused conflict? *(Some thought that he was trying to build a government, run by the wealthy, that was too powerful.)* Do you agree with this line of thinking? *(Answers may vary.)*

LESSON 1 REVIEW ANSWERS

1. Sample answer: Washington's presidency established precedents, such as the relationship between the president and cabinet.

2. Bonds issued during the Revolutionary War had been used to raise money, but many bonds had been sold to speculators. The bonds became a source of controversy when Hamilton proposed to pay the bonds in full.

3. They had to create departments within the executive branch (the cabinet), set up the court system, and add the Bill of Rights to the Constitution.

4. Hamilton proposed that the United States pay off its debt to other countries and individual citizens; he also created a national bank and promoted protective tariffs and national taxes.

5. Paragraphs should note that Washington was setting precedents with everything he did. The pattern he set might help or hurt the country for many years.

ANSWER, p. 251

✓ **PROGRESS CHECK** Many bondholders had sold their bonds to speculators. Opponents of the plan to pay off the bonds at full value feared that speculators would get rich. The original bondholders also felt betrayed by the government.

ENGAGE

Bellringer Discuss with students their prior knowledge of George Washington and his presidency. Tell students that in this lesson, they will learn about the challenges Washington and the nation faced, such as a violent protest against a tax on whiskey. **Ask: Have you heard of any recent protests against higher taxes or other legislation?** *(Students may refer to income tax reform, health care debates, or similar policies.)* **Have any of the protests been violent?** *(Answers may vary depending on current events.)*

TEACH & ASSESS

R Reading Skills

Explaining After students have read the text, discuss the events surrounding the Whiskey Rebellion. Ask students to explain why this armed protest was a concern for government leaders. **Ask: What did the government prove by using armed troops to put down the rebellion?** *(The government would use force when necessary to maintain order.)* AL

C Critical Thinking Skills

Determining Cause and Effect Remind students of the growing unrest among the American population during this time period. **Ask: What was the direct cause of the Whiskey Rebellion?** *(a tax on the manufacture and sale of whiskey)*

ANSWER, p. 252

TAKING NOTES: Treaty of Greenville—Native Americans gave up Ohio; Jay's Treaty—British withdrew from American soil but did not deal with impressment or interference with American trade; Pinckney's Treaty—Spain gave Americans navigation of the Mississippi River, trade rights at New Orleans.

---

netw⊚rks
There's More Online!

☑ **BIOGRAPHY** John Jay
☑ **GAME** Fill in the Blank
☑ **GRAPHIC ORGANIZER** Effects of Treaties
☑ **MAP** Native American Campaigns
☑ **PRIMARY SOURCE** Treaty of Greenville
☑ **VIDEO**

Lesson 2
Early Challenges

ESSENTIAL QUESTION *Why does conflict develop?*

IT MATTERS BECAUSE
George Washington's strong leadership brought stability to the young government.

Trouble in the New Nation

GUIDING QUESTION *What challenges on the frontier did the new government face?*

Washington faced difficult challenges while in office. Britain and France were pushing the United States to get more involved in their conflicts. President Washington stood firm against this pressure. Native Americans, aided by the British and Spanish, fought the westward advance of American settlers. In addition, there was growing unrest from within the American population.

The Whiskey Rebellion

The new government wanted to collect taxes on some products made in the United States. In 1791 Congress passed a tax on the manufacture and sale of whiskey, a type of alcohol made from grain. Western Pennsylvania farmers were especially upset by this tax. Their anger turned into violence in July 1794. An armed mob attacked tax collectors and burned down buildings. This protest, called the Whiskey Rebellion, alarmed government leaders. They viewed it as a challenge to the power of the new government. Washington sent federal troops to meet the challenge. His action sent a strong message to the public: The government would use force to **maintain** order.

(c) Archive Photos/Stock Montage/Getty Images, (r) The Granger Collection, NYC

Reading **HELPDESK** CCSS

Taking Notes: *Determining Cause and Effect*

As you read, use a diagram like this one to describe how the treaties mentioned in this lesson affected the United States. RH.6–8.5

252 *The Federalist Era*

Treaty		Effect
Treaty of Greenville	→	
Jay's Treaty	→	
Pinckney's Treaty	→	

Content Vocabulary (Tier 3 Words)
• **impressment**

---

netw⊚rks *Online Teaching Options*

VIDEO

George Washington

Making Connections Show the video. Then review the excerpts from Washington's Farewell Address in the textbook. Clarify any unfamiliar terms or concepts. AL ELL To extend the lesson, have students find a copy and read the whole speech. **Ask: What is Washington telling the nation?** *(that the country should remain neutral in foreign affairs and that political parties are a growing threat)* **What are some examples of these issues today?** *(Answers will vary.)* Visual/Spatial

See page 243D for other online activities.

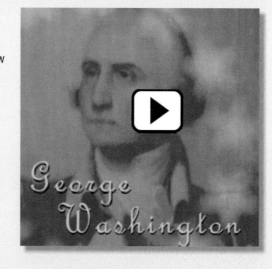

Challenges in the West

Washington worried about ongoing European interest in the Northwest Territory. The British and Spanish were trying to stir up Native American anger against American settlers in the region. To block these efforts, Washington signed treaties with Native American groups. Yet American settlers ignored the treaties and moved onto lands promised to Native Americans. Fighting broke out between the two groups.

Again, Washington decided to use force. He sent an army under General Arthur St. Clair to restore order in the Northwest Territory. In November 1791, St. Clair's army met a strong Native American force led by Little Turtle, a Miami chief. More than 600 U.S. soldiers died in the battle. It was the worst defeat U.S. forces had ever suffered against Native Americans.

Americans hoped an alliance with France would help them achieve full control in the West. The possibility of French involvement led Great Britain to take action. In 1794 the British urged Native Americans to destroy American settlements west of the Appalachians. The British also began building a new fort in Ohio.

Native Americans demanded that settlers who were living north of the Ohio River leave the area. In response, Washington sent Anthony Wayne, a Revolutionary War general, to the region.

R

Native American Campaigns 1791–1795

Northwest Territory

- Battle of Fallen Timbers 1794
- Fort Defiance
- Fort Miami (British)
- Fort Laurens
- Lake Erie
- N.Y.
- Pa.
- Wabash River
- Fort Recovery
- St. Clair's defeat 1791
- Treaty of Greenville Line, 1795
- Fort Greenville
- 40°N
- 0   50 miles
- 0   50 km
- Albers Equal-Area projection
- Fort Washington (Cincinnati)
- Ohio River
- Ky.
- Va.
- 84°W

N W E S

Key:
- Route of General Arthur St. Clair
- Route of General Anthony Wayne
- Land ceded by Native Americans
- Fort
- Battle

GEOGRAPHY CONNECTION

The United States fought with Native Americans in the Northwest Territory for control of land and resources.

1 PLACE In what present-day state was most of the land ceded by the Native Americans in the Treaty of Greenville?

2 CRITICAL THINKING
Speculating Why do you think the Native Americans were willing to make the Treaty of Greenville with the United States?

Academic Vocabulary (Tier 2 Words)

maintain to keep

Lesson 2 **253**

MAP

Native American Campaigns, 1791–1795

Analyzing Maps Use the interactive map to discuss the fighting between the Native Americans and American settlers. **Ask:** Why was Washington concerned about the European interest in the Northwest Territory? *(The British and the Spanish were trying to stir up Native American anger against American settlers.)* Where did most of the fighting take place? *(in Ohio)* Visual/Spatial

See page 243D for other online activities.

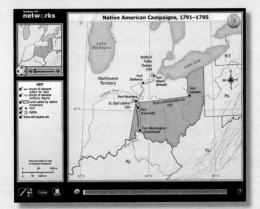

C1 Critical Thinking Skills

Analyzing Remind students that Americans were divided in their opinions regarding the French Revolution. **Ask:** Why did some Americans support the French Revolution? Why did others oppose it? (*Some supported it because of its similarity to America's own revolution, but others opposed its violence.*)

W Writing Skills

Paraphrasing Ask students to read the first paragraph under the section of the text titled, "Washington Struggles to Stay Neutral." Then instruct them to write a paragraph that paraphrases the information.

C2 Critical Thinking Skills

Comparing Create a list with students that compares aspects of Jay's Treaty to Pinckney's Treaty with Spain. Have student volunteers explain each treaty to create the list. **AL** **ELL**

BIOGRAPHY

John Jay (1745–1829)

John Jay attended college at the age of 14 and the First Continental Congress at the age of 28. Later, with Alexander Hamilton and James Madison, he wrote essays for *The Federalist* defending the Constitution.

George Washington appointed Jay the first chief justice of the United States in 1789. To avoid war with Great Britain, Jay negotiated Jay's Treaty. This unpopular treaty ruined his chances for the presidency.

▶ **CRITICAL THINKING**
Making Inferences What can you infer about Jay based on his accomplishments in life?

In August 1794, Wayne's army defeated more than 1,000 Native Americans under Shawnee chief Blue Jacket. The Battle of Fallen Timbers, near present-day Toledo, Ohio, crushed the Native Americans' hopes of keeping their land. In the Treaty of Greenville (1795), Native American leaders agreed to surrender most of the land in what is now Ohio.

✔ **PROGRESS CHECK**

Analyzing Why did Washington's efforts to gain the peaceful cooperation of Native Americans in the West fail?

Problems with Europe

GUIDING QUESTION *Why did Washington want to remain neutral in foreign conflict?*

In 1789 France erupted in revolution. Americans cheered at first as the French rose up against their king. The French struggle against royal tyranny was familiar to them. By 1793, however, the revolution had turned terribly violent. Some Americans were horrified by the bloodshed. Public opinion became divided.

When Britain and France went to war in 1793, some Americans sympathized with France. Others supported Britain. Washington hoped that the United States could stay neutral and not take either side.

Washington Struggles to Stay Neutral

Staying neutral proved difficult. The French tried to draw the United States into their conflict with Britain. They sent Edmond Genêt (zhuh•NAY) to ask American volunteers to attack British ships. President Washington **issued** the Proclamation of Neutrality, which prohibited Americans from fighting in the war. The proclamation also barred French and British warships from American ports.

Britain also challenged Washington's desire for neutrality. The British captured American ships that traded with the French. Then, they forced the American crews into the British navy. Americans were outraged by this practice of **impressment**.

Washington sent John Jay, chief justice of the United States, to discuss a solution with the British. The result of this negotiation was called Jay's Treaty. In the treaty, the British agreed to withdraw from American soil. There was no mention of impressment or British interference with American trade.

Archive Photos/Stock Montage/Getty Images

Reading **HELP**DESK (CCSS)

impressment seizing people against their will and forcing them to serve in the military or other public service

Academic Vocabulary (Tier 2 Words)
issue to deliver or hand out

Build Vocabulary: *Multiple Meaning Words*
The word *issue* can also be a noun, meaning "a troublesome subject," as in the sentence, "I brought up the issue to the rest of the class."

---

netw⊙rks   *Online Teaching Options*

GRAPHIC ORGANIZER

Taking Notes: *Determining Cause and Effect:* **Treaties and Their Effects**

Determining Cause and Effect Use the interactive graphic organizer to describe the treaties mentioned in this lesson and their effects on the growing nation. **Ask:** Who were the parties to these treaties? (*Greenville: the United States and Native American leaders; Jay's: the United States and Britain; Pinckney's: the United States and Spain.*) **AL** **ELL**

See page 243D for other online activities.

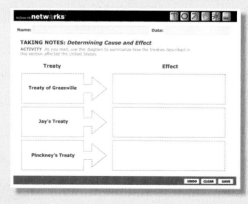

ANSWERS, p. 254

✔ **PROGRESS CHECK** Washington's efforts failed because white settlers ignored the treaties and moved onto Native Americans' land.

CRITICAL THINKING Jay was intelligent, ambitious, and very skilled.

Few Americans approved of this treaty. Washington also found fault with it but believed it would end the crisis. After fierce debate, the Senate approved Jay's Treaty in a close vote.

Pinckney's Treaty With Spain

Spanish leaders were nervous about Jay's Treaty. They feared that the United States and Great Britain would now work together against Spain in North America. Washington sent U.S. diplomat Thomas Pinckney to Spain to settle differences between the nations. In 1795 Pinckney's Treaty gave the Americans free navigation of the Mississippi River and the right to trade at New Orleans.

Washington Leaves Office

After eight years in office, Washington decided not to seek a third term as president. In his Farewell Address, Washington urged his fellow citizens to "observe good faith and justice toward all nations. ... It is our true policy to steer clear of permanent alliances." These parting words influenced the nation's foreign policy for more than 100 years.

Washington also warned against something he saw as a growing threat to the young nation: political parties. You will read about this threat in the next lesson.

When George Washington decided to step down after two terms as president, he set a precedent. No president served more than two terms until Franklin Roosevelt began his third term in 1941.

▶ CRITICAL THINKING
Analyzing Visuals What does this picture suggest about the public's feeling toward President Washington?

W

☑ **PROGRESS CHECK**

Explaining What was the significance of Jay's Treaty?

LESSON 2 REVIEW

Review Vocabulary (Tier 3 Words)

1. Use the word *impressment* in a sentence about the United States during Washington's presidency. RH.6–8.4

Answer the Guiding Questions

2. ***Describing*** Describe the Whiskey Rebellion and the government's actions in response to it. RH.6–8.2

3. ***Explaining*** What role did foreign nations play in President Washington's relations with Native American groups? RH.6–8.2

4. ***Summarizing*** What was Washington's approach to foreign policy, and why was it complicated? RH.6–8.2

5. **NARRATIVE** A tribute is a speech showing respect and gratitude. Write a one-paragraph tribute that you might have delivered on President George Washington's retirement. WHST.6–8.2, WHST.6–8.10

Lesson 2 **255**

W Writing Skills

Argument Have a student read aloud the words from George Washington's Farewell Address ("observe good faith . . . steer clear of permanent alliances"). Discuss these statements with the class. Define *alliances* and ensure students understand what the term "permanent alliances" means. Remind students of the meaning of neutrality. Then assign students to write paragraphs that argue either for or against *neutrality* as a foreign policy in general. Guide them in seeing the advantages and disadvantages of both approaches. **AL**

Have students complete the Lesson 2 Review.

CLOSE & REFLECT

Discussing Remind students that President Washington strove to have his young country remain neutral when it came to foreign wars. **Ask:** Why do you think it was important to Washington to keep America out of European affairs? *(Answers may vary.)*

LESSON 2 REVIEW ANSWERS

1. Sample answer: The British practice of impressment threatened to upset Washington's goal of neutrality.

2. Pennsylvania farmers attacked tax collectors and burned down buildings in July 1794. Washington decided to crush the rebellion and send a message that the government would use force to maintain order.

3. The presence of foreign nations encouraged the United States to seek peace with Native Americans and encouraged Native Americans to resist American settlement.

4. Washington hoped to keep the United States neutral, but the countries of Europe tried to lure the United States into their conflicts.

5. Answers will vary, but students should include Washington's leadership as the first president, his message that the federal government will protect order, and that the nation should avoid war if possible.

ANSWERS, p. 255

CRITICAL THINKING The public loved Washington and regarded him as a hero.

☑ PROGRESS CHECK Under Jay's Treaty, the British withdrew from American soil, but they did not deal with the issues of impressment or interference with trade. The treaty did end the crisis without war.

ENGAGE

Bellringer Discuss with students that today there are two major political parties, the Democrats and the Republicans. Point out that when the country first started, there were two different political parties, the Federalists and the Republicans. Tell students that in the upcoming lesson they will learn about these two parties and what they stood for.

TEACH & ASSESS

R1 Reading Skills

Identifying After students have read the text, discuss the history of political parties in the United States with the class. **Ask:** The supporters of which two leaders formed the first two political parties? *(Thomas Jefferson and Alexander Hamilton)* **AL**

R2 Reading Skills

Defining Ask for a volunteer to read the third paragraph on this page aloud to the class. Then, explain that the word *factions* can have different meanings. **Ask:** During the late 1700s, what did *factions* mean in American politics? *(political parties)* How is the word *factions* commonly used today? *(to refer to a smaller dissenting group within a larger group)* **ELL**

ANSWER, p. 256

TAKING NOTES: Role of federal government: Federalists—strong federal government, believed in "implied powers," representative government; Republicans—strict reading of the Constitution, feared strong federal government, ordinary people should participate in government

---

netw⊚rks
There's More Online!

☑ **CHARTS** Jefferson and Hamilton

☑ **GRAPHIC ORGANIZER** Role of Federal Government

☑ **PRIMARY SOURCE** Jefferson and the Constitution Political Cartoon

☑ **SLIDE SHOW** The Two-Party System

Lesson 3
The First Political Parties

ESSENTIAL QUESTION *How do governments change?*

IT MATTERS BECAUSE
Our nation's two-party political system developed from Americans taking opposing sides on political issues.

Opposing Parties

GUIDING QUESTION *How did different opinions lead to the first political parties?*

The American people generally admired President Washington and his service to the nation. Still, harsh attacks appeared from time to time in newspapers. One paper even called Washington "the scourge and the misfortune of his country."

Most of the attacks on Washington came from supporters of Thomas Jefferson. They hoped to weaken support for the policies of Alexander Hamilton, which the president seemed to favor. In fact, by 1796, the supporters of Jefferson and Hamilton were beginning to form the nation's first political parties.

At that time, many Americans thought political parties were harmful to good government. The Constitution made no mention of parties because its authors saw no good use for them. Washington disapproved of political parties, or "factions" as they were known. He warned that they would divide the nation.

To others, though, it seemed natural that people would disagree about issues. They also knew that people who hold similar views tend to band together.

Washington's cabinet was clearly divided on key issues. Alexander Hamilton and Thomas Jefferson had very different views. They disagreed on economic policy and foreign relations.

(l) Bettmann/Corbis, (cl) The Granger Collection, NYC, (cr) Christie's Images/SuperStock, (r) White House Historical Association

---

Reading HELPDESK **CCSS**

Taking Notes: *Comparing and Contrasting*

As you read, use a diagram like this one to compare and contrast the goals of the first two U.S. political parties. RH.6–8.5

256 *The Federalist Era*

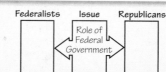

Federalists	Issue	Republicans
	Role of Federal Government	

Content Vocabulary (Tier 3 Words)
- partisan
- caucus
- alien
- sedition
- nullify
- states' rights

---

netw⊚rks *Online Teaching Options*

VIDEO

Electing the President: Political Parties

Making Connections View the video with students. The video defines the beginnings of American political parties, such as the Federalists and the Democratic-Republicans, and begins to identify how political parties affect presidential campaigning. Ask students to name the two major political parties in the United States today. *(Democrats and Republicans)* Point out that, although these two parties dominate, there are many other active parties in the United States. Challenge students to name some. *(Green, Libertarian, Constitution, etc.)*

See page 243E for other online activities.

They did not share the same opinion on the power of the federal government or on the meaning of the Constitution. Even Washington was **partisan** (PAHR·tuh·zuhn)—clearly favoring one faction. The president believed he stood above politics, but he usually supported Hamilton's views.

Political Parties Emerge

The differences found in Washington's cabinet also existed in Congress and among the public. They formed the basis for two **distinct** political parties that emerged at this time.

One party was the Federalists. Led by Hamilton, this group favored a strong federal government. They believed the Constitution gave government "implied" powers. These implied powers are not enumerated, or listed clearly in the Constitution. Instead, Federalists believed the enumerated powers imply the power to do other things. Federalists believed Congress could make all laws "necessary and proper" to carry out its enumerated powers.

The Democratic-Republicans, or Republicans, stood against the Federalists. Jefferson and Madison led this faction. They believed in a strict reading of the Constitution. They rejected the Federalist idea of implied powers. They believed congressional powers were limited to what is absolutely necessary to carry out the enumerated powers.

Debate over the national bank highlighted these differences. The Constitution gave Congress specific powers to do such things as issue and borrow money. To Hamilton, this implied that the federal government could create a bank to help with these tasks. Jefferson disagreed.

The Role of the People

The two parties also disagreed about the role of ordinary citizens in government. Federalists supported representative government, in which elected officials ruled in the people's name. They did not believe it was wise to let the public become too involved in politics.

Federalists thought that educated, wealthier men should hold public office. They did not trust ordinary people to make good decisions. In Hamilton's words, "The people are turbulent and changing; they seldom judge or determine right."

Bettmann/Corbis

Thinking Like a HISTORIAN

Analyzing Political Cartoons

Newspapers that supported Washington and Hamilton ridiculed Thomas Jefferson in print and in cartoons. In this cartoon, Jefferson is throwing the U.S. Constitution into a fire. The eagle is a symbol of the United States. What is the eagle trying to do in this cartoon? For more information about analyzing primary sources, read *Thinking Like a Historian*.

---

partisan firmly favoring one party or faction

Academic Vocabulary (Tier 2 Words)

distinct clearly different from the others

W Writing Skills

Informative/Explanatory Have students work in teams to write sentences comparing and contrasting the two parties' interpretation of the Constitution. Remind students that it may be helpful to organize their ideas in a two-column chart or other graphic organizer prior to writing their sentences. **AL** **ELL** Interpersonal

C Critical Thinking Skills

Analyzing Discuss with students the Federalists' belief that not just anyone should be allowed to hold a public office. **Ask:** What did Hamilton mean when he said, "The people are turbulent and changing; they seldom judge or determine right"? *(Possible answer: People become carried away with fads and new ideas. They do not know how to make the right decision.)* **BL**

V Visual Skills

Interpreting Have students review the political cartoon of Jefferson and the Constitution. **Ask:** What do you know about differences of opinion in the country from viewing this cartoon? *(People felt strongly about their different interpretations of the Constitution and were willing to ridicule politicians with different views.)* **BL** Visual/Spatial

---

CHART

Jefferson and Hamilton

Making Connections Use the interactive chart to discuss the topics Jefferson and Hamilton disagreed about with regard to key issues facing the young United States. **Ask:** What did many Americans think about political parties? *(Many Americans, including Washington, thought that political parties were harmful. Some people thought that they were to be avoided as much as a strong central government.)* Why do you think many Americans had this attitude? *(Possible answer: Political parties were not mentioned in the Constitution, and, like Washington, some people probably thought that political parties would divide the nation.)* Visual/Spatial

See page 243E for other online activities.

networks   **Jefferson and Hamilton**

There were few greater foes in the 1790s than Thomas Jefferson and Alexander Hamilton. Jefferson was the leader of the Anti-Federalists and represented the interests of rural Southerners. Hamilton was the leader of the Federalists and represented the interests of wealthy merchants. The debate between the two centered on the power of the federal government versus the power of state governments. The Federalists favored a strong central government; the Anti-Federalists pushed for states' rights.

Jefferson	Hamilton

ANSWER, p. 257

Thinking Like a Historian The eagle is stopping Jefferson from throwing the Constitution into the fire and destroying it.

The First Political Parties

C Critical Thinking Skills

Comparing Tell students to read the captions in the textbook that accompany the pictures of Jefferson and Hamilton. Point out the growing differences between the two men. Ask students to create a T-chart that illustrates what Jefferson and Hamilton thought about various issues. Students may use the textbook or outside sources. **AL**

R Reading Skills

Summarizing After students have read the text, have the class summarize the events and results of the election of 1796.
Ask:

- Which candidates were nominated to run for office in 1796? *(Federalists—John Adams and Charles Pinckney; Republicans—Thomas Jefferson and Aaron Burr)*
- What were the results of the election? *(John Adams won the presidency and Thomas Jefferson became the vice president.)*
- What was unusual about the outcome? *(John Adams was a Federalist and Thomas Jefferson was a Republican.)* **AL**

Content Background Knowledge

George Washington thought that factions were so dangerous that they could lead to tyranny:

"The alternate domination of one faction over another, sharpened by the spirit of revenge, natural to party dissension … leads at length to a more formal and permanent despotism. The disorders and miseries, which result, gradually incline the minds of men to seek security and repose in the absolute power of an individual; and sooner or later the chief of some prevailing faction … turns this disposition to the purposes of his own elevation, on the ruins of Public Liberty."

ANSWER, p. 258

✔ **PROGRESS CHECK** The election of 1796 was the first time that political parties were involved in a presidential election. Both Federalists and Republicans held caucuses to choose candidates.

Hamilton led the Federalist Party, which favored broad federal powers. They believed that wealthy, educated men should be elected to office and control the government.

C

Jefferson and the Republican Party wanted to limit federal powers and protect the powers of the states. They thought it was important for ordinary people to participate in government.

R

Reading **HELP**DESK **CCSS**

caucus a meeting of members of a political party to choose candidates for upcoming elections

Reading Strategy: *Identifying Points of View*

Most quotations express a person's point of view—what that person thinks or feels about a situation. Reread Hamilton's and Jefferson's quotations on the role of the people. Study the details. Try to restate the quotations in your own words. Then explain each person's point of view.

258 *The Federalist Era*

The Republicans feared a strong central government controlled by only a few people. They believed that democracy and liberty would be safe only if ordinary people took part fully in government. As Jefferson wrote in a letter, "I am not among those who fear the people. They, and not the rich, are our dependence [what we depend on] for continued freedom."

Washington's Reaction

The growing differences between the parties—and between Hamilton and Jefferson—troubled President Washington. He tried to get his two cabinet members to work out their differences. He wrote to Jefferson, trying to persuade him: "I . . . ardently wish that some line could be marked out by which both of you could walk."

Washington's efforts to get Jefferson and Hamilton to work together failed. The split was so strong that Jefferson left the cabinet and his job as secretary of state. Soon afterward, Hamilton resigned as secretary of the treasury. The rival groups and their points of view moved further apart. As the election of 1796 approached, the two parties each prepared to seek control of the presidency.

The Presidential Election of 1796

To prepare for the election, both parties held **caucuses** (KAW•kuhs•uhz). At these meetings, members of Congress and other leaders nominated, or chose, their parties' candidates for office.

Each party chose two presidential candidates, and the electors voted for any two. The Federalists chose John Adams and Charles Pinckney. The Republicans chose Thomas Jefferson and Aaron Burr. There was no candidate identified as a vice-presidential candidate on the ballot.

The Federalists carried the New England region. Republican strength lay in the Southern states. Adams got 71 electoral votes, winning the election. Jefferson finished second with 68 votes. Under the rules of the Constitution at that time, the person with the second-highest electoral vote total—Jefferson—became vice president. The administration that took office on March 4, 1797, had a Federalist president and a Republican vice president.

✔ **PROGRESS CHECK**

Contrasting How did the election of 1796 differ from the first presidential elections?

---

networks **Online Teaching Options**

WHITEBOARD ACTIVITY

The First Party System

Comparing and Contrasting Use the interactive whiteboard activity to discuss the creation of the first political parties. Drag and drop the information about the Federalists and the Republicans. **Ask: What is the basis for their disagreement?** *(the interpretation of the Constitution)* **Visual/Spatial**

See page 243E for other online activities.

networks** The First Party System

Directions: Read each statement. Decide if it applies to the Federalists or the Democratic-Republicans. Drag and drop the statement to the correct party.

Democratic-Republicans

Believed government had "implied" powers | Supported representative government | Believed in strict reading of Constitution | Led by Jefferson, opposed by Hamilton

Federalists

John Adams as President

GUIDING QUESTION *What important events occurred during the presidency of John Adams?*

John Adams spent most of his life in public service. He was well-known as one of Massachusetts's most active patriots in the period before and during the Revolutionary War. He served two terms as vice president under Washington before becoming president. His time in office, however, was troubled.

The XYZ Affair

The nation was in the middle of a dispute with France when Adams took office. The French viewed the 1794 Jay's Treaty as an American attempt to help the British in their war with France. To punish the United States, the French seized American ships that carried cargo to Britain.

President Adams sent a team to Paris to try to **resolve** the dispute in the fall of 1797. French officials chose not to meet with the Americans. Instead, the French sent three agents, who demanded a bribe and a loan for France from the Americans. The Americans refused.

When Adams learned what had happened, he was furious. The president urged Congress to prepare for war. In his report to Congress, Adams used the letters X, Y, and Z in place of the French agents' names. As a result, the event came to be called the XYZ affair.

Alien and Sedition Acts

When the public found out about the XYZ affair, many grew angry at foreign attempts to influence their government. They became more suspicious of **aliens**—residents who are not citizens. Many Europeans who had come to the United States in the 1790s supported the ideals of the French Revolution. Some Americans questioned whether these aliens would remain loyal if the United States went to war with France.

In response to these concerns, Federalists in 1798 passed the Alien and Sedition Acts. **Sedition** (sih·DIH·shuhn) means activities aimed at weakening the government. The Alien and Sedition Acts allowed the president to imprison aliens. The president could also deport—send out of the country—those thought to be dangerous. President Adams was a strong supporter of these laws.

---

alien a person living in a country who is not a citizen of that country

sedition activities aimed at weakening the established government by inciting resistance or rebellion to authority

Academic Vocabulary (Tier 2 Words)

resolve to find a solution; to settle a conflict

Connections to TODAY

Modern Political Parties

Today's Democratic Party started as the Democratic-Republican Party, which Thomas Jefferson and James Madison helped create in the 1790s. The Federalists no longer exist. The modern Republican Party was founded in the 1850s during the antislavery movement. These two political parties—Democrats and Republicans—now dominate the political process, filling most offices across the country. You can use the Internet to learn about the Democratic and Republican Parties of today.

C1 Critical Thinking Skills

Predicting Have students discuss what they have learned about John Adams from previous chapters. **Ask:** Based on this knowledge, how do you think he would fare as president? *(Possible answers: He had been involved in public service most of his life. He was probably well prepared for being president after having served as Washington's vice president.)*

C2 Critical Thinking Skills

Making Inferences Have students read the paragraphs under the heading "The XYZ Affair." **Ask:** Why do you think the French agents acted the way they did? *(Possible answers: They were probably told to act that way by the French foreign minister. The French were likely angry at the Americans because they thought the Americans were siding with Britain.)*

R Reading Skills

Explaining Using evidence from the text, ask students to explain the XYZ affair. Ask them to identify who was involved, what happened, and the outcome. **Ask:** Why was the scandal called the XYZ Affair? *(John Adams referred to the three French agents sent by the French government to demand a bribe and a loan from the Americans as X, Y, and Z.)* If time permits, ask students to think of another name that might have been created for this scandal. **AL**

IMAGE

The White House

Discussing Launch the interactive image of the early White House. Discuss with students the creation of the capital and the construction of the White House. **Ask:** Why is the White House significant to John Adams's presidency? *(Adams, like all presidents since 1800, lived in the White House. It is significant to his presidency because he was the first president to live there.)* **Visual/Spatial**

In 1790 George Washington signed an act of Congress stating that the U.S. federal government would be located on the Potomac River, in a district of no more than 10 square miles. We know this area today as Washington, D.C.
George Washington, along with city planner Pierre L'Enfant, chose the site for the president's house in the district at 1600 Pennsylvania Avenue. A contest was held to find the person who would build the house, and Irish architect James Hoban was chosen. Construction began in 1792 on what we know today as the White

See page 243E for other online activities.

The First Political Parties

C1 Critical Thinking Skills

Speculating Have students review the chart in the textbook on the Naturalization Act, the Alien Acts, and the Sedition Act. **Ask: Who do you think led the movement to allow states to overturn federal laws?** *(Students may say that Republicans, who were targeted by the acts, were probably the leaders of the effort to overturn laws such as these.)* **BL**

R Reading Skills

Explaining Have students use evidence from the text to explain the creation of the Virginia and Kentucky Resolutions as a response to the Alien and Sedition Acts. **Ask: Who drafted the Virginia and Kentucky Resolutions? Why?** *(James Madison and Thomas Jefferson drafted the Virginia and Kentucky Resolutions; they thought that the Alien and Sedition Acts violated the Constitution.)* **AL**

C2 Critical Thinking Skills

Analyzing Remind students that the Virginia and Kentucky Resolutions supported the principle of states' rights. **Ask: What is the principle of states' rights?** *(The powers of the federal government should be limited to those clearly granted to it by the Constitution.)* **AL** **ELL** **How is the power to nullify federal laws an example of states' rights?** *(The states claimed that laws such as the Alien and Sedition Acts were unconstitutional so they did not have to enforce them.)*

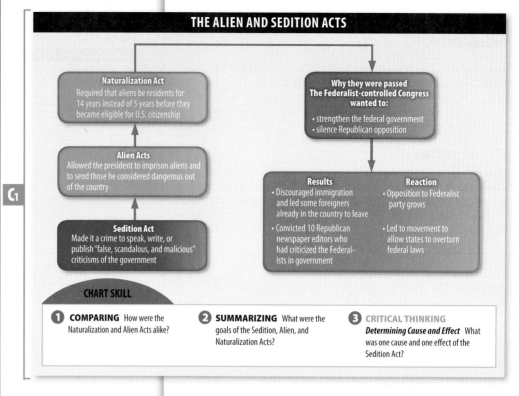

THE ALIEN AND SEDITION ACTS

C1

Naturalization Act
Required that aliens be residents for 14 years instead of 5 years before they became eligible for U.S. citizenship

Alien Acts
Allowed the president to imprison aliens and to send those he considered dangerous out of the country

Sedition Act
Made it a crime to speak, write, or publish "false, scandalous, and malicious" criticisms of the government

Why they were passed
The Federalist-controlled Congress wanted to:
• strengthen the federal government
• silence Republican opposition

Results
• Discouraged immigration and led some foreigners already in the country to leave
• Convicted 10 Republican newspaper editors who had criticized the Federalists in government

Reaction
• Opposition to Federalist party grows
• Led to movement to allow states to overturn federal laws

CHART SKILL

1. **COMPARING** How were the Naturalization and Alien Acts alike?

2. **SUMMARIZING** What were the goals of the Sedition, Alien, and Naturalization Acts?

3. **CRITICAL THINKING** *Determining Cause and Effect* What was one cause and one effect of the Sedition Act?

Domestic and Foreign Affairs

Democratic-Republicans saw the Alien and Sedition Acts as Federalist tyranny. They looked to the states to respond and protect people's liberties. Madison and Jefferson wrote statements of protest that the Virginia and Kentucky legislatures passed as resolutions.

R The Virginia and Kentucky Resolutions of 1798 and 1799 claimed that the Alien and Sedition Acts violated the Constitution. They declared that the states should not put them into action. The Kentucky Resolution further said that states could **nullify** (NUH•luh•fy)—legally overturn—federal laws they thought were unconstitutional.

C2 The resolutions supported the principle of **states' rights**. This principle held that the powers of the federal government were limited to those clearly granted by the Constitution. To

Reading **HELP**DESK **CCSS**

nullify to legally overturn
states' rights the idea that states should have all powers that the Constitution does not give to the federal government or forbid to the states

260 The Federalist Era

netw⊚rks *Online Teaching Options*

See page 243E for other online activities.

CHART

The Alien and Sedition Acts

Explaining Use the chart to discuss the Alien and Sedition Acts. Have volunteers explain the meanings of alien and sedition. *(aliens: residents who are not citizens; sedition: activities aimed at weakening the government)* **Ask: Why did Americans become more suspicious of aliens?** *(They were angry at foreign attempts to influence the government.)* **Why do you think the Sedition Acts lasted for such a short period?** *(Students may say that leaders realized that it could violate freedom of speech or that it was no longer needed after the treaty with France in 1800.)* **BL**

networks® The Alien and Sedition Acts

The Alien and Sedition Acts were signed into law by President John Adams in 1798. The acts were four laws passed by the Federalist-controlled Congress. The acts changed the number of years a person had to be a U.S. resident in order to be considered a citizen. The requirement increased from five to 14 years. The acts also allowed the president to imprison or deport illegal aliens and restrict negative speech about the U.S. government. These laws were intended to weaken the Democratic-Republican Party. Reaction to the Alien and Sedition Acts was largely negative. The acts helped contribute to the Democratic-Republican victory in the election of 1800.

THE ALIEN AND SEDITION ACTS

ANSWERS, p. 260

CHART SKILLS

1. Both dealt with aliens within the United States.

2. The acts were intended to strengthen the federal government and silence Republican opposition.

3. **CRITICAL THINKING** Possible answer: The XYZ Affair was one cause of the act; one of the results of the act was that immigration was discouraged.

Abigail Adams was the first First Lady to occupy the White House. She lived there while the building was still under construction. Adams found the unfinished East Room so large that she used it for hanging the family laundry.

prevent the federal government from becoming too powerful, the states should have all other powers not expressly forbidden to them. The issue of states' rights would remain an important issue in American politics for many years.

Meanwhile, the Federalists urged Adams to declare war on France. Adams, however, resisted this pressure. Instead, he sent a representative to seek peace with France.

In 1800 the French agreed to a treaty and stopped their attacks on American ships. Though it had benefits for the United States, the agreement with France was unpopular and hurt Adams's chance for reelection. Rather than cheering the agreement, Hamilton and his supporters opposed their own president. The Federalists were now split. This improved Democratic-Republican hopes for winning the presidency in the 1800 election.

☑ PROGRESS CHECK

Specifying What was important about the Virginia and Kentucky Resolutions of 1798 and 1799?

LESSON 3 REVIEW (CCSS)

Review Vocabulary (Tier 3 Words)

1. Use the following words in a sentence about the development of political parties. RH.6–8.4

    a. partisan   b. caucus

2. Use the following terms in a paragraph about the presidency of John Adams. RH.6–8.4, WHST.6–8.4

    a. alien   b. sedition
    c. nullify   d. states' rights

Answer the Guiding Questions

3. *Contrasting* What was the belief of those who opposed the formation of political parties? What was the belief of those who supported them? RH.6–8.5

4. *Recalling* What happened in the XYZ affair? RH.6–8.1

5. **ARGUMENT** Choose the candidate that you might have supported in the election of 1796 and make a campaign poster using words and illustrations to promote your candidate. WHST.6–8.1, WHST.6–8.10

Lesson 3   **261**

C Critical Thinking Skills

Determining Cause and Effect Describe to students why Adams was reluctant to declare war on France. **Ask:** What was the result of Adams sending a representative to seek peace with France? *(France agreed to the treaty and it had benefits to the United States, but it was unpopular and hurt Adams's chance at reelection.)* What was the effect on the upcoming election? *(The Federalist party was split, and this allowed Jefferson to have a better chance at winning the election.)*

Have students complete the Lesson 3 Review.

CLOSE & REFLECT

Review the beliefs and ideas of the Federalists and the Republicans of 1796. Ask students to compare the positions of those two parties with the positions of today's Democrats and Republicans.

LESSON 3 REVIEW ANSWERS

1. Possible answer: In the 1790s, more and more people became partisan, and political parties held caucuses to choose their own candidates for upcoming elections.

2. Possible answer: In response to a growing conflict with France, Adams and the Federalists in Congress passed laws that treated aliens harshly and that gave the federal government wide powers to combat sedition. Republicans opposed these laws and urged states to nullify them, thereby making what would become a key states' rights argument.

3. Those who opposed the formation of political parties, such as George Washington, believed that they were harmful to good government and would end up dividing the nation. Those who supported political parties, like Thomas Jefferson, believed that it was

natural for people to disagree about issues. They also suggested that people who hold similar views tend to band together.

4. The French seized American ships that carried cargo to Britain as a punishment for Jay's Treaty. Adams sent a delegation to Paris to try to end the dispute. The French, however, refused to meet with the Americans. Instead, France sent three agents—referred to as X, Y, and Z—who demanded a bribe and a loan for France. Adams refused and urged Congress to prepare for war.

5. Students' posters should use appropriate words and illustrations to promote the candidate they favor.

ANSWER, p. 261

☑ PROGRESS CHECK The resolutions both strongly supported the principle of states' rights. This principle stated that the powers of the federal government should be limited to those clearly spelled out in the Constitution.

CHAPTER REVIEW ACTIVITY

Have a volunteer create a two-column chart and write "Name" in the left column and "Role" in the right. Then lead a discussion that recalls the important individuals highlighted in the chapter. The volunteer should note their names and the roles they played in American history.

Name	Role
George Washington	First President
John Adams	First Vice President, Second President
Thomas Jefferson	Head of State Department
Alexander Hamilton	Head of Department of Treasury
John Jay	Chief Justice of the Supreme Court
James Madison	Powerful Democratic-Republican

REVIEW THE ENDURING UNDERSTANDING

Review this chapter's Enduring Understanding with students:

- *People, places, and ideas change over time.*

Now pose the following questions in a class discussion to apply this enduring understanding to the chapter.

Why was President George Washington so aware of precedents? *(As the first president, George Washington knew his actions and decisions would set traditions that would shape the nation's future. Because he knew he was setting precedents, he was very careful in what he said and did.)*

Why did George Washington use force to put down the Whiskey Rebellion? *(Washington wanted to send a strong message to the public that the new government would use force to maintain order.)*

What were factions, and how did they emerge? *(Factions were political parties. They first emerged when the supporters of Alexander Hamilton and the supporters of Thomas Jefferson, in Congress and among the public, expressed their disagreement about the powers of the government under the Constitution.)*

Write your answers on a separate piece of paper.

1 **Exploring the Essential Questions** RH.6–8.8, WHST.6–8.1
ARGUMENT Washington was the first of several generals who later became president. Think about this statement: A good general makes a good president. Is this an opinion or a fact? Do you agree or disagree? Explain.

2 **21st Century Skills** RH.6–8.5
COMPARING AND CONTRASTING Compare and contrast the views of the Federalists and the Democratic-Republicans.

3 **Thinking Like a Historian** WHST.6–8.1, WHST.6–8.10
DRAWING INFERENCES AND CONCLUSIONS In the first years of the United States under the Constitution, the first political parties started to develop. This ran against the hopes and expectations of many of the people who had written the Constitution. Write a brief essay in which you attempt to explain why the country may have been better off without political parties.

4 **GEOGRAPHY ACTIVITY**

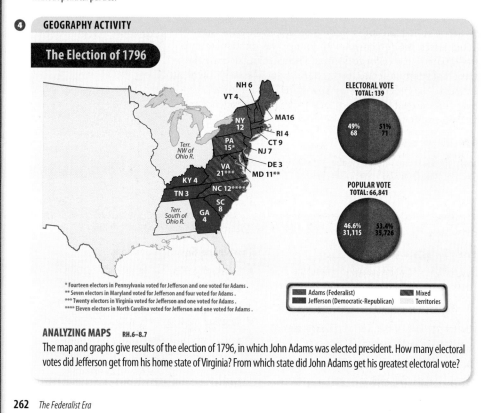

The Election of 1796

ELECTORAL VOTE TOTAL: 139

POPULAR VOTE TOTAL: 66,841

* Fourteen electors in Pennsylvania voted for Jefferson and one voted for Adams.
** Seven electors in Maryland voted for Jefferson and four voted for Adams.
*** Twenty electors in Virginia voted for Jefferson and one voted for Adams.
**** Eleven electors in North Carolina voted for Jefferson and one voted for Adams.

Adams (Federalist) Mixed
Jefferson (Democratic-Republican) Territories

ANALYZING MAPS RH.6–8.7
The map and graphs give results of the election of 1796, in which John Adams was elected president. How many electoral votes did Jefferson get from his home state of Virginia? From which state did John Adams get his greatest electoral vote?

ACTIVITIES ANSWERS

Exploring the Essential Questions

1 Answers will vary. It is an opinion but can be supported by examples. Answers should include an analysis of attributes of a good general, such as decisiveness, leadership, organization, ability to delegate, selecting good advisers, and so on, and note how these might contribute to or detract from a person being a good president. Students may also note skills that are not encouraged in a general but are necessary for a president, such as communicating with the public.

21st Century Skills

2 Students may note the following views:

Federalists	Both	Democratic-Republicans
Supported a National Bank, Supported representative government controlled by educated men, Believed in implied powers of the Constitution	Supported the Constitution and the Bill of Rights	Opposed a National Bank, Feared strong central government controlled by only a few people, Believed in a strict interpretation of the Constitution

REVIEW THE GUIDING QUESTIONS

Choose the best answer for each question.

RH.6–8.2
❶ With the Judiciary Act of 1789, Congress

   A. placed state courts under federal courts.

   B. established a federal court system.

   C. blocked state laws in favor of federal laws.

   D. named judges for all federal and state courts.

RH.6–8.2
❷ What was one reason Madison and Jefferson opposed the idea of a national bank?

   F. They believed it was unconstitutional for Congress to create a bank.

   G. They wanted each state to create and form its own bank.

   H. They feared that banking activities would threaten the purchase of municipal bonds.

   I. They considered bank practices, such as charging interest, to be unethical.

RH.6–8.1
❸ The Whiskey Rebellion was

   A. an armed uprising by farmers in Ohio.

   B. a violent slave rebellion in Virginia.

   C. a skirmish between U.S. soldiers and Native Americans in the Ohio Valley.

   D. a protest by Pennsylvania farmers over a new tax.

RH.6–8.1
❹ Pinckney's Treaty allowed the U.S. to

   F. purchase the state of Alaska.

   G. use the Mississippi River and trade in New Orleans.

   H. take over lands in Florida and Georgia.

   I. defend against the British impressment of sailors.

RH.6–8.2
❺ Which of the following is true about the Federalists?

   A. They supported representative government.

   B. They thought that there could never be too much democracy.

   C. They believed it was wise for the public to be involved in politics.

   D. Thomas Jefferson was their leader.

RH.6–8.2
❻ The Virginia and Kentucky Resolutions

   F. were drafted by Federalists opposing Republican uses of federal power.

   G. claimed that the Alien and Sedition Acts violated the Constitution.

   H. distributed land to settlers in Virginia and Kentucky.

   I. rejected the principle of states' rights stated in the Constitution.

263

ASSESSMENT ANSWERS
Review the Guiding Questions

❶ **B** The Judiciary Act left state laws and courts in place. It did not name judges. While federal courts had the power to rule on state laws, the state courts were not placed under federal courts.

❷ **F** Madison and Jefferson were Republicans who believed in a strict interpretation of the Constitution. The Constitution does not mention creation of a national bank; therefore, Madison and Jefferson considered it unconstitutional.

❸ **D** The Whiskey Rebellion took place in Pennsylvania and involved farmers who were angry about a new tax, not enslaved people (B) or Native Americans (C).

❹ **G** Pinckney's Treaty was with Spain and granted Americans free navigation on the Mississippi River and the right to trade at New Orleans. It was not related to Alaska, Florida, Georgia, or impressment.

❺ **A** Thomas Jefferson was the leader of the Republicans, not the Federalists (D). B and C describe Republican beliefs.

❻ **G** Republicans drafted the Virginia and Kentucky Resolutions in response to Federalist actions, not vice versa (F). The resolutions had nothing to do with the allocation of territory (H). The resolutions supported states' rights (I).

Thinking Like a Historian

❸ Essays may note that political parties can encourage divisiveness rather than compromise and that parties may serve to keep people apart rather than helping them to work for the best interests of the country.

Analyzing Maps

❹ Jefferson won 20 of Virginia's 21 electoral votes. Adams got his highest total of electoral votes in his home state of Massachusetts.

Analyzing Documents

7 **C** The passage does not mention money being set aside (A), U.S. interference on their lands (B), or the right to make war (D).

8 **F** The passage specifies that the sale of Native American land can only be to the United States, not to anyone else (G) or the highest bidder (H). The treaty is not related to profits (I).

Short Response

9 Two representatives are fighting. Other House members seem to be encouraging the fight.

10 The fight symbolizes the bitter differences between Republicans and Federalists, such as the dispute over the Alien and Sedition Acts.

Extended Response

11 Letters should discuss how differences of opinion on the proper role and powers of government divided the Washington Administration and led to the formation of two political parties. Letters should offer individual opinions about which view of government makes the most sense. Accept all reasonable responses.

DBQ ANALYZING DOCUMENTS

The following passage is taken from the Treaty of Greenville.

"The Indian tribes who have a right to those lands, are quietly to enjoy them, hunting, planting, and dwelling thereon, … but when those tribes … shall … sell their lands they are to be sold only to the United States; and until such sale, the United States will protect all the said Indian tribes … against all citizens of the United States. … "

—from the Treaty of Greenville, 1795

RH.6–8.2

7 **Identifying** What does the United States government promise Native Americans in this document?

A. Money will be set aside from the sale of their lands.

B. United States citizens will share Native American hunting lands.

C. They will be protected until their lands are sold.

D. They have the right to make war against others.

RH.6–8.6, RH.6–8.10

8 **Analyzing** How does this document control the sale of Native American lands?

F. Native Americans must sell their land only to the United States.

G. Native Americans cannot sell their land to anyone.

H. Native Americans are free to sell their lands to the highest bidder.

I. Native Americans must share the profits from selling their land.

SHORT RESPONSE

This 1798 cartoon shows an exchange between a Republican and Federalist over the Sedition Act.

RH.6–8.7, WHST.6–8.4

9 What is happening in the cartoon, and how are others reacting?

RH.6–8.7, WHST.6–8.4

10 What does the cartoon suggest about politics of the era?

EXTENDED RESPONSE

WHST.6–8.1, WHST.6–8.10

11 **Narrative** You are a citizen of the United States in 1796. It is a presidential election year. Write a letter to a friend in another country in which you describe the political events of the Washington Administration and the upcoming election. Offer your thoughts about the two new political parties.

Need Extra Help?

If You've Missed Question	1	2	3	4	5	6	7	8	9	10	11
Review Lesson	1	1	2	2	3	3	2	2	3	3	3

---

netw⊙rks   *Online Teaching Options*

Help students use the Skills Builder resources

Your students can practice important 21st Century skills such as geography, reading, writing, and critical thinking by using resources found in the Skills Builder tab of the online Student Learning Center. Resources include templates, handbooks, and slide shows. These same resources are also available in the Resource Library of the Teacher Lesson Center.

The Jefferson Era Planner

UNDERSTANDING BY DESIGN®

Enduring Understanding

- *People, places, and ideas change over time.*

Essential Questions

- *How do governments change?*
- *How does geography influence the way people live?*
- *Why does conflict develop?*

Predictable Misunderstandings

Students may think:

- *People elect the President directly.*
- *Presidential campaigns were quiet exercises in democracy.*
- *The Constitution lists all the powers of the federal government.*
- *The Supreme Court does not have much influence over the other branches of government.*

Assessment Evidence

Performance Tasks:

- *Hands-On Chapter Project*

Other Evidence:

- *Interactive Graphic Organizers*
- *What Do You Know? Activity*
- *21st Century Skills Activity*
- *Geography and History Activity*
- *Primary Source Activity*
- *Written Paragraphs*
- *Lesson Reviews*
- *Online Self-Check Quizzes*
- *Chapter Activities and Assessment*

NCSS Standards covered in "The Jefferson Era"

Learners will understand:

1   Culture

7. How people from different cultures develop different values and ways of interpreting experience

8. That language, behaviors, and beliefs of different cultures can both contribute to and pose barriers to cross-cultural understanding

2   Time, Continuity, and Change

1. The study of the past provides representation of the history of communities, nations, and the world

6. The origins and influences of social, cultural, political, and economic systems

7. The contributions of key persons, groups, and events from the past and their influence on the present

9. The influences of social, geographic, economic, and cultural factors on the history of local areas, states, nations, and the world

3   People, Places, and Environments

9. The use of a variety of maps, globes, graphic representations, and geospatial technologies to help investigate the relationships among people, places, and environments

5   Individuals, Groups, and Institutions

8. That when two or more groups with differing norms and beliefs interact, accommodation or conflict may result

SUGGESTED PACING GUIDE

Introducing the Chapter.............. 1 Day	Lesson 3 .... 2 Days
Lesson 1 .... 1 Day	Lesson 4 .... 2 Days
Lesson 2 .... 2 Days	Chapter Activities and Assessment...... 1 Day

TOTAL TIME   9 Days

Key for Using the Teacher Edition

SKILL-BASED ACTIVITIES

Types of skill activities found in the Teacher Edition.

V **Visual Skills** require students to analyze maps, graphs, charts, and photos.

R **Reading Skills** help students practice reading skills and master vocabulary.

W **Writing Skills** provide writing opportunities to help students comprehend the text.

C **Critical Thinking Skills** help students apply and extend what they have learned.

T **Technology Skills** require students to use digital tools effectively.

Letters are followed by a number when there is more than one of the same type of skill on the page.

DIFFERENTIATED INSTRUCTION

All activities are written for the on-level student unless otherwise marked with the leveled labels below.

BL **Beyond Level**
AL **Approaching Level**
ELL **English Language Learners**

All students benefit from activities that utilize different learning styles. Many activities are marked as below when a particular learning style is highlighted.

Intrapersonal	**Naturalist**
Logical/Mathematical	**Kinesthetic**
Visual/Spatial	**Auditory/Musical**
Verbal/Linguistic	**Interpersonal**

CHAPTER OPENER PLANNER

Students will know:

- how Jefferson won the election of 1800.
- the political and geographical changes that took place during Jefferson's presidency.
- why the United States entered the War of 1812.
- how the United States fared in the War of 1812.
- how the War of 1812 affected the nation.

Students will be able to:

- **compare and contrast** the election of 1800 with modern elections.
- **describe** how John Marshall affected the powers of the Supreme Court and the federal government.
- **identify and evaluate** how governments change.
- **locate** the Louisiana Purchase on a map and discuss the importance of the purchase.
- **determine cause and effect** in how the Haitian Revolution affected the United States.
- **analyze primary sources** to learn more about the Lewis and Clark expedition.
- **identify points of view** about the Louisiana Purchase, Native American rights, and the War of 1812.
- **analyze visuals and primary sources** to understand the war with Tripoli.
- **explain** why the United States was not prepared for war with Britain.
- **identify** the War Hawks.
- **describe and analyze** the events of the War of 1812.
- **explain** the origins of "The Star-Spangled Banner."

UNDERSTANDING
BY DESIGN®

☑ *Print Teaching Options*

V Visual Skills

☐ **P. 266** Students view a map of the United States in 1803. **AL** Interpersonal

☐ **P. 267** Students analyze a time line that shows events in the United States around Jefferson's presidency.
Visual/Spatial

☑ *Online Teaching Options*

V Visual Skills

☐ **MAP** **Louisiana Purchase and Westward Expansion**—Students trace the routes followed by Pike and Lewis and Clark.

☐ **TIME LINE** **America 1800 to 1816**—Students learn about key events in U.S. history during this time period.

☐ **WORLD ATLAS** Students can use this interactive map to identify regions of the world, learn about individual countries, locate political boundaries, measure distances, and much more.

☑ *Printable Digital Worksheets*

R Reading Skills

☐ **GRAPHIC NOVEL** *Election Deadlock*— The novel reports events of the election of 1800, when Jefferson and Burr tied for president.

Project-Based Learning

Hands-On Chapter Project

Biographical Cover Story

Students will identify people who influenced American government and expansion during the Jefferson era by writing a magazine cover story about Thomas Jefferson, James Madison, Robert Fulton, Meriwether Lewis, William Clark, or Tecumseh.

Technology Extension  edtechteacher
21st Century Learning

Online Discussion Forum

- Find an additional activity online that incorporates technology for this project.
- Visit the EdTechTeacher Web sites (included in the Technology Extension for this chapter) for more links, tutorials, and other resources.

Print Resources

ANCILLARY RESOURCES
These ancillaries are available for every chapter and lesson.

- **Reading Essentials and Study Guide Workbook** **AL** **ELL**
- **Chapter Tests and Lesson Quizzes Blackline Masters**

PRINTABLE DIGITAL WORKSHEETS
These printable digital worksheets are available for every chapter and lesson.

- **Hands-On Chapter Projects**
- **What Do You Know? activities**
- **Chapter Summaries (English and Spanish)**
- **Vocabulary Builder activities**
- **Guided Reading activities**

More Media Resources

SUGGESTED READING
Grade 6 reading level:

- *The Great Little Madison,* by Jean Fritz

Grade 7 reading level:

- *Crossing the Panther's Path,* by Elizabeth Alder

Grade 8 reading level:

- *Bold Journey: West with Lewis and Clark,* by Charles Bohner

A NEW PARTY IN POWER

Students will know:
- *how Jefferson won the election of 1800.*
- *the political and geographical changes that took place during Jefferson's presidency.*

Students will be able to:
- **compare and contrast** *the election of 1800 with modern elections.*
- **describe** *how John Marshall affected the powers of the Supreme Court and the federal government.*
- **identify and evaluate** *how governments change.*

UNDERSTANDING
BY DESIGN®

☑ *Print Teaching Options*

V Visual Skills

☐ **P. 269** Students analyze a map that shows the percentage of people who voted in 1800. **AL** Visual/Spatial

R Reading Skills

☐ **P. 269** Students draw conclusions about the tie between Jefferson and Burr in the election. **AL** **ELL**

☐ **P. 270** Students make a list of the different ways Jefferson reduced the role of the federal government. **AL** **ELL** Logical/Mathematical

☐ **P. 270** Students discuss the effect the Judiciary Act of 1801 had on Jefferson's presidency. **BL**

W Writing Skills

☐ **P. 269** Students write a narrative in which they imagine themselves as a modern-day politician who is trying to follow in Jefferson's footsteps as a frugal politician. **BL**

C Critical Thinking Skills

☐ **P. 268** Students research newspaper and magazine articles about current political campaigns and debates and compare them to those in 1800. **AL** **ELL** Visual/Spatial

☐ **P. 268** Students make a chart of examples of personal attacks in political campaigns they identify in articles or videos viewed online. **AL** **ELL** Visual/Spatial Auditory/Musical

☐ **P. 270** Students discuss why Jefferson was considered a Renaissance man. **AL** **ELL**

☐ **P. 271** Students infer how Jefferson may have felt about how the Supreme Court asserted its power as an equal branch of government. **BL** Interpersonal

☐ **P. 271** Students make predictions about how Native Americans may have felt about the Court's decision in *Worcester* v. *Georgia*. **BL**

☑ *Online Teaching Options*

V Visual Skills

VIDEO **President Thomas Jefferson**—Students view a video that describes Jefferson's election and some of his accomplishments as president.

MAP **The Presidential Election of 1800**—Students interact with the map to see voter preferences in the election of 1800.

R Reading Skills

GRAPHIC ORGANIZER **Taking Notes:** *Analyzing:* **Reducing the Role of Government**—Students record details on how the Republicans reduced the role of government.

BIOGRAPHY **Thomas Jefferson**—Students read about Jefferson's wide-ranging interests.

C Critical Thinking Skills

SLIDE SHOW **Monticello**—Students view the home Jefferson designed and built.

T Technology Skills

SELF-CHECK QUIZ **Lesson 1**—Students receive instant feedback on their mastery of lesson content.

☑ *Printable Digital Worksheets*

C Critical Thinking Skills

WORKSHEET **21st Century Skills Activity: Learning and Innovation: Identify Problems and Solutions**—Students examine the problem of a tied Electoral College and how Congress solved this problem.

THE LOUISIANA PURCHASE

Students will know:

- the political and geographical changes that took place during Jefferson's presidency.

Students will be able to:

- **locate** the Louisiana Purchase on a map and discuss the importance of the purchase.
- **determine cause and effect** in how the Haitian Revolution affected the United States.
- **analyze primary sources** to learn more about the Lewis and Clark expedition.

UNDERSTANDING BY DESIGN®

☑ *Print Teaching Options*

V Visual Skills

☐ **P. 273** Students locate the Mississippi River on a map of the United States in 1800 and discuss the importance of New Orleans. **AL** Visual/Spatial

☐ **P. 276** Students review a map of the Louisiana Territory compared with one of the current United States and determine the significance of the Louisiana Purchase. **AL** **ELL** Visual/Spatial

R Reading Skills

☐ **P. 272** Students describe the travels of the settlers. **AL** **ELL**

☐ **P. 273** Students discuss the effect changes in Spanish policy about the Mississippi River had on American trade.

☐ **P. 277** Students summarize the reasons for the duel between Hamilton and Burr.

W Writing Skills

☐ **P. 274** Students write a short paragraph making predictions of the effects of the Louisiana Purchase on the United States. **AL**

C Critical Thinking Skills

☐ **P. 274** Students discuss the role Santo Domingo had in the United States' purchase of the Louisiana Territory. Verbal/Linguistic Interpersonal

☐ **P. 274** Students identify concerns of President Jefferson by analyzing the questions he had relating to Lewis and Clark's expeditions. Interpersonal

☐ **P. 275** Students revisit maps of the Native American nations and imagine how the Native Americans felt about the westward movement of settlers.

☐ **P. 275** Students draw conclusions about the success of the Lewis and Clark expedition. **BL**

☐ **P. 276** Students describe the Federalist response to the Louisiana Purchase.

T Technology Skills

☐ **P. 272** Students search the Internet to find information to make maps showing Native American nations who lived in the Louisiana Territory in 1800. **BL** Interpersonal Verbal/Linguistic

☑ *Online Teaching Options*

V Visual Skills

☐ **MAP** **Louisiana Purchase and Westward Expansion**—Students trace the routes followed by Pike and Lewis and Clark.

☐ **BIOGRAPHY** **Zebulon Pike**—Students click to read biographical information about this American explorer and soldier.

☐ **IMAGE** **The Shoshone**—Students learn about the Snake Nation, the Native American group to which Sacagawea belonged.

R Reading Skills

☐ **GRAPHIC ORGANIZER** **Taking Notes:** *Describing:* **Lewis and Clark and Zebulon Pike**—Students describe the areas that Lewis and Clark and Zebulon Pike explored.

☐ **IMAGE** **Toussaint L'Ouverture**—Students read an extended biography of this Haitian freedom fighter.

☐ **BIOGRAPHY** **Sacagawea**—Students read biographical information about this Native American interpreter and guide for Lewis and Clark.

C Critical Thinking Skills

☐ **CHART** **Alexander Hamilton and Aaron Burr**—Students compare and contrast the backgrounds and opinions of these two men.

☐ **SLIDE SHOW** **The Lewis and Clark Expedition**—Students examine images and maps detailing events of the Lewis and Clark expedition.

T Technology Skills

☐ **SELF-CHECK QUIZ** **Lesson 2**—Students receive instant feedback on their mastery of lesson content.

☑ *Printable Digital Worksheets*

W Writing Skills

☐ **WORKSHEET** **Geography and History Activity: Understanding Human-Environment Interaction: Flora and Fauna of the Louisiana Purchase**—Students read and then write about the plants and animals Lewis and Clark encountered on their journey.

Students will know:
- why the United States entered the War of 1812.

Students will be able to:
- *identify points of view* about the Louisiana Purchase, Native American rights, and the War of 1812.
- *analyze visuals and primary sources* to understand the war with Tripoli.
- *explain* why the United States was not prepared for war with Britain.
- *identify* the War Hawks.

UNDERSTANDING
BY DESIGN®

☑ *Print Teaching Options*

V Visual Skills

☐ **P. 279** Students analyze an image of Decatur burning a captured pirate ship. **AL BL** Visual/Spatial

R Reading Skills

☐ **P. 278** Students explain the meaning of *tribute* today compared with its use by Barbary pirates. **AL ELL**

☐ **P. 280** Students discuss U.S. trade with both sides during the war between Britain and France in 1803.

☐ **P. 281** Students define *embargo* and discuss the Embargo Act of 1807 and the Nonintercourse Act. **AL ELL**

☐ **P. 282** Students summarize the major events of Thomas Jefferson's presidency. **BL**

☐ **P. 283** Students identify the role of Tenskwatawa in the history of westward expansion. **AL ELL**

☐ **P. 284** Students discuss the Battle of Tippecanoe and its long-lasting effects. **AL**

W Writing Skills

☐ **P. 280** Students write a narrative from the point of view of an American soldier forced to serve in the British navy. **BL** Verbal/Linguistic

☐ **P. 284** Students write a letter agreeing or disagreeing with the position of the War Hawks. **BL** Verbal/Linguistic

C Critical Thinking Skills

☐ **P. 278** Students imagine what some of the dangers were for American merchant ships.

☐ **P. 279** Students interpret the meaning of Decatur's words to the crew of the USS *Essex*. **BL** Verbal/Linguistic

☐ **P. 281** Students compare and contrast the Embargo Act and the Nonintercourse Act. **BL** Visual/Spatial

☐ **P. 282** Students determine the effect that Ohio statehood had on relations between white settlers and Native Americans. **AL**

☐ **P. 283** Students summarize Tecumseh's ideas about Native American land and relations with white Americans. **BL** Verbal/Linguistic

T Technology Skills

☐ **P. 280** Students create a bibliography of resources cited in their research of American soldiers' role in the British navy. Verbal/Linguistic

---

☑ *Online Teaching Options*

V Visual Skills

VIDEO **Tecumseh**—Students view a video that describes how Tecumseh united tribal people against the onrushing settlers of the frontier.

IMAGE **Stephen Decatur**—Students click to learn about this hero of the war against Tripoli.

R Reading Skills

GRAPHIC ORGANIZER **Taking Notes:** *Analyzing:* **Taking Action**—Students record the actions taken by the United States in three different situations.

IMAGE **Battle of Tippecanoe**—Students read about the defeat of Tecumseh at the hands of William Henry Harrison.

C Critical Thinking Skills

WHITEBOARD ACTIVITY **The War of 1812**—Students sequence events leading up to the War of 1812.

IMAGE **The *Chesapeake–Leopard* Affair**—Students click to learn details of the naval dust-up between the Americans and British.

T Technology Skills

SELF-CHECK QUIZ **Lesson 3**—Students receive instant feedback on their mastery of lesson content.

GAME **A Time of Conflict Identification Game**—Students review lesson vocabulary in this interactive game.

☑ *Printable Digital Worksheets*

R Reading Skills

WORKSHEET **Primary Source Activity: A Question of War with England**—Students analyze opinions for and against going to war with Great Britain.

THE WAR OF 1812

Students will know:
- how the United States fared in the War of 1812.
- how the War of 1812 affected the nation.

Students will be able to:
- *describe and analyze* the events of the War of 1812.
- *explain* the origins of "The Star-Spangled Banner."

UNDERSTANDING
BY DESIGN®

☑ *Print Teaching Options*

R Reading Skills

☐ **P. 285** Students summarize how the United States was unprepared for war with Britain. AL ELL

☐ **P. 286** Students discuss the strategic value of the Great Lakes in the War of 1812. AL ELL

☐ **P. 287** Students describe what happened when the British attacked Washington, D.C. AL ELL

☐ **P. 287** Students discuss the events that followed the attack on Washington, D.C. AL ELL

☐ **P. 288** Students discuss the end of the war and the Treaty of Ghent. AL ELL

☐ **P. 289** Students explain the impact of the War of 1812 on the Federalist Party. AL ELL

W Writing Skills

☐ **P. 289** Students write a narrative from the point of view of a Federalist who opposed the war. BL
Verbal/Linguistic

C Critical Thinking Skills

☐ **P. 286** Students identify the influence of Britain on the United States' movement toward war. AL ELL

☐ **P. 287** Students identify what effect the end of Britain's war with France had on the War of 1812. AL

☐ **P. 288** Students draw conclusions about the War of 1812 on Canadian history. BL

☐ **P. 288** Students make inferences on why war heroes have an advantage in political campaigns.

☑ *Online Teaching Options*

V Visual Skills

☐ **VIDEO** **History of United States Symbols: American Flag**—Students learn about the history of the American flag and how it represented the newly formed United States.

☐ **MAP** **The War of 1812**—Students identify the sites of major battles.

R Reading Skills

☐ **GRAPHIC ORGANIZER** **Taking Notes:** *Describing:* **Battle Outcomes**—Students record the outcomes of three important battles of the War of 1812.

☐ **BIOGRAPHY** **William Henry Harrison**—Students read the biography of this soldier and U.S. president.

☐ **BIOGRAPHY** **Dolley Madison**—Students read biographical information about the wife of the third president.

C Critical Thinking Skills

☐ **WHITEBOARD ACTIVITY** **Dates in History**—Students build a time line of important events from 1807 to 1815.

☐ **IMAGE** **The Battle of New Orleans**—Students consider this battle won by Andrew Jackson.

T Technology Skills

☐ **SELF-CHECK QUIZ** **Lesson 4**—Students receive instant feedback on their mastery of lesson content.

LESSON 1 A New Party in Power

Reading and Comprehension

This section focuses on the election of 1800, Jefferson's presidency, and the growing power of the Supreme Court. Explain to students that, similar to today, two parties in 1800 nominated candidates for president and vice president. Have students make a chart showing the two political parties and their respective candidates for the 1800 election. If you have time, make connections with the elections of today by having students make another chart that shows the parties and candidates for the most recent presidential election.

Text Evidence

In Jefferson's Inaugural Address, he said that one of his goals was "a wise and frugal government." Explain to students that "frugality" means staying on a budget and not spending too much. Have students skim the chapter and find evidence of Jefferson's commitment to frugality.

LESSON 2 The Louisiana Purchase

Reading and Comprehension

This section focuses on the Louisiana Purchase and the Lewis and Clark expedition. Have students make a map of North America, circa 1800, showing the United States, the Louisiana Territory, and the Spanish Territory. Then have them mark the travels of Lewis and Clark on the map.

Text Evidence

Tell students that President Jefferson was amazed when he had the opportunity to purchase the Louisiana Territory. Have students divide into pairs. One student in each pair should represent Napoleon, while the other should represent Jefferson. Have students write a short monologue for each man explaining the basis of his decision. Students should find supporting details for their monologues in the lesson subsection, "An Expanding Nation."

LESSON 3 A Time of Conflict

Reading and Comprehension

This lesson focuses on the period leading up to the war of 1812. Explain to students that Britain and France were at war in the early 1800s, but that the United States wanted to be able to trade with both countries. Have students skim the lesson and make a list of problems that arose as the United States tried to trade with both European countries. Remind students that in the early 1800s, trade was conducted via sea routes.

Text Evidence

Divide the class into groups, and have them make a time line showing events leading up to the War of 1812. Have students skim the lesson to find evidence of growing conflict between the United States and Great Britain.

LESSON 4 The War of 1812

Reading and Comprehension

This section covers the War of 1812. Tell students that at the beginning of the war, the United States was in a weak position. At some point in the war, events began to strengthen the United States. Have students skim the chapter to find events that made the United States stronger.

Text Evidence

Ask students to write a letter from the perspective of Dolley Madison, detailing the events that occurred when Washington, D.C., was attacked by British troops. Have students find details in the lesson to include in their letters.

Online Resources

Approaching Level Reader

Use this online lower-level text that corresponds directly to the text in the Student Edition. It includes a Spanish version.

Guided Reading Activities

This resource uses graphic organizers and guiding questions to help students with comprehension.

What Do You Know?

Use these worksheets to pre-assess student's background knowledge before they study the chapter.

Reading Essentials and Study Guide Workbook

This resource offers writing and reading activities for the approaching-level student. Also available in Spanish.

Self-Check Quizzes

This online assessment tool provides instant feedback for students to check their progress.

How Do I Help My Students
Review Skills Independently?

Students need to learn and implement a variety of skills in order to master social studies content. These skills include critical thinking; research and writing; reading maps, charts, and graphs; how to find resources on the Internet; how to create presentations, and so on. McGraw-Hill Education's networks™ platform enables students to choose a particular skill to practice or reinforce, at their own pace.

You can individualize your instruction by assigning a specific skill to a student who needs to learn or practice that skill. The networks™ Resource Library offers a series of Interactive Skill Lessons that guides your students independently through the process.

Step 1 **Log in to the Networks Student Center Dashboard**

- Tell your students to enter the ConnectEd portal and sign in to their social studies book.

- Use the username and password assigned to the student.

Step 2 **Look Through the Resource Library and the Skills Builder Section**

Step 3 **Choose Your Skill**

- Within the Resource library and the Skills Builder area are many different kinds of skills-related assets: Geography Skills, Economics Skills, Critical Thinking Skills, Research and Writing Skills, 21st Century Skills, and Building Projects and Presentation Skills.

- Select the asset that best suits your needs.

Step 4 **Open the Asset and Start Learning**

- Students click through the screens one at a time.

- The digital assets lead the user step-by-step through the skill being taught.

The Jefferson Era

1800–1816

ESSENTIAL QUESTIONS • *How do governments change?*
• *How does geography influence the way people live?* • *Why does conflict develop?*

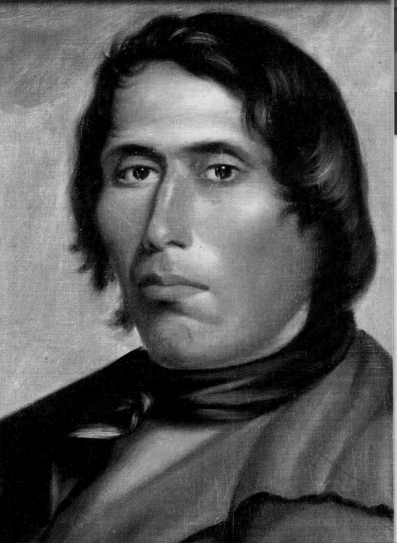

◄ *Shawnee leader Tecumseh rallied Native Americans to resist American settlement in the early 1800s.*

The Granger Collection, NYC

The Story Matters . . .

Shawnee leader Tecumseh grew up in what the Americans call the Northwest Territory. He fights to slow the advance of white settlers across the Appalachian Mountains. Tecumseh scoffs at the demands that his people give up their ancient homelands. "Sell a country!" he says. "Why not sell the air, the clouds and the great sea, as well as the earth?"

Tecumseh knows it will take the strength of many to stop the Americans. He hopes to build a great alliance of all the Native American groups in the region. Will he succeed in his plan?

265

ENGAGE

🔔 **Bellringer** Ask a volunteer to read "The Story Matters . . ." aloud. Then divide the class into two groups. Have one group write speeches from the point of view of Tecumseh, explaining why they believe that land cannot be sold and that the United States has no right to expand. Have the other group write speeches taking the opposite point of view, writing from the perspective of an American president. If you have time, have students stage a debate. **Ask:** How would you feel, or what would you think, if complete strangers—who might have nothing in common with you—arrived and began to settle land that you thought belonged to you? On the other hand, how would you feel if you were the settler and you thought you had every right to move with your family onto the new land? Tell the class that the tension between Native Americans and white settlers grew as the United States grew in size. It is only one of the conflicts they will learn about in this chapter. **BL** Verbal/Linguistic

Making Connections

Point out to students that Tecumseh's story is one about moving from one place to another. Have students reflect on occasions when they may have had to move or when they have lost friends to moves. Have students make a list of reasons why people sometimes think they must move. **Ask:** Do any of these reasons apply to Tecumseh and the Shawnee or to the settlers? Lead the class in a discussion of the connections between the reasons people moved in the 1800s and the reasons they move today.

Letter from the Author

Dear American History Teacher,

From 1789 to 1828, America became more democratic. The Founding Fathers had not anticipated political parties, but different ideas about government divided leaders and the public. As president, Jefferson reduced the size of the federal government. After purchasing the Louisiana Territory from the French, he named Lewis and Clark to lead an expedition of discovery. Differences between Great Britain and the United States prompted a renewal of hostilities in 1812. Although the war was short and inconclusive, a wave of patriotism washed over Americans when it ended.

Joyce Appleby

TEACH & ASSESS

Step Into the Place

V1 Visual Skills

Location Project the chapter opener map. Explain that this is the United States in 1803. **Ask: From what you know now, describe the differences between the United States in 1803 and the present-day United States.** As a class, discuss the Map Focus questions. **AL**

Have students read the events on the time line. **Ask: What names or events are familiar to you?** *(Students should recognize the name Tecumseh from the picture in the chapter opener. They are likely to have heard of the Supreme Court, Lewis and Clark, and Napoleon, though they may have limited knowledge of them.)* Ask students to share what they know about any of the names or events. Then have students choose one U.S. event and one world event. Ask them to formulate two questions that would help them learn more about each event. If time permits, students can research the answers to their questions. **AL** **Interpersonal**

Content Background Knowledge

- Lewis and Clark encountered nearly 50 different Native American nations on their way west.
- Lewis and Clark followed rivers as much as possible in part because they were hoping to find a "northwest passage" all the way through the continent that would facilitate trade with Asia. Jefferson also wanted a transportation network that would help to cement ties between the West and the rest of the United States. He was worried about the possibility that settlers in the West might someday secede.
- Jefferson did not announce the Louisiana Purchase to the public until just two days before Lewis and Clark set out.
- People in the United States who had never been west imagined that Lewis and Clark might find unicorns, giant mastodons, or giant beavers on their journey.

V2

ANSWERS, p. 266

Step Into the Place

1. Lewis and Clark traveled up the Missouri River through the northern part of the territory. They also explored the Oregon Territory, reaching the Pacific Ocean.
2. The Pike expedition traveled west until it reached the Rocky Mountains, when it turned south.
3. **CRITICAL THINKING** They had to cross several large rivers, such as the Missouri and the Columbia; face winter on the plains; and make their way through the Rocky Mountains.

Step Into the Time

At that time, the United States' relationship with Great Britain was one of conflict and confrontation.

Place and Time: America 1800 to 1816

During the Jefferson Era and the years immediately following it, the United States grew rapidly. The Louisiana Purchase roughly doubled the size of the country, and explorers probed the unknown lands beyond the frontier.

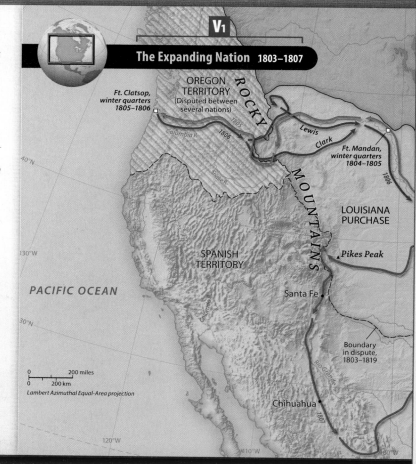

V1

The Expanding Nation 1803–1807

Ft. Clatsop, winter quarters 1805–1806

OREGON TERRITORY (Disputed between several nations)

Ft. Mandan, winter quarters 1804–1805

ROCKY MOUNTAINS

LOUISIANA PURCHASE

Pikes Peak

SPANISH TERRITORY

PACIFIC OCEAN

Santa Fe

Boundary in dispute, 1803–1819

Chihuahua

0   200 miles
0   200 km
Lambert Azimuthal Equal-Area projection

Step Into the Place

MAP FOCUS After the United States purchased the Louisiana Territory from France in 1803, it sent explorers into its new lands—and beyond.

1 **LOCATION** What part of the Louisiana Territory did Lewis and Clark explore? What other territory did they explore? RH.6–8.7

2 **MOVEMENT** In which direction did the Pike expedition travel when it started out? RH.6–8.7

3 **CRITICAL THINKING**
Analyzing What were the major geographic obstacles that Lewis and Clark encountered during their journey through the Louisiana Territory? RH.6–8.7

Step Into the Time

TIME LINE Based on the time line, what conclusions can you draw about the relationship between the United States and Britain in the early 1800s? RH.6–8.5, RH.6–8.7

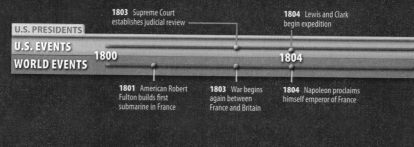

U.S. PRESIDENTS
U.S. EVENTS
WORLD EVENTS

1800

1804

1803 Supreme Court establishes judicial review

1804 Lewis and Clark begin expedition

1801 American Robert Fulton builds first submarine in France

1803 War begins again between France and Britain

1804 Napoleon proclaims himself emperor of France

266 *The Jefferson Era*

Project-Based Learning ✋

Hands-On Chapter Project

Biographical Cover Story

Students will work in groups to create a biographical magazine cover story about one of the following people: Thomas Jefferson, James Madison, Robert Fulton, Meriwether Lewis, William Clark, or Tecumseh. Students read about the topic in their textbook and conduct personal research on their subject, citing at least three sources. Then, student teams organize research and decide what to include in their article. Students work with their team to divide writing tasks and develop the article. Finally, students share their magazine cover story with the class and evaluate using a class-prepared rubric.

Technology Extension

Online Discussion Forum

Conduct an online chat or discussion to extend the classroom magazine cover story project. Through this activity, students can develop a deeper understanding of the major figures presented, pose opinions and questions, or take the role of a historical figure in a "meeting of the minds." Moderate the discussion to provide a student-centered approach to discussing the class content. Visit **networks** online to see the full project.

edtechteacher
21st Century Learning

networks
There's More Online!

☑ **MAP** Explore the interactive version of this map on NETWORKS.

☑ **TIME LINE** Explore the interactive version of this time line on NETWORKS.

BRITISH TERRITORY

Maine

Vt.
N.H.
New York
Mass.
R.I.
Conn.

Pennsylvania N.J.

Indiana Territory

Ohio

Md. Del.

St. Louis

Ohio R.

Virginia

Kentucky

North Carolina

Tennessee

South Carolina

Mississippi Territory

Georgia

Natchitoches

New Orleans

Spanish Florida

Disputed between U.S. and Spain, 1803–1819

Gulf of Mexico

Arkansas R.

Mississippi R.

Red R.

Brazos R.

Missouri R.

1805–1806

1804

1806

1800

ATLANTIC OCEAN

TROPIC OF CANCER

	United States, 1803
←	Lewis and Clark
←	Lewis and Clark return
→	Pike
□	Fort

Thomas Jefferson
1801–1809

1811 Tecumseh joins British forces after the Battle of Tippecanoe

1812 U.S. declares war on Britain

James Madison
1809–1817

1814 British forces burn Washington, D.C.

1815 Battle of New Orleans

1808

1812

1816

1809 Ecuador rebels against Spanish rule

1815 Napoleon is defeated at Waterloo

White House Historical Association

267

MAP

Nations of the World Atlas

Analyzing Maps Project the Interactive World Atlas on the whiteboard and select a world view. Point out Britain, France, and the Barbary States in northern Africa. Explain that these places will all affect the United States in the period students are about to study. **Visual/Spatial**

See page 265B for other online activities.

Step Into the Time

V₂ Visual Skills

Reading a Time Line Direct students' attention to the time line at the bottom of these two pages. Remind students that as of 1800, at the beginning of the time line, only 24 years had passed since the signing of the Declaration of Independence. The United States was still in its infancy as a country. **Ask: What traumatic event looms on the horizon shortly after the end of Jefferson's presidency?** *(War with Great Britain.)* Discuss with students the challenges of going to war again with Great Britain only a few years after having completed one war with the same country. **Visual/Spatial**

Content Background Knowledge

- In order to expand west, the young United States had to find a way to negotiate with the Native American nations who were already occupying that land. Native American nations are regarded as sovereign foreign nations, so the responsibility for declaring wars and signing peace treaties with them fell to Congress.

- British colonists, at first, and settlers from the United States (after the Revolution) did not always understand whose lands they were encroaching on when they moved west—and sometimes they signed treaties with the wrong nation, causing confusion and occasionally leading to violent conflicts. For example, the Iroquois ceded Shawnee land to the British in 1768 at the Treaty of Fort Stanwix, but the Shawnee did not recognize the Iroquois treaty.

- In addition, some Native American groups allied themselves with different nations. The Shawnee and many Mohawk fought on the side of the British in the American Revolution, but the Oneida and Tuscarora took the side of the American patriots. The Mohawk, Oneida, and Tuscarora were members of the Iroquois Confederacy, which never really recovered from the rift caused by the Revolution. These events affected U.S. relations with Native Americans for many years to come.

CLOSE & REFLECT

Problem-Solving Tell students that Lewis and Clark's expedition was a solution to a problem for President Jefferson. Jefferson needed to know what was in the West, but he could not send a large group because Congress would not authorize such a large expense. **Ask: What problems could Jefferson reasonably anticipate that Lewis and Clark would run into during their journey? How could they prepare for those problems?** *(Answers will vary but should indicate that Lewis and Clark would need food and supplies for the entire trip, that they would run into problems talking to people who spoke different languages, that they could get lost, etc.)* Lead the class in a discussion of the challenges faced by Lewis and Clark.

ENGAGE

Bellringer As a class, brainstorm a list of things students know about presidential campaigns and elections today. Write responses on the board. **Ask: What do candidates do to gain support and get their message to people? How is the president elected? How do people feel about presidential elections?** Clear up points of confusion. For example, explain that presidents are not elected directly by the people, but by the Electoral College. **AL ELL**

Tell students that they will be learning about the election of 1800. Encourage them to compare that election to elections today.

TEACH & ASSESS

C1 Critical Thinking Skills

Making Connections Have students research newspaper and magazine articles having to do with recent local and national elections. Encourage students to pay particular attention to articles that are related to how politicians run their campaigns. **Ask: What do you see in the campaigns of today that is different from the way politicians campaigned in 1800?** *(Answers may vary, but students should note that politicians today travel more and directly ask citizens to vote for them. Just like politicians today, though, politicians in 1800 formulated policy statements and tried to disseminate them to the public through forums such as newspapers.)* Encourage students to make connections between modern debates that are presented on television, in video format, and debates in the 1800s that took the form of competing letters to newspapers. **AL ELL Visual/Spatial**

C2 Critical Thinking Skills

Analyzing Have students go through the articles they have brought in about campaigns and highlight places where they find candidates engaging in personal attacks. You may wish to have students make a chart of attacks that occurred during different campaigns for the purpose of comparing and contrasting different elections. If your classroom technology permits, have students work with audiovisual equipment to save snippets of campaign videos or audio content as well as print media. **AL ELL Visual/Spatial Auditory/Musical**

ANSWER, p. 268

TAKING NOTES: Republicans reduced the size of government and the military, reduced military spending, and repealed federal internal taxes, focusing instead on customs duties.

netw⊙rks
There's More Online!

☑ **CHART/GRAPH** The Supreme Court—Then and Now

☑ **GRAPHIC ORGANIZER** Republicans and the Role of Government

☑ **MAP** The Election of 1800

☑ **SLIDE SHOW** Monticello

Lesson 1
A New Party in Power

ESSENTIAL QUESTION *How do governments change?*

IT MATTERS BECAUSE
In the election of 1800, the nation experienced a peaceful transfer of power from one party to the other.

The Election of 1800

GUIDING QUESTION *What did the election of 1800 show about the nature of politics?*

In the election of 1800, Federalists supported President Adams for a second term and Charles Pinckney for vice president. Republicans nominated Thomas Jefferson for president and Aaron Burr as his running mate.

The election campaign of 1800 was very different from the political campaigns we see today. Neither Adams nor Jefferson traveled around the country to gather support. Many thought direct campaigning improper for a person who would be president. Instead, hundreds of letters were sent to leading citizens and newspapers to make candidates' views public.

The campaign was bitterly fought. Each side made personal attacks against the other. For example, Federalists accused Jefferson, who believed in freedom of religion, of being "godless." Republicans warned that the Federalists favored the wealthy and would bring back monarchy.

The Vote Is Tied

Under the Constitution, voters in a presidential election are really electing groups of people called electors. These electors meet in what is known as the Electoral College. There they cast

(tc) Private Collection, Peter Newark American Pictures/Bridgeman Art Library; (tr) imagebroker/Alamy Images

---

Reading HELPDESK (CCSS)

Taking Notes: *Analyzing* RH.6–8.1
As you read, use a diagram like this one to analyze the ways in which the Republicans changed the government.

268 *The Jefferson Era*

Reducing the Role of Government

Content Vocabulary (Tier 3 Words)
• **customs duty**
• **jurisdiction**

---

netw⊙rks *Online Teaching Options*

VIDEO

President Thomas Jefferson

Citing Text Evidence As students watch the lesson video, have them take notes about major topics that come up, such as the concept of judicial review, the Barbary pirates, the Louisiana Purchase, and the Lewis and Clark expedition. Then have students use the information in the lesson to fact-check the information from the video. **AL ELL**

See page 265C for other online activities.

LEARN360
ENGAGE · ENRICH · EXCEL
A Division of APH Education, Inc.

A New Party in Power

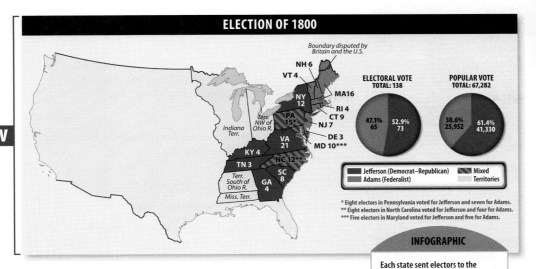

ELECTION OF 1800

Boundary disputed by Britain and the U.S.

NH 6
VT 4
MA 16
NY 12
RI 4
PA 15*
CT 9
NJ 7
Indiana Terr.
Terr. NW of Ohio R.
VA 21
DE 3
MD 10***
KY 4
TN 3
NC 12**
Terr. South of Ohio R.
SC 8
GA 4
Miss. Terr.

ELECTORAL VOTE TOTAL: 138
47.1% 65 / 52.9% 73

POPULAR VOTE TOTAL: 67,282
38.6% 25,952 / 61.4% 41,330

Jefferson (Democrat–Republican)
Adams (Federalist)
Mixed
Territories

* Eight electors in Pennsylvania voted for Jefferson and seven for Adams.
** Eight electors in North Carolina voted for Jefferson and four for Adams.
*** Five electors in Maryland voted for Jefferson and five for Adams.

INFOGRAPHIC

Each state sent electors to the Electoral College. Territories (shown in yellow) did not.

1 IDENTIFYING Which areas tended to support Adams?

2 CRITICAL THINKING *Drawing Conclusions* Why do you think Adams and Jefferson both had their support concentrated in particular regions of the country?

the ballots that actually elect the president and vice president. Each state has as many electoral votes as it has members of Congress.

At that time, the Constitution said that electors were to cast two ballots—without indicating which was for president and which was for vice president. The candidate with the majority of votes became president, and the candidate with the next-largest number of votes became vice president. In 1800, 73 electors cast their ballots for Jefferson and Burr. Each candidate, therefore, got the same number of votes. Because of the tie vote, the House of Representatives had to decide the election.

In the House, Federalists tried to keep Jefferson from becoming president by supporting Burr. For 35 ballots, the election remained tied. Finally, one Federalist decided not to vote for Burr.

Because no one wanted to see another tie between a presidential and vice-presidential candidate, Congress passed the Twelfth Amendment to the Constitution in 1803. From then on, electors cast one of their votes for president and the other for vice president.

Jefferson's Inauguration

On the day he became president, Jefferson dressed in his everyday clothes. He walked to the Senate to take the oath of office. President Adams did not attend.

Reading Strategy: *Predicting*

Good readers think ahead as they are reading. They predict, or guess, what might happen next. Find a good stopping place, like the bottom of this page, and ask yourself a question about what might happen next. For example, you might ask, "Since Jefferson was a Republican who had just defeated the Federalists, how might he change the government?" Try to answer your question, then read ahead to see whether your predictions are correct.

Lesson 1   **269**

V Visual Skills

Analyzing Images Direct students' attention to the map at the top of the page. Point out that in all elections, a certain percentage of adult citizens do not vote. **Ask:** Who can you think of who did not vote in the election of 1800? *(African Americans, women, people living in the western territories)* Looking at the pie charts, why do you think modern election volunteers work so hard to encourage people to vote? *(Students' answers should indicate that elections can sometimes be very close and that having more people vote can affect the outcome of an election.)* Why do the electoral vote and the popular vote not match? *(The electoral vote is based on the popular vote but is calculated differently.)* Continue to explore the data depicted in this image with the class.
AL Visual/Spatial

R Reading Skills

Drawing Conclusions After students have read the text, ask them to describe the tie between Jefferson and Burr in this election. **Ask:** What will prevent this kind of tie from happening again? *(The Twelfth Amendment states that electors must vote separately for the president and vice president.)*
AL **ELL**

W Writing Skills

Narrative Have students read the subsection titled "Jefferson's Inauguration" on this page and the next page. **Ask:** Do you see a connection between Jefferson's words in his Inaugural Address and his choice of what to wear and how to get to the inauguration? *(Students should note that Jefferson spoke about wanting a frugal government, and he chose to dress and transport himself frugally as well.)* Then have students write a narrative in which they present themselves as a modern day politician who is trying to follow in Jefferson's footsteps. Students should write a short speech calling for greater frugality in government and calling upon elected officials to follow Jefferson's example. **BL**

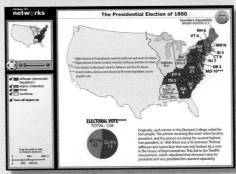

MAP

The Presidential Election of 1800

Comparing and Contrasting Have students look at the interactive map of the election of 1800 to discuss the events of that election. **Ask:** Do you think the country today has regions that tend to support certain candidates or parties? *(Recently, the country has often been divided into "red" states and "blue" states, or those that tend to vote for Republicans and those that tend to vote for Democrats.)* Why might there be regional differences in how people vote? *(People may choose to live in areas where their views are supported or may grow up with certain views because of where they live.)*
BL Visual/Spatial Interpersonal

See page 265C for other online activities.

ANSWERS, p. 269

INFOGRAPHIC

1. New England, the eastern mid-Atlantic States, and eastern North Carolina supported Adams.
2. **CRITICAL THINKING** Adams's supporters in New England and the mid-Atlantic states belonged to an industrial economy that supported a strong central government. Jefferson's supporters, mostly in the South, belonged to an agricultural economy that supported the idea of states' rights and limited central government.

R1 Reading Skills

Listing As students read the text, have them make a list of the different ways that Jefferson wanted to, and did, reduce the role of the federal government. **AL** **ELL**
Logical/Mathematical

R2 Reading Skills

Discussing After students read the text, discuss with them the Judiciary Act of 1801. **Ask:** How did this affect Jefferson's presidency? *(Adams blocked Jefferson from making appointments, and Jefferson's opposing political party now ran the court.)* **Ask:** Do you agree with Adams's actions? Why or why not? *(Students' answers will vary.)* Lead the class in a discussion of the ways in which presidents sometimes try to extend their power past an election that removes them from office. **BL**

C Critical Thinking Skills

Making Connections Explain that Jefferson was considered a "Renaissance man," a person with great curiosity who is accomplished in the arts and sciences, and is knowledgeable about many subjects. **Ask:** How is Jefferson's involvement in the construction of Monticello a good example of this idea? *(He designed the plans for his house.)* **AL** **ELL**

BIOGRAPHY

**Thomas Jefferson
(1743–1826)**

In addition to his many achievements in government and politics, Jefferson was a noted inventor and architect. His inventions include a plow that was twice as fast as older ones, a machine for making macaroni, and a device that encoded messages. He also designed the house on his plantation (Monticello) and founded the University of Virginia.

▶ CRITICAL THINKING
Analyzing Based on his interests and skills, what qualities do you think Jefferson might have had?

In his Inaugural Address, Jefferson outlined some of his goals, including "a wise and frugal government" and "the support of the state governments in all their rights." Jefferson believed a large federal government threatened liberty and that individual states could better protect freedom. He wanted to limit the power and size of the federal government.

✓ PROGRESS CHECK

Contrasting How did political campaigns and presidential inaugurations in Jefferson's day differ from those of today?

Jefferson as President

GUIDING QUESTION *What did Jefferson want to accomplish during his presidency?*

Thomas Jefferson had strong ideas about government and he surrounded himself with people who shared **similar** views. Jefferson and Albert Gallatin, secretary of the treasury, reduced the national debt and cut down on military expenses. Jefferson also limited the number of federal government workers to a few hundred people. At the same time, his government got rid of most federal taxes. They only collected **customs duties**, or taxes on imported goods. Under Jefferson, the government's income would come from customs duties and from the sale of western lands. He believed that these changes were needed to make the United States a great nation.

Judiciary Act of 1801

After the election and before Jefferson took office, the Federalists passed an act that set up a system of courts. John Adams used this act, the Judiciary Act of 1801, to make hundreds of appointments during his last days as president. Adams also asked John Marshall to serve as chief justice. Congress was then still under Federalist control and supported Adams's choices. In this way, Adams blocked Jefferson from making appointments and made sure the Federalists controlled the courts.

Adams's appointments could not take effect until these last-minute appointees, known as "midnight judges," received certain official papers, called commissions. When Jefferson became president, some of these appointees had not yet received their commissions. Jefferson told Secretary of State James Madison not to deliver them.

Private Collection, Peter Newark American Pictures/Bridgeman Art Library

Reading **HELP**DESK **CCSS**

customs duty tax collected on goods that are imported
jurisdiction the power or right to interpret and apply a law

Academic Vocabulary (Tier 2 Words)
similar sharing qualities, but not the same as; like
principle a fundamental, or basic, law or idea

270 *The Jefferson Era*

netw⊛rks *Online Teaching Options*

SLIDE SHOW

Monticello

Visualizing Use the interactive slide show of Monticello, Jefferson's home, to discuss the education and background of Thomas Jefferson and to introduce the idea of Jefferson as a "Renaissance man." **AL** Visual/Spatial

See page 265C for other online activities.

McGraw-Hill netw⊛rks™ — Monticello

Instead of a grand staircase, Jefferson designed stairways for Monticello that are elegant but narrow and hard to climb.

Thomas Jefferson Foundation

ANSWERS, p. 270

CRITICAL THINKING Jefferson was probably curious, open to new ideas, and creative.

✓ **PROGRESS CHECK** Candidates did not have today's means of communication. Candidates also did not travel to gain support; they used letter-writing campaigns instead. The inauguration was quite simple in contrast to the pomp and ceremony of today.

The Growing Power of the Supreme Court

Jefferson's home at Monticello in Charlottesville, Virginia, is considered an architectural masterpiece.

One of the appointees who did not get his commission was William Marbury. He asked the Supreme Court to force its delivery. The Court said it did not have the **jurisdiction** (jur•iss•DIK•shuhn)—the legal authority—to force delivery of Marbury's commission. Marbury had argued that an act of Congress gave the Court such authority, but the Court ruled that that act violated the Constitution.

The ruling in *Marbury* v. *Madison* affected much more than William Marbury's career. In his opinion, Chief Justice John Marshall established the three **principles** of judicial review: (1) the Constitution is the supreme law of the land; (2) the Constitution must be followed when there is a conflict with any other law; and (3) the judicial branch can declare laws unconstitutional. In short, Marshall claimed for the courts the power to find acts of other branches unconstitutional. Judicial review is a key check on the legislative and executive branches.

In his 34-year term as chief justice, Marshall helped broaden the power of the Court. He also expanded federal power at the expense of the states. In *McCulloch* v. *Maryland* (1819), the Court held that Congress does have implied powers and that states cannot tax the federal government. In *Gibbons* v. *Ogden* (1824), the Court held that federal law overrules state law in matters affecting more than one state. In *Worcester* v. *Georgia* (1832), the Court decided that states could not regulate Native Americans. Only the federal government had that power.

✓ **PROGRESS CHECK**

Explaining What was the significance of the *Marbury* v. *Madison* ruling?

imagebroker/Alamy Images

LESSON 1 REVIEW (CCSS)

Review Vocabulary (Tier 3 Words)

1. Write a sentence about the Jefferson administration that uses the term *customs duty*. RH.6–8.4

Answer the Guiding Questions

2. ***Contrasting*** How did the process of electing a president change after the election of 1800? RH.6–8.3

3. ***Discussing*** How did President Jefferson act on his beliefs about government? RH.6–8.1

4. ***Explaining*** Explain how the powers of the Supreme Court and federal law were extended by significant court cases during this period. RH.6–8.2

5. **INFORMATIVE/EXPLANATORY** During John Marshall's term on the Supreme Court, federal and Court power expanded. Write a paragraph contrasting these decisions with Thomas Jefferson's stated views on the proper size and power of the federal government. WHST.6–8.2, WHST.6–8.9

Lesson 1 **271**

LESSON 1 REVIEW ANSWERS

1. Possible answer: Because Jefferson believed in a *laissez-faire* approach to government, he got rid of all taxes except customs duties.

2. The Twelfth Amendment was passed to avoid the problems with a tie that occurred in the election of 1800. The amendment forces electors to vote for the president and vice president on separate ballots.

3. Jefferson describes a wise, frugal, and limited federal government. He acted on this by eliminating internal taxes and cutting the number of federal workers.

4. *Marbury* v. *Madison* confirmed the Court's power of judicial review and declared the other branches' acts unconstitutional. *McCulloch* v. *Maryland* recognized that Congress had implied powers and that states could not tax the federal government. *Gibbons* v. *Ogden*

held that federal law took precedence over state law in matters affecting more than one state. *Worcester* v. *Georgia* held that only the federal government can regulate Native Americans.

5. Students may mention that under Marshall, Supreme Court decisions expanded federal power at the expense of the states. In various decisions, the Court held that Congress has implied powers; that states cannot tax the federal government; that federal law overrules state law in matters affecting more than one state; and that only the federal government can regulate Native Americans. In contrast, Thomas Jefferson believed a large federal government threatened liberty and that individual states could better protect freedom. He wanted to limit the power and size of the federal government.

C1 Critical Thinking Skills

Drawing Conclusions Lead a discussion on how the Supreme Court asserted its power as an equal branch of government. **Ask: How did Chief Justice Marshall broaden federal powers with *McCulloch* v. *Maryland*?** *(This decision held that Congress has implied powers and that states cannot tax the federal government.)* **How did *Gibbons* v. *Ogden* affect federal law?** *(The Court held that federal law takes precedence over state law in matters affecting more than one state.)* **Given Jefferson's beliefs about government, how do you think he felt about these court decisions?** *(Jefferson believed in limiting the powers of the federal government and thought the states could better preserve liberty. He was probably opposed to these decisions, which broadened federal power at the expense of the states.)* In a class discussion, help students to understand that the Supreme Court did not always have as much power as it does today—its power evolved over time. **BL Interpersonal**

C2 Critical Thinking Skills

Predicting Consequences Point out that other Supreme Court decisions added to the power of the federal government. **Ask: What was the Court's decision in *Worcester* v. *Georgia*?** *(The Court ruled that only the federal government—not states—could regulate Native Americans.)* Have students predict how this ruling might affect Native Americans. To help them look at this social justice issue from other perspectives, ask how they would feel if another country tried to regulate Americans. **BL**

Have students complete the Lesson 1 Review.

CLOSE & REFLECT

Summarizing Discuss the essential question: *How do governments change?* **Ask: How did the United States government change from the election of 1800 through Jefferson's first term? Who was responsible for each change?** *(Answers may vary.)* In your discussion, encourage students to make connections between the election of 1800 and elections of today, and between decisions made by the Supreme Court in the early 1800s and decisions that are made today. You may wish to have students do a research project in which they choose to compare events from the two different eras either in a paper or research presentation to the class.

ANSWER, p. 271

✓ **PROGRESS CHECK** The Constitution is the supreme law of the land. It must be followed when another law conflicts with it, even a state law. Any unconstitutional law is nullified.

Chapter 10 **271**

ENGAGE

Bellringer Tell students that in the 1800s, pioneers moved westward seeking new land. Thomas Jefferson sent two major expeditions to explore the area west of the Mississippi River. Have students speculate what it would be like to explore a new territory. **Ask: What challenges might you face? What things might help you succeed? How might you feel about your journey? What do you think you would learn?** Write responses on the board. Have students compare their speculations with the experiences of the settlers and explorers in this lesson. **AL ELL**

TEACH & ASSESS

T Technology Skills

Researching on the Internet Have students use the Internet to research the Native American nations who lived in the Louisiana Territory in 1800. Then have them make maps to display in the classroom or on the class Web site, showing which nations lived in which areas or which languages were spoken where. **BL Interpersonal Verbal/Linguistic**

R Reading Skills

Describing Ask students to use details from the text to describe what the settlers' travels were like. **Ask: What kinds of routes did they travel? How did they travel? Why were rifles and axes so important?** *(They traveled muddy roads and through dense forests in Conestoga wagons. They carried rifles for hunting and protection and axes to help clear their way.)* **AL ELL**

---

net🌐works
There's More Online!

☑ **BIOGRAPHY**
• Toussaint L'Ouverture
• Zebulon Pike

☑ **CHART/GRAPH**
Alexander Hamilton and Aaron Burr

☑ **GRAPHIC ORGANIZER**
Exploring the West

☑ **MAP** Louisiana Purchase and Westward Expansion

☑ **SLIDE SHOW** Lewis and Clark

Lesson 2
The Louisiana Purchase

ESSENTIAL QUESTION *How does geography influence the way people live?*

IT MATTERS BECAUSE
The Louisiana Purchase changed the size and shape of the nation and helped hasten westward expansion.

Westward, Ho!

GUIDING QUESTION *How did Spain and France play a role in Americans moving west?*

In 1800 the territory of the United States extended as far west as the Mississippi River. The area west of the river—known as the Louisiana Territory—belonged to Spain. The Louisiana Territory was an enormous area of land, stretching south to the city of New Orleans and west to the Rocky Mountains. Its northern boundaries remained undefined.

During the early 1800s, Americans moved west in search of land and adventure. Pioneers, many of them farmers, traveled over the mountains into Kentucky and Tennessee. Many also set out for the less settled areas of the Northwest Territory. They made a long and exhausting journey over the Appalachian Mountains. Pioneers heading to the western lands had to travel along rough, muddy roads or cut their way through thick forests.

These westward-bound pioneers loaded their household goods into Conestoga (kah•neh•STOH•guh) wagons, sturdy vehicles topped with white canvas. The settlers traveled with their two most valued possessions: rifles and axes. They needed rifles for protection and to hunt animals for food. They used axes to cut paths for their wagons through the dense forests.

(l) North Wind Picture Archives / Alamy, (cl) Hulton Archive/Getty Images, (c) David David Gallery/SuperStock, (r) The Granger Collection, NYC

Reading HELPDESK (CCSS)

Taking Notes: *Describing* RH.6–8.1
As you read, use a diagram like this one to describe the areas that Lewis and Clark and Zebulon Pike explored.

Explorer		Area Explored
Lewis and Clark	→	
Zebulon Pike	→	

Content Vocabulary (Tier 3 Words)
• secede

272 *The Jefferson Era*

---

net🌐works *Online Teaching Options*

VIDEO

Jefferson's Vision of America

Recognizing Relationships Explain to students that in early American history, westward expansion was often associated with democratic politics. **Ask: Why do you think that the ideal of settlers supporting themselves and being independent was associated with democratic political philosophy?** *(Answers will vary.)* Encourage students to make connections between the ideas of rugged individualism and a tendency to put faith in the people rather than in authorities. **BL Visual/Spatial Verbal/Linguistic**

See page 265D for other online activities.

ANSWER, p. 272

TAKING NOTES: Lewis and Clark: explored from St. Louis westward to the Pacific Ocean, following a generally northern route; **Zebulon Pike:** explored the Upper Mississippi valley to Colorado and the northern Rio Grande to what is now southern Texas

Many of the pioneers set up farms along rivers that fed into the Upper Mississippi River. Farmers needed access to the Mississippi to transport their crops to markets. Their goods traveled down the Mississippi to New Orleans, where workers loaded them onto other ships bound for markets on the East Coast. The Spanish controlled the region, but they allowed the Americans to sail on the Lower Mississippi and trade in New Orleans. For the western farmers, this agreement was vital to their economic survival.

V

The French Threat

For some years, the Spanish allowed American goods to move freely in their territory. In 1802, the Spanish suddenly changed their policy, no longer allowing American goods to move into and beyond New Orleans. President Jefferson learned that Spain and France had secretly agreed to transfer the Louisiana Territory to France. Jefferson believed that France had also gained Florida in its secret agreement with Spain.

This news alarmed Jefferson. The agreement between Spain and France posed a serious threat to the United States. France's leader, Napoleon Bonaparte, had plans to create empires in Europe and the Americas. French control would put American trade along the Mississippi River at risk. Congress authorized Robert Livingston, the new minister to France, to offer as much as $2 million for New Orleans and West Florida in order to gain control of the territory.

R

Napoleon and Santo Domingo

Napoleon dreamed of a Western empire. He saw the Caribbean island of Santo Domingo as an important naval base from which he could control such an empire. Events in Santo Domingo, however, ended Napoleon's dream. Inspired by the ideas of the French Revolution, Toussaint L'Ouverture (too•SAN loo•vuhr•TOOR) led enslaved Africans and other laborers in Santo Domingo in a revolt against the island's plantation owners. After fierce fighting, the rebels won and declared the colony an independent republic. L'Ouverture established a new government.

In 1802, Napoleon sent troops to regain control of Santo Domingo, but they were not successful. By 1804, the French were driven out of Santo Domingo. The country took its original name, Haiti.

☑ **PROGRESS CHECK**

Explaining Explain why French control of the Louisiana Territory worried Jefferson.

When Toussaint L'Ouverture defeated the French in Haiti, France lost interest in Louisiana.

(b) North Wind Picture Archives / Alamy, (t) Brown Brothers

Build Vocabulary: *Word Origins*

The Conestoga wagon took its name from Conestoga, Pennsylvania, the town where it was first made.

V Visual Skills

Reading Maps Project the chapter opener map and have students locate the Mississippi River. Note that this was the western boundary of the United States in 1800. Have them locate New Orleans. **Ask:**

- **Who claimed this territory?** *(Spain)*
- **Where in this area did pioneers tend to settle? Why?** *(They settled along the river system that fed into the Mississippi River so they could move their goods to market.)*
- **Why was New Orleans an important city to settlers?** *(From there they could ship to East Coast markets.)*
- **What role did Spain play in the settlers' success?** *(Spain controlled New Orleans and allowed Americans to trade through the port.)* **AL** Visual/Spatial

R Reading Skills

Discussing After students have read the text, discuss with them the changes in Spanish policy about the Mississippi River and how it affected American trade. **Ask: How did the Spanish change their policy in 1802? Why did they make this change?** *(The Spanish stopped allowing American goods to move through or past New Orleans because they had a secret agreement to transfer the territory to France.)* **How did Jefferson react to the news?** *(Jefferson was concerned about how this would impact the American economy.)* **What did he do in response?** *(He had his minister to France try to buy New Orleans and West Florida.)* Lead students in a discussion of early American dependence on trade, helping students to understand the economic importance of trade networks.

IMAGE

Toussaint L'Ouverture

Summarizing Display the interactive image of Toussaint L'Ouverture. **Ask: What happened in 1802 in Santo Domingo?** *(Toussaint L'Ouverture was inspired by the French Revolution. He led fellow enslaved Africans and other laborers in a revolt against plantation owners.)* **What did the leaders of the Haitian Revolution hope to achieve?** *(They wanted to and were successful in gaining independence for Santo Domingo, which changed its name back to Haiti.)* Lead students in a discussion of the parallels between the American, French, and Haitian Revolutions. **BL** Visual/Spatial

See page 265D for other online activities.

McGraw-Hill **networks**

Toussaint L'Ouverture

Toussaint L'Ouverture was born into slavery in Haiti. His plantation overseer allowed him to learn to read and write, and he served as a coachman and house servant on the plantation. When he was in his thirties, Toussaint gained his freedom. Soon after, in 1791, a revolt against French rule broke out. The insurrection was put down, but by then the ideals of the French Revolution had spread throughout Haiti. Toussaint became commander-in-chief of the colony of Haiti. In that role, he established the country's first constitution, which ensured liberty and equality for all people, regardless of race or color. Back in France the emperor, Napoleon, felt threatened by Toussaint's popularity and had him captured. Toussaint died a prisoner in 1803. Still, the fight for independence continued, and Haiti freed itself from French rule in 1804.

ANSWER, p. 273

☑ **PROGRESS CHECK** Farmers needed to get their goods down the Mississippi River to New Orleans. If they could not, trade with East Coast markets would be cut off. Jefferson worried that the French would block farmers' shipments.

C1 Critical Thinking Skills

Determining Cause and Effect Discuss with students how Santo Domingo (Haiti) played a role in the United States buying the Louisiana Territory. **Ask: Why did Napoleon want to control the Louisiana Territory? Why was Santo Domingo an important part of Napoleon's plan for an empire?** *(Napoleon wanted to have an empire in the Americas. As part of this dream, he needed a naval base on Santo Domingo.)* **Ask: What effect did the rebellion have on the United States?** *(Napoleon sold the Louisiana Territory to the United States, and the country grew.)* **Why was Jefferson eager to make the deal? What worried him about it?** *(Jefferson wanted the land for settlement and access to the Mississippi River, but he wondered if he had the authority to buy new territory.)* Lead students in a discussion of how events in other countries can affect events within the United States. **Verbal/Linguistic Interpersonal**

W Writing Skills

Informative/Explanatory Have students make a list predicting the effects of the Louisiana Purchase on the United States. Use questions like these to spur thinking: **How much land was gained in the purchase? What will people do with the new land? What do they know about the land? How will the people react to the purchase?** Once students have written their lists, have them use the lists as the basis for a short paragraph about the Louisiana Purchase. After students finish this lesson, have them revisit their paragraphs to see how closely their predictions matched what actually occurred. **AL**

C2 Critical Thinking Skills

Identifying Problems Help students to look at the Lewis and Clark expedition from President Jefferson's point of view. **Ask: What did Jefferson hope to find out from Lewis and Clark once they had surveyed the land west of the Mississippi?** *(Jefferson hoped to find out about what people, plants, and animals were to be found there, whether there were locations for future forts, and whether there might be a water route across North America.)* **Do you notice a common theme in the questions Jefferson had about the new territory?** *(He wanted to know what resources were available in the Louisiana Territory that could benefit the United States.)* Encourage students to think about the expedition in a presidential way. Can they think of other questions that they would have had about the Louisiana Territory if they had been president? **Interpersonal**

An Expanding Nation

GUIDING QUESTION *How did the Louisiana Purchase open an area of settlement?*

C1 Napoleon had a problem: he needed money to finance his war against Britain. Without Santo Domingo, Napoleon had little use for Louisiana. In order to solve his money problem, he decided to sell the Louisiana Territory. A French official told U.S. representatives Robert Livingston and James Monroe that the entire Louisiana Territory was for sale. The offer took Livingston and Monroe by surprise. They did not have the **authority** to accept such an offer.

W The deal, however, was too good to pass up. The new territory would provide plenty of cheap land for farmers for future generations. It would also give the United States control of the Mississippi River, which would protect domestic shipping interests. These benefits convinced Livingston and Monroe to close the deal, even though they did not have authorization to buy the whole territory. After a few days of negotiation, the parties agreed on a price of $15 million.

Jefferson worried that such a large **purchase** might not be legal. The Constitution said nothing about acquiring new territory. By what authority could he buy the land? He thought of seeking a constitutional amendment, but he realized there was no time for such a step. Jefferson decided the government's treaty-making powers allowed the purchase of the new territory. The Senate approved the purchase in October 1803. The purchase of the Louisiana Territory doubled the size of the United States.

The Lewis and Clark Expedition

C2 Americans knew little about the land west of the Mississippi, and Jefferson wanted to learn more about the new territory he had just acquired. He persuaded Congress to sponsor an expedition to gather information about the new land. The expedition would document findings about the territory's people, plants, and animals and recommend sites for future forts.

The expedition had another goal: finding and mapping the fabled Northwest Passage, a water route across North America. In order to trade with Asia, Europeans had to sail around Africa. Because the trip was long and costly, European explorers searched, unsuccessfully, for a more direct route. Once the Americas were colonized, Americans and Europeans continued

Reading **HELP**DESK **CCSS**

Academic Vocabulary (Tier 2 Words)
authority the power to influence or command thought, opinion, or behavior
purchase the act of buying something

274 *The Jefferson Era*

Build Vocabulary: *Related Words*
Meriwether Lewis kept a journal—a record of the experiences, ideas, and thoughts he had during the expedition. The word *journalism* generally means the collection or presentation of the news, but in particular the direct presentation of facts or events without the writer's interpretation.

net⊛rks *Online Teaching Options*

SLIDE SHOW

The Lewis and Clark Expedition

Formulating Questions Have students review their lists of predictions they created regarding the Louisiana Purchase. Explain that the purchase opened much land up for settlement, but that not much was known about it. Then show students the Lewis and Clark slide show. Ask students to come up with three questions they'd like answered about the Lewis and Clark expedition. **AL ELL Visual/Spatial**

See page 265D for other online activities.

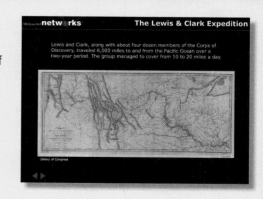
net⊛rks — The Lewis & Clark Expedition
Lewis and Clark, along with about four-dozen members of the Corps of Discovery, traveled 8,000 miles to and from the Pacific Ocean over a two-year period. The group managed to cover from 10 to 20 miles a day.

to sail around Africa or around the tip of South America in order to reach Asia. Finding a water route across North America became more important than ever.

Jefferson chose Meriwether Lewis, his 28-year-old private secretary, to head the expedition. Lewis joined the militia during the Whiskey Rebellion and had been in the army when Jefferson hired him as his private secretary in 1801. Jefferson apparently looked forward to one day sending out an expedition to explore the continent, and hired Lewis with that in mind. William Clark was co-leader of the expedition. Clark was 32 years old and a friend of Lewis's. Clark also brought along York, an enslaved African American and lifelong companion of Clark's. York was a key member of the expedition. He was especially helpful building ties with Native Americans, many of whom had never before seen an African American and were drawn to him.

Lewis and Clark were well-informed, amateur scientists. They also had experience doing business with Native Americans. Together they assembled a crew of expert sailors, gunsmiths, carpenters, scouts, and a cook. Two men of mixed Native American and French heritage served as interpreters.

In the spring of 1804, the expedition left St. Louis and worked its way up the Missouri River. On May 5, 1805, Lewis described what they encountered along the trail in his journal:

PRIMARY SOURCE

66 Buffalo Elk and goats or Antelopes feeding in every direction ... [T]he buffalo furnish us with fine veal and fat and beef. ... We have not been able to take any fish for some time past. The country is as yesterday beautiful in the extreme. 99
—from the journals of Lewis and Clark

The expedition encountered many Native American groups on the journey. A Shoshone woman named Sacagawea (SA•kuh•juh•WEE•uh) joined their group as a guide.

After 18 months and nearly 4,000 miles (6,437 km), Lewis and Clark reached the Pacific Ocean. They spent the winter there. Then they headed back east, returning in September 1806. The explorers had collected valuable information about people, plants, animals, and the geography of the West. Perhaps most important, their journey inspired people to move westward.

Sacagawea (c. 1788–1812?)

Sacagawea was the daughter of a Shoshone chief. Lewis and Clark hired her and her husband, a French Canadian fur trader, as interpreters. Sacagawea proved extremely valuable. She negotiated the purchase of horses, found edible plants, and made moccasins and clothing. According to Clark, her presence helped calm the fears of Native Americans the group met during their journey.

► CRITICAL THINKING
Speculating What challenges might the expedition have faced without Sacagawea?

C1

From 1804 to 1806, Meriwether Lewis and William Clark mapped and explored more than 7,000 miles (11,265 km).

C2

C1 Critical Thinking Skills

Identifying Points of View Have students revisit the maps of Native American nations or languages that they prepared earlier. Point out that Americans saw the Louisiana Purchase as an opening to new land. **Ask: Which Native American nations could Lewis and Clark have anticipated would be affected by American expansion?** *(Students' answers should reflect the nations that they found in their research.)* **How might Native Americans have seen the westward movement of settlers?** *(Possible answer: They might have been angry with people coming into and taking over their lands.)*

C2 Critical Thinking Skills

Drawing Conclusions Discuss the results of the Lewis and Clark expedition. **Ask: Did Lewis and Clark achieve their goals? What were the lasting effects of their work?** *(Lewis and Clark accomplished a great deal, although they did not find a water route to the Pacific. They charted large sections of the new land and provided valuable information about the people, plants, and animals in it. They inspired people to move westward.)* BL

IMAGE

The Shoshone

Making Connections Use the interactive image about the Shoshone people to discuss with students the Lewis and Clark expedition's need for guides and interpreters as they explored the Louisiana Territory. Remind students that Native Americans occupied the land. **Ask: Who was Sacagawea?** *(She was the daughter of a Shoshone chief who served as a guide and interpreter on the Lewis and Clark expedition.)* **Why might the daughter of a Shoshone chief be a good choice as a guide and translator?** *(Possible answer: She was probably familiar with some of the area.)* AL

See page 265D for other online activities.

McGraw-Hill **netw⊕rks**   The Shoshone

The Shoshone Indians, also known as the Snake Nation, lived in the lands both east and west of the Rocky Mountains. The tribes west of the Rockies lived in roofless grass huts and fished or hunted birds and rabbits. The eastern Shoshone lived in teepees and hunted buffalo. Shoshone families were nomadic and owned few belongings. Depending on the season, the men wore a simple breechcloth, while the women wore aprons, or pants, jackets, and capes made from animal hides. The spiritual leader of the Shoshone was the medicine man, who was believed to be a prophet with magical powers.

Hulton Archive/Getty Images

ANSWER, p. 275

CRITICAL THINKING The expedition might have faced language barriers, shortages of food or warm clothing, and problems with Native Americans.

C Critical Thinking Skills

Identifying Points of View Have students describe the Federalist response to the Louisiana Purchase. *(Federalists worried that they would lose power because the states created in the Louisiana Territory would probably be Republican.)* **Ask:** What did the Federalists in the Northeast plan to do? *(The New England states planned to secede.)* What steps did they take to secede? *(They included New York to increase chances of success and turned to Aaron Burr.)*

V Visual Skills

Interpreting Direct students' attention to the "Exploring the Louisiana Territory" map. Have students compare the United States with the area covered by the Louisiana Purchase and the Spanish Territory. **Ask:** Do you think that President Jefferson envisioned the United States someday spreading from sea to sea? Why or why not? *(Students' answers may vary.)* Lead students in a discussion of how vast an acquisition the Louisiana Purchase was, encouraging students to appreciate Jefferson's vision in considering expanding the country to more than twice the size it was when he became president. **AL** **ELL** Visual/Spatial

---

Pike's Expedition

Lewis and Clark were not the only people Jefferson sent to explore the wilderness. Lieutenant Zebulon Pike led two expeditions west between 1805 and 1807. He traveled through the Upper Mississippi River valley and into present-day Colorado. In Colorado, he found a snowcapped mountain he called Grand Peak, known today as Pikes Peak.

From Pike's travels, Americans learned about the Great Plains and Rocky Mountains. Pike also mapped part of the Rio Grande and traveled across northern Mexico and what is now southern Texas.

A Federalist Plan to Secede

C The Louisiana Purchase troubled Federalists in the Northeast. They feared the westward expansion would weaken New England's power in political and economic affairs. A group of

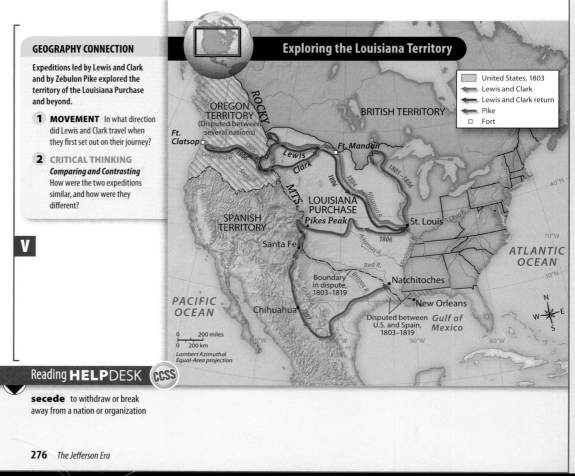

GEOGRAPHY CONNECTION

Expeditions led by Lewis and Clark and by Zebulon Pike explored the territory of the Louisiana Purchase and beyond.

1 MOVEMENT In what direction did Lewis and Clark travel when they first set out on their journey?

2 CRITICAL THINKING
Comparing and Contrasting
How were the two expeditions similar, and how were they different?

Exploring the Louisiana Territory

United States, 1803
Lewis and Clark
Lewis and Clark return
Pike
□ Fort

Reading **HELP**DESK **CCSS**

secede to withdraw or break away from a nation or organization

---

netw⊙rks *Online Teaching Options*

BIOGRAPHY

Zebulon Pike

Comparing and Contrasting Use the interactive image of Zebulon Pike to discuss the other explorers of the Louisiana Territory. **Ask:** Who was Zebulon Pike? *(an explorer who led expeditions west in 1805 and 1807)* Have students trace and discuss Pike's route. **AL** How was the purpose of Pike's expedition similar to the purpose of Lewis and Clark's expedition? How was it different? *(Pike also learned about the new land but traveled to a different part of the territory.)* Remind students that Pike mapped sections of Mexico and what is now Texas. **BL** Visual/Spatial

See page 265D for other online activities.

In 1813 Pike was promoted to brigadier general, and led American troops to victory against the British in York (now Toronto), Canada. He died at age 34 during the battle, as a result of rocks and other debris thrown up by a mine detonated by retreating British troops. Pikes Peak in Colorado is named for Zebulon Pike, even though he did not successfully climb it.

ANSWERS, p. 276

GEOGRAPHY CONNECTION

1 Lewis and Clark traveled north because they were looking for a northwest passage to Asia.

2 CRITICAL THINKING Both expeditions provided new information about the land, plants, animals, and inhabitants of the new territory. Each expedition covered different parts of the territory.

Federalists in Massachusetts plotted to **secede** (suh•SEED), or withdraw, from the Union. New England would become the "Northern Confederacy."

The plotters realized that if the confederacy were to last, it had to include New York as well as New England. The Massachusetts Federalists needed a powerful friend in New York who would support their plan. They turned to Aaron Burr.

Hamilton and Burr Duel

Alexander Hamilton was concerned about rumors of secession. He had never trusted Aaron Burr, and now he heard that Burr had secretly agreed to lead New York out of the Union. Hamilton accused Burr of plotting treason. Meanwhile, Burr was suffering setbacks in his political career. Blaming Hamilton for these troubles, Burr challenged him to a duel.

The two men—armed with pistols—met in Weehawken, New Jersey, in July 1804. Hamilton hated dueling, which was illegal but popular among upper-class Americans at the time. Hamilton pledged not to shoot at his rival, but Burr took no such pledge. He aimed to shoot Hamilton, and he was successful. Seriously wounded, Hamilton died the next day. Burr fled to avoid arrest.

After the duel, Aaron Burr fled to South Carolina. Never tried for Hamilton's death, Burr returned to Washington, D.C., and completed his term as vice president.

The Granger Collection, NYC

R

☑ **PROGRESS CHECK**

Drawing Conclusions Why was the Louisiana Purchase important for the United States?

LESSON 2 REVIEW (CCSS)

Review Vocabulary (Tier 3 Words)

1. Identify a word that means the opposite of *secede*. RH.6–8.4

Answer the Guiding Questions

2. *Explaining* How did the secret agreement between Spain and France over Louisiana affect American trade in the West? RH.6–8.2

3. *Identifying Cause and Effect* Name two effects of the Lewis and Clark expedition. RH.6–8.5

4. *Summarizing* How did the Federalists react to the Louisiana Purchase? Explain. RH.6–8.2

5. **NARRATIVE** Write a one-paragraph journal entry from the perspective of a participant of the Lewis and Clark expedition, explaining your feelings and expectations as you set out on your journey. WHST.6–8.1, WHST.6–8.10

Lesson 2   **277**

LESSON 2 REVIEW ANSWERS

1. Possible answers: join; combine; unite

2. Spain had transferred control of the Louisiana Territory to France but still controlled the port of New Orleans. Spain suddenly refused to let Americans use the port. This prevented settlers who depended on the Mississippi to ship their crops from being able to get their goods to East Coast markets and from receiving supplies.

3. The expedition gained useful information about the people, plants, animals, and geography of the new territory. It also inspired people to move westward.

4. The Federalists, mainly in New England, opposed the purchase because they feared that New England would lose political power.

5. Responses may mention Lewis, Clark, Sacagawea and her French Canadian husband, and York. The entry may mention a sense of adventure, animals seen, or the beautiful landscape.

R Reading Skills

Paraphrasing After students have read the text, have them describe in their own words the reason for the duel between Hamilton and Burr. **Ask: What did Hamilton and Burr disagree about?** (Hamilton accused Burr of plotting treason.) **What happened as a result of these differences?** (Burr challenged Hamilton to a duel; Hamilton was killed.) **What effect did this duel have on the Federalist Party and on America?** (The Federalist Party lost power; New England and New York did not secede.)

Content Background Knowledge

- Dueling was a common practice in America in 1804 and was legal in New Jersey at the time. Politicians and journalists were often challenged to duels. The duels did not always result in fatalities. Several early statesmen, including Benjamin Franklin and George Washington, were against dueling.

- Alexander Hamilton was in a total of 11 duels in his lifetime; Aaron Burr was in 2.

- This particular duel occurred because Burr thought that Hamilton was spreading rumors about him and insulting him on a personal level; the accusations of treason came from other parties, later, after Hamilton was dead.

- Burr was charged with murder in both New York and New Jersey for killing Hamilton and wrote to his daughter Theodosia that the two states were battling over "which shall have the honour of hanging the vice-president."

Have students complete the Lesson 2 Review.

CLOSE & REFLECT

Discuss with students what happened to Burr after the duel. **Ask: Why do you think the duel was a significant moment in U.S. history?** (Student answers may vary.) Have students support their answers.

ANSWER, p. 277

☑ **PROGRESS CHECK** The Louisiana Purchase greatly increased the size of the country, opened new land for settlement, and helped assure farmers access to East Coast markets via the Mississippi River and New Orleans.

ENGAGE

Bellringer Ask students what comes to mind when they hear the word *pirate*. Write ideas on the board. Then explain that pirates are people who commit piracy, or acts of theft, on the seas. Circle any students' ideas that fit this definition.

Tell students that in the late 1700s and early 1800s, pirates were active on the Barbary States of North Africa. Point out that pirates are still active today.

TEACH & ASSESS

C Critical Thinking Skills

Hypothesizing Explain that despite the success of American merchant ships, sailing the seas was dangerous. Have students hypothesize what some of the dangers were. Write ideas on the board.

R Reading Skills

Explaining Have students read the paragraph on tribute in the subsection, "Piracy on the Seas." **Ask: What is tribute?** *(protection money)* Ask students to explain the more common use of the word today, meaning "to show respect or honor." Remind students that while tribute can be given as a sign of respect, in the case of pirates, it is not. **AL** **ELL**

ANSWER, p. 278

TAKING NOTES: Demand for Tribute: war with Tripoli; **Attacks on the *Chesapeake:*** Embargo and Nonintercourse Acts; **Tecumseh's Confederation:** Battle of Tippecanoe

---

networks
There's More Online!

☑ **BIOGRAPHY**
Stephen Decatur

☑ **CHART/GRAPH**
U.S. Policies Leading to the War of 1812

☑ **GAME** Lesson Terms

☑ **GRAPHIC ORGANIZER**
U.S. Actions

☑ **VIDEO**

Lesson 3
A Time of Conflict

ESSENTIAL QUESTION *Why does conflict develop?*

IT MATTERS BECAUSE
As the United States grew, tensions emerged within and beyond the nation's borders.

American Ships on the High Seas

GUIDING QUESTION *How did the United States become involved in a conflict with Tripoli?*

In 1785 the ship *Empress of China* returned to New York from China. The ship's cargo of tea and silk sold for a great profit. The chance for similar profit inspired others to follow in the *Empress of China's* wake. Soon, American merchant ships were sailing regularly to China and India, as well as South America, Africa, and lands along the Mediterranean Sea.

In the mid-1790s, France and Britain were at war. French and British merchant ships stayed home to avoid capture by their enemies. American merchants took advantage of this opportunity. By 1800, the United States had almost 1,000 merchant ships trading around the world.

Piracy on the Seas

The practice of piracy, or robbery on the seas, made some foreign waters dangerous. Pirates from the Barbary States of North Africa—Morocco, Algiers, Tripoli, and Tunis—terrorized European ships sailing on the Mediterranean Sea.

The Barbary pirates demanded that governments pay **tribute,** or protection money, to allow their country's ships to pass safely. If tribute was not paid, the pirates attacked and took

(t) Courtesy of the Naval Historical Foundation, Washington, DC, (tcl) The Granger Collection, NYC, (c) Private Collection, Photo © Christie's Images/Bridgeman Art Library, (tcr) The Granger Collection, NYC, (tr) Getty Images

---

Reading HELPDESK (CCSS)

Taking Notes: *Analyzing* RH.6–8.1

As you read, use a diagram like this one to analyze the actions the U.S. took in response to each of the following situations.

	Action Taken
Demand for Tribute	
Attacks on the Chesapeake	
Tecumseh's Confederation	

Content Vocabulary (Tier 3 Words)
- **tribute**
- **neutral rights**
- **embargo**
- **nationalism**

278 *The Jefferson Era*

---

networks *Online Teaching Options*

VIDEO

Tecumseh

Finding the Main Idea Show the video about Tecumseh. Check to make sure that students understand the meaning of the word *prophet*. Have them speculate on why Tecumseh's brother might have been given this name. **Ask: Who was the Prophet?** *(Tecumseh's brother, who was also a leader of his tribe)* **AL** **ELL** Visual/Spatial

See page 265E for other online activities.

ships, and imprisoned their crews. European countries often paid this tribute. They believed that it was less expensive to pay the Barbary pirates than it was to go to war with them.

War With Tripoli

The Barbary States also demanded that the United States pay tribute. In 1801 the ruler of Tripoli asked the United States for even more money. When President Jefferson refused to pay, Tripoli declared war on the United States. In response, Jefferson sent ships to blockade Tripoli.

In 1804 pirates seized the U.S. warship *Philadelphia*. They towed the ship into Tripoli Harbor and threw the crew into jail. Stephen Decatur, a 25-year-old U.S. Navy captain, took action. He slipped into the heavily guarded harbor with a small raiding party. Decatur burned the captured ship to prevent the pirates from using it. A British admiral praised the deed as the "most bold and daring act of the age."

C

Stephen Decatur and crew attack one of Tripoli's gunboats.

▶ CRITICAL THINKING
Drawing Conclusions Why do you think Stephen Decatur was considered a national hero?

tribute money paid to a leader or state for protection

V

Lesson 3 **279**

C Critical Thinking Skills

Analyzing Primary Sources Share Decatur's words to the crew of the USS *Essex* with students: "We are now about to embark upon an expedition which may terminate in our sudden deaths, our perpetual slavery, or our immortal glory. The event is left for futurity to determine." Have students paraphrase the quote to make sure they understand the meaning. **Ask: What was Decatur's purpose in giving this speech?** *(Decatur was trying to get his men ready for a dangerous, but courageous, act.)* Ask students to infer what the outcome was. **BL** Verbal/Linguistic

V Visual Skills

Analyzing Visuals Have students look at the image of Decatur and his men to discuss Decatur burning the captured ship. **Ask: What is happening in the picture?** *(Decatur and his U.S. sailors are attacking a gunboat in Tripoli harbor. They appear to be doing well; several pirates can be seen falling or struggling.)* **If you were an American in 1804, how do you think you would react to this image?** *(An American at the time might be heartened to see Americans taking action against pirates. Those opposed to war might be disturbed by the image.)* If time permits, have students complete a project responding to the story of Decatur and his men in a creative way, by drawing or painting their own visual rendition of the story, or by writing a short story or poem about it. **AL BL** Visual/Spatial

---

IMAGE

Stephen Decatur

Identifying Discuss the war with Tripoli. Ask students if they had ever heard of Commodore Stephen Decatur before this lesson. Use the interactive image about Stephen Decatur to discuss his life and career. Explain that he was one of America's first naval heroes who had not fought in the American Revolution. **ELL** Visual/Spatial

See page 265E for other online activities.

McGraw-Hill **netw⊚rks**   **Stephen Decatur**

During the War of 1812 with Britain, while on the *President*, Decatur and his crew were surrounded by British ships and forced to surrender. Decatur was taken captive and brought to Bermuda. After peace was declared and Decatur was freed, he successfully fought a second war against the Barbary states of North Africa.

Courtesy of the Naval Historical Foundation, Washington, DC

ANSWER, p. 279

CRITICAL THINKING Decatur was a young man who made a daring move that helped end the war with Tripoli.

R Reading Skills

Discussing Ask students to use details from their text to explain the United States' position during the war between Britain and France in 1803. Have students explain how this position changed as the war progressed.

W Writing Skills

Narrative Have students compose a narrative written from the point of view of an American sailor who is unfairly impressed by the British and forced to serve in the British navy. The narrative could be addressed to a newspaper, to a British politician, to the captain of a warship, or it could be a letter written to someone at home explaining what happened. Have students do some historical research in order to flesh out their narratives with more authentic details. **BL** **Verbal/Linguistic**

T Technology Skills

Using and Citing Information As students research their narratives, have them keep track of sources. Provide students with a model for bibliographic citations, and have them provide a bibliography of sources at the end of their narratives. **Verbal/Linguistic**

ANSWER, p. 280

Thinking Like a Historian Americans were already angry about the British searching ships and impressing sailors. They were outraged that Britain would violate their neutral rights to the extent of firing on their ship.

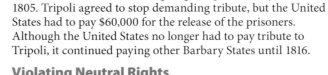

Thinking Like a
HISTORIAN

Predicting Consequences

As tensions between the United States and Great Britain worsened, the British warship *Leopard* attacked the American vessel *Chesapeake* off the coast of Virginia. How do you think the Americans people reacted to this violent conflict? For more information about predicting consequences, read *Thinking Like a Historian.*

R

Officers of the British ship *Leopard* impress American sailors from the *Chesapeake* in 1807.

Reading **HELP**DESK **CCSS**

neutral rights privileges or freedoms that are granted to nations that do not choose a side in a conflict
embargo a prohibition or blocking of trade with a certain country

Academic Vocabulary (Tier 2 Words)

react to act in response to something

280 *The Jefferson Era*

The war ended with the signing of a peace treaty in June 1805. Tripoli agreed to stop demanding tribute, but the United States had to pay $60,000 for the release of the prisoners. Although the United States no longer had to pay tribute to Tripoli, it continued paying other Barbary States until 1816.

Violating Neutral Rights

Thomas Jefferson won reelection in 1804. The nation was at peace—but trouble was brewing. Across the Atlantic Ocean, Great Britain and France were fighting a war that threatened to interfere with American trade.

When Britain and France went to war in 1803, the United States traded with both countries. By not taking sides in the war, the United States was able to continue with this trade. A nation not involved in a conflict enjoyed **neutral rights**, meaning its ships could sail the seas and not take sides.

American merchants prospered for two years. By 1805, however, Britain and France were each trying to block the other from trading with the United States. Britain blockaded the French coast and threatened to search all ships trading with France. France then announced that it would search and seize ships caught trading with Britain.

The British Abuse American Shipping

The British desperately needed sailors for their naval war. Many of their own sailors had deserted due to the terrible living conditions—hard labor, harsh treatment, and terrible food—in the British Royal Navy. British naval ships began stopping American ships to search for suspected British deserters. The British then forced these deserters to return to the British navy. This practice of forcing people to serve in the navy was called impressment (ihm•PREHS•muhnt).

While some of the sailors taken were deserters from the British navy, the British also impressed hundreds of native-born and naturalized American citizens.

W
T

The British often waited for American ships outside an American harbor, where they boarded and searched them. In June 1807, the British warship *Leopard* stopped the American vessel *Chesapeake* off the coast of Virginia. The *Leopard's* captain demanded to search the American ship for British deserters, but the *Chesapeake's* captain refused. In reply, the British opened fire, crippling the *Chesapeake* and killing three crew members.

The Granger Collection, NYC

---

netw⊚rks   *Online Teaching Options*

IMAGE

The *Chesapeake-Leopard* Affair

Analyzing Use the interactive image of the *Chesapeake-Leopard* affair to discuss the impressment of American sailors into the British Royal Navy. Have a volunteer describe the attempts of the British warship *Leopard* to stop the American vessel the *Chesapeake*. Discuss the demands made by *Leopard's* captain and the refusal of terms by *Chesapeake's* captain. Discuss the reaction by the British and the result of the attack. **AL** **ELL** **Visual/Spatial**

See page 265E for other online activities.

McGraw-Hill **netw⊚rks** The Chesapeake-Leopard Affair

Admiral Berkeley of the Royal Navy ordered that the Chesapeake be searched if it was encountered at sea. The HMS Leopard met up with the Chesapeake off the coast of Norfolk, Virginia.

The Granger Collection, NYC

When news of the attack spread, Americans **reacted** with an anti-British fury not seen since the Revolutionary War. Secretary of State James Madison called the attack an outrage. Many Americans demanded war against Britain, but President Jefferson wanted to avoid war.

More Problems for American Trade

When Britain violated America's neutral rights, Jefferson banned some trade with Britain. After the attack on the *Chesapeake*, he took stronger measures.

Congress passed the Embargo Act in December 1807. An **embargo** (ihm•BAHR•goh) prohibits trade with another country. The act targeted Great Britain, but the embargo banned imports from and exports to *all* foreign countries. Jefferson wanted to prevent Americans from using other countries as go-betweens for forbidden trade.

The embargo of 1807 was a disaster. With ships confined to their harbors, unemployment rose in New England. Without European markets, the South could not sell its tobacco or cotton. The price for wheat fell in the West, and river traffic stopped. Britain, meanwhile, simply bought needed goods from other countries. Congress repealed the Embargo Act in March 1809. In its place, it passed the Nonintercourse Act. This act, which prohibited trade only with Britain and France, was also unpopular and unsuccessful.

R

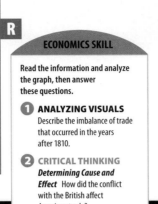

ECONOMICS SKILL

Read the information and analyze the graph, then answer these questions.

1 ANALYZING VISUALS
Describe the imbalance of trade that occurred in the years after 1810.

2 CRITICAL THINKING
Determining Cause and Effect How did the conflict with the British affect American trade?

C

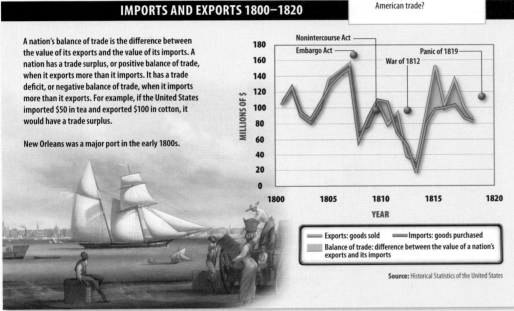

IMPORTS AND EXPORTS 1800–1820

A nation's balance of trade is the difference between the value of its exports and the value of its imports. A nation has a trade surplus, or positive balance of trade, when it exports more than it imports. It has a trade deficit, or negative balance of trade, when it imports more than it exports. For example, if the United States imported $50 in tea and exported $100 in cotton, it would have a trade surplus.

New Orleans was a major port in the early 1800s.

Nonintercourse Act
Embargo Act
War of 1812
Panic of 1819

MILLIONS OF $
180 160 140 120 100 80 60 40 20 0

YEAR
1800 1805 1810 1815 1820

— Exports: goods sold   — Imports: goods purchased
Balance of trade: difference between the value of a nation's exports and its imports

Source: Historical Statistics of the United States

Lesson 3   **281**

R Reading Skills

Defining After students have read the text, ask a volunteer to describe the Embargo Act of 1807 and the Nonintercourse Act. **Ask: What is an embargo?** *(a policy that prohibits trade with another country)* Explain that the Embargo Act targeted Great Britain, but that it banned exports to all foreign countries. **Ask: Why did Jefferson sign this act?** *(He wanted to prevent Americans from using other countries as go-betweens for illegal trade.)* Discuss the repeal of the act in 1809 and why it was repealed. **Ask: Between which groups were dealings not permitted under the Nonintercourse Act?** *(Trade was not permitted between the United States and Britain or France.)*
AL ELL

C Critical Thinking Skills

Comparing and Contrasting Have students compare and contrast the Embargo Act and the Nonintercourse Act. Be sure to discuss with students the policies of both acts, what they were designed to do, and whether they were successful. (Make sure that students understand why they were not successful.) Make a comparison chart or other organizer on the board to organize student answers. **BL Visual/Spatial**

GRAPHIC ORGANIZER

Chain of Events Flowchart

Listing Have students use the graphic organizer to fill in the events leading up to the War of 1812. Have students include both actions taken by the British and actions taken by the Americans. **AL**

See page 265E for other online activities.

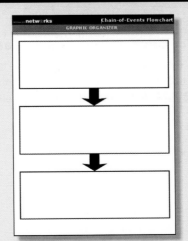

ANSWERS, p. 281

Economics Skill
1. The United States had a negative trade balance because it imported more than it exported.
2. **CRITICAL THINKING** The conflict with the British had a large negative effect on the U.S. economy. Both imports and exports dropped significantly between 1810 and 1815.

R Reading Skills

Summarizing Americans had to choose a new president in the election of 1808. Have students summarize the major events of Thomas Jefferson's presidency. **Ask: Why did Jefferson leave office?** *(He was following the precedent set by Washington.)* Ask them to compare the beginning of his term with the end of his term. **Ask: What changes occurred in the country's government?** *(Possible answer: Although Jefferson favored a less powerful federal government, a series of Supreme Court decisions strengthened it.)* **In its economy?** *(Possible answer: Jefferson's embargoes weakened the country's economy.)* **In its geography?** *(Possible answer: The Louisiana Purchase doubled the size of the country.)* **BL**

C Critical Thinking Skills

Determining Cause and Effect Emphasize the role of the Ohio River Valley in relations between U.S. settlers and Native Americans. **Ask: How did Ohio becoming a state affect relations between white settlers and Native Americans?** *(White settlers wanted more land in the Ohio Valley, but this land had been given to Native Americans by treaty.)* **AL**

Tecumseh called on Native Americans to unite in order to stop American expansion.

The Election of 1808

Jefferson, following Washington's precedent, made it clear that he would not be a candidate for a third term. The Republicans chose James Madison from Virginia as their candidate. The Federalists hoped that voter anger over the embargo would help them win. They nominated Charles Pinckney. Pinckney carried most of New England, but the Federalists gained little support from the other regions. Madison won the presidency with 122 electoral votes. Pinckney received just 47 votes.

R

☑ **PROGRESS CHECK**

Explaining Was the Embargo Act effective? Why?

War at Home and Abroad

GUIDING QUESTION *What issues challenged James Madison during his presidency?*

James Madison took office as president under unfavorable conditions. The nation was involved in the embargo crisis, and Britain continued to halt American ships. Cries for war with Britain grew louder.

War Looms

In 1810 Congress passed a new trade law. It would permit direct trade with either France or Britain, depending on which country first lifted its trade **restrictions**, or limits, against the United States. The British took no action, but Napoleon acted quickly, promising to end France's trade restrictions.

In spite of that promise, the French continued to seize and sell American ships. On the verge of war, Americans were divided only over who the enemy should be. Although angry over French actions, Madison believed Britain was the bigger threat to the United States.

Broken Treaties

C

Madison also received news about problems in the West. Ohio had become a state in 1803. White settlers wanted more land in the Ohio River valley. Native Americans had already given up millions of acres. Now the settlers were moving onto lands that were guaranteed to Native Americans by treaty.

The Granger Collection, NYC

Reading **HELP**DESK (CCSS)

nationalism a strong sense of devotion to one's country

Academic Vocabulary (Tier 2 Words)
restriction rule or regulation that limits something

---

netw⊙rks   *Online Teaching Options*

GAME

A Time of Conflict Identification Game

Assessing Have students play the interactive game to check their understanding of vocabulary terms from this lesson. **AL** **ELL** Verbal/Linguistic Interpersonal

See page 265E for other online activities.

ANSWER, p. 282

☑ **PROGRESS CHECK** The Embargo Act was a failure. Britain traded with other countries for goods, and the U.S. economy suffered greatly.

As tensions grew, some Native Americans renewed their contacts with British agents and fur traders in Canada. Other Native Americans pursued a new strategy. Tecumseh (tuh•KUHM•suh), a powerful Shawnee chief, tried to build a confederacy among Native American nations in the Northwest.

Tecumseh wanted to halt white movement into Native American lands. He believed that a strong alliance—with the backing of the British in Canada—could achieve that goal. Tecumseh also thought the treaties the U.S. government made with individual Native American nations were worthless. "The Great Spirit gave this great island to his red children," he said. No one nation, he believed, had the right to give it away.

Working alongside Tecumseh was his brother, Tenskwatawa (ten•skwah•TAH•wuh). Known as the Prophet, Tenskwatawa urged Native Americans to return to their ancient customs. His message gained a large following. He founded Prophetstown in northern Indiana, near where the Tippecanoe and Wabash Rivers meet.

R1

Tecumseh Meets the Governor

The governor of the Indiana Territory, William Henry Harrison, became alarmed by the growing power of the two Shawnee brothers. Fearing that they would form an alliance with the British, Harrison sent Tecumseh a letter. He warned Tecumseh that the United States had more warriors than all the Indian nations combined. Tecumseh replied to Harrison in person.

C1

The Prophet lacked his brother's military skill and was badly defeated in the Battle of Tippecanoe.

R2

PRIMARY SOURCE

C2

“ Since the peace was made, you have killed some Shawnees, Delawares and Winnebagoes. You have taken land from us and I do not see how we can remain at peace if you continue to do so. You try to force red people to do some injury. It is you that are pushing them on to some mischief. . . . You try to prevent the Indians from doing as they wish—to unite and let them consider their lands common property of the whole. ”

—from *The Centennial History of Oregon, 1811–1912,*
by Joseph Gaston

The Battle of Tippecanoe

Harrison attacked Prophetstown while Tecumseh was away trying to expand the confederacy. After more than two hours of battle, the Prophet's forces fled.

MPI/Getty Images

R1 Reading Skills

Explaining After students read the text, have them explain how westward expansion influenced Tecumseh's decision to join forces with the British. *(Tecumseh believed that a few Native American nations could not make binding agreements to give up land for all Native Americans. He felt that Harrison and other white Americans were pushing Native Americans toward rebellion. When Harrison attacked Prophetstown, Tecumseh decided to join forces with the British. He thought that a confederacy of Native Americans united with the British would be able to stop the westward movement of white settlers.)* **BL**

R2 Reading Skills

Stating Have students refer to the image of Tecumseh's brother, Tenskwatawa, on this page. **Ask:** What role did the Prophet play in the history of westward expansion? *(He encouraged Native Americans to return to their old customs and developed a strong following. He and his brother Tecumseh made a strong team. The Prophet founded Prophetstown, which Harrison attacked in the Battle of Tippecanoe.)* **AL ELL**

C1 Critical Thinking Skills

Comparing and Contrasting Have students compare Tecumseh's view with William Henry Harrison's view in regard to the broken treaties. Encourage students to analyze the primary sources in their text to identify Tecumseh's ideas. Students may work in pairs to create a brief dialogue between Tecumseh and Harrison. **BL Interpersonal**

C2 Critical Thinking Skills

Identifying Points of View Discuss with students the role that Tecumseh played in the war between Native Americans and the settlers. Have students read the primary source quotation in their textbook. Ask them to summarize Tecumseh's ideas about Native American land and relations with white Americans. **Ask:** What issue of social justice is Tecumseh raising? *(The issue is the Native Americans' rights to own land that they have lived on for generations in their own tradition.)* **BL Verbal/Linguistic**

WHITEBOARD ACTIVITY

The War of 1812

Sequencing Use the interactive whiteboard activity to discuss with students the events that led up to the War of 1812. Be sure to highlight the growing tensions between the British and the Americans over impressment and trade. Have students drag and drop their answers into the chart. Ask them to justify their responses for each using their own words. **AL ELL Visual/Spatial**

See page 265E for other online activities.

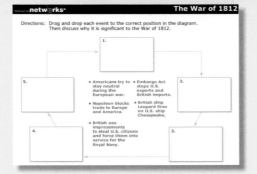

networks™   The War of 1812

Directions: Drag and drop each event to the correct position in the diagram. Then discuss why it is significant to the War of 1812.

A Time of Conflict

R Reading Skills

Explaining After students have read the text, explore the Battle of Tippecanoe with them. Have students explain who fought in the Battle of Tippecanoe and where it was fought. *(William Henry Harrison and his forces attacked Native Americans in Prophetstown on the Tippecanoe River.)* **Ask: What was the outcome of the battle?** *(Harrison and his forces won.)* **What longer-lasting effect did it have?** *(As a result of the battle, Tecumseh joined forces with the British.)* **AL**

W Writing Skills

Argument Discuss the War Hawks. **Ask: Who were the War Hawks?** *(young Republicans from the West and South who favored war with England)* **What were their goals?** *(Their goals were to gain territory and increase military spending. Pushing Madison to declare war would achieve both goals.)* **As the nation expanded, where did War Hawks want land?** *(Southern War Hawks wanted Spanish Florida. Western War Hawks wanted the fertile forests of southern Canada.)* **What roles did Henry Clay and John Calhoun play in the War Hawks?** *(They were the leaders. Henry Clay was from Kentucky and led the War Hawks in the West; John Calhoun was from South Carolina and led the War Hawks in the South.)* Have students imagine that they lived at this time. Have them write a short letter to a newspaper responding to the War Hawks' belief that their position was the most patriotic one, and agreeing or disagreeing with this position. **BL Verbal/Linguistic**

Have students complete the Lesson 3 Review.

CLOSE & REFLECT

Hypothesizing Discuss the backgrounds of Henry Clay and John Calhoun. Ask students if they think these two individuals might play an important role in American society in the future. Have them explain the reasons for their responses.

ANSWER, p. 284

☑ **PROGRESS CHECK** The British continued to seize and search U.S. ships. The British formed alliances with Native Americans. War Hawks increased pressure for war with Britain.

R The Battle of Tippecanoe was a victory for the Americans. Yet it came at a cost. After his people's defeat, Tecumseh joined forces with the British who, settlers believed, had supplied his confederacy with guns.

The War Hawks Call for War

W Meanwhile, President Madison faced demands for a more aggressive policy toward Britain. The loudest voices came from a group of young Republican congress members known as the War Hawks. Led by Henry Clay of Kentucky and John Calhoun of South Carolina, they represented the West and South.

The War Hawks supported increases in military spending and were driven by hunger for land. War Hawks from the West wanted the fertile forests of southern Canada, whereas the southerners wanted Spanish Florida. The War Hawks also wanted to expand the nation's power. Their **nationalism** (NA·shuh·nuh·lih·zuhm)—or loyalty to their country—appealed to a renewed American patriotism.

Not everyone, however, wanted war. The Federalists in the Northeast remained strongly opposed to it.

The Eve of War

By the spring of 1812, Madison knew that he could no longer avoid war with Britain. In a message to Congress on June 1, Madison asked them to declare war.

The British had already decided to end their policy of search and seizure of American ships. Unfortunately, news of Britain's change in policy did not reach Washington, D.C., until it was too late. Once set in motion, the war machine could not be stopped.

☑ **PROGRESS CHECK**

Summarizing List three factors that led to war with Britain.

LESSON 3 REVIEW (CCSS)

Review Vocabulary (Tier 3 Words)

1. How do *tribute* and *neutral rights* affect shipping? RH.6–8.4

2. Explain the significance of the following terms: RH.6–8.4
   a. embargo   **b.** nationalism

Answer the Guiding Questions

3. ***Explaining*** Explain why U.S. security was threatened as a result of the war between Britain and France. RH.6–8.2

4. ***Summarizing*** Why did conflict on the American frontier increase tensions between the United States and Britain? RH.6–8.2

5. ***Contrasting*** Describe how people from the South, Northeast, and West felt about going to war with Britain. RH.6–8.5

6. **ARGUMENT** Which of the challenges that the United States faced in this period do you feel was the most serious? Write a paragraph explaining your choice. WHST.6–8.1, WHST.6–8.10

284 *The Jefferson Era*

LESSON 3 REVIEW ANSWERS

1. Tribute is paid to protect ships, so it should promote shipping. Neutral rights allow ships to sail the seas without taking sides if their country is not involved in a conflict, which should also promote shipping and keep trade safe.

2. **a.** An embargo prohibits trade with certain nations.
   b. Nationalism—a strong sense of devotion to country—grew in the early 1800s. It was especially strong among the War Hawks, who were fueled by their hunger for more land and wanted the United States to expand into Florida and Canada. They also wanted to expand America's power in international affairs.

3. France and Britain seized and searched American ships. The British also impressed Americans into naval service.

4. As American settlers moved onto lands that had been given by treaties to Native Americans, Native Americans formed a confederacy to fight for their territory. This confederacy, headed by Tecumseh, turned to the British as allies. Once again, a conflict between the British and the Americans was looming.

5. People in different parts of the country held different attitudes about going to war. In the South and West, War Hawks wanted to go to war to get land and power. In the Northeast, Federalists opposed the war.

6. Essays should show an understanding of relations between Britain and the United States and France and the United States during Jefferson's presidency.

networks

There's More Online!

☑ **BIOGRAPHY**
Dolley Madison

☑ **GRAPHIC ORGANIZER**
Battles and Outcomes

☑ **MAP** The War of 1812

Lesson 4
The War of 1812

ESSENTIAL QUESTION *Why does conflict develop?*

IT MATTERS BECAUSE
The War of 1812 changed how Americans felt about their country and how other countries viewed the United States.

Defeats and Victories

GUIDING QUESTION *In what ways was the United States unprepared for war with Britain?*

When the war began, the War Hawks were confident the United States would achieve a quick victory over the British. In reality, though, the Americans were unprepared for war.

The fighting force was small and ill-prepared. The regular army had fewer than 12,000 soldiers, 5,000 of whom were new recruits. Added to that were the state militias, with between 50,000 and 100,000 poorly trained soldiers. Commanders who had served in the American Revolution were now too old to fight. In addition, not everyone supported the conflict. Some states opposed "Mr. Madison's War." The Americans also **underestimated,** or misjudged, the strength of the British and their Native American allies.

In July 1812, the war began. General William Hull led the American army from Detroit into Canada, where they met Tecumseh and his warriors. Fearing a massacre by the Native Americans, Hull surrendered Detroit to the British. Several other American attempts to invade Canada also ended in failure. General William Henry Harrison led one of these unsuccessful efforts. He decided that the Americans could make no headway as long as the British controlled Lake Erie.

R

(lt.) Collection of the New York Historical Society/Bridgeman Art Library/0285. (bcr) The Granger Collection, NYC. (tr) Stock Montage/Getty Images

Reading **HELP**DESK **CCSS**

Taking Notes: *Describing*

As you read, use a graphic organizer like the one shown here to record and describe each battle's outcome. RH.6–8.1

Battle	Outcome
Lake Erie →	
Washington, D.C →	
New Orleans →	

Content Vocabulary
• **frigate** (Tier 3 Words)

Academic Vocabulary (Tier 2)
underestimate to judge something below its actual value

Lesson 4 **285**

VIDEO

History of United States Symbols: American Flag

Analyzing Visuals Show students the video entitled "The History of the United States Symbols: The American Flag." Be sure that students understand why the American flag is a symbol of the United States. Have volunteers provide other examples of American symbols. **AL** **ELL** Visual/Spatial

See page 265F for other online activities.

ENGAGE

Bellringer Engage students in a discussion of their own secondhand experience with war. Ask for volunteers to tell the class about military-related news events that they have heard or read about or stories that they may have heard from veterans in their own families or in their circle of acquaintances. If time permits, arrange for students to interview veterans from their community. Explain that although the War of 1812 took place more than 200 years ago, the nation still faces questions of how best to protect its borders and how to prepare for war. These are ongoing issues that affect not only the nation as a whole, but also veterans and their families, who live in every community. **AL** **ELL** Interpersonal

TEACH & ASSESS

R Reading Skills

Summarizing Have students summarize how the United States was unprepared for war with Britain. *(limited number of soldiers and poorly trained militia; lack of young, experienced leaders; mixed public support; underestimation of the opponent)* Discuss how the lack of preparation led to the surrender of Detroit to the British. **AL** **ELL**

Making Connections

Discuss with students the experience of preparing for a physical challenge, such as a sports event, a dance recital, or a canoe trip. Help students to make connections between preparing for physical challenges that they may have experienced and preparing to go to war.

- Preparing for a physical challenge involves long hours of training and practice. Training and practicing increase the chances that the challenge will be met with success.
- Sports teams need to train together in order to play well in competition. They also need to have enough players, and preferably some extra players who can be cycled in as needed.
- Preparing for a challenge also requires dressing appropriately, bringing the necessary supplies, and being familiar with the environment of the challenge, such as the trails on a hiking trip or the layout of an obstacle course.
- Military units face all these issues: training together, having enough people and supplies, and being prepared for the terrain. Nations make preparations for war all the time so that they can be ready if the need arises, but this does not guarantee that those preparations will be adequate.

ANSWER, p. 285

TAKING NOTES: Lake Erie: Americans won control of the lake and access to Canada. **Washington, D.C.:** British soldiers seized the city and burned parts of it. **New Orleans:** Americans won a decisive victory, and Andrew Jackson became a hero.

R Reading Skills

Discussing As students read, ask them to note details about the strategic value of the Great Lakes in the War of 1812. **Ask:** Why were the Great Lakes important in the War of 1812? *(They were key to taking control of Canada.)* Which two leaders were unsuccessful in battles on or around the Great Lakes? *(Generals William Hull and William Henry Harrison)* Who finally beat the British navy and took control of Lake Erie? *(Oliver Hazard Perry)* Why was the battle of Lake Erie significant for America? *(Possible answer: It demonstrated the strength of the U.S. Navy.)* **AL** **ELL**

C Critical Thinking Skills

Making Connections Remind students that Britain was still at war with France. **Ask:** How did Britain's war with France influence the movement of the United States toward war? *(Britain violated American neutral rights while it was at war with France, angering the Americans.)* **AL** **ELL**

Making Connections

- During the War of 1812, the Creeks fought a civil war between villages that wanted to be allied with the United States (called White Sticks) and villages that wanted to attack the United States (called Red Sticks).
- The United States did not get involved in the Creek civil war until the Red Sticks attacked Fort Mims. This was the event that led General Andrew Jackson to lead troops to the Battle of Horseshoe Bend.
- After the Battle of Horseshoe Bend, the Creek nation was forced to give up 22 million acres of its land in Georgia and Alabama.

ANSWER, p. 286

☑ **PROGRESS CHECK** No, the United States was not prepared for the war when it started. (1) There were too few regular soldiers, and the state militias were untrained. (2) Some states opposed the war, and their militias were needed. (3) The British and their Native American allies were stronger than the United States realized.

U.S. Naval Strength

The U.S. Navy had three of the fastest **frigates** (FRIH • guhts), or warships, afloat. When the *Constitution* destroyed two British vessels early in the war, Americans rejoiced. Privateers, armed private ships, also captured many British vessels, boosting American morale.

Oliver Hazard Perry, commander of the Lake Erie naval forces, had his orders. He was to assemble a fleet and seize the lake from the British. The showdown came on September 10, 1813, when the British ships sailed out to face the Americans. In the bloody battle that followed, Perry and his ships destroyed the British naval force. After the battle, Perry sent General Harrison the message, "We have met the enemy and they are ours."

With Lake Erie in American hands, the British and their Native American allies tried to pull back from the Detroit area. Harrison and his troops cut them off. In the fierce Battle of the Thames, Tecumseh was killed.

American forces also attacked York (present-day Toronto), burning the parliament. Still, though America had won several victories by the end of 1813, Canada remained under British rule.

Defeat of the Creeks

Before his death in the Battle of the Thames, Tecumseh had talked with the Creeks in the Mississippi Territory about forming a confederation to fight the United States. With his death, hopes for such a confederation ended. The British-Native American alliance also came to an end.

In March 1814, Andrew Jackson led U.S. forces in an attack on the Creeks in the Battle of Horseshoe Bend. More than 550 Creek people died in that battle, and the Creeks were forced to give up most of their lands.

☑ **PROGRESS CHECK**

Evaluating Was the United States prepared to wage war? Explain.

The British Offensive

GUIDING QUESTION *Why were Americans instilled with national pride after the battle of New Orleans?*

Before fighting broke out with the United States, the British had already been at war with the French. Fighting two wars was difficult. Britain had to send soldiers and ships to both France

---

Reading HELPDESK (CCSS)

frigate a fast, medium-sized warship

Build Vocabulary: *Related Words*

The word *proceeded* in the quotation on the next page is similar to the word *preceded*. The prefixes *pro-* and *pre-* can both mean "before, or in front of." In this case *pro* means "forward," and the word *proceeded* means "to go forward." The word *preceded* means "to be or go in front of."

286 *The Jefferson Era*

---

networks   *Online Teaching Options*

BIOGRAPHY

William Henry Harrison

Discussing Use the interactive image of William Henry Harrison to discuss the events at the Battle of the Thames, and the death of Tecumseh and its impact on the Native Americans. **Ask:** What happened to Tecumseh in the Battle of the Thames? *(He was killed.)* How did this affect other Native Americans? *(His death ended hope of a permanent Native American confederation.)* **AL** **Visual/Spatial**

See page 265F for other online activities.

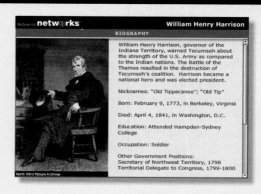

networks   **William Henry Harrison**
BIOGRAPHY

William Henry Harrison, governor of the Indiana Territory, warned Tecumseh about the strength of the U.S. Army as compared to the Indian nations. The Battle of the Thames resulted in the destruction of Tecumseh's coalition. Harrison became a national hero and was elected president.

Nicknames: "Old Tippecanoe"; "Old Tip"

Born: February 9, 1773, in Berkeley, Virginia

Died: April 4, 1841, in Washington, D.C.

Education: Attended Hampden-Sydney College

Occupation: Soldier

Other Government Positions: Secretary of Northwest Territory, 1798 Territorial Delegate to Congress, 1799-1800

North Wind Picture Archives

and the United States. In the spring of 1814, British fortunes began to improve. After winning the war against Napoleon, Britain was free to send more forces against the United States. **C**

In August 1814, the British sailed into Chesapeake Bay and launched an attack on Washington, D.C. British troops quickly overpowered the American militia on the outskirts of the city. Then they marched into the American capital. "They proceeded, without a moment's delay, to burn and destroy everything in the most distant degree connected with the government," reported a British officer. Among the buildings set ablaze were the Capitol and the president's mansion. Fortunately, a thunderstorm put out the fires before they could completely destroy the buildings. **R1**

The British did not try to hold Washington, D.C. Instead, they headed north to Baltimore. They attacked that city in mid-September, but the people of Baltimore were ready and held firm. A determined defense and fierce artillery fire from Fort McHenry in the harbor kept the British from entering the city. **R2**

As the bombs burst over Fort McHenry during the night of September 13, local attorney Francis Scott Key watched. The next morning he saw the American flag still flying over the fort. Deeply moved, Key wrote a poem that became known as "The Star-Spangled Banner." Congress designated "The Star-Spangled Banner" as the national anthem in 1931.

GEOGRAPHY CONNECTION

During the War of 1812, approximately 286,000 Americans fought the British, and an estimated 2,200 were killed in battle.

1 MOVEMENT Based on this map, from what three places did the British attack the Americans?

2 CRITICAL THINKING *Drawing Conclusions* Based on this map, in what area did the British have their greatest success? Explain your answer.

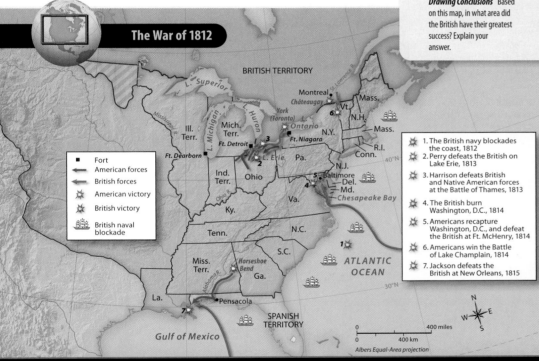

The War of 1812

1. The British navy blockades the coast, 1812
2. Perry defeats the British on Lake Erie, 1813
3. Harrison defeats British and Native American forces at the Battle of Thames, 1813
4. The British burn Washington, D.C., 1814
5. Americans recapture Washington, D.C., and defeat the British at Ft. McHenry, 1814
6. Americans win the Battle of Lake Champlain, 1814
7. Jackson defeats the British at New Orleans, 1815

Fort
American forces
British forces
American victory
British victory
British naval blockade

C Critical Thinking Skills

Identifying Points of View Ask students to think about the early events of the War of 1812. Have them speculate about how the British felt about the war up to this point. **Ask: How did the end of the war with France affect the War of 1812?** *(When Britain won the war with France, it was able to send more troops to fight the Americans.)* Have students speculate about how the British might want to proceed against the United States. **AL**

R1 Reading Skills

Describing Have students read about the attack on Washington, D.C. **Ask: What city did British troops attack?** *(Washington, D.C.)* Have students describe what happened when the British attacked Washington, D.C. *(The British captured the city and burned the Capitol and the president's mansion.)* Discuss with students how the burning of the capitol may have affected American morale. **AL ELL**

R2 Reading Skills

Discussing Ask students to take notes as they read the text. Then, have students discuss the events that occurred after the attack on Washington, D.C. **Ask: What did the British do next?** *(They attacked Baltimore.)* **What happened there?** *(They were defeated.)* Talk with students about how a local attorney named Francis Scott Key was inspired to write "The Star-Spangled Banner," which references the American flag that was displayed at Fort McHenry at the Battle of Baltimore. **AL ELL**

MAP

The War of 1812

Analyzing Discuss the importance of the Great Lakes in the War of 1812. Use the interactive map on the War of 1812 to discuss the location of the Great Lakes and their relation to the early battles. **AL ELL**
Visual/Spatial

See page 265F for other online activities.

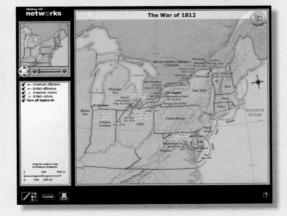

ANSWERS, p. 287

GEOGRAPHY CONNECTION

1 The British navy blockaded the East Coast and added support on Lake Erie, Lake Champlain, New Orleans, and Washington, D.C.

2 CRITICAL THINKING The British had their greatest success in the Chesapeake Bay area. There they attacked Washington, D.C. and burned the White House.

C1 Critical Thinking Skills

Drawing Conclusions Discuss the Battle of Lake Champlain with students. **Ask: How did the Battle of Lake Champlain affect the course of the war?** (*It convinced the British that it was not worth it to continue fighting.*) Have students consider how the War of 1812 affected Canadian history. Encourage students to turn back to other parts of the lesson if necessary. Discuss how Canadian history might have changed if the war had progressed differently from the way it did. **BL**

R Reading Skills

Discussing After students have read the text, begin a discussion with them about the end of the war and the Treaty of Ghent. **Ask: Why did the British decide to stop fighting?** (*The war was too costly.*) **What treaty ended the war?** (*the Treaty of Ghent*) **What did the treaty provide? What did it leave out?** (*The Treaty ended the war. It did not change any borders. It did not mention the impressment of sailors or neutral rights.*) **AL** **ELL**

C2 Critical Thinking Skills

Making Inferences Discuss the Battle of New Orleans. Point out that hundreds of British soldiers died in the battle, while Jackson's troops hid behind cotton bales that kept them safe. Discuss the outcome of this pivotal battle. **Ask: How did Jackson's fame during the War of 1812 help him later in life?** (*His victories made him a war hero, and he would eventually be elected president.*) **Ask: What other general from the War of 1812 became a U.S. president later in life?** (*William Henry Harrison*) Discuss with students why they think that war heroes often have an advantage in political campaigns.

BIOGRAPHY

Dolley Madison (1768–1849)

Dolley Payne Todd married James Madison in 1794, several years after the death of her first husband. While James Madison served as President Jefferson's secretary of state, Dolley acted as hostess for the widowed president. During the War of 1812 she showed remarkable bravery. In 1814 as the British approached the capital, she refused to leave the White House until she had packed up many valuable items, a painting of George Washington, and other priceless valuables.

▶ **CRITICAL THINKING**
Drawing Conclusions Why do you think Dolley Madison risked danger to save White House valuables?

Reading HELPDESK (CCSS)

Academic Vocabulary (Tier 2 Words)
goal something one is trying to accomplish

A Turning Point at Plattsburgh

While British forces were attacking Washington and Baltimore, British General Sir George Prevost was moving into New York from Canada. Leading more than 10,000 British soldiers, his **goal** was to capture Plattsburgh, a key city on the shore of Lake Champlain. An American naval force on the lake defeated the British fleet in September 1814. Fearing the Americans would surround them, the British retreated into Canada.

The Battle of Lake Champlain convinced the British that the war in North America was too costly and unnecessary. They had defeated Napoleon in Europe. To keep fighting the United States would result in little gain and was not worth the effort.

The End of the War

In December 1814, American and British representatives met in Ghent, Belgium, to sign a peace agreement. The Treaty of Ghent did not change any existing borders. There was no mention of the impressment of sailors. Even neutral rights had become a dead issue since Napoleon's defeat.

One final, ferocious battle occurred before word of the treaty reached the United States. On January 8, 1815, the British advanced on New Orleans. Waiting for them were Andrew Jackson and his troops. The redcoats were no match for Jackson's soldiers, who hid behind thick cotton bales. The bales absorbed the British bullets, while the British advancing in the open provided easy targets for American troops. In a short but gruesome battle, hundreds of British soldiers were killed. At the Battle of New Orleans, Americans achieved a decisive victory. Andrew Jackson became a hero whose fame would help him win the presidency in 1828.

Nationalism and New Respect

From the start, New England Federalists had opposed "Mr. Madison's War." These unhappy Federalists gathered in December 1814 at the Hartford Convention in Connecticut. A few favored secession, but most wanted to remain with the Union. To protect their interests, they made a list of proposed amendments to the Constitution.

Collection of the New-York Historical Society/Bridgeman Art Library

---

networks *Online Teaching Options*

BIOGRAPHY

Dolley Madison

Discussing Use the interactive image of Dolley Madison and give a brief account of how she saved priceless valuables in the White House from the British. **Ask: Why do you think she risked her life to save valuables in the White House from the British?** (*Answers may vary but could suggest that they were irreplaceable American treasures.*) **AL** **Visual/Spatial**

See page 265F for other online activities.

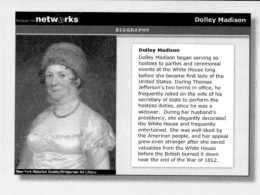

Dolley Madison

Dolley Madison began serving as hostess to parties and ceremonial events at the White House long before she became first lady of the United States. During Thomas Jefferson's two terms in office, he frequently relied on the wife of his secretary of state to perform the hostess duties, since he was a widower. During her husband's presidency, she elegantly decorated the White House and frequently entertained. She was well-liked by the American people, and her appeal grew even stronger after she saved valuables from the White House before the British burned it down near the end of the War of 1812.

New-York Historical Society/Bridgeman Art Library

ANSWER, p. 288

CRITICAL THINKING Dolley Madison was married to James Madison, one of the Framers of the Constitution. She had served President Jefferson as a hostess in the White House. She was a loyal and patriotic American who did not want the British to destroy American treasures.

The War of 1812

The Federalists' grievances seemed unpatriotic in the triumph following the war. The party lost the public's respect and disappeared as a political force, leaving only one significant political party. The War Hawks took over leadership of the Republican Party and carried on the Federalist belief in a strong national government. The War Hawks favored trade, western expansion, the energetic development of the economy, and a strong army and navy.

Americans felt a new sense of patriotism and a strong national identity after the War of 1812. The young nation also gained new respect from other nations around the world.

Although it took place after the peace treaty had been signed in Ghent, the Battle of New Orleans made Andrew Jackson (above) a national hero, easing his entrance into politics.

▶ CRITICAL THINKING
Speculating Why do you think military success often leads to political success?

☑ **PROGRESS CHECK**

Identifying Cause and Effect Identify three effects of the War of 1812.

LESSON 4 REVIEW (CCSS)

Review Vocabulary

1. Use the word *frigate* in a sentence about the developments of this era. RH.6–8.4

Answer the Guiding Questions

2. *Explaining* Why was the Battle of the Thames important for the United States in the War of 1812? RH.6–8.2

3. *Determining Cause and Effect* How did the outcome of the war affect the Federalist Party's efforts to change the Constitution? RH.6–8.5

4. *Summarizing* Describe how the War Hawks influenced the Republican Party after the War of 1812. RH.6–8.2

5. **ARGUMENT** Consider the causes and costs of the war, the Treaty of Ghent, and the impact of the war on the American people. Was the War of 1812 worth fighting? Did it help or hurt the young United States? State your opinion in a brief essay. WHST.6–8.1, WHST.6–8.4

Lesson 4   **289**

LESSON 4 REVIEW ANSWERS

1. The United States had some of the fastest frigates afloat, which represented a big advantage in the War of 1812.

2. Tecumseh was killed in the Battle of the Thames. Without Tecumseh's leadership, the Native American confederation that was opposed to the United States failed.

3. The Federalist Party lost power, and its ideas about constitutional amendments lost favor and support as nationalism grew following the war.

4. War Hawks took control of the party. They promoted strong national government, wanted to develop trade and the economy, pushed western expansion, and favored a strong military.

5. Student responses will vary, but students who say that the war helped may reflect the growth of patriotism and nationalism following the war and how those sentiments are represented by Key's poem. The United States also gained new respect from other nations around the world. Those who think the war hurt the country may reflect on the damage it did to the economy and trade, the loss of life, and the further poor and unfair treatment of Native Americans.

R Reading Skills

Explaining Remind students that the Federalists opposed the war. Then ask students to find details in the text that show how the Federalist party fared after the war. **Ask: How did the War of 1812 impact the Federalist Party?** *(They opposed the war from the start, so they wanted to protect their interests through amendments in the Constitution. They were viewed as unpatriotic in the aftermath of the war. The party lost the respect of the public and disappeared as a political force.)* Discuss how the collapse of the Federalists led to the rise of the War Hawks in the Republican Party. Discuss what aspects of government the War Hawks favored. **AL** **ELL**

W Writing Skills

Narrative Have students write a paragraph from the point of view of a Federalist who opposed the war. Students' paragraphs should indicate whether the Federalist continued to feel, even after the war, that the war was not a good idea, or whether events of the war caused a change of heart. **BL** **Verbal/Linguistic**

Have students complete the Lesson 4 Review.

CLOSE & REFLECT

Drawing Conclusions Discuss with students how the role of the United States in the world was different after the War of 1812.

ANSWERS, p. 289

CRITICAL THINKING People might think that individuals who have succeeded in the military are good leaders and dedicated to their country.

☑ PROGRESS CHECK The Federalist Party lost strength, American nationalism grew, and the United States gained status in the world.

CHAPTER REVIEW ACTIVITY

Ask students to think about ways people, places, and ideas have changed since the Jefferson Era. To spur thinking, ask questions like: **How do today's political campaigns differ from the campaign of 1800? How have relationships between white Americans and Native Americans changed over time? How has the geography of the United States changed since 1800?** Record students' responses in a T-chart on the interactive whiteboard. Label the left column "1800" and the right column "Today."

REVIEW THE ENDURING UNDERSTANDING

Review the chapter's Enduring Understanding with students.

* *People, places, and ideas can change over time.*

Now pose the following questions in a class discussion to apply these to the chapter.

How did the nation change geographically during the Jefferson era? *(The nation more than doubled in size with the Louisiana Purchase.)*

How did the nation change politically during the Jefferson era? *(The Federalist Party began to decline. The Supreme Court established judicial review and grew in power.)*

How did the nation change in terms of its standing in the world during the Jefferson Era? *(After the War of 1812, the young nation had new respect around the world.)*

ACTIVITIES ANSWERS

Exploring the Essential Questions

❶ The essay should address two major changes, such as the Louisiana Purchase, brewing conflicts with Native Americans, and growing conflicts and war with Britain. The Louisiana Purchase doubled the size of the nation and opened new lands for settlement. Conflicts with Native Americans grew as the United States expanded westward. Native Americans joined with the British against the United States, and tensions continued. The United States was not prepared for war against Britain but managed to win. The win increased American patriotism and international respect.

21st Century Skills

❷ Jefferson entered his presidency under the cloud of a close race (a tie). He tried to bridge the gap between parties but also instituted changes, such as cutting taxes and the size of the government. During his terms, he increased the size

---

CHAPTER 10 Activities CCSS

Write your answers on a separate piece of paper.

❶ **Exploring the Essential Questions** WHST.6–8.1, WHST.6–8.10
INFORMATIVE/EXPLANATORY What do you think were the two most significant changes in the United States during the Jefferson Era? Explain why you consider them important.

❷ **21st Century Skills** WHST.6–8.5, WHST.6–8.9
COMPARING AND CONTRASTING In a small group, discuss the similarities and differences between Jefferson's first term as president and Madison's first term as president. Consider the state of the nation and the challenges each man faced. Make a chart that summarizes the group's ideas.

❸ **Thinking Like a Historian** RH.6–8.5
UNDERSTANDING CAUSE AND EFFECT Significant changes occurred during Thomas Jefferson's presidency. Some of those changes still affect us today. Use a chart like the one shown below to identify changes and note modern effects of those changes.

	Geography	Civics and Government
Jefferson Era		
Today		

❹ **Visual Literacy** RH.6–8.7
ANALYZING POLITICAL CARTOONS During his presidency, Jefferson had to respond to British and French attacks on American shipping. Examine the political cartoon. What are Britain's King George and France's Napoleon Bonaparte doing? Explain whether the cartoon is critical or supportive of Jefferson and his response. Discuss whether political cartoons are an effective way of making comments about the government.

 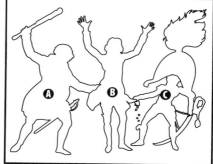

Ⓐ King George of England
Ⓑ Thomas Jefferson
Ⓒ Napoleon Bonaparte of France

The Granger Collection, NYC

---

of the nation dramatically. The country was much larger when Madison began his presidency. Jefferson faced war with Tripoli and got caught up in the war between France and Britain. When Madison began his term, the nation was on the brink of war and the economy had suffered because of the embargo instituted by Jefferson. He also faced conflicts with Native Americans.

Thinking Like a Historian

❸ **Geography: Jefferson Era**—The Louisiana Purchase roughly doubled the size of the nation. **Today**—The area of the Louisiana Purchase, then a territory, has become states. The Mississippi River is even more important to commerce today than it was in Jefferson's time. The Midwest and Great Plains areas are important parts of the nation today. **Civics and Government:**

Jefferson Era—After the election of 1800, the 12th Amendment to the Constitution changed the way the president was elected. Judicial review was established. **Today**—We continue to use the Electoral College, but electors cast one ballot for president and one for vice-president. The principles of judicial review still apply and are even more important today.

Visual Literacy

❹ King George and Napoleon are robbing Thomas Jefferson. The cartoon seems to be against Jefferson's embargo policy because it points out that attacks on American interests continue despite the policy. Political cartoons are one way of expressing opinions about government actions and other issues. How effective they are depends on the cleverness and skill of the political artist.

REVIEW THE GUIDING QUESTIONS
Choose the best answer for each question.

RH.6–8.4
❶ Which statement reflects a principle of judicial review?

A. State law takes precedence over federal law.

B. The Constitution is the supreme law of the land.

C. Laws that conflict with the Constitution may stand.

D. The executive branch must uphold the Constitution.

RH.6–8.2
❷ Which of the following factors influenced Napoleon's decision to sell the Louisiana Territory to the United States?

F. the westward movement of American settlers

G. his plans to invade Russia

H. the loss of a naval base in Santo Domingo

I. Spain's refusal to allow American goods to move into or past New Orleans

RH.6–8.2
❸ Why did Federalists oppose the Louisiana Purchase?

A. They thought it was too expensive, and they feared new taxes.

B. They worried about conflicts with Native Americans.

C. They were concerned that they would lose political power as new states were created.

D. They were afraid France would regret the sale and the nation would be forced into war with France.

RH.6–8.1
❹ What happened as a result of the Embargo Act of 1807?

F. It made the nation's economy stronger as Americans had to buy and sell more American goods.

G. It was effective in stopping Britain from violating America's neutral rights.

H. It forced Americans to find new markets for their goods.

I. It hurt the the U.S. economy by wiping out trade with other nations.

RH.6–8.2
❺ Why was the death of Tecumseh a setback for the British in the War of 1812?

A. It caused Tenskwatawa to side with the Americans.

B. Tecumseh was an ally of the British.

C. Tecumseh was an enemy of the French.

D. Tecumseh had a long history of besting Americans in battle.

RH.6–8.2
❻ Which of the following best describes an effect of the War of 1812?

F. The Federalist Party gained strength.

G. Other nations grew to despise the United States.

H. American patriotism weakened.

I. The United States gained status in the world.

291

Analyzing Documents

7 **C** Tecumseh does not believe in selling land, so A and D are incorrect. He wants Native Americans to keep land, so B is incorrect.

8 **H** Tecumseh believes that the land belongs to all Native Americans and therefore cannot be sold, so F and I are incorrect. There is no mention of Native Americans being misled, so G is incorrect.

Short Response

9 Both suggest disapproval of the policies of Jefferson and Madison. The first proposal shows dissatisfaction with the Embargo Act and the Nonintercourse Act. The second proposal shows the Federalists' dissatisfaction with the War of 1812; it appears that they believed the war was wrong because the country was not actually invaded and because the war did not reflect the wishes of a representative number of Americans.

10 Nationalism and patriotism grew after the war. In light of this national pride, the proposed amendments seemed unpatriotic. Limiting power to declare war after a successful war may have seemed misguided.

Extended Response

11 Possible answer: Jefferson supported a "wise and frugal" government. He also believed that a small federal government protected liberty and that states' rights should be protected. His ideas were similar to *laissez-faire*. Based on these ideals, Jefferson would likely limit the size and scope of the federal government. It is also likely that he would limit interference in the economy.

CHAPTER 10 **Assessment** (continued)

DBQ ANALYZING DOCUMENTS

"The only way to stop this evil [white settlement of Indians' land], is for all the red men to unite in claiming a common and equal right in the land as it was at first, and should be now—for it never was divided, but belongs to all. … Sell a country! Why not sell the air, the clouds, and the great sea, as well as the earth?"

—Tecumseh in a letter to President Harrison, 1810

RH.6–8.2, RH.6–8.10

7 **Identifying Main Ideas** What does Tecumseh suggest in this letter?

A. Native Americans should get a good price for selling their land.

B. Native Americans should give the land to white people.

C. Native Americans should work together to keep out white settlers.

D. Native Americans should sell the land and divide the profits equally.

RH.6–8.6

8 **Identifying Main Ideas** What does this letter suggest about Tecumseh's views of earlier Native American agreements to sell their land?

F. He supports these agreements.

G. He believes Native Americans were misled.

H. He believes they had no right to sell the land.

I. He believes the prices received for the land were too low.

SHORT RESPONSE

"Third.—Congress shall not have power to lay any embargo on the ships or vessels of the citizens of the United States, in the ports or harbors thereof, for more than sixty days."

"Fifth.—Congress shall not make or declare war, or authorize acts of hostility against any foreign nation, without the concurrence of two-thirds of both Houses, except such acts of hostility be in defense of the territories of the United States when actually invaded."

—Amendments to the Constitution Proposed by the Hartford Convention, 1814

RH.6–8.6, WHST.6–8.4

9 Do these changes suggest support or disapproval of the policies of Jefferson and Madison? Explain.

RH.6–8.9, WHST.6–8.4

10 Why did these amendments fall out of favor after the War of 1812?

EXTENDED RESPONSE

WHST.6–8.2, WHST.6–8.10

11 **Informative/Explanatory** Thomas Jefferson has just begun his first term as president of the United States. Write an article summarizing his views and explaining what you expect from his presidency.

Need Extra Help?

If You've Missed Question	1	2	3	4	5	6	7	8	9	10	11
Review Lesson	1	2	2	3	3	4	3	3	4	4	1

---

netw⊙rks *Online Teaching Options*

Using eAssessment

Use eAssessment to access and assign the publisher-made Lesson Quizzes & Chapter Tests electronically. You can also use eAssessment to create your own quizzes and tests from hundreds of available questions. eAssessment helps you design assessments that meet the needs of different types of learners. Follow the link in the *Assess* tab of your Teacher Lesson Center.

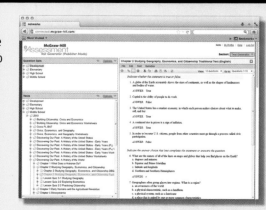

UNDERSTANDING BY DESIGN®

Enduring Understanding

- *The movement of people, goods, and ideas causes societies to change over time.*

Essential Questions

- *How does geography influence the way people live?*
- *Why does conflict develop?*

Predictable Misunderstandings

Students may think:

- *The United States' industrial growth was copied by other countries.*
- *The United States never experienced a period of nationalism between the American Revolution and the Civil War.*
- *The federal government has always had more power than state governments.*

Assessment Evidence

Performance Tasks:

- *Hands-On Chapter Project*

Other Evidence:

- *Interactive Graphic Organizers*
- *What Do You Know? activity*
- *Geography and History Activity*
- *Primary Source Activity*
- *America's Literature Questions*
- *Written Paragraphs*
- *Lesson Reviews*
- *Online Self-Check Quizzes*
- *Chapter Activities and Assessment*

SUGGESTED PACING GUIDE

Introducing the Chapter . . . . 1 day	Lesson 3 . . . . .2 days
Lesson 1 . . . . .2 days	*America's Literature* . . . . 1 day
Lesson 2 . . . . .2 days	Chapter Wrap-Up and Assessment . . . . . . 1 day

TOTAL TIME   9 Days

Key for Using the Teacher Edition

SKILL-BASED ACTIVITIES

Types of skill activities found in the Teacher Edition.

V **Visual Skills** require students to analyze maps, graphs, charts, and photos.

R **Reading Skills** help students practice reading skills and master vocabulary.

W **Writing Skills** provide writing opportunities to help students comprehend the text.

C **Critical Thinking Skills** help students apply and extend what they have learned.

T **Technology Skills** require students to use digital tools effectively.

Letters are followed by a number when there is more than one of the same type of skill on the page.

DIFFERENTIATED INSTRUCTION

All activities are written for the on-level student unless otherwise marked with the leveled labels below.

BL Beyond Level
AL Approaching Level
ELL English Language Learners

All students benefit from activities that utilize different learning styles. Many activities are marked as below when a particular learning style is highlighted.

Intrapersonal	Naturalist
Logical/Mathematical	Kinesthetic
Visual/Spatial	Auditory/Musical
Verbal/Linguistic	Interpersonal

NCSS STANDARDS covered in "Growth and Expansion"

Learners will understand:

3 PEOPLE, PLACES, AND ENVIRONMENTS

1. The theme of people, places, and environments involves the study of the relationships between human populations in different locations and geographic phenomena such as climate, vegetation, and natural resources

6. Patterns of demographic and political change, and cultural diffusion in the past and present (e.g., changing national boundaries, migration, and settlement, and the diffusion of and changes in customs and ideas)

7. Human modifications of the environment

5 INDIVIDUALS, GROUPS, AND INSTITUTIONS

4. That ways in which young people are socialized include similarities as well as differences across cultures

9. That groups and institutions influence culture in a variety of ways

7 PRODUCTION, DISTRIBUTION, AND CONSUMPTION

1. Individuals, government, and society experience scarcity because human wants and needs exceed what can be produced from available resources

4. Economic incentives affect people's behavior and may be regulated by rules or laws

5. That banks and other financial institutions channel funds from savers to borrowers and investors

7. How markets bring buyers and sellers together to exchange goods and services

8. How goods and services are allocated in a market economy through the influence of prices on decisions about production and consumption

8 SCIENCE, TECHNOLOGY, AND SOCIETY

1. Science is a result of empirical study of the natural world, and technology is the application of knowledge to accomplish tasks

4. Science and technology have had both positive and negative impacts upon individuals, societies, and the environment in the past and present

5. Science and technology have changed peoples' perceptions of the social and natural world, as well as their relationship to the land, economy and trade, their concept of security, and their major daily activities

CHAPTER OPENER PLANNER

Students will know:
- how technological improvements contributed to the Industrial Revolution and changed the ways people lived and worked.
- how improved transportation facilitated westward movement.
- how the unity and nationalism people felt after the War of 1812 changed to divisions over issues of economics and equality.

Students will be able to:
- **analyze** why industrial growth began in New England.
- **draw conclusions** about how the growth of factories contributed to the Industrial Revolution.
- **identify and evaluate** the elements of the free enterprise system.
- **compare** agriculture in the different regions of the country.
- **analyze** how cotton farming affected slavery.
- **identify and evaluate** modes of transportation during the Industrial Revolution.
- **analyze** the impact of the Erie Canal on transportation and industry.
- **analyze life in western settlements.**
- **compare** issues regarding the power of the federal government and states.
- **analyze and evaluate** the consequences of landmark Supreme Court decisions.
- **summarize** the Missouri Compromise.
- **analyze** the causes and effects of sectionalism.
- **identify points of view** of important leaders of the time period.

UNDERSTANDING
BY DESIGN

☑ *Print Teaching Options*

V Visual Skills

☐ **P. 294** Students review a map of U.S. industrial cities from 1800 to 1840 and discuss their proximity to rivers and canals. **AL** **ELL**

☐ **P. 295** Students analyze a time line of events in the United States from the late 1700s to the mid-1800s. **BL**

W Writing Skills

☐ **P. 294** Students pretend to be settlers traveling with Daniel Boone and write journal entries about their trip. **Intrapersonal** **BL**

T Technology Skills

☐ **P. 295** Students research industrial cities from the map at the beginning of the chapter and report on their findings. **BL**

☑ *Online Teaching Options*

V Visual Skills

☐ **MAP** **Growing Industrial Cities**—Students click on states to see whether they had industrial cities by 1840.

☐ **TIME LINE** **United States 1790–1840**—Students learn about key events in U.S. history during this time period.

☐ **WORLD ATLAS** Students can use this interactive map to identify regions of the world, learn about individual countries, locate political boundaries, measure distances, and much more.

☑ *Printable Digital Worksheets*

R Reading Skills

☐ **GRAPHIC NOVEL** *On Her Own*—A teenage girl moves to Lowell and learns what working in a factory is like.

Project-Based Learning

Hands-On Chapter Project

Create a Scrapbook
Small groups will each prepare one page of a scrapbook depicting topics dealing with U.S. growth and expansion, such as the development of transportation, the Industrial Revolution, or the Missouri Compromise. Groups will coordinate to produce a coherent and logical scrapbook.

Technology Extension

Create a Virtual Scrapbook
- Find an additional activity online that incorporates technology for this project.
- Visit the EdTechTeacher Web sites (included in the Technology Extension for this chapter) for more links, tutorials, and other resources.

Print Resources

ANCILLARY RESOURCES
These ancillaries are available for every chapter and lesson.
- **Reading Essentials and Study Guide Workbook** **AL** **ELL**
- **Chapter Tests and Lesson Quizzes Blackline Masters**

PRINTABLE DIGITAL WORKSHEETS
These printable digital worksheets are available for every chapter and lesson.
- **Hands-On Chapter Projects**
- **What Do You Know? activities**
- **Chapter Summaries (English and Spanish)**
- **Vocabulary Builder activities**
- **Guided Reading activities**

More Media Resources

SUGGESTED READING

Grade 6 reading level:
- *The Groundbreaking, Chance-Taking Life of George Washington Carver and Science and Invention in America,* by Cheryl Harness

Grade 7 reading level:
- *Robert Fulton,* by Elaine Landau

Grade 8 reading level:
- *Gibbons v. Ogden: Controlling Trade Between States (Landmark Supreme Court Cases),* by Isabel Simone Levinson

LESSON 1 PLANNER

A GROWING ECONOMY

Students will know:
- how technological improvements contributed to the Industrial Revolution and changed the ways people lived and worked.

Students will be able to:
- *analyze* why industrial growth began in New England.
- *draw conclusions* about how the growth of factories contributed to the Industrial Revolution.
- *identify and evaluate* the elements of the free enterprise system.
- *compare* agriculture in the different regions of the country.
- *analyze* how cotton farming affected slavery.

☑ Print Teaching Options

V Visual Skills

☐ **P. 297** Students analyze a photo of young factory workers from the 1840s. **ELL**

☐ **P. 299** Students interpret graphs about population distribution in 1820. **AL** **ELL** **BL** Visual/Spatial

☐ **P. 300** Students view an image of South Street in New York and make inferences about the development of cities.

R Reading Skills

☐ **P. 296** Students discuss the Industrial Revolution and its arrival in New England. **AL** **ELL**

☐ **P. 297** Students summarize the Industrial Revolution in the United States and name its new machines. **AL** **ELL**

☐ **P. 298** Students define and list examples of capitalism. **AL** **ELL**

☐ **P. 300** Students discuss the characteristics of a corporation.

☐ **P. 301** Students discuss waterways and explain why factory growth led to the development of cities.

W Writing Skills

☐ **P. 296** Students write about a technological device and the impact it has on their lives. **BL** Intrapersonal

☐ **P. 301** Students paraphrase a text to convey the author's meaning. Intrapersonal

C Critical Thinking Skills

☐ **P. 297** Students make inferences about the effect of patent laws passed by Congress in 1790. **AL** **ELL**

☐ **P. 298** Students analyze how businesses work in a free enterprise system. **AL** **ELL**

☐ **P. 299** Students make connections between agriculture and industry in the early 1800s. Logical/Mathematical

☐ **P. 299** Students compare and contrast types of farms in North America and their effect on agricultural growth.

☐ **P. 301** Students draw conclusions about what life was like in new cities and towns.

T Technology Skills

☐ **P. 298** Students research the Lowell factory workers and share their findings with the class.

☑ Online Teaching Options

V Visual Skills

☐ **VIDEO** **An Industrial Revolution in the Northern Region of the United States**—Students analyze the roots of the factory system and its effect on craftsmen and artisans.

☐ **IMAGE** **Water Mills**—Students analyze a diagram of the parts of a water mill in Lowell.

☐ **IMAGE** **South Street, New York**—Students view an image of this area developed by the Schermerhorns.

☐ **IMAGE** **Yellow Fever**—Students see why disease spread quickly in cities, such as Philadelphia.

R Reading Skills

☐ **GRAPHIC ORGANIZER** **Taking Notes:** *Finding the Main Idea:* **Free Enterprise System**—Students identify the major elements of the free enterprise system.

☐ **PRIMARY SOURCE ACTIVITY** **The Lowell Offering**—Students read an excerpt from and background about this monthly magazine published by working women.

C Critical Thinking Skills

☐ **WHITEBOARD ACTIVITY** **The Textile Industry**—Students organize characteristics of pre- and post-industrial revolution processes.

☐ **GRAPH** **Measuring Population**—Students click to see population growth over time.

T Technology Skills

☐ **SELF-CHECK QUIZ** **Lesson 1**—Students receive instant feedback on their mastery of lesson content.

☑ Printable Digital Worksheets

C Critical Thinking Skills

☐ **WORKSHEET** **Geography and History Activity: Understanding Human-Environment Interaction: Industrial Growth**—Students analyze a map and other information to determine why New England led the way to industrialization.

MOVING WEST

Students will know:
- *how improved transportation facilitated westward movement.*

Students will be able to:
- ***identify and evaluate*** *modes of transportation during the Industrial Revolution.*
- ***analyze*** *the impact of the Erie Canal on transportation and industry.*
- ***analyze*** *life in western settlements.*

UNDERSTANDING
BY DESIGN®

☑ *Print Teaching Options*

V Visual Skills

☐ **P. 306** Students view a painting of the Erie Canal and analyze the importance of waterways in the development of population centers. **Visual/Spatial**

R Reading Skills

☐ **P. 302** Students identify Daniel Boone and discuss his contribution to westward expansion. **BL**

☐ **P. 304** Students summarize the importance of the *Clermont* and steam power on waterways in the development of river travel.

☐ **P. 305** Students discuss reasons for the construction of the Erie Canal.

W Writing Skills

☐ **P. 303** Students write two paragraphs comparing and contrasting the types of roads during the Industrial Revolution with the types of roads we have today. **Logical/Mathematical**

☐ **P. 306** Students write two sentences that connect the painting of the Erie Canal to what they have learned about waterways. **AL** **ELL**

C Critical Thinking Skills

☐ **P. 303** Students contrast the different roads that were built due to the growth of cities and towns. **AL** **ELL**

☐ **P. 304** Students make predictions about the dangers a steamboat might encounter on the river. **AL** **ELL**

☐ **P. 307** Students make connections between river travel and the building of roads with the movement of westward expansion. **BL**

☐ **P. 307** Students infer what life in the West was like after the dramatic expansion west from 1800 to 1820. **BL**

T Technology Skills

☐ **P. 305** Students work in groups to research information about the Erie Canal on the Internet and report their findings to the class. **Interpersonal**

☑ *Online Teaching Options*

V Visual Skills

☐ **VIDEO** **Daniel Boone**—Students view a video about Daniel Boone and westward expansion.

☐ **MAP** **Canals, 1820–1860**—Students view the network of canals that crisscrossed the Northeast, Ohio, Indiana, and Illinois.

☐ **MAP** **The National Road, 1811–1837**—Students trace the route of the National Road.

R Reading Skills

☐ **GRAPHIC ORGANIZER** **Taking Notes:** *Sequencing:* **Developments in Transportation**—Students develop a time line to sequence major developments in transportation.

☐ **SLIDE SHOW** **The Erie Canal**—Students view slides of and read about the canal, its builder, and its modern counterpart.

C Critical Thinking Skills

☐ **SLIDE SHOW** **Pioneer Life**—Students examine the work and social lives of frontier families.

T Technology Skills

☐ **SELF-CHECK QUIZ** **Lesson 2**—Students receive instant feedback on their mastery of lesson content.

UNITY AND SECTIONALISM

Students will know:

- *how the unity and nationalism people felt after the War of 1812 changed to divisions over issues of economics and equality.*

Students will be able to:

- *compare* issues regarding the power of the federal government and states.
- *analyze and evaluate* the consequences of landmark Supreme Court decisions.
- *summarize* the Missouri Compromise.
- *analyze* the causes and effects of sectionalism.
- *identify* points of view of important leaders of the time period.

UNDERSTANDING BY DESIGN®

☑ *Print Teaching Options*

V Visual Skills

☐ **P. 311** Students make inferences about Henry Clay based on his picture and his words. `ELL` Visual/Spatial

☐ **P. 314** Students connect a painting of Mexican leaders to the information on the page. `ELL`

☐ **P. 315** Students discuss the roles of Miguel Hidalgo and Mexican leaders in the rebellion against the Spanish. Interpersonal

R Reading Skills

☐ **P. 308** Students discuss why the time after the War of 1812 was called "The Era of Good Feelings."

☐ **P. 309** Students summarize the main points about Clay's American System. `BL`

☐ **P. 311** Students list rulings on Supreme Court cases regarding power of the national government over states.

☐ **P. 312** Students summarize The Missouri Compromise. `AL` `ELL`

☐ **P. 315** Students explain why the Monroe Doctrine was issued.

W Writing Skills

☐ **P. 308** Students write about how the War of 1812 changed sentiments about central government. `BL`

☐ **P. 314** Students write a paragraph describing how General Andrew Jackson and Secretary of State Adams established U.S. rule in Florida. `AL` `ELL` Interpersonal

☐ **P. 315** Students write two sentences explaining the Monroe Doctrine in their own words. `AL` `ELL`

C Critical Thinking Skills

☐ **P. 309** Students connect Independence Day celebrations to feelings of nationalism. `AL` `ELL` Verbal/Linguistic

☐ **P. 310** Students discuss challenges facing the economy after the War of 1812. `AL` `ELL`

☐ **P. 313** Students infer why the United States entered agreements to rule out arms on the Great Lakes. `BL`

T Technology Skills

☐ **P. 314** Students make group presentations of Internet research about the Seminole people.

☑ *Online Teaching Options*

V Visual Skills

☐ `VIDEO` **President James Monroe and the Era of Good Feelings**—Students view a video that describes Monroe's leadership skills.

☐ `MAP` **The Missouri Compromise**—Students view a map that shows the areas designated as free and those open to slavery.

☐ `MAP` **Acquisition of Florida**—Students view areas of the South annexed between 1810 and 1819.

☐ `IMAGE` **Mexican Leaders Declaring Independence from Spain**—Students view an image of this historic event.

R Reading Skills

☐ `GRAPHIC ORGANIZER` **Taking Notes:** *Determining Cause and Effect:* **The Missouri Compromise**—Students show the effects of the Missouri Compromise on different areas.

☐ `BIOGRAPHY` **Henry Clay**—Students read a short biography of this statesman.

C Critical Thinking Skills

☐ `CHART` **The Seminole Wars**—Students click to reveal details about the three Seminole wars.

☐ `IMAGE` **The Second Bank of the United States**—Students click to learn about this bank, which was established in 1816.

T Technology Skills

☐ `SELF-CHECK QUIZ` **Lesson 3**—Students receive instant feedback on their mastery of lesson content.

☑ *Printable Digital Worksheets*

C Critical Thinking Skills

☐ `WORKSHEET` **Primary Source Activity: Why We Need a Protective Tariff**—Students analyze points of view on this topic.

INTERVENTION AND REMEDIATION STRATEGIES

LESSON 1 A Growing Economy

Reading and Comprehension

Ask students to skim the lesson and use context clues to write definitions for the vocabulary words. Then have them check their answers against a dictionary.

Text Evidence

Ask students to create a flowchart that depicts how a good product and a bad product will fare in a capitalistic economy. Points of reference are manufacturer, vendor, and customer. Then ask students to compare their answers to the text under the heading "Free Enterprise."

LESSON 2 Moving West

Reading and Comprehension

Explain that some words have multiple meanings. Point out the word *locks* and explain its different meanings. Ask students to skim the chapter for more multiple-meaning words.

Text Evidence

In groups, ask students to choose a mode of transportation of the time period (river, wilderness trails, roads, canals) and brainstorm the pros and cons of each one, using a T-chart. They should refer to the text as needed.

LESSON 3 Unity and Sectionalism

Reading and Comprehension

Divide the class into groups and ask each group to paraphrase a few paragraphs from this lesson and share their paraphrase with the class.

Text Evidence

Have students compare the fight for the independence of Mexico to the fight for U.S. independence. They can use the textbook and other sources to create a Venn diagram of similarities and differences.

Online Resources

Approaching Level Reader

Use this online lower-level text that corresponds directly to the text in the Student Edition. It includes a Spanish version.

Guided Reading Activities

This resource uses graphic organizers and guiding questions to help students with comprehension.

What Do You Know?

Use these worksheets to pre-assess student's background knowledge before they study the chapter.

Reading Essentials and Study Guide Workbook

This resource offers writing and reading activities for the approaching-level student. Also available in Spanish.

Self-Check Quizzes

This online assessment tool provides instant feedback for students to check their progress.

Growth and Expansion

1790–1840

ESSENTIAL QUESTIONS • How does geography influence the way people live?
• Why does conflict develop?

The Story Matters...

American settlers have always preferred to live on rivers and other waterways. In these days before railroads and automobiles, water is the fastest, easiest way to move goods. When nature fails to provide a waterway, Americans take out their shovels—and take matters into their own hands.

The Erie Canal stretches 363 miles (584 km) and connects the Great Lakes of the Midwest to the Atlantic Ocean in New York City. Horses or mules tow boats loaded with 30 tons (27 t) of goods in both directions. The Erie Canal cuts the cost of shipping goods along this route from $100 per ton to $10 per ton. It shows that Americans can overcome great obstacles in their expansion to the West.

◄ *The Erie Canal opened for business in 1825.*

Bettmann/CORBIS

293

ENGAGE

🔔 **Bellringer** Ask students to read "The Story Matters..." to themselves. Then discuss what it might have been like to work on building the Erie Canal. **Ask: What do you think the conditions were like for workers who built the Erie Canal?** Have a few students share their ideas. The Erie Canal changed the way goods were transported in the United States. **Ask: Which new inventions or methods do you use that have changed the way you work or play?** Have a few students share their stories. Tell the class that during the early 1800s U.S. industry and agriculture grew rapidly, allowing the country to grow and prosper. New states were admitted to the Union. Citizens felt a sense of nationalism shortly after the War of 1812, but soon the country became divided over conflicting ideas regarding economics and equality. **Interpersonal**

Making Connections

Use a map to explain that a canal connects bodies of water, in the case of the Erie Canal, the Great Lakes with the Atlantic Ocean. Ask students to describe some humanmade structures that enable travel, such as bridges or tunnels. They should list some structures in their city or neighborhood, and interested students may want to research famous canals, rivers, or tunnels.

Letter from the Author

Dear American History Teacher,

The theme of United States history during the first quarter of the nineteenth century was *growth* in territory, population, and economy. The Louisiana Purchase in 1803 doubled the size of the country, and the acquisition of Florida territory added another 70,000 square miles. In 1803 the American population was just under six million. By 1825, there were almost twelve million Americans. During these years, eight new states entered the Union. Rapid growth improved the standard of living, but it also created problems that threatened to tear apart the country.

James M. McPherson

TEACH & ASSESS

Step Into the Place

V1 Visual Skills

Location Ask students to look at the chapter opener map in the textbook. Remind students that it shows U.S. industrial cities from 1800 to 1840. Have students review the map. Tell students that river and canal travel helped create new industrial cities. As a class, discuss what attracted people to industrial cities and what life was like there. Have student volunteers analyze the map and name bodies of water located near industrial cities. As a class, discuss the Map Focus questions. **AL** **ELL**

W Writing Skills

Narrative Ask students to look at the painting of Daniel Boone and the settlers. Have them pretend to be one of the settlers and write a series of journal entries about their trip. **Intrapersonal** **BL**

Content Background Knowledge

Rivers were important for early civilizations, including the Mesopotamian, the Egyptian, and the Indus Valley. Rivers provided water for drinking, bathing, and irrigation; food; transportation; and fertile land after floods. Early American settlers chose to settle along rivers for these reasons, too.

ANSWERS, p. 294

Step Into the Place

1. Milwaukee, Chicago, Detroit, Cleveland, Buffalo, Rochester

2. Atlanta and New Orleans

3. **CRITICAL THINKING** Some regions, such as New England, saw industrial growth because the geography did not support large-scale agriculture but did include streams and rivers for waterpower and good harbors for ports. Other regions had rivers for shipping goods.

Step Into the Time
18 years

CHAPTER 11 (CCSS)
Place and Time: United States 1790 to 1840

In the early 1800s, United States industry and agriculture grew rapidly. Many Americans moved westward, created new settlements and cities, and improved methods of transportation.

Step Into the Place

MAP FOCUS During the early 1800s, industrialization grew. The map on the next page shows major industrial cities that emerged during this time.

1 **PLACE** Look at the map. Which cities near the Great Lakes saw industrial growth? RH.6–8.7

2 **LOCATION** Which industrial cities lie south of Virginia and Kentucky? RH.6–8.7

3 **CRITICAL THINKING** *Determining Cause and Effect* How do you think a region's geography influenced industrial growth in that region? RH.6–8.5

In 1818 General Andrew Jackson was ordered to stop the Native American raids coming from Florida. To accomplish this goal, he invaded areas of West Florida and Spanish East Florida. His actions helped Spain realize it could not defend or control Florida.

W

In the late 1700s, Daniel Boone helped lead American settlers into the lands beyond the Appalachian Mountains.

Step Into the Time

V2

TIME LINE Look at the time line. Agriculture and industry grew rapidly during this period. How many years after Robert Fulton designed the first practical steamboat did workers complete the Erie Canal? RH.6–8.5, RH.6–8.7

U.S. PRESIDENTS
U.S. EVENTS
WORLD EVENTS

1790 Washington, D.C., founded

1793 Eli Whitney invents cotton gin

George Washington 1789–1797
John Adams 1797–1801
Thomas Jefferson 1801–1809

1790

1800

1792 Russia invades Poland

1804 Haiti claims independence from France

294 *Growth and Expansion*

Project-Based Learning ✋

Hands-On Chapter Project

Create a Scrapbook

Small groups will each prepare one page of a scrapbook depicting U.S. growth and expansion. Ask groups of students to research a topic in their textbook (e.g., development of transportation, the Industrial Revolution, Missouri Compromise) and find maps, photos, or other visuals to create the scrapbook page. As a class, combine pages into a coherent and logical scrapbook. Each group will present its page to the class.

Technology Extension

Create a Virtual Scrapbook

Photo storing and virtual scrapbooks offer a creative method for presenting research about different locations and historical periods. Students can present information about simulated trips to close or faraway locations. The information can be embedded in existing Web pages or wikis and can be shared via social networking services. Students can collaborate online and create content material with their classmates as well.

Visit **networks** online to see the full project.

networks ☑ **MAP** Explore the interactive version of this map on NETWORKS. ☑ **TIME LINE** Explore the interactive version of this time line on NETWORKS.
There's More Online!

V₁   T

Growing Industrial Cities 1800–1840

Minnesota

L. Superior

Wisconsin

Iowa

Michigan

Milwaukee   Detroit

Illinois   Indiana   Ohio
Chicago   Cleveland
Cincinnati
St. Louis   Louisville   West Virginia
Missouri   Kentucky   Richmond
Virginia

Tennessee   North Carolina

Arkansas   South Carolina
Atlanta
Miss.   Alabama   Georgia

Louisiana   Florida
New Orleans

Vermont   Maine

New York   New Hampshire
Manchester   Lowell
Rochester   Mass.   Boston
Buffalo   Pawtucket
Conn.   Rhode Island
New York City
Pennsylvania   New Jersey
Pittsburgh   Philadelphia
Baltimore
Delaware
Maryland

ATLANTIC OCEAN

N
W   E
S

60°W
40°N
30°N

● Industrial city experiencing significant growth 1800-1840

0   400 miles
0   400 km
Lambert Azimuthal Equal-Area projection

1807 Robert Fulton designs first practical steamboat

James Madison 1809–1817

James Monroe 1817–1825

1825 Erie Canal completed

John Q. Adams 1825–1829

Andrew Jackson 1829–1837

Martin Van Buren 1837–1841

1810   1820   1830   1840

1814 Francis Scott Key writes poem that becomes national anthem

1815 Napoleon defeated at Battle of Waterloo

1820 Missouri Compromise passed

1823 Mexico becomes a republic

1840 Workers in Lowell, Massachusetts, begin publishing the *Lowell Offering*

295

Step Into the Time

V₂ Visual Skills

Interpreting Have students review the time line for the chapter. Explain that they will be studying events from the late 1700s to the mid-1800s. Tell students that in the early 1800s, the United States saw large population increases due to industrial growth. **Ask: Based on the information in the time line, what three events may have contributed to the industrial growth and expansion that happened during this period?** (*Answers may include invention of the cotton gin, 1793; the first practical steamboat, 1807; completion of Erie Canal, 1825.*) Ask students to discuss in pairs how these events might have contributed to expansion and growth. **BL**

T Technology Skills

Researching on the Internet Ask groups of students to research the cities on the map and determine what they manufactured during this time period. Students may report their findings to the class. **BL**

Content Background Knowledge

When the United States was a British colony, the British provided many manufactured goods to the colonies in exchange for raw materials. Industrialization decreased the need for costly imports from Great Britain and other countries because manufactured goods could be made close to home.

CLOSE & REFLECT

Ask students to write down three things they learned from this page, as well as three things they would like to know more about.

---

networks *Online Teaching Options*

WORKSHEET

What Do You Know? Activity: Growth and Expansion

Using Digital Tools Have students complete the Anticipation Guide activity before they study the chapter. Direct students to read each statement and respond to it by circling A for agree or D for disagree. Next take a class poll so that you can tailor your lessons to focus on students' misconceptions.

After students complete the chapter, have them reread their opinions and note if any have changed and why or why not. Ask students who changed their opinions to explain why they did so. (*Students should cite facts from the chapter.*) **Interpersonal** **AL**

See page 293B for other online activities.

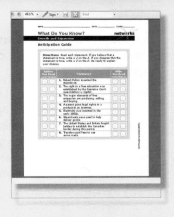

ENGAGE

Bellringer Call the attention of students to several technological innovations of the last few decades. Some examples are computers, barcodes used in the sale and purchase of products, cell phones, spacecraft, and radiation used in medical technology. Discuss how the recent innovations have changed lives. Tell students that the methods of making goods began to change in the late 1700s due to new technology. For example, machines were invented for cloth making in factories. **Ask:** How do you think the innovations of the 1700s revolution affected people? Did they affect people more or less than today's changes? *(Answers will vary, but accept any well-reasoned answer.)*

TEACH & ASSESS

W Writing Skills

Narrative Using the Bellringer as a springboard, ask students to write a paragraph about a technological item of choice. Have them explain how the item is used and how it makes a difference in their lives. **BL** Intrapersonal

R Reading Skills

Discussing After students have read the text, discuss with them how the Industrial Revolution developed before it reached the United States. Ask volunteers to describe what life during the start of the Industrial Revolution might have been like. Then, have a volunteer list the three reasons that New England became the central area for the start of the Industrial Revolution. **AL** **ELL**

networks
There's More Online!
☑ **GRAPHIC ORGANIZER**
Free Enterprise System
☑ **PRIMARY SOURCE**
Lowell Offering

Rural 92.8%

Lesson 1
A Growing Economy

ESSENTIAL QUESTION *How does geography influence the way people live?*

IT MATTERS BECAUSE
The Industrial Revolution of the late 1700s changed how people lived and worked.

Industrial Growth

GUIDING QUESTION *How did new technology affect the way things were made?*

W In colonial times, most Americans lived in the same place that they worked, which was usually a farm. When they wanted or needed something, they made it. Using their hands and simple tools, people made much of their own furniture, farm equipment, household items, and clothing.

In the mid-1700s, people began producing goods through new methods. In Great Britain, inventors built machines that did some of the work involved in cloth making, such as spinning thread. These new machines ran on the power of flowing water. British cloth makers built factories, called mills, along rivers. In the mills, they installed large numbers of machines. To tend the machines, mill owners paid people wages, regular payment of money in return for work. People began to leave their homes and farms to work in the mills and collect wages. This historic change is so important that it is known as the Industrial Revolution.

The Industrial Revolution in the United States

The Industrial Revolution reached the United States around 1800. Changes began in New England because of its geography. First, New England's poor soil made farming difficult. People

(cl) University of Massachusetts Lowell, Center for Lowell History, (tr) Archive Photos/Kean Collection/Getty Images

Reading HELPDESK (CCSS)

Taking Notes: *Finding the Main Idea* RH.6–8.1
Use a diagram like this one to identify the major elements of the free enterprise system.

Free enterprise system

Content Vocabulary (Tier 3 Words)
• **cotton gin**   • **capitalism**
• **interchangeable part** • **capital**
• **patent**   • **free enterprise**

296 *Growth and Expansion*

---

networks   *Online Teaching Options*

VIDEO

An Industrial Revolution in the Northern Region of the United States

Analyzing Visuals Divide the class into groups. Have them discuss the roles played by geographical and human resources at the beginning of the factory system. Have a volunteer from each group report findings to the class. *(Answers will vary but should include the important role of water resources, the grouping of people in one place for work, comparison/contrast between methods of factory workers and those of craftspeople.)* **AL** **ELL** **BL** Interpersonal

See page 293C for other online activities.

ANSWER, p. 296

TAKING NOTES: competition, profit, private property, economic freedom

willingly gave up farm work to earn wages elsewhere. Second, New England's many rivers and streams offered the waterpower needed to run factory machinery. Third, the area had many ports. These ports allowed the shipping in of raw materials, such as cotton, and the shipping out of finished goods, such as cloth.

New Inventions

At the heart of the Industrial Revolution was **technology.** First, new machines changed the way people made cloth. Inventions such as the water frame and spinning jenny spun thread, and the power loom wove the thread into cloth. Compared to making thread or cloth by hand, the machines saved time and money.

Other inventions followed. In 1793 Eli Whitney invented the **cotton gin.** The word *gin* is short for "engine." It quickly and easily removed the seeds from picked cotton and allowed a huge increase in cotton production.

Whitney later accepted the task of making 10,000 muskets in two years for the government. At that time, skilled workers made muskets and other items one at a time. They made each part individually, and each weapon was unlike any other. Whitney made musket parts in large numbers. Each part was identical to others of its type. Even unskilled workers could then assemble a musket quickly. Plus, if a musket broke, a soldier could quickly replace the bad part with another that fit. Whitney's idea of **interchangeable parts** changed manufacturing forever.

The Rise of Factories

In 1790 Congress passed a patent law to protect the rights of inventors. A **patent** gives an inventor the sole legal right to make money from an invention for a certain period of time.

The British also tried to protect their inventions. One law prohibited textile workers from sharing technology or leaving the country. Still, a few British workers brought these secrets to the United States. One such worker was Samuel Slater. He memorized the design of the machines used in the British factory in which he worked.

In the 1790s, Slater built copies in the United States of British machines that made cotton thread. Slater's mill marked an important step in the Industrial Revolution in the United States.

Francis Cabot Lowell improved on Slater's mill in 1814. Lowell's Massachusetts textile, or cloth, factory not only made thread, it also wove the thread into cloth. Lowell began the factory system, in which all manufacturing steps are combined in one place.

University of Massachusetts Lowell, Center for Lowell History

Thinking Like a HISTORIAN

Making Comparisons

Working in a factory was very different from working and living on a farm. Think about how working for wages changed the lives of people who had been used to making most of the goods they needed. How do you think life was different for the women in the picture below? For more about making comparisons, review *Thinking Like a Historian.*

R

These young factory workers from the 1840s, known as "Lowell Girls," lived and worked together.

V

---

cotton gin a machine that removes seeds from cotton fiber

interchangeable part a part of a machine or device that can be replaced by another, identical part

patent sole legal right to an invention and its profits

Academic Vocabulary (Tier 2 Words)

technology equipment that makes use of advanced knowledge and skill to solve a problem or do a task

Lesson 1   **297**

R Reading Skills

Summarizing Ask students to read the text and then summarize the Industrial Revolution in the United States. **Ask:** What were some machines that were invented during this time period? (*Answer may include the spinning jenny, the water frame, the power loom, and the cotton gin.*) **AL** **ELL** How did interchangeable parts play a role in these machines? (*It made machines that needed repair easier to fix.*)

V Visual Skills

Analyzing Images Have students view the photo of the young factory workers from the 1840s. **Ask:** How does the photo indicate that the Lowell Girls are workers? (*Possible answer: The women are holding objects that look like tools and are wearing aprons.*) **ELL**

C Critical Thinking Skills

Making Inferences Discuss with students Congress passing patent laws in 1790 to protect inventors. **Ask:** Why were patents important? (*They protected inventors' rights.*) Before patents, what were some difficulties inventors likely faced? (*Other people stole their ideas and made money from them.*) **AL** **ELL**

Content Background Knowledge

Lowell Mills Many people who came to the United States from other countries made a visit to the Lowell textile mills. Visitors were impressed by the powerful machinery, huge size of the mills, and workforce that consisted mostly of women. By 1840, 32 textile mills lined the waterways and employed some 8,000 workers.

IMAGE

Water Mills

Explaining Use the interactive image of water mills to discuss their role in the Industrial Revolution. Students can also review the diagram in the textbook to learn more. **Ask:** What is the source of the power in the mill? (*the power of flowing water, which turns a wheel*) Why do you think this system increased efficiency? (*It was not necessary to transport products to different locations for each step. Workers could perform every step in one place.*) **BL**

See page 293C for other online activities.

networks — Water Mills
LOWELL FACTORY SYSTEM

More Information

ANSWER, p. 297

Thinking Like a Historian Students should note that working in a factory was very different from working at home. The women probably also had to move away from the farm, leave their families, and buy what they needed instead of making it.

R ## Reading Skills

Defining Have students read the section "Free Enterprise" so that they can define the terms associated with capitalism. **Ask:** What is capitalism? *(an economic system in which people own property and decide what to do with it)* What types of things are considered capital? *(Possible answers: buildings, land, machines, money, and any other items used to create wealth)* **AL** **ELL**

C ## Critical Thinking Skills

Analyzing Identify the major elements of the free enterprise system. **Ask:** How do businesses work in a free enterprise system? *(Business owners produce the products they think will sell the best.)* **AL** **ELL**

T ## Technology Skills

Researching on the Internet Have students use the Internet to locate additional information about the Lowell factory workers. Ask them to create a list of their findings. Have volunteers share their lists with the class.

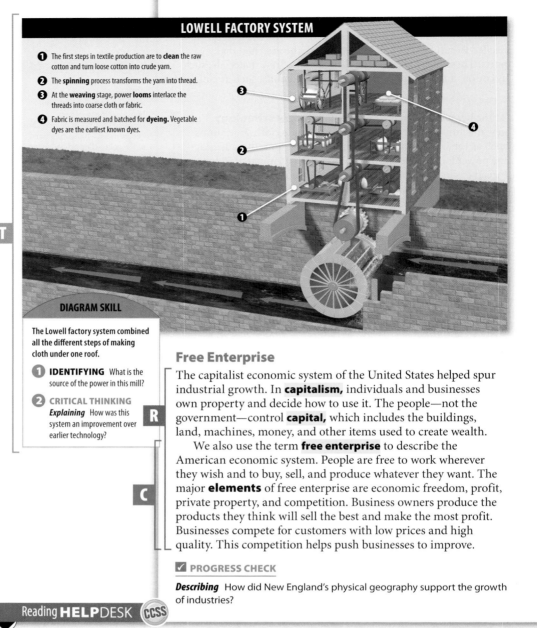

LOWELL FACTORY SYSTEM

❶ The first steps in textile production are to **clean** the raw cotton and turn loose cotton into crude yarn.

❷ The **spinning** process transforms the yarn into thread.

❸ At the **weaving** stage, power **looms** interlace the threads into coarse cloth or fabric.

❹ Fabric is measured and batched for **dyeing**. Vegetable dyes are the earliest known dyes.

T

DIAGRAM SKILL

The Lowell factory system combined all the different steps of making cloth under one roof.

❶ **IDENTIFYING** What is the source of the power in this mill?

❷ **CRITICAL THINKING**
Explaining How was this system an improvement over earlier technology?

R

Free Enterprise

The capitalist economic system of the United States helped spur industrial growth. In **capitalism,** individuals and businesses own property and decide how to use it. The people—not the government—control **capital,** which includes the buildings, land, machines, money, and other items used to create wealth.

We also use the term **free enterprise** to describe the American economic system. People are free to work wherever they wish and to buy, sell, and produce whatever they want. The major **elements** of free enterprise are economic freedom, profit, private property, and competition. Business owners produce the products they think will sell the best and make the most profit. Businesses compete for customers with low prices and high quality. This competition helps push businesses to improve.

C

☑ **PROGRESS CHECK**

Describing How did New England's physical geography support the growth of industries?

Reading **HELP**DESK **CCSS**

capitalism economic system in which people and companies own the means of production

capital money or other items, such as machines or buildings, used to create wealth

free enterprise a type of economy in which people are free to buy, sell, and produce whatever they want

netw❂rks *Online Teaching Options*

WHITEBOARD ACTIVITY

The Textile Industry

Comparing Use the interactive whiteboard activity with students to drag and drop information that compares the pre-Industrial Revolution process to the new process in the textile industry. Have students justify their responses in their own words. **AL** **ELL** Intrapersonal

See page 293C for other online activities.

ANSWERS, p. 298

DIAGRAM SKILL

1. the power of flowing water, which turns a wheel

2. **CRITICAL THINKING** By using water to power machines, mill owners could produce more goods more quickly and more cheaply.

☑ **PROGRESS CHECK** Farming was difficult, so there were more available workers; rivers and streams provided waterpower for machines; resources were located nearby; ports were available to ship goods.

Agriculture Grows

GUIDING QUESTION *Why did agriculture remain the leading occupation of Americans in the 1800s?*

While many New Englanders went to work in factories in the early 1800s, most Americans still lived and worked on farms. In the Northeast, farms were small, so a family could do all the necessary work. Farmers in the Northeast usually sold their products locally.

Agriculture moved west along with American settlers. Western farmers in the region north of the Ohio River found land that could support a thriving agriculture. Many of these farmers concentrated on raising pork and cash crops such as corn and wheat.

In the South, cotton production rose sharply. The demand for cotton grew steadily as textile factories appeared. In addition, the cotton gin allowed planters to grow cotton over a much wider area. Southern farmers seeking new land moved west to plant the valuable crop. Between 1790 and 1820, cotton production soared from 3,000 to 300,000 bales per year in the South.

The success and spread of cotton created a huge demand for enslaved workers. Trade in enslaved Africans expanded. Between 1790 and 1810, the number of enslaved Africans in the United States rose from about 700,000 to 1.2 million.

C2 As farmers moved west, the crops they planted varied according to the climate. While cotton was the common choice in the warmer South, grain crops such as wheat (shown here) and corn dominated the cooler areas to the north.

☑ **PROGRESS CHECK**

Determining Cause and Effect What are some of the significant effects of increased cotton production in the South?

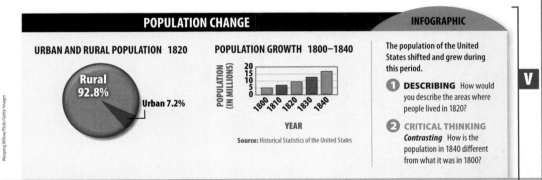

POPULATION CHANGE — INFOGRAPHIC

URBAN AND RURAL POPULATION 1820
Rural 92.8%
Urban 7.2%

POPULATION GROWTH 1800–1840
POPULATION (IN MILLIONS): 20, 15, 10, 5, 0
YEAR: 1800, 1810, 1820, 1830, 1840
Source: Historical Statistics of the United States

The population of the United States shifted and grew during this period.

1 **DESCRIBING** How would you describe the areas where people lived in 1820?

2 **CRITICAL THINKING** *Contrasting* How is the population in 1840 different from what it was in 1800?

Academic Vocabulary (Tier 2 Words)
element part of a larger whole

Lesson 1   **299**

CHAPTER 11, Lesson 1
A Growing Economy

C1 Critical Thinking Skills

Making Connections Tell students that even though many people worked in factories in the early 1800s (especially in New England), agriculture was still the main economic activity. As settlers moved west and acquired new land, more farms appeared. **Ask: Why did industrial growth begin in New England?** *(Farming was difficult in New England, so there were plenty of workers who were willing to work in factories. The area was also near many rivers and streams, which provided waterpower. The many ports made it easy to ship goods.)* **Logical/Mathematical**

C2 Critical Thinking Skills

Comparing and Contrasting Discuss with students the different types of farms in America and their effect on agricultural growth. **Ask: What were the differences between farms in the Northeast, West, and South?** *(In the Northeast, farms were small and family run. The products were sold locally. In the West, farmers mainly grew cash crops such as corn and wheat. They also raised pigs. In the South, cotton was a valuable crop and production was high.)* **What were the effects of the success of cotton?** *(More workers were needed, so slavery increased. There was a huge demand for enslaved workers.)*

V Visual Skills

Interpreting Review with students the circle and bar graphs about population change from the textbook. Be sure that students understand the difference between rural and urban. **AL** **ELL** **Ask: Where did most people live in 1820?** *(in rural areas)* **What was the most likely reason for this?** *(At this time, most people worked as farmers, so they lived in rural areas.)* **BL** **Visual/Spatial**

GRAPH

Measuring Population

Discussing Use the interactive graph to discuss measuring the population of the United States through the census. **Ask: When was the most recent census?** *(2010)*

See page 293C for other online activities.

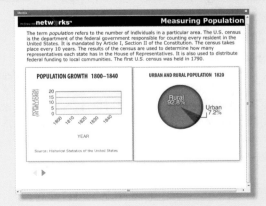

ANSWERS, p. 299

☑ **PROGRESS CHECK** Demand for enslaved African Americans increased, and trade in enslaved people became a big business.

INFOGRAPHIC

1. rural areas
2. **CRITICAL THINKING** It had grown from about 5 million to 17 million people.

V Visual Skills

Analyzing Images Use the image of South Street, New York, to discuss the development of cities and their design. **Ask: Where were cities likely to develop in the 1800s?** *(They developed where ships could reach them.)* **How would you describe city life based on the image?** *(Answers will vary but might include these: people were crowded together; commerce was a major feature; the seaport was the center of activity for city dwellers.)*

R Reading Skills

Defining Have students read the text, then discuss the definition and characteristics of a corporation. Discuss how a corporation is different from a business that only one or two people own. **Ask: What are corporations?** *(types of businesses that have many owners and are created according to certain laws)* **How did corporations become powerful and contribute to the success of industrialization?** *(They sold stock to raise money and to build factories so they were able to expand their business.)*

The area now known as the South Street Seaport in New York City offered hotels, restaurants, and businesses. The value of trade in the area increased from $84 million in 1825 to $146 million in 1836.

Economic Independence

GUIDING QUESTION *How did the growth of factories and trade affect cities?*

Small investors—such as shopkeepers, merchants, and farmers—provided the money necessary to build most new businesses. These people invested money in hopes of earning profits if the businesses were successful. Low taxes, minimum government regulations, and competition encouraged people to invest in new industries.

Growth of Corporations

In the 1830s, changes in the law paved the way for the growth of corporations. A corporation is a type of business that can have many owners. Because of their legal status, corporations can grow to a large size. They sell stock—shares of ownership in a company—to raise the money to build factories and expand their business. Large corporations began to appear in this era, and their great size helped drive industrialization.

Reading **HELP**DESK (CCSS)

Build Vocabulary: *Word Origins*

The word *corporation* comes from the Latin word *corpus,* which means "body." It is a group of people that acts together. A corporation continues to exist even after the people who first formed it have gone.

300 *Growth and Expansion*

netw⊙rks *Online Teaching Options*

IMAGE

Yellow Fever

Discussing Use the interactive image about yellow fever to discuss how disease spread quickly in cities, like this epidemic that spread in Philadelphia. **Ask: How does this information illustrate one of the dangers of living in the city?** *(When a lot of people live in close proximity, disease can spread. In this case, mosquitoes spread yellow fever from person to person.)* **BL** Logical/Mathematical

See page 293C for other online activities.

Cities Grow Up

The growth of factories and trade led to the growth of towns and cities. Many cities developed along rivers because factories could take advantage of the waterpower and easily ship goods to markets. Older cities such as New York, Boston, and Baltimore also grew as centers of commerce and trade.

Along New York City's South Street, shipping piers extended for 3 miles (5 km). One traveler wrote of the busy waterfront:

PRIMARY SOURCE

❝ Every thought, word, look, and action of the multitude seemed to be absorbed by commerce. ❞

—from *The Growing Years* by Margaret L. Coit

To the west, towns such as Pittsburgh, Cincinnati, and Louisville were located on major rivers. As farmers in the West shipped more products by water, these towns grew rapidly.

Cities and towns looked different from modern urban areas. They featured wood and brick buildings and unpaved streets. Barnyard animals often roamed freely. There were no sewers to carry away waste, so diseases such as cholera and yellow fever were a threat. Fire was another danger. Sparks from a fireplace could easily ignite wooden buildings. Fires could be disastrous since few cities had organized fire companies. Yet cities offered many opportunities, such as a variety of jobs and steady wages. As cities grew, residents built libraries, museums, and shops for people to enjoy during their leisure time. For many, the jobs and attractions of city life outweighed the dangers.

☑ **PROGRESS CHECK**

Analyzing Why were rivers important for the growth of cities?

LESSON 1 REVIEW (CCSS)

Review Vocabulary (Tier 3 Words)

1. Write a paragraph about Eli Whitney using the terms *cotton gin, patent,* and *interchangeable part.*
RH.6–8.4, WHST.6–8.4

2. Explain in a paragraph the connection between *capital, capitalism,* and *free enterprise.* RH.6–8.4, WHST.6–8.4

Answer the Guiding Questions

3. *Explaining* How did the introduction of factories change the way goods were made in the colonies?
RH.6–8.2

4. *Identifying* What economic activity was most widespread in the United States in the early 1800s?
RH.6–8.1

5. *Determining Cause and Effect* How did industrialization affect the way people lived in the United States? RH.6–8.5

6. **NARRATIVE** Imagine it is 1825 and you have recently moved from the family farm to New York City, where you work in a factory. Write a letter to a friend describing your new life. WHST.6–8.2, WHST.6–8.10

Lesson 1 **301**

LESSON 1 REVIEW ANSWERS

1. In 1793, Eli Whitney invented the cotton gin, for which he received a patent from the government. This machine quickly and efficiently removed the seeds from the cotton fiber. Whitney also pioneered the use of interchangeable parts, which could be put together quickly to make a complete product.

2. Capitalism, which is also sometimes referred to as free enterprise, is the economic system of the United States. With capitalism, individuals and businesses control capital and make decisions about its proper use.

3. Many steps that were originally done by hand could now be done by machine. Products could be made quickly, efficiently, and cheaply.

4. Farming remained the main economic activity. It moved west with settlement. Inventions such as the cotton gin encouraged planters to grow even more crops.

5. Many cities developed along rivers because factories could use waterpower and ship goods to other areas very easily.

6. Students' letters should contain details from the text, such as living conditions, work, and leisure time activities.

R Reading Skills

Explaining Direct students to read the text, and then ask a volunteer to explain the importance of waterways in moving goods from one place to another. **Ask: How did factory growth also lead to the development of cities?** *(Factories were also built along rivers to use waterpower to ship goods to other markets. The port areas became centers of commerce and trade.)*

W Writing Skills

Argument Use the primary source to develop students' ability to understand and paraphrase text. Have students write one or two sentences that convey, in their own words, the author's meaning. **Intrapersonal**

C Critical Thinking Skills

Drawing Conclusions Point out to students that towns and cities were growing rapidly in much of the country during this time. **Ask: What was life like in new cities and towns?** *(Life was difficult. The streets were unpaved and dangerous. The structures were often wooden, which made them fire hazards. There were no sewers, so waste and dirty water were in the street, causing disease. Cities did, however, offer opportunities such as jobs, libraries, museums, and shops.)*

Have students complete the Lesson 1 Review.

CLOSE & REFLECT

Listing Have the class list the ways industry changed American life in the early 1800s. Make a list on the board with the headings "Economy," "Family Life," and "Cities." Then ask students if any of these changes have continued into modern times.

ANSWER, p. 301

☑ **PROGRESS CHECK** Rivers provided a way for goods to be transported to markets and provided energy for factories.

ENGAGE

Bellringer Explain that people throughout history often settled near rivers. Use the chapter opener map to discuss the locations of industrial cities during the period. **Ask: Which industrial cities developed along rivers?** *(Pittsburgh, Cincinnati, Louisville, St. Louis)* **How did rivers help to promote early industrial growth?** *(Possible answers: transportation of goods and people; waterpower for machinery; water supply for people)* **Why might people who headed west want to locate rivers?** *(Rivers could provide water for agriculture, industrial development, transportation, and drinking.)* **ELL** Linguistic/Verbal

TEACH & ASSESS

R Reading Skills

Identifying Have students read the section "Daniel Boone and the Wilderness Road" to learn about how settlers moved west. Have students identify key people and ideas in the text. **Ask: Who was Daniel Boone?** *(He was an explorer and pioneer.)* **How did he contribute to westward exploration in the late 1700s?** *(He widened a Native American trail through the Appalachian Mountains called Warriors' Path. He explored all the way to Kentucky.)* **BL**

---

networks
There's More Online!

☑ **GRAPHIC ORGANIZER**
Transportation Developments

☑ **MAP**
• The National Road
• Canals 1820–1860

☑ **SLIDE SHOW**
The Erie Canal

☑ **VIDEO**

Lesson 2
Moving West

ESSENTIAL QUESTION *How does geography influence the way people live?*

IT MATTERS BECAUSE
Settling the West led to improvements in transportation that helped the nation grow and prosper.

Headed West

GUIDING QUESTION *What helped increase the movement of people and goods?*

In 1790 the first **census**—the official count of a population—**revealed** that there were nearly 4 million Americans. At that time, most of these people still lived in the narrow strip of land between the Appalachian Mountains and the Atlantic Ocean. That pattern, however, was changing. For years, a few rugged American settlers had been crossing the Appalachian Mountains and settling in western lands. Now, a steady stream of settlers began moving west.

Daniel Boone and the Wilderness Road

Explorer and pioneer Daniel Boone was among the early western pioneers. In 1769 he explored a Native American trail through the Appalachian Mountains. Called Warriors' Path, it led Boone through a break in the mountains—the Cumberland Gap. Beyond the gap lay the gentle hills of a land now called Kentucky. For two years, Boone explored the area's dense forests and lush meadows.

In 1775 Boone rounded up 30 skilled foresters to make the trail easier to cross for pioneers migrating west. Boone's crew widened Warriors' Path, cleared rocks from the Cumberland

(c) North Wind Picture Archives / Alamy, (c) Bettmann/Corbis, (r) Collection of the New-York Historical Society/Bridgeman Art Library

R

Reading HELPDESK **CCSS**

Taking Notes: *Sequencing* RH.6–8.5
Use a time line like this one to identify and place in chronological order the major developments in transportation during the early 1800s.

1800   1810   1820   1830

Content Vocabulary (Tier 3 Words)
• census   • canal
• turnpike   • lock

302 *Growth and Expansion*

---

networks *Online Teaching Options*

VIDEO

Daniel Boone

Using Visual Aids Use the video to discuss exploration that preceded westward expansion. **Ask: Why do you think Daniel Boone was regarded as a key figure in the history of exploration and expansion in the United States?** *(Answers will vary.)*

See page 293D for other online activities.

BBC Motion Gallery Education

ANSWER, p. 302

TAKING NOTES: 1807: Steamboat *Clermont* operates successfully; **1811:** Construction of the National Road begins; **1818:** First section of the National Road opens; **1825:** Erie Canal opens.

Gap, cut down trees in Kentucky, and marked the trail. The new Wilderness Road, as it came to be known, served as the main southern highway from the eastern states to the West. More than 100,000 people traveled it between 1775 and 1790.

Building Roadways

The nation needed good inland roads for travel and to ship goods. Private companies built many **turnpikes,** or toll roads. Tolls, or fees paid by travelers, helped pay the cost of building them. Many roads had a base of crushed stone. In some areas workers built "corduroy roads." These roads had a surface made up of logs laid side by side, like the ridges of corduroy cloth.

Ohio became a state in 1803. The new state asked the federal government to build a road to connect it with the East. In 1806 Congress approved funds for a national road to the West, though it took five more years for members to agree on the route.

Work on the project began in 1811 in Cumberland, Maryland. The start of the War of 1812 with Great Britain halted construction. As a result, the road's first section, which ran from Maryland to Wheeling in present-day West Virginia, did not open until 1818.

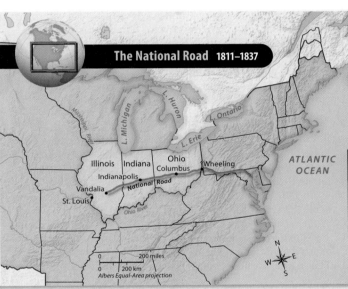

The National Road 1811–1837

POPULATION IN OHIO, INDIANA, AND ILLINOIS			
Year	Ohio	Indiana	Illinois
1800	45,465	5,641	—
1810	230,760	24,520	12,282
1820	581,434	147,178	55,211
1830	937,903	343,031	157,445

Source: United States Census

census the official count of a population
turnpike road on which tolls are collected

Academic Vocabulary (Tier 2 Words)
reveal to show

Lesson 2 **303**

Connections to TODAY

The National Road

Drivers today can follow a modern road that closely follows the route of the National Road. It is U.S. Route 40, which continues past the end of the original National Road all the way to Utah. The Internet also offers a great deal of information about the route and key points along it.

C

W

GEOGRAPHY CONNECTION

The National Road was the nation's first federally funded highway. When completed in 1837, the gravel road extended from the eastern seaboard to Vandalia, Illinois.

1 **MOVEMENT** What towns did the National Road pass through on its way to Vandalia?

2 **CRITICAL THINKING** **Speculating** In what ways do you think the National Road affected communities near which it passed?

C Critical Thinking Skills

Contrasting Explain to students that with the growth of cities and towns and the expansion west, the nation needed inland roads. **Ask:** **What were some differences between turnpikes, corduroy roads, and the National Road?** *(Turnpikes were toll roads. Travelers paid to use them, which helped pay the cost of building them. They were made from crushed stone. Some companies built corduroy roads, which were made up of logs laid side by side. The National Road was a government-funded road. It connected Ohio to the East.)* **AL** **ELL**

W Writing Skills

Argument Have students write two paragraphs in which they compare and contrast the types of roads during the period to the types of roads today. **Ask:** **How new is the idea of a toll road? Have the reasons for constructing roads changed between the 1800s and today?** **Logical/Mathematical**

Content Background Knowledge

Many new towns sprang up with the creation of the National Road. Traffic was heavy. The vehicles seen most often were the stagecoach and the Conestoga wagon. The stagecoach was fast—it could travel 60 to 70 miles in a day. The Conestoga wagon was yesterday's semitrailer truck. The "wagon stands," where travelers found lodging were yesterday's truck stops.

MAP

The National Road, 1811–1837

Analyzing Maps Display the interactive map of the National Road, and discuss with students how the road connected the coastline to the West. **Ask: What towns did the National Road pass through on the way to Vandalia, Illinois?** *(Columbus, Ohio, and Indianapolis, Indiana)* Point out the population chart next to the map in the textbook. **Ask: What was the population of Ohio in 1820?** *(581,434)* **AL** **How would you describe the population change in Indiana?** *(It grew rapidly.)* **How did the National Road play a role in the increase in population?** *(Because it was easier to travel due to the roads, more people moved west.)* **Visual/Spatial**

See page 293D for other online activities.

ANSWERS, p. 303

GEOGRAPHY CONNECTION

1 Columbus, Ohio, and Indianapolis, Indiana

2 **CRITICAL THINKING** Possible answer: Those communities grew and became centers of trade because people from the surrounding countryside came in order to take advantage of the road.

R Reading Skills

Summarizing After students have read the text, have a volunteer summarize the importance of the *Clermont* in the development of river travel. Discuss its significance in the use of steam power on waterways. **Ask: Why was river travel more popular than travel by road?** *(It was more comfortable, and river barges could carry more goods than a wagon.)* **What were the problems with river travel?** *(The early boats did not have the power to overcome currents and winds, and so traveling upstream was slow. All of the rivers flowed north to south, so you could not travel east to west.)* **What was Robert Fulton's role in solving these problems?** *(Fulton designed the steamboat, which had a very powerful engine that could travel upstream and against the wind.)* Remind students to use evidence from the text to support their responses.

C Critical Thinking Skills

Predicting Consequences Point out to students that tree branches and stumps are typically found in the rivers, and that water has to be placed in a container and heated to a very high temperature to create steam. **Ask: What kind of dangers might a steamboat encounter on the river?** *(An object in the river might snag the steamboat, causing damage or sinking; the steamboat might blow up if the steam is not watched carefully.)* **AL** **ELL**

Robert Fulton did not invent the technology of the steamboat, but his *Clermont* helped lead to the growth of steamboats in the United States. The 140-foot (43 m) *Clermont* was large, fast, and comfortable.

The route closely followed that of a military road George Washington had built in 1754. It eventually reached Ohio and then Vandalia, Illinois. Congress viewed the road as vital to military readiness but did not take on any other road-building projects.

Traveling on Rivers

River travel was far more comfortable than travel by road, which was often rough and bumpy. Also, boats or river barges could carry far larger loads of farm products or other goods.

River travel had two big drawbacks, however. First, most major rivers in the eastern **region** flowed in a north-south direction, while most people and goods were headed east or west. Second, while traveling downstream was easy, moving upstream against the current was slow.

In the 1780s and 1790s, boat captains were already using steam engines to power boats in quiet waters. These early engines, however, did not have enough power to overcome the strong currents and winds found in large rivers, lakes, or oceans.

The *Clermont*'s First Voyage

In 1802 Robert Livingston, a political and business leader, hired Robert Fulton to build a steamboat with a powerful engine. Livingston wanted the steamboat to carry cargo and passengers up the Hudson River from New York City to Albany.

In 1807 Fulton launched his steamboat, the *Clermont*. The boat made the 150-mile (241 km) trip from New York City to Albany in 32 hours. Using only sails, the trip would have taken four days.

The *Clermont* offered many comforts. Passengers could sit or stroll on deck or relax in sleeping compartments below deck. The engine was noisy, but its power provided a smooth ride.

Reading HELPDESK (CCSS)

canal an artificial waterway

lock separate compartment in which water levels rise and fall in order to raise or lower boats on a canal

Academic Vocabulary (Tier 2 Words)

region an area defined by a feature or characteristic

net**w**⊙rks *Online Teaching Options*

MAP

Canals, 1820–1860

Analyzing Maps Display the interactive map about the development of canals between 1820 and 1860 , and discuss the impact that canals had on business and travel. **Ask: What bodies of water did the Illinois and Michigan Canal connect?** *(Lake Michigan and the Illinois River)* **AL** **Why do you think so many of the canals were built north of the Ohio River and in the Northeast?** *(Those areas had more industrial development than the South.)* **BL**

See page 293D for other online activities.

Steamboats ushered in a new age of river travel. Shipping goods and moving people became cheaper and faster. Regular steamboat service began along the Mississippi River, between New Orleans and Natchez, Mississippi, in 1812. Steamboats also contributed to the growth of river cities such as Cincinnati and St. Louis. By 1850 some 700 steamboats were carrying cargo and passengers within the United States.

New Waterways

Steamboats improved transportation but were limited to major rivers. No such river linked the East and the West.

Business and government officials led by DeWitt Clinton in New York developed a plan to connect New York City with the Great Lakes region. They would build a **canal**—an artificial waterway—across the state. The canal would connect the Hudson River with Buffalo on Lake Erie. From these points, existing rivers and lakes could connect a much wider area.

The Erie Canal

Thousands of workers, many of them Irish immigrants, helped build the 363-mile (584 km) Erie Canal. Along the way they built a series of **locks**—separate compartments in which workers could raise or lower the water level. The locks worked like an escalator to raise and lower boats up and down hills.

Canal building was a hazardous task. Many workers died as a result of cave-ins or blasting accidents. Another threat was disease, which bred in the swamps where the workers toiled.

After more than eight years of hard work, the Erie Canal opened on October 26, 1825. Clinton, who was now governor of New York, boarded a barge in Buffalo and traveled on the canal to Albany. From there he sailed down the Hudson River to New York City. As crowds cheered, officials poured water from Lake Erie into the Atlantic Ocean.

R

T

> **GEOGRAPHY CONNECTION**
>
> The Erie Canal was just one of many canals built between 1820 and 1860.
>
> **1** **HUMAN-ENVIRONMENT INTERACTION** Which canal helped connect Lake Michigan to the Mississippi River?
>
> **2** **CRITICAL THINKING**
> *Making Inferences* Why do you think so many of the canals were built north of the Ohio River and in the Northeast?

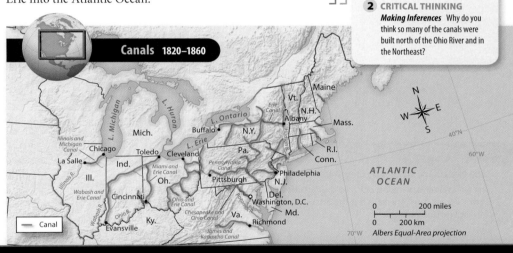

Canals 1820–1860

R Reading Skills

Discussing Ask students to take notes on the development of the Erie Canal as they read the text. Then, lead a class discussion about the construction of the Erie Canal. **Ask: Why was the Erie Canal built?** *(to connect Albany on the Hudson River to Buffalo on Lake Erie)*

T Technology Skills

Collaborating Divide the class into groups. Have them use the Internet to find information about the Erie Canal. Have a volunteer from each group report findings to the class. **Interpersonal**

Extend the discussion by asking students to raise their hands if they have replaced things they once used. **Ask: Why do people replace things?** *(Answers may vary but should include because they find something better or more useful.)* Point out that canals are not popular methods of transport today. **Ask: What might have caused canals to fall into disuse?** *(Answers should include the development of faster, less costly, and more convenient methods of transportation.)*

SLIDE SHOW

The Erie Canal

Analyzing Launch the interactive slide show to discuss the construction of the Erie Canal. **Ask: What were conditions like for the workers who built the canal?** *(Conditions were dangerous. Canal walls collapsed on workers, and others died in blasting accidents. Disease spread among workers.)* **How was the Erie Canal project financed?** *(It was financed by the State of New York and other investors.)* **What was Benjamin White's role in the project?** *(He created a cement that could be used underwater. This sped up the project and reduced cost.)*

See page 293D for other online activities.

netw⊕rks   The Erie Canal

Once investors saw the first section of the canal built, they were eager to lend money for its completion. It cost a total of about $7 million, which was soon repaid through toll charges. The cost of shipping cargo before the canal was built was about $100 per ton. After the canal was built, the cost fell to less than $10 per ton. Within 15 years, the Erie Canal was transporting almost one million tons of goods a year.

ANSWERS, p. 305

GEOGRAPHY CONNECTION

1 the Chicago and Michigan Canal

2 **CRITICAL THINKING** Those areas had more industrial development than the South, and they had more bodies of water near the industrial areas that could be connected by canals.

V Visual Skills

Analyzing Images Use the painting of the Erie Canal to discuss the importance of waterways in the development of population centers. **Ask: What do you see in the painting that demonstrates how the Erie Canal affected the communities along its length?** *(Answers should include comments about the presence of buildings and transport of goods by water.)* **Visual/Spatial**

W Writing Skills

Informative/Explanatory Review the text in the "Canal Travel Expands" section and recall the discussion of the painting. Have students write two sentences connecting the painting to what they have learned about the importance of waterways. **AL** **ELL**

The Erie Canal brought industry and economic growth to communities all along its length.

▶ **CRITICAL THINKING**
Analyzing Why do you think the canal helped populations grow?

Canal Travel Expands

At first, the Erie Canal did not allow steamboats because their powerful engines could cause damage to the canal's earthen banks. Instead, teams of mules or horses hauled the boats and barges. A two-horse team pulled a 100-ton (91 t) barge about 24 miles (39 km) in one day. This was fast compared with travel by wagon. In the 1840s, workers strengthened the canal banks so that steam tugboats could pull the barges.

The Erie Canal's success did not go unnoticed. By 1850 the country had more than 3,600 miles (5,794 km) of canals. Canals lowered shipping costs and brought prosperity to towns along their routes. They also linked regions of a growing country.

☑ **PROGRESS CHECK**

Finding the Main Idea Why were canals built?

The Move West Continues

GUIDING QUESTION *Why did Americans tend to settle near rivers?*

The United States added four new states between 1791 and 1803—Vermont, and the western states of Kentucky, Tennessee, and Ohio. Then, between 1816 and 1821, Indiana, Illinois, Mississippi, Alabama, and Missouri also became states.

Collection of the New-York Historical Society/Bridgeman Art Library

Reading **HELP**DESK (CCSS)

Build Vocabulary: *Multiple Meaning Words*
Some words with the same spelling and sound have more than one meaning. The word *lock* also means "a device for keeping something (door, window, box) closed and unable to open."

306 *Growth and Expansion*

---

netw⊙rks   *Online Teaching Options*

SLIDE SHOW

Pioneer Life

Making Connections Review with students the interactive slide show on daily pioneer life in the West. **Ask: What was life like for adults?** *(Life was difficult. Men and women worked alongside each other. The houses they built and tools they used were very simple. There were no services such as hospitals. The pioneers did manage to have fun at social gatherings.)* What was life probably like for children? *(The school did not have many books or resources, so children learned from the Bible or a simple spelling book. Children probably had to work hard alongside their parents to build cabins, make tools, and prepare meals.)*

See page 293D for other online activities.

ANSWERS, p. 306

CRITICAL THINKING The canal allowed businesses to prosper, hire workers, and attract newcomers.
☑ **PROGRESS CHECK** to create waterways where none naturally existed

The formation of new states reflected the dramatic growth of the region west of the Appalachians. In 1800 only 387,000 white settlers lived west of the Appalachian Mountains. By 1820 that number had grown to more than 2.4 million people. Ohio, for example, had only 45,000 settlers in 1800. By 1820 it had 581,000 residents.

Early pioneer families often settled in communities along the great rivers, such as the Ohio and the Mississippi. These waterways provided a highway for shipping crops and other goods to markets. The growth of canals also helped expand the area open to settlement. Canals allowed people to settle on lands farther from the large rivers.

People often preferred to settle with others from their original homes. It was mainly people from Tennessee and Kentucky who settled Indiana, for example. Michigan's pioneers came mostly from New England.

Western families often gathered together for social events. Men took part in sports such as wrestling. Women met for quilting and sewing parties. Both men and women took part in cornhuskings. These were gatherings where farm families shared the work of stripping the outer layers from corn.

Life in the West did not have many of the conveniences of Eastern town life. The pioneers had not traveled to the West to live a pampered life. They wanted to make new lives for themselves and their families.

At the same time, these new settlers brought with them many of the same hopes and dreams held by people in the East. In this way, the western migration of American pioneers helped spread an American culture and way of life.

☑ **PROGRESS CHECK**

Describing What was life like for families on the western frontier?

Connections to TODAY

Moving West

Americans have always been on the move, searching for new opportunities or better climates. In recent years, leading destinations for American migrants have been states such as Florida, Arizona, and Nevada. This migration pattern represents a long-standing trend of Americans leaving the Northeast and Midwest for the South, West, and Southwest.

LESSON 2 REVIEW CCSS

Review Vocabulary (Tier 3 Words)

1. Use each of these terms in a different sentence that explains the term's meaning. RH.6–8.4

   a. census   b. turnpike

2. Write a sentence that explains how canals and locks are related. RH.6–8.4

Answer the Guiding Questions

3. *Summarizing* What did Americans do in the late 1700s and early 1800s to improve the movement of people and goods? RH.6–8.2

4. *Describing* How did rivers play a role in the settlement of the West? RH.6–8.2

5. **INFORMATIVE/EXPLANATORY** Write a paragraph explaining how life in the West was different from life in the East. WHST.6–8.2, WHST.6–8.9

Lesson 2   **307**

CHAPTER 11, Lesson 2

C1 Critical Thinking Skills

Making Connections Explain to students that river travel and the building of roads and canals increased the movement of settlers westward. **Ask: What were the population trends between 1800 and 1820?** *(Most people lived east of the Appalachian Mountains around 1800. Only 378,000 white settlers lived west of the mountain chain at that time. By 1820, there were 2.4 million people living west of the Appalachians.)* **BL**

C2 Critical Thinking Skills

Making Inferences Remind students that there was a dramatic expansion west from 1800 to 1820. **Ask: What factors probably made life in the West difficult?** *(There were no buildings on the land. Everything had to be built from the ground up, so it was difficult work. Forests probably had to be cleared and roads built. There were no sewer systems and disease may have spread. People missed the places and people they had left behind.)* **BL**

Have students complete the Lesson 2 Review.

CLOSE & REFLECT

Discussing Remind students that roads and canals helped Americans move west to new areas. This helped change the shape of the geographic area occupied by U.S. citizens. Discuss which type of transportation was more important in expanding to the West—river and canal travel or travel on roads and trails.

LESSON 2 REVIEW ANSWERS

1. **a.** A census is the counting of a population. **b.** Many early roads were turnpikes, or toll roads.

2. Locks are separate compartments in which water levels are raised or lowered. They were built into canals and provided a way to raise and lower boats at places where canal elevation changed.

3. Private companies built turnpikes, and the federal government built the National Road. Inventors built steamboats, and governments and business leaders built canals.

4. Much Western settlement took place along major rivers, which made it possible for settlers to easily ship their crops and other goods to markets.

5. Life in the West did not include the conveniences of Eastern town life. The West was settled by people who did not seek comforts and conveniences but rather an opportunity to build a better life for themselves.

ANSWER, p. 307

☑ **PROGRESS CHECK** They settled with others from their home communities along rivers, gathered for social events and to share work, and lived without modern conveniences.

ENGAGE

Bellringer Tell students that the country's industry boomed, and the nation experienced a period called "The Era of Good Feelings" after the War of 1812. However, divisions began to take place between different groups. Have students speculate about the reasons that good feelings ran high in this era. Point out that they will learn in this lesson how the nation experienced a short period of unity and then began to divide over political policies.

TEACH & ASSESS

R Reading Skills

Discussing Direct students to read the text. Discuss why the era after the War of 1812 was called "The Era of Good Feelings," including the feeling of unity that swept the nation and how it affected the presidential election of 1812. **Ask: How was President James Monroe an example of this thinking?** *(He had been involved in politics since the revolution, so he represented an older time. Also, he wore old-fashioned clothes and represented a united country free of political strife.)*

W Writing Skills

Informative/Explanatory Have students write a paragraph explaining how the War of 1812 changed the way people felt about the role of the central government. On that basis, invite students to include comments about political parties today. *(Answers will vary, but students should recognize that the War of 1812 brought a growing sense of nationalism and support for central government.)* **BL**

ANSWER, p. 308

TAKING NOTES: Maine: admitted as a free state; **Missouri:** admitted as a slave state; **Louisiana Territory:** slavery banned north of a line running west from the southern boundary of Missouri

---

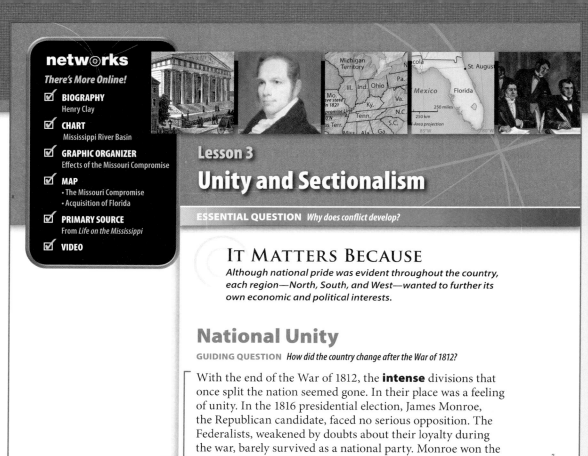

networks
There's More Online!

☑ **BIOGRAPHY**
Henry Clay

☑ **CHART**
Mississippi River Basin

☑ **GRAPHIC ORGANIZER**
Effects of the Missouri Compromise

☑ **MAP**
• The Missouri Compromise
• Acquisition of Florida

☑ **PRIMARY SOURCE**
From *Life on the Mississippi*

☑ **VIDEO**

Lesson 3
Unity and Sectionalism

ESSENTIAL QUESTION *Why does conflict develop?*

IT MATTERS BECAUSE
Although national pride was evident throughout the country, each region—North, South, and West—wanted to further its own economic and political interests.

National Unity

GUIDING QUESTION *How did the country change after the War of 1812?*

With the end of the War of 1812, the **intense** divisions that once split the nation seemed gone. In their place was a feeling of unity. In the 1816 presidential election, James Monroe, the Republican candidate, faced no serious opposition. The Federalists, weakened by doubts about their loyalty during the war, barely survived as a national party. Monroe won the election by an overwhelming margin.

A Boston newspaper called this time the Era of Good Feelings. The new president was a living, breathing symbol of this mood. Monroe had been involved in national politics since the American Revolution. He wore breeches, or knee-length pants, and powdered wigs—styles no longer in fashion. Yet with his sense of dignity, Monroe represented a united country, free of political strife.

Outgoing President James Madison's last message to Congress in 1817 expressed a growing nationalism, or strong loyalty to the nation. The War of 1812 had made clear that Jefferson's ideal of a limited central government could not meet the needs of a nation in times of crisis. Sounding more like a Federalist than a Republican,

Reading HELPDESK **CCSS**

Taking Notes: *Determining Cause and Effect*
Use a diagram like this one to show how the Missouri Compromise affected different parts of the country.
RH.6–8.5

308 *Growth and Expansion*

Maine	→	
Missouri	→	
Louisiana Territory	→	

Content Vocabulary (Tier 3 Words)
• sectionalism • interstate commerce
• monopoly • cede

---

networks *Online Teaching Options*

VIDEO

President James Monroe and the Era of Good Feelings

Using and Citing Information Use the video to discuss the period. Note that the video begins and ends with the same image. **Ask: Is "The People's Rights" an appropriate slogan to describe the Era of Good Feelings?** *(Answers will vary.)*

See page 293E for other online activities.

Madison urged the federal government to guide the growth of trade and industry. The large Republican majority in Congress agreed. The Republicans, who had once strongly supported states rights, now promoted federal power.

Henry Clay's American System

Henry Clay, a Republican and speaker of the house, proposed a nationalist program to help the nation grow. Clay's American System aimed to help the economy in each section of the country and increase the power of the federal government. Clay called for higher tariffs, a new Bank of the United States, and **internal** improvements, including the building of roads, bridges, and canals.

Not all congressional leaders agreed with Clay, and they did not accept all of his ideas. Congress did not spend much money on internal improvements, but other parts of the American System did become law.

The Second Bank of the United States

The charter for the First Bank of the United States expired in 1811, and Congress let the bank die. In 1816 the Republican majority in Congress brought the national bank back to life. President Madison signed the bill creating the Second Bank of the United States.

After the First Bank closed, many state banks had acted unwisely. They made too many loans and allowed too much money into circulation. These actions led to inflation, a rise in the prices of goods. As prices rose, American families could buy less and less with each dollar. The absence of a national bank also meant the federal government had no safe place to keep its funds. The Second Bank of the United States restored order to the money supply, helping American businesses to grow.

Competition From Britain

Another challenge facing the economy was a flood of British goods following the War of 1812. British factories often had more advanced technology and methods than American factories. The British turned out goods of higher quality and at a lower price than goods made in the United States. Naturally, buyers preferred these goods. By flooding the United States with their goods, the British hoped to keep American businesses from competing.

Congress created the Second Bank of the United States to restore order to the United States money supply. Today, the Federal Reserve System serves that same function.

▶ CRITICAL THINKING
Making Connections Is the idea of having a central bank for the nation consistent with the idea of free enterprise? Explain.

Academic Vocabulary (Tier 2 Words)
intense very strong
internal within the country

Lesson 3 **309**

C Critical Thinking Skills

Making Connections Use Independence Day celebrations to further discuss America's growing feelings of nationalism. **Ask: Why do you think Independence Day celebrations became popular during this period?** *(After victory in the War of 1812, people felt a strong sense of nationalism for their country. Celebrating independence was one way people showed their nationalism.)* Remind students that Independence Day was a day for celebration, but holidays are observed also to honor or reflect. **Ask: Which other national holidays are expressions of unity and patriotism?** *(Answers may include Presidents Day, Memorial Day, Flag Day, Veterans Day, or gatherings to remember the events of September 11, 2001.)* AL ELL Verbal/Linguistic

R Reading Skills

Summarizing After they read the text, have student volunteers summarize the key points about Clay's American System. *(higher tariffs, a new Bank of the United States, and internal improvements to the nation such as the building of roads, bridges, and canals)* **Ask: What was the purpose of the American System Clay proposed?** *(Clay wanted to improve the nation by helping the economy in each section and by increasing the power of the federal government.)* BL

Content Background Knowledge

- Congress had struggled since the earliest years of the United States to determine the powers of the federal government in developing the nation's economy.
- Clay's American System remains one of the most significant attempts of the federal government to balance agriculture, trade, and industry.

IMAGE

The Second Bank of the United States

Determining Cause and Effect Display the interactive image about the creation of the Second Bank of the United States and its importance to the U.S. financial system.

Ask: What was the result of the closure of the First Bank of the United States? *(State banks had fewer restrictions. They made too many loans and allowed too much money into circulation, which resulted in inflation.)* **How does a chartered bank help people with economic affairs?** *(It provides different types of savings accounts, keeps enough money to process transactions, and loans money to individuals and commercial borrowers.)* BL

See page 293E for other online activities.

ANSWER, p. 309

CRITICAL THINKING Possible answer: Yes. The bank provided stability to the money supply and allowed businesses to grow.

C Critical Thinking Skills

Analyzing Discuss with students the other challenges facing the economy after the War of 1812. **Ask: What impact did British goods have on the American economy?** *(There was a flood of British goods into the economy and with better factories that had advanced technology, the British produced more goods of higher quality at a lower price. American businesses could not compete.)* **What was the purpose of placing tariffs on imported goods?** *(The purpose was to promote American manufacturing. Imported European goods became more expensive because of the tariff that had to be paid.)* **AL** **ELL**

R Reading Skills

Identifying Direct students to read the section of the text titled "Growing Sectionalism." Ask students to identify how the interests in different parts of the country led to growing sectionalism in the United States. Have students define the term *sectionalism*. **AL** **ELL** **Ask: What were the three distinct sections of the country?** *(the North, the South, and the West)* **Who were the leaders of each section of the country in Congress?** *(North: Daniel Webster; South: John C. Calhoun; West: Henry Clay)* **AL** Divide the class into groups and have them brainstorm reasons that geography and economics might have encouraged each section to see itself as having different interests from the other sections. Then, working together as a class, make a list of these reasons on the whiteboard. **BL** **Interpersonal**

Thinking Like a HISTORIAN

Understanding Cause and Effect

The varying views toward tariffs in different regions of the country were the result of each region's unique economy. The South, for example, not only purchased manufactured goods from foreign nations, its planters also sold crops overseas. In addition to raising costs for Southern consumers, a protective tariff threatened to hurt foreign consumers of Southern cotton—and so the Southern planters themselves. For more about understanding cause and effect, review *Thinking Like a Historian.*

New Tariffs

American manufacturers called for high tariffs to protect their growing industries. To address this problem, Congress passed the Tariff of 1816. Unlike earlier revenue tariffs, which were meant to provide income for the federal government, this tariff was designed to protect American manufacturers from foreign competition by placing high taxes on imports. Merchants who paid the tariff on imported goods simply added the cost of the tariff to their prices. This made imported items more expensive for consumers and encouraged them to buy cheaper, American-made goods.

When Congress passed protective tariffs in 1818 and 1824 that were even higher than the Tariff of 1816, some Americans protested. Southerners were especially angry. They felt that the tariff protected Northern manufacturers at their expense. The South had few factories, so people there saw little benefit from high tariffs. What the Southern states did see were higher prices for the goods they had to buy.

Growing Sectionalism

The tariff dispute illustrated a growing **sectionalism** (SEHK·shuh·nuh·lih·zuhm)—differences in the goals and interests of different parts of the country. Such differences had existed since colonial times. Now, it seemed, they were growing sharper. In fact, they soon brought an end to the Era of Good Feelings.

In the early 1800s, three distinct sections developed in the United States—the North, the South, and the West. The North included New England and the Mid-Atlantic states. The South covered what is now the Southeast. The West included the area between the Appalachian Mountains and the Mississippi River. Geography, economics, and history all contributed to sectional differences and differing ways of life in the United States. As the differences grew deeper, however, people began to wonder whether sectionalism might divide the nation.

Each section of the country had a strong voice in Congress in the early 1800s. Henry Clay of Kentucky represented the West. John C. Calhoun of South Carolina spoke for Southern interests. Daniel Webster of Massachusetts protected the interests of New England. Each leader, although nationalist, remained concerned with protecting the interests of his own section of the country.

R

Reading **HELP**DESK (CCSS)

sectionalism rivalry based on the special interests of different areas

---

netw◉rks   *Online Teaching Options*

CHART

Graphic Organizer

Identifying Points of View Have students create a table graphic organizer about the growing sectionalism in the United States. Have them label the columns with "North," "South," and "West." Then have students fill in the organizers with information about each section's possible view on economics, history, politics, and expansion, as well as the names of the proponents for each section in Congress. **BL** **Visual/Spatial**

See page 293E for other online activities.

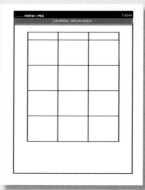

Nationalism and the Supreme Court

In three decisions in the early 1800s, the Supreme Court backed the powers of the national government over the states. During this time, Chief Justice John Marshall provided strong leadership.

In the case of *Fletcher* v. *Peck* in 1810, the Court ruled that courts could declare acts of a state government void if they violated provisions of the Constitution. Then, in 1819, the Court decided the case of *McCulloch* v. *Maryland*. It said that the state of Maryland could not tax the local office of the Bank of the United States because it was the property of the national government. Allowing such a tax, the Court said, would give states too much power over the national government.

The Court also ruled that the national bank was constitutional, even though the Constitution did not specifically give Congress the power to create a bank. Marshall observed that the Constitution specifically gave Congress power to issue money, borrow money, and collect taxes. Congress could also, he reasoned, do whatever was "necessary and proper" to carry out those powers.

In 1824 the Court again ruled in favor of federal government power in *Gibbons* v. *Ogden*. The state of New York had granted a **monopoly** (muh•NAH•puh•lee)—sole control of an industry—to a steamship operator running ships between New York and New Jersey. Under New York's law, no other operator could run steamboats on the same route. The Supreme Court said that only Congress had the power to make laws governing **interstate commerce,** or trade between states.

Missouri Statehood

In 1819 the Missouri Territory asked Congress for admission as a state. Most Missouri settlers had come from Kentucky and Tennessee, which allowed slavery. They believed slavery ought to be legal in Missouri.

Representative James Tallmadge proposed that Missouri gradually abolish slavery in order to be admitted to the Union. The House passed this plan, but the Senate blocked it.

At the time, the population in the North was slightly larger than in the slave states of the South. Consequently, the North had 105 members in the House of Representatives compared to the South's 81 members. Representation in the Senate was balanced, with 11 slave states and 11 free states. The addition of Missouri as a free state would put the South in the minority in both houses of Congress.

monopoly a market where there is only one provider
interstate commerce economic activity taking place between two or more states

Christie's Images/Bridgeman Art Library

BIOGRAPHY

Henry Clay (1777–1852)

Henry Clay had a long career in Congress that began when he was elected to fill a Senate vacancy when he was just 29, a year shy of the Constitution's age requirement. Clay's ability to resolve arguments earned him the nickname "The Great Compromiser." He believed strongly in the nation. In a speech on the Senate floor, he once said: "If the ... sad event of the dissolution [breaking up] of this Union is to happen, ... I shall not survive to behold the sad and heart-rending [upsetting] spectacle."

▶ **CRITICAL THINKING**
Analyzing Primary Sources How does Clay's statement reflect nationalist views?

R Reading Skills

Listing Make a chart with two columns and three rows on the whiteboard. List each of the Supreme Court cases in the first row. Then ask student volunteers to complete the chart by summarizing the Court's ruling on cases regarding the power of the national government over the states. Remind students to use details from their text. *(Fletcher v. Peck, 1810: Courts can declare acts of a state government void if they violate provisions of the Constitution; McCullough v. Maryland, 1819: State of Maryland could not tax the local office of the Bank of the United States because it was the property of the national government; Gibbons v. Ogden, 1824: Ruled in favor of federal government power, stating that New York could not make laws governing interstate commerce such as steamships running between New York and New Jersey.)* **Ask:** What effect did these rulings have on the power of the federal government? *(They increased its power.)*

C Critical Thinking Skills

Drawing Conclusions Explain that the admission of Missouri to the Union was a debated topic. Point out that Congressman James Tallmadge, Jr., failed to resolve the issue. **Ask:** Who settled Missouri, and what role did these settlers play in the debate about the admission of Missouri to the Union? *(The settlers came from Kentucky and Tennessee, which allowed slavery.)* **Ask:** What might have happened if Missouri became a state? *(It could have become a slave state and increased the sense of sectionalism.)*

V Visual Skills

Integrating Visual Information Have students read the "Biography" section on Henry Clay. **Ask:** How does the image of Henry Clay relate to the meaning of his words? *(He appears to be young; he expects the Union to last well past his time.)* ELL Visual/Spatial

---

MAP

The Missouri Compromise

Using Visual Aids Use the interactive map about the Missouri Compromise of 1820 to discuss the impact of this compromise on the United States. **Ask:** How many states developed from the compromise? *(two; Missouri and Maine)* What did it state about the Unorganized Territory? *(It permitted slavery south of the southern boundary of Missouri.)* Why was this only a temporary solution? *(When more states developed from new territories, the debate would continue.)*

See page 293E for other online activities.

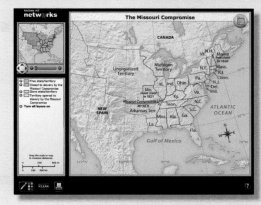

ANSWER, p. 311

CRITICAL THINKING Clay's statement reflects a belief in the strength and greatness of a union that should not be broken apart.

R Reading Skills

Summarizing Discuss with students the first paragraph of "The Missouri Compromise" section. Have volunteers take turns describing Henry Clay's proposal. *(Maine in the Northeast would enter the Union as a free state. Missouri would enter as a slave state. The balance of power in Congress would remain equal between North and South: 12 free states and 12 slave states.)* **AL** **ELL**

C Critical Thinking Skills

Identifying Central Issues Explain to students that the Missouri Compromise was an attempt to solve the problems related to the distribution of powers in Congress between the North and the South. **Ask: Why did Henry Clay propose a compromise for the admission of Missouri to statehood?** *(People who settled Missouri believed slavery ought to be legal in Missouri. The admission of Missouri as a slave state would have increased the power in Congress of the South against the North.)* **Why was the Missouri Compromise a temporary solution?** *(As settlers moved into western lands, more states could be added. If the problem of slavery remained unsolved, the balance of powers in Congress would continue to divide the nation.)*

GEOGRAPHY CONNECTION

Missouri's application for statehood sparked a national debate that led to the Missouri Compromise.

1 **REGION** Under the Missouri Compromise, was the Unorganized Territory open or closed to slavery?

2 **CRITICAL THINKING**
Analyzing Do you think the Missouri Compromise was a permanent solution to the question of slavery in new states? Explain.

The Missouri Compromise 1820

Free state/territory
Closed to slavery by the Missouri Compromise
Slave state/territory
Territory opened to slavery by the Missouri Compromise

The Missouri Compromise

R Debates in Congress heated to the boiling point. Fearing a split in the Union, Henry Clay suggested the Missouri Compromise. Clay proposed that Maine, in the Northeast, enter the Union as a free state. Missouri could then enter as a slave state. This would keep an even balance of power in the Senate—12 free states and 12 slave states.

The Missouri Compromise also addressed the question of slavery in the rest of the Louisiana Purchase territory. The compromise drew a line west from the southern boundary of Missouri—at 36°30' N latitude. The compromise blocked slavery north of the line but permitted it south of the line.

C The Missouri Compromise promised a temporary solution to sectional conflict. It did nothing to solve the basic problem, however. Americans who moved west took their different ways of life with them. White Southerners wanted to take an economy based on slavery to their new homes. Northerners believed in labor by free people and wanted to establish that in the West. It was a disagreement that seemed to have no peaceful solution.

☑ **PROGRESS CHECK**

Explaining Describe how the Supreme Court's decisions affected the power of the federal government.

Reading HELPDESK (CCSS)

Reading Strategy: *Summarizing*
When you summarize, you reduce the important content into short and simple form. Summarize the effects of the Missouri Compromise described on this page.

312 *Growth and Expansion*

ANSWERS, p. 312

GEOGRAPHY CONNECTION

1 closed to slavery by the Missouri Compromise

2 **CRITICAL THINKING** Possible answer: no, because there was much more land in North America that the United States would eventually acquire

☑ **PROGRESS CHECK** The Supreme Court strengthened the power of the federal government over the power of the states. Chief Justice John Marshall argued that the Constitution gives specific powers to the federal government, that take precedence over state government powers.

Reading Strategy By allowing Missouri to enter the Union as a slave state and dividing states that entered later at the 36°30' N latitude, the Missouri Compromise kept a balance of power in the Senate, provided a solution to the issue of slavery in the Louisiana Purchase territory, and promised a temporary solution to sectional conflict.

---

netw⊚rks   *Online Teaching Options*

GRAPHIC ORGANIZER

Taking Notes: *Determining Cause and Effect:* **The Missouri Compromise**

Using and Citing Information Use the interactive graphic organizer as students discuss how the Missouri Compromise affected different parts of the country. **AL** **ELL** **Ask: Who proposed the Missouri Compromise?** *(Henry Clay)* **What did it state?** *(Under the Missouri Compromise, Maine would enter the Union as a free state and Missouri would enter as a slave state. It also banned slavery in the territory north of a line running west from Missouri's southern border.)*

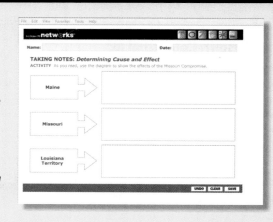

See page 293E for other online activities.

Foreign Affairs

GUIDING QUESTION *How did the United States define its role in the Americas?*

The War of 1812 heightened Americans' pride in their country. Americans also realized that the United States had to establish a new relationship with the "Old World"—the powers of Europe.

Relations with Britain

In the 1817 Rush-Bagot Agreement, the United States and Britain agreed to limit the number of armed naval vessels on the Great Lakes. Each country was to take apart or destroy other armed ships on the Great Lakes.

The Convention of 1818 set the northern boundary of the Louisiana Territory between the United States and Canada at the 49th parallel. The convention also created a secure border. Each country agreed to maintain its border without armed forces. Secretary of State John Quincy Adams also negotiated the right of Americans to settle in the Oregon Country.

Relations with Spain

Spain owned the colonies of East Florida and West Florida. In 1810 American settlers in West Florida rebelled against Spanish rule. The United States government then argued that West Florida was included in the Louisiana Purchase. In 1810 and 1812, the United States took control of sections of West Florida.

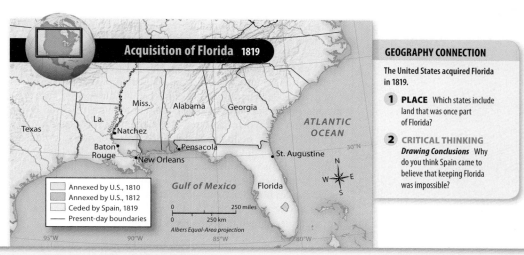

GEOGRAPHY CONNECTION

The United States acquired Florida in 1819.

1 PLACE Which states include land that was once part of Florida?

2 CRITICAL THINKING *Drawing Conclusions* Why do you think Spain came to believe that keeping Florida was impossible?

Reading in the Content Area: *Lines of Latitude*

The map on this page shows a single line running horizontally—a line of latitude, or a parallel. Marked 30°N, this line runs close to the city of St. Augustine in Florida. Further north, not shown on this map, is the 49th parallel. This line became the boundary between Canada and the Louisiana territory in 1818.

Lesson 3 **313**

C Critical Thinking Skills

Making Inferences Point out that the United States entered into agreements that ruled out the use of arms on the Great Lakes and at its border. **Ask: Why do you think the United States did this?** *(Answers may include national pride and the advantages of peace: The nation was young and had fewer resources for war than the "old powers of Europe"; the nation needed time to grow stronger; war would hamper industrial growth.)* BL

R Reading Skills

Identifying After students read the text on this page, refer them to the map of the Missouri Compromise again to discuss the boundaries established between the United States and British Canada after the War of 1812. **Ask: What did the Rush-Bagot Agreement do?** *(It limited the number of naval vessels on the Great Lakes and removed weapons along the border of the United States and Canada.)* **What was the border between the United States and Canada according to the Convention of 1818?** *(the 49th parallel)* Have students locate this boundary on the map. *(They will have to approximate this parallel based on the 40th and 50th parallels and the northern border of the Unorganized Territory.)* BL **What else did the Convention provide?** *(Americans could settle in the Oregon Country; the United States–Canada border would be maintained without the use of armed forces.)*

Content Background Knowledge

In 1565, the Spanish established at St. Augustine in Florida the first enduring settlement in the United States. This occurred more than 50 years before the Pilgrims landed at Plymouth Rock. The stone fortress called the Castillo San Marcos was built in the late 1600s as a defense against the British. Today, the Castillo San Marcos attracts many visitors.

MAP

Acquisition of Florida

Using Visual Aids Use the interactive map about the acquisition of Florida to discuss the territories still under Spanish control and the relationship between Spain and the United States. AL **Ask: Why was Spanish control of Florida a source of anger for white Southerners?** *(Enslaved Africans often ran away to Florida because they knew that Americans had no authority to capture them there.)* **What was the conflict created by the Louisiana Purchase of 1803?** *(Spain and the United States disagreed over whether West Florida was included in the Louisiana Purchase.)* **Visual/Spatial**

See page 293E for other online activities.

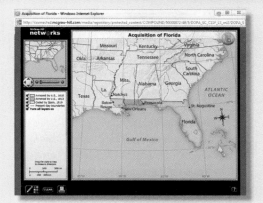

ANSWERS, p. 313

GEOGRAPHY CONNECTION

1 Louisiana, Mississippi, Alabama, and Florida

2 CRITICAL THINKING Possible answer: The land was nearly surrounded by the United States.

At this 1813 meeting, the Congress of Chilpancingo, Mexican leaders declared independence from Spain and drafted a constitution calling for a republican government. Mexico would finally achieve independence in 1821.

IMAGE ASSET MANAGEMENT/age FOTOSTOCK America

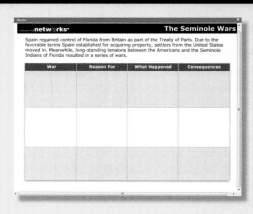

W Writing Skills

Informative/Explanatory Have students write a paragraph describing how General Andrew Jackson and Secretary of State Adams established U.S. rule in Florida. Point out that this was a process that occurred in a series of steps. Ask them to use words like *first, next, then,* and *finally* to indicate the order in which these steps happened. When students are finished, have them compare their work with a partner's to make sure their descriptions are complete. **AL ELL Interpersonal**

V Visual Skills

Integrating Visual Information Direct students' attention to the painting of the Mexican leaders. **Ask: How does the painting relate to the information on the page?** *(Students may mention specific actions taken by Mexican leaders and U.S. generals, but responses should involve recognition of the goal of both Mexico and the United States to throw off Spanish rule.)* **ELL**

T Technology Skills

Making Presentations Divide the class into several groups. Have them use the Internet to research the topic of the Seminole people. Have groups compare their findings in a class discussion.

The territory claimed by the United States reached west to the borders of Louisiana and Mississippi. Spain objected to losing part of West Florida but took no action against the United States.

Native Americans living in Spanish East Florida sometimes raided American settlements in Georgia. General Andrew Jackson was ordered to stop these Seminole raids. Jackson believed his order included pursuing the Seminoles into the Florida colonies. In the spring of 1818, another general, William McIntosh, led Creek allies against the Seminoles in Georgia. Meanwhile, Jackson followed fleeing Seminoles into Spanish West Florida. After pursuing the Seminoles, Jackson and his troops moved farther into West Florida. There they seized the Spanish forts at Pensacola and San Marcos. Secretary of State Adams had not authorized Jackson's actions, but he did nothing to stop them or to punish Jackson.

Jackson's raid demonstrated American military strength compared to that of Spain. Secretary of State Adams believed that the Spanish did not want war and wanted to settle the dispute. Adams was correct, and with the Adams-Onís Treaty of 1819, Spain **ceded,** or gave up control of, all claims and ownership to both East and West Florida. They also gave up claims to Oregon Country in the Pacific Northwest, while the United States agreed to Spanish control of Texas.

Reading **HELP**DESK (CCSS)

cede to transfer control of something

Reading in the Content Area: *Historical Maps*

Maps often use shading to show changes over time. To read a map of this type, point to each shaded area on the map as you read the map key. You may want to cover other areas, if possible.

314 *Growth and Expansion*

netw⊙rks *Online Teaching Options*

CHART

The Seminole Wars

Analyzing Maps, Graphs, Charts, Time Lines Use the interactive chart of the Seminole Wars to discuss how the Seminole fought to maintain their independence. **Ask: How were the Seminole involved in the U.S. acquisition of Florida?** *(Seminole raids in Georgia were one of the reasons Andrew Jackson invaded Florida in 1818.)* **What was the Adams-Onis Treaty?** *(a treaty between the United States and Spain that gave control of Florida to the United States)* **What did Spain keep in the treaty?** *(control of Texas)* **Visual/Spatial**

See page 293E for other online activities.

Spain Loses Power

Meanwhile, Spain was losing power elsewhere in its vast empire. In 1810 a priest named Miguel Hidalgo (ee • DAHL • goh) led a rebellion in Mexico. Hidalgo called for racial equality and the redistribution of land. The Spanish captured and executed Hidalgo, but by 1821 Mexico had gained its independence from Spain.

Simón Bolívar, also known as "the Liberator," led the independence movement that won freedom for the present-day countries of Venezuela, Colombia, Panama, Bolivia, and Ecuador. José de San Martín successfully achieved independence for Chile and Peru. By 1824 Spain had lost control of most of South America.

The Monroe Doctrine

In 1822 four European nations—France, Austria, Russia, and Prussia—discussed a plan to help Spain regain its American holdings. The possibility of increased European involvement in the Americas troubled President Monroe. There were also concerns about Russia's intentions for controlling land in the Northwest.

The president issued a statement on December 2, 1823: The United States would not get involved in the internal affairs or wars in Europe. It also would not interfere with any existing European colonies in the Americas. At the same time, the statement said, North and South America "are henceforth not to be considered as subjects for future colonization by any European powers." The Monroe Doctrine, as the statement came to be known, served as a clear warning to European nations to keep out of the Americas. It became a guiding force in American foreign policy in the decades ahead.

☑ **PROGRESS CHECK**

Summarizing Why did Spain finally give up Florida to the United States?

LESSON 3 REVIEW (CCSS)

Review Vocabulary (Tier 3 Words)

1. Use each of these terms in a sentence that explains the term's meaning. RH.6–8.4

   a. monopoly **b.** interstate commerce **c.** cede

2. What does the term *sectionalism* mean? RH.6–8.4

Answer the Guiding Questions

3. ***Explaining*** What factors contributed to the rise of nationalism in the 1810s? RH.6–8.2

4. ***Making Inferences*** Why was the Monroe Doctrine issued? RH.6–8.2

5. ***Listing*** What issues divided the country at the end of the Era of Good Feelings? RH.6–8.1

6. ***Describing*** How did the United States role in the world change in the early 1800s? RH.6–8.2

7. **ARGUMENT** Members of Congress agreed to the Missouri Compromise in an attempt to prevent serious conflict. Write a letter to a member of Congress arguing for or against this compromise. WHST.6–8.1, WHST.6–8.10

LESSON 3 REVIEW ANSWERS

1. **a.** If a company has a monopoly, it has total control of an industry in a certain market. **b.** Interstate commerce refers to business between two or more states. **c.** When Spain realized it could not hold on to Florida, it ceded the land to the United States.

2. Sectionalism is a rivalry based on the special interests of different geographical areas that may cause a division between the areas.

3. A sense of nationalism was present due to the lack of significant political divisions and due to pride over the nation's success in the war of 1812.

4. to keep the United States from getting involved in the internal affairs or wars of Europe, and to keep European countries from attempting further colonization in the Americas

5. slavery, states' rights, the need for tariffs, a national bank, internal improvements

6. The United States asserted its power by issuing the Monroe Doctrine, which stated that Spain and other European powers could not colonize any more land in the Americas.

7. Students' paragraphs should focus on the benefits or drawbacks of the compromise.

V Visual Skills

Integrating Visual Information Review with students how Spain began to lose most of its empire in North and South America. **Ask: Who was Miguel Hidalgo?** *(a priest who led a rebellion in Mexico, which led to Mexican independence from Spain)* Recall the painting in the textbook of Mexican leaders. Pair students to discuss the roles of Miguel Hidalgo and Mexican leaders in the rebellion of Mexico against the Spanish. **Interpersonal**

R Reading Skills

Explaining Have students read the section titled "The Monroe Doctrine," and then discuss with the class the reason that the Monroe Doctrine was issued. **Ask: Why did Monroe feel troubled by the mood in Europe?** *(In 1822 four European nations—France, Austria, Russia, and Prussia—discussed a plan to help Spain regain its American holdings.)* **What was the goal of the Monroe Doctrine?** *(It aimed to prevent European powers from becoming involved in the Americas.)* **What did the United States promise to do?** *(to stay out of Europe's internal affairs or wars and not interfere with any remaining European colonies in the Americas)*

W Writing Skills

Informative/Explanatory Have students write two sentences explaining the Monroe Doctrine in their own words. **AL** **ELL**

Have students complete the Lesson 3 Review.

CLOSE & REFLECT

Discussing Discuss with students the significance of the Monroe Doctrine. **Ask: What impact would this have on U.S. foreign affairs with Europe?** *(Students' answers will vary.)* **BL**

ANSWER, p. 315

☑ **PROGRESS CHECK** Spain was unable to maintain control of it and seemed likely to lose it by force.

ENGAGE

Bellringer Tell students that Mark Twain wrote about memories and experiences from his early life in *Life on the Mississippi*. Note that some of his writing, including this excerpt, describes changes that occurred after his early years. Use the image of the Mississippi River Basin to make a visual connection to what the students have read and what they will be learning about. Ask students to volunteer vivid memories from their earlier years. Then discuss the possibility of children in future years having similar memories or whether technological or other changes will make the same type of memories rare or impossible.

TEACH & ASSESS

C1 Critical Thinking Skills

Synthesizing Note to students that during the period covered in the excerpt, much of the Midwest was experiencing rapid economic and population growth. Some of that growth was related to better transportation for both people and goods. Ask students to consider the change from rafts traveling downstream on the Mississippi River to steamboats traveling quickly in both directions. Then ask students to list some reasons that the population of the Midwest grew so rapidly during this period. **BL**

C2 Critical Thinking Skills

Making Inferences Have students reread the description of the author and the information about the story. **Ask: From the description of the story, do you think everything in it will be strictly factual? Why or why not?** *(Humorous anecdotes and folktales may exaggerate certain events or people's actions.)* Note that Twain was well known for retelling folktales that may have been exaggerated or fictional. Students can write a short story from their lives and include a humorous anecdote. **Verbal/Linguistic**

Content Background Knowledge

Samuel Langhorne Clemens's pen name, Mark Twain, was related to his love for the Mississippi and its steamboats. The name means "mark number two," which refers to a mark on the line that measured the depth of the river. The second mark on this line indicated a depth of 12 feet, which was water that was deep enough for a steamboat.

AMERICA'S LITERATURE (CCSS)

Life on the Mississippi
by Mark Twain

Mark Twain used memories of his youth in writing *Life on the Mississippi*.

C2 Samuel Langhorne Clemens (1835–1910), known as Mark Twain, was born in Missouri. He spent his early years along the Mississippi River in the town of Hannibal.

Later, as a young man, Clemens trained as a river pilot's apprentice. He used his experiences as a basis for many of the stories in *Life on the Mississippi*. This book is a collection of humorous anecdotes and folktales, and it provides a glimpse into Twain's life before he became a famous author.

❝ *I remember the annual processions of mighty rafts that used to glide by Hannibal when I was a boy,—an acre or so of white, sweet-smelling boards in each raft, a crew of two dozen men or more . . .* **❞**

—from *Life on the Mississippi*

Steamboats carried passengers and cargo up and down the Mississippi.

C1

316 *Growth and Expansion*

(t) Archive.pix; (b) Library of Congress LC-DIG-pga-03028

---

netw⊙rks *Online Teaching Options*

VIDEO

Famous People, Incredible Lives: Mark Twain

Identifying Watch the video with students. **Ask: What are the best-known works of Mark Twain?** *(The Adventures of Tom Sawyer* and *The Adventures of Huckleberry Finn)* Ask students whether they have ever read a book by Mark Twain or seen a movie or television show based on one of his books. If so, have volunteers describe the story of what they read/watched and what they remember about its setting. **AL**

PRIMARY SOURCE

" Between La Salle's opening of the river and the time when it may be said to have become the vehicle of anything like a regular and active commerce, seven **sovereigns** had occupied the throne of England, America had become an independent nation. . . .

The river's earliest commerce was in great barges—keelboats, broadhorns. They floated and sailed from the upper rivers to New Orleans, changed cargoes there, and were **tediously** warped and poled back by hand. A voyage down and back sometimes occupied nine months. In time this commerce increased until it gave employment to hordes of rough and hardy men; rude, uneducated, brave, suffering terrific hardships with sailor-like **stoicism** . . . , heavy fighters, reckless fellows, every one, **elephantinely** jolly, foul-witted, **profane; prodigal** of their money, bankrupt at the end of the trip, fond of barbaric finery, **prodigious** braggarts; yet, in the main, honest, trustworthy, faithful to promises and duty, and often picturesquely **magnanimous.**

By and by the steamboat intruded. Then for fifteen or twenty years, these men continued to run their keelboats down-stream, and the steamers did all of the upstream business, the keelboatmen selling their boats in New Orleans, and returning home as deck passengers in the steamers.

But after a while the steamboats so increased in number and in speed that they were able to absorb the entire commerce; and then keelboating died a permanent death. The keelboatman became a deck hand, or a mate, or a pilot on the steamer; and when steamer-berths were not open to him, he took a berth on a Pittsburgh coal-flat, or on a pine-raft constructed in the forests up toward the sources of the Mississippi.

In the **heyday** of the steamboating prosperity, the river from end to end was flaked with coal-fleets and timber rafts, all managed by hand, and employing hosts of the rough characters whom I have been trying to describe. I remember the annual processions of mighty rafts that used to glide by Hannibal when I was a boy,—an acre or so of white, sweet-smelling boards in each raft, a crew of two dozen men or more, three or four wigwams scattered about the raft's vast level space for storm-quarters,—and I remember the rude ways and the tremendous talk of their big crews . . . for we used to swim out a quarter or third of a mile and get on these rafts and have a ride. "

[R]

[C1]

[C2]

Vocabulary

sovereign one who holds power
tedious boring
stoicism the quality of not reacting to pleasure or pain
elephantine having great size
profane not religious
prodigal wasteful
prodigious large in size or quantity
magnanimous noble, generous
heyday the peak of one's strength

Literary Element

Imagery is the use of descriptive and figurative language. It appeals to at least one of the five senses: hearing, seeing, tasting, smelling and touching. As you read, identify images that create a sensory experience. For example, how does Twain's description of the rafts appeal to your sense of smell?

Analyzing Literature | **DBQ**

1 **Analyzing** What does Twain think of the men who worked on the barges? RH.6–8.6

2 **Explaining** What happened to the keelboat operators once steamboats took over commerce on the river? RH.6–8.2

3 **Expressing** How does Twain describe his impressions of the rafts and men he saw as a young boy? Which senses do these images appeal to? RH.6–8.2, RH.6–8.10

Lesson 3 **317**

[C1] Critical Thinking Skills

Interpreting Point out that the words *elephantinely, prodigal, prodigious,* and *magnanimous* are all used to describe the personalities and actions of the men working on the keelboats. **Ask: Based on these words and Twain's descriptions, how do you think he felt about the workers on the keelboats?** *(They were almost larger than life, and Twain admired them.)* **Verbal/Linguistic**

[C2] Critical Thinking Skills

Determining Cause and Effect Ask students to identify the passage that describes the reasons that keelboating "died a permanent death." Compare the life of a keelboat worker to that of a steamboat worker. **Ask: How did the life of the keelboat workers change with the increase in steamboats?** *(They were forced to take different jobs on steamers or on rafts farther north.)* **[AL]** Ask students to think of other jobs that changed due to changing technologies. *(Answers may include weaving cloth and processing cotton)* **[BL]**

[R] Reading Skills

Describing Ask students to review the excerpt from *Life on the Mississippi.* **Ask: What do you learn about Mark Twain's life from this excerpt?** *(very little, except that he observed the river traffic closely and swam out to the rafts as a boy)* **Ask: What do you learn about Mark Twain's attitude toward the Mississippi River and the characters who traveled it?** *(Twain shows a great love for the river and for the people who made it busy and exciting during his early years.)* Discuss the Analyzing Literature questions as a class. **Visual/Spatial**

CLOSE & REFLECT

Remind students to make connections between the excerpt and the text in Lessons 1–3. Ask them to discuss ways that changes in transportation helped settlers move west and increased economic opportunities.

ANSWERS, p. 317

1. Twain thought they were rough, uneducated, and heavy drinkers, but they endured great hardships and were excellent workers.
2. The keelboat operators worked on the steamboats as deckhands, mates, or pilots. If there were no jobs on the steamboats, they worked on a Pittsburgh coal-flat or on a pine-raft constructed in the forests up toward the sources of the Mississippi.
3. He thought the rafts were mighty as they glided by him. They were made of sweet-smelling timber and had wigwams for shelter. The men "talked tremendously" and acted rudely. These images appeal to the sense of sight, sound, and smell.

PRIMARY SOURCE

Life on the Mississippi

Informative/Explanatory Explain to students that *imagery* is an important tool used by writers of both fiction and nonfiction. Ask students to identify other examples of imagery in the excerpt. **[BL]** Then have students write a short paragraph about their school, using references to at least three of the five senses. When they are finished, ask volunteers to share their paragraphs with the class.

netw⊕rks — Life on the Mississippi
ANALYZING PRIMARY SOURCES

One of the most famous descriptions of steamboats on the Mississippi River is Mark Twain's classic novel, *Life on the Mississippi*, published in 1883. In it, he describes what life was like on and around steamboats.

Library of Congress/LC-DIG-ppmsca-03526

" In the space of one hundred and seventy-six years the Lower Mississippi has shortened itself two hundred and forty-two miles. That is an average of a trifle over one mile and a third per year. Therefore, any calm person, who is not blind or idiotic, can see that in the Old Oölitic Silurian Period, just a million years ago next November, the Lower Mississippi River was upwards of one million three hundred thousand miles long, and stuck out over the Gulf of Mexico like a fishing-rod. And by the same token any person can see that seven hundred and forty- "

—from *Life on the Mississippi*, by Mark Twain

CHAPTER REVIEW ACTIVITY

On the board, have a volunteer create a web with five circles extending from the center circle. Students should write "The Industrial Revolution" in the center circle and label each of the other circles with the terms Agriculture, Transportation, Technology, Industry, and Leadership. Then lead a discussion that allows students to recall innovations in transportation and technology, trends in industry and agriculture, and important leaders of the Industrial Revolution in the late 1700s and early 1800s. A student volunteer should record answers in the chart.

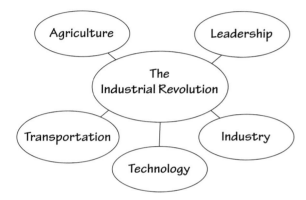

REVIEW THE ENDURING UNDERSTANDING

Review the chapter's Enduring Understanding with students.

- *The movement of people, goods, and ideas causes societies to change over time.*

Now pose the following questions in a class discussion to apply these to the chapter. **Ask: How did the Industrial Revolution affect the populations of farms and cities?** *(Students may respond that people left the farms to work in the cities. The population of rural areas decreased and the population of cities increased.)*

Ask: How did the increased demand for cotton cause a change in the population of the South? *(The increased demand for cotton increased the demand for enslaved people in the South.)*

Ask: What factors contributed to the westward expansion in the early 1800s? *(Settlers moved westward, first along the Wilderness Road. The construction of turnpikes also allowed the population to move west, as did river travel and the building of the Erie Canal.)*

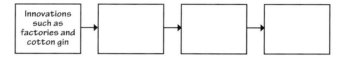

Write your answers on a separate piece of paper.

1 **Exploring the Essential Questions**   WHST.6–8.2, WHST.6–8.10
INFORMATIVE/EXPLANATORY How did the spread of the population in the United States over a wider area create challenges and tensions? Write an essay that answers this question.

2 **21st Century Skills**   RH.6–8.2, WHST.6–8.2
COMMUNICATION Review what you know about the process that resulted in Missouri statehood and the Missouri Compromise. Then, create a summary of the compromise that describes its key features and key contributors. Organize your findings in a diagram, or write an essay with headings that clearly communicate the information.

3 **Thinking Like a Historian**   RH.6–8.5
UNDERSTANDING CAUSE AND EFFECT Create a diagram such as the one below to explain the effects of innovations such as the factory system and the cotton gin on the South.

Innovations such as factories and cotton gin → □ → □ → □

4 **Visual Literacy**   RH.6–8.7
ANALYZING PAINTINGS This picture shows New York Governor DeWitt Clinton pouring water from Lake Erie into the Atlantic Ocean. What do you think is the meaning of Clinton's action?

The Granger Collection, NYC

318 *Growth and Expansion*

ACTIVITIES ANSWERS

Exploring the Essential Questions

1 Essays should explore the physical challenges of having people spread out over a large area—for example, how to move people and goods. Essays should also explore the rivalries that emerged as different areas pursued different interests.

21st Century Skills

2 Possible answer: Missouri wanted to become a state, and many residents wanted slavery. Congress did not support the extension of slavery. Southern states were concerned about admitting another free state for fear of tipping the balance of power to the North. The Missouri Compromise allowed for admission of Missouri as a slave state along with Maine as a free state. It also banned slavery in territories north of the southern border of Missouri but allowed it in areas south of that line.

REVIEW THE GUIDING QUESTIONS

Choose the best answer for each question.

RH.6–8.4
1 What was the significance of interchangeable parts?

A. It made farming less profitable.

B. It made it possible to produce items in large numbers.

C. It increased the demand for slave labor.

D. It undermined the factory system.

RH.6–8.4
2 The system in which all manufacturing steps are brought together in one place is called the

F. factory system.

G. patent system.

H. capital system.

I. corporation system.

RH.6–8.2
3 Why did pioneer families tend to settle in communities along major rivers?

A. Rivers provided easy escape routes in the event of Native American attack.

B. It was easier for them to travel east along the rivers.

C. Rivers provided opportunities for recreation.

D. They could ship their crops to market more easily.

RH.6–8.1
4 How was the National Road funded?

F. The federal government financed the road.

G. Private companies collected tolls from travelers.

H. Money was used from the canal fund.

I. Farmers were taxed on their crop production.

RH.6–8.2
5 In the mid-1800s, which group was least likely to support tariffs?

A. Northeastern factory owners

B. Southern planters

C. Westerners living on the frontier

D. free African Americans living in the North

RH.6–8.2
6 As a result of Andrew Jackson's 1818 actions in Florida,

F. the United States and Spain went to war.

G. East Florida was separated from West Florida.

H. Spain realized it could not maintain control of Florida.

I. Spain increased its presence in North America.

319

ASSESSMENT ANSWERS
Review the Guiding Questions

1 **B** Interchangeable parts made it possible to produce items in large numbers. It was not directly related to farming or slave labor. It supported the factory system.

2 **F** Patents, capital, and corporations are related to manufacturing, but the factory system refers specifically to bringing all the manufacturing steps together in one place.

3 **D** Rivers helped settlers ship their crops more easily. Rivers generally did not flow east and west, so B is not a correct answer. Neither A nor C are reasons for settlement along rivers.

4 **F** Ohio requested that the federal government construct the National Road to connect it to the East, and the government agreed.

5 **B** Southern planters purchased many of their goods from Europe, and they had little manufacturing to protect, so they would be least likely to support tariffs..

6 **H** Jackson's incursions pointed out Spain's weakness and inability to control its own territory. This led Spain to negotiate the handing over of Florida to the United States.

Thinking Like a Historian

3 Possible answers could include:

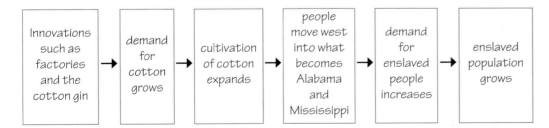

| Innovations such as factories and the cotton gin | → | demand for cotton grows | → | cultivation of cotton expands | → | people move west into what becomes Alabama and Mississippi | → | demand for enslaved people increases | → | enslaved population grows |

Visual Literacy

4 This action symbolizes the completion of the important link between the Great Lakes and the Atlantic Ocean, and the connections that canals bring to the country.

Analyzing Documents

7 **C** Answers A and B refer to domestic policies while answer D does not exist.

8 **F** The Monroe Doctrine pledges to respect existing colonies but resist any new involvement by European powers.

Short Response

9 The excerpt is attempting to settle the question of whether there will be slavery in lands from the Louisiana Purchase that may become states in the future.

10 Sectional rivalries were inflamed by the question of how to admit new states and deal with the question of slavery in new territories.

Extended Response

11 Students should describe the unifying forces such as expansionism, nationalism, optimism, and a belief in progress and self-improvement. Points of dispute may include slavery, tariffs, internal improvements, and states' rights.

DBQ **ANALYZING DOCUMENTS**

The following are the words of President James Monroe:

"With the existing colonies ... of any European power we have not interfered and shall not interfere. But with the [Latin American] governments who have declared their independence and maintained it ... we could not view any [involvement] for the purpose of oppressing them ... by any European power in any other light than as the [showing] of an unfriendly disposition toward the United States."

—James Monroe, speech to Congress, December 1823

RH.6–8.2, RH.6–8.10

7 **Identifying** In this statement, Monroe is issuing the

A. American Plan.   C. Monroe Doctrine.

B. Missouri Compromise.   D. Latin American Doctrine.

RH.6–8.6

8 **Identifying Central Issues** In this statement, Monroe pledges to

F. respect existing colonies but not new attempts to control Latin America.

G. open Latin America to colonization from European powers.

H. respect new European colonies but seek freedom for old ones.

I. be unfriendly toward Latin American governments.

SHORT RESPONSE

"Section 8. And be it further enacted, That in all that territory ceded by France to the United States, under the name of Louisiana, ... slavery and involuntary servitude ... shall be, and is hereby, forever prohibited."

—Missouri Compromise

RH.6–8.6, WHST.6–8.4

9 Describe the issue that this portion of the Missouri Compromise is seeking to resolve.

RH.6–8.9, WHST.6–8.4

10 Why was it necessary to make this agreement?

EXTENDED RESPONSE

WHST.6–8.2, WHST.6–8.9

11 **Informative/Explanatory** Describe the forces that tended to unify Americans in the early 1800s as well as some of the important points of disagreement.

Your essay should include the Industrial Revolution and the growth of American cities; the settlement of the western United States; transportation systems in the early and mid-1800s; sectional conflicts and the American System; and relations of the United States with foreign nations.

Need Extra Help?

If You've Missed Question	1	2	3	4	5	6	7	8	9	10	11
Review Lesson	1	1	2	2	3	3	3	3	3	3	1–3

---

netw⊙rks   *Online Teaching Options*

More Assessment Resources

The *Assess* tab in the online Teacher Lesson Center includes resources to help students improve their test-taking skills. It also contains many project-based rubrics to help you assess students' work.

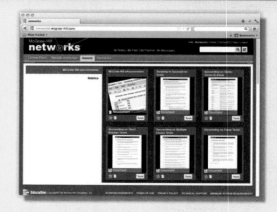

CHAPTER 12
The Jackson Era Planner

UNDERSTANDING BY DESIGN®

Enduring Understanding
- *People, places, and ideas change over time.*

Essential Questions
- *What are the characteristics of a leader?*
- *What are the consequences when cultures interact?*
- *How do governments change?*

Predictable Misunderstandings
Students may think:
- *Mudslinging in election campaigns is a modern campaign tactic.*
- *Issues that divided the North and South were related only to slavery.*
- *All eastern Native Americans resisted removal.*
- *Banks are personal savings and lending institutions that have little impact on the larger economy.*

Assessment Evidence
Performance Tasks:
- *Hands-On Chapter Project*

Other Evidence:
- *Interactive Graphic Organizers*
- *What Do You Know? activity*
- *Primary Source Activity*
- *Geography and History Activity*
- *21st Century Skills Activity*
- *Written Paragraphs*
- *Lesson Reviews*
- *Online Self-Check Quizzes*
- *Chapter Activities and Assessment*

Learners will understand:

3 People, Places, and Environments
6. Patterns of demographic and political change, and cultural diffusion in the past and present (e.g., changing national boundaries, migration, and settlement, and the diffusion of and changes in customs and ideas)
8. Factors that contribute to cooperation and conflict among peoples of the nation and world, including language, religion, and political beliefs

5 Individuals, Groups, and Institutions
8. That when two or more groups with differing norms and beliefs interact, accommodation or conflict may result

6 Power, Authority, and Governance
5. The ways in which governments meet the needs and wants of citizens, manage conflict, and establish order and society

7 Production, Distribution, and Consumption
3. The economic choices that people make have both present and future consequences
5. That banks and other financial institutions channel funds from savers to borrowers and investors

10 Civic Ideals and Practices
6. The origins and function of major institutions and practices developed to support democratic ideals and practices

SUGGESTED PACING GUIDE

Introducing the Chapter . . . . 1 Day	Lesson 3 . . . . 2 Days
Lesson 1 . . . . 2 Days	Chapter Activities and Assessment . . . . . .1 Days
Lesson 2 . . . . 2 Days	

TOTAL TIME   8 Days

Key for Using the Teacher Edition

SKILL-BASED ACTIVITIES

Types of skill activities found in the Teacher Edition.

V Visual Skills require students to analyze maps, graphs, charts, and photos.

R Reading Skills help students practice reading skills and master vocabulary.

W Writing Skills provide writing opportunities to help students comprehend the text.

C Critical Thinking Skills help students apply and extend what they have learned.

T Technology Skills require students to use digital tools effectively.

Letters are followed by a number when there is more than one of the same type of skill on the page.

DIFFERENTIATED INSTRUCTION

All activities are written for the on-level student unless otherwise marked with the leveled labels below.

BL Beyond Level
AL Approaching Level
ELL English Language Learners

All students benefit from activities that utilize different learning styles. Many activities are marked as below when a particular learning style is highlighted.

Intrapersonal	Naturalist
Logical/Mathematical	Kinesthetic
Visual/Spatial	Auditory/Musical
Verbal/Linguistic	Interpersonal

CHAPTER OPENER PLANNER

Students will know:

- the new ways of campaigning and their effect on the elections of 1824 and 1828.
- the debate over states' rights versus the rights of the federal government.
- the causes and consequences of the removal of eastern Native Americans.
- the reasons behind the closing of the national bank.

Students will be able to:

- **evaluate** the role of campaign tactics in elections of the early nineteenth century.
- **analyze** the conflict over tariffs as it relates to sectional divisions.
- **compare** the position of those who supported states' rights to those who wanted a stronger federal government.
- **assess** the impact of the policy of removal of the Native Americans to Indian Territory.
- **describe** the Seminoles' response to removal and how it differed from the responses of other Native American peoples of the time.
- **explain** Jackson's objections to the Bank of the United States.

UNDERSTANDING BY DESIGN®

☑ *Print Teaching Options*

V **Visual Skills**

☐ **P. 322** Students examine map key symbols and how they are used on a map. **AL** **BL** Visual/Spatial Interpersonal

☐ **P. 323** Students interpret a time line. Logical/Mathematical

T **Technology Skills**

☐ **P. 323** Students conduct Internet research on Native American groups and briefly summarize their findings. **AL** **ELL** Verbal/Linguistic

☑ *Online Teaching Options*

V **Visual Skills**

☐ **MAP** **The Removal of Native Americans, 1820–1840**—Students click on buttons to reveal the routes different Native American groups followed to Indian Territory.

☐ **TIME LINE** **The United States 1830s and 1840s**—Students learn about key events during this time period.

☐ **WORLD ATLAS** Students can use this interactive map to identify regions of the world, learn about individual countries, locate political boundaries, measure distances, and much more.

☑ *Printable Digital Worksheets*

R **Reading Skills**

☐ **GRAPHIC NOVEL** *Sequoya and the Cherokee Nation*—The novel recounts Cherokee attempts to adapt to white Americans' ways, their legal fight against forced relocation, and their journey on the Trail of Tears.

Project-Based Learning

Hands-On Chapter Project

Create a Political Campaign Ad

Student groups do research in order to create political advertisements with both print and audio components for one of the following candidates: Henry Clay, Andrew Jackson, or John Quincy Adams.

Technology Extension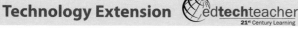

Create a Podcast
- Find an additional activity online that incorporates technology for this project.
- Visit the EdTechTeacher Web sites (included in the Technology Extension for this chapter) for more links, tutorials, and other resources.

Print Resources

ANCILLARY RESOURCES
These ancillaries are available for every chapter and lesson.

- **Reading Essentials and Study Guide Workbook** **AL** **ELL**
- **Chapter Tests and Lesson Quizzes Blackline Masters**

PRINTABLE DIGITAL WORKSHEETS
These printable digital worksheets are available for every chapter and lesson.

- **Hands-On Chapter Projects**
- **What Do You Know? activities**
- **Chapter Summaries (English and Spanish)**
- **Vocabulary Builder activities**
- **Guided Reading activities**

More Media Resources

SUGGESTED VIDEOS
Watch clips from the film *The Trail of Tears: Cherokee Legacy*.
- **Discuss:** What emotions do these scenes arouse about the treatment of Native Americans during the Jackson Era?
- **Discuss:** Can fictional movies capture historically accurate events?

(NOTE: Preview clips to ensure age-appropriateness.)

SUGGESTED READING
Grade 6 reading level:
- *Sequoyah: The Cherokee Man Who Gave His People Writing,* by James Rumford.

Grade 7 reading level:
- *Old Hickory: Andrew Jackson and the American People,* by Albert Marrin.

Grade 8 reading level:
- *First People: An Illustrated History of American Indians,* by David C. King.

LESSON **1** PLANNER

JACKSONIAN DEMOCRACY

Students will know:
- the new ways of campaigning and their effect on the elections of 1824 and 1828.
- the debate over states' rights versus the rights of the federal government.

Students will be able to:
- *evaluate* the role of campaign tactics in elections of the early nineteenth century.
- *analyze* the conflict over tariffs as it relates to sectional divisions.
- *compare* the position of those who supported states' rights to those who wanted a stronger federal government.

☑ *Print Teaching Options*

V Visual Skills

☐ **P. 324** Students make a graphic organizer. **AL** **ELL**

☐ **P. 325** Students analyze circle graphs. **BL** Visual/Spatial

☐ **P. 327** Students interpret an image and role play based on the image. **BL** Kinesthetic

R Reading Skills

☐ **P. 327** Students explore the idea of Jackson as a "common man." **AL** **ELL** Visual/Spatial

☐ **P. 327** Students discuss Jackson's promise to expand voting rights.

☐ **P. 329** Students analyze textual evidence to support a statement. **AL** **ELL** Verbal/Linguistic

W Writing Skills

☐ **P. 328** Students argue whether Jackson was a true war hero. Verbal/Linguistic

C Critical Thinking Skills

☐ **P. 325** Students interpret information. **AL** **ELL**

☐ **P. 326** Students draw conclusions about the 1828 election by looking at a map. **AL** **ELL**

☐ **P. 326** Students compare campaign innovations in 1828 to those of today. **AL** **ELL** **BL**

☐ **P. 328** Students describe the spoils system. **AL** **ELL** **BL**

☐ **P. 328** Students discuss tariffs.

T Technology Skills

☐ **P. 328** Students use digital sources to investigate Jackson's reputation. **BL**

☑ *Online Teaching Options*

V Visual Skills

☐ **VIDEO** **Old Hickory**—Students view a video that describes Andrew Jackson's presidency.

☐ **IMAGE** **Jackson's Inauguration**—Students click to reveal details of this first inauguration to be held on the east front portico of the U.S. Capitol.

☐ **MAP** **The Election of 1824**—Students click to reveal percentages of the vote received by each presidential candidate.

☐ **MAP** **The Election of 1828**—Students click to reveal percentages of the vote received by each presidential candidate.

R Reading Skills

☐ **GRAPHIC ORGANIZER** **Taking Notes:** *Comparing:* **The Election of 1928**—Students identify the views and supporters of each major candidate in the election of 1828.

☐ **BIOGRAPHY** **Andrew Jackson**—Students analyze the characteristics of Jackson that appealed to his supporters.

C Critical Thinking Skills

☐ **IMAGE** **The Nullification Crisis**—Students analyze a political cartoon that summarizes growing sectionalism over tariffs.

T Technology Skills

☐ **SELF-CHECK QUIZ** **Lesson 1**—Students receive instant feedback on their mastery of lesson content.

☑ *Printable Digital Worksheets*

C Critical Thinking Skills

☐ **WORKSHEET** **Primary Source Activity: Nullification**—Students analyze a statement by John C. Calhoun explaining South Carolina's position regarding tariffs.

CONFLICTS OVER LAND

Students will know:
- the causes and consequences of the removal of eastern Native Americans.

Students will be able to:
- **assess** the impact of the policy of removal of the Native Americans to Indian Territory.
- **describe** the Seminoles' response to removal and how it differed from the responses of other Native American peoples of the time.

UNDERSTANDING
BY DESIGN®

☑ *Print Teaching Options*

V **Visual Skills**

☐ **P. 331** Students analyze an illustration. **Visual/Spatial**

R **Reading Skills**

☐ **P. 331** Students discuss differences between state and federal governments and laws. **Verbal/Linguistic**

☐ **P. 333** Students discuss the Trail of Tears. **AL** **Intrapersonal**

☐ **P. 335** Students discuss the relocation of Native Americans.

☐ **P. 335** Students paraphrase the problem that the Five Civilized Tribes encountered when they arrived in the eastern half of Indian Territory. **AL** **ELL** **Verbal/Linguistic**

W **Writing Skills**

☐ **P. 332** Students discuss a painting depicting the Trail of Tears. **Verbal/Linguistic**

C **Critical Thinking Skills**

☐ **P. 330** Students examine cultural differences and biases. **BL**

☐ **P. 330** Students identify white settlers' point of view. **BL** **Interpersonal**

☐ **P. 332** Students examine how well the Cherokee adapted to white culture.

☐ **P. 333** Students determine why many Cherokee died as a result of their relocation. **AL** **ELL**

☐ **P. 334** Students compare the Seminoles' reaction to their relocation to that of the other Five Civilized Tribes. **BL**

☐ **P. 334** Students discuss why enslaved people would want to fight alongside the Seminoles. **BL** **Verbal/Linguistic**

☑ *Online Teaching Options*

V **Visual Skills**

☐ **VIDEO** **A Nation Divided**—Students consider the multi-ethnic origins of the Seminole people.

☐ **IMAGE** **The Seminole Wars**—Students click to reveal details of the three conflicts between the U.S. government and this Native American group.

R **Reading Skills**

☐ **GRAPHIC ORGANIZER** **Taking Notes:** *Describing:* **The Removal of Native Americans**—Students describe how the Cherokee and Seminoles resisted removal and the result.

☐ **PRIMARY SOURCE** **Walt Whitman**—Students learn of this famous poet and read an excerpt from the poem "Osceola."

C **Critical Thinking Skills**

☐ **WHITEBOARD ACTIVITY** **Forced Migration**—Students match Native American groups to their primary locations in 1830.

☐ **CHART** **Native American Removal**—Students click to reveal data on the number of people in different Native American groups forced to migrate to Indian Territory.

T **Technology Skills**

☐ **SELF-CHECK QUIZ** **Lesson 2**—Students receive instant feedback on their mastery of lesson content.

☑ *Printable Digital Worksheets*

C **Critical Thinking Skills**

☐ **WORKSHEET** **Geography and History Activity: Conflicts Over Land**—Students compare and contrast voluntary and forced migration.

JACKSON AND THE BANK

Students will know:
- the reasons behind the closing of the national bank.

Students will be able to:
- **explain** Jackson's objections to the Bank of the United States.

☑ Print Teaching Options

V Visual Skills

☐ **P. 338** Students analyze a political cartoon. **BL**
Visual/Spatial

R Reading Skills

☐ **P. 336** Students explain why Jackson disliked the Second Bank of the United States. **AL ELL**
Verbal/Linguistic

☐ **P. 337** Students discuss the plan of Henry Clay and Daniel Webster. **BL** Verbal/Linguistic

☐ **P. 338** Students explain Van Buren's *laissez-faire* approach to the Panic of 1837. **AL ELL**

☐ **P. 339** Students discuss voters' tendencies during times of financial crisis. **BL** Verbal/Linguistic

☐ **P. 340** Students identify the political parties and important attributes of the presidential candidates in 1840. **AL**

☐ **P. 341** Students discuss the problems the Whig Party had with John Tyler. **AL ELL** Verbal/Linguistic

☐ **P. 341** Students analyze Tyler's presidency.

W Writing Skills

☐ **P. 338** Students write an explanation of the Panic of 1837. **BL** Verbal/Linguistic

C Critical Thinking Skills

☐ **P. 337** Students analyze Jackson's actions after the veto of the renewal of the Second Bank of the United States' charter. **AL**

☐ **P. 338** Students discuss the political impact of the Panic of 1837 on the Democratic Party.

☐ **P. 340** Students compare the campaigns of Harrison and Van Buren. **AL ELL** Verbal/Linguistic

☐ **P. 340** Students discuss why Harrison's death in office was significant. **BL**

☑ Online Teaching Options

V Visual Skills

☐ **VIDEO** **The Second National Bank**—Students view a video that explains Jackson's strategies in weakening the Bank of the United States.

☐ **MAP** **The Election of 1836**—Students click to reveal percentages of the vote received by each presidential candidate.

☐ **MAP** **The Election of 1840**—Students click to reveal percentages of the vote received by each presidential candidate.

R Reading Skills

☐ **GRAPHIC ORGANIZER** **Taking Notes:** *Identifying:* **Bank of the United States Closes**—Students sequence actions taken by Jackson that caused the bank to close.

☐ **BIOGRAPHY** **William Henry Harrison**—Students review the characteristics that made this candidate attractive to his supporters.

C Critical Thinking Skills

☐ **POLITICAL CARTOON** **King Andrew I**—Students analyze a political cartoon that compares the actions of Jackson to that of a tyrannical king.

☐ **IMAGE** **The Panic of 1837**—Students analyze a political cartoon that describes how Jackson's banking policies led to the panic of 1837.

T Technology Skills

☐ **SELF-CHECK QUIZ** **Lesson 3**—Students receive instant feedback on their mastery of lesson content.

☑ Printable Digital Worksheets

W Writing Skills

☐ **WORKSHEET** **21st Century Skills Activity: Communication: Writing in Expository Style**—Students research and write about campaign literature.

INTERVENTION AND REMEDIATION STRATEGIES

LESSON 1 Jacksonian Democracy

Reading and Comprehension

Review the meaning of *connotation* if needed. Then have students find the highlighted vocabulary in the lesson and identify terms with potentially negative connotations (*mudslinging, spoils system*) and terms with neutral connotations (*plurality, majority, nominating convention*). Students may identify these terms as potentially negative or neutral: *favorite sons, bureaucracy.*

Text Evidence

Point out the title of the lesson, and have partners search through the lesson for text evidence showing how Andrew Jackson affected the way the federal government operated. As a whole group, review the information. Then have each student work independently to write a paragraph summarizing Jackson's effect.

LESSON 2 Conflicts Over Land

Reading and Comprehension

Have partners make a two-column chart to organize information about removing Native Americans. Students should list in the first column information related to white settlers' reasons for the removal and in the second column, the Native Americans' reasons against removal.

Text Evidence

Ask small groups of students to review the lesson to find major events in the Cherokee fight to stay on their land. Remind students to include dates that correspond to the events. Students can organize their information into a time line. Encourage students to discuss connections between the events.

LESSON 3 Jackson and the Bank

Reading and Comprehension

Help students review the major financial issues explored in this lesson. Provide these phrases as discussion starters: *powerful monopoly over loans, vetoed the Bank's charter, end of federal control over state banks, state-issued banknotes, and independent federal treasury.*

Text Evidence

Have students look for evidence in the text about the elections of 1836 and 1840. Ask students to name the presidential candidates, the factors that influenced each election, and the outcome of each election.

Online Resources

Approaching Level Reader

Use this online lower-level text that corresponds directly to the text in the Student Edition. It includes a Spanish version.

Guided Reading Activities

This resource uses graphic organizers and guiding questions to help students with comprehension.

What Do You Know?

Use these worksheets to pre-assess student's background knowledge before they study the chapter.

Reading Essentials and Study Guide Workbook

This resource offers writing and reading activities for the approaching-level student. Also available in Spanish.

Self-Check Quizzes

This online assessment tool provides instant feedback for students to check their progress.

The Jackson Era

1824–1845

ESSENTIAL QUESTIONS · *What are the characteristics of a leader?* · *What are the consequences when cultures interact?* · *How do governments change?*

◄ *This portrait of Seminole leader Osceola was painted shortly before his death in 1838.*

Superstock/Getty Images

321

networks

There's More Online about the people and events of the Jackson Era.

CHAPTER 12

Lesson 1
Jacksonian Democracy

Lesson 2
Conflicts Over Land

Lesson 3
Jackson and the Bank

The Story Matters . . .

He has put up a strong fight to save the land he believes the United States had promised his people. Now, weakened by illness, Osceola is ready for peace. He arrives at Fort Peyton carrying a white flag of truce. There, United States soldiers arrest Osceola and send him as a prisoner to a South Carolina fort.

At the fort, Osceola senses death approaching. He prepares by dressing in his finest clothes. Luckily for history, artist George Catlin is at the prison that day. He asks Osceola's permission to paint him in his fine clothing. Within days of sitting for this portrait, Osceola is dead.

In this chapter you will learn more about Osceola and the fight that he and other Native Americans waged against the United States to protect their land, rights, and freedom.

ENGAGE

🔔 **Bellringer** Read "The Story Matters . . ." aloud to the students. Call students' attention to the portrait of Osceola. Point out that photography was in its infancy in 1838, so portraits like this one are the only way we have of knowing what famous people in history looked like. Ask students if they know who this person is.

Ask: What can you tell about Osceola from the clothing he is wearing? *(Answers will vary, but students should note that he is not wearing stereotypical Native American clothing and seems to be dressed for a special occasion.)* **BL**

Then **ask: Why do you think Osceola agreed to have his portrait painted?** *(He knew he was sick and probably wanted to be remembered.)*

Ask students to identify where Osceola was when this portrait was painted and why he was there. *(in prison in South Carolina for waging war on the United States)* **BL**

Discuss with the class why Osceola went to war and whether his taking this action was justified. Tell students that in the 1830s and 1840s, nearly all Native Americans living in the eastern United States were forced to give up their lands and move west of the Mississippi River. Tell them that this removal, which some Native Americans called the Trail of Tears, is one of the events they will learn about in this chapter.

Making Connections

Native Americans wanted to keep their land, but they agreed to treaties that gave white settlers rights to the land. They did so to appease the settlers and hoped that the settlers would leave them alone on their remaining land.

If necessary, remind students that land was extremely important to Native Americans—they used natural resources to meet their basic needs of food, water, and shelter. **AL**

Encourage volunteers to discuss how they would handle pressure to give up something they value. Ask students how their responses might be different depending on the source of the pressure, for example, a younger sibling, a peer, or an adult acquaintance. **AL** **ELL** **Intrapersonal**

Letter from the Author

Dear American History Teacher,

Each generation rewrites history according to its own values. The reputation of Andrew Jackson has undergone considerable revision. Historians once focused on the spread of democracy in Jacksonian America and Jackson's fight with the Bank of the United States as an aristocratic institution. Recent interpretations have focused on Jackson's role in the removal of American Indians from their lands and on his ownership of enslaved people. Students need to know that history is not carved in stone. Historians sift through the records to explain the past as it relates to an ever-evolving present.

Donald A. Ritchie

TEACH & ASSESS

Step Into the Place

V1 Visual Skills

Analyzing Maps Before students begin, have them review the map key symbols and match each one with its corresponding routes on the map. If necessary, review the meaning of *ceded*. **AL**

Ask students to identify states that still had significant Native American populations in the 1820s and 1830s. **AL** Discuss the concepts of the West and the frontier in this period. Remind them that the frontier moved as white settlement expanded. Direct students' attention to the Native American lands on the map, and have them use the map key to identify the peoples who occupied these lands. **Ask:** Why might other Americans want Native Americans removed from these regions? *(Students may speculate about safety concerns or desire for Native Americans' lands.)* As a class, discuss the Map Focus questions. **BL** Visual/Spatial Interpersonal

Content Background Knowledge

- The Creek included people from a variety of groups.
- The Seminole were originally part of the Creek, but they split off into their own group.
- The name Seminole may have originated from *cimarron*, the Spanish word for runaway.
- The Freedman bands of the Seminole live in Oklahoma today, and they are descendants of formerly enslaved people.

V2

ANSWERS, p. 322

Step Into the Place
1. central and western Florida
2. They had to travel over water as well as land.
3. Because most were traveling by foot and by horse, it took a very long time; they would have had to protect themselves from various weather conditions and provide food and water for themselves along the way.
4. **CRITICAL THINKING** Those Native Americans settled in new land, which in the future would become states.

Step Into the Time
Spain transfers Florida to the United States in 1821; Peru gains independence in 1824, ending Spanish rule in South America.

Place and Time: United States 1820s to 1840s

As American settlement spread to the West, Americans came into conflict with the Native Americans who lived there. Over time, Native Americans were pushed even farther west.

Step Into the Place

MAP FOCUS During the Jackson Era, the Indian Removal Act forced the Seminole and other eastern Native Americans to move from their homelands to new homes west of the Mississippi River.

1 REGION Look at the map. In what part of Florida did the Seminole live? RH.6–8.7

2 MOVEMENT How did the removal route of the Seminole differ from that of the other groups? RH.6–8.7

3 HUMAN-ENVIRONMENT INTERACTION What kinds of challenges might Native Americans have encountered when traveling such long distances? RH.6–8.7

4 CRITICAL THINKING *Analyzing* How might the removal of the Native Americans have enabled greater expansion of the United States? RH.6–8.1

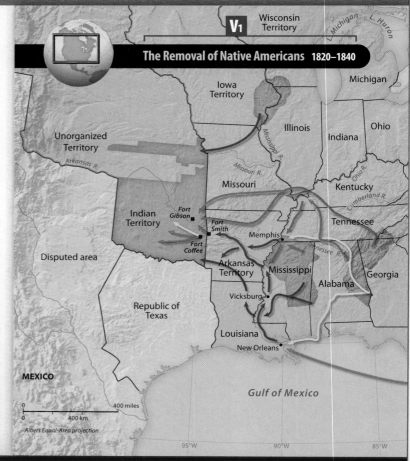

The Removal of Native Americans 1820–1840

Step Into the Time

TIME LINE Look at the time line. What events suggest a weakening of Spain's colonial empire in the Americas? RH.6–8.5, RH.6–8.7

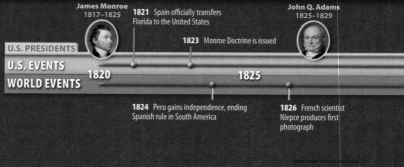

James Monroe 1817–1825

1821 Spain officially transfers Florida to the United States

1823 Monroe Doctrine is issued

John Q. Adams 1825–1829

U.S. PRESIDENTS
U.S. EVENTS
WORLD EVENTS

1820 — 1825

1824 Peru gains independence, ending Spanish rule in South America

1826 French scientist Niepce produces first photograph

322 *The Jackson Era*

Project-Based Learning N

Hands-On Chapter Project

Create a Political Campaign Ad

Have small groups create a political advertisement with both print and audio components for Henry Clay, Andrew Jackson, or John Quincy Adams. Tell groups to use at least three sources to identify the person's political platform and then use the Political Advertisement worksheet to create their advertisements. Give groups time to present their advertisement, and have them complete the Rubric Assessment. The full project and rubric are available online at **networks**.

Technology Extension

Create a Podcast

Have students use a recording device, such as a phone or computer to create a 45-second podcast of a political advertisement for their candidate. Begin by discussing the features of a successful advertisement, such as a clear voice and music or sound effects. Allow students time to write and refine their scripts before recording them. Provide them with resources to add music or sound effects, and then have students play their podcasts for the class.

edtechteacher
21st Century Learning

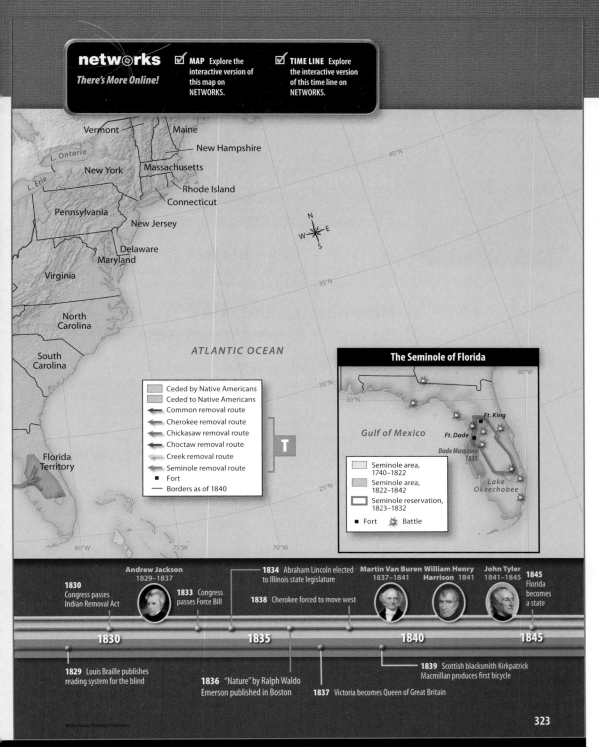

networks
There's More Online!
☑ MAP Explore the interactive version of this map on NETWORKS.
☑ TIME LINE Explore the interactive version of this time line on NETWORKS.

Legend (map)

- Ceded by Native Americans
- Ceded to Native Americans
- ← Common removal route
- ← Cherokee removal route
- ← Chickasaw removal route
- ← Choctaw removal route
- ← Creek removal route
- ← Seminole removal route
- ■ Fort
- — Borders as of 1840

The Seminole of Florida

- Ft. King
- Ft. Dade
- Dade Massacre 1835
- Lake Okeechobee

- Seminole area, 1740–1822
- Seminole area, 1822–1842
- Seminole reservation, 1823–1832
- ■ Fort
- ✴ Battle

Time line

1829 Louis Braille publishes reading system for the blind

1830 Congress passes Indian Removal Act

Andrew Jackson 1829–1837

1833 Congress passes Force Bill

1834 Abraham Lincoln elected to Illinois state legislature

1836 "Nature" by Ralph Waldo Emerson published in Boston

1837 Victoria becomes Queen of Great Britain

1838 Cherokee forced to move west

Martin Van Buren 1837–1841

William Henry Harrison 1841

John Tyler 1841–1845

1839 Scottish blacksmith Kirkpatrick Macmillan produces first bicycle

1845 Florida becomes a state

1830 — 1835 — 1840 — 1845

White House Historical Association

323

MAP

The Removal of Native Americans, 1820–1840

Discussing Ask students to discuss possible reasons that the routes were not direct. (*Student answers may vary but should demonstrate an understanding that topography affects travel. Some students may also mention the availability of natural resources such as food and water as influences on the route.*) **BL** **ELL** Have students measure the distance the Seminole traveled. **Ask:** How much of the journey was by water in the Gulf of Mexico? (*about 1,200 miles*) How much was by land? (*close to 1,000 miles*) Where did the part of the journey across the Gulf of Mexico end? (*New Orleans*) Which other group of Native Americans traveled over water? (*Creek*) **AL** Logical/Mathematical

See page 321B for other online activities.

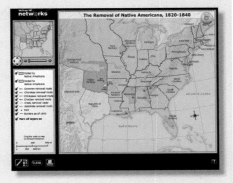

networks
The Removal of Native Americans, 1820–1840

Step Into the Time

V₂ Visual Skills

Analyzing Time Lines Have students look at the time line. **Ask:** What state is involved with both the beginning and ending events that frame this chapter? (*Both of these events involve Florida.*) About how long did it take for Florida to become a state after the United States acquired it from Spain? (*about 25 years*) Why was Florida an important acquisition? (*It extended the nation's frontier to its natural geographic borders to the south.*) How does the 1826 entry on the world time line relate to portraits like that of Osceola? (*Photographs would replace paintings.*) Logical/Mathematical

T Technology Skills

Researching on the Internet Organize students into five groups, and assign each group to research one of the five Native American groups removed from the Southeast. Students should use the Internet or a digital encyclopedia for their research and find out how the Native Americans made a living in their homeland and, if possible, the impact of the removal on their group's way of life. Reorganize students into new groups of five so that each group has one or two "experts" about each Native American group. Allow students time to share their expertise. Remind students to be brief as they summarize their findings. **AL** **ELL** Verbal/Linguistic

Content Background Knowledge

- About 300 Seminole were able to avoid removal to Indian Territory.
- Today about 2,000 descendants of these Native Americans live on six reservations around the state of Florida.
- The Seminole of Florida call themselves the "unconquered people."

CLOSE & REFLECT

To close the lesson, have students reflect on the lesson content by writing two short opinions about the removal, one from the perspective of a Native American and the other from the perspective of a white settler. Verbal/Linguistic

ENGAGE

Bellringer Before students begin this lesson, have them share what they know about elections at school or in their community. As needed, prompt students to discuss how candidates give voters information about their goals and ideas. Lead students to discuss how the candidates' desire to win can influence political advertising.

TEACH & ASSESS

V Visual Skills

Creating Visuals Have students create their own graphic organizer like that described in the Reading Help Desk so they can use it to compare the political parties discussed in this lesson. **AL ELL**

Making Connections

Tell the class that you are going to conduct an experiment with granting democracy in the classroom. Have each student choose a number between 1 and 10 and write it on a slip of paper. Next ask the students who have chosen 8 to raise their hands. Then tell the class that only those students are going to be allowed to vote. Discuss with the class whether or not the classroom is now democratic. *(Most students will recognize the lack of democracy.)*

ANSWER, p. 324

TAKING NOTES: *(Sample answers are provided for 1828.)* Party: National Republican; Candidate: Adams; Views: strong central government, build roads, a national bank to help shape the nation's economy; Supporters: merchants and well-off farmers. Party: Democratic; Candidate: Jackson; Views: states' rights and against tariffs on imports; Supporters: immigrants, big-city workers, people living on frontier.

networks
There's More Online!

☑ **BIOGRAPHY**
Andrew Jackson

☑ **GRAPHIC ORGANIZER**
Democrats and National Republicans

☑ **MAP**
• The Election of 1824
• The Election of 1828

☑ **VIDEO**

Lesson 1
Jacksonian Democracy

ESSENTIAL QUESTION *What are the characteristics of a leader?*

IT MATTERS BECAUSE
During the Jackson Era, the American democracy expanded and our modern political system began to take shape.

New Parties Emerge

GUIDING QUESTION *What new ways of campaigning appeared during the elections of 1824 and 1828?*

From 1816 to 1824, the United States had only one major political party. This was the Democratic Republican Party. The party was far from united. In 1824, four Democratic Republican candidates competed for the presidency. Party leaders chose William H. Crawford, a former senator from Georgia, to be their candidate. Three other candidates were **favorite sons**—that is, they received backing from their home states rather than the national party. Their views reflected the interests of their regions.

Two favorite sons, Andrew Jackson and Henry Clay, were from the West. Clay, of Kentucky, was Speaker of the House of Representatives. Jackson, of Tennessee, was a hero of the War of 1812. Raised in poverty, he claimed to speak for Americans who had been left out of politics. The third favorite son, John Quincy Adams of Massachusetts, was the son of former president John Adams. He was popular with merchants of the Northeast.

The House Chooses the President

In the election, Jackson received a **plurality** (pluh•RA•luh•tee) of the popular vote—the largest share. No candidate received a **majority,** or more than half, of the electoral votes.

(c) CORBIS SYGMA. (r) Bettmann/CORBIS

Reading HELPDESK **CCSS**

 V

Taking Notes: *Comparing*
As you read, use a diagram like this to compare political parties, their candidates, and their supporters.
RH.6–8.5

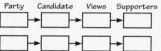

Party → Candidate → Views → Supporters

Content Vocabulary (Tier 3 Words)
• favorite son • mudslinging • nominating
• plurality • bureaucracy convention
• majority • spoils system

324 *The Jackson Era*

---

networks *Online Teaching Options*

VIDEO

Old Hickory

Discussing Provide an overview of Jacksonian Democracy by showing the video *The American President—The Candidate: The Power of the People, 1828–1837.* **AL ELL** Lead students in a discussion of the life events and character of Andrew Jackson. **Ask: How might having smallpox while in a concentration camp have affected Jackson?** *(Anyone who survived in those conditions must have been tough.)* **How does Jackson's defeat of the British at New Orleans fit with Jackson's nickname Old Hickory?** *(It's another example of his toughness, just like hickory wood is tough.)*

See page 321C for other online activities.

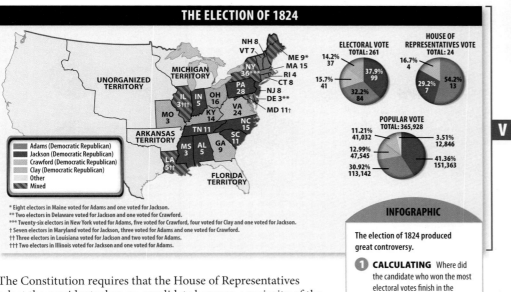

THE ELECTION OF 1824

Adams (Democratic Republican)
Jackson (Democratic Republican)
Crawford (Democratic Republican)
Clay (Democratic Republican)
Other
Mixed

ELECTORAL VOTE
TOTAL: 261
14.2% 37
15.7% 41
37.9% 99
32.2% 84

HOUSE OF REPRESENTATIVES VOTE
TOTAL: 24
16.7% 4
29.2% 7
54.2% 13

POPULAR VOTE
TOTAL: 365,928
11.21% 41,032
12.99% 47,545
30.92% 113,142
3.51% 12,846
41.36% 151,363

* Eight electors in Maine voted for Adams and one voted for Jackson.
** Two electors in Delaware voted for Jackson and one voted for Crawford.
*** Twenty-six electors in New York voted for Adams, five voted for Crawford, four voted for Clay and one voted for Jackson.
† Seven electors in Maryland voted for Jackson, three voted for Adams and one voted for Crawford.
†† Three electors in Louisiana voted for Jackson and two voted for Adams.
††† Two electors in Illinois voted for Jackson and one voted for Adams.

INFOGRAPHIC

The election of 1824 produced great controversy.

1 **CALCULATING** Where did the candidate who won the most electoral votes finish in the House vote?

2 **CRITICAL THINKING** *Drawing Conclusions* On what basis might Jackson have expected to win the presidency?

C The Constitution requires that the House of Representatives select the president when no candidate has won a majority of the electoral vote.

As the House prepared to vote, Clay met with Adams. Clay agreed to use his influence as Speaker to defeat Jackson. With Clay's help, the House chose Adams for president. Adams quickly named Clay to be secretary of state. In the past this office had been the stepping-stone to the presidency. Jackson's followers accused the two men of making a "corrupt bargain" and stealing the election.

Adams as President

Adams and Clay denied any wrongdoing. No one ever uncovered any evidence of a bargain. Still, the charge cast a shadow over Adams's presidency.

In his first message to Congress, Adams announced his plans. In addition to improving roads and waterways, he wanted to build a national university and support scientific research.

Adams's proposals upset his opponents. They wanted a more limited role for the federal government. It would be wrong, they believed, for government to spend money on such projects. Congress finally approved funds for improving rivers, harbors, and roads, but this was far less than Adams wanted.

favorite son a candidate for national office who has support mostly from his home state
plurality the largest number of something, but less than a majority
majority greater than half of a total number of something

Lesson 1 **325**

V Visual Skills

Analyzing Graphs Have students look at the information presented in the three circle graphs that are part of the map. **Ask: How could the difference between the popular and electoral votes be so large?** *(Accept reasonable responses. For example, when a candidate gets a small but significant number of votes in a state but does not win a majority of the votes, all of the states electoral votes may go to the candidate with the majority. If this happens in enough states, there could be a large difference between popular and electoral votes.)* **BL** **Visual/Spatial**

C Critical Thinking Skills

Analyzing Information Make sure students understand that if no candidate wins a majority of the electoral votes, the Constitution empowers the House of Representatives to choose the president. **AL** **ELL** **Ask: How did having four candidates make such a result more likely?** *(Each candidate had a strong base of support, but not enough for a majority.)* Students should understand the difference between a *majority* and a *plurality*.

Content Background Knowledge

The Electoral College is a compromise. Some of the Founding Fathers wanted the president to be elected by popular vote, and others wanted the president to be elected by Congress. To find the number of electors for a state, add the number of representatives (which is determined by the state's population) plus two, the number of senators in every state.

MAP

Presidential Election of 1824

Analyzing Maps Explain to students that there was only one major political party in the early 1820s. Call on a volunteer to identify it. Use the interactive map of the 1824 election from the textbook to discuss this election. **Ask: If there was only one political party, why were there four candidates for president in 1824?** *(States and regions supported their own candidates, called "favorite sons.")* **Who was the official party candidate in 1824?** *(William Crawford)* **AL** **Who were the other candidates and where were they from?** *(Jackson and Clay from the West—Tennessee and Kentucky, respectively— and Adams from Massachusetts in New England)* **Why did Andrew Jackson believe that he should have been elected president in 1824?** *(He won the most states, had the most popular votes, and had the most electoral votes.)*

See page 321C for other online activities.

ANSWERS, p. 325

INFOGRAPHIC
1. second
2. **CRITICAL THINKING** He won the most states, had the most popular votes, and had the most the electoral votes.

Jacksonian Democracy

G1 Critical Thinking Skills

Comparing and Contrasting Call students' attention to the map "The Election of 1828." **Ask: Which candidate had support from a larger number of states?** *(Jackson)* **Where were these states located?** *(on the frontier; in the West)* **AL ELL**

G2 Critical Thinking Skills

Comparing Have students compare innovations of the 1828 campaign, such as slogans, buttons, and rallies, to election campaigns today. *(Students should recognize and point out similarities between past and present.)* **Ask: What does mudslinging mean?** *(using gossip and lies to make an opponent look bad)* **AL ELL Why do you think the practice has this name?** *(Speculation should center on the concept of "dirt" or "mud.")* Have students identify similarities between mudslinging and today's negative campaigning. Ask students whether they think such tactics are effective in winning voter support. **BL Ask: Why was Jackson able to win easily in 1828 after losing to Adams in 1824?** *(Possible answers: Jackson's popularity in 1824 and the unusual nature of that election; unhappiness over Adams's performance and policies; campaign tactics, the expansion of voting rights, and Jackson's appeal to the "common man")*

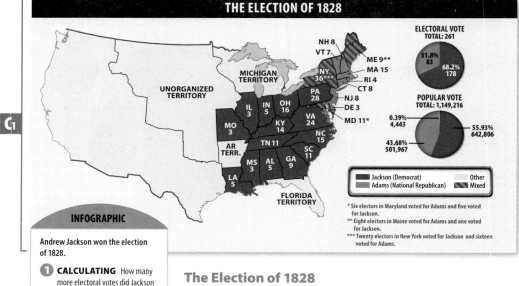

THE ELECTION OF 1828

G1

INFOGRAPHIC

Andrew Jackson won the election of 1828.

1 CALCULATING How many more electoral votes did Jackson get than he needed to win the election?

2 CRITICAL THINKING
Comparing How did having only two presidential candidates in 1828 affect the results of this election?

The Election of 1828

By 1828, the Democratic Republican Party had split. Jackson's supporters called themselves Democrats. The National Republicans supported Adams. Most Democrats favored states' rights and distrusted strong central government. The National Republicans wanted a strong central government. They supported measures such as building roads and a national bank to **facilitate** economic growth.

During the campaign, both sides resorted to **mudslinging,** or attempts to ruin their opponent's reputation with insults. The candidates also used slogans, buttons, and rallies. Such practices became a regular part of American political life.

G2 In the election, Jackson received most of the votes cast in the frontier states. He also received many votes in the South, where his support for states' rights was popular. John C. Calhoun of South Carolina, who had been Adams's vice president, switched parties to run with Jackson. Calhoun also supported states' rights. Jackson won the election easily. Shortly after the election, Jackson's supporters officially formed the Democratic Party.

✓ **PROGRESS CHECK**

Making Connections What practices of the 1828 election are still used today?

Reading **HELP**DESK **CCSS**

mudslinging a method in election campaigns that uses gossip and lies to make an opponent look bad

bureaucracy a system of government in which specialized tasks are carried out by appointed officials rather than by elected ones

Academic Vocabulary (Tier 2 Words)

facilitate to help make happen
participate to take part in

326 *The Jackson Era*

netw⊙rks *Online Teaching Options*

MAP

The Election of 1828— A Corrupt Bargain

Speculating Use the interactive image about the corrupt bargain to discuss Henry Clay throwing his support to John Quincy Adams and using his influence to help Adams be selected as president. **Ask: How did Clay influence the House of Representatives?** *(He was the Speaker and used his power to defeat Jackson.)*

See page 321C for other online activities.

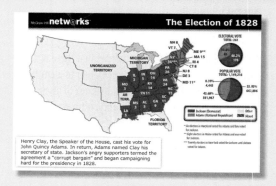

Henry Clay, the Speaker of the House, cast his vote for John Quincy Adams. In return, Adams named Clay his secretary of state. Jackson's angry supporters termed the agreement a "corrupt bargain" and began campaigning hard for the presidency in 1828.

ANSWERS, p. 326

INFOGRAPHIC

1. Jackson got 47 more than he needed. He needed 131, the majority of the 261 electoral vote total.

2. **CRITICAL THINKING** The electoral votes were not split among several candidates, guaranteeing that one candidate would have the majority.

✓ **PROGRESS CHECK** mudslinging, election slogans, rallies, campaign buttons, and events such as dinners

Jackson as President

GUIDING QUESTION *How did Andrew Jackson make the American political system more democratic?*

Andrew Jackson had qualities most Americans admired. He was a patriot, a self-made man, and a war hero. Thousands of ordinary people came to Washington for his inauguration. Later, many attended a White House reception.

Expanded Voting Rights

President Andrew Jackson promised "equal protection and equal benefits" for all Americans—at least, all white American men. Jackson's promise reflected the spirit of the times.

In the nation's early years, only men who owned property or paid taxes could vote. By the 1820s, many states had loosened these requirements. White male sharecroppers, factory workers, and others could now **participate** in the political process. By 1828, nearly all states let voters, rather than state legislatures, choose presidential electors. Women still could not vote. African Americans and Native Americans had few rights of any kind.

Making Government More Democratic

Democrats wanted to further open government to the people. They argued that ordinary citizens could do most government jobs. They were disturbed that the federal government had become a **bureaucracy** (byuh•RAH•kruh•see), a system in which nonelected officials carry out laws.

R1

R2

V

Andrew Jackson's supporters gather outside the White House hoping to shake hands with a president who seemed to be just like them.

▶ **CRITICAL THINKING**
Drawing Conclusions Why do you think people identified so closely with Andrew Jackson?

CORBIS SYGMA

McGraw-Hill **networks** | Jackson's Inauguration

The inaugural ball was a wild event, with Jackson's supporters packing rooms on the first floor of the White House. Furniture was broken as men with muddy boots stood on tables and chairs, hoping to get a glimpse of the new president.

CORBIS SYGMA

R1 **Reading Skills**

Finding the Main Idea Have students read the introduction on this page. Ask students to explain how Jackson was different from previous presidents of the country. **Ask: Why do you think so many people identified with Jackson?** *(Students may note that he came from a poor family and was a self-made man.)* Explore the concept of Jackson as a "common man" and why such an image might make a candidate appealing. **AL** **ELL** Visual/Spatial

R2 **Reading Skills**

Discussing Direct students to read the text. Then discuss with the class Jackson's promise to expand voting rights. **Ask: Who could participate in the political process at this time?** *(white males, with the inclusion of sharecroppers and factory workers)* **Who was excluded?** *(women, Native Americans, and African Americans)*

V **Visual Skills**

Interpreting Call students' attention to the image of the crowd gathered outside the White House on Inauguration Day in 1829. Have students look closely at the crowd and describe what they are wearing (winter clothes; some people are wearing fancy clothes, and others are wearing plain clothing). **Ask: What can you tell about the crowd from what they are wearing?** *(Students' answers will vary but should include that people with different levels of income attended the inauguration.)* **BL** Help students summarize what they have learned about Jackson and his supporters. Then have students work in small groups to role play what people in the crowd might have said or done during the inauguration. **Kinesthetic**

ANSWER, p. 327

CRITICAL THINKING He had qualities many people admired and identified with: patriotism, humble beginnings, self-reliance, resulting in prosperity, and success in war.

Jacksonian Democracy

C1 Critical Thinking Skills

Evaluating Describe the spoils system and who benefitted from it. **AL** **ELL** **Ask: Do you think the spoils system is truly democratic? Why or why not?** *(Answers will vary, but students should be able to defend their point of view.)* **BL**

T Technology Skills

Using Digital Tools Point out that the small biography of Jackson says he was a war hero. Have students use a digital encyclopedia or the Internet to find out why Jackson has this reputation. Ask students to identify the wars in which Jackson participated and the role he played in them. **BL**

W Writing Skills

Argument Ask students to take a position about whether or not Jackson was a true war hero and to use evidence from the text and from their research to support their position. **Verbal/Linguistic**

C2 Critical Thinking Skills

Identifying Central Issues Ask students to recall the definition of *tariff*. **Ask: Why did many Northerners support tariffs while many Southerners opposed them?** *(The tariff protected Northern industries from foreign imports. The South, which depended on trade with Europe, resented having to pay more for imported goods.)*

BIOGRAPHY

W **T**

Andrew Jackson (1767–1845)

Like many of his supporters, Andrew Jackson was born in a log cabin. A noted war hero, Jackson was called "Old Hickory" because he was said to be as tough as a hickory stick. Small farmers, craftspeople, and others who felt left out of the expanding American economy admired Jackson. They felt that his rise from a log cabin to the White House demonstrated the kind of success story possible only in the United States.

▶ **CRITICAL THINKING**
Making Inferences Why do you think voters would identify with a candidate who was from humble beginnings?

Soon after taking office in 1829, Jackson fired many federal workers and replaced them with his supporters. The fired employees protested. They charged that the president was acting like a tyrant.

C1 One Jackson supporter said: "To the victors belong the spoils." In other words, because Jackson had won the election, his supporters had the right to the spoils, or benefits, of victory. This practice of replacing current government employees with supporters of the winner is called the **spoils system.**

Jackson's supporters also abandoned the unpopular caucus system, in which top party leaders chose the party's candidates for office. Instead, parties began using **nominating conventions** (NAHM•ih•nayt•ing kuhn•VEN• shuhnz), where delegates from the states chose the party's presidential candidate. This system allowed many more people to participate in the selection of candidates.

✓ **PROGRESS CHECK**

Analyzing How did nominating conventions make government more democratic?

The Tariff Debate

GUIDING QUESTION *How did a fight over tariffs become a debate about states' rights versus federal rights?*

A tariff is a tax on imported goods. The high tariff on European manufactured goods was pleasing to Northeastern factory owners. Tariffs made European goods more expensive. This encouraged Americans to buy American-made goods. Southerners disliked the tariff. They had a profitable trade selling their cotton to Europe. They feared that taxing European goods might hurt this trade. In addition, tariffs meant higher prices for the goods they bought from their European trading partners.

In 1828 Congress had passed a very high tariff law. Vice President Calhoun claimed that a state had the right to nullify, or refuse to accept, a federal law if it was not in that state's best interests. President Jackson disagreed with this reasoning. He feared that nullification would destroy the Union.

C2

Bettmann/CORBIS

Reading **HELP**DESK (CCSS)

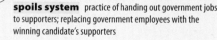

spoils system practice of handing out government jobs to supporters; replacing government employees with the winning candidate's supporters

nominating convention a meeting in which representative members of a political party choose candidates to run for important elected offices

---

netw⊙rks *Online Teaching Options*

IMAGE

The Nullification Crisis

Finding the Main Idea Read aloud the description of the political cartoon. Help students explore the text within the cartoon. Then call on one volunteer to state the reason the North wanted the tariffs and another volunteer to state the reason the South was opposed to them. A third volunteer can present Henry Clay's compromise. **ELL**

See page 321C for other online activities.

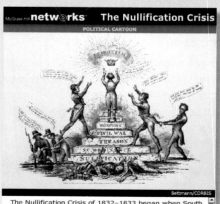

McGraw-Hill **netw⊙rks** The Nullification Crisis

POLITICAL CARTOON

Bettmann/CORBIS

The Nullification Crisis of 1832–1833 began when South Carolina nullified, or invalidated, the tariff acts of 1828 and 1832. South Carolina believed that these acts favored northern manufacturers over southern agricultural industries and were therefore

---

ANSWERS, p. 328

CRITICAL THINKING Such a candidate may understand ordinary people's concerns, and his success might make people think that they could rise above their humble situations.

✓ **PROGRESS CHECK** Conventions enabled more people to take part in the selection of candidates for elected office.

In 1830, at a Washington dinner marking Thomas Jefferson's birthday, Jackson had a chance to make his feelings on nullification known. He offered a toast. Looking directly at Calhoun, the president declared, "Our Union! It must be preserved!" Answering Jackson's challenge, the vice president rose with a toast of his own: "The Union, next to our liberty, most dear." To make sure his meaning was clear, Calhoun added, "It can only be preserved by respecting the rights of the states."

Not long after Jackson and Calhoun faced off at the dinner, Congress passed the Maysville Road bill. The bill provided federal funds for the building of a road in Kentucky. Jackson vetoed the bill. Jackson argued that because the road would be entirely within Kentucky, it should be a state project. In other words, the federal government should support only projects that benefited the entire nation.

In 1832 Congress passed a lower tariff. It was not enough to cool the protest. South Carolina passed the Nullification Act, declaring it would not pay "illegal" tariffs. The state threatened to secede, or break away, from the Union if the federal government interfered.

Jackson believed in a strong Union. He asked Congress to pass the Force Bill. This act allowed him to use the military to enforce federal law. South Carolina accepted the new tariff but nullified the Force Bill.

☑ **PROGRESS CHECK**

Making Inferences How might the workers at a factory in the Northeast react to the lowering of the tariff?

LESSON 1 REVIEW (CCSS)

Review Vocabulary (Tier 3 Words)

1. Show understanding of the following terms by using them in a sentence about the election of 1824. RH.6–8.4

   a. plurality   **b.** majority

2. Use the following terms in a sentence that illustrates how the terms are connected. RH.6–8.4

   a. bureaucracy   **b.** spoils system

Answer the Guiding Questions

3. *Evaluating* How do you think new election campaign methods affected American democracy? RH.6–8.1

4. *Analyzing* How did the election of 1828 show the growth of democracy? RH.6–8.1

5. *Explaining* How was the fight over tariffs related to the issue of states' rights? RH.6–8.2

6. **INFORMATIVE/EXPLANATORY** Andrew Jackson once said, "One man with courage makes a majority." Write a paragraph explaining what you think Jackson meant by this quote and how this idea influenced his leadership. RH.6–8.9, WHST.6–8.1

Lesson 1 **329**

LESSON 1 REVIEW ANSWERS

1. Sample sentence: Although Andrew Jackson won a plurality of the popular vote in the election of 1824, he was not the choice of a majority of voters.

2. Sample sentence: The spoils system fills a government bureaucracy with employees who supported the winning candidate for elected office.

3. The use of campaign buttons, slogans, and mass events like rallies stirred up public enthusiasm and excitement about elections. Combined with the expansion of voting rights, this involved more people in the political process.

4. Compared to 1824, many more voters participated in the election of 1828. In the same period, many states allowed more white males to vote.

5. To be effective, tariffs have to apply nationally. As importers of goods, the Southern states opposed tariffs and believed it was their right, as ratifiers of the Constitution, to not obey federal tariff laws.

6. Answers will vary, but students may point to Jackson's toughness and commitment to do what he thought was right, whether it was overcoming his loss in the 1824 election or his determination to enact tariffs despite opposition and the conflict over nullification that threatened the Union.

R **Reading Skills**

Explaining Direct students to the first sentence in the second paragraph that reads, "Not long after Jackson and Calhoun faced off at the dinner." **Ask: What evidence in the text supports this statement?** *(The two toasts showed their differences of opinion.)* **AL** **ELL** Verbal/Linguistic

Making Connections

Challenge students to recall the meaning of the term *states' rights*. *(rights and powers that are reserved for the states by the Constitution)* **AL** **ELL** Ask why Jackson, as a states' rights advocate, would have pushed Congress to pass the Force Bill, which empowered the federal government to use force to carry out federal laws in the states. Explore how Jackson's actions showed the characteristics of leadership. *(Students should recognize that he placed his duties to the nation as president ahead of is personal beliefs.)* **BL**

Have students complete the Lesson 1 Review.

CLOSE & REFLECT

Remind students that the title of this lesson is Jacksonian Democracy. **Ask: Do Jackson's policies and practices really hold true to the idea of democracy?** *(Students' answers may vary.)*

ANSWER, p. 329

☑ **PROGRESS CHECK** High tariffs make European goods more expensive for U.S. buyers. With lower tariffs, Americans might buy more European goods and fewer goods from Northeastern factories.

ENGAGE

Bellringer Ask students how they would feel if a government official told them that they had to move out of their home. Then have students discuss how they would feel if the reason was that another family wanted to live in their home. Tell students that in this lesson they will learn how most of the Native Americans remaining in the eastern United States were forced to move west in the 1820s and 1830s so that white settlers could have the Native Americans' land. Intrapersonal

TEACH & ASSESS

G1 Critical Thinking Skills

Recognizing Bias Remind students of the originally large cultural difference between the Native Americans in the Southeast and white settlers. Explain that Native Americans were most likely surprised by the cultural difference, but to get along with white settlers, several groups changed their lifestyles to be more like the white settlers. **Ask: What does the term *Five Civilized Tribes* reveal about the attitudes white settlers had toward Native Americans?** *(that they were generally inferior to white culture)* **Why do you think these Native Americans made such large changes in the way they lived?** *(Answers will vary and may include fitting in with the settlers or trying to stop the settlers from taking their land.)* **BL**

C2 Critical Thinking Skills

Identifying Points of View Remind students that sports teams, choirs, and other school groups often wear uniforms or very similar clothing. Students who are good friends often dress and behave in similar ways. Then **ask: If the Five Civilized Tribes had adopted white culture, why did many white Americans want them to move?** *(The white Americans wanted the land for themselves.)* **Why do you think adopting white culture wasn't enough to persuade white settlers to accept the Native Americans?** *(Students' answers will vary but may include that the settlers were greedy or that the Native Americans still seemed different from the settlers.)* **BL Interpersonal**

ANSWER, p. 330

TAKING NOTES: Cherokee: The Cherokee were unsuccessful in their efforts to negotiate with Georgia and the federal government, and moved west peacefully; **Seminole:** fought U.S. troops who were trying to remove them and were successful in delaying removal for a time.

---

net✪rks
There's More Online!

☑ **GRAPHIC ORGANIZER** Seminole and Cherokee Resistance

☑ **MAP** The Removal of Native Americans, 1820–1840

☑ **PRIMARY SOURCE** Osceola

☑ **VIDEO**

Lesson 2
Conflicts Over Land

ESSENTIAL QUESTION *What are the consequences when cultures interact?*

IT MATTERS BECAUSE

The forced removal and relocation of Native Americans in the 1830s largely ended the Native American presence in the eastern United States.

Removing Native Americans

GUIDING QUESTION *Why were Native Americans forced to abandon their land and move west?*

As the nation expanded west, many Native Americans still remained in the East. The Cherokee, Creek, Seminole, Chickasaw, and Choctaw peoples lived in Georgia, Alabama, Mississippi, and Florida. These groups had created successful farming communities that were much like many other American communities. As a result, Americans considered them "civilized" and referred to them as the "Five Civilized Tribes."

Though Americans recognized the success of the Five Civilized Tribes, they did not necessarily respect their rights. In fact, some white people wanted the Native Americans' lands for themselves. To make this possible, they wanted the **federal** government to force eastern Native Americans to **relocate** to lands west of the Mississippi River.

Andrew Jackson supported the white settlers' demand for Native American land. He had once fought the Creek and Seminole in Georgia and Florida to give the settlers more land. When he became president in 1829, he stated that he wanted to move all Native Americans to the Great Plains. Many people believed this region to be a wasteland

*© North Wind Picture Archives.
(c) Woolaroc Museum, Bartlesville, OK/SuperStock.
(r) Dennis MacDonald*

Reading HELPDESK **(ccss)**

Taking Notes: *Describing* RH.6–8.2

As you read, use a graphic organizer like this one to describe how each group of Native Americans resisted removal, and the result.

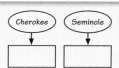

Content Vocabulary (Tier 3 Words)
• **relocate**

330 *The Jackson Era*

---

net✪rks *Online Teaching Options*

VIDEO

A Nation Divided

Identifying Points of View Have students view the video about the multi-ethnic origins of the Seminole people. Assign students to work in small groups. Have them identify the historical and present perspectives of "red Seminoles," "black Seminoles," and the Federal government and form their own opinions about the perspectives of these three groups.
Interpersonal Intrapersonal

See page 321D for other online activities.

BBC Motion Gallery Education

Like most people of the Americas in the early 1800s, the Seminole in this village lived off the land they farmed.

where American settlers would never want to live. Many people thought that if all Native Americans moved there, conflict with them would be ended.

The Cherokee Versus Georgia

In 1830 President Jackson pushed the Indian Removal Act through Congress. This law allowed the federal government to pay Native Americans to move west. Jackson then sent officials to make treaties with the Native Americans in the Southeast. In 1834 Congress established the Indian Territory. Most of the region was located in what is now the state of Oklahoma. This area was to be the new home for the Native Americans of the Southeast.

Most eastern Native American peoples felt forced to sell their land and move west. The Cherokee refused to do so. In treaties of the 1790s, the federal government had recognized the Cherokee as a separate nation. However, the state of Georgia, in which many Cherokee lived, refused to accept the Cherokee's status. In 1830 Georgia made Cherokee land part of the state. It also began to enforce state laws in the Cherokee Nation.

As pressure for relocation mounted, the Cherokee appealed to the American people:

PRIMARY SOURCE

66 We are aware, that some persons suppose it will be for our advantage to remove beyond the Mississippi.... Our people universally think otherwise.... We wish to remain on the land of our fathers. 99

—Appeal of the Cherokee Nation, 1830

North Wind Picture Archives

relocate to move to another place

Academic Vocabulary
federal relating to a national government (Tier 2)

Build Vocabulary: *Multiple Meaning Words*
The term *federal* applies to more than just the national government of the United States. It describes any system of government in which several smaller state or district governments unite but still keep control over their own internal affairs.

Lesson 2   **331**

This painting depicts the Cherokee on the Trail of Tears.

▶ **CRITICAL THINKING**
Analyzing Images What does this image suggest about the Native Americans' experience on the Trail of Tears? Use details from the painting to explain your answer.

W Writing Skills

Informative/Explanatory Have small groups of students discuss the painting of the Trail of Tears. Prompt them to look for different ways people traveled and carried their belongings, and to identify the weather or season. Then ask students to write a description of what they see in the painting.
Verbal/Linguistic

C Critical Thinking Skills

Drawing Conclusions Remind students that the Framers of the Constitution created three branches of government—the executive, legislative, and judicial. **Ask:** What was the Cherokee response to the order to leave their land? *(to go to the Supreme Court and sue for the right to remain on their land)* **Based on their response, how well did the Cherokee understand and adapt to white culture?** *(Answers will vary, but students should demonstrate comprehension of the fact that the Cherokee understood white culture well and had made major adaptations to fit in with it because they managed to figure out the legal system and win in the Supreme Court.)*

Content Background Knowledge

- Sequoyah, a Cherokee, invented a syllabary, a table of syllables, so that the Cherokee language could be written.
- The Cherokee had a written constitution.
- The *Cherokee Phoenix* was in Cherokee and English so that white settlers sympathetic to the Cherokee's situation could also read it.

Still, Georgia pressured the Cherokee. In response, the Cherokee turned to the U.S. Supreme Court. In *Worcester* v. *Georgia* (1832), Chief Justice John Marshall ruled that Georgia had no right to interfere with the Cherokee. President Jackson, who supported Georgia's efforts to remove the Cherokee, declared that he would ignore the Supreme Court's ruling. "John Marshall has made his decision," Jackson is said to have declared, "now let him enforce it." No one was willing or able to challenge the president's failure to enforce the Court's ruling.

The Trail of Tears

By 1835, the Cherokee were divided about what to do. That year the federal government convinced a small number of Cherokee—about 500 of them—to sign the Treaty of New Echota. In this treaty, the group agreed to give up all Cherokee land by 1838.

Cherokee Chief John Ross sent a protest to the U.S. Senate. Ross explained that the few Cherokee who signed the treaty did not speak for all the 17,000 Cherokee in the region. Many white Americans, including senators Daniel Webster and Henry Clay, also opposed the treaty as unfair. However, their pleas did not change the minds of President Jackson or the white settlers. In 1836 the Senate approved the treaty by a single vote.

Reading HELPDESK (CCSS)

Reading in the Content Area: *Bar Graphs*

Bar graphs often have vertical bars, but they may also appear with horizontal bars, as in the graph on the opposite page. In such graphs, the subject of each bar appears on the left. The item being measured—in this case, people—appears at the bottom of the graph.

332 *The Jackson Era*

---

netw⊙rks *Online Teaching Options*

IMAGE

The Seminole Wars

Comparing Use the interactive image about the Seminole Wars to have students compare the reaction of the Seminole to being pushed out of Florida to the reaction of the other Five Civilized Tribes.

See page 321D for other online activities.

This became known as the First Seminole War. In 1832 the U.S. government tried to force the Seminole into Indian Territory in Oklahoma. This started the Second Seminole War. Following the conflict, most Seminole moved to Indian Territory.

ANSWER, p. 332

CRITICAL THINKING Answers will vary. The painting shows that the groups were large and traveled by wagon, on horseback, and on foot. The soldier shows that they moved under guard. Students may also note the possessions carried in the wagons and the dejected postures and facial expressions on some of the figures.

When the treaty's 1838 deadline arrived, only about 2,000 Cherokee had moved west. Jackson's successor, President Martin Van Buren, ordered the army to move the rest of them. In May 1838, General Winfield Scott arrived in the Cherokee Nation with 7,000 troops to remove the remaining Cherokee by force. He told them that resistance and escape were hopeless. The Cherokee knew that fighting would lead to their destruction. Filled with sadness and anger, Cherokee leaders gave in.

Between June and December 1838, soldiers rounded up Cherokee in North Carolina, Georgia, Alabama, and Tennessee. Under guard, the Cherokee began their march to Indian Territory in the West.

The forced relocation of some 15,000 Cherokee was a terrible ordeal. Most people were not prepared for the journey. Trouble started even before they set out. As the Cherokee crowded in camps and awaited the command to begin their march, illness broke out. As many as 2,000 Cherokee died.

Once on the trail, the Cherokee suffered from hunger and from exposure to the weather. These conditions led to the deaths of another 2,000 people.

When the relocation was over, about one quarter of the Cherokee population was dead. The Cherokee came to call their forced journey west the Trail Where They Cried. Historians call it the Trail of Tears.

R

C

☑ PROGRESS CHECK

Assessing What was the purpose of the Indian Removal Act?

NATIVE AMERICAN REMOVAL

GRAPH SKILL

FORCED MIGRATION, 1830–1840

CHOCTAW

CREEK

CHICKASAW

CHEROKEE

SEMINOLE

| 0 | 5,000 | 10,000 | 15,000 | 20,000 |

NUMBER OF PEOPLE

After passage of the Indian Removal Act of 1830, the government began to force the Five Civilized Tribes living east of the Mississippi River to move to an area that was located in what is now part of the state of Oklahoma.

1 **CALCULATING** About how many Native Americans had to move to Indian Territory between 1830 and 1840?

2 **CRITICAL THINKING**
Drawing Inferences Which Native American groups in the South had the largest population in the early 1800s? How can you tell?

Lesson 2 **333**

R Reading Skills

Discussing After students have read the text on this page, discuss with them the forced relocation of the Cherokee, also known as the Trail of Tears. **Ask: How do you think the Native Americans felt about making this journey?** *(Answers will vary, but students will note that although the Native Americans tried to fight their removal, they were outnumbered and outmaneuvered. In addition to having to leave their homelands, the journey was long and difficult. They were subject to extreme weather conditions and a scarcity of food and water. Under these conditions, they would likely to feel sad and angry.)* **AL** **Intrapersonal**

C Critical Thinking Skills

Determining Cause and Effect Remind students that many Cherokee died as a result of the Indian Removal Act that President Jackson pushed through Congress. **Ask: What caused the death of so many Cherokee after they left their homes?** *(illness in the camps where they waited to begin the relocation and hunger and exposure as they walked west to Indian Territory)* **AL** **ELL**

GRAPHIC ORGANIZER

Taking Notes: *Describing:* The Removal of Native Americans

Describing Have students work with a partner and use the interactive graphic organizer to describe how Native American groups resisted removal. When students have completed their graphic organizers, have partners work with one or two other sets of partners to compare their notes. **AL** **ELL**

See page 321D for other online activities.

netw⊕rks

Name: _____ Date: _____

TAKING NOTES: *Describing*
ACTIVITY As you read, use the diagram to describe how each group of Native Americans resisted removal and the result.

Cherokee

Seminole

UNDO CLEAR SAVE

ANSWERS, p. 333

☑ **PROGRESS CHECK** to provide more good land for settlement of white Americans and end conflicts between white settlers and Native Americans

GRAPH SKILL
1. more than 40,000
2. **CRITICAL THINKING** The Creek and Cherokee; the graph shows that they had the largest numbers of people forced to migrate.

C₁ Critical Thinking Skills

Comparing Have students compare the reaction of the Seminole to being pushed out of Florida to the reaction of the other Five Civilized Tribes. **Ask: Why do you think the Seminole decided to fight?** (Answers may include variations in leadership, the experience of having lived under Spanish control, the influence of the Black Seminoles who feared a return to slavery, and the perception that they could successfully resist forced removal.) **BL**

C₂ Critical Thinking Skills

Identifying Points of View Discuss why escaped enslaved people would want to fight on the side of the Seminole. **Ask: How would the transfer of Florida from Spain to the United States have affected the Black Seminoles?** (Answers will vary but should suggest that it raised fears of being returned to slavery.) Discuss how these fears might have encouraged Black Seminoles to fight alongside the Seminole. **BL** Verbal/Linguistic

Making Connections

Explain to the class that when Europeans started colonizing North America, the Creek inhabited most of what is now the southeastern United States. Later, as American settlers pushed south, some Creek migrated into Spanish Florida. There they joined other Native Americans and became known as the *Seminole*, which, roughly translated, means "runaway." Point out that when Spain ceded Florida to the United States, life for the Seminole began to change.

Resistance and Removal

GUIDING QUESTION *Why did some Native Americans resist resettlement?*

C₁ Many Native American peoples did not want to give up their lands. However, the Seminole in Florida were the only group to successfully resist removal. They faced pressure in the early 1830s to sign treaties giving up their land, but the Seminole leader Osceola (ah•see•OH•luh) and his followers refused to leave. They decided to fight instead. Osceola was born a Creek but lived among the Seminole of Florida. "I will make the white man red with blood, and then blacken him in the sun and rain," Osceola vowed.

The Seminole Wars

In 1835 the U.S. Army arrived in Florida to force the removal of the Seminole. Instead, in December 1835, a group of Seminole attacked troops led by Major Francis Dade as they marched across central Florida. Only a few soldiers **survived.** The Dade Massacre prompted a call for additional troops to fight the Seminole.

C₂ Between 1835 and 1842, about 3,000 Seminole and African Americans known as Black Seminoles fought some 30,000 U.S. soldiers. The Black Seminoles were escaped slaves from Georgia and South Carolina. Some lived among the Seminole people. Others had built their own settlements. Like the Seminole, they did not want to move. One reason is that they feared the American soldiers would force them back into slavery. Together, the Seminole and Black Seminoles attacked white settlements along the Florida coast. They made surprise attacks and then retreated back into the forests and swamps.

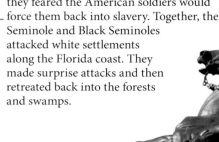

This statue of Osceola is located in Tallahassee, Florida.

Reading HELPDESK (CCSS)

Academic Vocabulary (Tier 2 Words)

survive to continue existing or living after nearly being destroyed

networks   *Online Teaching Options*

PRIMARY SOURCE

Walt Whitman

Analyzing Primary Sources Use the interactive primary source excerpt of Walt Whitman's poem about Osceola's death to discuss his importance to the Seminole. Have volunteers read the poem and describe Whitman's thoughts and feelings about Osceola. **BL**

See page 321D for other online activities.

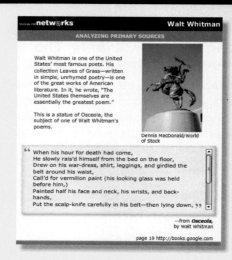

netw⊙rks   Walt Whitman

ANALYZING PRIMARY SOURCES

Walt Whitman is one of the United States' most famous poets. His collection Leaves of Grass—written in simple, unrhymed poetry—is one of the great works of American literature. In it, he wrote, "The United States themselves are essentially the greatest poem."

This is a statue of Osceola, the subject of one of Walt Whitman's poems.

Dennis MacDonald/World of Stock

" When his hour for death had come,
He slowly rais'd himself from the bed on the floor,
Drew on his war-dress, shirt, leggings, and girdled the belt around his waist,
Call'd for vermilion paint (his looking glass was held before him,)
Painted half his face and neck, his wrists, and back-hands,
Put the scalp-knife carefully in his belt—then lying down, "

—from *Osceola*, by Walt Whitman

page 19 http://books.google.com

The war cost the U.S. government over $20 million and the lives of more than 1,500 soldiers. Many Seminole also died. Others were captured and forced to move west. In 1842, with most of the surviving Seminole now in Indian Territory, the fighting stopped.

War broke out again in 1855 over what little land in Florida the Seminole had left. By 1858, the few remaining Seminole had escaped into the Everglades, where their descendants still live today.

Life in the West

By 1842, only a few scattered groups of Native Americans remained east of the Mississippi River. Most of them now lived in the West. They had given up more than 100 million acres of land. In return, they received about $68 million and 32 million acres west of the Mississippi. There they lived, organized by tribes, on reservations. Eventually, white settlement would extend into these areas as well.

The Five Civilized Tribes relocated in the eastern half of Indian Territory on lands already claimed by several Plains peoples, including the Osage, Comanche, and Kiowa. The U.S. Army built forts in the area and promised to protect the Five Civilized Tribes and maintain peace in the area. The Choctaw police force, known as the Lighthorsemen, also helped maintain order and public safety.

Settled in their new homes, the Five Civilized Tribes developed their own constitutions and governments. They built farms and schools. However, the disputes over removal that arose within each tribal group during the 1830s continued to divide the groups for years to come.

☑ **PROGRESS CHECK**

Analyzing What effect did the Native Americans' use of surprise attacks have on the Seminole Wars?

R1

R2

LESSON 2 REVIEW

Review Vocabulary (Tier 3 Words)

1. Use the term *relocate* to describe the relationship between the United States and Native Americans in the 1830s. RH.6–8.4

Answer the Guiding Questions

2. ***Explaining*** What reason did the government give for forcing the Native Americans to relocate? RH.6–8.2

3. ***Analyzing*** Why were the Cherokee forced to move in spite of the Supreme Court's ruling in *Worcester* v. *Georgia*? RH.6–8.1

4. ***Describing*** How did the Seminole resist removal? RH.6–8.2

5. **NARRATIVE** Write a diary entry as a Cherokee traveling to Indian Territory on the Trail of Tears. WHST.6–8.1, WHST.6–8.10

Lesson 2   **335**

LESSON 2 REVIEW ANSWERS

1. Possible answer: As American settlers moved onto Native American lands, the federal government put pressure on Native American groups to relocate to the West.

2. The government believed that if the Native Americans lived farther from the settlers, there would be less conflict between white settlers and Native Americans.

3. President Jackson ignored the Supreme Court's ruling and challenged the court to enforce it. No one did.

4. They refused to leave and used surprise attacks and quick retreats against the U.S. troops.

5. Diary entries will vary but should reflect the hardships of the journey and sorrow over the forced removal from and loss of their homeland.

R1 **Reading Skills**

Describing   After students have read the text on this page, ask them to describe the results of the removal of the Native Americans from their land. **Ask: How much land did the Five Civilized Tribes give up?** *(100 million acres)* **How much did they get in return from the government?** *($68 million and 32 million acres of land)*

R2 **Reading Skills**

Paraphrasing   Have students use details from the text to paraphrase the problem that the Five Civilized Tribes encountered when they arrived in the eastern half of Indian Territory. *(The land was already claimed by several Plains people.)* **Ask: What actions were taken to address this problem?** *(The U.S. Army built forts nearby, and the Choctaw police helped maintain order and public safety.)* **AL** **ELL**   Verbal/Linguistic

Have students complete the Lesson 2 Review.

CLOSE & REFLECT

Remind the class that many American citizens opposed the policy of removal. Encourage students to research, using either the library or the Internet, the current status of a Native American group discussed in this lesson. Be sure that students connect the impact of the forced migration to the group's current status. **Ask: Do you think the overall policy of Native American removal was fair? Why or why not?** *(Answers will vary, but students should be able to support their opinions with information from the lesson.)*

ANSWER, p. 335

☑ **PROGRESS CHECK**   The tactics made the war last longer because the Seminole were able to hold off the much larger U.S. forces.

ENGAGE

🔔 **Bellringer** Have students name some of the banks in their area. Explain to students that there is a Bank of the United States, but in 1832, there was turmoil about the purpose of that bank. Tell students that in this lesson, they will learn about the attempt to create the Second Bank of the United States and the political turmoil that arose from it.

TEACH & ASSESS

R Reading Skills

Explaining Ask volunteers to review Jackson's dislike for the Second Bank of the United States. Prompt students to support their explanations with evidence from their text. **Ask: Why did Andrew Jackson dislike Nicholas Biddle, the Bank's president?** *(Biddle was from a wealthy family, and Jackson prided himself on coming from nothing.)* **Which two major political opponents to Andrew Jackson were friends of Nicholas Biddle and supported the Bank?** *(Henry Clay and Daniel Webster)* AL ELL **Verbal/Linguistic**

Making Connections

The Bank was another sectional issue, with people in the Northeast generally favoring it and people in the South and West generally opposing it.

netw⊙rks
There's More Online!

☑ **GRAPHIC ORGANIZER**
The Bank War

☑ **MAP** Elections of 1836 and 1840

☑ **PRIMARY SOURCE**
• Jackson Political Cartoon
• Harrison Campaign Poster

Lesson 3
Jackson and the Bank

ESSENTIAL QUESTION *How do governments change?*

IT MATTERS BECAUSE

The ongoing struggle over the Bank of the United States represented the ongoing struggle over the role of the federal government.

Jackson's War Against the Bank

GUIDING QUESTION *What events occurred when President Jackson forced the National Bank to close?*

Andrew Jackson disliked the Second Bank of the United States long before he became president. Congress had set up the bank in 1816 to hold the federal government's money and to control the nation's money supply. Private bankers rather than elected officials ran the bank. Its president, Nicholas Biddle, represented everything Jackson disliked. Jackson prided himself on being a self-made western pioneer who had started with nothing. Biddle came from a wealthy Philadelphia family and had a good education and experience in financial matters.

In addition, the Bank's assigned duties made it a powerful **institution.** Many western settlers depended on being able to borrow money to run their farms. The Bank's strict policies made such loans difficult to obtain. Like many other westerners, Jackson viewed the Bank as a monopoly that favored wealthy Easterners and limited western growth.

The Bank and the Election of 1832

Jackson's opponents planned to use the Bank to defeat him in the 1832 presidential campaign. Senators Henry Clay and Daniel Webster were friends of Biddle. They persuaded Biddle to apply

© The Granger Collection, NYC. (c) Library of Congress Prints & Photographs Division, LC-USZ62-19198), (r) David J. & Janice L. Frent Collection/CORBIS

Reading HELPDESK CCSS

Taking Notes: *Identifying* RH.6–8.1
Use a chart like this one to identify the actions taken by President Jackson that put the Bank of the United States out of business.

Bank of United States Closes

Content Vocabulary (Tier 3 Words)
• **veto**

336 *The Jackson Era*

---

netw⊙rks *Online Teaching Options*

▶ **VIDEO**

The Second National Bank

Analyzing Discuss with students that Jackson's opponents planned to use the Bank against Jackson in the next presidential election. **Ask: What role did politics play in the conflict over the Bank?** *(Clay and Webster thought the Bank had the support of the American people and that Jackson would lose support if he vetoed the Bank's charter renewal. Clay wanted to run for president, and he and Webster thought that Jackson's veto would allow Clay to win the election.)* BL

See page 321E for other online activities.

ANSWER, p. 336

TAKING NOTES: [top] Jackson vetoes bill to renew Bank's charter; [middle] Jackson orders withdrawal of government money from the Bank; [lower] Jackson refuses to sign new Bank charter

early for a new charter—a government permit to run the Bank—even though the Bank's charter did not expire until 1836. They thought this would force Jackson to take action against the bank.

Clay and Webster believed the Bank had the support of the American people. They thought that if Jackson tried to **veto,** or reject, the renewal of the Bank's charter, he would lose support. Henry Clay wanted to run for president. He and Webster believed that Jackson's veto would help Clay defeat the president in the 1832 election.

Jackson was sick in bed when the bill to renew the Bank's charter came to him to sign. He told Secretary of State Martin Van Buren, "The bank is trying to kill me. But I will kill it." Jackson vetoed the bill. He argued that the Bank was unconstitutional despite the Supreme Court's decision to the contrary in *McCulloch* v. *Maryland* (1819).

Webster and Clay were right about one thing. The Bank did play a large part in the election of 1832. Instead of gaining support for Clay as president, however, their plan backfired. Most people supported Jackson's veto, and Jackson was reelected. Jackson then decided to "kill" the Bank even before its current charter ended. He ordered all government deposits withdrawn from the Bank and placed in smaller state banks. In 1836 he refused to sign a new charter for the Bank, and it closed.

The Panic of 1837

Jackson decided not to run for a third term in 1836. The Democrats chose Van Buren, Jackson's vice president during his second term. The Whigs, a new party that included former National Republicans and other anti-Jackson forces, were the opposition. The Whigs nominated three candidates. Each had support in a different part of the nation. The Whigs hoped this tactic would keep Van Buren from getting a majority of the electoral votes. Then the election would be decided by the House of Representatives, which the Whigs controlled. The Whigs' plan failed. Jackson's popularity and support helped Van Buren win both the popular and the electoral vote.

Van Buren had barely taken office when a financial panic hit the nation. The panic was in part an effect of Jackson's victory over the Bank of the United States. When the Bank ceased operations in 1836, control over state banks vanished.

The Granger Collection, NYC

BORN TO COMMAND.

OF VETO MEMORY.

HAD I BEEN CONSULTED.

KING ANDREW THE FIRST.

Jackson's opponents compared him to a bad king—a tyrant with too much power.

▶ **CRITICAL THINKING**
Analyzing Primary Sources What is the meaning of the documents that appear at Jackson's feet?

veto to reject a bill and prevent it from becoming law

Academic Vocabulary (Tier 2 Words)

institution an organization that has an important purpose in society

C Critical Thinking Skills

Analyzing Discuss Jackson's actions after the veto of the renewal of the Bank's charter. Explain to students that after his reelection in 1832, he "killed" the Bank before the current charter ended. Make sure students understand his role in ultimately shutting down the Bank. **Ask: What action did Jackson take to kill the Bank even before its charter expired?** (He withdrew the government's deposits from the Bank and placed them in state banks.) **AL**

R Reading Skills

Discussing After students have read the text, ask them to explain why Henry Clay and Daniel Webster were correct with regard to the importance of the Bank, yet wrong about the outcome. **Ask: Why was Clay's plan unsuccessful?** (He was wrong about the public's attitude toward the Bank and the public's support for Jackson's veto.) **BL** **Verbal/Linguistic**

King Andrew I

Discussing Use the interactive image entitled "King Andrew I" to discuss Jackson's veto of the bill to renew the Bank's charter and why people thought he exercised too much power. **Ask: How did some of the Bank's assigned duties make it a powerful institution?** (The Bank was in charge of loaning money but had established strict policies with regard to loans. This made it difficult for western settlers to borrow money to run their farms.) **BL** What were Jackson's objections to the Bank? (It was run by private bankers rather than elected officials. He viewed the Bank as a monopoly and thought its policies were biased in favor of wealthy people in the East and against western settlers.)

See page 321E for other online activities.

McGraw-Hill **networks**   **King Andrew I**

POLITICAL CARTOON

BORN TO COMMAND.

Following President Andrew Jackson's veto of the Bank bill, many of his opponents accused him of abusing the powers he was given as president. Some began referring to him as "King Andrew." This cartoon, by an unknown artist, shows Jackson as a tyrannical king, trampling the Constitution.

KING ANDREW THE FIRST.
The Granger Collection, NYC

ANSWER, p. 337

CRITICAL THINKING King Andrew I is standing on the torn-up pieces of the Constitution of the United States, meaning that he has no regard for the law. The cartoonist is charging the president with ignoring or violating the Constitution and abusing his executive power.

R Reading Skills

Explaining After they have read the text, ask students to explain why Van Buren took little action to ease the crisis. **Ask:** What economic principle did Van Buren believe in? *(laissez-faire)* Make sure everyone understands the term *laissez-faire* and that Van Buren's belief in this principle is what influenced his decisions with regards to the Panic of 1837. AL ELL

V Visual Skills

Analyzing Images Help students read the words in the speech balloons in the political cartoon. Explain that the word *huzza* means "hooray." Point out the figure who gives his name as the ghost of commerce. If needed, remind students that *commerce* means "buying and selling goods and services." **Ask:** Why is the ghost of commerce holding a paper that says "Repeal the Treasury Order"? *(because repealing the order would help strengthen the federal bank and prevent further bank crises)* BL Visual/Spatial

W Writing Skills

Informative/Explanatory Ask students to write an explanation of the 1837 financial panic that ended with the creation of the federal treasury in 1840. Remind students to put events in chronological order and to use words that signal cause-and-effect relationships. BL Verbal/Linguistic

C Critical Thinking Skills

Making Connections Discuss the political impact of the financial crisis on the Democratic Party. **Ask:** How did the Panic of 1837 help the Whig Party? *(People disagreed with Van Buren's actions, and this created a split in the Democratic Party, giving the Whigs the chance to win the presidency in 1840.)*

ANSWER, p. 338

✓ **PROGRESS CHECK** to provide a place to deposit government funds, to keep state and private banks from using those funds to back their notes, and to prevent future bank crises

---

Some of these banks began issuing huge amounts of banknotes. Concerned that these notes had little value, the government stopped accepting them as payment for purchasing public land. People began to question the value of their banknotes, leading to economic panic.

The Panic of 1837 led to a depression, a severe economic downturn. Land values dropped and banks failed. Thousands of businesses closed. Many workers lost their jobs, and farmers lost their land. In cities across the nation, many people could not afford food or rent.

President Van Buren did little to ease the crisis. He believed in the principle of *laissez-faire*—that government should interfere as little as possible in the nation's economy. However, Van Buren did persuade Congress to create an independent federal treasury in 1840. This meant that the government no longer had to deposit its money in private banks as it had been doing. It would keep its money in the federal treasury instead. This new system prevented state and private banks from using government money to back their banknotes. It helped prevent further bank crises.

Calling it a "second declaration of independence," Van Buren and his supporters hailed the passing of the federal treasury law. Still, members of Van Buren's own Democratic Party joined the Whigs in criticizing the act. The split in the Democratic Party gave the Whigs a chance to win the presidency in 1840.

This cartoon blames President Van Buren's policies for the Panic of 1837. Van Buren is standing, second from the right.

NEW EDITION OF MACBETH.   BANK-OH'S! GHOST.

Library of Congress Prints & Photographs Division, [LC-USZ62-19198]

✓ **PROGRESS CHECK**

Explaining What was the purpose of the new treasury system?

Reading **HELP**DESK CCSS

Build Vocabulary: *Word Origins*

The French term *laissez-faire* is a combination of a form of the verb *laisser*, which means "to let or allow," and the verb *faire*, meaning "to do." In translation, the phrase literally means "let them do." As a policy, it has been translated as "let them do as they please," referring to the people. In practice, it refers to giving the government the smallest role possible.

338 *The Jackson Era*

---

networks   *Online Teaching Options*

IMAGE

The Panic of 1837

Making Connections Explain to students that Van Buren was barely in office when the Panic of 1837 hit the nation. Be sure students connect Jackson's actions with regard to the Bank to the financial panic. **Ask:** What did the Panic of 1837 lead to? *(an economic depression, a drop in land values, failing banks, business closures, and loss of jobs)* AL ELL Remind students that Van Buren believed in the economic principle of *laissez-faire*. **Ask:** How did Van Buren's belief in *laissez-faire* influence his decisions with regard to the Panic of 1837? *(Van Buren took little action to ease the crisis.)* BL

See page 321E for other online activities.

The Panic of 1837

The Panic of 1837 was a financial crisis that severely damaged the U.S. economy. One of the main reasons for the economic downturn was President Jackson's decision to withdraw federal funds from the Bank of the United States. He then distributed these funds among state banks and private financial institutions. State banks began loaning large sums of money, leading to high inflation. Currency began to lose its value. Foreign investors did not want to accept American currency

The Whigs in Power

GUIDING QUESTION *What events occurred during the 1840s that led to the weakening of the Whig party?*

When Van Buren ran for reelection in 1840, Democrats had held the White House for 12 years. Now, with the country still in the depths of depression, the Whigs thought they had a chance to win the presidency.

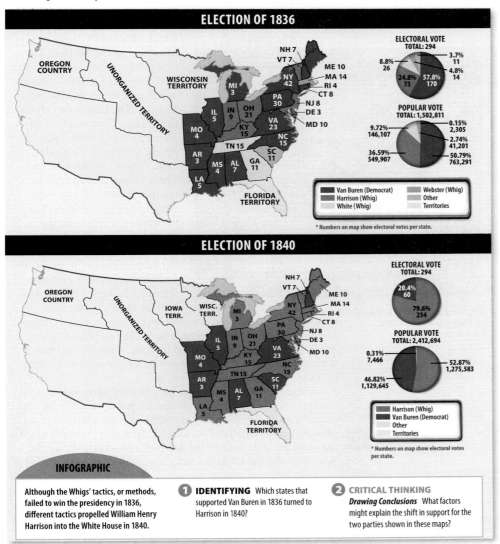

ELECTION OF 1836

ELECTORAL VOTE
TOTAL: 294

POPULAR VOTE
TOTAL: 1,502,811

Van Buren (Democrat)
Harrison (Whig)
White (Whig)
Webster (Whig)
Other
Territories

* Numbers on map show electoral votes per state.

ELECTION OF 1840

ELECTORAL VOTE
TOTAL: 294

POPULAR VOTE
TOTAL: 2,412,694

Harrison (Whig)
Van Buren (Democrat)
Other
Territories

* Numbers on map show electoral votes per state.

INFOGRAPHIC

Although the Whigs' tactics, or methods, failed to win the presidency in 1836, different tactics propelled William Henry Harrison into the White House in 1840.

1 **IDENTIFYING** Which states that supported Van Buren in 1836 turned to Harrison in 1840?

2 **CRITICAL THINKING**
Drawing Conclusions What factors might explain the shift in support for the two parties shown in these maps?

Lesson 3   **339**

R Reading Skills

Discussing As they read the text, ask students to speculate on how economic issues can impact an election. **Ask: Why do you think people make changes in their voting behavior during such times?** *(Answers will vary but should include that people often blame the party in power for the problem; people think that changing the party may change their own circumstances and help make things better for the country as a whole.)* **BL** **Verbal/Linguistic**

Making Connections

If possible, have students bring to class campaign literature from a recent election campaign. This literature may be either hard-copy brochures or printed out from candidates' Internet campaign sites. Point out that campaign literature is like an ad for a product. Both kinds of advertising are designed to persuade people to buy the product. Explain that in this case, the "product" is the candidate, and that people "buy the product" by giving the candidate their vote. **AL** **ELL**

Explain that historically, political advertising is not new. The media and methods of communication have changed drastically over the years, but the content and the objective are the same—to win votes for the candidate. Explain to students that political parties often used mudslinging as a method to persuade voters to vote against the other candidate. Have students recall the definition of *mudslinging* that they read in Lesson 1.

MAPS

The Election of 1836 and the Election of 1840

Analyzing Visuals Use the interactive maps to discuss the elections of 1836 and 1840. **Ask: Which party held the White House for 12 years before 1840?** *(the Democrats)*

See page 321E for other online activities.

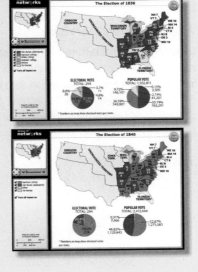

ANSWERS, p. 339

INFOGRAPHIC
1. Maine, Connecticut, Rhode Island, New York, Pennsylvania, Michigan, North Carolina, Mississippi, and Louisiana
2. **CRITICAL THINKING** Possible answers: public reaction to the Panic of 1837, the popularity and "common man" appeal of Harrison, or both

R Reading Skills

Identifying Write the names of the two 1840 presidential candidates on the board. Ask students to use details in the text to identify each candidate's political party and what they know about each candidate. *(Students should recognize: Martin Van Buren—Democrat and sitting president; William Henry Harrison—Whig and wealthy Ohioan)* **AL**

C1 Critical Thinking Skills

Comparing Compare with students the campaigns of Harrison and Van Buren. Remind students that Harrison portrayed himself as a war hero and simple frontiersman. **Ask: What was Harrison's actual background?** *(He was a wealthy Ohioan.)* **How did the Whigs and Harrison portray Van Buren?** *(They claimed he was a snob who was responsible for the depression.)* **AL** **ELL** Verbal/Linguistic

C2 Critical Thinking Skills

Analyzing Review with students Harrison's short-lived presidency. Discuss his death while in office. **Ask: Why was Harrison's death significant?** *(He was only in office for 32 days, his vice president became the youngest president in the history of the nation, and John Tyler became the first vice president to gain the presidency because of the death of the sitting president.)* **BL**

Content Background Knowledge

William Henry Harrison won this election by sweeping the Electoral College. Harrison's Inaugural Address lasted nearly two hours. Harrison was sixty-eight when he was elected. After standing in the cold without a coat, Harrison caught a chill, which developed into pneumonia. He died within a month of taking the oath of office and became the first president to die in office. The Whig Party would eventually dissolve after becoming divided over the issue of slavery and disappear by the 1850s.

ANSWER, p. 340

Reading Strategy Sample summary: The Whigs attacked Democrat Van Buren and portrayed their candidate, Harrison, as a "man of the people" to win the presidency in 1840.

The Log Cabin Campaign

To run against Van Buren, the Whigs united behind one of their 1836 candidates, William Henry Harrison. Like Andrew Jackson, Harrison was a hero of the War of 1812. John Tyler, a planter from Virginia, was Harrison's running mate. Harrison had first gained fame with his victory over Tecumseh's followers in the Battle of Tippecanoe in 1811. The Whigs made reference to this event in the campaign slogan: "Tippecanoe and Tyler Too."

Harrison needed the support of the workers and farmers who had voted for Jackson in order to win the election. The Whigs portrayed Harrison, who in reality was a wealthy Ohioan, as a simple frontiersman like Jackson. The Democrats attacked this image. They said that all Harrison was good for was sitting in front of a log cabin and collecting his military pension. These attacks played right into the hands of the Whigs, who adopted the log cabin as the **symbol** of their campaign.

During the campaign of 1840, the log cabin image appeared in paintings, banners, and political cartoons.

While presenting Harrison as a "man of the people," the Whigs portrayed Van Buren as a wealthy snob with perfume-scented whiskers. They blamed him for the depression and accused him of spending the people's money on expensive furniture for the White House. The Whigs' tactics and the effects of the depression seemed to work. A record number of voters turned out to elect Harrison by a wide margin, making him the first Whig president.

Inauguration day, 1841, was bitterly cold. Harrison insisted on delivering his long speech without a hat or coat. He died of pneumonia 32 days later. He served the shortest term of any president, and John Tyler became the first vice president to gain the presidency because of the death of a president. At age 50, Tyler was also the nation's youngest president up to that time.

David J. & Janice L. Frent Collection/CORBIS

Reading HELPDESK (CCSS)

Academic Vocabulary (Tier 2)

symbol a word or object that stands for something else

Reading Strategy: *Summarizing*

A summary is a short restatement of the ideas in a text. Summarizing helps you digest and remember the main points in what you have read. Read the text about the Log Cabin Campaign. On a separate sheet of paper, write one or two sentences that capture the main ideas about the campaign.

340 *The Jackson Era*

---

networks *Online Teaching Options*

BIOGRAPHY

William Henry Harrison

Comparing and Contrasting Use the interactive image of William Henry Harrison to discuss his background and his political campaign. **Ask: How did Harrison present himself to voters?** *(He claimed he was a man of the people and a war hero like Andrew Jackson.)* **BL**

McGraw-Hill **networks**

BIOGRAPHY

William Henry Harrison

William Henry Harrison was the Whig Party's nominee for President in 1840. Harrison's campaign slogan was, "Tippecanoe and Tyler Too!" Tippecanoe was a reference to Harrison's 1811 defeat of Tecumseh's Native American confederation near the Tippecanoe River in Indiana. Former Virginia Senator John Tyler was Harrison's vice presidential running mate. Harrison seemed to represent what Americans wanted in 1840—a common man who had served his country bravely in war.

David J. & Janice L. Frent Collection/CORBIS

See page 321E for other online activities.

John Tyler's Presidency

John Tyler won the vice presidential election as a Whig. However, he had once been a Democrat and had opposed many Whig policies. Whig party leaders had put him on the election ballot with Harrison mainly to attract Southern voters. Whig Party leaders Daniel Webster and Henry Clay had believed they could control Harrison and run the country behind the scenes. Harrison's death ruined that plan.

President Tyler vetoed several bills sponsored by Whigs in Congress. His lack of party loyalty outraged many Whigs. When he twice vetoed a bill to renew the charter of the Bank of the United States, all but one of his cabinet members resigned. Only Daniel Webster remained as secretary of state. Whig leaders actually expelled Tyler from the Whig Party.

The biggest success of the Tyler presidency came in the area of foreign relations. In 1842 the United States and Great Britain signed the Webster-Ashburton Treaty. This agreement settled a long dispute over the border between Maine and Canada and set a firm U.S.- Canadian boundary from Maine to Minnesota.

Except for opposing Tyler, the Whigs could not agree on their party's goals. Increasingly, they voted by region—North, South, and West—not party. This division may explain why the Whig candidate, Henry Clay, lost the election of 1844 to Democratic candidate James Polk. After only four years, the Whigs were out of power.

The Whigs elected just one more president, Zachary Taylor, in 1848. Taylor also died in office. By then, the Whig Party had become badly divided over the issue of slavery. By the early 1850s the party had nearly disappeared. Many Northern Whigs left the party and helped to form a new political party—the Republican Party that we have today.

R1

R2

☑ **PROGRESS CHECK**

Describing How did the Whigs lose power in the election of 1844?

LESSON 3 REVIEW (CCSS)

Review Vocabulary (Tier 3 Words)

1. Use the word *veto* in a sentence that demonstrates your understanding of the term. RH.6–8.4

Answer the Guiding Questions

2. *Identifying Cause and Effect* Describe the events that occurred as a result of the closing of the Second National Bank. RH.6–8.5

3. *Describing* Why did Tyler's policies differ from those of the Whig Party? RH.6–8.2

4. **ARGUMENT** Write a campaign slogan for Martin Van Buren and for William Henry Harrison that each man could have used on campaign signs to attract voter support in 1840. WHST.6–8.1, WHST.6–8.9

Lesson 3 **341**

LESSON 3 REVIEW ANSWERS

1. Possible answer: President Andrew Jackson fulfilled his pledge to kill the Bank of the United States by issuing a veto of the bill to renew its charter.

2. After the Second National Bank closed, smaller state and private banks failed, land values decreased, people lost their jobs, and an economic depression began.

3. Tyler had once been a Democrat and had opposed many Whig views. The party had paired him with Harrison mainly to attract Southern voters.

4. Slogans will vary but each might attempt to capitalize on the candidate's connection to Andrew Jackson and Jackson's voter appeal.

R1 **Reading Skills**

Citing Text Evidence Direct students to read the text and then cite the problems the Whig Party had with Tyler as the new president. **Ask: Why did the Whigs choose Tyler as Harrison's running mate?** *(He was from the South and they wanted to encourage Southerners to vote for Harrison.)* Point out that political parties still try to balance national tickets geographically. **AL** **ELL** **Verbal/Linguistic**

R2 **Reading Skills**

Describing After students have read the text, ask them to describe John Tyler's presidency. Remind them to cite examples used in the text. **Ask: What was Tyler's biggest accomplishment in office?** *(He settled a dispute with Great Britain over the boundary between the United States and Canada.)*

Have students complete the Lesson 3 Review.

CLOSE & REFLECT

Discuss the issues that split the Whigs and reflected the sectional differences among Americans. Lead students to create a list of these differences and a list of the other candidates of the Whig Party to use for review. Note that these differences soon splintered the Whig Party. Explain that out of that split emerged the Republican Party we have today.

ANSWER, p. 341

☑ **PROGRESS CHECK** The Whigs lost power because they could not agree on their party's goals and voted according to regional and sectional ties.

CHAPTER REVIEW ACTIVITY

Display a three-column chart like the one below. Then lead a discussion that requires students to contemplate the descriptions or ideas that would accurately complete the empty cells in the chart.

Jackson's Ideas	National Republican Party Ideas	Political Parties Today
1. Extend democracy to more citizens		
2. Strong Union, but limits to the role of the federal government		
3. Native Americans had no rights to land in the United States		

REVIEW THE ENDURING UNDERSTANDING

Review this chapter's Enduring Understanding with students:

• *People, places, and ideas change over time*

Now pose the following questions to help students apply this understanding to this chapter.

How did Americans' ideas about government and political parties change between 1824 and 1840? *(In 1824 there was only one political party, and four candidates from that party ran for president. Because no candidate received a majority, the House of Representatives decided the election. In 1828 there were two parties, and the election was decided in the Electoral College. By 1832 people wanted more say in the government, so presidential candidates were chosen at nominating conventions to which delegates were elected instead of by caucuses of party leaders. In 1836 a third party, the Whigs, was formed. People in this party hoped that by splitting the vote again, the presidential election would be decided in the House of Representatives, which they controlled. Their plan didn't work, and the Electoral College decided the election. By 1840 there were two parties again, and the Electoral College chose the president.*

Have students think back to previous chapters and the attitudes white settlers had toward Native Americans. **Ask: Did white settlers' attitudes toward Native Americans change?** *(Answers may vary, but accept reasonable answers that students*

can support.) **What caused white settlers to pressure the government to remove Native Americans?** *(White settlers wanted more land.)*

How did the United States change after Jackson "killed" the Second Bank of the United States, which controlled the nation's money supply? *(It caused a financial panic and depression. Many businesses failed and people lost their jobs. Many people struggled to pay for housing and food.)*

ACTIVITIES ANSWERS

Exploring the Essential Questions

❶ Answers will vary but should include references to Jackson's image as a "common man," his heroism in

Write your answers on a separate piece of paper.

❶ **Exploring the Essential Questions**   WHST.6–8.6, WHST.6–8.8
ARGUMENT   Why do you think Andrew Jackson was so popular in the 1820s and 1830s? Do you think he would be as popular a leader if he were president today? Research and examine information on the current and most recent past presidents. Then write an essay that examines Jackson's popularity and answers these questions.

❷ **21st Century Skills**   WHST.6–8.7, WHST.6–8.8
COMPARING AND CONTRASTING   Write an essay comparing the election of 1828 with a recent presidential election. Include information about how people got political information then and how they get it now.

❸ **Thinking Like a Historian**   WHST.6–8.6, WHST.6–8.8
MAKING COMPARISONS   Create a two-column chart in which you list Democrat Andrew Jackson's main ideas about government in one column and the ideas of the National Republican Party in the other column. Then research on the Internet the basic ideas of the Democratic and Republican parties today. Make a third column on your chart and check D or R to indicate which of Jackson's ideas would be more like the Democrats or Republicans of today.

Jackson's Ideas	National Republican Party Ideas	Political Parties Today

❹ **Visual Literacy**   RH.6–8.7
ANALYZING CAMPAIGN POSTERS   This poster advertises a meeting on behalf of presidential candidate William Henry Harrison. What is the image of Harrison portrayed in this poster? What elements contribute to producing that image?

battle, and his championing of "the people" against the "moneyed interests"—all timeless characteristics of charismatic populist leaders.

21st Century Skills

❷ Essays should include the idea that the 1828 campaign was one of the first to use mudslinging and that campaign rallies became a standard method of getting out voters. Students should also note that the media then were limited; media today are widespread, and the average person can easily check the accuracy of information.

REVIEW THE GUIDING QUESTIONS

Choose the best answer for each question.

RH.6–8.2

1 In the 1828 presidential election, Andrew Jackson's Democratic Party

   A. wanted a strong central government.

   B. supported setting up a national bank.

   C. favored states' rights.

   D. was dominated by wealthy merchants and farmers.

RH.6–8.2

2 Jackson's ideas about political rights and equality included

   F. all men.

   G. only white women and white men.

   H. everyone who lived in the United States.

   I. only white men.

RH.6–8.1

3 In the case of *Worcester* v. *Georgia* (1832), the United States Supreme Court ruled that

   A. Georgia had no right to interfere with the Cherokee.

   B. the spoils system was unconstitutional.

   C. the federal government had no authority over Native Americans.

   D. states had to support a national bank.

RH.6–8.2

4 Why was the removal of the Cherokee people from Tennessee and Georgia called the Trail of Tears?

   F. The Cherokee traveled mainly by water.

   G. The Cherokee left a trail so other Native Americans could find them.

   H. The Cherokee suffered and were unhappy when they had to leave their homeland.

   I. The Cherokee's trail disappeared after they left.

RH.6–8.2

5 Jackson attacked the Bank of the United States because

   A. it was being run by corrupt elected officials.

   B. it made too many loans to noncitizens.

   C. it financed foreign business deals that put Americans out of work.

   D. it was controlled by wealthy Easterners.

RH.6–8.1

6 One reason the Whigs won the presidential election of 1840 was that

   F. they made a "corrupt bargain" with Henry Clay to steal the presidency.

   G. the Democrats split over supporting Martin Van Buren.

   H. the depression caused by the Panic of 1837 had ended.

   I. they gained support from people who had supported Andrew Jackson.

343

ASSESSMENT ANSWERS

Review the Guiding Questions

1 **C** Jackson and the Democrats favored states' rights and mistrusted a strong central government. A is wrong because most Democrats favored limited central government. Many Democrats were Western and Southern farmers, who generally opposed the Bank, so B is incorrect. Settlers on the frontier, small farmers, and Southerners were more likely to favor the newly formed Democratic Party, not wealthy farmers and merchants; D is incorrect.

2 **I** Jackson's concept of who should be included did not extend to non-whites or women. Answer F is incorrect because African American men and Native American men were not included. Answer G is incorrect because women were not included. Answer H is incorrect because women, Native Americans, and African Americans did not have equal rights.

3 **A** Students should immediately eliminate choices B and D because they are not related to the court case. The Court has consistently held that the federal government—not the states—has authority over Native Americans.

4 **H** The Trail of Tears was so named because of the suffering of the Native Americans on their long journey to the Indian Territory. F is incorrect because most of the travel routes were by land. G is incorrect because they were not lost. I is incorrect because the trail followed established routes and so could not disappear.

5 **D** Jackson disliked the Bank for many reasons. One reason was his dislike for the people who controlled it: wealthy Easterners. Choice A is incorrect because the Bank was not run by elected officials. Choice B is wrong because the Bank restricted lending rather than expanding it. Choice C is incorrect because the Bank did not do this.

6 **I** In 1840 many of those who had supported Jackson—such as farmers and laborers—threw their support to Harrison. Choice F is incorrect because the "corrupt bargain" was related to the election of 1824. Choice G is incorrect because the Democrats did not split over Van Buren as their candidate. Choice H is wrong because the depression that followed the Panic of 1837 had not ended by 1840.

Thinking Like a Historian

3

Jackson's Ideas	National Republican Party Ideas	Political Parties Today
1. Extend democracy to more citizens	1. Protective tariffs are necessary	1. Extend democracy to more citizens [D]
2. Strong Union, but limits to the role of the federal government	2. Federal government should spend money to build roads and other public goods	2. Strong Union, but limits to the role of the federal government [R]

Visual Literacy

4 The poster portrays Harrison as a poor farmer and "common man." The elements used to portray this are the log cabin, Harrison working in the field as a farmer, his style of dress, and the banner calling him "The Farmer of North Bend."

Analyzing Documents

7 **B** **Making Inferences** Ross asserts that the Cherokee delegation who agreed to the treaty were "false and fraudulent" and not "the legal and accredited Delegation of the Cherokee people." There is nothing in the passage that supports answer A. C and D are wrong because Ross clearly does not like the treaty.

8 **H** **Summarizing** Ross states that the treaty is false and was therefore illegal, so answer F is incorrect. There is nothing in Ross's letter to support answers G and I.

Short Response

9 **Analyzing Primary Sources** that his people never accepted the idea of selling their land and moving to the West

10 **Analyzing Primary Sources** He does not trust the government because he asserts that it took his people's land without paying them for it.

Extended Response

11 **Expository Writing** Answers will vary, but essays should address the ethical issues of removal as well as note that it paved the way for other, further American development.

DBQ ANALYZING DOCUMENTS

John Ross, a chief of the Cherokee Nation, wrote the following in a letter to the House of Representatives in 1836:

> "A [false] Delegation, … proceeded to Washington City with this pretended treaty, and by the false and fraudulent representations [replaced] the legal and accredited Delegation of the Cherokee people, and obtained for this instrument, … the recognition of the United States Government. And now it is presented to us as a treaty, ratified by the Senate, and approved by the President."
>
> RH.6–8.6, RH.6–8.10

7 **Making Inferences** What does Ross feel about the treaty?

A. He thinks Congress made a mistake and will correct it.

B. He believes it was not negotiated by true representatives of his people.

C. He is happy that the treaty was ratified by the Senate.

D. He favors the treaty and wants Congress to recognize and enforce it.

RH.6–8.6

8 **Summarizing** Ross thinks the treaty is

F. a legal document.

G. the best the Cherokees can get.

H. false and illegal.

I. like previous U.S. treaties with the Cherokee.

SHORT RESPONSE

> "We had never sold our country. We never received any annuities [payments] from our American father! And we are determined to hold on to our village!"
>
> —Black Hawk, leader of a group of Sauk and Fox Native Americans

RH.6–8.6, WHST.6–8.1

9 What do you think Black Hawk means when he states that his people "never sold our country"?

RH.6–8.1, WHST.6–8.4

10 What does Black Hawk's statement suggest about Native Americans' level of trust toward the federal government?

EXTENDED RESPONSE

RH.6–8.9, WHST.6–8.1

11 **Informative/Explanatory** Use the two documents on this page and what you have learned in the chapter to write an essay evaluating the Indian Removal Act and its effect on America's development as a nation. Did it help the nation grow? Why or why not?

Need Extra Help?

If You've Missed Question	**1**	**2**	**3**	**4**	**5**	**6**	**7**	**8**	**9**	**10**	**11**
Review Lesson	1	1	2	2	3	3	2	2	2	2	2

---

netw⦿rks   *Online Teaching Options*

Help students use the Skills Builder resources

Your students can practice important 21st Century skills such as geography, reading, writing, and critical thinking by using resources found in the Skills Builder tab of the online Student Learning Center. Resources include templates, handbooks, and slide shows. These same resources are also available in the Resource Library of the Teacher Lesson Center.

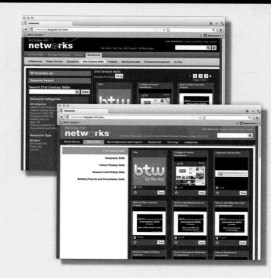

CHAPTER 13

Manifest Destiny Planner

UNDERSTANDING BY DESIGN®

Enduring Understanding

- *People, places, and ideas change over time.*

Essential Questions

- *How does geography influence the way people live?*
- *Why does conflict develop?*
- *How do new ideas change the way people live?*

Predictable Misunderstandings

Students may think:

- *Issues such as Manifest Destiny and Native American relations are easily understood.*
- *Traveling to Oregon along the Oregon Trail was not very challenging.*
- *Hollywood movies have accurately portrayed life in the West.*
- *The mix of cultures and nationalities in the West did not happen until contemporary times.*
- *A large number of people got rich during the California Gold Rush.*

Assessment Evidence

Performance Tasks:

- *Hands-On Chapter Project*

Other Evidence:

- *Interactive Graphic Organizers*
- *What Do You Know? activity*
- *Primary Source Activity*
- *Economics of History Activity*
- *Written Paragraphs*
- *What Do You Think? questions*
- *Lesson Reviews*
- *Online Self-Check Quizzes*
- *Chapter Activities and Assessment*

NCSS Standards covered in "Manifest Destiny"

Learners will understand:

2 Time, Continuity, and Change

3. That learning about the past requires the interpretation of sources, and that using varied sources provides the potential for a more balanced interpretive record of the past

4. That historical interpretations of the same event may differ on the basis of such factors as conflicting evidence from varied sources, national or cultural perspectives, and the point of view of the researcher

3 People, Places, and Environments

1. The theme of people, places, and environments involves the study of the relationships between human populations in different locations and geographic phenomena such as climate, vegetation, and natural resources

2. Concepts such as: location, region, place, migration, as well as human and physical systems

4. The roles of different kinds of population centers in a region or nation

5. The concept of regions identifies links between people in different locations according to specific criteria (e.g., physical, economic, social, cultural, or religious)

6. Patterns of demographic and political change, and cultural diffusion in the past and present (e.g., changing national boundaries, migration, and settlement, and the diffusion of and changes in customs and ideas)

7. Human modifications of the environment

8. Factors that contribute to cooperation and conflict among peoples of the nation and world, including language, religion, and political beliefs

9. The use of a variety of maps, globes, graphic representations, and geospatial technologies to help investigate the relationships among people, places, and environments

SUGGESTED PACING GUIDE

Introducing the Chapter	1 Day	Lesson 3	2 Days
Lesson 1	2 Days	Lesson 4	2 Days
Lesson 2	2 Days	Chapter Activities and Assessment	1 Day
Feature: What Do You Think?	1 Day		

TOTAL TIME   11 Days

Key for Using the Teacher Edition

SKILL-BASED ACTIVITIES

Types of skill activities found in the Teacher Edition.

V **Visual Skills** require students to analyze maps, graphs, charts, and photos.

R **Reading Skills** help students practice reading skills and master vocabulary.

W **Writing Skills** provide writing opportunities to help students comprehend the text.

C **Critical Thinking Skills** help students apply and extend what they have learned.

T **Technology Skills** require students to use digital tools effectively.

*Letters are followed by a number when there is more than one of the same type of skill on the page.

DIFFERENTIATED INSTRUCTION

All activities are written for the on-level student unless otherwise marked with the leveled labels below.

BL Beyond Level
AL Approaching Level
ELL English Language Learners

All students benefit from activities that utilize different learning styles. Many activities are marked as below when a particular learning style is highlighted.

Intrapersonal	Naturalist
Logical/Mathematical	Kinesthetic
Visual/Spatial	Auditory/Musical
Verbal/Linguistic	Interpersonal

CHAPTER OPENER PLANNER

Students will know:

- the ideas and the concepts of Manifest Destiny.
- how Florida, Texas, California, and Utah became states.
- the causes and results of the war with Mexico.
- how the Gold Rush affected California.
- why the Mormons settled in Utah.

Students will be able to:

- **analyze** why Americans wanted the land in the Oregon Country.
- **evaluate** the concept of and justifications for Manifest Destiny.
- **identify** the steps in the process of statehood for Florida.
- **identify** points of view in the War for Independence in Texas.
- **analyze** the importance and the impact of the Santa Fe Trail.
- **identify points of view** in the development of California's culture.
- **identify** the reasons behind the conflict between the United States and Mexico.
- **understand cause and effect** relationships that followed the discovery of gold in California.
- **identify** the Mormons and analyze why they settled in Utah.

UNDERSTANDING BY DESIGN®

☑ *Print Teaching Options*

V Visual Skills

☐ **P. 346** Students examine a map of territorial expansion.
Visual/Spatial Logical/Mathematical

☐ **P. 347** Students formulate questions about events in a time line. AL ELL Visual/Spatial

C Critical Thinking Skills

☐ **P. 347** Students make inferences about events that occurred in the 1800s by examining a time line.
Visual/Spatial

☑ *Online Teaching Options*

V Visual Skills

☐ **MAP** **Territorial Expansion 1800–1853**—Students click to reveal the extent of land ceded to, purchased by, or annexed by the United States during this time period.

☐ **TIME LINE** **North America 1810–1850**—Students learn about key events during this time period.

☐ **WORLD ATLAS** Students can use this interactive map to identify regions of the world, learn about individual countries, locate political boundaries, measure distances, and much more.

☑ *Printable Digital Worksheets*

R Reading Skills

☐ **GRAPHIC NOVEL** *From Sea to Shining Sea*—A father and son attend a speech given by the president about the spread of the United States from the Atlantic Ocean to the Pacific.

Project-Based Learning

Hands-On Chapter Project

Manifest Destiny

Students conduct personal research and develop arguments regarding the causes and consequences of U.S. westward expansion and the conflict surrounding the acquisition of territory for statehood.

Technology Extension edtechteacher
21st Century Learning

Online Concept Mapping Tools

- Find an additional activity online that incorporates technology for this project.
- Visit the EdTechTeacher Web sites (included in the Technology Extension for this chapter) for more links, tutorials, and other resources.

Print Resources

ANCILLARY RESOURCES

These ancillaries are available for every chapter and lesson.

- **Reading Essentials and Study Guide Workbook** AL ELL
- **Chapter Tests and Lesson Quizzes Blackline Masters**

PRINTABLE DIGITAL WORKSHEETS

These printable digital worksheets are available for every chapter and lesson.

- **Hands-On Chapter Projects**
- **What Do You Know? activities**
- **Chapter Summaries (English and Spanish)**
- **Vocabulary Builder activities**
- **Guided Reading activities**

More Media Resources

SUGGESTED VIDEOS

Watch clips of movies about westward expansion such as The Alamo: Thirteen Days to Glory (1987)

- **Ask:** Did this film make the story of the Alamo more real to you? Why or why not?
- **Ask:** Can fictional movies capture historically accurate events?

(NOTE: Preview clips for age-appropriateness.)

SUGGESTED READING

Grade 6 reading level:

- *The Coast Mappers,* by Taylor Morrison

Grade 7 reading level:

- *Away to the Goldfields!,* by Pat Derby

Grade 8 reading level:

- *Narcissa Whitman and a Faithful History of the Oregon Trail,* by Cheryl Harness

Students will know:
- the ideas and the concepts of Manifest Destiny.
- how Florida, Texas, California, and Utah became states.

Students will be able to:
- *analyze* why Americans wanted the land in the Oregon Country.
- *evaluate* the concept of and justifications for Manifest Destiny.

UNDERSTANDING
BY DESIGN®

☑ *Print Teaching Options*

V Visual Skills

☐ **P. 351** Students discuss variations in climate and the challenges faced by settlers moving between climate zones. **Visual/Spatial**

R Reading Skills

☐ **P. 348** Students locate the Oregon Country and identify the states that were formed from the land in this region. **AL** **ELL** **Visual/Spatial**

☐ **P. 348** Students summarize the effects of the Adams-Onís Treaty. **AL** **ELL**

☐ **P. 349** Students reflect on the role of mountain men.

☐ **P. 350** Students discuss the lives of the Cayuse before and after western settlement.

☐ **P. 351** Students examine why settlers were drawn to Oregon and why they all took the same trail.

☐ **P. 352** Students learn the different definitions of the word *mission* and discuss the mission of the United States during colonial times. **AL** **ELL**

☐ **P. 352** Students analyze the significance of westward expansion to Polk's election.

W Writing Skills

☐ **P. 351** Students write a paragraph describing what they consider the mission of the United States. **BL** **Verbal/Linguistic**

C Critical Thinking Skills

☐ **P. 349** Students discuss the problems that arise from joint occupation. **BL**

☐ **P. 350** Students discuss the roles of mountain men in western settlement.

☐ **P. 350** Students identify possible motivations settlers had for moving west. **AL** **ELL**

☐ **P. 352** Students examine the phrase "Manifest Destiny."

☑ *Online Teaching Options*

V Visual Skills

☐ **VIDEO** **Oregon: The Oregon Trail**—Students view various artists' murals that depict the pioneers that followed the trail to Oregon Country.

☐ **IMAGE** **The Fur Trade**—Students view an image of a beaver hat as they read interesting facts about the fur trade.

☐ **MAP** **Oregon Country, 1846**—Students trace the route of the Oregon Trail from Independence, Missouri to Champoeg in Oregon Country.

☐ **MAP** **Territorial Expansion, 1800–1853**—Students identify territories added to the United States during this period.

R Reading Skills

☐ **GRAPHIC ORGANIZER** **Taking Notes:** *Sequencing:* **Time Line Sequencing**—Students list key events from 1819 to 1846.

☐ **PRIMARY SOURCE** **Osborne Russell: Journal of a Trapper**—Students read an excerpt from Osborne Russell's journal.

C Critical Thinking Skills

☐ **IMAGE** **The Whitman Massacre**—Students read how this event resulted in Oregon's becoming a territory.

T Technology Skills

☐ **SELF-CHECK QUIZ** **Lesson 1**—Students receive instant feedback on their mastery of lesson content.

☑ *Printable Digital Worksheets*

C Critical Thinking Skills

☐ **WORKSHEET** **Primary Source Activity: Life on the Trail**—Students analyze and react to three excerpts from the writings of Catherine Sager Pringle, who traveled the trail when she was a child.

STATEHOOD FOR FLORIDA AND TEXAS

Students will know:
- how Florida, Texas, California, and Utah became states.

Students will be able to:
- *identify* the steps in the process of statehood for Florida.
- *identify* points of view in the War for Independence in Texas.

UNDERSTANDING
BY DESIGN™

☑ *Print Teaching Options*

V **Visual Skills**

☐ **P. 356** Students examine a map that shows how the Texas war for independence progressed. **Visual/Spatial**

R **Reading Skills**

☐ **P. 353** Students explain the history of Florida's becoming an American territory.

☐ **P. 354** Students discuss the growth of Florida and the conditions for statehood.

☐ **P. 354** Students examine the question of slavery as it pertained to Florida's becoming a state. **AL**

☐ **P. 355** Students discuss American settlement of Texas and the resulting tensions with Mexico.

☐ **P. 356** Students discuss the temporary government and the battles that led to indpendence for the Republic of Texas.

☐ **P. 357** Students discuss the annexation of Texas and consider how ideas can change history.

W **Writing Skills**

☐ **P. 356** Students write a short essay describing a historical event from their own lives. **AL**

C **Critical Thinking Skills**

☐ **P. 353** Students discuss the development of agriculture in Florida.

☐ **P. 354** Students explore the importance of Congress' desire to maintain an equal number of free and slave states. **BL**

☑ *Online Teaching Options*

V **Visual Skills**

☐ **VIDEO** **Davy Crockett and the Alamo**—Students witness the struggle as Crockett, Jim Bowie, William B. Travis, and others fight for independence from Mexico.

☐ **MAP** **Texas War for Independence, 1835–1836**—Students view the locations of battles in this 18-month-long war.

☐ **SLIDE SHOW** **Remember the Alamo**—Students view visuals and read extended text to understand the history of this mission.

R **Reading Skills**

☐ **GRAPHIC ORGANIZER** **Taking Notes:** *Sequencing:* **Key Events in Texas History**—Students list key events in Texas history on a time line.

☐ **BIOGRAPHY** **The Tejano People**—Students read biographies of two Texans of Mexican or Latin-American descent.

☐ **BIOGRAPHY** **Davy Crockett**—Students view a picture and read biographical information on Crockett.

C **Critical Thinking Skills**

☐ **SLIDE SHOW** **Florida's Capitol Buildings**—Students compare and contrast several buildings that have housed Florida's legislators.

T **Technology Skills**

☐ **SELF-CHECK QUIZ** **Lesson 2**—Students receive instant feedback on their mastery of lesson content.

WAR WITH MEXICO

Students will know:
- *how Florida, Texas, California, and Utah became states.*
- *the causes and results of the war with Mexico.*

Students will be able to:
- *analyze the importance and the impact of the Santa Fe Trail.*
- *identify points of view in the development of California's culture.*
- *identify the reasons behind the conflict between the United States and Mexico.*

UNDERSTANDING
BY DESIGN®

☑ *Print Teaching Options*

V Visual Skills

☐ **P. 361** Students analyze a map of the Santa Fe Trail.
Logical/Mathematical Visual/Spatial

☐ **P. 363** Students compare the distances involved in the acquisition of Texas and California. **AL** **ELL**
Visual/Spatial Logical/Mathematical

R Reading Skills

☐ **P. 360** Students discuss the New Mexico Territory and the states that were created from it. **AL**

☐ **P. 360** Students identify William Becknell and the opening of the Santa Fe Trail. **AL**

☐ **P. 361** Students summarize the influence of Spanish culture on the development of California.

☐ **P. 362** Students discuss how ranch culture affected relations between Mexico and Native Americans.

☐ **P. 363** Students describe the uprising in California. **AL** **ELL**

☐ **P. 364** Students discuss the Treaty of Guadalupe Hidalgo and reflect on the effects of the war with Mexico.

W Writing Skills

☐ **P. 362** Students adopt the role of an 1800s politician and write a speech arguing for/against going to war with Mexico. **BL** Verbal/Linguistic

C Critical Thinking Skills

☐ **P. 360** Students contrast Spanish and Mexican relations with Americans regarding New Mexico.

☐ **P. 362** Students examine the reasons the United States wanted to expand into California.

T Technology Skills

☐ **P. 363** Students research the progress of the Mexican War and make a display showing what they have learned.
Visual/Spatial Interpersonal

☑ *Online Teaching Options*

V Visual Skills

☐ **VIDEO** **California's Early History**—Students journey through California's history, from its native inhabitants and the establishment of missions to statehood in 1850.

☐ **MAP** **War With Mexico, 1846–1848**—Students view routes traveled by American troops during the war with Mexico.

R Reading Skills

☐ **GRAPHIC ORGANIZER** **Taking Notes:** *Describing:* **Individual Achievements**—Students describe the achievements of Becknell, Frémont, and Scott.

☐ **BIOGRAPHY** **John C. Frémont**—Students read a biography of this mapmaker who helped explore and settle the West.

C Critical Thinking Skills

☐ **MAP** **The Santa Fe Trail**—Students click to trace the route of this trail and see superimposed present-day state borders.

☐ **PRIMARY SOURCE** **The Bear Flag**—Students read the portion of the *General Laws of the State of California* that describes the California state flag.

T Technology Skills

☐ **SELF-CHECK QUIZ** **Lesson 3**—Students receive instant feedback on their mastery of lesson content.

CALIFORNIA AND UTAH

Students will know:
- *how the Gold Rush affected California.*
- *why the Mormons settled in Utah.*

Students will be able to:
- *understand cause and effect* relationships that followed the discovery of gold in California.
- *identify* the Mormons and analyze why they settled in Utah.

UNDERSTANDING BY DESIGN®

☑ *Print Teaching Options*

V Visual Skills

- ☐ **P. 366** Students analyze the landscape of California. **ELL** Visual/Spatial

- ☐ **P. 368** Students analyze an image that depicts Joseph Smith's death. **BL** Visual/Spatial

R Reading Skills

- ☐ **P. 365** Students discuss the value of gold and describe why the forty-niners rushed to California. Verbal/Linguistic

- ☐ **P. 365** Students discuss the life of a forty-niner. **AL** **ELL** Kinesthetic

- ☐ **P. 367** Students describe the life of a miner living in a Gold Rush mining camp. Verbal/Linguistic

- ☐ **P. 368** Students discuss the controversy surrounding Mormom beliefs and ideas.

- ☐ **P. 368** Students explain the reasons why Mormons were forced to move from place to place.

W Writing Skills

- ☐ **P. 366** Students examine the pros and cons of Californios becoming U.S. citizens.

C Critical Thinking Skills

- ☐ **P. 366** Students speculate on how forty-niners who didn't find gold could make a living in California. **BL** Interpersonal

- ☐ **P. 366** Students discuss the effects of the California Gold Rush.

- ☐ **P. 367** Students explore how the Land Law of 1851 affected Californios.

- ☐ **P. 367** Students consider the effects of the California Gold Rush and the Southern states' opposition to California's statehood.

- ☐ **P. 368** Students analyze Joseph Smith's ideas about an ideal society. **AL** **ELL**

- ☐ **P. 369** Students examine the settlement of Utah.

- ☐ **P. 369** Students discuss the reasons it took a long time for Utah to become a state.

☑ *Online Teaching Options*

V Visual Skills

- ☐ **VIDEO** **Diverse Population in the West**—Students view a video that details Brigham Young leading the Mormons westward to Utah and the influx of formerly enslaved people seeking a better life in the West.

R Reading Skills

- ☐ **GRAPHIC ORGANIZER** **Taking Notes:** *Describing:* **Settling California and Utah**—Students identify the roles of different groups in the settlement of California and Utah.

- ☐ **BIOGRAPHY** **Mariano Guadalupe Vallejo**—Students read biographical information on this early California leader.

- ☐ **PRIMARY SOURCE** **The Gold Rush**—Students analyze a primary source excerpt about the odds of people striking it rich in the California Gold Rush.

C Critical Thinking Skills

- ☐ **GRAPH** **San Francisco Population Growth**—Students click to reveal data on the change in population of San Francisco between 1820 and 1900.

T Technology Skills

- ☐ **SELF-CHECK QUIZ** **Lesson 4**—Students receive instant feedback on their mastery of lesson content.

☑ *Printable Digital Worksheets*

C Critical Thinking Skills

- ☐ **WORKSHEET** **Economics of History Activity: Manifest Destiny: Boomtown Economics**—Students understand the causes of inflation in boomtowns.

LESSON 1 The Oregon Country

Reading and Comprehension

This section focuses on the acquisition of the Oregon Country. Have students make a map showing the United States as it was in 1846 and the Oregon Country. Then have them add the Oregon Trail to the map.

Text Evidence

The United States was able to acquire the Oregon Country through negotiation and treaties, without having to go to war again with a European power. Have students go through the chapter and make a list of the names and dates of the treaties in question.

LESSON 2 Statehood for Florida and Texas

Reading and Comprehension

This section covers the process by which Florida and Texas became states. Have students find Florida and Texas on the maps they made for Lesson 1. Then have them add labels to the maps explaining what events happened to cause these states to end up joining the Union.

Text Evidence

Tell students that Texas, like the United States, declared itself independent and went through a period of independence as a sovereign nation. Have students skim through the chapter until they find the section on the Lone Star Republic. Then have students write a short paragraph explaining what happened when Texas became independent.

LESSON 3 War With Mexico

Reading and Comprehension

This section focuses on the war with Mexico and the events leading up to it. Have students make a time line delineating the events that caused tension between the United States and Mexico, the events that occurred during the war, and the end of the war.

Text Evidence

Have students go through the chapter looking for quotations to add to their time lines as annotations. Students should be able to find four quotes: one by William Becknell, one by Jedediah Smith, one by John C. Frémont, and one by President Polk.

LESSON 4 California and Utah

Reading and Comprehension

This section covers the Gold Rush in California and the migration of Mormon settlers to Utah. Have students make a migration chart listing both groups, detailing their reasons for leaving home to go to a new place, and explaining the challenges they found when they arrived.

Text Evidence

Point out to students that the Mormon settlers in Utah met the forty-niners who were rushing to California to mine for gold. Have students write a dialogue in which a forty-niner tries to convince a Mormon settler to come along to California. How would the Mormon settler reply? What arguments would the forty-niner use to try to convince the Mormon settler? Have students look through the chapter to find details to use in their dialogues. If time permits, have them work in pairs and present their dialogues to the class.

Online Resources

Approaching Level Reader

Use this online lower-level text that corresponds directly to the text in the Student Edition. It includes a Spanish version.

Guided Reading Activities

This resource uses graphic organizers and guiding questions to help students with comprehension.

What Do You Know?

Use these worksheets to pre-assess student's background knowledge before they study the chapter.

Reading Essentials and Study Guide Workbook

This resource offers writing and reading activities for the approaching-level student. Also available in Spanish.

Self-Check Quizzes

This online assessment tool provides instant feedback for students to check their progress.

How Do I Use
Google Earth™ and
Google Maps™?

Google Earth is a powerful map, image, and information delivery system that you can use to enrich your teaching. Students respond positively to Google Earth because its dynamic display of imagery and data is what they expect in today's classroom. Most students are probably already familiar with Google Earth from using it on their own home computers and mobile devices.

Strategy 1

Use Google Earth's tour function to build a virtual field trip through your community.

- Using Google Earth, your students can create pre-programmed field trips to significant civic buildings in their community.

- Information about each building and its role in the community can be programmed into the field trip.

- This assignment will help students strengthen their mapping skills, improve their understanding of directions, and provide them with practice on organizing and presenting information.

NASA Earth Observatory image by Robert Simmon with data courtesy of the NASA/NOAA GOES Project Science team

Strategy 2

Track climate change or the effects of human actions on the environment.

- Google Earth statistics and data overlays can transform maps into valuable information centers.

- Students can build layered maps to illustrate projects and support discussions about concepts they are learning in the classroom.

Strategy 3

Use Google Earth to prompt discussions on current events or to create a historical sense of place.

- If you like to incorporate real-world events in your social studies classroom, Google Earth provides a powerful tool to show students where events are taking place.

- Google Earth can also provide dynamic before and after views of historical locations. Some locations are linked to historic images which will help you stimulate discussion of how places have changed over time.

Note: The resources available on Google Earth™ and Google Maps™ were not created by McGraw-Hill Education. These resources should be viewed before presenting in a classroom or assigning to students, to determine if they are on-level and appropriate.

Manifest Destiny

1818–1853

ESSENTIAL QUESTIONS · *How does geography influence the way people live?* · *Why does conflict develop?* · *How do new ideas change the way people live?*

The Story Matters . . .

The six-month trip to the Oregon Country in the Northwest is hard and dangerous. Pioneers in "wagon trains" of up to 100 wagons wade or swim across swift rivers, climb steep mountains, face severe storms, and risk conflict with Native Americans.

Still, 12,000 people make the journey along the Oregon Trail in the 1840s. What prize lures them? Many, made poor by an economic crisis in 1837, are drawn by stories of rich land in Oregon.

These pioneers are also part of something bigger than themselves. They are helping the nation fulfill its "Manifest Destiny"—the idea that the United States should stretch from sea to shining sea.

◄ *Settlers traveled by wagon train along the Oregon Trail.*

The Granger Collection, NYC

345

ENGAGE

🔔 **Bellringer** Ask students to read "The Story Matters . . ." to themselves. Discuss with students what it must have been like to be a young person on the six-month journey to Oregon and the Northwest. Use the following questions to discuss the migration westward. **Ask: Many Americans traveled west on the Oregon Trail in search of a new life. Who else in American history traveled a long way for a new life?** *(Possible answer: the Pilgrims/Puritans and others who came to the United States from Britain and Europe)* **How might the stories of these early "pioneers" have inspired the people of the 1800s to set out for a new place?** *(The early settlers were brave and worked very hard. The travelers in the 1800s may have thought, "If they can do it, I can do it.")* Encourage students to think about why people moved west, and why they move from one place to another in general. **Ask: What factors influenced those who moved west?** *(financial hardship, the desire for more land, adventure, and so on)* **What factors influence those who come to the United States today?** *(financial hardship, the desire for freedom from bad governments or persecution, and so on)*

Making Connections

Remind students that every community has a history. Discuss the history of your local community with students. Tell students that most communities develop in fits and spurts, with waves of settlers arriving during certain periods. Usually, when a wave of settlers arrives, it is because a group of people all have common reasons for moving to an area.

- Did any settlers arrive in, or depart from, your area as a part of the movement west? Or was your community settled at a different time?
- When people moved to your area, what were their reasons for doing so?
- What was your area like before it became part of the United States?

Letter from the Author

Dear American History Teacher,

As the United States economy grew rapidly in the four decades preceding the Civil War, the American people exhibited a restless energy to move and settle every corner of the continent. Many Americans had come to believe that it was the God-given mission of the United States to expand its boundaries, even if this involved violating long-standing treaties or encroaching on the territory of other nations. The United States expanded its western boundaries to the Oregon coast and then into the American Southwest and vastly expanded the size of the United States.

Albert S. Broussard

TEACH & ASSESS

Step Into the Place

V1 Visual Skills

Analyzing Maps Direct students' attention to the Territorial Expansion map. Locate present-day Missouri and Oregon. Explain that most of the travelers started their journey at the western border of Missouri, near the Missouri River. Remind students that some people made the journey because they had been hit hard by the 1837 economic crisis. Other people were excited about the land and a new life in Oregon. Have students look at the map scale. **Ask: How far is it from Missouri to Fort Oregon Country?** *(about 1,400 miles)* **What is the terrain between those two points?** *(rugged mountains, plains)* **Why do you think someone would want to make this long journey?** *(for adventure, to start a new life, to get away from a place the person does not like)* As a class, discuss the Map Focus questions. **Visual/Spatial Logical/Mathematical**

Content Background Knowledge

- The Oregon Country was originally claimed by Spain, Great Britain, Russia, and the United States. The U.S. claim was based on the journeys of Lewis and Clark, and on the trading posts set up by John Jacob Astor's Pacific Fur Company. Great Britain's claim was based on Captain James Cook's travels along the Columbia River. Spain ceded its claim to the United States in 1819. The dispute between the U.S. and Great Britain was finally resolved by treaty in 1846.
- In 1823 President Monroe established the Monroe Doctrine, warning European powers not to meddle in the Western hemisphere.
- President James Polk presided over the largest expansion of U.S. territory up to that time, including the 1845 annexation of Texas, the treaty with Great Britain over the Oregon Country (see above), and the conclusion of the Mexican-American War in 1848.

ANSWERS, p. 346

Step Into the Place
1. Mexico
2. The original states of 1800. The population, cities, and industry had had the most time to develop.
3. **CRITICAL THINKING** Possible answer: Native Americans lost more and more of their lands to settlers.

Step Into the Time
Possible answer: There may be a relationship between Texans fighting the Battle of the Alamo, Texas becoming a state, and Congress declaring war on Mexico, because Texas was at one time part of Mexico.

346

In the first half of the 1800s, the United States greatly expanded its territory. By 1853, it stretched clear across the continent, from coast to coast.

Step Into the Place

MAP FOCUS Note that the area controlled by the United States more than doubled in size during this period.

1. **REGION** After the Louisiana Purchase, from which country did the United States gain the most territory? RH.6–8.7

2. **PLACE** Which area of the country do you think was most densely populated in 1853? Why? RH.6–8.7

3. **CRITICAL THINKING**
Speculating As the United States grew, how do you think Native Americans were affected? RH.6–8.7

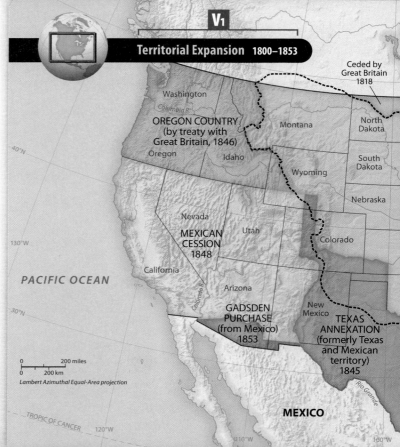

V1
Territorial Expansion 1800–1853

Ceded by Great Britain 1818

Washington
OREGON COUNTRY (by treaty with Great Britain, 1846)
Oregon — Idaho
Montana
North Dakota
South Dakota
Wyoming
Nebraska
Nevada — Utah
MEXICAN CESSION 1848
Colorado
California
PACIFIC OCEAN
Arizona
New Mexico
GADSDEN PURCHASE (from Mexico) 1853
TEXAS ANNEXATION (formerly Texas and Mexican territory) 1845

0   200 miles
0   200 km
Lambert Azimuthal Equal-Area projection

TROPIC OF CANCER

MEXICO

Step Into the Time

TIME LINE Identify events on the U.S. Events time line that you think might be related to one another, and explain how you think they may be related. RH.6–8.5, RH6–8.7

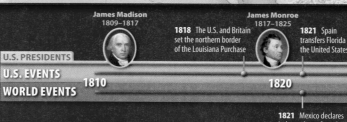

U.S. PRESIDENTS

U.S. EVENTS

WORLD EVENTS

James Madison 1809–1817

James Monroe 1817–1825

1810

1818 The U.S. and Britain set the northern border of the Louisiana Purchase

1821 Spain transfers Florida to the United States

1820

1821 Mexico declares independence from Spain

346 *Manifest Destiny*

Project-Based Learning 🖐

Hands-On Chapter Project

Manifest Destiny

This project is for students to learn about the causes and consequences of U.S. westward expansion and the conflict surrounding the acquisition of territory for statehood. Students will read about the topic in their textbook; conduct personal research on the topic, citing at least three sources; develop arguments to support their position; outline a list of points to frame their debate; draft a constructive speech for the beginning of the debate; draft a rebuttal based on the points the other side is likely to raise; rehearse their speeches; and debate in front of the class and/or an audience.

Technology Extension

Online Concept Mapping Tools

Have students gather information for a debate about westward expansion in the United States, and organize their arguments using the online concept mapping, or mind-mapping, tool. Teams can then work with online concept-mapping tools to prepare for their debate. Students will begin the assignment by gathering information about their topic. Next, they can begin formulating their arguments. Each student needs to have an account with an online concept-mapping program.

edtechteacher
21st Century Learning

networks
There's More Online!

☑ **MAP** Explore the interactive version of this map on NETWORKS.

☑ **TIME LINE** Explore the interactive version of this time line on NETWORKS.

BRITISH TERRITORY

Ceded by Great Britain 1842

Ceded by Great Britain 1842

Vermont   Maine

L. Superior

40°N

60°W

New Hampshire
Massachusetts

L. Michigan   L. Huron

L. Ontario   New York

Wisconsin   Michigan   L. Erie

Rhode Island
Connecticut

Minnesota

Pennsylvania

New Jersey

Iowa

Indiana   Ohio

Delaware

Illinois   Ohio R.   Maryland

ATLANTIC OCEAN

Missouri R.   Missouri

W. Va.   Virginia

Kansas

UNITED STATES
(Treaty of Paris, 1783)

Kentucky

30°N

LOUISIANA
PURCHASE
1803

North Carolina

ORIGINAL
THIRTEEN STATES
and Controlled
Territories)

Arkansas

Tennessee

Okla.

South Carolina

Miss.   Alabama   Georgia

Louisiana

Texas

Present day state boundaries

Original extent of the
Louisiana Purchase 1803

FLORIDA
CESSION
(Ceded by Spain,
1819–1821)

Florida

Gulf of Mexico

90°W   80°W   70°W   30°N   60°W

1824 Russia gives up its claim to land south of Alaska

John Q. Adams 1825–1829

Andrew Jackson 1829–1837

1836 Texans fight Battle of the Alamo

Martin Van Buren 1837–1841

William Henry Harrison 1841

John Tyler 1841–1845

James Polk 1845–1849

1846 Congress declares war on Mexico

Zachary Taylor 1849–1850

1830   1840   1850

1826 First Burmese War ends

1830 France invades Algeria

1839 Opium War begins between Britain and China

1842 Treaty of Nanking gives Hong Kong to Great Britain

1846 Neptune discovered

1840s Americans in large numbers follow the Oregon Trail

1849 California Gold Rush begins

1845 Florida and Texas become states

1845 Blight destroys Ireland's potato crop

White House Historical Association

347

Step Into the Time

C Critical Thinking Skills

Making Inferences Have students review the time line for the chapter. Explain that they will be studying events from 1821 to 1850. **Ask: During the 1800s, new beginnings and new ideas were occurring all over the world. What were three of these events?** *(Possible answers: Mexico's independence from Spain, the French invasion of Algeria, and the discovery of the planet Neptune)* **What new beginnings were going on in the United States at this time?** *(new states, the Great Migration, the Gold Rush)* **Visual/Spatial**

V2 Visual Skills

Reading a Time Line Although students have not yet read about the events on the chapter time line, encourage them to look at the time line and formulate questions about it. Brainstorm as a class to find out which events students would like to learn more about. Encourage students to keep a copy of their lists handy as they read through the chapter. When students come to answers for each question, they should note the answers next to the question. **AL ELL Visual/Spatial**

Content Background Knowledge

- Students may be aware of Mexico's declaration of independence from Spain if they have celebrated Mexican Independence Day, September 16.

C

CLOSE & REFLECT

Ask students if they believe in the concept of destiny, or fate. Do they think that individual people have destinies? Can groups of people, or cultures, have destinies? What about countries? Tell students that the idea that a country could have a destiny was common in the 1800s and that they will learn more about this belief, and its consequences, in this chapter.

IMAGE

Place and Time: North America 1853

Reading a Time Line Have students use the interactive time line to find out even more information about each event. Ask students whether the interactive time line answers their questions about each event. If not, encourage students to conduct additional research to find out the rest of the story. **AL ELL Visual/Spatial**

See page 345B for other online activities.

North America 1853

ENGAGE

🔔 **Bellringer** Turn to the chapter opener map and focus on the original thirteen colonies. Tell students to look at the map scale. With a ruler, measure the distance from the western border of the colonies to the Atlantic coast at three different locations. Average the numbers. **Ask:** On average, what was the distance from the western border of the colonies to the coast? *(less than 200 miles)* Where is the western border of the United States now? *(the Pacific Ocean)* Point out the large area in the middle of the country, and tell students that they will learn about westward expansion into the Oregon Country in this lesson.

TEACH & ASSESS

R1 Reading Skills

Identifying Ask for a student volunteer to read the first paragraph on this page aloud to the class. As a class, discuss the location of this new territory and have students find this area on a present-day map of the United States. **Ask:** What present-day states are included in the Oregon Country? *(Oregon, Washington, and Idaho, parts of Montana and Wyoming)* Part of what other modern country is included? *(Canada)* Remind students that these additions to the country were part of the results of Jefferson's Louisiana Purchase. **AL** **ELL** **Visual/Spatial**

R2 Reading Skills

Summarizing After students have read the text, have them summarize the role of the Adams-Onís Treaty in the Oregon Country and the nations that claimed territory in the West. **Ask:** Which countries gave up their claims on western territory? *(Spain and Russia)* How did Secretary of State John Quincy Adams end the Spanish occupation in the West? *(with the Adams-Onís Treaty)* How did the treaty limit the Spanish claim on territory? *(Spain gave up its claim to land north of the northern border of California.)* **AL** **ELL**

networks
There's More Online!

☑ **CHART** Oregon Trail Facts
☑ **GRAPHIC ORGANIZER** Event Time Line 1819–1846
☑ **MAP** Oregon Country
☑ **PRIMARY SOURCE** Osborne Russell, trapper

Lesson 1
The Oregon Country

ESSENTIAL QUESTION *How does geography influence the way people live?*

IT MATTERS BECAUSE
Thousands of pioneers moved west, adding their struggles and triumphs to the American story.

Rivalry in the Northwest

GUIDING QUESTION *Why did Americans want to control the Oregon Country?*

R1 The Oregon Country was a huge area located north of California, between the Pacific Ocean and the Rocky Mountains. It included all of what are now Oregon, Washington, and Idaho, **plus** parts of Montana and Wyoming. The region also contained about half of what is now the Canadian province of British Columbia.

In the early 1800s, four nations claimed the vast, rugged land known as the Oregon Country. The United States based its claim on Robert Gray's discovery of the Columbia River in 1792 and the Lewis and Clark expedition. Great Britain had explored the Columbia River. Spain controlled California, and Russia had settlements south from Alaska into Oregon.

Adams-Onís Treaty

R2 Many Americans wanted control of Oregon in order to gain **access** to the Pacific Ocean. In 1819 Secretary of State John Quincy Adams got Spain to approve the Adams-Onís Treaty. The Spanish agreed to set the limits of their territory at what is now California's northern border and to give up all claims to Oregon. In 1824 Russia also gave up its claim to the land south of Alaska.

Reading **HELP**DESK (CCSS)

Taking Notes: *Sequencing* RH.6–8.5
As you read, list key events on a time line such as this one.

1819	1825	1836	1846

Content Vocabulary *(Tier 3 Words)*
• joint occupation • prairie schooner
• mountain man   • Manifest Destiny
• emigrant

348 *Manifest Destiny*

---

networks *Online Teaching Options*

VIDEO

Oregon: The Oregon Trail

Creating Visuals Have students create their own murals like the ones depicted in the video, either individually or as a class project. Choose a particular place along the Oregon Trail to focus on with the murals. Encourage students to research and include authentic historical details in their murals. **AL** **ELL** **Visual/Spatial** **Interpersonal**

See page 345C for other online activities.

ANSWER, p. 348

TAKING NOTES: 1819: Adams-Onís Treaty; 1825: President Adams proposes division of Oregon; 1836: early settlers move; 1846: Britain agrees to U.S. border at 49°N latitude.

Dealing with Great Britain was more complicated. In 1818 Adams worked out an agreement with Britain for **joint occupation.** This meant that people from both the United States and Great Britain could settle there. When Adams became president in 1825, he proposed that the two nations divide Oregon along the 49° N line of latitude. Britain refused, and the countries extended the joint occupation.

Mountain Men in Oregon

Fur traders had been the first Americans to take up the challenge of living in the Oregon Country. They came to trap beaver, whose skins were in great demand in Europe. The British established trading posts in the region, as did merchant John Jacob Astor of New York. In 1808 Astor organized the American Fur Company. The country's leading fur company, it traded on the East Coast, in the Pacific Northwest, and in China.

At first the fur merchants traded with the Native Americans. Gradually others joined the trade. These tough, independent men spent most of their time in the Rocky Mountains and were known as **mountain men.** Many had Native American wives. They lived in buffalo-skin lodges and dressed in fringed buckskin pants, moccasins, and beads.

Over time, the mountain men could no longer make a living by trapping. Overtrapping limited the amount of pelts available, and changes in fashion reduced demand for pelts. Some moved to Oregon and settled on farms.

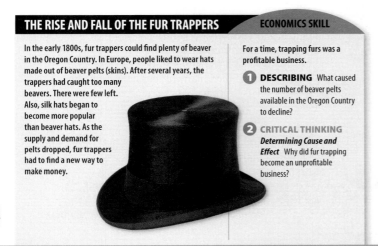

THE RISE AND FALL OF THE FUR TRAPPERS   ECONOMICS SKILL

In the early 1800s, fur trappers could find plenty of beaver in the Oregon Country. In Europe, people liked to wear hats made out of beaver pelts (skins). After several years, the trappers had caught too many beavers. There were few left. Also, silk hats began to become more popular than beaver hats. As the supply and demand for pelts dropped, fur trappers had to find a new way to make money.

For a time, trapping furs was a profitable business.

1. **DESCRIBING** What caused the number of beaver pelts available in the Oregon Country to decline?

2. **CRITICAL THINKING** *Determining Cause and Effect* Why did fur trapping become an unprofitable business?

joint occupation situation in which people from two countries can occupy an area
mountain man an adventurer of the American West

Academic Vocabulary (Tier 2 Words)

plus in addition to
access a way into something or someplace

Lesson 1   **349**

C Critical Thinking Skills

Identifying Problems Discuss with students the meaning of the term "joint occupation." **Ask: What problems do you think could arise as the result of two countries agreeing to share a territory through a policy of joint occupation?** *(There could be conflicts later as to which country would have jurisdiction over the laws in that territory or over which country the residents of that territory would be considered citizens of.)* **Ask: Do you think that a joint occupation is likely to be a permanent or a temporary solution to a dispute over territory?** *(Answers will vary.)* Discuss with students the use of diplomacy and negotiation in working out agreements of this type between countries. BL

R Reading Skills

Explaining Ask students to cite text evidence to explain the role of mountain men and their importance to the development of the Oregon Country. **Ask: What did mountain men do for a living?** *(They trapped beaver and sold the skins, or pelts.)* Reflect with students about what kinds of personal characteristics the mountain men must have had in order to make their living in this way.

PRIMARY SOURCE

Osborne Russell: Journal of a Trapper

Analyzing Primary Sources Use the interactive primary source excerpt by Osborne Russell to further discuss the fur trade and the lives of the mountain men as trappers. **Ask: What happened to the mountain men?** *(They overtrapped the animals in the territory, which limited the number of pelts available, and they had to find other employment.)* AL Visual/Spatial

See page 345C for other online activities.

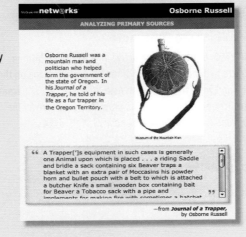

McGraw Hill **netw⊚rks**   **Osborne Russell**

ANALYZING PRIMARY SOURCES

Osborne Russell was a mountain man and politician who helped form the government of the state of Oregon. In his *Journal of a Trapper*, he told of his life as a fur trapper in the Oregon Territory.

Museum of the Mountain Man

❝ A Trapper['']s equipment in such cases is generally one Animal upon which is placed . . . a riding Saddle and bridle a sack containing six Beaver traps a blanket with an extra pair of Moccasins his powder horn and bullet pouch with a belt to which is attached a butcher Knife a small wooden box containing bait for Beaver a Tobacco sack with a pipe and implements for making fire with sometimes a hatchet ❞

—from *Journal of a Trapper,* by Osborne Russell

ANSWERS, p. 349

ECONOMICS SKILL

1. Overtrapping limited the number of pelts available.
2. **CRITICAL THINKING** The availability of beaver pelts made it harder to supply them at about the same time that fashions changed and silk hats became popular. As demand for beaver hats fell, prices dropped, and it became too expensive to find pelts.

Making Connections Discuss with students the lives of the mountain men after they could no longer make a living as trappers. Note that some moved to Oregon to become farmers but that others became guides. **Ask: How did the mountain men play a vital role in western settlement?** *(They carved out the east-to-west passages that allowed people to travel, and they helped to develop the Oregon Trail, the California Trail, and the Santa Fe Trail.)*

R Reading Skills

Discussing Have students read the section titled "Marcus and Narcissa Whitman." Then, lead a class discussion on the lives of the Cayuse before and after western settlement. **Ask: What happened at the mission that caused the Cayuse to attack?** *(An epidemic of measles was brought by the new settlers and children died.)* Continue the class discussion to highlight the intended and unintended effects of settlement on the Native Americans who already lived in the West.

C2 Critical Thinking Skills

Speculating Remind students that in the "Great Migration," American settlers continued to move west in spite of violence and hardship. Also remind students that economic troubles at home were one reason that Americans began moving west. **Ask: What may be other reasons people chose to move west?** Lead a class discussion of settlers' motivations in moving west. **AL ELL**

C1 With their knowledge of the western lands, several mountain men, such as Jim Bridger and Kit Carson, found work as guides. They led the parties of settlers now streaming west. Beginning in the 1830s, the mountain men carved out several east-to-west passages that played a vital role in western settlement. The most popular route was the Oregon Trail. Others included the California Trail and the Santa Fe Trail.

✅ **PROGRESS CHECK**

Identifying What did America gain from the Adams-Onís Treaty?

Oregon and Manifest Destiny

GUIDING QUESTION *What is Manifest Destiny?*

In the 1830s, Americans began traveling to the Oregon Country to settle. Economic troubles in the East and reports of Oregon's fertile land drew many people.

Marcus and Narcissa Whitman

Among the first settlers were Dr. Marcus Whitman and his wife, Narcissa. They were missionaries who went to Oregon in 1836 and built a mission among the Cayuse people near the present site of Walla Walla, Washington. They wanted to provide medical care and convert the Cayuse to Christianity.

The new settlers unknowingly brought measles to the mission. Native Americans had never been exposed to this disease. An epidemic killed many of the Cayuse children. The Cayuse blamed the Whitmans. They attacked the mission in November 1847 and killed the Whitmans and 11 others.

Along the Oregon Trail

C2 The Whitman massacre was a shocking event, but it did little to stop the flood of pioneers on their way to Oregon. Drawn by reports of fertile Oregon land, and driven by economic hard times in the East, many Americans took to the trail. These pioneers were called **emigrants**—people who leave their country—because they left the United States to go to Oregon.

Before the 1847 Cayuse attack, the Whitman Mission was a popular stopping point for settlers traveling along the Oregon Trail.

▶ **CRITICAL THINKING**
Drawing Conclusions Based on this picture, what do you think the Whitman Mission offered travelers on the way to the Oregon Country?

Courtesy National Park Service

Reading **HELP**DESK **CCSS**

emigrant person who leaves his or her country to live somewhere else
prairie schooner a canvas-covered wagon used by pioneers in the mid-1800s

---

netw⊙rks   *Online Teaching Options*

IMAGE

The Whitman Massacre

Analyzing Display the interactive image of the Whitman massacre to discuss the effect of the Whitman mission on the region and western settlement. **Ask: Why did the Whitmans go to Oregon?** *(They wanted to provide medical care for the Cayuse and convert them to Christianity.)* **AL ELL**
Visual/Spatial

See page 345C for other online activities.

McGraw Hill **netw⊙rks**   The Whitman Massacre

Twelve jurors found them guilty, and they were hanged and buried in unmarked graves.

Courtesy National Park Service

ANSWERS, p. 350

✅ **PROGRESS CHECK** access to the Pacific Ocean, the Oregon territory northward from the northern border of California
CRITICAL THINKING There were few places to stop along the way, and the mission provided medical care and a place to rest.

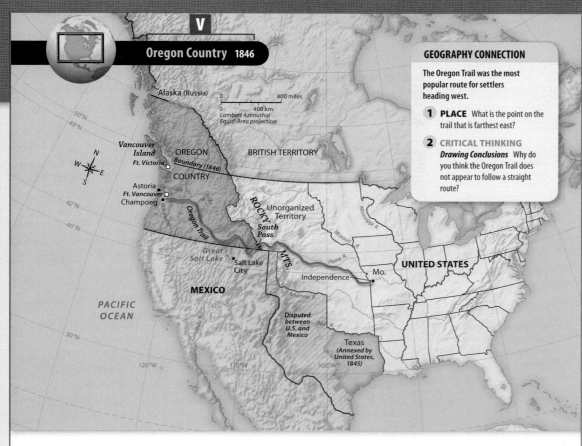

Oregon Country 1846

Alaska (Russia)

0   400 miles
0   400 km
Lambert Azimuthal
Equal-Area projection

Vancouver Island
Ft. Victoria

OREGON Boundary (1846)
COUNTRY

Astoria
Ft. Vancouver
Champoeg

Oregon Trail

South Pass

Great Salt Lake

Salt Lake City

Independence

BRITISH TERRITORY

Unorganized Territory

ROCKY MTS.

Platte R.

Missouri R.

Mississippi R.

UNITED STATES

Mo.

Arkansas R.

MEXICO

PACIFIC OCEAN

Disputed between U.S. and Mexico

Texas (Annexed by United States, 1845)

GEOGRAPHY CONNECTION

The Oregon Trail was the most popular route for settlers heading west.

1 PLACE What is the point on the trail that is farthest east?

2 CRITICAL THINKING
Drawing Conclusions Why do you think the Oregon Trail does not appear to follow a straight route?

In 1843 about a thousand emigrants made the journey. Tens of thousands more would follow in the years ahead. Before the difficult 2,000-mile (3,219 km) journey, these pioneers packed all their belongings. They stuffed their canvas-covered wagons with supplies. From a distance these wagons looked like schooners, or ships at sea, and people called them **prairie schooners.** Gathering in Independence or other towns in Missouri, the pioneers followed the Oregon Trail across the Great Plains, along the Platte River, and through the South Pass of the Rocky Mountains. Then they turned north and west along the Snake and Columbia Rivers into the Oregon Country.

R

America Seeks Its Manifest Destiny

Since colonial times, many Americans had believed their nation's mission should be to serve as a model of freedom and democracy. In the 1800s that vision changed.

W

Lesson 1   **351**

V Visual Skills

Analyzing Maps Remind students that weather and climate can vary tremendously from one geographic region to another. Have students research the differences in climate between Missouri and Oregon. **Ask: What differences in climate did settlers have to adjust to after traveling such a vast distance?** Lead a class discussion of the challenges of moving at a time when it was not possible to forecast the weather in a faraway place. **Visual/Spatial**

R Reading Skills

Explaining After students have read the text, explain that the events of the Whitman massacre did not deter new settlers. **Ask: What drew pioneers to Oregon?** *(fertile land and an escape from hard times in the East)* **Ask: Why do you think that the settlers all followed the same trail? Why didn't each go his or her own way?** *(It was easier and safer to follow a trail that had been used by others.)*

W Writing Skills

Argument Ask students what they consider the nation's mission to be. Have students write a paragraph stating what they consider the to be the current mission of the United States. Encourage students to include details explaining how they expect the United States to carry out its mission. **BL Verbal/Linguistic**

MAP

Oregon Country, 1846

Analyzing Visuals Return to the interactive map of Oregon Country to discuss the hardships on the Oregon Trail. Have volunteers describe what the journey was like across the Oregon Trail. **Ask: How many miles did they travel?** *(2,000)* **What kinds of hardships and challenges would you predict they might face?** *(harsh terrain, long journeys in wagons, Native American groups who did not want to give up their land)* **What did they travel in?** *(a wagon, also called a prairie schooner)* **Why was it given that name?** *(The wagons looked like ships at sea when crossing the plains.)* **AL ELL Visual/Spatial Logical/Mathematical**

See page 345C for other online activities.

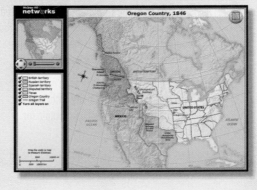

netw*rks

Oregon Country, 1846

ANSWERS, p. 351

1. Independence, Missouri
2. **CRITICAL THINKING** It might have changed directions as it followed easier routes along or around natural obstacles, such as rivers and mountains.

The Oregon Country

R1 Reading Skills

Defining Have a student volunteer read the section aloud. Then, explain the different meanings of the word *mission*. Ask students if they have encountered this word in any other context. **Ask: Which definition is meant when talking about the "mission" of the United States?** *(objective or purpose)* **What did the United States say its mission was in colonial times?** *(to serve as a model of freedom for the world)* **What did that mission become as people began to move west?** *(to spread freedom by occupying the entire continent)* **AL** **ELL**

C Critical Thinking Skills

Making Connections Discuss the newspaper excerpt from the textbook and editor John O'Sullivan's use of the term "Manifest Destiny" to describe this national mission. **Ask: What did O'Sullivan mean by this phrase?** *(that the United States was destined by God to extend its boundaries all the way to the Pacific Ocean)* Have students consider whether they agree or disagree with O'Sullivan's use of this phrase. Ask for volunteers to share their opinions with the class.

R2 Reading Skills

Explaining Direct students to read the section. Then, explain that presidential candidate James K. Polk decided to make westward expansion his main campaign issue against Whig opponent Henry Clay. **Ask: What does the slogan "Fifty-Four Forty or Fight" mean?** *(Either Britain would grant the United States that line of latitude as a border or there would be war.)* **How did that slogan help get James K. Polk elected?** *(Most of the voters were in favor of expansion, so they voted for Polk.)* **What happened?** *(The United States and Britain compromised and agreed to make the border the forty-ninth line of latitude.)*

Have students complete the Lesson 1 Review.

CLOSE & REFLECT

Speculating Point out that most people did not move west for the express purpose of driving Native Americans and others out of their land. The people who moved west did so for different reasons. Identify some of the motives people had for moving west. Lead a class discussion of some positive results and some negative results of these motives.

ANSWERS, p. 352

Thinking Like a Historian The emigrants to Oregon were pushed by poor economic conditions and pulled by the promise of new opportunities and fertile land in Oregon.

✔ **PROGRESS CHECK** Polk was a strong supporter of Manifest Destiny and believed that America should own all of Oregon. Henry Clay did not take a strong stand on the issue. Since most Americans agreed with Polk, he won the election.

Thinking Like a HISTORIAN R1

Understanding Cause and Effect

Push-pull factors are reasons for people to leave one area and move to another area. Push factors—such as lack of economic activity or a natural disaster such as a hurricane or flood—drive people away from an area. Pull factors—such as a desirable climate or the opportunity to own land—attract people to an area.

What were the push and pull factors affecting emigrants to Oregon? For more about understanding cause and effect, review *Thinking Like a Historian.*

Manifest Destiny the belief that the United States was destined by God to extend its boundaries to the Pacific Ocean

Many believed that the nation's mission was to spread freedom by settling the entire continent. In 1819 John Quincy Adams expressed what many Americans were thinking when he said expansion to the Pacific was as certain as the Mississippi River flowing to the sea.

In the 1840s, New York newspaper editor John O'Sullivan expressed in more specific words the idea of a national mission. O'Sullivan declared it was America's "**Manifest Destiny** to overspread and to possess the whole of the continent which Providence has given us." O'Sullivan meant that the United States was clearly destined—set apart for a special purpose—by God to extend its boundaries all the way to the Pacific Ocean. **C**

"Fifty-Four Forty or Fight"

Many Americans wanted the United States to take over all of Oregon. In the 1844 presidential election, James K. Polk, the Democratic nominee, supported this desire. Democrats used the slogan "Fifty-Four Forty or Fight," referring to the line of latitude they believed should be the nation's northern border in Oregon. **R2**

Polk's Whig opponent, Henry Clay, did not take a strong position on the Oregon issue. Polk won the election because Whig support was not united behind Clay.

A firm believer in Manifest Destiny, Polk was focused on acquiring Oregon. Britain would not accept a border at 54°40' N latitude. In 1846 the two countries compromised. They set the border at 49° N latitude. It was the same boundary the British had rejected 21 years before.

✔ **PROGRESS CHECK**

Summarizing How did Polk's views differ from Clay's in the 1844 election?

LESSON 1 REVIEW (CCSS)

Review Vocabulary (Tier 3 Words)

1. Using the following words, write sentences that describe settlers traveling on the Oregon Trail. RH.6–8.4
   a. Manifest Destiny   b. emigrant
   c. prairie schooner

Answer the Guiding Questions

2. *Specifying* Which nations claimed the Oregon Country? How did John Quincy Adams resolve the claims? RH.6–8.1

3. *Explaining* In what way was the Oregon Trail part of Manifest Destiny? RH.6–8.2

4. *Defining* What did "Fifty-Four Forty or Fight" mean? RH.6–8.4

5. *Analyzing* During the 1840s, more Americans than British settled in the Oregon Country. How do you think this settlement influenced negotiations with the British over the territory? RH.6–8.1

6. ARGUMENT You are a scout in the 1830s who makes a living by guiding settlers to Oregon. Write a two-paragraph "advertisement" telling people why they should move to Oregon and why they should choose you to guide them. WHST.6–8.1, WHST.6–8.10

LESSON 1 REVIEW ANSWERS

1. Possible answer: Many immigrants from the United States believed in Manifest Destiny. They faced great challenges when they traveled the Oregon Trail in prairie schooners, or covered wagons.

2. The United States, Spain, and Britain. Adams negotiated the Adams-Onís Treaty with Spain, and he came to an agreement with Britain for joint occupation.

3. It was one of the main trails people used to travel east to west and spread out over the continent.

4. "Fifty-Four Forty" was the line of latitude that the United States wanted as the northern border of Oregon. If the British did not agree to this, the Americans said they would fight for it.

5. Since Americans occupied more territory in the Oregon Country, the American position was stronger than the British claim, leading the British to compromise.

6. Advertisements should be imaginative, promote the scout's expertise, and show an understanding of the facts.

networks
There's More Online!

- ☑ **BIOGRAPHY** Davy Crockett
- ☑ **CHART** Florida's Capitol Buildings
- ☑ **GRAPHIC ORGANIZER** Texas History Time Line
- ☑ **MAP** Texas War for Independence
- ☑ **SLIDE SHOW** The Alamo
- ☑ **VIDEO**

Lesson 2
Statehood for Florida and Texas

ESSENTIAL QUESTION *Why does conflict develop?*

IT MATTERS BECAUSE
Through conflict and negotiations, the United States acquired Florida and Texas.

Florida

GUIDING QUESTION *How did Florida become a state?*

When Spain transferred Florida to the United States on July 17, 1821, Florida became an American territory. Under the terms of the Northwest Ordinance of 1787, Florida had an appointed territorial governor, a territorial legislature, and a nonvoting delegate to the United States Congress.

Tallahassee became the territorial capital in 1824. The capital was located about midway between St. Augustine and Pensacola, Florida's major cities at that time. Not counting Native Americans, fewer than 8,000 people lived in the territory, including enslaved people. Later, as news of the area's fertile land spread, thousands of new settlers streamed into Florida.

Many planters from Virginia, Georgia, and the Carolinas had worn out their soil with years of heavy use. They left their old plantations for new land in Florida. Here, the planters **established** cotton and tobacco plantations, especially in northern Florida and the narrow strip in the northwest called the Panhandle. In addition, small farms and cattle ranches dotted the region of central Florida. The leading planters of northern Florida played a major role in the government and politics of the area.

R

C

(l) State Archives of Florida; (c) Bettmann/CORBIS; (c) Archives and Information Services Division, Texas State Library and Archives Commission; (c) Burstein Collection/CORBIS; (r) Texas State Library & Archives Commission

Reading **HELP**DESK (CCSS)

Taking Notes: *Sequencing* RH.6–8.5
As you read, list key events on a time line like this one.

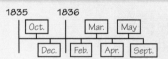

Content Vocabulary (Tier 3 Words)
- **Tejano**
- **annex**
- **decree**
- **barricade**

Lesson 2 **353**

VIDEO

Davy Crockett and the Alamo

Narrative As students watch the lesson video, have them take notes about Davy Crockett and the Alamo. Then have students write a short narrative from the point of view of Davy Crockett—the narrative that Crockett might have written home to his family if he had survived long enough to do so. **BL** Verbal/Linguistic

See page 345D for other online activities.

ENGAGE

🔔 **Bellringer** Have students write what they think about when they hear the names "Florida" and "Texas." Then ask several volunteers to read their lists. Ask if anyone wrote "part of Spanish Empire." Tell students that in this lesson they will learn how Florida and Texas both became states.

TEACH & ASSESS

R Reading Skills

Explaining Have students read the first paragraph on this page. Then, explain to them that although people began moving to the Oregon territory in the 1830s, another territory—Florida—was on its way to becoming a state earlier than that. **Ask:** What document made Florida a territory? *(the Northwest Ordinance of 1787)* When did Florida become an American Territory? *(1821)* What country claimed Florida before then? *(Spain)* Lead a class discussion of developments in Florida after 1821.

C Critical Thinking Skills

Making Connections Discuss with students the development of plantations in Northern Florida and farms in Central Florida. **Ask:** What group of people moved to Florida from Southern states? *(planters)* Why did they decide to move to Florida? *(These planters had worn out their soil with years of heavy use. They heard about fertile land in Florida.)*

ANSWER, p. 353

TAKING NOTES: October 1835: battle between Texas and Mexico in Gonzales; December 1835: Texans freed San Antonio; February 1836: Battle of the Alamo; March 1836: Texas declares independence; April 1836: Texans attack Mexican troops at San Jacinto; May 1836: Santa Anna signs treaty with Texas; September 1836: Texas elects Sam Houston president and asks for U.S. annexation.

R1 Reading Skills

Discussing After students have read the text, lead a class discussion about the growth of the Florida territory and the conditions for statehood. **Ask: How many people lived in Florida in 1837?** *(48,000)* **What type of government did the Florida constitution provide?** *(governor elected for four years, a General Assembly)* Discuss with students that statehood was not automatic for territories that wanted to become states—territories had to satisfy a number of conditions to become a state.

R2 Reading Skills

Explaining Ask students to cite text evidence as they explain why the question of slavery in Florida had to be answered before it was made a state. **Ask: What did the Florida constitution say about slavery?** *(It allowed slavery.)* **What members of the population of Florida were allowed to vote on whether or not to become a state?** *(white men over 21)* **What did Congress want to do with regard to slavery?** *(Congress wanted to keep a balance of slave and free states.)* **How was this issue settled?** *(When Iowa became a free state, Florida became a slave state.)* **AL**

C Critical Thinking Skills

Identifying Central Issues Discuss with students the fact that Florida had to wait for statehood until another state was ready to be admitted to the Union as a free state. **Ask: What can you conclude from the fact that Congress wanted to keep an equal balance of slave and free states?** *(Slavery was a contentious issue; the country was about equally divided on the subject of whether slavery should be allowed in a free country or not.)* **What event in the nation's history is foreshadowed by the nation's struggle to maintain a balance between free and slave states?** *(The Civil War)* Lead a discussion on the nature of compromise in politics and the attempt to avoid war by making compromises. **BL**

ANSWER, p. 354

✔**PROGRESS CHECK** People from the Southern states had exhausted the soil on their cotton and tobacco plantations, so they went to Florida to start new ones.

The Territory Grows

R1 In 1837 the census for the territory of Florida reported that 48,000 people lived there. Enslaved people made up about one-half of Florida's population. Officials organized a vote to determine if Floridians wanted to form a state. Only white men over 21 years of age voted in this election. These voters chose to seek statehood. Now Floridians had to draw up a state constitution and submit it to the U.S. Congress.

R2 Florida voters chose 56 people to attend the constitutional convention in St. Joseph, a small port city on the Gulf Coast. The first constitution provided for a governor elected for four years and an elected General Assembly, or legislature. The constitution also allowed slavery and called for a system of public schools. The delegates approved the constitution on January 11, 1839. Florida then sent the document to the U.S. Congress for final approval, or ratification.

C Florida's desire to enter the Union as a slave state caused some difficulty. Congress had long struggled to maintain an equal balance between slave and free states. As a result, it would take six years for Congress to act on Florida's wish. Congress had to wait until another territory was ready to become a free state.

Statehood for Florida

Iowa finally emerged as a free state candidate. With the question of slavery **removed,** President John Tyler signed the Florida statehood bill. Florida became the twenty-seventh state in the United States on March 3, 1845. The next year, Iowa became a free state. Thus, the balance between the slave and free states in the nation remained the same in Congress.

✔ **PROGRESS CHECK**

Determining Cause and Effect What caused the population of Florida to grow?

The new capital in Tallahassee was chosen because it was about halfway between Florida's major cities at the time. This building was the second capitol, and it was in use from 1826 to 1839.

Reading **HELP**DESK **CCSS**

Academic Vocabulary (Tier 2 Words)
establish to set up or create
remove to take away

354 *Manifest Destiny*

---

net**w**orks   *Online Teaching Options*

SLIDE SHOW

Florida's Capitol Buildings

Analyzing Visuals Discuss with students the changes that have been made to the Florida state capitol building over the years. **Ask: What was the capital of the Florida territory?** *(Tallahassee)* Use the interactive slide show of the state capitol building to discuss how Tallahassee and this building have changed over time. Ask student volunteers to do research on the state capitol and present their findings to the class. **AL ELL Visual/Spatial**

See page 345D for other online activities.

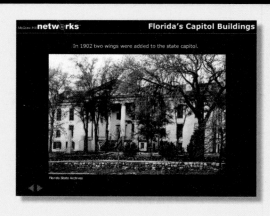

McGraw Hill net**w**orks   Florida's Capitol Buildings

In 1902 two wings were added to the state capitol.

Florida State Archives

Texts

GUIDING QUESTION *How did Texas become a state?*

In 1821 Mexico won independence from Spain. Mexico controlled the land that is now Texas. At the time, the non-Native American population of Texas was about 3,000. Most of these people were **Tejanos** (tay•HAH•nohs), or Mexicans who claimed Texas as their home. Wishing to increase settlement, Mexico offered vast tracts of land to people who would agree to bring families to settle there—as citizens of Mexico. Stephen F. Austin brought 300 American families to settle in Texas. Austin's success made him a leader among the American settlers.

At first, Mexico encouraged Americans to settle in Texas. Before long, Americans greatly outnumbered Tejanos. Tensions with Mexico developed when Americans refused to follow Mexico's rules. These included learning Spanish and becoming Catholic. Many Americans also had enslaved African Americans, which Mexico threatened to ban. In 1830 Mexico issued a **decree**, or official order, closing its borders to further immigration. American settlers, led by Austin and Sam Houston, tried to make peace with Mexican leaders. These efforts failed. Texans—including Americans and Tejanos—began planning to break away from Mexico.

In 1835 the conflict grew violent. Mexican General Antonio López de Santa Anna took an army into Texas to punish the rebels. In December of that year, the Texans captured the city of San Antonio from a larger Mexican force. Santa Anna was enraged. His army reached San Antonio in late February 1836. There it found a small Texan force **barricaded**, or blocked off, inside a mission building called the Alamo.

The Alamo

The Texans had only about 180 soldiers to take on Santa Anna's army of several thousand. The Texans did have brave leaders, however, including folk hero Davy Crockett, commander William B. Travis, and a tough Texan named Jim Bowie.

Santa Anna hoped the fall of the Alamo would show the Texans their cause was hopeless. Instead, Texans rallied to the cry "Remember the Alamo!"

R

Alamo defenders were inspired by their leader, William Barret Travis.

Tejano a Texan of Latin American, often Mexican, descent
decree official order
barricade to block off

(t) Bettmann/CORBIS;
(b) Archives and Information Services Division, Texas State Library and Archives Commission

R Reading Skills

Specifying Direct students to read the text. Then, discuss with the class American settlement in Texas and explain how tensions with Mexico developed. **Ask: Why did American settlers come to Texas?** *(Mexico offered land if they came.)* **Who led the American settlers to Texas?** *(Stephen Austin)* **Who tried to make peace with Mexican leaders?** *(Stephen Austin and Sam Houston)* **Why did Mexico issue a decree closing the border to further immigration?** *(Americans did not want to follow Mexico's rules, such as learning Spanish and becoming Catholic.)*

Making Connections

Have students recall that like Florida, part of Texas was also once claimed by Spain. Ask students if any of them have ever been to Texas. If someone has, ask them to volunteer to tell the class what it was like. Explain some of the ways that Spanish and Mexican culture have been central in Texas life. Tell students that in this section they will learn about how Texas declared independence from Mexico and eventually became a state.

Content Background Knowledge

- The defenders of the Alamo knew that their position was a tenuous one and that they would be lucky to survive. They knew they could not survive without more men and wrote asking for reinforcements.
- General Sam Houston wanted the Alamo to be abandoned and blown up to make it useless to Mexican troops. But Bowie, in particular, thought that the Alamo was a critical outpost between the Mexican army and Anglo settlements.
- Santa Anna's officers were startled when he gave the order to storm the Alamo—they thought that it would make better military sense to starve the garrison out. During the storming of the Alamo, Mexican troops sustained about 600 casualties.
- Santa Anna allowed noncombatant women and children to leave the Alamo safety afterward. He provided each with a blanket and two dollars, and made sure that they were escorted safely through the front lines.

The Tejano People

Identifying Discuss with students Mexico's independence from Spain and the Mexican control of the land that is now Texas. Use the interactive image of the Tejano people, and discuss the contributions they made to Texas. **Ask: Who were the Tejanos?** *(Mexican citizens who lived in Texas)*
AL **ELL** Visual/Spatial

See page 345D for other online activities.

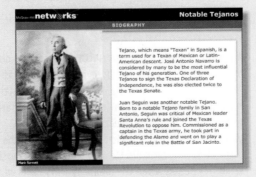

McGraw-Hill **networks** — Notable Tejanos
BIOGRAPHY

Tejano, which means "Texan" in Spanish, is a term used for a Texan of Mexican or Latin-American descent. José Antonio Navarro is considered by many to be the most influential Tejano of his generation. One of three Tejanos to sign the Texas Declaration of Independence, he was also elected twice to the Texas Senate.

Juan Seguín was another notable Tejano. Born to a notable Tejano family in San Antonio, Seguín was critical of Mexican leader Santa Anna's rule and joined the Texas Revolution to oppose him. Commissioned as a captain in the Texas army, he took part in defending the Alamo and went on to play a significant role in the Battle of San Jacinto.

W Writing Skills

Narrative Discuss how the Battle of the Alamo was a terrible defeat but became an inspiration and later led to a victory. **Ask: How did this happen?** *(It inspired the Texans to keep fighting until they won their independence.)* **What battle cry did it inspire?** *("Remember the Alamo!")* Have students write a short essay describing a historical event or an event from their own lives that they find inspiring, and explain why. **AL**

R Reading Skills

Locating Have students read the section titled "Texas Declares Its Independence." Then, lead a class discussion about the temporary government of the Republic of Texas. **Ask: Who did the government name governor when the Republic was established?** *(Sam Houston)* Display the interactive map of the Texas War for Independence from the textbook. Locate and discuss all the battles that led to independence. **How did San Jacinto play a role in the final victory for the Republic of Texas?** *(It was the site of a surprise attack that killed 600 soldiers and captured Santa Anna.)*

V Visual Skills

Reading a Map Direct students' attention to the map at the bottom of this page. **Ask: Why do you think that the defenders of the Alamo believed it had so much strategic importance?** *(because it was on the way to other communities)* **Why might it have been important to control the coast?** *(because the coast is the gateway to the sea, which can be used as a transportation route for trade purposes)* Lead students in a discussion of how the Texas war for independence progressed, using the map as a reference. **Visual/Spatial**

ANSWERS, p. 356

CRITICAL THINKING Crockett served in Congress and also on the frontier, helping to win independence for Texas.

GEOGRAPHY CONNECTION

1 Battle of San Jacinto

2 **CRITICAL THINKING** The Mexicans were the aggressors, sending troops into Texas and marching to meet the Texans in battle.

BIOGRAPHY

Davy Crockett (1786–1836)

Davy Crockett was born in Tennessee and became known as a bear hunter, soldier, and scout. Stories of his daring deeds turned him into a folk hero. He served three terms in Congress and moved to Texas after he was defeated for re-election. He joined the Texas army to fight against Mexico and fought to the death at the Alamo.

▶ **CRITICAL THINKING**
Summarizing What were Crockett's major contributions to the United States?

GEOGRAPHY CONNECTION

Texas became an independent republic after winning its independence from Mexico.

1 **LOCATION** What battle took place northeast of Brazoria?

2 **CRITICAL THINKING**
Drawing Conclusions Which side was the aggressor in this war? Explain your answer.

Reading HELPDESK (CCSS)

annex to add a territory to one's own territory

356 *Manifest Destiny*

For 13 long days, through several attacks, the defenders of the Alamo kept Santa Anna's army at bay with rifle fire. On March 6, 1836, Mexican cannon fire smashed the Alamo's walls.

The Mexican army was too large to hold back. They entered the fortress, killing all the defenders, including Travis, Crockett, Bowie, and a number of Tejanos. Only a few women and children and some servants survived to tell of the battle.

The Alamo defenders had been defeated, but they had bought the Texans time to gather troops and supplies. They had also provided the Texans with a rallying cry: "Remember the Alamo!" **W**

Texas Declares Its Independence

During the siege at the Alamo, Texan leaders met at the town of Washington-on-the-Brazos. Among them were a number of Tejanos, who were also unhappy with Mexican rule. On March 2, 1836—four days before the fall of the Alamo—they declared independence from Mexico. They then established the Republic of Texas.

Texan leaders set up a temporary government. This government named Sam Houston commander in chief of the Texan forces. Houston gathered an army of about 900 at San Jacinto (san juh•SIHN•toh), near the site of present-day Houston. Santa Anna camped nearby with an army of more than 1,300. On April 21, the Texans launched a surprise attack, shouting, "Remember the Alamo!" They killed more

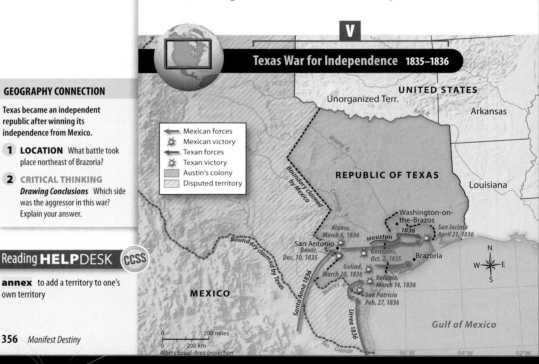

Texas War for Independence 1835–1836

- Mexican forces
- Mexican victory
- Texan forces
- Texan victory
- Austin's colony
- Disputed territory

UNITED STATES
Unorganized Terr.
Arkansas
REPUBLIC OF TEXAS
Louisiana
MEXICO
Gulf of Mexico

Washington-on-the-Brazos
San Jacinto, April 21, 1836
Alamo, March 6, 1836
San Antonio Bexar, Dec. 10, 1835
Houston
Gonzales, Oct. 2, 1835
Brazoria
Goliad, March 20, 1836
Refugio, March 14, 1836
San Patricio, Feb. 27, 1836

0   200 miles
0   200 km
Albers Equal-Area projection

(c) Burstein Collection/CORBIS

---

netw⊙rks *Online Teaching Options*

SLIDE SHOW

Remember the Alamo

Analyzing Visuals Use the interactive slide show to discuss the Alamo and the battle fought there. **Ask: What is the Alamo?** *(It is an old mission building.)* **During the battle, how many soldiers did the Texans have in comparison to Santa Anna's army?** *(about 180 soldiers to several thousand)* Use slides 3 and 4 to discuss the events of the battle. **Ask: How long did the fighting last?** *(13 days)* **What happened when the Mexican army entered the fortress?** *(They killed the defenders, including Davy Crockett and Jim Bowie. Only a few survived.)* **AL ELL Visual/Spatial**

On February 23, 1836, Santa Anna and his army stormed the Alamo after a twelve-day siege. Nearly all the Alamo's defenders and more than 600 Mexican soldiers were killed. Santa Anna claimed victory.

North Wind Picture Archives

See page 345D for other online activities.

than 600 soldiers and captured about 700 more—including Santa Anna. On May 14, 1836, Santa Anna signed a treaty that recognized the independence of Texas.

The Lone Star Republic

In September 1836, Texans elected Sam Houston as their president. Mirabeau Lamar, who had fought at the Battle of San Jacinto, served as vice president. Houston sent a delegation to Washington, D.C., to ask the United States to **annex,** or take control of, Texas.

Andrew Jackson, however, refused their request. The addition of another slave state would upset the balance of slave and free states in Congress. For the moment, Texas would remain an independent country.

Texas Becomes a State

Many Texans wanted to join the United States. Southerners favored Texas annexation, but Northerners opposed admitting another slave state to the Union. President Martin Van Buren did not want to inflame the slavery issue or risk war with Mexico. He put off the question of annexing Texas. John Tyler, who became president in 1841, supported Texas annexation. The Senate remained divided over the slavery issue and failed to ratify the annexation treaty.

The situation changed with the 1844 presidential campaign. Manifest Destiny was a popular idea at the time. The South wanted Texas. The North favored gaining all of Oregon. Candidate James K. Polk supported both actions. After Polk won, Congress passed a resolution to annex Texas. In 1845 Texas joined the Union.

☑ **PROGRESS CHECK**

Identifying Central Issues Why did it take a long time for the United States to annex Texas?

R

Juan Seguín (above) and José Antonio Navarro were Tejanos who supported and worked for an independent Texas.

(t) Mark Burnett,
(b) Texas State Library & Archives Commission

LESSON 2 REVIEW (CCSS)

Review Vocabulary (Tier 3 Words)

1. Explain the significance of the following terms in Texas history. RH.6–8.4

   a. Tejano   **b.** annex
   c. decree   **d.** barricade

Answer the Guiding Questions

2. ***Explaining*** What factor explained Florida's six-year wait to have its request for statehood approved? RH.6–8.1

3. ***Specifying*** Why was the Battle of San Jacinto important? RH.6–8.2

4. ***Making Connections*** How did the battle at the Alamo help the cause of Texas independence? RH.6–8.2

5. **ARGUMENT** Imagine you live in 1840 and are trying to encourage American settlement in Florida. Write an advertisement that might attract settlers to this land. WHST.6–8.1, WHST.6–8.9

Lesson 2   **357**

R **Reading Skills**

Listing After students have read the text, work together as a class to create a list of the four presidents who were elected before Texas was finally annexed in 1845. Include their names, the years they were in office, and why they chose not to annex Texas. **Ask: How did the issue of slavery affect the annexation of Texas?** *(Texas was not annexed right away because when it became a state, it would upset the balance between slave and free states.)* **What changed when James K. Polk was elected?** *(People saw Texas as a part of Manifest Destiny. The North saw that free states would be created from the Oregon Territory.)* Discuss with students how an idea can change history. Polk's election did not change anything about the facts related to Texas statehood, but people were beginning to look at the situation with different ideas in mind.

Have students complete the Lesson 2 Review.

CLOSE & REFLECT

Speculating Have students speculate about what would have happened if Texas had remained part of Mexico. **Ask: What language would Texans speak?** *(Spanish)* **What would be their relationship with the United States?** *(Texas would not be a part of the United States but would be part of Mexico.)* **What customs might be different?** *(Answers will vary, but students might mention such differences as changes in holidays. For example, holidays such as the Fourth of July and Veterans' Day would not be celebrated, and Halloween would be celebrated as the Day of the Dead.)*

LESSON 2 REVIEW ANSWERS

1. **a.** Tejanos were people from Mexico who had settled in Texas. **b.** The United States annexed Texas. **c.** The Mexican government issued a decree in 1830 that Americans could no longer settle in Texas. **d.** The defenders of the Alamo barricaded themselves inside the structure.

2. Florida wanted to enter the Union as a slave state, and Congress waited until there was a free state ready to enter the union to maintain the balance.

3. At that battle, the Texans captured Santa Anna and forced him to sign a treaty recognizing Texan independence.

4. The sacrifice of the men at the Alamo inspired the rest of the Texas soldiers to be even braver and stronger as they fought for independence.

5. Possible answers might include the availability of land that is good for growing crops such as cotton, the climate, and also the state's recent growth.

ANSWER, p. 357

☑ **PROGRESS CHECK** It would have become a slave state and upset the balance of slave and free states. There was also a risk of war with Mexico.

ENGAGE

Bellringer Discuss the authors of these excerpts with students. **Ask: Who was Albert Gallatin?** *(a long-time public servant)* **Who was John L. O'Sullivan?** *(a magazine editor)* Encourage students to find out more information about these two men, using the Internet to extend the lesson.

TEACH & ASSESS

R Reading Skills

Defining Have volunteers read the excerpt from Gallatin aloud. Pause and define terms as necessary to help all students understand what he is saying. Have students list the words that they do not know the meanings of, and then ask volunteers to look up the meanings and explain the words to the class.
AL **ELL**

W Writing Skills

Argument Have students write a paraphrase of the argument made by Gallatin. Ask several students to read their paraphrases aloud. **Ask: Does Gallatin support or oppose Manifest Destiny?** *(oppose)* **What arguments does he use to support his opinion?** *(He says that it is wrong for anyone to think that he is born superior to anyone else and that democracy does not support taking over land from Mexicans. In a democracy all are supposed to be equal.)*

What Do You Think? CCSS

Was Manifest Destiny Justified?

In 1845 a magazine editor named John L. O'Sullivan declared that it was the "manifest destiny" of the United States to expand westward to the Pacific Ocean. Manifest Destiny did have its opponents, however. Long-time public servant Albert Gallatin expressed his opposition to Manifest Destiny.

No

PRIMARY SOURCE

ALBERT GALLATIN

R
W

❝ It is said, that the people of the United States have an hereditary superiority of race over the Mexicans, which gives them the right to **subjugate** and keep in bondage the inferior nation. . . .

Is it compatible with the principle of Democracy, which rejects every hereditary claim of individuals, to admit an hereditary superiority of races? . . . At this time the claim is but a pretext for covering and justifying unjust **usurpation** and unbounded ambition. . . .

Among ourselves, the most ignorant, the most inferior, either in physical or mental faculties, is recognized as having equal rights, and he has an equal vote with any one, however superior to him in all those respects. This is founded on the **immutable** principle that no one man is born with the right of governing another man. ❞

Emigrants often packed their wagons so full that they had to make the long trip on foot.

358 *Manifest Destiny*

(t) Bettmann/CORBIS, (b) The Granger Collection, NYC

---

networks *Online Teaching Options*

MAP

Territorial Expansion 1800–1853

Analyzing Maps Have students add layers to the map one at a time to see how Manifest Destiny unfolded in practice. Point out to students that some of these additions to the United States were acquired peacefully, such as the area ceded by Britain in 1842. Some, however, were acquired by force, such as the area ceded in the Mexican Cession, ending the war with Mexico. **AL** **ELL** **Visual/Spatial**

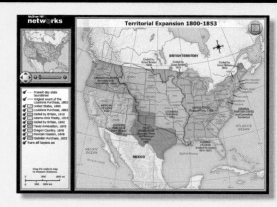

Texans celebrate as Texas becomes the 28th state in December 1845.

Yes

PRIMARY SOURCE

JOHN L. O'SULLIVAN

R
W

*(l) Bettmann/CORBIS,
(b) The Granger Collection, NYC*

> ❝ Texas is now ours. Already, before these words are written, her Convention has undoubtedly ratified the acceptance, by her Congress, of our **proffered** invitation into the Union. . . . The next session of Congress will see the representatives of the new young State in their places in both our halls of national legislation, side by side with those of the old Thirteen. . . .
>
> Other nations have undertaken to intrude themselves [into the question of Texas. They have come] between us and the proper parties to the case, in a spirit of hostile intervention against us, for the avowed object of thwarting our policy and hampering our power, limiting our greatness and checking the fulfillment of our manifest destiny to overspread the continent allotted by Providence for the free development of our yearly multiplying millions. ❞

Vocabulary

subjugate conquer

usurpation an unjust seizing of power

immutable does not change

proffered present for acceptance

What Do You Think? **DBQ**

❶ Summarizing According to O'Sullivan, what was Manifest Destiny? RH.6–8.6

❷ Analyzing What does Albert Gallatin think is the real motive underlying the idea of Manifest Destiny? RH.6–8.6

❸ Contrasting How do you think O'Sullivan might have responded to Gallatin's claims about the true motives of Manifest Destiny? RH.6–8.6, RH.6–8.10

C

Lesson 2 **359**

How to Recognize Historical Perspectives

Identifying Points of View Before having students read the excerpts, you may wish to make use of the Interactive Skills slide show, "How to Recognize Historical Perspectives." This slide show will walk students through the process of understanding the context for a historical statement. Have students follow the steps in the slide show to help them understand the context in which these statements are made about Manifest Destiny. **AL** **ELL** **Visual/Spatial Verbal/Linguistic**

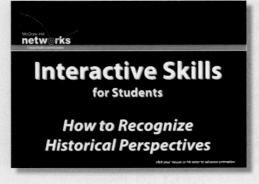

R Reading Skills

Paraphrasing Have students try to orally paraphrase the argument made by O'Sullivan. **Ask: Does O'Sullivan support or oppose Manifest Destiny?** *(support)* **What phrases tell you what he thinks about those who opposed making Texas a state?** *(Possible answers: He says it was a hostile intervention, that they were "thwarting our policy, hampering our power, limiting our greatness.")* **AL** **ELL**

W Writing Skills

Informative/Explanatory Reread O'Sullivan's definition of Manifest Destiny, ". . . our manifest destiny to overspread the continent allotted by Providence for the free development of our yearly multiplying millions." Ask students to write a definition of Manifest Destiny in their own words. Ask volunteers to write their definitions on the board and choose the definition that best reflects what students have learned. **AL** **ELL**

C Critical Thinking Skills

Defending As a class, discuss the answers to the What Do You Think? questions. Then divide the class into two groups and have each present arguments in a mock debate. Finally, take a class poll to see which side of the debate students would have supported at that time.

CLOSE & REFLECT

Discuss what the United States might be like today if Americans had not believed in Manifest Destiny and if the government had not followed policies that fulfilled that destiny.

ANSWERS, p. 359

1. Manifest Destiny was the God-given right of the United States to expand to the Pacific Ocean and become a great nation.
2. Gallatin believes the motivation is the unjust seizure of power and limitless ambition.
3. Possible answer: O'Sullivan might have argued that the United States' growing population needed more territory for expansion and that it was the nation's right to grow in size, power, and greatness.

ENGAGE

🔔 **Bellringer** In the early 1800s, a person in North America would be most likely to hear Spanish spoken in the Southwest. Today, however, Spanish is spoken in many parts of the United States, and many students may speak Spanish themselves. Ask for volunteers to name cities and states in which Spanish is often spoken. *(Answers may vary but could include not only the Southwestern states, but also major metropolitan areas such as New York City and Chicago.)* Then ask for volunteers to name other languages that are often spoken by bilingual members of your local community. Tell students that in this lesson, they will learn about areas of the country that, to this day, have a strong Spanish influence both in language and culture.

TEACH & ASSESS

R1 Reading Skills

Discussing After students have read the text, lead a class discussion about the area of the New Mexico Territory. Point out to students that the New Mexico Territory included more than just the present-day state of New Mexico. **Ask: What states developed from this territory?** *(New Mexico, Arizona, Nevada, Utah, and parts of Colorado and Wyoming)* Lead a discussion in which you review the various territories students have studied thus far in the book. Ask for volunteers to point out the differences between territories and the states that were eventually formed from them. **AL**

C Critical Thinking Skills

Contrasting Have students contrast Spanish and Mexican relations with Americans regarding New Mexico. **Ask: How was the Mexican attitude toward American settlers different from the Spanish attitude?** *(The Spanish did not want Americans to settle in New Mexico. Mexicans did.)* **Why did Mexico welcome Americans?** *(They thought increased trade would help their economy.)* Lead a discussion of the reasons that different governments might regard the same action (settlement) in different ways.

R2 Reading Skills

Identifying Have a student volunteer read the last paragraph on this page aloud. **Ask: Who was William Becknell?** *(a U.S. trader)* **What did he do?** *(opened the Santa Fe Trail)* **AL**

ANSWER, p. 360

TAKING NOTES: William Becknell: first American trader to reach Santa Fe; **John C. Frémont:** mapmaker who wrote about California's climate and resources; formed the Bear Flag Republic; **Winfield Scott:** army general who captured Veracruz, Mexico

---

netw⊚rks
There's More Online!

☑ **BIOGRAPHY**
John C. Frémont

☑ **GRAPHIC ORGANIZER** Individual Achievements

☑ **MAP**
• Santa Fe Trail
• War With Mexico

☑ **PRIMARY SOURCE**
The Bear Flag

☑ **VIDEO**

Lesson 3
War With Mexico

ESSENTIAL QUESTION *Why does conflict develop?*

IT MATTERS BECAUSE
Mexican lands in the West became part of the United States.

The New Mexico Territory

GUIDING QUESTION *How did the Santa Fe Trail benefit the New Mexico Territory?*

R1 In the early 1800s, the land called New Mexico was a vast region between the Texas and California territories. It included all of the land that is now the states of New Mexico, Arizona, Nevada, and Utah and parts of Colorado and Wyoming. Native Americans had lived in the area for thousands of years. Spanish conquistadors, or soldiers, arrived in the late 1500s. They made the region part of Spain's American colonies. In 1610 the Spanish founded the settlement of Santa Fe. Spanish missionaries soon followed the conquistadors into the area.

C Mexico—including New Mexico—won its independence from Spain in 1821. Before that time, the Spanish had tried to keep Americans away from Santa Fe. They feared that Americans would want to take over the area. The new Mexican government, however, welcomed American traders. Mexico hoped trade would boost the economy.

R2 William Becknell, the first American trader to reach Santa Fe, arrived in 1821. Becknell's route came to be known as the Santa Fe Trail. It was a big improvement over the trails that existed in the dry and rugged area at that time. As Becknell wrote: "I avoided the so much dreaded sand hills, where adventurers have frequently been forced to drink the blood of their mules, to allay [relieve] their thirst."

(c) The Granger Collection, NYC. (r) Photodisc/Getty Images

Reading **HELP**DESK (CCSS)

Taking Notes: *Describing* RH.6–8.1
As you read, describe the achievements of each individual in a chart like this one.

	Achievements
William Becknell	
John C. Frémont	
Winfield Scott	

Content Vocabulary (Tier 3 Words)
• **rancho**
• **ranchero**

360 *Manifest Destiny*

---

netw⊚rks *Online Teaching Options*

VIDEO

California's Early History

Analyzing Visuals Show the Learn360 video about California's early history to give students a brief overview of California from its earliest inhabitants to about the time of the Gold Rush. Then lead a discussion of California's diverse historical and cultural background. **Ask: What different cultures have been a part of California's history?** *(Native American nations, Spanish explorers and missionaries, Mexican ranchers, and eventually settlers from the United States)* **AL** **ELL** Visual/Spatial

See page 345E for other online activities.

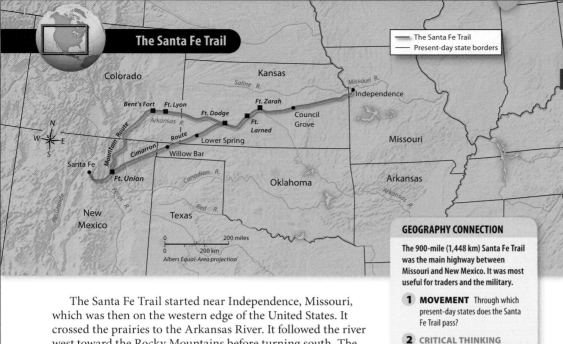

The Santa Fe Trail

The Santa Fe Trail — Present-day state borders

Colorado
Kansas
Saline R.
Missouri R.
Independence
Bent's Fort · Ft. Lyon
Ft. Zarah
Ft. Dodge
Council Grove
Mountain Route
Arkansas R.
Route
Ft. Larned
Missouri
Cimarron
Lower Spring
Willow Bar
Santa Fe
Pecos R.
Ft. Union
Canadian R.
Oklahoma
Arkansas
Arkansas R.
Rio Grande
New Mexico
Texas
Red R.

0   200 miles
0   200 km
Albers Equal-Area projection

The Santa Fe Trail started near Independence, Missouri, which was then on the western edge of the United States. It crossed the prairies to the Arkansas River. It followed the river west toward the Rocky Mountains before turning south. The trail was mostly flat, and Becknell used wagons to transport his goods.

Other Americans soon followed Becknell. The Santa Fe Trail became a busy trade route. As trade with New Mexico increased, Americans began settling in the area. Some began to believe that acquiring New Mexico was part of American Manifest Destiny.

☑ **PROGRESS CHECK**

Describing How did William Becknell influence the American settlement of New Mexico?

California's Spanish Culture

GUIDING QUESTION *How did the culture of California develop?*

Spanish explorers and missionaries from Mexico settled California in the 1700s. Captain Gaspar de Portolá and Father Junípero Serra (hoo•NIP•uh•roh   SEHR•uh) began a chain of missions that eventually extended from San Diego to Sonoma.

The missions aimed to convert Native Americans to Christianity and the Spanish way of life. Native Americans learned to farm, and they worked at weaving and other crafts. American mountain man Jedediah Smith described the missions as "large farming and [cattle-ranching] establishments."

Lesson 3   **361**

R

GEOGRAPHY CONNECTION

The 900-mile (1,448 km) Santa Fe Trail was the main highway between Missouri and New Mexico. It was most useful for traders and the military.

1 **MOVEMENT** Through which present-day states does the Santa Fe Trail pass?

2 **CRITICAL THINKING** *Drawing Conclusions* Why do you think Independence, Missouri, is the starting point for the trail?

V

V Visual Skills

Reading a Map   Direct students' attention to the map of the Santa Fe Trail. Remind students that in 1821, the United States did not have the transportation infrastructure that it has today. **Ask:** **Why do you think that so much of the trail follows the Arkansas River?** *(Settlers needed water and may have been able to use part of the river as transportation. In addition, following the river made it easier to avoid getting lost.)* **Ask:** **Can you think of any reasons that some settlers would prefer the mountain route?** *(They may have felt safer from possible attack in the mountains, where the terrain would provide some concealment.)* Have students calculate the approximate distance of the trail based on the map scale. **Logical/Mathematical   Visual/Spatial**

R Reading Skills

Summarizing   Ask students to read the section titled "California's Spanish Culture." Then, have them summarize the influence of Spanish culture on the development of California, specifically the missions. **Ask:** **How did the missions affect the culture of California?** *(They were established all along California and they aimed to convert Native Americans to Christianity and the Spanish way of life.)*

Content Background Knowledge

- By the 1850s, the goods shipped along the Santa Fe Trail were worth about $5 million per year. Wagons carried calico, leather, hardware, clothing, furs, and coins. The trail remained in use as a trade route until the Atchison, Topeka and Santa Fe Railroad came through, making the trail unnecessary.

- Wagon trains could choose from two options: the Mountain Branch, which was longer, or the Cimarron Cutoff, which took them through the Cimarron Desert.

- Wagon trains did not know, when they met Native American groups, whether these groups would be friendly or not. They had to be ready to form a protective corral in case of a raid but also had to be ready to trade with friendly parties.

MAP

The Santa Fe Trail

Analyzing Maps   Refer students to the interactive map of the Santa Fe Trail. **Ask:** **Who used the Santa Fe Trail and why did they use it?** *(Traders used the Santa Fe Trail to transport goods.)* **Why did more Americans begin settling in the New Mexico Territory?** *(They began to consider acquiring New Mexico as part of Manifest Destiny.)* Have students compare this map with the interactive map of the Oregon Trail in Lesson 1. **Ask:** **Which trail would you rather follow? Why?** *(Most students will say they would rather follow the Santa Fe Trail because it is shorter and probably easier to travel. Students might know that New Mexico is warmer and sunnier than Oregon.)* Tell students that in this lesson they will learn how the Santa Fe Trail opened another part of the West, leading to the New Mexico Territory. **AL** **ELL** **Visual/Spatial**

See page 345E for other online activities.

networks
The Santa Fe Trail

ANSWERS, p. 361

GEOGRAPHY CONNECTION

1 Missouri, Kansas, Oklahoma, Colorado, and New Mexico

2 **CRITICAL THINKING** There were other roads and waterways that provided transportation from the east up to that point.

☑ **PROGRESS CHECK** He was the first American to arrive in New Mexico using a new route, the Santa Fe Trail, to bring goods to trade. Other Americans began to use the trail and to settle in New Mexico.

R Reading Skills

Discussing Direct students to read the first paragraph on this page. Then, **ask: What happened to mission lands that belonged to Mexico?** *(They became ranchos.)* **How did this affect the Native Americans?** *(They worked the ranchos in return for food and shelter, and were treated almost like enslaved people by the rancheros.)* Lead a class discussion on how ranch culture may have affected relations between Mexico and Native Americans.

C Critical Thinking Skills

Analyzing Tell students that wars do not always start because of a just cause. Sometimes they start because the governments of the countries in question hope to accomplish something, such as acquire additional territory. **Ask: Why did more Americans become interested in settling in California?** *(They were attracted by the climate for farming/ranching and began to consider the Mexican state a part of Manifest Destiny.)* **Why did many Americans think that California would be a good addition to the United States?** *(good farmland and resources; access to the Pacific Ocean; the United States would be safely bounded by the ocean instead of a foreign country)* Discuss with students what options were available to the United States if it wanted to expand its territory into California.

W Writing Skills

Argument Have students write a speech in which they take on the role of a politician of the 1800s and argue that the United States should, or should not, go to war with Mexico. Have students support their views with evidence from the text. **Ask: What played a role in the tension between the two countries?** *(disagreement over the Texas border)* **What disagreement over California intensified tensions?** *(The United States wanted California, but Mexico did not want to sell it.)* When students have written their speeches, have them present the speeches to the class, or hold a debate. **BL** **Verbal/Linguistic**

ANSWERS, p. 362

✓ PROGRESS CHECK It had a mild climate and vast natural resources. It also bordered the Pacific Ocean. Americans thought that this would be a safer border than a foreign country and would open trade to East Asia.

CRITICAL THINKING The Mexican government could not provide a settled and stable government, which was reflected in their treatment of California settlers.

BIOGRAPHY

John C. Frémont (1813–1890)

John C. Frémont was a mapmaker who helped explore and settle the West. He led his third expedition to California in 1845. The United States was close to war with Mexico because of the conflict over Texas. In June 1846, he encouraged a small group of Americans during the Bear Flag Revolt. Frémont later wrote that he saw their actions as "movements with the view of establishing a settled and stable government, which may give security to their persons and property."

▶ **CRITICAL THINKING**
Drawing Conclusions Based on Frémont's quotation, how do you think the Mexican government treated American settlers?

After Mexico won independence from Spain in 1821, California became a Mexican state. Mexicans bought mission lands and set up huge ranches, or **ranchos.** Native Americans worked the land in return for food and shelter. **Rancheros**—ranch owners—treated Native Americans almost like slaves.

In the 1840s, more Americans reached California. John C. Frémont, an army officer, wrote of the region's mild climate and vast natural **resources.** Americans began to talk about adding California to the Union. They argued that the nation would then be safely bordered by the Pacific Ocean rather than by a foreign country. Shippers also hoped to build seaports on the Pacific coast for trade with East Asia.

✓ PROGRESS CHECK

Explaining Why did Americans want to make California part of the United States?

Conflict Begins

GUIDING QUESTION *Why did war break out between the United States and Mexico?*

President James K. Polk was determined to get the California and New Mexico territories from Mexico. After Mexico refused to sell the lands, Polk planned to gain them through war. To **justify** a war, Polk hoped to get Mexico to strike first.

Relations between the two countries were not friendly. The two nations disagreed about where the Texas-Mexico border was. The United States said that the Rio Grande formed the border. Mexico claimed that the border lay along the Nueces (nu•AY•sehs) River, 150 miles (241 km) farther north.

Polk sent a representative, John Slidell, to Mexico to propose a deal. Slidell could offer $30 million for California and New Mexico as long as Mexico accepted the Rio Grande as the Texas border. The United States would also pay what Mexico owed to American citizens. Mexican leaders refused to discuss the offer. They announced that they intended to reclaim Texas for Mexico.

To bring pressure, Polk ordered General Zachary Taylor to lead U.S. forces into the disputed area on the Rio Grande. To Mexican leaders, Taylor's action was an invasion of their country. On April 25, 1846, Mexican troops attacked Taylor's forces. President Polk told Congress that Mexico had "invaded our territory and shed American blood upon the American soil." On May 13, Congress passed a declaration of war against Mexico.

Reading **HELP**DESK **CCSS**

rancho ranch, especially the large estates set up by Mexicans in the American West
ranchero rancher, owner of a rancho

Academic Vocabulary (Tier 2 Words)

resource something that can be used for benefit, especially land, minerals, and water
justify to provide an explanation for

362 *Manifest Destiny*

netw**o**rks *Online Teaching Options*

MAP

War With Mexico, 1846–1848

Analyzing Maps Display the interactive map about the war with Mexico. Point out the disputed area north of the Rio Grande. Have students follow the course of the war using the interactive map. **Ask: How many U.S. victories are shown on the map?** *(ten)* **How many Mexican victories are shown?** *(one)* **Where did the last battle take place?** *(Mexico City)* **Ask: How do you think the U.S. naval blockade affected the course of the war?** *(The naval blockade made it hard for Mexico to trade with other countries. At best it could only trade with its southern neighbors.)* **AL** **ELL** **Visual/Spatial Logical/Mathematical**

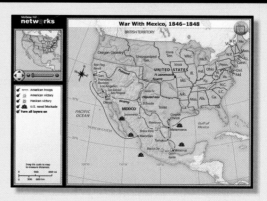

See page 345E for other online activities.

A War Plan

Polk planned to defeat Mexico by accomplishing three goals. First, the United States would drive Mexican forces out of Texas. Second, it would seize New Mexico and California. Finally, American forces would advance into Mexico and capture the capital, Mexico City.

By 1847, Zachary Taylor had accomplished the first goal. His army had captured all the important towns in the border area between Mexico and Texas. General Stephen Kearney made progress toward the second goal by marching his troops down the Santa Fe Trail. They captured New Mexico's capital, Santa Fe, in 1846 after the Mexican governor fled. Kearney then turned toward California.

T

California Uprising

R

Even before war with Mexico officially began, American settlers in northern California had begun an uprising. They were encouraged by American general John C. Frémont. The settlers had little trouble overcoming the weak official Mexican presence in the territory. On June 14, 1846, the Americans declared California independent. They renamed it the Bear Flag Republic. The name came from the flag the rebels had made for their new nation.

GEOGRAPHY CONNECTION

War between the United States and Mexico broke out in 1846 near the Rio Grande. Polk's party, the Democrats, generally supported the war. Many Whigs did not, calling Polk's actions unnecessary and unjust. Northerners accused Democrats of waging war to gain territory for the spread of slavery.

1 LOCATION Which battle was a Mexican victory?

2 CRITICAL THINKING
Making Inferences What information on the map can you use to infer which side won the war?

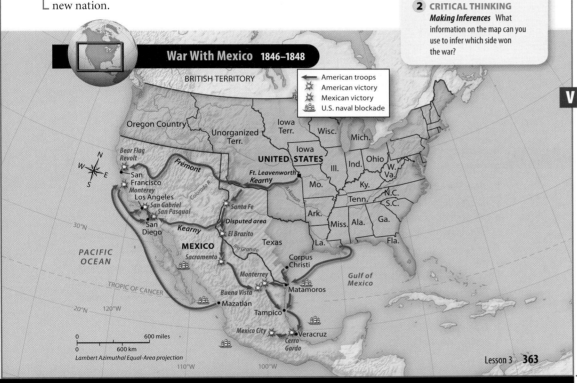

War With Mexico 1846–1848

BRITISH TERRITORY

- American troops
- American victory
- Mexican victory
- U.S. naval blockade

Oregon Country
Iowa Terr.
Unorganized Terr.
Wisc.
Mich.
Bear Flag Revolt
Frémont
San Francisco
Monterey
Los Angeles
San Gabriel
San Pasqual
San Diego
Kearny
UNITED STATES
Iowa
Ft. Leavenworth Kearny
Ill.
Ind.
Ohio
W. Va.
Mo.
Ky.
Santa Fe
Colorado R.
Ark.
Tenn.
N.C.
Disputed area
Miss.
Ala.
Ga.
El Brazito
Texas
La.
Fla.
S.C.
Rio Grande
MEXICO
PACIFIC OCEAN
Sacramento
Corpus Christi
TROPIC OF CANCER
Monterrey
Gulf of Mexico
Buena Vista
Matamoros
Mazatlán
Tampico
Mexico City
Veracruz
Cerro Gordo

30°N
20°N
120°W
110°W
100°W

0   600 miles
0   600 km
Lambert Azimuthal Equal-Area projection

Lesson 3   **363**

T Technology Skills

Researching on the Internet Have students research the progress of the Mexican War on the Internet, adding to the details that they have learned in the text. Have students focus on the roles played by President Polk and by Zachary Taylor. Then have students make a display about the Mexican War for the classroom or for the class Web site. **Visual/Spatial Interpersonal**

R Reading Skills

Describing Ask students to use text evidence to describe the uprising in California and Frémont's role in the uprising. **Ask: What was the result of the uprising?** (*California declared its independence as the Bear Flag Republic.*) **What action did the United States take to claim the Bear Flag Republic as part of the United States?** (*Soon after California declared its independence, the United States sent navy ships to the ports of San Francisco and San Diego.*) **AL ELL**

V Visual Skills

Analyzing Maps Have students compare the distances involved in the acquisition of Texas and California with the distances involved in the states that were already part of the Union. **Ask: Which area is larger?** (*The area acquired in the Mexican War.*) **AL ELL Visual/Spatial Logical/Mathematical**

V

PRIMARY SOURCE

The Bear Flag

Analyzing Primary Sources Use the primary source excerpt to discuss the creation of the Bear Flag and how it represents the state of California. **Ask: Where did the idea for the Bear Flag come from?** (*It was the flag the rebels used to represent their new nation.*) **Visual/Spatial AL ELL**

See page 345E for other online activities.

netw@rks   The Bear Flag

ANALYZING PRIMARY SOURCES

The California legislature recognized the bear flag as the official state flag in 1911. Like those of Hawaii and Texas, the California flag is unusual because it features a design used by a formerly independent country.

CALIFORNIA REPUBLIC

PhotoDisc/Getty Images

" Section 1. The bear flag is hereby selected and adopted as the state flag of California.

Sec 2. The said bear flag shall consist of a flag of a length equal to one and one-half the width thereof; the upper five-sixths of the width thereof to be a white field, and the lower sixth of the width thereof "

—from *General Laws of the State of California*, Edited by James H. Deering

ANSWERS, p. 363

GEOGRAPHY CONNECTION

1 San Pasqual, in California

2 CRITICAL THINKING The United States won nearly all the battles, including the ones deep in what is Mexico today.

R Reading Skills

Naming Direct students to read the section titled "Peace Terms." Then, lead a class discussion about the treaty that finally ended the war with Mexico. **Ask: What present-day states did the United States acquire through the Treaty of Guadalupe Hidalgo?** *(California, Nevada, and Utah, as well as most of Arizona and New Mexico and parts of Colorado and Wyoming)* **Where did the treaty say the Mexican/United States border was?** *(the Rio Grande)* **As a result of this treaty, what did the United States finally get that it had wanted for a long time?** *(access to the Pacific Ocean)* Encourage students to reflect on how much the size of the country had changed as the result of one conflict.

Have students complete the Lesson 3 Review.

CLOSE & REFLECT

Lead the class in a discussion of how the war with Mexico fits into the idea of Manifest Destiny, despite the violent steps taken to gain territory. Ask students if they think that the war with Mexico was worth it.

Connections to
TODAY
The California Bear Flag
The state flag of California today is based on the bear flag created during the Bear Flag Revolt in 1846.

The Bear Flag Republic did not exist for long. Within a month, American warships arrived at the ports of San Francisco and San Diego to claim the republic for the United States.

Mexico still refused to surrender, even though it had lost New Mexico, California, and Texas. President Polk sent General Winfield Scott and his troops to attack Mexico City. They landed in the port of Veracruz and captured it after three weeks of fighting. They still needed to travel 300 miles (483 km) to Mexico City, fighting Mexican troops along the way.

Finally, in September 1847, six months after Scott's forces landed in Veracruz, they captured Mexico's capital. Polk's plan for the war had succeeded.

Peace Terms

Defeated on February 2, 1848, Mexico's leaders signed the Treaty of Guadalupe Hidalgo (GWAH·duh·loop he·DAHL·goh). Mexico gave the United States more than 500,000 square miles (1,295,000 sq. km) of territory—what are now the states of California, Nevada, and Utah, as well as most of Arizona and New Mexico and parts of Colorado and Wyoming. Mexico accepted the Rio Grande as its border with Texas. In return, the United States paid Mexico $15 million and assumed $3.25 million in debts Mexico owed American citizens.

With Oregon and the former Mexican territories under the American flag, the dream of Manifest Destiny had been realized. The question of whether the new lands should allow slavery, however, would lead the country toward another bloody conflict.

☑ **PROGRESS CHECK**

Describing What did America gain from the Mexican War?

LESSON 3 REVIEW (CCSS)

Review Vocabulary (Tier 3 Words)

1. Describe the settlements established by the Spanish and by Mexicans in California using the following words. RH.6–8.4

   a. rancho **b.** ranchero

Answer the Guiding Questions

2. *Specifying* What was the main purpose of the Santa Fe Trail? RH.6–8.1

3. *Explaining* Why did Americans want to acquire California? RH.6–8.2

4. *Identifying* What was the source of the conflict between the United States and Mexico before they went to war? RH.6–8.1

5. *Analyzing* Describe how trade contributed to United States territorial growth. RH.6–8.2

6. **INFORMATIVE/EXPLANATORY** Write a brief national anthem for the Bear Flag Republic. Include details meant to inspire pride among its citizens. WHST.6–8.9, WHST.6–8.10

364 *Manifest Destiny*

LESSON 3 REVIEW ANSWERS

1. Possible answer: Mexican settlers established huge estates in California called ranchos. The estate owners were called rancheros.

2. the transportation of goods for sale

3. They thought the Pacific Ocean was a safer border than a foreign country. California also had great resources.

4. President Polk considered California a part of Manifest Destiny even though it belonged to Mexico. He tried to buy it, but Mexico would not sell. Mexico still considered Texas a part of that nation and disagreed with the United States over the location of the southern border of Texas.

5. Mexico opened Santa Fe to trade. When the Santa Fe Trail became a popular American trade route, American settlers followed.

6. Possible answer: Free now/the Bear Flag Republic stands/our future is in our own hands/ever always we are free/our republic by the sea.

ANSWER, p. 364

☑ **PROGRESS CHECK** It gained the areas of California, Nevada, Utah, most of Arizona and New Mexico, and parts of Colorado and Wyoming. Mexico also agreed to make the Rio Grande the southern border of Texas.

netw⚡rks
There's More Online!

- ☑ **BIOGRAPHY**
  Mariano G. Vallejo
- ☑ **GRAPH** San Francisco
  Population Growth
- ☑ **GRAPHIC ORGANIZER**
  Roles in the West
- ☑ **PRIMARY SOURCE**
  Gold Rush Letter
- ☑ **VIDEO**

Lesson 4
California and Utah

ESSENTIAL QUESTION *How do new ideas change the way people live?*

IT MATTERS BECAUSE
Through the treaty ending the war with Mexico, the United States controlled Texas, California, and what was then New Mexico territory.

California Gold Rush

GUIDING QUESTION *How did the discovery of gold help California?*

When gold was discovered at Sutter's Mill in 1848, people from all over the world traveled to California in search of riches. Those who arrived in 1849 were called **forty-niners.** As one official reported, "The farmers have thrown aside their plows, the lawyers their briefs, the doctors their pills, the priests their prayer books, and all are now digging gold." Some people arrived by sea. Others traveled on the Oregon Trail or the Santa Fe Trail.

Americans made up about 80 percent of the forty-niners. Others came from Mexico, South America, Europe, and Australia. About 300 men arrived from China, the first large group of Asian immigrants to settle in America. Although some eventually returned to China, others remained and established California's Chinese American community.

The Californios

The Treaty of Guadalupe Hidalgo ended the war with Mexico and made Californios—Mexicans living in California—citizens of the United States. The treaty also guaranteed them the rights to their lands. The Land Law of 1851, however, established a group of reviewers who examined the Californios' land rights.

R2

R1

(l) Bettmann/CORBIS, (cl) North Wind Picture Archives, (c) Government Transfer: US DOTT, USM, (r) North Wind Picture Archives

---

Reading HELP DESK (CCSS)

Taking Notes: *Describing* RH.6–8.1

As you read, take notes in a chart like this one. Describe what each person or group did and what their roles were in the settlement of California and Utah.

Forty-Niners	Role
Mormons	Role
Brigham Young	Role

Content Vocabulary
- forty-niner
- boomtown
- vigilante (Tier 3)

Lesson 4 **365**

VIDEO

Diverse Population in the West

Differentiating Show the Learn360 video about the diverse population in the West to help students understand that not only the Mormons but others, too, were seeking to make a new life in the West. Many people chose to move; others were left little choice. Clarify any unfamiliar terms or concepts. **AL** **ELL**

See page 345F for other online activities.

ENGAGE

🔔 **Bellringer** Lead a discussion of the present-day states of California and Utah by asking volunteers what they know about the people and the natural resources in each state. Then have students preview the lesson. **Ask: What groups of people do you think you will learn about in this lesson?** *(Possible answers: Californios, forty-niners, and Mormons)* Ask students what they already know about any of these groups. Students may know about the Gold Rush and the forty-niners, for example. Tell students that they will study each of these groups as they move through this lesson.

TEACH & ASSESS

R1 Reading Skills

Describing Direct students to read the section titled "California Gold Rush." Explain to the class that one reason gold is a precious metal is its rarity. **Ask: Why did the forty-niners rush to California?** *(to find gold, because it was easy to find gold there)* Then have students turn to a partner and describe people who became forty-niners. *(people with many kinds of backgrounds; farmers, lawyers, doctors, and priests; people from the United States, Mexico, South America, Europe, Australia, and China)* Encourage them to use details from the text to support their answers. **Verbal/Linguistic**

R2 Reading Skills

Discussing After students have read the text, discuss the life of a forty-niner with the class. **Ask: Why were the miners called forty-niners?** *(because that was the year they came to California to look for gold)* **What kind of experience did a person typically have in mining?** *(Most had no experience in mining.)* Have a volunteer describe and then act out how a miner would "pan" for gold. Finally, discuss the development of boomtowns due to miners and their needs for supplies, housing, food, and entertainment. Make sure everyone understands the term *boomtown*. **AL** **ELL** **Kinesthetic**

ANSWER, p. 365

TAKING NOTES: William Becknell: first American trader to reach Santa Fe; John C. Frémont: mapmaker who wrote about California's climate and resources; formed the Bear Flag Republic; Winfield Scott: army general who captured Veracruz, Mexico

366

V Visual Skills

Analyzing Images Call students' attention to the image at the top of the page. Discuss the landscape shown in this part of California. If needed, call students' attention to the natural resources *(trees, water, stone)*. **ELL** **Visual/Spatial**

C1 Critical Thinking Skills

Speculating Ask a volunteer to read aloud the image's caption. Have students work in groups of three or four and discuss whether forty-niners who didn't find gold might be able to make a living in this part of California. After a few minutes of group work, have students share their ideas with the rest of the class. **BL** **Interpersonal**

W Writing Skills

Informative/Explanatory Ask students to discuss reasons Californios might like being U.S. citizens and reasons they might dislike it. Then have students write a brief essay describing the pros and cons of being citizens. Encourage students to explain what happened in 1851 that might change Californios' attitudes about being subject to laws of the United States. *(The 1851 Land Law said if a new settler claimed a Californio's land, the parties had to go to court and the Californio had to prove that he or she owned the land.)*

C2 Critical Thinking Skills

Determining Cause and Effect Discuss with students the location of Sutter's Mill in relation to the developed cities in Gold Rush Era California. **Ask: What happened when people rushed to California to search for gold?** *(Communities sprang up overnight.)*

C1 A few forty-niners became rich from their work on the hillsides and streams of California, but most gained little or nothing.

V

W When a new settler claimed land that was held by a Californio, the two parties would go to court. There, it was the Californio who had to prove his or her ownership of the land. Some Californios were able to prove their claims. Many others lost their cases and their land.

The Life of a Forty-Niner

C2 As people rushed to a new area to look for gold, they built new communities. Towns and small cities appeared almost overnight. One site on the Yuba River had only two houses in September 1849. A year later, a miner arrived to find a bustling town of 1,000 people "with a large number of hotels, stores, groceries, bakeries, and ... gambling houses."

Cities also flourished during the Gold Rush. As ships arrived daily with gold seekers, San Francisco became a **boomtown,** growing quickly from a tiny village to a city of about 20,000 people.

Most forty-niners had no experience in mining. Whenever they heard that gold had been discovered at a particular site, they rushed to it and attacked the hillsides with pickaxes and shovels. They spent hours bent over streambeds, "panning" for gold dust and nuggets. Panning involved gently swirling water and gravel in a pan in order to remove dirt and, perhaps, reveal a small speck of gold.

Bettmann/CORBIS

Reading HELPDESK **CCSS**

forty-niner fortune-seeker who came to California during the Gold Rush
boomtown a fast-growing community

366 *Manifest Destiny*

---

netw⊙rks   *Online Teaching Options*

PRIMARY SOURCE

The Gold Rush

Analyzing Primary Sources Use the interactive primary source excerpt to discuss the discovery of gold at Sutter's Mill in 1848. **Ask: What does the miner say will happen to many who come?** *(They will get sick and die or not have enough money to get home.)* **Do you think this miner would encourage others to come to California? Why or why not?** *(Possible answer: No, he describes many negative aspects of life.)* **BL**

See page 345F for other online activities.

netw⊙rks   **The Gold Rush**
ANALYZING PRIMARY SOURCES

The most famous gold strike took place at Sutter's Mill in 1848 when James W. Marshall and John Sutter discovered gold near the Sacramento River in California. They tried their best to keep their discovery a secret, but soon thousands of people hoping to strike it rich descended on California.

Bettmann/CORBIS

" Many, very many, that come here meet with bad success & thousands will leave their bones here. Others will lose their health, contract diseases that they will carry to their graves with them. Some will have to beg their way home, & probably one half that come here will never make enough to carry them back. But this does not alter the fact about the gold "

—from *The California Gold Rush, 1849,* by S. Shufelt

The California Gold Rush more than doubled the world's supply of gold. For all their hard work, however, very few forty-niners achieved lasting wealth. Most found little or no gold. Many of those who did find gold lost their riches through gambling or wild spending.

Boomtown merchants, however, made huge profits. They could charge whatever they liked for food and other essential items because there were no other nearby stores that sold these products. For example, an immigrant named Levi Strauss sold the miners sturdy pants made of denim. His "Levi's" made him rich.

Gold Rush Society

Mining camps contained men of all backgrounds but few women. Lonely and suffering hardships, many men spent their free hours drinking, gambling, and fighting. Mining towns had no police or prisons. As a result, citizens known as **vigilantes** (vih·juh·LAN·teez) formed committees to protect themselves. Vigilantes took the law into their own hands and acted as police, judge, jury, and sometimes executioner.

R

Economic and Political Progress

The Gold Rush had lasting effects on California. Agriculture, shipping, and trade grew to meet the demand for food and other goods. Many people who had arrived looking for gold stayed to farm or run a business.

Rapid growth brought the need for better government. In 1849, Californians applied for statehood and wrote a **constitution.** The constitution's ban on slavery, however, caused a crisis in Congress. Southern states opposed California's admission. Congress eventually worked out a compromise by which California became a free state in 1850.

C2

☑ **PROGRESS CHECK**

Determining Cause and Effect How did the California Gold Rush lead to the expansion of cities?

A Religious Refuge in Utah

GUIDING QUESTION *Why did the Mormons settle in Utah?*

While the Gold Rush was transforming California, change was also taking place in nearby Utah. There, Mormons, or members of the Church of Jesus Christ of Latter-day Saints, were building a new community and fulfilling their vision of the godly life.

North Wind Picture Archives

North Wind Picture Archives

vigilante person who acts as police, judge, and jury without formal legal authority

Academic Vocabulary (Tier 2 Words)

constitution a list of laws supporting a government

Lesson 4 **367**

BIOGRAPHY

Mariano G. Vallejo
(1808–1890)

Mariano G. Vallejo was born in Monterey, California, to Mexican parents. He served in the Mexican military, but he was often critical of the Mexican government. After California became part of the United States, he took part in the convention that wrote California's constitution. After statehood, Vallejo served in the state senate and acted as a leader of the state's Californio population. Still, like many other Californios, Vallejo wound up losing much of his California land.

C1

▶ **CRITICAL THINKING**
Speculating Why do you think Californios considered Vallejo to be a leader of their interests in California?

R Reading Skills

Describing Have students review the section about the Gold Rush society. Have volunteers describe the life of a miner who lived in a Gold Rush mining camp. Be sure students understand that life was very difficult and that the men suffered from loneliness and hardship. **Ask: How did some of the men spend their free time?** *(drinking, gambling, fighting)* **Verbal/Linguistic**

C1 Critical Thinking Skills

Reasoning Ask a volunteer to state how the Land Law of 1851 affected Californios, such as Mariano G. Vallejo. **Ask: Do you think Vallejo was treated fairly? Why or why not?** *(Students' answers will vary. Accept any well-reasoned answer.)* **Do you think something like that could happen to someone today? Why or why not?** *(Students' answers will vary. Accept any well-reasoned answer.)*

C2 Critical Thinking Skills

Making Connections Explain that when a large number of people move into an area, as they did during the California Gold Rush, their arrival causes large changes. **Ask: How did California respond to the problems of sudden growth of the region?** *(wrote a constitution and applied for statehood)* **Why did the Southern states oppose statehood for California?** *(The constitution banned slavery and the Southern states did not want another free state to enter the Union.)* Tell students that California was admitted later in the year as part of the Compromise of 1850, which they will read about in a later chapter of their textbook.

See page 345F for other online activities.

GRAPH

San Francisco Population Growth

Analyzing Graphs Use the interactive graph to discuss the population growth of San Francisco, which was a boomtown during the Gold Rush. **Ask: How did the population of San Francisco change between 1850 and 1900?** *(It grew by more than 300,000 people.)* **AL** **What problems might a city experience by gaining so many people in a short time?** *(not enough resources or housing, disagreements and violence among the people, deciding who makes the rules for the people, and so on)* **BL** **Logical/Mathematic**

netw⊙rks | **San Francisco Population Growth**

The Gold Rush was responsible for encouraging people to move to San Francisco in the mid- to late-1800s. This incredible population growth led to California becoming a state in 1850.

POPULATION OF SAN FRANCISCO, CA

Year	Population
1820	350
1830	21,000
1860	56,802
1870	149,473
1880	233,959
1890	298,997
1900	342,782

YEAR

ANSWERS, p. 367

CRITICAL THINKING He had lived in California all his life, and he had taken part in the transition of California to statehood.

☑ **PROGRESS CHECK** Gold miners needed supplies, so merchants settled in the cities. As more people arrived to find gold, stores, hotels, and gambling houses opened. People who did not find gold often stayed in the cities or became farmers.

C Critical Thinking Skills

Analyzing Joseph Smith told people about his visions. **Ask: What did he hope to achieve by this?** *(He hoped to use the visions to achieve an ideal society.)* Discuss with students some of the practices Smith thought would lead to this society. **Which one angered people?** *(the idea of polygamy, or marriage to more than one wife)* **AL** **ELL**

R1 Reading Skills

Citing Text Evidence After students have read the text, remind them that some of the early European settlers in North America left Europe to find a place where they could practice their religion freely and live according to their own customs. In fact, the first amendment to the Constitution protects religious rights. **Ask: Why were Mormon ideas controversial?** *(Smith published a book called* The Book of Mormon *and claimed that it was a translation from golden plates. He also claimed that the plates told of the coming of Christ. This contradicts other Christian religions and angered many people.)* Have students cite evidence from the text to support their answers.

R2 Reading Skills

Explaining Ask for a student volunteer to read the text aloud. Then, lead a class discussion about the formation of the Mormon community in New York. **Ask: Why were the Mormons forced to move from place to place?** *(People disagreed with their religious beliefs and practices, especially the belief that a man could have more than one wife.)* Ask students to speculate why Smith and his followers left New York instead of waging a battle in the courts.

V Visual Skills

Analyzing Images Discuss the death of Joseph Smith with students. Have students look at the image of the shooting and describe the conditions under which Joseph Smith was held. Ask students whether they think the picture accurately portrays the conditions in the jail where Smith was held, and have them give reasons to support their answers. **BL** **Visual/Spatial**

The Mormons Move On

The Church of Jesus Christ of Latter-day Saints was among a number of religious movements that sprang up during the religious awakenings of the 1830s and 1840s. The founder of the Mormon Church was Joseph Smith, a New Englander living in western New York. Smith said that he had received visions that led him to build a new church. He began preaching Mormon ideas in 1830.

Smith published *The Book of Mormon* that year, announcing that it was a translation of words written on golden plates that he had received from an angel. The text told of the coming of the Christ and the need to build a kingdom on Earth to receive him.

Smith hoped to use his visions to build an ideal society. He believed that property should be held in common, rather than belong to individuals. He also supported polygamy, the idea that a man could have more than one wife. This angered a large number of people. Mormons eventually gave up this practice.

Joseph Smith formed a community in New York, but neighbors disapproved of the Mormons' religion and forced them to leave. The Mormons eventually settled in Illinois. In 1839 they bought the town of Commerce, Illinois, and renamed it Nauvoo. Nauvoo became a prosperous community.

Still, the Mormons continued to suffer persecution, or mistreatment because of their beliefs. In 1844 a mob of local residents killed Joseph Smith. After Smith's death, Brigham Young took over as head of the Mormons. Young decided that the Mormons should move again to escape persecution and find religious freedom. This time, the Mormons would move west to the Great Salt Lake in present-day Utah. Although part of Mexico at the time, no Mexicans had settled in the region because of its harsh terrain.

Joseph Smith was killed while being held in an Illinois jail.

North Wind Picture Archives

Reading HELPDESK (CCSS)

Academic Vocabulary (Tier 2 Words)
incorporate to include, absorb

networks *Online Teaching Options*

WORKSHEET

Economics of History Activity: Manifest Destiny: Boomtown Economics

Analyzing Information Have students complete the Economics of History Activity worksheet entitled "Boomtown Economics" as a homework assignment.

See page 345F for other online activities.

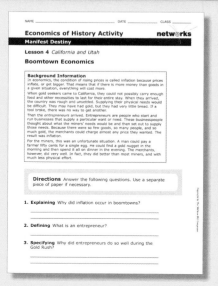

NAME _____ DATE _____ CLASS _____

Economics of History Activity **networks**
Manifest Destiny

Lesson 4 *California and Utah*
Boomtown Economics

Background Information
In economics, the condition of rising prices is called inflation because prices inflate, or get bigger. That means that if there is more money than goods in a given situation, everything will cost more.

When gold seekers came to California, they could not possibly carry enough food and other necessities to last for their entire stay. When they arrived, the country was rough and unsettled. Supplying their physical needs would be difficult. They may have had gold, but they had very little bread. If a tool broke, there was no way to get another.

Then the entrepreneurs arrived. Entrepreneurs are people who start and run businesses that supply a particular want or need. These businesspeople thought about what the miners' needs would be and then set out to supply those needs. Because there were so few goods, so many people, and so much gold, the merchants could charge almost any price they wanted. The result was inflation.

For the miners, this was an unfortunate situation. A man could pay a farmer fifty cents for a single egg. He could find a gold nugget in the morning and then spend it all on dinner in the evening. The merchants, however, did very well. In fact, they did better than most miners, and with much less physical effort.

Directions Answer the following questions. Use a separate piece of paper if necessary.

1. **Explaining** Why did inflation occur in boomtowns?

2. **Defining** What is an entrepreneur?

3. **Specifying** Why did entrepreneurs do so well during the Gold Rush?

A Haven in the Desert

The Mormon migration began in 1846. About 12,000 Mormons made the trek in the largest single migration in American history. The Mormons' route became known as the Mormon Trail and served as a valuable route to the western United States.

In 1847 the Mormons finally reached the Great Salt Lake. There, Young declared that the Mormons would build a new settlement. The Mormons staked a claim on the dry, wild land they called Deseret. Soon they had set up farming communities.

Mormons minted coins and printed paper money in the 1840s and 1850s.

At first life was difficult for the settlers. The Mormons, however, made Deseret flourish through hard work and determination. They carefully planned towns, such as Salt Lake City, and built irrigation canals for their farms. They taxed property and regulated the use of water, timber, and other resources. Mormons also founded industries so they could be self-sufficient. Mormon merchants sold supplies to the forty-niners who passed through Utah on their way to California.

In 1848 the United States acquired the Salt Lake area from Mexico after the Mexican War. In 1850 Congress established the Utah Territory. Brigham Young was named governor.

By 1860 there were many Mormon communities, but Utah was not easily **incorporated** into the United States. Problems included the Mormon practice of polygamy and frequent conflicts with federal officials. In 1857 and 1858, war almost broke out between the Mormons and the United States Army. Utah did not become a state until 1896, after the Mormons officially gave up the practice of polygamy.

C1

C2

Government Transfer: US DOTT, USM

☑ **PROGRESS CHECK**

Summarizing Why did the Mormons have to keep moving from one place to another?

LESSON 4 REVIEW

Review Vocabulary (Tier 3 Words)

1. Define each of the following words or terms, then use them to write a paragraph about the Gold Rush. RH.6–8.4, WHST.6–8.4

   a. forty-niner   **b.** boomtown   **c.** vigilante

Answer the Guiding Questions

2. *Explaining* Why was California's entry into the Union delayed? RH.6–8.2

3. *Explaining* What did Joseph Smith believe was the goal for Mormons? RH.6–8.2

4. *Making Connections* How did the Gold Rush affect California's population? RH.6–8.5

5. *Listing* Make a list of reasons that Deseret was able to flourish. RH.6–8.1

6. **INFORMATIVE/EXPLANATORY** Consider the challenges and opportunities facing a forty-niner. What kinds of qualities do you think this kind of person would have to possess? WHST.6–8.1, WHST.6–8.9

Lesson 4   **369**

C1 Critical Thinking Skills

Making Connections Explain that people who move choose to settle in a place that they think will meet their needs. Often people choose to live in places where food, water, and other resources are plentiful. **Ask:** Why do you think Brigham Young decided that his people should settle in Utah? *(It was far away from people who might persecute them.)* How many people traveled to Utah with Young? *(12,000)* What is unusual about this number? *(It was the largest single migration in American history.)*

C2 Critical Thinking Skills

Determining Cause and Effect Point out to students that Utah was made a territory in 1848, but it did not become a state until 1896. **Ask:** Why did it take so long to achieve statehood? *(The Mormons held different beliefs from most Americans and often had conflicts with federal authorities.)* What did the Mormons have to give up for Utah to become a state? *(the practice of polygamy)*

Have students complete the Lesson 4 Review.

CLOSE & REFLECT

Review with students the number of states created out of the new territories developed during westward expansion. Ask volunteers to describe how much land was now a part of America due to Manifest Destiny.

ANSWER, p. 369
☑ **PROGRESS CHECK** Some people did not like the Mormons' religious beliefs, especially the belief in having more than one wife.

LESSON 4 REVIEW ANSWERS

1. **a.** A forty-niner was a fortune hunter who went to California during the Gold Rush. **b.** A boomtown was a fast-growing community. **c.** Vigilantes were individuals who took the law into their own hands, acting as police, judge, jury, and sometimes executioner. The arrival of the forty-niners in large numbers created boomtowns in California. The difficulty in providing services and protecting law and order in these towns led to the rise of vigilantes.

2. The South did not want another free (non-slave) state to enter the Union.

3. He thought that the Mormons should prepare a kingdom for the coming of Christ. Smith hoped the preparations would result in an ideal society. Students may also mention that he believed that all property should belong to everyone and that a man could have more than one wife.

4. The population grew quickly and became more diverse as people came from China and other countries to find gold.

5. The people of Deseret worked very hard. They farmed using irrigation. They planned their cities, collected taxes, used resources wisely, and founded industries. They also sold supplies to people who were traveling to California.

6. Possible answer: A person would have to be willing to put up with hardship, be a risk taker, and be highly motivated by the possibility of wealth.

CHAPTER REVIEW ACTIVITY

Have a student volunteer create a three-column chart, with the columns labeled "Area," "Before the Move West," and "After the Move West." In the first column, ask the volunteer to write: Texas, California, and Oregon. Lead a class discussion to complete the chart. Possible answers are given below. Encourage students to use their own words to complete the chart.

Area	Before the Move West	After the Move West
Texas	belonged to Mexico	became a state
California	small, mostly Spanish population	large, widely varied population
Oregon	home of Native Americans and fur trappers	home of farmers, merchants, and others

REVIEW THE ENDURING UNDERSTANDING

Review the chapter's Enduring Understanding with students.

• *People, places, and ideas change over time.*

Now pose the following questions in a class discussion to apply this to the chapter.

How did the mountain men adapt to life in the Oregon Country? *(Mountain men made a living by trapping the beaver there and later by serving as guides in the country they had come to learn. They traded with the Native Americans; many had Native American wives. They lived in buffalo-skin lodges and dressed in fringed buckskin pants, moccasins, and beads.)*

Why did Mexico come to regret encouraging Americans to settle in Mexican Texas? *(Because the settlers did not adapt to Mexican ways and rules. They failed to learn Spanish, convert to Catholicism, and respect Mexican opposition to slavery.)*

Do you think Spanish settlers had a greater effect on Native American culture in California, or did Native American culture have a greater effect on Spanish settlers? Why? *(Spanish settlers had a greater effect on Native American culture in California. Spanish missions attempted to convert Native Americans to farming and Christianity, and rancheros treated Native American workers almost like enslaved people.)*

What were some of the elements of the society that the forty-niners created in California? *(Many lived in boomtowns, where drinking, gambling, and fighting were common. Vigilante committees formed to provide some semblance of law and order.)*

Write your answers on a separate piece of paper.

1 Exploring the Essential Questions WHST.6–8.2, WHST.6–8.9
INFORMATIVE/EXPLANATORY Use examples from the history of Texas and the experiences of the Mormons to illustrate how geography, conflict, and new ideas change the way people live.

2 21st Century Skills RH.6–8.5
SEQUENCING EVENTS Put the following events on a time line in chronological (time) order: Florida becomes a state, the Adams-Onís Treaty, gold is discovered in California, the election of President James K. Polk, the battle of the Alamo, the Mormons reach the Great Salt Lake.

3 Thinking Like a Historian RH.6–8.5
PREDICTING CONSEQUENCES Imagine a large, uninhabited area in the Florida Panhandle. How would the environment change if Southern planters from other states came and settled there? Create a graphic organizer like the one below, and write the changes in the boxes provided.

4 Visual Literacy RH.6–8.7
ANALYZING PAINTINGS This painting shows a group of Mormons on the Mormon Trail to Utah in the 1850s. How does this painting portray the Mormons? What kind of life does the painting suggest the Mormons will be living when they reach their destination?

North Wind Picture Archives

370 *Manifest Destiny*

ACTIVITIES ANSWERS

Exploring the Essential Questions

1 Answers should include the conflict between Texas and Mexico over the border, the problems caused by the new ideas of Mormonism, and the Mormon migration to and survival in the desert.

21st Century Skills

2 the Adams-Onís Treaty, the battle of the Alamo, the election of James K. Polk, Florida becomes a state, Mormons reach the Great Salt Lake, gold is discovered in California

Thinking Like a Historian

3 Possible answers include:

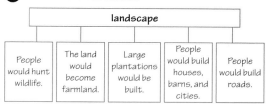

Visual Literacy

4 The painting shows the Mormons as determined, committed people who are willing to endure much to pursue their dream. The painting suggests that life will be difficult, with few comforts. The Mormons are able to bring only that which they can push or pull across the plains themselves.

REVIEW THE GUIDING QUESTIONS

Choose the best answer for each question.

RH.6–8.2
1 Which of these is a reason that many Americans believed in Manifest Destiny?

A. They did not want to speak Spanish.

B. They liked to wear clothes made from beaver skins.

C. They believed it was God's plan for the country.

D. They did not like the British.

RH.6–8.1
2 Which of these people was the biggest supporter of Manifest Destiny?

F. John Quincy Adams

G. Henry Clay

H. John Tyler

I. James K. Polk

RH.6–8.2
3 What was the main problem that delayed the statehood of Texas and Florida?

A. Congress wanted to keep a balance of slave and free states in the Union.

B. Neither one had a large enough population.

C. They had no organized government.

D. They were in continual conflict with neighboring territories.

RH.6–8.2
4 The Santa Fe Trail

F. was a disputed area between the United States and Mexico.

G. began as a route for bringing trade goods from the western edge of the United States to the territory of New Mexico.

H. was used by emigrants to get to Oregon.

I. was part of the Bear Flag Republic.

RH.6–8.2
5 The population of California increased quickly after

A. the arrival of the Chinese.

B. people learned that they could get there by water.

C. the discovery of gold.

D. people heard about the mild climate.

RH.6–8.1
6 The Mormons used irrigation to water crops at

F. Deseret.

G. California missions.

H. Sutter's Mill.

I. boomtowns in California.

371

ASSESSMENT ANSWERS
Review the Guiding Questions

1 **C** Students should realize that speaking Spanish was an issue when Mexico controlled Texas, and beaver skins are related to mountain men. Joint occupation reduced conflict with the British. C is the only answer that has to do with an actual reason for the belief.

2 **I** John Quincy Adams was president before the idea of Manifest Destiny became widely popular. Henry Clay and John Tyler were not known for their support of this issue. James K. Polk, however, made Manifest Destiny a big part of his winning presidential campaign.

3 **A** Texas and Florida both wanted to be slave states. They had to wait until a territory wanted to enter as a free state. The other three choices are all false for both states.

4 **G** The first person to use the Santa Fe Trail was a merchant, and other merchants followed with their goods. The trail was not a major point of dispute and was not used to get to California, which was also called the Bear Flag Republic.

5 **C** The Gold Rush brought thousands of new people to California. The other choices also increased the population, but the Gold Rush was the biggest factor.

6 **F** Deseret was what the Mormons called their Utah community. New York was the original place the Mormons lived. The California missions and boomtowns were part of California, not Utah.

Analyzing Documents

7 **A** Clayton was not interested in wealth, and he was committed to his faith. He wanted to live among the Mormons to avoid persecution.

8 **H** He was not drawn to wealth and power, and he wanted to live in peace with other Mormons.

Short Response

9 Senator Corwin states that Southerners would expect to be allowed to bring their slavery to the new territory with them. They would not expect to "expend their blood" in the war and then be unable to continue their way of life.

10 Students should support their positions with valid reasons.

Extended Response

11 Answers will vary but should include the following basic views: Polk: destiny of the United States to control the continent; Santa Anna: way for the United States to take Mexican lands; Native American: way for the United States to take land from Native Americans; mountain man: provides opportunities for Americans to explore and take advantage of economic opportunities.

DBQ **ANALYZING DOCUMENTS**

William Clayton, a Mormon emigrant, wrote the following in 1847:

"When I commune [discuss] with my own heart and ask myself whether I would choose to dwell here in this wild-looking country amongst the Saints [Mormons] surrounded by friends, though poor, … or dwell amongst the gentiles [in this context, non-Mormons] with all their wealth … to be eternally mobbed, harassed, hunted, our best men murdered … give me the quiet wilderness and my family to associate with."

RH.6–8.2, RH.6–8.10

7 **Analyzing Primary Sources** What choice did William Clayton make?

A. to live in the wild country, even though he would be poor

B. to gain wealth and good things

C. to reject his faith

D. to suffer persecution

RH.6–8.6

8 **Drawing Conclusions** What was his reason for that choice?

F. He wanted to become powerful in the church.

G. He looked forward to a life of adventure.

H. He wanted to live quietly with people of his own faith.

I. He wanted to become a saint.

SHORT RESPONSE

"I allude to the question of slavery. Opposition to its further extension … is a deeply rooted determination … in what we call the non-slaveholding states. … How is it in the South? Can it be expected that they should expend in common their blood and their treasure in the acquisition of immense territory, and then willingly forego the right to carry thither [there] their slaves, and inhabit the conquered country … ? Sir, I know the feelings and opinions of the South … ."

—Senator Thomas Corwin, 1847, in a speech on the Mexican War

RH.6–8.2, WHST.6–8.4

9 Based on the excerpt, what does Senator Corwin expect Southern whites to do if the United States wins the Mexican War?

RH.6–8.6, WHST.6–8.4

10 Do you think Corwin is for or against the war? Explain.

EXTENDED RESPONSE

RH.6–8.6, WHST.6–8.1

11 **Informative/Explanatory** Write four separate reactions to the idea of Manifest Destiny from the perspective of each of these people: James K. Polk, General Santa Anna, a Native American of the Plains, a mountain man.

Need Extra Help?

If You've Missed Question	1	2	3	4	5	6	7	8	9	10	11
Review Lesson	1	1	2	3	4	4	4	4	3	3	1–4

---

networks   *Online Teaching Options*

Using eAssessment

Use eAssessment to access and assign the publisher-made Lesson Quizzes & Chapter Tests electronically. You can also use eAssessment to create your own quizzes and tests from hundreds of available questions. eAssessment helps you design assessments that meet the needs of different types of learners. Follow the link in the *Assess* tab of your Teacher Lesson Center.

CHAPTER 14
North and South Planner

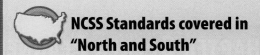
UNDERSTANDING BY DESIGN®

Enduring Understanding
- *Economic systems shape relationships in society.*

Essential Questions
- *How does technology change the way people live?*
- *How do people adapt to their environment?*
- *Why do people make economic choices?*

Predictable Misunderstandings
Students may think:
- *Most Southerners owned slaves and operated large plantations.*
- *The impact of technological advancements was limited to the Northern industrial states.*

Assessment Evidence
Performance Tasks:
- *Hands-On Chapter Project*

Other Evidence:
- *Interactive Graphic Organizers*
- *What Do You Know? activity*
- *Geography and History Activity*
- *Primary Source Activity*
- *Written Paragraphs*
- *Lesson Reviews*
- *Online Self-Check Quizzes*
- *Chapter Activities and Assessment*

Learners will understand:

1 Culture
  2. Concepts such as beliefs, values, institutions, cohesion, diversity, accommodation, adaptation, assimilation, and dissonance

2 Time, Continuity, and Change
  9. The influences of social, geographic, economic, and cultural factors on the history of local areas, states, nations, and the world

3 People, Places, and Environments
  4 The roles of different kinds of population centers in a region or nation

7 Production, Distribution, and Consumption
  3. The economic choices that people make have both present and future consequences
  4. Economic incentives affect people's behavior and may be regulated by rules or laws

8 Science, Technology, and Society
  4. Science and technology have had both positive and negative impacts upon individuals, societies, and the environment in the past and present
  5. Science and technology have changed people's perceptions of the social and natural world, as well as their relationship to the land, economy and trade, their concept of security, and their major daily activities
  8. Science and technology sometimes create ethical issues that test our standards and values

SUGGESTED PACING GUIDE

Introducing the Chapter	1 Day	
Lesson 1	2 Days	
Lesson 2	2 Days	
Lesson 3	1 Day	
Lesson 4	2 Days	
Chapter Activities and Assessment	1 Day	

TOTAL TIME   9 Days

Key for Using the Teacher Edition

SKILL-BASED ACTIVITIES

Types of skill activities found in the Teacher Edition.

V Visual Skills require students to analyze maps, graphs, charts, and photos.

R Reading Skills help students practice reading skills and master vocabulary.

W Writing Skills provide writing opportunities to help students comprehend the text.

C Critical Thinking Skills help students apply and extend what they have learned.

T Technology Skills require students to use digital tools effectively.

Letters are followed by a number when there is more than one of the same type of skill on the page.

DIFFERENTIATED INSTRUCTION

All activities are written for the on-level student unless otherwise marked with the leveled labels below.

BL Beyond Level
AL Approaching Level
ELL English Language Learners

All students benefit from activities that utilize different learning styles. Many activities are marked as below when a particular learning style is highlighted.

Intrapersonal	Naturalist
Logical/Mathematical	Kinesthetic
Visual/Spatial	Auditory/Musical
Verbal/Linguistic	Interpersonal

CHAPTER OPENER PLANNER

Students will know:

- the causes and consequences of the nineteenth-century transportation revolution.
- the impact of technological advancements on the agricultural economy and slave labor.
- the various immigrant groups that came to the United States during the early 1800s and their contributions.
- the reasons various urban centers developed during the 1800s.
- the differences between the economies of the North and South.
- the influence of individuals on social and political developments in the South.
- the role of slavery in the development of sectional conflict.

Students will be able to:

- **identify and evaluate** how the innovations in industry, travel, and communications changed the lives of Americans in the 1800s.
- **understand cause and effect relationships** between immigration and its impact on cities and industry in the North.
- **analyze and compare** the economies of the North and South.
- **analyze and describe** the living conditions of enslaved African Americans in the South and the unique culture they developed.

UNDERSTANDING BY DESIGN®

☑ *Print Teaching Options*

V Visual Skills

☐ **P. 374** Students consider the extent of the United States in 1840 and discuss the desire to move west.
Visual/Spatial

R Reading Skills

☐ **P. 375** Students identify important events in U.S. history between 1820 and 1860. **AL** **Visual/Spatial**

☑ *Online Teaching Options*

V Visual Skills

☐ **MAP** **Territorial Expansion 1840**—Students click to view the extent of the states, territories, unorganized territory, and foreign areas in 1840.

☐ **WORLD ATLAS** Students can use this interactive map to identify regions of the world, learn about individual countries, locate political boundaries, measure distances, and much more.

C Critical Thinking Skills

☐ **TIME LINE** **The United States 1820 to 1860**—Students consider key events during this time period.

☑ *Printable Digital Worksheets*

R Reading Skills

☐ **GRAPHIC NOVEL** *Strangers on a Train*—A Portuguese businessman travels to Raleigh, NC, looking for investment opportunities. On the train, a family from the North and a man from the South try to convince the businessman to invest in their region of the country.

Project-Based Learning

Hands-On Chapter Project

Illustrated Encyclopedia Entry

Student groups will do independent research to create an encyclopedia entry about one of the following: clipper ships, the *Tom Thumb*, Erie Canal, Morse code, cotton gin, or plantations. Entries will include maps, photos, or other visuals and cite at least three references.

Technology Extension

Create Glogster Posters

- Find an additional activity online that incorporates technology for this project.
- Visit the EdTechTeacher Web sites (included in the Technology Extension for this chapter) for more links, tutorials, and other resources.

Print Resources

ANCILLARY RESOURCES

These ancillaries are available for every chapter and lesson.

- **Reading Essentials and Study Guide Workbook** **AL** **ELL**
- **Chapter Tests and Lesson Quizzes Blackline Masters**

PRINTABLE DIGITAL WORKSHEETS

These printable digital worksheets are available for every chapter and lesson.

- **Hands-On Chapter Projects**
- **What Do You Know? activities**
- **Chapter Summaries (English and Spanish)**
- **Vocabulary Builder activities**
- **Guided Reading activities**

More Media Resources

SUGGESTED READING

Grade 6 reading level:

- *So Far From Home: The Diary of Mary Driscoll, an Irish Mill Girl,* by Barry Denenberg

Grade 7 reading level:

- *Rebels Against Slavery: American Slave Revolts,* by Patricia C. McKissack and Fredrick L. McKissack

Grade 8 reading level:

- *True North: A Novel of the Underground Railroad,* by Kathryn Lasky

LESSON 1 PLANNER

THE INDUSTRIAL NORTH

Students will know:
- the causes and consequences of the nineteenth-century transportation revolution.
- the impact of technological advancements on the agricultural economy and slave labor.
- the differences between the economies of the North and South.

Students will be able to:
- **identify and evaluate** how the innovations in industry, travel, and communications changed the lives of Americans in the 1800s.
- **analyze and compare** the economies of the North and South.

UNDERSTANDING BY DESIGN®

☑ *Print Teaching Options*

V Visual Skills

☐ **P. 379** Students trace the route of the SS *Central America* and the location of its sinking. **AL** **BL** Visual/Spatial

R Reading Skills

☐ **P. 376** Students define *innovation*. **ELL**

☐ **P. 377** Students identify improvements in manufacturing in the Northeast and explain how they helped the region's economy.

☐ **P. 378** Students explore the expansion of the railroads by calculating the increase in the amount of track.

☐ **P. 378** Students explain how railroads and canals transformed trade. **BL**

☐ **P. 381** Students explain how the steel-tipped plow changed farming.

☐ **P. 381** Students discuss McCormick's mechanical reaper and its effects on the Midwestern economy. **AL**

W Writing Skills

☐ **P. 380** Students write paragraphs explaining the effects of farming innovations on the settlement of the Midwest.

C Critical Thinking Skills

☐ **P. 376** Students consider how the invention of the sewing machine transformed the textile industry.

☐ **P. 377** Students describe aspects of the canals built between 1800 and 1850.

☐ **P. 379** Students identify the changes put into place after the Great Train Wreck of 1856. **AL**

☐ **P. 380** Students discuss modern innovations in transportation and communication.

☐ **P. 381** Students consider the impact the mechanical reaper had on farmers. **BL**

☑ *Online Teaching Options*

V Visual Skills

☐ **VIDEO** **Life at the Beginning of the 20th Century: Communication**—Students view a video that describes the means of communication available to middle class people at the turn of the century.

☐ **IMAGE** **The Steamboat**—Students click to reveal facts about this transportation innovation.

☐ **MAP** **Major Railroads, 1860**—Students view the major rail lines in place in the United States in 1860.

R Reading Skills

☐ **GRAPHIC ORGANIZER** **Taking Notes: *Determining Cause and Effect*: Development of Industrialization**—Students describe the three phases of the development of industrialization in the North.

☐ **BIOGRAPHY** **Donald McKay**—Students read about this shipbuilder.

☐ **BIOGRAPHY** **John Deere**—Students read about this builder of steel plows.

C Critical Thinking Skills

☐ **WHITEBOARD ACTIVITY** **Morse Code**—Students decode a word presented in Morse code.

T Technology Skills

☐ **SELF-CHECK QUIZ** **Lesson 1**—Students receive instant feedback on their mastery of lesson content.

PEOPLE OF THE NORTH

Students will know:
- the various immigrant groups that came to the United States during the early 1800s and their contributions.
- the reasons various urban centers developed during the 1800s.

Students will be able to:
- **understand cause and effect** relationships between immigration and its impact on cities and industry in the North.

UNDERSTANDING BY DESIGN®

☑ *Print Teaching Options*

V Visual Skills

☐ **P. 384** Students identify the location of several Midwest cities and analyze why they became centers of trade. **AL** **BL** Visual/Spatial

☐ **P. 385** Students interpret a circle graph on immigration. Logical/Mathematical

☐ **P. 386** Students identify the change in immigrants as a percentage of the population over time. Visual/Spatial

R Reading Skills

☐ **P. 382** Students discuss the establishment of the factory system.

☐ **P. 383** Students explain the meaning and purpose of a trade union.

☐ **P. 383** Students describe the discriminatory practices toward African Americans in the North.

☐ **P. 384** Students describe how women were treated in the workplace.

☐ **P. 386** Students identify groups who resented the arrival of immigrants. **AL** **ELL** **BL**

W Writing Skills

☐ **P. 385** Students respond to the question: How did your family end up in the city in which you live?

C Critical Thinking Skills

☐ **P. 382** Students list the problems people dealt with when working in a factory and consider why these conditions existed. **AL**

☐ **P. 383** Students infer how strikes affect businesses. **ELL** **BL**

☐ **P. 384** Students discuss successful African American businesspeople.

☐ **P. 384** Students explain the effect of industry on the growth of cities.

T Technology Skills

☐ **P. 383** Students work in groups to make a slide presentation showing working conditions for children in factories and mills in the early 1800s. **BL** Interpersonal

☑ *Online Teaching Options*

V Visual Skills

☐ **VIDEO** **Labor Struggle—They Dared Not Stop Working**—Students view a video that describes the working conditions of wage laborers.

☐ **SLIDE SHOW** **Lewis Hine and Child Labor**—Students click to see a sampling of the photos Hine took of children working in sweatshops and as farm laborers.

R Reading Skills

☐ **GRAPHIC ORGANIZER** **Taking Notes:** *Identifying:* **Growth of Cities**—Students record two reasons for the growth of cities.

☐ **PRIMARY SOURCE** **Life as a Lowell Girl**—Students analyze an excerpt from Harriet H. Robinson's autobiography, in which she describes the working conditions for children in the mills of Lowell, Massachusetts.

C Critical Thinking Skills

☐ **GRAPH** **U.S. Immigration in the Mid-1800s**—Students click to reveal data about the immigrants who came to America during this period.

☐ **GRAPH** **Immigrants as a Percentage of Population**—Students click to reveal a line graph that traces trends in immigration to the United States in each decade between 1821 and 2000.

T Technology Skills

☐ **SELF-CHECK QUIZ** **Lesson 2**—Students receive instant feedback on their mastery of lesson content.

☑ *Printable Digital Worksheets*

C Critical Thinking Skills

☐ **WORKSHEET** **Geography and History Activity: A Landscape for Industry**—Students analyze the geographic factors that helped the development of industry in New England beginning around 1800.

SOUTHERN COTTON KINGDOM

Students will know:
- the differences between the economies of the North and South.

Students will be able to:
- **analyze and compare** the economies of the North and South.

☑ *Print Teaching Options*

V Visual Skills

☐ **P. 388** Students analyze a map to understand the dramatic increase in cotton production in a short period of time. **ELL** Visual/Spatial

☐ **P. 389** Students interpret graphs about cotton production as a percentage of U.S. exports. **ELL** Visual/Spatial

R Reading Skills

☐ **P. 387** Students describe the Southern economy in 1850.

☐ **P. 387** Students list the Southern crops grown in colonial times.

☐ **P. 390** Students explain how Southerners transported their goods to market. **AL**

W Writing Skills

☐ **P. 390** Students imagine they are Gregg or Anderson as they write a letter to other Southern leaders to argue why the South should develop industry. **Intrapersonal**

C Critical Thinking Skills

☐ **P. 387** Students consider the effect of the slow process of cotton harvesting and how this affected profits.

☐ **P. 388** Students identify the effect the cotton gin had on productivity. **BL** Logical/Mathematical

☐ **P. 389** Students identify how the boom in cotton production affected the growth of industry in the South. **AL BL**

☐ **P. 389** Students consider the reasons why industries did not develop in the South. **BL**

☐ **P. 390** Students discuss the impact of the short, disconnected rail lines present in the South.

☑ *Online Teaching Options*

V Visual Skills

☐ **VIDEO** **The South and Regional Economics of the United States**—Students see how the regional economy of the South relied primarily on cotton plantations, which led to political and economic instability in the mid-nineteenth century.

☐ **MAP** **Cotton Production, 1820–1860**—Students view a color-coded map that shows the increase in cotton producing areas between 1820 and 1860.

☐ **IMAGE** **The Cotton Gin**—Students click to reveal facts about Eli Whitney's invention.

☐ **MAP** **Major Railroads, 1860**—Students view the major rail lines in place in the United States in 1860.

R Reading Skills

☐ **GRAPHIC ORGANIZER** **Taking Notes:** *Determining Cause and Effect:* **Cotton Production and Industrial Growth**—Students show reasons that cotton production grew at the same time industrial growth remained slow in the South.

☐ **BIOGRAPHY** **Elias Howe**—Students read about the inventor of the first sewing machine.

C Critical Thinking Skills

☐ **GRAPH** **Cotton Production**—Student click to graphically see the difference in the amount of cotton a worker could produce before and after the advent of the cotton gin.

T Technology Skills

☐ **SELF-CHECK QUIZ** **Lesson 3**—Students receive instant feedback on their mastery of lesson content.

PEOPLE OF THE SOUTH

Students will know:
- the influence of individuals on social and political developments in the South.
- the role of slavery in the development of sectional conflict.

Students will be able to:
- **analyze and describe** the living conditions of enslaved African Americans in the South and the unique culture they developed.

UNDERSTANDING
BY DESIGN®

☑ *Print Teaching Options*

V Visual Skills

☐ **P. 392** Students analyze why an uprising of enslaved African Americans would have posed a threat to white Southerners. **BL** Visual/Spatial

R Reading Skills

☐ **P. 391** Students list the four categories that most white Southerners fit into during this time period. **AL**

☐ **P. 392** Students discuss how wealth was counted by plantation owners.

☐ **P. 393** Students explain the responsibilities of plantation wives. **AL** **BL**

☐ **P. 394** Students describe the characteristics of life for enslaved people.

☐ **P. 395** Students summarize Nat Turner's Rebellion. **AL** **ELL**

☐ **P. 396** Students discuss the Underground Railroad. **AL** **ELL**

☐ **P. 397** Students list the ways in which the rights of free African Americans were limited.

W Writing Skills

☐ **P. 396** Students explain how the Nat Turner Rebellion and the Underground Railroad were both factors that led to the Civil War. **BL**

C Critical Thinking Skills

☐ **P. 391** Students list the differences between yeomen farmers and tenant farmers. **ELL**

☐ **P. 392** Students compare the operations of plantations with those of factories. **BL**

☐ **P. 393** Students make a graphic organizer to describe and review the work that was done on plantations.
Intrapersonal

☐ **P. 393** Students consider the effect of separation on members of a family that was enslaved. **BL**
Intrapersonal

☐ **P. 394** Students contrast work songs and spirituals.
Auditory/Musical

☐ **P. 395** Students consider why white Southerners may have wished to keep enslaved people illiterate.

☐ **P. 397** Students link the lack of public education to increased illiteracy in the South. **ELL**

☑ *Online Teaching Options*

V Visual Skills

☐ **VIDEO** **Secrets of the Underground Railroad**—Students view a video shot from the perspective of an enslaved person escaping on the Underground Railroad.

☐ **IMAGE** **Slave Codes**—Students view some of the state laws that enslaved people were required to follow.

☐ **IMAGE** **Underground Railroad Routes**—Students click to learn facts about the routes enslaved people followed to freedom.

R Reading Skills

☐ **GRAPHIC ORGANIZER** **Taking Notes: *Describing:* Working on a Plantation**—Students describe the work that was done on a Southern plantation.

☐ **SLIDE SHOW** **Songs of Freedom**—Students read lyrics and explanations of African American songs of freedom.

☐ **PRIMARY SOURCE** **American Slavery As It Is**—Students read an excerpt from this book of firsthand accounts of slavery compiled by Theodore Weld.

☐ **BIOGRAPHY** **Harriet Tubman**—Students read a biography of this conductor on the Underground Railroad.

C Critical Thinking Skills

☐ **WHITEBOARD ACTIVITY** **Life on a Plantation**—Students categorize types of work done on a plantation.

☐ **CHART** **U.S. Population, 1860**—Students click to reveal free versus enslaved populations for each state listed in the 1860 census.

☐ **PRIMARY SOURCE** **Harriet Jacobs**—Students read an excerpt from *Incidents in the Life of a Slave Girl* by Harriet Jacobs.

☐ **SLIDE SHOW** **Plantation Living Quarters**—Students contrast the homes of plantation owners and those of people they held enslaved.

T Technology Skills

☐ **SELF-CHECK QUIZ** **Lesson 4**—Students receive instant feedback on their mastery of lesson content.

☑ *Printable Digital Worksheets*

R Reading Skills

☐ **WORKSHEET** **Primary Source Activity: A Life in Slavery**—Students analyze two primary sources that describe the conditions of enslaved people.

INTERVENTION AND REMEDIATION STRATEGIES

LESSON 1 The Industrial North

Reading and Comprehension

Have students create an outline of the lesson. They can use the major heads as outline topics. They should include all main ideas for each topic.

Text Evidence

Ask students to do research to learn more about Morse code. Encourage them to write a short message in Morse code and read other students' messages.

LESSON 2 People of the North

Reading and Comprehension

Have students write sentences using each of the lesson content vocabulary words. Sentences should show a clear understanding of the words' meanings

Text Evidence

Have students do research about the origin of trade unions. Ask them to list the rights workers gained by joining trade unions.

LESSON 3 Southern Cotton Kingdom

Reading and Comprehension

Ask students to summarize the reasons that industry developed more slowly in the South than in the North.

Text Evidence

Remind students that the cotton gin helped workers process 50 times more cotton each day than they could by hand. Have students create a line graph showing this increase.

LESSON 4 People of the South

Reading and Comprehension

Have students make a graphic organizer showing the characteristics of the four categories of Southerners: yeoman, tenant farmer, rural poor, and plantation owner

Text Evidence

Have students research the Underground Railroad and write a fictional narrative of an enslaved person who runs away. Encourage students to include details from their research in their narratives.

Online Resources

Approaching Level Reader

Use this online lower-level text that corresponds directly to the text in the Student Edition. It includes a Spanish version.

Guided Reading Activities

This resource uses graphic organizers and guiding questions to help students with comprehension.

What Do You Know?

Use these worksheets to pre-assess student's background knowledge before they study the chapter.

Reading Essentials and Study Guide Workbook

This resource offers writing and reading activities for the approaching-level student. Also available in Spanish.

Self-Check Quizzes

This online assessment tool provides instant feedback for students to check their progress.

How Do I Help With
Multimedia Presentations?

Students are quite comfortable operating computers and digital devices. They spend much of their time using these tools to consume entertainment and information. Not all students, however, are as familiar with how to effectively use computers as tools. In their professional life, they will often need to create digital presentations.

Tip 1 — Don't focus on the platform. Focus on the content being presented.

- There are many different digital platforms that you can point students towards as the environment in which they build their online presentations. Do research and find the platform that you understand. This will allow you to clearly explain how to use the platform to your class.

- What you want your students to learn is the proper techniques required to build effective online presentations. Help them learn to consider the following design choices as they make their multimedia presentation.

- **What sort of background image works best?** Encourage students to pick a background image that represents the content topic they are presenting, but one that is not too "busy" or distracting to the content, which should be the focal point.

- **How should they incorporate audio or video elements?** There is a temptation with online media to overload the presentation with audio or video that could not be used as easily in traditional two-dimensional presentations. But these dynamic content tools should be used sparingly to provide maximum impact. The presentation should not be "blinking" and "shouting" for attention.

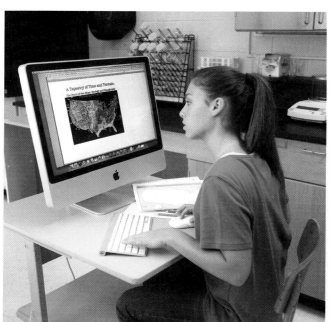

Hutchings Photography/Digital Light Source

Tip 2 — Don't forget to do the research!

- Students must be careful that they don't get so involved in building their multimedia environment that they forget to spend an equal (or larger) amount of time researching the topic. This is especially true when learning a new platform with lots of tools and options. A presentation is no good if there is no content.

Tip 3 — Show some examples of good models.

- Creating a multimedia presentation might seem overwhelming to students, especially ones that are focused on learning the content being presented or trying to learn how to use digital platforms. So, make it more understandable by displaying some models that show what you expect the students to create.

- Finding good models helps the students begin visualizing how to begin their own project. Also, take the time to explain details of the models that make them a good example. Allow time for students to review the models and ask you questions.

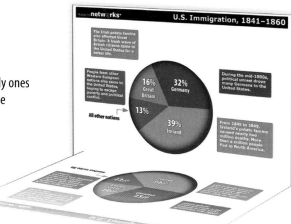

North and South

1820–1860

ESSENTIAL QUESTIONS • How does technology change the way people live?
• How do people adapt to their environment? • Why do people make economic choices?

◄ These women worked in one of the many booming industries of the North—a mill in Lowell, Massachusetts.

The Granger Collection, New York

networks

There's More Online about the North and South in the first half of the 1800s.

CHAPTER 14

The Story Matters . . .

These women are like many other workers at the mills of Lowell, Massachusetts. They have come to earn wages and to live in the comfortable company town mill-owners have built. At Lowell, the women can earn good wages and enjoy the cultural offerings designed to help them grow into fine, upstanding members of society.

The women hear that other factories do less for their workers. Also, more and more immigrants are arriving each day. The immigrants are hungry—and willing to work longer hours for lower wages. Things are changing at Lowell. These women are wondering what the future holds for them and the rapidly industrializing North.

373

ENGAGE

🔔 **Bellringer** Ask students how much they know about the North and South in the mid-1800s. Have students write answers to the following questions about the time period to test their knowledge. **Ask:**

- What was the telegraph?
- What were working conditions like in early factories in the North in the mid-1800s?
- What were the lives of enslaved people like in the South?

Tell students they will learn the answers to these questions and more as they read the chapter. After students complete the chapter, have them reread their answers, add more detail, and circle any information that was not accurate.

Making Connections

Read "The Story Matters . . ." aloud to students. Then discuss what it might have been like to be a young worker in a factory such as the one at Lowell. **Ask: What kind of conditions on a job would you consider unfair or horrible? What would make living conditions in a boardinghouse unpleasant?**

Have a few students describe their ideas about horrible working conditions and unpleasant living conditions. Then **ask: What action would you take if you started a job with safe and pleasant conditions, and then the conditions got worse? Would you talk to your boss individually, or would you form a group with other workers who also wanted changes?**

Tell students that some workers today belong to organized groups called unions and that union workers sometimes go on strike, or refuse to work, to try to force employers to make changes. Tell interested students to do research on the Internet for recent strike actions by workers or actions involving unions taken by states. **Intrapersonal**

Letter from the Author

Dear American History Teacher,

As you discuss the sectional strains between 1820 and 1861, the most obvious difference will be the presence of slavery in the South, yet the North also practiced slavery on a smaller scale. Northern states had already started to abolish slavery, so slave labor never became an integral part of the North's economy. The Northern economy was more diversified than the Southern economy. Two results of northern industrialization were the rapid growth of cities and a larger population. Inventions also transformed the South. The cotton gin increased cotton production and drove demand for land and enslaved people.

Albert S. Broussard

TEACH & ASSESS

Step Into the Place

V Visual Skills

Analyzing Maps Direct students to the chapter opener map. Explain that this map shows how the United States looked in 1840 and that the 10 cities shown were the largest cities at that time. Have student volunteers analyze the map, explaining the key. Remind students that the desire to expand westward existed as far back as the colonial era. Have students recall some of the reasons that Americans wanted to expand westward during that time. Explain how similar reasons continued to influence westward expansion during the mid-1800s. As a class, discuss the Map Focus questions. **Visual/Spatial**

Content Background Knowledge

- Some of the first settlers to move west did so around 1841 along the northern part of the United States in what would later be called the Oregon Trail.
- The explosion population in the Western territories due to the Gold Rush sparked renewed interest in a transcontinental railroad, which finally began construction around 1860.

ANSWERS, p. 374

Step Into the Place
1. along the Atlantic coast, west to the Mississippi River
2. mostly in the Northeast and Mid-Atlantic areas
3. **CRITICAL THINKING** Possible answer: They were the oldest established cities. They were industrial cities and had jobs, good transportation, and resources.

Step Into the Time
Possible answer: The Irish famine influenced immigration to the United States. Students might also suggest that the discovery of gold sparked some immigration.

Chapter 14 CCSS

Place and Time: United States 1820 to 1860

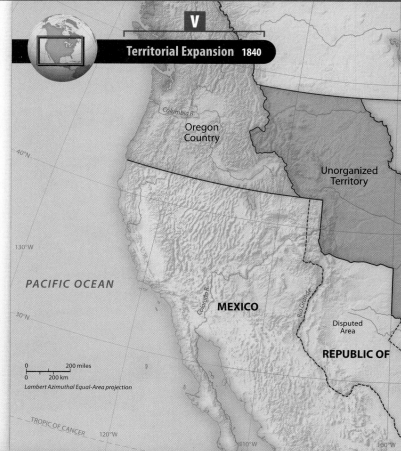

The United States is an expanding nation in 1840. Settlement has moved westward, and new cities and industries are emerging in the North and South.

V Territorial Expansion 1840

Step Into the Place

MAP FOCUS This is how the United States looked in 1840. Some areas were states, some were still territories, and some belonged to foreign nations. The 10 cities shown were the 10 largest cities at that time.

1 REGION In what regions of the country are all the organized states located? RH.6–8.7

2 LOCATION Where are the largest cities located? RH.6–8.7

3 CRITICAL THINKING *Drawing Conclusions* What factors do you think helped these cities grow? RH.6–8.7

Step Into the Time

TIME LINE Review the time line. Identify an event on the time line that might help explain the growing immigration to the United States during this era. Explain your answer. RH.6–8.5, RH.6–8.7

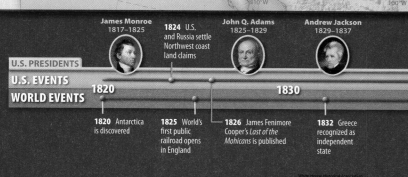

U.S. PRESIDENTS

James Monroe 1817–1825

John Q. Adams 1825–1829

Andrew Jackson 1829–1837

U.S. EVENTS

WORLD EVENTS 1820   1830

1824 U.S. and Russia settle Northwest coast land claims

1820 Antarctica is discovered

1825 World's first public railroad opens in England

1826 James Fenimore Cooper's *Last of the Mohicans* is published

1832 Greece recognized as independent state

374 *North and South*

R

Project-Based Learning ✋

Hands-On Chapter Project

Illustrated Encyclopedia Entry

Groups will create an encyclopedia entry about one of the following: clipper ships, the *Tom Thumb*, Erie Canal, Morse code, cotton gin, or plantations. Students will read about the topic in their textbook and conduct research in groups, citing at least three sources. Then they will find maps, photos, or other visuals, decide what to include, organize the details, and create the entry. Have students display and discuss their encyclopedia entries in class.

Technology Extension

Create Glogster Posters

Students can create Glogster posters, or "Glogs," which are online multimedia posters, to represent their understanding of how geography and regional differences shaped the development of various advances in the North and the South. To learn more about creating and setting up this type of project, visit the Glogster page at EdTechTeacher's Teaching History with Technology site: http://thwt.org/posters.html.

edtechteacher
21st Century Learning

BRITISH TERRITORY

L. Superior

Iowa Territory

Wisconsin Territory

L. Michigan

L. Huron

Mich.

L. Ontario

L. Erie

Maine

Vt. N.H.

New York

Albany

Boston

Mass.

R.I.

New York Brooklyn Conn.

Pennsylvania

Philadelphia N.J.

Northern Liberties

Baltimore Del.

Md.

Illinois

Ind.

Ohio

Cincinnati

Missouri

Kentucky

Virginia

Tennessee

North Carolina

Ark.

Miss.

Ala.

Georgia

South Carolina

Charleston

TEXAS

La.

New Orleans

Florida Territory

Gulf of Mexico

ATLANTIC OCEAN

Legend:
- States
- Territories
- Unorganized Territory
- Claimed areas
- Foreign areas
- - - - Disputed boundary

Time line:

1834 McCormick reaper is patented

Martin Van Buren 1837–1841

William Henry Harrison 1841

John Tyler 1841–1845

James Polk 1845–1849

Zachary Taylor 1849–1850

Millard Fillmore 1850–1853

Franklin Pierce 1853–1857

James Buchanan 1857–1861

1840   1850   1860

1845 Ireland experiences famine

1848 James Marshall discovers gold in California

1851 Gold discovered in Australia

1857 Sepoy Rebellion begins in India

375

Step Into the Time

R Reading Skills

Identifying Have students review the time line for the chapter. Explain that they will be studying events from about 1820 to 1860. Tell them that this was a time of both industrial revolution and population growth in the United States. **Ask:**

- **What invention contributed to the change in agricultural practices in the South and the West?** *(In 1834, the McCormick reaper was patented.)*
- **What event on the time line indicates an advance in transportation?** *(The world's first public railroad opened in England in 1825.)* **AL** **Visual/Spatial**

CLOSE & REFLECT

Ask students to look again at the map, the time line, and the Hands-On Chapter Project, and choose a topic that they would like to learn more about. Tell students that they will have the opportunity to learn more about these topics in the lessons that follow.

World Atlas

Integrating Visual Information Ask students to identify place names on the time line. **Ask: What names of places or countries do you see on the World Events time line?** *(Antarctica, England, Greece, Ireland, Australia, India)*

Ask students to locate these places on the interactive map and mark the locations. **AL** Have students research some of the events on the time line and provide a short summary of what happened. **BL** **Visual/Spatial**

See page 373B for other online activities.

ENGAGE

Bellringer Ask students how often they have traveled by train and how often they use e-mail or text messaging. Discuss with students how these items have a significant and daily impact on their lives. Then have students turn to a partner and discuss how their lives would be different if they did not have these items. Tell students that in this lesson they will be learning about the impact of new innovations in technology and industry on the lives of Americans. **Intrapersonal**

TEACH & ASSESS

R Reading Skills

Defining Have a student volunteer read the first paragraph of the lesson aloud. **Ask:**

- What is an innovation? *(a new idea or method, an improvement, an advance)*
- What are some examples of modern innovations in the ways we travel and communicate? *(faster trains, cell phones, e-mail, instant messaging)* **ELL**

C Critical Thinking Skills

Determining Cause and Effect Using the example of cloth, determine the three phases of industrialization. Then discuss how the invention of the sewing machine by Elias Howe transformed the textile industry even further. **Ask:**

- How was clothing made before the invention of mass production and the sewing machine? *(It was all handmade.)*
- How did the invention of the sewing machine change the clothing industry? *(Workers could make clothing in large quantities.)*

ANSWER, p. 376

TAKING NOTES: Phase 1: Manufacturers made products by dividing tasks among workers. **Phase 2:** Manufacturers built factories to bring specialized workers together. **Phase 3:** Workers used machinery to perform some of their work.

---

networks
There's More Online!
☑ **BIOGRAPHY**
John Deere
☑ **GRAPHIC ORGANIZER**
Phases of Industrialization
☑ **MAP** Major Railroads 1860s

Lesson 1
The Industrial North

ESSENTIAL QUESTION *How does technology change the way people live?*

IT MATTERS BECAUSE
Industry and innovation expanded the North's economy and power.

Technology and Industry

GUIDING QUESTION *How did technology and industry change during the 1800s?*

R The early years of the 1800s saw much **innovation** in industry and technology. The ways in which Americans worked, traveled, and communicated underwent great change. The new ways of living affected the whole nation, but their effects were most dramatic in the North.

Three Phases of Industrialization

C Before industrialization, workers made most goods one item at a time, from start to finish. To make clothes, a woman might spin the thread, weave the cloth, then cut and sew the fabric. Industrialization changed that way of working.

The North's industrialization took place in three phases. During the first phase, employers divided jobs into smaller steps. For example, one worker would spin thread—and nothing else. Another worker wove cloth. Each worker specialized in one step and became an expert in it. Two specialized workers could produce more cloth than if each worker did both tasks.

During the second phase of industrialization, entrepreneurs built factories to bring specialized workers together. This allowed the product to move quickly from one worker to the next.

*(l) Ann Ronan Picture Library/ Heritage-Images/The Image Works
(r) The Granger Collection, NYC*

Reading HELPDESK (CCSS)

Taking Notes: *Determining Cause and Effect*
As you read, use a diagram like the one shown to describe the three phases of the development of industrialization in the North. RH.6–8.5

Development of Industrialization
Phase 1
Phase 2
Phase 3

Content Vocabulary (Tier 3 Words)
- clipper ship
- telegraph
- Morse code

376 *North and South*

---

networks *Online Teaching Options*

VIDEO

Life at the Beginning of the 20th Century: Communication

Predicting Consequences Explain to students that they are going to watch a video about communication at the beginning of the 20th century. Tell them that as they watch, they should make a list of the innovations shown in the video. After students watch the video, ask them to share the innovations on their lists (telegram, telephones). Then have small groups predict the consequences the innovations shown in the video will have on people's lives.

See page 373C for other online activities.

In the third phase, workers used machines to complete tasks. For example, machines called looms wove cloth using the power of flowing water. The machines worked much faster than any human could. The worker's job changed from weaving to tending the machine.

Mass production of cloth began in New England in the early 1800s. Then, Elias Howe invented the sewing machine in 1846. Workers could now make clothing in mass quantities by using machine-made fabrics and sewing machines.

Similar changes were transforming other industries and affecting the North's economy. By 1860, the Northeast's factories made at least two-thirds of the country's manufactured goods.

Changing Transportation

Improvements in transportation contributed to the success of the new American industries. Between 1800 and 1850, crews built thousands of miles of roads and canals. By connecting lakes and rivers, canals opened new shipping routes. In 1807 inventor Robert Fulton launched his first steamboat, the *Clermont*, on the Hudson River. Steamboats made fast upstream travel possible. They carried goods and passengers more cheaply and quickly along inland waterways than flatboats or sail-powered vessels did.

In the 1840s, builders began to widen and deepen canals to make space for steamboats. By 1860, about 3,000 steamboats traveled the country's major rivers and canals, as well as the Great Lakes. This encouraged the growth of cities such as Cincinnati, Buffalo, and Chicago.

Sailing technology also improved in the 1840s. The new clipper ships featured tall sails and sleek hulls. They could sail 300 miles (483 km) per day, as fast as most steamships at that time. **Clipper ships** got their name because they "clipped" time from long journeys. Before the clippers, the voyage from New York to Great Britain took about 21 to 28 days. A clipper ship could usually cut that time in half.

In 1851 the *Flying Cloud*, a famed clipper ship, sailed from New York City to San Francisco in 89 days.

Ann Ronan Picture Library/ Heritage-Images/The Image Works

clipper ship ship with sleek hulls and tall sails that "clipped" time from long journeys

Academic Vocabulary (Tier 2 Words)

innovation a new development or invention

Lesson 1 **377**

R Reading Skills

Citing Text Evidence Ask students to use evidence from the text to identify two inventions that had a great impact on manufacturing in the Northeast. *(the loom and the sewing machine)* **Ask:** How did the introduction of these machines affect the economy of the North? *(The loom and the sewing machine allowed workers to mass-produce fabric and clothing, so the Northern factories made and sold more goods. This helped the economy grow and flourish.)*

C Critical Thinking Skills

Explaining After students read the section titled "Changing Transportation," discuss with them the canals and roads that were built between 1800 and 1850. **Ask:**

- Why did builders begin widening the canals? *(to make room for the new ships being developed)*
- What was the effect of the canals on American cities? *(They helped American cities to grow by allowing steamboats to carry goods and passengers to the cities.).*

Content Background Knowledge

Though Robert Fulton is credited for creating the first commercial steamboat in 1807, he invented two other important and exciting things. In 1800, Napoleon Bonaparte, the future leader of France, gave Fulton the go-ahead to test his design of the first submarine, which he was able to submerge twenty-five feet. Fulton also created an early version of "torpedoes," which were at that time merely underwater mines, for the British Navy.

GRAPHIC ORGANIZER

Taking Notes: *Determining Cause and Effect:* Development of Industrialization

Creating a Cause and Effect Chart Use the interactive graphic organizer to describe the three phases of industrialization. Have a volunteer provide an example of a finished product, and using the three phases of industrialization, move through the process of developing that finished product. **Ask:** How would dividing jobs into smaller steps be beneficial? *(It would produce "experts" at each step of the job and speed up the individual processes of each phase.)*

See page 373C for other online activities.

TAKING NOTES: *Determining Cause and Effect*
ACTIVITY As you read, use the diagram below to describe the three phases of the development of industrialization in the North.

Development of Industrialization

Phase 1

Phase 2

Phase 3

R1 Reading Skills

Calculating Direct students to read the section titled "The Railroads Arrive." Ask a volunteer to describe the first railroads. Discuss what the first railroads were used for and Peter Cooper's invention of the first steam-powered passenger locomotive, the *Tom Thumb*. **Ask:**

- **How many miles of track did the United States have in 1840?** *(almost 3,000)*
- **How many more miles of track did it have by 1860?** *(28,000)*
- **What do these numbers tell us about the U.S. railroads?** *(That the railroad was growing very quickly during this time period.)*

R2 Reading Skills

Explaining After students have read the text, lead a class discussion about how railways and canals transformed trade in the 1800s. **BL** Explain that the impact of improved transportation was mostly felt in western areas. **Ask: How did canals and railroads transform trade in this region?** *(Goods moved directly from the Midwest to the East; they moved faster and more cheaply; new industries developed as more people moved into the area.)*

The Railroads Arrive

The first railroads in the United States ran along short stretches of track that connected mines with nearby rivers. Horses pulled these early trains. The first steam-powered passenger locomotive began running in Britain in 1829.

A year later, Peter Cooper designed and built the first American steam-powered locomotive. The *Tom Thumb*, as it was called, got off to a slow start. It actually lost a race staged against a horse-drawn train when its engine failed. Before long, however, engineers had improved the technology. By 1840, steam locomotives were pulling trains in the United States. In 1840 the United States had almost 3,000 miles (4,828 km) of railroad track. By 1860, the nation's tracks totaled about 31,000 miles (49,890 km), mostly in the North and Midwest.

The new rail lines connected many cities. One line linked the cities of New York and Buffalo. Another connected Philadelphia and Pittsburgh. Railway builders connected these eastern lines to lines being built farther west in Ohio, Indiana, and Illinois. By 1860, the nation's railroads formed a network that united the Midwest and the East.

Moving Goods and People

The impact of improved transportation was felt deeply in the western areas of the country. Before canals and railroads, farmers sent their crops down the Mississippi River to New Orleans. From there, goods sailed to the East Coast or to other countries. This took a considerable amount of time and often caused goods to be more expensive.

Railways and canals **transformed** trade in these regions. The opening of the Erie Canal in 1825 and later the railroad networks allowed grain, livestock, and dairy products to move directly from the Midwest to the East. Improvements in transportation provided benefits to both businesses and consumers. Farmers and manufacturers could now move goods faster and more cheaply. As a result, consumers could purchase them at lower prices than in the past.

The railroads also played an important role in the settlement of the Midwest and the growth of its industry. Fast, affordable train travel brought people into Ohio, Indiana, and Illinois. The populations of these states grew. New towns and industries developed as more people moved into the area.

Reading HELPDESK (CCSS)

telegraph a device that used electric signals to send messages

Academic Vocabulary
transform to change significantly (Tier 2 Words)

Build Vocabulary: *Multiple Meaning Words*
The word *engineer* has many meanings. As a verb, it can mean to use science and math to make certain complex products. As a noun, it often means someone who applies those skills—for example, someone who builds buildings or electrical systems. The word also refers to the people who operate and drive trains.

378 *North and South*

netw⊙rks *Online Teaching Options*

IMAGE

The Steamboat

Making Connections Use the interactive image of the steamboat to discuss the importance of this new technology. Discuss Robert Fulton and his steamboat, the *Clermont*. **Ask:**

- **What was the relationship between steamboats and snagboats?** *(Steamboats could be damaged by hitting snags on the river bottoms; snagboats patrolled the rivers and cleared out snags.)*
- **How did the invention of the steamboat lead to the growth of cities?** *(Builders began to widen and deepen canals to make space for steamboats. By 1860, about 3,000 steamboats traveled the country's major rivers and canals, as well as the Great Lakes. This encouraged the growth of cities.)*

McGraw-Hill **netw⊙rks** The Steamboat

Steamboats sometimes hit snags and debris on the river bottom, which could pierce the hull and capsize the vessel. Snagboats, like the Montgomery, were developed to patrol the rivers and clear out potential snags.

Mike Simons/CORBIS

See page 373C for other online activities.

Progress with Problems

As more people moved more quickly along railways and waterways, the possibility of disaster also increased. Some tragic events occurred.

The SS *Central America* was a 270-foot side-wheel steamer that carried passengers and cargo between New York and the Central American country of Panama. The ship traveled one part of a widely traveled route between the East Coast and California. In September 1857, the *Central America* was carrying a full load of passengers and a large amount of gold when it steamed into a hurricane. The ship sank off the coast of the Carolinas, and hundreds of people drowned.

The Great Train Wreck of 1856 occurred between Camp Hill and Fort Washington, Pennsylvania, on July 17, 1856. Two trains slammed head-on into each other. An estimated 60 people were killed, and more than 100 were injured. At that point in time, it was considered one of the worst accidents in railroad history. The tragic news horrified the nation. Newspapers demanded that railroad companies improve their methods and equipment and make the safety of passengers their first concern.

C

Communications Breakthroughs

The growth of industry and the new pace of travel created a need for faster methods of communication. The **telegraph** (teh•luh•graf)—a device that used electric signals to send messages—filled that need.

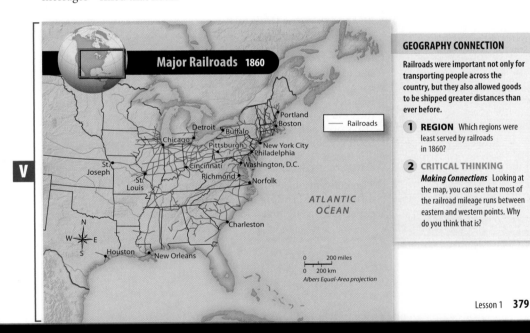

V

Major Railroads 1860

— Railroads

Portland
Boston
Detroit
Buffalo
Chicago
Pittsburgh
New York City
Philadelphia
Cincinnati
Washington, D.C.
St. Joseph
Richmond
St. Louis
Norfolk

ATLANTIC OCEAN

Charleston

Houston
New Orleans

N W E S

0   200 miles
0   200 km
Albers Equal-Area projection

GEOGRAPHY CONNECTION

Railroads were important not only for transporting people across the country, but they also allowed goods to be shipped greater distances than ever before.

1 REGION Which regions were least served by railroads in 1860?

2 CRITICAL THINKING
Making Connections Looking at the map, you can see that most of the railroad mileage runs between eastern and western points. Why do you think that is?

V Visual Skills

Reading a Map Discuss that even progress had problems. Ask students to describe the route of the steamship SS *Central America* and the place of its accident. *(The SS Central America traveled between New York and Panama, in Central America. In September 1857, it sank with a load of passengers and gold in a hurricane off the coast of the Carolinas.)* **BL** Have students use the map in their textbook to locate New York and use their finger to trace the route downward to the coast of the Carolinas where this ship sank. **AL** **Visual/Spatial**

C Critical Thinking Skills

Determining Cause and Effect Discuss the events surrounding the Great Train Wreck of 1856. **Ask: What changes were called for after the Great Train Wreck of 1856?** *(Railroad companies had to improve their methods and equipment, and make the safety of passengers their first concern.)* **AL**

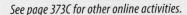

MAP

Major Railroads, 1860

Specifying Use the interactive map about the major railroads in 1860 to further discuss with students the growth and development of the railroads. **Ask:**

- **Which regions were connected by the railroads by 1860?** *(the East and the Midwest)* **ELL**
- **Which region might have an advantage for transporting goods and people more easily? Why?** *(the North because it had more railroad tracks)* **AL** **Visual/Spatial**

See page 373C for other online activities.

ANSWERS, p. 379

GEOGRAPHY CONNECTION

1 the South and the West

2 **CRITICAL THINKING** Most rivers ran north and south. Railroads enabled fast and efficient transportation between western areas and eastern areas.

C Critical Thinking Skills

Making Connections As a class, discuss the innovations in transportation and communication in the 1800s. **Ask: What innovations in transportation and communication have been made recently?** *(Students could suggest hybrid cars, electric cars, smartphones, text messaging, Skype, and instant messaging.)* Have students debate which innovations had the greater impact on people's lives: the innovations of the 1800s or the innovations of today.

W Writing Skills

Informative/Explanatory Have partners discuss why few farmers were willing to settle in the Great Plains west of Missouri. Make sure students recognize that the land in this area, and in areas like Ohio and Kentucky, had very hard soil that was too difficult to farm. Then have students each write a paragraph explaining the effects of farming innovations on the settlement of the Midwest. Ask partners to read their paragraphs to each other and compare their responses.

BIOGRAPHY

John Deere (1804–1886)

John Deere was born in Vermont. He trained as a blacksmith but found it difficult to make a living in his home state. He traveled to the state of Illinois in the 1830s. There he learned that farmers were having a difficult time plowing the region's rich but sticky soil with the rough iron plows of the day. Deere began making a polished steel plow that performed much better. Within 10 years, Deere was selling 1,000 plows per year. He was quoted as saying, "I will never put my name on a product that does not have in it the best that is in me."

▶ **CRITICAL THINKING**
Drawing Conclusions What can you conclude about the benefit of Deere's invention for his farmer customers?

Reading HELPDESK (CCSS)

Morse code a system of dots and dashes that represent the alphabet

---

Samuel Morse, an American inventor, developed a system for sending coded messages instantly along electrical wires. After Morse showed his system could send messages over a short distance, Congress gave him money to test the device over a wider area. Morse strung wires between Washington, D.C., and Baltimore, Maryland. On May 24, 1844, he was ready to try out his system. A crowd of people watched as Morse tapped out the words "What hath God wrought" on his telegraph system. A few moments later, the operator in Baltimore sent the same message back in reply. Morse's telegraph had worked!

Telegraph operators sent messages quickly by using **Morse code.** This code uses different arrangements of short and long signals—dots and dashes—to represent letters of the alphabet. Telegraph companies formed, and workers put up telegraph lines across the country. By 1852, there were about 23,000 miles (37,015 km) of telegraph lines in the United States.

The telegraph allowed information to be communicated in minutes rather than days. People could quickly learn about news and events from other areas of the United States. The telegraph also allowed businesses to become more efficient with production and shipping.

✓ **PROGRESS CHECK**

Explaining How did canals and railways transform trade in the interior of the United States?

Farming Innovations

GUIDING QUESTION *What changes made agriculture more profitable in the 1830s?*

In the early 1800s, few farmers were willing to settle in the treeless Great Plains west of Missouri, Iowa, and Minnesota. Even areas of mixed forest and prairie west of Ohio and Kentucky seemed too difficult for farming. Settlers worried that their old plows could not break the prairie's matted sod. They also worried that the soil would not be fertile enough to support fields of crops.

Advancements in Agriculture

Three inventions of the 1830s helped farmers overcome difficulties in farming the land. As a result, settlement expanded throughout wider areas of the Midwest.

The Granger Collection, NYC

---

netw⊙rks *Online Teaching Options*

Morse Code

Speculating Have students work in pairs to use the interactive whiteboard activity, "Morse Code." Tell students they are about to see an example of how Morse code is translated into text. Suggest to students that they uncover only one letter at a time to see if they can guess the word. *(HELP)* Ask students to speculate about how the ability to send this message quickly changed life for people in the 1800s.

See page 373C for other online activities.

netw⊙rks° **Morse Code**

In Morse code, each letter of the alphabet is represented by a combination of dots (.) and dashes (—). A dot means a short beep, and a dash means a long beep. With these beeps, a sender can send a message by spelling out words.

Directions: Click on the Morse code to reveal each letter in the message.

●●●●　　●　　●—●●　　●—●—

ANSWERS, p. 380

✓ **PROGRESS CHECK** They created a more direct way to get from the East Coast to the Midwest, greatly improving trade in the nation's interior.

CRITICAL THINKING The success of Deere's sales shows that the steel-tipped plow helped his customers be more successful as farmers by allowing them to plow more easily and raise more crops.

One of these inventions was the steel-tipped plow developed by John Deere in 1837. This allowed farmers to cut through the hard-packed prairie sod. Knowing that they would be able to farm the land on the prairies helped people make the decision to move west. Equally important to the transformation of farming were the mechanical reaper, which sped up the harvesting of wheat, and the thresher, which quickly separated the grain from the stalk. Each of these innovations reduced the labor required for farming.

R1

McCormick's Reaper

Cyrus McCormick was the genius behind the invention of the mechanical reaper. Before this invention, farmers had harvested grain with handheld cutting tools. McCormick's reaper greatly increased the amount of crop a farmer could harvest. Because farmers could harvest more wheat, they could plant more of it. Growing wheat became profitable. Raising wheat became and would remain the main economic activity on the Midwestern prairies.

C

R2

New machines and the ease of access to railroads allowed farmers to plant more acres with cash crops. Midwestern farmers grew wheat and shipped it east by train and canal barge. Northeast and Middle Atlantic farmers increased their production of fruits and vegetables.

In spite of improvements in agriculture, the North was steadily becoming more industrial and urban. Agriculture in the region was still growing, but industry was growing faster.

☑ **PROGRESS CHECK**

Identifying What innovation sped up the harvesting of wheat?

LESSON 1 REVIEW (CCSS)

Review Vocabulary (Tier 3 Words)

1. Use these two words in a sentence that shows their importance to American life in the early 1800s. RH.6–8.4

   a. telegraph   **b.** Morse code

Answer the Guiding Questions

2. ***Explaining*** How was water transportation improved in the 1800s? RH.6–8.2

3. ***Summarizing*** How were messages sent by telegraph? RH.6–8.2

4. ***Identifying*** List innovations in farming methods in the 1830s. RH.6–8.1

5. **ARGUMENT** Which individual do you think created the invention with the greatest impact on the nation's development, and why? WHST.6–8.1, WHST.6–8.9

- Samuel Morse
- John Deere
- Cyrus McCormick

Lesson 1   **381**

LESSON 1 REVIEW ANSWERS

1. Possible answer: The invention of the telegraph enabled the almost immediate transmission of messages in Morse code.

2. Both the steamship and clipper ships increased the speed and lowered the cost of carrying goods and passengers.

3. The telegraph used electric signals as dots and dashes to send messages instantly along wires. It provided a faster way of communicating over great distances.

4. steel-tipped plow, mechanical reaper, thresher

5. Paragraphs should include persuasive reasons to support the individual and invention chosen as having the greatest impact.

R1 **Reading Skills**

Discussing Ask for a student volunteer to read the first paragraph on this page aloud. Then, ask students if they are familiar with the name John Deere or what his name is associated with. Guide a discussion about the invention of the steel-tipped plow. **Ask: How did farmers benefit from the invention of the steel-tipped plow?** *(This plow easily cut through the hard-packed prairie sod and reduced the labor required for farming on the prairies).*

R2 **Reading Skills**

Identifying Have students read the text about McCormick's reaper. Then, **ask: Who was Cyrus McCormick?** *(He was an inventor.)* **What invention did he create that made the harvesting, or gathering, of wheat faster?** *(the mechanical reaper)* Discuss the function of the reaper, why it was a modern improvement over handheld cutting tools, and how it affected the economy of the Midwest. **AL**

C **Critical Thinking Skills**

Determining Cause and Effect Review the farming innovations discussed in this lesson. Be sure students understand that these specialized machines allowed people to move and settle in new areas and also allowed for increased production of a crop. **Ask: What impact did the invention of the mechanical reaper have on farmers?** *(Because farmers could harvest more wheat with the reaper, they could plant more of it. Growing wheat became more profitable in more places.)* **BL**

Have students complete the Lesson 1 Review.

CLOSE & REFLECT

Making Connections Remind students that these farming innovations were easier to use than earlier tools, which made farming more productive. Have volunteers name some technologies or devices that they use on a daily basis that allow them to be more productive. Encourage students to research how those items were invented.

ANSWER, p. 381

☑ **PROGRESS CHECK** the mechanical reaper

ENGAGE

Bellringer Ask students if they have ever worked to earn some money, and have them discuss the jobs they did. Then ask if they thought their pay was fair. If some students thought their pay was unfair, have volunteers describe how they could have negotiated a higher salary. Tell students that in this lesson they will learn how workers negotiated to improve factory conditions. **Intrapersonal**

TEACH & ASSESS

R Reading Skills

Discussing Direct students to read the first paragraph on this page. Then, lead a class discussion about the establishment of the factory system. Explain that the factory system combined several steps of an item's production under one roof and that machines took over more and more production of goods. **Ask:** What did factories in the factory system begin to produce? *(fabric, clothing, shoes, watches, guns, sewing machines, and other machinery)*

C Critical Thinking Skills

Drawing Conclusions Discuss the range of problems that people dealt with when working in a factory. Have students refer to their textbooks to create a list that they can use for later review. **Ask:**

- What was the average number of hours worked per day in Northern factories in 1840? *(11.4 hours)* **AL**
- Why do you think factory owners would allow their employees to work long hours under unsafe conditions? *(The long hours created larger profits, and factory owners were more concerned with that than with the safety of employees. Also, no regulations or laws were in place to prevent the unsafe conditions, so the factory owners could do whatever they wanted.)*

ANSWER, p. 382

TAKING NOTES: growth of industry, immigration

networks
There's More Online!

☑ **CHART/GRAPH**
 • Immigration Sources
 • Immigration, 1820–1860

☑ **GRAPHIC ORGANIZER**
 Growth of Cities

☑ **PRIMARY SOURCE** Life in Lowell

☑ **SLIDE SHOW** Child Labor

Lesson 2
People of the North

ESSENTIAL QUESTION *How do people adapt to their environment?*

IT MATTERS BECAUSE

Industrialization in the North changed the way people lived and worked as well as where they lived and worked.

The Factories of the North

GUIDING QUESTION *Why did many Americans push for reform in the workplace during this era?*

R The factory system combined several steps of an item's production under one roof. In the mid-1800s, machines took over more and more manufacturing tasks. The range of goods manufactured this way also increased. American factories began to turn out everything from fabric and clothing to shoes, watches, guns, sewing machines, and agricultural machinery.

Conditions for Factory Workers

Working conditions worsened as the factory system developed. Employees worked long hours. By 1840, the average workday was 11.4 hours. Longer days caused fatigue—and on-the-job accidents. Many factory machines had rapidly moving belts and **C** other parts. These belts had no shields for protection, and many workers, especially children, suffered injuries from these belts. Belts were just one of the many hazards of factory work.

 Employees often worked under harsh conditions. In the summer, factories were hot and stifling. The machines gave off heat, and there was no such thing as air-conditioning at that time. Likewise, in the winter workers were often cold because most factories had no heating.

(l) North Wind Picture Archives, (c) The Granger Collection, NYC

Reading HELPDESK **CCSS**

Taking Notes: *Identifying* RH.6–8.2
As you read, use a diagram like the one here to list two reasons that cities grew.

Growth of Cities

Content Vocabulary (Tier 3 Words)
- **trade union**
- **strike**
- **prejudice**
- **discrimination**
- **famine**
- **nativist**

382 *North and South*

---

networks *Online Teaching Options*

VIDEO

Labor Struggle—They Dared Not Stop Working

Speculating Before students watch the video, ask them to think about the title, "They Dared Not Stop Working." **Ask:** Why do you think people would be afraid to stop working? *(Answers will vary.)* Challenge students to predict what they will see and hear in the video that might answer that question. After students watch the video, guide them in comparing what they predicted they would see with what the video described.

See page 373D for other online activities.

No laws existed to control working conditions or protect workers. Factory owners were often more concerned about profits than about employees' comfort and safety.

Child labor was also a serious problem. Children in factories often worked six days a week and 12 hours or more a day. The work was dangerous and hard. Young workers tended machines in mills and worked underground in coal mines. Reformers called for laws to regulate child labor, shorten work hours, and improve conditions. Many years passed before child labor regulations became law.

Workers' Attempts to Organize

Workers tried various ways to gain better conditions in the workplace. By the 1830s, they began organizing into unions. Skilled workers formed **trade unions.** These were groups of workers with the same trade, or skill. The idea was that by working together, union members would have more power than they would as individuals.

In New York City, skilled workers wanted to receive higher wages and limit their workday to 10 hours. Groups of skilled workers formed the General Trades Union of the City of New York. The workers staged a series of **strikes** in the mid-1830s. A strike is a refusal to work in order to put pressure on employers.

Going on strike was illegal in the early 1800s. In addition to the threat of losing their jobs, workers who went on strike faced punishment for breaking the law. In 1842 a Massachusetts court ruled that workers did have the right to strike. However, workers would not receive other legal rights for many more years.

African Americans in the North

In the North, slavery had largely disappeared by the 1830s. Still, racial **prejudice** (PREH•juh•duhs)—an unfair opinion of a group—and **discrimination** (dihs•krih•muh•NAY•shuhn)—unfair treatment of a group—remained. White men in New York no longer had to own property in order to vote. Few African Americans enjoyed this right. Rhode Island and Pennsylvania passed laws to keep African Americans from voting.

In addition, most **communities** in the North did not allow African Americans to attend public schools. Many communities also kept them from using other public services. African Americans often had to attend poor-quality schools and go to hospitals that were reserved only for them.

North Wind Picture Archives

Manufacturers often hired children because they could pay children lower wages than adult workers.

trade union group of workers with the same trade, or skill

strike a work stoppage by employees as a protest against an employer

prejudice an unfair opinion not based on facts

discrimination unfair treatment

Academic Vocabulary (Tier 2 Words)

community group of people who live in the same area

Lesson 2 **383**

T Technology Skills

Making Presentations Have a group research working conditions for children in factories and mills in the early 1800s, including information about dangerous conditions, work hours, and wages. Have the group report their findings in a presentation. **BL** Interpersonal

R1 Reading Skills

Explaining Have students read the section titled "Workers' Attempts to Organize." Then, explain to the class that workers began to try different ways to improve conditions in the workplace. **Ask:** *What is a trade union? (a group of workers with the same trade, or skill) Why would workers join a trade union? (by working together, they would have more power to make changes than they would if they were working individually)*

C Critical Thinking Skills

Making Inferences Discuss with students how the General Trades Union of the City of New York organized strikes to put pressure on employers. **Ask:**

- **What is a strike?** *(a refusal to work)* **ELL** **How might a strike put pressure on employers?** *(Employers lose money when their employees are not working. They have fewer products to sell.)* **BL**
- **Why was going on strike a potential problem for employees?** *(It was illegal and they could lose their jobs.)* Have partners role-play a discussion between a factory worker and a factory owner about whether workers should have the right to strike.

R2 Reading Skills

Specifying After students have read the text, explain that even though slavery had disappeared in the North by 1830, African Americans in the North still faced discrimination. **Ask:** *What difficulties did African Americans face in the North? (They faced poverty, prejudice, and discrimination. They often could not attend public schools or use other public services.)*

Content Background Knowledge

- *The AFRO* is the longest-running African-American newspaper. It was founded in 1892 and has continued to run well into the 21st century.
- The social reformer Frederick Douglass started an African American newspaper called *The North Star*. The newspaper expressed an abolitionist viewpoint in the years before the Civil War.

Lewis Hine and Child Labor

Making Inferences Use the slide show "Lewis Hine and Child Labor" to discuss with students the extreme working conditions for children in the mid-1800s and why the laws to regulate child labor were not passed for many years. **Ask:** **Under what conditions did children work in Northern factories?** *(They often worked six days a week and 12 or more hours a day. The work was dangerous and hard.)* **Why did it take so long for child labor to be regulated?** *(Students may say that the public was not aware of the children's working conditions until people like Hine started to document them.)*

See page 373D for other online activities.

McGraw Hill **netw⊚rks**   Lewis Hine

Children had long worked on farms and in factories, but the dangerous conditions did not receive much attention until the early 1900s. In this photo, two young boys are working in a Georgia cotton mill.

Library of Congress

G1 Critical Thinking Skills

Making Inferences Discuss with the students the success in the business world achieved by African Americans. Discuss the establishment of the first African American newspaper by Samuel Cornish and John Russwurm. **Ask: Why is Macon B. Allen an example of African American success?** *(He was the first African American to be a licensed lawyer.)*

Ask students to use what they have learned about the lives of African Americans in the North to make an inference about why Macon B. Allen wanted to become a lawyer.

R Reading Skills

Describing Ask students to read the section on women workers. Explain that women also faced discrimination in the workplace. **Ask: How were women discriminated against in the workplace?** *(Employers paid women less than male workers. Men kept women from joining unions.)*

Discuss the creation of the Lowell Female Labor Reform Organization, what it hoped to achieve, and how it paved the way for later movements in the fight for equality.

C2 Critical Thinking Skills

Determing Cause and Effect Discuss with students the impact of industry on the growth of cities in the early to mid-1800s. **Ask: What effect did industrialization have on cities?** *(Factories were usually in urban areas. Because factories drew workers, Northern cities grew in size in the early 1800s. By the mid-1800s, cities along rivers became centers of trade.)*

V Visual Skills

Analyzing Maps Discuss the importance of location on the growth of port cities between 1820 and 1840. Display a map on the whiteboard and have students identify the location of St. Louis; then mark that location. Discuss the location and the region in which it is located. **AL** Have students do the same for Pittsburgh, Cincinnati, and Louisville. **BL** **Ask: How did the location of St. Louis, Pittsburgh, Cincinnati, and Louisville help them grow into cities?** *(Because of their location on waterways, these cities became centers of trade that linked Midwestern farmers with cities of the Northeast.)* **BL** **Visual/Spatial**

ANSWER, p. 384

✔ **PROGRESS CHECK** Conditions got worse; workers labored long hours under uncomfortable and often dangerous conditions.

The women who worked at the Lowell mills communicated—and shared grievances—through a publication called the *Lowell Offering*. It included creative works on many topics, including the hardships facing factory workers.

In the business world, a few African Americans found success. In New York City, Samuel Cornish and John B. Russwurm founded *Freedom's Journal*, the first African American newspaper, in 1827. In 1845 Macon B. Allen became the first African American **licensed,** or given official authority, to practice law in the United States. Most African Americans, however, lived in poverty in the mid-1800s. **G1**

Women Workers

Women also faced discrimination in the workplace. Employers often paid women half as much as they paid male workers. Men kept women from joining unions and wanted them kept out of the workplace.

In the 1830s and 1840s, some female workers tried to organize. Sarah G. Bagley, a weaver from Massachusetts, founded the Lowell Female Labor Reform Organization. In 1845 her group petitioned for a 10-hour workday. Because most of the workers were women, the legislature did not consider the petition. However, movements like the one Sarah Bagley led paved the way for later movements to help working women. **R**

✔ **PROGRESS CHECK**

Describing How did conditions for workers change as the factory system developed?

The Growth of Cities

GUIDING QUESTION *What challenges did European immigrants face in Northern cities?*

Industrialization had a big impact on cities. Factories were usually in urban areas. Because factories drew workers, Northern cities grew in size in the early 1800s. **C2**

Urban Populations Grow

Some major cities developed between 1820 and 1840 from Midwestern villages located along rivers. St. Louis sits on the banks of the Mississippi River just south of where that river meets the Illinois and Missouri Rivers. By the mid-1800s, steamboats from north and south lined up along the docks of St. Louis. Pittsburgh, Cincinnati, and Louisville also profited from their locations on waterways. These cities became centers of trade that linked Midwest farmers with cities of the Northeast. **V**

The Granger Collection, NYC

Reading HELPDESK (CCSS)

famine an extreme shortage of food
nativist person opposed to immigration

Academic Vocabulary (Tier 2 Words)

license to give an official authority to do something

---

netw☉rks   *Online Teaching Options*

PRIMARY SOURCE

Life as a Lowell Girl

Analyzing Primary Sources Use the interactive primary source excerpt from Harriet Robinson to discuss life as a Lowell Girl and early factory labor in New England. Have volunteers point out words that describe the harsh conditions faced by women in the factory system. Then encourage students to summarize the text in their own words. **Ask: Would you have joined a union if you were working in this era? Why or why not?** *(Answers may vary.)*

See page 373D for other online activities.

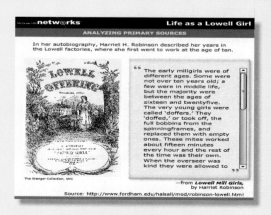

netw☉rks   Life as a Lowell Girl
ANALYZING PRIMARY SOURCES

In her autobiography, Harriet H. Robinson described her years in the Lowell factories, where she first went to work at the age of ten.

"The early millgirls were of different ages. Some were not over ten years old; a few were in middle life, but the majority were between the ages of sixteen and twentyfive. The very young girls were called 'doffers.' They 'doffed,' or took off, the full bobbins from the spinningframes, and replaced them with empty ones. These mites worked about fifteen minutes every hour and the rest of the time was their own. When the overseer was kind they were allowed to"

The Granger Collection, NYC

—from *Lowell Mill Girls*, by Harriet Robinson

Source: http://www.fordham.edu/halsall/mod/robinson-lowell.html

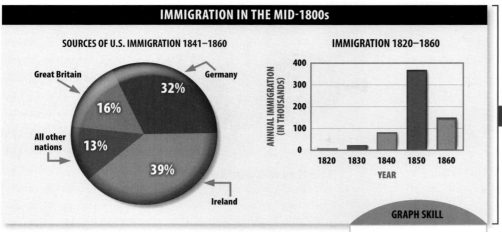

IMMIGRATION IN THE MID-1800s

SOURCES OF U.S. IMMIGRATION 1841–1860

- Great Britain **16%**
- Germany **32%**
- All other nations **13%**
- Ireland **39%**

IMMIGRATION 1820–1860

ANNUAL IMMIGRATION (IN THOUSANDS)

400 / 300 / 200 / 100 / 0

1820 1830 1840 1850 1860

YEAR

GRAPH SKILL

Immigrants came to the United States from different countries in the mid-1800s.

1 CALCULATING What share of immigrants came from Great Britain and Ireland combined between 1841 and 1860?

2 CRITICAL THINKING *Drawing Conclusions* What can you conclude about Germany and Ireland during this time based on this information?

Increased Immigration

Between the years 1840 and 1860, immigration to the United States grew sharply. The greatest number of immigrants came from Ireland. A plant disease, the potato blight, destroyed most of the Irish food supply in the 1840s. The people of Ireland faced **famine,** an extreme shortage of food. More than a million people died during what was called the Great Irish Famine. Another 1.5 million Irish emigrants—people who leave their home to move elsewhere—left for the United States between 1846 and 1860.

The second largest group of immigrants in the United States between 1820 and 1860 came from Germany. Some sought work and opportunity. Others fled to escape political problems at home.

Immigration's Impact

European immigrants brought languages, customs, religions, and traditions to their new country. Some of their ways of living changed American culture.

Immigrants Face Prejudice

In the 1830s and 1840s, some people began to resist immigration. They were known as **nativists** (NAY•tih•vihsts). Nativists believed that immigration threatened the future of "native"—American-born—citizens. They often blamed immigrants for problems in society. Some nativists accused immigrants of taking jobs from "real" Americans and were angry that immigrants would work for lower wages. Others accused immigrants of bringing crime and disease to U.S. cities.

Lesson 2 **385**

V Visual Skills

Analyzing Graphs Direct students to look at the "Sources of U.S. Immigration 1841–1860" circle graph at the top of this page. Ask students to determine which countries most immigrants came from in the mid-1880s. *(Ireland and Germany)* Have partners discuss the reasons for immigration from each country. **Ask: Who had the largest percentage of immigration?** *(the Irish)* **Logical/Mathematical**

W Writing Skills

Informative/Explanatory Review the reasons that German and Irish immigrants came to the United States between 1820 and 1860. Explain to students that there are many reasons that people move to various places. Distribute an index card to each student. **Ask: How did your family end up in the city in which you live?**

Have students write a one-paragraph answer to the question on the index card. Collect the cards and choose a few to read to the class.

Immigration to the United States, by Decade

Analyzing Graphs Explain to students that since 1860, the number of immigrants to the United States has tended to rise and fall, often reflecting the impact of world events. Present the interactive line graph that shows immigration to the United States between 1820 and 1860. **Ask:**

- **Why did immigration spike in 1850?** *(famine in Ireland and political unrest in Germany)* **AL** **ELL**
- **Why did immigration decline again in 1860?** *(Possible answer: Conditions may have become better in Ireland and Germany, so people did not have reasons to leave those countries.)*
- **What impact did immigrants have on cities?** *(They increased the population of cities. They brought languages, customs, religions, and traditions to their new country. Some of their ways of living changed the character of American life.)* **ELL** **Logical/Mathematical**

See page 373D for other online activities.

.netw rks· Immigration to the United States, by Decade

Since 1860, the number of immigrants to the United States has tended to rise and fall, often reflecting the impact of world events.

NUMBER OF IMMIGRANTS

10,000,000 / 9,000,000 / 8,000,000 / 7,000,000 / 6,000,000 / 5,000,000 / 4,000,000 / 3,000,000 / 2,000,000 / 1,000,000 / 0

YEAR

ANSWERS, p. 385

GRAPH SKILL

1. about 55 percent
2. **CRITICAL THINKING** There were likely strong "push" factors in those countries that encouraged emigration because those countries were sending immigrants at a much higher rate than other nations.

V Visual Skills

Analyzing Graphs Review the circle graph about immigrants as a percentage of the population. **Ask: What happened to the immigrant population between 1820 and 1860?** *(It grew from less than 1 percent in 1820 to 13 percent in 1860.)* Help students understand that even though there was growth in the immigrant population, it was still small in comparison to American citizens. **Visual/Spatial**

R Reading Skills

Identifying Direct students to read the section titled "The Know-Nothing Party." Then, discuss with the class the fact that some Americans resented the arrival of the new immigrants. **Ask: Who was against immigration?** *(people called nativists, who believed that immigrants threatened the future of "native," or American-born, citizens)* **AL**

Discuss with students that nativists blamed immigrants for the problems in society and feared that they would take jobs and work for lower wages. **Ask:**

- **What actions did the nativists take to have their opinions heard?** *(They formed a political party called the Know-Nothing Party and called for stricter citizenship laws.)*
- **What was inconsistent about the nativists' viewpoint?** *(They ignored the fact that their ancestors were immigrants.)* **BL** **ELL**

Have students complete the Lesson 2 Review.

CLOSE & REFLECT

Making Connections Remind students that immigration during the 1800s affected the culture of the United States. Ask students to name their favorite foods. Encourage them to research the origins of their favorite foods and beverages. **AL** **ELL**

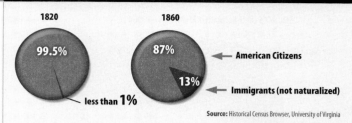

GRAPH SKILL

Immigration to the United States had a noticeable effect on the country's population.

1 CALCULATING How much larger was the immigrant population as a share of the overall population in 1860 compared to 1820?

2 CRITICAL THINKING *Speculating* How might a nativist react to this information?

IMMIGRANTS AS A PERCENTAGE OF POPULATION

1820 — 99.5% / less than 1%

1860 — 87% ← American Citizens / 13% ← Immigrants (not naturalized)

Source: Historical Census Browser, University of Virginia

The Know-Nothing Party

In 1849 nativists formed a new political party. Because party members often answered questions about their group with the statement "I know nothing," the party came to be known as the Know-Nothing Party. The Know-Nothings called for stricter citizenship laws. In 1854 the Know-Nothings became known as the American Party.

PRIMARY SOURCE

❝ Americans must rule America; and to this end native-born citizens should be selected for all State, Federal and municipal offices of government employment, in preference to all others. ❞

—American Party platform, from the American National Convention, 1856

✓ **PROGRESS CHECK**

Identifying From which two nations did most immigrants come in the mid-1800s?

LESSON 2 REVIEW (CCSS)

Review Vocabulary (Tier 3 Words)

1. Use these terms in a sentence that explains their meaning. RH.6–8.4
   a. trade union   b. strike

2. Write a brief statement about life in the mid-1800s using the following terms. RH.6–8.4
   a. prejudice   b. discrimination
   c. famine   d. nativist   e. emigrant

Answer the Guiding Questions

3. *Listing* What were some of the early attempts at work reform in the North? RH.6–8.1

4. *Discussing* Why did some Americans object to immigration? RH.6–8.2

5. *Explaining* What were conditions like for African Americans in the North in the mid-1800s? RH.6–8.2

6. **NARRATIVE** Take the role of a young person working in a factory in the North in the mid-1800s. Write a letter in which you tell a friend what you like and dislike about your job. WHST.6–8.1, WHST.6–8.10

LESSON 2 REVIEW ANSWERS

1. Possible answer: As industrialization expanded factories, skilled workers formed trade unions to press their demands, and some workers organized strikes in an effort to force employers to improve wages or conditions.

2. Possible answer: Immigration rose sharply in the early and mid-1800s. A major cause was the famine in Ireland. Many Irish emigrants went to the United States. Many immigrants faced prejudice and discrimination as nativists reacted with alarm to the growing immigrant presence.

3. formation of trade unions, organization of unskilled workers, strikes, formation of the Lowell Female Labor Reform Organization

4. Some Americans—"nativists"—feared that immigrants were changing the character of the United States too much; they accused immigrants of taking "their" jobs, were upset that immigrants worked for lower wages, and accused immigrants of bringing crime and disease.

5. Possible answer: Even though slavery had ended in the North, African Americans were discriminated against. A few succeeded in business, but most lived in poverty.

6. Students' letters should reflect some of the typical working conditions of the era.

ANSWERS, p. 386

GRAPH SKILL

1. It was more than 13 times larger.
2. **CRITICAL THINKING** A nativist might be alarmed to see that the immigrant influence was growing so rapidly.

✓ **PROGRESS CHECK** Ireland and Germany

South Carolina

Georgia

Florida

1840

51.6%

Lesson 3
Southern Cotton Kingdom

ESSENTIAL QUESTION *Why do people make economic choices?*

IT MATTERS BECAUSE

The demand for cotton deepened the white South's commitment to slavery and a slave-based economy.

Rise of the Cotton Kingdom

GUIDING QUESTION *How were the economies of the South and North different?*

In the early years of the United States, the South had an economy based almost entirely on farming, despite the fact that settlers had developed only a small part of the region. Most Southerners lived in the Upper South, an area along the Atlantic coast in Maryland, Virginia, and North Carolina. A few people had also settled in Georgia and South Carolina.

By 1850, the South had changed. Its population had spread inland to the Deep South. This region includes Georgia and South Carolina, as well as Alabama, Mississippi, Louisiana, and Texas. The economy of the South was thriving. That economy depended, however, on slavery. In fact, slavery grew stronger than ever in the South, while it all but disappeared in the North.

R1

Cotton Is King

Southern planters grew mainly rice, indigo, and tobacco in colonial times. After the American Revolution, demand for these crops decreased. European mills now wanted Southern cotton.

R2

Raising a cotton crop took a large amount of time and labor. After the harvest, workers had to carefully separate the plant's sticky seeds from the cotton fibers.

C

(c) SSPL/The Image Works

Reading **HELP**DESK **CCSS**

Taking Notes: *Determining Cause and Effect*

As you read, use a diagram like this one to show the reasons cotton production grew but industrial growth was slower in the South. RH.6–8.5

Cotton   Industry

Content Vocabulary
- **productivity**
- **domestic slave trade** (Tier 3 Words)

Lesson 3 **387**

The South and Regional Economics of the United States

Comparing and Contrasting Explain to students that, historically, regional industries and resources in the United States have affected the growth of local economies. Play the video about the regional economies of Silicon Valley and of the South in the 1800s. Make a chart with students showing the similarities and differences between the two economies. *(Similarities: Both dependent on one type of product, both confined to a single regional area. Differences: The South's economy was based on cotton, while Silicon Valley's economy is based on technology. The South's economy was dependent upon slave labor, while Silicon Valley's economy is not.)*

See page 373E for other online activities.

LEARN360
ENGAGE · ENRICH · EXCEL
A Division of APH Education, Inc.

ENGAGE

Bellringer Have students look briefly at the clothes they are wearing. **Ask: What fabric is your favorite T-shirt made of?** Invite students to name as many products as they can in one minute—besides clothing—that can be made from cotton (e.g., towels, bandages, sheets, tablecloths). Tell them they are going to discuss the importance of cotton production in the South. Intrapersonal

TEACH & ASSESS

R1 Reading Skills

Finding the Main Idea Discuss with students that in the early years of the United States, the South had an economy based on farming. Be sure to explain that most of these farmers lived in the Upper South in colonies like Maryland, Virginia, and North Carolina. Direct students to read the two paragraphs under the heading "Rise of the Cotton Kingdom" on this page. **Ask: How had the South changed by 1850?** *(The population had spread to an area known as the Deep South.)* Have a volunteer list the states that make up the region of the Deep South. Discuss with students that the economy was thriving, but it was dependent on slavery.

R2 Reading Skills

Listing Ask for a student volunteer to read the text aloud. Point out to the class that cotton was not the sole Southern crop. **Ask: What crops did Southern planters grow in colonial times?** *(rice, indigo, and tobacco)* Explain to students that after the Revolutionary War the demand for these crops decreased because European mills wanted Southern cotton.

C Critical Thinking Skills

Determining Cause and Effect Discuss with students that raising a cotton crop took a lot of time and labor. **Ask: How was the cotton processed?** *(Workers had to carefully separate the plant's sticky seeds from the cotton fibers.)* Be sure students understand that this slow process led to a smaller amount of cotton that they could sell to European mills, affecting the profit that a farmer could make.

ANSWER, p. 387

TAKING NOTES: Cotton: 1. boom in cotton sales **2.** ready source of labor—enslaved African Americans; **Industry: 1.** boom in cotton sales (agriculture was more profitable) **2.** small market for manufactured goods; lack of interest in industry

V Visual Skills

Analyzing Maps Use the map about cotton production from 1820 to 1860 to discuss the impact of the cotton gin on the production of cotton in the Upper South and Deep South. Have students compare the two shaded areas on the map and analyze the dramatic change in cotton production that occurred in a short amount of time. **Ask: Why do you think more farmers switched to growing cotton?** *(Answers may vary but should suggest that because of the increase in productivity that resulted from the cotton gin, farmers may have believed that they could make larger profits by growing and producing cotton.)* **ELL** Visual/Spatial

C Critical Thinking Skills

Determining Cause and Effect Discuss the effects of the cotton gin. **Ask: What effect did the cotton gin have on productivity?** *(Workers could process 50 times more cotton each day using the cotton gin than they could by hand.)*

Explain to students that this dramatic increase in productivity did have consequences. Discuss that because productivity encouraged farmers in other areas to grow cotton, the demand for slave labor spread into the Deep South and also increased. Be sure students understand that the increase in cotton productivity created the need for slave labor. Ask a student to represent this information on a graph, and explain the concept of *direct proportion*. **Logical/Mathematical** Explain that the Upper South became a center for the sale and transport of enslaved people. Explain that this became known as the domestic slave trade. **BL**

Content Background Knowledge

The cotton gin made plantation owners rich, but eventually made Eli Whitney bankrupt. Numerous lawsuits and a lack of a patent led to his monetary downfall, leading him to say to a business partner, "My situation makes me perfectly miserable."

ANSWERS, p. 388

GEOGRAPHY CONNECTION

1 the Deep South
2 **CRITICAL THINKING** It might increase the value of enslaved people overall, create a demand for those people, and encourage the trading of enslaved people within the United States.

✓**PROGRESS CHECK** It made cotton production more profitable for Southern planters, increased the need for slave labor, and helped lead to an expanding internal slave trade.

388

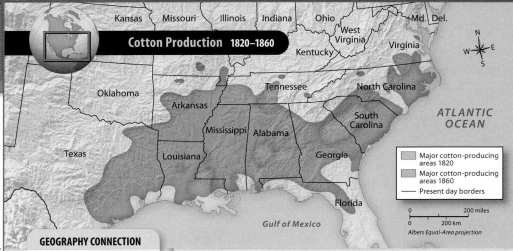

Cotton Production 1820–1860

GEOGRAPHY CONNECTION

Agriculture was very profitable in the South. By 1860, much of the South was devoted to raising cotton.

1 **REGION** In which region did cotton expand most, the Upper South or Deep South?

2 **CRITICAL THINKING** *Making Connections* How might the expansion of slavery in the Deep South affect slavery in the Upper South?

Eli Whitney solved this problem with his invention of the cotton gin in 1793. Whitney's gin quickly and easily removed seeds from cotton fibers. With a cotton gin, **productivity** (proh·duhk·TIH·vuh·tee)—the amount a worker can produce in a given time—shot up. The cotton gin helped workers **process** 50 times more cotton each day than they could by hand.

The use of the cotton gin had important **consequences.** It encouraged farmers to grow more cotton in more places. Because Southern planters relied on enslaved workers to plant and pick their cotton, the demand for slave labor increased. Slavery spread across a larger area of the South.

By 1860, the Deep South and Upper South remained agricultural, but each region concentrated on different crops. The Upper South grew more tobacco, hemp, wheat, and vegetables. The Deep South produced more cotton, as well as rice and sugarcane.

Because more workers were needed to produce cotton and sugar, the sale of enslaved Africans became a big business. The Upper South became a center for the sale and transport of enslaved people. This trade became known as the **domestic slave trade.**

✓ **PROGRESS CHECK**

Describing What effect did the cotton gin have on the South's economy?

Reading HELPDESK (CCSS)

productivity a measure of how much a worker can produce with a given amount of time and effort
domestic slave trade the trade of enslaved people among states of the United States

Academic Vocabulary (Tier 2 Words)
process to prepare
consequence result

388 *North and South*

netw⊙rks   *Online Teaching Options*

IMAGE

The Cotton Gin

Explaining Use the interactive image of the cotton gin to help students understand how the invention worked. **Ask: How did the cotton gin work?** *(A crank pulled the cotton through a set of metal teeth, which caught the seeds. A rotating brush then pulled the cotton lint off the teeth, separating the plant's sticky seeds from the cotton fibers.)* **AL**

Be sure to explain to students that this simple machine increased productivity by decreasing the time spent processing the cotton, allowing more time for more cotton to be processed. Be sure to connect this information to the three phases of industrialization and the use of specialized machines to increase production.

See page 373E for other online activities.

The Cotton Gin
A rotating brush then pulled the clean cotton off the teeth.
Private Collection, Peter Newark American Pictures/Bridgeman Art Library

Southern Industry

GUIDING QUESTION *Why did industry develop slowly in the South?*

Industry developed more slowly in the South than in the North. Why was this so? One reason was the boom in cotton. Agriculture, especially cotton farming, produced great profits. Building new industry is costly. Planters would have had to sell enslaved people or land to raise the money to build factories. They chose instead to invest in profitable agriculture—including enslaved Africans.

In addition, the market for manufactured goods in the South was small. Enslaved people, who made up a large share of the population, had no money to buy goods. This limited local market discouraged industries from developing.

For these reasons, some white Southerners simply did not want industry. One Texas politician, Louis Wigfall, summed up that Southern point of view:

PRIMARY SOURCE

66 We want no manufactures: we desire no trading, no mechanical or manufacturing classes. As long as we have our rice, our sugar, our tobacco and our cotton, we can command wealth to purchase all we want. 99

—quoted in *Louis T. Wigfall, Southern Fire-Eater*

INCREASES IN PRODUCTIVITY

New inventions helped increase worker productivity in the 1800s. Increased productivity meant farmers could grow more cotton to sell. By the mid-1800s, cotton made up more than one-half of U.S. exports.

Elias Howe's sewing machine drove up worker productivity by enabling workers to make large amounts of clothing in a day.

SSPL/The Image Works

COTTON PRODUCTION AS A PERCENTAGE OF U.S. EXPORTS

1800	1820
7.1%	32%

1840	1860
51.6%	57.5%

Source: Historical Statistics of the United States

ECONOMICS SKILL

Cotton's role in the economy of the South—and the nation—increased in the 1800s.

1 CONTRASTING How did cotton's share of the U.S. export market change between 1800 and 1860?

2 CRITICAL THINKING
Determining Cause and Effect How do you think increases in productivity affected the demand for enslaved labor? Explain.

BIOGRAPHY

Elias Howe

Making Connections Use the interactive image of Elias Howe to discuss his invention of the sewing machine. Use the information contained on the slide to discuss how it worked. Discuss with students that, like the cotton gin, the sewing machine sped up the time it took to do something that was originally done by hand. Have students recall the information about the sewing machine that was discussed in Lesson 1 with regard to its role in the factory system, the three phases of industrialization, and the process of manufacturing clothing. Discuss how increased productivity in growing cotton is connected to the increased productivity in the manufacture of clothing. **BL**

See page 373E for other online activities.

McGraw Hill **netw⊚rks**   **Elias Howe**
BIOGRAPHY

Elias Howe invented the first sewing machine. He spent his childhood in Massachusetts and apprenticed for a mechanic in a textile factory. In 1845, Howe created his first sewing machine. In a public demonstration, Howe showed that his machine was five times faster than sewing by hand. Howe's machine had a curved eye-pointed needle that moved in an arc as it moved the thread through the fabric. It then interlocked with a second thread on the other side.

SSPL/The Image Works

C1 Critical Thinking Skills

Determining Cause and Effect Discuss with students that industry developed at a much slower pace in the South than in the North. **Ask: How did the boom in cotton production affect the growth of industry in the South?** *(Answers may vary but should suggest that the boom in cotton production discouraged the growth of industry because people in the South believed that their economy based on agriculture was strong and produced enough profit.)*

Explain that a reason industry was slow to develop in the South was because building new industry was expensive. **AL** Ask students to research reasons that cotton did well in the South. **BL**

C2 Critical Thinking Skills

Analyzing Explain to students that because a large share of the Southern population had no money with which to buy goods, the market for manufactured goods was small. Discuss how this discouraged industries from developing in the South. Be sure students make the connection that while the agricultural economy was dependent on slavery, an industrial economy would be dependent on those enslaved people being free, earning a wage, and purchasing goods. **BL**

V Visual Skills

Analyzing Graphs Have students examine the circle graphs about cotton production as a percentage of U.S. exports. Encourage students to notice that as productivity increased, so did the export of cotton to other countries. Discuss with students how drastically the graphs change in a very small amount of time. Be sure to connect this information with the development of the cotton gin and the consequence of an increase in slave labor. **ELL Visual/Spatial**

ANSWERS, p. 389

ECONOMICS SKILL

1. Cotton went from about 7 percent of U.S. exports in 1800 to almost 58 percent of exports in 1860.
2. **CRITICAL THINKING** Increased productivity created greater demand for enslaved labor because cotton was more profitable. Even though, or because, technology made growing cotton more efficient, more enslaved labor was needed, and the slave trade increased in the South.

Southern Cotton Kingdom

W Writing Skills

Argument Discuss with students that while most white Southerners did not want industry in the South, some Southern leaders, like William Gregg and Joseph Reid Anderson, did. **Ask: Why did these Southern leaders want to develop industry?** *(They thought the South relied too much on agriculture and depended too much on the North for industrial goods. They believed development of industry would encourage the economy in the Upper South to grow.)*

Ask students to imagine that they are Gregg or Anderson. Have them write a letter to other Southern leaders in which they argue why the South should develop industry. **Intrapersonal**

R Reading Skills

Explaining Have students read the text and remind them that the production of goods is only one part of supplying what consumers need. **Ask: How did most farmers transport goods in the South?** *(on natural waterways)* **AL** Be sure to explain that most Southern towns were located on coasts or along rivers because canals were scarce and roads were poor. Have students speculate how the construction of canals and the improvement of roads may have changed economic development in the South.

C Critical Thinking Skills

Determining Cause and Effect Discuss that Southern rail lines were short, local, and not connected to each other or to the North. **Ask: How did this impact the growth of cities and industry in the South?** *(Southern cities grew more slowly than Northern cities. Students should suggest that if the railroads in the South had been more like those in the North, the South would have experienced a growth in commerce and settlement—a positive impact on the Southern economy.)*

Have students complete the Lesson 3 Review.

CLOSE & REFLECT

Refer students to the quote by Louis Wigfall in their textbooks. Examine his statement and have volunteers describe his point of view in their own words. **Ask: How did this point of view hold back development?** *(Answers may vary but should suggest that without industry, the South could not move forward and be equal to the North. Answers could also suggest that Wigfall's quote does not take into account factors that affect crops, such as drought or diseases, which could dramatically impact the South's agricultural economy.)*

ANSWER, p. 390

✓ **PROGRESS CHECK** Slavery slowed major changes to the Southern economy. White planters' investment in enslaved people reduced the amount of money available for investment in other industries.

Factories in the South

W Some Southern leaders wanted to develop industry in the region. They thought that the South depended too much on the North for manufactured goods. These leaders also argued that factories would improve the economy of the Upper South.

William Gregg of South Carolina shared this view. He opened his own textile factory. Georgia's Augustin Clayton also went into textiles, opening a cotton mill. In Virginia, Joseph Reid Anderson made Tredegar Iron Works one of the nation's leading iron producers. The Alabama Iron Works also included a sawmill for producing lumber. These industries, however, were not typical of the South.

Southern Transportation

R In general, farmers and the few manufacturers of the South relied on natural waterways to transport their goods. Most towns were located on coasts or along rivers because canals were scarce and roads were poor.

Southern rail lines were short, local, and not linked together. C The South had fewer railroads than the North. This caused Southern cities to grow more slowly than Northern cities, where railways were major routes of commerce and settlement. The rail networks in the North also gave Northern manufacturers an advantage over their Southern competitors. Lower shipping costs allowed Northerners to charge less for their goods. By 1860, only about one-third of the nation's rail lines lay within the South. This rail shortage would hurt the South in the years to come.

✓ **PROGRESS CHECK**

Explaining How did slavery affect the development of the Southern economy?

LESSON 3 REVIEW

Review Vocabulary (Tier 3 Words)

1. Use these two words in a sentence in a way that shows their meaning and relationship. RH.6–8.4
   a. productivity   b. domestic slave trade

Answer the Guiding Questions

2. *Comparing* Discuss ways the economies of the Upper South and the Deep South became dependent on each other around 1860. RH.6–8.5

3. *Explaining* How did some Southerners contribute to industrial growth in the region? RH.6–8.2

4. *Identifying* What were the barriers to Southern transportation? RH.6–8.1

5. **ARGUMENT** Look again at the words of Texas politician Louis Wigfall, who said, "We want no manufactures." Add a second paragraph to this quotation that explains why, in words you imagine Wigfall might use, he opposes industry for the South. RH.6–8.6, WHST.6–8.1

LESSON 3 REVIEW ANSWERS

1. Possible answer: The increase in productivity made possible by the cotton gin increased the demand for enslaved African Americans and spurred the domestic slave trade.

2. The economies of both areas depended on agriculture rather than industry and relied on enslaved workers. The Deep South needed more enslaved workers, and the Upper South became the center of an expanded internal slave trade.

3. by opening industrial facilities such as cotton mills and iron manufacturing factories

4. lack of canals; poor roads; short, local rail lines

5. Students might give reasons such as favorable growing conditions in the South, strong demand for the South's agricultural products, and confidence that the South's agricultural economy will continue to prosper. The tone should reflect the strength of the politician's convictions.

networks
There's More Online!

- ☑ **BIOGRAPHY**
  Harriet Tubman
- ☑ **GRAPHIC ORGANIZER**
  Working on a Plantation
- ☑ **PRIMARY SOURCE**
  American Slavery As It Is
- ☑ **VIDEO**

Lesson 4
People of the South

ESSENTIAL QUESTION *How do people adapt to their environment?*

IT MATTERS BECAUSE

Enslaved Africans faced many hardships but were able to establish family lives, religious beliefs, and a distinct culture.

Southern Agriculture

GUIDING QUESTION *How were Southern farms different from Southern plantations?*

Slavery was at the heart of the Southern economy, but that did not mean that every white person owned large numbers of enslaved people. White society in the South was complex and had many levels. Most white Southerners fit into one of four categories: yeomen, tenant farmer, rural poor, or plantation owner.

Small Farmers and the Rural Poor

Most white people in the South were **yeomen** (YOH•muhn), farmers who generally owned small farms of 50 to 200 acres (20–81 ha). These yeomen lived mostly in the Upper South and in the hilly areas of the Deep South. They did not practice plantation-style agriculture. They grew crops to use themselves and to trade with local merchants. Yeomen generally owned few or no enslaved African Americans.

Another group of Southern whites worked as tenant farmers. They rented land from property owners.

These classes of white Southerners made up the majority of the white population of the South. They lived in simple homes—cottages or log cabins. The poorest of these groups lived in crude cabins.

R

C

Reading **HELP**DESK **CCSS**

Taking Notes: *Describing* RH.6–8.2
As you read, use a diagram like the one here to describe the work that was done on Southern plantations.

Working on a Plantation

Content Vocabulary (Tier 3 Words)
- yeoman
- overseer
- spiritual
- slave codes
- Underground Railroad
- literacy

Lesson 4 **391**

(Image credits, left margin:) (l) Collection of the New York Historical Society/Bridgeman Art Library; (cl) CORBIS; (c) Carlos Barria/Reuters/CORBIS; (cr) CORBIS; (r) CHM/UIG/Universal Images Group/age fotostock

---

🔔 **Bellringer** Use the two images of plantation living quarters (on the next page and later in the lesson) to introduce this lesson about the people of the South. **Ask: How would you contrast these living quarters?** *(The plantation looks large and grand; the slave cabin looks small and plain.)* **AL** **ELL** Discuss with students that not all farmers in the South owned plantations and enslaved people. Tell students that in this lesson they will learn about the different people in the South, how agriculture influenced their lives, and the growth of Southern cities.

TEACH & ASSESS

R Reading Skills

Listing Have a student volunteeer read the first paragraph on this page aloud. Explain that although slavery was a critical part of the Southern economy, many Southerners did not own enslaved people. Ask students to list the four categories that most white Southerners fit into during this time. *(yeomen, tenant farmer, rural poor, plantation owner)* **AL**

C Critical Thinking Skills

Contrasting Create a list with students that compares the differences between yeomen farmers and tenant farmers. Discuss with students that yeomen farmers owned small farms and lived mostly in the Upper South and in the hilly areas of the Deep South. Be sure students know that they grew crops that they traded with local merchants and had few or no slaves. Then, discuss with students the life of the tenant farmer. Explain that tenant farmers rented land from property owners and that this group made up the majority of the population of the South. Discuss that they lived in simple homes and that they were proudly independent. **ELL**

VIDEO

Secrets of the Underground Railroad

Evaluating Tell students they will watch a video about a fictional person who was running away from slavery. After students watch "Secrets of the Underground Railroad," ask pairs of students to discuss the challenges faced by the runaway slave. Have each student write an answer to the question: What was the most difficult part of an enslaved person's escape? Ask volunteers to share their answers with the class.

See page 373F for other online activities.

(Video still shows LEARN360 — ENGAGE · ENRICH · EXCEL)

ANSWER, p. 391

TAKING NOTES: domestic work—cleaning house, laundry, sewing, cooking, serving meals; **pasture work**—tending to livestock; **fieldwork**—planting, tending, and harvesting crops; **trade work**—blacksmithing, carpentry, shoemaking, weaving

People of the South

V Visual Skills

Analyzing Graphs Have students review the graph "Southern Population 1860" in their textbook. **Ask: Why was a rebellion of enslaved people a threat to white Southerners?** *(There were nearly 4 million enslaved people—about 34 percent of the Southern population. A widespread rebellion would have been hard to stop.)* **BL** Visual/Spatial

R Reading Skills

Discussing Direct students to read the text. Guide a class discussion about the farm of a plantation owner. Encourage students to compare this information to the information about the yeoman and the tenant farmers. Remind them that a large plantation was made up of several thousand acres of land. **Ask: How did plantation owners measure their wealth?** *(by the amount of land they owned and the number of enslaved people they had)*

C1 Critical Thinking Skills

Analyzing Discuss with students that like a business or a factory, the major goal of a plantation was to make a profit. **Ask:**

- **What is one way that plantation owners could operate their plantations like a factory in order to make a profit?** *(Plantation owners could keep their fixed costs as low as possible and keep those costs stable over time.)* **BL**
- **Who would be directly affected by plantation owners' efforts to keep their fixed costs as low as possible? Why?** *(Enslaved workers because they were a fixed cost.)*

C2 Critical Thinking Skills

Making Connections Ask students if they understand the concept of supply and demand. Briefly explain to students the economic theory of supply and demand as it relates to cotton. Discuss that cotton prices can change year after year depending on the market and the amount of supply generated by Southern farmers. Discuss that a change in the demand for or supply of cotton can affect cotton prices and can lead to a good year or a bad year for the farmer. Also discuss with students that the price of the cotton affects the farmer's profits, which can also mean the difference between a successful year and a bad one. **BL**

ANSWERS, p. 392

GRAPH SKILL

1. 34 percent
2. **CRITICAL THINKING** White Southerners did not allow enslaved people to learn to read and write; they broke up their families. Owners also relied on intimidation and fear to control the enslaved people.

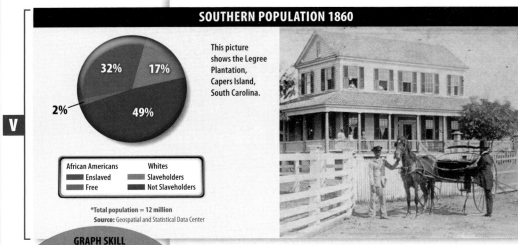

SOUTHERN POPULATION 1860

32% 17%
2% 49%

This picture shows the Legree Plantation, Capers Island, South Carolina.

African Americans
- Enslaved
- Free

Whites
- Slaveholders
- Not Slaveholders

*Total population = 12 million
Source: Geospatial and Statistical Data Center

GRAPH SKILL

In 1860 about 400,000 households in the South held enslaved workers. Nearly 4 million African Americans remained in slavery.

1 IDENTIFYING What percentage of the total Southern population was African American?

2 CRITICAL THINKING *Making Inferences* Given the size of the African American population, how do you think white Southerners were able to control African Americans?

These rural poor were often stubborn and independent. Though they were looked down upon by many, they were proud of their ability to provide for their families.

A few free African Americans also held enslaved workers. Some free African Americans bought members of their own families to free them, although others worked their enslaved workers in the same manner as white Southern planters.

Plantation Owners

The larger plantations covered several thousand acres. In addition to the land they owned, plantation owners measured their wealth by the number of enslaved people they had. In 1860 only about 4 percent of slaveholders held 20 or more enslaved workers.

Earning profits was the main goal for owners of large plantations. To make a profit, they needed to bring in more money than they spent to run their plantations.

Large plantations had fixed costs. These are operating costs that remain much the same year after year. For example, the cost of housing and feeding workers is a fixed cost. There is no easy way to reduce a fixed cost.

On the other hand, the price of cotton changed from season to season. A change in price often meant the difference between a successful year for a plantation and a bad one.

Collection of the New-York Historical Society/Bridgeman Art Library

Reading HELPDESK (CCSS)

yeoman farmer who owns a small farm

Reading in the Content Area: *Circle Graphs*
Circle graphs show how a whole is divided into parts. In the graph above, what is the whole being shown, and what is the largest share of that whole?

---

netw⊙rks   *Online Teaching Options*

CHART

U.S. Population, 1860

Analyzing Charts Before students use the chart "U.S. Population 1860," ask them to make a prediction about how the populations of enslaved people in Northern and Southern states will differ. *(Students should expect that Southern states will have much higher populations of enslaved people.)* Have students interact with the chart by first clicking on the Northern states and determining whether their predictions were correct. Then have students click on the Southern states. **Ask: What do you notice about the free and enslaved populations in Alabama, Louisiana, Georgia, Mississippi, and South Carolina?** *(The free and enslaved populations are nearly equal.)* **In which states were the enslaved populations greater than the free populations?** *(Mississippi and South Carolina)*

See page 373F for other online activities.

networks **U.S. Population, 1860**

In 1860 nearly 4 million people lived in slavery. Here are the results of the 1860 United States census. They show the population of free and enslaved people in each state.

Plantation owners—who were almost always men—traveled often in order to ensure fair dealings with traders. Their wives often led difficult and lonely lives. They took charge of their households and supervised the buildings. They watched over the enslaved domestic workers and sometimes tended to them when they became ill. Women also often kept the plantation's financial records.

Keeping a plantation running involved many tasks. Some enslaved people cleaned the house, cooked, did laundry and sewing, and served meals. Others were trained as blacksmiths, carpenters, shoemakers, or weavers. Still others tended livestock. Most enslaved African Americans, however, were field hands. They worked from sunrise to sunset to plant, tend, and harvest crops. An **overseer** (OH•vuhr•see•uhr), or plantation manager, supervised them.

✓ **PROGRESS CHECK**

Identifying What group made up the largest number of whites in the South?

The Lives of Enslaved People

GUIDING QUESTION *How did enslaved African Americans try to cope with their lack of freedom?*

The fate of most enslaved African Americans was hardship and misery. They worked hard, earned no money, and had little hope of freedom. They lived with the threat that an owner could sell them or members of their family without warning. In the face of these brutal conditions, enslaved African Americans tried to build stability. They kept up their family lives as best they could. They developed a culture all their own that blended African and American elements. They came up with clever ways to resist slavery.

African American Family Life

The law did not recognize slave marriages. Still, enslaved people did marry and raise families, which provided comfort and support. Uncertainty and danger, however, were always present. There were no laws or customs that would stop a slaveholder from breaking a family apart. If a slaveholder chose to—or if the slaveholder died—families could be and often were separated.

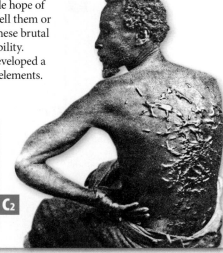

The punishments used against enslaved people included whipping, which could leave terrible scars.

overseer plantation manager

Lesson 4 **393**

R **Reading Skills**

Explaining Have students review the text about plantation wives. Explain that plantation owners often spent a good deal of time traveling to get the best price for their goods, which frequently left their wives in charge of the plantations. **AL** **Ask:**

- What were some of the responsibilities of plantation wives? *(They took charge of their households and supervised the buildings. They watched over the enslaved domestic workers. They often kept the plantation's financial records.)*
- Why do you think plantation wives learned to keep the financial records? *(The owners were away much of the time, and their wives were capable of doing the records.)* **BL**

C₁ **Critical Thinking Skills**

Comparing and Contrasting Have students make a graphic organizer to describe and review the work that was done on Southern plantations. Have partners use the graphic organizer to compare and contrast the tasks done by plantation owners, their wives, and African Americans on a plantation. Then ask students to relate this division of labor to their own households. **Intrapersonal**

C₂ **Critical Thinking Skills**

Determining Cause and Effect Discuss with students that the law did not recognize the marriage between two enslaved people. Explain that in spite of this, many African Americans did marry and raise families for support and comfort. Discuss that there were no laws that prevented the slaveholder from separating a family. **Ask:** What did enslaved people do in response to the threat of having a parent sold or a family broken up? *(In response, they set up a network of relatives and friends who would step in to help raise children who were left behind if they were separated from their parents. These networks became a source of strength.)* Ask students how they might react under similar circumstances. **BL** **Intrapersonal**

GRAPHIC ORGANIZER

Taking Notes: *Describing:* Working on a Plantation

Identifying Use the interactive graphic organizer to discuss and identify the variety of tasks that needed to be performed in order to keep a plantation running. Have students drag and drop the answers into the appropriate area and have them justify their responses. *(Domestic work: cleaning house, serving meals, laundry, sewing, cooking; Pasture work: tending to livestock; Fieldwork: harvesting crops, planting crops, tending crops; Trade work: blacksmithing, carpentry, shoemaking, weaving cloth)*

See page 373F for other online activities.

mcgraw-hill**networks**

Name: Date:

TAKING NOTES: *Describing*
ACTIVITY As you read, use the diagram to describe the work that was done on a plantation in the South.

Working on a Plantation

UNDO   CLEAR   SAVE

ANSWER, p. 393

✓ **PROGRESS CHECK** yeomen

R **Reading Skills**

Describing Direct students to read the first paragraph on this page. Then, lead a class discussion about the life and fate of an enslaved African American who worked on a plantation. **Ask:** What were some characteristics of life for enslaved people on plantations? *(They worked hard, earned no money, and had little hope of freedom. They lived with the threat that an owner could sell them or members of their family without warning.)*

Discuss with students that in these brutal conditions, enslaved African Americans tried to build stability by keeping up their family lives and creating a culture that blended African and American elements.

C **Critical Thinking Skills**

Contrasting Discuss how the work song, or field holler, and the call-and-response song were ways for the African Americans to pass the time and set a tempo for their work. Contrast these two with the spiritual, which helped enslaved people express their joy in their religion but their sadness in their suffering. Ask students to research and find recordings of some of these songs. **Auditory/Musical**

─ Connections to ─
TODAY

American Music

From the rhythmic patterns and themes of work songs and spirituals arose a new musical form—the blues. The blues influenced later styles, including jazz, rock and roll, and rap.

Wynton Marsalis is a modern-day jazz musician whose music has its roots in work songs and spirituals.

R

In the face of this threat, enslaved people set up a network of relatives and friends. If an owner sold a father or mother, an aunt, an uncle, or a close friend stepped in to raise the children left behind. These networks were a source of strength in the lives of enslaved people. Large, close-knit extended families became an important part of African American culture.

African American Culture

In 1808 Congress banned the import of slaves. Slavery remained **legal,** but traders could no longer purchase enslaved people from other countries. Some illegal slave trading continued, but by 1860, almost all the enslaved people in the South had been born there.

Though most enslaved people were born in the United States, they tried to preserve African customs. They passed traditional African folk stories on to their children. They performed African music and dance.

Enslaved people also drew on African rhythms to create musical forms that were uniquely American. One form was the work song, or field holler. A worker led a rhythmic call-and-response song, which sometimes included shouts and moans. The beat set the tempo for their work in the fields.

African American Religion

C

Many enslaved African Americans followed traditional African religious beliefs and practices. Others, however, accepted the Christian religion that was dominant in the United States. Christianity became for enslaved people a religion of hope and resistance. Enslaved people prayed for their freedom. They expressed their beliefs in **spirituals,** African American religious folk songs. The spiritual below, for example, refers to the biblical story of Daniel, whom God saved from being eaten by lions:

> **PRIMARY SOURCE**
>
> ❝ Didn't my Lord deliver Daniel
> Deliver Daniel, deliver Daniel
> Didn't my Lord deliver Daniel
> An' why not-a every man. ❞
>
> —from *Didn't My Lord Deliver Daniel*

Carlos Barria/Reuters/CORBIS

Reading **HELP**DESK **CCSS**

spiritual an African American religious folk song

Academic Vocabulary (Tier 2 Words)

legal permitted by law

netw⊙rks *Online Teaching Options*

SLIDE SHOW

Songs of Freedom

Discussing Discuss with students that though most enslaved people were born in America, they tried to preserve African customs. Explain that they did this through African folk stories and African music and dance. Explain that African Americans drew on African rhythms to create unique musical forms. Use the interactive slide show to discuss the three different types of songs sung by enslaved people. **AL** **ELL** **Ask:** What was the purpose of the three types of songs? *(Work songs set a tempo for fieldwork; spirituals helped enslaved people express their feelings; recreational songs were just for pleasure.)* **Auditory/Musical**

See page 373F for other online activities.

On large plantations, enslaved people might live in small communities such as this.

Spirituals helped enslaved people express joy—but also sadness about their suffering here on Earth. Enslaved people also used spirituals as a way to communicate secretly among themselves.

Slave Codes

The **slave codes,** sometimes called black codes or Negro Laws, were laws in the Southern states that controlled enslaved people. Such laws had existed since colonial times.

One purpose of the codes was to prevent what white Southerners dreaded most—a slave rebellion. For this reason, slave codes prohibited enslaved people from gathering in large groups. The codes also required enslaved people to have written passes before leaving the slaveholder's property.

The slave codes made teaching enslaved people to read or write a crime. White Southerners feared that an educated enslaved person might start a revolt. They thought an enslaved person who could not read and write was less likely to rebel.

C

Copper slave tags identified enslaved workers when they were away from their home plantation.

▶ CRITICAL THINKING
Drawing Conclusions Why do you think enslaved Africans might need identification tags when they were away from their plantations?

Fighting Back

R

Enslaved African Americans did sometimes rebel openly against their owners. One who did was Nat Turner.

Turner, who had taught himself to read and write, was a popular religious leader among the enslaved people in his area. In 1831 he led a group of followers on a **brief,** violent rampage in Southhampton County, Virginia. Turner and his followers killed at least 55 whites.

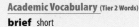

slave codes laws in a Southern state that controlled enslaved people

Academic Vocabulary (Tier 2 Words)
brief short

C Critical Thinking Skills

Making Inferences Ask students to think about why white Southerners thought an enslaved person who could not read or write was less likely to rebel. Have small groups discuss why an enslaved person who was educated might be more likely to start a revolt. Have a volunteer from each group share their answers with the class.

R Reading Skills

Summarizing Ask students to read the subsection titled "Fighting Back." Then, ask them to summarize Nat Turner's Rebellion. **Ask:**

- **What were the consequences of Nat Turner's Rebellion?** *(White mobs killed about 100 African Americans and also passed more severe slave codes.)*
- **What effect do you think the reaction of whites would have on further attempts at violent rebellion?** *(Students may say that it would discourage further attempts because the outcome did not help enslaved people.)* Encourage students to research to find more details about the rebellion. AL ELL

IMAGE

Slave Codes

Specifying Use the interactive image of slave codes to discuss with students how these laws in the Southern states controlled the enslaved population. **Ask: What was the main purpose of the slave codes?** *(to prevent rebellion)* **What were some provisions of the slave codes?** *(The codes prohibited enslaved people from gathering in large groups, required enslaved people to have written passes before leaving the slaveholder's property, and made teaching enslaved people to read or write a crime.)* Discuss with students that many Southerners felt that an educated enslaved person might start a revolt and that preventing them from learning would make them less likely to rebel. AL

See page 373F for other online activities.

McGraw-Hill **netw⊘rks** — Slave Codes

Each slave state had a set of laws called slave codes. These were laws that enslaved people were required to follow.

All slave codes had certain laws in common:

A person with ANY amount of African ancestry was classified as

North Wind Picture Archives

ANSWER, p. 395

CRITICAL THINKING The tags might prevent someone from stealing the enslaved African American and might help others identify where the enslaved person belonged in the event he or she ran away.

R Reading Skills

Identifying After students have read the text, guide a class discussion about the role of the Underground Railroad routes in assisting enslaved African Americans in their escape to freedom. **Ask:** What was the Underground Railroad? *(a network of "safe houses" owned by people who were against slavery)* **AL** **ELL** What kinds of people were helping enslaved people who had escaped? *(members of the African American community, including formerly enslaved people such as Harriet Tubman; Northerners who opposed slavery)*

W Writing Skills

Informative/Explanatory Have students write a response to the following question: **Ask:** How were both the Nat Turner Rebellion and the Underground Railroad factors that led to the Civil War? *(Possible answer: The response of white Southerners to the rebellion—passing more severe slave codes—showed how deeply entrenched their position on slavery was. The Underground Railroad made many Northerners sympathetic to the plight of enslaved people and probably showed Southerners that the North would not allow the practice of slavery to continue.)* **BL** Have student volunteers read their responses to the class.

Content Background Knowledge

Some people believed that rebellion and war were the only ways slavery could be stopped. John Brown, a famous abolitionist who was sentenced to death in 1859 for his attack on Harper's Ferry in Virginia, wrote these prophetic words shortly before his hanging: ". . . the crimes of this guilty, land: will never be purged away; but with Blood."

BIOGRAPHY

**Harriet Tubman
(c. 1820–1913)**

Harriet Tubman was born into slavery in Maryland. She escaped in 1849 and fled to Philadelphia. The following year Tubman returned to free her family. This began a career during which she made 19 trips to the slaveholding South and helped about 300 slaves escape to freedom. During the Civil War, Tubman helped the Union Army. In June 1863, she led a squad of African American soldiers on a South Carolina mission the led to the freeing of 800 enslaved African Americans. After the war, Tubman became an active women's suffragist and created the Home for the Aged in Auburn, New York. She died there in 1913.

▶ **CRITICAL THINKING**
Drawing Conclusions Why do you think Tubman was willing to risk her own freedom to help free other enslaved African Americans?

Reading **HELP**DESK (CCSS)

Underground Railroad a system of cooperation to aid and house enslaved people who had escaped
literacy the ability to read and write

Two months after the uprising began, authorities captured and hanged Turner. Still, his rebellion terrified white Southerners. White mobs killed dozens of African Americans, many of whom had nothing to do with the rebellion. Whites also passed more severe slave codes, making life under slavery even harsher.

Armed revolts such as Turner's were rare because enslaved African Americans realized they had little chance of winning. For the most part, enslaved people resisted slavery by working slowly or by pretending to be ill. Sometimes they might set fire to a plantation building or break tools. Such acts helped enslaved African Americans cope with their lack of freedom. Even if they were not free, they could strike back at the slaveholders.

Escaping Slavery

Enslaved people also resisted by running away from their owners. Often their goal was to find relatives on other plantations. Sometimes they left to escape punishment.

Less often, enslaved African Americans tried to run away to freedom in the North. Getting to the North was very difficult. Among those who succeeded were Harriet Tubman and Frederick Douglass, two African American leaders.

Most who succeeded escaped from the Upper South. A runaway might receive aid from the **Underground Railroad,** a network of "safe houses" owned by people opposed to slavery.

Moses Grandy, who did escape, spoke about the hardships runaways faced:

PRIMARY SOURCE

❝ They hide themselves during the day in the woods and swamps; at night they travel. . . . In these dangerous journeys they are guided by the north-star, for they only know that the land of freedom is in the north. ❞

—from *Narrative of the Life of Moses Grandy*

The big danger, of course, was capture. Most runaways were caught and returned to their owners. The owners punished them severely, usually by whipping.

✓ **PROGRESS CHECK**

Explaining How did the African American spirituals develop?

---

netw⊙rks *Online Teaching Options*

PRIMARY SOURCE

American Slavery As It Is

Analyzing Present the interactive primary source excerpt from *American Slavery As It Is*. Have students read the excerpt to determine why Theodore Weld and the Grimke sisters felt the need to compile firsthand accounts of slavery. **Ask:** Why do you think they felt the need to compile these narratives? *(They felt that if the stories could be told, the horrors would be enough to stop slavery.)* **BL** Have students debate whether firsthand accounts of injustice can make people change their behavior.

See page 373F for other online activities.

netw⊙rks | American Slavery As It Is

ANALYZING PRIMARY SOURCES

Theodore Weld, along with his wife Angelina Grimké and her sister Sarah Grimké, compiled American Slavery As It Is: Testimony of a Thousand Witnesses. The book was published by the American Anti-Slavery Society and illustrated the horrors of American slavery. It includes a series of first-hand accounts and personal narratives from both freedmen and white abolitionists.

❝ The scenes that I have witnessed are enough to harrow up [disturb] the soul; but could the slave be permitted to tell the story of his sufferings, which no white man, not linked with slavery, is allowed to know, the land would vomit out the horrible system, slaveholders and all, if they would not unclinch their grasp upon their defenceless victims. ❞

—from *American Slavery As It Is,* by Nehemiah Caulkins

ANSWERS, p. 396

CRITICAL THINKING She felt that the cause of freedom for enslaved African Americans was extremely important. She had been born into slavery and escaped, so she knew how it felt to be enslaved and also to be free.

✓ **PROGRESS CHECK** African American spirituals developed as a way to communicate secretly and to combine prayer with grieving about suffering.

Southern Cities

GUIDING QUESTION *What changes did urbanization introduce in the South by the mid-1800s?*

Though mostly agricultural, the South had several large cities by the mid-1800s, including Baltimore and New Orleans. The 10 largest cities in the South were either seaports or river ports. Cities located where the region's few railroads crossed paths also began to grow. These included Chattanooga, Montgomery, and Atlanta. **R1**

Free African Americans formed their own communities in Southern cities. They practiced trades and founded churches and institutions, yet their rights were limited. Most states did not allow them to move from state to state. Free African Americans did not share equally in economic and political life. **R2**

In the early 1800s, there were no statewide public school systems in the South. People who could afford to do so sent their children to private schools. By the mid-1800s, however, education was growing. North Carolina and Kentucky set up and ran public schools. **C**

The South lagged behind other parts of the country in **literacy** (LIH•tuh•ruh•see), the ability to read and write. One reason was that the South was thinly populated. A school would have to serve a wide area, and many families were unwilling or unable to send children great distances to school. Many Southerners also believed education was a private matter.

✅ **PROGRESS CHECK**

Identifying What factors made possible the growth of the few Southern cities?

LESSON 4 REVIEW (CCSS)

Review Vocabulary (Tier 3 Words)

1. Use the following words in a brief paragraph about slavery in the South. RH.6–8.4, WHST.6–8.4

  a. overseer   **b.** slave codes

  c. spiritual   **d.** Underground Railroad

2. Explain the significance of the following terms: RH.6–8.4

  a. yeoman   **b.** literacy

Answer the Guiding Questions

3. ***Discussing*** How did the family structure of enslaved African Americans help them survive life under slavery? RH.6–8.2

4. ***Explaining*** How did African American culture develop in cities in the South? RH.6–8.2

5. **NARRATIVE** From the perspective of an enslaved person, write about whether it is worth the risk to seek freedom. WHST.6–8.1, WHST.6–8.10

Lesson 4   **397**

LESSON 4 REVIEW ANSWERS

1. Possible answer: Enslaved African Americans faced difficult lives of hard work under the control of an overseer. They were subject to strict slave codes. They coped by building a culture that included spirituals. A few slaves escaped to freedom with the aid of the Underground Railroad.

2. Yeomen owned land and grew crops for their own use and for profit. Literacy—the ability to read and write—lagged in the South compared to the North.

3. Families were broken up as people were sold, but extended families of relatives and friends provided stability.

4. African Americans formed their own communities in Southern cities, where they practiced trades and founded churches and institutions.

5. Students' thoughts and discussion should explore and reflect the hopes for freedom and risks of trying to escape.

R1 Reading Skills

Discussing Ask for a volunteer to read the first paragraph on this page aloud. Then, lead a class discussion on the growth of Southern cities, including the factors that encouraged their growth. **Ask: What did the 10 largest cities in the South have in common?** *(they were all near the water and were either seaports or river ports)* Be sure students understand the importance of location on the development of a place.

R2 Reading Skills

Listing After students have read the text, discuss the lives of free African Americans in Southern cities. Have partners list the ways in which the rights of free African Americans were limited. *(They could not move from state to state. They did not share equally in economic or political life. They did not have access to public schools.)* Ask volunteers to share items from their list with the class.

C Critical Thinking Skills

Determining Cause and Effect Discuss with students that there were no statewide public school laws in the South in the early 1800s. Discuss how this lack of public education caused the South to lag behind other parts of the country in literacy. **Ask:**

* **What is literacy?** *(the ability to read and write)* **ELL**
* **What were the reasons for this lack of public education?** *(Because the population was spread out over large areas, families would have to send their children great distances to school. Also, many Southerners believed that education was a private matter.)*

Have students complete the Lesson 4 Review.

CLOSE & REFLECT

Have students summarize the ways in which African Americans in the South resisted slavery. *(working slowly, pretending to be ill, running away, armed revolt)* Have students debate which methods carried the most risk and the most reward for enslaved people.

ANSWER, p. 397

✅ **PROGRESS CHECK** These cities were located on the water—on the seacoast or on a river—or at the crossroads of railways.

Activities Answers

CHAPTER REVIEW ACTIVITY

Make a three-column chart on the board similar to the one shown below. Then lead a discussion that allows students to recall the key points of the differing economic and transportation systems that developed in the North and South during the first half of the 1800s and the different people who worked in each region at that time. A student volunteer should note these points on the chart.

Indicator	North	South
Economy	Industrial economy; new technology helps grow industry.	Agricultural economy; invention of cotton gin makes cotton production very profitable; other industry develops slowly.
Transportation	Canals and railroads are built.	Natural waterways used for shipping; fewer railroads built than in the North.
Labor	Immigrants, especially from Ireland and Germany, work in factories.	White Southerners owned farms; demand for enslaved African Americans on plantations grows due to increased demand for cotton.

REVIEW THE ENDURING UNDERSTANDING

Review the chapter's Enduring Understanding with students.

- *Economic systems shape relationships in society.*

Now pose the following questions in a class discussion to apply these to the chapter.

Ask: **How did the construction of canals and railroads affect the economic expansion of the United States?** *(Canals allowed bigger ships to move across the country, bringing passengers and goods to cities in the West. Cities along the routes of these canals and rivers expanded. Railroads also carried goods and people to faraway places, making it possible for more people to live in the western territories.)*

How did immigration change the United States between 1820–1860? *(Large numbers of immigrants, mainly from Ireland*

Write your answers on a separate piece of paper.

1 Exploring the Essential Questions WHST.6–8.2, WHST.6–8.9
INFORMATIVE/EXPLANATORY Describe how improved transportation affected trade for farmers and manufacturers in the Midwest. Use examples from the chapter to help you organize your essay.

2 21st Century Skills WHST.6–8.2, WHST.6–8.8
USING BAR GRAPHS Use this chapter and information from outside sources to collect data about the number of enslaved African Americans in the United States between 1800 and 1860. Create a series of bar graphs showing the changes in the enslaved population. Write a paragraph that explains what factors are behind the information shown in the graphs.

3 Thinking Like a Historian RH.6–8.5
UNDERSTANDING CAUSE AND EFFECT Use a diagram like this one to show and briefly describe the factors that encouraged the growing settlement of the Midwest in the early and mid-1800s.

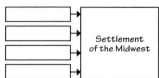

Settlement of the Midwest

4 Visual Literacy RH.6–8.7
ANALYZING POLITICAL CARTOONS Many Irish immigrants journeyed to the United States in the mid-1800s. Castle Garden was the processing facility for immigrants at that time. According to this cartoon, how do the British feel about the migration? How do you know?

A UNCLE SAM (UNITED STATES)	C JOHN BULL (BRITAIN)
B IRISH IMMIGRANTS	D BRITISH LION

---

and Germany, came to the United States, bringing their culture and language with them. Immigration led to discrimination and prejudice, as some American-born citizens feared that immigrants would take their jobs.)*

ACTIVITIES ANSWERS

Exploring the Essential Questions

1 The newly constructed canals and the growing railroad system provided farmers and manufacturers in the Midwest with a more direct and less expensive route for shipping goods to the East. This meant goods could be sold at lower prices, which benefited both sellers and buyers.

21st Century Skills

2 Students' bar graphs should provide accurate data about the number of enslaved African Americans in the United States between 1800 and 1860, and should show how that population changed over time. Their paragraphs should discuss such factors as the rise of the cotton kingdom and the subsequent increased demand for enslaved labor, as well as the growing reliance in the South and in the nation on cotton as a key export product.

Thinking Like a Historian

3 steamboats, railroads, canals, farming technology

REVIEW THE GUIDING QUESTIONS

Choose the best answer for each question.

RH.6–8.2
1 What happened in the first phase of industrialization in the North?

A. Factory workers used machinery to perform some work.

B. Manufacturers made products by dividing the tasks among the workers.

C. Waterpower and steam power were used to produce more products in less time.

D. Manufacturers built factories to bring specialized workers together.

RH.6–8.4
2 The Underground Railroad helped enslaved people who

F. wanted to smuggle enslaved people from Africa into the United States.

G. wanted to expand transportation routes in the South.

H. had escaped from their owners.

I. were too weak to walk.

RH.6–8.1
3 The American Party was once called the Know-Nothing Party because

A. party members knew nothing about the important issues.

B. party members did not support education.

C. party members responded to questions about the group by saying, "I know nothing."

D. party members were mainly Catholics who knew nothing about Protestants.

RH.6–8.1
4 Which of the following inventions were most important to the growth of cities in the interior of the United States?

F. the clipper ship and telegraph

G. the cotton gin and Underground Railroad

H. the locomotive and steamship

I. the sewing machine and the slave codes

RH.6–8.2
5 What was the main reason that the Southern economy remained largely agricultural?

A. Southerners did not know how to start industries.

B. Cotton sales were very profitable.

C. Southerners refused to work in factories.

D. There were no railroads in the South.

RH.6–8.4
6 The largest group of white people in the South were

F. yeomen.　　　　　　H. enslaved.

G. tenant farmers.　　　I. plantation owners.

399

ASSESSMENT ANSWERS

Review the Guiding Questions

1 **B** Advise students to look for clues to the sequence of events. Choice B describes specialization, so it must occur before specialized workers are brought together in factories (choice D). This sequence also eliminates choices A and C, which involve factories.

2 **H** Remind students that the Underground Railroad was not really a railroad, which eliminates choices G and I. F is incorrect because enslaved people did not smuggle enslaved people into the United States; they were trying to help enslaved people escape slavery in the South.

3 **C** Remind students that this party began as a secret, anti-Catholic society. This information eliminates choice D and suggests choice C as the likely answer.

4 **H** The cotton gin had an impact on the South, not the interior of the country. This eliminates choice G. The slave codes were not an invention, eliminating choice I. Both the locomotive and steamship, choice H, made transportation of goods and people to the interior faster.

5 **B** Remind students that under capitalism, people conduct business to make a profit. When a business is especially profitable, as cotton production was in the South, a large portion of the people in that area will go into that business and will continue to invest in it instead of investing in other types of businesses.

6 **F** Remind students that only a small portion of white Southerners owned large farms, eliminating choice I.

Visual Literacy

4 The British do not want immigrants to go; John Bull is trying to hold back an immigrant, and the lion looks sad.

Analyzing Documents

7 C Students should see that companies must have been concerned about the power of unions if they made workers agree not to join them. The contract shows that companies were worried that unions had the power to delay work and harm the company's interests.

8 H Employers held all the power by stating what they would pay for the job and requiring that employees not join labor unions. This was causing conflict.

Short Response

9 They were ignorant and easily controlled by priests.

10 that all "ignorant foreigner" Catholics would vote as priests told them to vote

Extended Response

11 Students' writing should compare conditions in the North and South, and use this comparison to support their decisions about where to settle.

DBQ ANALYZING DOCUMENTS

The following is an excerpt from a work contract from around 1830.

"We ... agree to work for such wages per week, and prices by the job, as the≈Company may see fit to pay. ...We also agree not to be engaged in any [labor union], whereby the work may be [delayed], or the company's interest in any work [harmed]."

Source: Cocheco Manufacturing Company

RH.6–8.6, RH.6–8.10

7 Making Inferences This excerpt suggests that labor unions at this time

A. were not very active.

B. did not have many members.

C. were a cause of worry for employers.

D. were not helpful to employees.

RH.6–8.2

8 Drawing Conclusions What does this contract suggest about the relationship between employees and employers in factories in the early 1800s?

F. The relationship was close.

G. Employers had deep respect for their workers.

H. There was conflict between workers and employers.

I. Employers were having trouble getting enough people to take their factory jobs.

SHORT RESPONSE

A Southern newspaper publisher wrote the following in 1856.

"Every Roman Catholic in the known world is under the absolute control of the Catholic Priesthood. ... And it is ... this power of the Priesthood to control the Catholic community, and cause a vast multitude of ignorant foreigners to vote as a unit."

Source: William G. Brownlow, *Americanism Contrasted with Foreignism, Romanism, and Bogus Democracy*

RH.6–8.6, WHST.6–8.4

9 What did the writer believe about Catholic immigrants to the United States?

RH.6–8.8, WHST.6–8.4

10 What did the writer find dangerous about Catholics being controlled by priests?

EXTENDED RESPONSE

WHST.6–8.1, WHST.6–8.9

11 Argument Take the role of an immigrant to America in 1840. Would you decide to settle in the North or the South? Describe the conditions in both sections of the country that led to your decision.

Need Extra Help?

If You've Missed Question	❶	❷	❸	❹	❺	❻	❼	❽	❾	❿	⓫
Review Lesson	1	4	2	1	3	4	2	2	2	2	1–4

---

netw⊙rks *Online Teaching Options*

More Assessment Resources

The *Assess* tab in the online Teacher Lesson Center includes resources to help students improve their test-taking skills. It also contains many project-based rubrics to help you assess students' work.

The Spirit of Reform Planner

UNDERSTANDING BY DESIGN®

Enduring Understanding

- *People, places, and ideas change over time.*

Essential Questions

- *Why do societies change?*
- *What motivates people to act?*
- *How do new ideas change the way people live?*

Predictable Misunderstandings

Students may think:

- *Religious movements had little effect on early American society.*
- *The abolition movement did not begin until just before the Civil War.*
- *All Northerners supported abolition.*
- *Men and women always had the same educational opportunities.*
- *Men and women had the same legal rights in early American society.*

Assessment Evidence

Performance Tasks:

- *Hands-On Chapter Project*

Other Evidence:

- *Interactive Graphic Organizers*
- *What Do You Know? Activity*
- *Geography and History Activity*
- *21st Century Skills Activity*
- *Primary Source Activity*
- *America's Literature Questions*
- *Written Paragraphs*
- *Lesson Reviews*
- *Online Self-Check Quizzes*
- *Chapter Activities and Assessment*

Learners will understand:

2 TIME, CONTINUITY, AND CHANGE

7. The contributions of key persons, groups, and events from the past and their influence on the present

10 CIVIC IDEALS AND PRACTICES

1. The theme of civic ideals and practices helps us to learn about and know how to work for the betterment of society

2. Concepts and ideals such as: individual dignity, liberty, justice, equality, individual rights, responsibility, majority and minority rights, and civil dissent

3. Key practices involving the rights and responsibilities of citizenship and the exercise of citizenship (e.g., respecting the rule of law and due process, voting, serving on a jury, researching issues, making informed judgments, expressing views on issues, and collaborating with others to take civic action)

5. Key documents and excerpts from key sources that define and support democratic ideals and practices (e.g., the U.S. Declaration of Independence, the U.S. Constitution, the Gettysburg Address, the Letter from Birmingham Jail; and international documents such as the Declaration of the Rights of Man and the Universal Declaration of the Rights of Children)

SUGGESTED PACING GUIDE

Introducing the Chapter . . . . 1 day	Lesson 3 . . . . 2 days
Lesson 1 . . . . 2 days	America's Literature . . . . 1 day
Lesson 2 . . . . 2 days	Chapter Wrap-Up and Assessment . . . . . . 1 day

TOTAL TIME   9 Days

Key for Using the Teacher Edition

SKILL-BASED ACTIVITIES

Types of skill activities found in the Teacher Edition.

V **Visual Skills** require students to analyze maps, graphs, charts, and photos.

R **Reading Skills** help students practice reading skills and master vocabulary.

W **Writing Skills** provide writing opportunities to help students comprehend the text.

C **Critical Thinking Skills** help students apply and extend what they have learned.

T **Technology Skills** require students to use digital tools effectively.

Letters are followed by a number when there is more than one of the same type of skill on the page.

DIFFERENTIATED INSTRUCTION

All activities are written for the on-level student unless otherwise marked with the leveled labels below.

BL **Beyond Level**
AL **Approaching Level**
ELL **English Language Learners**

All students benefit from activities that utilize different learning styles. Many activities are marked as below when a particular learning style is highlighted.

Intrapersonal	Naturalist
Logical/Mathematical	Kinesthetic
Visual/Spatial	Auditory/Musical
Verbal/Linguistic	Interpersonal

CHAPTER OPENER PLANNER

Students will know:

- the influence of various individuals on social and political developments in the United States.
- the growth of social reform movements between 1820 and 1860.
- the development of the abolitionist movement and its impact.
- what the women's movement fought for and what the results were.

Students will be able to:

- **explain** how the Second Great Awakening led to an interest in social reform.
- **identify and analyze** major reform movements and who led them.
- **identify** transcendentalist authors and describe their work.
- **trace** the development of the abolitionist movement.
- **identify** abolitionist leaders and their actions.
- **contrast** the arguments for and against abolition.
- **analyze** the impact of the Seneca Falls Convention on the women's reform movement.
- **identify and analyze** changes in education for women.
- **evaluate** the result of how women's rights in marriage, family, and careers expanded.

UNDERSTANDING
BY DESIGN™

☑ *Print Teaching Options*

V Visual Skills

☐ **P. 402** Students analyze a map of the Underground Railroad and slave regions of the United States.

☐ **P. 403** Students analyze images on a time line to preview events between 1820 and 1860 that will be covered in the chapter.

☑ *Online Teaching Options*

V Visual Skills

☐ **MAP** **Slavery in the United States**—Students view a color-coded map representing slaveholding and non-slaveholding regions in the United States.

☐ **TIME LINE** **United States 1820 to 1860**—Students learn about key events during this time period.

☐ **WORLD ATLAS** Students can use this interactive map to identify regions of the world, learn about individual countries, locate political boundaries, measure distances, and much more.

☑ *Printable Digital Worksheets*

R Reading Skills

☐ **GRAPHIC NOVEL** *Seeing the Light*—This novel tells the story of a husband and wife who are just average Americans struggling with the decision to help escaped African Americans on the Underground Railroad.

Project-Based Learning

Hands-On Chapter Project

Reform Speech Reenactment
To identify how certain leaders changed the way people thought, students will research an inspiring speech by an important abolitionist, such as Sojourner Truth, Frederick Douglass, William Lloyd Garrison, or Harriet Tubman. They will present a reenactment of the speech, using their own words.

Technology Extension

Working With Word Clouds
- Find an additional activity online that incorporates technology for this project.
- Visit the EdTechTeacher Web sites (included in the Technology Extension for this chapter) for more links, tutorials, and other resources.

Print Resources

ANCILLARY RESOURCES
These ancillaries are available for every chapter and lesson.

- **Reading Essentials and Study Guide Workbook** **AL** **ELL**
- **Chapter Tests and Lesson Quizzes Blackline Masters**

PRINTABLE DIGITAL WORKSHEETS
These printable digital worksheets are available for every chapter and lesson.

- **Hands-On Chapter Projects**
- **What Do You Know? activities**
- **Chapter Summaries (English and Spanish)**
- **Vocabulary Builder activities**
- **Guided Reading activities**

More Media Resources

SUGGESTED VIDEOS
Watch clips of films about the reform era, such as *Underground Railroad (History Channel)* and *Not for Ourselves Alone: The Story of Elizabeth Cady Stanton & Susan B. Anthony (PBS)*.

- **Ask:** How do documentary films help you understand a historical era?

(NOTE: Preview clips for age-appropriateness.)

SUGGESTED READING
Grade 6 reading level:
- *Breaking the Chains: The Crusade of Dorothea Lynde Dix,* by Penny Coleman

Grade 7 reading level:
- *Sojourner Truth: Speaking Up for Freedom (Voices for Freedom: Abolitionist Heroes),* by Geoffrey M. Horn

Grade 8 reading level:
- *Elizabeth Blackwell: The First Woman Doctor,* by Frances Sabin

SOCIAL REFORM

Students will know:
- the influence of various individuals on social and political developments in the United States.
- the growth of social reform movements between 1820 and 1860.

Students will be able to:
- *explain* how the Second Great Awakening led to an interest in social reform.
- *identify and analyze* major reform movements and who led them.
- *identify* transcendentalist authors and describe their work.

UNDERSTANDING
BY DESIGN®

☑ *Print Teaching Options*

V Visual Skills

☐ **P. 406** Students analyze a painting of a classroom and compare it with their own. **Visual/Spatial**

R Reading Skills

☐ **P. 404** Students discuss the importance of revival to spreading religious interest in the 1800s.

☐ **P. 405** Students discuss aspects of the temperance movement. **AL ELL**

☐ **P. 406** Students identify the reasons for education reform. **AL**

☐ **P. 406** Students assess the impact of various social reformers. **AL ELL**

W Writing Skills

☐ **P. 405** Students write a paragraph explaining how religious revivals led to reforms. **Verbal/Linguistic**

C Critical Thinking Skills

☐ **P. 404** Students answer questions about the *Autobiography of Rev. James B. Finley.*

☐ **P. 407** Students synthesize information about American thinking in the 1800s. **BL**

☑ *Online Teaching Options*

V Visual Skills

☐ **VIDEO** **Romanticism in Art and Literature**—Students examine the effects of romanticism on literature and art, exemplified in paintings by the Hudson River School and the writings of Thoreau.

☐ **IMAGE** **The American School for the Deaf**—Students examine the history of this school founded in Hartford, Connecticut.

R Reading Skills

☐ **GRAPHIC ORGANIZER** **Taking Notes:** *Identifying:* **Reformers' Contributions**—Students identify the contributions of Gallaudet and Dix.

☐ **BIOGRAPHY** **Dorothea Dix**—Students read a biography of this woman who spearheaded reforms in the treatment of the mentally ill.

C Critical Thinking Skills

☐ **POLITICAL CARTOON** **Temperance**—Students analyze a political cartoon that supported the temperance movement.

☐ **PRIMARY SOURCE** **Lyman Beecher**—Students analyze an excerpt from a speech by Beecher in which he supports the abolition of slavery.

T Technology Skills

☐ **SELF-CHECK QUIZ** **Lesson 1**—Students receive instant feedback on their mastery of lesson content.

☑ *Printable Digital Worksheets*

C Critical Thinking Skills

☐ **WORKSHEET** **Geography and History Activity: Understanding Region: Religion and Reform**—Students analyze the effect on society of the Second Great Awakening, which stressed taking moral action against wrongdoing.

THE ABOLITIONISTS

Students will know:
- the influence of various individuals on social and political developments in the United States.
- the development of the abolitionist movement and its impact.

Students will be able to:
- **trace** the development of the abolitionist movement.
- **identify** abolitionist leaders and their actions.
- **contrast** the arguments for and against abolition.

UNDERSTANDING
BY DESIGN®

☑ *Print Teaching Options*

V Visual Skills

☐ **P. 410** Students create graphic organizers to list the five abolitionists mentioned. **AL** **ELL** Visual/Spatial

R Reading Skills

☐ **P. 408** Students observe a presentation on the meaning, etymology, and synonyms for the word *abolitionist*.

☐ **P. 409** Students discuss the use of farm labor in the South. **BL** **ELL** Verbal/Linguistic

☐ **P. 411** Students describe the efforts of African American abolitionists.

☐ **P. 412** Students summarize what they know about the Underground Railroad. **AL** **ELL**

☐ **P. 413** Students discuss the reasons for Northern opposition to abolition.

W Writing Skills

☐ **P. 411** Students study a painting and write a description about it. **BL** Verbal/Linguistic

C Critical Thinking Skills

☐ **P. 408** Students contrast the views about slavery between the Northern and Southern states. **BL**

☐ **P. 409** Students discuss the establishment of the American Colonization Society.

☐ **P. 410** Students list the accomplishments of abolitionists and make inferences about the growth of the abolitionist movement between 1832 and 1838. **BL** **ELL**

☐ **P. 413** Students make connections between Senator Hammond's speech and other opinions of those who supported slavery.

T Technology Skills

☐ **P. 412** Students map the Underground Railroad using the Internet and art-related software. Visual/Spatial

☐ **P. 414** Students research three primary source examples of both abolitionist and anti-abolitionist arguments.

☑ *Online Teaching Options*

V Visual Skills

☐ **VIDEO** **Uncle Tom's Cabin**—Students view a video that explains how the Fugitive Slave Law inspired Harriet Beecher Stowe to write a book that became a literary phenomenon.

☐ **MAP** **Liberia**—Students locate this African nation.

☐ **MAP** **Slavery in the United States**—Students view the routes taken by people fleeing slavery.

☐ **IMAGE** **Freedom's Journal**—Students view a page from the first newspaper owned and operated by African Americans in the United States.

R Reading Skills

☐ **GRAPHIC ORGANIZER** **Taking Notes: *Identifying*: Abolitionists**—Students identify five abolitionists and their roles in the movement.

☐ **BIOGRAPHY** **Elijah Lovejoy**—Students read of the life and death of this newspaper editor who wrote against slavery.

☐ **BIOGRAPHY** **Sojourner Truth**—Students read a biography of this formerly enslaved woman who traveled the country calling for an end to slavery.

C Critical Thinking Skills

☐ **WHITEBOARD ACTIVITY** **The Life of Frederick Douglass**—Students sequence events in Douglass's life.

☐ **GRAPH** **Slavery in the United States**—Students trace the growth in the number of enslaved people in the United States between 1800 and 1860.

☐ **PRIMARY SOURCE** **Frederick Douglass**—Students analyze an excerpt from the preface to Douglass's book.

T Technology Skills

☐ **SELF-CHECK QUIZ** **Lesson 2**—Students receive instant feedback on their mastery of lesson content.

Students will know:

- the influence of various individuals on social and political developments in the United States.
- what the women's movement fought for and what the results were.

Students will be able to:

- **analyze** the impact of the Seneca Falls Convention on the women's reform movement.
- **identify and analyze** changes in education for women.
- **evaluate** the result of how women's rights in marriage, family, and careers expanded.

UNDERSTANDING
BY DESIGN®

☑ *Print Teaching Options*

V Visual Skills

☐ **P. 416** Students conduct research on Mary Lyon and Maria Mitchell and create time lines of their lives. **Visual/Spatial**

R Reading Skills

☐ **P. 415** Students analyze the significance of the Seneca Falls Convention. **AL**

☐ **P. 418** Students discuss the educational goals of Emma Willard. **AL**

W Writing Skills

☐ **P. 417** Students write a one-page essay about the Women's Rights Convention. **Verbal/Linguistic**

C Critical Thinking Skills

☐ **P. 416** Students read aloud from the Declaration of Sentiments and evaluate which statement would influence them to support or oppose it. **AL** **ELL** **BL** **Auditory/Musical**

☐ **P. 417** Students infer why Susan B. Anthony might think that coeducation would be important if women had the right to vote. **BL**

☐ **P. 418** Students make inferences about the ideas of early champions of women's education.

☐ **P. 419** Students analyze the effect the women's movement had on marriage and family laws.

☐ **P. 419** Students make generalizations about how Elizabeth Blackwell's success as a doctor made it easier for other women to become doctors.

T Technology Skills

☐ **P. 417** Students conduct searches on the Internet for images of Elizabeth Cady Stanton and Susan B. Anthony. **Visual/Spatial**

☐ **P. 418** Students use Google Maps Street View to see if they can locate a building from a painting. **Interpersonal Visual/Spatial Logical/Mathematical**

☑ *Online Teaching Options*

V Visual Skills

☐ **VIDEO** **Elizabeth Cady Stanton and Susan B. Anthony**—Students view a video that describes how these two women argued for women's rights and the abolition of slavery.

R Reading Skills

☐ **GRAPHIC ORGANIZER** **Taking Notes:** *Summarizing:* **Individual Contributions to Women's Rights**—Students summarize the contributions of three women reformers.

C Critical Thinking Skills

☐ **BIOGRAPHY** **Maria Mitchell**—Students reflect on the accomplishments of the first professional female astronomer in the United States.

☐ **BIOGRAPHY** **Mary Lyon**—Students consider the accomplishments of this teacher who founded Mount Holyoke Female Seminary.

T Technology Skills

☐ **SELF-CHECK QUIZ** **Lesson 3**—Students receive instant feedback on their mastery of lesson content.

☑ *Printable Digital Worksheets*

W Writing Skills

☐ **WORKSHEET** **21st Century Skills Activity: Critical Thinking and Problem Solving: Drawing Inferences and Conclusions**—Students write about the effects of Thoreau's work on later leaders.

INTERVENTION AND REMEDIATION STRATEGIES

LESSON 1 Social Reform

Reading and Comprehension

Direct students to create a list of all the words in boldface in the lesson. Have students identify each word's basic etymology. Students should explain how this knowledge will help them remember the meaning of each word.

Text Evidence

Direct students to identify three important individuals discussed in the lesson. For each, have students construct sentences that start "I believe . . ." and accurately convey each historical figure's point of view.

LESSON 2 The Abolitionists

Reading and Comprehension

Have students ask and answer six questions about abolitionists using the question words (*who, what, where, when, why,* and *how*).

Text Evidence

Have students write alternate captions for the images in the lesson. Their captions should be fact-based, relying on information from the text.

LESSON 3 The Women's Movement

Reading and Comprehension

Ask students to make lists that summarize the most important facts about the Seneca Falls Convention.

Text Evidence

Challenge students to write an imaginary but history-based dialogue between Elizabeth Cady Stanton and Susan B. Anthony.

Online Resources

Approaching Level Reader

Use this online lower-level text that corresponds directly to the text in the Student Edition. It includes a Spanish version.

Guided Reading Activities

This resource uses graphic organizers and guiding questions to help students with comprehension.

What Do You Know?

Use these worksheets to pre-assess student's background knowledge before they study the chapter.

Reading Essentials and Study Guide Workbook

This resource offers writing and reading activities for the approaching-level student. Also available in Spanish.

Self-Check Quizzes

This online assessment tool provides instant feedback for students to check their progress.

The Spirit of Reform

1820–1860

ESSENTIAL QUESTIONS • Why do societies change?
• What motivates people to act? • How do new ideas change the way people live?

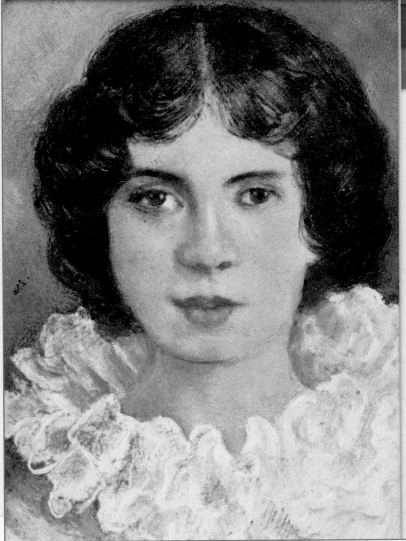

◄ *Emily Dickinson was a brilliant poet of the mid-1800s.*

The Granger Collection, NYC

401

networks

There's More Online about the issues that American reformers tackled in the mid-1800s.

CHAPTER 15

The Story Matters . . .

Young Emily Dickinson excels at school, especially in Latin, science, and writing. Dickinson even takes the then-unusual step of attending college for a year, but she finds its strict rules unsuited for her creative energy.

As an adult, she spends less and less time in public. After the age of 40, she dresses only in white. She does not travel and chooses not to meet most visitors. She spends much of her time writing, eventually producing 1,800 brilliant gems of poetry. She is a literary pioneer—though few people at the time know it. Only 10 of her poems ever appear in print during her lifetime. Only in death is she recognized among the era's many women of achievement.

ENGAGE

Bellringer Lead a class discussion about the idea of social change. Elicit examples from students, and ask them to evaluate their own time. **Ask: Do you think we are living through a time of great social change? Why or why not?** *(Answers will vary but should be explained.)* **Do you think it's more interesting to learn about times when there was a lot of change happening or more peaceful times? Why?** *(Answers will vary.)* Explain that they are about to read about an exciting period of American history when life changed for lots of people.

Making Connections

Ask a volunteer to read "The Story Matters . . ." aloud. Then discuss the educational opportunities Dickinson had and whether she might have continued in college if more opportunities had been available to her. **Ask:**

- **Why do you think few of her poems were published while she was alive?** *(Students might note her shyness and that it may have been difficult to get a woman's poems published.)*
- **How might Dickinson's life and poetry have been changed if she had continued her education, or would it have changed? For example, would her poems have been as famous or would she have written as many poems? Why or why not?** *(Answers will vary, but any answer well supported by good reasons is acceptable.)* Tell the class that in this chapter they will learn more about how women worked to increase their opportunities for education and careers, and to expand their legal rights. Then tell students that this chapter is about reform and change.
- **Do you know anyone who tried to change a situation they thought was unfair? How did they do it?** *(Answers will depend on student experiences.)*

Letter from the Author

Dear American History Teacher,

The four decades preceding the Civil War were an energetic age for American reformers. These reformers touched every area of American society, and many were driven by strong moral and religious convictions. The abolitionist movement overshadowed all reform movements, as men and women dedicated their lives to abolishing slavery. Other reformers made people aware of the treatment of the mentally challenged, developed a new system to teach those with hearing impairments, and worked to improve the plight of women. This era also witnessed strides in the education of women.

Albert S. Broussard

TEACH & ASSESS

Step Into the Place

V1 Visual Skills

Analyzing Maps Direct students to the map of the Underground Railroad and slave regions of the United States. Ask students to recall examples of how slavery affected African Americans and of the views that people in the North and South had about the institution of slavery. Ask students if they recall the names of any people who were involved in the abolition movement. Have students select a state from the map and read its name aloud. Then ask them if the state was originally a slave or free state. Have students explain how this status might have affected the lives of African Americans living or traveling there. Then as a class, discuss the Map Focus questions.

Content Background Knowledge

Nobody knows exactly how many slaves escaped along the routes of the Underground Railroad shown on this map. The number was never high enough to threaten slavery as an economic institution, but it was certainly high enough to cause widespread consternation in the South. Historians estimate the number of escapees as anywhere from a few hundred to one thousand per year.

Place and Time: United States 1820 to 1860

During this period, many men and women, including whites and African Americans, worked to abolish slavery. Other people wanted to reform laws and customs that limited women's choices and created harsh conditions for the poor and people with disabilities.

Step Into the Place

MAP FOCUS One of the main reforms people sought in the mid-1800s was the abolition of slavery. Reformers also tried to help enslaved people escape to freedom in the North or outside the country. Some of the routes to freedom are noted on the map.

1 **LOCATION** On the map, locate the cities of Toledo, Cleveland, and Buffalo. Why do you think these cities became important points for people trying to escape slavery? RH.6–8.7

2 **CRITICAL THINKING**
   Speculating Why do you think some enslaved people traveled to Canada instead of stopping when they reached a free Northern state? RH.6–8.7

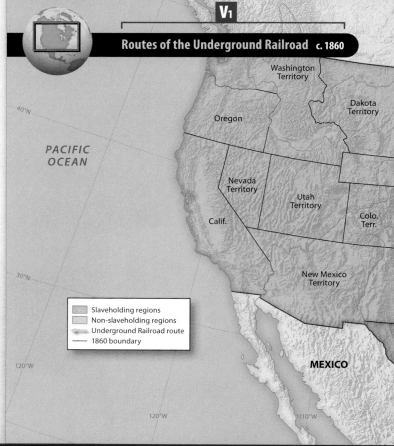

V1

Routes of the Underground Railroad c. 1860

Washington Territory
Dakota Territory
Oregon
PACIFIC OCEAN
Nevada Territory
Utah Territory
Calif.
Colo. Terr.
New Mexico Territory
MEXICO

40°N
30°N
120°W
120°W
110°W

- Slaveholding regions
- Non-slaveholding regions
- Underground Railroad route
- 1860 boundary

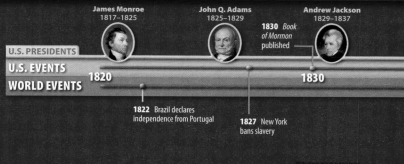

Step Into the Time

V2 **TIME LINE** Look at the time line. Who was president when New York banned slavery? RH.6–8.5, RH.6–8.7

U.S. PRESIDENTS
U.S. EVENTS
WORLD EVENTS

James Monroe 1817–1825
John Q. Adams 1825–1829
Andrew Jackson 1829–1837

1830 *Book of Mormon published*

1820
1830

1822 Brazil declares independence from Portugal
1827 New York bans slavery

402   *The Spirit of Reform*

Project-Based Learning ✋

Hands-On Chapter Project

Reform Speech Reenactment

To identify how certain leaders changed the way people thought, students will research a speech and reenact a scene about it in their own words. Students will read about the topic in their textbook and select an inspiring speech by an important abolitionist, such as Sojourner Truth, Frederick Douglass, William Lloyd Garrison, or Harriet Tubman. They will then research the reformer and his or her speech, and find photos or other visuals to enhance their presentation. They will organize their research, plan the presentation (including any costumes or props they plan to include), and present their reenactment.

Technology Extension

Working With Word Clouds

Word clouds introduce a unique element to your classroom, can be created quickly, and require only Internet access. Put simply, word cloud creation tools highlight the most frequently used words in a text or Web site and present them in various sizes, colors, and fonts. The largest words in a word cloud represent the most commonly used words in the original text source. Have students prepare word clouds using the text from the speech they chose for reenactment.

edtechteacher
21st Century Learning

ANSWERS, p. 402

Step Into the Place

1. These cities are close to Canada, and Canada was a final destination for enslaved people.

2. CRITICAL THINKING They would have less chance of being captured if they went all the way to Canada.

Step Into the Time
John Quincy Adams

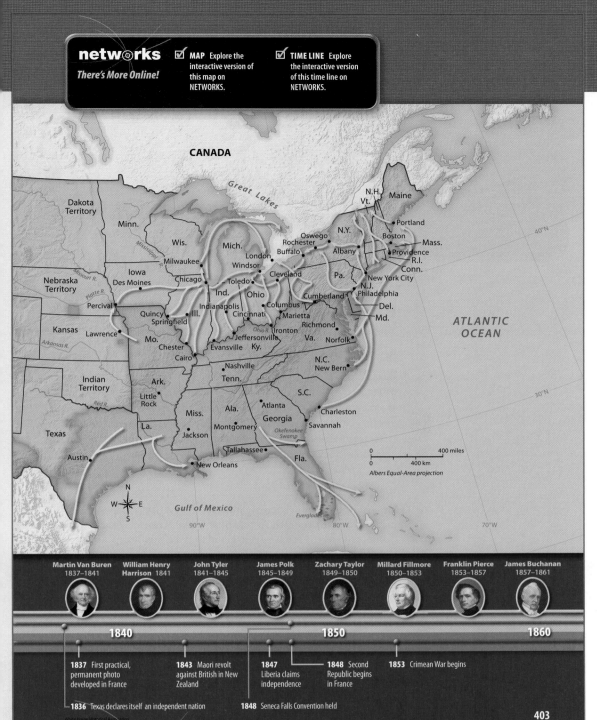

CANADA

Dakota Territory

Minn.

Wis.

Mich.

N.H.
Vt.
Maine

Iowa
Des Moines

Nebraska Territory

Milwaukee

London
Windsor

Oswego
Rochester
Buffalo

N.Y.

Portland

Boston
Mass.
Providence
R.I.
Conn.

40°N

Chicago

Toledo

Cleveland

Pa.

Albany

Percival

Ind.

Ohio

New York City
N.J.
Philadelphia

Kansas

Quincy
Springfield
Ill.

Indianapolis
Columbus

Cincinnati
Marietta

Cumberland

Del.
Md.

ATLANTIC
OCEAN

Lawrence

Mo.
Chester

Jeffersonville
Evansville
Ky.
Ohio R.
Ironton

Richmond
Va.
Norfolk

Cairo

Nashville
Tenn.

N.C.
New Bern

Indian Territory

Ark.
Little Rock

Red R.

Miss.
Ala.

S.C.

Atlanta
Georgia

Charleston
Savannah

30°N

Texas

La.
Jackson

Montgomery

Okefenokee Swamp

Austin

Tallahassee
Fla.

New Orleans

0   400 miles
0   400 km
Albers Equal-Area projection

N
W   E
S

Gulf of Mexico

Everglades

90°W   80°W   70°W

Great Lakes

Mississippi R.

Missouri R.

Platte R.

Arkansas R.

| Martin Van Buren 1837–1841 | William Henry Harrison 1841 | John Tyler 1841–1845 | James Polk 1845–1849 | Zachary Taylor 1849–1850 | Millard Fillmore 1850–1853 | Franklin Pierce 1853–1857 | James Buchanan 1857–1861 |

1840   1850   1860

1837 First practical, permanent photo developed in France

1843 Maori revolt against British in New Zealand

1847 Liberia claims independence

1848 Second Republic begins in France

1853 Crimean War begins

1836 Texas declares itself an independent nation

1848 Seneca Falls Convention held

White House Historical Association

403

Step Into the Time

V₂ Visual Skills

Analyzing Time Lines Use the images on the time line to preview some of the events covered in the chapter. Have students review the time line for the chapter. Note that they will be studying events from 1820 to 1860. **Ask: Based on the information listed in the time line for 1827, what can you infer about views toward slavery in the 1800s?** *(Views were changing. At least one state had changed its laws to ban slavery after previously allowing it.)*

Content Background Knowledge

The United States changed a great deal between 1820 and 1860:

- In 1820, the population was 9.6 million. By 1860, it had more than tripled, to 31.4 million.

- In 1820, there were 61 places with populations greater than 2,500. In 1860, there were 392.

- In 1820, only about 7 percent of Americans lived in cities. By 1860, almost 20 percent did.

CLOSE & REFLECT

Call on individual students to state aloud what they anticipate the main ideas of this chapter will be.

---

networks
There's More Online!

☑ **MAP** Explore the interactive version of this map on NETWORKS.

☑ **TIME LINE** Explore the interactive version of this time line on NETWORKS.

networks *Online Teaching Options*

WORKSHEET

What Do You Know? Activity: The Spirit of Reform

Assessing Have students complete the What Do You Know? activity before they study the chapter. Direct students to categorize each term to the best of their knowledge. If they are unsure, they should make educated guesses or logical inferences.

After students complete the chapter, have them complete the activity again to see if their knowledge has grown.

See page 401B for other online activities.

ENGAGE

Bellringer Have students brainstorm a list of people they know who work to help people and the types of help that they provide. List them in a chart, and help students identify with the values or beliefs that may motivate them. Discuss what values or beliefs these people may have in common. Tell students that some social reformers of the 1800s had strong religious views. **Ask: How do you think these views might influence their willingness to help others?** *(Students might recognize that most major religions value helping others.)* Tell students that this lesson will cover reformers of the 1800s. They will find out if their predictions are correct.

TEACH & ASSESS

C Critical Thinking Skills

Analyzing Primary Sources Read, or have a student read, the primary source to the class. **Ask: What is the source of this quotation?** *(the* Autobiography of Rev. James B. Finley*)* **What do you think the rest of his book would be like?** *(Answers will vary. The rest is probably about his various experiences as a religious leader in 19th-century America.)*

R Reading Skills

Discussing After students have read the text, discuss with them the importance of a revival to spreading religious interest in the 1800s. **Ask: Why was this wave of religious interest called the Second Great Awakening?** *(The First Great Awakening spread in the mid-1700s.)*

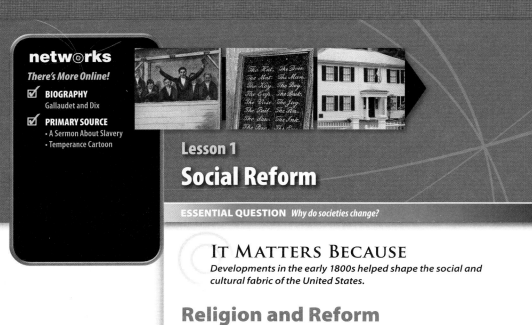

net works
There's More Online!
☑ **BIOGRAPHY**
Gallaudet and Dix
☑ **PRIMARY SOURCE**
• A Sermon About Slavery
• Temperance Cartoon

Lesson 1
Social Reform

ESSENTIAL QUESTION *Why do societies change?*

IT MATTERS BECAUSE
Developments in the early 1800s helped shape the social and cultural fabric of the United States.

Religion and Reform

GUIDING QUESTION *What was the effect of the Second Great Awakening?*

Reverend James B. Finley described the scene this way:

> **PRIMARY SOURCE**
>
> ❝ The noise was like the roar of Niagara [Falls]. The vast sea of human beings seemed to be agitated as if by a storm. ... Some of the people were singing, others praying, some crying for mercy. ... While witnessing these scenes, a peculiarly strange sensation, such as I had never felt before, came over me. My heart beat tumultuously [violently], my knees trembled, my lip quivered, and I felt as though I must fall to the ground. ❞
>
> —from *Autobiography of Rev. James B. Finley*

Finley was describing an early nineteenth-century religious meeting called a **revival.** At this time, people traveled great distances to hear preachers speak and to pray, sing, weep, and shout. This wave of religious interest—known as the Second Great Awakening—stirred the nation. The first Great Awakening had spread through the colonies in the mid-1700s.

Also at this time, a new spirit of reform took hold in the United States. This spirit brought changes to American religion, education, and literature. Some reformers sought to improve society by forming

Reading HELP DESK (CCSS)

Taking Notes: *Identifying* RH.6–8.1
As you read, use a diagram like this one to identify the reformers' contributions.

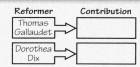

Reformer		Contribution
Thomas Gallaudet	→	
Dorothea Dix	→	

Content Vocabulary (Tier 3 Words)
• revival   • normal school
• utopia   • civil disobedience
• temperance

404 *The Spirit of Reform*

---

net works *Online Teaching Options*

(l) The Granger Collection, NYC;
(c) The Granger Collection, NYC;
(r) David Lyons/Alamy

VIDEO

Romanticism in Art and Literature

Explaining Explain that many people today see nature as a source of inspiration and therefore feel the need to take responsibility for it, but that people have not always felt this way. Show the video about romanticism in art. **Ask: How might the spirit of reform in the 1800s have changed people's views about their relationship to nature?** *(Students might recognize that attitudes of reform may instill in people a sense of respect for nature.)* Explain that the social reform movement affected America's literature and art. **Visual/Spatial**

See page 401C for other online activities.

ANSWER, p. 404

TAKING NOTES: Gallaudet: developed a method to educate people who were hearing impaired, opened the Hartford School for the Deaf; **Dix:** educated the public about poor conditions for prisoners and the mentally ill

utopias (yu·TOH·pee·uhs)—communities based on a vision of the perfect society. Most of these communities did not last. A few groups, such as the Mormons, did form lasting communities.

The Impact of Religion

Attending revivals often made men and women eager to reform their own lives and the world. Some people became involved in missionary work or social reform movements. Among those movements was the push to ban alcohol.

Connecticut minister Lyman Beecher was a leader of this movement. He wanted to protect society from "rum-selling, tippling folk, infidels, and ruff-scuff." Beecher and other reformers called for **temperance**, or drinking little or no alcohol. They used **lectures**, pamphlets, and revival-style rallies to warn people of the dangers of liquor.

The temperance movement persuaded Maine and some other states to outlaw the manufacture and sale of alcohol. States later repealed most of these laws.

Changing Education

Reformers also wanted to improve education. Most schools had little money, and many teachers lacked training. Some people opposed the idea of compulsory, or required, education.

Religious revivals could attract thousands of people for days of prayers and song.

▶ CRITICAL THINKING
Analyzing Images Who are the people standing and sitting on the platform?

revival religious meeting
utopia community based on a vision of the perfect society

temperance drinking little or no alcohol

Academic Vocabulary (Tier 2 Words)

lecture speech meant to provide information, similar to what a teacher presents

Lesson 1   **405**

The Granger Collection, NYC

W Writing Skills

Informative/Explanatory Discuss with students the relationship between religious revival and the spirit of reform that occurred during this period. Have students write a paragraph explaining how religious revivals led to reforms. Ask volunteers to share their explanations. **Verbal/Linguistic**

R Reading Skills

Identifying Direct students to read the section titled "The Impact of Religion." Lead students in a discussion about the temperance movement. **Ask:** Who was Lyman Beecher? *(a Connecticut minister who was the leader of the temperance movement)* Explain to students that Beecher supported other causes, such as abolition.

Point out that the word *temper* can mean "control" or "moderate." **Ask:** How did temperance reformers want to change society? *(They wanted people to control or moderate the consumption of alcohol.)* **AL** **ELL**

PRIMARY SOURCE

Lyman Beecher

Identifying Central Issues Display the primary source excerpt from Lyman Beecher's lecture on the abolition of slavery. Have a volunteer read it aloud. **Ask:** Why would listeners be inspired by it? *(Beecher was a compelling speaker.)* Encourage students to use the Internet to find a Beecher temperance sermon. **BL**

See page 401C for other online activities.

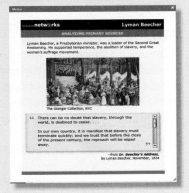

ANSWER, p. 405

CRITICAL THINKING preachers, song leaders, and revival leaders

R1 Reading Skills

Identifying Direct students to read the section on education reform. Discuss with students the reasons for education reform. **Ask: What did Horace Mann do to change education?** *(persuaded Massachusetts to start schools for teacher training)* **Which group did Samuel Gridley Howe help?** *(Howe helped people who were visually impaired by heading the Perkins Institute for the Blind.)* **AL**

V Visual Skills

Analyzing Visuals Have students study the classroom shown in the painting and then look around their own classroom. **Ask: What is somewhat similar? What is very different?** *(Answers will vary.)* **Visual/Spatial**

R2 Reading Skills

Discussing After students have read the section on reform, ask them to list each of the reformers mentioned. After each name, ask students to summarize the reforms each individual enacted. Finally, have students assess the impact of each reform on today's society. Help students see the lasting contributions of these reforms by examining evidence of their legacies in today's society. **AL ELL**

In addition, some groups faced barriers to schooling. Parents often kept girls at home. They thought someone who was likely to become a wife and mother did not need much education. Many schools also denied African Americans the right to attend.

Massachusetts lawyer Horace Mann was a leader of educational reform. He believed education was a key to wealth and economic opportunity for all. Partly because of his efforts, in 1839 Massachusetts founded the nation's first state-supported **normal school**—a school for training high school graduates to become teachers. Other states soon adopted Mann's reforms.

New colleges and universities opened their doors during the age of reform. Most of them admitted only white men, but other groups also began winning access to higher education. Oberlin College of Ohio, for example, was founded in 1833. The college admitted both women and African Americans.

Helping People with Disabilities

Reformers also focused on teaching people with disabilities. Thomas Gallaudet (ga•luh•DEHT) developed a method to teach those with hearing impairments. He opened the Hartford School for the Deaf in Connecticut in 1817. At that same time, Samuel Gridley Howe was helping people with vision impairments. He printed books using an alphabet created by Louis Braille, which used raised letters a person could "read" with his or her fingers. Howe headed the Perkins Institute, a school for the visually impaired in Boston.

Schoolteacher Dorothea Dix began visiting prisons in 1841. She found some prisoners chained to the walls with little or no clothing, often in unheated cells. Dix also learned that some inmates were guilty of no crime. Instead, they were suffering from mental illnesses. Dix made it her life's work to educate the public about the poor conditions for prisoners and the mentally ill.

This picture shows students with hearing impairments receiving specialized instruction. The education of people with disabilities greatly advanced during the early and mid-1800s.

The Granger Collection, NYC

✓ **PROGRESS CHECK**

Describing How did Samuel Howe help people with vision impairments?

Reading HELPDESK (CCSS)

normal school state-supported school for training high school graduates to become teachers

civil disobedience refusing to obey laws considered unjust

Academic Vocabulary (Tier 2 Words)

author writer of books, articles, or other written works

---

netw⊚rks   *Online Teaching Options*

BIOGRAPHY

Dorothea Dix

Discussing Use the interactive image to discuss the contributions of Dorothea Dix to the improvement of prisons and treatment for the mentally ill. **Ask: How did she discover this problem?** *(She visited prisons and witnessed the problems.)* **Interpersonal**

See page 401C for other online activities.

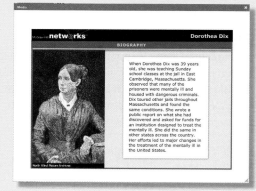

netw⊚rks   Dorothea Dix
BIOGRAPHY

When Dorothea Dix was 39 years old, she was teaching Sunday school classes at the jail in East Cambridge, Massachusetts. She observed that many of the prisoners were mentally ill and housed with dangerous criminals. Dix toured other jails throughout Massachusetts and found the same conditions. She wrote a public report on what she had discovered and asked for funds for an institution designed to treat the mentally ill. She did the same in other states across the country. Her efforts led to major changes in the treatment of the mentally ill in the United States.

North Wind Picture Archives

ANSWER, p. 406

✓ **PROGRESS CHECK** Howe developed a system of raised letters that people with sight impairments could read with their fingers.

Culture Changes

GUIDING QUESTION *What type of American literature emerged in the 1820s?*

Art and literature of the time reflected the changes in society and culture. American **authors** and artists developed their own style and explored American themes.

Writers such as Margaret Fuller, Ralph Waldo Emerson, and Henry David Thoreau stressed the relationship between humans and nature and the importance of the individual conscience. This literary movement was known as Transcendentalism. In his works, Emerson urged people to listen to the inner voice of conscience and to overcome prejudice. Thoreau practiced **civil disobedience** (dihs•uh•BEE•dee•uhns)—refusal to obey laws he found unjust. For example, Thoreau went to jail in 1846 rather than pay a tax to support the Mexican American War.

In poetry, Henry Wadsworth Longfellow wrote narrative, or story, poems such as the *Song of Hiawatha*. Walt Whitman captured the new American spirit and confidence in his *Leaves of Grass*. Emily Dickinson wrote hundreds of simple, deeply personal poems, many of which celebrated the natural world.

American artists also explored American topics and developed a purely American style. Beginning in the 1820s, a group of landscape painters known as the Hudson River School focused on scenes of the Hudson River Valley. Print-makers Nathaniel Currier and James Merritt Ives created popular prints that celebrated holidays, sporting events, and rural life.

Ralph Waldo Emerson's house in Concord, Massachusetts, was a gathering place for many of the leaders of the Transcendentalist movement.

David Lyons/Alamy

☑ **PROGRESS CHECK**

Describing How did the spirit of reform influence American authors?

LESSON 1 REVIEW

Review Vocabulary (Tier 3 Words)

1. Examine the three terms below. Then write a sentence or two explaining how these terms were related to each other during the period of social reform. RH.6–8.4

   a. revival   b. utopia   c. temperance

Answer the Guiding Questions

2. *Analyzing* What was the relationship between the Second Great Awakening and the reform movements of the early 1800s? RH.6–8.1

3. *Explaining* What themes did the transcendentalists focus on in their writings? RH.6–8.2

4. *Comparing and Contrasting* How was the work of Dorothea Dix similar to that of Thomas Gallaudet? How was it different? RH.6–8.5

5. **ARGUMENT** Create a brochure about the newly established Oberlin College to send to potential students. Explain why the college differs from others, and describe the advantages of this college experience. WHST.6–8.2, WHST.6–8.9

Lesson 1   **407**

LESSON 1 REVIEW ANSWERS

1. Sample answer: Many reformers attended revivals where religious beliefs were strong. Some tried to create utopias, or perfect societies. Others went to lectures about temperance, or refusing alcohol.

2. The Second Great Awakening encouraged people to examine the need for reform in themselves and in society.

3. The themes included the relationship between humans and nature, and the importance of the individual conscience.

4. Both worked to protect people with disabilities. Dix focused on the mentally ill while Gallaudet focused on those with hearing impairments.

5. Students' brochures will differ. Answers should mention that men, women, and African Americans are all welcome as members of the student body.

C Critical Thinking Skills

Synthesizing Discuss the changes in American thinking during the 1800s. **Ask: What is civil disobedience?** *(refusing to obey laws you consider unjust)* **What was Thoreau's point in refusing to pay his taxes?** *(He practiced civil disobedience. He argued that the Mexican War was wrong and he should not have to help pay for it.)* **Where did Emerson advise people to look for guidance on their behavior?** *(He told them to listen to their conscience.)* **In what way did both these thinkers want people to transcend?** *(They wanted people to separate themselves from the rules of society and think for themselves.)* **BL**

Have students complete the Lesson 1 Review.

CLOSE & REFLECT

Making Connections Research a poem by Emily Dickinson, and then read the poem aloud to the students. **Ask: How does Dickinson's poem represent transcendentalist ideas?** *(Answers may vary but should be based on the poem that is read aloud to the students.)* Have students write a four-line poem on one of the themes of the transcendentalists. **Intrapersonal Verbal/Linguistic**

ANSWER, p. 407

☑ **PROGRESS CHECK** It inspired work on the relationship between humans and nature, individual conscience, and the injustice of slavery.

ENGAGE

Bellringer Tell students that at one time smoking cigarettes was common and acceptable in restaurants, hospitals, and on airplanes. **Ask: What do you think of this behavior?** *(Students will likely think this behavior is totally unacceptable.)* Point out that ideas once accepted as normal can later seem totally ridiculous or unacceptable, and vice versa. **What do you think happens to make people change their views about what is acceptable?** *(Students will probably comment that some people object to the behavior and over time more and more people see that objecting makes sense.)* Lead students to understand that attempts to change accepted behaviors can lead to tension and conflict. Tell students that they will be learning about efforts to abolish, or end, slavery in the United States. **What conflicts might result from those efforts?** *(People who wanted to keep slavery, such as plantation owners, probably got angry with those who wanted to end it.)*

TEACH & ASSESS

R Reading Skills

Defining After reading the text aloud, direct a student to give a mini-presentation to the class about the word *abolitionist*. The student should define it, give its etymology, and identify several synonyms.

C Critical Thinking Skills

Contrasting Discuss the growing antislavery sentiment. **Ask: How did views about slavery differ in the Northern and Southern states?** *(The Northern states had banned, or ended, slavery by the early 1800s. Slavery continued in the South.)* **BL What role did the reform movement play in these changing views?** *(The reform movement encouraged the antislavery movement.)*

ANSWER, p. 408

TAKING NOTES: Answers may include: **William Lloyd Garrison:** editor of *The Liberator*; **Sarah and Angelina Grimké:** lectured and wrote against slavery; **David Walker:** wrote an argument against slavery; **Frederick Douglass:** influential speaker, editor; **Sojourner Truth:** powerful speaker; **Harriet Tubman:** worked on Underground Railroad; **Elijah Lovejoy:** editor of antislavery newspaper

---

networks
There's More Online!

☑ **BIOGRAPHY**
Sojourner Truth

☑ **GRAPH** Slavery in the United States

☑ **GRAPHIC ORGANIZER**
Prominent Abolitionists

☑ **MAP** Liberia

☑ **SLIDE SHOW** Farm Labor in the United States

☑ **VIDEO**

Lesson 2
The Abolitionists

ESSENTIAL QUESTION *What motivates people to act?*

IT MATTERS BECAUSE
The growing demands of abolitionists helped deepen the divide between North and South.

The Start of the Abolition Movement

GUIDING QUESTION *How did Americans' attitudes toward slavery change?*

R Among the reformers of the early 1800s were **abolitionists** (a·buh·LIH·shuhn·ihsts), who sought the end of slavery. Though their voices were growing, their cause was not a new one.

The Early Movement

Even before the Revolution, some Americans had tried to limit or end slavery. Early antislavery societies generally believed slavery had to be ended gradually. First they wanted to stop the slave trade. Then they would phase out slavery itself. Supporters believed that ending slavery gradually would give the South's economy time to adjust to the loss of enslaved labor.

At the Constitutional Convention in 1787, delegates debated slavery and its future. The delegates reached a compromise, allowing each state to decide whether to allow the practice.

By the early 1800s, the Northern states had officially ended slavery there. The practice continued in the South. In fact, the rise of the Cotton Kingdom increased the use of enslaved labor.

C The reform movement of the early and mid-1800s gave new life to the antislavery cause. A growing number of Americans were coming to believe slavery was wrong and that the practice should end.

(d) The Granger Collection, NYC, (c) Library of Congress, Prints & Photographs Division, LC-USZ62-119343, (l) North Wind Picture Archives

Reading **HELP**DESK **CCSS**

Taking Notes: *Identifying* RH.6–8.1
As you read, use a diagram like this one to identify five abolitionists. Below each name, write a brief description of his or her role in the movement.

Abolitionists

Content Vocabulary (Tier 3 Words)
• abolitionist

408 *The Spirit of Reform*

---

networks *Online Teaching Options*

VIDEO

Uncle Tom's Cabin

Analyzing Show students the video about Harriet Beecher Stowe and her motivations to write *Uncle Tom's Cabin*. Clarify any unfamiliar words or concepts. **AL ELL Ask: Why do you think Stowe wrote *Uncle Tom's Cabin*?** *(She wanted to expose the cruelty and injustice of slavery.)* Brainstorm ideas with students for writing a fictional account of overcoming difficult circumstances. **Verbal/Linguistic**

See page 401D for other online activities.

Many who led the antislavery movement came from the Quaker faith. One Quaker, Benjamin Lundy, founded a newspaper in Ohio in 1821 called the *Genius of Universal Emancipation*. Its purpose was to spread the abolitionist message. "I heard the wail of the captive," he wrote. "I felt his pang of distress, and the iron entered my soul."

R

The Colonization Plan

There were many barriers to ending slavery. Many white Northerners still supported the practice. Even some white abolitionists worried about the effect free African Americans would have on society. They did not like the idea of hundreds of thousands of former enslaved people living in the United States.

In 1816 a group of powerful whites formed the American Colonization Society. They planned to send free African Americans to Africa to start new lives. The society raised money to send free African Americans out of the country. Some went to the west coast of Africa, where the society acquired land for a colony. The first settlers arrived in Liberia ("place of freedom") in 1822. In 1847 Liberia declared itself an independent republic.

The American Colonization Society did not stop the growth of slavery. It helped resettle only about 10,000 African Americans by the mid-1860s. Only a few African Americans wanted to go to Africa, while most wanted to be free in America.

C

☑ PROGRESS CHECK

Identifying What was the purpose of the American Colonization Society?

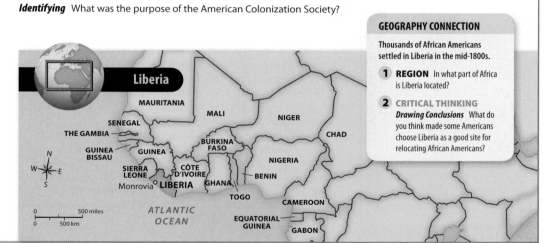

GEOGRAPHY CONNECTION

Thousands of African Americans settled in Liberia in the mid-1800s.

1 REGION In what part of Africa is Liberia located?

2 CRITICAL THINKING
Drawing Conclusions What do you think made some Americans choose Liberia as a good site for relocating African Americans?

abolitionist person who sought the end of slavery in the United States in the early 1800s

R Reading Skills

Discussing Remind students that those early efforts emphasized gradual freeing of enslaved persons. Review the use of farm labor in the South. **Ask: What do you know about farm labor in the South?** (*Enslaved farm labor had been used for many years. The Southern economy depended on it.*) **What do you think life was like for enslaved children?** (*Life was very hard. They did physical work, often in inhospitable conditions.*) **BL** Have a volunteer read the quotation from the textbook by Benjamin Lundy aloud. **Ask: How does his statement predict that the abolition movement was likely to become stronger?** (*He uses strong words to describe slavery: wail, pang, distress.*) **ELL** **Verbal/ Linguistic**

C Critical Thinking Skills

Evaluating Discuss the establishment of the American Colonization Society. **Ask: What successes and failures did the Society experience?** (*They freed and resettled some enslaved workers but most did not want to leave America.*) **For an enslaved person, what were some advantages and disadvantages of going to Liberia?** (*Advantages: freedom, chance for self-rule; Disadvantages: unknown land*)

Content Background Knowledge

Liberia still exists as a country.
• It is the oldest republic in sub-Saharan Africa.
• Liberia's population is about 3.5 million.
• Liberia covers 43,000 square miles; about the size of Virginia.
• The capital city, Monrovia, is named for James Monroe.

GRAPH

Slavery in the United States

Synthesizing Use the interactive graph to discuss the increase in slavery in the United States. Have students study this interactive graph. **Ask: What does the graph show?** (*the number of enslaved people in the United States during the period 1800 to 1860*) **AL** **What trend does the graph show?** (*a steady growth in the slave population between 1800 and 1860*) **How might abolitionists have used this information?** (*They might have used it to show that slavery was growing.*) **BL** **Visual/Spatial**

See page 401D for other online activities.

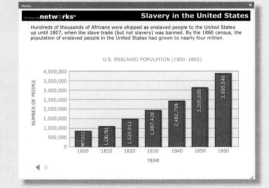

ANSWERS, p. 409

GEOGRAPHY CONNECTION

1 It is located in the western part of the continent.

2 CRITICAL THINKING Possible answer: Perhaps they believed African Americans would prosper on their ancestors' continent. Others may have thought it best for them to be far from the United States.

☑ PROGRESS CHECK The Society sought to send free African Americans to live in Africa—in part to address concerns about the presence of free African Americans in American society.

Chapter 15 409

V **Visual Skills**

Creating Charts Have students create graphic organizers as they move through this part of the lesson to list the five abolitionists mentioned in this section. Be sure students highlight their roles as well. **AL** **ELL** Visual/Spatial

C **Critical Thinking Skills**

Making Inferences Discuss the influence of abolitionists like William Lloyd Garrison and the Grimké sisters on the antislavery movement. Have students create a list of their accomplishments. *(Garrison started an antislavery newspaper and the New England and American Anti-Slavery societies. The Grimké sisters used their inheritance to free enslaved workers and published a book of collected accounts of slavery that raised awareness.)* **BL** **Ask:** What evidence suggests that the abolitionist movement grew between 1832 and 1838? *(The antislavery societies of 1832 had more than 1,000 chapters by 1838. The Grimkés' book was very effective in its time.)* **ELL**

The Movement Builds Strength

GUIDING QUESTION *Why did the reform movement gain momentum?*

Gradualism and colonization remained the main goals of antislavery groups until the 1830s. At this time, abolitionists began arguing that enslaved African Americans should be freed immediately. Slavery became America's most pressing social issue.

Making the Case Against Slavery

Massachusetts abolitionist William Lloyd Garrison had a great influence on the antislavery movement. In 1831 he started a newspaper called *The Liberator*.

Garrison was one of the first white abolitionists to call for an immediate end to slavery. He rejected a slow, gradual approach. In the first issue of *The Liberator*, he wrote, "I *will be* as harsh as truth, and as uncompromising as justice. ... I will not retreat a single inch—AND I WILL BE HEARD."

Garrison was heard. He attracted enough followers to start the New England Anti-Slavery Society in 1832 and the American Anti-Slavery Society the next year. By 1838, the groups Garrison started had more than 1,000 local branches.

Sarah and Angelina Grimké were two other early abolitionists. The sisters were born in South Carolina to a wealthy slaveholding family. They both moved to Philadelphia in 1832. While living in the North, the Grimké sisters spoke out for both abolition and women's rights.

To show their commitment to abolition, the Grimkés asked their mother to give them their family inheritance early. Instead of money or land, the sisters wanted several of the family's enslaved workers. The sisters immediately freed them.

The Grimkés, along with Angelina's husband Theodore Weld, wrote *American Slavery As It Is* in 1839. This book collected firsthand stories of life under slavery. The book was one of the most powerful abolitionist publications of its time.

Harriet Beecher Stowe was another writer who made a major impact on public opinion. Her 1852 novel, *Uncle Tom's Cabin*, became a wildly popular best-seller. The book portrayed slavery as a cruel and brutal system. Some people, however, strongly opposed the book and its message. Sale of *Uncle Tom's Cabin* was banned in the South.

Reading **HELP**DESK **CCSS**

Reading Strategy: *Summarizing*
When you summarize a reading, you find the main idea of the passage and restate it in your own words. Read about the work of William Lloyd Garrison. On a separate sheet of paper, summarize the information in one or two sentences.

---

netw⊙rks *Online Teaching Options*

WHITEBOARD ACTIVITY

The Life of Frederick Douglass

Sequencing Use the interactive whiteboard activity to sequence events in Frederick Douglass's life as a way to discuss his views with students. **Ask:** What seems to be the main goal of Douglass's life? *(the abolition of slavery)* Why did some people find Douglass's ideas controversial? *(He advocated full equality with whites.)* Extend the discussion by having students use the interactive flow chart to sequence events in Douglass's life as a way to understand how his views grew out of experience. Visual/Spatial

See page 401D for other online activities.

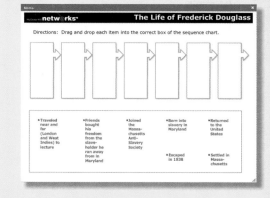

ANSWER, p. 410

Reading Strategy Garrison was a leading abolitionist who demanded an immediate end to slavery. He expressed his views in a publication called *The Liberator*.

African American Abolitionists

Free African Americans in the North especially supported the goal of abolition. Most lived in poverty in cities and had trouble getting good jobs and decent housing. They were often subject to violent attacks. Yet these African Americans were proud of their freedom. They sought to help those who remained enslaved.

African Americans helped organize and lead the American Anti-Slavery Society. They subscribed to *The Liberator*. They also did their own writing and publishing. In 1827 Samuel Cornish and John Russwurm started the country's first African American newspaper *Freedom's Journal*.

Born free in North Carolina and settling in Boston, writer David Walker published a powerful pamphlet against slavery. He challenged African Americans to rebel and overthrow slavery. He wrote, "America is more our country than it is the whites'—we have enriched it with our blood and tears."

In 1830 free African American leaders held a convention in Philadelphia. Delegates met "to devise ways and means for the bettering of our condition." They discussed starting an African American college and encouraging free African Americans to move to Canada.

The Role of Frederick Douglass

Frederick Douglass is the best-known African American abolitionist. Born into slavery in Maryland, Douglass escaped in 1838. He settled first in Massachusetts.

R

Frederick Douglass speaks while disorder breaks out at this 1860 abolitionist meeting in Boston, Massachusetts.

▶ **CRITICAL THINKING**
Drawing Conclusions Why do you think this abolitionist meeting in a northern city became disorderly?

The Granger Collection, NYC

R Reading Skills

Describing After students have read the selection, have a volunteer describe the efforts of African American abolitionists.
Ask: How did free African Americans feel about slavery? *(They wanted to help those who were enslaved.)* What are some ways that African Americans worked to end slavery? *(They started and read antislavery newspapers. They started and joined antislavery organizations. They wrote and published articles against slavery. They met to organize their efforts.)*

W Writing Skills

Narrative Invite students to closely study the painting. Have them use it as a prompt for a writing exercise. Students can write a description of the painting as a whole or a description of one of the individuals in the painting. Some students may want to try their hand at expressing the meaning or message of the painting in poetry. **BL** Verbal/Linguistic

W

IMAGE

Freedom's Journal

Discussing Use the interactive image to discuss the creation of *Freedom's Journal* and other antislavery newspapers. **Ask:** Why was Freedom's Journal a significant publication? *(It was one of the first antislavery newspapers and was created by African Americans.)*

See page 401D for other online activities.

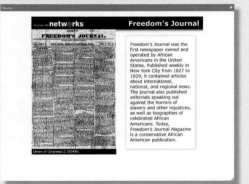

networks — Freedom's Journal

FREEDOM'S JOURNAL

Freedom's Journal was the first newspaper owned and operated by African Americans in the United States. Published weekly in New York City from 1827 to 1829, it contained articles about international, national, and regional news. The journal also published editorials speaking out against the horrors of slavery and other injustices, as well as biographies of celebrated African Americans. Today, *Freedom's Journal Magazine* is a conservative African American publication.

Library of Congress/LC-2(2930E)

ANSWER, p. 411

CRITICAL THINKING Possible answer: Abolition was an emotional topic, and even abolitionists disagreed over how to abolish slavery.

T Technology Skills

Analyzing Data Divide the class into groups. Ask each group to research the routes of the Underground Railroad. Have each group create an illustrated map of the Underground Railroad. The map should show major routes but also be illustrated with such things as stations and passengers. Encourage the student to evaluate images from the Internet and art-related software for use in the map. **Visual/Spatial**

R Reading Skills

Summarizing Ask students to use details from the text to review Harriet Tubman's role in the Underground Railroad.
Ask: What was the Underground Railroad? *(a system of secret routes for helping enslaved people escape to free states or Canada)* Explain that members of the Underground Railroad used railroad terminology as code names for people and places. Create a two-column chart with students that explains the meaning of these four terms: *Underground Railroad, conductor, passenger,* and *station.* **AL** **ELL**

BIOGRAPHY

Sojourner Truth (1797–1883)

Sojourner Truth was a powerful voice for abolition. Truth worked with William Lloyd Garrison, Frederick Douglass, and others to bring about the end of slavery. She traveled throughout the North and spoke about her experiences in slavery. Sojourner Truth was also an active supporter of the women's rights movement.

▶ **CRITICAL THINKING**
Making Connections Why do you think Sojourner Truth later became involved with the women's rights movement?

As a runaway, Douglass faced the danger of capture and a return to slavery. Still, he joined the Massachusetts Anti-Slavery Society. He traveled widely to speak at abolitionist meetings. He even appeared at events in London and the West Indies. Douglass was a powerful speaker who often moved listeners to tears. He also edited the antislavery newspaper *North Star*.

Douglass made his home in the United States because he believed abolitionists must fight slavery at its source. He insisted that African Americans receive not just freedom but full equality with whites as well. In 1847 friends helped Douglass buy his freedom from the slaveholder from whom he had fled in Maryland.

Sojourner Truth

"I was born a slave in Ulster County, New York," Isabella Baumfree began when she told her story to audiences. After a childhood and youth filled with hardship, she escaped in 1826. Then, she officially gained her freedom in 1827 when New York banned slavery. Baumfree later settled in New York City with her two youngest children. In 1843 Baumfree chose a new name. In the biography *Sojourner Truth: Slave, Prophet, Legend*, she explained: "The Lord [named] me Sojourner ... Truth, because I was to declare the truth to the people."

The Underground Railroad

Abolitionists sometimes risked prison and death to help African Americans escape slavery. They helped create a network of escape **routes** from the South to the North called the Underground Railroad.

Underground Railroad "passengers"—that is, escaping African Americans—traveled by night, often on foot. The North Star guided them in the direction of freedom. During the day they rested at "stations"—barns, basements, and attics—until the next night. The railroad's "conductors" were whites and African Americans who guided the runaways to freedom in the northern United States or Canada. Harriet Tubman was the most famous conductor.

The Underground Railroad helped as many as 100,000 enslaved people escape. It gave hope to many more.

✓ **PROGRESS CHECK**

Identifying What were Underground Railroad "stations"?

Library of Congress, Prints & Photographs Division, LC-USZ62-119343

Reading **HELP**DESK **CCSS**

Build Vocabulary: *Origins of Sayings*

"Underground Railroad" is a metaphor. A metaphor describes one thing by calling it something else. Readers imagine a train track that is literally underground. This helps them understand that the Underground Railroad was a method for moving people that was not visible to the public.

412 *The Spirit of Reform*

Academic Vocabulary (Tier 2 Words)

route line of travel

---

networks   *Online Teaching Options*

MAP

Slavery in the United States

Analyzing Visuals Use the map to point out the various Underground Railroad routes. Discuss with students the reasons for the Underground Railroad and how it functioned. **AL** **Ask:** What route might an escaped slave take to get from Charleston, South Carolina, to Canada? *(travel from Charleston to Philadelphia by sea; then travel to Buffalo through Rochester; then cross the border to Canada)* **Visual/Spatial**

See page 401D for other online activities.

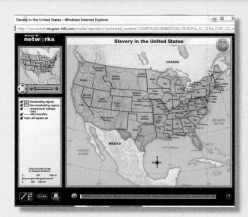

ANSWERS, p. 412

CRITICAL THINKING Answers may vary but should suggest that Truth may have found a similarity between the abolitionist movement and the women's rights movement.

✓ **PROGRESS CHECK** places such as barns, basements, and attics where "passengers" (escaping African Americans) stayed during the daytime

Reaction to the Abolitionists

GUIDING QUESTION *Who opposed the abolition of slavery?*

Abolitionists stirred strong reactions. Most white Southerners believed abolition threatened their way of life, which required enslaved labor.

Even in the North, only a few white people supported abolition. Many white Northerners worried that freed African Americans would never blend into American society. Others feared that abolitionists could begin a war between the North and South.

Opposition to abolitionism sometimes led to violence. In Philadelphia a bloody race riot followed the burning of an antislavery group's headquarters. Police had to jail William Lloyd Garrison to protect him from a Boston mob.

Elijah Lovejoy in Illinois was not so lucky. Angry whites invaded his antislavery newspaper offices and wrecked his presses three times. Three times Lovejoy installed new presses. The fourth time the mob attacked, it set fire to the building. When Lovejoy came out of the blazing building, someone shot and killed him.

The White South Reacts

White Southerners fought abolitionism with arguments in defense of slavery. They claimed that slavery was necessary to the Southern economy and had allowed Southern whites to reach a high level of culture. As anti-abolitionist Senator James Henry Hammond said in an 1858 speech to Congress: "In all social systems there must be a class to do the menial duties, to perform the drudgery of life. … Such a class you must have, or you would not have that other class which leads progress, civilization, and refinement."

The John Rankin House, located along the Ohio River, was a station stop on the Underground Railroad. The Reverend John Rankin, along with his wife and children, assisted hundreds escaping from slavery.

Columbus Dispatch/Renee Sauer/AP Images

R Reading Skills

Summarizing Ask student volunteers to summarize the reasons for Northern opposition to abolition. Remind students to use details from the text. *(threat to social order—African Americans would not blend in, might start a war, might take jobs belonging to whites)* **Ask:** **Which of these reasons do you think the Northerners felt were the most justified?** *(Answers may vary but could suggest that their worries about war were justified.)* **Why might Northerners fear employers hiring African Americans instead of white workers?** *(African Americans would likely work for lower wages because they had been working for no wages.)*

C Critical Thinking Skills

Making Connections Invite a volunteer to read aloud the excerpt in the textbook from Senator Hammond's speech. **Ask:** **What Southern pro-slavery argument does Hammond make?** *(He argues that African Americans are an inferior race suited only for life's menial tasks and that they are better off under the care of white people.)* **How does this connect to the other opinions of those who supported slavery?** *(It echoes a racist idea that African Americans are inferior and will not blend into American life.)* **How does it contrast with the ideas of the abolitionists?** *(They believed that African Americans were equal and deserved to be free and to live independent lives.)*

BIOGRAPHY

Elijah Lovejoy

Determining Cause and Effect Using the interactive image of Elijah Lovejoy, review with students the violence that broke out in the North because of the abolitionist movement. **Ask:** **Why do you think angry whites wrecked Elijah Lovejoy's presses over and over?** *(They wanted him to stop speaking out against slavery, but he obviously kept replacing the presses.)* **What finally happened to Lovejoy?** *(He was shot and killed when he came out of his burning office.)* **AL**

See page 401D for other online activities.

networks   Elijah Lovejoy
BIOGRAPHY

When Lovejoy tried to save his business, he was shot. Lovejoy's death affected many people who opposed slavery and strengthened the abolitionist cause.

North Wind Picture Archives

ANSWER, p. 413

CRITICAL THINKING They were angry over ideas he published in his newspaper, and they tried to stop him from publishing.

T Technology Skills

Researching on the Internet Direct a pair of students to conduct Internet research to find three primary source examples (posters, sermons, essays, etc.) of abolitionist arguments. Direct a second pair to find primary source examples of anti-abolitionist arguments. The two pairs should organize the Web sites using folders or an online tool and make them available to the class.

Have students complete the Lesson 2 Review.

CLOSE & REFLECT

Contrasting Have students make a two-column chart. Ask them to use the chart to contrast the views of abolitionists and Southerners who opposed abolition. Have students use contrasting language to write three sentences based on their chart. **AL** **ELL** Verbal/Linguistic

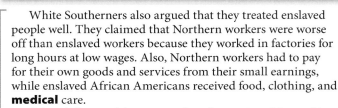

In 1837 a mob attacked and killed newspaper editor Elijah Lovejoy.

▶ CRITICAL THINKING
Explaining Why did anti-abolitionists attack Elijah Lovejoy?

Academic Vocabulary (Tier 2 Words)
medical relating to medicine and help given to people who are sick or injured

White Southerners also argued that they treated enslaved people well. They claimed that Northern workers were worse off than enslaved workers because they worked in factories for long hours at low wages. Also, Northern workers had to pay for their own goods and services from their small earnings, while enslaved African Americans received food, clothing, and **medical** care.

Other defenses of slavery were based on racism. Many whites believed that African Americans were better off under white care than on their own.

The conflict between pro-slavery and antislavery groups continued to mount. At the same time, a new women's rights movement was growing.

☑ PROGRESS CHECK

Identifying Points of View How did many Southerners defend the institution of slavery?

North Wind Picture Archives

LESSON 2 REVIEW (CCSS)

Review Vocabulary (Tier 3 Words)

1. Use the term *abolitionist* in a sentence about the mid-1800s. RH.6–8.4

Answer the Guiding Questions

2. *Identifying Points of View* What concern about ending slavery did the American Colonization Society seek to address? RH.6–8.6

3. *Discussing* How did African Americans help the abolitionist movement gain strength? RH.6–8.2

4. *Comparing and Contrasting* How did Northerners and Southerners view abolition differently? RH.6–8.6

5. **NARRATIVE** Take the role of a conductor on the Underground Railroad. Write an explanation for why you are willing to help African Americans escape from slavery to freedom. WHST.6–8.1, WHST.6–8.10

414 *The Spirit of Reform*

LESSON 2 REVIEW ANSWERS

1. In the mid-1800s, many abolitionists supported the Underground Railroad, a network that helped enslaved African Americans escape to freedom.

2. The Society sought to send free African Americans out of the country, in part to address concerns about the impact of large numbers of free African Americans on American society.

3. They organized and directed the American Anti-Slavery Society, ran antislavery newspapers, wrote and spoke against slavery, and served as conductors on the Underground Railroad.

4. Many Southerners believed that abolition threatened their way of life, which depended on enslaved labor. Many Northerners opposed abolition as well. They feared that ending slavery would upset the social order, tear the nation apart, and take jobs away from whites. Other Northerners believed that slavery was wrong and supported abolition.

5. Explanations should note reasons that a person would oppose slavery and why the Underground Railroad was a way to help.

ANSWER, p. 414

☑ **PROGRESS CHECK** Southerners claimed slavery was essential to the Southern economy. They argued that enslaved people were treated well because they were given food, clothing, shelter, and medical care. They also argued that African Americans would not survive as well on their own.

networks

There's More Online!

☑ **GRAPHIC ORGANIZER**
Women's Rights Leaders

☑ **PRIMARY SOURCE**
William Lloyd Garrison
on Frederick Douglass

☑ **TIME LINE** Opportunity and
Achievement for Women

☑ **VIDEO**

Lesson 3
The Women's Movement

ESSENTIAL QUESTION *How do new ideas change the way people live?*

IT MATTERS BECAUSE

Women began the long quest for expanded rights, including the right to vote, in the mid-1800s.

Reform for Women

GUIDING QUESTION *What did women do to win equal rights?*

For women such as Lucretia Mott, causes such as abolition and women's rights were linked. Like many other women reformers, Mott was a Quaker. Quaker women enjoyed an unusual degree of equality in their communities. Mott was actively involved in helping runaway enslaved workers. She organized the Philadelphia Female Anti-Slavery Society. At an antislavery convention in London, Mott met Elizabeth Cady Stanton. The two found they also shared an interest in women's rights.

The Seneca Falls Convention

In July 1848, Stanton and Mott helped organize the first women's rights convention in Seneca Falls, New York. About 300 people, including 40 men, attended.

A highlight of the convention was debate over a Declaration of Sentiments and Resolutions. These resolutions called for an end to laws that discriminated against women. They also demanded that women be allowed to enter the all-male world of trades, professions, and businesses. The most controversial issue, however, was the call for woman **suffrage,** or the right to vote in elections.

R

Reading **HELP**DESK (CCSS)

Taking Notes: *Summarizing* RH.6–8.2

As you read, use a diagram like this one to summarize the contributions each individual made to the women's movement.

Individual	Contribution
Lucretia Mott →	
Elizabeth Cady Stanton →	
Susan B. Anthony →	

Content Vocabulary (Tier 3 Words)
• **suffrage**
• **coeducation**

Lesson 3   **415**

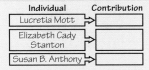

VIDEO

Elizabeth Cady Stanton and Susan B. Anthony

Discussing Use the video to discuss the relationship between Susan B. Anthony and Elizabeth Cady Stanton. Clarify any unfamiliar terms or concepts. **AL** **ELL** **Ask:** How did they meet? *(at a temperance rally)* Have a volunteer describe the friendship that grew from a passion for women's rights and temperance. **Visual/ Spatial Verbal/Linguistic Interpersonal**

See page 401E for other online activities.

ENGAGE

🔔 **Bellringer** Have students look around and count the number of girls in your class. *(Answers will vary from none in a boys' school, to all students in a girls' school, or a mix in a typical classroom.)* Use students' answers to point out that at one time most American classrooms had few or no girls or women in them. Help students to further explore the contrast. **Ask: How might school be different if the number of girls was different from what it is in your classroom?** *(Answers will vary depending on the classroom, but students should recognize that girls can have an effect on classroom learning.)* Tell students that they will be learning about the efforts that reformers made in the 1800s to gain educational and other opportunities for American women.

TEACH & ASSESS

R Reading Skills

Analyzing Direct a volunteer to read the text about the Seneca Falls Convention. Ask the class to explain the significance of the event. **Ask: What were the main issues discussed at the convention?** *(laws to end discrimination against women, access to career opportunities, and the right to vote)* **What positions did Lucretia Mott and Elizabeth Cady Stanton take on the convention's demand for woman suffrage?** *(Stanton argued for demanding suffrage, while Mott argued against this.)* **AL**

Making Connections

Explain to students that the United States has done an excellent job of preserving historical sites and interpreting them for the public. The site of the Seneca Falls Convention is one. Today, people from all over the world visit the Women's Rights National Historical Park in Seneca Falls, New York. Two chief attractions of the park are Wesleyan Chapel, where the convention was held, and the Elizabeth Cady Stanton House. Suggest to students that, when they get older, they make a point of visiting such national treasures.

ANSWER, p. 415

TAKING NOTES: Mott: organized Philadelphia's Female Anti-Slavery Society and first women's rights convention. **Stanton:** helped organize first women's rights convention; had woman suffrage included in the Declaration of Sentiments and Resolutions; helped lead the women's movement. **Anthony:** called for equal pay, college training for girls, and suffrage; helped lead the women's movement

The Women's Movement

V Visual Skills

Creating Time Lines Have interested students conduct research on Mary Lyon and Maria Mitchell, and create time lines of these two pioneering women's lives. **Visual/Spatial**

C Critical Thinking Skills

Evaluating Have volunteers take turns reading aloud each of the four paragraphs in the textbook from the Declaration of Sentiments. After each paragraph, pause to review difficult vocabulary. **AL ELL Ask: Which statement in the Declaration would most influence you to support or oppose it?** *(Students may indicate that a phrase such as "all men and women are created equal" won their support. Or they may have found the statement that "the history of mankind is a history of repeated injuries . . . on the part of man toward woman" to be too strong an assertion, thereby turning them against the Declaration.)* **BL Auditory/Musical**

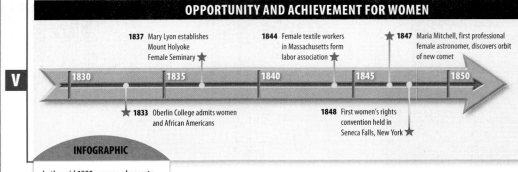

OPPORTUNITY AND ACHIEVEMENT FOR WOMEN

V

1837 Mary Lyon establishes Mount Holyoke Female Seminary ★

1844 Female textile workers in Massachusetts form labor association ★

1847 Maria Mitchell, first professional female astronomer, discovers orbit of new comet ★

1830   1835   1840   1845   1850

★ **1833** Oberlin College admits women and African Americans

1848 First women's rights convention held in Seneca Falls, New York ★

INFOGRAPHIC

In the mid-1800s, women began to argue for—and earn—their own rights and an equal place in society.

1 IDENTIFYING Which items on the time line reflect growing opportunities for women to learn and gain skills?

2 CRITICAL THINKING *Analyzing* Which items on the time line suggest women were using their education to achieve great things?

Elizabeth Stanton insisted the resolutions include a demand for woman suffrage. Some delegates worried that the idea was too radical. Mott told her friend, "Lizzie, thee will make us ridiculous." Standing with Stanton, Frederick Douglass argued powerfully for women's right to vote. After a heated debate, the convention voted to include in their declaration the demand for woman suffrage in the United States.

The Seneca Falls Declaration

The first women's rights convention called for women's equality and for their right to vote, to speak publicly, and to run for office. The convention issued a Declaration of Sentiments and Resolutions modeled on the Declaration of Independence. Just as Thomas Jefferson had in 1776, women are announcing the need for revolutionary change based on a claim of basic rights:

PRIMARY SOURCE

C

❝ When, in the course of human events, it becomes necessary for one portion of the family of man to assume among the people of the earth a position different from that which they have hitherto [before] occupied, but one to which the laws of nature and of nature's God entitle them, a decent respect to the opinions of mankind requires that they should declare the causes that impel them to such a course. ❞

In this passage, two important words—*and women*—are added to Thomas Jefferson's famous phrase:

❝ We hold these truths to be self-evident: that all men and women are created equal; that they are endowed by their Creator with certain inalienable rights; that among these are life, liberty, and the pursuit of happiness. . . . ❞

Reading HELPDESK (CCSS)

suffrage the right to vote

---

netw☉rks   *Online Teaching Options*

GRAPHIC ORGANIZER

Taking Notes: *Summarizing:* Individual Contributions to Women's Rights

As students move through the lesson, use the interactive graphic organizer to identify individuals and their contributions to women's rights. **AL ELL Visual/Spatial**

See page 401E for other online activities.

ANSWERS, p. 416

INFOGRAPHIC

1. The admission of women to Oberlin and the opening of Mount Holyoke indicate women were gaining new opportunities.

2. CRITICAL THINKING The achievements of the Massachusetts female textile workers, the Seneca Falls Convention, and Maria Mitchell suggest women were beginning to use their educations to achieve great things.

The women's declaration called for an end to laws that discriminated against women. It demanded that women be free to enter the all-male world of trades, professions, and businesses.

❝The history of mankind is a history of repeated injuries and [wrongful takings of power] on the part of man toward woman, having in direct object the establishment of an absolute tyranny over her. To prove this, let facts be submitted to a candid world. . . .

Now, in view of this entire [withholding of rights] of one-half the people of this country, their social and religious degradation,—in view of the unjust laws above mentioned, and because women do feel themselves aggrieved, oppressed, and fraudulently deprived of their most sacred rights, we insist that they have immediate admission to all the rights and privileges which belong to them as citizens of the United States. ❞

—Seneca Falls Convention Declaration of Sentiments

W

The Women's Movement Grows

The Seneca Falls Convention helped launch a wider movement. In the years to come, reformers held several national conventions, with the first taking place in Worcester, Massachusetts, in 1850. Both male and female reformers joined the cause.

Among the movement's leaders was Susan B. Anthony. Anthony was the daughter of a Quaker abolitionist. She called for equal pay and college training for women, and **coeducation** (coh·eh·juh·KAY·shuhn)—the teaching of males and females together. Anthony also organized the country's first women's temperance association, the Daughters of Temperance. Anthony met Elizabeth Cady Stanton at a temperance meeting in 1851. They became lifelong friends and partners in the struggle for women's rights and suffrage.

Opportunities for women increased greatly in the late 1800s. Beginning with Wyoming in 1890, several states granted woman suffrage. Yet not until 1920 and the Nineteenth Amendment to the Constitution did women gain the right to vote everywhere.

C

Elizabeth Cady Stanton (left), seen here with Susan B. Anthony, was an organizer of the Seneca Falls Convention.

T

☑ PROGRESS CHECK

Describing What is suffrage?

coeducation the teaching of males and females together

National Portrait Gallery, Smithsonian Institution/Art Resource, NY

Lesson 3 **417**

W Writing Skills

Informative/Explanatory Assign a student the task of learning more about the first National Women's Rights Convention. The student should conduct library and Internet research in order to gather enough information to write a one-page informative essay about the convention. The essay should answer at least these questions: Where was the convention held? Who organized and attended it? What was their agenda? Make sure the student writes an introduction and a conclusion, and uses paragraphs correctly. **Verbal/Linguistic**

C Critical Thinking Skills

Identifying Points of View Review the information about Susan B. Anthony. Explain that Anthony also championed coeducation and other women's rights issues. **Ask: Why might Susan B. Anthony think that coeducation would be important if women were to have the right to vote?** *(Women would need an education and to be informed in order to exercise their voting rights effectively.)* **BL**

T Technology Skills

Researching on the Internet Have students conduct image searches on the Internet for more images of Elizabeth Cady Stanton and Susan B. Anthony. Discuss the photographs, paintings, and drawings with them. Ask students, based on their knowledge of what these women accomplished, which images seem to best capture the women's personalities. **Visual/Spatial**

WORKSHEET

21st Century Skills Activity: The Spirit of Reform

Analyzing Have students complete this activity. Urge students to paraphrase for understanding and to use in-text definitions, their textbook, or a dictionary to define unfamiliar words. **AL** **ELL**

To extend the lesson, have the students compare the rules in this activity to the Declaration of the Rights of Women for differences. **BL** **Verbal/Linguistic**

See page 401E for other online activities.

ANSWER, p. 417

☑ PROGRESS CHECK Suffrage is the right to vote.

Making Inferences Discuss the Milwaukee College for Women and its curriculum. **Ask: Why might society have been willing to accept the ideas of early champions of women's education, such as Catherine Beecher?** (*Beecher advocated women's education but only to prepare women for their traditional roles. This idea did not seem radical, so it might have been more acceptable.*)

R Reading Skills

Discussing Have students read the text, then discuss with them the educational goals of Emma Willard. **Ask: What did she study?** (*science and math*) **What subjects did the Troy Female Seminary teach women?** (*math, history, geography, physics, and homemaking*) **AL**

T Technology Skills

Using Digital Tools Challenge students to cooperate in using Google Maps Street View to see if they can locate the building in the painting. **Interpersonal Visual/Spatial Logical/Mathematical**

Maria Mitchell was the first woman to work as a professional astronomer. "It seems to me that the needle is the chain of woman. ... Emancipate her from the 'stitch, stitch, stitch,' ... and she would have time for studies which would engross as the needle never can."

▶ **CRITICAL THINKING**
Paraphrasing Restate the quote from Mitchell above using your own words.

Women Make Gains

GUIDING QUESTION *In what areas did women make progress in achieving equality?*

Pioneers in women's education began to call for more opportunity. Early champions such as Catherine Beecher believed that women should be educated for their traditional roles in life. The Milwaukee College for Women used Beecher's ideas "to train women to be healthful, intelligent, and successful wives, mothers, and housekeepers." **C**

Other people thought that women could be trained to be **capable** teachers and to fill other professional roles. These pioneers broke down the barriers to female education and helped other women do the same.

One of these pioneers, Emma Willard, educated herself in subjects considered suitable only for males, such as science and mathematics. In 1821 Willard set up the Troy Female Seminary in upstate New York. Willard's seminary taught mathematics, history, geography, and physics, as well as the usual homemaking subjects. **R**

Mary Lyon, after working as a teacher for 20 years, began raising funds to open a women's college. She established Mount Holyoke Female Seminary in Massachusetts in 1837, modeling its curriculum on that of nearby Amherst College. Lyon became the school's first principal, believing that "the great secret ... is female education."

T

Mount Holyoke Female Seminary in South Hadley, Massachusetts, was the first women's college in the United States.

▶ **CRITICAL THINKING**
Analyzing Primary Sources What do you think Lyon meant when she referred to women's education as "the great secret"?

Reading **HELP**DESK **CCSS**

Academic Vocabulary (Tier 2 Words)
capable skillful
ministry the job of a religious leader

netw⊙rks   *Online Teaching Options*

BIOGRAPHY

Maria Mitchell

Making Connections Use the interactive image of Maria Mitchell to discuss the first professional female astronomer. **Ask: What is the importance of Mitchell's accomplishment?** (*She was one of many women who opened the door to fields previously reserved for men.*) **How does this connect to the Seneca Falls Convention?** (*Without it, she may never have had the opportunity to pursue her love of astronomy.*)

See page 401E for other online activities.

netw⊙rks   **Maria Mitchell**
BIOGRAPHY

Maria Mitchell was the first professional female astronomer in the United States. She grew up in Nantucket, Massachusetts, where she attended school and became interested in astronomy. She regularly used her father's telescope to observe the night sky. In October 1847, Mitchell discovered the orbit of a new comet. The following year she became the first woman elected to the American Academy of Arts and Sciences. Mitchell spent the rest of her life devoted to the study of astronomy.

ANSWERS, p. 418

CRITICAL THINKING Mitchell may have meant that sewing (doing "women's work") kept women from ever achieving anything significant and that freeing women from the needle would allow them to do really interesting things.

CRITICAL THINKING Lyon may have meant that education was the key for women to achieve many great things in life.

Marriage and the Family

Prior to the mid-1800s, women had few rights. They depended on men for support. Anything a woman owned became the property of her husband if she married. She had few options if she was in an unhappy or abusive relationship.

During the mid- to late-1800s, women made some gains **C1** in marriage and property laws. New York, Pennsylvania, Indiana, Wisconsin, Mississippi, and the new state of California recognized the right of married women to own property.

Some states passed laws allowing divorced women to share guardianship of their children with their former husbands. Indiana was the first of several states that allowed women to seek divorce if their husbands abused alcohol.

Breaking Barriers

In the 1800s, women had few career choices. They could become elementary teachers—often at lower wages than a male teacher received. Jobs in professions dominated by men were even more difficult. Women had to struggle to become doctors or work in the **ministry**. Some strong-minded women succeeded.

Elizabeth Blackwell tried and failed repeatedly to get into medical school. Finally accepted by Geneva College in New York, Blackwell graduated first in her class and achieved fame as a doctor. **C2**

Maria Mitchell was another groundbreaking woman. Mitchell received an education from her father. In 1847 she became the first person to discover a comet with a telescope. The next year, she became the first woman elected to the American Academy of Arts and Sciences. In 1865 Mitchell joined the faculty of Vassar College.

Women's gains in the 1800s were remarkable—but far from complete. Women remained limited by social customs and expectations. In fact, women had just begun the long struggle to achieve their goal of equality.

☑ PROGRESS CHECK

Describing What gains did women make in the field of education?

Connections to TODAY

Women's Colleges

Mount Holyoke is one of the Seven Sisters—a group of outstanding colleges founded to educate women. Today, Mount Holyoke and several of the Seven Sisters still provide a woman-only educational experience. Some of the Seven Sisters now admit men.

LESSON 3 REVIEW (CCSS)

Review Vocabulary (Tier 3 Words)

1. Explain ways that *suffrage* and *coeducation* could offer women in the 1800s new ways to participate in society. RH.6–8.4

Answer the Guiding Questions

2. *Analyzing* What did the Seneca Falls Convention do to help the women's movement grow? RH.6–8.1

3. *Explaining* Describe the rights within marriage that women gained in the 1800s. RH.6–8.1

4. **ARGUMENT** What arguments might a woman have used to support suffrage? You are a female pioneer traveling west. Write a paragraph explaining why women should have the right to vote. WHST.6–8.1, WHST.6–8.9

Lesson 3   419

CHAPTER 15, Lesson 3
The Women's Movement

C1 Critical Thinking Skills

Analyzing Discuss progress that the women's movement made in reforming marriage and family laws. **Ask: Before the mid-1800s, who became guardian of the children after a divorce? By the late 1800s?** *(the husband; both parents shared custody)* Have students list other effects that the women's movement had on marriage and family law. *(Some states allowed married women to own property or divorce husbands who abused alcohol.)*

C2 Critical Thinking Skills

Making Generalizations Discuss Elizabeth Blackwell's success as a doctor. **Ask: How might Blackwell's success as a doctor make it easier for other women to become doctors?** *(People saw that women could be good doctors, so they may have become more open to the idea.)*

Have students complete the Lesson 3 Review.

CLOSE & REFLECT

Summarizing As a class, summarize the individuals and accomplishments discussed in this section.

LESSON 3 REVIEW ANSWERS

1. Suffrage offered women the right to vote and express their views in politics. Coeducation offered women the chance to attend educational institutions previously available only to men.

2. Possible answer: The convention brought together people with common goals for women's rights so they could share ideas on how to achieve the goals and bring public attention to the issues.

3. In some states, married women could own property, share child guardianship in the case of divorce, and divorce if their husbands abused alcohol.

4. Students' paragraphs should support their argument for suffrage.

ANSWER, p. 419

☑ **PROGRESS CHECK** Gains included the establishment of colleges for women and the study of subjects considered traditionally "male," such as science and mathematics.

ENGAGE

Bellringer Ask students if they ever tell stories from their lives to help people better understand their views about the world. *(Answers may include that students sometimes share stories with new friends or with a teacher when getting to know each other or to explain a decision.)* **Ask**: What do you think makes you want to share life stories with others? *(Students may say that they want to feel known or that they want others to understand their hopes, fears, or frustrations.)* Tell students they will read a selection by a man who wants to share his experiences with the world to help people understand the impact of slavery.

TEACH & ASSESS

V Visual Skills

Creating Maps Direct a small group of students to create a "life map" for Frederick Douglass. Using a map of the United States as a base, students should do some research and annotate the map to show key places in Douglass's life (where he was born, where he lived, where he gave important speeches, etc.). **Visual/Spatial**

AMERICA'S LITERATURE ⒸⒸⓈⓈ

Narrative of the Life of Frederick Douglass, an American Slave

Frederick Douglass

V Frederick Douglass (c. 1818–1895) was born and raised in slavery in Maryland. One of his owners broke the law by teaching Douglass to read and write. Frederick escaped from slavery in 1838 and made his way to freedom in the North. There he began to speak against slavery.

This passage comes from Chapter 1 of Frederick Douglass's autobiography. He wrote the autobiography because many people doubted his story. They heard him speak against slavery and thought he spoke too well to have been a slave. Douglass decided to tell his life story as a way to quiet these critics.

Frederick Douglass escaped a life of slavery to become a leading abolitionist.

420 *The Spirit of Reform*

netw⊙rks *Online Teaching Options*

LECTURE SLIDE

Frederick Douglass

Making Presentations Assign a pair of students to prepare an introduction to *Narrative of the Life of Frederick Douglass, an American Slave*. They should display the bulleted list of the highlights of Frederick Douglass's life for the class and offer at least one detail for each of the major points. **Visual/ Spatial Interpersonal**

Frederick Douglass

Frederick Douglass
- Born and raised in slavery in Maryland
- Learned to read and write
- Escaped from slavery in 1838
- Settled in Massachusetts
- Joined the Massachusetts Anti-Slavery Society
- Began to travel and speak out against slavery
- Edited the antislavery newspaper "North Star"
- Published his autobiography, *Narrative of the Life of Frederick Douglass, an American Slave*
- Bought his freedom in 1847

PRIMARY SOURCE

" I was born in Tuckahoe, near Hillsborough, and about twelve miles from Easton, in Talbot County, Maryland. I have no accurate knowledge of my age, never having seen any authentic record containing it. By far the larger part of the slaves know as little of their ages as horses know of theirs, and it is the wish of most masters within my knowledge to keep their slaves thus ignorant. I do not remember to have ever met a slave who could tell of his birthday. They seldom come nearer to it than planting-time, harvest-time, cherry-time, spring-time, or fall-time. A want of information concerning my own was a source of unhappiness to me even during childhood. The white children could tell their ages. I could not tell why I ought to be deprived of the same privilege. I was not allowed to make any inquiries of my master concerning it. . . . The nearest estimate I can give makes me now between twenty-seven and twenty-eight years of age. I come to this, from hearing my master say, some time during 1835, I was about seventeen years old. . . .

My mother and I were separated when I was but an infant—before I knew her as my mother. It is a common custom, in the part of Maryland from which I ran away, to part children from their mothers at a very early age. Frequently, before the child has reached its twelfth month, its mother is taken from it, and hired out on some farm a considerable distance off, and the child is placed under the care of an old woman, too old for field labor. For what this separation is done, I do not know, unless it be to **hinder** the development of the child's affection toward its mother, and to blunt and destroy the natural affection of the mother for the child. This is the inevitable result.

I never saw my mother, to know her as such, more than four or five times in my life; and each of these times was very short in duration, and at night. She was hired by a Mr. Stewart, who lived about twelve miles from my home. She made her journeys to see me in the night, traveling the whole distance on foot, after the performance of her day's work. She was a field hand, and a whipping is the penalty of not being in the field at sunrise . . . I do not recollect of ever seeing my mother by the light of day. . . . Death soon ended what little [relationship] we could have while she lived, and with it her hardships and suffering. She died when I was about seven years old . . . I was not allowed to be present during her illness, at her death, or burial. . . . Never having enjoyed, to any considerable extent, her soothing presence, her tender and watchful care, I received the **tidings** of her death with much the same emotions I should have probably felt at the death of a stranger. "

Literary Element

First-Person Point of View occurs when a story's narrator tells his or her own experiences. First-person narrators use the pronouns *I, me,* and *we.* These narrators tell readers a lot about their own experience but very little about the experiences of other people or characters in their stories. As you read, think about what you learn because Douglass tells his own story—and what you don't learn.

Vocabulary

hinder
prevent

tidings
news

Analyzing Literature   **DBQ**

❶ *Recalling* How old was Frederick Douglass when he wrote this narrative? RH.6–8.1, RH.6–8.10

❷ *Analyzing* How does Douglass feel about his age? Explain. RH.6–8.6

❸ *Making Inferences* How does Douglass feel about his mother and her death? Explain. RH.6–8.6

Lesson 3   **421**

G1 **Critical Thinking Skills**

Making Inferences Have students reread the first paragraph. **Ask:** **Why might slaveholders want enslaved people to be ignorant of their ages?** *(Answers may include that preventing enslaved people from having this kind of personal knowledge was a way to make them less human.)* **How did young Frederick feel about not knowing his age?** *(He thought it was unfair that white children knew their ages and he did not know his.)*

R **Reading Skills**

Summarizing Have students reread the section that begins with Douglass's separation from his mother. **Ask:** **Why were Frederick and his mother separated?** *(It was the custom for enslaved women and children to be separated early.)* **What possible reason does Frederick give for this separation?** *(He thinks slaveholders might want to keep mother and child from being too attached to each other.)*

G2 **Critical Thinking Skills**

Interpreting With students, reread the paragraph beginning with Douglass's statement that he very seldom saw his mother. **Ask:** **What does Frederick's mother have to do to visit him?** *(She has to walk all night and lose a night's sleep to visit him and be back in the fields by light of day.)* **What does this suggest about her feelings toward Frederick, despite their separation?** *(She loved him very much.)*

CLOSE & REFLECT

Have students write personal and private journal entries in which they record the feelings and emotions they felt while reading about Douglass's childhood and his relationship with his mother.

PRIMARY SOURCE

Frederick Douglass

Making Connections Use the interactive primary source to discuss the excerpt from the preface of Douglass's book. Ask volunteers to read the excerpt aloud and find words and phrases that detail how highly Garrison thought of Douglass. **AL** **ELL** **Ask:** **How does the preface relate to Douglass's reasons for writing his autobiography?** *(Douglass wrote it because many people doubted his story. Garrison is stating that the account is true.)* **BL** Verbal/ Linguistic

ANSWERS, p. 421

1. He does not know because he never learned his birthday; he estimates 27 or 28 years old.

2. He is upset that he does not know his age. It makes him feel less important than the white children, who all know their birthdays.

3. He feels very little about his mother or her death. They were separated when he was an infant so he had no chance to form a loving relationship with her.

CHAPTER REVIEW ACTIVITY

Have a student volunteer create a chart on the board and write "Issues" as the title of the left column boxes and "Reforms" as the title of the right column boxes. Then lead a discussion that allows students to recall changes to American society that occurred during this era. The student volunteer should note these features in the chart.

Issues	Reforms
Education	(Sample answers) Normal schools founded to train teachers. Many new colleges, some for women, founded. Schools for the disabled created.
Slavery	Public views against slavery spread. Opposition to abolitionists also spread.
Literature	American style of literature and art developed. Writers were influenced by spirit of reform.
Women's Rights	Some states granted woman suffrage. Women gained rights to own property and divorce in some states. Women gained some career opportunities.

REVIEW THE ENDURING UNDERSTANDING

Review the chapter's Enduring Understanding with students.

• *People, places, and ideas change over time.*

Now pose the following questions in a class discussion to apply these to the chapter.

How did religion lead to reform during the early 1800s? *(Attending revivals often made men and women eager to reform their own lives and the world. Some people became involved in missionary work or social reform movements.)*

What arguments did people opposed to the abolitionists use? *(that abolition threatened white Southerners' way of life, which required enslaved labor; that freed African Americans would never blend into American society; that abolitionists could begin a war between the North and South; that slavery was necessary to the Southern economy and had allowed Southern whites to reach a high level of culture)*

Why would many historians say that July 1848 marked the birth of a very big change in American society? *(because it was then that the first women's rights convention was held in Seneca Falls, New York, thus launching the women's movement)*

Write your answers on a separate piece of paper.

1 **Exploring the Essential Questions** WHST.6–8.1, WHST.6–8.10

INFORMATIVE/EXPLANATORY Take on the role of a mid-1800s reformer and explain your goals for American society. Write an essay in which you describe the changes you hope to achieve and the challenges you face in getting people to change their ideas over time.

2 **21st Century Skills** WHST.6–8.1, WHST.6–8.9

DRAWING INFERENCES AND CONCLUSIONS Review the chapter for information about the reasons that people opposed abolition, temperance, and women's rights. Then select a current problem or injustice that you feel deeply about. Use the information from the chapter to draw conclusions about who in society today might be opposed to your cause and why.

3 **Thinking Like a Historian** RH.6–8.2, RH.6–8.5

UNDERSTANDING CAUSE AND EFFECT Review the events related to the Second Great Awakening. Create a diagram like the one to the right to show some changes that resulted from this period of reform. Add additional spokes if you need to. Then explain the role that religion had in promoting these reforms.

Second Great Awakening

4 **Visual Literacy** RH.6–8.7

ANALYZING PAINTINGS This picture is called *The Hunters' Shanty in the Adirondacks,* by Currier and Ives. Describe the subject of this painting. What kind of feeling or mood do you think the artists are trying to create? Is it an appealing image? Explain.

Corbis

422 *The Spirit of Reform*

ACTIVITIES ANSWERS

Exploring the Essential Questions

1 Essays should be written in first person from the viewpoint of a reformer in one of the movements of the mid-1800s. Students should clearly state the movement's goals, the challenges facing the movement as it tries to change people's ideas, and realistic ways to overcome those challenges.

21st Century Skills

2 Students' conclusions should rest on factual and accurate information from the chapter and logical links between the concerns of historical reformers from the chapter and the current concern that students have identified.

REVIEW THE GUIDING QUESTIONS
Choose the best answer for each question.

RH.6–8.4
1 A major subject of transcendentalist literature was
  A. realism.
  B. the importance of inner knowledge and individual conscience.
  C. anti-abolitionism.
  D. the relationship between humans and technology.

RH.6–8.4
2 What was the main goal of the temperance reformers?
  F. improve public schools
  G. increase church attendance
  H. reduce alcohol drinking
  I. teach the hearing impaired

RH.6–8.2
3 Which of the following arguments did pro-slavery Southerners use against abolitionists?
  A. Many abolitionists were also secretly slaveholders.
  B. Slave labor was essential to the South, allowing Southern whites to reach a high level of culture.
  C. Abolitionists only wanted to free enslaved workers so that they could work in Northern factories.
  D. Abolitionists wanted to steal Southerners' farms.

RH.6–8.1
4 What happened at the Seneca Falls Convention in 1848?
  F. Delegates called for an end to child labor.
  G. Delegates passed a resolution in favor of voting rights for all African Americans.
  H. Delegates demanded that women be given the right to vote.
  I. Delegates petitioned the states to add an Equal Rights Amendment to the Constitution.

RH.6–8.1
5 William Lloyd Garrison influenced the antislavery movement by
  A. using inherited money to buy and free enslaved workers.
  B. starting the American Anti-Slavery Society.
  C. giving speeches about his experiences as an enslaved man.
  D. publishing an African American newspaper.

RH.6–8.1
6 How did the Troy Female Seminary improve women's education?
  F. It was open to African American men.
  G. It taught them housekeeping skills.
  H. It allowed them to study with men.
  I. It taught subjects such as science.

423

ASSESSMENT ANSWERS
Review the Guiding Questions

1 **B** Students can narrow the possible choices by recalling that many writers reflected the reform spirit of their time.

2 **H** Remind students that temperance refers to "tempering," or moderating, behavior by drinking little or no alcohol. Thus H is correct.

3 **B** Students can eliminate choice A by recognizing that most abolitionists were in the North, where slavery was mostly gone. They can eliminate choice C by recalling that some Northerners opposed abolition because they feared African Americans would take their jobs.

4 **H** Remind students that the Seneca Falls Convention was about women's rights, eliminating choices F and G. The Equal Rights Amendment was a late twentieth century issue.

5 **B** Students can narrow their choices by remembering that William Lloyd Garrison was a white man, which rules out choices C and D.

6 **I** Point out the words "Female" and "women's" in the question. This should help students rule out choices F and H (a Female Seminary is only for women). They can then recognize that learning science is an improvement in education over the teaching of more traditional housekeeping skills.

Thinking Like a Historian

3 Graphic organizers should include reforms resulting from the Second Great Awakening, such as utopian communities, temperance laws, new colleges including the first normal school, techniques for teaching people with disabilities, and better conditions for prisoners and the mentally ill. Students' explanations should recognize that the revival of religious spirit inspired people to reform their own lives and address the ills of society.

Visual Literacy

4 The painting is of a hunter's cabin in the mountains. It looks like the men are bringing an animal they have killed back to the cabin. The artist is probably trying to evoke feelings of tranquility and peace due to the environment. The artist could also be encouraging the viewer to recognize the hard work of frontier life. Because the environment looks peaceful, some students may suggest that it is an appealing image.

Analyzing Documents

7 **C** Students should rule out choice D, which is about Massachusetts. They should use the word "divided" in the passage to rule out choice B and the word "theory" in the passage and question to recognize that the focus of each theory is the status of people *within* that society.

8 **F** Clarify that the word equalizer means "something that causes equality." Direct students to look in the passage for "what causes equality." This should lead them to choice F.

Short Response

9 The passage echoes the words of the Declaration of Independence. It uses many of the same phrases.

10 The temperance society might have used this style to gain attention and to associate their cause with the widely respected principles stated in the Declaration.

Extended Response

11 Students' essays should explore the roots, goals, and accomplishments of the social reform, education reform, and women's rights movements, and should be well supported with examples.

DBQ ANALYZING DOCUMENTS

Horace Mann wrote this excerpt in an 1848 report.

> "According to the European theory, men are divided into classes,—some to toil and earn, others to seize and enjoy. According to the Massachusetts theory, all are to have an equal chance for earning, and equal security in the enjoyment of what they earn. ... Education, then, beyond all other devices of human origin, is the great equalizer of the conditions of men."

> —from "Report No. 12 of the Massachusetts School Board"

RH.6–8.2, RH.6–8.10

7 **Analyzing** Which describes the European theory according to Mann?

A. People in Europe are better than others.

B. Everyone has an equal chance.

C. Opportunity is determined at birth.

D. Massachusetts has good laws.

RH.6–8.5, RH.6–8.6

8 **Understanding Cause and Effect** According to Mann, what is the greatest cause of equality among men?

F. education   H. class at birth

G. job security   I. where you were born

SHORT RESPONSE

This statement reflected the goals of the temperance movement.

> "We hold these truths to be self-evident; that all men are created temperate [without the need to drink alcohol]; that they are endowed by their Creator with certain natural and innocent desires; that among these are the appetite for cold water and the pursuit of happiness!"

> —from *Manifesto of the Washington Total Abstinence Societies,* 1841

RH.6–8.1, WHST.6–8.4

9 Which American document does this passage imitate? How can you tell?

RH.6–8.6, WHST.6–8.4

10 Why do you think the writers chose this style? Explain.

EXTENDED RESPONSE

WHST.6–8.2, WHST.6–8.10

11 **Informative/Explanatory** Write a short essay that describes the roots, goals, and accomplishments of the social reform, education reform, and women's rights movements. Explain the similarities and differences. Give an example of a change each movement achieved that affects your life today.

Need Extra Help?

If You've Missed Question	1	2	3	4	5	6	7	8	9	10	11
Review Lesson	1	1	2	3	2	3	1	1	1	1	1–3

---

networks   *Online Teaching Options*

Help students use the Skills Builder resources

Your students can practice important 21st Century skills such as geography, reading, writing, and critical thinking by using resources found in the Skills Builder tab of the online Student Learning Center. Resources include templates, handbooks, and slide shows. These same resources are also available in the Resource Library of the Teacher Lesson Center.

CHAPTER 16
Toward Civil War Planner

UNDERSTANDING BY DESIGN®

Enduring Understanding
• *People, places, and ideas change over time.*

Essential Questions
• *Why does conflict develop?*

Predictable Misunderstandings

Students may think:
• *Secession happened quickly.*
• *There have always been only two parties in the U.S. political system.*
• *All Southerners supported secession and all Northerners wanted the South to secede.*

Assessment Evidence

Performance Tasks:
• *Hands-On Chapter Project*

Other Evidence:
• *Interactive Graphic Organizers*
• *What Do You Know? activity*
• *Geography and History Activity*
• *Primary Source Activity*
• *21st Century Skills Activity*
• *What Do You Think? questions*
• *Class discussion answers about slavery and secession*
• *Written Paragraphs*
• *Online Self-Check Quizzes*
• *Lesson Reviews*
• *Chapter Activities and Assessment*

SUGGESTED PACING GUIDE

Introducing the Chapter . . . . 1 day	Lesson 3 . . . . 2 day
Lesson 1 . . . . .2 days	*What Do You Think?* . . . . .1 days
Lesson 2 . . . . .2 days	Chapter Wrap-Up and Assessment . . . . . . 1 day

TOTAL TIME   9 Days

Key for Using the Teacher Edition

SKILL-BASED ACTIVITIES

Types of skill activities found in the Teacher Edition.

V Visual Skills require students to analyze maps, graphs, charts, and photos.

R Reading Skills help students practice reading skills and master vocabulary.

W Writing Skills provide writing opportunities to help students comprehend the text.

C Critical Thinking Skills help students apply and extend what they have learned.

T Technology Skills require students to use digital tools effectively.

Letters are followed by a number when there is more than one of the same type of skill on the page.

DIFFERENTIATED INSTRUCTION

All activities are written for the on-level student unless otherwise marked with the leveled labels below.

BL Beyond Level
AL Approaching Level
ELL English Language Learners

All students benefit from activities that utilize different learning styles. Many activities are marked as below when a particular learning style is highlighted.

Intrapersonal	Naturalist
Logical/Mathematical	Kinesthetic
Visual/Spatial	Auditory/Musical
Verbal/Linguistic	Interpersonal

Learners will understand:

2 TIME, CONTINUITY, AND CHANGE

3. That learning about the past requires the interpretation of sources, and that using varied sources provides the potential for a more balanced interpretive record of the past

4. That historical interpretations of the same event may differ on the basis of such factors as conflicting evidence from varied sources, national or cultural perspectives, and the point of view of the researcher

7. The contributions of key persons, groups, and events from the past and their influence on the present

9. The influences of social, geographic, economic, and cultural factors on the history of local areas, states, nations, and the world

5 INDIVIDUALS, GROUPS, AND INSTITUTIONS

2. Concepts such as: mores, norms, status, role, socialization, ethnocentrism, cultural diffusion, competition, cooperation, conflict, race, ethnicity, and gender

7. That institutions may promote or undermine social conformity

8. That when two or more groups with differing norms and beliefs interact, accommodation or conflict may result

6 POWER, AUTHORITY, AND GOVERNANCE

5. The ways in which governments meet the needs and wants of citizens, manage conflict, and establish order and society

10 CIVIC IDEALS AND PRACTICES

7. Key past and present issues involving democratic ideals and practices, as well as the perspectives of various stakeholders in proposing possible solutions to these issues

CHAPTER OPENER PLANNER

Students will know:

- *what compromises involving the issues of slavery and the admission of new states were made or attempted and why they failed.*
- *how slavery contributed to the division of the nation.*
- *the events that led to the Civil War.*

Students will be able to:

- *determine the causes that led to the division of the nation.*
- *discuss and evaluate the political compromises that were made because of slavery.*
- *draw conclusions about the Kansas-Nebraska Act.*
- *analyze the new political party and its role in government.*
- *identify and evaluate the importance of the Dred Scott v. Sandford decision.*
- *evaluate the importance of the election of 1860.*
- *analyze the significance of the attack on Fort Sumter.*
- *analyze and compare arguments about whether or not the South had the right to secede.*

UNDERSTANDING
BY DESIGN®

☑ *Print Teaching Options*

V Visual Skills

☐ **P. 426** Students view a photograph of Fort Sumter and describe its location. **Visual/Spatial**

☐ **P. 427** Students view a map of the United States and analyze whether states are Union free states, Union slave states, or seceding slave states. **Visual/Spatial**

C Critical Thinking Skills

☐ **P. 426** Students evaluate a claim made in a poster advertising *Uncle Tom's Cabin*. **Logical/Mathematical**

☐ **P. 427** Students refer to a map and draw conclusions about why the Civil War was called a war between the North and the South. **Visual/Spatial**

☑ *Online Teaching Options*

V Visual Skills

☐ **MAP** **A Nation Divided 1861**—Students classify states as Union free, Union slave, or seceding and identify the Union territories.

☐ **TIME LINE** **United States 1840 to 1861**—Students learn about key events during this time period.

☐ **WORLD ATLAS** Students can use this interactive map to identify regions of the world, learn about individual countries, locate political boundaries, measure distances, and much more.

Project-Based Learning

Hands-On Chapter Project

Toward Civil War

Students will demonstrate an understanding of how conflict between the states led to war by assuming the role of an army general and presenting a motivating speech to his soldiers. The speech should explain why they are there and what winning the war would accomplish, as well as inspire them to victory.

Technology Extension

Social Bookmarking

- Find an additional activity online that incorporates technology for this project.
- Visit the EdTechTeacher Web sites (included in the Technology Extension for this chapter) for more links, tutorials, and other resources.

Print Resources

ANCILLARY RESOURCES

These ancillaries are available for every chapter and lesson.

- **Reading Essentials and Study Guide Workbook** **AL ELL**
- **Chapter Tests and Lesson Quizzes Blackline Masters**

PRINTABLE DIGITAL WORKSHEETS

These printable digital worksheets are available for every chapter and lesson.

- **Hands-On Chapter Projects**
- **What Do You Know? activities**
- **Chapter Summaries (English and Spanish)**
- **Vocabulary Builder activities**
- **Guided Reading activities**

More Media Resources

SUGGESTED READING

Grade 6 reading level:

- *Vinnie and Abraham,* by Dawn FitzGerald
- *Fort Sumter (We the People),* by Michael Burgan

Grade 7 reading level:

- *Dred Scott v. Sanford (Great Supreme Court Decisions),* by Tim McNeese
- *5,000 Miles To Freedom: Ellen And William Craft's Flight From Slavery,* by Judith Bloom Fradin and Dennis Brindell Fradin

Grade 8 reading level:

- *John Brown (Leaders of the Civil War Era),* by Jon Sterngass
- *The Dred Scott Case: Slavery and Citizenship,* by D.J. Herda

Students will know:
- *what compromises involving the issues of slavery and the admission of new states were made or attempted and why they failed.*

Students will be able to:
- *determine the causes that led to the division of the nation.*
- *discuss and evaluate the political compromises that were made because of slavery.*
- *draw conclusions about the Kansas-Nebraska Act.*

UNDERSTANDING
BY DESIGN®

☑ Print Teaching Options

V Visual Skills

☐ **P. 431** Students view a legend on a pair of maps to determine whether a territory is either open or closed to slaveholding. **Visual/Spatial Logical/Mathematical**

R Reading Skills

☐ **P. 428** Students define the word *compromise*. **AL ELL Verbal/Linguistic**

☐ **P. 428** Students cite examples in the text to explain the issues that led to the Mexican War.

☐ **P. 429** Students identify why Southerners protested the Wilmot Proviso. **AL**

☐ **P. 429** Student volunteers summarize Senator Calhoun's proposal. **BL**

☐ **P. 432** Students discuss the effect of the Kansas-Nebraska Act.

W Writing Skills

☐ **P. 430** Students write letters expressing differing points of view about Senator Henry Clay's suggested compromise.

C Critical Thinking Skills

☐ **P. 430** Students identify differing points of view about slavery. **AL ELL**

☐ **P. 431** Students contrast a map showing the Compromise of 1850 with a map showing the Kansas-Nebraska Act of 1854. **Visual/Spatial**

☐ **P. 432** Students draw conclusions about the results of the Kansas-Nebraska Act and the events in Kansas.

☑ Online Teaching Options

V Visual Skills

☐ **VIDEO** **An Economic Panic and the Missouri Compromise**—Students view a video that traces slavery issues that threatened the Union and considers how the Missouri Compromise delayed the threat.

☐ **MAP** **New Territories of the United States, 1848**—Students identify territories gained from Mexico.

☐ **IMAGE** **The Free-Soil Party**—Students view an image of the candidates from the Free-Soil Party and learn about the party's history.

☐ **IMAGE** **Underground Railroad**—Students view a painting of the courageous "conductors" who aided enslaved people in their escape to freedom.

R Reading Skills

☐ **GRAPHIC ORGANIZER** **Taking Notes: *Describing:* The Kansas-Nebraska Act**—Students summarize reactions to the Kansas-Nebraska Act.

☐ **PRIMARY SOURCE** **Stephen Douglas**—Students analyze Douglas's position regarding slavery in the territories and states.

C Critical Thinking Skills

☐ **IMAGE** **Charles Sumner**—Students analyze a political cartoon showing the altercation between Sumner and his nephew.

☐ **MAP** **The Compromise of 1850; Kansas-Nebraska Act, 1854**—Students compare and contrast slave holdings in U.S. territories in 1850 and 1854.

T Technology Skills

☐ **SELF-CHECK QUIZ** **Lesson 1**—Students receive instant feedback on their mastery of lesson content.

☑ Printable Digital Worksheets

V Visual Skills

☐ **WORKSHEET** **Geography and History Activity: Toward Civil War: The Search for Compromise: Expansion of Slavery**—Students analyze maps to better understand the spread of slavery in the United States.

CHALLENGES TO SLAVERY

Students will know:
- *how slavery contributed to the division of the nation.*

Students will be able to:
- **analyze** *the new political party and its role in government.*
- **identify and evaluate** *the importance of the Dred Scott v. Sandford decision.*

UNDERSTANDING
BY DESIGN®

☑ *Print Teaching Options*

V Visual Skills

☐ **P. 434** Students analyze a map showing the results of the election of 1856. **Visual/Spatial Logical/Mathematical**

☐ **P. 437** Students analyze an image of one of the Lincoln-Douglas debates. **BL** **Visual/Spatial**

R Reading Skills

☐ **P. 433** Students discuss the Congressional election of 1854. **AL** **ELL**

☐ **P. 434** Students identify troubles in Millard Fillmore's campaign with the American Party.

☐ **P. 435** Students summarize Chief Justice Roger Taney's comments about Dred Scott, Congress, the Missouri Compromise, and popular sovereignty and identify the impact of the *Dred Scott* decision on abolishing slavery in the United States.

☐ **P. 436** Students debate *popular sovereignty* as if they were assuming the roles of Douglas and Lincoln. **BL** **Verbal/Linguistic**

☐ **P. 437** Students paraphrase John Brown's statement to the Virginia Court and identify any unfamiliar words in the text. **ELL**

W Writing Skills

☐ **P. 437** Students write a summary of the events that occurred at Harpers Ferry, Virginia.

C Critical Thinking Skills

☐ **P. 434** Students list the parties, candidates, platforms, and results of the 1856 presidential election.

☐ **P. 435** Students make connections between the appellate court process and Dred Scott's case. **BL**

☐ **P. 436** Students make inferences about Abraham Lincoln's possible reasons for challenging Stephen A. Douglas in the Illinois Senate race. **BL**

☐ **P. 438** Students define the word *martyr* and discuss what Northerners thought of John Brown's conviction.

T Technology Skills

☐ **P. 436** Students work in small groups to research information to contribute to a documentary that describes one or more of the Lincoln-Douglas debates. **Auditory/Musical Interpersonal Visual/Spatial**

☑ *Online Teaching Options*

V Visual Skills

☐ **VIDEO** **Young People of the South**—Students learn of cousins Edward and Lucy through their letters as they correspond about conditions in the North and South.

☐ **MAP** **Presidential Election of 1856**—Students compare the electoral and popular vote for Buchanan, Frémont, and Fillmore.

R Reading Skills

☐ **GRAPHIC ORGANIZER** **Taking Notes:** *Describing:* **Party Platforms**—Students record each party's candidate and platform in the 1856 presidential election.

☐ **IMAGE** *Dred Scott v. Sandford*—Students explore this landmark Supreme Court decision.

☐ **IMAGE** **Abraham Lincoln**—Students read a biography summarizing Lincoln's life before he was elected president.

C Critical Thinking Skills

☐ **PRIMARY SOURCE** **John Brown**—Students analyze an excerpt from an essay by Henry David Thoreau.

T Technology Skills

☐ **SELF-CHECK QUIZ** **Lesson 2**—Students receive instant feedback on their mastery of lesson content.

☑ *Printable Digital Worksheets*

R Reading Skills

☐ **WORKSHEET** **Primary Source Activity: Toward Civil War: Challenges to Slavery: Speaking on Slavery**—Students react to excerpts from the first Lincoln-Douglas debate.

Students will know:
- the events that led to the Civil War.

Students will be able to:
- **evaluate** the importance of the election of 1860.
- **analyze** the significance of the attack on Fort Sumter.
- **analyze and compare** arguments about whether or not the South had the right to secede.

UNDERSTANDING BY DESIGN®

☑ *Print Teaching Options*

V Visual Skills

☐ **P. 439** Students take notes about the major events between November 1860 and March 1861 using a graphic organizer. **Visual/Spatial**

☐ **P. 441** Students identify, on a map, the states that seceded before April 1861. **Visual/Spatial**

☐ **P. 442** Students analyze a political cartoon. **Visual/Spatial**

R Reading Skills

☐ **P. 439** Students define and discuss the meanings of the words *secede* and *secession*. **AL ELL**

☐ **P. 440** Students discuss promises made by the Republican Party and the reaction of Southerners. **BL**

☐ **P. 440** Students identify the efforts of Senator Crittenden to keep the South from seceding.

☐ **P. 443** Students describe Fort Sumter and its role in the Civil War.

☐ **P. 443** Students summarize the events of the attack on Fort Sumter and the immediate aftermath.

W Writing Skills

☐ **P. 439** Students write a paragraph comparing and contrasting the candidates of the 1858 Illinois Senate election—Lincoln and Douglas. **BL**

C Critical Thinking Skills

☐ **P. 441** Students compare and contrast the reactions of the Northerners and Southerners to the idea of secession. **AL ELL**

☐ **P. 442** Students speculate on how Lincoln may have felt while giving his Inaugural Address.

☐ **P. 443** Students draw conclusions about the reasons behind some of the events that happened at Fort Sumter. **BL**

☑ *Online Teaching Options*

V Visual Skills

☐ **VIDEO** **Abraham Lincoln's Campaign for President**—Students listen to one of Lincoln's campaign speeches and identify sectional concerns that polarized the Democratic Party in the election of 1860.

☐ **IMAGE** **Supporting Secession**—Students view a secession ribbon worn by some white Southerners.

☐ **MAP** **Seceding States, 1860–1861**—Students view the sequence of the secession of the 11 Southern states.

R Reading Skills

☐ **GRAPHIC ORGANIZER** **Taking Notes: *Sequencing*: Secession and War**—Students list the major events of November 1860 through March 1861 on a time line.

☐ **IMAGE** **Jefferson Davis**—Students read facts about the president of the Confederacy.

C Critical Thinking Skills

☐ **WHITEBOARD ACTIVITY** **Toward Civil War**—Students drag and drop events to build a time line for the years 1820 to 1864.

☐ **POLITICAL CARTOON** **Secessionists Leaving the Union**—Students analyze the components of a political cartoon.

T Technology Skills

☐ **SELF-CHECK QUIZ** **Lesson 3**—Students receive instant feedback on their mastery of lesson content.

☑ *Printable Digital Worksheets*

C Critical Thinking Skills

☐ **WORKSHEET** **21st Century Skills Activity: Toward Civil War: Secession and War: Critical Thinking And Problem Solving: Distinguishing Fact from Opinion**—Students analyze statements and determine if they are fact or opinion.

INTERVENTION AND REMEDIATION STRATEGIES

LESSON 1 The Search for Compromise

Reading and Comprehension

Fugitive and *ruffian* are words that can apply in many contexts. As a class, review how these words are used in the lesson and the definitions provided in the text. Lead a discussion of other contexts in which these words might be used. At the end of the discussion, allow time for students to write sentences that use the words in another context.

Text Evidence

Have partners review the lesson, looking for events that threatened the balance between free and slave states. Students should record the event and date in the first column of a two-column chart and the way the issue was resolved in the second column.

LESSON 2 Challenges to Slavery

Reading and Comprehension

Provide students with the names of the political parties from this chapter (Democrat, Whig, Free-Soilers, Republican, American/Know-Nothing),and help them create a flowchart showing how the parties are related. Indicate for each party whether it supported slavery (S) or supported freedom (F) for African Americans. Note that some parties had members who favored slavery and others who favored freedom.

Text Evidence

Have students work in small groups to conduct additional research into the facts of *Dred Scott v. Sandford*. Students should develop a list of points for each side of the case. If time permits, assign each group to present one side of the case. After all groups give their evidence, discuss the Supreme Court decision.

LESSON 3 Secession and War

Reading and Comprehension

Have partners look for causes and effects in this lesson. Provide them with a list of signal words and phrases such as *so, because, although, while,* and *as a result.* Remind students that some causes and effects do not include signal words. Allow time for students to share the causes and effects they found.

Text Evidence

Ask students to work in groups of at least five and prepare a brief skit showing the events that led to the fight at Fort Sumter. Tell groups that they should choose members to play Lincoln, the commander of Fort Sumter, Governor Pickens, Jefferson Davis, and a commander in the Confederate forces that attacked the fort. Allow time for each group to present their skit.

Online Resources

Approaching Level Reader

Use this online lower-level text that corresponds directly to the text in the Student Edition. It includes a Spanish version.

Guided Reading Activities

This resource uses graphic organizers and guiding questions to help students with comprehension.

What Do You Know?

Use these worksheets to pre-assess student's background knowledge before they study the chapter.

Reading Essentials and Study Guide Workbook

This resource offers writing and reading activities for the approaching-level student. Also available in Spanish.

Self-Check Quizzes

This online assessment tool provides instant feedback for students to check their progress.

Toward Civil War

1840–1861

ESSENTIAL QUESTION · *Why does conflict develop?*

◄ *Dred Scott was at the center of a controversial Supreme Court ruling in the 1850s.*

The Granger Collection, NYC

425

---

networks

There's More Online about the people and events that led the nation into civil war.

CHAPTER 16

Lesson 1
The Search for Compromise

Lesson 2
Challenges to Slavery

Lesson 3
Secession and War

The Story Matters...

His is a complicated story that raises many questions about slavery and freedom. Dred Scott was born into slavery in Virginia. He has been bought and sold like a piece of furniture. He has been taken against his will to live in many places—including, for a time, a place where slavery is illegal. Now Scott is wondering: Did his time in "free" territory turn him into a free man? He decides to take his question to a court for a judge to decide.

Other people wonder if Scott—an enslaved African American—even has the right to go to court.

The answers to these questions are of great interest to the people of the United States. Emotions run high as the debate over slavery rages.

ENGAGE

Bellringer Ask a volunteer to read "The Story Matters..." aloud. Discuss what Dred Scott's early life must have been like—born into slavery, moving from place to place, being bought and sold, and living in places over which he had no control. He was not even considered a human being by some people. Does a person born into slavery have the right to be free if he has lived as a free man? Does he even have the right to ask that question in court? Then **ask:** Who was Dred Scott? *(an enslaved African American)* Why did he believe he should be a free man and no longer enslaved? *(because he had lived in free territory where slavery was illegal)* Tell students that in this chapter, they will discover what happened to Dred Scott and how slavery led to the dividing of the United States into two separate nations. **Interpersonal**

Making Connections

Most students will be familiar with the idea that decisions about where to live are made for them by their parents or other adults. Ask students to discuss how their parents or other family members might respond to being told where they could live and work.

Continue to help students make connections with Dred Scott's experience by discussing how the rules that apply to someone are sometimes different depending on the circumstances. For example, are the rules for weekends and school days the same in their family? If students spend time with grandparents or other relatives, are the rules the same as when students are at home? If the rules are different, how are they different? Ask volunteers to share other situations in which the rules are different.

Letter from the Author

Dear American History Teacher,

Hardly anyone in America would have predicted in the 1820s that the nation would fight a divisive civil war between 1861 and 1865. The Missouri Compromise defined a geographical boundary between slave and free states, and established a set of conditions for whether future states admitted to the Union would permit slavery. By the 1850s, in the wake of the Mexican War, the vast expansion of new American territory had reopened the slavery debate. The Compromise of 1850 represented the last great compromise of the pre-Civil War era, an ambitious attempt to keep the peace.

Albert S. Broussard

TEACH & ASSESS

Step Into the Place

V1 Visual Skills

Analyzing Images Have students view the photograph of Fort Sumter and describe its location. **Ask: Why is this location a good place for a fort?** *(Accept reasonable responses, such as hard for enemies to sneak up on it; stops enemies before they get closer to where people live.)* **Visual/Spatial**

C1 Critical Thinking Skills

Evaluating Ask students to find the poster advertising *Uncle Tom's Cabin*. Call on a volunteer to read aloud the last line on the poster. Have students use the sales figures provided in Content Background Knowledge to discuss whether this claim is an exaggeration. **Logical/Mathematical**

Content Background Knowledge

- *Uncle Tom's Cabin* was first published in a weekly newspaper. Each week between June 5, 1851, and April 1, 1852, another section of the story was published.
- By the time the novel was available in book form, demand was great. In the United States 10,000 copies of it were sold in the first week and 300,000 copies in the first year.
- When Harriet Beecher Stowe, the author, discovered she and her husband were employing a woman who had escaped from slavery, they helped the woman find freedom in Canada.

The divide between North and South, which had been deepening for decades, split wide following the election of 1860. States of the South decided they must break away from the Union and form their own nation.

V1

Step Into the Place

MAP FOCUS The map shows the states that seceded from the Union.

1. **REGION** To which side did the states in the far West belong? RH.6–8.7

2. **LOCATION** Describe the location of the Union slave states relative to the other Union states and the seceding states. RH.6–8.7

3. **CRITICAL THINKING**
   Speculating How do you think the location of the Union slave states affected their decision not to secede? RH.6–8.7

135,000 SETS, 270,000 VOLUMES SOLD.

UNCLE TOM'S CABIN

FOR SALE HERE.

AN EDITION FOR THE MILLION, COMPLETE IN 1 Vol. PRICE 37 1-2 CENTS.
" IN GERMAN, IN 1 Vol. PRICE 50 CENTS.
" IN 2 Vols. CLOTH, 6 PLATES. PRICE $1.50.
SUPERB ILLUSTRATED EDITION, IN 1 Vol. WITH 153 ENGRAVINGS,
PRICES FROM $2.50 TO $5.00.

The Greatest Book of the Age.

C1

After the Southern states seceded, Union attempts to maintain control of Fort Sumter at Charleston, South Carolina, triggered armed conflict. The first shots of the Civil War were fired here on April 12, 1861.

This pictures shows a scene from the book *Uncle Tom's Cabin*. The book played a powerful role in an increasingly emotional debate over slavery in the 1850s.

Step Into the Time

TIME LINE Look at the time line. Which world event suggests that other nations were also debating the issue of slavery? RH.6–8.5, RH.6–8.7

U.S. PRESIDENTS	William Henry Harrison 1841	John Tyler 1841–1845	James Polk 1845–1849
U.S. EVENTS	1840	1845 1846 Congress establishes the Smithsonian Institution	
WORLD EVENTS			

1843 Charles Dickens's *A Christmas Carol* published
1845 Many Irish emigrate to escape famine
1848 Marx publishes *The Communist Manifesto*

Project-Based Learning ✋

Hands-On Chapter Project

Toward Civil War

Students should choose an issue that they read about in the textbook and research it, using more than three sources. Have students take a position on the issue and then prepare a speech that an army general would give to motivate troops. Suggest that students include the reason the soldiers are fighting and the results when their side is victorious. Give students time to rehearse their presentation before giving it to the class.

Technology Extension

Social Bookmarking

If students are not already familiar with social bookmarking tools, introduce them to one of your choice from the Social Bookmarking page of Teaching History with Technology: http://www.thwt.org/socialbookmark.html. (For rubrics to evaluate Web sites, check http://thwt.org/research.html.) Have students search for and bookmark sites that are related to the Underground Railroad or abolitionism. In a shared document, have students contribute a brief description of each link they choose.

edtechteacher
21st Century Learning

ANSWERS, p. 426

Step Into the Place

1. the Union

2. between the Union free states and the seceding states, bordering both

3. **CRITICAL THINKING** Students may suggest that the Union slave states were on the border of the Union and were culturally very similar to the North, or that their residents feared those states would become battlegrounds if the North and South went to war.

Step Into the Time
Possible answer: The serfs of Russia, who were similar to enslaved African Americans, were set free in 1861.

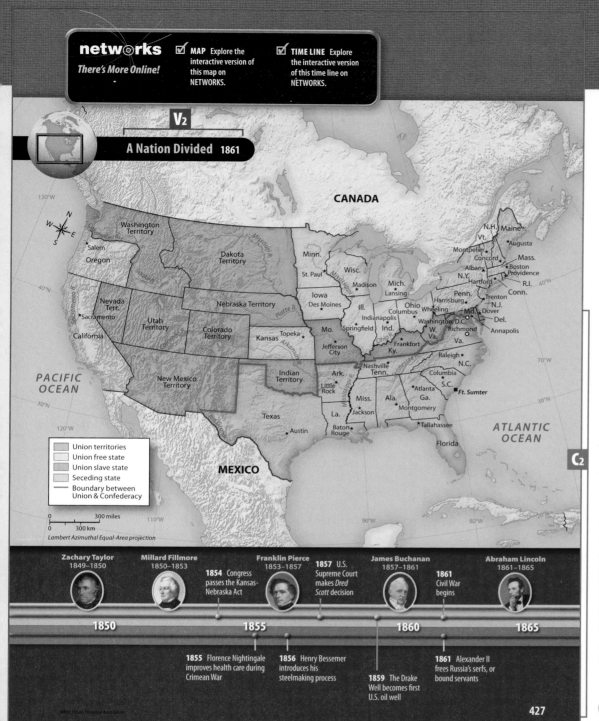

networks
There's More Online!

☑ **MAP** Explore the interactive version of this map on NETWORKS.

☑ **TIME LINE** Explore the interactive version of this time line on NETWORKS.

V₂

A Nation Divided 1861

Step Into the Time

V₂ Visual Skills

Analyzing Maps Refer students to the map. Point out the map key, review its use, and ask a volunteer to explain this key. Ask students to locate various states and say whether they are Union free states, Union slave states, or seceding slave states. Then have students study the map and the Map Focus questions on the facing page. As a class, answer the Map Focus questions. **Visual/Spatial**

C₂ Critical Thinking Skills

Drawing Conclusions Have students refer to the map, paying particular attention to the boundary between the Union and Confederacy. **Ask: Why was the Civil War called a war between the North and the South?** *(because one side—the Union—was composed of states in the northern part of the United States, and the other side—the Confederacy—included only states from the southern part of the country)* Next, have students relate the start of the war to other world events by responding to the time line question on the facing page. **Visual/Spatial**

Content Background Knowledge

- The Confederate States of America had three capital cities. The first was Montgomery, Alabama.
- Because of the heat and mosquitoes in that city, the capital was moved to Richmond, Virginia, which was the capital for almost four years.
- After Richmond was burned by Union forces, Danville, Virginia, became the capital for the final eight days of the Confederacy.

CLOSE & REFLECT

Tell students that people on each side of the Civil War had strong feelings about the underlying reasons for the war. These strong feelings sometimes divided families, resulting in family members facing each other on the battlefield. Have students begin a KWL chart by writing what they know and what they want to learn in the corresponding columns of the chart.

Map Key

- Union territories
- Union free state
- Union slave state
- Seceding state
- Boundary between Union & Confederacy

0   300 miles
0   300 km
Lambert Azimuthal Equal-Area projection

Time Line

Zachary Taylor 1849–1850

Millard Fillmore 1850–1853

1854 Congress passes the Kansas-Nebraska Act

Franklin Pierce 1853–1857

1857 U.S. Supreme Court makes *Dred Scott* decision

James Buchanan 1857–1861

1861 Civil War begins

Abraham Lincoln 1861–1865

1850   1855   1860   1865

1855 Florence Nightingale improves health care during Crimean War

1856 Henry Bessemer introduces his steelmaking process

1859 The Drake Well becomes first U.S. oil well

1861 Alexander II frees Russia's serfs, or bound servants

427

WORKSHEET

What Do You Know? Activity: Toward Civil War

Have students complete the K-W-L chart activity about the causes of the Civil War before they read the chapter. Direct them to write in the first column what they already know about what caused the U.S. Civil War and in the second column the questions they want answered about the war's causes. Use students' entries to help tailor your lessons and discussions to students' needs.

See page 425B for other online activities.

ENGAGE

🔔 **Bellringer** Have students role-play the following scenario in pairs: Tell them to imagine that they are planning to have lunch. One wants to go to a burger place. The other one does not want a burger: he or she wants pizza. They just cannot agree and instead must find a solution that will make both of them happy. After pairs solve the problem, have them share their solutions. Point out solutions that feature compromise and how each student in those pairs has given up something. Tell students they will learn how people and Congress tried to find compromises when it came to the issue of slavery.

TEACH & ASSESS

R1 Reading Skills

Determining Word Meanings Read aloud the title of this lesson. Write the word *compromise* on the board. Point out the Latin prefix *com* (which means "together") and the verb *promittere* (which means "to promise"). Have students use these clues to determine what *compromise* means. Invite volunteers to share their ideas with the class. **AL** **ELL** Verbal/Linguistic

R2 Reading Skills

Citing Text Evidence Explain that several issues led to the Mexican War. Have students cite the issues identified on this page of the text. Invite volunteers to list them on the board. *(Texas joined the Union; the Texas-Mexico boundary was disputed; President Polk failed to purchase California and New Mexico from the Mexican government.)*

ANSWER, p. 428

TAKING NOTES: Antislavery: opposed; the law repealed the Missouri Compromise that established the territory as free. **Pro-slavery:** supported; expected slavery supporters from Missouri to settle the territory and vote to keep slavery legal there

---

---

networks
There's More Online!

☑ **GRAPHIC ORGANIZER**
The Kansas-Nebraska Act

☑ **MAP** Sectionalism and Slavery

☑ **PRIMARY SOURCE** A Defense of the Kansas-Nebraska Act

R1

Lesson 1
The Search for Compromise

ESSENTIAL QUESTION *Why does conflict develop?*

IT MATTERS BECAUSE
The decision whether to allow slavery in new territories was a heated issue that divided the nation.

Political Conflict Over Slavery

GUIDING QUESTION *What political compromises were made because of slavery?*

The question of slavery had long fueled debate in the United States. Each time this debate flared, the nation's leaders struck some form of compromise.

For example, in 1820 the Missouri Compromise preserved the balance between slave and free states in the Senate. It also brought about a temporary stop in the debate over slavery.

New Territory Brings New Debates

In the 1840s, the debate over slavery in new territories erupted again. In 1844 the Democrats nominated James K. Polk of Tennessee for president and called for the annexation of Texas at the earliest possible time. After Polk's election, Texas was admitted to the Union in December 1845.

Texas's entry into the Union angered the Mexican government. Matters worsened when the two countries disputed the boundary between Texas and Mexico. At the same time, support was growing in the South for taking over California and New Mexico. President Polk tried to buy these territories from the Mexican government, but failed. All these issues helped lead to the Mexican War.

R2

(c) Smithsonian American Art Museum, Washington, DC/Art Resource, NY

Reading **HELP**DESK **CCSS**

Taking Notes: *Describing* RH.6–8.1
As you read, use a diagram like the one shown to note reactions to the Kansas-Nebraska Act. Explain the reasons for these reactions.

Kansas-Nebraska Act	
Antislavery:	Pro-slavery:

Content Vocabulary (Tier 3 Words)
- fugitive
- civil war
- secede
- border ruffian

428 *Toward Civil War*

---

networks **Online Teaching Options**

VIDEO

An Economic Panic and the Missouri Compromise

Discussing Have students watch the video and then discuss the use of the word *compromise*. **Ask: What are examples of compromise mentioned in the video?** *(Spain got Texas in exchange for giving Florida and Louisiana to the United States; government used compromises to avoid the question of slavery; admission of Maine led to Missouri Compromise.)*
Visual/Spatial Interpersonal

See page 425C for other online activities.

New Territories of the United States 1848

Territory Ceded By Mexico 1848

UNITED STATES

36°30'N Latitude

PACIFIC OCEAN

TEXAS

ATLANTIC OCEAN

MEXICO

Gulf of Mexico

0   300 miles
0   300 km
Albers Equal-Area projection   110°W   100°W

GEOGRAPHY CONNECTION

The territory of the United States expanded in the mid-1800s.

1 LOCATION How might location play a part in whether New Mexico and California became slave or free states?

2 CRITICAL THINKING *Explaining* How does this map help explain the growing divide over slavery in the United States?

Differing Views

Soon after the war with Mexico began, Representative David Wilmot of Pennsylvania introduced the Wilmot Proviso. This proposal would ban slavery in any lands the United States might acquire from Mexico.

R1

Southerners protested. They wanted the new territory to remain open to slavery. Senator John C. Calhoun of South Carolina offered another idea, saying that neither Congress nor any territorial government could ban slavery from a territory or **regulate** it.

R2

Neither bill passed, but both caused heated debate. By the 1848 presidential election, the United States had taken California and New Mexico from Mexico but took no action on slavery in those territories.

In 1848 the Whigs picked General Zachary Taylor as their presidential candidate. The Democrats chose Senator Lewis Cass of Michigan. Both candidates ignored the slavery issue, which angered some voters.

Those who opposed slavery left their parties and formed the Free-Soil Party. Its slogan was "Free Soil, Free Speech, Free Labor, and Free Men." The party chose former president Martin Van Buren as its candidate. Taylor won, but the Free-Soil Party gained several seats in Congress.

Academic Vocabulary (Tier 2 Words)

regulate to control

CHAPTER 16, Lesson 1
The Search for Compromise

R1 Reading Skills

Identifying After students read the text, ask them to identify David Wilmot. *(Students should note that Wilmot was a representative from Pennsylvania who introduced the Wilmot Proviso.)* Have students describe the Wilmot Proviso. *(The Wilmot Proviso was a plan to ban slavery in any lands acquired from Mexico.)* **Ask:** Why did Southerners protest the Proviso? *(They wanted California and New Mexico open to slavery.)* **AL**

R2 Reading Skills

Summarizing Direct students to read the passage. Ask students to summarize Senator Calhoun's proposal, using details from the text. *(Answers will vary, but should show an accurate understanding of the proposal.)* Discuss how this proposal and the Wilmot Proviso caused debate. Point out that no action was taken regarding the future of slavery in those territories at the time. **BL**

MAP

New Territories of the United States, 1848

Analyzing Use the interactive map showing the new territories gained after the Mexican War. Recall with students the policies established by the Missouri Compromise of 1820 and its role in the debate over slavery. **Ask:** How did the Mexican War change the landscape? *(The United States gained Texas, California, and other new territories.)* **Visual/Spatial**

See page 425C for other online activities.

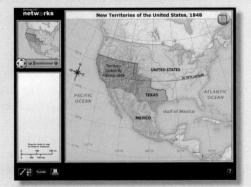

ANSWERS, p. 429

GEOGRAPHY CONNECTION

1 It depended on whether the location was north or south of 36°30'N latitude, the line set in the Missouri Compromise as the limit of slavery.

2 CRITICAL THINKING Answers might include that the 36°30'N latitude line created a clear division between North and South.

C Critical Thinking Skills

Identifying Points of View Tell students that opposition to slavery in the United States was growing, especially in the free states. Explain that abolitionists were people who wanted to abolish, or end, slavery. **Ask: Why would the South want a national fugitive slave law?** *(to require all states to return runaway slaves)* Make sure all students understand the word *fugitive.* Discuss the reactions of Northerners to the law. **Ask: Do you think people were justified in their opposition to the law?** *(Students should support their answers with facts from the lesson.)* Point out how Northern juries reacted to the law. **AL** **ELL**

W Writing Skills

Argument Have pairs of students write letters expressing differing points of view about the compromise that Senator Henry Clay suggested. One student should write a letter in favor of the compromise and address it to Senator John Calhoun, and the other should write a letter against the compromise and address it to Senator Henry Clay.

James Michael Newell painted this mural, *The Underground Railroad,* in the post office of Dolgeville, New York, in 1940.

▶ **CRITICAL THINKING**
Analyzing Visuals What methods does the painter use to show the danger and difficulties facing the runaway family?

A New Compromise

C Concerned over growing abolitionism, Southerners wanted a strong national **fugitive** (FYOO·juh·tihv), or runaway, slave law. Such a law would require every state to return runaway slaves.

In 1849 California applied to become a state—without slavery. If California became a free state, however, slave states would be outvoted in the Senate. Even worse, antislavery groups wanted to ban slavery in Washington, D.C. Southerners talked about **seceding** (sih·SEED·ihng) from, or leaving, the Union.

W In 1850 Senator Henry Clay of Kentucky suggested a compromise. California would be a free state, but other new territories would have no limits on slavery. In addition, the slave trade, but not slavery itself, would be illegal in Washington, D.C. Clay also pushed for a stronger fugitive slave law.

A heated debate took place in Congress. Senator Calhoun opposed Clay's plan. Senator Daniel Webster supported it. Then President Taylor, who was against Clay's plan, died unexpectedly. Vice President Millard Fillmore, who favored the plan, became president.

Senator Stephen A. Douglas of Illinois solved the problem. He divided Clay's plan into parts, each to be voted on separately. Fillmore had several Whigs abstain, or not vote, on the parts they opposed. In the end, Congress passed the Compromise of 1850.

Smithsonian American Art Museum, Washington, DC/Art Resource, NY

Reading **HELP**DESK **CCSS**

fugitive person who is running away from legal authority
secede to officially leave an organization

Academic Vocabulary (Tier 2 Words)
network interconnected system

netw⊙rks   *Online Teaching Options*

IMAGE

The Free-Soil Party

Analyzing Discuss the presidential race of 1848. Click on the interactive image to find out about the election and the Free-Soil Party. Discuss the selection of Zachary Taylor by the Whigs and Lewis Cass by Democrats. **Ask: Why do you think the Whig and Democratic candidates ignored the issue of slavery in their campaigns?** *(Possible answer: They were afraid to lose voters on one side or the other.)* **How did voters react to this tactic?** *(Many voters left the party they had been a member of and formed a new party.)*

See page 425C for other online activities.

McGraw-Hill **netw⊙rks**   **The Free-Soil Party**

The Free-Soil Party was a minor political party in the United States prior to the Civil War. The party opposed the extension of slavery into the newly acquired western territories of the United States. The slogan of the Free-Soil Party was "Free Soil, Free Speech, Free Labor, and Free Men." The party's ideas were popular with small farmers, merchants, and mill workers, among others. The Republican Party, which also opposed slavery, absorbed the Free-Soil Party in 1854.

The Granger Collection, NYC

ANSWER, p. 430

CRITICAL THINKING Possible answers: The darkness emphasizes that people had to travel only at night; some people are entering a cave or a tunnel; one man is waving good-bye, another one is reading a map; the family seems serious, worried, or focused on their trip.

The Fugitive Slave Act

Part of the Compromise of 1850 was the Fugitive Slave Act. Anyone who helped a fugitive could be fined or imprisoned. Some Northerners refused to obey the new law. In his 1849 essay "Civil Disobedience," Henry David Thoreau wrote that if the law "requires you to be the agent [cause] of injustice to another, then I say, break the law." Northern juries refused to convict people accused of breaking the new law. People gave money to buy freedom for enslaved people. Free African Americans and whites formed a **network,** or interconnected system, called the Underground Railroad to help runaways find their way to freedom. Democrat Franklin Pierce became president in 1853. He intended to enforce the Fugitive Slave Act.

✓ PROGRESS CHECK

Explaining Who formed the Free-Soil Party and why?

The Kansas-Nebraska Act

GUIDING QUESTION *What is the Kansas-Nebraska Act?*

In 1854 Senator Stephen A. Douglas of Illinois introduced a bill to settle the issue of slavery in the territories. It organized the region west of Missouri and Iowa as the territories of Kansas and Nebraska. Both were north of 36°30' N latitude, the line that limited slavery. Before the law they would have been free, giving the free states more votes in the Senate and angering the South.

Douglas hoped to make his plan acceptable to both the North and South. He proposed repealing the Missouri Compromise and letting the voters in each territory vote on whether to allow slavery. He called his proposal "popular sovereignty."

GEOGRAPHY CONNECTION

As the United States grew, so did the debate over slaveholding.

1 PLACE Which territories did not allow slavery in 1854?

2 CRITICAL THINKING
Analyzing Which side in the slavery debate lost territory because of the Kansas-Nebraska Act in 1854?

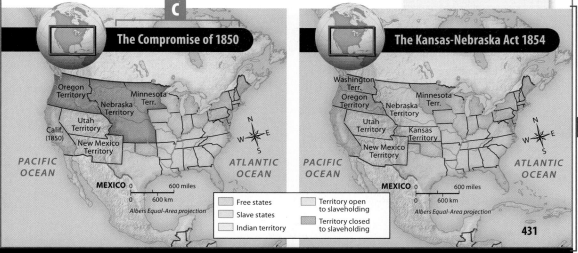

The Compromise of 1850

The Kansas-Nebraska Act 1854

- Free states
- Slave states
- Indian territory
- Territory open to slaveholding
- Territory closed to slaveholding

431

Washington Terr. • Oregon Territory • Minnesota Terr. • Nebraska Territory • Utah Territory • Kansas Territory • New Mexico Territory • PACIFIC OCEAN • ATLANTIC OCEAN • MEXICO • 0 600 miles • 0 600 km • Albers Equal-Area projection

Stephen Douglas

Analyzing Primary Sources Use the primary source excerpt to discuss Stephen Douglas and his introduction of the Kansas-Nebraska Act. **Ask: Who was Stephen Douglas?** *(He was a senator from Illinois.)* **What role did he play in the Compromise of 1850?** *(He divided Clay's plan into parts, which made it easier to pass.)* **BL** Ask: **How did Douglas want to please both the North and the South?** *(He wanted to repeal the Missouri Compromise and institute popular sovereignty, where citizens choose for themselves whether to have slavery.)*

See page 425C for other online activities.

V Visual Skills

Reading a Map Have students look at the legend for the two maps and identify the colors that indicate a territory is either open or closed to slaveholding. *(orange, closed; tan, open)* Ask students to create two circle graphs that record the distribution of the states in 1850 and 1854. **Visual/Spatial Logical/Mathematical**

C Critical Thinking Skills

Contrasting Explain that the Compromise of 1850 was in effect when the Kansas-Nebraska Act was proposed. Ask students to contrast the map showing the Compromise of 1850 with the map showing the Kansas-Nebraska Act of 1854. **Visual/Spatial**

Content Background Knowledge

- Henry David Thoreau was a philosopher and the author of *Walden*.
- He was an active participant in the Underground Railroad.
- In his essay "Civil Disobedience," he argues for a better government by saying that a government that has lost the consent of the people whom it governs should be changed.
- A just government, Thoreau argues, must be in agreement with the conscience of the individuals.

ANSWERS, p. 431

✓ PROGRESS CHECK antislavery Democrats and Whigs, because their parties refused to take a stand on slavery in the territories

GEOGRAPHY CONNECTION

1 Minnesota, Washington, Oregon

2 CRITICAL THINKING the antislavery side

R Reading Skills

Discussing Ask a student to summarize the effect of the Kansas-Nebraska Act. *(removed the Missouri Compromise and let each territory vote on slavery)* Ask another student to explain how Douglas planned to please both the North and the South. *(He wanted to repeal the Missouri Compromise and institute popular sovereignty, where citizens choose for themselves whether to have slavery.)* **Ask: Why were Northerners opposed to repealing the Missouri Compromise?** *(Repeal would allow slavery in areas that had been free for years.)* **Why did Southerners like the idea of popular sovereignty?** *(They expected that Kansas would be settled mostly by slaveholders from Missouri who would vote to make Kansas a slave state.)*

C Critical Thinking Skills

Drawing Conclusions Discuss the results of the Kansas-Nebraska Act and the events in Kansas. **Ask: How did the two sides react to the debate, including the border ruffians?** *(People rushed to Kansas to vote.)* **Why did they feel that heading to Kansas would be effective?** *(They could influence the vote for slavery in Kansas.)*

Have students complete the Lesson 1 Review.

CLOSE & REFLECT

Give students time to review the KWL chart they started at the beginning of the lesson and add or revise information as needed. Then have students recall the role-playing activity they performed at the beginning of the lesson. **Ask: Did any of the pairs not reach a compromise on burgers versus pizza?** *(Students can raise hands to answer.)* **Why was it hard to compromise?** *(Students' answers may vary.)*

ANSWER, p. 432

✓ **PROGRESS CHECK** Pro-slavery and antislavery supporters rushed to Kansas, where pro-slavery laws were passed. Antislavery supporters set up a rival government. Both sides were armed. An antislavery attack provoked a response from pro-slavery supporters, and people died.

border ruffian armed pro-slavery supporter who crossed the border from Missouri to vote in Kansas
civil war conflict between citizens of the same country

This idea, which is central to the American system of government, means that the people are the source of all government power. Douglas's *popular sovereignty* came to mean a particular method for deciding the question of slavery in a place.

R   Northerners protested. The plan allowed slavery in areas that had been free for years. Southerners supported the bill. They expected Kansas to be settled mostly by slaveholders from Missouri. They would, of course, vote to keep slavery legal. With some support from Northern Democrats and the backing of President Pierce, the Kansas-Nebraska Act passed in 1854.

Conflict in Kansas

C   Supporters of both sides rushed to Kansas. Armed pro-slavery supporters known as **border ruffians** (BOHR·duhr RUH·fee·uhns) crossed the border from Missouri just to vote. When elections took place, only about 1,500 voters lived in Kansas, but more than 6,000 people voted. The pro-slavery group won.

Kansas established laws supporting slavery. Slavery opponents refused to accept the laws. They armed themselves, held their own elections, and adopted a constitution banning slavery. By January 1856, Kansas had two rival governments.

In May 1856, slavery supporters attacked the town of Lawrence, an antislavery stronghold. Antislavery forces retaliated. John Brown led an attack that killed five supporters of slavery. Newspapers wrote about "Bleeding Kansas" and "the Civil War in Kansas." A **civil war** is war between citizens of the same country. In October 1856, federal troops arrived to stop the bloodshed.

✓ **PROGRESS CHECK**

Identifying Cause and Effect What events led to "Bleeding Kansas"?

LESSON 1 REVIEW

Review Vocabulary (Tier 3 Words)

1. Explain the significance of the following terms. RH.6–8.4
   a. fugitive   **b.** secede

2. Use the following terms in a short paragraph about Kansas in the 1850s. RH.6–8.4, WHST.6–8.4
   a. border ruffians   **b.** civil war

Answer the Guiding Questions

3. *Describing* How did the Compromise of 1850 address the question of slavery? RH.6–8.2

4. *Analyzing* What was the Wilmot Proviso? Why was it so controversial? RH.6–8.1

5. *Explaining* How did Stephen Douglas help win approval of the Compromise of 1850? RH.6–8.2

6. *Listing* What were some ways that Northerners defied the Fugitive Slave Act? RH.6–8.1

7. **ARGUMENT** Write a dialogue between two people in Nebraska who are expressing their views on the issue of popular sovereignty. Have one person defend the policy and the other oppose it. WHST.6–8.1, WHST.6–8.10

432   *Toward Civil War*

LESSON 1 REVIEW ANSWERS

1. Possible answer: When the federal government refused to enforce the return of fugitive slaves, Southern states considered seceding.

2. Possible answer: To support slavery, armed border ruffians crossed from Missouri into Kansas to vote. With their help, Kansas became a slave state. Antislavery citizens in Kansas then held their own vote and set up a rival government. This increased violence, leading to a state of civil war.

3. Key components of the compromise were that California became a free state but future states were to have no limit on slavery.

4. The Wilmot Proviso was a proposal to ban slavery in any lands acquired from Mexico. Southerners wanted the California and New Mexico territories to be open to slavery.

5. Stephen Douglas divided Clay's plan into parts that members of Congress could vote on separately.

6. Northerners ran the Underground Railroad, tried to rescue pursued or captured African Americans, gave funds to buy freedom for enslaved persons, and refused to convict lawbreakers.

7. Students' dialogues should clearly represent the arguments both for and against the issue of popular sovereignty; one or both sides may want to include the idea of states being able to determine for themselves how to handle important issues.

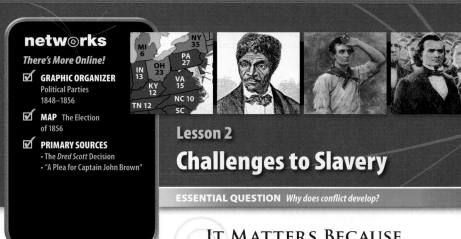

networks
There's More Online!

☑ **GRAPHIC ORGANIZER**
Political Parties
1848–1856

☑ **MAP** The Election
of 1856

☑ **PRIMARY SOURCES**
• The *Dred Scott* Decision
• "A Plea for Captain John Brown"

Lesson 2
Challenges to Slavery

ESSENTIAL QUESTION *Why does conflict develop?*

IT MATTERS BECAUSE
As feelings over slavery intensified, the chance for compromise disappeared.

Birth of the Republican Party

GUIDING QUESTION *How did a new political party affect the challenges to slavery?*

After the Kansas-Nebraska Act, the Democratic Party began to divide along sectional lines. Northern Democrats left the party. Differing views over slavery also split the Whig Party.

The 1854 Congressional Elections

Antislavery Whigs and Democrats joined with Free-Soilers to form the Republican Party. One of the party's major goals was the banning of slavery in new territories. In 1854 the Republicans chose candidates to challenge the pro-slavery Whigs and Democrats in state and congressional elections.

The Republicans quickly showed strength in the North. In the election, they won control of the House of Representatives and several state governments. Unlike the Republicans, almost three-fourths of the Democratic candidates from free states lost in 1854.

In contrast, Republican candidates received almost no support in the South. At the same time, the Democrats, having lost members in the North, were becoming a largely Southern party. This division would be even more apparent in the presidential election of 1856.

R

Reading **HELP**DESK **CCSS**

Taking Notes: *Describing* RH.6–8.2

As you read, use a diagram like the one shown to note each party's candidate and platform in the 1856 presidential election. Also record the election result.

Republican: ⎯ Platform:
Democrat: ⎯ Platform:
American Party: ⎯ Platform:
Election Result:

Content Vocabulary (Tier 3 Words)
• **arsenal**
• **martyr**

Lesson 2 **433**

(c) CORBIS, (c) MPI/Archive Photos/Getty Images, (c) Fotosearch/Archive Photos/Getty Images, (r) Mary Evans Picture Library/The Image Works

VIDEO

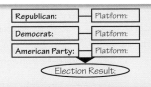

Young People of the South

Comparing and Contrasting Ask half the class to create a compare-and-contrast chart that looks at the lives of young men and women during the 1850s. Instruct the other half to create a chart that compares and contrasts life in the South to life in the North. After students watch the video, lead a discussion about how the lives of young people in the South were similar to and different from the lives of young people in the North. Be sure to include a discussion of enslaved young people. **Interpersonal Visual/Spatial**

See page 425D for other online activities.

Young People of the South

ENGAGE

Bellringer Lead a discussion of the political process in America, and help students understand that it often takes place between only two political parties. Explain that third parties can cause problems for the other two parties. Recall with students how some Democrats and Whigs left their parties to form the Free-Soil Party, which won a few seats in Congress. **Ask: Do you know of any third parties from recent political campaigns?** *(Students may mention the Green party, the Independent party, and so forth.)* Discuss how such candidates draw votes away from the two major parties but often bring important issues to the public's attention.

TEACH & ASSESS

R Reading Skills

Discussing After students have read the text, discuss with them the Congressional election of 1854. Direct students to make a list of the political parties in that election, including the sectional split that affected the Democratic Party. Make sure the list shows the Democrats, the Whigs, the Republicans, the American Party, and the Free-Soil Party. Ask students to save the list to compare to the parties in the 1856 presidential election. **Ask: Why did individuals from the Whigs and Democrats join the Free-Soilers?** *(They were most likely antislavery supporters and so were the Free-Soilers; individuals from both parties were disappointed that their parties and candidates were not addressing the issue of slavery.)* **What was the new Republican Party's stand on slavery?** *(The new Republican Party wanted to leave slavery where it existed and then ban any further expansion of slavery.)* **AL** **ELL**

ANSWER, p. 433

TAKING NOTES: Republican: John C. Frémont, free territories; **Democrat:** James Buchanan, popular sovereignty; **American Party:** Millard Fillmore, anti-immigrant; **Election Result:** Buchanan elected

Challenges to Slavery

V Visual Skills

Analyzing Maps Have students look at the map showing the results of the election of 1856. Explain that the verb *carry* can refer to winning a state's electoral votes. **Ask: Without counting, which candidate carried the most states?** *(Buchanan)* **Which carried the fewest?** *(Fillmore)* **How can you tell?** *(Most of the map with votes is blue; there's almost no yellow. The map key shows how the colors relate to the candidates.)* Then have students look at the circle graphs. **How many more popular votes did Buchanan get than Fillmore?** *(484,472)* **How many more electoral votes did Buchanan get than Fillmore?** *(166)* Lead a discussion of the reasons for the wide difference between the popular vote margin and the margin in the Electoral College. **Visual/Spatial Logical/Mathematical**

C Critical Thinking Skills

Analyzing Discuss the different parties' platforms in the 1856 presidential election. Create a three-column table on the whiteboard, and work with students to list in it the parties, candidates, platforms, and results of the election. **Ask: Who was John C. Frémont?** *(a famous explorer of the West)* **Why did the Democrats and Buchanan endorse popular sovereignty?** *(The Democrats wanted to appeal to Southern whites.)* **What weakened the position of the American Party?** *(They refused to call for the repeal of the Kansas-Nebraska Act and lost Northern supporters.)* Compare the information about the 1856 election with the list of information about the election of 1854 created earlier in the lesson.

R Reading Skills

Identifying As students read the text, remind them that Millard Fillmore was in favor of the 1850 plan that allowed California to be a free state and that allowed slavery in new territories. **Ask: Who was Millard Fillmore?** *(He was vice president and became president after Tyler's death.)* Discuss troubles in Fillmore's campaign with the American Party.

ANSWERS, p. 434

INFOGRAPHIC

1. Frémont was most successful in the Northeast; in that region, he lost in Pennsylvania and New Jersey.
2. **CRITICAL THINKING** Possible answer: yes, because most states are shaded blue

✓ **PROGRESS CHECK** to join together former Whigs and Democrats and Free-Soilers who opposed the spread of slavery to new territories

---

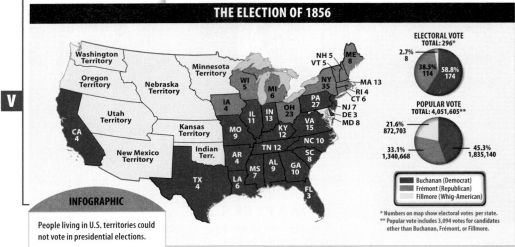

THE ELECTION OF 1856

ELECTORAL VOTE TOTAL: 296*
2.7% 8
38.5% 114
58.8% 174

POPULAR VOTE TOTAL: 4,051,605**
21.6% 872,703
33.1% 1,340,668
45.3% 1,835,140

Buchanan (Democrat)
Frémont (Republican)
Fillmore (Whig-American)

* Numbers on map show electoral votes per state.
** Popular vote includes 3,094 votes for candidates other than Buchanan, Frémont, or Fillmore.

INFOGRAPHIC

People living in U.S. territories could not vote in presidential elections.

1 **IDENTIFYING** In which region was Frémont most successful? Which states in that region did he not win?

2 **CRITICAL THINKING** *Drawing Conclusions* A landslide is an overwhelming victory. Do you think Buchanan's victory was a landslide? Why or why not?

The Presidential Election of 1856

The Whig Party, torn apart over slavery, did not offer a candidate in 1856. Republicans chose Californian John C. Frémont, a famed western explorer. The party platform called for free territories. Its campaign slogan was "Free soil, Free speech, and Frémont."

The Democratic Party nominated James Buchanan of Pennsylvania. He was a diplomat and former member of Congress. Buchanan tried to appeal to Southern whites. The Democratic Party endorsed the idea of popular sovereignty.

The American Party, or Know-Nothings, grew quickly between 1853 and 1856 by attacking immigrants. The party nominated former president Millard Fillmore as its candidate. Yet this party was also divided over the issue of the Kansas-Nebraska Act. When the Know-Nothings refused to call for a repeal of the act, many northern supporters left the party.

The vote in 1856 was divided along **rigid** sectional lines. Buchanan took all Southern states except Maryland. Frémont won 11 of the 16 free states but did not get any electoral votes from south of the Mason-Dixon Line. With 174 electoral votes compared to 114 for Frémont and 8 for Fillmore, Buchanan won.

✓ **PROGRESS CHECK**

Explaining Why did the Republican Party form?

Reading **HELP**DESK **CCSS**

Reading Strategy: *Context Clues*
When you find an unknown word, look at surrounding text for clues to the meaning. Clues to the meaning of the unknown word may be:

434 *Toward Civil War*

• a definition: The word is defined immediately following its use.
• a synonym: A word or expression that has the same meaning as another word or expression. (For example, huge, big, and enormous are synonyms.)
• inference: Hints are given to help you figure out the meaning.

---

netw⊙rks *Online Teaching Options*

MAP

Presidential Election of 1856

Synthesizing As a class, study the interactive map and chart showing the election results of 1856. Ask students to describe in their own words the division of presidential votes along sectional lines and the breakdown of popular and electoral votes. **AL Verbal/Linguistic Logical/Mathematical**

See page 425D for other online activities.

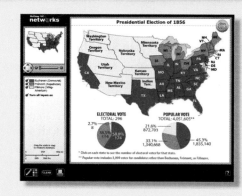

Dred Scott v. Sandford

GUIDING QUESTION *Why was the Dred Scott case important?*

Dred Scott was an enslaved African American bought by a doctor in Missouri, a slave state. In the 1830s, the doctor moved with Scott to Illinois, a free state, then to the Wisconsin Territory. The Northwest Ordinance of 1787 banned slavery there. Later the doctor returned with Scott to Missouri.

In 1846 antislavery lawyers helped Scott sue for his freedom. Scott claimed he should be free since he had lived in areas where slavery was illegal. Eleven years later, the case reached the Supreme Court. At issue was Scott's status, but the case also gave the Court a chance to rule on the question of slavery itself.

The Court Rules

Chief Justice Roger B. Taney (TAW•nee) wrote the Court's opinion: Dred Scott was still an enslaved person. As such, he was not a citizen and had no right to bring a lawsuit. Taney wrote that living on free soil did not make Scott free. A slave was property. The Fifth Amendment prohibited the taking of property without "due process."

Finally, Taney wrote that Congress had no power to ban slavery. The Missouri Compromise, that banned slavery north of 36°30' N latitude, was unconstitutional, and so was popular sovereignty. Not even voters could ban slavery because it would mean taking someone's property. In effect, Taney said that the Constitution protected slavery.

Reaction to the Decision

The Court's decision upheld what many white Southerners believed: Nothing could legally stop slavery. It ruled limiting the spread of slavery, the Republicans' main issue, unconstitutional.

Republicans and other antislavery groups were outraged. They called the decision "a wicked and false judgment" and "the greatest crime" ever committed in the nation's courts.

✓ PROGRESS CHECK

Explaining Why did the *Dred Scott* decision say voters could not ban slavery?

Academic Vocabulary (Tier 2 Words)

rigid firm and inflexible

Many newspapers announced the *Dred Scott* decision on their front pages. Scott is pictured at bottom left, next to a picture of his wife.

▶ **CRITICAL THINKING**
Analyzing Visuals Do these images present a positive view of Scott? Explain your answer.

Lesson 2 **435**

C **Critical Thinking Skills**

Making Connections Review this background information with students: A case must first go to a district court; if that verdict is appealed, the case goes to the Court of Appeals, where it may be sent back to the district court or may be ruled on. The process through which the case may be appealed to the Supreme Court can take several years. **Ask: Why do you think it took so long for Scott's case to reach the Supreme Court?** *(Answers may vary.)* **BL Why did this case attract so much attention?** *(The outcome might influence the question of slavery itself.)*

R **Reading Skills**

Summarizing After students have read the text, ask a volunteer to review the details of the Dred Scott case. Have students summarize Chief Justice Roger Taney's comments about Scott, Congress, the Missouri Compromise, and popular sovereignty. Point out how serious it was that Taney's decision meant that the Constitution protected slavery. **Ask: What impact did the *Dred Scott* decision have on abolishing slavery in the United States?** *(Students may suggest that the movement to abolish slavery was slowed because slavery was now protected by the Constitution.)*

Discuss reactions from both the North and the South with regard to the *Dred Scott* decision. **Ask: How did the Republicans and other antislavery groups react?** *(They felt it was a false judgment and that a great crime had been committed by the court.)*

IMAGE

Dred Scott v. Sandford

Identifying Use the interactive image about Dred Scott's background to discuss with students why he sued for his freedom. Be sure to use the information on the slide to discuss key points in his life that would be used in the case. Point out how long it took the case to reach the Supreme Court.
Visual/Spatial

See page 425D for other online activities.

ANSWERS, p. 435

CRITICAL THINKING Possible answer: Yes, because they show him well dressed and well groomed; also, he is pictured as a family man.

✓ PROGRESS CHECK It would be like taking someone's property without due process, which is unconstitutional. The Supreme Court, in the *Dred Scott* case, essentially ruled that slavery was constitutional and that a mere act of the voters or Congress, such as the Missouri Compromise, could not outlaw slavery. To outlaw slavery would take an amendment to the Constitution.

C Critical Thinking Skills

Making Inferences Point out that Abraham Lincoln challenged Stephen A. Douglas to a series of debates when they were candidates for the Illinois Senate. Lead a discussion of Lincoln's possible reasons for this challenge. Write students' ideas on the board. **BL**

T Technology Skills

Collaborating Have students work in small groups to research and contribute to a documentary that describes one or more of the Lincoln-Douglas debates. Encourage students to find primary sources such as photographs and maps to include in their presentation. If possible, students should find music of the time period. Alternatively, students may want to add sound effects, including crowd noise and applause. Allow time for students to view each group's presentation. Some groups may want to record voice-overs describing the visuals. Group members may also record themselves reading quotes from the debate. **Auditory/Musical Interpersonal Visual/Spatial**

R Reading Skills

Applying Call on a volunteer to review the meaning of *popular sovereignty.* Then ask students to state the positions of Douglas and Lincoln on this issue. Record their answers in a two-column chart. Have student pairs debate the issue, with one partner assuming the role of Douglas and the other of Lincoln. **BL** **Verbal/Linguistic**

Making Connections

Discuss how debating and campaigning have become a more important part of the political process. Make sure that students know the meaning of the term *debate.* **Ask: Have you ever seen a political debate in person or on TV?** *(Answers may vary.)* If so, have students give their impressions. Discuss the methods candidates use when they campaign. Ask students whom they would vote for based on the debate they saw.

ANSWER, p. 436

CRITICAL THINKING Possible answer: The debate about slavery was becoming more intense, and Lincoln's views appealed to many voters. In addition, Lincoln won the reputation as a man of clear thinking and great persuasion.

BIOGRAPHY

Abraham Lincoln (1809–1865)

Just a few years before becoming a national leader, Lincoln was relatively unknown. From a poor rural family, Lincoln knew the importance of education to success. As a young man, he had mostly taught himself and in time became a lawyer. Lincoln was intensely opposed to slavery. He served in the Illinois state legislature and the U. S. Congress. In 1858, he ran for the Senate against Stephen A. Douglas. Although Lincoln lost the election, he gained national attention as a leading Northern voice against slavery.

▶ **CRITICAL THINKING**
Speculating Why do you think Lincoln won fame in spite of losing the race for the Senate?

Reading **HELP**DESK **CCSS**

Academic Vocabulary (Tier 2 Words)
topic subject of discussion

Lincoln and Douglas

GUIDING QUESTION *How did Abraham Lincoln and Stephen A. Douglas play a role in the challenges to slavery?*

The Illinois Senate race of 1858 was the center of national attention. The contest pitted the current senator, Democrat Stephen A. Douglas, against a rising star in the Republican Party named Abraham Lincoln.

People considered Douglas a possible candidate for president in the 1860 election. Lincoln, far less known outside of his state, challenged Douglas to a series of debates. Douglas reluctantly agreed.

The Lincoln-Douglas Debates

Lincoln and Douglas debated seven times. The face-offs took place in Illinois cities and villages during August, September, and October of 1858. Thousands of spectators came to the debates. Newspapers provided wide coverage. The main **topic,** or subject of discussion, was slavery.

During the debate at Freeport, Lincoln pressed Douglas about his views on popular sovereignty. Lincoln asked whether the people of a territory could legally exclude slavery before becoming a state.

Douglas replied that voters could exclude slavery by refusing to pass laws that protected the rights of slaveholders. Douglas's response, which became known as the Freeport Doctrine, satisfied antislavery followers, but it cost Douglas support in the South.

Douglas claimed that Lincoln wanted African Americans to be fully equal to whites. Lincoln denied this. Still, Lincoln insisted that African Americans should enjoy rights and freedoms:

PRIMARY SOURCE

❝ But in the right to eat the bread . . . which his own hand earns, [an African American] is my equal and the equal of [Senator] Douglas, and the equal of every living man. ❞

—Abraham Lincoln, August 21, 1858

The real issue, Lincoln said, was "between the men who think slavery a wrong and those who do not think it wrong. The Republican Party think it wrong."

---

netw⊙rks *Online Teaching Options*

LECTURE SLIDE

Lincoln-Douglas Debates

Listing Display the slide show about the Lincoln-Douglas debates. After discussing the differences between the two men, create a list with students of their opinions as expressed in the debates. **Ask: What was the main topic of the debates?** *(slavery)* **What other topics were debated?** *(popular sovereignty, slavery in the new territories, and voting rights)* **What is the Freeport Doctrine?** *(A reply by Douglas pertaining to the question of slavery in the new territories. He stated that voters could exclude slavery by refusing to pass laws that protected the rights of slaveholders. It satisfied antislavery voters but lost Douglas support in the South.)*

See page 425D for other online activities.

netw⊙rks **Lincoln-Douglas Debates**

The Lincoln-Douglas Debates
- Lincoln and Douglas debated seven times in the fall of 1858.
- The main topic was slavery: Lincoln challenged Douglas's view on popular sovereignty. Douglas challenged Lincoln on African American rights.
- Douglas won the election; Lincoln won national attention.

Following the debates, Douglas won a narrow victory in the election. Lincoln lost but did not come away empty-handed. He gained a national reputation as a man of clear thinking who could argue with force and persuasion.

John Brown and Harpers Ferry

After the 1858 election, Southerners felt threatened by Republicans. Then, an act of violence added to their fears.

On October 16, 1859, the abolitionist John Brown led a group on a raid on Harpers Ferry, Virginia. His target was a federal **arsenal** (AHRS•nuhl), a storage site for weapons. Brown hoped to arm enslaved African Americans and start a revolt against slaveholders. Abolitionists had paid for the raid.

> **PRIMARY SOURCE**
>
> ❝ Now if . . . I should forfeit my life for the furtherance of the ends of justice and MINGLE MY BLOOD . . . with the blood of millions in this slave country whose rights are disregarded by wicked, cruel, and unjust enactments—I submit; so LET IT BE DONE. ❞
>
> —John Brown's statement to the Virginia Court

W

R

The Lincoln-Douglas debates have been described as "the most famous war of words in history."

▶ CRITICAL THINKING
Analyzing Visuals How does the artist of this picture portray the audience of the debate?

arsenal a place to store weapons and military equipment
martyr a person who dies for a great cause

Lesson 2   **437**

V Visual Skills

Analyzing Images Have students describe the image of the debate. **Ask: Where is the debate being held?** *(outside, maybe in a park)* **What might be the reason for this location?** *(The debates were very popular, and the crowds may have been too large to fit in the available buildings.)* **BL** Visual/Spatial

V

W Writing Skills

Informative/Explanatory Have students write a summary of the events that occurred at Harpers Ferry, Virginia, why John Brown chose that target, and what he hoped to achieve.

R Reading Skills

Paraphrasing Call on a volunteer to read aloud John Brown's statement to the Virginia Court. Have students identify any words that are unfamiliar and discuss their meanings. Then ask students to paraphrase Brown's statement. **ELL**

> **PRIMARY SOURCE**

John Brown

Analyzing Primary Sources Use the interactive primary source excerpt by Henry David Thoreau about John Brown. First, discuss Thoreau's opinion of Brown based on the excerpt. Then, discuss the reactions of both Northerners and Southerners to his death. **Ask: What was the reaction of abolitionists to Brown's death? How did white Southerners react?** *(Brown's death rallied abolitionists, which frightened white Southerners; they thought that there was a Northern conspiracy against them.)*

See page 425D for other online activities.

ANSWER, p. 437

CRITICAL THINKING as a mixed group: men and women, adults and children, people in fine clothing and people in working clothes

Chapter 16   437

Challenges to Slavery

C Critical Thinking Skills

Assessing Point out the vocabulary word *martyr* and ask a volunteer to define the word. **Ask: What did Northerners think of John Brown's conviction for treason and death by hanging?** *(Some thought his use of violence was wrong, and others thought he was a martyr.)* Have students turn to a partner and share their opinions of John Brown's actions.

Content Background Knowledge

- Abraham Lincoln was born in Kentucky in a one-room log cabin. His father could not read and the family was very poor. It was Lincoln's stepmother who encouraged his education. After leaving home at the age of 21, he became a clerk in a general store and helped those who could not read or write. He began his political career by running for state legislature. During his political career, he would take several risks and blur party lines.

- Stephen Douglas left his home state of Vermont at 20 to head to Illinois. He immediately began practicing law and was a great admirer of Andrew Jackson. His political career started small, first by joining the General Assembly; but in 10 short years, Douglas was a senator. While he was victorious in his senatorial campaign, he lost the election of 1860. After Lincoln's victory, Douglas would appeal to the South to stop the secessionist movement, with no success.

Have students complete the Lesson 2 Review.

CLOSE & REFLECT

Remind students that the lesson ends with these words: "The nation was on the brink of disaster." Explain that the word *brink* means "edge." **Ask: Who or what do you think could possibly stop the nation from falling over that brink? What kind of compromise would help? What if there is no way to find a compromise?** Encourage students to contribute suggestions that might have worked to prevent the Civil War.

ANSWERS, p. 438

CRITICAL THINKING Brown's actions were controversial because they went outside the law to make a moral statement.

☑ **PROGRESS CHECK** to take weapons to give to enslaved African Americans and start a rebellion against slaveholders

---

Colonel Robert E. Lee and federal troops crushed Brown's raid. More than half of Brown's group, including two of his sons, died in the fighting. Lee's troops captured Brown and his surviving men.

► CRITICAL THINKING
Analyzing Primary Sources
Why do you think Brown's raids were so controversial in the United States of the late 1850s?

Mary Evans Picture Library/The Image Works

Local citizens and federal troops defeated Brown's raid. Tried and convicted of treason and murder, Brown received a death sentence. His hanging shook the North. Some antislavery Northerners rejected Brown's use of violence. Others saw him as a **martyr** (MAHR•tuhr)—a person who dies for a cause.

John Brown's death rallied abolitionists. When white Southerners learned of Brown's abolitionist ties, their fears of a great Northern conspiracy against them were confirmed. The nation was on the brink of disaster.

☑ PROGRESS CHECK

Identifying Why did John Brown raid the arsenal at Harpers Ferry?

LESSON 2 REVIEW (CCSS)

Review Vocabulary (Tier 3 Words)

1. Use the word *arsenal* in a sentence about Harpers Ferry. RH.6–8.4

2. Explain the meaning of *martyr* as it relates to John Brown. RH.6–8.4

Answer the Guiding Questions

3. *Specifying* What issue led to the formation of the Republican Party, and what stand did the party take on the issue? RH.6–8.1

4. *Explaining* What reasons did Taney give for why he believed Dred Scott was an enslaved person? RH.6–8.1

5. *Identifying* How did the Lincoln-Douglas debates benefit Lincoln? RH.6–8.2

6. *Making Inferences* Why do you think the raid on Harpers Ferry by just a few men was so threatening to Southerners? RH.6–8.1

7. ARGUMENT Imagine you live at the time of John Brown's raid on Harpers Ferry. Write a letter to the editor of a local paper expressing your feelings about his methods. WHST.6–8.1, WHST.6–8.10

LESSON 2 REVIEW ANSWERS

1. Possible answer: John Brown led a raid on the arsenal at Harper's Ferry because he wanted to use the weapons to arm slaves.

2. Possible answer: After his execution, some abolitionists considered John Brown a martyr for their cause.

3. Slavery in the territories; the Republicans opposed it.

4. Taney stated that because a slave was considered to be property, if a slave lived on free soil that did not make that person free.

5. By skillfully debating the more prominent Douglas, Lincoln gained a national reputation.

6. Answers might include: Abolitionists backed the raid, so it seemed like part of a bigger conspiracy against the South. In addition, the idea of enslaved people with guns was probably terrifying to slaveholders.

7. Letters should either agree or disagree with John Brown's plans and his raid on the arsenal, and should state facts and arguments that support the students' opinions.

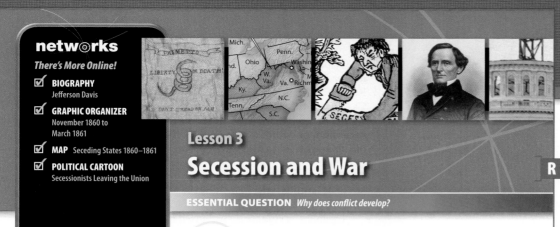

networks
There's More Online!

☑ **BIOGRAPHY**
Jefferson Davis

☑ **GRAPHIC ORGANIZER**
November 1860 to
March 1861

☑ **MAP** Seceding States 1860–1861

☑ **POLITICAL CARTOON**
Secessionists Leaving the Union

Lesson 3
Secession and War

R

ESSENTIAL QUESTION *Why does conflict develop?*

IT MATTERS BECAUSE
When Abraham Lincoln was elected president, the Southern states decided to break away from the Union.

The 1860 Election

GUIDING QUESTION *What was the importance of the election of 1860?*

In the presidential election of 1860, the big question was whether the Union would continue to exist. Regional differences divided the nation.

The issue of slavery split the Democratic Party. Northern Democrats supported popular sovereignty. They nominated Stephen Douglas. Southern Democrats vowed to uphold slavery. Their candidate was John C. Breckinridge.

Moderates from the North and South formed the Constitutional Union Party. The Constitutional Unionists took no position on slavery. They chose John Bell as their candidate.

The Republicans nominated Abraham Lincoln. They wanted to leave slavery alone where it existed—but also to ban it in the territories. Still, white Southerners feared that a Republican victory would promote slave revolts as well as interfere with slavery.

With the Democrats divided, Lincoln won a clear majority of electoral votes. Voting followed sectional lines. Lincoln's name did not even appear on the ballot in most Southern states. He won every Northern state, however. So in effect, the more populous North outvoted the South.

W

Reading **HELP**DESK **CCSS**

Taking Notes: *Sequencing* RH.6–8.5
As you read, list the major events on a time line like the one shown.

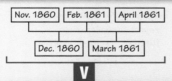

Nov. 1860 | Feb. 1861 | April 1861
Dec. 1860 | March 1861

Content Vocabulary (Tier 3 Words)
• secession
• states' rights

V

Lesson 3   **439**

VIDEO

Abraham Lincoln's Campaign for President

Contrasting When Lincoln rose to speak at Harvard, the audience was surprised at how awkward he looked. However, when he began to speak, they became interested. Have students share their opinions of the excerpts of Lincoln's speeches in this video. **Ask: How were Lincoln's campaign managers different from Lincoln?** *(They made many promises, but Lincoln did not want to make deals before he was elected.)*
Interpersonal

See page 425E for other online activities.

ENGAGE

Bellringer Ask students to imagine a situation in which a group of children are playing soccer or basketball. Explain that the ball belongs to one of the children and that the child becomes unhappy with the game. She decides to take her ball and go home. **Ask: How do you think the other children feel? Do you think the person with the ball is justified in leaving the game and taking the ball?** *(Answers will vary, but students should provide reasons for their answers.)* After students share their thoughts, explain that they will discover how fear in the South that slavery would be ended or restricted grew to a point where some states believed that the only choice they had was to leave the Union.

TEACH & ASSESS

R Reading Skills

Defining Call on a volunteer to read aloud the title of the lesson. Write the words *secede* and *secession* on the board. Invite volunteers to infer the words' meanings and how the two words are related to each other. **AL** **ELL**

W Writing Skills

Informative/Explanatory When discussing the 1860 presidential election, remind students that the candidates in the 1858 Illinois Senate election were Lincoln and Douglas, and that slavery was a divisive issue in that race. Then have students write one paragraph explaining how the two candidates were similar and one paragraph explaining how they were different. **BL**

V Visual Skills

Integrating Visual Information Point out the graphic organizer at the bottom of the page. Direct students to take notes about the major events between November 1860 and March 1861, making sure to include dates. Lead a discussion of how sequencing their notes on a time line can help students understand how the events may be related. **Visual/Spatial**

ANSWER, p. 439

TAKING NOTES: Nov. 1860: Lincoln elected president; **Dec. 1860:** South Carolina secedes; **Feb. 1861:** Confederacy formed; **March 1861:** Lincoln's Inaugural Address; **April 1861:** attack on Fort Sumter begins Civil War.

Secession and War

R1 Reading Skills

Discussing Call on a volunteer to read aloud the subheading at the top of the page. **Ask:**

- **What can you infer from the subheading about the text that follows?** *(The text will describe a disagreement between sides that want to work out their differences.)*

- **What was the Republican position on slavery?** *(They wanted to leave it where it already existed but ban it in the new territories.)* Discuss with students the reaction by Southern states to this Republican promise.

- **What did Southerners think would happen?** *(Southerners thought that Republicans would not protect their rights and that they would ban slavery everywhere.)* Discuss how the Republican promise and the South's reaction finally led to secession.

- **Which state seceded first?** *(South Carolina)*

- **What do you think South Carolina could have done instead of seceding?** *(Possible answers: met with Lincoln to get his promise in writing; boycotted Northern goods; refused to pay federal taxes without a guarantee of freedom for the state to continue slaveholding)* **BL**

R2 Reading Skills

Identifying Have a volunteer read the text aloud. Call students' attention to Senator Crittenden and his efforts to keep the South from seceding. **Ask: Who was John Crittenden?** *(He was a senator from Kentucky.)* **What compromise did Senator Crittenden offer to prevent states from seceding?** *(He proposed constitutional amendments that included protecting slavery south of the Missouri Compromise line.)* **Did he succeed?** *(No; six more states seceded.)*

Looking for Compromise

R1 The Republicans had promised not to stop slavery where it already existed. Yet white Southerners did not trust the Republicans to protect their rights. On December 20, 1860, South Carolina voted to secede from the Union.

In other Southern states, leaders debated the question of **secession,** or withdrawal from the Union. Meanwhile, members of Congress tried to find ways to prevent it. Senator John Crittenden of Kentucky suggested a series of amendments to the Constitution. They included a protection for slavery south of 36°30′ N latitude—the line set by the Missouri Compromise—in all territories "now held or hereafter acquired."

R2 Republicans **rejected,** or refused to accept, Crittenden's idea. They had just won an election by promising to stop slavery's spread into any territories. "Now we are told …" Lincoln wrote, "the government shall be broken up unless we surrender to those we have beaten."

Leaders in the South also rejected the plan. "We spit upon every plan to compromise," exclaimed one Southern leader. "No human power can save the Union," wrote another.

The Confederacy Established

By February 1861, Texas, Louisiana, Mississippi, Alabama, Florida, and Georgia had joined South Carolina and seceded. Delegates from these states met to form a new nation. Calling themselves the Confederate States of America, they chose Jefferson Davis as their president.

Southerners used **states' rights** to **justify** secession. Each state, they argued, had voluntarily chosen to enter the Union. They defined the Constitution as a contract among the independent states. They believed the national government had broken the contract by refusing to enforce the Fugitive Slave Act and by denying Southern states equal rights in the territories. As a result, Southerners argued, the states had a right to leave the Union.

The Public Reacts to Secession

Not all white Southerners welcomed secession. Church bells rang and some people celebrated in the streets. To other Southerners, the idea of secession was alarming. Virginian Robert E. Lee expressed concern about the future. "I only see that a fearful calamity is upon us," he wrote.

Some Southerners wore ribbons like this to show their support for secession from the Union. The ribbons carried slogans, such as this one used in the American Revolution—"Liberty or Death."

▶ **CRITICAL THINKING**
Analyzing Why do you think secessionists used the same slogans as those used in the Revolutionary War?

Chicago Historical Society

Reading **HELP**DESK **CCSS**

secession withdrawal
states' rights theory that individual states are independent and have the right to control their most important affairs

Academic Vocabulary (Tier 2 Words)

reject to refuse to accept
justify to find reasons to support

netw⊙rks   *Online Teaching Options*

IMAGE

Supporting Secession

Explaining Use the interactive image of the secession ribbons to discuss secession. **Ask: What does it mean to secede?** *(to leave or break away from)* **Why would Southerners want to wear ribbons like the ones shown?** *(to show support for secession)*

See page 425E for other online activities.

McGraw-Hill **netw⊙rks**   **Supporting Secession**

Secession means "separation from the Union." Some white southerners wore ribbons like this one to show their support for separating from the United States. The ribbons featured mottoes, or well-known expressions, from the American Revolution.

Chicago Historical Society

ANSWER, p. 440

CRITICAL THINKING Possible answer: During the Revolution, the mottoes indicated the Patriots' desire for liberty from Britain, even at the expense of their lives. The secessionists compared their cause to that of the Patriots.

Some Northerners approved of the Southern secession. If the Union could survive only by giving in to slavery, they declared, then let the Union be destroyed. Still, most Northerners believed that the Union had to be preserved. As Lincoln put it, the issue was "whether in a free government the minority have the right to break up the government whenever they choose."

Lincoln Takes Over

As always, several months passed between the November election and the start of the new president's term. Buchanan would remain in office until March 4, 1861. In December 1860, Buchanan sent a message to Congress. He said that the Southern states had no right to secede from the Union. He added that he had no power to stop them from doing so.

As Lincoln prepared for his inauguration, people throughout the United States wondered what he would say and do. They wondered, too, what would happen in Virginia, North Carolina, Kentucky, Tennessee, Missouri, Delaware, Maryland, and Arkansas. These slave states had not yet seceded, but their decisions were not final. If the United States used force against the Confederates, the remaining slave states also might secede.

GEOGRAPHY CONNECTION

Some slaveholding states and territories did not secede from the Union.

1. **LOCATION** Which states seceded before the attack on Fort Sumter? Which seceded after the attack on Fort Sumter?

2. **CRITICAL THINKING**
Speculating Which side controlled more territory, and how might the answer affect a military conflict between the two sides?

Seceding States 1860–1861

West Virginia separated from Virginia in 1861 and was admitted to the Union in 1863.

South Carolina was the first state to secede from the Union.

In February 1861, delegates met in Alabama to form the Confederate States of America.

Legend:
- Union territories
- Union free state
- Union slave state
- Slave state seceding before siege of Ft. Sumter, April 1861
- Slave state seceding after siege of Ft. Sumter, April 1861
- Boundary between Union & Confederacy

0 600 miles
0 600 km
Lambert Azimuthal Equal-Area projection

441

Secession and War

C Critical Thinking Skills

Comparing and Contrasting Remind students that most Southerners welcomed secession, but some found it alarming. Call on a volunteer to explain the Northerners' reactions. *(Some Northerners approved of secession, but most wanted to restore the Union.)* Have students create compare-and-contrast sentences to describe these reactions to secession. **AL** **ELL**

V Visual Skills

Analyzing Maps Have students refer to the map legend to identify the states that seceded before April 1861. *(TX, LA, MS, AL, GA, FL, SC)* **Ask: What do Missouri, Kentucky, and West Virginia have in common?** *(allowed slavery and were in the Union)* **If slave states were in the Union, what can you infer about the conflict between the North and South?** *(It was not only about slavery.)* Explain that the issue of states' rights was also a factor leading to the Civil War. **Visual/Spatial**

Content Background Knowledge

- The president of the Confederate States of America was Jefferson Davis. He was born in Kentucky but soon moved to the frontier of Mississippi.

- He was a commander during the Mexican War and served in the United States Senate. President Franklin Pierce named him Secretary of War in 1853.

- Davis was inaugurated president of the Confederacy in 1861, and in 1865, at the end of the Civil War, he was captured, charged with treason, and imprisoned for two years.

MAP

Seceding States, 1860–1861

Locating Display the interactive map of seceding states. Ask students to identify the states that seceded before April 1861. Use the map to display those states. **AL** **Ask: How many states had seceded by February 1861?** *(six)* **AL** **Ask: What name did the Southern states take after they seceded?** *(Confederate States of America)* **What was the main reason the South gave for secession?** *(states' rights)* Discuss the South's justifications for the creation of the Confederate States of America. **BL**

See page 425E for other online activities.

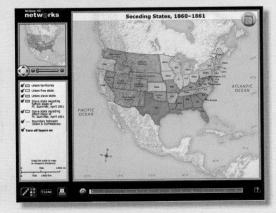

Seceding States, 1860–1861

ANSWERS, p. 441

GEOGRAPHY CONNECTION

1. Before—Texas, Louisiana, Mississippi, Alabama, Georgia, Florida, South Carolina; After—Virginia, North Carolina, Tennessee, Arkansas

2. **CRITICAL THINKING** The Union controlled more territory. This might give the Union advantages such as more resources to support the war effort and a greater population from which to draw soldiers.

V Visual Skills

Analyzing Images Discuss the political cartoon. Invite volunteers to explain some of the symbolism that is present in the drawing. Then **ask: What can you tell from the expressions on the men's faces?** *(Accept reasonable answers. Some students may say that the men are determined, but they don't look very happy about having to secede from the Union.)* **Visual/Spatial**

C Critical Thinking Skills

Speculating Have students recall the situation facing Lincoln on Inauguration Day. Remind students of the lesson video they watched and the manner in which the actors read Lincoln's lines. Have partners take turns reading aloud the excerpts from Lincoln's First Inaugural Address quietly but with appropriate pauses and feeling. **Ask: How do you think Lincoln felt? Would you have given the same speech he gave?** *(Answers will vary.)*

This cartoon was created in 1861, just before the Civil War began. At that time, secession was breaking apart the United States.

1 **INTERPRETING** What do the men in the cartoon represent?

2 **CRITICAL THINKING**
Drawing a Conclusion What do you think the cartoonist is predicting will happen because of the men's action?

V

SECESSIONISTS LEAVING THE UNION

In his Inaugural Address, Lincoln spoke to the seceding states directly. He said that he could not allow secession and that "the Union of these States is perpetual [forever]." He vowed to hold federal property in the South, including a number of forts and military installations, and to enforce the laws of the United States. At the same time, Lincoln pleaded with the South:

C

PRIMARY SOURCE

❝ In your hands, my dissatisfied fellow countrymen, and not in mine, is the momentous issue of *civil war*. The Government will not assail you. You can have no conflict without being yourselves the aggressors....

... We are not *enemies*, but *friends. We must not be enemies.* Though passion may have strained, it must not break our bonds of affection. ❞

—Abraham Lincoln, First Inaugural Address

☑ **PROGRESS CHECK**

Explaining What was John Crittenden's proposal to save the Union?

Reading **HELP**DESK CCSS

Build Vocabulary: *Word Parts*

The suffix -*ist* on the word *cartoonist* tells you that a cartoonist is a person. The same is true of the words *pianist* (a person who plays the piano) and *essayist* (a person who writes essays). Can you think of other examples with the suffix -*ist*?

442 *Toward Civil War*

---

netw⊙rks *Online Teaching Options*

POLITICAL CARTOON

Secessionists Leaving the Union

Interpreting Have students study the political cartoon in the interactive image. **Ask: Who do the men represent?** *(The men could represent Southern states.)* **What is the significance of cutting the branch from the tree?** *(a permanent break from the Union)* **Visual/Spatial**

See page 425E for other online activities.

POLITICAL CARTOON

SECESSIONISTS LEAVING THE UNION
The Granger Collection, NYC

ANSWERS, p. 442

1. states that are seceding
2. **CRITICAL THINKING** Secession will hurt the states that secede far more than it will hurt the Union. The states (branches) will die if cut off from the Union (trunk and roots).

☑ **PROGRESS CHECK** He proposed amendments to the Constitution that included protecting slavery south of 36°30'N latitude—the line set by the Missouri Compromise—in all current or future territories.

Build Vocabulary Possible answers: abolitionist, secessionist, cyclist, violinist, dramatist, and so forth

Fighting at Fort Sumter

GUIDING QUESTION *What did the attack on Fort Sumter signify?*

The day after taking office, Lincoln received a message from the commander of Fort Sumter, a U.S. fort on an island guarding Charleston Harbor. The message warned that the fort was low on supplies and the Confederates demanded its surrender.

Lincoln responded in a message to Governor Francis Pickens of South Carolina that he was sending an unarmed group to the fort with supplies. He promised Union forces would not "throw in men, arms, or ammunition" unless they were fired upon.

Jefferson Davis ordered his forces to attack Fort Sumter before the Union supplies could arrive. Confederate guns opened fire on April 12, 1861. Union captain Abner Doubleday witnessed the attack from inside the fort:

PRIMARY SOURCE

❝ Showers of balls ... and shells poured into the fort in one incessant stream, causing great flakes of masonry to fall in all directions. ❞

—quoted in *Fort Sumter*

Meanwhile, high seas kept Union ships from reaching the fort. Facing a hopeless situation, the Union surrendered the fort on April 14. Despite heavy bombardment, no one had died.

With the loss of Fort Sumter, Lincoln decided he had to act. He issued a call for troops. Volunteers quickly signed up. In reaction to Lincoln's call, Virginia, North Carolina, Tennessee, and Arkansas voted to join the Confederacy. The Civil War had begun.

☑ **PROGRESS CHECK**

Explaining Why did Lincoln decide not to send armed troops to Fort Sumter?

LESSON 3 REVIEW

Review Vocabulary (Tier 3 Words)

1. Use the word *secession* in a sentence about Florida. RH.6–8.4
2. Explain the meaning of *states' rights* as it relates to the U.S. Constitution. RH.6–8.4

Answer the Guiding Questions

3. *Specifying* What did South Carolina do after Lincoln won the election of 1860? Why? RH.6–8.1
4. *Explaining* What was the impact of the attack on Fort Sumter? RH.6–8.2

5. *Drawing Conclusions* What was President Lincoln's priority when he took office in March 1861? RH.6–8.2
6. *Analyzing* What role did the idea of states' rights play in the Civil War? RH.6–8.1
7. **INFORMATIVE/EXPLANATORY** Write a brief newspaper article about the attack on Fort Sumter that describes the battle in an objective way, without bias for one side or the other. WHST.6–8.2, WHST.6–8.9

Lesson 3   **443**

LESSON 3 REVIEW ANSWERS

1. Possible answer: Florida was one of the first six states to join South Carolina in secession.

2. Southern states argued that the states' rights guaranteed to them under the U.S. Constitution included the right to secede from the Union.

3. South Carolina seceded; many Southerners did not trust a Republican administration to protect their rights.

4. It turned the North–South dispute into a conflict—a civil war—and brought more Southern states into the Confederacy.

5. Lincoln was determined to preserve the Union by opposing secession. He hoped to prevent war.

6. Many people in the South believed the Constitution was a voluntary contract between states and that the contract had been broken because the federal government violated the rights of some states; therefore, individual states (the Southern states) had the right to secede.

7. Each article should provide an objective description of the attack on Fort Sumter.

R1 Reading Skills

Describing Before students read the text, tell them that in this section they will learn about the event that started the Civil War. After students read the section, direct them to the aerial photograph of Fort Sumter in the chapter opener. Then discuss the fort's location and readiness for war. **Ask: Was the fort in Union or Confederate territory?** *(Confederate)* **What message did Lincoln receive from Fort Sumter?** *(The fort was low on supplies, and the Confederates wanted to surrender.)* **How did Lincoln respond?** *(He sent a note to the governor of South Carolina telling him that he was sending unarmed men to deliver supplies to the fort.)*

C Critical Thinking Skills

Drawing Conclusions Discuss Lincoln's actions so far with regard to Fort Sumter. **Do you think Lincoln knew that the Confederates would fire first?** *(Answers might include: Yes; he was sending people into Confederate territory. No; he thought that because he was sending unarmed men that the Southerners would know the Union meant no harm.)* **BL Why do you think Jefferson Davis ordered an attack?** *(to beat the arrival of Union supplies)* **What was the result?** *(The Confederacy won the victory, and the Union had to surrender.)*

R2 Reading Skills

Summarizing Have students use details from the text to summarize the events of the attack on Fort Sumter, the surrender of the Union to the Confederacy, Lincoln's immediate call for troops, and the secession of four more states.

Have students complete the Lesson 3 Review.

CLOSE & REFLECT

Prompt students to discuss the beginning of the Civil War by asking whether they think the Civil War was inevitable. **Ask: Can you think of any way it could have been stopped?** *(Students' answers may vary.)* Discuss the pros and cons of their suggestions.

ANSWER, p. 443

☑ **PROGRESS CHECK** Lincoln did not want to be the one to start a war. He let the Confederacy make the decision to begin the conflict.

ENGAGE

Bellringer Lead a discussion of the ways students resolve disagreements. **Ask: Is it always possible to resolve disagreements? Why or why not?** *(Answers will vary.)* Tell students that they will read excerpts from the inauguration speeches of President Abraham Lincoln and Confederate President Jefferson Davis. Ask students to predict what they think each leader will say as his main argument to support his point of view.

TEACH & ASSESS

R Reading Skills

Paraphrasing Have a volunteer read the background information aloud. Discuss the background of each president before discussing their speeches. **Verbal/Linguistic**

G1 Critical Thinking Skills

Analyzing Have students read Davis's position to themselves. Help them with challenging vocabulary as needed. Then have volunteers explain Davis's argument in their own words. **AL ELL Ask: Were the opinions in Davis's speech justified? Why or why not? What do you think was the strongest point of Davis's argument?** *(Answers will vary depending on what students think of his opinions. They should support their answers with information from Davis's speech.)*

C2 Critical Thinking Skills

Analyzing Primary Sources Point out that Jefferson Davis used a quotation from the Preamble to the U.S. Constitution in his speech. Call on a volunteer to read the quotation aloud. **Ask: Why does Davis also refer to the Declaration of Independence?** *(He makes a comparison between the founding of the United States, which was based on the fact that the British government no longer met the needs of colonists in North America, and the founding of the Confederate States of America, which was based on the fact that the U.S. government no longer met the needs of many people living in the South.)*

What Do You Think? CCSS

Did the South Have the Right to Secede?

R

When Abraham Lincoln began his first term as president on March 4, 1861, seven Southern states had already voted to secede from the Union and formed the Confederate States of America.

The Confederacy's president, Jefferson Davis, had taken office earlier, on February 18, 1861. Each man's inauguration address presented a different view on whether any state had the right to secede.

Yes

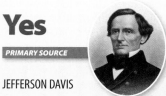

PRIMARY SOURCE

JEFFERSON DAVIS

G1

C2

❝ Our present position . . . illustrates the American idea that government rests upon the consent of the governed, and that it is the right of the people to alter or abolish a government whenever it becomes destructive of the ends for which it was established. The declared purpose of the compact of Union from which we have withdrawn was t o 'establish justice, insure domestic tranquility, to provide for the common defence, to promote the general welfare, and to secure the blessings of liberty for ourselves and our posterity'; and when in the judgment of the sovereign States now comprising this Confederacy it [no longer meets] the purposes for which it was **ordained**, and ceased to answer the ends for which it was established, a peaceful appeal to the ballot box declared that, so far as they are concerned, the government created by that compact should cease to exist. In this they merely asserted a right which the Declaration of Independence of July 4, 1776, defined to be inalienable. ❞

—Jefferson Davis

(l) Stock Montage/Archive Photos/Getty Images, (b) Bettmann/CORBIS

Jefferson Davis's inauguration took place at the capitol in Montgomery, Alabama.

444

---

netw⊙rks   *Online Teaching Options*

GRAPHIC ORGANIZER

Problem-Solution Chart

Analyzing Have students use the graphic organizer to identify the problems Davis raises in his speech and the solutions he offers. *(Problem: The government no longer meets the purposes for which it was formed. Solution: Such a government should cease to exist.)* **Visual/Spatial**

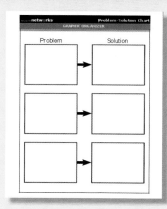

Abraham Lincoln's inauguration took place at the United States Capitol in Washington, D.C.

V

V Visual Skills

Analyzing Images Have students use the caption of the photograph to identify the location of Lincoln's inauguration. *(U.S. Capitol)* **Ask: How is this location similar to the location where Jefferson Davis delivered his inaugural address?** *(They are both capitols.)* **What do you notice about the U.S. Capitol?** *(under construction)* Have students answer the questions that follow the feature. **Visual/Spatial**

R Reading Skills

Discussing Ask student volunteers to read Lincoln's position aloud to the class. Divide the paragraphs among the student volunteers. Discuss Lincoln's vivid use of language in the excerpt. Have students note some examples. **AL** **ELL** **Ask: What was Lincoln's opinion? What do you think was the strongest part of Lincoln's argument?** *(Answers will vary depending on students' viewpoints about his opinion. They should support their answers with information from the primary source.)*

CLOSE & REFLECT

Have students write a two-paragraph essay that presents their opinion about whether the South had the right to secede. Encourage students to share their work. If time permits, invite volunteers with opposing views to hold a mock debate.

No

PRIMARY SOURCE

ABRAHAM LINCOLN

❝ The [president] derives all his authority from the people, and they have referred none upon him to fix terms for the separation of the States. The people themselves can do this if also they choose, but the executive as such has nothing to do with it. His duty is to **administer** the present government as it came to his hands and to transmit it **unimpaired** by him to his successor. . . .

. . . The mystic chords of memory, stretching from every battlefield and patriot grave to every living heart and hearthstone all over this broad land, will yet swell the chorus of the Union, when again touched, as surely they will be, by the better angels of our nature. ❞

—Abraham Lincoln

Vocabulary

ordained
established

administer
manage, direct

unimpaired
not harmed, not damaged

What Do You Think?	**DBQ**

1 *Identifying* What are Abraham Lincoln's and Jefferson Davis's basic arguments against or in favor of secession? RH.6–8.6

2 *Making Inferences* What issue seems most important to Lincoln? To Davis? RH.6–8.2

3 *Evaluating* In your opinion, which of the two makes the more powerful appeal to emotions? Explain your answer in a short essay. RH.6–8.8

Lesson 3 **445**

(t) Library of Congress [LC-USZC4-4581], (b) Stock Montage/Archive Photos/Getty Images

GRAPHIC ORGANIZER

Vertical Main Idea Graphic Organizer

Finding the Main Idea Give each student a copy of the graphic organizer, and have partners find the main idea in each leader's inaugural address. One partner should complete the graphic organizer for Davis and the other for Lincoln. Tell students that they may not find supporting details to write in every box on the graphic organizer. **Visual/Spatial**

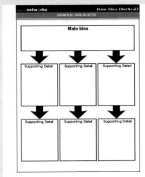

ANSWERS, p. 445

1. Lincoln believes that as chief executive, he must preserve the government as it was when he took office; he does not believe the people gave him the authority to allow secession. Davis believes the South had the right to secede from the Union because Southerners were no longer willing to consent to be governed by it.
2. Lincoln wants to keep the Union as is; Davis wants to keep what he sees as the rights of Southerners to choose their own government.
3. Students' essays should include evidence from either quote to explain their views.

CHAPTER REVIEW ACTIVITY

Have students use a simple flow chart like the one below. Then lead a discussion that allows students to complete the chart. As needed, students may add boxes for additional events.

Event 1 → Event 2 → Event 3

REVIEW THE ENDURING UNDERSTANDING

Review the chapter's Enduring Understanding with students.

• *People, places, and ideas change over time.*

Now pose the following questions in a class discussion to apply this to the chapter.

In the early years of the republic, few people were against slavery. Why do you think slavery became such a divisive issue in the mid-1800s? *(Accept reasonable responses. Some students may say that Northerners may have believed that enslaved people were people who should have the same rights as others. Some students may say that Northerners were influenced by economics: because farms in the North were much smaller than those in the South, there was less of a need for farm labor. The publication of* Uncle Tom's Cabin *also may have raised awareness among Northerners.)*

What are some of the reasons that the United States added territories and new states during the 1800s? *(Accept reasonable answers. Some students may point to Manifest Destiny—the belief that the country was destined to expand to the West Coast. Others may say that as the population of the United States grew, people needed more land so they moved westward. Some students may say that the residents of Texas may have decided that being independent had fewer benefits than being part of a larger country.)*

During the Lincoln-Douglas debates, Lincoln denied that he wanted African Americans to have the same rights as whites. However, five years later, Lincoln freed enslaved people in the United States. What do you think caused Lincoln to express such different beliefs? *(Accept reasonable answers. Some students may point out that during a political campaign candidates may be influenced by popular opinion to say something they don't believe, but once Lincoln became president, he was less influenced by popular opinion. Other students may say that Lincoln acted strategically and that he freed the slaves to create more pressure on the South. Some students may say that Lincoln thought more deeply about the issue or that abolitionists were able to persuade him that slavery was wrong.)*

Write your answers on a separate piece of paper.

❶ **Exploring the Essential Question**   WHST.6–8.1, WHST.6–8.9
INFORMATIVE/EXPLANATORY Make a list of five important events you read about in this chapter. Select the two events you think did the most to increase the conflict between the North and South. Write an essay in which you explain how these events led to war.

❷ **21st Century Skills**   WHST.6–8.5, WHST.6–8.8
IDENTIFYING PROBLEMS AND SOLUTIONS Working with a small group, think of a controversial issue that is a source of disagreement among the public today. Possible examples include health care reform or immigration reform. Research opposite sides of the issue; then work together to come up with a list of compromises that might make the solution to this problem acceptable to different sides.

❸ **Thinking Like a Historian**   RH.6–8.1
PREDICTING CONSEQUENCES What do you think would have happened to the Confederacy if Lincoln had made no effort to prevent it from seceding? Provide reasons to support your answer.

❹ **Visual Literacy**   RH.6–8.7
COMPARING ARTIFACTS Below are campaign posters produced during political campaigns. The poster on the left is from a presidential campaign from the mid-1800s; the poster on the right is from more recent times. What features do the two items share in common? How are they different from one another?

ACTIVITIES ANSWERS

Exploring the Essential Question

❶ Students' essays will vary depending on the two events chosen. Accept any essay that explains in a logical manner how the two events led to war.

21st Century Skills

❷ Each student should take part in the small-group activity, which may follow a cooperative learning structure. Students should take part in selecting the issue and in generating a list of possible compromises.

Thinking Like a Historian

❸ Accept any answer a student can justify. Answers may include: There might not have been a Civil War; the United States might have split into two separate countries permanently; slavery would have continued in the Confederacy.

REVIEW THE GUIDING QUESTIONS

Choose the best answer for each question.

RH.6–8.1
1 Which of the following was a proposal to ban slavery in any lands acquired from Mexico?

A. Compromise of 1850

B. Wilmot Proviso

C. Missouri Compromise

D. Freeport Doctrine

RH.6–8.2
2 What resulted from the Fugitive Slave Act?

F. Passage of the law stopped violence in Kansas.

G. Most Northerners respected slaveholders' rights.

H. Abolitionists were jailed in the North.

I. The law convinced many Northerners to help runaways.

RH.6–8.1
3 The Supreme Court's *Dred Scott* decision stated that

A. enslaved persons could bring lawsuits.

B. the slave trade should be abolished.

C. Congress had no power to ban slavery in any territory.

D. the Missouri Compromise was constitutional.

RH.6–8.1
4 Which was included in the Republican Party platform in the election of 1860?

F. The question of slavery should be decided by popular sovereignty.

G. In a free society, the minority has the right to break up the government.

H. Slavery should be left where it existed but be excluded from the territories.

I. Slavery should be protected in all territories south of 36°30′ N latitude.

RH.6–8.1
5 The armed pro-slavery groups of Missourians who went to Kansas to vote were called

A. Kansas Crusaders.

B. Border Breakers.

C. Missouri Militia.

D. Border Ruffians.

RH.6–8.1
6 What event officially started the Civil War?

F. the raid on Harpers Ferry

G. the attack on Fort Sumter

H. the burning of Lawrence, Kansas

I. the election of Abraham Lincoln

447

ASSESSMENT ANSWERS
Review the Guiding Questions

1 **B** Choice A is not correct because the Compromise of 1850 proposed that California be a free state but that slavery not be limited in other territories acquired from Mexico. The Missouri Compromise was before the Mexican War, so C is not correct. The Freeport Doctrine left the decision about slavery up to voters. Only the Wilmot Proviso, Choice B, would have banned slavery in all territories acquired from Mexico.

2 **I** Students should recall that the Fugitive Slave Act required all citizens to help catch runaways and made it a criminal offense to help fugitives. Many people in the North, who disagreed with slavery, would not obey the law, so choice I is correct.

3 **C** Students should eliminate choice A because the decision stated that enslaved people could not bring lawsuits, choice B because *Dred Scott* did not have to do with the slave trade, and choice D because the decision stated the compromise was unconstitutional. The decision said that Congress had no power to prohibit slavery anywhere. Choice C is correct.

4 **H** The Republicans, while pledging to keep slavery from spreading, promised not to disturb it where it already existed in the hopes of keeping the Union together. This should lead students to select choice H.

5 **D** The border-jumping voters were called *border ruffians* because they were armed and came to Kansas to cause trouble. Choices A, B, and C are not correct.

6 **G** Choices F, H, and I all contributed to the unrest that led to the outbreak of war, but the Civil War did not begin until one group of citizens (the Confederacy) attacked another (the Union) at Fort Sumter. Therefore, choice G is the correct one.

Visual Literacy

4 Similarities may include: Both use pictures of the candidate and the red, white, and blue of the flag (or the flag itself). Differences may include: The poster from the mid-1800s uses drawings of the candidates for both president and vice president, while the newer poster shows a photo of the presidential candidate only; the older poster shows images evoking U.S. ideals, while the newer one shows excited supporters of the candidate.

Analyzing Documents

7 **D** Based on the map key, Kentucky and Missouri were Union slave states in 1860.

8 **F** Because only one Union slave state borders the Mississippi River, G is not correct. Because none are in New England, H is incorrect, and because none are below Alabama, I can be eliminated, leaving F the only possible answer.

Short Response

9 He probably did not think their actions were legal because he says the voters "claimed" the right.

10 He is suggesting that the elections have been corrupted by the influence of people moving into the territory for the sole purpose of affecting the election.

Extended Response

11 Journal entries should include support from the chapter content about Dred Scott's life, the Dred Scott case, and the Supreme Court's decision in the case, as well as background information about the conditions in which enslaved persons lived.

CHAPTER 16 **Assessment** *(continued)*

DBQ ANALYZING DOCUMENTS
RH.6–8.7

7 **Identifying** According to the map, in 1860 Kentucky and Missouri were both

A. Confederate states.

B. Union free states.

C. Union territories.

D. Union slave states.

RH.6–8.7

8 **Making Generalizations** What generalization can you make about the Union slave states?

F. They share a border with free states to the north.

G. They all border the Mississippi River.

H. They are all in New England.

I. They are farther south than Alabama.

Map key:
- Union Territories
- Union free state
- Union slave state
- Slave state seceding before Fort Sumter, April 1861
- Slave state seceding after Fort Sumter, April 1861
- Boundary between Union and Confederacy

SHORT RESPONSE

Erastus D. Ladd described voters from Missouri crossing the border to vote in an 1855 election in Kansas.

"They claimed to have a legal right to vote in the Territory [Kansas], and that they were residents by virtue of their being then in the Territory. They said they were free to confess that they came from Missouri; that they lived in Missouri, and voted as Missourians."

Source: Albert Bushnell Hart, *Source-Book of American History*

RH.6–8.6, WHST.6–8.4

9 Did Ladd think the actions of these voters were legal? Explain your answer.

RH.6–8.2, WHST.6–8.4

10 What is Ladd suggesting about the elections in Kansas?

EXTENDED RESPONSE
WHST.6–8.1, WHST.6–8.10

11 **Narrative** Take the role of an African American living in the United States in the 1850s. Write a journal entry expressing your thoughts after the *Dred Scott* decision is issued.

Need Extra Help?

If You've Missed Question	1	2	3	4	5	6	7	8	9	10	11
Review Lesson	1	1	2	3	1	3	3	1	1	1	2

---

netw🌐rks *Online Teaching Options*

Using eAssessment

Use eAssessment to access and assign the publisher-made Lesson Quizzes & Chapter Tests electronically. You can also use eAssessment to create your own quizzes and tests from hundreds of available questions. eAssessment helps you design assessments that meet the needs of different types of learners. Follow the link in the *Assess* tab of your Teacher Lesson Center.

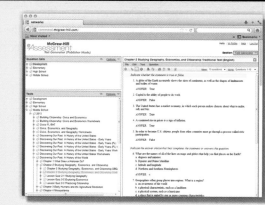

CHAPTER 17
The Civil War Planner

UNDERSTANDING BY DESIGN®

Enduring Understanding
- *Conflict can lead to change.*

Essential Questions
- *Why does conflict develop?*

Predictable Misunderstandings

Students may think:
- *The Emancipation Proclamation immediately freed all enslaved people.*
- *There were more American military deaths in other conflicts, such as the World Wars.*

Assessment Evidence

Performance Tasks:
- *Hands-On Chapter Project*

Other Evidence:
- *Interactive Graphic Organizer*
- *What Do You Know? activity*
- *Economics of History Activity*
- *21st Century Skills Activity*
- *Primary Source Activities*
- *America's Literature Questions*
- *Written Paragraphs*
- *Online Self-Check Quizzes*
- *Lesson Reviews*
- *Chapter Activities and Assessment*

SUGGESTED PACING GUIDE

Introducing the Chapter . . . . 1 day	America's Literature . . . . 1 day
Lesson 1 . . . . 2 days	Lesson 4 . . . . 2 days
Lesson 2 . . . . 2 days	Lesson 5 . . . . 2 days
Lesson 3 . . . . 2 days	Chapter Wrap-Up and Assessment . . . . . . 1 day

TOTAL TIME   13 Days

Key for Using the Teacher Edition

SKILL-BASED ACTIVITIES

Types of skill activities found in the Teacher Edition.

V **Visual Skills** require students to analyze maps, graphs, charts, and photos.

R **Reading Skills** help students practice reading skills and master vocabulary.

W **Writing Skills** provide writing opportunities to help students comprehend the text.

C **Critical Thinking Skills** help students apply and extend what they have learned.

T **Technology Skills** require students to use digital tools effectively.

Letters are followed by a number when there is more than one of the same type of skill on the page.

DIFFERENTIATED INSTRUCTION

All activities are written for the on-level student unless otherwise marked with the leveled labels below.

BL Beyond Level
AL Approaching Level
ELL English Language Learners

All students benefit from activities that utilize different learning styles. Many activities are marked as below when a particular learning style is highlighted.

Intrapersonal	Naturalist
Logical/Mathematical	Kinesthetic
Visual/Spatial	Auditory/Musical
Verbal/Linguistic	Interpersonal

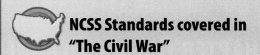

NCSS Standards covered in "The Civil War"

Learners will understand:

2   TIME, CONTINUITY, AND CHANGE

1. The study of the past provides representation of the history of communities, nations, and the world

2. Concepts such as: chronology, causality, change, conflict, complexity, multiple perspectives, primary and secondary sources, and cause and effect

5. Key historical periods and patterns of change within and across cultures (e.g., the rise and fall of ancient civilizations, the development of technology, the rise of modern nation-states, and the establishment and breakdown of colonial systems)

7. The contributions of key persons, groups, and events from the past and their influence on the present

3   People, Places, and Environments

8. Factors that contribute to cooperation and conflict among peoples of the nation and world, including language, religion, and political beliefs

9. The use of a variety of maps, globes, graphic representations, and geospatial technologies to help investigate the relationships among people, places, and environments

4   INDIVIDUALS, GROUPS, AND INSTITUTIONS

1. This theme helps us know how individuals are members of groups and institutions, and influence and shape those groups and institutions

3. Institutions are created to respond to changing individual and group needs

7. That institutions may promote or undermine social conformity

7   PRODUCTION, DISTRIBUTION, AND CONSUMPTION

1. Individuals, government, and society experience scarcity because human wants and needs exceed what can be produced from available resources

CHAPTER OPENER PLANNER

Students will know:
- the goals and strategies, strengths and weaknesses of the North and the South.
- major battles of the early part of the American Civil War.
- the debate leading up to, and the results of, Lincoln's Emancipation Proclamation.
- how the Civil War affected the roles of women, politics, and the economies of the North and South.
- major battles and turning points of the American Civil War.
- the events that ended the Civil War.

Students will be able to:
- ***identify and evaluate*** the goals of both the North and the South.
- ***compare*** the strengths and weaknesses of the North and the South.
- ***explain*** how the Union responded to defeats in the East in 1862.
- ***evaluate*** the effect of the Emancipation Proclamation.
- ***identify*** the changes in lifestyle during the Civil War.
- ***describe*** the conditions of the hospitals and the prison camps during the Civil War.
- ***analyze*** political and economic changes that occurred during the war.
- ***explain*** why the South seemed to be winning the war.
- ***analyze*** why the Battle of Gettysburg was a turning point in the war.
- ***evaluate*** the idea of total war and how it affected the South.
- ***identify and analyze*** the events that ended the Civil War.

UNDERSTANDING
BY DESIGN®

☑ *Print Teaching Options*

V Visual Skills

☐ **P. 450** Students review a map and name some Confederate states, Union states, and Union territories. **AL** **ELL** **Visual/Spatial**

☐ **P. 451** Students review events on a time line and make inferences as to why the events were included. **Visual/Spatial**

C Critical Thinking Skills

☐ **P. 450** Students infer why some states banded together to form the Confederate States of America.

☐ **P. 451** Students look at a time line of events from 1861 to 1865 and draw conclusions about what might have led to the end of the Civil War.

☑ *Online Teaching Options*

V Visual Skills

☐ **MAP** **The Civil War 1861–1865**—Students compare the land holdings of the Union and Confederate states.

☐ **TIME LINE** **United States 1861–1865**—Students learn about key events during the Civil War period.

☐ **WORLD ATLAS** Students can use this interactive map to identify regions of the world, learn about individual countries, locate political boundaries, measure distances, and much more.

Project-Based Learning

Hands-On Chapter Project

The Civil War
Student groups will describe the experiences and events of the Civil War by creating a visual display about a group or individual.

Technology Extension ✎edtechteacher
21st Century Learning

Civil War Web Site
- Find an additional activity online that incorporates technology for this project.
- Visit the EdTechTeacher Web sites (included in the Technology Extension for this chapter) for more links, tutorials, and other resources.

Print Resources

ANCILLARY RESOURCES
These ancillaries are available for every chapter and lesson.
- **Reading Essentials and Study Guide Workbook** **AL** **ELL**
- **Chapter Tests and Lesson Quizzes Blackline Masters**

PRINTABLE DIGITAL WORKSHEETS
These printable digital worksheets are available for every chapter and lesson.
- **Hands-On Chapter Projects**
- **What Do You Know? activities**
- **Chapter Summaries (English and Spanish)**
- **Vocabulary Builder activities**
- **Guided Reading activities**

More Media Resources

SUGGESTED VIDEOS
Watch clips from popular culture films about the Civil War, such as ***Gone with the Wind, Cold Mountain,*** or the 1993 miniseries ***Gettysburg.***
- **Discuss:** What can we learn about historical events from fictional movies?
- **Discuss:** Can fictional movies capture historical events accurately?

(NOTE: Preview clips for age-appropriateness.)

SUGGESTED READING 📖
Grade 6 reading level:
- ***Civil War on Sunday,*** by Mary Pope Osborne

Grade 7 reading level:
- ***The Boys' War: Confederate and Union Soldiers Talk About the Civil War,*** by Jim Murphy

Grade 8 reading level:
- ***Harriet Tubman: Conductor of the Underground Railroad,*** by Ann Petry

LESSON **1** PLANNER

THE TWO SIDES

Students will know:
- the goals and strategies, strengths and weaknesses of the North and the South.

Students will be able to:
- **identify and evaluate** the goals of both the North and the South.
- **compare** the strengths and weaknesses of the North and the South.

☑ *Print Teaching Options*

V Visual Skills

☐ **P. 455** Students view a photo of two soldiers and identify how the caption relates to the photo.
Visual/Spatial

R Reading Skills

☐ **P. 452** Students identify the boundaries of the North and the South and discuss the border states. **AL** **ELL**

☐ **P. 452** Students summarize the importance of border states to both the North and the South. **BL**

☐ **P. 453** Students specify the goals of the North and the South in the Civil War. **AL**

☐ **P. 456** Students discuss the approaches of the North and the South regarding the participation of African Americans in the Civil War.

☐ **P. 457** Students identify reasons why soldiers may have *deserted* the war. **AL** **ELL**

W Writing Skills

☐ **P. 457** Students write a letter from the point of view of a soldier in the Civil War writing home from the battlefront.

C Critical Thinking Skills

☐ **P. 453** Students analyze the advantages and disadvantages of the North and the South at the start of the war.

☐ **P. 454** Students discuss the strategies of the Confederate forces and the Union forces for winning the war and make predictions about the effectiveness of the strategies. **AL** **ELL** **BL**

☐ **P. 455** Students think about how differing points of view on the war may have affected families. **Intrpersonal**

☐ **P. 456** Students make connections between the reasons people enlisted in the armed forces during the Civil War with the reasons people may enlist today. **AL** **ELL**

T Technology Skills

☐ **P. 454** Students use the Internet to research and write a brief statement on how Abraham Lincoln viewed the South at the beginning of the war. **BL**

☑ *Online Teaching Options*

V Visual Skills

☐ **VIDEO** **The North and South Mobilize for War**—Students learn why both sides thought the war would be short and discover what kept Europe out of the war.

☐ **SLIDE SHOW** **Civil War Casualties**—Students view paintings and photographs of Civil War battles, wounded, and dead.

☐ **IMAGE** **Artillery**—Students click to learn about large-caliber weapons.

R Reading Skills

☐ **GRAPHIC ORGANIZER** **Taking Notes: *Comparing and Contrasting:* The North and the South**—Students list similarities and differences between the North and the South.

☐ **SLIDE SHOW** **Army Organization**—Students learn about troop organization from single soldier to squad, platoon, brigade, division, and finally corps.

☐ **IMAGE** **African Americans in the Civil War**—Students read about the 180,000 soldiers of African descent who served in the Union army.

C Critical Thinking Skills

☐ **WHITEBOARD ACTIVITY** **Resources of the North and South**—Students categorize advantages held by each side before the war.

☐ **CHART** **Army Salaries**—Students compare army salaries across four wars and prices for items during the Civil War.

☐ **SLIDE SHOW** **Railroads in the Civil War**—Students analyze how differences in the railroads in the North and South affected their ability to move troops and material.

T Technology Skills

☐ **SELF-CHECK QUIZ** **Lesson 1**—Students receive instant feedback on their mastery of lesson content.

EARLY YEARS OF THE WAR

Students will know:
- major battles of the early part of the American Civil War.
- the debate leading up to, and the results of, Lincoln's Emancipation Proclamation.

Students will be able to:
- **explain** how the Union responded to defeats in the East in 1862.
- **evaluate** the effect of the Emancipation Proclamation.

UNDERSTANDING
BY DESIGN®

☑ *Print Teaching Options*

V Visual Skills

☐ **P. 459** Students discuss how the image of the *Virginia* helps to identify the purpose of the *ironclad*. **ELL**
Visual/Spatial

☐ **P. 461** Students analyze a map of the war in the West between 1862 and 1865. Visual/Spatial

R Reading Skills

☐ **P. 458** Students explain the significance of the Battle of Bull Run. **AL** **BL**

☐ **P. 459** Students identify the role of General Ulysses S. Grant in the capture of Fort Henry and the surrender of Fort Donelson. **ELL**

☐ **P. 460** Students discuss the significance of the capture of New Orleans to the Union cause.

☐ **P. 464** Students discuss the Emancipation Proclamation.

W Writing Skills

☐ **P. 461** Students write journal entries discussing how it might have felt to be a resident of New Orleans as the North gained control of the region.

☐ **P. 462** Students write a newspaper editorial from the point of view of either the North or the South in response to the Union defeat at Chancellorsville, Virginia. **BL** Interpersonal

☐ **P. 464** Students write a brief paragraph explaining why they agree or disagree with Lincoln's judgment about his place in history.

C Critical Thinking Skills

☐ **P. 458** Students evaluate President Lincoln's reasons for ordering a blockade of Confederate ports and how this set the stage for fighting at sea. **ELL**

☐ **P. 460** Students make generalizations about the Confederates' battle strategy. **BL**

☐ **P. 462** Students identify the point of view of President Lincoln and that of the Confederates regarding the Union defeat at Chancellorsville, Virginia.

T Technology Skills

☐ **P. 463** Students collaborate with each other to research the influence of abolitionists on the end of slavery. **BL** Interpersonal

☑ *Online Teaching Options*

V Visual Skills

☐ **VIDEO** **Lincoln's Great Speeches**—The impact of the Emancipation Proclamation and Gettysburg Address is examined.

☐ **IMAGE** **Ironclads**—Students learn more about the *USS Merrimack*.

☐ **MAP** **The War in the West 1862–1863**—Students locate major battles along the Mississippi River.

☐ **MAP** **War in the East 1862–1863**—Students trace Union and Confederate troop movement in Virginia, Maryland, and Pennsylvania.

R Reading Skills

☐ **GRAPHIC ORGANIZER** **Taking Notes:** *Sequencing:* **Civil War Battles**—Students record on a time line major battles, the date they occurred, the location, and the victor.

☐ **IMAGE** **Robert E. Lee**—Students read of the life and accomplishments of this Southern general.

☐ **PRIMARY SOURCE** **Virginia and Monitor**—Students read a first-hand account of the battle between these two ships that ended in a draw.

☐ **PRIMARY SOURCE** **The Emancipation Proclamation**—Students read an excerpt of this document that freed enslaved persons within the areas loyal to the Confederacy.

C Critical Thinking Skills

☐ **CHART** **Advantages of Ironclads**—Students identify the advantages of ironclad ships.

☐ **SLIDE SHOW** **The Battle of Antietam**—Students analyze visuals and text that describe the bloodiest single-day battle in American history.

T Technology Skills

☐ **SELF-CHECK QUIZ** **Lesson 2**—Students receive instant feedback on their mastery of lesson content.

☐ **GAME** **Fill in the Blank Game: Early Years of the War**—Students complete sentences to review lesson content.

LIFE DURING THE CIVIL WAR

Students will know:
- how the Civil War affected the roles of women, politics, and the economies of the North and South.

Students will be able to:
- **identify** the changes in lifestyle during the Civil War.
- **describe** the conditions of the hospitals and the prison camps during the Civil War.
- **analyze** political and economic changes that occurred during the war.

UNDERSTANDING BY DESIGN®

☑ Print Teaching Options

V Visual Skills

☐ **P. 466** Students analyze a photograph of Frances Clayton. **Visual/Spatial**

☐ **P. 467** Students look at a photo of a hospital during the Civil War and contrast it with hospitals of today. **BL Visual/Spatial**

☐ **P. 471** Students analyze a graph that shows inflation. **Visual/Spatial Logical/Mathematical**

R Reading Skills

☐ **P. 465** Students create a Venn diagram to identify the ways the war affected the home front . **AL Visual/Spatial**

☐ **P. 466** Students describe how the daily lives of women changed during the Civil War. **AL**

☐ **P. 469** Students discuss the phrase *habeas corpus* and the reasons why it was suspended during the Civil War. **AL ELL**

☐ **P. 470** Students discuss the protests against the draft after participating in an activity where they await their name to be called. **Kinesthetic**

W Writing Skills

☐ **P. 466** Students research and write a description of women soldiers in the Civil War.

C Critical Thinking Skills

☐ **P. 465** Students contrast how the South suffered compared to the North as a result of the war. **AL**

☐ **P. 468** Students make inferences about how soldiers from any country may feel towards prisoners of war. **BL**

☐ **P. 468** Students compare the conditions at the Andersonville prison camps with those at Elmira.

☐ **P. 469** Students compare and contrast the similarities and differences between hospitals and surgical practices in the days of the Civil War and now. **AL ELL Verbal/Linguistic**

☐ **P. 471** Students compare and contrast the effect the war had on the economies of the North and the South.

T Technology Skills

☐ **P. 467** Students work in small groups and use a social bookmarking service to research and share information about Dorothea Dix. **Interpersonal**

☑ Online Teaching Options

V Visual Skills

☐ **VIDEO Clara Barton**—Students view a video that describes the work of this founder of the Red Cross.

☐ **IMAGE Andersonville Prison**—Students learn of the conditions at this Confederate prison in central Georgia.

☐ **IMAGE Amputation Kit**—Students examine the tools used by doctors during the war.

R Reading Skills

☐ **GRAPHIC ORGANIZER Taking Notes: *Identifying*: Women of the North and the South**—Students identify contributions of women to the war effort.

☐ **SLIDE SHOW Women Take Charge**—Students read about women who took an active role to change society.

☐ **SLIDE SHOW Dorothea Dix**—Students view scenes and read of the accomplishments of this social reformer.

C Critical Thinking Skills

☐ **GRAPH Greenbacks**— Students analyze the effect of inflation on purchasing power.

☐ **POLITICAL CARTOON Civil War Political Cartoons**—Students analyze visuals and text in order to consider opinions held during the war.

☐ **SLIDE SHOW Roles of Women in War**—Students compare and contrast roles of women during the Civil War and now.

T Technology Skills

☐ **SELF-CHECK QUIZ Lesson 3**—Students receive instant feedback on their mastery of lesson content.

☑ Printable Digital Worksheets

W Writing Skills

☐ **WORKSHEET 21st Century Skills Activity: The Civil War: Life During the Civil War: Communication: Write a Letter**—Students write a personal letter.

THE STRAIN OF WAR

Students will know:
- *major battles and turning points of the American Civil War.*

Students will be able to:
- *explain* why the South seemed to be winning the war.
- *analyze* why the Battle of Gettysburg was a turning point in the war.

UNDERSTANDING
BY DESIGN®

☑ *Print Teaching Options*

V Visual Skills

☐ **P. 478** Students analyze a map of the Battle of Gettysburg. **Visual/Spatial**

R Reading Skills

☐ **P. 474** Students explain the events of the Battle of Fredericksburg and its aftermath. **BL**

☐ **P. 475** Students discuss the Southern victory at Chancellorsville and the effect that losing Stonewall Jackson had on the morale of the Confederacy. **AL** **ELL**

☐ **P. 475** Students create lists of Union commanders discussed in the text. **AL**

☐ **P. 476** Students discuss possible reasons why African Americans would have been willing to put themselves in such danger to fight for the Union.

☐ **P. 477** Students discuss the establishment of the 54th Massachusetts Regiment and its record in battle.

☐ **P. 479** Students summarize the events of the third day of the Battle of Gettysburg.

☐ **P. 480** Students determine the meaning of the word *casualties* as it relates to war. **AL** **ELL**

W Writing Skills

☐ **P. 477** Students write either a brief history of the 54th Massachusetts Regiment or a short biography of Colonel Robert Gould Shaw. **BL**

C Critical Thinking Skills

☐ **P. 476** Students identify the different points of view on African American soldiers enlisting in the Civil War. **AL** **ELL**

☐ **P. 477** Students contrast the leadership qualities of the Union and Confederate leaders.

☐ **P. 478** Students create a graphic organizer that highlights the elements of the Battle of Gettysburg that they knew prior to reading and add to it as they learn more. **AL**

☐ **P. 479** Students identify Vicksburg as an important city for the Union's strategy. **AL**

☑ *Online Teaching Options*

V Visual Skills

☐ **VIDEO** **The Gettysburg Address**—Students view a video that recounts the delivery of this address by Lincoln, which dedicated the battlefield at Gettysburg as a war memorial in 1863.

☐ **IMAGE** **Trench Warfare**—Students click to understand how trench warfare was conducted.

☐ **MAP** **The Battle of Gettysburg, Day 3**—Students view the deployment and movement of troops on this bloody day of the Civil War.

R Reading Skills

☐ **GRAPHIC ORGANIZER** **Taking Notes:** *Categorizing:* **Union and Confederate Victories**—Students identify which side won each victory in the Civil War.

☐ **PRIMARY SOURCE** **Thomas Jonathan "Stonewall" Jackson**—Students read of the life and accomplishments of this Confederate general.

C Critical Thinking Skills

☐ **PRIMARY SOURCE** **Recruiting of African American Soldiers**—Students analyze a recruitment poster.

T Technology Skills

☐ **SELF-CHECK QUIZ** **Lesson 4**—Students receive instant feedback on their mastery of lesson content.

☐ **GAME** **The Strain of War Crossword Puzzle**—Students solve clues to review lesson content.

☑ *Printable Digital Worksheets*

W Writing Skills

☐ **WORKSHEET** **Primary Source Activity: The Civil War: The Strain of War: Lincoln's Gettysburg Address**—Students write their own evaluation of Lincoln's speech.

Students will know:
- the events that ended the Civil War.

Students will be able to:
- *evaluate* the idea of total war and how it affected the South.
- *identify* and analyze the events that ended the Civil War.

UNDERSTANDING
BY DESIGN®

☑ *Print Teaching Options*

V Visual Skills

☐ **P. 483** Students analyze a map of the final battles of the Civil War. **Visual/Spatial**

☐ **P. 486** Students analyze information in a graph that shows death tolls in major U.S. wars. **AL ELL Visual/ Spatial Logical/Mathematical**

R Reading Skills

☐ **P. 481** Students identify what it means to close in on something and what that subheading suggests about who won the war. **AL ELL**

☐ **P. 482** Students cite text evidence to support the claim that Grant's move south toward Richmond represented the "six bloodiest weeks of the war."

☐ **P. 483** Students assess the meaning of "total war."

☐ **P. 483** Students discuss Sherman's march to Atlanta while Grant laid siege to Petersburg.

☐ **P. 484** Students identify important elements of the war at sea. **BL**

☐ **P. 485** Students explain why the Confederates evacuated Richmond rather than stay and fight.

☐ **P. 487** Students discuss the surrender of the Confederacy at Appomattox Court House.

W Writing Skills

☐ **P. 482** Students argue their position on whether or not Ulysses S. Grant was a practical man. **Verbal/Linguistic**

C Critical Thinking Skills

☐ **P. 481** Students evaluate why Lincoln chose Ulysses S. Grant to command the Union army.

☐ **P. 482** Students speculate as to why Grant was called a "butcher" and why Lincoln did not replace him. **AL ELL**

☐ **P. 483** Students discuss Grant's actions at Petersburg and state whether they thought Lincoln's appointment of Grant was a good one.

☐ **P. 484** Students theorize what might have happened if Lincoln had not won reelection in 1864. **BL**

☐ **P. 485** Students analyze and assess Sherman's total war strategy. **BL**

☐ **P. 486** Students analyze primary sources to show that the Union army was both ruthless and compassionate.

☑ *Online Teaching Options*

V Visual Skills

☐ **VIDEO Sherman's March to the Sea**—Students learn the cost of "total war."

☐ **MAP The Final Battles, 1864–1865**—Students view troop movements in the South, recounting the final battles, which were mostly won by Union forces.

☐ **SLIDE SHOW Richmond**—Students view scenes of this city that played an important role in both the American Revolution and the Civil War.

R Reading Skills

☐ **GRAPHIC ORGANIZER Taking Notes: *Determining Cause and Effect:* The Civil War Ends**—Students sequence the chain of events that led to the end of the war.

☐ **IMAGE William Tecumseh Sherman**—Students read of this Union general's life and accomplishments.

☐ **PRIMARY SOURCE Grant's Strategy**—Students read an excerpt from a letter written by Grant describing his strategy for Union troops in the spring of 1864.

C Critical Thinking Skills

☐ **GRAPH Costs of War**—Students compare American battle deaths over eight wars.

☐ **CHART Costs of War**—Students click to see the monetary cost of seven wars both at the time and in today's dollars.

T Technology Skills

☐ **SELF-CHECK QUIZ Lesson 5**—Students receive instant feedback on their mastery of lesson content.

☐ **GAME The War's Final Stages Concentration Game**—Students match terms and definitions to review lesson vocabulary.

☑ *Printable Digital Worksheets*

C Critical Thinking Skills

☐ **WORKSHEET Primary Source Activity: The Civil War: The War's Final Stages: Lincoln's Inaugural Addresses**—Students analyze excerpts from Lincoln's two inaugural addresses.

INTERVENTION AND REMEDIATION STRATEGIES

LESSON 1 The Two Sides

Reading and Comprehension

Ask students to locate the graphs in the lesson and point out ideas and sentences in the text that they support.

Text Evidence

Have students create a T-chart summarizing the two sides in the Civil War conflict. They may use outside resources or base their chart solely on the text.

LESSON 2 Early Years of the War

Reading and Comprehension

Have students locate each of the Content Vocabulary words in the lesson and use context clues in the text to write a definition for each word.

Text Evidence

Ask each student to write two questions about the lesson and then exchange them with another student, who will search the text for the answer.

LESSON 3 Life During the Civil War

Reading and Comprehension

Ask each student to choose and summarize a paragraph in the lesson, stating in his or her own words the main ideas represented in the text.

Text Evidence

Ask students to create a Venn diagram comparing and contrasting modern medical practices and instruments with those during the Civil War. Students should use their text to confirm their diagrams.

LESSON 4 The Strains of War

Reading and Comprehension

Ask students to skim the text, looking for quotations. Have them tell how each quotation contributes to the overall meaning of the paragraph.

Text Evidence

Divide the class into groups and ask them to create a time line of the events in this lesson. They may want to include any other interesting events that happened during the time, too.

LESSON 5 The War's Final Stages

Reading and Comprehension

Ask students to read the last section of the lesson, "The Toll of War," and skim the chapter to determine what the work of Reconstruction might involve.

Text Evidence

Have students create a map with the locations of the final battles of the conflict, as well as the location of the surrender. Students should use their text and outside sources to provide specific dates.

Online Resources

Approaching Level Reader

Use this online lower-level text that corresponds directly to the text in the Student Edition. It includes a Spanish version.

Guided Reading Activities

This resource uses graphic organizers and guiding questions to help students with comprehension.

What Do You Know?

Use these worksheets to pre-assess student's background knowledge before they study the chapter.

Reading Essentials and Study Guide Workbook

This resource offers writing and reading activities for the approaching-level student. Also available in Spanish.

Self-Check Quizzes

This online assessment tool provides instant feedback for students to check their progress.

The Civil War

1861–1865

ESSENTIAL QUESTION *Why does conflict develop?*

◄ *Abraham Lincoln was president during the nation's greatest crisis.*

Library of Congress [LC-DIG-ppmsca-19241]

The Story Matters . . .

In November 1860, voters elect a self-educated lawyer from Illinois named Abraham Lincoln to be president of the United States. Even before Lincoln is inaugurated, South Carolina and six other Southern states secede from the Union. As he waits to take office, Lincoln sees the nation he is to lead spiral downward toward civil war—a war that will prove to be the deadliest in U.S. history.

Lincoln does not give up. He believes "[a] house divided against itself cannot stand," and he guides the nation until it is once again united.

ENGAGE

Bellringer Ask groups of students to jot down on self-stick notes words or phrases related to the Civil War, using the textbook or personal knowledge. Then ask each group to place the notes on the board, grouped by topic. Discuss the topics as they are placed. Then have individual students write down and turn in two questions that they would like to have answered during the lesson.

Making Connections

Have students read "The Story Matters . . ." to themselves. Ask them what they think of when they hear the name "Abraham Lincoln" or of what events his name reminds them. *(Possible answers: was a president, Honest Abe, emancipation, the Civil War)* Write their responses on the board. **Ask: How do you think Abraham Lincoln's plans for handling the problems facing the United States had to change when states began seceding before he was even sworn in?** *(Discuss responses and use them to introduce the chapter.)* Tell students that in this chapter, they will learn about many of the struggles that Lincoln faced as president during the Civil War.

Letter from the Author

Dear American History Teacher,

The Civil War remains the most divisive war in American history. Abraham Lincoln entered the White House at an advanced stage of the sectional crisis, but it was his leadership, vision, and determination to keep the Union together that made a profound difference in the war's outcome. Enslaved African Americans interpreted the Civil War as a war of liberation, despite President Lincoln's initial statement that the war had nothing to do with slavery. By the war's conclusion, however, slavery would be abolished.

Albert S. Broussard

TEACH & ASSESS

Step Into the Place

V1 Visual Skills

Reading a Map Review the parts of the map with students, pointing out the key and the colors that indicate regions. Ask students to name some Confederate states, Union states, and Union territories. Assist students who may be colorblind by using crosshatching to help them distinguish the different regions. **AL** **ELL** Visual/Spatial

C1 Critical Thinking Skills

Determining Cause and Effect Ask students to consider what they learned about the area in green. **Ask:**

* Why do you think these states banded together to form the Confederate States of America? *(Student responses may include that these states all grew cotton and used slave labor to harvest it.)*
* Why do you think there are no Confederate territories? *(Students answers will vary.)*

Content Background Knowledge

Point out that before regions joined the Union, they were known as *territories*. Point out the territories in orange on the map. The names of the territories often became the names of the states once they joined the Union. Some territories, however, became multiple states. Point to *Indian Territory* and ask students what its modern name is. *(Oklahoma)* Students may want to list the names of the territories and the states they became.

ANSWERS, p. 450

Step Into the Place
1. Kentucky, Maryland, Pennsylvania
2. Possible answer: The Confederate capital, Richmond, is in Virginia.
3. **CRITICAL THINKING** Possible answer: The Northern army was stronger, or the North kept attacking the Confederacy to force it to return to the Union.

Step Into the Time
The Emancipation Proclamation was issued in 1862, three years before the war ended in 1865.

Place and Time: United States 1861 to 1865

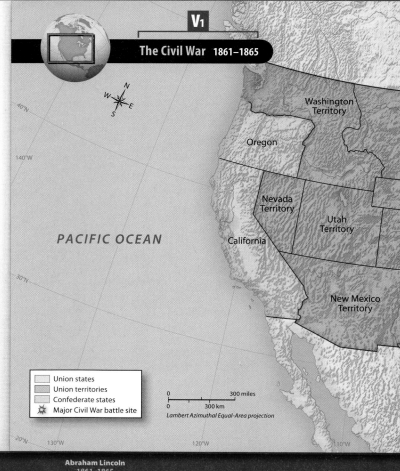

In December 1860, South Carolina announced that it was seceding from the United States. Within a few months, six other states had followed South Carolina out of the Union. After the battle at Fort Sumter, a total of 11 Southern states joined together in the Confederate States of America.

Step Into the Place

MAP FOCUS In 1861 soldiers fired the first shots of the Civil War. Armies of the Confederacy and the Union did battle in locations all across the country.

1 LOCATION On this map, which Union states have Civil War battle sites? RH.6–8.7

2 PLACE What clue can you find on the map that might explain why so many battles took place in Virginia? RH.6–8.7

3 CRITICAL THINKING
Drawing Conclusions Why do you think most of the battles of the Civil War took place in the Confederate states? RH.6–8.7

The Civil War 1861–1865

Washington Territory

Oregon

Nevada Territory

California

Utah Territory

New Mexico Territory

PACIFIC OCEAN

☐ Union states
☐ Union territories
☐ Confederate states
✴ Major Civil War battle site

| 0 | 300 miles |
| 0 | 300 km |

Lambert Azimuthal Equal-Area projection

Step Into the Time

Abraham Lincoln
1861–1865

V2 C2
TIME LINE Look at the time line. For how many years after the Emancipation Proclamation did the Civil War continue? RH.6–8.5, RH.6–8.7

U.S. PRESIDENTS
U.S. EVENTS
WORLD EVENTS

1861 | 1862

1861 Robert E. Lee takes command of Virginia's Confederate forces

1862 International Red Cross established (American Red Cross organized 10 years later)

450 *The Civil War*

White House Historical Association

Project-Based Learning

Hands-On Chapter Project

The Cilvil War

Students learn about the experiences and events of the Civil War by creating a visual display about a chosen group or individual. They will read about their group or individual in their textbook and brainstorm a list of words and phrases that describe what life was like for their group or individual. Have students locate primary and secondary source images and meet in groups to select and arrange images for their display. Then have them add text and assemble the display. Have them create a plaque that includes a title and a paragraph summarizing what life was like for their group or individual during the Civil War.

Technology Extension

Civil War Web Site

Students will design a Web site that illustrates life during the Civil War. They will understand how to organize the Web site, make it accessible online, and address a wider audience. This authentic experience will capture the minds of your students as they put themselves in the shoes of historical Web site designers. Even though students will be working in small groups to complete sections of the site, their efforts can be combined for a collaborative class production.

edtechteacher
21st Century Learning

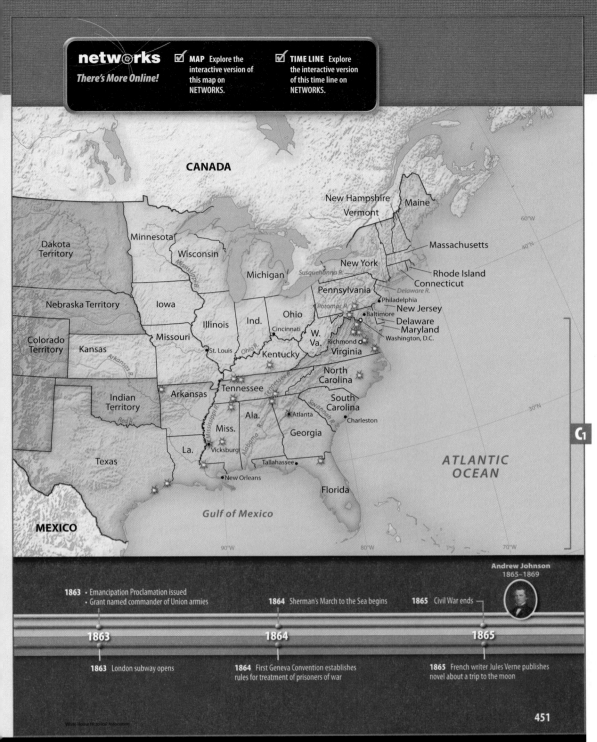

CANADA

New Hampshire
Maine
Vermont
Minnesota
Dakota Territory
Massachusetts
Wisconsin
New York
Rhode Island
Michigan
Connecticut
Pennsylvania
Philadelphia
Nebraska Territory
Iowa
New Jersey
Delaware
Ohio
Illinois
Ind.
Maryland
Cincinnati
Washington, D.C.
Colorado Territory
W. Va.
Missouri
St. Louis
Richmond
Kansas
Kentucky
Virginia
North Carolina
Arkansas
Tennessee
Indian Territory
South Carolina
Ala.
Atlanta
Miss.
Charleston
Georgia
La.
Vicksburg
Texas
Tallahassee
ATLANTIC OCEAN
New Orleans
Florida
Gulf of Mexico
MEXICO

1863 • Emancipation Proclamation issued
• Grant named commander of Union armies
1864 Sherman's March to the Sea begins
1865 Civil War ends

Andrew Johnson
1865–1869

1863   **1864**   **1865**

1863 London subway opens
1864 First Geneva Convention establishes rules for treatment of prisoners of war
1865 French writer Jules Verne publishes novel about a trip to the moon

White House Historical Association

451

Step Into the Time

V₂ Visual Skills

Integrating Visual Information Ask students to look at the time line and review the events listed there. **Ask:**

• Why might the author have chosen to include these events, especially those in Europe? *(Student responses will vary; accept and discuss responses.)*
• Are there events that you would have included on the time line? *(Student responses will vary.)*
Visual/Spatial

C₂ Critical Thinking Skills

Drawing Conclusions Have students review the time line for the chapter. Explain that they will be studying events from 1861 to 1865. **Ask:** Based on the information in the time line, what event might have led to the end of the war? *(Grant being named as commander of the Union armies and/or Sherman's March to the Sea)*

Content Background Knowledge

The London subway, also known as the Tube, was a product of the Industrial Revolution. When it first opened in 1836, it was an above-ground line. Work began on the underground line in 1860. In 1863 the line opened to the public, and it had 38,000 passengers on its first day.

CLOSE & REFLECT

Collect students' questions from the Bellringer activity and use them to construct a KWL chart. While students, especially those in major battleground states, may know quite a bit about the Civil War, ask them to incorporate new facts into the chart or to correct misconceptions.

The Civil War, 1861-1865

Location Project the interactive Chapter Opener map on the whiteboard. Point out the Union states, the Confederate states, and the border states on the map. Ask students if they know of any famous battle sites from the Civil War, and point out their locations on the map. Point out important physical features, such as the Mississippi River and its tributaries, along with the port cities. Ask students if they can think of reasons that these might become important during the war. Have students study the key to the map. Then, as a class, discuss the Map Focus questions.

See page 449B for other online activities.

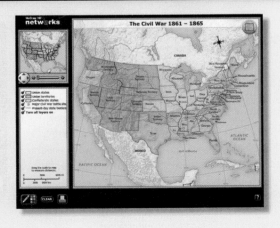

The Civil War 1861 – 1865

ENGAGE

🔔 **Bellringer** Discuss with students problems that can develop within families or between friends when they disagree. **Ask: How is a country like a family?** *(Possible answers: The people share a government like children share parents. The country's laws are like parents' rules.)* Discuss with students what can happen when members of a family have strong disagreements. Explain that the disagreements between the Northern and the Southern states divided the country and even divided families.

TEACH & ASSESS

R1 Reading Skills

Identifying As a class, use the Chapter Opener map to identify the boundaries of the North and the South. Then, have students read the text and guide a class discussion about these states. **Ask:**

- **Which states were considered the "border" states?** *(West Virginia, Maryland, Kentucky, and Missouri)* **Why are they called "border" states?** *(because they are along the border between North and South, where the two parts of the country touch one another)* **AL** **ELL**
- **What ties did people in the border states have to the North and the South?** *(People had ties to both sides in the border states. Because slavery was still legal in these states, some were loyal to the South, while others probably identified more with the North. Those who had family in other states may have felt divided loyalties, too.)*

R2 Reading Skills

Summarizing Direct students to read the section titled "Division in the Border States." As a class, discuss the importance of the border states to both the North and the South. Discuss what each state would bring to the cause of either the North or the South. **Ask: Which border state was most important to the Union?** *(Maryland)* **Why?** *(Washington, D.C., was located within the state. If the Confederacy held Maryland, the Union's capital would be surrounded.)* **BL**

ANSWER, p. 452

TAKING NOTES: North: large population, resources, offensive strategy; **South:** smaller population, fewer resources, defensive strategy; **Overlapping:** confident, expected quick victory, determined

---

---

netw⊛rks
There's More Online!

☑ **CHART** Army Salaries

☑ **GRAPHIC ORGANIZER**
Comparing North and South

☑ **SLIDE SHOW**
- Army Organization
- Civil War Casualties

Lesson 1
The Two Sides

ESSENTIAL QUESTION *Why does conflict develop?*

IT MATTERS BECAUSE
Both the North and the South had strengths and weaknesses that helped determine their military strategies.

Two Very Different Sides

GUIDING QUESTION *What were the goals and strategies of the North and the South?*

The war divided many families. Neither side imagined, however, that the four years of fighting would lead to so much suffering. By the end of the war, 600,000 Americans had lost their lives. Many thousands more were wounded in battle.

Division in the Border States

For most states, choosing sides in the Civil War was easy. The **border states** of Delaware, Maryland, Kentucky, and Missouri, however, were bitterly divided. Slavery existed in all four states, though it was generally not as widespread as in the Confederate states. All four of these states had close ties to the North and the South.

The border states were vital to the **strategy** of the Union. Missouri could control parts of the Mississippi River and major routes to the West. Kentucky controlled the Ohio River. Delaware was close to the key Union city of Philadelphia. Maryland, perhaps the most important of the border states, was close to Richmond, the Confederate capital. Most significantly, Washington, D.C., lay within the state. If Maryland seceded, the North's capital would be surrounded.

R1 **R2**

(l) Bettmann/CORBIS, (c) Library of Congress, (r) North Wind Picture Archives, (r) StockTrek/SuperStock

Reading HELP DESK (CCSS)

Taking Notes: *Comparing and Contrasting*
As you read, note the differences and similarities between the North and the South in a Venn diagram like this one. **RH.6–8.5**

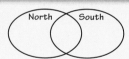
North   South

Content Vocabulary (Tier 3 Words)
- **border state**
- **enlist**

452 *The Civil War*

---

netw⊛rks *Online Teaching Options*

VIDEO

The North and South Mobilize for War

Collaborating Before sharing the video, ask students what they know about the Civil War. **Ask: Why did the Civil War begin? Which historical figures took part? How did women play a role?** After viewing, divide the class into groups to analyze how the video answered these questions. Then have a volunteer from each group present findings in a panel discussion before the class. **Interpersonal**

See page 449C for other online activities.

President Lincoln worked tirelessly to keep the four border states in the Union. In September 1861, he wrote:

❝ I think to lose Kentucky is nearly the same as to lose the whole game.... We would as well consent to separation at once, including the surrender of this capitol. ❞

—from *Abraham Lincoln: His Speeches and Writings*

In the end, Lincoln was successful. Still, many border state residents supported the Confederacy. The president had to work hard to restrain these opponents of the war.

Strengths and Weaknesses

When the war began, each side had advantages and disadvantages compared to the other. How each side used its strengths and weaknesses would determine the war's outcome.

The North had a larger population and more resources than the South. The South had other advantages, such as excellent military leaders and a strong fighting spirit. Also, because most of the war was fought in the South, the Confederacy knew the land and had the will to defend it.

 C

The Goals of War

Each side had different goals in fighting the Civil War. The Confederacy wanted to be an independent nation. To do this, it did not have to invade the North or destroy the Union army. It just needed to fight hard enough and long enough to convince Northerners that the war was not worth its cost.

 R

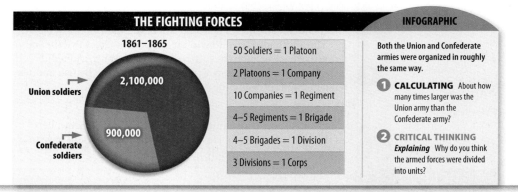

THE FIGHTING FORCES

INFOGRAPHIC

1861–1865

- Union soldiers → 2,100,000
- Confederate soldiers → 900,000

50 Soldiers = 1 Platoon
2 Platoons = 1 Company
10 Companies = 1 Regiment
4–5 Regiments = 1 Brigade
4–5 Brigades = 1 Division
3 Divisions = 1 Corps

Both the Union and Confederate armies were organized in roughly the same way.

1 **CALCULATING** About how many times larger was the Union army than the Confederate army?

2 **CRITICAL THINKING** *Explaining* Why do you think the armed forces were divided into units?

border state state on the border between the North and South: Delaware, Maryland, Kentucky, and Missouri

Academic Vocabulary (Tier 2 Words)
strategy a careful plan or method

Army Organization

Evaluating Use the interactive slide show about army organization to discuss the fighting forces for both the Union and Confederacy. **Ask:**

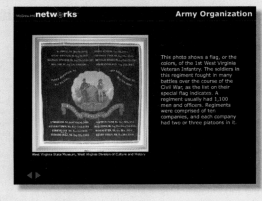

Mc Graw-Hill **netw⊕rks**   **Army Organization**

This photo shows a flag, or the colors, of the 1st West Virginia Veteran Infantry. The soldiers in this regiment fought in many battles over the course of the Civil War, as the list on their special flag indicates. A regiment usually had 1,100 men and officers. Regiments were comprised of ten companies, and each company had two or three platoons in it.

West Virginia State Museum, West Virginia Division of Culture and History

- Why was this organization considered the most effective in waging war? *(Dividing the armed forces into units made it easier to organize the movements and activities of the soldiers.)* Have students refer to the pie chart in their textbooks to find out how many soldiers fought on each side during the Civil War.

- How many more soldiers did the Union have than the Confederacy? *(1,200,000 more soldiers)* **Visual/ Spatial**

See page 449C for other online activities.

C Critical Thinking Skills

Analyzing Discuss with students the advantages and disadvantages of the North and the South at the start of the war. **Ask: Do you think one side entered the war stronger than the other?** *(Possible answers: the North appeared stronger because it had more troops and resources: the South had an advantage because of its strong leaders and knowledge of the terrain; each side had strengths and weaknesses that balanced each other out.)*

R Reading Skills

Specifying Have a student volunteer to read aloud the Goals of War section which continues on the following page. Then, discuss with students the goals of the North and South concerning the war. **Ask:**

- **What was the primary goal of the North?** *(to restore the Union)*
- **What was the South's main goal?** *(to be an independent nation)*

Write these answers on the board. Consider keeping them up throughout the chapter so students can refer to them. **AL**

Content Background Knowledge

Lincoln's earliest memories were of his farm chores at the Knob Creek farm in Kentucky, where he lived from ages two to eight. He also recalled his mother who read to him, the birth and death of a baby brother, and rain that washed away a garden he had planted with his sister the day before. There Lincoln first saw African Americans being taken south to become slaves. The Lincolns moved to Indiana in 1816.

ANSWERS, p. 453

INFOGRAPHIC

1. The Union army was about 2 1/3 times larger than the Confederate army.

2. **CRITICAL THINKING** This organization of forces was considered the most effective in waging war.

The Two Sides

T Technology Skills

Using and Citing Information Direct students' attention to the quotation by Abraham Lincoln. **Ask: What do you think Abraham Lincoln was most concerned about as president of the United States during the Civil War?** *(preserving the United States as one nation without the loss of the South)* Have groups of students use the Internet to research and write a brief statement on how Lincoln viewed the South at the beginning of the war. Ask a representative from each group to report findings to the class. **BL**

C Critical Thinking Skills

Predicting Consequences Make sure everyone understands the meaning of the word *strategy*. **AL** **ELL** Discuss the strategies of the Confederate forces and the Union forces for winning the war, including the Anaconda Plan. **Ask: Which side do you think had the greater advantage at the start of the war?** *(Answers may vary.)* **What was the Anaconda Plan?** *(It was a strategy in which the Union would blockade Southern ports. This would keep the Confederacy from exporting its cotton crop and give control of the Mississippi River to the North.)* **Ask: Which strategy seemed more likely to succeed?** *(Possible answer: The Union's strategy seemed more likely to succeed because the Union had greater military resources to carry out its strategy.)* **BL**

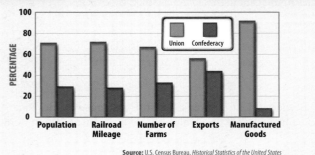

GRAPH SKILL

RESOURCES IN THE NORTH AND SOUTH

The North and South went into the war with very different strengths and weaknesses.

1 SUMMARIZING How would you summarize the status of the North and South at the start of the war?

2 CRITICAL THINKING *Comparing* In what areas did the North have the greatest advantage over the South?

Source: U.S. Census Bureau, *Historical Statistics of the United States*

In **contrast,** the North wanted to restore the Union. Its forces had to invade the South and force the breakaway states to give up their quest for independence. Although slavery helped drive a wedge between Northerners and Southerners, President Lincoln's original aim was not to defeat slavery. He wrote in 1862:

T

> **PRIMARY SOURCE**
>
> ❝ If I could save the Union without freeing *any* slave I would do it, and if I could save it by freeing *all* the slaves I would do it; and if I could save it by freeing some and leaving others alone I would also do that. ❞
>
> —from *Abraham Lincoln: His Speeches and Writings*

Confederate Strategies

The Confederacy's basic strategy was to conduct a defensive war. This meant that it would hold as much territory as possible. Southerners felt that if they showed determination to be independent, Northerners would tire of the war.

C

The South also tried to win the support of Great Britain and France, whose economies suffered when the war disrupted the export of Southern cotton. Southerners hoped the British and French might pressure the North to end the war.

Union Strategies

The North's war plan came from General Winfield Scott, hero of the war with Mexico. He knew that the North would have to defeat the South completely.

Reading **HELP**DESK **CCSS**

enlist to formally join a military force

Academic Vocabulary (Tier 2 Words)

contrast to compare with respect to differences

Reading in the Content Area: *Bar Graphs*

Bar graphs are often used to compare and contrast information about two groups. The large bars and different colors make them easy to read and interpret.

454 *The Civil War*

---

netw⊙rks *Online Teaching Options*

WHITEBOARD ACTIVITY

Resources of the North and South

Comparing and Contrasting Use the interactive whiteboard activity with students to compare and contrast the resources in the North and the South. Ask students to define and give examples of resources. Have volunteers drag and drop the information into the appropriate box and justify their choices. **Ask: Based on this activity, which side seems to have the advantage?** *(Answers may vary but could suggest the North based solely on resources available.)* **Logical/Mathematical**

See page 449C for other online activities.

netw⊙rks™   **Resources of the North and South**

Directions: Both the North and South had resources at their disposal at the beginning of the war. Drag each item to match the side that had the greater use of this resource or advantage.

Item Bank	North	South
railroads		
most fighting on home terrain		
offensive role		
defensive role		
larger population		
excellent military leaders		
soldiers called Yankees		
control of Mississippi River		

ANSWERS, p. 454

GRAPH SKILL

1. The North had more of everything than the South did.

2. CRITICAL THINKING manufactured goods and railroad mileage

To do this, Scott proposed the so-called Anaconda Plan, which took its name from a type of snake that squeezes its prey to death. First, the Union would blockade, or close, Southern ports. This strategy would keep supplies from reaching the Confederacy and prevent the South from exporting its cotton crop. Second, the North would seek to gain control of the Mississippi River. This would split the Confederacy in two and cut Southern supply lines. Another goal of the Union forces was the capture of Richmond, Virginia—the Confederate capital.

✅ **PROGRESS CHECK**

Explaining Why did the South use a defensive strategy?

Americans Against Americans

GUIDING QUESTION *What was war like for the soldiers of the North and the South?*

The Civil War was more than a war between the states. It turned brother against brother and neighbor against neighbor. Kentucky senator John Crittenden had two sons who became generals. One fought for the Confederacy, the other for the Union. Even President Lincoln's wife, Mary Todd Lincoln, had relatives in the Confederate army.

Men of all ages rushed to **enlist** (ihn·LIHST) in, or join, the Union or Confederate army. Some did so out of patriotism. Others thought they would be called cowards if they did not serve. Still others were looking for excitement. The sister of William Stone of Louisiana wrote that her brother was eager:

PRIMARY SOURCE

❝ to be off to Virginia [to join the Confederate army]. He so fears that the fighting will be over before he can get there. ❞

—from *Brokenburn: The Journal of Kate Stone*

Though the average Civil War soldier was in his mid-20s, many recruits on both sides were hardly adults. Tens of thousands of soldiers were under 18. Some were younger than 14. To get into the army, many teenagers ran away from home or lied about their ages.

Although teenage boys were accepted into service, one group of men was not allowed to fight in the early days of the war. The Union refused at first to let free African Americans enlist. Union leaders worried that white troops would not accept African American soldiers.

Though they fought bitterly, the two sides in the Civil War shared close bonds. Often families had soldiers on each side of the conflict.

455

McGraw Hill networks African Americans in the Civil War

Roughly 180,000 soldiers of African descent served in the Union Army during the Civil War. Official enlistment of African Americans did not begin until after the Emancipation Proclamation in 1862. This was because most white military officials believed that African Americans would not make good soldiers. The Negro Regiments, as the regiments of African Americans were called, proved the white military officials wrong. Highly effective and courageous, African American soldiers made up 10 percent of the Union Army by the end of the war.

Library of Congress/LC-DIG-ppmsca-27027

Nearly a fifth of African American soldiers lost their lives for the Union cause during the Civil War.

The Two Sides

R Reading Skills

Stating After students have read the text, discuss the approaches of the North and the South in regards to the participation of African Americans in the Civil War. **Ask: What policy change took place during the war, and which side made that change?** *(The Union army admitted African American soldiers.)*

C Critical Thinking Skills

Making Connections Discuss the number of people who went to war for both the Union and the Confederacy. Remind students that some of the soldiers who enlisted during the Civil War were not much older than they and their classmates are. Make sure everyone understands the word *enlist*. **AL ELL** Discuss the reasons so many people enlisted, including young people seeking excitement or patriotism. **Ask: For what reasons do you think people enlist in the armed forces today?** *(Possible responses: patriotism, desire for excitement, training and educational opportunities)*

$100 BOUNTY
$13 PAY PER MONTH
$6 STATE PAY for MARRIED MEN
$4 STATE PAY for SINGLE MEN
$3.50 PER MONTH FOR CLOTHES
BOARD & RATIONS FOUND.
THE
BRYAN GUARDS!
Attached to the GLORY LEGION, Colonel William Bryan, now encamped at Beverly. A few more
ACTIVE YOUNG MEN WANTED
TO FILL THIS COMPANY.
TO be MUSTERED IN AND PROCEED TO CAMP AT ONCE
RECRUITING STATION,
ZIMMERMAN'S, SECOND ST
Between Market and Plum Sts.
CAMDEN, N. JERSEY.
CAPT. R. GRAHAM CLARKE.

A SOLDIER'S PAY

		ARMY SALARIES (MONTHLY)		
Rank	**Civil War**	**World War II 1942**	**Vietnam War 1965**	**Iraq War 2007**
Private	*$13	$50	$85	$1,203–1,543.20
Corporal	$14	$66	$210	$1,699.50
Sergeant	$17	$78	$261	$1,854–2,339.10
Sergeant Major	$21	$138	$486	$4,110

*Until 1864, African Americans in the Civil War were paid only $7 per month
Source: Bureau of Economic Analysis; Princeton Review; www.militaryfactory.com

To get more men to enlist, Union recruiters put up posters offering a sign-up bonus, or bounty.

CHART SKILL

Although many volunteered to serve, soldiers in both the Union and Confederate armies received monthly pay. Compare their pay rates to those in later wars.

R

1 DESCRIBING What happens to a soldier's pay as he or she moves up in rank?

2 CRITICAL THINKING
Making Connections Name some items you could buy today with a Civil War private's monthly salary.

Later in the war, the Union army changed this policy. The Confederacy refused to consider having African Americans fight until the war's final, desperate days. They did not want to give enslaved people weapons.

High Hopes

When the war began, each side expected a quick victory. Northerners could not imagine the Confederates holding out for long against the Union's greater resources. Confederates believed the North could never subdue the fighting spirit of the South. Both sides were wrong. In the end, the war lasted far longer than most Americans could have guessed.

Who Were the Soldiers?

Soldiers came from every region of the country and all walks of life. Most came from farms. Almost half of the North's troops and more than 60 percent of the South's had owned or worked on farms.

C By the summer of 1861, the Confederate army had about 112,000 soldiers. They were sometimes called Rebels. The Union had about 187,000 soldiers, also known as Yankees. By the end of the war, about 900,000 men fought for the Confederacy and about 2.1 million men bore arms for the Union. The Union army included just under 200,000 African Americans. About 10,000 Mexican Americans served in the war.

Library of Congress

Reading HELPDESK (CCSS)

Reading Strategy: *Finding the Main Idea*
Paragraphs and sections have main ideas and details that support that main idea. Make an outline of the section "A Soldier's Life" by writing down the main idea and listing the supporting details under it.

---

networks *Online Teaching Options*

CHART

Army Salaries

Calculating Use the interactive chart on army salaries and expenses to discuss with students the pay Civil War soldiers received. **Ask: Do you think soldiers were paid enough to support themselves? Their families?** *(Answers should include information from the chart.)* **Logical/Mathematical BL**

See page 449C for other online activities

Media
networks· Army Salaries
Click on the chart to see a comparison of army salaries during four wars. Army salaries have changed dramatically since the Civil War. The $13 in 1864 would have been worth about $177 in 2007 – a small salary!

	ARMY SALARIES (MONTHLY)			
Rank	**Civil War**	**World War II 1942**	**Vietnam War 1965**	**Iraq War 2007**
Private				
Corporal				
Sergeant				
Sergeant Major				

*Until 1864, African Americans in the Civil War were paid only $7 per month
Source: Bureau of Economic Analysis; Princeton Review; www.militaryfactory.com

Prices for Items During the Civil War

Look at the salary chart and the chart that shows prices for items during the Civil War. Civil War soldiers had to replace any of the clothing they lost out of their own pay.

ANSWERS, p. 456

CHART SKILL

1. Pay goes up.

2. **CRITICAL THINKING** Answers will vary; students should realize that $13/month by today's standards would not buy very much.

A Soldier's Life

Soldiers of the North and the South described what they saw and how they felt in letters to family and friends. Many wrote about their boredom, discomfort, sickness, fear, and horror.

Most of the time the soldiers lived in camps. Camp life had its pleasant moments of songs, stories, letters from home, and baseball games. At other times, a soldier's life was a dull routine of drills, bad food, marches, and rain.

Between battles, soldiers on both sides sometimes forgot they were enemies. A private described his wartime experiences:

PRIMARY SOURCE

❝ A part of Co [company] K and some of the enemy came together and stacked arms and talked for a long time. Our men cooked coffee and treated them and [afterward] ... each one took up his position again and they began to fire at each other again, but not as hard as before. ❞

—from *The Life of Billy Yank*

R

The Horrors of War

In spite of fleeting moments of calm, the reality of war was always close by. Thousands of casualties overwhelmed medical facilities. After the Battle of Shiloh, the wounded lay in the rain for more than 24 hours waiting for treatment. A soldier recalled, "Many had died there, and others were in the last agonies as we passed. Their groans and cries were heartrending."

Faced with these terrible realities, many men deserted. About one of every eleven Union soldiers and one of every eight Confederates ran away because of fear, hunger, or sickness.

W

☑ **PROGRESS CHECK**

Comparing and Contrasting How did the expectations of the war compare with the reality for both sides?

THEN

The picture above shows a Union artillery unit during the Civil War. The photograph below shows a U.S. artillery unit in Iraq in 2010.

NOW

▶ **CRITICAL THINKING**
Comparing and Contrasting How is the artillery that soldiers used during the Civil War like the artillery they use today? How is it different?

(l) North Wind Picture Archives, (b) StockTrek/SuperStock

Summarizing Direct students to read the text. Then, lead a class discussion about the life of a soldier and the horrors of war that soldiers suffered. Introduce the term *desert*. **AL ELL** **Ask:** **Why did many men desert?** *(They deserted to escape the harsh realities of war: hunger, sickness, danger.)*

W **Writing Skills**

Narrative Have students recall what they have learned about the horrors of war. Remind them that the high hopes of a quick end to the war were dashed. Then ask students to write a letter home from the point of view of a soldier from either side during the Civil War. The letter should comment about hardships and speculate about why the war has lasted so long. Pair students to read and discuss each other's letters.

Have students complete the Lesson 1 Review.

CLOSE & REFLECT

Direct students' attention to the images of artillery. Discuss how changing military technology can affect the way a war is fought.

LESSON 1 REVIEW (CCSS)

Review Vocabulary (Tier 3 Words)

1. Use the following terms in sentences about the Civil War that demonstrate your understanding of the terms. RH.6–8.4

   a. border state   **b.** enlist

Answer the Guiding Questions

2. **Contrasting** How was the North's strategy different from the South's? RH.6–8.5

3. **Comparing and Contrasting** Compare and contrast attitudes in the Union and the Confederacy about enlisting African American soldiers. RH.6–8.5

4. **Evaluating** What was the goal of the Anaconda Plan? RH.6–8.2

5. **ARGUMENT** You are a young Southern or Northern man in 1861. You have left home to join the army. Write a letter to your family explaining your reasons for joining the Union or Confederate army. WHST.6–8.1, WHST.6–8.10

Lesson 1   **457**

LESSON 1 REVIEW ANSWERS

1. Possible answer: **a.** President Lincoln was anxious to ensure that the border states, slave states that bordered the Union and the Confederacy, stayed loyal to the Union. **b.** Many young men from all across the nation enlisted to fight in the Civil War.

2. The North's goal was to invade the South to try to prevent the South from leaving the Union; the South's strategy was to defend its territory until the North gave up.

3. At first, neither side allowed African American soldiers to enlist in the army. Later in the war, the Union army accepted African Americans, but the Confederate army still did not want to arm enslaved people.

4. The goal of the Anaconda Plan was to choke off the South's economic resources by blockading the South's ports and controlling the Mississippi River.

5. Letters should reflect an understanding of the reasons young men and boys were so eager to fight the war on both sides.

ANSWERS, p. 457

CRITICAL THINKING Possible answer: Like today's artillery, Civil War artillery was mounted on vehicles. However, at that time, the vehicles were carts pulled by horses or by soldiers on foot, while today's artillery is pulled by or mounted on motorized vehicles.

☑ **PROGRESS CHECK** Both sides expected the war to end quickly, and many soldiers enlisted out of a sense of adventure. In reality, the war lasted longer than anyone had expected, and many soldiers deserted out of fear, hunger, and sickness.

ENGAGE

🔔 **Bellringer** Have students predict the outcome of the first battle of the Civil War, based on the strengths and weaknesses of the North and the South discussed in Lesson 1. **Ask: Which side do you think will have better success in the war?** (*Answers will vary. Students may say that in the early years of the war it was difficult to predict who would prevail but that the South seemed to have the advantage.*)

TEACH & ASSESS

C Critical Thinking Skills

Evaluating Discuss with students the reasons President Lincoln might have ordered a blockade of Confederate ports at the outset of the war. Make sure students understand the meaning of *blockade*. **ELL** **Ask: Why did the blockade set the stage for fighting at sea as well as on land?** (*Answers will vary but students should recognize that the blockade deprived the Confederacy of communication and supplies by ship. The blockade also prevented other nations from trade with the South.*)

R Reading Skills

Explaining After students have read the section, review with them the events of the Battle of Bull Run. **Ask:**

- **How did General Thomas "Stonewall" Jackson get his nickname?** (*He held his position "like a stone wall" during the Battle of Bull Run.*)
- **How does this reflect the spirit of the Confederate army during the war?** (*The Confederate army had a strong fighting spirit, which turned out to be a major advantage.*) **BL**
- **How did the Battle of Bull Run affect the North's view of the war?** (*They were surprised to have lost. It made them realize that the war might not be won as easily as they had expected.*) **AL**
- **How did President Lincoln respond to the Confederate victory at Bull Run?** (*He called for a million more men to enlist as soldiers for three years.*) **AL**

ANSWER, p. 458

TAKING NOTES: **July 1861:** Confederates win First Battle of Bull Run; **February 1862:** Union captures Fort Henry; **March 1862:** Virginia and Monitor clash at sea; **April 1862:** Union wins Battle of Shiloh; **April 1862:** Union navy takes New Orleans; **May 1862:** Union takes control of Corinth, Mississippi; **June 1862:** Memphis falls to the Union; **September 1862:** Union wins Battle of Antietam; **May 1863:** Confederates win at Chancellorsville

---

netw⊙rks
There's More Online!

☑ **BIOGRAPHY**
   Robert E. Lee

☑ **GRAPHIC ORGANIZER**
   Civil War Battles

☑ **MAP** • War in the West
   • War in the East

☑ **PRIMARY SOURCE**
   Report on the Battle of Ironclads

☑ **SLIDE SHOW** The Battle
   of Antietam

☑ **VIDEO**

Lesson 2
Early Years of the War

ESSENTIAL QUESTION *Why does conflict develop?*

IT MATTERS BECAUSE
Neither side gained a strong advantage during the war's early years.

War on Land and at Sea

GUIDING QUESTION *What was the outcome of the first major battle of the war?*

While the Union and the Confederacy mobilized their armies, the Union navy began operations against the South. In April 1861, President Lincoln announced a blockade of all Confederate ports. The stage was set for fighting at sea as well as on land.

First Battle of Bull Run

Tension mounted in the summer of 1861, leading to the first major battle of the Civil War. On July 21, about 30,000 Union troops commanded by General Irvin McDowell attacked a smaller Confederate force led by General P.G.T. Beauregard.

The fighting took place in northern Virginia, near a small river called Bull Run. Hundreds of spectators from Washington, D.C., watched the battle from a few miles away.

Both sides lacked battle experience. At first, the Yankees drove the Confederates back. Then the Rebels rallied, inspired by General Thomas Jackson. Another Confederate general noted that Jackson was holding his position "like a stone wall." This earned him the nickname "Stonewall" Jackson. The Confederates then unleashed a savage counterattack that broke the Union lines. As they retreated, Union troops ran into civilians fleeing in panic.

(l) Library of Congress/0810 1, (c) Bettmann/CORBIS, (r) SuperStock/SuperStock,

Reading HELPDESK (CCSS)

Taking Notes: *Sequencing* RH.6–8.5
As you read about the early Civil War battles, note them on a time line, and take notes on what happened during each of them.

1861   1862   1862

458   The Civil War

Content Vocabulary (Tier 3 Words)
- **tributary**   • **Emancipation**
- **ironclad**   **Proclamation**
- **casualty**

---

netw⊙rks   *Online Teaching Options*

VIDEO

Lincoln's Great Speeches

Finding the Main Idea Discuss the video with students. Point out that the Emancipation Proclamation and the Gettysburg Address followed an incredible loss of life on both sides. **Ask: What was the significance of the Emancipation Proclamation for the Union and the Confederacy, Great Britain, and Europe?** (*Answers should indicate students' recognition that the Emancipation Proclamation changed the nature of the Civil War. The war became a battle for freedom for all people, everywhere.*) **Visual/Spatial**

See page 449D for other online activities.

The loss shocked Northerners, who now realized that the war could be long and difficult. President Lincoln named a new general, George B. McClellan, to head the Union army in the East—called the Army of the Potomac—and to train the troops.

Although dismayed over Bull Run, President Lincoln was also determined. He put out a call for more army volunteers. He signed two bills requesting a total of 1 million soldiers to serve for three years. In addition, victories in the West would soon give a boost to Northern spirits and also increase enlistment.

Control of the West

In the West, the major Union goal was to control the Mississippi River and its **tributaries** (TRIH•byuh•tehr•eez), the smaller rivers that fed it. With control of the river, Union ships could prevent Louisiana, Arkansas, and Texas from supplying the eastern Confederacy. Union gunboats and troops would also be able to use the rivers to move into the heart of the South.

R The battle for the rivers began in February 1862. Union forces captured Fort Henry on the Tennessee River. Naval commander Andrew Foote and army general Ulysses S. Grant led the assault. Soon afterward, Grant and Foote moved against Fort Donelson on the Cumberland River. The Confederates realized they had no chance of saving the fort. They asked Grant what terms he would give them to surrender. Grant replied, "No terms except an unconditional and immediate surrender can be accepted." "Unconditional Surrender" Grant became the North's new hero.

A Battle Between Ironclads

The Union blockade of Confederate ports posed a real threat to the Confederacy. Southerners hoped to break it with a secret weapon—the *Merrimack*. The *Merrimack* was a damaged frigate that had been **abandoned** by the Union. The Confederates rebuilt the wooden ship and covered it with iron. They renamed their new **ironclad** (EYE•uhrn•klad) the *Virginia*.

To create the *Virginia*, the Confederate navy took what remained of a burned Union warship, covered it in iron, and equipped it with 10 guns. On its bow they placed an iron ram so the ship could steer into another ship and puncture its hull.

V On March 8, 1862, the *Virginia* attacked Union ships in the Chesapeake Bay. Union shells just bounced off its sides. Some Union leaders feared the *Virginia* would destroy the Union navy, steam up the Potomac River, and bombard Washington, D.C.

By this time, however, the North had an ironclad of its own. The *Monitor* rushed southward to face the *Virginia*. On March 9, the two ironclads met in battle. Neither ship won, but the stirring clash raised spirits in both the North and the South.

tributary stream or smaller river that feeds into a larger river

ironclad a warship equipped with iron plating for protection

Academic Vocabulary (Tier 2 Words)

abandon to leave behind or give up

Lesson 2 **459**

R Reading Skills

Identifying Direct students to read the text. Then, lead a class discussion about the role of General Ulysses S. Grant in the capture of Fort Henry and the surrender of Fort Donelson. Ask students to explain the term *unconditional*. **ELL** **Ask:**

- **How did General Grant get the nickname "Unconditional Surrender Grant"?** *(He got the nickname because his initials were "U.S." and he told the South he would accept only unconditional surrender of Fort Donelson.)*
- **How do you think this affected the morale of the North?** *(It probably increased support for the war and made the North feel they had a strong leader in the West.)*

V Visual Skills

Integrating Visual Information Discuss with students the transformation of the *Merrimack* into the *Virginia*. Make sure that students understand the meaning of *ironclad*. **Ask: How does the image of the *Virginia* help to identify the purpose of the ironclad?** *(Answers may include the usefulness of the battering ram in war.)* **ELL** **Visual/ Spatial**

Content Background Knowledge

Inventors, mechanics, and engineers built the USS *Monitor*, an example of how 19th-century industrial power had grown. The revolving turret was 22 feet in diameter and weighed 140 tons. The *Monitor's* wreck site was found in 1973 off the North Carolina coast. Congress later designated the site as the first National Marine Sanctuary. Parts of the *Monitor*, including its turret, have been recovered and are conserved today in Newport News, Virginia.

Virginia and *Monitor*

Analyzing Primary Sources Use the interactive primary source excerpt that describes the ironclad battle. Discuss the significance of this battle. *(Both ironclad ships were virtually indestructible so neither side won, but both sides felt stronger as a result of the battle.)* **BL** **Ask: What is the Union name for the CSS *Virginia*?** *(the Merrimack)*

See page 449D for other online activities.

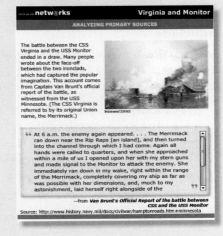

netw@rks Virginia and Monitor

ANALYZING PRIMARY SOURCES

The battle between the CSS Virginia and the USS Monitor ended in a draw. Many people wrote about the face-off between the two ironclads, which had captured the popular imagination. This account comes from Captain Van Brunt's official report of the battle, as witnessed from the USS Minnesota. (The CSS Virginia is referred to by its original Union name, the Merrimack.)

"At 6 a.m. the enemy again appeared. . . . The Merrimack ran down near the Rip Raps [an island], and then turned into the channel through which I had come. Again all hands were called to quarters, and when she approached within a mile of us I opened upon her with my stern guns and made signal to the Monitor to attack the enemy. She immediately ran down in my wake, right within the range of the Merrimack, completely covering my ship as far as was possible with her dimensions, and, much to my astonishment, laid herself right alongside of the

—from *Van Brunt's Official Report of the battle between CSS and the USS Monitor*
Source: http://www.history.navy.mil/docs/civilwar/hamptonroads.htm#minnesota

Early Years of the War

C Critical Thinking Skills

Making Generalizations Discuss with students the events and significance of the Battle of Shiloh. **Ask:**

- **What can you conclude about the Confederates' battle strategy?** *(Students might suggest that striking first is a good tactic because it can surprise the enemy; reinforcements can change a battle's outcome.)* **BL**
- **Did this strategy work?** *(No; the South lost the Battle of Shiloh.)*

R Reading Skills

Discussing Ask students to read the subsection titled "Capturing New Orleans." Then, discuss with them the capture of New Orleans and its significance to the Union cause. **Ask:**

- **What was the significance of Farragut's capture of New Orleans?** *(The South could no longer use the Mississippi to transport its goods.)*
- **What do you think the goal of most military innovations is?** *(to make it possible to destroy the other side with as little risk to your side as possible)*

Just two months after their March 1862 battle, the crew of the *Virginia* (on the right) destroyed their ship rather than let it fall into Union hands. The *Monitor* sank in a storm in December 1862.

▶ **CRITICAL THINKING**
Analyzing Visuals Why do you think neither ship was able to seriously damage the other?

The Battle of Shiloh

Meanwhile, in the West, General Grant and about 40,000 troops headed south toward Corinth, Mississippi, a major railroad junction. In early April 1862, the Union army camped at Pittsburg Landing, 20 miles (32 km) from Corinth, near Shiloh Church. Additional Union forces joined Grant from Nashville.

Confederate leaders decided to strike before more troops arrived to **reinforce** the Union. Early on the morning of April 6, Generals Albert Sidney Johnston and P.G.T. Beauregard led Confederate forces in a surprise attack. The battle lasted two days. It was a narrow victory for the Union, but the losses were enormous. Together, the two armies suffered more than 23,000 **casualties** (KA•zhuhl•teez)—people killed, wounded, captured, or missing.

After Shiloh, Union troops laid siege to Corinth, forcing the Confederates to withdraw. The Union army occupied the town on May 30. Memphis, Tennessee, fell to Union forces on June 6. The North seemed well on its way to controlling the Mississippi River.

Capturing New Orleans

A few weeks after Shiloh, the North won another key victory. On April 25, 1862, Union naval forces under David Farragut captured New Orleans, Louisiana, the largest city in the South. Farragut, who was of Spanish descent, grew up in the South but remained loyal to the Union. The capture of New Orleans meant

Reading **HELP**DESK **CCSS**

casualty a soldier who is killed, wounded, captured, or missing in battle

Academic Vocabulary (Tier 2 Words)
reinforce to make stronger

Bettmann/CORBIS

netw**o**rks *Online Teaching Options*

IMAGE

Ironclads

Analyzing Visuals Use the interactive images of the ironclads to discuss their creation and their importance to the war. **Ask:**

- **Why were they called ironclads?** *(Their hulls were clad, or covered, in iron, a strong metal.)* **AL** **ELL**
- **What was the purpose of covering ships in iron?** *(It made them stronger and less likely to be destroyed by enemy fire.)*

See page 449D for other online activities.

On its bow the Confederates placed an iron ram so that the ship could steer into a hostile ship and puncture, or make a hole in, its hull.

Ironclads

ANSWER, p. 460

CRITICAL THINKING The shells just bounced off the sides of the ironclads. Both ships were covered in iron, so they were evenly matched.

that the Confederacy could no longer use the Mississippi River to carry its goods to sea. The city's fall also left the Confederate stronghold of Vicksburg, Mississippi, as the only major obstacle to the Union's strategy in the West.

☑ **PROGRESS CHECK**

Explaining How did the loss of New Orleans affect the Confederacy?

War in the Eastern States

GUIDING QUESTION *How did the Union respond to important defeats in the East in 1862?*

While the two sides fought for control of Tennessee and the Mississippi River, the Union was trying to capture the Confederate capital at Richmond, Virginia. Close to the Union, Richmond was vulnerable to attack. Confederate armies fought hard to defend it. Confederate forces in the East enjoyed much more success than their western counterparts.

Confederate Victories

Southern victories in the East were largely the result of the leadership of Robert E. Lee and Stonewall Jackson. The two generals knew the terrain and could move forces quickly. They were also expert at inspiring troops. As a result, Confederate forces managed to defeat much larger Union forces.

GEOGRAPHY CONNECTION

Gaining control of the West was a key part of the Union's war strategy.

1 PLACE Where did the South win battles in the West?

2 CRITICAL THINKING
Making Inferences What important cities remained for the North to capture after 1863?

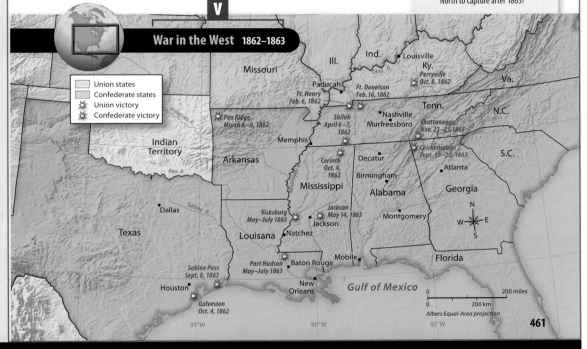

War in the West 1862–1863

Union states
Confederate states
☆ Union victory
✪ Confederate victory

461

W Writing Skills

Narrative Have students write journal entries describing how it might have felt to be a resident of New Orleans or another community along the Mississippi as the North gained control of this region. Ask students to share their journal entries with the class if time permits.

V Visual Skills

Analyzing Maps Point students to the map. **Ask:**

- **Which side had gained the advantage in the West by the middle of 1862?** *(the North)*
- **Why do you think so?** *(because the Union had gained control over much of the Mississippi River)*
- **Why do you think the South did not surrender at this point in the war?** *(Answers may vary, but students may suggest that the South remained determined to fight and that they still had hope of holding back the Union in the East. Also, they might have hoped that England and France would help them.)* **Visual/Spatial**

GAME

Fill in the Blank Game: Early Years of the War

Reviewing Display the interactive game. Lead students in filling in the blanks to review the events of the lesson. Review the pronunciation of words like *tributary, casualty,* and *Emancipation* with students who may be struggling. Point out that "Stonewall" Jackson's name contains the words *stone* and *wall,* just like sentence #3. Give students hints or reminders about the lesson. **AL ELL**
Verbal/Linguistic

See page 449D for other online activities.

ANSWERS, p. 461

☑ **PROGRESS CHECK** It stopped the Confederacy from moving goods down the river to the sea.

GEOGRAPHY CONNECTION

1 Sabine Pass in Texas and Chickamauga in Georgia

2 CRITICAL THINKING Students should identify New Orleans and Mobile as important port cities the North needed to control.

C Critical Thinking Skills

Identifying Points of View Direct students to the quotes from Lincoln regarding the Union defeat at Chancellorsville, Virginia. **Ask:**

- **What was Lincoln's response to the Confederate victories?** *(He was worried about how people would react in the North.)*
- **What was the Confederate response?** *(President Davis became more confident and urged General Lee to invade Maryland, which was Union territory.)*

W Writing Skills

Argument Have students reread Lincoln's comment: "What will the country say!" Then divide the class into two groups, one to represent the point of view of the North and the other the point of view of the South. Tell students to imagine that they are newspaper editors reacting to the Union defeat at Chancellorsville, Virginia. Allow them to work in pairs to write a few sentences for an editorial about the defeat. They should compose a headline for their editorial. Have students share their editorials with the class. **BL** **Interpersonal**

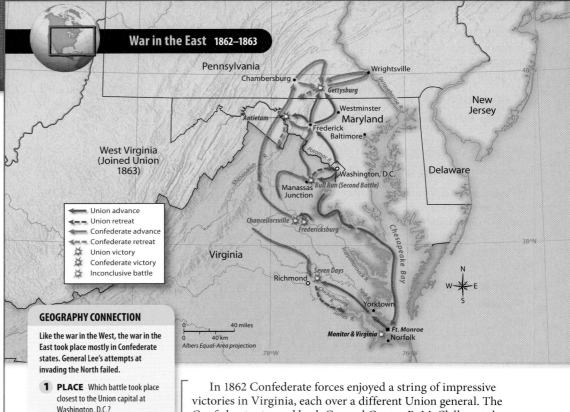

War in the East 1862–1863

Union advance
Union retreat
Confederate advance
Confederate retreat
Union victory
Confederate victory
Inconclusive battle

GEOGRAPHY CONNECTION

Like the war in the West, the war in the East took place mostly in Confederate states. General Lee's attempts at invading the North failed.

1 PLACE Which battle took place closest to the Union capital at Washington, D.C.?

2 CRITICAL THINKING
Making Generalizations What does this map suggest about the difficulty of invading enemy territory? Explain your answer. **W**

In 1862 Confederate forces enjoyed a string of impressive victories in Virginia, each over a different Union general. The Confederates turned back General George B. McClellan at the Seven Days' Battle, General John Pope at the Second Battle of Bull Run, and General Ambrose Burnside at Fredericksburg. In May 1863, at Chancellorsville, Virginia, Lee's army defeated a Union force twice its size. "My God, my God," Lincoln said when he learned of the defeat, "What will the country say!" The mood in the Union grew grim.

Lee Invades Maryland

Confederate president Jefferson Davis urged Lee to move his troops into western Maryland—Union territory. His goal was to move into Pennsylvania and to bring the war deeper into the Northern states. Though he knew McClellan was following him with a sizable force, Lee's forces crossed into Maryland and began the invasion of Union territory. **C**

Reading **HELP**DESK **CCSS**

Reading Strategy: *Taking Notes*

Taking notes about what you are reading can help you remember facts and prepare effectively for tests. As you read the section "War in the Eastern States," make a list of each battle, the date, the location, and which side won.

462 *The Civil War*

---

netw⊙rks   *Online Teaching Options*

MAP

War in the East 1862–1863

Locating Use the interactive map about the war in the East, and have students locate Washington, D.C., the Union capital, and Richmond, Virginia, the Confederate capital. During the discussion, use the map to illustrate the movement of troops to key battle sites described in the lesson. **Ask: How far apart are Richmond and Washington, D.C.?** *(about 100 miles)* **What battles did the Confederates win in the East in 1862?** *(Seven Days' Battle, the Second Battle of Bull Run, Fredericksburg, and Chancellorsville)* **Visual/ Spatial** **AL**

See page 449D for other online activities.

ANSWERS, p. 462

GEOGRAPHY CONNECTION

1 Battle of Bull Run

2 CRITICAL THINKING It seems it is very difficult to invade enemy territory successfully. The map shows that the Union tended to lose when its troops fought in the Confederacy and Confederate troops lost when fighting in Union territory.

The Battle of Antietam

Once in Maryland, Lee split his army into four parts. To confuse McClellan, he ordered each part to move in a different direction. Lee's plan never had a chance to work. A Confederate officer lost his copy of the orders describing it. Two Union soldiers found the orders and brought them to McClellan.

McClellan did not attack immediately. This gave Lee time to gather his troops. On September 17, 1862, the two sides met at a place called Antietam (an·TEE·tum) near Sharpsburg, Maryland.

Antietam was a key victory for the Union. It was also the deadliest single day of fighting in the war. About 6,000 soldiers died. About 17,000 more suffered wounds. Because of the great losses, Lee retreated to Virginia after the battle. For the time being, his strategy of invading the North had failed.

✔ **PROGRESS CHECK**

Summarizing What was the outcome of the Battle of Antietam?

The Emancipation Proclamation

GUIDING QUESTION *What was the effect of the Emancipation Proclamation?*

At first, Lincoln viewed the Civil War as a battle for the Union, not a fight against slavery. As the war went on, Lincoln changed the way he thought about the role of slavery in the war.

The Debate Over Ending Slavery

Lincoln hated slavery, yet he was reluctant to make the Civil War a battle to end it. Early in the war, Lincoln hesitated to move against slavery for fear of losing the border states. Even many white Northerners who disapproved of slavery were not eager to risk their lives to end it.

Meanwhile, abolitionists, including Frederick Douglass and newspaper editor Horace Greeley, urged Lincoln to make the war a fight to end slavery. The abolitionists described slavery as a moral wrong that needed to be abolished. They also pointed out that slavery was the root of the divisions between North and South. Finally, they argued that if Lincoln presented the war as a fight to abolish slavery, Britain and France would be less willing to support the South. Confederate hopes were increasingly linked to this European support.

R

T

SuperStock/SuperStock

Emancipation Proclamation
decree issued by President Lincoln freeing enslaved people in those parts of the Confederacy still in rebellion on January 1, 1863

Lesson 2   **463**

BIOGRAPHY

Robert E. Lee (1807–1870)

Robert Edward Lee came from a leading Virginia family. He attended West Point Academy and graduated second in his class in 1829. Lee was still in the United States Army and stationed in Texas in 1861 when that state seceded from the Union. He returned to Virginia. Soon after his return, Virginia voted to secede from the Union. Lee resigned from the U.S. Army and became commander of Virginia's military forces.

▶ **CRITICAL THINKING**
Drawing Conclusions What factor apparently caused Lee to leave the United States Army? Explain your answer.

Library of Congress/LC-US262-2276

R Reading Skills

Identifying Have students read the section about the Empancipation Proclamation. Then, ask students to use evidence from the text to identify the two sides in the debate to end slavery. **Ask: Why was Lincoln hesitant to free enslaved African Americans?** *(He was worried about losing the support of the border states.)*

T Technology Skills

Collaborating Point out that Frederick Douglass and Horace Greeley were abolitionists. Pair students to use the Internet to learn more about these or other abolitionists and their influence on the move to end slavery. Have pairs give short presentations to the class on what they learned. **BL** **Interpersonal**

Content Background Knowledge

- A bugler and private in the Union army named Johnny Cook was 15 years old when he won the Medal of Honor for his actions at Antietam.
- The son of Robert E. Lee, Robert Jr., was a private with an artillery unit that fought at Antietam.
- Lincoln issued his preliminary Emancipation Proclamation just days after the Battle of Antietam.

SLIDE SHOW

The Battle of Antietam

Analyzing Visuals Use the interactive slide show to discuss the Battle of Antietam and its significance to the war. **Ask: Why is Antietam significant?** *(It was an important victory for the Union, and it was the deadliest single day of fighting in the war.)* **What might have happened if Lee's orders had not been found?** *(McClellan would not have known Lee's plans and that his army was split. Lee's strategy might have succeeded. If Confederates had won Antietam, they might have continued to advance in the North.)* **BL**

See page 449D for other online activities.

Abraham Lincoln was photographed visiting the Union camp at the battlefield on October 3, 1862. On the following day, the Emancipation Proclamation was published in the nation's newspapers.

ANSWERS, p. 463

✔ **PROGRESS CHECK** Lee retreated to Virginia, abandoning his attempt to invade the North.

CRITICAL THINKING Possible answer: Lee remained in the U.S. Army until Virginia seceded. He apparently was more loyal to Virginia than to either the United States or the Confederacy itself.

Early Years of the War

R Reading Skills

Discussing Direct students to read the section titled "A Call for Emancipation." Then, begin a class discussion about the Emancipation Proclamation. **Ask:**

- **How could Lincoln free the South's enslaved people if the Constitution did not give him the power to do so?** *(The enslaved people were considered property, and he could seize property from the enemy in wartime.)*
- **What is the date of the Emancipation Proclamation?** *(September 22, 1862)*
- **On what date did it take effect?** *(January 1, 1863)*

W Writing Skills

Argument Direct students' attention to the primary source quotation by Abraham Lincoln. Have a volunteer read it to the class. Ask students to write a brief paragraph explaining why they agree or disagree with Lincoln's judgment about his place in history.

Have students complete the Lesson 2 Review.

CLOSE & REFLECT

Have volunteers name the battles won by each side in the early years of the war to review the content of the lesson with students. **Ask: Which side do you think gained an advantage in the early years of the war?** *(Possible responses: Neither side gained a strong advantage.)* As a class, discuss the reasons that neither side gained a strong advantage during the war.

A Call for Emancipation

The Constitution did not give Lincoln the power to end slavery, but it did give him the power to take property from an enemy in wartime. By law, enslaved people were considered property. On September 22, 1862, Lincoln announced that he would issue the **Emancipation Proclamation** (ih·mant·suh·PAY·shuhn prah·kluh·MAY·shuhn). This decree freed all enslaved people in rebel-held territory on January 1, 1863. **R**

The Emancipation Proclamation did not change the lives of all enslaved people overnight. For example, enslaved people living in the loyal border states remained in bondage. Others remained under the direct control of their holders in the South and would have to wait for a Union victory before gaining their freedom.

Yet the Emancipation Proclamation had a strong impact. With it, the government declared slavery to be wrong. It was clear that a Union victory would end slavery in the United States.

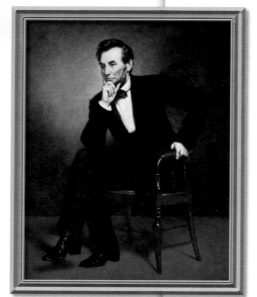

Lincoln's Emancipation Proclamation sent a clear message to enslaved people and the Confederacy about the future of slavery.

W

PRIMARY SOURCE

❝ I never in my life felt more certain that I am doing right than I do in signing this paper. . . . If my name ever goes into history it will be for this act, and my whole soul is in it. ❞

—Abraham Lincoln, 1863

☑ **PROGRESS CHECK**

Explaining How did the Emancipation Proclamation change the focus of the war?

LESSON 2 REVIEW (CCSS)

Review Vocabulary (Tier 3 Words)

1. Identify the significance of the following terms to the subject of the Civil War. RH.6–8.4

   a. tributary   **b.** ironclad   **c.** casualty

Answer the Guiding Questions

2. *Analyzing* Why was the outcome of the Battle of Bull Run surprising to Northerners? RH.6–8.1

3. *Explaining* Why was it important for the Confederacy to defend Richmond? RH.6–8.2

4. *Evaluating* How did the Emancipation Proclamation affect enslaved people in the South? RH.6–8.2

5. **ARGUMENT** Choose one of Douglass' and Greeley's arguments for making abolition an aim of the war. Write a short paragraph expanding on the argument. WHST.6–8.1, WHST.6–8.9

464 *The Civil War*

LESSON 2 REVIEW ANSWERS

1. Possible answers: **a.** The Union fought to control tributaries to the Mississippi River, which was essential to Confederate strength. **b.** The battle between the *Monitor* and the *Virginia* was the first-ever battle between ironclads. **c.** The Battle of Shiloh led to a horrifying number of casualties.

2. Northerners had expected that the war would be easy to win and were surprised that they lost the first battle.

3. Richmond was the capital of the Confederacy, so it was a matter of pride to defend it as long as possible.

4. Although the Proclamation did not immediately free the slaves, it sent the message that the government was taking a stand against slavery.

5. Answers will vary. Supporting arguments should be based on facts and logical ideas.

ANSWER, p. 464

☑ **PROGRESS CHECK** The Emancipation Proclamation made the abolition of slavery an official government policy and the focal point of the war between the North and South

networks
There's More Online!

☑ **GRAPHIC ORGANIZER**
Women's Contributions to the War

☑ **SLIDE SHOW**
• Civil War Political Cartoons
• Roles of Women in the War
• Dorothea Dix

Lesson 3
Life During the Civil War

ESSENTIAL QUESTION *Why does conflict develop?*

IT MATTERS BECAUSE
Those who lived through the Civil War experienced many challenges and hardships.

A Different Way of Life

GUIDING QUESTION *How did life change during the Civil War?*

When the Civil War began, many young people left their homes to serve in the military. This meant leaving family and friends, and jobs or school.

Almost everyone who stayed home was touched in some way by the war. Only about half of the school-age children attended school because many had to stay home to help their families. Schools closed during the war in some areas, especially those near battles and skirmishes. Many schools and churches served instead as hospitals for the wounded.

R

Hardships in the South

Although the war affected everyone, life in the South changed most dramatically. Both armies spent the majority of their time on Southern soil. Because the fighting took place there, the South suffered the most destruction. Southerners who lived in the paths of marching armies lost their crops and sometimes their homes. Thousands of Southern civilians became refugees—people displaced by war.

Even those who lived outside the war zones suffered. As the war dragged on, many areas faced shortages of food and everyday supplies. Common household items became scarce.

C

Reading **HELP**DESK ⓒⓒⓢⓢ

Taking Notes: *Identifying* RH.6–8.1

As you read, complete a diagram like this one to catalog the ways that women in the North and the South contributed to the war effort.

[Diagram: Women's Contributions]

Content Vocabulary (Tier 3 Words)
• habeas corpus
• draft
• bounty

VIDEO

Clara Barton

Discuss Lead students in a discussion of Clara Barton's life. **Ask:**

• **What are some of Clara Barton's accomplishments?** *(caring for injured soldiers during the Civil War, helping families of Civil War soldiers find their family members and identify their dead, founding and serving as president of the American Red Cross)*

• **What can you tell about her character?** *(Answers will vary, but students may say that she was compassionate, responsible, a hard worker, and a good leader.)* **Intrapersonal**

See page 449E for other online activities.

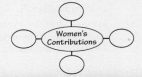
LEARN360
ENGAGE · ENRICH · EXCEL
A Division of AIM Education, Inc.

ENGAGE

Bellringer Ask students to suggest other events that have affected the daily lives of large numbers of people. *(Possible answers: Pearl Harbor, the attack on 9/11, other terrorist attacks, assassinations or attempted assassinations, deaths of famous people, and other significant events in history)* Tell students that in this lesson they will learn how the Civil War affected the daily lives of all Americans.

TEACH & ASSESS

R Reading Skills

Identifying After students have read the section, guide a class discussion about the ways the war affected the home front in the North and in the South. On the whiteboard, create a Venn diagram to identify the changes at home for both sides. **AL** **Ask:**

• **What did school-aged children do during the war?** *(Many of them stayed home to help the family because schools were closed.)*

• **How were schools and churches used during the war?** *(as hospitals for the wounded)* Then lead a discussion of what students would think about living under these circumstances **Visual/Spatial**

C Critical Thinking Skills

Contrasting Help students understand that the South suffered more as a result of the war. **Ask:**

• **Do you think that these changes affected the North or the South more?** *(the South)*

• **How did life change in the South during the war?** *(Students should recognize that the South faced the additional hardships of losing their homes, crops, and land to the Union, as well as shortages of food and other supplies.)* **AL**

ANSWER, p. 465

TAKING NOTES: Possible answers: spying, nursing, teaching, managing businesses and farms

V Visual Skills

Analyzing Images Have students look at the photograph of Frances Clayton and read the caption. **Ask: Why did women disguise themselves and fight in war?** *(Accept reasonable answers. Some students may say that women would not have been allowed to fight if they had not been disguised; other students may say that many women were used to working at jobs that were just as physically demanding as men's jobs, so they joined the war.)* **Visual/Spatial**

W Writing Skills

Informative/Explanatory Have students research and write a description of other female soldiers in the Civil War. Students may want to search for information about Sarah Edmonds Seelye, Albert D.J. Cashier, Elizabeth Niles, Mary Galloway, Frances Hook, Madame Collier, or Florina Budwin.

R Reading Skills

Describing Direct students to read the text. Then, explain that daily life changed dramatically during the Civil War. Have students describe roles women took on during the war. *(At home, they kept farms and businesses running; on the battlefield, they nursed the sick and wounded; some even became spies or disguised themselves as men so that they could enlist as soldiers.)* **AL**

V

W Frances Clayton disguised herself as a man to fight in the Civil War. As many as 400 other women did the same.

R

As one observer noted, the South depended on the outside world "for everything from a hairpin to a toothpick, and from a cradle to a coffin." Most people had to learn to do without.

☑ PROGRESS CHECK

Summarizing Why did many children stop going to school during the Civil War?

New Roles for Women

GUIDING QUESTION *What were the new roles for women in the Civil War?*

Against the advice of family and friends, Kate Cumming, a young woman from Mobile, Alabama, left home to begin a career as a nurse with the Confederate Army of the Mississippi. Cumming was one of the many women whose lives changed because of the Civil War.

In both the North and the South, women kept the farms and factories going. They ran offices, taught school, and kept government records. Women suffered the stress of having husbands away at war and the pain of losing family members. They struggled to keep their families together. With little money available, they cut back on expenses and went without many things they were used to.

Caring for the Wounded

In the Civil War, thousands of women on both sides served as nurses. The idea of women nurses on the battlefield was a relatively new one. Many doctors did not welcome them. They said that women were too delicate for the bloody work of wartime hospitals. Some men also felt it was improper for women to tend the bodies of men they did not know.

Strong-minded women disregarded these objections. Serving with the Union army, Mary Edwards Walker became the first female army surgeon and later received the Congressional Medal of Honor. Dorothea Dix helped persuade officials to let women work as nurses. She became the superintendent of nurses for the Union army and recruited large numbers of women to serve. Another Northerner, Clara Barton, became famous for her work helping wounded soldiers. In the South, Sally Tompkins set up a hospital for soldiers in Richmond, Virginia. Tompkins held the rank of captain in the Confederate army and was the only female officer in the Confederate forces.

Reading **HELP**DESK (CCSS)

Build Vocabulary: *Related Words*
The word *spy*, which means "to watch secretly," is related to the word *espionage*, which means "spying."

Reading Strategy: *Finding the Main Idea*
As you read "New Roles for Women," jot down the main idea in each paragraph in your notebook. Using your notes, write a sentence that summarizes this section.

netw⊙rks *Online Teaching Options*

SLIDE SHOW

Women Take Charge

Analyzing Use the interactive slide show about women and social reform to show how Dorothea Dix and Clara Barton played roles in helping the ill and wounded during the Civil War. **Ask: Why did doctors think women should not serve as nurses on the battlefield?** *(They thought it was improper for women to tend to men they did not know and that women were too delicate for work on the battlefields.)* Explain that women's roles in war have changed, and currently women have many more choices about the work they do during wartime.

See page 449E for other online activities.

McGraw-Hill **netw⊙rks** **Women Take Charge**

Dorothea Dix was a pioneering social reformer of the mid-1800s. She observed the horrific conditions of mental institutions, where the sick were imprisoned with criminals, without heat or privacy or treatment. She devoted her life to reform legislation and to building new mental hospitals.

Wikimedia/The Boston Antatheaeum

ANSWER, p. 466

☑ **PROGRESS CHECK** They stayed home to help their families. Also, many schools served as hospitals.

The women who served in wartime hospitals came face to face with terrible brutality. After the Battle of Shiloh, Kate Cumming wrote, "Nothing that I had ever heard or read had given me the faintest idea of the horrors witnessed here."

Spying

Women on both sides served as spies. For example, Rose O'Neal Greenhow entertained Union leaders in Washington, D.C. From them, she gathered information about Union plans and passed it to the South. Greenhow eventually was caught and convicted of treason—the crime of betraying one's country. Belle Boyd of Front Royal, Virginia, informed Confederate generals of Union troop movements in the Shenandoah River valley.

Harriet Tubman, a leading "conductor" on the Underground Railroad, also served as a spy and scout for the Union. In 1863 Tubman led a mission that freed many enslaved people and disrupted Southern supply lines.

Some women disguised themselves as men and became soldiers. Loreta Janeta Velázquez fought for the South at the First Battle of Bull Run and at the Battle of Shiloh. She later became a Confederate spy.

☑ PROGRESS CHECK

Explaining Why did some people object to women working as nurses during the war?

R In 1861 Dorothea Dix became superintendent of woman nurses for the Union army. Part of her job was to set up military hospitals like the brick building shown here. Dix served till the end of the war without pay.

(t) North Wind Picture Archives,
(b) Medford Historical Society Collection/CORBIS

Lesson 3   467

R Reading Skills

Discussing Discuss female spies, such as Rose O'Neal Greenhow, Belle Boyd, Harriet Tubman, and Loreta Janeta Velázquez. Ask students to use evidence from the text to explain the impact of these spies on both the Union and the Confederacy. Have students work in pairs to organize their notes on these important women in a chart. **Interpersonal**

T Technology Skills

Collaborating Have students work in small groups and use a social bookmarking service to research and share information about the life of Dorothea Dix. If time permits, groups can prepare a presentation about Dorothea Dix and her accomplishments. **Interpersonal**

V Visual Skills

Interpreting Ask students to look at the photograph of the hospital and contrast it with the hospitals of today. **Ask: What might the tents be for?** *(Answers may vary, but students should identify purposes related to the hospital., such as a triage site for patients or a place to temporarily store the deceased.)* **BL** **Visual/Spatial**

SLIDE SHOW

Roles of Women in War

Making Connections Use the interactive slide show about women's roles in wartime to discuss the role of women in the Civil War and modern society. Compare the slideshow to the textbook and indicate any new information in the slides. **ELL**

See page 449E for other online activities.

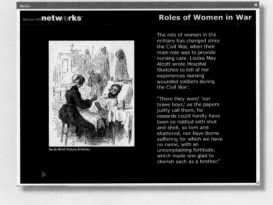

ANSWER, p. 467

☑ PROGRESS CHECK They felt the work was too bloody for women, and that it was inappropriate for women to tend to men they didn't know.

Critical Thinking Skills **G₁**

Making Inferences Call on a volunteer to read aloud the first sentence under the subheading "Prisoners of War."

- Lead a discussion of the reasons each side was ambivalent about its prisoners.
- Help students conclude that in a civil war the two sides have many commonalities, which could lead to sympathy.
- Ask students whether they think soldiers from different countries would have a similar reaction to their prisoners. *(Accept reasonable responses. Some students may realize that people on different sides of an issue can still feel sympathy at a human level. Other students may concentrate on the differences between the two sides and say that a sympathetic response is less likely when two countries fight each other.)* **BL**

Reading Skills **R**

Explaining Ask students to read the remainder of the section on prisons and prisoners of war. Then, lead a class discussion about the creation of prison camps during the war. **Ask: How were prisoners dealt with at first?** *(The sides exchanged them.)* **Why were prison camps established?** *(because of issues such as Confederate treatment of African American soldiers)*

Critical Thinking Skills **G₂**

Comparing After discussing the Andersonville prison with students, compare the conditions at that prison camp to the conditions at Elmira. **Ask: How did conditions at Andersonville compare with those at Elmira?** *(Conditions were similar at both prisons—little to eat, dirty water, poor facilities.)*

The Captured and the Wounded

GUIDING QUESTION *What were the conditions of hospitals and prison camps during the Civil War?*

For many soldiers, battle could be a terrifying experience. For those with wounds or for those taken prisoner, the misery was just beginning.

Prisoners of War

G₁
R
Each side treated its enemy soldiers with a mixture of sympathy and hostility. At first the two sides exchanged prisoners. After this system broke down over issues such as Confederate treatment of African American prisoners, each side set up prison camps. A prisoner typically kept his blanket and a cup or canteen. These possessions were all he had during his imprisonment. Food shortages made the suffering worse. Volunteers **distributed** bread and soup to the wounded. In the prisons, though, there was little or nothing to eat.

G₂
Andersonville prison opened in Georgia in early 1864. It was built to hold 10,000 prisoners. By August, 33,000 crammed its grounds. The men slept in shallow holes dug in the ground. All they received to eat each day was a teaspoon of salt, three tablespoons of beans, and eight ounces of cornmeal. They drank and cooked with water from a stream that also served as a sewer. Almost 13,000 Union prisoners died there, mostly from disease.

The Union prison in Elmira, New York, was no better. Captured soldiers from the South suffered through the winter months without blankets and warm clothes. The hospital was located in a flooded basement. A pond within the compound served as both toilet and garbage dump. Almost one quarter of all prisoners at Elmira died.

Field Hospitals

Surgeons set up hospitals near battlefields. There, with bullets and cannonballs flying by, they bandaged wounds and amputated limbs. Nurse Kate Cumming recalled:

PRIMARY SOURCE

❝ We have to walk, and when we give the men anything kneel, in blood and water; but we think nothing of it. ❞

—from *Kate: The Journal of a Confederate Nurse*

In the Civil War, more than 2,000 women served as nurses in hospitals on both sides. Most were volunteers.

Reading **HELP**DESK **CCSS**

Academic Vocabulary (Tier 2)

distribute to hand out, spread around

Reading Strategy: *Context Clues*

When you find an unknown word, look at surrounding text for clues to the meaning. Clues may be:
- The word is defined immediately following its use.
- A synonym or an antonym is used that explains the meaning.
- Hints appear in the surrounding passage to help you figure out the meaning.

---

netw⊙rks *Online Teaching Options*

IMAGE

Andersonville Prison

Describing Show students the image of Andersonville prison to discuss the prison camps created during the Civil War. **Ask: What were prisoners allowed to keep?** *(a blanket, cup, or canteen)* **AL** **Where did prisoners sleep at Andersonville?** *(in shallow holes dug in the ground)* **What other hardships did they endure?** *(They had very little to eat and had to drink from a stream that was also a sewer.)* **AL** **Visual/Spatial**

See page 449E for other online activities.

McGraw-Hill netw⊙rks™   Andersonville Prison

The cemetery at Andersonville is now a national cemetery, serving as a memorial to all prisoners of war.

Library of Congress/LC-USZC4-10808

Disease was another medical threat. Crowded together in camps and drinking unclean water, many soldiers got sick. Disease spread quickly—and could be deadly. Some regiments lost half their men to illness before they ever went into battle.

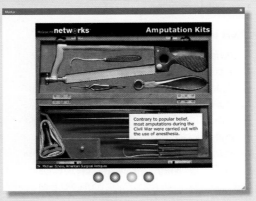

Doctors in the Civil War did not have many modern medicines. To prevent deadly infections, they often amputated wounded limbs with tools such as these.

✅ **PROGRESS CHECK**

Explaining Why were prison camps set up?

Political and Economic Change

GUIDING QUESTION *What political and economic changes occurred during the Civil War?*

In the South, many white people opposed the war. The fighting was costly not just in terms of lives lost or damaged, but in food, material, and money. Everywhere, people suffered from shortages. Bread riots broke out throughout the South as hungry people took to the streets. In Richmond, a group of mostly women and children gathered peacefully to protest but soon started smashing shop windows and stealing food.

In the North, the Democratic Party was split down the middle. War Democrats supported the war while criticizing Lincoln's handling of it. Peace Democrats argued for an immediate end to fighting and a reunion of the states through negotiation. Most Peace Democrats came from the Midwestern states of Ohio, Illinois, and Indiana. Critics of the Peace Democrats called them Copperheads. A copperhead is a type of deadly snake. Rather than take offense, the Copperheads proudly embraced this label. They wore copper pennies as badges on their clothing.

As in the South, some Northerners who opposed the war discouraged people from enlisting. A few even helped Confederate prisoners of war escape. Opponents claimed that the Peace Democrats encouraged the South to keep fighting. They said the war dragged on because Confederates believed the Peace Democrats would eventually prevail in the North.

Jail Without Trial

As a way of dealing with war opponents in the North, President Lincoln suspended **habeas corpus** (HAY•bee•uhs KAWR•puhs)—a legal process that helps ensure the government has a legal right to keep someone in jail. The Constitution says government can suspend habeas corpus, but only "when in cases of rebellion or invasion, the public safety may require it."

Dr. Michael Echols, American Surgical Antiques

C1 Critical Thinking Skills

Comparing Point students to the photograph of the nurse and patient in a Civil War hospital on the previous page. Then have students use the language of comparing and contrasting to discuss similarities and differences between hospitals and surgical practices in the days of the Civil War and now. **AL ELL** Verbal/Linguistic

C2 Critical Thinking Skills

Identifying Central Issues Review the facts about the War Democrats and the Peace Democrats, including their opinions about the war. **Ask: Why were the Peace Democrats called "Copperheads"?** *(Because they were viewed as traitors, they were nicknamed after the venomous snake.)* Discuss the reasons some people thought that opposing the war was unpatriotic.

R Reading Skills

Discussing Have students read the section titled "Jail Without Trial." Tell students that *habeas corpus* is a Latin phrase meaning "you should have the body." **AL ELL** Then, remind students that the U.S. Constitution allows the president to suspend habeas corpus. (You may want students to refer to the copy of the Constitution in their textbook to find the exact language.) Ask students to use evidence from the text to explain the reasons that Presidents Lincoln and Davis suspended habeas corpus during the Civil War. Ask students whether they agree or disagree with their decision.

IMAGE

Amputation Kits

Discussing Use the interactive image of an amputation kit to introduce and discuss with students the horrible conditions in field hospitals, along with the lack of modern medical treatments. **Ask: What was a major threat in these hospitals?** *(disease)* Then read from the textbook the excerpt by Kate Cumming to provide students with a firsthand description of the conditions the soldiers faced. **Ask: What risks did surgeons face?** *(Hospitals on battlefields were dangerous because of flying bullets and cannonballs.)*

See page 449E for other online activities.

McGraw **netw⊙rks**   Amputation Kits

Contrary to popular belief, most amputations during the Civil War were carried out with the use of anesthesia.

Dr. Michael Echols, American Surgical Antiques

○ ○ ○ ○

ANSWER, p. 469

✅ **PROGRESS CHECK** Prison camps became necessary when the system of exchanging prisoners broke down because of issues such as Confederate treatment of African American soldiers.

Life During the Civil War

R1 Reading Skills

Defining Provide students with a dictionary and discuss the multiple meanings of the word *draft*. Invite volunteers to use each form of the word in a sentence. Then have students identify the meaning that is used in the textbook. **AL** **ELL**

C Critical Thinking Skills

Determining Cause and Effect Discuss with students the creation of draft laws, which required men to join and serve for three years. **Ask:** **Why do you think this policy angered poor people in America?** *(Because wealthy individuals could buy a substitute to replace them and they would not have to serve. Also, if a man paid $300, he did not have to serve. Poor people often did not have these options available to them.)*

R2 Reading Skills

Illustrating After students have read the section about the draft law, have them write their name on a slip of paper and put the papers into a container. Ask for a volunteer to draw 10 names out of the container and read the names aloud. As students hear their name, they should stand and walk to the front of the classroom. **Ask:** **What were you thinking as you waited to hear your name?** *(Accept reasonable answers.)* Use this activity as a springboard to discuss the protests against the draft during the Civil War. **Kinesthetic**

Content Background Knowledge

- Although there was no official draft during the colonial period, states were required to have militias.
- During the Revolutionary War, cash and other incentives failed to recruit enough soldiers. President Washington tried to institute a draft, but Congress rejected this idea.
- In later wars, including the War of 1812, the Spanish-American War, and World Wars I and II, the draft was in effect.
- Young men were also drafted to serve during the Vietnam War, and the protests against the draft rivaled those protesting the draft during the Civil War.
- Currently, service in the armed forces is voluntary.

ANSWER, p. 470

CRITICAL THINKING Because the snakes are attacking Lady Liberty, the cartoon suggests the Copperheads are a threat to U.S. citizens' liberty.

A Northern newspaper ran this cartoon in 1863. It shows Lady Liberty warding off an attack of the Peace Democrats, or Copperheads.

▶ **CRITICAL THINKING**
Analyzing Images What does this cartoon suggest about the artist's view of Copperheads? Explain your answer.

THE COPPERHEAD PARTY.—IN FAVOR OF A VIGOROUS PROSECUTION OF PEACE!

With this act, Lincoln's government was able to jail thousands of Northerners without putting them on trial. Some of these people were likely traitors to the Union. Others did nothing more than use their right of free speech to criticize the government.

In the South, President Davis also suspended habeas corpus. He, too, believed he needed to deal harshly with opponents of the war. Still, Davis's action upset many loyal supporters.

Draft Laws

R1 Both the North and the South had trouble getting troops to sign up. In 1862 the Confederate Congress passed a **draft** that required able-bodied white men between ages 18 and 35 to serve for three years. Later the requirement included men from ages 17 to 50. Several exceptions were allowed. A man with enough money could hire a **substitute** to serve for him. Later, a man with 20 or more enslaved people did not have to serve.

C At first, the North offered a **bounty** (BAUN•tee), or a sum of money, to encourage volunteers. In March 1863, it also passed a draft. Men aged 20 to 45 had to register. As in the South, a man could avoid the draft by hiring a substitute or paying $300. Many workers earned less than $500 a year and could not afford these options. In the North and the South, people complained it was "a rich man's war and a poor man's fight."

People rioted to protest the draft in several Northern cities.
R2 The New York City draft riots in July 1863 were the worst. As the first names were drawn, rioters attacked government and military buildings. Then mobs turned their attacks against

Reading **HELP**DESK **CCSS**

habeas corpus a legal writ, or order, that guarantees a prisoner the right to be heard in court
draft a system of selecting people for required military service
bounty reward or payment

470 *The Civil War*

Visual Vocabulary
greenback
paper money issued by the United States government

Academic Vocabulary (Tier 2 Words)
substitute an alternate or replacement

---

networks *Online Teaching Options*

POLITICAL CARTOON

Civil War Political Cartoons

Analyzing Visuals Use the interactive slide show about political cartoons to discuss both political unrest and civil unrest that occurred during the war.
Ask: **How does the cartoonist make fun of Abraham Lincoln?** *(shows Lincoln avoiding the hard question about the loss of young soldiers)* **What is the message of the cartoon of the two soldiers who have lost a leg?** *(The soldiers have a common experience and can be respectful of each other even though they are from different races.)*
Visual/Spatial

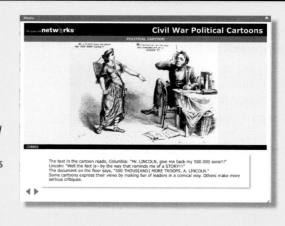

See page 449E for other online activities.

African Americans. Many white workers had opposed the Emancipation Proclamation, fearing freed African Americans would take their jobs. After four days, more than 100 people were dead. Federal troops finally stopped the riots.

War and the Economy

The war strained the economies of the North and the South. However, the North, with its greater resources, was better able to cope with the costs of the war.

The two sides had three ways of paying for the war. First, they borrowed money. Second, they passed new taxes, including income taxes. Third, they printed money. Northern bills became known as **greenbacks** because of their color.

In the North, industry profited from the war effort. It made guns, ammunition, shoes, and uniforms. Farmers prospered, too. They sold their crops to feed the troops. Because goods were in high demand, prices went up—faster than workers' wages. This inflation caused hardship for working people.

The white South felt the economic strain even more sharply than the North. Many of the battles of the Civil War took place on Confederate soil, destroying farmland and railroad lines. The Union naval blockade prevented the shipping of trade goods. Vital materials could not reach the Confederacy. Salt was in such short supply that women scraped the floors of smokehouses to recover it. Food shortages led to riots in Atlanta, Richmond, and other cities.

The South also suffered much worse inflation. As early as 1862, citizens were begging Confederate leaders for help.

☑ **PROGRESS CHECK**

Comparing How did the war affect the economy in the North and South?

Thinking Like a —
HISTORIAN

Analyzing and Interpreting Information

Inflation, a rise in prices, hurts people by reducing the buying power of money. The graph below shows that with just 3.5 percent inflation, the buying power of $1,000 drops sharply. In 20 years, the $1,000 will have about half its original buying power. To learn more about analyzing and interpreting information, review *Thinking Like a Historian.*

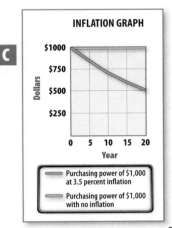

INFLATION GRAPH

Dollars: $1000, $750, $500, $250
Year: 0, 5, 10, 15, 20

— Purchasing power of $1,000 at 3.5 percent inflation
— Purchasing power of $1,000 with no inflation

V Visual Skills

Analyzing Graphs Discuss the slope of the line in the inflation graph *(negative)* and that it shows that inflation reduces the buying power of money. **Ask: At 3.5% inflation, which is shown in the graph, how much is $1,000 worth after 10 years?** *(a little less than $750; about $725)*
Visual/Spatial   Logical/Mathematical

R Reading Skills

Identifying Have students review the text. Explain to students that wars are expensive because each side has to feed, house, and equip its troops. **Ask:**

- **How did the North and South pay for the war?** *(borrowed money, raised taxes, printed money)*
- **Why do you think they called the Union money greenbacks?** *(because of its green color)* Point out that U.S. paper money is still green.

C Critical Thinking Skills

Comparing and Contrasting Discuss how the war affected the economies of the North and South. **Ask:**

- **How did the North's economy fare during the war?** *(Northern industry and farms prospered because they produced supplies for the Union.)*
- **How did the South's economy fare?** *(The South's economy suffered because the blockade prevented the South from selling cotton and other goods, and obtaining needed supplies.)*
- **How did the South's economic woes affect support for the war?** *(They increased opposition to the war, and there were riots throughout the South.)*

Have students complete the Lesson 3 Review.

LESSON 3 REVIEW ⓒⒸⓈⓈ

Review Vocabulary (Tier 3 Words)

1. Use each of these terms in a complete sentence that explains the term's meaning. RH.6–8.4

   a. habeas corpus   **b.** draft   **c.** bounty

Answer the Guiding Questions

2. ***Explaining*** How did the roles of women change during the Civil War? RH.6–8.2

3. ***Evaluating*** How did the Civil War affect children? RH.6–8.2

4. ***Comparing*** What challenges and threats did prisoners and wounded soldiers face? RH.6–8.2

5. ***Summarizing*** Who were the Copperheads? What was their position on fighting the war? RH.6–8.1

6. **ARGUMENT** President Lincoln and President Davis suspended habeas corpus to deal with opponents of the war. Do you think suspending civil liberties is justified in some situations? Write a short essay in which you state and defend your position. WHST.6–8.1, WHST.6–8.10

LESSON 3 REVIEW ANSWERS

1. Possible answers: **a.** Both sides in the Civil War suspended habeas corpus as a way of dealing with dissent. **b.** Drafting men helped ensure a steady supply of soldiers for the war effort. **c.** To encourage enlistment, the North offered bounties.

2. Women took on more roles at home and became nurses for the first time on the battlefield.

3. Many children stopped going to school to help at home, and many schools were closed.

4. Prisoners and the wounded faced challenges from shortages of medicine and supplies, and from threats of disease because of conditions in prisons and field hospitals.

5. The Copperheads were "Peace" Democrats from the North who were against the war.

6. Students should use logical, fact-based arguments in defending their positions.

CLOSE & REFLECT

As a class, discuss the reasons for the social, political, and economic changes that took place during the Civil War. **Ask: Do you think any of these changes would have occurred if there had not been a war?** *(Students may suggest that some social changes, such as roles for women, may have occurred even if there had not been a war, but that others, such as economic woes, were a direct effect of the war.)*

ANSWER, p. 471

☑ **PROGRESS CHECK** In the North, industry and farming prospered. In the South, the economy was very strained by the war. Both sides suffered inflation, but inflation was much worse in the South.

ENGAGE

🔔 **Bellringer** Have students read the background information on *Across Five Aprils*. Tell students that this novel is an example of historical fiction. **Ask: How can authors create realistic fictional accounts of historical times and events?** *(by researching the time, including realistic facts and details)*

TEACH & ASSESS

C Critical Thinking Skills

Drawing Conclusions Remind students that during the Civil War, there were no televisions, radios, cell phones, or computers. Have them suggest ways that people communicated with each other or heard news about events in the country. *(Possible answers: letters, newspapers, word of mouth from travelers)* **Ask: How do you think Tom's mother and brother felt about getting a letter from him? How might they have felt after reading his letter? Why?** *(Answers may vary, but students should use their understanding of the reading and of the chapter to explain their answers.)* **ELL** **Interpersonal**

V Visual Skills

Analyzing Images Discuss the image at the bottom of the page with students. Ask them to write three sentences using descriptive adjectives to tell someone about the image. Share the sentences with the class. **Visual/Spatial, Verbal/Linguistic**

Content Background Knowledge

Point out the following details in the image at the bottom of the page:

• Union soldiers wore blue uniforms; Confederates wore gray.
• Soldiers carried rifles called *bayonets*. These guns had a sharp knife on the end that was used for close-range fighting.
• Troops also used cannons, as you can see in the lower right of the image.
• Mounted soldiers, called *cavalry,* also fought. The word *cavalry* is related to the French word for horse rider, *chevalier.*

AMERICA'S LITERATURE CCSS

Across Five Aprils
by Irene Hunt

Irene Hunt (1907–2001) was born in Pontiac, Illinois, more than 40 years after the Civil War ended. Her father died when she was seven years old. Hunt graduated from the University of Illinois in 1939. She taught French and English in Illinois public schools until she retired to write full-time in 1969. She wrote many books for young people and won a Newberry Medal for her second novel, *Up a Road Slowly.* Hunt died in 2001.

First published in 1965, *Across Five Aprils* was Irene Hunt's first novel. It is the story of Jethro Creighton, a nine-year-old boy living in Indiana during the Civil War. In this excerpt, he and his mother are at home when a letter arrives from one of Jethro's older brothers, who is fighting for the Union.

A Union soldier might wear a cap like this.

> **❝I miss yore good cookin Ma. You tell Jeth that bein a soljer aint so much.❞**
>
> —from Irene Hunt's *Across Five Aprils*

In February 1862, Brigadier General Ulysses S. Grant demanded and received unconditional surrender of Confederate Fort Donelson on the Cumberland River.

472   *The Civil War*

---

netw⊙rks   *Online Teaching Options*

SLIDE SHOW

How to Distinguish Fact from Opinion

Distinguishing Fact from Opinion View the resource with students to review fact and opinion. **Ask: What is a fact?** *(a statement that can be proven)* **What is an opinion?** *(a statement based on beliefs and values)* Make a two-column chart on the board, and ask students to identify statements of fact and statements of opinion in the reading selection. *(Answers will vary.)*

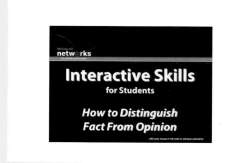

netw⊙rks
Interactive Skills
for Students

*How to Distinguish
Fact From Opinion*

C

" Finally one day Ed Turner brought them a letter from Tom. Ed looked pinched with cold after his long drive, but he wouldn't stop for coffee.

"A fam'ly needs to be alone when one of these letters comes," he said in answer to Ellen's invitation. "I'd be pleased if you'd let me know what the boy has to say—later on when Matt has the time to drop over."

Jenny had gone with her father to see about some **stock,** and Jethro was alone in the cabin with his mother. When Ed Turner was gone, she handed the letter to Jethro.

"My hands is shakin', Son," she said. They were, indeed, but both she and the boy knew that the real reason she was forced to hand the letter over was the fact that she could not read.

The envelope was crumpled and stained, the letter written in pencil in a round, childish hand. It was probably among the first three or four letters that young Tom had ever written.

Dere Fokes:

I take pencle in hand to let you no that Eb and me is alright.

I expect you no by now how we took Fort Henry down here. Mebby I oughtnt say we took it becus it was the ironclads that done it. Old admiral Foote had what it took and he give the rebs a **dressin down** but some of his iron-clads got hit hard. A boy I no was on the Essex and he was burned so bad he dide when that boat got nocked out of the fite.

Us boys didn't do much fitin at Fort Henry but at Donelson I can tell you we made up fer it. We had done a foolish thing on our way to Donelson and I will rite you about it. When we was marchin tord the fort the weather was like a hot april day back home. We was feelin set-up about Fort Henry and when some of the boys got tard of carryin hevey blanket rolls they jest up and throwed em away. Then more and more of us acted like crazy fools and we throwed away hevey cotes and things to make our lodes a littel liter. As soon as we got to Donelson the wether turned cold as Billy Sideways and some of the boys that was sick or bad hurt they froze to deth in the snow. Things was awful bad with so many kilt and others froze. I felt sick when I looked at them and so I am, not so proud about Donelson as mebby I ought to be. I miss yore good cookin Ma. You tell Jeth that bein a soljer aint so much.

yrs truley
Tom "

Vocabulary

stock
livestock

dressin down
(incorrect spelling of "dressing down")
a serious punishment or scolding

Literary Element

Dialect refers to the language, speech patterns, spelling, grammar, and sounds used by people from a particular area or from a particular social or economic group. As you read, note the ways Irene Hunt uses dialect to reveal information about her characters. If you have trouble following the dialect, try reading the text aloud.

W

Analyzing Literature DBQ

1 **Explaining** Why didn't Ed Turner accept Mrs. Creighton's invitation to stay for coffee? **RH.6–8.2**

2 **Analyzing** What does the dialect used in Tom's letter reveal about him? Use examples from the text to support your answer. **RH.6–8.1**

3 **Interpreting** What has Tom learned about the reality of war? **RH.6–8.6**

Lesson 3 **473**

C Critical Thinking Skills

Making Connections Ask volunteers to read the excerpt two paragraphs at a time aloud to the class. Clarify any confusion over meaning. **AL** **ELL** **Ask: Do you recognize any names, places, or events from your textbook?** *(Students should recognize Admiral Foote, Fort Henry, and Fort Donelson.)*

Discuss dialect as a literary feature. Ask students if they have read any other books with characters that speak in dialect. Refer to the other Features in the textbook to identify dialect. **Ask: Why would the authors choose to use dialect in this and other texts?** *(Answers may vary, based on the text. In this instance dialect makes the character more believable. It also gives a quality of innocence to Tom.)*

W Writing Skills

Narrative Have students read the explanation of dialect under Literary Element. Ask students to write a letter back to Tom from his mother, using dialect.

Content Background Knowledge

Tom's letter mentions Donelson; this fort was the site of a major battle of the war. The Union had retreated and the Confederates, in confusion, pulled back. General Ulysses S. Grant ordered a counterattack and went on to win. The capture of Fort Donelson on February 16, 1862, helped propel Grant to hero status. He was made a major general and later won the presidency.

CLOSE & REFLECT

Encourage students to read *Across Five Aprils* in its entirety to gain more perspective on what life was like during the Civil War. You may also wish to suggest other books on the subject, such as those listed as "More Media Resources" for this chapter.

MAP

The Civil War 1861-1865

Creating Maps Display the Civil War map for students. Based on Tom's letter and the information given in the Feature, have students trace on the interactive map a probable route for Tom from his home to the locations where he fought.
Visual/Spatial **ELL** **AL**

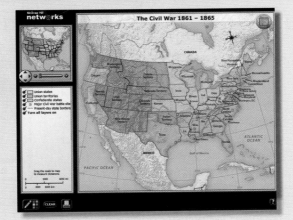

ANSWERS, p. 473

1. He knew she would want to be alone after reading the letter from her son.

2. Possible answer: Tom's grammar and spelling reveal that he has not had much education. Although he can write, he spells many words incorrectly, such as "deth," "wether," and "mebby."

3. Students should suggest that Tom has learned that war is dangerous and sad, even when battles are won.

ENGAGE

Bellringer Review the events of the war so far. Ask students if they can recall the Anaconda Plan and the goals of this strategy. **Ask:**

- **By the end of 1862, what had the North accomplished toward its "Anaconda Plan"?** *(The Union controlled most of the Mississippi and had blockaded most ports.)*
- **How had this affected the South?** *(The South's economy was strained because getting supplies and exporting cotton was difficult, and the South was suffering from the destruction of its farms and homes.)*

TEACH & ASSESS

R Reading Skills

Explaining Direct students to read the section titled "The Battle of Fredericksburg." Discuss with students the events of the battle and its aftermath. **Ask:**

- **How did Lee's troops manage to defeat Burnside?** *(Lee anticipated Burnside's movement and was able to intercept Burnside's troops from a protected position before the Union got to Richmond.)*
- **Why did Lee's forces dig trenches at Fredericksburg?** *(They dug them on hillsides south of the town so they could fire down on the enemy.)* **BL**

ANSWER, p. 474

TAKING NOTES: Union Victories: Gettysburg, Vicksburg, Port Hudson; **Confederate Victories:** Fredericksburg, Chancellorsville

---

networks

There's More Online!

☑ **BIOGRAPHY**
"Stonewall" Jackson

☑ **GAME**

☑ **GRAPHIC ORGANIZER**
Union and Confederate Victories

☑ **MAP** The Battle of Gettysburg, Day 3

☑ **PRIMARY SOURCE**
• Obituary of Stonewall Jackson
• Union Recruitment Poster

Lesson 4
The Strain of War

ESSENTIAL QUESTION *Why does conflict develop?*

IT MATTERS BECAUSE
Union victories at Gettysburg and Vicksburg marked a turning point in the war.

Southern Victories

GUIDING QUESTION *What factors contributed to the early success of the Confederate forces?*

The military leadership of Generals Robert E. Lee and Stonewall Jackson was a key factor in the Confederates' military success in the East. With their knowledge of the land and ability to inspire troops, these two generals often defeated larger Union forces.

The Battle of Fredericksburg

After Antietam, Robert E. Lee moved his army out of Maryland into Virginia. This encouraged the newly named Union commander, General Ambrose Burnside, to march his troops toward the Confederate capital at Richmond. Lee intercepted the Union army near Fredericksburg. Lee's forces dug trenches in hills south of the town. This gave them the advantage of higher ground from which to fight. On December 13, 1862, Union forces attacked. Lee's **entrenched** (ihn•TREHNCHT) troops drove them back with heavy losses. Devastated, Burnside resigned.

Victory at Chancellorsville

In May 1863, Lee met Union forces led by General Joseph Hooker in the Battle of Chancellorsville. General Lee again showed daring and a brilliant command of tactics. Although Hooker had

(l) North Wind Picture Archives, (cl) Archive Photos/Getty Images, (c) Kean Collection/Getty Images, (r) The Granger Collection, NYC

Reading HELPDESK CCSS

Taking Notes: *Categorizing* RH.6–8.1
As you read, use a chart like this one to keep track of who won which battles.

Union Victories	Confederate Victories

Content Vocabulary (Tier 3 Words)
• **entrench**
• **flank**

474 *The Civil War*

---

networks *Online Teaching Options*

VIDEO

The Gettysburg Address

Determining Central Ideas Show the video about the Gettysburg Address. Answer any questions that students may have about the video. **Ask: What are the main themes of the Gettysburg Address?** *(the question of whether the nation will survive; hope that the Union will be restored so the soldiers did not die in vain; honoring those fallen in battle)* **Why was the Gettysburg Address so effective?** *(Possible answer: Although it was short, it used memorable language to address important themes like the survival of the Union and the need to honor those fallen in battle.)* **BL**

See page 449F for other online activities.

twice as many men, Lee divided his forces. Some Confederate troops confronted the main Union force. Others under the leadership of Stonewall Jackson secretly marched to a spot at the far end of the Union line. The risky plan worked perfectly. Jackson's army surprised the Union force with a crushing attack on its **flank** (FLANGK), or side. Lee struck from the front. Caught between the two Confederate forces, Hooker eventually withdrew his men.

The Confederate victory came at a high cost. In the confusion of battle, Confederate soldiers fired on and wounded Stonewall Jackson by mistake. Surgeons amputated Jackson's arm, prompting Lee to say, "He has lost his left arm, and I have lost my right." Worse, Jackson developed pneumonia. After a week of suffering, he died. His death cost the South one of its great leaders. It also affected the morale of its army and its citizens.

Problems With Union Leadership

In contrast, Union leadership in the East disappointed the president. In less than a year, a frustrated Lincoln saw three different generals try and fail to lead the Union to victory.

The first, Major General George McClellan, commanded the Union forces at the Battle of Antietam in March 1862. Although he was expert at preparing for battle, he was overly careful and slow to act. Said Lincoln, "If McClellan doesn't want to use the army, I'd like to borrow it for a while." The last straw came when, after victory at Antietam, McClellan failed to obey Lincoln's order to follow the retreating Confederate troops and destroy them.

Lincoln pushed his next commander, General Ambrose Burnside, to take aggressive action. Burnside quickly lost the president's favor after his crushing loss at Fredericksburg.

Next, Lincoln appointed Major General Joseph Hooker, who had often been critical of other generals. Hooker's attitude matched the president's. "May God have mercy on General Lee, for I will have none," he declared. Despite Hooker's confidence, Lee's much smaller army crushed Hooker's forces at Chancellorsville. Hooker soon resigned.

Lincoln's next commander needed to prove himself quickly. Major General George Meade took command three days before one of the war's great battles, at Gettysburg, Pennsylvania.

✓ PROGRESS CHECK

Explaining Why was Lincoln frustrated with the Union generals?

North Wind Picture Archives

BIOGRAPHY

Thomas Jonathan "Stonewall" Jackson (1824–1863)

Thomas Jackson was born in Virginia. At the age of 18, he moved north to attend the military academy at West Point. He went on to a short and unremarkable career in the United States Army. During the 1850s, he taught at the Virginia Military Institute. At that time, he showed more interest in art than in war. When the Civil War started, Jackson was not widely known in the military. That changed at the First Battle of Bull Run, when Jackson won his nickname "Stonewall." By 1863 he had become one of the Confederacy's top leaders.

▶ CRITICAL THINKING
Speculating What does Jackson's nickname—Stonewall—suggest about his personal qualities?

---

entrench to place within a trench, or ditch, for defense; to place in a strong defensive position
flank the side or edge of a military formation

Build Vocabulary: *Metaphor*

Entrench is often used metaphorically to refer to ideas that are firmly held and cannot be easily changed. Here's an example: "Thanks to my parents, the belief that I would succeed as long as I studied hard became entrenched in my mind."

Lesson 4 **475**

R1 Reading Skills

Discussing After students have read the text, discuss the Southern victory at Chancellorsville. Ask a volunteer to describe how Lee divided Hooker's forces. Instruct the student to draw a diagram to illustrate this strategy. Be sure to discuss the attacks from both the front and the flank.

Make sure that everyone understands the term *flank*. Invite a second volunteer to locate the word in a text and define it for the class. **AL ELL**

Finally, point out that although the Confederates won the battle at Chancellorsville, they lost one of their great leaders, Stonewall Jackson. **Ask: What was the effect of the loss of Stonewall Jackson?** *(It deprived Lee of his most valuable officer and affected the morale of the Confederate army and citizens.)*

R2 Reading Skills

Listing Remind students that keeping notes in list form while reading can help them isolate important events or people in the text. Have students create lists to keep track of the Union commanders discussed in this section. **AL**

Content Background Knowledge

Thomas Jonathan Jackson earned his nickname "Stonewall" during the First Battle of Manassas, in 1861. Another Confederate general, so the story goes, shouted, "There is Jackson, standing like a stone wall! Rally behind the Virginians!"

PRIMARY SOURCE

Stonewall Jackson

Explaining Show students the interactive primary source excerpt of the obituary of Thomas "Stonewall" Jackson to discuss his life and the cause of his death. **Ask: How did Jackson die?** *(He was wounded, and his arm was amputated, which resulted in his death.)* **ELL**

See page 449F for other online activities.

McGraw-Hill **networks** — Stonewall Jackson
ANALYZING PRIMARY SOURCES

After Stonewall Jackson's death in 1863, the northern magazine *Harper's Weekly* published an obituary about him. Read the obituary. What characteristics of Stonewall Jackson does it reveal?

Northwind Picture Archives

❝ GEN. STONEWALL JACKSON.
WE publish herewith a portrait of the late THOMAS JEFFERSON JACKSON, better known as "Stonewall Jackson," in his lifetime a Lieutenant-General in the rebel army.
He was born about the year 1826, in Lewis County, Virginia, and entered West Point in 1842. He ❞

—from *Harper's Weekly: General Stonewall Jackson (May 30, 1863),* by Harper's Weekly

Source: http://www.sonofthesouth.net/leefoundation/civil-war/1863/may/death-stonewall-jackson.htm

---

ANSWERS, p. 475

CRITICAL THINKING His nickname suggests that he is stubborn and unmoving, and that he will not give up.

✓ **PROGRESS CHECK** Lincoln was frustrated because they were not acting aggressively enough.

C Critical Thinking Skills

Identifying Points of View Review Union and Confederate policies regarding the enlistment of African Americans. Remind students of the meaning of *enlist.* **AL** **ELL** **Ask: What were attitudes toward African American soldiers in the Civil War?** (*In the North, African Americans were allowed to enlist, but many whites thought they would not make good soldiers. Confederate soldiers hated the African American soldiers and fired more aggressively at them in battle. In the South, African Americans could not enlist, but they often accompanied white slave owners to battle and performed many tasks to support Confederate troops.*)

R Reading Skills

Discussing After students have read the selection, discuss why African Americans would have been willing to put themselves in such danger to fight for the Union. Ask students to explain the tough position that these soldiers were placed in. **Ask:**

- **How did the Union feel about all-African American regiments?** (*They doubted their fighting ability and some resented them.*)
- **What about the South?** (*Many troops hated them and would focus attacks on African American regiments.*)

Connections to
TODAY

African American Soldiers

Beginning with the Revolutionary War, African Americans have had a long history of serving with distinction in the U.S. military. When the draft ended in 1973, African American enrollment in the armed forces increased. Today, African Americans make up about 17 percent of the active forces and 15 percent of the Reserves and National Guard.

The Union army actively recruited African Americans through posters like this.

Reading **HELP**DESK (CCSS)

Academic Vocabulary (Tier 2 Words)
reverse to go in the opposite direction

African Americans in the Civil War

GUIDING QUESTION *What role did African Americans play in military efforts?*

At first, both the North and the South barred African Americans from serving in their armies. As time passed, the North relaxed its rules.

Excluded in the South

Even though African Americans made up more than 30 percent of the smaller Southern population, Confederate leaders would not allow them to enlist. Only in the last days of the war, when defeat drew near, did they consider it. Confederate leaders feared that once armed, African American soldiers would attack their fellow troops or even begin a general revolt.

Enlisted in the North

At first, President Lincoln resisted calls to enlist African Americans in the Union army. He feared that such a policy would be unpopular in the border states.

By 1862, though, it was clear that the North needed more soldiers in order to defeat the Confederacy. Many African Americans were eager to fight. As a result, Congress decided to **reverse** past policy and allow the formation of all-African American regiments.

These new Union soldiers were in a tough position. Many white Union regiments doubted their fighting ability. Others resented them. Many Southern troops also especially hated the Union's African American soldiers. They often focused their fiercest fire on African American regiments.

Despite this, African Americans joined. By the end of the war, they made up about 10 percent of the Union army. Some were freed people from the North. Others had fled enslavement in the South. These men fought hard and effectively, too. As one white Union officer wrote about an all-African American Kansas regiment:

PRIMARY SOURCE

66 They make better soldiers in every respect than any troops I have ever had under my command. 99

—Union General James G. Blunt

Archive Photos/Getty Images

---

networks   *Online Teaching Options*

PRIMARY SOURCE

Recruiting African American Soldiers

Analyzing Use the interactive image of the poster designed to recruit African Americans to discuss the requirements to enlist. **Ask: What was required of African Americans who wanted to enlist?** (*They had to be literate.*) **What does this poster tell you about attitudes toward African Americans in the North?** (*Students should realize that although slavery was banned in the North, racism still existed, and many whites still did not see African Americans as equals.*) **BL** **How did Union attitudes change toward African American soldiers?** (*They learned that they fought just as well as their white counterparts.*)

See page 449F for other online activities.

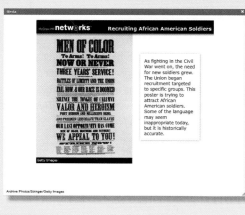

COME AND JOIN US BROTHERS.

PUBLISHED BY THE SUPERVISORY COMMITTEE FOR RECRUITING COLORED REGIMENTS
1210 CHESTNUT ST. PHILADELPHIA.

This picture, showing troops in a camp near Philadelphia, served as a Union recruiting poster.

▶ CRITICAL THINKING
Analyzing Visuals What do you think is the purpose of this poster? Explain your answer.

The 54th Massachusetts

The best-known African American regiment was the 54th Massachusetts. Founded in 1863, the 54th was under the command of Colonel Robert Gould Shaw, who came from a Boston abolitionist family. Later that year, the 54th served on the front lines in an assault on Fort Wagner in South Carolina. Confederate gunfire caused nearly 300 casualties in the 54th alone, including Colonel Shaw. Though the Union could not capture the fort, the 54th became famous for the courage and sacrifice of its members. It would also serve with distinction in other battles, such as the Battle of Olustee in Florida.

☑ PROGRESS CHECK

Determining Cause and Effect Why did Lincoln hesitate to enlist African Americans?

The Tide Turns

GUIDING QUESTION *How was the Battle of Gettysburg a turning point in the war?*

In spring of 1863, the Confederates had the upper hand. Their victory at Chancellorsville ruined Union plans to attack Richmond. Lee was emboldened. He decided to take the war once more into the North, hoping to impress France and Britain.

The Confederate strategy was similar to that of the colonies in the Revolutionary War. Though far outnumbered, the colonies won the support of France—and the war. Now, France and Britain missed the goods, especially cotton, that Southern planters had once supplied. If the Confederates appeared to be winning, those nations might help their cause.

Lesson 4 **477**

R Reading Skills

Discussing Direct students to read the section titled "The 54th Massachusetts." Discuss with students the establishment of the 54th Massachusetts Regiment and its record in battle. Have a volunteer describe the events at Fort Wagner in South Carolina, including the casualties and the loss of Colonel Robert Gould Shaw.

W Writing Skills

Informative/Explanatory Assign students the task of writing a brief history of the 54th Massachusetts Regiment or a short biography of its commander, Colonel Robert Gould Shaw. If students choose to write a biography, review with them the kinds of information that are usually included in a biographical text. **BL**

C Critical Thinking Skills

Contrasting Lead students in a brief discussion of the importance of good leadership, not only for strategy, but for inspiring people to support a cause. **Ask:**

- What leadership qualities did Lee and Jackson have that the Union leaders seemed to lack? *(Possible response: The Confederate leaders made bold strategic moves, while the Northern leaders seemed slow to act.)*
- What do you think the Union needed in order to win the war? *(Possible response: The Union needed an effective military leader who would lead them to victory.)*

Content Background Knowledge

Frederick Douglass's sons, Charles and Lewis, joined the 54th Massachusetts Regiment in April 1863.

MAP

The War in the East 1862-1863

Analyzing Maps Use the interactive map in the textbook about the war in the East to point out locations of major battles in Virginia and Maryland covered in this lesson. **AL** Visual/Spatial **Ask:** Which two generals became key factors in Southern victories in this area? *(Robert E. Lee and Thomas "Stonewall" Jackson)*

See page 449F for other online activities.

networks
War in the East 1862 - 1863

ANSWERS, p. 477

CRITICAL THINKING Possible answer: Its purpose is to encourage African Americans to join the Union army. At the top of the poster, it reads, "Come and Join Us Brothers." The picture shows African American soldiers in Union army uniforms.

☑ PROGRESS CHECK He did not want to risk losing the support of the border states.

Chapter 17 477

V Visual Skills

Analyzing Maps Direct students' attention to the map. Discuss with students the events of the first day of the battle at Gettysburg, including the Union retreat to Cemetery Ridge and the arrival of reinforcements. Have students locate Cemetery Ridge on the map. Then discuss the events of the second day, including the battles at Big Round Top and Little Round Top. Have students locate these two hills on the map. **Ask: What were the results of these battles?** *(Southern generals tried to drive Union forces from the hills, but the Union troops held their ground.)* **Visual/Spatial**

C Critical Thinking Skills

Organizing Ask students to recall what they may know about the Battle of Gettysburg either from reading on their own, previous history classes, or what they may have seen in movies or on television. Have students create a graphic organizer that highlights the elements that students already know about. They should modify this organizer while moving through this section. **AL**

GEOGRAPHY CONNECTION

After two days of heavy fighting at Gettysburg, the Confederates mounted a heavy attack on the Union lines.

1 LOCATION Where did the Confederates concentrate their attack?

2 CRITICAL THINKING
Drawing Conclusions What about the Union position as shown on this map might have given Union forces an advantage?

The Battle of Gettysburg, Day 3

C The Battle of Gettysburg

In July 1863, a small town in southern Pennsylvania became the site of one of the most decisive battles in the Civil War. Gettysburg was not a capital, a key port, or the location of a fort. It was almost an accident that such serious fighting took place there.

The Confederates entered the town looking for supplies. General Lee hoped to avoid fighting in a landscape he did not know well. It was there, however, that he **encountered** the enemy. When Lee's troops crawled out of Gettysburg four grueling days later, they had suffered 25,000 casualties. The Union—the victor—lost 23,000.

The battle started at 7:30 A.M. on July 1. Outnumbered Union troops retreated to a section of high ground called Cemetery Ridge. Reinforcements arrived for both sides. On the second day of fighting, Southern generals tried to drive Union forces from hills named Round Top and Little Round Top. In furious fighting, Union forces under General George Meade held their positions.

Reading **HELP**DESK (CCSS)

Academic Vocabulary (Tier 2 Words)
encounter to meet; to come face-to-face with

networks *Online Teaching Options*

MAP

The Battle of Gettysburg, Day 3

Analyzing Maps Use the interactive map of the Battle of Gettysburg and explain that this map shows the movement of Confederate and Union troops on the third day of this battle. **AL** Discuss with students the background and events of this significant three-day battle. Have students use the map to locate events in the battle as you discuss them. **Visual/Spatial**

See page 449F for other online activities.

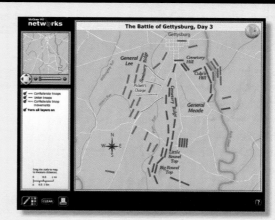

ANSWERS, p. 478

GEOGRAPHY CONNECTION

1 Cemetery Ridge

2 **CRITICAL THINKING** They were on high ground (on Cemetery Ridge, Culp's Hill, Little Round Top, and Big Round Top) and above rivers. This meant that Confederate troops had to cross the rivers and then fight uphill while being fired on from above.

The next day, Lee ordered an attack designed to "create a panic and virtually destroy the [Union] army." First, the Confederates fired nearly 140 cannons at the Union lines. Then, General George Pickett led thousands of Confederate troops in an attack on the Union's position at Cemetery Ridge. Putting themselves directly in the line of fire, they advanced across open land in what came to be remembered as Pickett's Charge.

At first, it seemed that Pickett's Charge might work. The Confederates broke the first line of Union defense. In the end, however, half of those who started the attack lay dead or wounded on the ground. Lee later wrote, "The army did all it could. I fear I required of it impossibilities."

Gettysburg ended the Confederates' hope of gaining help from Britain and France. The South had hoped to receive two ironclads from the British and use them to sweep Union shipping from the Atlantic. However, in October 1863, the British government decided not to release the ships.

The Siege of Vicksburg

On July 4, the day that Lee retreated from Gettysburg, the Confederacy suffered another major blow. The important river city of Vicksburg, Mississippi, fell under the control of Union troops led by Ulysses S. Grant.

Grant had first attacked Vicksburg in April. His army surrounded the 30,000 Confederate troops there. In May Grant began a siege of the town, preventing food and supplies from reaching the Confederates. Union gunships on the river supported Grant's 77,000 troops by firing thousands of shells into the city.

R

C

This painting shows Union forces fighting their way to the Confederate lines at Vicksburg, Mississippi, in May 1863.

▶ **CRITICAL THINKING**
Analyzing Visuals Do you think this painting was meant for a Union audience or a Confederate audience? Explain your answer.

The Granger Collection, NYC

R **Reading Skills**

Summarizing After students read the text, ask them to summarize Pickett's Charge. **Ask:**

- **Why did the Confederates think that Pickett's Charge would work?** *(They broke the first line of Union defense.)*
- **What was the eventual result?** *(Half the men who started the battle lay dead or wounded in the field when it ended.)*
- **How did Gettysburg affect the course of the war?** *(It was a significant Union victory after several Confederate ones. It also ended the Confederates' hope of getting help from Britain and France.)*

C **Critical Thinking Skills**

Identifying Central Issues Discuss with students the events of the siege at Vicksburg and Vicksburg's eventual fall. **Ask:** **Why was Vicksburg an important city for the Union's strategy?** *(because of its location along the Mississippi River)* After students have read the text on the following page, point out that winning Vicksburg paved the way for the Union's complete control of the Mississippi River, finally achieving the Anaconda Plan.

Primary Source Activity: The Civil War: The Strain of War: Lincoln's Gettysburg Address

Analyzing You may wish to assign the Primary Source Activity worksheet on the Gettysburg Address as homework. **Verbal/Linguistic**

See page 449F for other online activities.

ANSWER, p. 479

CRITICAL THINKING The painting was probably meant for a Union audience because the American flag is a focal point in the painting, and the image seems to show Union soldiers overwhelming a Confederate position

R Reading Skills

Determining Word Meanings Read the sentence in the text that includes the word *casualties*. Ensure that students understand that casualties of war include both people who are killed and people who are injured. To monitor understanding, have students use the word in a new sentence. **AL** **ELL**

Content Background Knowledge

Today, the battlefield is preserved as Gettysburg National Military Park. One of the attractions is the Gettysburg Cyclorama. A cyclorama is a circular picture of a 360-degree scene, viewed from inside. The Gettysburg Cyclorama is 359 feet long and 27 feet high, and depicts the fury of the turning point of the battle.

Have students complete the Lesson 4 Review.

CLOSE & REFLECT

Discuss with students how the Battle of Gettysburg and the fall of Vicksburg helped to hasten the end of the war. **Ask: Who had the advantage in the war by the end of the summer of 1863?** *(Students should realize that the Union had gained the advantage after defeating the Confederates at Gettysburg and Vicksburg.)*

R The siege lasted 47 days. There were more than 9,000 Confederate and 10,000 Union casualties, and many soldiers died of disease or starvation. Despite heavy losses of soldiers, fewer than 20 citizens of Vicksburg were killed in the long siege.

A few days after Vicksburg fell, the Confederacy lost Port Hudson in Louisiana, its last stronghold on the Mississippi River. The Union had split the South in two. Arkansas, Louisiana, and Texas were now cut off. The tide of the Civil War had turned.

Lincoln's Address at Gettysburg

On November 19, 1863, officials and citizens gathered to dedicate the Soldiers' National Cemetery at Gettysburg. At the ceremony, former governor of Massachusetts Edward Everett delivered a two-hour speech. After him, President Abraham Lincoln spoke for about two minutes. In 272 words, Lincoln honored the soldiers and their cause, and stated his vision for the country.

PRIMARY SOURCE

❝ These dead shall not have died in vain. . . . Government of the people, by the people, for the people shall not perish from the earth. ❞

—from the Gettysburg Address

Reactions to Lincoln's Gettysburg Address were mixed. Everett, along with the *New York Times, Chicago Tribune,* and *Springfield* (Mass.) *Republican,* thought the speech was a success. The *Republican* wrote, "His little speech is a perfect gem; deep in feeling, compact in thought and expression, and tasteful . . . in every word and comma." It remains one of the most enduring and powerful speeches in American history.

☑ **PROGRESS CHECK**

Summarizing How did the events at Vicksburg change the tide of the war?

LESSON 4 REVIEW CCSS

Review Vocabulary (Tier 3 Words)

1. Use the following terms in sentences about the Civil War. RH.6–8.4

  a. entrench **b.** flank

Answer the Guiding Questions

2. *Explaining* Why was the Battle of Chancellorsville important? RH.6–8.2

3. *Making Inferences* Why do you think some leaders called for African Americans to be allowed to fight in the Civil War? RH.6–8.2

4. *Evaluating* Why was Gettysburg a turning point for the South? RH.6–8.2

5. NARRATIVE You are a soldier who fought at Gettysburg. Write a letter to a loved one at home, describing the battle scene, how you felt, and what the outcome was. WHST.6–8.2, WHST.6–8.10

LESSON 4 REVIEW ANSWERS

1. Possible answers: **a.** Lee's entrenched soldiers were able to defeat the Union forces at Fredericksburg. **b.** Stonewall Jackson attacked the Union flank at Chancellorsville.

2. Chancellorsville was important because it was a strategic victory for the Confederacy, but the Confederacy lost a key general when Stonewall Jackson was injured in the battle and died.

3. It would allow the Union army to add many soldiers; African Americans wanted to end slavery and would be motivated to fight.

4. Losing Gettysburg cost the South the possibility of support from Britain and France.

5. Students' letters should reflect the information they have learned in this chapter.

ANSWER, p. 480

☑ **PROGRESS CHECK** The events at Vicksburg led to the success of the Union's strategy of splitting the South in two.

networks
There's More Online!

☑ **BIOGRAPHY**
Ulysses S. Grant

☑ **CHART/GRAPH**
The Cost of U.S. Wars

☑ **GRAPHIC ORGANIZER**
Events Leading to the End of War

☑ **MAP** The Final Battles

☑ **PRIMARY SOURCE**
Grant's Strategy for Spring 1864

☑ **SLIDE SHOW** Richmond

☑ **VIDEO**

Lesson 5
The War's Final Stages

ESSENTIAL QUESTION *Why does conflict develop?*

IT MATTERS BECAUSE
With each side determined to win, the bloodiest months of the Civil War were still to come.

The Union Closes In

R

GUIDING QUESTION *What events occurred at the end of the war?*

By 1864 Union forces had the South surrounded. Union ships blocked the Confederate coast, reducing the trade goods getting out and supplies getting in. The Union also controlled the Mississippi River, cutting off the western Confederate states from those in the East. The South seemed ready to fall—if the Union could come up with the right plan of attack. General Grant would be the one to draw up such a plan.

General Grant Takes Charge

Ulysses S. Grant had been only an average student. He failed as a farmer and in business. Yet he became a brilliant soldier. He led Union troops to victory at Shiloh and Vicksburg and at another key battle in Chattanooga, Tennessee. In March 1864, President Lincoln put General Grant in charge of all the Union armies.

President Lincoln liked that Grant was a man of action. Now in charge, Grant wasted little time coming up with a plan to finish the war. He would deliver killing blows from all sides. His armies would move on to Richmond, the Confederate capital. At the same time, General William Tecumseh Sherman would lead attacks across the Deep South.

C

(l) Library of Congress/LC-USZC4-678, (c) Bettmann/CORBIS, (r) Library of Congress LC-B8184-10575

Reading **HELP**DESK (CCSS)

Taking Notes: *Determining Cause and Effect*
As you read, keep track of the chain of events that led to the end of the Civil War using a diagram like this one.
RH.6–8.5

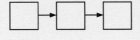

Content Vocabulary (Tier 3 Words)
• **resistance**
• **total war**

Lesson 5 **481**

VIDEO

Sherman's March to the Sea and the Battles of Richmond and Petersburg

Describing As Grant led forces against Lee in Virginia, Union General Sherman began his march of destruction from Atlanta to Savannah. Have students gauge the effect of the southern campaign on the slave population. Then ask students to examine both Grant's and Lee's battle strategies in Virginia.

See page 449G for other online activities.

ENGAGE

🔔 **Bellringer** Discuss the war up until this point. Have students raise their hands if they know the end results of the war. *(Most students know the Union won the Civil War. Have them speculate about events that might bring the end about.)*

• **Ask:** How do you think soldiers and civilians were probably feeling about the war by this time? *(Possible answers: Everyone was sick and tired of war and fear and disease. Everyone probably just wanted it to be over. Too many people had died.)*

• Tell students that in this lesson they will learn about the events that took place in the war's final stages.

TEACH & ASSESS

R Reading Skills

Identifying Explain to students that headings and subheadings can often provide clues to what a section of text may be about. Ask a volunteer to read aloud the first heading in this lesson. **Ask:** What does it mean to close in on something? *(Accept reasonable responses, such as "come nearer to try to get something.")* Then ask students what this subheading suggests about which side won the war. **AL** **ELL**

C Critical Thinking Skills

Evaluating Discuss Lincoln's appointment of Ulysses S. Grant to lead the Union army. **Ask:** Why did Lincoln choose Grant to command the Union army? *(Grant had won victories at Shiloh, Vicksburg, and Chattanooga. Lincoln also liked that he was a man of action.)*

ANSWER, p. 481

TAKING NOTES: Grant takes charge > Wilderness Campaign > Farragut blockades Mobile Bay > Sherman takes Atlanta > Lincoln is reelected > Sherman's March to the Sea > Grant takes Petersburg > Richmond falls > Lee surrenders

W Writing Skills

Argument Have students skim the biography of Ulysses S. Grant and identify phrases that indicate the general's character and personality. *(not interested in military service, wanted chance at further education, fearless soldier, strategy seemed ruthless)* Then ask students to take a position about whether Grant was a practical man or not. Students should express their position and use information from the biography and the rest of the chapter to defend it. **Verbal/Linguistic**

R Reading Skills

Citing Text Evidence Ask a volunteer to read aloud the first paragraph below the subheading "Grant Moves South Toward Richmond." Point out the phrase "six bloodiest weeks of the war." Then have students find text evidence on this page that supports this statement. *(Grant lost 17,000 men in the Battle of the Wilderness; brushfires burned alive 200 wounded men; Grant lost 50,000 of his troops in 30 days.)* Encourage students to continue looking for text evidence in descriptions of the next two battles.

C Critical Thinking Skills

Speculating Point out that the Union lost about 50,000 troops during this campaign and that as a result, many in the North called Grant a butcher. **Ask:**

- **Why do you think they called Grant a "butcher"?** *(because so many men died on the battlefields on the way to Richmond, but Grant would not stop)* **AL** **ELL**
- **Why did Lincoln not replace Grant?** *(Lincoln knew Grant would not give up until the war was won.)*

BIOGRAPHY

Ulysses S. Grant (1822–1885)

Ulysses S. Grant was born and raised in Georgetown, Ohio. As a young man, his father pressured him to attend the U.S. Military Academy at West Point. Grant was not interested in military service, but he went because it was his only chance at further education. Yet Grant became a fearless soldier and an expert rider at a time when soldiers rode horses in battle. Grant's military strategy seemed ruthless at times, but he said, "I have never advocated [war] except as a means of peace."

▶ **CRITICAL THINKING**
Explaining What do you think Grant meant in the quotation?

Reading **HELP**DESK CCSS

Academic Vocabulary (Tier 2 Words)
series events that occur one after the other

482 *The Civil War*

Grant soon put his strategy into action. In May and June of 1864, Grant's army confronted Lee's smaller force in a **series** of three battles near Richmond, Virginia. These were the Battles of the Wilderness, Spotsylvania Court House, and Cold Harbor. At each battle, Confederate lines held at first, but Grant quickly renewed the attack. "Whatever happens, there will be no turning back," Grant promised Lincoln. He was determined to march southward, attacking Lee's forces relentlessly and in spite of heavy losses until the Confederacy surrendered.

Grant Moves South Toward Richmond

The Wilderness was a densely wooded area about halfway between Washington, D.C., and Richmond, Virginia. Here, on May 5, 1864, the six bloodiest weeks of the war began. For two days, Union and Confederate forces struggled among a tangle of trees through which they could hardly see. A Union private said, "It was a blind and bloody hunt to the death."

At the Battle of the Wilderness, Lee had only about 60,000 men, while Grant had more than 100,000. Both sides suffered huge casualties. Grant, who lost 17,000 men, cried in his tent at the end of the second day. Meanwhile, brushfires raged through the forest. The fires burned alive 200 wounded men. On the morning of the third day, with no clear winner, Grant moved his forces south toward Richmond.

The next battles took place at nearby Spotsylvania Court House and at Cold Harbor. On June 2, the night before the third battle began, a Union general observed that men were "writing their names and home addresses on slips of paper and pinning them to the backs of their coats" to help people identify their bodies. The war seemed hopeless. Grant, however, was determined. He explained to the White House, "I propose to fight it out on this line, if it takes all summer."

In a space of 30 days, Grant lost 50,000 of his troops. His critics in the North called him a "butcher." Lincoln, however, stood by his general. "I can't spare this man," Lincoln is reported to have said. "He fights." As he fought, the Confederates were also losing men—losses their smaller army could not survive.

Siege at Petersburg

Grant made steady progress. He next arrived at Petersburg, a railroad center vital to the Confederate movement of troops and supplies. If Grant could take Petersburg, Richmond would be

Library of Congress LC-USZC4-678

---

networks *Online Teaching Options*

PRIMARY SOURCE

Grant's Strategy

Analyzing Primary Sources Show students the interactive primary source excerpt of the letter from Grant to General Sherman that discusses his strategy for the war. **Ask:**

- **What was Grant's strategy?** *(He would move his armies on to Richmond, and Sherman would lead his troops across the Deep South.)*
- **What adjectives describe Grant's strategy for winning the war?** *(Possible responses: aggressive, bold, confident, nervy)* **AL** **ELL**

See page 449G for other online activities.

ANSWER, p. 482

CRITICAL THINKING He meant that he believed in being ruthless in war only because it was the fastest means to achieve peace.

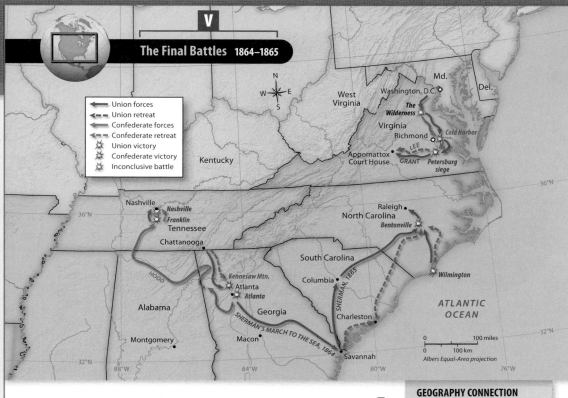

The Final Battles 1864–1865

Union forces
Union retreat
Confederate forces
Confederate retreat
Union victory
Confederate victory
Inconclusive battle

cut off from the rest of the Confederacy. Grant laid siege. The Confederates defended the city, but they could not break the Union's grip. Trains brought food and more troops to the Union side. The Confederates could get neither. Determined, they refused to give up.

Sherman in Georgia

Meanwhile, William Tecumseh Sherman headed for Georgia. In early July, his troops circled Atlanta. There they faced the brilliant Confederate general, John Hood. Hood's forces put up major **resistance** (rih·ZIHS·tuhnts). Sherman laid siege, finally forcing Hood to abandon the city on September 1. Among white Southerners, the mood became desperate as the prospect of defeat became more certain. Mary Chesnut, a South Carolinian who kept a diary throughout the war, wrote, "There is no hope, but we will try to have no fear."

resistance refusal to give in

GEOGRAPHY CONNECTION

During the final year of the war, Union troops moved through the heart of the Confederacy.

1 LOCATION Where did Sherman's March to the Sea begin and end?

2 CRITICAL THINKING
Analyzing Visuals What information on the map helps explain why Sherman was able to cause such destruction on his March to the Sea?

Lesson 5 **483**

V Visual Skills

Analyzing Maps Have students review the map legend. **Ask:**

- **Which side retreated more during 1864–1865?** *(Confederate)*
- **How can you tell?** *(because of the number of dashed red lines and absence of dashed blue lines. Red shows Confederate troops, blue shows Union troops, and a dashed line shows retreat.)* **Visual/Spatial**

C Critical Thinking Skills

Making Connections Direct students to the text that discusses Grant's actions at Petersburg. **Ask: Do you think Lincoln made a good choice in Ulysses S. Grant? Why or why not?** *(Possible answer: yes, because he had an aggressive strategy that ultimately succeeded)*

R Reading Skills

Expressing Direct students to read the section titled "Sherman in Georgia." Tell students that while Grant laid siege to Petersburg, Sherman marched to Atlanta. **Ask:**

- **How long did General Hood's troops resist Sherman's siege?** *(more than a month)*
- **Why was Sherman's capture of Atlanta important?** *(It was important to the morale of the North; it also gave him access to the heart of the Confederacy.)*
- **What was the mood in the South after Atlanta's fall?** *(desperate)*

MAP

The Final Battles, 1864–1865

Analyzing Maps Use the interactive map of the war's final battles from the textbook to discuss the final stages of the war. Have students locate the battles of the Wilderness, Spotsylvania Court House, and Cold Harbor. Show students the movement of Grant's troops to Petersburg on the map. **Ask:**

- **Why was Petersburg an important target?** *(If the Union captured Petersburg, Richmond would be completely cut off from the Confederacy.)*
- **Why didn't Grant just attack Richmond directly?** *(because the Confederates tried to stop him from reaching the city)*

See page 449G for other online activities.

ANSWERS, p. 483

GEOGRAPHY CONNECTION

1 Sherman's March to the Sea began in Atlanta and ended in Savannah, Georgia.

2 CRITICAL THINKING There was no significant Confederate force left to attack or stop him.

R Reading Skills

Identifying Before students read the selection, remind them that the war was still continuing at sea as well. **Ask:**

- **Who led the Union navy in 1864?** *(David Farragut)* Discuss Farragut's background. Point out that he joined the navy when he was about the same age as the students in class. Discuss his role in the Civil War and the events at Mobile Bay.

- **Why was Mobile Bay an important naval target?** *(It was the last port east of the Mississippi that the Union had not blocked.)* **BL**

Direct students to cite evidence from the text to support their responses.

C Critical Thinking Skills

Theorizing Have students recall the divisions between the Peace Democrats and the War Democrats, as well as the opposition to the war in the North. Remind students that many thought Lincoln would lose the election of 1864. **Ask:**

- **If Lincoln had lost his reelection bid, how would this have affected the outcome of the Civil War?** *(The Union might have stopped its aggressive attack and allowed the Confederacy to secede.)* **BL**

- **How did the successes in Atlanta and Mobile Bay help Lincoln win the election?** *(They boosted morale and support for the war in the North, which in turn boosted support for Lincoln.)*

- **What did Congress do in response to the election results?** *(It passed the Thirteenth Amendment, which banned slavery in the United States.)*

Farragut Blockades Mobile Bay

David Farragut led the U.S. Navy to some of its greatest victories in the Civil War.

R The highest-ranking officer in the Union navy was David Farragut. The son of a Spanish military man, Farragut had joined the navy when he was only 12 years old. In August 1864, he led a fleet of 18 ships through a narrow channel into Mobile Bay in Alabama. His mission was to gain control of the bay. Faced with stiff resistance, Farragut prepared for battle. To make sure he had a good view, he climbed high into the ship's rigging and had himself tied in place.

The Confederates had forts on both sides of the channel, and they had mined the water with torpedoes. Unwilling to back down, Farragut shouted his famous order: "Damn the torpedoes, full speed ahead!" The mission succeeded in blocking the last Southern port east of the Mississippi.

The Election of 1864

In the North, opposition to the war grew stronger through much of 1864. It seemed unlikely that Lincoln could win reelection in November. His loss could mean an end to the war and recognition of the Confederacy as an independent country. White Southerners clung to this hope.

After Union troops captured Atlanta and blocked Mobile Bay, however, weary Northerners began to believe again that victory **C** was possible. In November, President Lincoln won a second term. He took 55 percent of the popular vote and 212 to 21 electoral votes over the Democratic candidate, General George B. McClellan.

Many **interpreted** Lincoln's reelection as a clear sign from the voters: They wanted a permanent end to slavery. On January 31, 1865, Congress passed the Thirteenth Amendment, which banned slavery in the United States.

☑ **PROGRESS CHECK**

Explaining Why did it seem unlikely that Lincoln would be reelected in the early part of 1864?

The War Ends

GUIDING QUESTION *What is total war?*

From the beginning of the war, a goal of the Union was to capture the Confederate capital at Richmond. Petersburg had been the last roadblock in Grant's path. After a nine-month siege, Grant finally drove Lee's army out of that city. Jefferson Davis knew that Richmond was doomed.

Bettmann/CORBIS

Reading **HELP**DESK (CCSS)

total war a strategy of bringing war to the entire society, not just the military

Academic Vocabulary (Tier 2 Words)

interpret to find meaning in something

networks   *Online Teaching Options*

WORKSHEET

Primary Source Activity: The Civil War: The War's Final Stages: Lincoln's Inaugural Address

Analyzing Primary Sources Remind students that when Lincoln first became president, the country was on the verge of war. When he was reelected, that war was almost finished. Tell them that these circumstances are reflected in his two Inaugural Addresses. Make sure that all students understand the term *inaugural*. **AL** **ELL** Assign the Primary Source Activity worksheet on Lincoln's Inaugural Addresses as homework.

See page 449G for other online activities.

ANSWER, p. 484

☑ **PROGRESS CHECK** Opposition to the war made Lincoln's reelection unlikely.

Sherman's March to the Sea

Still, the Confederacy fought on. The Union was determined to break the South's will to continue the fight. To break this will, Sherman burned much of the city of Atlanta in November 1864. Sherman then had his troops march across Georgia toward the Atlantic, burning cities and crops as they went. This trail of destruction is known as Sherman's March to the Sea.

Sherman continued his march through the Carolinas to join Grant's forces near Richmond. Union troops took food, tore up railroad lines and fields, and killed livestock. General Sherman's march was part of a strategy called **total war.** Total war involves targeting not only the enemy's army, but also its land and people. Sherman hoped that by bringing the horrors of the war to the Southern population, he could help end the war.

White Southerners were outraged by Sherman's march. Thousands of African Americans, however, left their plantations to follow the protection of his army. For them, the March to the Sea was a march to freedom.

Richmond Falls

Meanwhile, Grant continued the siege of Petersburg. Lee and his troops defended the town, but sickness, casualties, and desertion weakened them. Finally, on April 2, 1865, the Confederate lines broke and Lee withdrew.

Word of Lee's retreat soon reached the Confederate president. As the Union army marched toward Richmond, Davis and his cabinet prepared to leave. They gathered documents and ordered that bridges and weapons useful to the enemy be burned. Then they fled the city. An observer wrote:

PRIMARY SOURCE

"The trains came and went, wagons, vehicles, and horsemen rumbled and dashed to and fro. . . . As night came on . . . rioting and robbing took place. "

—from *Battles and Leaders of the Civil War*

The armory, with its stores of ammunition, exploded. Boom after boom rang through the city, and fires raged out of control.

On April 3, President Lincoln visited the captured town of Petersburg. Later, Lincoln confided to naval officer David Porter, "Thank God I have lived to see this. It seems to me that I have been dreaming a horrid nightmare for four years, and now the nightmare is gone."

President Lincoln, his son Tad, and a group of military officials arrived in Richmond on April 4 to tour the fallen Confederate capital. As Lincoln walked through the streets, joyful African Americans followed—singing, laughing, and reaching out to touch the president.

When the Union army marched into the Confederate capital after the 11-month siege, they found the city in ruins and still burning.

Lesson 5 **485**

R1 Reading Skills

Defining After students have read the text, point out that Sherman's March to the Sea is considered the first use of the strategy of "total war" in modern times.

- **Ask:** What is "total war"? *(the total destruction of the land and the people)*

Suggest that students periodically refer to the map from earlier in this chapter to trace Sherman's progress through the South.

C Critical Thinking Skills

Analyzing Lead students in analyzing and assessing Sherman's total war strategy. Discuss the destruction of Atlanta and Sherman's March to the Sea. Point out that Sherman's strategy to bring terror to the Southern people was deliberate. **Ask:**

- Why did General Sherman want to bring total war to the South? *(The Union was determined to break the will of the South.)*
- How did Southerners feel about Sherman's March to the Sea? *(Possible answer: White Southerners were horrified and desperate, but African Americans were jubilant.)* Make sure students remember that African Americans left their plantations to follow Sherman's army.
- What do you think the long-term effects of Sherman's total war strategy would be? *(Possible answers: high cost of rebuilding the South; bitterness of Southerners toward Northerners)* **BL**

R2 Reading Skills

Explaining Direct students to read the section titled: "Richmond Falls." Remind students that capturing Richmond was part of the North's original strategy. Point out that the Union army was finally nearing this goal in March 1865. Rather than fight, the Confederates fled the city. **Ask:** Why did Confederates evacuate Richmond? *(They knew it was hopeless to stay and fight.)*

GRAPHIC ORGANIZER

Taking Notes: *Determining Cause and Effect:* **The Civil War Ends**

Organizing Have students use the interactive graphic organizer to summarize the chain of events that led up to the end of the war. After students have completed the graphic organizer, have small groups of students discuss the events. Encourage students to revise their graphic organizers if needed. **AL** **ELL**

See page 449G for other online activities.

V Visual Skills

Analyzing Visuals Discuss the information in the graph. **Ask:** **By how much did the deaths in the Civil War exceed the deaths in World War II?** *(113,000)* **AL** **ELL** Lead a discussion of the reason for the large number of deaths in this war. *(Students may realize that all the deaths were American because the United States was not fighting another country; they may also point to lack of food and supplies. Some students may mention infection and the difficulty of treating severe wounds with the medical knowledge available at the time.)* **Visual/Spatial** **Logical/Mathematical**

C Critical Thinking Skills

Analyzing Primary Sources Discuss with students that the Union forces were ruthless as they marched through the South. **Ask:** **What evidence in the primary source shows a more compassionate side of the Union army?** *(allowed hungry people to help themselves to whatever was in the warehouses)* Lead students to understand that because the war was clearly over, the Union soldiers had no need to continue their ruthlessness.

Content Background Knowledge

- The total Union casualties were 359,528 deaths and 25,175 wounded.
- On the Confederate side the casualties were 258,000 deaths and 225,000 wounded.
- Many public structures, homes, farms, and railroad tracks in Southern cities were destroyed. The war cost billions of dollars and left many in debt.
- The Union was saved and the federal government was strengthened.
- Slavery was over and millions of African Americans were free.

ANSWERS, p. 486

GRAPH SKILL

1. 213,000 more Americans died in the Civil War than in World War II.

2. **CRITICAL THINKING** The war was not against other peoples; the soldiers on both sides were Americans. Also, the war was fought entirely on American soil.

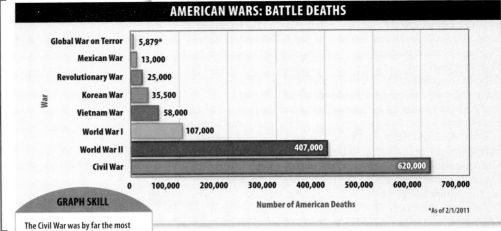

AMERICAN WARS: BATTLE DEATHS

War	Number of American Deaths
Global War on Terror	5,879*
Mexican War	13,000
Revolutionary War	25,000
Korean War	35,500
Vietnam War	58,000
World War I	107,000
World War II	407,000
Civil War	620,000

*As of 2/1/2011

GRAPH SKILL

The Civil War was by far the most costly war in terms of lives lost of any conflict in American history.

1. **CALCULATING** How many more Americans died in the Civil War than in the second-most-costly war?

2. **CRITICAL THINKING** *Analyzing* What makes the Civil War different from the other wars in this graph besides the higher number of war dead?

When one man knelt down to thank him, Lincoln told him, "Don't kneel to me. You must kneel to God only, and thank Him for your freedom."

At the home of Confederate president Davis, Lincoln sat wearily for a while on a chair in the president's office. After visiting two prisons for Confederate prisoners, Lincoln replied to a question about what to do with captured Confederates: "If I were in your place, I'd let 'em up easy, let 'em up easy."

As a child, Dallas Tucker witnessed the arrival of Union troops in his hometown of Richmond, Virginia. He later recalled:

PRIMARY SOURCE

❝[There was] a tremendous shock, which rocked the house and rattled the windows. At first we thought it was an earthquake, but very soon concluded … it must be an explosion of some kind. … It was, in fact, the blowing up of the government powder magazine just beyond the city limits. … Richmond was on fire. … In sheer despair, warehouse after warehouse was thrown open, and the gathered crowd of hungry, despairing people were told to go in and help themselves.

… Just as I reached the Washington Monument, I [saw] the troops entering [Capital] Square. … It was then only a few minutes later … that I saw the United States flag appear on the flag-pole above, where the Stars and Bars [the Confederate flag] had floated for years.❞

— Reverend Dallas Tucker, writing in the *Richmond Dispatch,* February 3, 1902

Reading HELPDESK **CCSS**

Build Vocabulary: *Word Origins*

The word *compassion* was first used in the fourteenth century. Its origin is a compound word from Latin: *compati*. The prefix *com* means "with," and the root *pati* means "suffer" or "bear."

486 *The Civil War*

networks *Online Teaching Options*

GAME

Concentration Game: The War's Final Stages

Summarizing Display the interactive game for this chapter, and encourage students to take turns matching the cards to review the characters and concepts of this lesson.

See page 449G for other online activities.

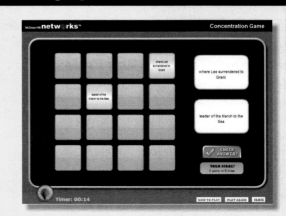

A Meeting at Appomattox Court House

The formal end of the war came on April 9, 1865. Two days earlier, Grant had asked Lee to surrender, writing, "The result of last week must convince you of the hopelessness of further resistance." At first, Lee had believed he must fight on. Then, the Union captured the train carrying food to his starving troops and completely surrounded his army. Lee knew it was over.

Grant met with Lee in a small Virginia town called Appomattox Court House. The two men shook hands and talked a little. Then Grant offered his terms: Lee's officers could keep their small firearms, and any soldier with a horse could keep it. No one would disturb the soldiers as they made their way home. Grant also gave 25,000 rations to feed Lee's troops. America's deadliest war ended with dignity and compassion.

The Toll of War

More lives were lost in the Civil War than in any other conflict in American history. The war cost billions of dollars and left many Southern cities and farms in ruins.

The North's victory saved the Union. The war also made clear that the national government was more powerful than the states. Finally, the war freed millions of African Americans. As you will read, however, the end of slavery left unsettled many of the problems that newly freed African Americans were to face.

Many questions remained. No one yet knew how to bring the Southern states back into the Union, nor what the status of African Americans would be in Southern society. Americans would struggle to answer these questions in the years ahead—an era known as Reconstruction.

Nearly 4 million people served in the military forces during the Civil War.

✓ PROGRESS CHECK

Explaining Why did General Lee finally surrender?

R Reading Skills

Discussing Have students skim the first two paragraphs about the Confederacy's surrender at Appomattox Court House. Point out that it took place a week after the fall of Richmond. **Ask:**

- **Why did Lee finally surrender?** *(There was little hope of the South winning. To keep fighting would have meant sacrificing more lives in vain.)*
- **What were the terms of the surrender?** *(Grant gave rations to the Confederate troops, and Confederate officers were allowed to keep their small firearms. Any soldier with a horse was allowed to keep it, and the troops were allowed to make their way home undisturbed.)*

Have students complete the Lesson 5 Review.

CLOSE & REFLECT

Discuss with students conditions in the South at the end of the war. Ask them how they think Southerners felt about Northerners and about the Union victory. **Ask: What difficulties do you think the U.S. government faced when it tried to rebuild the South after the war?** *(Possible answers: People would be angry and would resist change. Without slavery, other methods of farming plantations had to be found. Southern cities would have to be rebuilt.)*

LESSON 5 REVIEW CCSS

Review Vocabulary (Tier 3 Words)

1. How did total war affect civilians of the Confederacy? RH.6–8.4

Answer the Guiding Questions

2. ***Explaining*** How did events on the battlefield affect Lincoln's reelection? RH.6–8.2

3. ***Identifying Cause and Effect*** Why did Sherman burn and destroy the South's land? RH.6–8.5

4. ***Evaluating*** Why did the war leave the U.S. government stronger than ever before? RH.6–8.2

5. **NARRATIVE** You are a reporter covering Lee's army at the time of his surrender. Write a brief article describing the events surrounding his meeting with Grant. WHST.6–8.2, WHST.6–8.4

Lesson 5   **487**

LESSON 5 REVIEW ANSWERS

1. Possible answer: Total war involved destruction of Southern towns, railroads, farms, crops, and plantations, which caused great hardship for the Confederacy.

2. Lincoln's chances for reelection were slim while the North was losing major battles during most of 1864. However, the North started winning and Lincoln was reelected.

3. The Union was determined to break the will of the South. Total war was a deliberate strategy by the North to deprive the South of resources and to end the conflict.

4. The war and its outcome showed that the federal government was more powerful than the individual states or even a group of states.

5. Students' responses should include facts from the lesson content, as well as interpretation of those facts.

ANSWER, p. 487

✓ PROGRESS CHECK Lee knew he was surrounded and that there was no hope any longer of the Confederacy winning the war.

CHAPTER REVIEW ACTIVITY

On the board, have students create a flowchart. Tell them that they will be charting the course of major events beginning, during, and ending the Civil War. Because this is a flowchart, and not a time line, remind students that they should keep cause and effect in mind and show how one event flows, or is caused, by another.

Ask a volunteer to write one key event in the chart. Then ask another volunteer to write the event that followed from the first event. Continue until you have reached the entry for the end of the Civil War.

REVIEW THE ENDURING UNDERSTANDING

Review the chapter's Enduring Understanding with students.

• *Conflict can lead to change*

Now pose the following questions in a class discussion to apply this enduring understanding to the chapter.

How did the Civil War lead to changes in population, and what problems might this present for the country? *(There would be fewer men to work the fields due to war casualties and no slaves to work the cotton fields.)*

How might the outcome of the conflict have changed the nation as a whole if the South had won? *(The United States of America would be a separate country from the Confederate States of America. The states would also have been granted more power than the federal government, and the Constitution would have been weakened.)*

Besides changing the population and strengthening the federal government, what other effects did the Civil War have on the country? *(freed slaves, destroyed cities, much money spent, difficulty of reintegrating states into the Union)*

ACTIVITIES ANSWERS

Exploring the Essential Questions

❶ Students should correctly describe how civilians in the North and the South participated in and affected the war effort. They should discuss the contributions of both men and women, such as women replacing men on farms and in the workplace, and civilians working as nurses and spies, as well as in other capacities. Some civilians also opposed the war and the draft.

CHAPTER 17 Activities CCSS

Write your answers on a separate piece of paper.

❶ **Exploring the Essential Question** WHST.6–8.2, WHST.6–8.9
INFORMATIVE/EXPLANATORY Write a short essay that describes the impact civilians had on the war effort. Include references to the North and the South.

❷ **21st Century Skills** WHST.6–8.1, WHST.6–8.10
COMMUNICATING Assume the point of view of an adviser to President Lincoln. Write an argument in favor of enlisting African Americans in the Union cause.

❸ **Thinking Like a Historian** WHST.6–8.1, WHST.6–8.9
DRAWING INFERENCES AND CONCLUSIONS Based on the events leading up to the end of the war, how do you think soldiers on each side felt about Lee's surrender at Appomattox? How might enslaved African Americans have felt? Write a paragraph that addresses these questions.

❹ **Visual Literacy** RH.6–8.7
ANALYZING POLITICAL CARTOONS Look at the images and read the caption of this cartoon. What do the men on either side of Lincoln represent? What are the "two difficulties" the president faces?

LINCOLN'S TWO DIFFICULTIES.
Lin. "WHAT? NO MONEY! NO MEN!"

21st Century Skills

❷ Arguments should identify the benefits to the Union of an increased pool of soldiers, a highly motivated group of willing fighters; also the possible benefit of the statement such a decision would make about the rights and capabilities of African Americans..

Thinking Like a Historian

❸ Soldiers on both sides may have been relieved that the long war was over; Confederate soldiers may have been frustrated at surrendering or fearful of how they would be treated. Enslaved African Americans may have felt relief at being free, perhaps confusion about what to do, and/or hostility toward or from former slaveholders.

Visual Literacy

❹ The cartoon shows Lincoln learning that he does not have enough money (from the man on the left) or soldiers (from the man on the right) to fight the Civil War. Lincoln had to find ways to raise revenue and add soldiers to the military.

REVIEW THE GUIDING QUESTIONS

Choose the best answer for each question.

RH.6–8.1
❶ What was one advantage the Southern states had during the Civil War?

   A. They received military support from Britain and France.

   B. The largest weapons factories were located in the South.

   C. They were more familiar with the places where most battles occurred.

   D. Most people in the North and South supported the Confederacy's effort to form an independent country.

RH.6–8.1
❷ Gaining control of the Mississippi River enabled the Union to

   F. surround the Confederacy.

   G. force the Confederacy to surrender.

   H. defeat the Confederate forces at Gettysburg.

   I. split the Confederacy into smaller parts.

RH.6–8.2
❸ During the war, the economy of the Confederacy was

   A. severely strained by the Union blockade and the destruction of Southern land and property.

   B. unchanged because most of the battles took place on Northern soil.

   C. strengthened due to inflation.

   D. strengthened by bounties paid to army recruits.

RH.6–8.1
❹ Which of the following is one advantage the Union had over the South?

   F. They had greater numbers of troops.

   G. They knew the terrain better than the Southern troops did.

   H. They had stronger military leadership.

   I. They had a strong fighting spirit.

RH.6–8.1
❺ The city of Atlanta was burned

   A. as the result of an accident caused by Union troops marching through.

   B. as part of Sherman's total war strategy.

   C. by Confederate troops trying to stop Union forces from taking the city.

   D. after a freak lightning strike set the docks on fire.

RH.6–8.2
❻ Control of the sea was significant during the Civil War because

   F. the Union was able to block France and Britain's attempts to send arms to the Confederacy.

   G. the Union was able to cut off the Confederates' ability to export goods.

   H. the Confederacy was able to stop the Union from trading with Europe.

   I. President Lincoln was a former navy officer.

489

ASSESSMENT ANSWERS
Review the Guiding Questions

❶ **C** The Confederacy hoped to get support from Britain and France but never did. The country was divided on the Confederacy's plan. The North housed most of the weapons factories. C is the only correct response.

❷ **I** Gaining control of the Mississippi achieved a key goal for the Union: to split the Confederacy and cut off supply lines. The Union could never have surrounded the Confederacy. The Union did force the Confederacy to surrender, but not just because it controlled the Mississippi. Gettysburg had nothing to do with controlling the Mississippi River.

❸ **A** The Confederacy's economy suffered as a result of the war. This was made even worse because most battles took place on Confederate soil, which makes all the other answers incorrect.

❹ **F** Answers G, H and I apply to Confederate troops, not Union troops. The Union had more soldiers.

❺ **B** Sherman burned the city of Atlanta before his March to the Sea as part of his total war strategy. Answers A and D are wrong because the burning of Atlanta was an intentional act by Sherman and the Union, which also makes answer C wrong.

❻ **G** Naval blockades were part of the Union's strategy to block Southern ports so that the South could not export goods. I is incorrect: Lincoln was never in the navy. F is wrong because the South was never able to secure the assistance of France and Britain. H is wrong because the South was never able to blockade any Union ports or trade with Europe.

Analyzing Documents

7 B Douglass wanted African Americans to have equal citizenship and felt that if they fought in the war, they would earn this right. Answers A, C, and D are wrong because Douglass was focused on ways in which African Americans could achieve equality with whites. B is the only answer that relates to that goal.

8 I Douglass's primary goal was not for African Americans to have a greater role in the military but to have a greater role in society, so he likely focused on citizenship. Answer F may or may not have been true, but it is not a reasonable inference from this excerpt. Answer G might look like a reasonable inference, but the tone of Douglass's statement supports the inference that African Americans already deserve citizenship and that enlisting and fighting is undeniable proof of that fact, not something they have to do to earn citizenship. H is not supported by anything in the statement.

Short Response

9 Lincoln argues that people are morally obligated to take care of each other. He also believes that by taking care of those who were hurt by the war, peace will replace any anger and resentment people might have.

10 to honor the people affected by the war and to unite the country

Extended Response

11 Responses will vary. Students' predictions should be based on their knowledge of the central issues of the Civil War and an understanding of social studies.

DBQ ANALYZING DOCUMENTS

Frederick Douglass led the movement to allow African American men to enlist in the Union armed forces.

> *"Once let the black man get upon his person the brass letters U.S. . . . and a musket on his shoulder and bullets in his pocket, and there is no power on earth that can deny that he has earned the right to citizenship."*
>
> —from James M. McPherson, *Battle Cry of Freedom*

RH.6–8.2
7 Identifying Main Ideas How does Douglass think enlisting will help African Americans?

A. He believes they would enjoy having a uniform to wear.

B. He believes that it will earn African Americans the right to citizenship.

C. He thinks that only African Americans can free enslaved people.

D. Serving in the army will give them the experience to fight slaveholders.

RH.6–8.6
8 Making Inferences From this excerpt, you can infer that Douglass believes that African Americans

F. have not earned the right to citizenship.

G. must fight to prove themselves worthy of citizenship.

H. will prove to be an unstoppable force in battle.

I. already deserve citizenship.

SHORT RESPONSE

> *"With malice toward none, with charity for all, with firmness in the right as God gives us to see the right, let us strive on to finish the work we are in, to bind up the nation's wounds, to care for him who shall have borne the battle and for his widow and his orphan—to do all which may achieve and cherish a just and lasting peace among ourselves and with all nations."*
>
> —from Abraham Lincoln's Second Inaugural Address

RH.6–8.2, WHST.6–8.4
9 State two reasons Lincoln did not focus on Union victory in the war.

RH.6–8.6, WHST.6–8.4
10 What do you think Lincoln's main goal is in this speech?

EXTENDED RESPONSE

WHST.6–8.1, WHST.6–8.10
11 Informative/Explanatory Write an essay predicting what will happen in the United States in the years following the war.

Need Extra Help?

If You've Missed Question	**1**	**2**	**3**	**4**	**5**	**6**	**7**	**8**	**9**	**10**	**11**
Review Lesson	1	2, 4	3	1	5	2	4	4	5	5	1–5

---

netw☉rks   *Online Teaching Options*

More Assessment Resources

The *Assess* tab in the online Teacher Lesson Center includes resources to help students improve their test-taking skills. It also contains many project-based rubrics to help you assess students' work.

UNDERSTANDING BY DESIGN®

Enduring Understanding
- *People, places, and ideas change over time.*

Essential Question
- *How do new ideas change the way people live?*

Predictable Misunderstandings
Students may think:
- *The nation was quickly and easily reunited after the Civil War.*
- *The South recovered and healed after the Civil War.*
- *The end of slavery greatly improved life for African Americans in the South.*
- *African Americans were denied the right to vote until the civil rights movement of the 1960s.*

Assessment Evidence
Performance Tasks:
- *Hands-On Chapter Project*

Other Evidence:
- *Interactive Graphic Organizers*
- *What Do You Know? activity*
- *Primary Source Activity*
- *Geography and History Activity*
- *Economics of History Activity*
- *21st Century Skills Activity*
- *Lesson Reviews*
- *Online Self-Check Quizzes*
- *Chapter Activities and Assessment*

SUGGESTED PACING GUIDE

Introducing the Chapter	1 day	Lesson 3	1 day
Lesson 1	1 day	Lesson 4	2 days
Lesson 2	2 days	Chapter Wrap-Up and Assessment	1 day

TOTAL TIME   8 Days

Key for Using the Teacher Edition

SKILL-BASED ACTIVITIES

Types of skill activities found in the Teacher Edition.

V Visual Skills require students to analyze maps, graphs, charts, and photos.

R Reading Skills help students practice reading skills and master vocabulary.

W Writing Skills provide writing opportunities to help students comprehend the text.

C Critical Thinking Skills help students apply and extend what they have learned.

T Technology Skills require students to use digital tools effectively.

*Letters are followed by a number when there is more than one of the same type of skill on the page.

DIFFERENTIATED INSTRUCTION

All activities are written for the on-level student unless otherwise marked with the leveled labels below.

BL Beyond Level
AL Approaching Level
ELL English Language Learners

All students benefit from activities that utilize different learning styles. Many activities are marked as below when a particular learning style is highlighted.

Intrapersonal	Naturalist
Logical/Mathematical	Kinesthetic
Visual/Spatial	Auditory/Musical
Verbal/Linguistic	Interpersonal

NCSS Standards covered in "The Reconstruction Era"

Learners will understand:

3 PEOPLE, PLACES, AND ENVIRONMENTS

4. The roles of different kinds of population centers in a region or nation

5. The concept of regions identifies links between people in different locations according to specific criteria (e.g., physical, economic, social, cultural, or religious)

6 POWER, AUTHORITY, AND GOVERNANCE

1. Rights are guaranteed in the U.S. Constitution, the supreme law of the land

2. Fundamental ideas that are the foundation of American constitutional democracy (including those of the U.S. Constitution, popular sovereignty, the rule of law, separation of powers, checks and balances, minority rights, the separation of church and state, and Federalism)

3. Fundamental values of constitutional democracy (e.g., the common good, liberty, justice, equality, and individual dignity)

4. The ideologies and structures of political systems that differ from those of the United States

5. The ways in which governments meet the needs and wants of citizens, manage conflict, and establish order and society

7 PRODUCTION, DISTRIBUTION, AND CONSUMPTION

3. The economic choices that people make have both present and future consequences

4. Economic incentives affect people's behavior and may be regulated by rules or laws

10 CIVIC IDEALS AND PRACTICES

1. The theme of civic ideals and practices helps us to learn about and know how to work for the betterment of society

2. Concepts and ideals such as: individual dignity, liberty, justice, equality, individual rights, responsibility, majority and minority rights, and civil dissent

3. Key practices involving the rights and responsibilities of citizenship and the exercise of citizenship (e.g., respecting the rule of law and due process, voting, serving on a jury, researching issues, making informed judgments, expressing views on issues, and collaborating with others to take civic action)

CHAPTER OPENER PLANNER

Students will know:

- *the different plans for Reconstruction and what Radical Reconstruction meant.*
- *how Reconstruction affected politics, economics, and society in the South.*
- *how rights of freed African Americans changed during Reconstruction and in the post-Reconstruction Era.*
- *the successes and failures of Reconstruction in the South.*

Students will be able to:

- **compare and contrast** *plans for Reconstruction.*
- **evaluate** *the effectiveness of the Freedmen's Bureau.*
- **analyze** *black codes and the federal government's responses to them.*
- **evaluate** *Radical Reconstruction.*
- **identify** *important individuals and groups that played a role in Reconstruction.*
- **describe and analyze** *what life was like for African Americans in the South during Reconstruction.*
- **analyze** *the significance of the election of 1876 and the end of Reconstruction.*

UNDERSTANDING BY DESIGN®

☑ *Print Teaching Options*

V **Visual Skills**

☐ **P. 492** Students analyze a map of the United States during the Reconstruction Era. **Visual/Spatial**

☐ **P. 493** Students read a time line and identify important events in the Reconstruction Era. **Visual/Spatial Logical/Mathematical**

C **Critical Thinking Skills**

☐ **P. 493** Students make inferences about what was achieved by the end of Reconstruction in 1877.

☑ *Online Teaching Options*

V **Visual Skills**

☐ **MAP** **Place and Time: The United States During the Reconstruction Era**—Students view the makeup of the United States during this time.

☐ **TIME LINE** **Place and Time: United States 1865–1896**—Students learn about key events during the Reconstruction Era.

☐ **WORLD ATLAS** Students can use this interactive map to identify regions of the world, learn about individual countries, locate political boundaries, measure distances, and much more.

☑ *Printable Digital Worksheets*

R **Reading Skills**

☐ **GRAPHIC NOVEL** **The Impeachment of Andrew Johnson**—Students read about the debate over whether to impeach the president.

Project-Based Learning

Hands-On Chapter Project

Political Cartoon

Students demonstrate understanding of factors that led to the impeachment of President Andrew Johnson by creating a political cartoon. They will review information about Andrew Johnson's presidency, use the Political Cartoon worksheet to brainstorm ideas for their cartoon, create their cartoon, and present their cartoon to the class.

Technology Extension

Political Cartoon Video

- Find an additional activity online that incorporates technology for this project.
- Visit the EdTechTeacher Web sites (included in the Technology Extension for this chapter) for more links, tutorials, and other resources.

Print Resources

ANCILLARY RESOURCES

These ancillaries are available for every chapter and lesson.

- **Reading Essentials and Study Guide Workbook** **AL** **ELL**
- **Chapter Tests and Lesson Quizzes Blackline Masters**

PRINTABLE DIGITAL WORKSHEETS

These printable digital worksheets are available for every chapter and lesson.

- **Hands-On Chapter Projects**
- **What Do You Know? activities**
- **Chapter Summaries (English and Spanish)**
- **Vocabulary Builder activities**
- **Guided Reading activities**

More Media Resources

SUGGESTED VIDEOS

Show appropriate clips of popular culture films made about the aftermath of the Civil War, such as **Gone With the Wind** and **Cold Mountain**.

- **Discuss:** What challenges might civilians and soldiers on the losing side of a war face? *(mistreatment, poverty, homelessness, despair, and so on)*

(NOTE: Preview clips for age-appropriateness.)

SUGGESTED READING 📚

Grade 6 reading level:

- **The Buffalo Soldier,** by Sherry Garland

Grade 7 reading level:

- **Frederick Douglass: For the Great Family of Man,** by Peter Burchard

Grade 8 reading level:

- **Blind Boone: Piano Prodigy,** by Madge Harrah

Students will know:
- *the different plans for Reconstruction and what Radical Reconstruction meant.*

Students will be able to:
- *compare and contrast* plans for Reconstruction.
- *evaluate* the effectiveness of the Freedmen's Bureau.
- *identify* important individuals and groups that played a role in Reconstruction.

UNDERSTANDING
BY DESIGN®

☑ *Print Teaching Options*

R Reading Skills

☐ **P. 494** Students discuss Lincoln's Ten Percent Plan. AL ELL

☐ **P. 496** Students identify the three main requirements each state had to meet to rejoin the Union.

☐ **P. 497** Students discuss the Reconstruction plan under President Johnson.

W Writing Skills

☐ **P. 497** Students write an essay about how Lincoln's assassination changed the course of history. BL
Verbal/Linguistic

C Critical Thinking Skills

☐ **P. 495** Students differentiate the options the Union had for dealing with formerly Confederate states after the war. BL

☐ **P. 496** Students draw conclusions about the successes and failures of the Freedman's Bureau.

☑ *Online Teaching Options*

V Visual Skills

☐ **VIDEO** **Reconstructing the Southern States**—Students examine the physical, economic, and psychological consequences of the war in the South to both whites and blacks.

☐ **SLIDE SHOW** **Lincoln's Funeral**—Students view images of Lincoln's funeral train.

R Reading Skills

☐ **GRAPHIC ORGANIZER** **Taking Notes:** *Summarizing:* **Reconstruction Plans**—Students write short summaries of three plans for Reconstruction.

C Critical Thinking Skills

☐ **SLIDE SHOW** **Reconstruction in the South**—Students analyze images of damage in Southern states and evaluate how it would affect Reconstruction.

T Technology Skills

☐ **SELF-CHECK QUIZ** **Lesson 1**—Students receive instant feedback on their mastery of lesson content.

☑ *Printable Digital Worksheets*

C Critical Thinking Skills

☐ **WORKSHEET** **Primary Source Activity: The Reconstruction Era: Planning Reconstruction: "Cause of Attack: None Whatever"**—Students analyze cases of attacks on African Americans following the Civil War.

THE RADICALS TAKE CONTROL

Students will know:
- how Reconstruction affected politics, economics, and society in the South.

Students will be able to:
- *analyze* black codes and the federal government's responses to them.
- *evaluate* Radical Reconstruction.
- *identify* important individuals and groups that played a role in Reconstruction.

UNDERSTANDING
BY DESIGN®

☑ *Print Teaching Options*

V Visual Skills

☐ **P. 501** Students analyze a map showing Reconstruction military districts and identify the states belonging to each.
Visual/Spatial

R Reading Skills

☐ **P. 499** Students discuss the Civil Rights Act of 1866 and the rights it tried to protect.

☐ **P. 499** Students create a list identifying the core disagreements between President Johnson and the Radical Republicans over the Civil Rights Act of 1866.

☐ **P. 500** Students discuss the impact of the Fourteenth Amendment. **AL** **ELL**

☐ **P. 501** Students identify the period known as "Radical Reconstruction."

☐ **P. 502** Students discuss the impeachment trial of Andrew Johnson. **AL** **ELL**

☐ **P. 503** Students summarize what happened after Johnson was impeached.

W Writing Skills

☐ **P. 500** Students write a short essay explaining the importance of "due process" and "equal protection."
Verbal/Linguistic

C Critical Thinking Skills

☐ **P. 498** Students determine the effect of the black codes on daily life in the South. **AL**

☐ **P. 499** Students list the ways Radical Republicans increased the power of the federal government and discuss why this was necessary. **BL**

☐ **P. 502** Students determine the cause of Johnson's impeachment.

☐ **P. 503** Students identify what needs to happen after passing a law before change can happen.

T Technology Skills

☐ **P. 500** Students work in small groups to research the Internet to find current or recent court cases in which the Fourteenth Amendment plays a role. **BL** **Interpersonal**

☑ *Online Teaching Options*

V Visual Skills

☐ **VIDEO** **The Aftermath of War**—Students consider the political battles that raged over the granting of civil rights to African Americans.

☐ **MAP** **Reconstruction Military Districts**—Students view the five military districts made up of the ten states that did not ratify the Fourteenth Amendment.

R Reading Skills

☐ **GRAPHIC ORGANIZER** **Taking Notes: *Determining Cause and Effect:* The Fourteenth and Fifteenth Amendments**—Students record the impact of the Fourteenth and Fifteenth Amendments on African Americans.

C Critical Thinking Skills

☐ **CHART** **Radical Republicans**—Students compare facts about two Radical Republicans who urged equal treatment for African Americans.

☐ **SLIDE SHOW** **The Memphis Riots**—Students view images of race riots in Memphis and New Orleans.

T Technology Skills

☐ **SELF-CHECK QUIZ** **Lesson 2**—Students receive instant feedback on their mastery of lesson content.

Students will know:
- how rights of freed African Americans changed during Reconstruction and in the post-Reconstruction Era.

Students will be able to:
- *describe and analyze* what life was like for African Americans in the South during Reconstruction.

UNDERSTANDING BY DESIGN®

☑ *Print Teaching Options*

R   Reading Skills

☐ **P. 504** Students make a list of positive developments that suggested African Americans would have more political power than ever before. **AL**

☐ **P. 506** Students discuss the economic challenges that African Americans faced during Reconstruction.

☐ **P. 506** Students identify the challenges African Americans faced from terrorist groups during Reconstruction. **AL**

☐ **P. 507** Students discuss the creation of public schools and the gains of African Americans in higher education after Reconstruction.

W   Writing Skills

☐ **P. 505** Students write an essay explaining the differences between the scalawags and the carpetbaggers.
Verbal/Linguistic

C   Critical Thinking Skills

☐ **P. 504** Students draw conclusions about what happens when three different groups are vying for power. **BL**

☐ **P. 505** Students create a two-column list to compare and contrast the scalawags and carpetbaggers.

☐ **P. 506** Students make predictions of possible consequences that arise when citizens do not obey the law.

☐ **P. 507** Students compare and contrast sharecropping and slavery. **AL** **ELL**

☑ *Online Teaching Options*

V   Visual Skills

☐ **VIDEO** **African-American Gains and Losses During Reconstruction**—Students examine corruption in new state governments and explore former slaves' gains in family and education, and losses through sharecropping and debt.

R   Reading Skills

☐ **GRAPHIC ORGANIZER** **Taking Notes:** *Classifying:* **Improvements in Education**—Students describe improvements in the education of African Americans in the South.

C   Critical Thinking Skills

☐ **GRAPH** **African Americans in Congress**—Students click to reveal the numbers of African Americans in Congress from 1869 to 2009.

☐ **GRAPH** **Literacy Rates**—Students click to reveal falling illiteracy rates from 1870 to 1979.

T   Technology Skills

☐ **SELF-CHECK QUIZ** **Lesson 3**—Students receive instant feedback on their mastery of lesson content.

☑ *Printable Digital Worksheets*

V   Visual Skills

☐ **WORKSHEET** **21st Century Skills Activity: The Reconstruction Era: The South During Reconstruction: Analyze Primary Sources: Photographs**—Students analyze photographs of sharecroppers.

THE POST-RECONSTRUCTION ERA

Students will know:
- the successes and failures of Reconstruction in the South.

Students will be able to:
- **analyze** the significance of the election of 1876 and the end of Reconstruction.

UNDERSTANDING
BY DESIGN®

☑ *Print Teaching Options*

V Visual Skills

☐ **P. 509** Students view a map of the election of 1876 and determine which states had the most influence due to the Electoral College. **Visual/Spatial** **Logical/Mathematical**

☐ **P. 510** Students analyze a chart showing industry in the South. **BL** **Logical/Mathematical** **Visual/Spatial**

R Reading Skills

☐ **P. 508** Students discuss how lack of political experience affected Ulysses S. Grant's presidency.

☐ **P. 508** Students explain why control by the Democrats was considered negative.

☐ **P. 510** Students discuss the desire to change Southern agriculture and industry.

☐ **P. 511** Students describe problems faced by sharecroppers. **AL** **ELL**

☐ **P. 512** Students make a list summarizing ways white Southerners denied African Americans their right to vote.

☐ **P. 512** Students explain the creation of Jim Crow laws.

☐ **P. 513** Students explain why formerly enslaved people that left the South were called "Exodusters." **ELL**

☐ **P. 513** Students define the meaning of "buffalo soldiers." **Verbal/Linguistic**

W Writing Skills

☐ **P. 513** Students write a narrative speech that Frederick Douglass may have given in response to the events that occurred during Reconstruction. **BL** **Verbal/Linguistic**

C Critical Thinking Skills

☐ **P. 510** Students make predictions about the effect of living under martial law during major transitions.

☐ **P. 511** Students analyze the effects of dividing up large plantation estates into smaller farms.

☐ **P. 512** Students make connections between lynching and the lack of due process. **BL**

T Technology Skills

☐ **P. 509** Students analyze biases by news media in the coverage of the elections of 1876 and 2000. **BL** **Visual/Spatial**

☑ *Online Teaching Options*

V Visual Skills

☐ **VIDEO** **President Rutherford B. Hayes, Southern Manufacturing, and Booker T. Washington**—Students learn how Hayes won the election of 1876, how the South began to embrace manufacturing, and the stand Booker T. Washington took on education and rights of African Americans.

☐ **MAP** **Election of 1876**—Students compare the vote for the candidates in 1876.

R Reading Skills

☐ **GRAPHIC ORGANIZER** **Taking Notes:** *Summarizing:* **The New South**—Students summarize the "New South's" goals for agriculture and manufacturing.

☐ **IMAGE** **Disenfranchisement**—Students read how some Southerners tried to keep African Americans away from the polls.

C Critical Thinking Skills

☐ **SLIDE SHOW** **Industry in the New South**—Students examine images that describe the growth of the textile industry in the South.

☐ **PRIMARY SOURCE** **Sharecropping**—Students analyze an excerpt from a sharecropping contract.

T Technology Skills

☐ **SELF-CHECK QUIZ** **Lesson 4**—Students receive instant feedback on their mastery of lesson content.

☑ *Printable Digital Worksheets*

C Critical Thinking Skills

☐ **WORKSHEET** **Geography And History Activity: The Reconstruction Era: The Post-Reconstruction Era: Understanding Movement: The Exodusters**—Students examine the story of African Americans fleeing to Kansas to escape the oppression of the South.

INTERVENTION AND REMEDIATION STRATEGIES

LESSON 1   Planning Reconstruction

Reading and Comprehension

Have students locate key words or phrases that describe the following leaders and what they supported: Lincoln, Johnson, and Stevens.

Text Evidence

This lesson presents three agendas for Reconstruction: Lincoln's Ten Percent plan, the Radical Republicans' plan, and Johnson's plan. Help students make a chart comparing and contrasting the three plans, using evidence from the lesson.

LESSON 2   The Radicals Take Control

Reading and Comprehension

Most of the attempts made by Radical Republicans to protect civil rights were legislative. Have students skim through the lesson, making a list of the laws that were passed during this time and how each affected civil rights.

Text Evidence

Have the students review the measures taken to protect African American rights. Ask them to choose the measure they think was most effective and write a paragraph that defends their choice. Have them share with the class.

LESSON 3   The South During Reconstruction

Reading and Comprehension

Have students make a chart of the positive (African Americans in government, establishment of schools, etc.) and negative (accusations of corruption, denial of credit, violence) changes that occurred during this time.

Text Evidence

Tell students that the changes discussed in this lesson fall into three areas: changes in government, changes related to the economy, and social changes. Have students revisit the chapter, making a list or chart showing which changes fall into which category.

LESSON 4   The Post-Reconstruction Era

Reading and Comprehension

Have students read the second paragraph on the first page of Lesson 4. Point out words like *plague, crisis, severe,* and *fear*. Explain that these words set a negative tone for this paragraph. Ask students to find similar words that contribute to tone in this lesson.

Text Evidence

Ask students to construct a time line of events in the chapter. They should conduct research and add relevant information from outside the textbook as well.

Online Resources

Approaching Level Reader

Use this online lower-level text that corresponds directly to the text in the Student Edition. It includes a Spanish version.

Guided Reading Activities

This resource uses graphic organizers and guiding questions to help students with comprehension.

What Do You Know?

Use these worksheets to pre-assess student's background knowledge before they study the chapter.

Reading Essentials and Study Guide Workbook

This resource offers writing and reading activities for the approaching-level student. Also available in Spanish.

Self-Check Quizzes

This online assessment tool provides instant feedback for students to check their progress.

How Do I Teach with
Maps, Graphs, and Charts?

Maps, graphs, and charts are important visual tools that present and combine information to help students understand relationships and draw conclusions. Visual tools are useful because they enable you to condense large amounts of information into a relatively small graphic.

Strategy 1 Focusing on the Important Parts of Maps

- Read the **title,** which identifies the general topic of the map.

- Study all symbols in the **map key, or legend,** and find examples of each one on the map.

- Check the **scale,** which shows the relationship between the unit of measure on the map (miles or kilometers), and a unit of measure (such as inches or centimeters) that students can use to determine distance.

- Find the **compass rose** for cardinal directions.

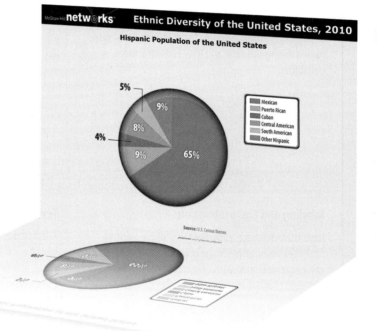

Strategy 2 Understanding Types of Graphs

- **Bar graphs** show how two or more subjects or statistics compare. They provide information along two sides or axes. In most cases, the label on one axis shows quantity or percent. The label on the opposite axis shows the categories of data being compared.

- **Line graphs** show change over time. Like a bar graph, the data is shown over two axes. The horizontal axis usually shows passing time. The vertical axis shows quantity or amount. Sometimes more than one set of data is shown in a line graph to show how those data sets compare over the time period.

- **Circle graphs** show how each part or percentage relates to a whole.

- **Pictographs** use rows of symbols to represent a different amount of data. A pictograph is also useful for making comparisons.

Strategy 3 Types of Charts

- **Tables** show information, including numerical data, in columns and rows to ease comparison. Labels are usually located at the top of each column and on the left-hand side of the table.

- **Diagrams** are specialized drawings that may show steps in a process; point out parts of an object, organization, or idea; or explain how something works. Arrows or lines may join parts of a figure to show the relationship between parts.

The Reconstruction Era

1865–1896

ESSENTIAL QUESTION: *How do new ideas change the way people live?*

◄ *In the years leading up to the Civil War and after, Frederick Douglass was a leading voice for African American rights.*

Bettmann/CORBIS

networks

There's More Online about events of the Reconstruction era.

CHAPTER 18

The Story Matters . . .

Frederick Douglass has done as much as any American in winning freedom for African Americans. Formerly enslaved, Douglass became a powerful voice for the abolitionist cause. During the Civil War, he shared his advice with President Lincoln himself. Now, he is looking forward to the rebuilding of the nation—Reconstruction. He says, "Whether the tremendous war so heroically fought and so victoriously ended shall pass into history a miserable failure . . . must be determined one way or another by the present session of Congress." In this chapter, you will read about Congress's response to Douglass's challenge.

ENGAGE

Bellringer As students read "The Story Matters . . ." to themselves have them recall what they learned earlier about Frederick Douglass and the end of the Civil War. **Ask:**

- Do you think that the Union victory in the Civil War ended discrimination against African Americans? *(Answers may vary, but students should suggest that it did not.)*
- What do you think Douglass hoped would happen during Reconstruction? *(Douglass probably hoped that laws and attitudes toward African Americans would change and that people would realize that African Americans should have equality.)* Discuss with students what "reconstructing" the South might involve and how large a job it might be. **Ask:**
- How long do you think it would take to restore the South to pre-war levels? *(Answers will vary but should reflect that the job would be difficult and would take a long time.)*

Making Connections

Have students interview members of their families or people in the community who remember the civil rights movement of the 1960s. If possible, record the interviews using a digital camera and add them to the class Web site. Have students ask questions about segregation and desegregation, protests, and tactics of violence and intimidation. Alternatively, have a member of the community come in as a guest speaker to discuss these issues with the class. Remind students that the struggle for civil rights began during Reconstruction.

491

Letter from the Author

Dear American History Teacher,

During the era of Reconstruction, Americans were attempting to rebuild following a catastrophic war. Restoring the eleven states that had seceded from the Union would be fraught with controversy, and neither the president nor congressional leaders agreed immediately on the best policy. Reconstruction also comprised a legal revolution for enslaved people. Congress passed three constitutional amendments to recognize their new status as free people and to protect their civil rights. Not since the passage of the Bill of Rights had so many amendments been added to the Constitution in such a short period of time.

Albert S. Broussard

TEACH & ASSESS

Step Into the Place

V1 Visual Skills

Analyzing Maps Show students the Chapter Opener map and ask volunteers to describe what it shows. **Ask: What can you infer from the existence of "military districts" in the former Confederacy?** After students have suggested answers, note that although united in victory, people in the North were divided about how the South should be treated after the Civil War. On one hand, Southerners were viewed as fellow Americans, defeated but deserving mercy and assistance. On the other, they were seen as a conquered enemy, many of whom were bitter in defeat and who should be punished. **Visual/Spatial**

As a class, discuss the Map Focus questions.

Content Background Knowledge

- In the last speech President Lincoln gave, on April 11, 1865, he said that some African Americans should be given the right to vote, especially those who were "very intelligent" or who had served in the Union army.

- Southern states did not lack educated African American leaders. African American political leadership in the South during Reconstruction included previously enslaved persons who had been freed before the war, ministers, artisans, and Civil War veterans.

- Many African Americans hoped to be provided with land after the Civil War because the federal government had taken control of many former plantations. But in 1865, President Johnson ordered that Southern land still in the possession of the federal government should be returned to its former owners.

ANSWERS, p. 492

Step Into the Place
1. Tennessee

2. the states of Nebraska, Nevada, and California, and the Utah and Wyoming Territories; Because the railroad passed through these places, the people in each one would benefit directly and quickly from the changes this transportation improvement brought.

3. **CRITICAL THINKING** Responses may suggest that the federal government's plan to bring the Southern states under control and require them to accept the nation's laws was more difficult in some states than in others.

Step Into the Time
1867; Reconstruction lasted 10 more years, ending in 1877.

Place and Time: United States 1865 to 1896

After the Civil War, the federal government faced the task of putting the nation back together. At the same time, the nation continued to grow and confront a variety of challenges all across the continent.

Step Into the Place

MAP FOCUS The federal government admitted Southern states back into the Union, and the nation sought to establish control of the West.

1 **PLACE** Which former Confederate state was the first to rejoin the Union? RH.6–8.7

2 **HUMAN-ENVIRONMENT INTERACTION** Which states and territories are likely to be impacted by completion of the transcontinental railroad? Explain your answer. RH.6–8.7

3 **CRITICAL THINKING**
Making Inferences Why do you think different states reentered the Union at different times? RH.6–8.7

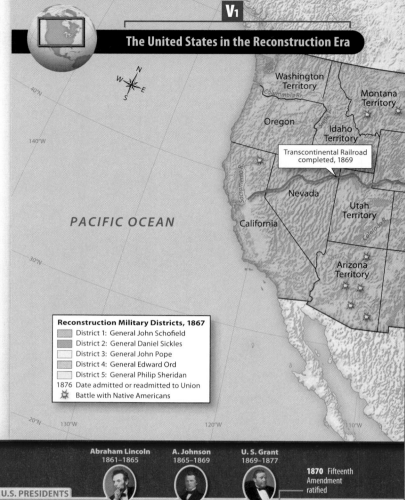

V1 The United States in the Reconstruction Era

Washington Territory
Oregon
Montana Territory
Idaho Territory

Transcontinental Railroad completed, 1869

Nevada
Utah Territory
California

PACIFIC OCEAN

Arizona Territory

Reconstruction Military Districts, 1867
District 1: General John Schofield
District 2: General Daniel Sickles
District 3: General John Pope
District 4: General Edward Ord
District 5: General Philip Sheridan
1876 Date admitted or readmitted to Union
✸ Battle with Native Americans

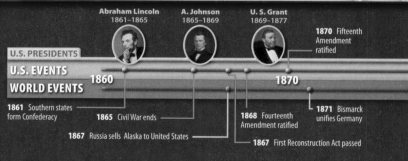

Step Into the Time

V2 **TIME LINE** Look at the time line. When was the First Reconstruction Act passed? How much longer did Reconstruction last? RH.6–8.5, RH.6–8.7

Abraham Lincoln 1861–1865
A. Johnson 1865–1869
U. S. Grant 1869–1877

U.S. PRESIDENTS
U.S. EVENTS
WORLD EVENTS

1860
1870

1870 Fifteenth Amendment ratified

1861 Southern states form Confederacy
1865 Civil War ends
1867 Russia sells Alaska to United States
1868 Fourteenth Amendment ratified
1867 First Reconstruction Act passed
1871 Bismarck unifies Germany

492 *The Reconstruction Era*

Project-Based Learning ✋

Hands-On Chapter Project

Political Cartoon
Students demonstrate understanding of factors that led to the impeachment of President Andrew Johnson by creating a political cartoon. They will review information about Andrew Johnson's presidency and related political issues in their textbook, use the Political Cartoon worksheet to brainstorm possible ideas for their cartoon, choose an idea and create their cartoon, meet with the teacher to discuss their cartoon, and present their cartoon to the class.

Technology Extension

Political Cartoon Video
Have students create political cartoons on paper and then turn them into flip-book style videos with audio narration. You can record the videos using a digital camera or even a cell phone and then import the images into a video editing program. When the videos are complete, you may wish to upload them to the class Web site or an online video hosting service. Encourage students to watch each other's projects and leave comments and analysis.

edtechteacher
21st Century Learning

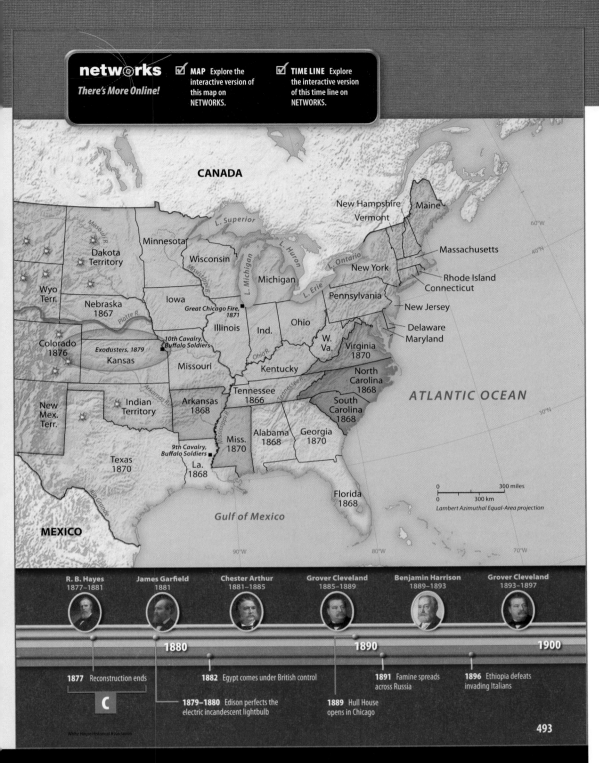

Step Into the Time

V₂ Visual Skills

Reading a Time Line Ask students to study the events on the blue U.S. time line. Have volunteers determine how long Reconstruction lasted after the Civil War and compare that time span to the length of the war itself. *(Reconstruction lasted about 12 years, or about three times the length of the Civil War.)* **Visual/Spatial Logical/Mathematical**

C Critical Thinking Skills

Speculating Have students find the date 1877 on the time line. **Ask: What happened in 1877?** *(Reconstruction ended.)* **Do you think that all of the goals of Reconstruction had been achieved by 1877? Why or why not?** *(Student answers will vary.)* Lead a class discussion of the pace of societal change.

Content Background Knowledge

- During the 1870s, many Radical Republicans began to give up their ideals of a racially equal society.
- By 1900, the South had a new racial system in place, featuring race and class segregation and the use of terrorist tactics of intimidation by violent groups such as the Ku Klux Klan.
- Despite the gains that were lost, the newly passed amendments to the Constitution remained law, although they were not to be enforced until the civil rights movement of the 1960s (which is sometimes called the "second Reconstruction"). Radical Republican leader Charles Sumner, envisioning the future use of these amendments, called them "sleeping giants."

CLOSE & REFLECT

Speculating Have students return to the words of Frederick Douglass: "Whether the tremendous war so heroically fought and so victoriously ended shall pass into history a miserable failure . . . must be determined one way or another by the present session of Congress." **Ask: Do you think Douglass will be pleased or disappointed with the results of Reconstruction?** Tell students that as they study this chapter they will learn about what Congress did during Reconstruction and how those actions affected the entire country.

See page 491B for other online activities.

WORKSHEET

What Do You Know? Activity: The Reconstruction Era—KWL Chart

Listing Have students fill out the KWL chart about Reconstruction. Before they study the chapter, have them complete columns 1 and 2. List student responses on the board. Maintain and refer to the lists as appropriate during the teaching of this chapter's lessons.

When students complete the chapter, have them fill out the third column of the chart. Then use those responses to have students evaluate the two lists on the board.

ENGAGE

🔔 **Bellringer** Tell students that the Civil War can be thought of as an event that shattered the nation. Have students think of other events that make people feel "shattered." List responses on the board. Explain that for an individual, "shattering" events are often stressful experiences such as moving, changing jobs or schools, or losing a loved one through a death or divorce. Communities, too, can experience stressful events, such as wars, famines, recessions, and natural disasters. **Ask: How do people and communities recover after such events? What plans and actions do they have to take in order to recover?**

TEACH & ASSESS

R Reading Skills

Discussing After they have read the text, discuss with students Lincoln's Ten Percent Plan and what it required of Southern states. **Ask: How did Lincoln feel about punishing the Southern states after the war?** *(He did not want to punish the South. He believed that punishment would get little done and would slow the nation's healing process.)*

Discuss offering amnesty to those who would swear loyalty to the Union. **Ask: How many states created governments under the Ten Percent Plan?** *(three: Louisiana, Arkansas, and Tennessee)* **AL** **ELL**

Making Connections

Some students may remember or may have heard stories of locally devastating events such as tornadoes, hurricanes, or other natural or man-made disasters. Have students interview members of the community about how they responded to these events. Then have students interview each other to find out what they learned about communities in recovery.

ANSWER, p. 494

TAKING NOTES: Lincoln's plan: the Ten Percent Plan: when 10 percent of the voters in the state take an oath of loyalty, the state can form a new state government, adopt a constitution that bans slavery, and send representatives to Congress; **Radical Republicans:** the Wade-Davis bill: a majority of the state's white male adults had to pledge loyalty, only white males who had not fought against the Union could vote for representatives, all new state constitutions had to ban slavery; **Johnson's plan:** amnesty for most Southerners who swore loyalty, pardons by appeal for leaders, outlaw slavery, ratify Thirteenth Amendment

---

networks
There's More Online!

☑ **GRAPHIC ORGANIZER**
Reconstruction Plans

☑ **SLIDE SHOW**
• Reconstruction in the South
• Lincoln's Funeral Procession

Lesson 1
Planning Reconstruction

ESSENTIAL QUESTION *How do new ideas change the way people live?*

IT MATTERS BECAUSE
Plans for Reconstruction after the Civil War proved difficult and divisive.

The Reconstruction Debate

GUIDING QUESTION *Why did leaders disagree about the South rejoining the Union?*

The Confederate states tried and failed to break away from the United States. Now, they had to rejoin that Union. In addition, the war left the South's economy and society in ruins. It would take much effort to restore the states that had experienced so much destruction during the war.

The task of rebuilding the former Confederate states and readmitting them to the Union was called **Reconstruction** (ree•kuhn•STRUHK•shuhn). The president and members of Congress had different ideas about how to achieve these goals. The debate over Reconstruction led to bitter conflict in the years following the Civil War.

Lincoln's Ten Percent Plan

President Lincoln offered the first plan for bringing Southern states back into the Union. In December 1863, while the Civil War still raged, Lincoln presented his ideas. Lincoln's plan required voters in each Southern state to take an oath of loyalty to the Union. When 10 percent of the voters in a state had taken the oath, the state could form a new state government. The state would also be required to adopt a new constitution that banned

Reading **HELP**DESK (CCSS)

Taking Notes: *Summarizing* RH.6–8.2

Using a graphic organizer like the one shown here, write short summaries of the Reconstruction plans proposed by Abraham Lincoln, the Radical Republicans, and Andrew Johnson.

494 *The Reconstruction Era*

```
        Lincoln
           |
     Reconstruction
      /         \
  Radicals    Johnson
```

Content Vocabulary (Tier 3 Words)
• Reconstruction
• amnesty

---

networks *Online Teaching Options*

VIDEO

Reconstructing the Southern States

Discussing Show students the lesson video entitled "Reconstructing the Southern States." Discuss the consequences of the war in the South to both African Americans and whites. Ask students if they think any real "reconstruction" took place in the time frame discussed in this lesson. **AL** **ELL** **Visual/Spatial**

See page 491C for other online activities.

slavery. Once a state had met these conditions, it could send representatives to Congress. Lincoln's proposal was known as the Ten Percent Plan.

Lincoln did not want to punish the South after the war ended. He believed that punishment would accomplish little and would slow the nation's healing from the war. Lincoln wanted to see white Southerners who supported the Union take charge of their state governments. He offered **amnesty** (AM•nuh•stee)—forgiveness for any crimes committed—to those who would swear loyalty to the Union. Only Confederate leaders would not be offered amnesty.

In 1864, three states—Louisiana, Arkansas, and Tennessee—set up new governments under Lincoln's plan. Congress, however, was not willing to accept the new states. It refused to seat their senators and representatives.

The Radical Republicans

Some members of Congress thought Lincoln's plan went too easy on the South. A group of Republican representatives favored a more **radical** approach to Reconstruction. This group was known as the Radical Republicans, or the Radicals. Radical leader Thaddeus Stevens said that Southern institutions "must be broken up and relaid, or all our blood and treasure have been spent in vain." The Radicals were powerful. The Republican Party controlled Congress, and the Radicals had much influence in the party. Congress could—and did—vote to deny seats to any state that sought to reenter the Union under Lincoln's plan.

C The city of Richmond, Virginia, shown here, was the capital of the Confederacy and an industrial center.

▶ **CRITICAL THINKING**
Determining Cause and Effect What challenges do you think this type of destruction presented to the economy of Virginia?

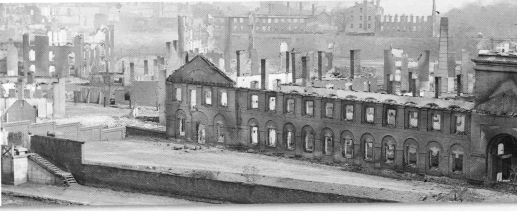
Library of Congress [LC-DIG-cwpb-03370]

Reconstruction the period of rebuilding the South and readmitting Southern states into the Union
amnesty the granting of a pardon to a large number of persons

Academic Vocabulary (Tier 2 Words)
radical extreme

Lesson 1 **495**

C Critical Thinking Skills

Differentiating Have volunteers explain the more radical approach to Reconstruction that Republicans in Congress wanted. **Ask:**

- **How did the Radical Republicans influence Congress and the addition of states under Lincoln's plan?** *(The Republicans were in control of Congress and the Radical Republicans had influence in the party. They denied seats to states coming into Congress under Lincoln's plan.)*
- **Why do you think the Radical Republicans felt so strongly that their Reconstruction plan was best?** *(Answers will vary, but students might say that the Radical Republicans were very committed to repair the damage caused by the institution of slavery or that the Radical Republicans did not trust the South not to take up arms against the Union again.)*

Lead a discussion of the different options the Union had for dealing with formerly Confederate states after the war. Encourage students to find their own points of view and defend them in the discussion. **BL**

Content Background Knowledge

- During the war, the Radical Republicans were committed to abolishing slavery and, afterward, were determined to see that formerly enslaved persons were treated equally and allowed to vote.
- Although the Radical Republicans were committed to ending slavery during the Civil War, Lincoln's primary aim was not emancipation of enslaved persons but restoration of the Union.
- Although the Radical Republicans were united in their approach to slavery, they were often divided on other issues.

SLIDE SHOW

Reconstruction in the South

Discussing Display the slide show, which shows photos of the devastation. **Ask: What was the condition of the South at the end of the Civil War?** *(The South was devastated: cities lay in ruins, railroads had been destroyed, and the economy and society were deeply damaged.)* **Ask: Given what you have just seen, what policies do you think the North should make toward the South now that the war has ended?** *(Answers will vary.)*

See page 491C for other online activities.

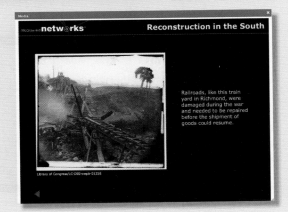
Media
McGraw-Hill **networks**   Reconstruction in the South

Railroads, like this train yard in Richmond, were damaged during the war and needed to be repaired before the shipment of goods could resume.

Library of Congress/LC-DIG-cwpb-01258

ANSWER, p. 495

CRITICAL THINKING The massive destruction to a city makes reconstruction very expensive and would be a huge burden on the state's economy.

Identifying Ask a volunteer to read the text aloud. Discuss the passage of the Wade-Davis Bill in July 1864. Ask students to identify the three main requirements each state had to meet to rejoin the Union. Then discuss Lincoln's pocket veto of the bill. **Ask: What were Lincoln's goals?** *(He wanted the state governments to be established quickly and for rebuilding to get underway.)*

Lead a discussion in which you build connections between students' own perspectives on how Reconstruction should be handled and the position that Lincoln took.

C Critical Thinking Skills

Drawing Conclusions Discuss the creation of the Freedmen's Bureau with students. **Ask:**

- **Do you think the Freedmen's Bureau accomplished its purpose? Why or why not?** *(Answers will vary but should be supported by facts and good arguments.)*
- **What do you think the greatest contribution of the Freedmen's Bureau was?** *(Possible answers: building schools; providing food, clothing, and medical care)*

Acting on his sympathies for the Confederacy, John Wilkes Booth assassinated President Lincoln on April 14, 1865. Lincoln had had less than a week to celebrate the Union victory.

▶ **CRITICAL THINKING**
Analyzing Images How does the artist use actions of the people in this picture to create a mood? Explain your answer.

In July 1864, Congress passed its plan for Reconstruction. The Wade-Davis Bill stated that to rejoin the Union, a state must meet three requirements. First, a majority of the state's white male adults had to pledge loyalty to the Union. Second, only white males who swore they had not fought against the Union could vote for delegates to a state constitutional convention. Third, all new state constitutions had to ban slavery. The bill also barred former Confederates from holding public office.

Lincoln objected to the harshness of this plan. Lincoln wanted new state governments to be quickly established and the rebuilding of the South to get underway. Because Congress was about to end its session, he was able to "pocket veto" the bill: He refused to sign it, and the bill died after Congress adjourned. Still, the Wade-Davis Bill made President Lincoln realize that he would have to compromise with the Radicals.

Founding the Freedmen's Bureau

In March 1865, Lincoln and Congress together created the Freedmen's Bureau. Its main purpose was to help African Americans **adjust** to life after slavery. The Freedmen's Bureau provided food, clothing, and medical care to poor Southerners, especially those freed from slavery. It set up schools, some staffed with teachers from the North. The bureau helped some people get their own land to farm or find work for fair pay.

☑ **PROGRESS CHECK**

Listing What were the three requirements for rejoining the Union stated in the Wade-Davis Bill?

Reading **HELP**DESK **CCSS**

Academic Vocabulary (Tier 2 Words)
adjust to become more suited to new conditions

Library of Congress/3b52661

---

netw⊙rks *Online Teaching Options*

GRAPHIC ORGANIZER

Taking Notes: *Summarizing:* Reconstruction Plans

Summarizing Have students use the interactive graphic organizer to summarize the Reconstruction plans of Abraham Lincoln, Andrew Johnson, and the Radical Republicans. You may wish to organize the class into three groups, and have each group provide details of a different plan. **Visual/Spatial**

See page 491C for other online activities.

ANSWERS, p. 496

CRITICAL THINKING Booth's anger and determination show in his face. The flash of the gun is a violent flare. The army officer attempts vainly to stop the gunman, while Mrs. Lincoln and her female companion express horror. President Lincoln's posture portrays helplessness and adds to the horror of the image.

☑ **PROGRESS CHECK** A majority of the white men in the state had to swear loyalty to the Union; only white males who swore they had not fought against the Union could vote for delegates to a state constitutional convention; all new state constitutions had to ban slavery.

Johnson's Reconstruction Plan

GUIDING QUESTION *How did Lincoln's assassination change the plans for the South rejoining the Union?*

Events took a dramatic turn on the night of April 14, 1865. As the president enjoyed a play at Ford's Theater in Washington, D.C., actor and Confederate sympathizer John Wilkes Booth shot Lincoln in the head. Hours later, Lincoln died.

News of the president's assassination swept across the nation. African Americans mourned the death of the man who helped bring an end to slavery. White Northerners grieved for the president who had restored the Union.

Vice President Andrew Johnson became president. Although he was a Southerner, Johnson had supported the Union during the Civil War. Johnson had his own ideas about rebuilding the South. His Reconstruction plan gave amnesty to most Southerners who swore loyalty to the Union. However, high-ranking Confederates could receive pardons only by appealing to the president. This part of his plan was meant to humiliate Confederate leaders. He believed that they had tricked other Southerners into secession. Johnson also opposed equal rights for African Americans. "White men alone must manage the South," he stated.

President Johnson's plan did require that Southern states outlaw slavery before they could rejoin the Union. They also had to ratify the Thirteenth Amendment to the Constitution. Passed by Congress in January 1865, the Thirteenth Amendment abolished slavery in the United States. By the end of 1865, all former Confederate states except Texas had set up new governments under Johnson's plan. These newly reformed states were now ready to rejoin the Union.

☑ **PROGRESS CHECK**

Specifying What did the Thirteenth Amendment accomplish?

Thinking Like a HISTORIAN

Analyzing Primary Sources

In his Second Inaugural Address, President Lincoln said: "With malice toward none, with charity for all, with firmness in the right as God gives us to see the right, let us strive on to finish the work we are in, to bind up the nation's wounds." Lincoln wanted the South to be treated with compassion. Explain how Reconstruction might have been different if Lincoln had not been assassinated. For more about analyzing primary sources, review *Thinking Like a Historian.*

LESSON 1 REVIEW (ccss)

Review Vocabulary (Tier 3 Words)
1. Explain the meaning of the term *Reconstruction*. RH.6–8.4
2. Use the word *amnesty* in a sentence. RH.6–8.4

Answer the Guiding Questions
3. *Explaining* What was the nature of the disagreement about the terms under which former Confederate states might rejoin the Union after the Civil War? RH.6–8.2

4. *Speculating* How would Lincoln's assassination affect the debate over Reconstruction? RH.6–8.2

5. **INFORMATIVE/EXPLANATORY** You have been hired by the newly formed Freedmen's Bureau to promote the new organization. Write a brief description of the bureau, its work, and why it is important to the future of the nation. WHST.6–8.2, WHST.6–8.9

Lesson 1 **497**

LESSON 1 REVIEW ANSWERS

1. Answers should mention that Reconstruction was the period of rebuilding the South and readmitting Southern states to the Union.

2. Possible answer: Vice President Johnson believed in granting amnesty to Southerners who swore loyalty to the Union.

3. Some leaders thought that the South should be punished for seceding from the Union while others favored granting amnesty. Congress refused to recognize representatives from states readmitted under Lincoln's plan. Congress demanded that voters in Southern states swear loyalty to the Union, swear they had not fought against the Union in the Civil War, and ban slavery in their new state constitutions. Leaders

disagreed about the rights of formerly enslaved people and about the best plan for governing the South.

4. There would likely be less support for a compromise solution. Radical Republicans and the new president, Andrew Johnson, had very different views on Reconstruction.

5. Students' descriptions will vary but should include information about who can be helped by the Bureau, how they can be helped, and the benefits to the nation of providing schools and other help.

TEACH & ASSESS

W Writing Skills

Informative/Explanatory Discuss how Lincoln's assassination changed the course of history. **Ask:**

- **How was President Lincoln killed?** *(He was shot by John Wilkes Booth while watching a play at Ford's Theater in Washington, D.C.)*
- **Who succeeded him as president?** *(Andrew Johnson)*
- **How did people react to Lincoln's death?** *(with shock, mourning, and sadness)*

Have students write a short essay explaining how Lincoln's death affected the nation as a whole. If time permits, have students do additional research on Johnson and Lincoln, and extend their essays by comparing and contrasting the two men and their leadership styles. **BL** **Verbal/Linguistic**

R Reading Skills

Listing After students read the text, discuss Johnson becoming president and his Reconstruction plan. Discuss the ratification of the Thirteenth Amendment. **Ask:**

- **What did the Thirteenth Amendment do?** *(It abolished slavery in the United States.)*
- **How many states were ready to rejoin the Union by the end of 1865?** *(all except Texas)*

Remind students that before the Civil War, Congress had to admit new states to the Union in a balanced way, with a slave state for every free state. Discuss with students how the process of becoming a state changed as the result of the Civil War. Point out that the post-war political changes also affected people traveling between the North and the South.

Have students complete the Lesson 1 Review.

CLOSE & REFLECT

Identifying Central Issues Encourage students to reflect on the central issues facing the nation after the Civil War. **Ask:** **What do you think were the main issues that Congress needed to address during Reconstruction?** *(Answers might include equal rights for formerly enslaved people, concerns about the potential for another civil war, rebuilding areas that were devastated by war, and rebuilding the economy.)* Have students make their own graphic organizer or mind map that shows how they perceive the issues facing the nation at this point in time.

ANSWERS, p. 497

Thinking Like a Historian Possible answer: Lincoln would have been willing to compromise and would not have punished or humiliated former Confederate leaders.

☑ **PROGRESS CHECK** It abolished slavery throughout the United States.

ENGAGE

 Bellringer Discuss the concept of fairness with students.

- Ask students if they have ever experienced any situation that they thought was unfair or in which they thought that their basic rights were not being respected. Encourage students to share strategies that they used to defend their rights or to react against situations that they believed to be unjust.
- Then recall with students that Andrew Johnson became president after Lincoln's assassination. Discuss that the new Confederate states began creating new governments based on his Reconstruction plan. Ask students to recall Johnson's ideas about Reconstruction. **Ask: Do you think Johnson's plans for Reconstruction were fair? Why or why not?**
- Tell students that in this lesson they will learn about attempts to protect the rights of newly freed African Americans as the Radical Republicans take control of government.

TEACH & ASSESS

C Critical Thinking Skills

Determining Cause and Effect Discuss some of the black codes created by Southern states. **Ask:**

- **What were black codes?** (laws passed right after the Civil War in the South that severely restricted the rights of formerly enslaved people)
- **How did the black codes impact African Americans?** (Students should suggest that the black codes took away rights they had just gained and had a negative impact on their lives.) Lead a discussion of the many ways in which the black codes affected daily life in the South. **AL**

ANSWER, p. 498

TAKING NOTES: Fourteenth Amendment: African Americans gained full citizenship, and the principles of equal protection and due process were intended to protect their rights; **Fifteenth Amendment:** African American men gained the right to vote.

---

netw⊙rks
There's More Online!

☑ **CHART/GRAPH** Radical Republicans

☑ **GRAPHIC ORGANIZER** The Fourteenth and Fifteenth Amendments

☑ **MAP** Reconstruction Military Districts

☑ **SLIDE SHOW** Violence in the South

☑ **VIDEO**

Lesson 2
The Radicals Take Control

ESSENTIAL QUESTION *How do new ideas change the way people live?*

IT MATTERS BECAUSE
Reconstruction under the Radical Republicans advocated rights for African Americans and harsh treatment of former Confederates.

Protecting African Americans' Rights

GUIDING QUESTION *How did the North attempt to assist African Americans in the South?*

In 1865 former Confederate states began creating new governments based on President Johnson's plan. These states elected leaders to again represent them in the Congress. When the new senators and representatives arrived in Washington, D.C., Congress would not seat them. The Radical Republicans were not willing to readmit the Southern states on Johnson's easy terms. Radicals were determined to make the former Confederacy's return to the Union difficult for the white South.

Black Codes and Civil Rights

Events in the South strengthened the Radicals' determination. By early 1866, legislatures in the Southern states had passed laws called **black codes.** These laws were designed to help control the newly freed African Americans. Some black codes made it illegal for African Americans to own or rent farms. The laws also made it easy for white employers to take advantage of African American workers. Some black codes allowed officials to fine or

© Stock Montage/Archive Photos/Getty Images
(c) North Wind Picture Archives
(c) North Wind Picture Archives

Reading HELPDESK **CCSS**

Taking Notes: *Determining Cause and Effect*
As you read, take notes on the impact of the Fourteenth and Fifteenth Amendments on African Americans. Use a diagram like the one shown here to organize your notes. **RH.6–8.5**

498 *The Reconstruction Era*

Fourteenth Amendment → ☐

Fifteenth Amendment → ☐

Content Vocabulary (Tier 3 Words)
- black codes
- override
- impeach

---

netw⊙rks *Online Teaching Options*

VIDEO

The Aftermath of War

Identifying Central Issues Explain to students that after the Civil War, the perspectives of different groups on the subject of race varied widely. Though the Civil War was over, the political system itself became a new battleground. **Ask: What did states' rights have to do with the rights of African Americans?** *(The Southern states still wanted to limit the rights of African Americans, while the federal government was trying to protect the rights of African Americans. As a result, the federal and state governments came into conflict.)* Discuss the ways in which the political arena can be a battleground for people trying to protect the rights of a minority group.

See page 491D for other online activities.

even arrest African Americans who did not have jobs. To freed men and women and their supporters, life under the black codes was little better than slavery.

At the same time, Congress tried to protect the rights of the South's African Americans. In 1866 it passed a bill that gave the Freedmen's Bureau new powers. The Bureau could now set up special courts to try persons charged with violating African Americans' rights. African Americans could sit on the juries in these courts and judge accused white Southerners.

To combat the black codes, Radical Republicans pushed the Civil Rights Act of 1866 through Congress. This law gave the federal government power to get involved in state affairs to protect African Americans' rights. It also granted citizenship to African Americans. This act was meant to counter the Supreme Court decision in the 1857 case *Dred Scott* v. *Sandford*. The Supreme Court had ruled that African Americans were not citizens.

President Johnson vetoed both bills. He claimed that the federal government was exceeding its authority. Johnson also argued that both bills were unconstitutional. He reasoned that they had been passed by a Congress that did not include representatives from all the states. By raising this issue, he was warning that he would veto any law passed by a Congress in which the South was not represented.

Republicans in Congress were able to **override,** or defeat, both vetoes, and the bills became law. Radical Republicans began to see that Congress and Johnson would not be able to work together on Reconstruction. They gave up hope of compromising with the president and began to create their own plan for dealing with the South.

The Fourteenth Amendment

Congress did worry that the courts might overturn the Civil Rights Act. It proposed another amendment to the Constitution, which the states ratified in 1868. The Thirteenth Amendment had ended slavery. The Fourteenth Amendment took the next step by stating that:

PRIMARY SOURCE

❝ All persons born or naturalized in the United States, and subject to the jurisdiction thereof, are citizens of the United States and of the State wherein they reside. ❞

—the Fourteenth Amendment

Radical Republicans such as Charles Sumner of Massachusetts were determined not only to rebuild the South but also to remake Southern society.

black codes laws passed in the South just after the Civil War aimed at controlling freed men and women, and allowing plantation owners to take advantage of African American workers
override to reject or defeat something that has already been decided

Stock Montage/Archive Photos/Getty Images

Lesson 2 **499**

R1 **Reading Skills**

Discussing After students read the passage, discuss with the class the passing of the Civil Rights Act of 1866 and what rights it tried to protect. **Ask:**

- What was the Civil Rights Act designed to combat? *(the black codes)*
- What did the act do? *(It gave the federal government power to get involved with state affairs to protect African Americans and gave full citizenship to African Americans.)*

Discuss with students why the federal government needed to get involved in order to protect African Americans.

C **Critical Thinking Skills**

Reasoning Point out to students that, like the Civil Rights Act of 1866, most of the reforms enacted by the Radical Republicans involved increasing the power of the federal government over the states. As students read this lesson, have them make a list of the ways in which the Radical Republicans increased the power of the federal government. Then discuss with students why it was necessary to increase federal power in order to reconstruct the South. **BL**

R2 **Reading Skills**

Listing Have students read the text, then describe Johnson's response to the Civil Rights Act of 1866. **Ask: How did Johnson respond to the act?** *(He vetoed it.)* **What did Congress do?** *(overrode the veto)*

Create a list with students identifying the core disagreements between President Johnson and the Radical Republicans. **Ask: What was the result of these disagreements?** *(It became clear that Congress would not be able to work with the president, so it came up with its own plans for dealing with the South.)*

Lead a discussion of some of the problems that can arise when Congress and the president disagree with each other. Encourage students to pay attention to the news and notice when Congress and the president support each other on various issues and when they do not.

R Reading Skills

Discussing Have students read the text, then discuss with them the impact of the Fourteenth Amendment. **Ask:** What did the Fourteenth Amendment achieve? *(It gave full citizenship to all people born in the United States; it stated that no state could take away a citizen's life, liberty, or property without due process of the law.)*

Explain that "due process" of law is a complicated legal concept. "Due process" means that a citizen accused of a crime must be allowed to have all the benefit of the procedures that are normally included in the legal process, for example, the right to a trial by jury. Discuss with students how the Fourteenth Amendment protects Americans today from abuses by state governments. **AL** **ELL**

T Technology Skills

Researching on the Internet Have students work in small groups to search through online newspapers, magazines, and databases to find current or recent court cases in which the Fourteenth Amendment plays a role. Have each group pick a different case to present to the class. **BL** **Interpersonal**

W Writing Skills

Informative/Explanatory Continue your discussion with students of the phrases "due process of law" and "equal protection of the laws." **Ask:** How do "due process" and "equal protection" affect citizens today? Have students answer the question by writing a short essay explaining why these phrases in the Constitution continue to be important today. **Verbal/Linguistic**

Connections to TODAY

The Fourteenth Amendment

The Fourteenth Amendment aimed to preserve the rights of formerly enslaved people. Today it protects the rights of all Americans from abuse by state governments. Before the Fourteenth Amendment, the Bill of Rights applied only to actions of the federal government. For example, the First Amendment prevented the federal government from denying freedom of religion—but not a state government. Over time, the Supreme Court has used the Fourteenth Amendment to apply many Bill of Rights protections to state governments, too.

White mobs killed nearly 50 African Americans and burned their homes, churches, and schools in Memphis, Tennessee, in May 1866. Reactions to such violence helped Republicans win an overwhelming victory in the 1866 elections.

▶ **CRITICAL THINKING**
Making Connections Why would such violent acts have helped Republicans win elections?

This language protected the citizenship extended to African Americans by the Civil Rights Act of 1866. It guaranteed that citizenship could not later be taken away by passing another law. The amendment made it clear that if a state barred any adult male citizen from voting, that state could lose some representation in Congress.

Another part of the Fourteenth Amendment said that no state could take a person's life, liberty, or property "without due process of law." It stated that every person was entitled to "equal protection of the laws." It also **excluded** former Confederate leaders from holding any national or state office unless Congress had pardoned them.

Some people considered amending the Constitution to protect African Americans to be an extreme measure. Increasing violence toward African Americans across the South convinced moderate Republicans that an amendment was necessary. Congress required that the Southern states ratify the Fourteenth Amendment as another condition of rejoining the Union. Because most refused to do so at first, this delayed the amendment's ratification until 1868.

✔ **PROGRESS CHECK**

Defining Identify two key features of the Civil Rights Act of 1866.

North Wind Picture Archives

Reading HELPDESK (CCSS)

Academic Vocabulary (Tier 2 Words)

exclude to prevent from being involved in something

500 *The Reconstruction Era*

---

networks *Online Teaching Options*

SLIDE SHOW

The Memphis Riots

Discussing Display the interactive slide show about the Memphis riots to discuss that violence increased in the South because of the Fourteenth Amendment. **Ask:** How did members of Congress react to this violence? *(They realized that the amendment was necessary and made ratifying it a requirement to rejoin the Union.)* Discuss with students whether or not they think that an amendment to the Constitution has the capacity to prevent race riots. **AL** **Visual/Spatial**

See page 491D for other online activities.

ANSWERS, p. 500

CRITICAL THINKING Violence would have caused many voters to support Republican plans to deal harshly with white Southerners and protect Southern African Americans.

✔ **PROGRESS CHECK** The act overturned the black codes, gave full citizenship to African Americans, and gave the federal government the power to get involved in state affairs to protect African Americans' rights.

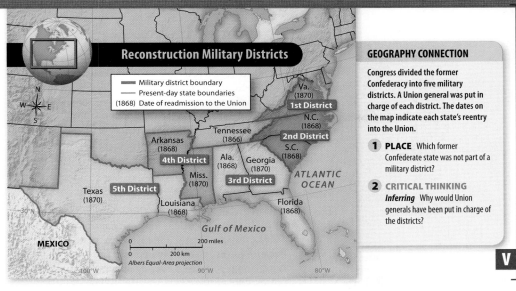

Reconstruction Military Districts

Military district boundary
Present-day state boundaries
(1868) Date of readmission to the Union

Va. (1870) — 1st District
N.C. (1868)
Tennessee (1866) — 2nd District
Arkansas (1868) — 4th District
S.C. (1868)
Ala. (1868)
Georgia (1870) — 3rd District
Miss. (1870)
Texas (1870) — 5th District
Louisiana (1868)
Florida (1868)

ATLANTIC OCEAN

Gulf of Mexico

MEXICO

0   200 miles
0   200 km
Albers Equal-Area projection

V

Radical Republicans in Charge

GUIDING QUESTION *What elements were included in the Radical Republican idea of Reconstruction?*

President Johnson campaigned against the Radical Republicans in the congressional elections of 1866. He attacked the Fourteenth Amendment and made it a major issue in the campaign. Many Northerners disliked Johnson's tone. Some feared the clashes between whites and African Americans that were taking place in the South. Voters rejected Johnson's views, and the Republicans won an overwhelming majority in Congress. This meant that Johnson could no longer prevent them from overriding his vetoes. A period known as Radical Reconstruction began.

The Reconstruction Acts

By 1867, 10 of the former Confederate states had not ratified the Fourteenth Amendment. In response, Congress passed the First Reconstruction Act. This law required that those states form new governments. Only Tennessee, which had ratified the amendment, kept its government and rejoined the Union.

R

The act divided the 10 defiant states into five military districts. Each district would be governed by an army general until new state governments were formed. Former Confederate leaders were banned from serving in these new governments. Each state also had to submit a new state constitution to Congress for approval. Finally, the act guaranteed African American men the right to vote in state elections. A Second Reconstruction Act empowered the army to register voters in each district and to help organize state constitutional conventions.

V Visual Skills

Analyzing Maps Direct students' attention to the map at the top of the page. **Ask: Which states took the longest to be readmitted to the Union?** *(Virginia, Georgia, Mississippi, and Texas)* Have students make a chart showing the five military districts and listing which states were included in each. **Visual/Spatial**

R Reading Skills

Identifying After students have read the text, discuss with them the tension that was building between Andrew Johnson and the Radical Republicans. Have volunteers provide examples. Then discuss the period known as "Radical Reconstruction." Ask students to identify when this period began. *(It began when the Republicans won an overwhelming majority of Congress in 1866.)* **Ask: What did the Radical Republicans do to put their Reconstruction program into practice?** *(passed the Reconstruction Acts)*

CHART

Graphic Organizer: Tree Diagram

Summarizing Have students use the tree diagram graphic organizer to summarize the requirements placed on formerly Confederate states by the Reconstruction Acts. Encourage students to use one branch of the tree to cover the military districts, one branch for the new state constitutions, and one branch for elections. **Visual/Spatial**

See page 491D for other online activities.

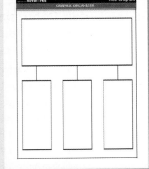

The Radicals Take Control

C Critical Thinking Skills

Determining Cause and Effect   Discuss how the tensions between the two parties continued to grow. Explain how Johnson violated the Tenure of Office Act and the steps that led to his impeachment. **Ask: How did Johnson react to this challenge of the Tenure of Office Act?** *(He first suspended Stanton and then fired him without the Senate's approval.)* **Ask: Why did Johnson want to fire Stanton?** *(because Stanton supported Radical Reconstruction)* **Ask: What other actions did Johnson take that angered the Radical Republicans?** *(He appointed people that the Radicals were opposed to to command military districts.)* **What was the result of Johnson's actions?** *(The House of Representatives voted to impeach him.)*

R Reading Skills

Explaining   Direct students to read the section on the impeachment trial of Andrew Johnson. Have students explain the key points of this passage. **Ask:**

- **What does** *impeach* **mean?** *(to formally charge with wrongdoing)* Make sure that students understand that being impeached is being accused; it is not being tried and found guilty.
- **How long did the trial last?** *(three months)* Have volunteers explain Johnson's defense and his critics.
- **What was the result of the trial?** *(The Senate did not get the two-thirds majority needed to convict him.)*
- **Do you think Johnson deserved to be impeached?** *(Possible answers: Yes, he knowingly broke a law. No, the impeachment was politically motivated.)* **AL** **ELL**

Many white Southerners refused to take part in the elections for constitutional conventions and new state governments. Thousands of newly registered African Americans did cast ballots. These developments favored the Republicans, who took control of Southern state governments. By 1868, Alabama, Arkansas, Florida, Georgia, Louisiana, North Carolina, and South Carolina had set up new governments, ratified the Fourteenth Amendment, and rejoined the Union. By 1870, the remaining three states—Mississippi, Virginia, and Texas—had also been readmitted.

Impeaching the President

The Constitution makes the president the commander in chief of the military. This gave President Johnson control over the military governors created by the First Reconstruction Act.

Because Johnson strongly opposed the Reconstruction Acts, Congress passed a series of laws to limit his power. One of these laws was the Tenure of Office Act. This law stated that the president could not remove government officials, including members of his own cabinet, without the Senate's approval. Congress wanted to protect Secretary of War Edwin Stanton. Stanton was the cabinet official in charge of the military and a supporter of Radical Reconstruction.

Tensions between Johnson and the Radical Republicans continued to grow. In August 1867, while Congress was not in session, Johnson **suspended** Stanton—temporarily stopped him from working—without the Senate's approval. When the Senate met again, it refused to approve the suspension. Johnson then fired Stanton. This action deliberately violated the Tenure of Office Act. Johnson also appointed people the Radical Republicans opposed to command some of the military districts in the South.

The House of Representatives voted to **impeach** (ihm‧PEECH) President Johnson—that is, formally charge him with wrongdoing. In 1868 the case went to the Senate for a trial. The trial lasted almost three months. Johnson's defenders claimed that the president had exercised his right to challenge laws he considered unconstitutional. They argued that the House had impeached Johnson for political reasons. Johnson's critics said that Congress had supreme power to make the laws and that Johnson's use of the veto interfered with that power.

This ticket entitled the holder to attend the impeachment trial of President Johnson.

▶ CRITICAL THINKING
Speculating   Why might Johnson's conviction and removal have weakened the office of president?

North Wind Picture Archives

Reading **HELP**DESK   CCSS

impeach   to formally charge a public official with misconduct in office

Academic Vocabulary (Tier 2 Words)

suspend   to stop temporarily

net**works**   *Online Teaching Options*

GRAPHIC ORGANIZER

Taking Notes: *Determining Cause and Effect:* **The Fourteenth and Fifteenth Amendments**

Summarizing   Display the graphic organizer. **Ask: What did the Fourteenth Amendment achieve?** *(It stated that no state could take away a citizen's life, liberty, or property without due process of the law.)* **What did the Fifteenth Amendment achieve?** *(It stated that the right to vote could not be denied to any male citizen based on "race, color, or previous condition of servitude.")*

See page 491D for other online activities.

ANSWER, p. 502

CRITICAL THINKING   It could have set a pattern for removing future presidents from office for purely political reasons or differences.

The Senate did not get the two-thirds majority it needed to convict President Johnson. Some moderate Republicans supported the president, arguing that he should not be removed from office for political reasons. As a result, Johnson remained president until Lincoln's second term ended in 1869. During that time, President Johnson did little to interfere with Congress's Reconstruction plans.

The Fifteenth Amendment

Most Southern states had rejoined the Union by the time the presidential election of 1868 drew near. Most Americans hoped that the turbulent period of Reconstruction was over. The Republican Party rejected Johnson and instead nominated Civil War hero Ulysses S. Grant. The Democrats chose New York governor Horatio Seymour as their candidate. Most African American voters supported Grant, and he won the presidency. The election results also showed that voters continued to support Radical Reconstruction.

Congress took one more major step in Reconstruction in 1869 when it proposed the Fifteenth Amendment. This amendment guaranteed that state and federal governments could not deny the right to vote to any male citizen because of "race, color, or previous condition of servitude."

When the states ratified the Fifteenth Amendment in 1870, Republicans thought their job was largely done. They believed that they had succeeded in giving African American men the right to vote. They also thought the power of the vote would allow African Americans to better protect themselves against unfair treatment by white people. Both beliefs would prove to be too optimistic.

☑ **PROGRESS CHECK**

Describing How did Congress organize the South during Reconstruction?

LESSON 2 REVIEW (CCSS)

Review Vocabulary (Tier 3 Words)

1. Define each of the following terms, then use each term in a sentence. RH.6–8.4

   a. suspend   **b.** impeach   **c.** override

Answer the Guiding Questions

2. ***Describing*** What threats did African Americans continue to face in the South, and what measures did Congress take to deal with these threats? RH.6–8.2

3. ***Analyzing*** What measures did the Radical Republicans take to make Reconstruction harder for the white South? RH.6–8.1

4. **ARGUMENT** Assume the role of President Andrew Johnson. Write a short speech to give at your trial, explaining why senators should not convict you of wrongdoing. WHST.6–8.1, WHST.6–8.10

Lesson 2 **503**

R Reading Skills

Summarizing Have students use details from the text to summarize the events after Johnson's impeachment. **Ask:** What happened after Johnson was impeached? *(He remained president until Lincoln's second term ended in 1869.)*

Tell students that the Senate was only one vote short of the two-thirds majority that would have convicted Johnson. Explain that despite their failure to remove Johnson from office, the Radical Republicans were still powerful. In the next election, voters elected Civil War General Ulysses S. Grant, who supported Radical Reconstruction, as president.

C Critical Thinking Skills

Identifying Problems Tell students that passing a law does not always bring about immediate change. **Ask:** What tools do you think the government would have to use to enforce the Fifteenth Amendment? *(Answers may vary but should indicate that the government would have to enforce the law for it to have any effect.)* Lead students in a discussion of what it means to have laws and why laws matter to people in a free society.

Have students complete the Lesson 2 Review.

CLOSE & REFLECT

Synthesizing Explain to students that the *honor system* refers to trust in people to not be dishonest. Explain that laws, in part, depend on the honor system. If citizens do not take it upon themselves to obey the law, it will not function properly as a law. It is not possible or desirable in a free society for law enforcement to be everywhere all the time, forcing people to obey the law. Lead students in a discussion of what the honor system means in a society bound by law, and encourage them to reflect on how the honor system may have operated, or failed to operate, during Reconstruction.

LESSON 2 REVIEW ANSWERS

1. The president can suspend the activities of his cabinet members. Under the Constitution, the House has the power to impeach the president. Congress can override a president's veto if it can get enough votes.

2. Possible answers: Southern states passed black codes, which restricted the rights of African Americans. Congress passed laws furthering the rights of African Americans, including the Freedmen's Bureau bill, the Civil Rights Act of 1866, and the Fourteenth and Fifteenth Amendments.

3. Dividing the South into military districts, banning former Confederate leaders from office, requiring Southern states to write new state constitutions and ratify the Fourteenth Amendment, and passing the Fifteenth Amendment all carried out the Radical Republicans' goal of reshaping Southern society.

4. Speeches might note that the veto is a presidential power granted by the Constitution and that limiting the president's ability to remove his secretary of war, as well as any other members of his own cabinet, is purely political and unreasonable, as well as unconstitutional.

ANSWER, p. 503

☑ **PROGRESS CHECK** The South was organized into five military districts, each run by a Union general.

ENGAGE

Bellringer Discuss the idea of power with students. Ask students who has power in their lives and why. Does that power ever change hands? Explain to students that politics is about power: who has it, who does not, and how power shifts from one area to another. In democratically elected governments, different parties struggle for power, and power changes hands on a regular basis. Then discuss with students that during Reconstruction, Republicans controlled Southern politics. Discuss the groups that supported the Republicans in state government, including African Americans. Tell students that in this lesson they will learn about life and politics in the South during Reconstruction.

TEACH & ASSESS

C Critical Thinking Skills

Drawing Conclusions Tell students that when there are three groups vying for power, one of those groups can often tip the balance of power in favor of one of the other groups. Have students consider the groups who were vying for power in the Reconstruction of the South: African Americans, white Southerners, and white newcomers from the North. **Ask:**

- Which group do you think would be most likely to tip the balance of power? *(white newcomers from the North)*
- What do you think will happen if that group ceases to be active in Southern politics? *(The balance of power would be at risk of shifting back.)* Lead the class in a discussion of the shifting power dynamics in the South during Reconstruction. **BL**

R Reading Skills

Citing Text Evidence Direct students to read the text. Tell students that some scholars have called the beginning of Reconstruction a very hopeful time for African Americans. Have students make a list of positive developments that suggested that African Americans would have more political power than ever before. Remind students to support their responses with evidence from the text. **AL**

ANSWER, p. 504

TAKING NOTES: new public school systems for both races; academies offering advanced education to African Americans

---

networks
There's More Online!

☑ **CHART/GRAPH**
 • Illiteracy Rates
 • African Americans in Congress

☑ **GRAPHIC ORGANIZER**
 Improvements in Education

Lesson 3
The South During Reconstruction

ESSENTIAL QUESTION *How do new ideas change the way people live?*

IT MATTERS BECAUSE
Reconstruction brought significant—but not necessarily lasting—change to the South.

Republicans in Charge

GUIDING QUESTION *How were African Americans discouraged from participating in civic life in the South?*

C Republicans controlled Southern politics during the Reconstruction period. Groups in charge of state governments supported the Republican Party. These groups included African Americans, some white Southerners, and white newcomers from the North.

African Americans in Government

R Though they had fewer rights than white Southerners, African Americans greatly influenced Southern politics. During Reconstruction, African Americans played important roles as voters and as elected officials. In some states their votes helped produce victories for Republican candidates—including African American candidates. For a short time, African Americans held the majority in the lower house of the South Carolina legislature. Overall, the number of African Americans holding top positions in most Southern states during Reconstruction was small. African Americans did not control any state government. At the national level, 16 African Americans served in the House of Representatives and 2 served in the Senate between 1869 and 1880.

(l) Library of Congress/264952(l); (c & r) The Granger Collection, NYC

Reading HELPDESK **CCSS**

Taking Notes: *Classifying* RH.6–8.1
As you read, use a diagram like the one shown here to describe improvements in the education of African Americans in the South during Reconstruction.

Improvements in Education

Content Vocabulary (Tier 3 Words)
- scalawag   • sharecropping
- corruption
- integrate

504 *The Reconstruction Era*

---

networks *Online Teaching Options*

VIDEO

African-American Gains and Losses During Reconstruction

Making Connections After students watch the lesson video, discuss the life of sharecroppers with them. **Ask:** How did sharecropping work? *(Landowners traded access to land and tools to formerly enslaved persons in return for a share of the crop.)* What was unfair about sharecropping? *(Landowners charged an unreasonable amount of money for renting tools and other necessary items, and then charged exorbitant interest on the loans.)* Tell students that many people today also are working to pay off debt. Lead a discussion of how it is possible for debt itself to "enslave" a person.

See page 491E for other online activities.

At the center of this picture of leading Reconstruction politicians is Frederick Douglass. Beside him are Hiram Revels (right), who in 1870 became the first African American elected to the United States Senate, and Blanche K. Bruce, who became the first African American to serve a full term in the Senate.

▶ **CRITICAL THINKING**
Making Inferences Why do you think Douglass appears at the center of this picture?

Carpetbaggers and Scalawags

Some Southern whites supported the Republican Party. These were often pro-Union business leaders and farmers who had not owned enslaved people. Former Confederates who held resentment against those who had been pro-Union called these people **scalawags** (SKA•lih•wagz), a term meaning "scoundrel" or "worthless rascal."

Republicans also had the support of many Northern whites who moved to the South after the war. White Southerners called these Northerners carpetbaggers. The term referred to cheap suitcases made of carpet fabric—what white Southerners might have thought untrustworthy newcomers might carry. White Southerners were suspicious of the Northerners' intentions. Some carpetbaggers were dishonest people looking to take advantage of the South's difficulties, but most were not. Many sincerely wanted to help rebuild the South.

White Southerners accused Reconstruction governments of **corruption** (kuh•RUHP•shuhn)—dishonest or illegal actions. Some officials did make money illegally. Yet there is no evidence that corruption in the South was greater than in the North.

C **W**

scalawag name given by former Confederates to Southern whites who supported Republican Reconstruction of the South
corruption dishonest or illegal actions

Build Vocabulary: *Word Origins*

Today the term *carpetbagger* is used to criticize candidates who run for office in a place where they have not lived for long.

C Critical Thinking Skills

Comparing and Contrasting Have students compare and contrast the characteristics of the scalawags and carpetbaggers. Create a two-column list with students for them to use as a comparison chart. **Ask:**

- **Who were the scalawags?** *(southern whites who supported Republican Reconstruction)*
- **What kind of people were typical scalawags?** *(business leaders and farmers who had not owned enslaved people)*
- **Who were the carpetbaggers?** *(Northern whites who moved to the South after the war)*
- **Why do you think they moved to the South?** *(Possible answers: for personal opportunity, to help rebuild the South)*
- **How were scalawags and carpetbaggers similar? How were they different?** *(Possible answers: They were similar because they were white, Republican, lived in the South, and were opposed by those who were against Reconstruction. They were different because carpetbaggers moved from the North while scalawags were already Southerners.)*

W Writing Skills

Informative/Explanatory Have students write an essay explaining the similarities and differences between the carpetbaggers and the scalawags. Have them use the comparison/contrast chart as a resource in developing their essays. Encourage students to cite textual evidence to support their statements. **Verbal/Linguistic**

GRAPH

African Americans in Congress

Analyzing Graphs Use the interactive graph to discuss the growth of African Americans in Congress. Discuss the number of representatives in Congress between 1869 and 1880. **Ask:** How would you describe the trend of African Americans serving in Congress between the Civil War and 1900? *(Answers may vary but should point out the immediate increase of, then the lack of, representatives. Students should also point out the steady increase since 1929.)* **Visual/Spatial Logical/Mathematical**

See page 491E for other online activities.

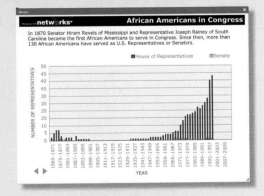

African Americans in Congress

In 1870 Senator Hiram Revels of Mississippi and Representative Joseph Rainey of South Carolina became the first African Americans to serve in Congress. Since then, more than 130 African Americans have served as U.S. Representatives or Senators.

■House of Representatives ■Senate

ANSWER, p. 505

CRITICAL THINKING Douglass had led the fight for African American rights for many years.

R1 Reading Skills

Discussing After students have read the paragraph, discuss the economic challenges that African Americans faced during Reconstruction. Remind students that employers and landowners were unwilling to provide jobs and land, and that many Southerners resented African Americans having rights. **Ask: Why was it a problem for store owners to refuse to offer credit to African Americans?** *(Answers will vary but should indicate that refusing to offer credit meant that newly freed persons who did not have any money saved did not have a chance to earn money for themselves. Sharecroppers needed tools to work with in order to be able to produce crops from the land.)*

Lead students in a discussion of the challenges faced by sharecroppers in the South, and encourage students to think about how they would handle these challenges if placed in such a situation.

R2 Reading Skills

Identifying After students have read the text, ask a volunteer to identify the daily challenges that African Americans faced during Reconstruction from terrorist groups using fear and violence to intimidate. **Ask: What was the Ku Klux Klan?** *(a secret society that used fear and violence to intimidate African Americans and oppose Republican rule)* Discuss how the Ku Klux Klan was an especially serious threat to the lives of freed people in the South because they used violence and fear to deny African Americans their rights. **AL**

C Critical Thinking Skills

Predicting Consequences Point out to students that making changes in the laws was one of the main tools used by Republicans for changing society during Reconstruction. **Ask:**

- **What is the main weakness of using laws as a tool for bringing about societal change?** *(Laws are only as strong as citizens' willingness to act in accordance with them. If citizens do not obey the laws and other citizens do not enforce the laws, then the laws do little good.)*
- **How is the political system and government affected when citizens do not obey the law?** *(The government is weakened, and so are the laws.)* Lead the class in a discussion of the role of law in society.

ANSWER, p. 506

✓ **PROGRESS CHECK** Many Southerners viewed carpetbaggers and Republican officials as corrupt, and they resented the scalawags who supported them.

This picture shows a school for African American children in Charleston, South Carolina.

Resistance to Reconstruction

Life during Reconstruction was difficult for African Americans. Most Southern whites did not want African Americans to have more rights. White landowners often refused to rent land to freed people. Store owners refused them **credit.** Many employers would not hire them. Many of the jobs available to African Americans were those that whites were unwilling to do.

A more serious danger to the freed people in the South was secret societies such as the Ku Klux Klan. These groups used fear and violence to deny rights to freed men and women. Disguising themselves in white sheets and hoods, Klan members threatened, beat, and killed thousands of African Americans and the whites who supported them. Klan members burned African American homes, schools, and churches. Many Democrats, planters, and other white Southerners supported the Klan. Some saw violence as a way to oppose Republican rule.

In 1870 and 1871, Congress passed several laws to try to stop the growing Klan violence. These laws were not always effective. White Southerners often refused to testify against those in their own communities who attacked African Americans and their white supporters.

☑ **PROGRESS CHECK**

Explaining Why did many Southerners resent scalawags and carpetbaggers?

The Granger Collection, NYC

Reading **HELP**DESK (CCSS)

integrate to unite, or to blend into a united whole
sharecropping system of farming in which a farmer works land for an owner who provides equipment and seeds and receives a share of the crop

Academic Vocabulary (Tier 2 Words)

credit a loan, or the ability to pay for a good or service at a future time rather than at the time of purchase
academy a school or college for special training

506 The Reconstruction Era

netw⊙rks   *Online Teaching Options*

GRAPH

Literacy Rates

Making Connections Use the interactive graph of literacy rates to discuss improvements in the education of African Americans. **Ask: About what percent of African Americans were illiterate in 1870?** *(about 80 percent)* **How did conditions in the South affect this figure?** *(Students should recall that it was illegal to educate slaves.)* **What conclusion can you draw from this graph about education reforms during the Reconstruction Era?** *(Reforms reduced the illiteracy rate among African Americans after Reconstruction.)* **Mathematical/Logical Visual/Spatial**

See page 491E for other online activities.

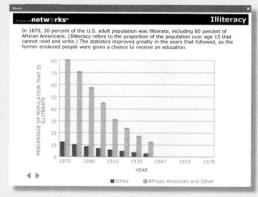

netw⊙rks™   Illiteracy

In 1870, 20 percent of the U.S. adult population was illiterate, including 80 percent of African Americans. (Illiteracy refers to the proportion of the population over age 15 that cannot read and write.) The statistics improved greatly in the years that followed, as the former enslaved people were given a chance to receive an education.

■ White ▨ African American and Other

Education and Farming

GUIDING QUESTION *What were some improvements and some limitations for African Americans?*

During the early days of Reconstruction, African Americans built their own schools. Many Northerners came south to teach. In the 1870s, Reconstruction governments created public schools for both races. Soon about 50 percent of white children and 40 percent of African American children attended school in the South.

African Americans also made gains in higher education. Northerners set up **academies** in the South. These academies grew into a network of colleges and universities for African Americans.

African American and white students usually went to different schools. Few states had laws requiring schools to be **integrated** (IHN·tuh·grayt·uhd). Schools that are integrated have both white and African American students. Often, integration laws were not enforced.

In addition to education, freed people wanted farmland. Having their own land would enable them to support their families. Some African Americans bought land with the help of the Freedmen's Bank. Many freed people, however, had no choice but to farm on land owned by whites.

In the **sharecropping** (SHEHR·krah·peeng) system, landowners rented land to sharecroppers, or farmers. Sharecroppers gave a percentage of their crops to the landowner. Landowners often demanded an unfairly large percentage that left sharecroppers with almost nothing to support themselves. For many, sharecropping was little better than slavery.

☑ **PROGRESS CHECK**

Describing How did sharecroppers get land to farm?

LESSON 3 REVIEW

Review Vocabulary (Tier 3 Words)

1. Use the following terms in sentences that illustrate the meaning of these terms. RH.6–8.4

   a. integrate   **b.** sharecropping

2. How are the terms *corruption* and *scalawag* connected? RH.6–8.4

Answer the Guiding Questions

3. ***Explaining*** In what ways was life during Reconstruction difficult for African Americans? RH.6–8.2

4. ***Describing*** How did education improve in the South during Reconstruction? RH.6–8.2

5. **INFORMATIVE/EXPLANATORY** Charlotte Forten was an African American who moved from the North to teach freed children in South Carolina. Of her students, she wrote, "The long, dark night of the Past, with all its sorrows and its fears, was forgotten; and for the Future—the eyes of these freed children see no clouds in it." Write an explanation of what you think Forten meant. RH.9–8.9, WHST.6–8.1

Lesson 3 **507**

LESSON 3 REVIEW ANSWERS

1. Possible answers: Most states did not integrate black and white students in schools. In the sharecropping system, some landowners demanded too large a share of the crops.

2. Many Southerners believed the Republican governments to be guilty of corruption and blamed the scalawags for supporting them.

3. Answers should note that African Americans found little support from whites; employment, fair wages, land, and credit were hard to obtain; and violence by the Ku Klux Klan was always a threat.

4. Republican governments created public school systems for both whites and African Americans, although these schools were very rarely integrated. Missionary groups created academies to provide special training for African Americans.

5. Explanations will vary but should suggest that Forten believed the end of slavery, along with the educational opportunities that Reconstruction offered, provided a bright future for the South's African American children.

R Reading Skills

Discussing Have students use evidence from the text to discuss the creation of public schools and African Americans' gains in higher education after Reconstruction. Remind students that before the Civil War, it was illegal in most of the South to teach African Americans to read and write. **Ask: How many children attended school in the South after Reconstruction?** *(about 50 percent of white children and 40 percent of African American children)*

Lead the class in a discussion of the importance of education and the changes that occurred in education during Reconstruction.

C Critical Thinking Skills

Comparing and Contrasting Students may have already picked up the meaning of sharecropping, but direct their attention to the last paragraph of this lesson to find a definition of the term. **Ask: What is sharecropping?** *(a system in which a farmer works land for an owner who provides supplies and seeds, and then receives a share of the crop)*

Discuss the policies and agreements for sharecropping. **Ask: Were sharecropping agreements fair?** *(Sharecropping agreements were typically unfair and could be compared to slavery.)*

Discuss with students the similarities and differences between the conditions under which sharecroppers worked and the working conditions of slavery. **AL** **ELL**

Have students complete the Lesson 3 Review.

CLOSE & REFLECT

Speculating Discuss which aspects of Reconstruction were beneficial to African Americans and which aspects were detrimental. Discuss how Reconstruction policies might have been different if President Lincoln had lived.

ANSWER, p. 507

☑ **PROGRESS CHECK** Landowners rented land and provided supplies to sharecroppers in exchange for a share of the crop.

ENGAGE

Bellringer Review what students have learned about Reconstruction so far. **Ask: What event marked the beginning of Reconstruction?** *(the Union victory in the Civil War)* **What was Reconstruction?** *(the period of rebuilding the South after the Civil War and the plans for bringing Southern states back into the Union)* **What would you say was being "reconstructed," or rebuilt?** *(the Union; the country)* **How would people know when the Reconstruction was finished, or complete?** *(Answers will vary.)*

TEACH & ASSESS

R1 Reading Skills

Discussing Direct students to read the text. Ask students why Grant's lack of political experience may have led to the corruption and scandal that affected his presidency. **Ask: How did scandal and the Panic of 1873 hurt the Republican party?** *(By 1874, the Republicans had lost and the Democrats had regained control of Congress.)*

R2 Reading Skills

Explaining Ask students to read the text and then to use evidence from their reading to support this statement: Southern Democrats worked hard to regain control of state government but did so in ways that were detrimental to society. **Ask: How was control by the Democrats something negative?** *(They used terror against voters and then called themselves "redeemers.")*

ANSWER, p. 508

TAKING NOTES: Industry: a strong industrial economy based on the region's abundant coal, iron, tobacco, cotton, and lumber; **Agriculture:** small, profitable farms raising a variety of crops rather than large plantations devoted to cotton

---

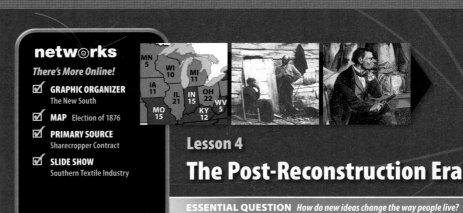

net⊚rks
There's More Online!

☑ **GRAPHIC ORGANIZER**
The New South

☑ **MAP** Election of 1876

☑ **PRIMARY SOURCE**
Sharecropper Contract

☑ **SLIDE SHOW**
Southern Textile Industry

Lesson 4
The Post-Reconstruction Era

ESSENTIAL QUESTION *How do new ideas change the way people live?*

IT MATTERS BECAUSE
After Reconstruction, a "New South" emerged, but African Americans steadily lost freedoms.

Reconstruction Ends

GUIDING QUESTION *How did Democrats regain control of Southern governments?*

As a general, Ulysses S. Grant had led the North to victory in the Civil War. His reputation as a war hero carried him into the White House in the election of 1868 and to reelection in 1872. Unfortunately, Grant had little experience in politics.

Scandal and corruption plagued Grant's presidency. In addition, a severe economic depression began during his second term. A crisis arose when a powerful banking firm declared bankruptcy. This triggered a wave of fear known as the Panic of 1873. It set off a depression that lasted much of the decade.

The depression and the scandals in the Grant administration hurt the Republican Party. In the 1874 congressional elections, the Democrats won back control of the House of Representatives. Democrats also made gains in the Senate. These changes cost the Radical Republicans much of their power.

Meanwhile, Southern Democrats worked hard to regain control of their state governments. They got help from groups such as the Ku Klux Klan, which terrorized African Americans and other Republican voters. The Democrats who came to power in the South called themselves "redeemers." They claimed to have redeemed, or saved, their states from "black Republican" rule.

(L & I The Granger Collection, NYC)

Reading **HELP**DESK **CCSS**

Taking Notes: *Summarizing* RH.6–8.2

As you read, use a diagram like this one to summarize the main ideas about the New South.

508 *The Reconstruction Era*

```
        The New South
       /            \
  Goal for        Goal for
  Industry:       Agriculture:
```

Content Vocabulary (Tier 3 Words)
- **poll tax**
- **literacy test**
- **grandfather clause**
- **segregation**
- **lynching**

---

net⊚rks *Online Teaching Options*

VIDEO

President Rutherford B Hayes, Southern Manufacturing, and Booker T. Washington

Making Comparisons Discuss with students which aspect of Reconstruction was more important, politics or the economy. **Ask: What role did Booker T. Washington play in helping to integrate African Americans into the economy?** *(He promoted education for African Americans and encouraged them to focus on the economy as their first priority.)* Lead students in a debate of the two potentially conflicting priorities for Reconstruction: the economy and politics. Ask students which they think is more important and why. **Interpersonal**

See page 491F for other online activities.

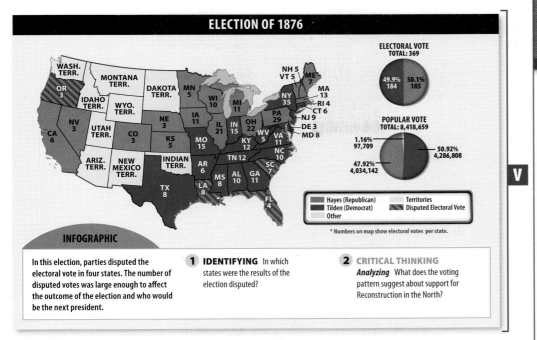

ELECTION OF 1876

INFOGRAPHIC

In this election, parties disputed the electoral vote in four states. The number of disputed votes was large enough to affect the outcome of the election and who would be the next president.

1 IDENTIFYING In which states were the results of the election disputed?

2 CRITICAL THINKING *Analyzing* What does the voting pattern suggest about support for Reconstruction in the North?

The Election of 1876

Republicans attempted to keep control of the White House by choosing Ohio Governor Rutherford B. Hayes as their candidate for president in 1876. Hayes held moderate views on Reconstruction. Republicans hoped he would appeal to voters in both the North and the South.

Hayes ran against Democrat Samuel Tilden, the governor of New York, in a very close election. Neither got a majority of the electoral votes, mainly because of confusing election returns from three Southern states. These states—Florida, South Carolina, and Louisiana—were still under Republican rule. Republicans insisted that many voters in these states favored Hayes, but their votes had not been counted. Congress named a **commission** to decide which candidate should receive the disputed electoral votes. The commission recommended giving them all to Hayes. Doing this would make Hayes president by one electoral vote.

Connections to TODAY

The Election of 2000

A voting dispute in Florida also affected the 2000 presidential election. An extremely close vote count led to a bitter dispute between Republican George W. Bush and Democrat Al Gore over whether and how to recount the ballots. The dispute kept either party from gaining enough electoral votes to win the election. This time, a U.S. Supreme Court ruling helped make Bush the winner and president.

Academic Vocabulary (Tier 2 Words)

commission a group of officials chosen for a specific responsibility

Lesson 4 **509**

MAP

Election of 1876

Analyzing Maps Use the interactive map to discuss the results of the 1876 presidential election. **Ask: What things about the presidential election of 1876 are significant?** *(The election was very close, and its outcome was disputed. A commission and a political deal resolved the issue. The Republican Hayes would be named president. In exchange, the Republicans promised to remove Union troops from the South.)* **What marked the end of Reconstruction?** *(the departure of Union troops from the South in 1877)* **Visual/Spatial**

See page 491F for other online activities.

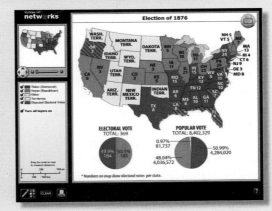

The Post-Reconstruction Era

V Visual Skills

Analyzing Charts Direct students' attention to the chart at the top of the page. Discuss the increase in manufacturing in the South during the 40 years from 1860 to 1900. Have students pick two or three states and calculate the differences between their increases. Then have students show the growth in manufacturing for the states they chose on a graph. **BL** Logical/Mathematical Visual/Spatial

C Critical Thinking Skills

Predicting Consequences Discuss with students President Hayes's withdrawal of federal troops from the South. **Ask: What effect do you think the withdrawal of troops had on the South?** *(Answers may vary but might include improvement of morale among white Southerners, but increased risk of violence and intimidation for African American Southerners.)* Lead a class discussion of the ways in which living under martial law can affect a society that is going through major transitions.

R Reading Skills

Discussing After students read the text, ask them to explain the desire to change Southern agriculture and industry. **Ask:**

- **What did the advocates of the "New South" envision?** *(replacing cotton plantations with smaller farms that grew a greater variety of crops)*
- **What actually occurred?** *(When estates were divided, the land often went to sharecropping and tenant farming, neither of which was profitable.)*
- **Why do you think that advocates of Southern agriculture used the phrase "New South" to promote their ideas?** *(They wanted to make the idea sound positive and to ignite the patriotism of Southerners. They were also connecting with the idea that the South would "rise again" but this time economically.)*

ECONOMICS SKILL

INDUSTRY IN THE NEW SOUTH

Before the Civil War, the backbone of the Southern economy was agriculture. It remained so through the rest of the nineteenth century, though industry in the region made dramatic gains.

1 CALCULATING About how many more manufacturing establishments did Florida have in 1900 than in 1860?

2 CRITICAL THINKING
Analyzing Which two Southern states experienced the greatest growth in manufacturing between 1860 and 1900? Explain.

State	MANUFACTURING IN THE SOUTHERN STATES 1860–1900*		
	1860	1880	1900
Alabama	1,459	2,070	5,602
Arkansas	518	1,202	4,794
Florida	185	426	2,056
Georgia	1,890	3,593	7,504
Louisiana	1,744	1,553	4,350
Mississippi	976	1,479	4,772
North Carolina	3,689	3,802	7,226
South Carolina	1,230	2,078	3,762
Tennessee	2,572	4,326	8,016
Texas	983	2,996	12,289
TOTAL	**15,246**	**23,525**	**60,371**

* Number of manufacturing establishments

To ensure that Congress accepted this **outcome,** Republicans made many promises to the Democrats. One of these was a pledge to withdraw the troops who had been stationed in the South since the end of the Civil War. Shortly after Hayes took office in 1877, the last troops left the South.

Rise of the "New South"

By the 1880s, forward-looking Southerners were convinced that their region must develop an industrial economy. They argued that the South had lost the Civil War because its industry did not match the North's. Atlanta newspaper editor Henry Grady headed a group that urged Southerners to "out-Yankee the Yankees" and build a "New South." This "New South" would have industries based on the region's coal, iron, tobacco, cotton, and lumber resources. Southerners would create this new economy by embracing a spirit of hard work and regional pride.

Southern industry made great gains in the 1880s. Textile mills sprang up across the region. The American Tobacco Company, developed largely by James Duke of North Carolina, came to control nearly all of the tobacco manufacturing in the country. By 1890, the South produced nearly 20 percent of the nation's

---

Reading **HELP**DESK **CCSS**

poll tax a tax a person must pay in order to vote

Academic Vocabulary *(Tier 2 Words)*

outcome the effect or result of an action or event

---

netw⊙rks *Online Teaching Options*

SLIDE SHOW

Industry in the New South

Analyzing Visuals Use the slide show about Southern industry to discuss the growth of an industrial economy in the South. **Ask: What industries would the "New South" be based on?** *(Possible answers: coal, iron, tobacco, cotton, and lumber)* Discuss the growth of the textile industry and the railroad system.
Visual/Spatial

See page 491F for other online activities.

ANSWERS, p. 510

ECONOMICS SKILL

1. almost 2,000 more

2. CRITICAL THINKING Florida and Texas; each had more than 10 times as many manufacturing establishments in 1900 as it had in 1860.

iron and steel. Much of the industry was in Alabama, near deposits of iron ore. In Florida, port cities Jacksonville and Pensacola prospered because of strong demand for lumber and other products.

The South possessed a cheap and reliable supply of labor. A railroad-building boom also helped development. By 1870, the railroad system, destroyed by the war, was nearly rebuilt. Between 1880 and 1890, track mileage more than doubled.

The New South's Rural Economy

In spite of these gains, the South did not develop an industrial economy as strong as the North's. Agriculture remained the South's main economic activity.

Supporters of the New South hoped to promote small, profitable farms that grew a variety of crops instead of relying on cotton. A different economy emerged, however. Many landowners held on to their large estates. When estates were divided, much of the land went to sharecropping and tenant farming. Neither of these activities was profitable.

Debt also caused problems. Poor farmers used credit to buy supplies. Merchants who provided credit also charged high prices, and farmers' debts rose. To repay debts, farmers turned to cash crops. As in the past, the main cash crop was cotton. Higher cotton production drove cotton prices down. Lower prices led farmers to plant even more cotton. The growth of sharecropping and the heavy reliance on a single cash crop helped prevent improvements in the conditions of Southern farmers.

C

R

By 1880, a third of the South's farmers were sharecroppers or tenant farmers, systems that helped keep African Americans in a condition not much better than slavery.

☑ **PROGRESS CHECK**

Describing Why did Southern industry grow in the late 1800s?

A Divided Society

GUIDING QUESTION *Why did freedom for African Americans become a distant dream after Reconstruction ended?*

As Reconstruction ended, African Americans' dreams for justice faded. Laws passed by the redeemer governments denied Southern African Americans many of their newly won rights.

Voting Restrictions

The Fifteenth Amendment barred a state from denying someone the right to vote because of race. White Southern leaders found ways to get around the amendment. One way was by requiring a **poll tax,** a fee required for voting. Many African Americans could not afford to pay the tax, so they could not vote.

The Granger Collection, NYC

C Critical Thinking Skills

Determining Cause and Effect Clarify with students what the effects were of dividing up large plantation estates into smaller farms. **Ask:** What were some of the results of this? *(Most of the land went toward sharecropping or tenant farming, which was not profitable for the landowners or the farmers.)* Discuss with students the differences between what supporters of a small farm system hoped would happen and what actually did happen.

R Reading Skills

Describing Before students read, ensure that students understand that sharecroppers are also tenant farmers—they pay to farm another's land—but a particular type of tenant farmer who pays rent with a percentage of the crops. After students have read the passage, **ask:** What problems did this system create for sharecroppers? *(Farmers became reliant on one cash crop in an attempt to pay their debts and then spiraled into more debt when that one crop, cotton, did not always do well in the market.)* Tell students that sharecropping became widespread in the South during and after Reconstruction. **AL** **ELL**

Sharecropping

Analyzing Primary Sources Use the interactive primary source excerpt of the sharecropper contract to discuss how one-sided this contract is in the landowners' favor. Point out how unforeseen events—a bad crop, illness, a drop in crop prices—could force the sharecropper to farm additional years. Sharecroppers often became locked into an endless cycle of debt. **Ask:** How did this make sharecropping much like slavery? *(Through debt, sharecroppers were bound to their landlords like enslaved people.)* **BL** Visual/Spatial

See page 491F for other online activities.

ANSWER, p. 511

☑ **PROGRESS CHECK** Leaders favored industrial development; the South had abundant resources and a cheap and reliable labor supply. A railroad boom also contributed.

R1 Reading Skills

Summarizing After students have read the text, direct them to make a list summarizing ways white Southerners denied African Americans their right to vote. **Ask: What are three things Southern whites used to limit African Americans' voting rights, and how did each work?** *(Poll taxes made voting unaffordable. Literacy tests proved impossible for people who were uneducated. Grandfather clauses ruled out freed slaves or their offspring because African Americans could not vote before 1867.)* Be sure students understand that these voting restrictions further oppressed African Americans.

R2 Reading Skills

Explaining Have students use evidence from the text to explain the creation of the Jim Crow laws and how they worked. **Ask: What segregation law was upheld by the Supreme Court?** *(Plessy v. Ferguson)* Discuss the idea of "separate but equal," how separate facilities were hardly equal for African Americans, and the long-term impact of segregation.

C Critical Thinking Skills

Making Connections Remind students of the concept of "due process of law" introduced in Lesson 3. **Ask: If someone who is suspected of a crime is lynched, what has happened to due process of law?** *(Victims of lynchings were denied due process of law, both in terms of their own rights and because the lynch mobs were not brought to justice.)* Discuss with students the effects of state-sanctioned violence on a democratic society. **BL**

After Reconstruction, white Southern leaders used a variety of means to deny African Americans their right to vote.

Another means of denying voting rights was the **literacy test** (LIH·tuh·ruh·see TEHST). This approach required potential voters to read and explain difficult parts of state constitutions or the federal Constitution. Because most Southern African Americans had little education, literacy tests prevented many from voting.

Both poll taxes and literacy tests also kept some whites from voting. To prevent this, some states passed **grandfather clauses** (GRAND·fah·thuhr KLAHZ·ihz). These laws allowed people to vote if their fathers or grandfathers had voted before Reconstruction. Because African Americans could not vote until 1867, they were excluded. Such laws and the constant threat of violence caused African American voting to decline sharply.

Jim Crow Laws

By the late 1800s, segregation had also become common across the South. **Segregation** (seh·grih·GAY·shuhn) is separation of the races. Southern states passed so-called Jim Crow laws that required African Americans and whites to be separated in almost every public place. In 1896 the Supreme Court upheld segregation laws in *Plessy* v. *Ferguson*. The case involved a Louisiana law that required separate sections on trains for African Americans and whites. The Court ruled that segregation was legal as long as African Americans had access to public places equal to those of whites.

In practice, the separate facilities for African Americans were far from equal. Southern states spent much more money on schools and other facilities for whites than on those for African Americans. Still, this "separate but equal" doctrine gave legal support to segregation for more than 50 years.

Violence against African Americans also rose. One form of violence was **lynching** (LIHN·cheeng), in which angry mobs killed people by hanging them. Some African Americans were lynched because they were suspected of crimes—others because they did not act as whites thought they should.

Reading **HELP**DESK **CCSS**

literacy test a method used to prevent African Americans from voting by requiring prospective voters to read and write at a specified level

grandfather clause a device that allowed persons to vote if their fathers or grandfathers had voted before Reconstruction began

segregation the separation or isolation of a race, class, or group

lynching putting to death by the illegal action of a mob

512 *The Reconstruction Era*

netw⊙rks *Online Teaching Options*

IMAGE

Disenfranchisement

Defining Display the image of African Americans being turned away from a polling place to discuss disenfranchisement. Click on the image and have a volunteer read the definition of disenfranchisement. **AL** **ELL** Visual/Spatial

See page 491F for other online activities.

McGraw net**w⊙rks** Disenfranchisement

Disenfranchisement refers to actions that prevent people from voting. The Fifteenth Amendment prohibited disenfranchisement on the basis of race or prior enslavement. Southern states who were still against voting rights for all Americans came up with a variety of ways to keep African Americans away from the polls. These included acts of violence, charging a poll tax, stuffing ballot boxes, and requiring voters to take a literacy test.

Exodusters and Buffalo Soldiers

Formerly enslaved people began to leave the South during Reconstruction. They called themselves "Exodusters." This name came from the biblical book of Exodus, which describes the Israelites' escape from slavery in Egypt.

During the exodus of the 1870s, more than 20,000 African Americans migrated to Kansas. They hoped their journey would take them far from the poverty that they experienced in the South. Other African Americans escaped the South by becoming soldiers. They served in segregated army units and fought in the western Indian Wars from 1867 until 1896. According to legend, the men were called "buffalo soldiers" by the Apache and Cheyenne. The soldiers adopted the name as a sign of honor and respect. Units of Buffalo Soldiers answered the nation's call to arms not only in the West, but also in Cuba, the Philippines, Hawaii, and Mexico.

Reconstruction's Impact

Reconstruction was a success in some ways and a failure in others. It helped the South rebuild its economy. Yet much of the South remained agricultural and economically poor. African Americans gained greater equality and shared power in government, but their advances did not last. In the words of the great African American writer and civil rights leader W.E.B. Du Bois, "The slave went free; stood a brief moment in the sun; then moved back again toward slavery." Yet the seeds of freedom and equality had been planted. For a long time, African Americans struggled to gain their full rights. **W**

✅ **PROGRESS CHECK**

Explaining What were Jim Crow laws?

LESSON 4 REVIEW (CCSS)

Review Vocabulary (Tier 3 Words)

1. Explain the meaning of the terms by using them in a sentence. RH.6–8.4

   a. literacy test   b. poll tax

2. What was the purpose of grandfather clauses? RH.6–8.4

Answer the Guiding Questions

3. *Describing* In what ways was the economy of the New South different from—and similar to—the economy of the past? RH.6–8.5

4. *Summarizing* How did Democrats regain control of Southern governments from the Republican Party? RH.6–8.2

5. *Explaining* Why did freedom for African Americans become a distant dream after Reconstruction ended? RH.6–8.2

6. INFORMATIVE/EXPLANATORY How did the South after Reconstruction compare to the South before the Civil War? Write a paragraph that answers this question. WHST.6–8.2, WHST.6–8.4

Lesson 4   **513**

LESSON 4 REVIEW ANSWERS

1. Possible answer: If African Americans could not read and had no money, literacy tests and poll taxes would keep them from voting.

2. Grandfather clauses were used to prevent African Americans from voting while providing a way for poor and uneducated whites to vote.

3. Answers should include that although industrial growth had taken place in the "new" South, the main economic activity of the South was still agriculture, as it had been before.

4. Answers should summarize lesson information about how Democrats took control of Southern governments. Possible responses: Americans lost confidence in the Republican Party after scandals and an economic

depression, and more voters began supporting the Democrats.

5. Possible answer: Racism, unfair laws, violence, and discrimination all grew worse after Reconstruction. This prevented African Americans from exercising their rights, kept them separate from whites, and controlled them through fear and intimidation.

6. Answers will vary but should note the end of slavery and the industrialization that characterized the New South as the major differences, but that despite their new-found freedom, conditions for African Americans were little changed once Reconstruction ended.

R1 **Reading Skills**

Explaining Ask students to use details from the text to explain why African Americans who migrated to Kansas were called "Exodusters." Discuss the troubles these people were hoping to escape. **ELL**

R2 **Reading Skills**

Defining Have a volunteer read the text that describes the army units called "buffalo soldiers." Discuss that these segregated army units fought in the western Indian Wars, and this name was adopted as a sign of honor. If time permits, have students do research on other segregated army units that fought in the nation's future wars and present their research to the class. **Verbal/Linguistic**

W **Writing Skills**

Narrative Have students turn back to the words of Frederick Douglass in *The Story Matters* on the chapter opener page. **Ask: Would Douglass consider Reconstruction to be a success or a "miserable failure"?** Have students write their answer in Douglass's own voice, in the form of a narrative speech that Douglass might give in reaction to events during Reconstruction. If time permits, you may want to encourage students to refer to the actual words of Douglass, which they can find online or in the library. **BL** **Verbal/Linguistic**

Have students complete the Lesson 4 Review.

CLOSE & REFLECT

Listing Work with students to develop a list that analyzes the successes, failures, and impacts of the Reconstruction Era. Read the quote in the textbook by W.E.B. DuBois to students, and analyze the quote in relation to the hardships and successes in the fight for civil rights. **Ask: Do you think Reconstruction was successful?** *(Answers may vary.)*

ANSWER, p. 513

✅ **PROGRESS CHECK** Florida and Texas; each had more than 10 times as many manufacturing establishments in 1900 as it had in 1860.

CHAPTER REVIEW ACTIVITY

Write "to bind up the nation's wounds" on the board. Tell students that this is what Abraham Lincoln thought needed to be done once the Civil War was over. Work with students to categorize strategies used during Reconstruction according to which were effective and which were not effective in healing the nation.

Lead a class discussion in which students evaluate Reconstruction from the perspective of healing a wounded nation. **Ask: Did Reconstruction bind up the nation's wounds?** *(Students' answers will vary but should reflect that even for the 12 years when Reconstruction was supposed to be taking place, old and new disagreements kept the nation from binding up its wounds. When Reconstruction ended, the anger and bitterness made healing the nation even more difficult.)*

Strategies "to bind up the nation's wounds"	
Effective	Not Effective

REVIEW THE ENDURING UNDERSTANDING

Review the chapter's Enduring Understanding with students.

- *People, places, and ideas change over time.*

Now pose the following questions in a class discussion to apply this enduring understanding to the chapter.

How did the plans of Presidents Lincoln and Johnson differ from the plans that the Radical Republicans had for Reconstruction? *(Lincoln wanted to allow states to form a new state government once 10% of voters had taken an oath of loyalty to the Union and once the state had adopted a new constitution banning slavery. The Radical Republicans wanted to require a majority of white male adults to take the loyalty oath, ban former Confederates from holding public office or voting for delegates to a state constitutional convention, and require that slavery be banned. Johnson was opposed to equal rights for African Americans and wanted to pardon most Confederates.)*

How did the Constitution change during Reconstruction? *(The Fourteenth and Fifteenth Amendments were passed, making all persons citizens if they were born or naturalized in the United States, mandating due process of law and equal protection under the law, and banning state and federal governments from denying citizens the right to vote based on "race, color, or previous condition of servitude.")*

Write your answers on a separate piece of paper.

1 **Exploring the Essential Question**   WHST.6–8.1, WHST.6–8.10
INFORMATIVE/EXPLANATORY Would Reconstruction have taken a different course if Lincoln had not been assassinated? Write an essay to explain your answer.

2 **21st Century Skills**   RH.6–8.5, WHST.6–8.1
INFORMATION LITERACY Review this chapter and draw a time line of key events during Reconstruction. Identify the event that you think had the most impact and write a short essay justifying your choice.

3 **Thinking Like a Historian**   RH.6–8.5
MAKING COMPARISONS How were poll taxes and literacy tests similar? How were they different?

4 **Visual Literacy**   RH.6–8.7, WHST.6–8.4
ANALYZING PHOTOGRAPHS Look at the image of workers processing tobacco. Write a caption for the image that explains what is happening and how it reflects the new realities of the post-Civil War South.

CORBIS

514   *The Reconstruction Era*

By the time that Reconstruction was over, had the goals of the Radical Republicans and others who advocated racial equality been achieved? *(No, by the end of Reconstruction the early gains in the area of racial equality had been rolled back again, and a new system of racial segregation, Jim Crow laws, violence, and intimidation was in place.)*

ACTIVITIES ANSWERS

Exploring the Essential Question

1 Students' essays should recognize and cite examples of the political, economic, and social changes that Reconstruction brought to the South and how they all might have been different had Lincoln not been killed.

21st Century Skills

2 Students' time lines should include the key events from the era, including elections, laws passed, and so on. Essays should be factually accurate and demonstrate reasoned judgment as well as an understanding of the political, social, and/or economic dynamics of the Reconstruction Era.

REVIEW THE GUIDING QUESTIONS

Choose the best answer for each question.

RH.6–8.2

1 Which was a reason that Northern leaders disagreed over the South rejoining the Union?

A. Some leaders wanted the South to pay for damage done during the Civil War.

B. Some leaders wanted harsher treatment of the South for leaving the Union.

C. Some leaders wanted to keep slavery legal in the South.

D. Some leaders felt that allowing Southern states back into the Union would delay westward expansion.

RH.6–8.1

2 Which of the following protected the rights of African Americans in the South?

F. the Civil Rights Act of 1866   H. Jim Crow laws

G. black codes   I. sharecropping and tenant farming

RH.6–8.4

3 Which of the following was a method used by state governments to prevent African Americans from voting?

A. the Ten Percent Plan

B. the Wade-Davis bill

C. the Freedmen's Bureau

D. literacy tests

RH.6–8.1

4 Which of the following brought major improvement to the lives of African Americans in the South?

F. sharecropping

G. the Fourteenth Amendment

H. segregation laws

I. redeemer governments

RH.6–8.2

5 How did the scandals surrounding the Grant administration and the Panic of 1873 affect politics in the United States?

A. Democrats regained control of Southern governments.

B. Republicans retained control of Southern governments.

C. President Grant was impeached.

D. Jim Crow laws were enforced.

RH.6–8.4

6 For many African Americans in the South, sharecropping was

F. forbidden to them.

G. highly profitable.

H. more desirable that factory work.

I. not much better than slavery.

515

CHAPTER ASSESSMENT
Review the Guiding Questions

1 **B** The issue of the South paying for war damages did not come up. The slavery issue was decided by the war. Westward expansion was not an issue.

2 **F** The Civil Rights Act of 1866 was a response to black codes. Jim Crow laws were segregation laws that were passed later in the century. Sharecropping and tenant farming were economic arrangements that were generally harmful to African Americans.

3 **D** The Ten Percent Plan was Lincoln's plan for Reconstruction. The Freedmen's Bureau was established to help African Americans adjust to life after slavery. The Wade-Davis bill was Congress's alternative to Lincoln's Reconstruction plan.

4 **G** The Fourteenth Amendment gave full citizenship to all people born in the United States. The sharecropping system and segregation laws were detrimental to African Americans. Redeemer governments were Southern state governments opposed to equal rights for African Americans.

5 **A** Grant was a Republican, so the scandals and Panic benefited Democrats.

6 **I** Sharecropping was not forbidden to African Americans. It was not profitable either. Factory work paid better. Most African Americans found that sharecropping was not much better than slavery.

Thinking Like a Historian

3 Poll taxes levied a tax on voters; literacy tests forced prospective voters to show they could read. Both were aimed at limiting the voting rights of African Americans; both also blocked some poor whites from voting.

Visual Literacy

4 Captions will vary but should recognize that these workers were all probably formerly enslaved and that the formerly enslaved people provided the South with a large number of workers who were willing to work for low wages, which allowed for expansion of Southern industries like this one.

Analyzing Documents

7 **A** The laws provided schools and textbooks for African Americans, so choice B is incorrect. Choices C and D were often the effect of such laws, but they were not the laws' stated intent. The intent was to enforce separation of the races in schools.

8 **G** The law provided that textbooks not be exchanged between white and African American schools. It did not deny African American schools textbooks, new textbooks, nor the money to buy them.

Short Response

9 Bruce thought most African Americans would earn their living as farmers in the South, but he also saw that a number would seek their places in the fields of letters, arts, science, and the professions, and that others would be employed in mechanical pursuits.

10 Bruce expressed the belief that African Americans loved their country.

Extended Response

11 Answers will vary but should demonstrate reasoned judgment and show an understanding of the dynamics of the Reconstruction Era. Students should support their assessment with facts from the chapter.

CHAPTER 18 Assessment (continued)

DBQ ANALYZING DOCUMENTS

The following are examples of Jim Crow laws in the South.

"The schools for white children and the schools for negro children shall be conducted separately." (Florida)

"Books shall not be interchangeable between the white and colored schools, but shall continue to be used by the race first using them." (North Carolina)

—Martin Luther King, Jr., National Historic Site

RH.6–8.6
7 **Specifying** Which statement best represents the purpose of these laws?

A. The laws forced separation of the races.

B. The laws denied African Americans any access to schools.

C. The laws required inferior facilities for African Americans.

D. The laws made it difficult for African Americans to get an education.

RH.6–8.2
8 **Analyzing** Which of the following was an effect of the North Carolina law?

F. African American schools were not permitted to have textbooks.

G. White schools could not give textbooks to African American schools.

H. Only white schools received new textbooks.

I. No money was set aside to buy textbooks for African American schools.

SHORT RESPONSE

"I have confidence ... in the endurance, capacity and destiny of my people [African Americans]. We will ... seek our places, sometimes in the field of letters, arts, science and the professions. More frequently mechanical pursuits will attract and elicit our efforts; more still of my people will find employment ... as the cultivators of the soil. The bulk of this people—by surroundings, habits, adaptation, and choice will continue to find their homes in the South. ... Whatever our ultimate position in the ... republic ... we will not forget our instincts for freedom nor our love for country."

—Senator Blanche K. Bruce, from a speech in 1876

RH.6–8.2, WHST.6–8.4
9 How did Bruce expect most African Americans to earn a living?

RH.6–8.6, WHST.6–8.4
10 According to Bruce, how did African Americans feel about their country?

EXTENDED RESPONSE

WHST.6–8.1, WHST.6–8.9
11 **Informative/Explanatory** What do you think was Reconstruction's greatest success? What was its greatest failure? Explain your answer.

Need Extra Help?

If You've Missed Question	**1**	**2**	**3**	**4**	**5**	**6**	**7**	**8**	**9**	**10**	**11**
Review Lesson	1	2	4	2	4	3	4	4	3	3	1-4

---

networks   *Online Teaching Options*

Help students use the Skills Builder resources

Your students can practice important 21st Century skills such as geography, reading, writing, and critical thinking by using resources found in the Skills Builder tab of the online Student Learning Center. Resources include templates, handbooks, and slide shows. These same resources are also available in the Resource Library of the Teacher Lesson Center.

GLOSSARY/GLOSARIO

- Content vocabulary are words that relate to American history content.
- Words that have an asterisk (*) are academic vocabulary. They help you understand your school subjects.
- All vocabulary words are **boldfaced** or highlighted in yellow in your textbook.

abandon • amend

ENGLISH	A	ESPAÑOL
abandon to give up; to leave behind (p. 178; p. 459)		***abandonar*** rendirse; dejar atrás (pág. 178; pág. 459)
abolitionist person who sought the end of slavery in the United States in the early and mid-1800s (pp. 408–409)		**abolicionista** persona que buscaba el fin de la esclavitud a principios y mediados del siglo XIX en Estados Unidos (págs. 408–409)
academy a school or college for special training (pp. 506–507)		***academia*** escuela o universidad donde se brinda enseñanza especializada (págs. 506–507)
access a way into something or someplace (pp. 348–349)		***acceso*** entrada a un objeto o un lugar (págs. 348–349)
accumulate to build up or collect (p. 250)		***acumular*** juntar o reunir (pág. 250)
acquire to get possession or control of (pp. 31–32)		***adquirir*** tomar posesión o control de algo (págs. 31–32)
adapt to change in response to a new set of conditions (p. 97)		***adaptarse*** cambiar como respuesta a una nueva serie de condiciones (pág. 97)
adjust to become more suited to new conditions (p. 496)		***ajustarse*** hacerse más apropiado para una nueva condición (pág. 496)
administer manage; direct (p. 445)		***administrar*** gerenciar; dirigir (pág. 445)
administrate to carry out (p. 213)		***administrar*** llevar a cabo (pág. 213)
advocate to support (pp. 126–127)		***defender*** respaldar (págs. 126–127)
aid to help (p. 152)		***ayudar*** auxiliar (pág. 152)
alien a person living in a country who is not a citizen of that country (p. 259)		**extranjero** persona que vive en un país sin ser ciudadano de ese país (pág. 259)
allay to reduce in strength (p. 91)		***mitigar*** perder fuerza (pág. 91)
alliance a partnership; system in which countries agree to defend each other or to advance common causes (p. 102)		**alianza** sociedad; sistema en el cual los países acuerdan defenderse mutuamente o promover causas comunes (pág. 102)
alter to change (pp. 38–39)		***alterar*** cambiar (págs. 38–39)
ambush an attack in which the attacker hides and surprises the enemy (p. 168)		**emboscada** ofensiva en el que el atacante se esconde y sorprende al enemigo (pág. 168)
amend to change or revise (p. 188)		***enmendar*** cambiar o modificar (pág. 188)

amendment a change, correction, or improvement added to a document (pp. 198–199)

amnesty the granting of a pardon to a large number of persons (p. 495)

*****animosity** hostility; ill will; hatred (p. 127)

annex to add a territory to one's own territory (pp. 356–357)

apprentice a person who learns a trade from a skilled craftsperson (p. 97)

*****approach** to get closer to something (p. 123)

archaeology the study of material remains of ancient peoples (pp. 4–5)

armada a fleet of warships (p. 50)

arsenal a place to store weapons and military equipment (p. 437)

artifact a tool, weapon, or other object left behind by early peoples (pp. 4–5)

astrolabe an instrument used to plan a course, using the stars (pp. 30–31)

*****author** writer of books, articles, or other works (pp. 406–407)

*****authority** the power to influence or command thought, opinion, or behavior (p. 274)

enmienda cambio, corrección o mejora que se hace a un documento (págs. 198–199)

amnistía perdón otorgado a un gran número de personas (pág. 495)

*****animosidad** hostilidad; antipatía; odio (pág. 127)

anexar agregar un territorio al propio (págs. 356–357)

aprendiz persona que aprende un oficio de un artesano experto (pág. 97)

*****aproximarse** acercarse a algo (pág. 123)

arqueología estudio de los restos materiales de pueblos antiguos (págs. 4–5)

armada flota de barcos de guerra (pág. 50)

arsenal lugar para almacenar armas y equipo militar (pág. 437)

artefacto instrumento, arma u otro objeto dejado por los pueblos primitivos (págs. 4–5)

astrolabio instrumento usado para planear un recorrido valiéndose de las estrellas (págs. 31–32)

*****autor** escritor de libros, artículos u otras obras (págs. 406–407)

*****autoridad** facultad de influir o imponer la forma de pensar, opinar o comportarse (pág. 274)

B

barricade to block off (p. 355)

bicameral having two separate lawmaking chambers (p. 177)

black codes laws passed in the South just after the Civil War aimed at controlling freed men and women, and allowing plantation owners to take advantage of African American workers (pp. 498–499)

blockade actions that keeps a country from communicating and trading with other nations (p. 159)

bond certificate that promises to repay borrowed money with interest by a certain date (pp. 248–249)

boomtown a fast-growing community (p. 366)

barricada bloqueo (pág. 355)

bicameral que tiene dos cámaras legislativas separadas (pág. 177)

códigos negros leyes aprobadas en el Sur después de la Guerra Civil, cuyo objetivo era controlar a los hombres y mujeres libertos, y permitir a los dueños de las plantaciones aprovecharse de los trabajadores afroamericanos (págs. 498–499)

bloqueo acción que evita que un país se comunique y comercie con otras naciones (pág. 159)

bono certificado en el que se promete pagar un préstamo con intereses en una fecha determinada (págs. 248–249)

ciudad en auge comunidad de rápido crecimiento (pág. 366)

border ruffian armed supporter of slavery who crossed the border from Missouri to vote in Kansas during the mid-1850s (p. 432)

bandido de la frontera individuo armado, partidario de la esclavitud, que cruzaba la frontera desde Missouri para votar en Kansas, a mediados de la década de 1850 (pág. 432)

border state state between the North and South that was divided over whether to remain in the Union or join the Confederacy: Delaware, Maryland, Kentucky, and Missouri (pp. 452–453)

estado fronterizo estado entre el Norte y el Sur que estaba dividido con respecto a si debía permanecer en la Unión o incorporarse a la Confederación: Delaware, Maryland, Kentucky y Missouri (págs. 452–453)

bounty reward or payment (p. 470)

recompensa retribución o pago (pág. 470)

boycott to refuse to buy items in order to protest or to force acceptance of one's terms (pp. 114–115)

boicot negarse a comprar productos para protestar o con el fin de presionar para que acepten las condiciones de una persona (págs. 114–115)

*brief short (p. 395)

*breve corto (pág. 395)

bureaucracy a system of government in which specialized tasks are carried out by appointed officials rather than by elected ones (pp. 326–327)

burocracia sistema de gobierno en el cual algunas tareas especializadas son realizadas por funcionarios designados, no elegidos (págs. 326–327)

burgess elected representative to an assembly (pp. 62–63)

burgués representante elegido a una asamblea (págs. 62–63)

C

cabinet a group of advisors to a president (p. 247)

gabinete grupo de asesores de un presidente (pág. 247)

canal an artificial waterway (pp. 304–305)

canal vía fluvial artificial (págs. 304–305)

*capable skillful (p. 418)

*capaz hábil (pág. 418)

cape a point of land that sticks out into water, much like a peninsula (p. 36)

cabo punta de tierra que sobresale en el agua, semejante a una península (pág. 36)

capital money or other resources used to create wealth (p. 298)

capital dinero y demás recursos usados para generar riquezas (pág. 298)

carbon dating a scientific method of determining the age of an artifact (pp. 6–7)

datación por carbono método científico para determinar la edad de un artefacto (págs. 6–7)

cash crop a crop raised for sale in markets (p. 85)

cultivo para la venta cultivo realizado para su venta en el mercado (pág. 85)

casualty a soldier who is killed, wounded, captured, or missing in battle (p. 460)

baja soldado que es asesinado, herido, capturado o desaparecido en combate (pág. 460)

caucus a meeting of members of a political party to choose candidates for upcoming elections (p. 258)

asamblea partidista reunión de miembros de un partido político para elegir candidatos a las próximas elecciones (pág. 258)

cede to transfer control of something (p. 314)

ceder transferir el control de algo (pág. 314)

census the official count of a population (pp. 302–303)

censo conteo oficial de una población (págs. 302–303)

Glossary/Glosario

Glossary/Glosario

*channel a long, narrow gutter or groove (p. 16)

charter a document granting the holder the right to settle a colony (p. 61)

checks and balances a system by which each branch of government limits the powers of other branches so that one branch does not become too powerful (p. 197)

circumnavigate to travel completely around something (pp. 40–41)

civic virtue the democratic ideas, practices, and values that are at the heart of citizenship in a free society (p. 100)

civil disobedience refusing to obey laws considered unjust as a nonviolent way to push for change (pp. 406–407)

civil war conflict between citizens of the same country (p. 432)

civilization highly developed society (pp. 8–9)

clan a group of people who have a common ancestor (p. 20)

classical related to the culture of ancient Greece and Rome (p. 29)

*clause a special condition in a formal document (pp. 180–181)

clipper ship a fast ship with sleek hulls and tall sails that "clipped" time from long journeys (p. 377)

coeducation the teaching of male and female students together (p. 417)

*commission a group of officials chosen for a specific responsibility (p. 509)

committee of correspondence an organization that spread political ideas and information through Britain's American colonies (p. 117)

*community group of people who live in the same area (p. 383)

compass an instrument that shows the direction of magnetic north (pp. 30–31)

*complex highly detailed (pp. 8–9)

*compromise a settlement of a dispute or disagreement reached by each side giving up some of what it wants in order to reach an agreement (p. 190; p. 250)

*canal surco largo y estrecho (pág. 16)

carta constitucional documento que da al tenedor el derecho a establecer una colonia (pág. 61)

equilibrio de poderes sistema en el cual cada rama del gobierno limita los poderes de las otras ramas de manera que ninguna se vuelva demasiado poderosa (pág. 197)

circunnavegar viajar rodeando por completo algo (págs. 40–41)

virtud cívica ideas, prácticas y valores democráticos que son fundamentales para la ciudadanía en una sociedad libre (pág. 100)

desobediencia civil negativa a obedecer las leyes que se consideran injustas como una forma no violenta de presionar para que haya un cambio (págs. 406–407)

guerra civil conflicto entre ciudadanos del mismo país (pág. 432)

civilización sociedad altamente desarrollada (págs. 8–9)

clan grupo de personas que tienen un ancestro común (pág. 20)

clásico relativo a la cultura de la Grecia antigua y Roma (pág. 29)

*cláusula condición especial en un documento formal (págs. 180–181)

navío rápido barco rápido con cascos pulidos y mástiles altos que "ahorraba" tiempo en viajes largos (pág. 377)

coeducación sistema en el que se enseña a hombres y mujeres en la misma institución (pág. 417)

*comisión grupo de funcionarios escogidos para una responsabilidad específica (pág. 509)

comité de correspondencia organización que difundía ideas políticas e información en las colonias americanas de Gran Bretaña (pág. 117)

*comunidad grupo de personas que viven en la misma área (pág. 383)

brújula instrumento que muestra la dirección del norte magnético (págs. 30–31)

*complejo sumamente detallado (págs. 8–9)

*compromiso resolución de una disputa o discrepancia a la que se llega cuando cada parte renuncia a algo de lo que desea para llegar a un acuerdo (pág. 190; pág. 250)

*concurrence agreement (p. 193)

concurrent power power shared by the states and federal government (p. 207)

conquistador Spanish explorer in the Americas during the 1500s (pp. 42–43)

*consequence effect or result of (p. 388)

constitution a detailed written plan for a government; a list of basic laws that support a government (p. 76; p. 367)

*contact when two or more groups or objects come together (pp. 43–44)

*contradict to go against or state the opposite (p. 208)

*contrast to compare in terms of differences (p. 454)

*convention a formal or official meeting (p. 187)

*convert to change from one belief, form, or use to another (p. 102)

corruption dishonest or illegal actions (p. 505)

cotton gin a machine that removes seeds from cotton fiber (p. 297)

*credit a loan, or the ability to pay for a good or service at a future time rather than at the time of the purchase (p. 506)

Crusade one of a series of expeditions Europeans made to regain control of Christian holy sites in the Middle East from the A.D. 1000s to the 1200s (pp. 28–29)

culture a people's shared values, beliefs, traditions, and behaviors (pp. 6–7)

customs duty tax collected on goods that are imported (p. 270)

*concurrencia acuerdo (pág. 193)

poder concurrente poder que comparten los gobiernos estatales y el gobierno federal (pág. 207)

conquistador explorador español de América durante el siglo XVI (págs. 42–43)

*consecuencia efecto o resultado (pág. 388)

Constitución plan escrito y detallado de un gobierno; conjunto de leyes básicas que respaldan un gobierno (pág. 76; pág. 367)

*hacer contacto cuando dos o más grupos u objetos se acercan (págs. 43–44)

*contradecir ir en contra o afirmar lo contrario (pág. 208)

*contrastar comparar diferencias (pág. 454)

*convención reunión formal u oficial (pág. 187)

*convertir cambiar de una creencia, forma o uso a otro (pág. 102)

corrupción acciones deshonestas o ilegales (pág. 505)

almarrá máquina que elimina las semillas de la fibra de algodón (pág. 297)

*crédito préstamo, o capacidad de pagar un bien o servicio en el futuro, no en el momento de la compra (pág. 506)

Cruzada una de una serie de expediciones europeas llevadas a cabo para recuperar el control de los lugares sagrados cristianos en el Medio Oriente entre los siglos XI y XIII A.D (págs. 28–29)

cultura valores, creencias, tradiciones y comportamientos que comparte un pueblo (págs. 6–7)

arancel aduanero impuesto que se cobra a los bienes importados (pág. 270)

D

*debate a discussion by opposing points of view (pp. 130–131)

debtor person or country that owes money (pp. 76–77)

decree an order given by a person in authority (p. 355)

*debate controversia en la que se presentan puntos de vista opuestos (págs. 130–131)

*deudor persona o país que debe dinero (págs. 76–77)

decreto orden impartida por una persona que tiene autoridad (pág. 355)

Glossary/Glosario

depreciate to fall in value (p. 182)

depression a period when economic activity slows and unemployment increases (pp. 184–185)

*****desert** to leave without permission or intent to come back (p. 154)

*****devote** to commit oneself or one's resources to something (p. 38)

*****diminish** to reduce, make smaller (pp. 214–215)

*****discipline** the ability to follow rules and procedures (p. 130)

discrimination unfair treatment based on prejudice against a certain group (p. 383)

*****distinct** clearly different from the others (p. 257)

*****distribute** to hand out; spread around (p. 468)

diversity variety, such as of ethnic or national groups (p. 85)

domestic slave trade the trade of enslaved people among states in the United States (p. 388)

*****dominate** to control (p. 74–75)

draft a system of selecting people for required military service (p. 470)

*****dress down** a serious punishment or scolding (p. 473)

due process the legal rules and procedures established by law and guaranteed by the Constitution that the government must observe before depriving a person of life, liberty, or property (p. 214)

E

effigy a mocking figure representing an unpopular individual (pp. 114–115)

Electoral College a group of people named by each state legislature to select the president and vice president (pp. 196–197)

*****element** part of a larger whole (pp. 298–299)

depreciar perder valor (pág. 182)

depresión periodo en el cual la actividad económica disminuye y el desempleo aumenta (págs. 184–185)

*****desertar** abandonar sin permiso ni intención de regresar (pág. 154)

*****dedicar** comprometerse a sí mismo o comprometer los recursos propios en algo (pág. 38)

*****disminuir** reducir, hacer más pequeño (págs. 214–215)

*****disciplina** capacidad de seguir reglas y procedimientos (pág. 130)

discriminación trato injusto basado en un prejuicio contra un grupo determinado (pág. 383)

*****distinto** claramente diferente de los demás (pág. 257)

*****distribuir** entregar; dispersar (pág. 468)

diversidad variedad, por ejemplo de grupos étnicos o nacionales (pág. 85)

comercio interno de esclavos comercio de personas esclavizadas entre los estados de Estados Unidos (pág. 388)

*****dominar** controlar (págs. 74–75)

reclutamiento sistema de selección de personas para el servicio militar obligatorio (pág. 470)

*****reprimenda** castigo o represión severos (pág. 473)

debido proceso reglas y procedimientos establecidos por la ley y que avala la Constitución, que el gobierno debe cumplir antes de privar a una persona de la vida, la libertad o la propiedad (pág. 214)

efigie figura burlesca que representa a un individuo impopular (págs. 114–115)

colegio electoral grupo de personas designado por el órgano legislativo de cada estado con el fin de elegir al presidente y al vicepresidente (págs. 196–197)

*****elemento** parte de un todo (págs. 298–299)

*elephantine having great size (p. 317)

Emancipation Proclamation decree issued by President Abraham Lincoln freeing slaves in those parts of the Confederacy still in rebellion on January 1, 1863 (pp. 463–464)

embargo a prohibition or blocking of trade with a certain country (pp. 280–281)

emigrant person who leaves his or her country to live elsewhere (p. 350)

*emphasis placing of stress or special importance on something (p. 99)

*encounter to meet, come face-to-face with (p. 117; p. 478)

*enforce to apply a rule or law; to carry out by force (p. 67)

enlist to formally join a military force (p. 454)

entrench to place within a trench, or ditch, for defense; to place in a strong defensive position (pp. 474–475)

enumerated power power specifically given Congress in the Constitution (p. 207)

epidemic an illness that affects large numbers of people (pp. 96–97)

equal protection the equal application of the law regardless of a person's race, religion, political beliefs, or other qualities (p. 214)

*establish to set up or create (pp. 353–354)

*estate a large area of land that has one owner (p. 74)

*estimate a rough calculation of a number (pp. 6–7)

*ethnic of or relating to national, tribal, racial, religious, language, or cultural background (p. 70)

*exclude to prevent from being involved in something; to shut out (p. 500)

executive branch the branch of government that executes, or carries out, the law and that is headed by the president (pp. 196–197)

*expand to increase in size or number (pp. 62–63)

---

*elefantino de gran tamaño (pág. 317)

Proclamación de la Emancipación decreto expedido por el presidente Abraham Lincoln el 1o. de enero de 1863 ordenando liberar a los esclavos de las regiones de la Confederación que aún estaban sublevadas (págs. 463–464)

embargo prohibición o bloqueo del comercio con un país determinado (págs. 280–281)

emigrante persona que abandona su país para vivir en otro lugar (pág. 350)

*enfatizar resaltar o dar especial importancia a algo (pág. 99)

*encontrar reunirse, estar frente a frente (pág. 117; pág. 478)

*hacer cumplir aplicar una regla o ley; llevar a cabo una acción mediante el uso de la fuerza (pág. 67)

enlistarse unirse formalmente a una fuerza militar (pág. 454)

atrincherarse situarse dentro de una trinchera, o zanja, para defenderse; ubicarse en una fuerte posición de defensa (págs. 474–475)

poder enumerado poder conferido específicamente al Congreso en la Constitución (pág. 207)

epidemia enfermedad que afecta a un gran número de personas (págs. 96–97)

igualdad ante la ley la misma aplicación de la ley sin importar la raza, la religión, las creencias políticas u otras cualidades (pág. 214)

*establecer instaurar o crear (págs. 353–354)

*finca gran extensión de tierra que tiene un único propietario (pág. 74)

*estimado cálculo aproximado de un número (págs. 6–7)

*étnico perteneciente o relativo al origen nacional, tribal, racial, religioso, lingüístico o cultural (pág. 70)

*excluir evitar involucrarse en algo; dejar fuera (pág. 500)

poder ejecutivo rama del gobierno que ejecuta, o hace cumplir, las leyes y que está encabezada por el presidente (págs. 196–197)

*ampliar aumentar de tamaño o número (págs. 62–63)

Glossary/Glossario

export to sell goods to other countries; a good made in one country and then sold to another (p. 94)

exportar vender bienes a otros países; bien que se produce en un país y se vende a otro (pág. 94)

F

facilitate to help make happen (p. 326)

facilitar ayudar a que suceda (pág. 326)

famine an extreme shortage of food (pp. 384–385)

hambruna escasez extrema de alimentos (págs. 384–385)

favorite son a candidate for national office who has support mostly from his home state (pp. 324–325)

hijo predilecto candidato para un cargo nacional que tiene el respaldo de su estado de origen (págs. 324–325)

*federal relating to a national government (pp. 330–331)

*federal relativo al gobierno nacional (págs. 330–331)

federalism a form of government in which power is divided between the federal, or national, government and state government (p. 195)

federalismo forma de gobierno en la cual el poder se divide entre el gobierno federal o nacional y el gobierno estatal (pág. 195)

federation a government that links and unites different groups (p. 19)

federación gobierno que vincula y une a diferentes grupos (pág. 19)

flank the side or edge of a military formation (p. 475)

flanco lado o borde de una formación militar (pág. 475)

forty-niner fortune seeker who came to California during the Gold Rush of 1849 (pp. 365–366)

los del cuarenta y nueve buscadores de fortuna que llegaron a California durante la Fiebre del Oro de 1849 (págs. 365–366)

*found to start; to establish (p. 46)

*fundar iniciar; establecer (pág.46)

free enterprise a type of economy where people and businesses are free to buy, sell, and produce whatever they want, with a minimum of government intervention (p. 298)

libre empresa tipo de economía en el cual las personas y las empresas son libres de comprar, vender y producir lo que quieren, con una intervención gubernamental mínima (pág. 298)

frigate a warship (p. 286)

fragata barco de guerra (pág. 286)

fugitive person who is running away from legal authority (p. 430)

fugitivo persona que se encuentra huyendo de las autoridades (pág. 430)

*function to be in action; to operate (pp. 71–72)

*funcionar estar en acción; operar (págs. 71–72)

G

*goal something one is trying to accomplish (p. 288)

*meta algo que se trata de alcanzar (pág. 288)

grandfather clause part of southern state constitutions after the Civil War that placed high literacy and property requirements on voters whose fathers and grandfathers did not vote before 1867 (p. 512)

cláusula del abuelo parte de las constituciones estatales sureñas después de la Guerra Civil que fijaba exigentes requisitos de alfabetismo y propiedad a los electores cuyos padres y abuelos no votaban antes de 1867 (pág. 512)

H

habeas corpus court order that requires police to bring a prisoner to court to explain why they are holding the person (pp. 469–470)

hábeas corpus orden judicial que exige que la policía traiga a un prisionero ante un tribunal para explicar por qué ha sido detenido (págs. 469–470)

headright a 50-acre grant of land given to colonial settlers who paid their own way (pp. 62–63)

concesión de tierras por cabeza 50 acres de tierra que se entregaban a los colonos, quienes pagaban a su manera (págs. 62–63)

*heyday the peak of one's strength (p. 317)

*apogeo cima de la fortaleza de una persona (pág. 317)

hieroglyphics a form of writing that uses symbols or pictures to represent things, ideas, and sounds (p. 9)

jeroglífico forma de escritura que usa símbolos o imágenes que representan cosas, ideas y sonidos (pág. 9)

*hinder to prevent (p. 421)

*dificultar evitar (pág. 421)

I

immigration the permanent movement of people into a country from other countries (pp. 96–97)

inmigración desplazamiento permanente hacia un país de personas de otros países (págs. 96–97)

immunity resistance of an organism to infection or disease (p. 43)

inmunidad resistencia de un organismo a infecciones y enfermedades (pág. 43)

*immutable does not change (pp. 358–359)

*inmutable que no cambia (págs. 358–359)

*impact an effect (p. 160)

*impacto efecto (pág. 160)

impeach to formally charge a public official with misconduct in office (p. 502)

recusar denunciar formalmente a un funcionario público por mala conducta en el ejercicio de su cargo (pág. 502)

implied power authority not specifically mentioned in the Constitution but suggested in its language (pp. 210–211)

poder implícito autoridad que no se menciona específicamente en la Constitución pero se sugiere en su redacción (págs. 210–211)

import to bring in goods from foreign countries (pp. 94–95)

importar traer productos de otros países (págs. 94–95)

*impose to force on others (p. 93)

*imponer obligar a otros (pág. 93)

impressment seizing people against their will and forcing them to serve in the military or other public service (p. 254)

leva reclutamiento de personas contra su voluntad para obligarlas a servir en el Ejército o en otra entidad pública (pág. 254)

*incorporate to include, absorb (pp. 368–369)

*incorporar incluir, absorber (págs. 368–369)

indentured servant laborer who agrees to work without pay for a certain period of time in exchange for passage to America (pp. 73–74)

sirviente por contrato trabajador que acuerda trabajar sin un salario durante cierto tiempo a cambio de transporte hacia América (págs. 73–74)

*infallibly without fail (p. 127)

*infaliblemente sin falla (pág. 127)

Glossary/Glosario

inflation when it takes more and more money to buy the same amount of goods; a continuous rise in prices of goods and services (p. 156)

inflación cuando se necesita cada vez más dinero para comprar la misma cantidad de bienes; aumento continuo en el precio de bienes y servicios (pág. 156)

*innovation a new development or invention (pp. 376–377)

*innovación nuevo desarrollo o invento (págs. 376–377)

*institution an organization that has an important purpose in society (pp. 336–337)

*institución organización que tiene un propósito importante en la sociedad (págs. 336–337)

integrate to unite, or to blend into a united whole (pp. 506–507)

integrar unir o mezclar en una unidad (págs. 506–507)

*intense very strong (pp. 308–309)

*intenso muy fuerte (págs. 308–309)

interchangeable part a part of a machine or device that can be replaced by another, identical part (p. 297)

parte intercambiable parte de una máquina o aparato que se puede reemplazar por otra; parte idéntica (pág. 297)

*internal within the country (p. 309)

*interno dentro del país (pág. 309)

*interpret to explain the meaning of something (p. 484)

*interpretar explicar el significado de algo (pág. 484)

interstate commerce economic activity taking place between two or more states (p. 311)

comercio interestatal actividad económica que tiene lugar entre dos o más estados (pág. 311)

*investigate to search for facts and other information about something (p. 61)

*investigar buscar hechos y otra información sobre algo (pág. 61)

*involve to include (p. 210)

*implicar incluir (pág. 210)

ironclad a warship equipped with iron plating for protection (p. 459)

acorazado barco de guerra equipado con capa de hierro para su protección (pág. 459)

Iroquois Confederacy a group of Native American nations in eastern North America joined together under one general government (p. 102)

Confederación Iroquesa grupo de naciones indígenas americanas del este de Norteamérica que se unieron bajo un gobierno general (pág. 102)

irrigate to supply water to crops by artificial means (p. 16)

irrigar suministrar agua a los cultivos por medios artificiales (pág. 16)

*issue a subject that people have different views about; to deliver or hand out (pp. 156–157; p. 254)

*asunto tema sobre el cual las personas tienen diferentes perspectivas; el término en inglés "issue" también significa "expedir" o "entregar" (págs. 156–157; pág. 254)

J

joint occupation the control and settlement of an area by two or more countries or groups (p. 349)

ocupación compartida control y establecimiento de un área por parte de dos o más países o grupos (pág. 349)

joint-stock company a business in which investors buy stock in return for a share of its future profits (p. 62)

sociedad por acciones empresa en la cual los inversionistas compran acciones a cambio de una parte en sus ganancias futuras (pág. 62)

judicial branch the branch of government that interprets the law; it includes courts that settle disputes and questions of the law (p. 197)

poder judicial rama del gobierno que interpreta las leyes; incluye los tribunales que resuelven las disputas y los asuntos relacionados con la ley (pág. 197)

judicial review power of the Supreme Court to say whether any federal, state, or local law or government action goes against the Constitution (p. 213)

revisión judicial facultad de la Corte Suprema de declarar si una ley federal, estatal o local, o una acción del gobierno van en contra de la Constitución (pág. 213)

jurisdiction a court's power or right to hear and decide cases (pp. 270–271)

jurisdicción facultad o derecho que tiene un tribunal de oír los casos y decidir sobre ellos (págs. 270–271)

*justify to provide an explanation for; to find reasons to support (p. 362; p. 440)

*justificar dar una explicación; hallar razones para sustentar (pág. 362; pág. 440)

L

*lecture speech meant to provide information, similar to what a teacher presents (p. 405)

*conferencia discurso que busca proporcionar información, similar a una presentación de un profesor (pág. 405)

*legal permitted by law (p. 394)

*legal permitido por la ley (pág. 394)

legislative branch the lawmaking branch of government (pp. 196–197)

poder legislativo rama del gobierno encargada de crear las leyes (págs. 196–197)

*license to give official authority to do something (p. 384)

*autorizar conferir autoridad oficial para hacer algo (pág. 384)

limited government idea that a government may only use the powers given to it by the people (p. 207)

gobierno limitado idea según la cual un gobierno solo puede usar los poderes que le confiere el pueblo (pág. 207)

*link to connect (p. 10)

*vincular conectar a (pág. 10)

literacy the ability to read and write (pp. 396–397)

alfabetismo capacidad de leer y escribir (págs. 396–397)

literacy test a method used to prevent African Americans from voting by requiring prospective voters to read and write at a specific level (p. 512)

prueba de alfabetismo método usado para evitar que los afroamericanos voten exigiendo que los posibles electores lean y escriban a un nivel específico (pág. 512)

lock in a canal, separate compartment with gates at each end used in which water levels rise and fall in order to raise or lower boats (pp. 304–305)

esclusa en un canal, compartimento separado con puertas en los extremos en el cual el nivel del agua sube y baja para que los barcos se levanten o desciendan (págs. 304–305)

Loyalist an American colonist who remained loyal to Britain and opposed the war for independence (pp. 124–125)

leal colono americano que permanecía fiel a Gran Bretaña y se oponía a la guerra de independencia (págs. 124–125)

lynching putting to death by the illegal action of a mob (p. 512)

linchar provocar la muerte mediante la acción ilegal de una turba (pág. 512)

M

magnanimous noble; generous (p. 317)

magnánimo noble; generoso (pág. 317)

*maintain to keep or uphold (pp. 252–253)

maize a variety of corn (pp. 6–7)

majority a number that is more than 50 percent of the total (pp. 324–325)

Manifest Destiny the belief popular in the United States during the 1800s that the country must extend its boundaries to the Pacific Ocean (p. 352)

manumission the freeing of individual enslaved persons (p. 186)

martyr a person who sacrifices his or her life for a principle or cause (pp. 437–438)

*medical relating to medicine; help given to people who are sick or injured (p. 414)

mercantilism an economic theory that a nation's power depends on its ability to increase wealth by increasing exports and receiving precious metals (p. 94)

mercenary paid soldier who serves in the armed forces of a foreign country (p. 146)

migration the movement of a large number of people into a new area (p. 6)

militia a military force made of ordinary citizens who are trained to fight in emergencies (p. 102)

*ministry the office and duties of a religious leader (p. 418–419)

minuteman a civilian during Revolutionary era who was ready to fight with only one minute's notice (p. 122)

mission a religious community where farming was carried out and Native Americans were converted to Christianity (pp. 45–46)

monopoly a market where there is only one provider of a good or service (p. 311)

Morse code a system for sending messages that uses a series of dots and dashes to represent the letters of the alphabet, numbers, and punctuation (p. 380)

mosque a Muslim house of worship (pp. 32–33)

mountain man an adventurer of the American West (p. 349)

*mantener conservar o sostener (págs. 252–253)

maíz elote (págs. 6–7)

mayoría número superior al 50 por ciento del total (págs. 324–325)

Destino Manifiesto creencia popular en Estados Unidos durante el siglo XIX según la cual el país debía ampliar sus fronteras hacia el océano Pacífico (pág. 352)

manumisión liberación de personas esclavizadas (pág. 186)

mártir persona que sacrifica su vida por un principio o una causa (págs. 437–438)

*médico relativo a la medicina; ayuda que se brinda a los enfermos y heridos (pág. 414)

mercantilismo teoría económica según la cual el poderío de una nación depende de su capacidad de aumentar sus riquezas incrementando las exportaciones y recibiendo metales preciosos (pág. 94)

mercenario soldado remunerado que sirve en las fuerzas armadas de un país extranjero (pág. 146)

migración desplazamiento de un gran número de personas en un área nueva (pág. 6)

milicia fuerza militar compuesta por ciudadanos comunes que están entrenados para combatir en situaciones de emergencia (pág. 102)

*ministerio cargo y deberes de un líder religioso (págs. 418–419)

miliciano civil que estaba listo para combatir en cuestión de minutos durante el periodo revolucionario (pág. 122)

misión comunidad religiosa donde se practicaba la agricultura y los indígenas americanos se convertían al cristianismo (págs. 45–46)

monopolio mercado en el que solo hay un proveedor de un bien o servicio (pág. 311)

código morse sistema de transmisión de mensajes que consta de una serie de puntos y rayas para representar las letras del abecedario, los números y la puntuación (pág. 380)

mezquita casa musulmana de adoración (págs. 32–33)

hombre de montaña aventurero del oeste americano (pág. 349)

mudslinging a method in election campaigns that uses gossip and lies to make an opponent look bad (p. 326)

calumnia método de las campañas electorales en el que se usan el rumor y las mentiras para hacer quedar mal al adversario (pág. 326)

--- N ---

nationalism a strong sense of devotion to one's country (p. 282; p. 284)

nacionalismo fuerte sentido de devoción al país propio (pág. 282; pág.284)

nativist person opposed to immigration (pp. 384–385)

nativista persona que se opone a la inmigración (págs. 384–385)

naturalization the process of becoming a citizen of another country (pp. 214–215)

naturalización proceso para hacerse ciudadano de otro país (págs. 214–215)

*network interconnected system (pp. 430–431)

*red sistema interconectado (págs. 430–431)

*neutral taking no side (p. 102)

*neutral que no toma partido (pág. 102)

neutral rights privileges or freedoms that are granted to nations that do not choose a side in a conflict (p. 280)

derechos neutrales privilegios o libertades que se otorgan a naciones que no toman partido en un conflicto (pág. 280)

nomad a person who moves from place to place (p. 6)

nómada persona que se traslada de un lugar a otro (pág. 6)

nominating convention a meeting in which representative members of a political party choose candidates to run for important elected offices (p. 328)

convención de nominación reunión en la cual los representantes de un partido político eligen candidatos para importantes cargos de elección (pág. 328)

normal school state-supported school for training high school graduates to become teachers (p. 406)

escuela normal escuela apoyada por el Estado en la que se educa a los estudiantes de secundaria para que sean profesores (pág. 406)

Northwest Passage a much-sought sea route between the Atlantic and Pacific Oceans, located along the north coast of North America (pp. 50–51)

Paso del Noroeste ruta marítima muy buscada entre los océanos Atlántico y Pacífico, localizada en la costa norte de América del Norte (págs. 50–51)

nullify to legally overturn; to cancel (p. 260)

anular invalidar legalmente; cancelar (pág. 260)

--- O ---

*occupy to move into and take control of a place, especially by force (pp. 116–117)

*ocupar desplazarse a un lugar y tomar control de él, en especial mediante un enfrentamiento entre fuerzas (págs. 116–117)

*ordained established (p. 445)

*ordenado establecido (pág. 445)

ordinance a law or regulation (p. 180)

ordenanza ley o norma (pág. 180)

*outcome the effect or result of an action or event (p. 510)

*resultado efecto o producto de una acción o un evento (pág. 510)

override to reject or defeat something that has already been decided (p. 499)

anular rechazar o derrotar algo que ya se ha decidido (pág. 499)

Glossary/Glosario

overseer a plantation manager (p. 393)

supervisor administrador de una plantación (pág. 393)

--- **P** ---

pacifists people opposed to the use of war or violence to settle disputes (p. 71)

pacifista persona que se opone al uso de la guerra o la violencia para resolver disputas (pág. 71)

*participate to take part in (pp. 326–327)

*participar tomar parte (págs. 326–327)

partisan firmly favoring one party or faction (p. 257)

partidario que favorece firmemente un partido o facción (pág. 257)

patent sole legal right to an invention and its profits (p. 297)

patente derecho legal exclusivo sobre un invento y las ganancias que este produce (pág. 297)

Patriot American colonist who favored American independence (pp. 124–125)

patriota colono americano partidario de la independencia americana (págs. 124–125)

patroon landowner in the Dutch colonies who ruled over large areas of land (pp. 69–70)

patrón terrateniente de las colonias holandesas que dominaba grandes áreas de tierra (págs. 69–70)

persecute to mistreat a person or group on the basis of their beliefs (pp. 64–65)

perseguir maltratar a una persona o un grupo por sus creencias (págs. 64–65)

petition a formal request for government action (p. 129)

petición solicitud formal de una acción gubernamental (pág. 129)

pilgrimage a journey to a holy place (pp. 32–33)

peregrinación viaje a un lugar sagrado (págs. 32–33)

plantation a large farm (pp. 46–47)

plantación granja grande (págs. 46–47)

plurality the largest number of something, but less than a majority (pp. 324–325)

pluralidad mayor número de algo, inferior a la mayoría (págs. 324–325)

*plus in addition to (pp. 348–349)

*además en adición (págs. 348–349)

*policy a statement of ideals or plan of action (pp. 67–68)

*política declaración de ideales o plan de acción (págs. 67–68)

poll tax a tax a person must pay in order to vote (pp. 510–511)

impuesto al sufragio impuesto que una persona debe pagar para votar (págs. 510–511)

popular sovereignty the belief that government is subject to the will of the people (pp. 206–207)

soberanía popular creencia de que el gobierno está sujeto a la voluntad del pueblo (págs. 206–207)

*pose to present; to offer (pp. 52–53)

*plantear presentar; ofrecer (págs. 52–53)

prairie schooner a canvas-covered wagon used by pioneers in the mid-1800s (pp. 350–351)

carromato vagón cubierto de lona que usaban los pioneros a mediados del siglo XIX (págs. 350–351)

preamble the introduction to a formal document that often tells why the document was written (p. 132)

preámbulo introducción a un documento formal que con frecuencia indica por qué se escribió (pág. 132)

precedent something done or said that becomes an example for others to follow (pp. 246–247)

precedente algo que se hace o se dice y se vuelve un ejemplo para los demás (págs. 246–247)

prejudice an unfair opinion not based on facts (p. 383)

prejuicio opinión injusta que no se basa en los hechos (pág. 383)

presidio a fort (pp. 45–46)

presidio fuerte (págs. 45–46)

*previous earlier (pp. 146–147)

*previo anterior (págs. 146–147)

*principal most important (p. 86)

*principal lo más importante (pág. 86)

*principle a fundamental, or basic, law or idea (pp. 270–271)

*principio ley o idea fundamental o básica (págs. 270–271)

privateer a privately owned ship outfitted with weapons (p. 159)

corsario barco privado equipado con armamento (pág.159)

*process to prepare (p. 388)

*procesar preparar (pág. 388)

*prodigal wasteful (p. 317)

*derrochador despilfarrador (pág. 317)

*prodigious large in size or quantity (p. 317)

*prodigioso de gran tamaño o cantidad (pág. 317)

productivity a measure of how much a worker can produce within a given amount of time and effort (p. 388)

productividad medida de cuánto puede producir un trabajador en una cantidad de tiempo y con un esfuerzo determinados (pág. 388)

*profane not religious (p. 317)

*profano no religioso (pág. 317)

*proffer to present for acceptance (p. 359)

*proponer presentar para su aceptación (pág. 359)

*prohibit to prevent or forbid (pp. 112–113)

*prohibir evitar o proscribir (págs. 112–113)

propaganda ideas or information intentionally spread to harm or help a cause (p. 117)

propaganda ideas o información que se difunden intencionalmente para perjudicar o apoyar una causa (pág. 117)

proportional having the proper size in relation to other objects or items (p. 188)

proporcional que tiene el tamaño apropiado en relación con otros objetos o elementos (pág. 188)

Protestantism a form of Christianity that began in opposition to the Catholic Church (pp. 49–50)

protestantismo forma del cristianismo que nació en oposición a la Iglesia católica (págs. 49–50)

*pueblo a communal Native American structure; a town in Spanish-ruled lands (p. 16; p. 46)

*pueblo ciudad en tierras bajo el dominio español (pág. 16; pág. 46)

*purchase the act of buying something (p. 274)

*comprar acción de adquirir algo (pág. 274)

*pursue to proceed with (p. 167)

*proseguir continuar (pág. 167)

R

*radical extreme (p. 495)

*radical extremo (pág. 495)

ranchero a Mexican ranch owner (p. 362)

ranchero propietario de un rancho mexicano (pág. 362)

rancho a ranch, especially the large estates set up by Mexicans in the American West (p. 362)

ratify to vote approval of (p. 167)

*****react** to act in response to something (pp. 280–281)

rebellion open defiance of authority (pp. 116–117)

reconciliation settlement; understanding (pp. 126–127)

Reconstruction the period of rebuilding the South after the Civil War and readmitting the former Confederate states into the Union (pp. 494–495)

recruit to enlist in the military (p. 146)

*****Reformation** a sixteenth-century religious movement rejecting or changing some Roman Catholic teachings and practices and establishing the Protestant Churches (pp. 49–50)

*****reformation** change (p. 193)

*****region** an area defined by a feature or characteristic (p. 304)

*****regulate** to control or govern (p. 429)

*****reinforce** to make stronger (p. 460)

*****reject** to refuse to accept (p. 440)

*****relinquish** to give up (pp. 192–193)

relocate to move to another place (pp. 330–331)

*****rely** to depend upon (p. 86)

*****remove** to take away (p. 354)

Renaissance a reawaking of culture and intellectual curiosity in Europe from the 1300s to the 1600s (p. 30)

*****renounce** to give up; to abandon (pp. 126–127)

repeal to cancel an act or law (pp. 114–115)

representative government a system in which citizens elect a smaller group to make laws and conduct government on their behalf (p. 93)

republic a government in which citizens rule through elected representatives (p. 177)

reserved power authority belonging only to the states (p. 207)

rancho hacienda, en especial las grandes propiedades que los mexicanos establecieron en el oeste de Estados Unidos (pág. 362)

ratificar aprobar por votación (pág. 167)

*****reaccionar** actuar en respuesta a algo (págs. 280–281)

rebelión desafío abierto a la autoridad (págs. 116–117)

reconciliación acuerdo; entendimiento (págs. 126-127)

Reconstrucción periodo de reconstrucción del Sur después de la Guerra Civil y readmisión de los antiguos estados confederados en la Unión (págs. 494–495)

reclutar enlistar en las fuerzas militares (pág. 146)

*****Reforma** movimiento religioso del siglo XVI que rechazó o modificó algunas enseñanzas y prácticas de la Iglesia católica romana y estableció las iglesias protestantes (págs. 49–50)

*****reforma** cambio (pág. 193)

*****región** área definida por un rasgo o característica (pág. 304)

*****regular** controlar o gobernar (pág. 429)

*****reforzar** fortalecer (pág. 460)

*****rechazar** rehusarse a aceptar (pág. 440)

*****abdicar** ceder (págs. 192–193)

reubicar trasladar a otro lugar (págs. 330–331)

*****confiar** depender (pág. 86)

*****quitar** sacar (pág. 354)

Renacimiento renacer de la cultura y la curiosidad intelectual en Europa entre los siglos XIV y XVII (pág. 30)

*****renunciar** ceder, abandonar (págs. 126–127)

revocar cancelar un acto o una ley (págs. 114–115)

gobierno representativo sistema en el cual los ciudadanos eligen un grupo más pequeño para que legisle y dirija el gobierno en su nombre (pág. 93)

república gobierno en el cual los ciudadanos gobiernan por medio de representantes elegidos (pág. 177)

poder reservado autoridad que pertenece solo a los estados (pág. 207)

*reside to exist or live in (p. 197)

resistance refusal to give in (p. 483)

resolution an official expression of opinion by a group (pp. 114–115)

*resolve to find a solution; to settle a conflict (p. 259)

*resource something that can be used for benefit, especially land, minerals, and water (p. 362)

*restriction rule or regulation that limits something (p. 282)

*reveal to show (pp. 302–303)

revenue incoming money from taxes or other sources (pp. 112–113)

*revere to deeply love and respect (pp. 192–193)

reverse to go in the opposite direction (p. 476)

revival religious meeting (pp. 404–405)

*rigid firm and inflexible (pp. 434–435)

*route line of travel (p. 412)

*residir existir o vivir en un lugar (pág. 197)

resistencia negativa a darse por vencido (pág. 483)

resolución expresión oficial de la opinión por parte de un grupo (págs. 114–115)

*resolver hallar una solución; dirimir un conflicto (pág. 259)

*recurso algo que se puede usar para obtener beneficios, en especial tierra, minerales y agua (pág. 362)

*restricción norma o regulación que limita algo (pág. 282)

*revelar mostrar (págs. 302–303)

renta dinero que ingresa por concepto de impuestos o de otras fuentes (págs. 112–113)

*reverenciar amar y respetar profundamente (págs. 192–193)

invertir ir en la dirección contraria (pág. 476)

asamblea evangélica encuentro religioso (págs. 404–405)

*rígido firme e inflexible (págs. 434–435)

*ruta línea de viaje (pág. 412)

S

scalawag name given by former Confederates to Southern whites who supported Republican Reconstruction of the South (p. 505)

secede to withdraw or break away from a nation or organization; to officially leave an organization (pp. 276–277; p. 430)

secession withdrawal; to leave the Union (p. 440)

sectionalism rivalry based on the special interests of different areas (p. 310)

sedition activities aimed at weakening the established government by inciting resistance or rebellion to authority (p. 259)

segregation the separation or isolation of a race, class, or group (p. 512)

separation of powers the division of authority among executive, legislative, and judicial branches to make sure no one branch has too much power (p. 208)

bribón nombre dado por los antiguos confederados a los blancos sureños que apoyaban la reconstrucción republicana del Sur (pág. 505)

separarse retirarse o apartarse de una nación u organización; dejar oficialmente una organización (págs. 276–277; pág. 430)

secesión retiro; acción de abandonar la Unión (pág. 440)

faccionalismo rivalidad que surge de tener intereses en áreas diferentes (pág. 310)

sedición actividades que buscan debilitar el gobierno establecido incitando a la resistencia o a la rebelión contra la autoridad (pág. 259)

segregación separación o aislamiento de una raza, clase o grupo (pág. 512)

separación de poderes división de la autoridad entre las ramas ejecutiva, legislativa y judicial para garantizar que ninguna de ellas tenga demasiado poder (pág. 208)

Glossary/Glosario

*series events that occur one after the other (p. 482)

sharecropping system of farming in which a farmer works land for an owner who provides equipment and seeds and receives a share of the crop (pp. 506–507)

siege attempt to force surrender by blocking the movement of people or goods into or out of a place (p. 165)

*similar sharing qualities, but not the same as; like (p. 270)

slave codes rules focusing on the behavior and punishment of enslaved people; laws in Southern states that controlled enslaved people (pp. 88–89; p. 395)

*so-called known as (p. 124)

*source a supply (pp. 6–7)

*sovereign one who holds power (p. 317)

spiritual an African American religious folk song (p. 394)

spoils system practice of rewarding government jobs to political supporters; replacing government employees with the winning candidate's supporters (p. 328)

states' rights the idea that states should have all powers that the Constitution does not give to the federal government or forbid to the states; theory that individual states are independent and have the right to control their most important affairs (p. 260; p. 440)

*status rank or place as compared to others (pp. 132–133)

*stock livestock (p. 473)

*stoicism the quality of not reacting to pleasure or pain (p. 317)

strait a narrow passage of water between larger bodies of water (p. 5)

*strategy a plan of action; a careful plan or method (p.165; pp. 452–453)

strike a work stoppage by employees as a protest against an employer (p. 383)

*structure a building (p. 16)

*subjugate conquer (pp. 358–359)

*serie eventos que ocurren uno tras otro (pág. 482)

aparcería sistema en el cual un agricultor trabaja la tierra para un propietario que suministra el equipo y las semillas y recibe una parte de la cosecha (págs. 506–507)

sitio intento de obligar al enemigo a rendirse bloqueando el movimiento de personas y bienes desde y hacia un lugar (pág. 165)

*similar que comparte cualidades pero no es igual; parecido (pág. 270)

códigos esclavistas reglas que se enfocaban en la conducta de los esclavos y los castigos que recibían; leyes de los estados del Sur que controlaban a los esclavos (págs. 88–89; pág. 395)

*llamado conocido como (pág. 124)

*fuente suministro (págs. 6–7)

*soberano quien ostenta el poder (pág. 317)

espiritual canción tradicional religiosa afroamericana (pág. 394)

sistema de botín práctica de recompensar con cargos en el gobierno a los seguidores políticos; reemplazar a los empleados del gobierno por los seguidores del candidato ganador (pág. 328)

derechos de los estados idea de que los estados deberían tener todas las facultades que la Constitución no le confiere al gobierno federal o les prohíbe a estos; teoría según la cual los estados individuales son independientes y tienen derecho a controlar sus asuntos más importantes (pág. 260; pág. 440)

*estatus posición o lugar en comparación con otros (págs. 132–133)

*ganado semovientes (pág. 473)

*estoicismo cualidad de no reaccionar frente al placer o el dolor (pág. 317)

estrecho paso de agua angosto entre grandes masas de agua (pág. 5)

*estrategia plan de acción; plan o método cuidadosos (pág. 165; págs. 452–453)

huelga interrupción del trabajo por parte de los empleados como protesta contra el empleador (pág. 383)

*estructura construcción (pág. 16)

*subyugar conquistar (págs. 358–359)

subsistence farming producing just enough to meet immediate needs (pp. 84–85)

agricultura de subsistencia producir solo lo suficiente para satisfacer las necesidades inmediatas (págs. 84–85)

*substitute an alternate or replacement (p. 470)

*sustituto alternativa o reemplazo (pág. 470)

suffrage the right to vote (pp. 415–416)

sufragio derecho al voto (págs. 415–416)

*survive to continue existing or living after nearly being destroyed (p. 334)

*sobrevivir seguir existiendo o vivir después de haber estado a punto de ser destruido (pág. 334)

*suspend to temporarily set aside or stop operation of something (p. 93; p. 502)

*suspender dejar de lado o detener temporalmente el funcionamiento de algo (pág. 93; pág. 502)

*sustain to suffer or experience (pp. 162–163)

*soportar sufrir o experimentar (págs. 162–163)

*symbol a word or object that stands for something else (p. 340)

*símbolo palabra u objeto que representa otra cosa (pág. 340)

T

technology the use of scientific knowledge for practical purposes (p. 30; p. 297)

tecnología uso del conocimiento científico para propósitos prácticos (pág. 30; pág. 297)

*tedious boring (p. 317)

*tedioso aburrido (pág. 317)

Tejano a Texan of Latin American, often Mexican, descent (p. 355)

tejano descendiente texano de un latinoamericano, por lo general mexicano (pág. 355)

telegraph a device that used electric signals to send messages (pp. 378–379)

telégrafo aparato que envía mensajes mediante señales eléctricas (págs. 378–379)

temperance drinking little or no alcohol (p. 405)

abstinencia beber poco o nada de alcohol (pág. 405)

tenant farmer a farmer who pays a landowner an annual rent and worked for that person for a fixed number of days each year (pp. 52–53)

granjero arrendatario granjero que paga a un terrateniente una renta anual y trabaja para él un número determinado de días al año (págs. 52–53)

terrace a broad platform of flat land cut into a slope (p. 12)

terraza plataforma ancha de tierra plana excavada en una pendiente (pág. 12)

theocracy a society that is ruled by religious leaders (p. 9)

teocracia sociedad gobernada por líderes religiosos (pág. 9)

*tidings news (p. 421)

*novedades noticias (pág. 421)

tolerance the ability to accept and respect different views or behaviors (p. 67)

tolerancia capacidad de aceptar y respetar puntos de vista o comportamientos diferentes (pág. 67)

*topic subject of discussion (p. 436)

*asunto tema de análisis (pág. 436)

*torrent fast-moving liquid (p. 127)

*torrente líquido que corre rápidamente (pág. 127)

total war a strategy of bringing war to the entire society, not just the military (pp. 484–485)

guerra total estrategia de llevar la guerra a toda la sociedad, no solo al estamento militar (págs. 484–-485)

trade union group of workers with the same trade, or skill (p. 383)

sindicato grupo de trabajadores con el mismo oficio o destreza (pág. 383)

*tradition a long-standing cultural belief and practice (pp. 194–195)

*tradición creencia o práctica cultural de larga data (págs. 194–195)

*transfer to move (p. 146)

*transferir mover (pág. 146)

*transform to change significantly (p. 378)

*transformar cambiar significativamente (pág. 378)

triangular trade pattern of trade that developed in colonial times among the Americas, Africa, and Europe (p. 88)

comercio triangular patrón de comercio desarrollado durante la Colonia entre América, África y Europa (pág. 88)

tributary stream or smaller river that feeds into a large river (p. 459)

tributario corriente de agua o río pequeño que desemboca en un río más grande (pág. 459)

tribute money paid to a leader or state for protection (pp. 278–279)

tributo dinero que se paga a un líder o Estado para obtener protección (págs. 278–279)

turnpike a road that one must pay to use (p. 303)

autopista de peaje camino por el que se debe pagar para su uso (pág. 303)

U

*underestimate to judge something below its actual value (p. 285)

*subestimar juzgar algo por debajo de su valor real (pág. 285)

Underground Railroad a system of cooperation to aid and house enslaved people who had escaped (p. 396)

Tren Clandestino sistema de cooperación para ayudar y albergar a los esclavos que habían escapado (pág. 396)

*uniform identical; unchanging (p. 247)

*uniforme idéntico; constante (pág. 247)

*unimpaired not harmed; not damaged (p. 445)

*intacto que no se ha deteriorado; sin daño (pág. 445)

*usurpation an unjust seizing of power (pp. 358–359)

*usurpación toma injusta del poder (págs. 358–359)

utopia community based on a vision of a perfect society (p. 405)

utopía comunidad basada en una visión de una sociedad perfecta (pág. 405)

V

veto to reject a bill and prevent if from becoming law (p. 337)

vetar rechazar un proyecto y evitar que se convierta en ley (pág. 337)

*victual food (p. 91)

*víveres alimento (pág. 91)

vigilante person who acts as police, judge, and jury without formal legal authority (p. 367)

vigilante persona que actúa como policía, juez y jurado sin autoridad legal formal (pág. 367)

*violate to disregard or go against (p. 114)

*violar ignorar o ir en contra (pág. 114)

W

*widespread over a wide area (p. 50)

writ of assistance court document allowing customs officers to enter any location to search for smuggled goods (p. 113)

*generalizado en un área amplia (pág. 50)

interdicto de despojo documento judicial que permite a los funcionarios de aduana entrar a un lugar en busca de productos de contrabando (pág. 113)

Y

yeoman a farmer who owns a small farm (pp. 391–392)

pequeño terrateniente agricultor que posee una granja pequeña (págs. 391–392)

Glossary/Glosario

The following abbreviations are used in the index: m=map, c=chart, p=photograph or picture, g=graph, crt=cartoon, ptg=painting, q=quote

Index

Index

Index

Index